T0139198

# American Volunteer Police

## Mobilizing for Security

# American Volunteer Police

## Mobilizing for Security

**Martin Alan Greenberg**

**CRC Press**
Taylor & Francis Group
Boca Raton London New York

CRC Press is an imprint of the
Taylor & Francis Group, an **informa** business

CRC Press
Taylor & Francis Group
6000 Broken Sound Parkway NW, Suite 300
Boca Raton, FL 33487-2742

© 2015 by Taylor & Francis Group, LLC
CRC Press is an imprint of Taylor & Francis Group, an Informa business

No claim to original U.S. Government works

Printed on acid-free paper
Version Date: 20140912

International Standard Book Number-13: 978-1-4822-3254-7 (Hardback)

---

**Library of Congress Cataloging-in-Publication Data**

---

Greenberg, Martin Alan.
American volunteer police : mobilizing for security / Martin Alan Greenberg.
pages cm
Includes bibliographical references and index.
ISBN 978-1-4822-3254-7 (hardcover : alk. paper) 1. Auxiliary police--United States.
2. Volunteer workers in law enforcement--United States. 3. Crime prevention--United States. I. Title.

HV8139.G74 2015
363.2--dc23                                                                              2014033185

---

**Visit the Taylor & Francis Web site at**
**http://www.taylorandfrancis.com**

**and the CRC Press Web site at**
**http://www.crcpress.com**

*This book is dedicated to*

*the memories of*

*Gwen Elliott and John T. Gobble Jr.*

*Gwendolyn J. "Gwen" Elliott was a trailblazing champion for the rights of women, children, the elderly, minorities, and crime victims in her role as a Pittsburgh police commander. In the early 1970s, she was among the group of mothers who founded the Center for Victims of Violence and Crime. In 2002, the year she retired from the Pittsburgh force after 26 years, she founded Gwen's Girls, the first county nonprofit organization dedicated solely to the needs of at-risk girls aged 8–18 years.*

*John T. Gobble Jr. was the founding director of Point Park University's criminal justice programs and a remarkably gifted educator, mentor, and friend who motivated hundreds of students to succeed because of his caring attitude.*

*Both John and Gwen were visionaries who worked hard to make Pittsburgh a better place to live and to work.*

# Contents

## Section I

### OVERVIEW OF VOLUNTEER POLICING

## Section II
### SPECIAL ISSUES IN VOLUNTEER POLICING

## 8  Youth Involvement in Police Work                                  199

## 9  Youth Involvement in Public Safety and Security at the Federal Level                                              235

# Preface

According to the Federal Bureau of Investigation's *Uniform Crime Reports*, although the violent crime rate has been falling since 1992, it is still more than twice as great as it was in 1960. At the same time that the complexity and burden of police work have been evolving, agency budgets have failed to keep pace with such developments. However, there has been a fascinating trend with respect to the use of police volunteers. Since the end of World War I, the use of mostly unpaid volunteers in sworn or non-sworn capacities has become standard practice in many police departments, including in those of New York City, Washington, D.C., Detroit, and Los Angeles.

Three states lead the nation with respect to the total number of volunteer police officers: Ohio, Florida, and California. Over the years, training for these volunteers has vastly improved, and thorough background investigations are conducted for candidates. For example, all new California reserve police officers are required to attend a basic police academy as mandated by the California State Commission on Peace Officer Standards and Training (POST). The training requirement is the same academy program required of all regular full-time officers. Furthermore, in agencies that meet the standards of the Commission on Accreditation for Law Enforcement Agencies (CALEA), sworn volunteer police officers are required to receive the same training as regular police officers. The intent of this book is to document these trends.

A search on the Web can reveal much about the current status of many of these units. I hope that readers will want to learn more about the augmentation of first responder organizations through the recruitment and training of volunteers and will browse the Web to keep abreast of developments. Various Web sites are cited throughout the book. Readers should keep in mind that these online addresses were only current during the preparation of this book.

This work seeks to introduce the reader to the most current and relevant materials concerning modern units of volunteer police. It highlights what average Americans have done and are currently doing to safeguard their communities. The contributions of volunteers at all levels of government are presented. The materials should be of value to volunteer first responders, youth workers, educators, public officials, organizations, institutions, or private individuals concerned about contemporary public safety issues. In particular, students, urban planners, and emergency public safety administrators should discover within the book essential information about the past, present, and future roles of citizen participation in public safety.

In addition to describing a wide range of contemporary activities performed by volunteer police, this book also offers several recommendations toward utilizing qualified citizens in the following new roles: (1) serving as educators and supplemental staff for the prevention of human trafficking and worker exploitation; (2) serving as language interpreters to assist both documented and undocumented immigrants; (3) leading rescue teams to assist the homeless; (4) aiding youth and other users of community centers; (5) assisting school resource officers; (6) delivering crime prevention presentations to diverse community groups, especially in urban neighborhoods; and (7) augmenting border patrol security in a new federal auxiliary program.

This book is designed to serve as either a reference work or a textbook for courses dealing with public safety and security issues. Given the new responsibilities of the nation's law enforcement establishment, the need for augmenting police services through the use of qualified volunteers has never been greater.

# Acknowledgments

Every book involves the assistance of a number of persons. I have had the very capable assistance of Joselyn Banks-Kyle, who served as the book's project coordinator, and Carolyn Spence, the acquisitions editor at CRC Press, a Taylor & Francis Company. In addition, I am very grateful for the permission to reprint Sections 16.3 and 16.4 from the Standards for Law Enforcement Agencies along with the manual's definition of "Reserve" and "Auxiliary" found in Appendix A of this book. The Commission on Accreditation for Law Enforcement Agencies, Inc. (CALEA®) is the registered copyright holder of the materials republished in Appendix A. The materials in this appendix are from *Standards for Law Enforcement Agencies* (©2006, update 5.17 from August 2013; all rights reserved).

I have been able to reach out to a number of law enforcement professionals, activists, historical societies, and scholars for assistance with this book. The following individuals were especially helpful in permitting the use of the various photographs included in this book: Officer Scott L. Harris, Public Information Officer/Explorer Post Advisor, Visalia Office of the California Highway Patrol; Donna Conley, Westbrook (Maine) Historical Society; Dave Griffin, president, Maynard (Massachusetts) Historical Society; Roberta Weintraub, founder of the Los Angeles Police Academy Magnet Schools and founder/executive director, Police Orientation Preparation Program; Michael Kovacsev, Acting Assistant Chief, St. Petersburg Police Department, Investigative Services Bureau; Ken and Patricia Driscoll and their creative and invaluable Web site located at BaltimoreCityPoliceHistory.com; Lt. Joseph Gruver, Cheltenham (Pennsylvania) Township Police Department; Auxiliary Colonel Arthur Wilson, Ohio State Highway Patrol Auxiliary; Michael Suess, chief, Oshkosh (Wisconsin) Auxiliary Police; Zachary Feder, New York City Parks and Recreation; Mark A. Elkins, president, New York City Parks Auxiliary Mounted Unit; and Russ Malone, City Clerk and Clerk of the Waltham City Council in Massachusetts.

For specific textual materials, special thanks are due to: Erick Hoffman, Glenn J. Kearney, president, New York State Association of Auxiliary Police, Inc. (NYSAAP); Philip Franckel, counsel, NYSAAP; James D. Brown, associate director, CALEA; and Bonnie Bucqueroux, Michigan State University. Bucqueroux was the associate director of the National Center for Community Policing at Michigan State University's School of Criminal Justice and currently teaches at Michigan State University's School of Journalism.

# Author

Martin Alan Greenberg is the director of research and education for the New York State Association of Auxiliary Police, Inc. He was formerly a professor and administrator of several different criminal justice and law enforcement programs at a variety of colleges and universities including: Virginia Union University, Point Park University (Pittsburgh, Pennsylvania), the University of Hawaii at Hilo, Arkansas State University, and the State University of New York at Ulster. He holds four graduate degrees in criminal justice and law, including a PhD from the City University of New York and a JD from New York Law School. He is the past chair of the Security and Crime Prevention Section of the Academy of Criminal Justice Sciences and holds lifetime board certification in security management. His experiences also include service as senior court officer, probation officer, campus security assistant, and judicial clerk. He is the author of four books and received an honorable discharge recognizing 12 years of service in the New York City Auxiliary Police Force, having obtained the volunteer rank of auxiliary deputy inspector.

# Overview of Volunteer Policing

# I

# Introduction

The fall of Rome occurred over 300 years. That is longer than any democracy, including our own, has survived. As wondrous as it is, we can never take our democracy for granted. It can only survive as long as we, its citizens, are willing to nurture, to defend, and to tend it.

—**Bob Schieffer**
*CBS News, Chief Washington Correspondent, The Citadel,*
*Corps of Cadets, Commencement Address, May 8, 2010*

One of the most pressing crises facing America is the need to balance the various protections offered by the U.S. Constitution concerning individual freedom with public safety. This book is premised on the idea that the unending march of a wide variety of daily crime incidents and continuing threats to national security require the attention of full-time practitioners and qualified members of the general public. Both groups need to contend with these problems by adhering to the rule of law.

The combination of public servants and qualified citizens is needed to address such issues as: guarding borders in order to prevent the entry of illegal aliens, illicit drugs, and possible terrorists; reducing the carnage on our nation's highways; delivering antigun violence programs; supplementing the efforts to enforce "quality of life" laws and ordinances; curtailing human trafficking; and preparing for the radiological "dirty bomb" that could kill thousands. Other potential threats include: the explosion of tank cars carrying chlorine and phosgene gas and the release of plague bacteria in an American city or in Mexico City, resulting in a flood of refugees into the United States.

Nearly 30,000 American lives are lost to gun violence each year—a number far higher than in any other developed country. Since 1963, more Americans have died by gunfire than those perished in combat during the whole of the twentieth century. Gun violence reaches across borders and jurisdictions and compromises the safety of everyone along the way (IACP and Joyce Foundation 2008). No community or person in America is immune. According to Ronald C. Ruecker, the former president of the International Association of Chiefs of Police (IACP) and currently the assistant director of the Federal Bureau of Investigation's (FBI) Office of Law Enforcement Coordination (OLEC), "Every citizen in this country must stop accepting outrageous levels of gun violence in our streets, our schools, and our homes, and we must work with our fellow citizens as well as law enforcement and elected officials to put an end to this continuing tragedy" (Ruecker 2008, 6). These actual and potential threats should be of great importance to all Americans.

This chapter reviews current threats to national security and the need for volunteer preparedness. It also considers highlights in the development of citizen-based law enforcement officers in the United Kingdom and the United States. A brief overview of the office of sheriff is included. A final section summarizes the contents of the remaining chapters of this book.

## National Security and Preparedness

About 100 years ago, a now famous poster first appeared on the cover of *Leslie's Weekly*. An illustration of Uncle Sam (as seen in Figure 1.1) appears with a pointed finger and he is declaring "I want you ...." In subsequent

**Figure 1.1** Illustration of Uncle Sam.

times of crisis, similar posters were designed again featuring Uncle Sam or depicting uniformed soldiers or citizens who had answered their nation's call for service. The need for everyday Americans to answer the call for service remains, although the types of threats have changed.

During the wars of the twentieth century, individuals who were not eligible for military service were encouraged (sometimes pressured) to participate in some type of civilian defense work (fire auxiliary, air raid wardens, auxiliary police, communications, etc.). By the time of the Korean War and the advent of the Cold War, our forebears were constructing and stocking bomb shelters in their backyards and basements. At the same time, children practiced ducking under their desks at school. This was family life in the new era of the A-bomb. This was the homeland defense of yesteryear.

Members of al-Qaeda first attacked the World Trade Center in 1993. The more recent events of September 11, 2001, should encourage all Americans to reconsider their own safety and security. Today, it is not fear of an atomic attack from a superpower that is driving the U.S. foreign and domestic security policy but the fear of a suitcase dirty bomb or some other stealth weapon of mass destruction. Although "al Qaeda has suffered a confusing mix of setbacks and advances ... it's worth reflecting on the many advances al Qaeda has made since 9/11, and on its impressive resilience" (Byman 2011).

Following the September 11 attacks, the federal government focused its energies on providing new measures to protect the nation from future terrorist attacks. The attacks led to a series of government actions aimed at countering the new threat of large-scale terrorism, including the establishment of a cabinet-level Department of Homeland Security. The FBI was not merged into the new department, but it has been reorganized in view of several instances of faulty intelligence gathering. For example, Coleen Rowley, the former chief legal adviser in the FBI's Minneapolis field office, wrote a 13-page letter to the director of the FBI that said that FBI headquarters stymied her efforts in the summer of 2001 to investigate Zacarias Moussaoui, who was eventually charged and convicted as a conspirator in the September 11 attacks. She testified before a Senate panel in June 2002 regarding her concerns. In addition, a memo from an agent in the bureau's Phoenix office came to light. The memo was prepared in July 2001, but it was never acted upon. It had urged FBI headquarters to investigate a group of Middle Eastern men training at U.S. flight schools.

Rowley's letter, a copy of which was also sent to key congressional leaders, was made public when lawmakers began grappling with the question of why the nation's vaunted intelligence apparatus was unable to "connect the dots." Some believed the clues dated back nearly a decade. In 1994, for example, a "test bomb" was detonated aboard a Philippine Airlines jet, which exposed an al-Qaeda plot to blow up more than a dozen jets over the Pacific. In 2000, the Central Intelligence Agency (CIA) began noting increased signs of terrorist activities abroad. In the spring of 2001, specific threats were received by the White House from intelligence sources that said a Middle Eastern terrorist group could potentially attack U.S. interests overseas. Subsequently, U.S. troops were deployed to Afghanistan and then to Iraq. Both interventions took more than double the length of time U.S. forces fought in World War II. The long-term nature of these overseas deployments and possible future ones has raised valid questions about the need for more resources for homeland defense.

Although many American citizens may be unaware or simply complacent about a new kind of war, one in which they may be combatants and targets, U.S. governmental efforts to protect citizens are moving forward. In April 2005, an antiterrorism drill was conducted involving hundreds of people in Canada, the United Kingdom, and the United States. The Canadian component of the simulation was titled "Exercise Triple Play," while the United States conducted "TOPOFF 3." The fictional scenario included the release of a pneumonic plague in New Jersey by a terrorist group and a chemical explosion in Connecticut. Canadian authorities were called upon to deal with victims and perpetrators heading into their country. In the scenario, a fictional senior official requested a plan to restrict the movement of people in New Brunswick, where a luxury ship was carrying victims of the New Jersey incident. The drill revealed a major logistical error—the request was ignored, and no contingency planning occurred!

Although this particular drill revealed significant glitches with antiterrorism planning, it provided a much-needed learning experience for our nation and one of its closest allies. It clearly demonstrated the fact that the United States and Canada need to create a revised civil defense program. Both nations need to ascertain the best ways to become mobilized to defend themselves against internal and external threats.

The events of September 11 have led to some concern about the relative responsibilities of individuals, localities, states, and the federal government to fund and implement protective and recovery programs. Moreover, the havoc of hurricanes, such as Katrina and Sandy, has renewed discussions in this regard. For the most part, the concept of disaster preparedness or even the need for the sharing of "self-help" defense methods has been a very low profile affair. Nonetheless, one of the easiest ways to tap the American citizenry's willingness to serve in the aftermath of September 11 is the formation of block watch and community emergency response teams (CERT).[1] Citizen volunteers can help their community's public safety by serving as the eyes and ears of their local police. In addition, the very presence of such teams will also help to decrease physical and social disorder.

It must be appreciated that although homeland defense recruitment efforts can garner publicity when calls for participation are made by high-ranking officials, local defense relies mostly on local initiatives. The general public should be participating in its own defense. However, the goal of recruiting Americans by the millions to assist with homeland defense has not been accomplished. According to Amitai Etzioni (professor at George Washington University), the problem has been twofold: "The Citizen Corps has only two problems: its name and its size. The name means nothing. It could be about getting people to vote, serve on juries, or remember to renew their passports. For some reason, the obvious title—Homeland Protection Corps—has been avoided….Overall, the Citizen Corps has not caught the eye or imagination of the public and is largely unknown…." (Etzioni 2002, 9).

Nonetheless, since Professor Etzioni's opinion article was published, the Web site pages for the Citizen Corps have been revised and new features have appeared. A new "Ready" campaign has been launched and a host of free independent study courses have been posted. (Information about the courses can be found at: http://www.ready.gov/citizen-corpstraining/fema-independent-study-courses.) Moreover, materials about new partner and affiliate programs have been posted providing a clearer pathway for learning about the existence of various types of volunteer opportunities. (Links to 11 of these opportunities can be found at: http://www.ready.gov/volunteer.)

Many citizen law enforcement officers are already serving in unsung units of volunteer police throughout the United States. They are our neighbors, friends, and relatives. They may be bankers, construction workers, teachers, clerks, physicians, and from many other occupations. They fly aircraft and operate boats as part of their duties. They patrol the streets of our eastern cities, the open spaces of the West, and protect our natural resources.[2] Citizens perform law enforcement duties in many countries. There are volunteer citizen peace officers in Canada, Finland, Germany, Holland, Hong Kong, Russia, Israel, South Africa, Singapore, Switzerland, Malaysia, and the United Kingdom (England, Wales, Scotland and Northern Ireland) (Hoffman 2014).

The term "reserve" includes many types of law enforcement officers. Typically, reserve or auxiliary police officers receive their authority for law enforcement by virtue of common law, case law, or statute. They may be entirely volunteer (unpaid) or part-time salaried officers. They may work intermittently for several hours a month or for 40 hours a week for a few months of the year. A number of shore communities on the U.S. East Coast use seasonal peace officers or non-sworn security rangers who work during the summer months.[3] The important distinction between reserve and career law enforcement officers (also called "regular officers") is that the reserve or auxiliary officer's employment, if paid, is not the person's primary source of income; rather such officers (if paid) are usually compensated on a per diem basis. Moreover, these part-time officers are usually not provided with health insurance or pension benefits (Hoffman 2014).

The titles of citizen police officers are varied. Titles include: auxiliary, reserve, special, part-time, supernumerary, and seasonal. In many instances, reserves are not distinguished by any title. One example is the title of "constable." Constables serve in numerous localities throughout the United States. Many constables are not full-time employees and do not receive health benefits or pensions. In Pennsylvania, constables work on a fee basis (collect fees for serving eviction orders, etc.). Many police departments and sheriff offices use paid part-time officers, but there is no difference in the title from a career officer (Hoffman 2014).

## Special Constables in the United Kingdom

Citizen law enforcement officers were deployed long before the concept of modern policing took hold in the mid- to late nineteenth century. In these earlier times, such officers were known by a variety of titles, and they had an interesting array of duties and responsibilities. Depending on the era, all adult males were at one time required to keep the peace. For example, they raised a "hue and cry" when there was danger. "In the event of a crime, every man had to join in the 'hue and cry'—summoning aid and joining the pursuit of anyone who resisted arrest or escaped from custody" (Levy 1999, 136). One early group as far back as the tenth century in Britain was known as *constabulus* or count of the stable. Although at first they had a military role, their duties evolved into what today would be considered police duties. Some of these early police or "constables of the manor" were unpaid peace officers who were appointed by the manor court (i.e., selected by the local lord who owned the largest estate). They kept the king's peace, executed warrants, transported prisoners, removed "vagabonds," and set up procedures so that a "hue and cry" could be raised when necessary. Such procedures evolved into the use of villagers who acted as watchmen during the evening hours. Some of the more unpleasant duties of the manor constables were punishing lawbreakers (many were punished for not attending church!) by executing sentences such as dunking in the village pond and whipping. As Britain became more populated, the manor constable evolved into the parish constable. Manor constables as well as parish constables were unpaid peace officers. In addition, the parish constable worked with the justice of the peace (Hoffman 2014).

The unpaid parish constable still exists in Great Britain to this day. They are now called "special constables" and serve in all 43 police forces in Great Britain and Wales. The office of special constable has existed for more than 180 years, since the Special Constable Act of 1831. The act allowed the justice of the peace to "conscript men to combat riot and social unrest." This act was updated in 1914, 1923, and 1964. Special constables played an important role in protecting the public during the Blitz (bombing of Britain) during World War II. Many died in the line of duty (Hoffman 2014). The special constabulary is a voluntary body drawn mainly from the community served by each local force. Specials have full police powers and carry out a range of police work under the supervision and support of regular officers. Specials give a few hours of service each week, typically evenings and weekends. The specials have a key role in the reduction of crime and fear of crime and make a vital contribution to addressing local policing problems. They are volunteer police officers who work with regular police colleagues and other police staff, making an important contribution to the work of the wider police family.

Important new regulations for the special constables came into being in August 2012 and can be viewed at: http://www.legislation.gov.uk/uksi/2012/1961/contents/made. They amend the Special Constables Regulations of 1965 by inserting provisions about: the biometric vetting of candidates for appointment as special constables; the testing of special constables and candidates for substance misuse; and the notification and approval of business interests held by special constables, candidates, and their relatives. The new provisions are effectively identical to those applicable to regular police officers. In recent years, the number of special constables in England and Wales has increased. In 2012, there were more than 20,000 special constables in Home Office forces in England and Wales. This represented a 10.4% increase on the previous year's figures and an important indication of the value of special constables in supporting their regular colleagues in policing (College of Policing 2014).

## Overview of Police History in the United States

The history of regular policing in the United States can be roughly divided into four different periods based on the dominance of a particular strategy of policing. In 1805, New Orleans inaugurated a distinctive paramilitary model of policing, and this style was duplicated in "Deep South cities with large slave concentrations" (Rousey 1997, 4). During the first few decades of the nineteenth century, military style policing was in vogue in New Orleans, Richmond, Mobile, Savannah, and Charleston (Rousey 1997, 11–39). The southern military model can be said to represent the first era of modern policing. Rousey (1997, 39) concluded that the military style of policing was used in the South because "policemen who looked like soldiers probably helped ameliorate the deep anxieties many whites harbored about the dangers of slave crime and revolt." The second period consisted of the ending of the Deep South military model and the beginning of the adoption of a civil style of urban policing during the 1840s, continuing through the Progressive Period, and ending after the first third of the twentieth century.

The third period took place from the 1930s through the late 1970s. The years since the latter period comprise the fourth era. Kelling and Moore (1988) have referred to eras two, three, and four as: (1) the political era; (2) the reform era; and (3) the community problem solving or community policing era, respectively. The political era was so named because of the existence of close ties between police and politics. The reform era resulted in reaction to the first era. The reform era has now given way to a period emphasizing community policing strategies (Hartmann 1988).

## Office of the Sheriff

The position of sheriff evolved from the "shire-reeve" or headman of the shire, which means county. These officers worked primarily for the king serving "writs" (civil papers and warrants) and collecting tax. They were appointed by the king and, in many instances, it was a very lucrative occupation. Persons either bought or inherited the office of sheriff. They kept a portion of the taxes collected. They also were the direct representative of the king and wielded enormous power. They had very little to do with the day-to-day peacekeeping in the villages and towns. The sheriffs in early British history were viewed by the common people as "oppressors" rather than as "protectors." The sheriff could raise a posse under the common law concept known as *posse commitatus* or "power of the county" (not to be confused with the law in the United States entitled the Posse Commitatus Act of 1878, which generally prohibits the use of the military for direct enforcement of civilian law). The British common law allowed the sheriff to call on citizens to act as volunteer peace officers. They helped keep the peace in times of unrest and apprehended fleeing lawbreakers (Hoffman 2014). About "midway through the sixteenth century until the present time, the office of sheriff in England has had little political clout or government importance compared to the wealth of power that it once had during medieval times. The position of justice of the peace had relieved the last vestiges of the position's former judicial duties" (Buffardi 1998, 17).

The office of the sheriff is the oldest office under the system of common law in the United States and is an integral part of government in all states. In New York State, the office of sheriff is the oldest constitutional law enforcement officer of the county. In addition, the sheriff is charged with maintaining the peace in all municipalities, villages, and townships within his jurisdiction and the care and custody of persons pending court action. The sheriff also serves as the chief executive officer of the courts in some counties. The powers and the duties of the sheriff are embodied in the constitution of each state. There are more than 3,000 sheriffs in the United States who are elected officials; typically, the term of office is four years, and sheriffs are expected to be devoted to their duties full-time and to not hold any other public office. President Grover Cleveland began his political career as the sheriff of Erie County, New York, in 1871. He went on to become mayor of the city of Buffalo, governor of the state of New York, and then president (Erie County Sheriff's Office 2014).[4]

## Overview of Volunteer Police History in the United States

The history of volunteer policing may be divided into slightly more diverse periods than those provided for regular policing. The epochs have some degree of overlap. They include: (1) the lay justice period, consisting of the Native American military societies, the militia (including slave patrols), and the constable and watch systems of the colonial settlements, which extended up until the establishment of unified day and night watches in the 1840s; (2) the vigilant era, consisting of the detective societies and posses (including slave patrols) of the nineteenth century as well as the rise of a score of anti-vice societies during the last quarter of the nineteenth century; (3) the spy era (including operatives from the Anti-Saloon League and the American Protective League, as well as charity workers) during the Progressive Era and World War I; (4) the transformation era between 1920 and 1941 (when special purpose units evolved into general purpose police reserve units); and finally, (5) the assimilation era, when civil defense and other varieties of volunteer police became integrated parts of the community policing strategy of many police departments (Greenberg 2005).

The offices of constable and sheriff were imported to the United States during colonial times. In 1651, the colony of Virginia provided for the selection of a sheriff who could summon a posse. The American colonies also had constables. Most were volunteer peace officers appointed by village leaders. Like their British counterparts, they were responsible for keeping the peace and arresting lawbreakers who were then brought before the local justices of the peace. In 1634, in Plymouth, Massachusetts, the constables were responsible for weights and measures, land surveys, and announcing marriages. During the War of 1812, a Maryland posse arrested several British soldiers for disorderly conduct and placed them in the custody of the sheriff. The leader of the posse was captured by the British and imprisoned beneath the decks of a British warship. One of the negotiators for his release was Francis Scott Key. The first peace officer to be killed in the line of duty was Constable Darius Quimby of New York. Constable Quimby was gunned down in 1791 (Hoffman 2014).

As America expanded westward, so did the use of citizens for peace officer work. There were posses of volunteer peace officers that worked for the sheriff. They were per diem part-time deputies, constables, and marshals.

It was not unusual for a person to get a one-day appointment as a deputy sheriff, constable, or marshal to find a lawbreaker and bring him to justice. In the late 1800s, Theodore Roosevelt served as a part-time deputy sheriff. There were also special U.S. Deputy Marshals, appointed by the U.S. Marshal. Special deputy marshals worked for a pittance and sometimes for nothing to protect the citizens in the territories (which were not yet states) from roving bands of outlaws and to administer justice for the federal district courts. Some of these volunteers and part-time lawmen died in the line of duty (Hoffman 2014).

In the 1940s, during World War II, many communities across the United States created auxiliary police units for civil defense purposes (see Chapter 4). Some counties and municipalities authorized their auxiliary units to provide law enforcement services. This happened in those communities that had lost manpower to the military and that needed extra protection at strategic facilities. The 1950s, 1960s, and 1970s saw a growth in citizen law enforcement in the United States. Membership in volunteer police units reflected the composition of each jurisdiction's population. In America's segregated regions, even volunteer organizations formed for the public good reflected social and cultural biases (e.g., see photos of the two squads of Baltimore Auxiliary Police in Figures 1.2 and 1.3).

**Figure 1.2** In the city of Baltimore, the auxiliary police were first organized in 1941. However, integration within the Baltimore Police Department did not take place until 1966. Thus, two separate auxiliary police units were maintained for about 25 years. Photo, ca. 1960. (Photo used with permission of Retired Detective Ken Driscoll at BaltimoreCityPoliceHistory.com.)

**Figure 1.3** Baltimore Auxiliary Police segregated unit. Photo, ca. 1960. (Photo used with permission of Retired Detective Ken Driscoll at BaltimoreCityPoliceHistory.com.)

By the 1980s, the use of the "civil defense" banner was replaced by the title of "emergency management."[5] However, in the 1980s, there was a decline in the number of programs and volunteer officers due to economic, social, and political changes. After the events of September 11, 2001, there was, at least briefly, a renewed interest in volunteer law enforcement (Hoffman 2014). Although homeland security has become an important national topic and many people would like to become involved, the necessity of maintaining at least two streams of income from both husband and wife can impede participation. In order to encourage recruitment of public safety volunteers, the IACP has hosted a federally funded Web site that features the activities of many citizen law enforcement units. Registration at this site is entirely voluntary. The IACP plans to upgrade their online services in 2014.

The legal authority of citizen police widely varies inasmuch as there are thousands of law enforcement agencies in the United States (see Chapter 10). The training ranges from the same that career peace officers receive (which is usually four to seven months of full-time instruction) to a few hours per week. Some volunteer officers are armed and some are not. Some have the same law enforcement arrest powers as career peace officers; some have limited arrest powers (Hoffman 2014).

Volunteer police serve at all levels of government. However, those at the federal level tend to be in youth programs (such as Explorer posts), seasonal workers, or in such semi-military organizations as the Civil Air Patrol and the Coast Guard Auxiliary. At the local and county levels, volunteer officers are an established part of law enforcement. In recent years, the police agencies in Los Angeles, California; Phoenix, Arizona; and Dallas, Texas, have expanded their reserve programs. In some states, many local municipalities have only part-time police. In a few states, there are reserve state conservation and game enforcement officers as well as auxiliary state police and reserve highway patrol officers. There are even college and university reserve police. One example of reserve law enforcement at the federal level is the use of seasonal U.S. park rangers (Hoffman 2014).

Although the future of reserve law enforcement is unknown, across the nation and the globe, law enforcement agencies are using volunteers to supplement regular police services. Moreover, the need for citizen participation in the fight against terror and crime has increased.

## New Developments in Volunteer Policing

In April 2007, a two-day national firearm violence summit was held in Chicago. It was designed and sponsored by the IACP and the Joyce Foundation. The summit had 120 participants. An ad hoc advisory group composed of law enforcement, community health, and academic experts guided the planning and the preparation for the summit. The efforts of the attendees and advisory group led to the development of a comprehensive firearm violence reduction strategy. The final summit report presented a total of 39 recommendations, grouped into three major policy areas: keeping communities safe, preventing and solving gun crime, and keeping police officers safe. A summary of the report was published in *The Police Chief* magazine in April 2008. The report is entitled: "Taking a Stand: Reducing Gun Violence in Our Communities" (see IACP and Joyce Foundation 2008).

Recommendations 2, 3, and 4 of the final summit report are most appropriate for involving members of volunteer police units. Recommendation 2 states: "Law enforcement agencies and their partners should work to identify and implement effective education and prevention programs focused on youth at risk of gun violence" (see IACP and Joyce Foundation 2007, 11). The third recommendation states: "Law enforcement agencies and their partners should work to develop and implement education campaigns targeted at gun owners" (see IACP and Joyce Foundation 2007, 11). The fourth recommendation states: "Law enforcement leaders should devote resources and personnel to establishing and sustaining partnerships with community leaders to combat gun violence" (see IACP and Joyce Foundation 2007, 12). Together these three recommendations appear to represent a clear mandate for including qualified volunteer police in the delivery of a variety of educational programs to reduce the risk of gun violence.

The members of volunteer police units consist of thousands of citizen "partners" who have already made a major commitment in their lives to assist law enforcement and who stand ready to engage in further efforts to promote public safety.

Another important development is the new Commission on Accreditation for Law Enforcement Agencies, Inc. (CALEA) standards concerning the use of volunteer police. CALEA Standard 16.4.1 requires that agencies seeking the commission's national accreditation must have a written directive that establishes and describes the agency's auxiliary program, which includes a statement that auxiliaries are not sworn officers and a description of the duties of auxiliaries, including their role and scope in authority. Standard 16.4.3 states that "If auxiliaries wear uniforms, the uniforms clearly distinguish them from sworn officers." As part of the accreditation process, the CALEA standards also specify that every member of a volunteer or paid reserve force must complete the same training as a full-time certified police officer. Thus far, only 4% of the 18,000 non-federal law enforcement agencies in the United States have earned CALEA accreditation (Carder 2013). These standards are quite relevant to the future of volunteer policing because they demonstrate a distinction between the two major types of contemporary volunteer police: auxiliaries and reserves. Moreover, in several jurisdictions (Kansas City, Connecticut State Police, etc.), these particular new national training standards for police department accreditation have been used as the principal justifications for phasing out the use of existing volunteer police units. On the contrary, in addition to enlisting the services of volunteer police in antigun violence campaigns, police agencies seeking national accreditation and those interested in maintaining either type of volunteer police program should consider the programs proposed in Chapters 2, 11, and 12 of this book.

A third important development in the field of volunteer policing concerns the youth enrolled in Law Enforcement Explorer units. Since 1998, Explorer programs have been a cooperative venture with Learning for Life, an association affiliated with the Boy Scouts of America (BSA). Over the past few decades, hundreds of police agencies have established Explorer posts designed to give young men and women between the ages of 14 and 21, a chance to develop leadership skills and to learn about the wide range of law enforcement careers. In fact, according to John Anthony, national director of Learning for Life, there are more than 2,000 law enforcement posts across the country with 35,000 members (Steinhauer 2009). A new certification program exists for Law Enforcement Explorer posts. On a voluntary basis, each police agency or related organization now has an opportunity to have its Explorer basic or advance training programs recognized by the national office of the Explorer program (see Chapter 8 for more details). The new Explorer training standards are bound to promote a greater pool of qualified candidates for regular and volunteer police units.

Furthermore, these police candidates could also be tapped for assistance with antigun violence campaigns.

A fourth factor that is an encouraging development despite some very early criticism was the creation of the Citizen Corps itself. In January 2002, the president of the United States launched Citizen Corps to capture the spirit of service that emerged throughout our communities following the terrorist attacks of September 11, 2001. Citizen Corps was created to assist in coordinating volunteer activities to help communities better prepare to respond to any emergency situation. It provides opportunities for people to participate in a range of measures to make their families, their homes, and their communities safer from the threats of crime, terrorism, and disasters of all kinds. Citizen Corps is coordinated nationally by the Department of Homeland Security's Federal Emergency Management Agency. A few of its various initiatives have been indicated here.

In this day and age, there maybe a few reasons for not favoring the establishment and expansion of more volunteer police units. Perhaps the main one is that volunteers might replace regular full-time first responders. Police leadership can do much to dispel this type of fear. It is also critical that police officials in charge of their agencies and desirous of having effective volunteer police units know how to work with people, especially in groups (King 1960). With about 4,500 auxiliary police officers in New York City and perhaps as many as 200,000 or more nationwide, it is appropriate that qualified units of volunteer police play a significant role on behalf of homeland security and related concerns. Throughout this book, the term "volunteer police" is used to refer to authorized permanent groups that perform one or more police functions in an overt manner for little or no salary (Greenberg 2001).[6]

## Chapter Overviews

Chapter 2 addresses the present-day need for citizen mobilization to enhance public safety related to national security as well as local quality of life concerns. It includes materials about local and national organizations. Historical information about militia forces is discussed. At the national level, the roles of the Corporation for National and Community Service (CNCS) and the Federal Emergency Management Agency (FEMA) Corps are outlined.

Chapter 3 presents an overview of the early history of volunteer police involving such groups as Native American military societies; militia units; slave patrols; the watch and ward; the posse and anti-horse thief society members; vice-suppression societies; boy police; and early volunteer caseworkers. In addition, this chapter presents materials concerning the largest volunteer domestic spy organization in the nation's history—the American Protective League.

Chapter 4 examines seven different auxiliary and reserve volunteer police units. They have distinctive names, but a lack of consistency in the use of unit titles makes it difficult to ascribe specific characteristics to each category. Nevertheless, a trend appears to have developed with respect to the use of titles in certain parts of the United States, especially within several New England states and in California. The seven units discussed are: the Buffalo (New York) Police Reserve; Brentwood (California) Reserve Police; the Cheltenham Township (Pennsylvania) Auxiliary Police; the Los Angeles (California) Reserve Police; the New York City Auxiliary Police; the New York City Parks Mounted Auxiliary Unit; and the Albemarle County (Virginia) Auxiliary Police.

Chapter 5 reviews the origins of several state police agencies as well as events associated with the development of auxiliary or reserve state police units to supplement the strength of their parent organization. The agencies examined are those of Alabama, Arizona, Connecticut, Florida, New Hampshire, Ohio, South Carolina, and Vermont. In addition, the events associated with the sudden demise of one historic regional volunteer police group are presented. This happened in 2005, when the Pennsylvania House of Representatives voted 198–0 to repeal the charter of a 133-year-old volunteer police unit known as the "State Police of Crawford and Erie Counties." The unit was established by legislation passed in 1872. The initial law set up a volunteer force to arrest horse thieves during a time when the nearest organized police force was across the state in Philadelphia, hundreds of miles to the east. The group provided traffic and crowd control at community events in the two counties. In the year prior to its ending, the organization had 100 active members and provided more than 4,000 hours of volunteer service.

Chapter 6 highlights the following national (nonprofit) and federal organizations: the Metropolitan Police Reserve Corps, the Civil Air Patrol, the U.S. Power Squadrons, the U.S. Coast Guard Auxiliary, and the FEMA Reserves. In addition, a proposal to consider the establishment of a Border Patrol Auxiliary is considered. The chapter begins with background materials about the nature of the federal government and some historical aspects related to a federal role in public safety.

Chapter 7 describes the nature and purpose of a variety of non-sworn or non-peace officer roles and involvement in groups such as: chaplains; Citizens Assisting Pasadena Police (CAPP Patrol); equestrians; Community Response to Eradicate and Deter Identity Theft (CREDIT); Missing Persons Unit (MPU); Pawn Detail; Criminal Investigations Division's Victim Assistance; records and traffic sections; general volunteers; and the Youth Accountability Board. In addition, brief reviews of a variety of adult citizen police academy programs are presented as well as their advantages and disadvantages. Following this information, a new role is proposed for qualified members of volunteer police units to serve as "neighborhood police academy" instructors.

Chapter 8 focuses on the establishment of various prominent local youth programs: youth (junior) police academies; junior police programs (e.g., P.A.L., Explorers, and cadets); school safety patrols; police academy magnet schools; and youth courts. The origins and purposes of the various programs are described, and recommendations concerning future trends are discussed. One of the newest models for the delivery of police education and training for youth, the Police Orientation and Preparation Program (POPP), is reviewed. This chapter also addresses the topics of liability and insurance as well as youth protection from abuse. Reportedly, many law enforcement officers serving at the federal, state, county, and local levels have been motivated to undertake their careers due to their experiences as Explorers.

Chapter 9 also deals with the development and activities of youth involvement with law enforcement work but focuses on the national level. The following current federal law enforcement or military related youth initiatives are reviewed: Senior (college level) Reserve Officer Training Corps (ROTC) units; the Coast Guard's College Student Pre-commissioning Initiative (CSPI) program; Junior ROTC units; FEMA Corps; U.S. Navy Sea Cadets; and the Civil Air Patrol Cadet Program. The nature of the federal Law Enforcement Explorer Leadership academies and Explorer posts are examined. For historical perspective, the civilian military training camps of past generations are described. In addition, a few federal internship programs are reviewed.

Chapter 10 considers the wide range of legal rights and responsibilities associated with volunteer police work as well as a discussion regarding the nature, problems, and issues associated with the creation of police/citizen partnerships. In particular, the following topics are covered: the status and authority of volunteer police; sovereign immunity and the public duty doctrines; indemnification in claims of negligence; the Law Enforcement Officers Safety Act of 2004 (LEOSA); The Volunteer Protection Act; and the impact of CALEA standards on volunteer policing. Chapter 12 also continues the discussion of CALEA standards.

Chapter 11 considers the important role that volunteer police and other concerned individuals may play in the prevention of human trafficking and worker exploitation. Human trafficking is considered to be one of the fastest growing criminal industries in the world. This chapter indicates the various types of existing human slavery (contract, chattel, etc.) and describes a citizen's role in the prevention of human trafficking. In addition, the purposes of the Trafficking Victims Protection Act of 2000 and the definition for human trafficking established by the Palermo Protocol are provided.

Chapter 12 concludes the book's discussions regarding America's volunteer police by reviewing a few of the emerging trends for citizens willing to undertake the duties of part-time volunteer police. Several new roles for volunteer police are identified involving school safety, the protection of the homeless, and immigration issues. Qualified unit members should also be able to conduct a variety of school-based crime prevention educational programs such as Drug Abuse Resistance Education (D.A.R.E.), Gang Resistance Education and Training (G.R.E.A.T.), or antiviolence and bullying classes. They can also conduct workshops devoted to the prevention of carjacking and to how to respond in the event of active shooters. In addition, a new program is proposed with a focus on training college students to be fully certified reserve police officers in conjunction with their undergraduate studies.

## Summary

Volunteer police can serve many roles—for example, protecting against the illegal entry of terrorists, reducing highway fatalities, delivering antigun violence programs, curtailing human trafficking, enforcing quality of life statutes, and limiting the damages caused by the potential use of a weapon of mass destruction. With respect to national security and preparedness, the events of September 11, 2001, have led to new concerns about the relative responsibilities of individuals, localities, states, and the federal government to fund and implement protective and recovery programs. Ongoing threats relating to natural disasters require advance planning. The availability of cadres of CERT units and other types of volunteers is essential for aiding in the immediate aftermath of hurricanes, floods, and tornadoes.

The titles of citizen police officers are varied. They include auxiliary, reserve, special, part-time, supernumerary, and seasonal. In the United Kingdom, the volunteer police are known as "special constables." Important new rules governing the appointment of special constables have been established, and these are effectively identical to those applicable to regular police officers. There are about 20,000 specials performing routine patrol duties alongside regular constables in the United Kingdom. In the United States, the terms "reserves" or "auxiliaries" refer to citizen volunteer police officers. They became prominent when organized into various units during World War I and World War II, although unpaid "posse" members had been recruited in frontier towns during the nineteenth century. The offices of constable and sheriff were imported to the United States during colonial times. In the United States, the modern position of sheriff is an adaptation of the earlier role of the shire-reeve or sheriff in the United Kingdom. Sheriffs are still authorized to summon "the power of the county" (i.e., those able-bodied people who may be needed in times of distress).

The history of volunteer police can be divided into five epochs having some degree of overlap, including from earliest to latest: the lay justice period featuring the Native American military societies, the militia, and so forth; the vigilant era consisting of the detective societies and posses; the spy era during the Progressive Era and World War I; the transformation era between 1920 and 1941; and the assimilation era when civil defense and other varieties of volunteer police become an integrated part of the community policing strategy of many police departments. Volunteer police serve at all levels of government. However, those at the federal level tend to serve in youth programs, such as Explorer posts, or in such semi-military organizations as the Civil Air Patrol and the Coast Guard Auxiliary. There are also an interesting range of seasonal positions at the federal level.

There have been several important developments in the field of volunteer policing in recent years. The first has to do with new opportunities for volunteer police to participate as coequals with regular police in the initiation and delivery of antigun violence programs. This can be inferred from several recommendations found in the report prepared by the IACP and the Joyce Foundation. However, whether this will take place in any community is at the discretion of police administrators. A second opportunity is presented by the new CALEA standards concerning the use of volunteer police. These standards can be used to upgrade the training of volunteer police, and they can also serve as a catalyst for police agencies to assign new responsibilities to members of their volunteer police units. However, several agencies have thus far demonstrated an unwillingness to take this opportunity to enhance their sworn volunteer programs and have instead opted to eliminate them on fiscal grounds. Third, a new national certification program has been instituted to recognize those Law Enforcement Explorer programs that are adhering to specific guidelines with respect to their basic or advance training programs.

## Review Questions

1. Identify at least four activities that citizens can undertake to assist in the improvement of public safety.
2. Search online for recent articles concerning al-Qaeda. State your findings.
3. Distinguish between volunteer reserve and career law enforcement officers.
4. Indicate several highlights regarding the history of volunteer policing.
5. Discuss the evolution of the position of sheriff in the United Kingdom.
6. Search online to find any examples of volunteer police being used for the activities you identified in response to question one. Present your findings.
7. Contrast the historical periods associated with the development of volunteer policing with those of regular policing.
8. Important new rules governing the appointment of special constables have been established in the United Kingdom. What is the nature or purpose of these rules?

9. State the author's definition of volunteer police. Is it appropriate? Discuss.
10. Search the Citizen Corps Web page (at: http://www.ready.gov/volunteer). Use the links at this Web page to browse various homeland defense volunteer opportunities and discuss at least two programs that caught your attention.

## Notes

1. There are more than 2,200 official CERT programs registered at: http://www.citizencorps.fema.gov/cc/CertRegWizard.do. "The Community Emergency Response Team (CERT) Program educates people about disaster preparedness for hazards that may impact their area and trains them in basic disaster response skills, such as fire safety, light search and rescue, team organization, and disaster medical operations. Using the training learned in the classroom and during exercises, CERT members can assist others in their neighborhood or workplace following an event when professional responders are not immediately available to help. CERT members also are encouraged to support emergency response agencies by taking a more active role in emergency preparedness projects in their community" (CERT 2014).
2. In 1981, the U.S. Congress authorized the Natural Resources Conservation Service (NRCS), formerly the Soil Conservation Service, to accept volunteers aged 14 and above to increase soil and water conservation efforts and to do this by working closely with Soil and Water Conservation Districts. Referred to as the "Earth Team," volunteers work side by side with professionals from NRCS, helping to protect and conserve the Earth's natural resources. A list of the types of jobs volunteers do is located at: http://www.nrcs.usda.gov/wps/portal/nrcs/main/sc/people/volunteers/
3. For example, the New York State Park Police hire seasonal State Park and Recreation Public Safety Rangers (PSR). PSRs provide general public safety services throughout the state in support of the state park police. This is a seasonal-only position, generally from late May to Labor Day. PSRs are subject to the provisions of the Security Guard Act of 1993, are unarmed, and have neither peace nor police officer status. PSRs are assigned to patrol park facilities and grounds, maintain order, enforce park ordinances/regulations, and answer questions from park patrons. On a situational basis, incumbents may also assist with search and rescue operations and marine patrol. For more information, go to: http://nysparks.com/employment/park-police/default.aspx
4. An interesting U.S. Supreme Court Case involving whether a county sheriff is representing the state or the county when he acts in a law enforcement capacity was decided in *McMillian v. Monroe County*, AL, 520 U.S. 781 (1997). Petitioner McMillian sued Monroe County, AL, under 42 U.S.C. § 1983 for allegedly unconstitutional actions taken by the Monroe County sheriff. If the sheriff's actions constituted county "policy," then the county is liable for them. The parties agreed that the sheriff is a "policymaker" for § 1983 purposes, but

they disagreed about whether he is a policymaker for Monroe County or for the state of Alabama. In affirming the Court of Appeals for the Eleventh Circuit's dismissal of petitioner's § 1983 claims against Monroe County, the court held as to the actions involved in this case that the sheriff represented the state of Alabama and is therefore not a county policymaker. An important factor in the court's decision was the fact that the Alabama's Constitution, adopted in 1901, states that "the executive department shall consist of a governor, lieutenant governor, attorney general, state auditor, secretary of state, state treasurer, superintendent of education, commissioner of agriculture and industries, and a sheriff for each county" (Article V, Section 12, 520 U.S. 787). Moreover, the Alabama Supreme Court had already declared "unequivocally that sheriffs are state officers, and that tort claims brought against sheriffs based on their officials [sic] acts therefore constitute suits against the State, not suits against the sheriff's county" (520 U.S. 789). The court also used a historical analysis in coming to its conclusion. Chief Justice Rehnquist declared: "[The] petitioner's disagreement with the concept that 'county sheriffs' may actually be state officials is simply a disagreement with the ancient understanding of what it has meant to be a sheriff" (520 U.S. 795). The *McMillian* decision involved a 5–4 vote with Justices Stevens, Souter, Ginsburg, and Breyer dissenting.

5. The most significant and earliest instance of federal involvement in disaster relief occurred in 1803 when a series of fires swept through the port city of Portsmouth, NH. In response to the disaster, Congress passed legislation that provided relief for Portsmouth merchants, the Congressional Act of 1803. In the decades to follow, until the middle of the twentieth century, Congress dealt with each new disaster with special legislation adopted on a case-by-case basis. During the 1930s, the federal government incorporated disaster relief as part of its wide-reaching legislation to rebuild the U.S. economy. By the middle of the decade, laws were in place that provided federal funds for the reconstruction of public facilities, highways, and bridges damaged by natural disasters. During the 1950s, emergency management was dominated by wartime civil defense activities that the government believed would prepare the nation for a possible nuclear attack. A series of massive hurricanes and earthquakes during the 1960s and early 1970s served to focus public attention on natural disaster relief. In 1974, the Disaster Relief Act was enacted, establishing a process for presidential declarations of national disasters (Origins 2014).

Despite these changes, emergency and disaster activities remained fragmented. More than 100 federal agencies were involved in some aspect of these efforts, while state and local governments had many parallel programs and policies. The need to centralize federal emergency functions was made even more acute by the much publicized Three Mile Island nuclear power plant accident in 1978. In 1979, President Jimmy Carter signed an executive order to create FEMA. FEMA absorbed a host of disaster-related agencies, including the Federal Insurance Administration, the National Fire Prevention and Control Administration, the National Weather Service Community Preparedness Program, and the Federal Disaster Assistance Administration. It also assumed responsibility for civil defense (Origins 2014). Hence, the civil defense banner gave way to the new umbrella branding provided by the phrase: "emergency management."

In March 2003, FEMA joined 22 other federal agencies, programs, and offices in becoming the U.S. Department of Homeland Security. The new department brought a coordinated approach to national security from emergencies and disasters—natural and manmade. In 2006, President George W. Bush signed into law the Post-Katrina Emergency Reform Act. The act significantly reorganized FEMA, providing it with substantial new authority to remedy gaps that became apparent in the response to Hurricane Katrina in August 2005, the most devastating natural disaster in U.S. history, and included a more robust preparedness mission for FEMA (FEMA 2014).

6. This definition is not as robust as the one the author used in a previous work, but it is offered here for the sake of brevity. In the longer version, volunteer police are defined as: "Individuals who are members of a permanent organization (or one established during wartime mobilization) authorized by either governmental or societal action for the purpose of performing one or more functions of policing in an overt manner (i.e., functions that go beyond surveillance or communications work) for minimal or no salary" (Greenberg 2005, 14).

# References

Buffardi, H. S. (1998). History of the office of the sheriff. Retrieved January 27, 2014 from http://www.co.ulster.ny.us/sheriff/admin/history/toc.htm

Byman, D. L. (2011). The history of al Qaeda. Retrieved January 26, 2014 from http://www.brookings.edu/research/opinions/2011/09/01-al-qaeda-history-byman

Carder, D. (2013, October 30). Police disband reserve force. Retrieved June 22, 2014 from http://ottawaherald.com/news/103113reserve

CERT. (2014). Community Emergency Response Teams. Retrieved January 26, 2014 from http://www.fema.gov/community-emergency-response-teams

College of Policing. (2014). Special Constabulary. Retrieved January 26, 2014 from http://www.college.police.uk/en/10040.htm

Erie County Sheriff's Office. (2014). History. Retrieved January 27, 2014 from http://www2.erie.gov/sheriff/index.php?q = history

Etzioni, A. (2002, July 25). Mobilize America's foot soldiers. *The Christian Science Monitor*, p. 9.

FEMA. (2014). About the agency: History. Retrieved January 28, 2014 from http://www.fema.gov/about-agency

Greenberg, M. A. (2005). *Citizens defending America: From colonial times to the age of terrorism*. Pittsburgh, PA: University of Pittsburgh Press.

Greenberg, M. A. (2001). *The evolution of volunteer police in America*. Ph.D. diss., City University of New York/John day College of Criminal Justice.

Hartmann, F. X. (1988). *Debating the evolution of American policing* (Perspectives on Policing, No. 5). Washington, DC: U.S. Government Printing Office.

Hoffman, E. (2014). A history of reserve law enforcement. Retrieved January 26, 2014 from http://www.reservepolice.org/History_of_Reserves.htm

IACP and Joyce Foundation. (2008). IACP and Joyce Foundation summit and report: Taking a stand: Reducing gun violence in our communities. *The Police Chief*, 75(4), 26–34.

IACP and Joyce Foundation. (2007). Taking a stand: Reducing gun violence in our communities; A report from the International Association of Chiefs of Police 2007 Great Lakes Summit on Gun Violence. Retrieved June 22, 2014 from http://research.policyarchive.org/96387.pdf

Kelling, G., and Moore, M. (1988). *The evolving strategy of policing* (Perspectives on Policing, No. 4). Washington, DC: National Institute of Justice and Harvard University.

King, E. M. (1960). *The auxiliary police unit*. Springfield, IL: Charles C. Thomas.

Levy, L. W. (1999). *Origins of the bill of rights*. New Haven, CT: Yale University Press.

Origins. (2014). Origins of U.S. emergency management. Retrieved January 28, 2014 from http://online.annamaria.edu/emergencymanagementhistory.asp

Rousey, D. C. (1997). *Policing the southern city: New Orleans, 1805–1889*. Baton Rouge, LA: Louisiana State University Press.

Ruecker, R. C. (2008). President's message: The need to take a stand against gun violence. *The Police Chief, 75*(4), 6.

Steinhauer, J. (2009, May 14). Scouts train to fight terrorists, and more. *New York Times*, p. A1.

# Mobilizing for Security  2

The ordinary, loyal, and decent citizens are themselves a priceless asset in combating terrorism if only they can be mobilized to help the government and security forces.
—**Paul Wilkinson**
*(1986, 25)*

We live in an age where catastrophic events often seem to be inevitable. As if worldwide wars of aggression and episodes of massive genocides were not enough during the twentieth century, the twenty-first century has already witnessed a wide range of manmade disasters because of terrorist actions. In addition, scores of floods, tsunamis, tornadoes, and other climatic events have produced mass casualties. In the United States, many disasters and mass casualty events are generally handled at the local level. At such times, the first few hours of response by the affected community will be critical. In brief, communities must look to themselves and adjoining communities for survival assistance. The formal agencies of response will be needed as well as those at the "grassroots" level. The latter consists of "community groups, such as civic organizations, religious groups, Boy/Girl Scout troops, and high school sport teams, among others. These groups provide ... social support for participation in the planning and response effort that will help individuals stay engaged over time, even during times of perceived 'low risk' when apathy about preparedness can become pervasive" (Joint Commission 2005, v).

It is a human desire to want to be safe and feel secure in everyday activities. In the United States, such a sense of security also includes being safe from the fear of arbitrary government intrusion or the intrusion of others. Under the U.S. system of justice, the police are the guardians of not only our safety but also our freedom. Today, most Americans feel it is altogether appropriate to rely on police agencies and their full-time sworn officers to effectively deal with any wrongdoers within the parameters set out by the criminal justice system. Americans trust that the police will be able to enforce the law and at the same time be respectful of the rights of the accused.

Fire departments have long depended on volunteers to accomplish their missions, but the duties and capacities of volunteer police are not generally known. However, since the end of World War II, the use of unpaid volunteers in sworn or non-sworn capacities has become standard practice in many police departments, including those in New York City, Washington, DC, Detroit,[1] and Los Angeles. This chapter explores why such volunteers are needed to enhance public safety for national security as well as for local quality of life concerns. It includes materials about local and national organizations. At the national level, the roles of the Corporation for National and Community Service, the Civil Air Patrol (CAP), and the Coast Guard are briefly considered. Greater details about federal and volunteer police relationships are presented in Chapter 6.

## Militia

The U.S. Army traces the military organization we know today as the National Guard to a declaration made on December 13, 1636. On this date, the Massachusetts General Court in Salem, for the first time in the history of the North American continent, established that all able-bodied men between the ages of 16 and 60 were required to join the militia. The North, South, and East Regiments were established (Boehm 2012).

Every American colony except Pennsylvania organized a militia system during the seventeenth century. Generally, militia companies consisted of all free adult white males. Militia members were required to provide their own weapons, to keep them in good order, and to attend regular drills. The power to muster militia units was given to local militia officers because "the threat of surprise attack and the isolation of many localities made that power essential" (Cress 1982, 4). Militia officers were either elected by militia members, local assemblies or officials, and/or appointed by the colonial governor. By the middle of the eighteenth century, the militia had ceased to be a viable citizen army that could be mustered for frontier defense or other military requirements. According to Cress (1982, 7), "instead of a citizen army, colonists relied on special fighting forces manned by draftees and volunteers and officered by British regulars or American colonists holding commissions outside the militia establishment." However, in the North, the militia registry was used for the purpose of organizing night watch duty among community members (Cress 1982). During times of public disorder, units of the militia were called upon. In the North and the South, the militia was used to maintain the institution of slavery (Cress 1982).

In South Carolina, the repression of African Americans was codified between 1690 and 1740. These codes restricted almost all aspects of life including freedom of movement, religious worship, and work habits. They were enforced by the sheriff, the constable, and the slave patrol (Henderson 1976). For a complete review of the topic of slave patrols, Sally Hadden's book entitled *Slave Patrols: Law and Violence in Virginia and the Carolinas* (Harvard University Press 2001) is recommended.

Militia members not only helped to fill the ranks of the night watch and slave patrols but militia membership also provided a sense of affiliation and identification with one's settlement, town, and county. In general, this was of critical importance not only for general peacekeeping but also for survival. However, in the indigenous region (backcountry) of South Carolina, the lack of sufficient means for mobilization or even a court system contributed to the rise of a vigilante organization known as the "Regulators." In the mid-1700s, due to wilderness conditions, an area that was only 30–40 miles away from a population center—such as Charleston—was referred to as the backcountry. The Regulators were "a group of law-abiding citizens who organized patrols and tried members of criminal bands and others deemed to have committed crimes" (Johnson and Wolfe 1996, 121). In 1769, with the passage of the Circuit Court Act, the Regulator movement faded into history (Regulators 2014). There was also a "Regulator" movement in North Carolina that tried to effect governmental changes in the 1760s due to the abuse of local officials. After the American colonies obtained independence, various national militia laws were adopted—the first in 1792. The greatest reforms took place in 1903 and 1908. These laws repealed the Militia Act of 1792 and divided the militia into two groups: the Reserve Militia, defined as all able-bodied men between 18 and 45, and the Organized Militia, defined as state units receiving federal support. The latter became the National Guard of today (Donnelly 2001). Additional materials about the history of the militia and vigilantes are presented in Chapter 3.

Slavery divided the nation until the conclusion of the Civil War. But it was replaced by Jim Crow laws that fostered segregation and second class citizenship for black Americans that continued until new national civil rights laws were enforced. "Jim Crow was the name of the racial caste system which operated primarily, but not exclusively in southern and border states, between 1877 and the mid-1960s. Jim Crow was more than a series of rigid anti-black laws. It was a way of life. Under Jim Crow, African Americans were relegated to the status of second class citizens. Jim Crow represented the legitimization of anti-black racism" (Pilgrim 2012). In 1896, the U.S. Supreme Court affirmed a segregation law in Louisiana in the case of *Plessy v. Ferguson*. "Plessy gave Jim Crow states a legal way to ignore their constitutional obligations to their black citizens" (Pilgrim 2012). The *Plessy* decision set the precedent that "separate" facilities for blacks and whites were constitutional as long as they were "equal." The "separate but equal" doctrine was quickly extended to cover many areas of public life, such as restaurants, theaters, restrooms, and public schools. The doctrine was a fiction because facilities for blacks were always inferior to those for whites. Not until 1954, in the equally important Supreme Court decision of *Brown v. Board of Education of Topeka*, would the "separate but equal" doctrine be struck down.

## Civil Defense

During World War II, the most ubiquitous form of volunteer police were the members of various civilian defense units. For example, volunteers in the War Emergency Radio Service were able to transform the basic automobile radio of that era into a shortwave War Emergency Radio Service set, permitting the auxiliary police communications officers to maintain constant two-way contact with their control centers. Thousands of volunteers also served in the Air Raid Protective Service and the Auxiliary Police Service. The members of these services played a unique role in guarding the various points where saboteurs might hope to operate, especially around gas tanks, power houses, telephone exchanges, and water works.

Although the end of World War II was greeted with spontaneous celebrations, especially after the defeat of Nazi Germany, America's reliance on atomic weaponry to end the war with Japan was to cast a mushroom cloud over all Americans and the rest of the world. As a result of the Cold War, American citizens had to face the fact that any hope of survival would be dependent upon some degree of luck and their own survival skills and degree of preparations. In case of nuclear attack, many Americans would not only become targets but also combatants. It was the Federal Civil Defense Administration's job to encourage citizens to adapt to their nuclear present and future. Many of the same types of civilian defense services established during World War II were resurrected for this new era.

Since 1959, during the time of the Cold War, there has been an auxiliary police force in Oshkosh, Wisconsin (see Figure 2.1). It began as an auxiliary police/civil defense organization to assist the Oshkosh Police Department at all public functions involving large numbers of people, as well as to assist in

**Figure 2.1** The Oshkosh (Wisconsin) Auxiliary Police Color Guard was established in May 2000. Color Guard unit coordinator Auxiliary Captain Scott Footit appears at the far left. Various services are provided by the auxiliary police. For example, during the school year, they deploy a radar speed trailer at school zones throughout Oshkosh. The first class of recruits graduated from their academy in April 1959. There are currently 40 members in the volunteer police force, and there have been more than 380 auxiliary officers in the group. Nine members have become police officers in the Oshkosh Police Department. (Courtesy of the Oshkosh Auxiliary Police, Wisconsin and used with permission.)

any disasters or emergency situations within the city. The primary function at that time was a civil defense role. During the 1960s—at the height of the Cold War era, unit membership was as high as 70–80 members. All association with the civil defense function was eliminated in the 1970s as the auxiliary police organization's role evolved (Oshkosh Auxiliary Police 2011).

Today, a sudden and potentially devastating incident may arise due to terrorist actions. During World War I and World War II, and during the era of the Cold War (about 1947 to 1991), Americans were also beset by threats to homeland security. These concerns became even weightier after the Soviets acquired atomic capabilities in 1949. The fears expressed since 1945—that the next war might result in the end of civilization—seemed to be coming closer to reality. This new threat ushered in the Cold War and the reinstitution of civil defense planning efforts. Posters and pamphlets advocated parental readiness, and children were taught to "duck and cover" by the cartoon character Bert the Turtle (as seen in Figure 2.2).

In 1956, a 16-minute film produced by the Radio-Keith-Orpheum (RKO) Corporation for the Federal Civil Defense Administration (FCDA) highlighted the main threat to American safety and security during the Cold War—nuclear attack. The film discusses how the United States was built on the spirit of neighborliness and cooperation. The narrator explains that cooperation is required for survival of a nuclear attack and the key to survival is to be organized through civil defense. The film provides a brief view of the National Civil Defense Administration, headquartered in Battle Creek, Michigan, and then explores the volunteer work that has to be done at the local level to accomplish the goals of civil defense. In this film, the Berks County Civil Defense unit (which includes the city of Reading, Pennsylvania) is presented as a model program for other communities. In the aftermath of an attack, armed auxiliary police officers would maintain order.

**Figure 2.2** "Bert the Turtle" illustration from 1951 pamphlet published by the U.S. Federal Civil Defense Administration.

"The people of Reading work together in a remarkable display of patriotism, public spirit, community pride, personal responsibility, and mutual assistance" (Oakes 1995, 4). The film is entitled *Alert Today—Alive Tomorrow*. A 9-minute clip from this film is available online at: http://www.youtube.com/watch?v=c3ZnNsVyWMA.

## Quality of Life Matters

The threat of nuclear attack has greatly diminished since the collapse of the Soviet Union in 1991. Today, many law enforcement agencies are facing a variety of new responsibilities relating to gun violence, human trafficking, cybercrimes, homeland security, domestic abuse, and immigration enforcement. Moreover, the public is expecting excellence in all areas of service, including public nuisances. The term "quality of life offenses" is generally used to describe conduct that demoralizes community residents and business people because it involves acts that create physical disorder (e.g., graffiti or vandalism) or that reflect social decay (e.g., prostitution). These behaviors may be merely minor annoyances to some people, but they can be major problems for the community. These acts may also be accompanied by nuisances that affect the community's health and safety, such as noise and public urination. Although they are generally not serious enough to result in felony charges or to be the focus of large-scale enforcement operations, these misdemeanors and violations cause a great deal of misery to community residents. Such offenders need to be held accountable, but it is also important to offer them the assistance they need to avoid further criminal conduct.

As a response, police patrols have been directed toward many quality of life matters, such as prostitution and vandalism, and less than 15% of police time is being devoted to more serious law enforcement initiatives (Manning 1995). For example, in 2013, Jeffrey Blackwell was appointed chief of police in Cincinnati, Ohio. (Blackwell had been the deputy chief of police in Columbus and had 26 years of service experience.) His main concerns were to reduce crime and the fear of crime. Based on the findings of the community-oriented policing model, he announced plans to focus on quality of life issues, such as lighting in alleys, abandoned needles, graffiti, trash, loud noise, and teenage problems (Smith 2013). Police Chief Blackwell pointed out that police "have to get to know folks in their community by name—and not just the bad ones" (Smith 2013). Quality of life concerns the public, and members of the public are needed to relate information to the police about suspicious behavior.

Using volunteers to help supplement sworn staff is a possible way for law enforcement agencies to continue to enhance the safety of the community when police agencies are losing manpower. Community safety is promoted by having additional resources available to contend with quality of life matters, to increase the efficiency of sworn personnel, and to strengthen linkages between citizens and police. The North Miami Beach Police Department Neighborhood Services and Inspections (NSI) unit has taken volunteerism to a new level by using police recruits from local academies to volunteer their time to gain experience in the field. The NSI Community Policing Cadet Program allows "these cadets [to] patrol the city for quality of life issues, offering a valuable service—providing free services to the agency" (Alqadi 2011). Subsequently, in May 2012, Detroit's police chief announced an "Enhanced Police Reserve Program." The program made it a requirement that any person who applies to become a Detroit police officer must first serve as an active reservist. At the time, Police Chief Ralph Godbee said the department had about 240 reserve officers, but the goal was to recruit 200–250 more (Hackney 2012).[1]

In a paper concerning the design of a restorative community justice model, Bonnie Bucqueroux (2004) presents a three-phase plan. The first phase involves the synthesis of the diverse reform pieces of the existing justice systems. The second requires the branches and agencies within the justice apparatus to transform themselves by becoming learning labs or organizations, willing to change their nature from "an expert, command-and-control model to participatory management where managers act as coaches who nurture a climate that promotes innovation" (Bucqueroux 2004). The third phase focuses on the community "so that they become full partners in the process of merging formal and informal social control into a unified, community-based approach. Agencies and organizations also need to embrace the model of collaboration, open communication, and participatory management that they want communities to mirror" (Bucqueroux 2004). The third phase calls for the engagement of community participants in order that America's rate of incarceration (the highest in the world) and its crime rates can be reduced. The full utilization of the energies and talents of the American populous should be employed by the agencies of the justice system. For many years, this resource has been neglected, and communities continue to suffer. Box 2.1 reveals an episode of such neglect, but it also indicates how it might be overcome.

## Volunteer Police Mobilization at the Local Level

Fortunately, since the end of World War I, the use of unpaid volunteers in sworn or non-sworn capacities has become standard practice in many police departments, including those in New York City; Washington, DC; Detroit; and Los Angeles. However, greater participation is still needed. The resources for planning and responding to natural disasters, potential terrorist attacks, and quality of life matters can be greatly enhanced through the recruitment,

## BOX 2.1   A REALITY CHECK

The importance of involving the community in all phases of decision making cannot be overstated. I well remember the time a community resident, let's call her "Mary," stopped a meeting with local police dead in its tracks. "I have been coming to these meetings for months now. And I appreciate all your hard work. But I still see the same problem outside my window each day at noon." What Mary saw each day during the summer was a 12-year-old prostitute plying her trade.

The young girl would ride her bike in a circle in the intersection of the quiet residential neighborhood where Mary had lived for many decades. The girl's adult male pimp would sit on the curb, waiting to negotiate with customers. Mary would watch businessmen come by during their lunch hour. They would pay the girl's pimp, the girl would climb into the man's car, from which she would emerge a few minutes later. Mary often called police, but even when patrol cars arrived quickly, the girl and her pimp would always spot them coming and disappear.

Not only did Mary's story underscore the importance of dealing with the community's priorities, it also reminds us that the system alone can never have all the answers. Police, prosecutors, and courts can play a role in arresting and prosecuting the girl's pimp. Clearly, she and her family also need professional interventions and services. But there are important roles that the community can play in saving at-risk kids. This can mean recruiting neighborhood residents into a community patrol that can intervene when the girl and her pimp show up, with the police as protector. Saving kids one by one could also mean finding new ways for women in the community to play the role of formal and informal advisors and mentors, again with the system playing a role in setting up opportunities for old and young to form supportive relationships.

Engaging the community is not just a nice thing to do, it is the most effective way of addressing the underlying conditions that allow problems like child prostitution to persist. Given sufficient structure, support, and funding, our communities can function as learning labs, a place where professionals and community residents can work together to make the most of collaborative strategies.

*Source:* Bucqueroux, B., 2004, Restorative community justice: A comprehensive approach to reducing crime and violence in our culture. Available at: http://www.policing.com/articles/rcj.html. With permission.

selection, and training of qualified volunteer police. Opportunities currently exist and should be made more widely available to permit auxiliary and reserve volunteer police to perform a wide range of quality of life crime prevention and enforcement activities.

In a number of jurisdictions, auxiliary police are not authorized or trained to conduct quality of life enforcement duties or are not even able to issue summonses for parking violations. For example, New York City auxiliary police officers may only engage in traffic control, beat patrols, and provide security at public events. A few youthful auxiliaries may work in plainclothes under direct supervision of vice enforcement or precinct conditions unit supervisors. They are trained to attempt to purchase alcohol, box cutters, and other items that are not permitted to be displayed or sold to minors in licensed premises. Such undercover operations take place at restaurants, bars, and liquor and grocery stores based on community complaints. Relevant summonses are issued by borough vice and precinct conditions units using such auxiliary police (Kelly et al. 2008). Clearly, deciding to add responsibilities for volunteers requires imagination on the part of police leadership. However, this is a characteristic that Drucker (1990) warns can become suppressed in volunteer organizations.

On the contrary, due to shrinking budgets, various police officials have found that volunteers are indispensable in dealing with low-level offenses because they allow their full-time sworn officers to focus on more pressing crimes and more violent criminals. For example, Fresno's police chief, Jerry Dyer, whose department has lost more than 300 employees in recent years, has stated: "We had the option to either stop handling those calls or do it in a different manner … I've always operated under the premise of no risk, no success. And in this instance, I felt we really didn't have very much to lose" (McKinley 2011). The Fresno, California, volunteers handle nonviolent crimes such as petty theft, stolen vehicles, and vandalism that is not gang-related.

Other chiefs facing budget problems are also using volunteers. In Mesa, Arizona, a Phoenix suburb, 10 volunteers have been trained to process crime scenes, dust for fingerprints, and even swab for DNA. In addition, volunteers supplement Mesa's sworn police force by on-scene processing of subjects who have been arrested for drunk driving. This processing includes fingerprinting and photographing the suspect and taking blood and urine samples. Volunteers work out of a specially equipped van, which responds to the location of the arrest for the processing. Program supervisor Sgt. Bill Peters stated: "I only have eight police officers for DUIs in a city of 440,000 people. If it weren't for the volunteers, I'd have to pull officers off the road to do the things the volunteers do. The volunteers are just as responsible as officers in keeping citizens safe from drunk drivers" (Worton 2003, 13). In Pasadena, California, a team of retirees is working to reduce identity theft. According to

Officer Celestine Ratliff, the volunteer liaison for the Charlotte-Mecklenburg Police Department in North Carolina, "citizens are more receptive to our volunteers than to our officers" (McKinley 2011).

## Volunteer Police Mobilization at the National Level

In addition, volunteers are also needed to perform important law enforcement–related functions at the federal level. For example, the U.S. Coast Guard lacks the personnel and resources to fill critical gaps in its safety and security missions without help from its volunteer arm, the Coast Guard Auxiliary. It is for this reason that Homeland Security and Coast Guard leaders have become dependent on the Auxiliary to achieve a number of Coast Guard missions, a reliance that has become more tenuous because Auxiliary membership has dropped about 21% since 2003 to the current 28,635. This trend is in sharp contrast to membership trends in other large volunteer groups in the United States. For example, Dooris (2008) indicated that Coast Guard Auxiliary membership is declining even though membership in the CAP is rising.

Notwithstanding the decrease in enrollments in the Coast Guard Auxiliary, Americans are volunteering at record numbers; although there has been a moderate decline since 2005 (Dooris 2008). In 2011, an estimated 64.3 million Americans (more than one in four adults) volunteered through a formal organization, an increase of 1.5 million from 2010. The 7.9 billion hours these individuals volunteered is valued at $171 billion. Among citizens who volunteered through an organization, the top activities included fundraising or selling items to raise money (26.2%); collecting, preparing, distributing, or serving food (23.6%); engaging in general labor or transportation (20.3%); or tutoring or teaching (18.2%) (Volunteering 2013).

At one time, America's leading national civilian voluntary program was the Civilian Conservation Corps (locations of work camps are indicated in Figure 2.3). Formed in March 1933, the Civilian Conservation Corps (CCC) was one of the first New Deal programs. It was a public works project intended to promote environmental conservation and to build good citizens through vigorous, disciplined outdoor labor. President Franklin Roosevelt believed that this civilian "tree army" would relieve the rural unemployed and keep youth "off the city street corners." The CCC operated under the supervision of the U.S. Army. Camp commanders had disciplinary powers, and corpsmen were required to address superiors as "sir." By September 1935, more than 500,000 young men had lived in CCC camps, most staying from six months to a year. In all, nearly 3 million young men participated in the CCC (Foner and Garraty 1991).

Today, individuals aged 14 and above can still volunteer for conservation purposes. Volunteer positions are available within the Natural Resources

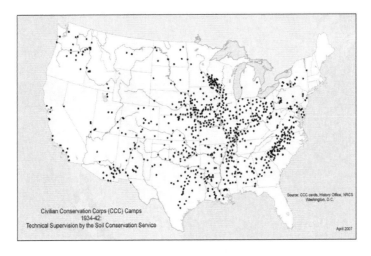

Civilian Conservation Corps (CCC) Camps
1934-42
Technical Supervision by the Soil Conservation Service

Source: CCC cards, History Office, NRCS
Washington, D.C.

April 2007

**Figure 2.3** Location of Civilian Conservation Corps Camps, 1934–1942.

Conservation Service (NRCS), a division of the U.S. Department of Agriculture. NRCS partners with conservation groups and others to ensure private lands are conserved, restored, and more resilient to environmental challenges such as climate change. Working side-by-side with farmers and ranchers, the NRCS identifies natural resource concerns, such as soil erosion and water quality issues, and develops unique conservation plans for restoring and protecting resources. There are more than 19,000 volunteers who are considered an integral part of the NRCS agency, and they serve in every state (USDA Volunteers 2014).

Today, the leading federal agency devoted to encouraging Americans to volunteer is the Corporation for National and Community Service (CNCS). It is the nation's largest grant maker for service and volunteering, playing a critical role in strengthening America's nonprofit sector. CNCS's board of directors and chief executive officer are appointed by the president and confirmed by the senate. The chief executive officer oversees the agency, which includes about 600 employees operating throughout the United States and its territories (About CNCS 2013). Established in 1993, the CNCS has engaged more than 5 million Americans in service through its four core programs: Senior Corps, AmeriCorps, Federal Emergency Management (FEMA) Corps, and the Social Innovation Fund. AmeriCorps is often referred to as "the domestic Peace Corps." AmeriCorps and the Peace Corps are committed to service, and both offer challenging and rewarding full-time opportunities. Peace Corps assignments are all overseas, and AmeriCorps members serve only in the United States. Although Peace Corps volunteers serve for two years, assignments in AmeriCorps usually last 10 months to one year. Unlike the Peace Corps, some AmeriCorps projects may have part-time opportunities (FAQs 2013).

AmeriCorps has several service tracks including: AmeriCorps National Civilian Community Corps (NCCC) and AmeriCorps Volunteers in Service to America (VISTA). AmeriCorps NCCC is a residential, team-based, national service program that engages young adults aged 18–24 in full-time service. VISTA is the national service program designed specifically to fight poverty. Authorized in 1964 and founded in 1965, VISTA was incorporated into the AmeriCorps network of programs in 1993 (FAQs 2013).

FEMA Corps is a service track within AmeriCorps NCCC. It began in 2012 in order to strengthen the nation's ability to respond to and recover from disasters while expanding career opportunities for young people aged 18–24. Appendix B presents a modern era time line of nonmilitary national service initiatives. Because a specific federal program directly involving America's local or state police volunteers does not exist, the time line does not include any information about the rise of such volunteers since the World War II era. Nevertheless, the International Association of Chiefs of Police (IACP) has found a vast increase in the number of volunteers that are being used by American law enforcement agencies to perform police duties since 2004. A recent estimate of the number of police volunteers is well above 200,000. In fact, numerous U.S. police agencies have some type of volunteer worker. There are more than 2,000 such volunteers according to the IACP (U.S. Department of Justice 2011). The U.S. Bureau of Justice Assistance, under its Local Law Enforcement Block Grant Program, has awarded grants to police agencies for projects involving partnerships between community organizations and local law enforcement agencies to prevent crime in business districts, on school grounds, and around high-risk areas such as abortion clinics; for hiring additional police officers and purchasing necessary equipment to increase the effectiveness of police departments; for partnerships between social agencies and local law enforcement that combat domestic violence and child abuse; and for the development of computer systems that allow fingerprint identification, the maintenance of criminal history records, and so forth.[2] (Interested persons can search http://Grants.gov for federal grants by keywords or by more specific criteria. All discretionary grants offered by the 26 federal grant-making agencies can be found on this Web site.) Perhaps the best opportunity for a governmental agency or non profit organization to obtain funding related to a volunteer police project is through the AmeriCorps State and National Grant Competitions.

## Civilianization

Clearly, the establishment of full-time police forces has not abated the need for supplemental volunteers and paid personnel. Most local and state police agencies in the United States recruit and train salaried civilian employees.

These efforts shift some of the duties typically reserved for sworn staff to civilian employees as a means of cost savings. The term civilianization generally refers to a law enforcement agency's hiring of non-sworn personnel in order to replace or supplement its current sworn staff (Forst 2000). By utilizing civilians to perform duties typically undertaken by sworn staff, police departments are able to save money primarily through lower pay, reduced training requirements, and smaller overhead requirements. According to one study, entitled *The Privatization and Civilization of Policing*, estimates from New York City indicate the average cost of a civilian employee is about one-third to one-half that of a sworn officer, even when they are performing the same functions (Forst 2000). In Oklahoma City, civilians working as part-time police ambassadors take on some of the light duties formally performed by police, such as giving directions or working special events (Loren 2010). The Mesa, Arizona, Police Department has begun using civilians for everything from crime scene processing to fraud investigations. They created a team of nine civilian investigators who are paid 30–40% less than an officer. In 2010, the unit handled about 50% of all burglary calls (Adams 2011).

In addition, since America's entry into World War II, the use of unpaid volunteers in sworn or non-sworn capacities has become a standard practice in many police departments. The titles of such volunteers varied throughout the twentieth century but, by the second half of the century, there emerged two distinctive categories for unpaid or low-paid volunteers: *auxiliary* and *reserve*. The titles *reserve deputy sheriff*, *reserve posse member*, and *reserve officer* are more common throughout the western and mid-western regions of the United States, while the designation *auxiliary police officer* appears to be in common usage in the eastern regions.

Irrespective of the specific title in use, there are volunteer units in every state. However, three states lead the nation with respect to the total number of sworn volunteer police officers: Ohio, Florida, and California. Over the years, training for these volunteers has vastly improved, and complete background investigations are usually conducted for candidates. For example, all new California reserve police officers are required to attend a basic police academy, as mandated by the California State Commission on Peace Officer Standards and Training (POST). Significantly, the training requirement for full-service volunteer reserve police officers in California is the same academy program required of all regular full-time officers.[3]

It is therefore somewhat surprising, given their numbers, that only one well known and national initiative has been undertaken to help recruit and otherwise publicize the existence of local volunteer police in the United States. The Volunteers in Police Service (VIPS) program is managed by the IACP with financial support from the Bureau of Justice Assistance. The goal of the VIPS Program is to enhance the capacity of state and local law enforcement to use volunteers. A variety of volunteer management tools can be found on a newly revised VIPS Web site. Citizens who wish to volunteer their time and skills with a law enforcement agency can find Information for contacting program coordinators.

More federal initiatives are needed to coordinate or at least assist in the training of additional police volunteers in case of a national, regional, or state emergency.[4] In fact, only a handful of states have initiated volunteer state police units. Yet assuming sufficient numbers, carefully trained and screened volunteer police could be deployed to reduce the yearly slaughter due to traffic accidents; to help secure homeless shelters and aid America's homeless population; to present antibullying and antiviolence programs to increase school safety and security[5]; to control human trafficking; and to tend to a host of matters involving everyday quality of life concerns. Several of these initiatives and recommendations are addressed in Chapters 11 and 12. It is again important to state that in this book, the terms "volunteer police" or "police volunteer" are used to refer to authorized permanent groups that undertake one or more police functions in an overt manner for little or no salary. In most cases, volunteer police are unpaid, and they pay for their own uniforms and personal equipment.

## Counterterrorism Planning

Since the catastrophic events of September 11, federal and local authorities have been very reluctant to mobilize the community in such a way that the United States could be said to possess a new security force—the people of America—aligned and prepared to stop terrorists before they strike. Preferences in this regard still emphasize the military or semi-military establishment.

Guarding against future acts of domestic terrorism should be a number one concern of all Americans. By the end of the 1990s, President Clinton was urging the country "to get the very best ideas we can to try to strengthen this country's hand against terrorism" (quoted in Purdum 1996). At that time, several experts in the field commented that the problem of countering terrorism is complicated by the nature of America's open society, its large and diverse population, and the simmering hostility and anger felt by some groups in our society. Jeff Beatty, a terrorism expert who worked on security planning for the Olympic Games in Los Angeles in 1984 and in Barcelona in 1992, observed: "In the counterterrorism business, if you're investigating, you've already lost the battle. The key is stopping an attack beforehand. Terrorists build practice bombs and conduct casing and rehearsal activity that may be suspicious. Citizens need to chip in with additional eyes and ears to report suspicious activity. To win the war, we need an organization and tools designed from the ground up to beat terrorism worldwide" (Greenberg and Cooper 1996). A similar view was offered by Robbie Friedmann, another

Olympic security consultant, who stated: "The community should be called on to help law enforcement do their job. It's common sense. There are more of them than security personnel" (Greenberg and Cooper 1996).

At the federal level, the United States has two major volunteer organizations that could be given a greater role in the prevention of terrorism—the CAP and the Coast Guard Auxiliary. The CAP (as seen in Figures 2.4 and 2.5) was conceived in the late 1930s by legendary New Jersey aviation advocate Gill Robb Wilson, who foresaw aviation's role in war and general aviation's potential to supplement America's military operations. With the help of Fiorello La Guardia, the Mayor of New York, the new CAP was

**Figure 2.4** Students of the Incident Command System School, Civil Air Patrol National Emergency Services Academy (NESA) conduct a tabletop exercise on search and rescue response and operations planning at Camp Atterbury, Edinburgh, Indiana, July 25, 2013. The Incident Command System School of NESA covers the skills required to be a leader and operate in a command post and operations management role. (Courtesy of Ashley Roy, Atterbury-Muscatatuck Public Affairs, Edinburgh, Indiana.)

**Figure 2.5** Civil Air Patrol Master Sgt. Nathan Baker (left), CAP Staff Sgt. Troy Henson (center), and U.S. Air Force Staff Sgt. Angelito Cooper (right) pose with informational brochures following the CAP Clovis High Plains Composite Squadron change of command, May 28, 2013. The CAP organization was established as the official auxiliary of the Air Force in 1948 and was charged with three primary mission areas: aerospace education, cadet programs, and emergency services. (Courtesy of U.S. Air Force photo/Senior Airman Whitney Tucker.)

established on December 1, 1941, just days before the Japanese attacked Pearl Harbor. During World War II, the civilian group's mission expanded when German submarines began to prey on American ships off the U.S. coast and CAP planes began carrying bombs and depth charges. The CAP coastal patrol flew 24 million miles, found 173 submarines, attacked 57, hit 10, and sank two. By presidential executive order, CAP became an auxiliary of the Army Air Forces in 1943. A German commander later confirmed that coastal U-boat operations were withdrawn from the United States "because of those damned little red and yellow airplanes" (Congressional Record 2012). In all, CAP flew a half-million hours during the war, and 64 CAP aviators lost their lives in the line of duty. The U.S. Air Force was created as an independent armed service in 1947, and CAP was designated as its official civilian auxiliary the following year. CAP currently has 60,000 members and three main missions: to develop its cadets, to educate Americans on the importance of aviation and space, and to perform lifesaving humanitarian missions (History of Civil Air Patrol 2014).

Since its creation by Congress in 1939, the U.S. Coast Guard Auxiliary has served as the civilian, nonmilitary component of the Coast Guard. Today, more than 28,000 volunteer men and women of the Auxiliary are active on the waterways and in classrooms in more than 2,000 cities and towns across the nation. Each year, its members save nearly 500 lives, assist some 15,000 boaters in distress, conduct more than 150,000 courtesy safety examinations of recreational vessels, and teach more than 500,000 students in boating and water safety courses (Membership 2014).

The traditional roles of police include law enforcement, crime prevention, order maintenance, delivery of services, and the protection of civil liberties and rights. Terrorism involves the commission of a violent act for the purpose of making some kind of political statement. The most important role that local volunteer police can provide to help prevent terrorism is engaging in routine community safety and security patrols. Various experts have asserted that the U.S. Justice Department has neither the power nor the resources to effectively prevent terrorism. Moreover, even with stricter controls, surveillance, and other security measures in confined spaces such as buildings and airports, a particular act of terrorism may be impossible to stop. Philip Stern, a New York-based terrorism expert, has noted that Israel has survived because it has mobilized its citizens into a variety of professional and volunteer protective services (Greenberg and Cooper 1996). Alertness for suspicious behavior and objects and the reporting of such suspicions are critical to thwarting terrorist attacks. Appendix C provides a list prepared by the Federal Bureau of Investigation (FBI) of suspicious activities that should be reported. See Box 2.2 for a list of volunteer opportunities involving citizens in the prevention of terrorism.

**BOX 2.2   CITIZEN PARTICIPATION
OPPORTUNITIES IN TERRORISM PREVENTION**

- Citizen Corps Councils, which help drive local citizen participation by coordinating Citizen Corps programs, developing community action plans, assessing possible threats, and identifying local resources
- The Community Emergency Response Team (CERT), which is a training program that prepares people in neighborhoods, the workplace, and schools to take a more active role in emergency management planning and to prepare themselves and others for disasters
- An expanded Neighborhood Watch Program, which incorporates terrorism prevention and education into its existing crime prevention mission
- Volunteers in Police Service, who provide support for resource-constrained police departments by using civilian volunteers to free up more law enforcement professionals for frontline duty
- The Medical Reserve Corps, which coordinates volunteer health professionals during large-scale emergencies to assist emergency response teams, provide care to victims with less serious injuries, and to remove other burdens that inhibit the effectiveness of physicians and nurses in a major crisis

Since 1996, the State and Local Anti-Terrorism Training (SLATT) program has been funded by the U.S. Department of Justice, Bureau of Justice Assistance. It has trained more than 120,000 state, local, and tribal law enforcement officers in classes designed to help recognize and prevent terrorist attacks. Both on-site and online instruction is provided. The SLATT program provides specialized multiagency antiterrorism detection, investigation, and interdiction training and related services at no cost to U.S. law enforcement officers (SLATT 2014).

In the United States, the police and the citizens they serve must realize that their combined efforts are needed to combat terrorism. The resulting synergism can accomplish much more than their isolated individual efforts. Citizens need to be included in governmental planning to combat terrorism. Their additional eyes and ears could help to report suspicious behavior. Remember again Beatty's observation that, in the realm of terrorism, if you are reacting to an emergency, such as a bombing, you have already lost the battle—and maybe the war.

However, the idea of calling upon the community for assistance is often seen as a last resort, and when the call has gone out it is typically limited to asking citizens to respond to a toll-free hotline or to an e-mail address. Not surprisingly, the police may receive numerous calls that have little validity or value. Furthermore, although reserves and auxiliary units have been recruited by many police agencies, they are sometimes viewed as competitors because patrol officers feel that their jobs are threatened by unpaid volunteers.

Despite such drawbacks, there are several ways in which auxiliary police or reserves could be used in a day-to-day way for the purpose of promoting counterterrorism. For starters, the federal government could officially recognize the potential contributions of volunteer police by establishing a special training division at one or more of its training centers. Such centers would teach appropriate reporting techniques, crime prevention, and surveillance skills. Further, state governments could establish and train auxiliary police units for the specific purpose of screening employees in sabotage-prone industries, such as transportation workers and those working in ports and in fuel depots. Auxiliaries with appropriate training also could be assigned to teach crime prevention skills to the general public at Citizen Police Academies.

The armed forces including the National Guard are vital to U.S. security, but so much needs to be done. America needs to consider a new composite security force of qualified citizens, organized into largely civilian-based units such as CAP, the Coast Guard Auxiliary, and state and local auxiliary/reserve police units. The establishment of a fully trained volunteer Border Patrol reserve should also be implemented. The regular use of this new force would appear to be a natural type of counterterrorism strategy. Chapter 6 provides additional details regarding a proposal to establish a U.S. Border Patrol Auxiliary. If governments were to recognize their potential, the current forces marshaled against terrorism could be greatly enlarged. Moreover, this new combination of the American people and governmental organizations should be able to accomplish what they could not have achieved alone—establishing a much safer America with full regard to the dignity and freedom of all. Herman Melville once wrote: "We cannot live for ourselves alone. Our lives are connected by a thousand invisible threads, and along these sympathetic fibers, our actions run as causes and return to us as results" (Joint Commission 2005, 1). "The invisible threads that connect individuals, as described by Melville, must be pulled together to create a surviving community fabric" (Joint Commission 2005, 1).

Thus far, American planning has refrained from drawing upon the types of organizational structure developed as a result of its civilian mobilization during the World War II and Cold War eras. Nonetheless, it has maintained and, in some cases, enhanced the duties and responsibilities of existing volunteer units. America's reluctance to mobilize all of its citizen resources may be due to the fact that the creation of previous civil defense programs not only disrupted the lives of most Americans but produced new dilemmas about the degree to which civilian society should be militarized to defend itself against internal and external threats. Conflicts arose about the relative responsibilities of states and citizens to fund and implement home front security programs. The federal government had attempted to popularize and privatize military preparedness. The doctrine of "self-help" defense demanded that citizens become autonomous rather than rely on the federal government for protection. In many ways, during these earlier eras, families were expected to reconstitute themselves as paramilitary units that could quash subversion from within and absorb attack from without (McEnaney 2000).

Despite a considerable amount of planning at various levels of government, there still appears to be a lot more to do to mobilize the nation. Throughout the history of the United States, various conflicts have arisen regarding the use of average Americans as resources for community safety. Some of the earliest efforts in this regard are chronicled in the following chapter.

## Summary

In colonial America, the militia served as a source of personnel for the earliest night watches as well as for southern slave patrols. A Regulator movement developed in the 1760s in South Carolina involving groups interested in establishing law and order. Slavery divided the nation until the conclusion of the Civil War. But it was replaced by Jim Crow laws that fostered segregation and second class citizenship for black Americans that continued until new national civil rights laws were enforced. New national laws in 1903 and 1908 created the Organized Militia, which became known as the National Guard.

This chapter also presented several ways volunteer police may be used for the purpose of countering terrorism and advancing public safety. For example, at the time of disasters, the efforts of both formal and informal agencies of response will be needed. The latter consists of community groups, such as civic organizations, religious groups, and Boy/Girl Scout troops. At such times, the CERT and volunteer police units will play important roles.

Carefully trained and screened volunteer police can also be deployed to deal with everyday problems. They can help to reduce the yearly slaughter due to traffic accidents, help to keep homeless shelters safe, present antibullying and violence programs to increase school safety and security, control human trafficking, and tend to a host of matters involving everyday quality of life concerns.

Guarding against future acts of domestic terrorism should be the number one concern of all Americans. At the federal level, the United States has two major volunteer organizations that could be given a greater role in the prevention of terrorism: the CAP and the Coast Guard Auxiliary. In addition, the federal government could officially recognize the potential contributions of volunteer police by establishing a special training division at one or more of its training centers. At the local level, states and police departments could allow auxiliaries with appropriate training to teach crime prevention skills to the general public at Citizen Police Academies. Moreover, federal and state agencies could establish and train auxiliary police units for the specific purpose of screening employees in sabotage-prone industries, such as ports, passenger transportation hubs, and fuel depots.

## Review Questions

1. View the 9-min. clip from the film entitled *Alert Today—Alive Tomorrow*. Discuss whether any aspects of this film might be considered relevant today.
2. Provide at least two examples of "quality of life" crimes or problems.
3. Do you believe it is appropriate to require police academy cadets to engage in active street patrols in their free time or for police applicants to be required to serve as reserve officers? Discuss.
4. Discuss the pros and cons of using volunteer police to enforce low-level or misdemeanor crimes.
5. Visit the Web site for the Corporation for National and Community Service (CNCS) and determine if any of its four core programs have any new announcements. Describe your findings.
6. What do the CCC camps of the 1930s and today's NRCS volunteers have in common?
7. What do paid civilian police employees have in common with volunteer police officers?
8. The SLATT program provides an on-site training schedule and online training modules at no charge to law enforcement officers. Discuss the pros and cons of having this training available to volunteer police.
9. State at least two ways the federal government could augment the capacity of auxiliary police or reserves for the purpose of promoting counterterrorism.
10. Explain the role of the Civil Air Patrol during World War II.
11. Indicate the three main tasks of today's Civil Air Patrol.
12. Discuss why Americans were instructed at the height of the Cold War to prepare for possible roles as combatants.
13. Read the full article on the building of a Restorative Community Justice model by Bonnie Bucqueroux (2004). Based on your reading, discuss the value of creating "learning organizations."

# Notes

1. The program also will allow retired officers to serve as reservists. Those officers would be able to maintain their state law enforcement certification, which expires after two years of inactivity. Reserve officers are volunteers who are trained and uniformed and who carry weapons and have full power to make arrests under the direction of a sworn Detroit police officer. Chief Godbee said the reserve officers will be used for special events where foot patrols are necessary and to help in various precincts. "We acknowledge challenges in public safety relative to resources, and this is a huge untapped resource," Godbee said. "We have a ready pool of people who have expressed a desire to be a Detroit police officer, but at times when we're not hiring, we need to leverage that energy and that desire, and it also gives us an assessment period to see if they really will fit in with our Police Department" (Hackney 2012).

2. A major exception was the funding of the VIPS Web site under the management of the IACP. In addition, the federal government has funded numerous initiatives involving local crime prevention programs. Grants have been available to police agencies since 1966 through the Office of Justice Programs. Typically, this funding has been accomplished through "block grants" that have been allotted to states or local governments such as counties and municipalities. Block grants are widely applied for by police agencies because of the low match (10%), accessibility, and diversity of the grants. These have been an important channel for funding some local volunteer police efforts. Sometimes these programs may have assisted in the establishment of volunteer police units. The Department of Justice usually dispenses these local law enforcement block grants; in past years, the focus has been on adding new officers to the rosters of agencies. In turn, these officers are now available to train and supervise volunteer police. The CERT Program is federally supported. In recent years, death benefits for the families of volunteer police officers killed in the line of duty have also been provided as well as programs to protect women from violence under the sponsorship of nonprofit organizations. Police departments are receiving federal aid for school resource officers, Drug Abuse Resistance Education (DARE) programs, driving under the influence (DUI) awareness and enforcement programs, and many others (Van Etten 1996). In the 1990s, due to the advent of new computer technology, many departments applied for block grants to equip their squad cars with new laptops. For example, the Pacifica (CA) Police Department obtained state block grants to replace older dispatch and communication systems. The older systems had required such long searches that officers were either unable to use them or spent excessive time on the computer rather than on their beat. Laptop computers were mounted in each vehicle to allow officers to make electronic reports from their vehicles while maintaining their presence in the community. In addition, a radar warning trailer was purchased and used on streets throughout the city to educate and warn citizens of the speed at which they were traveling (Pacifica 2014).

3. In addition to satisfying state POST standards, police agencies seeking recognition for excellence may apply to the Commission on Accreditation for Law Enforcement Agencies, Inc. (CALEA). Significantly, under their standards, sworn volunteer police officers must receive the same training as regular police officers.

In 1973, the first recommended standards for reserve officers appeared in the *Report on Police* presented by the National Advisory Commission on Criminal Justice Standards and Goals. The National Advisory Commission recommended that every state immediately establish minimum standards for reserve officer training and selection. In particular, the commission urged that reserve training programs meet or exceed state standards that regulate the training of regular, part-time, or reserve officers. Significantly, standards for auxiliaries were omitted. Yet, the fact remains that in some jurisdictions, auxiliary police officers may still be used the same as reserves. Presently, however, progress appears to be in the direction of both auxiliaries and reserves achieving sworn status and training parity with regular police, thus making the two titles equivalent. An example of this trend has occurred in the state of Virginia. Virginia State Code 15.2-1731 provides for the use of auxiliary officers. Consequently, the city of Williamsburg, VA, has declared that the term "auxiliary" is synonymous with "reserve" for compliance with CALEA Standards (see Rosenberg 1998).

4. In a state emergency, it is customary for the governor of the state to call upon the state's National Guard. This happens during hurricanes, wildfires, floods, and numerous other disasters. If necessary, missions will be prioritized and other state's National Guard and Department of Defense resources for special capability may be called upon. However, in any emergency, speed means life. The availability of volunteer police for similar purposes could be increased if the existing federal Reserve Officer Training Corps (ROTC) programs were authorized to accept not only potential military officer candidates but also reserve police officer candidates. This could be done with the cooperation of county sheriff agencies. In essence, after a certain amount of ROTC training, qualified college students could move into a law enforcement track conducted by the local office of the sheriff.

5. A recent national study released by Brown University reveals that large numbers of students are still being seriously hurt while on school grounds. Each year more than 90,000 schoolchildren suffer "intentional" injuries severe enough to land them in the emergency room. According to Patrick Tolan, a professor at the University of Virginia, part of the solution may be increased monitoring of the students (Carroll 2014).

# References

About CNCS. (2013). About us: Who we are. Retrieved October 9, 2013 from http://www.nationalservice.gov/about/who-we-are

Adams, P. (2011, April 5). Arizona police force turns to civilian investigators. *BBC News*. Retrieved January 20, 2014 from www.bbc.co.uk/news/world-us-canada-12754776

Alqadi, N. (2011, October). Building relationships and solving problems in North Miami. *Community Policing Dispatch, 4*(10). Retrieved from http://www.cops.usdoj.gov/html/ dispatch/10-2011/North-Miami-Beach.asp.

Boehm, B. (2012). National Guard celebrates 376th birthday. Retrieved January 21, 2014 from http://www.army.mil/article/92912/

Bucqueroux, B. (2004, March). Restorative community justice: A comprehensive approach to reducing crime and violence in our culture. Retrieved January 27, 2014 from http://www.policing.com/articles/rcj.html

Carroll, L. (2014). School violence lands more than 90,000 a year in the ER, study finds. Retrieved January 13, 2014 from http://www.nbcnews.com/health/school-violence-lands-more-90-000-year-er-study-finds-2D11898820

Congressional Record. (2012, May 10). Awarding a Congressing gold medal to members of the Civil Air Patrol. Retrieved June 23, 2014 from http://www.gpo.gov/fdsys/pkg/CREC-2012-05-10/pdf/CREC-2012-05-10-pt1-PgS3071.pdf#page=1

Cress, L. D. (1982). *Citizens in arms: The army and the militia in American society to the War of 1812.* Chapel Hill, NC: University of North Carolina Press.

Donnelly, W. M. (2001). The Root reforms and the National Guard. Retrieved January 21, 2014 from http://www.history.army.mil/documents/1901/Root-NG.htm

Dooris, M. D. (2008). Enhancing recruitment and retention of volunteers in the U.S. Coast Guard Auxiliary. Master's thesis, Naval Postgraduate School.

Drucker, P. F. (1990). *Managing the nonprofit organization: Principles and practices.* New York: HarperCollins.

FAQs. (2013). Frequently asked questions (FAQs). Retrieved October 9, 2013 from http://www.nationalservice.gov/about/frequently-asked-questions-faqs#12454

Foner, E., and Garraty, J. A. (1991). *The reader's companion to American history.* New York: Houghton Mifflin Harcourt.

Forst, B. (2000). The privatization and civilization of policing. In C. M. Friel (Ed.), *Boundary changes in criminal justice organizations: Criminal justice 2000* (pp. 19–79). Vol. 2. Washington, DC: National Institute of Justice. NCJ 182409.

Greenberg, M., and Cooper, K. (1996, November 15). Unused secret weapon against terrorism. *Law Enforcement News.* Retrieved January 20, 2014 from http://www.lib.jjay.cuny.edu/len/96/15nov/html/forum.html

Hackney, S. (2012, May 11). Millage, volunteer police part of Detroit's public safety plan. *Detroit Free Press.* Retrieved January 21, 2014 from http://www.freep.com/article/20120511/NEWS01/205110438/Millage-volunteer-police-officers-part-of-Detroit-s-public-safety-plan?odyssey=nav|head

Henderson, W. C. (1976). The slave court system in Spartanburg County. In *The proceedings of the South Carolina Historical Association* (pp. 24–38). Columbia, SC.

History of Civil Air Patrol. (2014). Retrieved January 20, 2014 from http://vawg.cap.gov/history.html

Johnson, H. A., and Wolfe, N. T. (1996). *History of criminal justice.* (Rev. ed.). Cincinnati, OH: Anderson.

Joint Commission. (2005). *Standing together: An emergency planning guide for America's communities.* Oakbrook Terrace, IL: Joint Commission on Accreditation of Healthcare Organizations.

Kelly, R. W., Grasso, G. A., Esposito, J. J., Giannelli, R. J., and Maroulis, A. J. (2008, April). Auxiliary police program overview. Retrieved November 11, 2013 from http://www.nyc.gov/html/nypd/downloads/pdf/careers/nypd_auxiliary_police_overview_2008.pdf

Loren, J. (2010, February 3). Stimulus money used to save police jobs. *WorldNow and KWTV.* Retrieved June 23, 2014 from http://www.news9.com/story/11930579/stimulus-money-used-to-save-police-jobs

Manning, P. K. (1995). The police: Mandate, strategies, and appearances. In V. E. Kappeler (Ed.) *The police & society: Touchstone readings* (pp. 97–126). Mt. Prospect, IL: Waveland Press.

McEnaney, L. (2000). *Civil defense begins at home: Militarization meets everyday life in the fifties.* Princeton, NJ: Princeton University Press.

McKinley, J. (2011, March 1). Police department turn to volunteers. *New York Times.* Retrieved January 13, 2014 from http://www.nytimes.com/2011/03/02/us/02volunteers.html?pagewanted=all&_r=0

Membership. (2014). What is the Coast Guard Auxiliary? Retrieved January 20, 2014 from http://wow.uscgaux.info/content.php?unit = 092&category = units

Oakes, G. (1995). *The imaginary war: Civil defense and American Cold War culture.* New York: Oxford University Press.

Oshkosh Auxiliary Police. (2011). Program description. Retrieved January 31, 2014 from http://www.policevolunteers.org/programs/?fa = dis_pro_detail&id = 409

Pacifica. (2014). Pacifica police history. Retrieved January 20, 2014 from http://www.cityofpacifica.org/depts/police/history.asp

Pilgrim, D. (2012). What was Jim Crow? Retrieved January 21, 2014 from http://www.ferris.edu/jimcrow/what.htm

Purdum, T. S. (1996, July 30). Bomb at the Olympics: Legislation; bipartisan panel to frame an anti-terrorism package. Retrieved June 23, 2014 from http://www.nytimes.com/1996/07/30/us/bomb-olympics-legislation-bipartisan-panel-frame-anti-terrorism-package.html

Regulators. (2014). Lesson 8: The Regulators. Retrieved January 21, 2014 from http://www.scetv.org/education/emedia/guides/The%20Palmetto%20Special/lesson8.pdf

Rosenberg, P. (1998, March 7). Volunteer police force proposed. Retrieved June 23, 2014 from http://articles.dailypress.com/1998-03-07/news/9803070035_1_auxiliary-officers-volunteer-police-officers-police-leaders

SLATT. (2014). State and Local Anti-Terrorism Training Program (SLATT). Retrieved January 21, 2014 from http://www.iir.com/WhatWeDo/Criminal_Justice_Training/SLATT/

Smith, C. B. (2013, October 10). New chief's priorities fit with city's policing progress. Retrieved October 12, 2013 from http://news.cincinnati.com/article/20131011/NEWS01/310110048?gcheck=1&nclick_check=1

USDA Volunteers. (2014). Message from NRCS Chief Jason Weller. Retrieved January 21, 2014 from http://www.nrcs.usda.gov/wps/portal/nrcs/main/national/people/volunteers/

U.S. Air Force. (2014, May 19). Civil Air Patrol WWII members' gold medal journey new website tells their stories, describes their service. Retrieved June 23, 2014 from http://www.af.mil/News/ArticleDisplay/tabid/223/Article/484868/civil-air-patrol-wwii members-gold-medal-journey-new-website-tells-their-storie.aspx

U.S. Department of Justice. (2011, October). *The impact of the economic downturn on American police agencies.* Washington, DC: U.S. Department of Justice, Office of Community Oriented Policing Services.

Van Etten, J. (1996). The impact of grants on police agencies. Retrieved January 20, 2014 from http://www.fdle.state.fl.us/Content/getdoc/b34d43a0-b789-41e4-aad1-4ce6a61ac4df/VanEtten.aspx

Volunteering. (2013). Volunteering in America. Retrieved October 9, 2013 from http://www.nationalservice.gov/impact-our-nation/research-and-reports/ volunteering-america

Wilkinson, P. (1986). Terrorism versus liberal democracy: The problems of response. In W. Gutteridge (Ed.), *The new terrorism* (pp. 3–28). London: Mansell Publishing.

Worton, S. (2003, September). *Volunteers in police work: A study of the benefits to law enforcement agencies.* An applied research project submitted as part of the School of Police Staff and Command Program, Eastern Michigan University. Retrieved January 20, 2014 from http://www.emich.edu/cerns/downloads/ papers/PoliceStaff/Police%20Personnel%20(e.g.,%20Selection,%20%20 Promotion)/Volunteers%20in%20Police%20Work.pdf

# The Early History of Volunteer Police

# 3

Policing, like all professions, learns from experience. It follows then that as modern police executives search for more effective strategies of policing, they will be guided by the lessons of police history.

—**George L. Kelling and Mark H. Moore**
*(1988)*

In England, prior to 1829, law enforcement slowly evolved from the basic concept of preserving the "King's Peace" by mutual responsibility (Anglo-Saxon era, 550 to 1066) to the use of various constables and the keeping of a "watch and ward." The King's Peace refers to the general protection of persons and property secured in medieval times to large areas and later to the entire royal domain by the law administered by authority of the British monarch. In the ninth century, during the reign of King Alfred the Great, the office of "shire-reeve" was developed to maintain law and order within a shire (equivalent to a modern-day county).[1]

In 1066, the Norman conquest of England was led by William the Conqueror, Duke of Normandy. This was a pivotal event in English history. It largely removed the native ruling class, replacing it with a foreign, French-speaking monarchy, aristocracy, and clerical hierarchy. This, in turn, brought about a transformation of the English language and the culture of England in a new era often referred to as Norman England (Norman Conquest 2013). Every man in Norman England had to be part of a frank-pledge. In this system, every man belonged to a group of ten men who were responsible for the conduct of each member of the group. This was not only a system of law enforcement, but it was a system of mutual protection. "It was very important to belong somewhere and be protected by others, to be removed from this could be very dangerous indeed" (Sherwood Forest Archaeology Project 2014).

The office of constable and the keeping of a "watch and ward" were officially set forth in the Statute of Winchester of 1285 (Seth 1961). In the late 1600s, local justices of the peace were empowered to appoint additional or "special" parish constables (Critchley 1967; Leon 1991). Prior to the nineteenth century, it was generally considered an unpaid compulsory obligation to serve as a tithingman (a member of the frank-pledge who was elected to preside over the tithing), constable, or a member of the watch and ward (Prassel 1972). Today, approximately 14,000 "special constables" serve as unpaid volunteer police throughout the United Kingdom.[2]

## Native American Societies

In America, the most dramatic advances in the utilization of volunteer police have taken place in recent times, but before the arrival of the first colonists to the New World, Native Americans were already engaged in maintaining order in their communities. One scholar has indicated that Native American societies maintained order through clearly defined customs "enforced by public opinion and religious sanctions" (Hagan 1966, 16). Nearly everyone knew and respected the customs and beliefs of their tribe. Such conformity was possible because the "tribes were homogeneous units—linguistically, religiously, economically, and politically" (Deloria and Lytle 1983, xi). By the time of the arrival of the European settlers, many tribes had founded numerous societies and cults to preserve order in camp and "to foster a military spirit among themselves and the rest of the tribe, since war was a matter of survival" (Mails 1973, 46). The Plains Indians instituted honorary military societies to police their annual reunion ceremonies and buffalo hunts. Similar societies were operated year-round by the Cheyenne and the Teton Sioux (Hagan 1966).

The Sioux maintained an organized system of volunteer police known as the *akicitas*. Various authors also refer to these groups as either "warrior societies," "policing societies," or "whip-bearers" (Humphrey 1942; Hassrick 1964; Hoxie 1986). Members lived in their own separate tents when the band was on the move, and they were supported by tribal contributions. Each band usually had several such societies that a young warrior could join. The *akicita* societies helped to ensure law and order. Members were selected by the tribal leader or a council of leaders at the spring gathering of the various Sioux bands. Because their authority was derived from a particular council or chief, bands were accountable to them. Their assignments could last just for the duration of the summer hunts or throughout the year. During the communal hunting activities, the members of these policing societies kept noise levels down, performed scouting missions to ensure security, repressed the tendency for some hunters to act overzealously, and helped prevent others from falling behind. Moreover, society members might also question individuals in order to learn the identity of trouble markers (Barker 1994).

Members of the Sioux volunteer policing societies could also be called upon by the tribal council to carry out various types of punishment but only as a last resort. Such punishments could involve the destruction of property (shelters, rifles, etc.), corporal punishment, and banishment (Barker 1994). When several societies were selected, the various duties of each group would be rotated to ensure that as many young warriors as possible could have an equal chance at performing the most important duties (Barker 1994).

Prior to 1838 (when they were forcibly moved to Oklahoma), the Cherokee Indians lived in what is now the state of Georgia.[3] They adopted many of the customs of their white neighbors—perhaps because of their location.

The Cherokees (one of the Five Civilized Tribes) were "admired and respected by the settlers because of their apparent willingness to acculturate" (Barker 1994, 40). In 1808, they instituted a system of appointed sheriffs and a group of quasi-police/militia they called the "lighthorse." These men enforced the first written legal code adopted by an Indian tribe (Hagan 1966). The lighthorse were small companies, each consisting of four privates and two officers who patrolled on horseback. Barker (1994, 36) referred to the Cherokee's lighthorse-men and the *akicitas* of the Sioux as "the first 'police departments' in America."

## Watch and Ward

Volunteers served as America's first police officers as well as the organizers of the first police agencies (Garry 1980). Prior to American independence, justice in the colonies was administered by lay judges, community residents, militia and watch members, foreign soldiers, clergymen, constables, various administrative officers (e.g., governors, sheriffs, and constables), and by legis-lative assemblies. An important legacy of the colonial period was a system of petty courts manned by laymen (e.g., rural justices of the peace). In America's seaport towns, a constable was elected for each ward and a nighttime patrol called "the watch" was instituted. The earliest watch organizations relied on local citizen participation or on the use of paid substitutes.

During colonial times, "watch and ward committees" were established in New England, and they represented an early version of citizen patrols. The Dutch settlement of New Amsterdam, which later became New York, "created a burgher watch in 1643, one year after it was founded, but did not pay them until 1712" (Bayley 1985, 32). The governor of New Amsterdam, Peter Stuyvesant, also created the first American volunteer fire department in 1648. Eventually, either elected or appointed constables, sheriffs, marshals, and watches were established in every settlement (Bayley 1985). Initially, constable work was the communal responsibility of all adult males, and fines could be levied for refusing to assume this obligation (Walker 1998). In the South, during the colonial and antebellum periods, slave patrol laws were adopted. These patrols initially recruited militia members in order to maintain the institution of slavery.

## The Militia

America's use of militias and town watches can be traced to thirteenth-century England and the reign of Henry III. He mandated that all his male subjects aged 15–50 own a weapon other than a knife so that they could stand guard to preserve the peace.

One of the earliest uses of an organized militia came in 1636 when militia companies were formed in the Massachusetts Bay Colony to protect against attacks by Native Americans. "Colonial militiamen defended the colonies and participated in expeditions against Indians and the French until the War of Independence" (Stentiford 2002, 6).

During the Revolutionary War, "militia augmented Washington's Continental Army, as well as enforced revolutionary discipline among the populace, clearly demonstrating the dual roles of militia during wartime of fighting the enemy and in stabilizing the homefront" (Stentiford 2002, 6). The existence of militia is referred to in the U.S. Constitution (see Article I, Article II, and the Second Amendment). It is of considerable importance that the framers of the Constitution "intended that the militia would be called into federal service when needed [since] Article II, section 3 established the president as the commander-in-chief of the militia when in federal service" (Stentiford 2002, 11).

The Militia Act of 1792 required most free white males between the ages of 18 and 45 to arm themselves and attend regular drills. However, "neither the federal government nor the states enforced the law....[and] in the years following the War of 1812, the militia as an institution fell into disuse. Few Americans, including Congressmen, saw any need for citizens to waste time drilling when no danger threatened and more profitable pursuits beckoned" (Stentiford 2002, 7).

At one time, George Washington served in a British militia unit and decades later Abraham Lincoln was chosen to lead a militia company during the Black Hawk War. When the famous French aristocrat Alexis de Tocqueville traveled in America (1831–1832), he was impressed by the fact that Americans had formed many voluntary associations. He noted that this ability to form self-help groups provided the basis and strength for maintaining democracy in America. Nevertheless, not all such organizations had egalitarian or noble purposes. In the South, slaves were controlled through a system of slave patrols that relied on the militia model to preserve the slave system.[4]

Changes in the militia's role of providing an external defense coincided with a need for internal protection of America's growing seaports and other centers of commerce. In general, the seaports needed increased security because of higher population and the transient nature of seaport life (Johnson and Wolfe 1996). In New York and in parts of New England, the militia was directly connected with the provision of police services as a result of the formation of the night watch. By statute, the militia was used "as the organizational base for distributing night-watch duty among the citizenry" (Cress 1982, 7). In addition, in times of emergency, the militia could be called upon to restore order in conjunction with the *posse comitatus*. In both the North and the South, the militia was used to maintain the institution of slavery, such as in 1741, when the New York City militia suppressed a slave revolt (Cress 1982).

Over time, the militia tradition developed into today's well-known concept of the "citizen soldier" who serves the nation in peacetime and in war as a volunteer member of the National Guard. Members of the New York Army National Guard were called to active duty after September 11, 2001, to provide security at airports, bridges, and train stations (Debnam 2003).

## The New Police

During the two or three decades just prior to the Civil War, most eastern U.S. port cities abandoned the informal system of "watch and ward" (a system involving separate organizations for evening and day patrols). A wave of urban riots took place in this period, and many persons feared that America's experiment with democratic institutions was threatened. The establishment of the London Metropolitan Police Force in 1829 served as a convenient model for reform (Walker 1976).

However, the initial establishment of unified day and night salaried police departments did not result in any panacea for crime. It also did not serve as a guarantee that democratic traditions or that the rule of law would be respected, especially with regard to the protection of minority citizens and their rights. The new police forces excluded minority group members. Moreover, between 1882 and 1969, more than 4,700 people—mostly black—were lynched in the United States (Perloff 2000). Furthermore, a census bureau study conducted in 1973 found that in the five largest U.S. cities, "blacks were much more likely than whites to be the victims of robbery and burglary, in some cases by a ratio of nearly two to one" (Wilson 1975, 34). In the United States, the high point of this crisis was reached in the late 1960s when civil protests and riots erupted in more than 100 cities (Travis 1995). Ultimately only through the peaceful efforts of courageous civil rights leaders and demonstrators did it become possible for U.S. deputy marshals and National Guardsmen to be deployed in the South to enforce federal court orders for integration in schools and public accommodations, thereby initiating significant legal procedures to end the era of "Jim Crow."

## The Posse

Due to a lack of records, it is not certain when the first American sheriff took office. However, various sources indicate that Captain William Stone was appointed sheriff in Virginia's Accomac Shire in 1634 (Buffardi 1998; Henry County Sheriff 2010; Scott 2013). Virginia's first counties were established that same year, and it is probable that one or more of these counties appointed a sheriff. In Maryland, the St. Mary's County Sheriff's Office can document that its first sheriff was appointed in 1637. In 1776, the position of sheriff became an elective office under Maryland's new constitution (St. Mary's County Sheriff 2013). By custom and law, one of the powers extended to a sheriff is the ability to select able-bodied individuals to help capture suspected criminals. The posse comitatus (or the "power of the county") refers to an ancient British common law right empowering sheriffs to summon the assistance of any citizen in time of civil disorder. In America, this right was put into statutory form and extended to other types of peace officers and to most magistrates (Prassel 1972). "Much of the philosophy of law regarding citizen's arrest powers are founded in the posse comitatus premise" (Buffardi 1998).

During the nineteenth century, the institution of the "posse" developed as America expanded to its Pacific Coast boundary. Klockars (1985, 22) refers to the use of the posse as a form of "obligatory avocational policing" because an individual could be arrested for failure to serve when called upon.

There are probably hundreds of interesting stories about the activities of posses. One of the earliest cases of note took place during the War of 1812. The sheriff's office of Prince George's County in Maryland was involved in an incident that resulted in the writing of the national anthem. "When the British army marched on Washington they passed through Upper Marlboro. The local residents cooperated with the invading army and the British Commander saw to it that no major damage was done to local property. After the battle of Bladensburg and the burning of Washington, the British army marched back through Upper Marlboro. This time some of the British soldiers looted local farms and were arrested by a Sheriff's Posse. The stragglers were placed in the county jail" (Oertly 2013). When the British commander learned of the arrests of his soldiers, he ordered the arrest of Dr. William Beam and other sheriff's posse members. They were taken aboard a British warship. Several notable officials of the U.S. Government were selected to negotiate their release, including a talented young lawyer. While the give and take of the bargaining was taking place over a period of a few days, the young lawyer, "Francis Scott Key witnessed an attack on Fort McHenry. Standing on the deck of an American ship, Key looked through a telescope and observed the fighting. Seeing that the American flag was still there meant that the British had failed in their attack on Baltimore. He was so overwhelmed by the sight that he was inspired to express his feelings in verse which was to become 'The Star Spangled Banner'" (Buffardi 1998).

The founder of the modern detective and security guard industry was also a posse member. In fact, the career of Allan Pinkerton and the eventual establishment of an entire new industry might be traced to the year 1847 when Pinkerton was searching on a tiny island for any wood he could use for his barrel-making business. His curiosity was aroused when he discovered the remains of a cooking fire. As a member of a sheriff's posse, Pinkerton later returned to the island to arrest a group of counterfeiters, and he engaged in the seizure of the evidence of their illegal activities. As a result of this event, Pinkerton's reputation led him to other local crime detective work. Eventually, he was appointed to a variety of law enforcement roles including deputy sheriff, becoming the first detective in Chicago, and being appointed as a special agent for the U.S. Postal Service. The latter position involved investigating thefts from post offices in Chicago. In 1861, Pinkerton safely escorted President-elect Abraham Lincoln to his first inauguration while Pinkerton's operatives protected the train route (Horan 1967).

Over time it became possible for posse members to be reimbursed for their services. For example, in the early spring of 1886, just as the ice was beginning to break up on the Little Missouri River in present-day North Dakota, three thieves stole a boat from its mooring at a local ranch and took it downriver. The boat belonged to a part-time deputy sheriff in Billings County. He chased after them with his ranch hands and made three arrests. Under the laws of the Dakota Territory, as a deputy sheriff, he received a fee for making the three arrests, and he was also compensated for the hundreds of miles traveled—a total of some $50. The rancher and deputy sheriff was Theodore Roosevelt (Roosevelt Pursues 2013). When President McKinley died from an assassin's bullet on September 14, 1901, Vice President Roosevelt—the former Dakota Territory cattle rancher—became president of the United States.

Today, most states still have laws that require the average citizen to come to the aid of a police officer when requested. During the nineteenth century, some northeastern and midwestern states passed laws authorizing the establishment of various protective, detective, or anti-horse thief associations. The charters of these groups provided for the preselection of posses to chase and apprehend wrongdoers. In addition, a number of societies were established to oversee the selection and distribution of private welfare aid.

## The Volunteers

According to Stentiford (2002), a new institution arose in 1806 that supplanted the use of the militia during wartime. Known simply as "the Volunteers," these usually were companies and regiments recruited at the local level. "The men from each company elected their officers; the governor of the state appointed the regimental officers; and the regiment was then mustered into federal service for an agreed-upon period" (Stentiford 2002, 7–8). These types of voluntary military organizations existed throughout the nineteenth century and assisted state governments in strike breaking, riot control, and in disaster relief. Their existence obviated the need to enforce the Militia Act of 1792. In essence, they represented a body of self-selected men derived from the unorganized militia, who "formed or joined companies out of patriotism, from fear of slave uprisings ... or as a way of establishing social and political contacts, but not out of legal obligation" (Stentiford 2002, 8). Abraham Lincoln served in such a company during the Black Hawk War, and Theodore Roosevelt led his volunteer "Rough Riders" during the Spanish-American War.

Many volunteer companies were recruited during the Civil War and may have suffered high rates of loss because of their inexperience. Stentiford (2002, 11) notes that toward the end of the nineteenth century, "the resurgent organized militia—or as it was increasingly called, the National Guard—began to wrest from the Volunteers the official role as the nation's second line of defense. Unlike Volunteers, National Guard units trained during peacetime."

## Friendly Visitors

During the nineteenth century, several types of specialized volunteer law enforcement organizations appeared in America. As early as the 1830s, Alexis de Tocqueville (1805–1859)—the French aristocrat who visited the United States to study its people and institutions—discerned a trend in American society for the establishment of a variety of voluntary associations. Many of these organizations were not solely of the amateur soldier variety but rather were concerned with the welfare of diverse immigrant groups. By 1878, in Philadelphia alone, "there were some 800 such groups of one kind or another in existence" (Trattner 1989, 85). The growth in their number created a need for the establishment of umbrella associations known as charity organization societies. They did not directly dispense relief but instead served as clearinghouses for the registration, screening, and referral of applicants in need of charity. The largest organization of this type existed in New York City. Initially, the New York Charity Organization Society (COS) relied upon a corps of volunteers known as the "friendly visitors" to perform home visits (Trattner 1989). While they helped families contend with relief agencies, their intimate knowledge of family life could be used to ensure that families were conforming to the norms of the era (Katz 1996).

After a time, the New York COS was unable to recruit all the volunteers needed for its special type of charitable work. Initially, it created a Committee on Mendicancy, "which hired 'Special Agents' who were empowered by the city to arrest beggars" (Burrows and Wallace 1999, 1160). Eventually, additional agents were hired to conduct the everyday role of serving as "friendly visitors." Over time, the roles of the first social workers directly sprang from the nature of the duties of the field workers of the charity organization societies. Thus, by the second decade of the twentieth century, the caseworker was, in essence, "a trained, professional friendly visitor" (Katz 1996, 171).

## Vigilantes

In the United States, various types of vigilante organizations were common in the nineteenth century. Richard Maxwell Brown, one of America's leading scholars on the subject, defined vigilantism as "organized, extralegal movements, the members of which take the law into their own hands" (Brown 1975, 95–66). Karmen (1990, 357) has clarified this classic statement by indicating that "vigilantes don't 'take' the law; they break the law. They don't act in self-defense, which is legal; they react aggressively, which is illegal." Historically, two of the most well-known episodes of vigilantism took place in California and Montana.

The San Francisco Committee of Vigilance (or simply "The San Francisco Vigilantes") was formed in 1851 in order to reduce government corruption and the extremely high crime rate during the California Gold Rush. The San Francisco Vigilantes were well-organized and forced several officials to resign on grounds of corruption. The Montana Vigilantes was a group of men who aimed to restore order in the small but lawless community of western Montana in 1860. These vigilante groups have been both praised and condemned. However, they were organized for the specific purpose of reducing crime and corruption.

Two of the most infamous types of vigilante organizations arose after the Civil War—the Ku Klux Klan and the White Caps. The Klan was formed to counter any efforts by southern blacks to achieve racial equality. The White Caps were concerned with the control of morality (wife beaters, prostitutes, drunkards, poor providers, etc.). Both groups wore masks. However, whereas the Klan was known for lynching, the White Caps relied on whipping to fulfill their goals (Brown 1971; Friedman 1993).

In numerous ways, the activities of extra legal vigilante groups represented the antithesis of the modern-day role of volunteer police. Generally, vigilante groups deviated from the traditional and contemporary democratic hallmarks of voluntary community service because they went about their business without regard to individual rights and liberties. Furthermore, these groups lacked any statutory authority when they engaged in punitive activities.

In contrast, the evolving role of volunteer police appears to be deeply rooted in the American democratic spirit. This spirit is best characterized by its concern for free speech, religious tolerance, universal suffrage, and other egalitarian concepts such as hiring and promotion based on merit. On the other hand, the evolution of volunteer police has had an undemocratic side, especially when it has been linked to other branches of government that have abused the rights of citizens. In particular, this occurred when slave patrols were used to control slaves in the South and later, during World War I, when the federal government condoned the use of thousands of volunteer citizen spies for the purposes of identifying draft evaders

**Figure 3.1** In this photograph, 40,000 members of the Ku Klux Klan march down Pennsylvania Avenue on August 8, 1925. (Courtesy of Prints and Photographs Division, Library of Congress.)

and suspected anarchists. These volunteer spies were part of a giant civic organization known as the American Protective League (APL).

The first decades of the twentieth century saw a rebirth of the Ku Klux Klan after its having been dormant for 50 years. Although there was no actual connection with the original Ku Klux Klan of the post–Civil War Reconstruction period, the new organization (founded in 1915) adapted its rituals and dress (Slosson 1958, 308). It was not uncommon to see white-robed and masked figures in both southern and northern states (Sullivan 1939). On one occasion, Klan members marched down Pennsylvania Avenue in the heart of the nation's capital (as seen in Figure 3.1).

## Boy Police

Since at least the time of World War I, there have been several types of law enforcement programs involving American youth. In the second decade of the twentieth century, various articles about the use of "junior police" or "boy police" appeared in such popular national periodicals as *The Literary Digest*, *The Survey*, and *The Outlook*. A few of the earliest programs were established in California, Iowa, Ohio, and New York. Figure 3.2 presents a page from an early twentieth-century catalog displaying a variety of school patrol

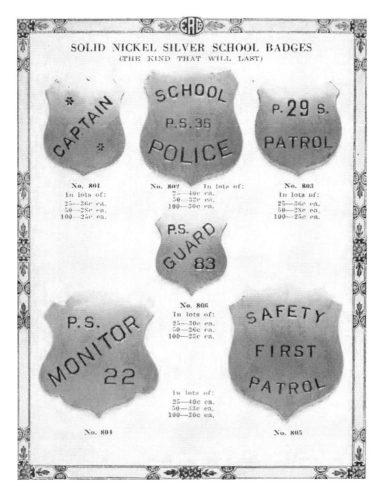

**Figure 3.2** Early twentieth-century catalog page of student badges.

badges worn by students. The participants were encouraged to lead healthy lives and to engage in various projects related to community service. It is interesting to note that on some occasions arrests were made under the direction and initiative of members of the New York City Junior Police. For example, in 1914, a 13-year-old member of the junior police, Sergeant Louis Goldstein of the Fifteenth Precinct, caused the arrest of a storeowner who was charged with conducting an illegal lottery. Young Sergeant Goldstein provided testimony about the incident in the Court of Special Sessions of the city of New York. After the defendant realized the strength of the evidence against him, he pleaded guilty. Furthermore, this was not the first arrest in which Goldstein had participated. On a previous occasion, he encountered two men breaking into a display case. Each man received a jail sentence of six months. For this arrest, Goldstein was promoted to sergeant (Boy Police of New York 1915).

By the mid-1920s, some of these groups had been either transformed or replaced by school safety patrols and the establishment of Police Athletic Leagues (PALs). Junior police activities also morphed into the Law Enforcement Explorer program, administered on a national level by Learning for Life, an affiliate of the Boy Scouts of America. Law enforcement or police explorers are usually between the ages of 14 and 20.

The growth of youth safety patrols was triggered in the 1920s when the popularity of the automobile led to a rise in traffic fatalities among children aged 5–14. In 1926, the city fathers of Newark, New Jersey, took stock of their nine-year-old safety patrol program. They found that no serious injuries had taken place since its implementation (Rosseland 1926). In 1923, the Honolulu sheriff swore in 33 members of the Boy Scouts of America as "junior traffic police officers" (Honolulu Police Department 2000). By 1932, there were approximately 10,000 safety patrol units involving 200,000 boys in 1,800 cities and towns (Guarding Five Million Children 1932; Schoolboy Patrols Approved by the President 1933). Two future presidents of the United States, Jimmy Carter and Bill Clinton, were safety patrollers. In addition, Rudolph Giuliani, New York City's former Mayor, *Time Magazine's* "Person of the Year 2001," was also a safety patroller. Additional materials about youth involvement in public safety at both the local and national levels are presented in Chapters 8 and 9.

## Vice and Alcohol Suppression Societies

There were also groups that were mainly concerned with the morals of the immigrants who were arriving daily from Europe during the latter part of the nineteenth century and the first two decades of the twentieth. Thousands of migrant, working class families settled in the largest U.S. cities, establishing densely packed ethnic neighborhoods. Conditions in these neighborhoods were often poor, with crowding and lack of proper sanitation compounding problems such as infant mortality, substance abuse, and crime. In Chicago, "improper sanitation led to high rates of disease, such as smallpox and tuberculosis. Working conditions were unsafe in the many 'sweatshops,' mills, and slaughterhouses where immigrant men and women sought employment" (Frances Willard 2013, 35). One of the earliest organizations of this type was the New York Society for the Suppression of Vice. Its agents identified and prosecuted vendors of pornography and birth control for more than 40 years (Hovey 1998).

Another group focused on the detection and prosecution of liquor law violators. The Anti-Saloon League (ASL) began operations in the 1890s. Its earliest agenda "was not to advocate prohibition in the broad sense, but was to rally the divided temperance forces for the more modest task of saloon suppression" (Timberlake 1963, 127). Private detectives were employed by the League and, by 1908, it had participated in more than 31,000 cases involving liquor law enforcement. Such groups worked in parallel with or in place of local police. The ASL-sponsored prosecutions and the use of private detectives in order to obtain evidence against local violators of temperance legislation. These actions were deemed necessary because of the laxity or disinterest of public officials in pursuing such offenders. Saloons were also associated with gambling and prostitution.

At the end of the nineteenth century, one national women's organization was particularly concerned with a reduction in the consumption of liquor as well as the curtailment of prostitution. The Women's Christian Temperance Union (WCTU) pursued its efforts under the banner of "home protection," perhaps in early recognition of the fact that the greatest threat to "homeland security" is the breakdown of the family. The WCTU's main accomplishment was in establishing "laws in every state compelling some form of Temperance Instruction in the public schools" (Gusfield 1963, 86). "Organizations like the WCTU faced a difficult challenge in their efforts to close down these drinking establishments. The city of Chicago, in the late 1800s, derived a significant portion of its revenues from the sale of liquor licenses, and the political establishment was committed to seeing that the saloons stayed open. Chicago politics during this period were often corrupt, and local ward bosses received payoffs from saloon owners in exchange for allowing them to operate on Sundays" (Frances Willard 2013, 34).

## The American Protective League

The APL was active during U.S. involvement in World War I. Albert M. Briggs, a Chicago advertising executive, founded the APL. Briggs promised personnel and automobiles that could be used by the Justice Department at the discretion of the chief of its Bureau of Investigation (Jensen 1968). The Bureau of Investigation was the forerunner of the Federal Bureau of Investigation. This was a time when funds and departmental equipment were in short supply. Briggs made a persuasive case, and the APL was authorized by the U.S. Department of Justice to carry out the following duties: protection of property, reporting of disloyal or suspicious persons and activities, locating draft violators, assisting in the arrest of deserters, and enforcing vice and liquor law regulations in areas around naval and army bases. More than 200,000 citizens were recruited for this organization, and historians have acknowledged that the APL was the largest spy network ever authorized by the U.S. government. Numbered metal badges were sold by the League to help identify its members and to raise funds for the organization's administration. Their most notorious activities involved investigating and reporting

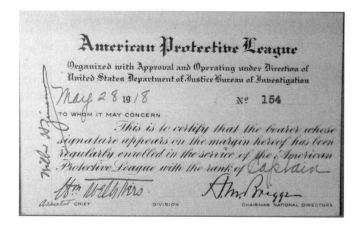

**Figure 3.3** American Protective League membership card, ca. 1918.

"disloyal and seditious utterances" (Hough 1919, 120) and participating in raids where volunteer APL agents joined with police personnel in rounding up suspected draft evaders. Figure 3.3 displays an APL membership card.

Members of the APL were not sworn in as peace officers and did not have any powers beyond that of a private citizen. Membership also did not confer any special authorization to carry firearms beyond that extended to private citizens by local laws. Moreover, members were not exempted from Selective Service regulations, and they were instructed to avoid making any claims that they were government officers. However, they were permitted to state when conducting investigations that they were doing so "for the Department of Justice" (Hough 1919, 499). In addition, they were organized along a chain of command involving a local chief, an assistant chief, inspectors, captains, lieutenants, and general members (Hough 1919).

The tactics used by the APL to stifle dissent and members' participation in various raids to find draft evaders were condemned by liberal leaders, but in the main, their practices led to little public outcry. The Justice Department decided to disband the League at the end of World War I.

## Citizen Home Defense Leagues, Home Guards, State Guards

At the time of World War I, many cities established citizen home defense leagues as well as state and home guard organizations to provide homeland security. State and home guard units were organized to fill the vacuum left when the National Guard was called upon for active military service; home or citizen defense leagues were instituted by some large city police chiefs concerned about both natural and man-made disasters. For example, in 1916 in New York City, nearly 21,000 citizens were recruited out of concern that the war in Europe would deplete police ranks and reduce the number of available personnel for guarding vital resources (i.e., reservoirs, bridges, transportation lines, etc.). The volunteers were asked to perform routine patrol duties and to participate in training programs. In 1918, New York City's Home Defense League was reorganized into a police reserve organization.

By 1917, various states (e.g., Massachusetts, Connecticut etc.) had established military state units to fill the void left by the induction of all or part of the National Guard into the regular army. Such units were named the "State Guard" to indicate the statewide obligation of the forces (Stentiford 2002, 23). They "provided needed services to their states during disasters, the 'Spanish Influenza' epidemic in 1918, and periods of civil unrest. By contrast, in the poorer and more rural Deep South, governors and state adjutants general reacted with indifference or hostility to locally created home guards. Lacking uniforms, support, or encouragement, southern home guardsmen contributed little service to the states" (Stentiford 2002, 23).

In Missouri, a state-directed Home Guard was also established. "At its peak, the Missouri Home Guard consisted of five regiments, six separate battalions, and sixteen separate companies…. The Home Guard contained six thousand men, mostly in the infantry" (Stentiford 2002, 37). The recruitment of such a force was facilitated by the existence of the Missouri Militia Act of 1908. This foresighted state law specifically authorized the governor to create a replacement militia for the National Guard when it left the state. One regiment of the Missouri Guard based in Kansas City was successful in controlling labor unrest during a general strike of workers that lasted six days. Between emergency the units of the Home Guard engaged in training exercises.

The municipality-based citizen defense leagues should not be confused with home and state guard organizations. According to Stentiford (2002, xi–xii), the home guard is "an organized militia of a town, city, county, or state, without a federal obligation. These units are usually liable for service within the jurisdiction of the government that recruited them." The units of the state guard were usually forces that "had a statewide obligation and depended on the local and state resources rather than federal…" (Stentiford 2002, xi–xii). Stentiford notes that such terms may have slightly different meanings depending on context and year.

## Summary

Generally, Native American military societies, constables, watch members, and slave patrollers share the following attributes membership in a permanent organization or one established during wartime mobilization organized by governmental or societal action undertaking one or more police functions and serving in an overt manner for minimal or no salary.

The early constables and watch members were looked upon as part of a permanent organization for the purpose of maintaining the order and safety of a city's inhabitants. They were selected through governmental procedures (initially from the ranks of the local militia) and eventually were rewarded by being able to receive fees or a minimal salary for their services. In a similar fashion, the members of the southern slave patrols also were selected and were provided with small stipends. Finally, the Native American military societies were permanent organizations until they were required to disband by congressional mandate. They performed a wide range of peacekeeping and tribal functions. Because these groups could also punish violators for tribal custom transgressions, they performed a necessary role involving the use of proactive enforcement methods. Their members shared in the communal ownership of property and sometimes received extra gifts for their services. All three groups carried out their protective functions in an overt manner.

In colonial America, the duties of watchmen and constables were numerous; in the absence of any other frontline support groups, they were the primary law enforcers of their era. Their duties expanded and became more difficult as towns grew and when crime became a more frequent concern. Peak (1997) has noted that when their increased responsibilities became more demanding, many began to evade their duties whenever possible.

The advent of slavery gave rise to the creation of slave patrols whose members did not hesitate to use punitive means to carry out their duties. Yanochik (1997) has pointed out that the slave patrollers were merely one variety of a growing band of "specialists" that included salaried sheriffs and constables. He implies that what was important was not so much the nature of the "specific" duties being performed, but rather that the population at large was no longer being looked to for order maintenance. A differentiation in roles between the ordinary citizen and officers of the law had now begun.

Thus, prior to America's independence, justice was administered on the Great Plains by Native American military societies. In the eastern and coastal colonies, justice was administered by various combinations of lay judges, community residents (e.g., regulators or posse members), militia, slave patrols, foreign soldiers, clergymen, constables, watch members, various administrative officers (e.g., governors, sheriffs), and by legislative assemblies. An important legacy of the colonial period was a system of petty courts manned by laymen (e.g., rural justices of the peace). Town courts are a major feature of the modern American justice system.

During the late nineteenth century, several organizations were established to halt the distribution of pornography and birth control information (e.g., the New York Society for the Suppression of Vice). A substantial part of the history of the ASL and its volunteer police had to do with the phenomenon of American saloon life. "In the five or six decades before 1920, the saloon was an almost ubiquitous structure on the American landscape" (Engelmann 1979, 3). The ASL's attorneys and private investigators, although privately retained, performed the essential police functions of surveillance, investigation, arrest, and prosecution. Members volunteered for their assignments and, after arrests were made, their activities were publicized when the attorneys and their private investigators had to appear in court.

Charity organization societies used a system of "friendly visitors" who were middle- and upper-class women with leisure time who would visit aid recipients to help them achieve independence as quickly as possible. The societies that recruited these volunteers did not dispense any relief but rather coordinated its dispensation through cooperating churches and private associations.

Several pioneering youth programs were developed at the start of the twentieth century. In general, the junior police and safety patrollers engaged in a limited number of service-oriented projects, such as serving as school crossing guards, performing crowd control at special events, and working as security escorts. If a crime occurred in their presence, their duty was to call for assistance.

At the outset of World War I, various home defense leagues were established by police departments in such cities as New York, Chicago, and Berkeley, California. The largest of these was in New York City. Its chief purpose was to serve as a source of additional police workers during any emergency. In addition, the APL was founded by Albert M. Briggs, an outdoor advertising executive. Briggs was able to convince the head of the U.S. Department of Justice's Chicago office about the League's value. He offered a volunteer solution to the problem of investigating suspected German agents at a time when funds and departmental equipment were in short supply. Briggs promised personnel and automobiles that could be used by the Justice Department at the discretion of the chief of its Bureau of Investigation (Jensen 1968). Unlike many of the members of the ASL, all of the APL members involved in law enforcement activities were unpaid volunteers. However, both groups were proactive or aggressive in their approach to their assignments, and they performed a variety of special purpose police functions. Members of the APL conducted investigations for various federal agencies, especially the U.S. Department of Justice.

Unlike their volunteer specialist counterparts, the regular urban police of the post–Civil War era were preoccupied with maintaining their political appointments as well as performing a variety of non-law enforcement roles including supervision of elections, censoring of movies, operation of lodging homes in the basements of police stations, provision of emergency ambulances, disposal of confiscated liquor, and the inspection of boilers, tenements, markets, and factories (Fogelson 1977). These responsibilities and concerns no doubt contributed to the ability of the ASL and APL operatives to undertake specific law enforcement functions.

## Review Questions

1. Discuss how Native Americans engaged in maintaining order in their communities.
2. The Sioux maintained an organized system of volunteer police known as the *akicitas*. Describe their role.
3. List who administered justice in the colonies prior to America's independence.
4. State the origin of the use of militias and town watches in America.
5. Explain why the militia as an institution fell into disuse after the War of 1812.
6. Identify the modern version of the militia.
7. Who and which made it possible for U.S. deputy marshals and National Guardsman to be deployed in the South to enforce federal court orders for integration of schools and public accommodations?
8. Describe the origin of caseworkers or social workers.
9. Identify two pre–Civil War and two post–Civil War vigilante groups.
10. Do you believe that 15-year-olds should be able to make arrests as part of a youth police group? Discuss.
11. What fact or facts contributed to the rise of youth safety patrols?
12. What were some of the issues that affected working class, urban families in the late 1800s?
13. Describe the activities of the Anti-Saloon League.
14. List the types of duties that the APL was authorized by the U.S. Department of Justice to carry out.
15. What activities preoccupied the urban police so that ASL and APL operatives were needed to carry out specific law enforcement functions?

## Notes

1. "In early England, the land was divided into geographic areas between a few individual kings—these geographic areas were called shires. Within each shire there was an individual called a reeve, which meant guardian. This individual was originally selected by the serfs to be their informal social and governmental leader. The kings observed how influential this individual was within the serf community and soon incorporated that position into the governmental structure. The reeve soon became the King's appointed representative to protect the King's interest and act as mediator with people of his

particular shire. Through time and usage the words shire and reeve came together to be shire-reeve, guardian of the shire and eventually the word sheriff, as we know it today" (Scott 2013).

2. In the United Kingdom, the role of special constables has evolved from the performance of limited service on special occasions (especially during national emergencies) to routine neighborhood patrol assignments. In addition, the police force of the city of London and the Metropolitan Police use specials to conduct neighborhood self-defense classes. In Wiltshire, specials coordinate the neighborhood watch program. In 1986, there were more than 16,000 special constables in England and Wales, just under a third of whom were women (Conference on Special Constables 1987).

3. In 2013, a memorial wall to honor members of the Cherokee Nation who were forcibly removed from their native homeland was dedicated at the Cherokee Removal Memorial Park in Birchwood, TN. The location was selected because it is along the "Trail of Tears." Here, 9,000 Native Americans crossed a river and, at this stage of their journey, "they knew their homeland was gone forever" (Phipps 2013). Nancy Williams, park manager for the Cherokee Removal Memorial Park, said the Trail of Tears was much more brutal than people would like to think. Native Americans were forced to march in the worst winter on record in Tennessee (Phipps 2013).

4. Important treatments of slave patrols are found in several doctoral dissertations. Henry (1968) studied patrols in South Carolina from their origins in the late 1600s until 1860. He discusses the legal status and punishment of slaves, the role of the overseer, the patrol system, slave insurrections, and a variety of other aspects related to the lives of southern slaves, runaway slaves, and freed slaves. Hadden's study (1993) is divided into six parts including the origins of slave patrols, organization and administration, methods of appointment and compensation, routine functions of slave patrols, responses in time of crisis, and facts related to patrols during the Civil War and at the war's conclusion. In her discussion of the reasons for the formation of the original patrol groups, Hadden draws upon Henry's discussion of the origins of slave patrols in the late seventeenth and eighteenth centuries. Her dissertation includes an interesting epilogue concerning the legacy of patrols with respect to the establishment of regular police systems as well as the founding of the Ku Klux Klan. Subsequently, Hadden's dissertation was revised and published as *Slave Patrols: Law and Violence in Virginia and the Carolinas.* Currently, this volume is the most definitive work on this subject. Yanochik (1997) presents three essays regarding the economics of slavery. His second essay examines the economic effects of the slave patrol system. He considers some of the legal aspects of patrols as well as the personal characteristics of the individuals serving on them. He concludes that slave patrols acted as a subsidy to slave owners and that this served to lower the cost of using slave labor. Slavery served as a profitable mode of labor utilization in the South, in part due to the fact that the costs of maintaining slave labor would have been higher for the slave owner if the full cost of policing slaves had fallen on them. Green (1997) explores the relationship between slave patrols in South Carolina and the police in northern industrial centers. He notes the similarity in their features as well as the reasons for their existence. He found that "each law enforcement apparatus acted to protect the interests of the dominant economic class" (Green 1997, 121).

# References

Barker, M. L. (1994). *American Indian tribal police: An overview and case study.* Unpublished doctoral dissertation, State University of New York, Albany.

Bayley, D. H. (1985). *Patterns of policing: A comparative international analysis.* New Brunswick, NJ: Rutgers University Press.

Boy Police of New York. (1915, July 28). *The Outlook*, pp. 706–708.

Brown, R. M. (1971). Legal and behavioral perspectives on American vigilantism. In D. Fleming and B. Bailyn (Eds.), *Perspectives in American history Vol. 5* (pp. 95–144). Cambridge, NY: Charles Warren Center for Studies in American History, Harvard University.

Brown, R. M. (1975). *Strain of violence: Historical studies of American violence and vigilantism.* New York: Oxford University Press.

Buffardi, H. C. (1998). The history of the office of sheriff. Retrieved November 9, 2013 from http://www.correctionhistory.org/html/chronicl/sheriff/ch10.htm

Burrows, E., and Wallace, M. (1999). *A history of New York City to 1898.* New York: Oxford University Press.

Conference on Special Constables. (1987). *Report of the conference on special constables.* London: Home Department.

Critchley, T. (1967). *A history of police in England and Wales.* London: Constable & Co.

Cress, L. D. (1982). *Citizens in arms: The army and the militia in American society to the war of 1812.* Chapel Hill, NC: University of North Carolina Press.

Debnam, B. (2003, June 29). Minutemen and the Declaration: Citizen soldiers. *TV Plus-The Sunday Gazette Supplement*, pp. 21–24.

Deloria, V., Jr., and Lytle, C. (1983). *American Indian, American justice.* Austin, TX: University of Texas Press.

Engelmann, L. (1979). *Intemperance: The lost war against liquor.* New York: Free Press.

Fogelson, R. (1977). *Big-city police.* Cambridge, MA: Harvard University Press.

Friedman, L. M. (1993). *Crime and punishment in American history.* New York: Basic Books.

Garry, E. (1980). *Volunteers in the criminal justice system: A literature review and selected bibliography.* Washington, DC: U.S. Department of Justice, National Institute of Justice.

Green, E. (1997). *Origins of American policing: Slave patrols in South Carolina from colonial times to 1865.* Unpublished doctoral dissertation, Howard University, Washington, DC.

Guarding Five Million Children. (1932, September). *School Life*, pp. 7 & 18.

Gusfield, J. R. (1963). *Symbolic crusade: Status politics and the American temperance movement.* Urbana, IL: University of Illinois Press.

Hadden, S. E. (1993). *Law enforcement in a new nation: Slave patrols and public authority in the old south, 1700–1865.* Unpublished doctoral dissertation, Harvard University, Cambridge, MA.

Hadden, S. E. (2001). *Slave patrols: Law and violence in Virginia and the Carolinas.* Cambridge, MA: Harvard University Press.

Hagan, W. (1966). *Indian police and judges: Experiments in acculturation and control.* New Haven, CT: Yale University Press.

Hassrick, R. (1964). *The Sioux: Life and customs of a warrior society.* Norman, OK: University of Oklahoma Press.

Henry, M. A. (1968). *The police control of the slave in South Carolina*. New York: Negro Universities Press. (Original work presented as a doctoral dissertation to Vanderbilt University in 1913).

Henry County Sheriff. (2010). A brief history of the office of sheriff. Retrieved November 9, 2013 from http://www.henrycountysheriff.net/SheriffsofHenry County/HistoryoftheOfficeoftheSheriff/tabid/208/Default.aspx

Honolulu Police Department. (2000). Junior police officers. Retrieved July 30, 2000 from http://www.honolulupd.org/history/museum/mu15.htm

Horan, J. D. (1967). *The Pinkertons: The detective dynasty that made history*. New York: Crown.

Hough, E. (1919). *The web*. Chicago: Reilly & Lee.

Hovey, E. B. (1998). *Stamping out smut: The enforcement of obscenity laws, 1872–1915*. Unpublished doctoral dissertation, Columbia University, New York.

Hoxie, F. (1986). Towards a new North American Indian legal history. *American Journal of Legal History, 30*, 351–352.

Humphrey, N. (1942). Police and tribal welfare in Plains and Indian culture. *Journal of Criminal Law and Criminology, 33*, 147–161.

Jensen, J. M. (1968). *The price of vigilance*. Chicago: Rand McNally.

Johnson, H. A., and Wolfe, N. T. (1996). *History of criminal justice* (Rev. ed.). Cincinnati, OH: Anderson.

Karmen, A. (1990). *Crime victims: An introduction to victimology* (Rev. ed.). Pacific Grove, CA: Brooks/Cole.

Katz, M. B. (1996). *In the shadow of the poorhouse: A social history of welfare in America* (Rev. ed.). New York: Basic Books.

Kelling, G. L., and Moore, M. H. (1988). *The evolving strategy of policing*. Washington, DC: U.S. Department of Justice, National Institute of Justice. Retrieved February 28, 2014 from https://ncjrs.gov/pdffiles1/nij/114213.pdf

Klockars, C. (1985). *The idea of police*. Beverly Hills, CA: Sage.

Leon, C. K. (1991). *Special constables: An historical and contemporary survey*. Unpublished doctoral dissertation, University of Bath, Bath, UK.

Mails, T. (1973). *Dog soldiers, bear men and buffalo women: A study of the societies and cults of the Plains Indians*. Upper Saddle River, NJ: Galahad Books.

Norman Conquest. (2013). Norman conquest of England. Retrieved November 9, 2013 from https://www.princeton.edu/~achaney/tmve/wiki100k/docs/Norman_conquest_of_England.html

Oertly, L. (2013). The fascinating history of the office of the sheriff, 1696–1996. Retrieved November 9, 2013 from http://www.pghistory.org/PG/PG300/sherifhist.html

Peak, K. J. (1997). *Policing America: Methods, issues, challenges* (2nd ed.). Upper Saddle River, NJ: Prentice Hall.

Perloff, R. (2000, January 16). The horror that was lynching. *New York Sunday Times*, sec. 4, p. 16.

Phipps, S. (2013, October 23). Dedication of Cherokee Removal Memorial Wall concludes 25-year project. Retrieved November 6, 2013 from http://www.nooga.com/163965/dedication-of-cherokee-removal-memorial-wall-concludes-25-year-project/

Prassel, F. (1972). *The western peace officer*. Norman: The University of Oklahoma Press.

Roosevelt Pursues. (2013). Roosevelt pursues the boat thieves. Retrieved November 8, 2013 from http://www.nps.gov/thro/historyculture/roosevelt-pursues-boat-thieves.htm

Rosseland, F. M. (1926, November). Nine years without an injury to children on their way to or from school. *American City*, p. 684.

Schoolboy Patrols Approved by the President. (1933, October). *American City*, p. 70.

Scott, R. (2013). 'ROOTS': An historical perspective of the office of sheriff. Retrieved November 9, 2013 from http://www.sheriffs.org/content/office-sheriff

Seth, R. (1961). *The specials: The story of the special constabulary in England, Wales and Scotland*. London: Victor Gollancz.

Sherwood Forest Archaeology Project. (2014). Outlaws. Retrieved June 23, 2014 from http://sherwoodforesthistory.blogspot.com/p/outlaws-villains.html

Slosson, P. (1958). *The great crusade and after: 1914–1928*. Chicago: Quadrangle Paperbacks. (Original work published in 1930).

Stentiford, B. M. (2002). *The American Home Guard: The state militia in the twentieth century*. College Station, TX: Texas A & M University Press.

St. Mary's County Sheriff. (2013). Sheriffs' office history. Retrieved November 9, 2013 from http://www.firstsheriff.com/sheriffofficehistory.asp

Sullivan, M. (1939). *Our times 1900–1925*. New York: Charles Scribner's Sons.

Timberlake, J. H. (1963). *Prohibition and the progressive movement 1900–1920*. Cambridge, MA: Harvard University Press.

Trattner, W. I. (1989). *From poor law to welfare state: A history of social welfare in America* (4th ed.). New York: The Free Press.

Travis, L. F. (1995). *Introduction to criminal justice* (2nd ed.). Cincinnati, OH: Anderson.

Walker, S. (1976). The urban police in American history: A review of the literature. *Journal of Police Science and Administration, 4*(3), 252.

Walker, S. (1998). *Popular justice: A history of American criminal justice* (Rev. ed.). New York: Oxford University Press.

Willard, F. (2013). Frances Willard and the Woman's Christian Temperance Union, 1874–1898. Retrieved November 8, 2013 from http://www.franceswillardhouse.org/uploads/HST391-Project-2-finished_-_printer.pdf

Wilson, J. Q. (1975). *Thinking about crime*. New York: Basic Books.

Yanochik, M. A. (1997). *Essays on the economics of slavery*. Unpublished doctoral dissertation, Auburn University, Alabama.

# Auxiliaries and Reserves
## Volunteer Police Generalists

4

> Volunteering is the ultimate exercise in Democracy. In an election, you vote once—when you volunteer, you vote for your community every day.

**—Deputy Inspector Phylis S. Byrne**
*Commanding Officer, New York City Police Department Patrol Service Bureau's Auxiliary Police Section (NYC Press Release 2012)*

The International Association of Police Chiefs (IAPC) has listed more than 2,000 volunteer programs involving more than 200,000 citizens helping to augment police services (U.S. Department of Justice 2011). The existence of so many programs and participants is reminiscent of earlier times in U.S. history when citizen support and participation in community activities, such as the justice system, was viewed as a necessity in a democratic society. In those earlier times, it was commonplace for community residents to look after one another. Since the entry of the United States into World War II, there has been a resurgence of interest in civic participation. For example, many community residents throughout the United States are policing themselves through the establishment of "neighborhood watch" groups. They are selecting block captains, engaging in neighborhood surveillance, holding regularly scheduled safety meetings, and sometimes engaging in organized patrols. Local and national organizations concerned with public safety have benefitted from this renewed spirit of civic engagement. For example, at the national level, the all-volunteer Civil Air Patrol (CAP) has resources that are almost unparalleled by any other civilian search and rescue organization in the world today, including America's largest privately owned fleet of single engine aircraft and the world's largest privately owned shortwave radio network. Within six months of the Cadet CAP Program's inception in 1942, more than 20,000 youth had joined across the country (Blascovich 2013). In more recent years, new groups known as Community Emergency Response Team (CERT) volunteers have been recruited and trained at the local level. CERT teams support their local communities by assisting in emergency preparedness and response and by educating their communities about emergency preparedness. New York City (NYC) has more than 1,500 active CERT volunteers, and there are more than 3,500 CERT programs in the United States (NYC Press Release 2012).[1]

This chapter looks at seven different auxiliary and reserve volunteer police units. They have distinctive names, but a lack of consistency in the use of unit titles makes it difficult to ascribe specific characteristics to each category. Nevertheless, a trend appears to have developed with respect to the use of titles in certain parts of the United States, especially within several New England states and in California. The seven units discussed are: the Buffalo (New York) Police Reserve; the Brentwood (California) Reserve Police; the Cheltenham Township (Pennsylvania) Auxiliary Police; the Los Angeles (California) Reserve Police; the NYC Auxiliary Police; the NYC Parks Department Mounted Auxiliary Unit, Inc.; and the Albemarle County (Virginia) Auxiliary Police. According to Judge George Edwards, without such support, "the police tend to become an alien force imposing its power on a resentful population" (Greenberg 1984, 47). In addition, some details regarding the city of Miami's volunteer police are presented because its police department houses both auxiliary and reserve police units. However, tenuous, some distinctions, mostly regional in nature with respect to the two most common titles—reserve and auxiliary—can be discerned by examining aspects of volunteer law enforcement programs.

## The Origins of Auxiliary and Reserve Police

The first white settlement in New York took place at the southern end of the island of Manhattan in about 1610. The area was known as Fort Amsterdam and was controlled by the Dutch East India Company. The Dutch settlement of New Amsterdam "created a burgher watch in 1643, one year after it was founded, but did not pay them until 1712" (Bayley 1985, 32). The English took possession of this region in 1664 and renamed it New York in honor of the Duke of York. Eventually, either elected or appointed constables, marshals, or watches were established in every settlement (Bayley 1985, 32).

Before whistles and radios, law enforcement used wooden rattles and their distinct noise to signal for help, even into the nineteenth century (Early Days 2012). The watchmen patrolled using their wooden rattles to warn people of threats or fires. The patrols also carried green lanterns from sunset until dawn. They hung their lanterns on a hook by the front door of the watch house to show they were on the job. Today, green lights are still placed outside the entrances of some police stations as a symbol that the "watch" is present and vigilant. In the decades between the American Revolution and the Civil War, the growth of population and industrialization eventually led to the unification of day and night watches to form municipal police departments. Philadelphia had accomplished such a unification in 1833, and by 1845, NYC had merged its two police forces. At the same time, London's new Metropolitan Police (established in 1829) served as a model for the effectiveness of a centralized and preventive type of police force.

Nonetheless, the establishment of such full-time police forces has not diminished the need for supplemental personnel, especially in rural areas where the only available police may be faraway. Today, most local and state police agencies in the United States recruit and train civilian employees. In addition, since the end of World War I, the use of unpaid volunteers in sworn or non-sworn capacities has become a standard practice in many police departments. Some of the titles of such volunteers have included special deputy, reserve deputy sheriff, reserve posse member, supernumerary, and reserve officer. However, by the second half of the twentieth century, there emerged two distinctive categories for unpaid or minimally paid volunteers: auxiliary and reserve. In some ways, these volunteer police may remind us of the old watch and ward committees that existed in the early settlements of New England.

Generally, the "auxiliary police officer" is an individual who wears a police uniform but does not possess regular police authority. The "reserve police officer" wears a police uniform and usually does possess regular police officer powers while in uniform and on duty. Some very clear exceptions exist to this general conclusion, and a few of these are considered here. Auxiliaries and reserves are required to conform to departmental rules and regulations, to undergo recruit and in-service training, and to participate in prescribed activities on a regular basis in order to maintain their positions. In most jurisdictions, they are uncompensated except for a clothing allowance and participation in state workmen's compensation programs. Their primary job is to serve as a deterrent to crime. It is generally believed that if a person bent on crime spots a uniformed officer on the street, he or she will think twice about committing a crime. If auxiliaries spot something wrong, they are instructed to call the stationhouse or use their walkie-talkies to call for immediate help.

The Miami (Florida) Police Department recruits and deploys both reserve and auxiliary officers. Candidates for positions as auxiliary or reserve police officers have different selection and training requirements. For example, auxiliaries must successfully complete a minimum of 272 hours of training consisting of a prerequisite course, which includes the 48-hour Medical First Responder Training Course; a weapons course; and various defensive tactics and high-liability training courses. There is also an optional 32-hour Vehicle Operations Training Course that may be required. On the contrary, reserve officers must satisfy all of the eligibility requirements established for full-time police officers as well as the minimum departmental requirements established by Florida's Criminal Justice Standards and Training Commission. The auxiliary serves without compensation assisting full-time or part-time officers and may—under the direct supervision of a full-time law enforcement officer—arrest and perform law enforcement functions. Reserve police officers have enhanced authority and are is considered part-time law enforcement officers Miami's reserve officers may be employed or appointed less than full-time, with or without compensation with the authority to bear arms and make arrests and whose primary responsibility is the prevention and detection of crime or the enforcement of penal, criminal, traffic, or highway laws of the state. At the Miami Police Department, both auxiliary police officers and reserve police officers are required to receive training on the use of force and to successfully complete annual firearms qualifications (Miami PD 2014).

In an odd twist of fate, an existing auxiliary police force in Los Angeles was upgraded to a reserve police program at the end of World War II. However, in NYC, a reserve force active in the 1920s was disbanded about a decade prior to America's entry into World War II. During World War II, NYC established a short-lived organization of volunteer police known as the "City Patrol Corps." Later, it created its present-day auxiliary program. During the wartime period, when enlistment in the armed forces acutely depleted the ranks of qualified full-time police recruits, many cities and towns throughout the United States turned to local residents to supplement the shortage of full-time police officers. Throughout the country, tens of thousands of citizens volunteered their services as civilian defense auxiliary police and as air raid wardens.

Today, NYC's auxiliary program involves approximately 4,500 auxiliary police officers. Their most distinctive feature is the star-shaped badge they have been issued since the late 1960s. This huge force, the largest of its kind in the United States, is trained to use radios to call for help. They receive about 64 hours of classroom instruction stretched over several months. They are armed only with a police nightstick but face the same risks as any regular full-time police officer. According to James Mitts, the volunteer commanding officer of the 125-member auxiliary unit at the 109th Precinct in Flushing, Queens, "We tell our people, 'Don't get into foot pursuits to apprehend somebody'" (Barron and Kilgannon 2007, p. 5). NYC auxiliary officers are repeatedly told that they are not police officers, only private citizens who act as "the eyes and ears" of the police department. On the contrary, Los Angeles's 700 police reserve officers receive hundreds of hours of instruction, and their volunteer police officers are armed and given additional instruction in order to carry out police duties that include making felony arrests.

## NYC and Buffalo

Prior to America's entry into World War I, long-standing suspicions about the need for a standing army contributed to debate about the need for troop and equipment buildups. Many residents of the rural South and West opposed military expansion. However, a compromise was accepted by President Wilson that resulted in the passage of the National Defense

Act of 1916[2] (Tindall and Shi 2007). Although the U.S. Congress debated the need for such legislation, New York State and several cities led the way for protection on the home front.

The city of Buffalo, New York, was incorporated in 1832. By the time of World War I, it had a population of about 450,000 and a police force of about 800 regular officers that were assigned to 15 police stations. In place of the muddy roads of earlier days, Buffalo now had more than 600 miles of paved streets with about 30,000 automobiles. Seventeen different railroads, 13 of them trunk lines, entered the city. It had 2,500 manufacturing plants. Buffalo also had easy access to water transportation (being located at the foot of Lake Erie and the terminus of the state's barge canal transport system); it ranked high on the nation's list of industrial cities. It also had 66 public and 40 parochial schools, three colleges and the University of Buffalo, 19 hospitals, and six English daily newspapers. In short, Buffalo was an American city with critical infrastructure that was important to protect during wartime (Sweeney 1920).

On April 2, 1917, President Woodrow Wilson appeared before a joint session of the U.S. Congress to request a declaration of war against Germany. Wilson cited Germany's violation of its pledge to suspend unrestricted submarine warfare in the North Atlantic and the Mediterranean and its attempts to entice Mexico into an alliance against the United States as his reasons for declaring war.[3] On April 4, 1917, the U.S. Senate voted in support of the measure. The House concurred two days later. The United States later declared war on Austria-Hungary on December 7, 1917 (Office of the Historian 2014).

Many people in the United States had not been inclined to go to war with Germany, but state and local governments in many parts of the nation abruptly took steps to mobilize for the war effort upon learning of Wilson's war message. Thus, 12 days after Congress approved President Wilson's request, Mayor Louis P. Fuhrmann called for the creation of a reserve police force for the protection of life and property within the city of Buffalo. He asked for citizens "to act as volunteer policemen, so that in case of extreme emergencies, where a large number of policemen were needed, the reserve would be ready and willing to offer their services as special policemen" (Sweeney 1920, 430).

The reserve force received no compensation from the city of Buffalo. Members were issued a badge, baton, and patrol box keys. They "were organized and existed purely for the patriotic purpose of serving their city in case of riots or uprising, and when the members of the Police Department were detailed to protect the great water front which contained hundreds of storehouses and grain elevators, the Police Reserve after daily toil in banks, offices, and in the shops, patrolled the streets of the city in the absence of the regular police. The Police Reserve was a very active organization until long after the signing of the Armistice. They assisted the Department in disposing of a great many Liberty Bonds and War Savings Stamps, assisted the Red Cross to keep order at parades, and helped with election day and registration day details…. They were required to attend meetings at the station house once each week for the purpose of being instructed in the proper method of performing police duties, and observing rules and regulations, laws and ordinances. They were drilled in the military drills of the U.S. Army, received lectures from the training school instructor, and were ready to give efficient service when called upon, as was proven by the many meritorious arrests made by their members" (Sweeney 1920, 430). During the 1950s and 1960s, the Buffalo Police Department coordinated a civil defense auxiliary police program.[4] A successor organization now exists in the city of Buffalo, and it consists of a small group of uncompensated volunteers (about 45) who routinely maintain security at more than 40 events a year. Some of these events include: Winterfest at Delaware Park, the Shamrock Run, the fourth of July celebration at Riverside Park, and National Night Out. The events the "Buffalo Police Reserves" attend are first cleared through the city's police commissioner and then voted on by its membership before being accepted as an event or function to perform (Buffalo Police Reserves 2014a). A nonrefundable application fee is paid by potential members. Membership requirements include U.S. citizenship; being at least 20 years of age; the possession of a New York State driver's license; and satisfactory criminal history, drug testing, and physician physical fitness reports (Buffalo Police Reserves 2014b).

At the same time that the first Buffalo Police Reserve was being organized, Mayor Fuhrmann instituted a separate organization known as the Volunteer Patrol League. Members of the League were required to furnish their automobiles for patrol purposes in the city's residential districts. Also as a consequence of wartime preparation, in New York State, each county (pursuant to directives from New York's governor and the state's adjutant general) was required to establish a Home Defense Committee. These county committees formed additional committees to carry out their responsibilities, one of which was to organize and equip a Home Defense Corps. In due course, Erie County succeeded in establishing such an organization consisting of 12 companies in Buffalo and one each in the communities of Tonawanda, Kenmore, Depew, and East Aurora. The average number of men in a company was 80, making a total of 1,280. It was soon renamed the Home Defense Reserve. Officers for each company were selected based on prior military organization experience. In general, membership was composed of individuals who were either beyond draft age or too young to be conscripted. The companies participated in drills and helped with Liberty Loan campaigns. Over time, many members who remained on the home front joined the state militia or the state guard (Sweeney 1920).

By May 1916, 8,000 citizens in NYC had been enrolled into a "Citizens Home Defense League," Within two additional months that number had reached 21,000. It was also during this period when an early forerunner to today's Law Enforcement Explorer Posts and Police Athletic Leagues was established in NYC. It was known as the "junior police." At its peak, NYC's junior police program had enrolled approximately 6,000 boys between the ages of 11 and 15. By 1919, the "Citizens Home Defense League" had become a reserve force, and a state law was passed in 1920 that reorganized this group into a permanent adjunct to the police force with full police powers when on active duty. These assignments were curtailed in the late 1920s, and the reserves were formally abolished by order of the city's police commissioner in 1934 (Greenberg 1984).

When the United States entered World War II, Mayor Fiorello LaGuardia created a new type of auxiliary police force, the "City Patrol Corps." By 1942, this emergency auxiliary police force was in full operation, and by 1943, it had 32 companies with a total of nearly 4,500 volunteers. Its last patrol was on August 30, 1945; one month later it was officially demobilized. The corps helped to preserve the city's infrastructure and prevented crime during a significant period of world upheaval (Greenberg 1984).

Figure 4.1 is a photo of the front and rear covers of a 1942 "Civil Defense Index" booklet. Its pages offered information to civilians on the home front. Survival-related advice was given for air raids, blackouts, bombs, poison gas, as well as first aid situations. The rear cover (right side as seen in Figure 4.1)

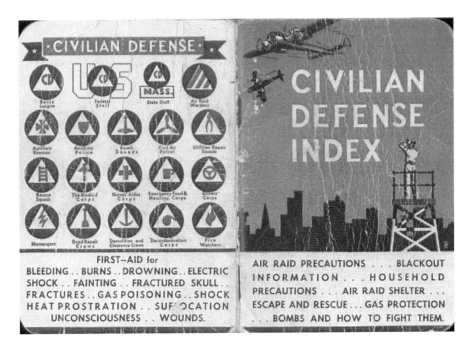

**Figure 4.1** Photo of the front and rear covers of a 1942 *Civil Defense Index* booklet.

indicates the various units of civilian defense in which Americans were urged to enroll.

At the start of the Korean War, Congress passed Public Law No. 920 (entitled The Civil Defense Act of 1950), which authorized a Federal Civil Defense Program. This law provided a plan for the protection of life and property in the United States in the event of a national emergency, such as a nuclear attack. The responsibility for civil defense was vested in the states and their political subdivisions. The New York State Legislature followed the recommendations of the federal government and, in 1951, enacted the New York State Defense Emergency Act, which empowered the city of New York to create a civil defense program. This act, which is still in force, requires cities in New York State to recruit, train, and equip volunteers who will act as an adjunct to the regular police departments in the event of a civil defense emergency or natural disaster. In the final organization chart, NYC's defenses were divided into five volunteer divisions: police emergency, fire, public works, health, and emergency welfare. Currently, auxiliaries throughout the state function by virtue of the 1951 statute, and their routine patrols and assignments are officially considered training exercises (Greenberg 1984). However, as can be observed from the foregoing discussion, the origin of NYC's present-day auxiliary police program can be traced to several earlier volunteer defense groups.

In counties and cities throughout New York State during the 1950s, units of auxiliary police were organized under the various local community civil defense units, which were each headed by a local volunteer director. Nassau County is immediately east of NYC, within the New York metropolitan area. After World War II, training for auxiliaries in Nassau County consisted largely of an inspector from the Nassau County Police Department (NCPD) occasionally stopping by at an auxiliary police meeting. In the 1960s, the NCPD took responsibility for the program by detailing a deputy inspector to the county civil defense agency to serve as the head of the county's auxiliary program. Later, the county's commissioner of police ordered that each auxiliary police officer attend an approved 23-session Nassau County Police Department Basic Training Course. Eventually, the NCPD took over responsibility for county-level oversight and direction. In the 1970s, their duties changed, reflecting concerns about safety. The auxiliary police were used as "eyes and ears" against crime. They were also used for various community- and county-sponsored events. They assisted the police department with traffic and crowd control, allowing regular police to devote more attention to emergencies and other duties.[5]

In 1967, John V. Lindsay, the Mayor of NYC, signed Executive Order #51. In that order, the NYC Police Department was given full responsibility for the city's auxiliary police. Executive Order No. 38 (August 29, 1975) continued this responsibility. The second order was sparked by a period of turmoil in the ranks of regular and volunteer police. Throughout much of the 1980s, the auxiliary program moved along with little fanfare or further controversy. On occasion, however, there was enlightening press coverage. For example, in 1988, the *New York Times* reported that the "auxiliaries span the city's social order, from Wall Street professionals to high-school drop-outs. They are held up by Police Commissioner Benjamin Ward and other police officials as an example of what civilians can do to help maintain order" (Hays 1988, p. 30). Members must be between the ages of 17 and 63 in order to patrol; persons over 63 may apply for administrative duties. (See Box 4.1 for the current requirements for membership.)

A Housing Auxiliary Police program was started in 1992 as a pilot project. Subsequently, this program expanded to the residents of the housing developments throughout the city. Auxiliaries patrol in each of nine Housing

---

**BOX 4.1   NEW YORK CITY AUXILIARY
POLICE MEMBERSHIP REQUIREMENTS**

- At least age 17
- Be in good health
- Proof of good character and satisfactory background
- Must comply with zero tolerance department drug policy
- Able to read and write English
- Be a U.S. citizen, lawful permanent resident, or authorized to work in the United States
- Live in New York City or live in one of the six authorized surrounding counties (Nassau, Suffolk, Westchester, Rockland, Orange, and Putnam) and work within New York City
- Must possess a valid New York State driver's license or New York State identification card
- A minimum of 144 hours of duty per fiscal year is required. Must comply with zero tolerance Department drug policy (Careers 2014)
- Never been convicted of a felony or have a previous arrest record that would prevent acceptance (Careers 2014; Kelly et al. 2008, 2, 5)

*Source:* Careers, 2014, Careers – Auxiliary police, available at: http://www. nyc.gov/html/nypd/html/careers/auxiliary_police.shtml; Kelly, R. W. et al., 2008, Auxiliary police program overview, available at: http://www. nyc.gov/html/nypd/downloads/pdf/careers/nypd_auxiliary_police_ overview_2008.pdf

Police Service Areas and are used for crime prevention, community events, and administrative functions. They attend tenant association and youth meetings to coordinate perimeter and lobby patrols and to address such specific concerns as gang-related activity.

The NYC Transit District auxiliary police crime deterrent program started in 2000, also as a pilot project in one area. In July 2005, this program expanded to include all 12 Transit Districts. Auxiliaries assigned to transit (subway) patrols center their activities at the entrances and exits, stairs leading to and from stations, mezzanine areas, and in street areas in the immediate vicinity of subway stations. This initiative was related to the 2005 London transit bombings. If medically qualified, transit auxiliaries may respond to common medical emergency calls in the transit system if they are near to the transit location. The main functions of the Transit auxiliary police primarily remain within the subway system.

NYC auxiliaries are also assigned to harbor, highway, headquarters, and special task units. In all of these units as well as in each of the city's 76 patrol precincts, members are supervised by officers of the regular police as well as superiors within the auxiliary police ranks.

Auxiliary police officers in NYC, unlike many of their counterparts in upstate New York, are not permitted to carry a sidearm on duty, even if independently licensed to carry a firearm. This restriction may have contributed to a major tragedy that occurred more than halfway into the first decade of the twenty-first century. Sixth Precinct Auxiliary Police Officers Eugene Marshalik (age 19) and Nicholas T. Pekearo (age 28) were killed in March 2007 by a gunman who had first fired upon and killed a pizzeria employee in Greenwich Village. The gunman then shot the two on-duty auxiliaries at close range. They were the seventh and eighth NYC auxiliary officers killed while on duty in the auxiliary force's modern-day history (which commenced during the Korean War era). Their deaths alone were tragic enough, but the matter became more heartbreaking with an initial decision by the federal government to deny death benefits for their families under the Public Safety Officers Benefits (PSOB) program. The federal government's representatives claimed that although the officers were killed in the line of duty, their lack of peace officer status when they were killed made them ineligible. The federal government came under heavy criticism for denying the benefits, and NYC Police Commissioner Raymond Kelly and U.S. Senator Charles Schumer made personal appeals to the Department of Justice on behalf of the stricken families. In a NYC Police Department (NYPD) press release, Kelly stated: "The City of New York has already awarded the death benefits available to Auxiliary Police Officers. It only makes sense that the Department of Justice follow suit and recognize Eugene and Nicholas as public safety officers within the meaning of the law. This was a wrong-headed decision. It needs to be reversed" (NYPD 2008). In March 2008, Kelly testified before an administrative hearing judge. At the appeal hearing, Commissioner Kelly stated that the killer had "made the calculated decision to specifically target Officers Pekearo and Marshalik because of their affiliation with the NYPD. It was the officers' willingness to continue to be the eyes and ears of the NYPD that led to these tragic results" (Gendar et al. 2008, p. 6). With respect to the U. S. Justice Department's reasoning in its original decision denying benefits, Kelly stated: "It's a hyper technical interpretation. Every citizen has arrest powers. You can arrest for a felony in any crime that takes place in your presence" (Gendar et al. 2008, p. 6). Finally, after much additional publicity, U.S. Attorney General Michael Mukasey reversed the original ruling and approved the death benefits.[6]

Two years later and more than 16 years after another NYPD auxiliary officer was slain trying to apprehend a gunman in the Bronx, the government granted a line-of-duty death benefit to the family of Milton Clarke. The Justice Department had repeatedly refused to grant the monetary award under the PSOB program to the Clarke family because auxiliaries are not considered peace officers. Clarke was off duty, working in his auto repair shop on December 1, 1993, when he heard the nearby sound of shots fired; he retrieved his licensed handgun. A 47-year-old father of five, Clarke ran in the direction of the gunfire and was immediately shot in the chest by a gunman who had wounded another man (Marzulli 2010). The precedent of the earlier award of benefits no doubt led to the payment of the claim instituted by the Clarke family.

In March 2007, less than two weeks after the unarmed volunteers were killed, Mayor Bloomberg vowed to provide bulletproof vests to each of the city's 4,500 auxiliaries.[7] In addition, a committee was selected to review the auxiliary program at the request of Commissioner Kelly. The report was supposed to be completed in 90 days.[8] About a year later, a report was released by the NYPD. The report began with these statements: "The Department has made it clear that the Auxiliary Police Program is one of the best vehicles offered for involving the citizenry and community in promoting public safety through their personal participation. Ranking superior officers of the NYPD have favorably evaluated the Auxiliary Police Program. Commanding Officers are encouraged to fully utilize this valuable personnel resource" (Kelly et al. 2008, 2).

The review report revealed some information that was not generally known to the public. For example, some auxiliaries participate in "quality of life" enforcement initiatives. The participants must be between the ages of 18 and 20½ and are given specialized training at the auxiliary police headquarters by members of the Organized Crime Control Bureau (OCCB) Vice Enforcement Unit and auxiliary police headquarters staff in safety, tactics, and integrity. They work in plainclothes under the direct supervision of the vice enforcement or precinct conditions unit supervisor. They are trained to attempt to purchase alcohol, box cutters, and other items that are not permitted to be displayed or sold to minors in licensed premises. Acting on community complaints, such undercover operations take place at restaurants, bars, and liquor and grocery stores. Each year summonses are issued by borough vice and precinct conditions units using auxiliary police (Kelly et al. 2008, 8, 17).

For a number of years, there were opportunities to participate in bicycle units in various commands. The bicycles were obtained through community donations or from the Community Policing Unit. Candidates for this assignment attended the department's bicycle training course conducted by the Police Academy Driver Training Unit at Floyd Bennett Field (Kelly et al. 2008). In 2011, apparently as a result of an unfavorable New York State Department of Labor investigation concerning the city's auxiliary program, the Auxiliary Bike Patrol Program was suspended. At that time, there was concern that an auxiliary officer's wooden nightstick might get stuck in bicycle wheels as volunteer police pedaled (Auer 2011).

Many auxiliaries would like to receive training in the use of pepper spray, to have peace officer status, and to see a state law passed to make it a felony to assault an auxiliary officer. In addition, just a few weeks after the March 2007 deaths of the auxiliary officers, City Councilman David Weprin created a ten-point plan—with the help of auxiliary officers—to improve the program. One of the points included the "full restoration of the Auxiliary Emergency Service Unit (AESU) name and function in order to allow auxiliary officers to properly serve as the auxiliary arm/adjunct of the NYPD Emergencies Services Unit as was originally mandated upon its creation in 1950" (Auxiliary Officers Assistance Plan 2007).[9]

A useful summary of NYC's Auxiliary Police program can be found at: http://cttfauxiliary.com/page5. This Web page indicates that, in 2010, funding for protective vests (Level IIIA vests, the same used by full-time officers) for the auxiliaries was no longer available in the NYPD budget. However, every Police Precinct, Housing Police Service Area, and Transit District had a pool of "loaner" vests for new auxiliary officers to use while on patrol.

There has been some confusion over the "peace officer" status of NYC auxiliaries. However, a 2008 program review report prepared by the leadership of the NYPD clearly states: "Auxiliary Police Officers are neither Police Officers nor Peace Officers (except during an emergency under 2.20 Criminal Procedure Law). They do not carry firearms and [have] no power of arrest beyond that of a private citizen" (Kelly et al. 2008, 2). In addition, the report also explains that: "In the event of an emergency, legislation exists which enables the Police Commissioner, Mayor, and/or New York State Legislature to confer Peace Officer status upon Auxiliary Police. Pursuant to Section 2.20 of the Criminal Procedure Law, Auxiliary Officers may be given Peace Officer status. This limited authority is only valid during a period of imminent or actual attack by enemy forces, or during official duties. The principal function that Auxiliaries would perform during this period would be to direct and control traffic" (Kelly et al. 2008, 3). Yet, several unofficial New York auxiliary police Web sites state that these volunteers are "NYS certified peace officers." Some of these sites refer to the fact that NYC auxiliaries are registered as "part-time peace officers" with a state agency. It needs to be understood that the New York State Division of Criminal Justice Services does not certify police or peace officers but merely maintains a database of employed officers and their training records.

## Los Angeles Police Reserve Corps

California has many reserve police programs, and one of the most significant is the Los Angeles Police Reserve Corps. It is the state's largest volunteer police program with approximately 700 members. Its roots extend deep into the history of California and include meeting the need to recruit civil defense auxiliary police during World War II. During the post-war years, after the program's formal establishment by the Los Angeles (LA) City Council in 1947, its membership reached nearly 2,500. At that time, the reserve force paid for their own equipment and uniforms, much like the NYC auxiliaries. Today, police equipment and uniforms are provided. Unlike their NYC counterparts, the LA reserves' physical and medical membership qualifications were upgraded to be equivalent to that of regular LA police officers. Gradually, training requirements were also expanded so that the standards required by the California Commission on Peace Officer Standards and Training (POST) were met. Training classes are held evenings and weekends. Today, the LA police reserves are divided into three levels of membership.

Level III Reserve Officers are assigned duties at the front desk, with area detectives, and in community relations. Level III Reserve Officers receive approximately 240 hours of professional classroom instruction and must be at least 18 at the time of application for membership. Level III Reserve Officers also receive approximately 26 hours of basic self-defense training including wrist locks, twist locks, kicks, and other techniques at the lower end of the department's use-of-force scale. Physical fitness exercises are used to prepare recruits for self-defense training. Level III members are not eligible to carry firearms until their twenty-first birthday (Reserve Police Officer Program 2013).

Level I and II Reserve Officers receive additional training and must be at least 21 at the time of application. Level II Reserve Officers receive approximately 250 hours of professional classroom instruction. Level I Reserve Officers receive approximately 340 hours of professional classroom instruction. They receive approximately 72 hours of self-defense training. This training includes techniques available within the higher end of the department's use-of-force scale. Physical training includes weight training, calisthenics, and running. The additional hours of training are needed because Level I and II Reserve Officers perform the same functions as regular, full-time police officers. They are armed, uniformed peace officers who work in police vehicles along with full-time police officers (Reserve Police Officer Program 2013). After graduating from the academy, Level I and II Reserve Officers are required to work a minimum of 32 hours every two 28-day deployment periods, and they must attend mandatory monthly reserve officer meetings.

Today, the LA reserves tend to be older than new regular police recruits, and they come from all walks of life. During the day, they may be attorneys, small business owners, government employees, homemakers, retirees, or even city council members. Moreover, like most reserves and auxiliaries located elsewhere, their primary reasons for joining stem from their desire to make the community a better and safer place to live. All reserve officers undergo an exhaustive selection process, including a detailed background check, and are held to the high standards set by the department. As a result, they are looked upon favorably by full-time officers who often ask to work with reservists. One of the first acts performed by Charlie Beck when he became the new Los Angeles Police Department (LAPD) chief of police was to recognize volunteers who serve the community as members of the police reserves. As part of the LAPD's Financial Counseling Team, Attorney Doug Neistat was among those honored for their service. Neistat serves as a specialist reserve officer, working with departmental employees and their families and providing free legal assistance—especially in the areas of bankruptcy and insolvency. Volunteer Police Officer Neistat has served as an LAPD reserve officer since 1998 (Of Counsel 2010).

Like their full-time officer counterparts, LA reserves wear the same badge and have the same gun and the same uniform. They may progress to greater levels of responsibility by meeting additional training requirements. However, although NYC city auxiliaries wear the same uniform as regular officers, their star-shaped badges can distinguish them and none are permitted to carry a firearm while performing their duties. There is a promotional system for NYC auxiliaries, but it does not include the ability to carry out routine law enforcement duties. Some of the youngest auxiliaries may be assigned to undercover operations in order to make underage beverage or cigarette purchases, but it is a very small number. An entry-level LA reservist must work alongside a full-time officer and participate in special events such as festivals and art walks. LA volunteer officers with special qualifications have the opportunity to use their skills for the benefit of the public. For example, an individual with years of legal experience may be assigned as a reserve detective to help the LAPD investigate white-collar crime (Hillard 2011). On the contrary, NYC auxiliaries seldom have opportunities to work alongside full-time officers unless they have reached the higher ranks, such as captain and above.[10] In such cases, these auxiliaries will work closely with their regular precinct auxiliary coordinators in order to help in administrative matters. NYC auxiliary members seeking promotion to ranks of sergeant and above must complete additional training courses.

## Brentwood Reserve Police

The city of Brentwood lies 325 miles north of Los Angeles and 32 miles east of Oakland, California. Brentwood has long been known for its crops of cherries, apricots, plums, peaches, and corn; however, the city has become more of a residential community in the last few decades. The Brentwood Police Department was established in 1948 and services an area of approximately 14 square miles. Prior to its establishment, an elected constable held law and order responsibility. The city is comprised of about 52,000 residents and is divided into four separate patrol beats. With a starting salary of approximately $75,000, the department currently has 62 sworn police officers and another 17 civilian support staff. In addition to its permanent staff, there are approximately 20 police volunteer citizens (Brentwood Police Department 2013). The Brentwood Police Department is in the process of reestablishing a reserve police unit. The department had a strong reserve police program dating back to the 1960s, providing the community with an auxiliary unit of trained and competent volunteer police officers. These officers were used to supplement the department's regular personnel and historically were used for special events, prisoner transports, and in emergencies. In June 2013, the city council voted to recruit a maximum of 10 reserve officers to assist with prisoner transports, traffic control, and public event security under the supervision of sworn officers (Szymanski 2013).

The new reserves will have to satisfy all the hiring qualifications and standards of full-time police officers. They would be expected to work a minimum of 20 hours a month after completing three training modules at the Contra Costa County Regional Police Academy. As Level II volunteer police, they would have the same authority as sworn officers. The city had an active force in the 1980s when the number of reserves outnumbered the full-time police. However, the population of this bedroom community has steadily grown, and the reserves are needed to transport prisoners and cover the local jail, especially on busy Friday nights. In return for their service, volunteers will be provided with all necessary equipment, a $25 monthly uniform cleaning allowance, $100 per court appearance, and an additional $100 for every weekend they agree to be on-call to transport arrestees to the Contra Costa County Detention Facility in Martinez. The program is expected to cost the city an estimated $153,000 a year (Szymanski 2013).

During the 1980s and 1990s, Brentwood had an average of 15 reserve officers, but attrition, retirements, and a lack of qualified candidates are said to have caused the program to be disbanded in 2006. Recently, law enforcement agencies, including the Contra Costa Office of the Sheriff, have started to recruit or create new reserve units (Szymanski 2013).

## New York City Park Volunteer Units

In various western and midwestern states, volunteers who own their own horses and are interested in policing or participating in ceremonial events have become members of sheriff posse mounted units. Many of these units often appear wearing their distinctive regalia in various parades, such as the annual Tournament of Roses parade held in Pasadena, California. NYC's Central Park is patrolled by the NYPD's 22nd Precinct (also known as the Central Park Precinct) and the NYC Parks Enforcement Patrol (PEP) unit. Central Park was designed in 1858 by Fredrick Law Olmstead and Calvert Vaux, and it became the nation's first man-made public park. The park is made up of approximately 840 acres, 150 acres of water and 690 acres of land. It is 2.5 miles long and 0.5 mile wide. There are 58 miles of pedestrian paths, six miles of vehicle drives, and almost five miles of bridle paths. Two different volunteer auxiliaries in mounted units have performed public safety patrols in Central Park since the early 1950s. The first mounted auxiliary patrols were under the supervision of the NYPD, but in recent years, a different organizational unit has been under the command of the city's Parks Department.

In 1955, the Central Park Auxiliary Police unit had 75 members, and 50 of them carried pistols as part of their participation in the unit's gun club. The majority of these auxiliaries patrolled on foot or drove their own cars and motorcycles in order to police the park from 8 p.m. to midnight. In those days, members who choose to patrol on horseback provided their own horses or rented them from a nearby stable for two dollars a tour (Hudson 1955). In a 1974 interview, Auxiliary Inspector Joseph Siegel, an original member of the auxiliary mounted troop, indicated that during World War II he patrolled on horseback in Central Park as a member of the City Patrol Corps. He was instrumental in starting an auxiliary police mounted unit when the city's current auxiliary police force was organized during the Korean War era (Carmody 1974). In 1973, this unit was given added strength when 26 new members—including a night club singer, an economist, a computer programmer, several lawyers and business executives, and Michael Burke, the president of Madison Square Garden—completed the NYPD's riding school in Pelham Bay Park (City's First Auxiliary 1973). By the following year, the unit had grown and was patrolling in various city parks including Manhattan's theater district. In addition, a small uniform allowance became available to help with the cost of uniforms and equipment, but all mounts were provided by the NYPD. However, by the 1980s, unit members were again providing their own mounts (Buder 1980).

In September 1980, the Parks Department established its own full time professional and salaried unit of mounted riders that began park patrols in NYC; they were known as mounted rangers. This contingent joined a new paid urban park ranger force that had been created the previous year to patrol on foot and in vehicles. The mounted rangers were only assigned to daylight patrols (Goodman 1980).

Less well-known is the volunteer mounted auxiliary unit of the NYC Parks Department, which deploys experienced riders to conduct patrols to educate the public and to enforce park rules in Central Park in Manhattan, in Van Cortlandt Park in the Bronx, and in other parks throughout the city (as seen in Figures 4.2 through 4.4). The auxiliary unit serves to deter, identify, and report illegal or unsafe activities and is an informational resource for the public. It raises sufficient funds to pay for itself (Auxiliary Mounted 2013; Karni 2011). In this way, they supplement the services of the full-time, salaried, mounted PEP officers (Z. Feder, personal communication, February 5, 2014).

The mounted volunteers of the city's Parks Department help with crowd control during parades, shut down illegal barbecues, find lost children, and

**Figure 4.2** Members of the NYC Parks Department Mounted Auxiliary Unit on patrol, ca. 2013. (Used with the permission of the NYC Parks Department Mounted Auxiliary Unit, Inc.)

**Figure 4.3** Member of the NYC Parks, Department Mounted Auxiliary Unit on patrol in winter, ca. 2013. (Used with the permission of the NYC Parks Department Mounted Auxiliary Unit, Inc.)

**Figure 4.4** Member of the NYC Parks Department Mounted Auxiliary Unit, ca. 2013. (Used with the permission of the NYC Parks Department Mounted Auxiliary Unit, Inc.)

report crime to police. For these purposes, the city's Parks Department owns four 1,800-pound Clydesdales and currently has 50 volunteers on its roster, all of whom are required to serve a minimum of 48 hours per year, including a minimum of six patrols and at least one special event. According to Mark Elkins, the president of the unit since 2006, "Central Park is an interesting beat. To the south, it's mostly interacting with tourists and making them feel more secure. To the north, there are areas that are heavily wooded and impenetrable except by horse" (Karni 2011).

The Parks Department auxiliary unit was founded in 1996. After being tested on riding skills, potential members are rigorously trained on policies, procedures, and communications before going out on patrol. Riding instruction is not provided. Members assist the PEP officers of the city's Department of Parks and Recreation. PEP officers are certified New York State Peace Officers and NYC Special Patrolmen. The NYC Parks Department Mounted Auxiliary volunteers serve as "eyes and ears" for the Parks Department, patrolling on horseback in areas inaccessible by vehicles, to ensure the safety of park patrons and the preservation of animals, plants, and natural resources. They also advise the public on park rules, provide directions and information, and assist those who are injured, lost, or victims of crime (Auxiliary Mounted 2013).

## Cheltenham Township Auxiliary Police

Cheltenham Township covers an area of just over 9 square miles in eastern Pennsylvania. Cheltenham Township, as it exists today, is the product of more than 300 years of history and is known as Philadelphia's first suburb. The township is about 13 miles due north of Philadelphia and is governed by a board of commissioners who appoint the township's manager. The township's police department is located in Elkins Park. Its surrounding areas were developed around early mill establishments located next to a creek. Tookany Creek provided industrial opportunities for early settlers and entrepreneurs. As the mills prospered, small villages containing workers' housing and supporting businesses grew up around them. By the early twentieth century, most of the mills had been abandoned and demolished, but they had been the original reason for the settlement of the region (Cheltenham 2014d).

According to the 2010 U.S. Census, slightly more than half of the township's population is white and a quarter black. Their median age is 40, and more than half of the adult population have earned a bachelor's degree or higher. According to the 2000 U.S. Census, about 80% of its labor force is engaged in white-collar occupations and about 60% of all of the township's workers had an annual income exceeding $50,000 (Cheltenham 2014c).

The Township Board of Commissioners created the Cheltenham Police Department in February 1903, with an authorized strength of one police chief and "not more than seven officers." In those days, duties included patrolling the small villages, large estates, and open countryside comprising the township. Today, the Cheltenham Township Police Department is the third largest police department in Montgomery County, Pennsylvania. The department serves a population of approximately 37,000 residents and responded to more than 25,000 calls for service in 2008. The 84-member Cheltenham Township Police Department maintains round-the-clock street patrols, investigates crimes and serious accidents, conducts traffic studies, maintains special situation units, and offers safety education and crime prevention programs for community groups (e.g., the Drug Abuse Resistance Education, or DARE, officers teach school children about substance abuse avoidance). A mobile mini-station van and bicycle patrols are among the tools used by the agency's Community Policing Unit (Cheltenham 2014a).

In addition to its regular sworn police officers, the Cheltenham Township Police Department is assisted by volunteers who comprise an Auxiliary Police unit that assists at the scenes of serious accidents, fires, other emergencies and special events; they volunteer hundreds of hours of crowd and traffic control service each year (as seen in Figures 4.5 and 4.6). There is a Student Intern Program, a volunteer Chaplain's Program, and a volunteer residential Town Watch, equipped with cellular phones. The Town Watch members conduct mobile patrols of their neighborhoods and are alert for suspicious activity, functioning as additional trained "eyes and ears" for the police department (Cheltenham 2014a).

**Figure 4.5** Auxiliary officer on traffic post at a special event. (Used with the permission of the Cheltenham (PA) Township Police Department.)

**Figure 4.6** Auxiliary officer providing assistance to transit system bus driver at a special event. (Used with the permission of the Cheltenham (PA) Township Police Department.)

The Cheltenham Township Volunteer Auxiliary Police unit was formed in the mid-1950s. Auxiliary police officers are equipped with uniforms similar to those worn by regular officers. Though not armed, they are authorized to use police vehicles and police band radio communications equipment. The organization has assisted the police department with traffic and crowd control at various community events, such as the Community Harvest Festival and Sundays in the Park. By handling these responsibilities, auxiliary officers free Cheltenham police for regular patrol duties. Like other emergency services of the township, auxiliary police are available 24 hours a day. Training of the volunteer police is provided by members of the police department, supplemented by outside sources. Requirements for membership include being 18 years of age and a resident, for at least six months, of Cheltenham Township or any of 15 different other Montgomery County townships or boroughs (Cheltenham 2014b).

In February 2005, the Cheltenham Police Department introduced a Chaplain's Program to better serve the community and to help with difficult assignments. The program may strengthen relationships between the police and the community. It may also improve communication between police and local religious groups in the township. The program started with five local religious leaders representing various faiths and currently has seven volunteer chaplains active in the program. As trained counselors, the chaplains are available to offer support to residents in need, such as comforting grieving families during death notifications. Chaplains participate in ride-along shifts with regular police officers and may help to defuse potential problems that may arise. As a result of their close working relations with police, the volunteer police chaplains have developed a bond with agency personnel and are available to them as needed. In addition, the chaplains can help put residents in touch with representatives of many faiths if the need arises (Cheltenham 2014e).

## Albemarle County (Virginia) Auxiliary Police

Albemarle County is in central Virginia and contains the homes of three of America's earliest presidents. Its 726 square miles rest at the foot of the Blue Ridge Mountains, situated approximately 110 miles southwest of Washington, D.C., and 70 miles west of Richmond. Its main city is Charlottesville, where the Monticello estate of Thomas Jefferson, America's third president, is located. Monticello annually attracts nearly 440,000 visitors. Charlottesville is an independent city enclave entirely surrounded by the county. Ash Lawn–Highland was the home of James Monroe, the fifth president of the United States and the author of the Monroe Doctrine; it is located two miles from Monticello. Montpelier, in Orange, Virginia, was the estate of James Madison, the fourth president of the United States and widely recognized as the "Father of the Constitution." When the Constitution was sent to the states for ratification, Madison (along with Alexander Hamilton and John Jay) wrote essays arguing in favor of the new form of government. First printed in New York newspapers, the essays were later published as *The Federalist*. The essays not only influenced the ratification debates but continue to influence legal thinking today.

The county currently employs 119 paid police officers, but in January 2014, it added six unpaid auxiliary officers and plans to recruit about a dozen more. The new unit was organized due to the initiative of the county's police chief, Col. Steve Sellers. He urged that it was a way to relieve the burden of some routine and administrative tasks of his regular officers. Sellers had been satisfied with the effort of the other police volunteers in his department and were aware that many other counties in Virginia have auxiliary forces.[11] In fact, all six members of the new unit had been members of the agency's Volunteers in Police Service (VIPS) program when they were selected to become auxiliary officers. Sellers said the new unit of auxiliary officers represents a cultural change to his department. He told the new volunteer officers that they would be "pioneers, ambassadors, and partners" in the department (Albemarle 2014).

Virginia's Department of Criminal Justice Services maintains standards for training volunteer police at three different levels, with the lowest level not trained in firearms. The two upper levels may be armed, with the highest level required to attend the 19-week police academy just like a paid officer.

The six new officers all entered their volunteer service at the lowest level. They will aid with tasks such as crime prevention programs, house safety checks, and traffic direction at special events. They are not armed with firearms and would rarely, if ever, respond to incidents such as robberies or domestic disputes without being accompanied by a full-time officer. Outfitting the first six auxiliary officers is costing $8,400, an amount that was included in the department's current fiscal year budget (Albemarle 2014).

## Summary

This chapter has briefly highlighted seven units of volunteer police: the Albemarle County Auxiliary Police, the Buffalo Police Reserve, the Brentwood Reserve Police, the Cheltenham Township Auxiliary Police, the Los Angeles Reserve Police, the NYC Auxiliary Police, and the NYC Parks Department Mounted Auxiliary Unit.

It took many centuries for paid professional crime fighters to arrive on the scene in all regions of America. Therefore, some persons believe that returning to citizen involvement in policing, especially in urban areas, is a step backward rather than forward. America no longer needs to use citizen posses as it once did during the era of western lawlessness associated with the 1850s' Gold Rush. How can volunteers act as a "professional force" functioning 24 hours a day in order to deliver services and provide law and order?

The answer to this question can be traced to America's involvement in two world wars during the twentieth century. In those periods, many leaders and citizens believed that there was a profound need for additional security on the home front. Thereafter, the threat of nuclear attack spurred additional planning for citizen mobilization. Subsequently, urban and suburban police departments found value in maintaining their civil defense forces for crime prevention assignments. Regional distinctions appear to have arisen because the central and western regions of the United States were developed last and have had to cope with fewer public resources than the eastern third of the nation. The same can be said of some wilderness and mountainous regions of the East. These regions had to depend upon greater civilian involvement in peacekeeping for a longer time, and they tended to vest greater authority in their volunteer police. In the South, slave owners established slave patrols consisting of private citizens. The title of "auxiliary police" was part of the World War II and Korean War lexicons and remains in general use throughout the eastern half of the United States. In Virginia, the term "auxiliary police" dates back to at least the World War II era, but the title is not necessarily reflective of the broad scope of the powers of current members of volunteer police units who may progress through different classification levels. Moreover, citizen support of and participation in the justice system can take a variety of other forms nationwide: citizen watch member, VIPS administrative aide, CERT member, chaplain and just a few examples.

Reserve and auxiliary officers coexist in the Miami Police Department to assist the police force in the provision of emergency services and other functions. Both types of volunteer officers attend training opportunities and work alongside regular officers. However, the auxiliary is provided with somewhat less training and has less law enforcement responsibilities than reserve members. In particular, reserve officers must meet the same eligibility requirements and POST training standards as regular full-time officers.

During the 1950s and 1960s, the Buffalo Police Department coordinated a civil defense auxiliary police program. More recently, a "Buffalo Police Reserves" unit has been established with the approval of the city's police commissioner and mayor. It consists of a small group of uncompensated volunteers who routinely volunteer to maintain security at selected events of their own choosing and with the approval of Buffalo's police commissioner. At the time of America's entry into World War I, the city of Buffalo established its first Buffalo Police Reserve for the purpose of protecting the city in case of large disorders and when the members of the Police Department were detailed to protect the great water front which contained hundreds of storehouses and grain elevators.... They assisted the Department in disposing of a great many Liberty Bonds and War Savings Stamps, assisted the Red Cross to keep order at parades, and helped with election day and registration day details.... (Sweeney 1920, 430). They had the powers of special policemen and were assigned to each of the city's 15 precincts, but eventually the organization was phased out.

Today, most large urban police departments require huge budgets, the latest scientific aids, and the most up-to-date administrative techniques for the supervision of hundreds of employees. In the case of NYC, the police force is numbered in the tens of thousands. NYC volunteer and unsalaried police officers are unarmed, except for a straight nightstick. However, members of the volunteer force are exposed to the same dangers as regular officers. In 2007, auxiliary officers Marshalik and Pekearo of the 6th Precinct were shot to death in the line of duty. NYC auxiliaries are instructed to observe, report, and wait until full-fledged police officers arrive at the scene of a crime. Marshalik and Pekearo did not possess the necessary equipment to defend themselves when an armed and dangerous felon approached. In addition, it can be argued that the basic auxiliary training course of about 64 hours spread over a 16-week period is insufficient for the nature of their work.

The reserve police on America's West Coast (e.g., the LAPD Reserve) have quite a different set of training standards. They are provided with hundreds of hours of training. In the LAPD Reserves, volunteer police officers who go on patrol are Level II or I officers. Level II officers have approximately

460 hours of training, while Level I officers have approximately 800 hours of training. LAPD reserve officers are peace officers who have the same power and authority as full-time officers. Consequently, LAPD reserve officers are allowed to do certain things NYC auxiliary officers are not allowed to do, such as write tickets or make traffic stops.

The Brentwood Police Department is in the process of reestablishing its Reserve Police Officer Program. The police department had a strong Reserve Police Officer Program as far back as the 1960s, but it was demobilized in 2006. Due to a changed economic climate and an increase in population growth, there is renewed interest in reestablishing the program. It is planned that newly trained and qualified reserve officers will be assigned to provide support services such as prisoner transports, traffic control, and public event security.

The New York City Parks Department Mounted Auxiliary Unit, founded in 1996, is a group of private citizens who assist the PEP officers of the city's Department of Parks and Recreation. The full-time regular PEP officers are certified New York State Peace Officers and NYC Special Patrolmen. As non-sworn volunteers, the auxiliary officers serve as "eyes and ears" for the Parks Department, patrolling on horseback in areas inaccessible by vehicles to ensure the safety of park patrons and the preservation of animals, plants, and natural resources. Accepted mounted auxiliary unit candidates are trained in PEP policies and procedures, as well as park rules and regulations and the proper use of equipment.

The Cheltenham Township Volunteer Auxiliary Police unit was formed in the mid-1950s. Their auxiliary police officers are equipped with uniforms similar to those worn by regular officers. Though not armed, they are authorized to use police vehicles and police band radio communications equipment. The organization has assisted the police department with traffic and crowd control at various community events. The Cheltenham Police Department also conducts a Chaplain's Program to help with difficult assignments and to strengthen relationships between the police and the community.

The Albemarle County Auxiliary Police unit is the newest organization highlighted. The first group of their recruits will have limited police functions, but in the state of Virginia, it is possible for more highly trained volunteer police to assume the full range of law enforcement responsibilities. Its three different classifications of volunteer police appear to be comparable to the system used in California.

Currently, the "reserve police" title is more common in the western regions of the United States, and the "auxiliary" title is most common in the eastern half of the country. Nonetheless, in earlier times when the "reserve" title was used in the eastern region (e.g., during the 1920s in Buffalo and NYC), the volunteer officers had arrest authority comparable to regular officers. It is imperative that, irrespective of the type of auxiliary or reserve program established, it is essential that the unit's policies are consistent with the highest standards of human rights in order to preserve our nation's democratic heritage. Part II of this book discusses the various activities of volunteer youth police groups and critical issues, and it touches upon several new types of possible assignments. Volunteer police are capable of undertaking new roles, and they are in a unique position to augment the delivery of existing police functions and programs.

## Review Questions

1. State a generalization about the authority of auxiliary and reserve police officers.
2. Provide at least one exception to the generalization you stated in response to the first question.
3. Why was there a need for volunteer police during WW II? Discuss.
4. Contrast the nature of the work of Buffalo's first Police Reserve Force with that of its second and ongoing "police reserves" force.
5. What was the "Volunteer Patrol League"?
6. Who comprised the membership of Buffalo's Home Defense Reserve, and how did it come into existence?
7. What historical events led up to the origin of NYC's present-day auxiliary police program?
8. At the time of the publication of this book, there was confusion among some online contributors about the exact nature of the "peace officer" status of NYC auxiliary police officers. The lack of "peace officer" status was the main reason for an initial refusal by the U.S. Department of Justice to award death benefits to the families of three slain auxiliaries. Research the current nature of these issues and discuss your findings.
9. State at least two advantages and two disadvantages concerning the assignment of volunteer police to work alongside regular officers.
10. This chapter indicated that one California police department was revising a reserve police program and one Virginia police department had recently instituted its first auxiliary police program. Do you believe that either of these types of programs will encounter resistance from regular police? In your discussion, consider the nature of these two programs.
11. Is there a volunteer police force in your hometown? If so, research and present information about the nature of the program.
12. The author of this book theorizes that there exist particular regional differences among volunteer police units in the United States. How could a study be designed to test this theory?

# Notes

1. The Community Emergency Response Team (CERT) idea was first developed in 1985 by the city of Los Angeles Fire Department. It was established because citizens would probably have to work together during the early stages of a disaster. The Los Angeles CERT training proved to be so beneficial that the Federal Emergency Management Agency (FEMA) decided the program should be made available to communities across the United States. In 1994, FEMA and the Los Angeles Fire Department expanded the CERT curriculum. And, in 2003, FEMA's Citizen Corps Council adopted CERT as a primary way to encourage people to volunteer to make their communities safer, stronger, and better prepared to respond to emergencies. There are currently more than 3,500 active CERT programs in the United States. In January 2012, Deputy Inspector Byrne spoke at a graduation ceremony for more than 100 new (CERT) volunteers (NYC Press Release 2012).

2. "The National Defense Act of 1916 expanded the regular federal army from 90,000 to 175,000 and permitted gradual enlargement to 223,000. It also increased the National Guard to 440,000, made provision for training, and gave federal funds for summer training camps for civilians" (Tindall and Shi 2007, 941).

3. On January 19, 1917, British naval intelligence intercepted and decrypted a telegram sent by German Foreign Minister Arthur Zimmerman to the German Ambassador in Mexico City. The "Zimmerman Telegram" promised the Mexican government that Germany would help Mexico recover the territory it had ceded to the United States following the Mexican-American War. In return for this assistance, the Germans asked for Mexican support in the war. The British had initially not shared the news of the Zimmerman Telegram with U.S. officials because they did not want the Germans to discover that British code breakers had cracked the German code. However, following Germany's resumption of unrestricted submarine warfare in February, the British decided to use the note to help sway American official and public opinion about joining the war (Office of the Historian 2014).

4. The Cold War centered on the threat of a nuclear exchange between the Union of Soviet Socialist Republics (USSR) and the United States. It was the Federal Civil Defense Administration's job to encourage citizens to adapt to their nuclear present and future. Civil defense media showed fathers building bomb shelters and mothers stocking them while the children practiced ducking under their desks at school. This was family life in the new era of the A-bomb. This was civil defense, and it turned the front lawn into the front line. The reliance on atomic weaponry as a centerpiece of U.S. foreign policy cast a mushroom cloud over everyday life. American citizens now had to imagine a new kind of war, one in which they were both combatants and targets. According to McEnaney (2000), the creation of America's civil defense program produced new dilemmas about the degree to which civilian society should be militarized to defend itself against internal and external threats. Conflicts arose about the relative responsibilities of state and citizen to fund and implement a home front security program. Today's security conflicts center on the debate between gun control advocates and those who would defend the right of all law-abiding citizens to possess firearms.

5. An important case, *Fitzgibbons vs. The County of Nassau, et al.*, held that counties and cities in New York State were fully liable for the actions taken by their auxiliary police. Previously, the State's Defense Emergency Act gave blanket immunity for the auxiliary's actions.

6. It is also likely that a Justice Department report critical of how the department reviewed each claim for benefits greatly impacted the decision by the Justice Department to reverse its previous decision in the case. The 103-page report was prepared by the Inspector General's Office, which oversees the Justice Department. The report indicated that the claims filed by families of those seeking compensation were processed far too slowly and that Justice Department officials responsible for reviewing claims too "narrowly interpreted" terms of the act in at least 19 cases filed in the first year after the act went into effect (Parascandola 2008). Moreover, John Hyland, president of the Auxiliary Police Benevolent Association of the City of New York, Inc., had pointed out that there had been a prior precedent. In fact, the families of two on-duty NYC auxiliary officers killed by a drunken driver in the Bronx in 1989 were awarded benefits. Relatives of Sgts. Noel Faide and Larry Cohen were initially denied but won on appeal. Hyland stated: "It's been done before. It should almost be automatic" (Gendar et al. 2008, p. 6).

7. As of September 2010, the issuance of the vests remained an issue among the largest municipal volunteer police force in the United States. An initial complement of vests was received in February 2008, but many new volunteers were receiving ill-fitting loaner vests. Deputy Inspector Kim Royster, an NYPD spokeswoman, acknowledged that new members of the auxiliary force are no longer getting new vests. She stated that "all auxiliary officers wear vests while out on patrol. If they don't have a vest assigned to them, they must wear a loaner vest" (Weichselbaum 2010, p. 13). "A police source said each of the vests costs about $580 and that the NYPD hoped to one day return to issuing new vests to auxiliary cops. No timetable has been set" (Weichselbaum 2010, p. 13).

8. By early March 2008, no report was released. However, a high-ranking member of the NYPD, Assistant Chief Michael Collins, said the committee had handed down its recommendations within 90 days as required. He indicated that he did not know why the report was never presented to the city council but that all recommendations have been implemented, including centralization of training under the police academy, issuance of bullet resistant vests to nearly 2,000 auxiliaries, and requiring the NYPD recruitment office to take over recruiting tasks from the auxiliary division. John Hyland, president of the auxiliary union, indicated the training of auxiliary cops is improving, but more must be done. Marshalik and Pekearo never called for help on their radios after the shooter had first punched Marshalik. Instead, they tailed the gunman. According to Hyland, "You can't ask them, why didn't you make the call so you assume why; it's really scary when you think about it, and the radio is their lifeline...." (White 2008). Hyland also indicated that most auxiliary cops are discouraged from using their radios and are told by supervisors to use cell or pay phones (White 2008). The long awaited report was presented by the NYPD the following month and is available online at: http://www.nyc.gov/html/nypd/downloads/pdf/careers/nypd_auxiliary_police_overview_2008.pdf.

9. In addition to the restoration of the various units of the NYPD AESU, the plan proposed by City Councilmember David Weprin involved equipping NYC's auxiliary officers with: (1) bulletproof vests, (2) mace, (3) expandable nightsticks,

(4) protective masks, and (5) automatic external defibrillators for all AESUs who are already authorized by the NYPD for its use. Legislation for (1) increased penalties for attacking and/or injuring auxiliary police officers by granting auxiliary officers the status of "peace officer while on duty" (auxiliary members will be requalified as "NYC Special Patrolmen," a status that exists in the NYC Administrative Code and the NYS Criminal Procedure Law, such a change in status will automatically bring with it an increased range of penalties for injury to an auxiliary officer); (2) appropriate benefits for disabled auxiliary officers and their families; (3) mandated regular reporting by the NYPD to the city council on auxiliary program statistics such as equipment, vehicles, training, hours, and number of personnel; and (4) improved and increased training and self-defense classes for auxiliary officers to be administered by police academy instructors (Auxiliary Officers Assistance Plan 2007).

10. During times of disaster, auxiliaries have played and can play major roles in search and rescue efforts as well as a variety of other assignments. Such efforts require close cooperation between full-time first responders as well as part-time first responders, such as volunteer police. "Most disasters and mass casualty events are experienced locally; in this country, incidents are generally handled at the lowest possible jurisdictional level. When significant events occur, the 'intrusive reality' is that small, rural, and suburban communities in the United States may be on their own for 24 to 72 hours before help arrives from regional, state, and federal sources" (Joint Commission 2005, 1). The New York State Association of Auxiliary Police, Inc., published a special tenth anniversary issue of their newsletter devoted to the contributions of auxiliary police during the aftermath of the collapse of the World Trade Center Towers on September 11, 2001. The issue is available at: http://www.auxiliary-police.org/newsletter.pdf.

11. For example, the Chesterfield County (VA) Auxiliary Police program began as part of the civil defense program during the 1950s. Its 22 members exercise full police powers, perform patrols with regular department officers, and provide assistance in cases of civil unrest, natural disasters, or missing person's searches. They perform traffic enforcement measures, respond to crimes, maintain security at crime scenes, and investigate citizen complaints. This valuable unit also patrols assigned areas during public events, such as the annual Chesterfield County Fair, and during the holiday season at shopping centers and business areas. In 2008, Chesterfield auxiliary officers made 384 arrests, worked 42 special assignments, and served a plethora of summonses. Chesterfield police estimate that auxiliary volunteers donate 11,105 hours each year, saving the county $224,876 annually. Participants are provided the same training that regular police recruits receive. However, it is stretched over a longer period of time because the auxiliary recruits are volunteers who attend part-time; the regular recruits attend full-time (Burchett 2010).

# References

Albemarle. (2014, January 3). Albemarle swears in first auxiliary police officers. *The Daily Progress*. Retrieved January 18, 2014 from http://www.dailyprogress.com/news/local/albemarle-swears-in-first-auxiliary-police-officers/article_fe5a08c2-74e1-11e3-8331-001a4bcf6878.html

Auer, D. (2011, November 12). An auxiliary farce. *New York Post*. Retrieved November 11, 2013 from http://nypost.com/2011/11/12/an-auxiliary-farce/

Auxiliary Mounted. (2013). Who are we? Retrieved November 16, 2013 from http://www.auxparksmtd.org/faqs.html

Auxiliary Officers Assistance Plan. (2007, March 26). Retrieved November 14, 2013 from http://www.gothamgazette.com/index.php/open-government/3516-auxiliary-officers-assistance-plan

Barron, J. and Kilgannon, C. (2007, March 16). Rampage in Greenwich Village; auxiliary officers know the limitations, and the dangers, when they volunteer. *New York Times*, p. 5.

Bayley, D. H. (1985). *Patterns of policing: A comparative international analysis*. New Brunswick, NJ: Rutgers University Press.

Blascovich, L. (Ed.). (2013, April). Introduction the Civil Air Patrol. Retrieved January 17, 2014 from http://www.capmembers.com/media/cms/P050_005_C3E62FDD0BD80.pdf

Brentwood Police Department. (2013). About us. Retrieved November 15, 2013 from http://www.brentwoodca.gov/department/pd/index.cfm

Buder, L. (1980, December 28). Expanded auxiliary unit annoys city police union. *New York Times*, p. 36.

Buffalo Police Reserves. (2014a). Retrieved January 15, 2014 from http://buffalopolicereserves.com/information.htm

Buffalo Police Reserves. (2014b). Buffalo Police reserve requirement. Retrieved January 15, 2014 from http://buffalopolicereserves.com/apply.htm

Burchett, M. (2010, January 6). Auxiliary police help in Colonial Heights, Chesterfield. Retrieved January 20, 2014 from http://progress-index.com/news/auxiliary-police-help-in-colonial-heights-chesterfield-1.528186

Careers. (2014). Careers – Auxiliary police. Retrieved January 18, 2014 from http://www.nyc.gov/html/nypd/html/careers/auxiliary_police.shtml

Carmody, D. (1974, November 30). 100 volunteer mounties ride herd on park crime: 100 volunteer mounties in the parks organized in 1951. *New York Times*, pp. 33 & 49.

Cheltenham. (2014a). About us. Retrieved January 14, 2014 from http://www.cheltenhamtownship.org/pView.aspx?id = 3125&catid =29

Cheltenham. (2014b). Auxiliary police unit. Retrieved January 14, 2014 from http://www.cheltenhamtownship.org/pView.aspx?id = 3126&catid =29

Cheltenham. (2014c). Demographics. Retrieved January 14, 2014 from http://www.cheltenhamtownship.org/pView.aspx?id = 2448&catid =25

Cheltenham. (2014d). Early industrial development. Retrieved January 14, 2014 from http://www.cheltenhamtownship.org/pView.aspx?id = 3008&catid =25

Cheltenham. (2014e). Police chaplain. Retrieved January 14, 2014 from http://www.cheltenhamtownship.org/pview.aspx?id = 3094&catID =29

City's First Auxiliary. (1973, September 9). City's first auxiliary mounted policemen will help patrol parks: Took horsemanship course. *New York Times*, p. 57.

Early Days. (2012, April). The early days of American law enforcement: The watch. *Insider*, 4(4). Retrieved November 10, 2013 from http://www.nleomf.org/museum/news/newsletters/online-insider/2012/April-2012/early-days-american-law-enforcement-april-2012.html

Gendar, A., White, M. and Connor, T. (2008, March 27). Fed official shuns key evidence to gain benefits for slain auxiliary cops. *New York Daily News*, p. 6.

Goodman, G., Jr. (1980, September 13). Mounted rangers begin patrol of parks. *New York Times*, p. 25.

Greenberg, M. (1984). *Auxiliary police: The citizen's role in public safety*. Westport, CT: Greenwood Press.

Hays, C. L. (1988, August 20). Unpaid eyes and ears of the police. *New York Times*, p. 30.

Hillard, G. (2011, May 19). In tight times, L.A. relies on volunteer police. Retrieved January 12, 2012 from http://www.npr.org/2011/05/19/136436405/in-tight-times-l-a-relies-on-volunteer-police

Hudson, E. (1955, August 28). Volunteer force aids park police. *New York Times*, p. 60.

Joint Commission. (2005). *Standing together: An emergency planning guide for America's communities*. Oakbrook Terrace, IL: Joint Commission on Accreditation of Healthcare Organizations.

Karni, A. (2011, December 25). Mounting interest in civilian park patrol. *New York Post*. Retrieved November 13, 2013 from http://nypost.com/2011/12/25/mounting-interest-in-civilian-park-patrol/

Kelly, R. W., Grasso, G. A., Esposito, J. J., Giannelli, R. J. and Maroulis, A. J. (2008, April). Auxiliary police program overview. Retrieved November 11, 2013 from http://www.nyc.gov/html/nypd/downloads/pdf/careers/nypd_auxiliary_police_overview_2008.pdf

LAPD (2013). Reserve police officer program. Retrieved November 14, 2013 from http://www.lapdonline.org/join_the_team/content_basic_view/542

Marzulli, J. (2010, June 25). Justice Department grants benefits 17 years late for auxiliary cop Milton Clarke's family. *New York Daily News*, p. 26.

McEnaney, L. (2000). *Civil defense begins at home: Militarization meets everyday life in the fifties*. Princeton, NJ: Princeton University Press.

Miami PD. (2014). Community involvement. Retrieved January 15, 2014 from http://www.miami-police.org/COMMUNITY_INVOLVEMENT.HTML

NYC Press Release. (2012, January 12). Retrieved January 17, 2014 from http://www.nyc.gov/portal/site/nycgov/menuitem.c0935b9a57bb4ef3daf2f1c701c789a0/index.jsp?pageID = mayor_press_release&catID = 1194

NYPD (2008). New York City Police Commissioner Raymond W. Kelly and U.S. Senator Charles E. Schumer urge Department of Justice to approve death benefits for auxiliary police officers. NYPD Press Release No. 2008-11. Retrieved November 12, 2013 from http://www.nyc.gov/html/nypd/html/pr/pr_2008_011.shtml

Of Counsel. (2010, March 26). Of counsel Doug Neistat receives LAPD commendation. Retrieved June 15, 2010 from http://www.greenbass.com/newsdetail.aspx?id=6

Office of the Historian. (2014). Milestones: 1914–1920 – American entry into World War I, 1917. Retrieved January 16, 2014 from http://history.state.gov/milestones/1914-1920/wwi

Parascandola, R. (2008, April 1). Report may help death benefits case for auxiliary cops. Retrieved November 12, 2013 from http://www.newsday.com/long-island/report-may-help-death-benefits-case-for-auxiliary-cops-1.881568

Sweeney, D. J. (1920). *History of Buffalo and Erie County, 1914–1919*. Buffalo, NY: Committee of One Hundred.

Szymanski, K. (2013, July 4). Brentwood to bring back police reserves program. Retrieved November 15, 2013 from http://www.thepress.net/view/full_story/23045301/article-Brentwood-to-bring-back-police-reserves-program

Tindall, G. B. and Shi, D. E. (2007). *America: A narrative history, Vol. 2* (7th ed.). New York: W.W. Norton.

U.S. Department of Justice. (2011, October). *The impact of the economic downturn on American police agencies.* Washington, DC: U.S. Department of Justice, Office of Community Oriented Policing Services.

Weichselbaum, S. (2010, September 16). NYPD auxiliary officers at risk because they aren't getting best protection, say union officials. *New York Daily News,* p. 13.

White, M. (2008, March 9). Family blames lack of training for slain auxiliary cop tragedy 1 year ago. *New York Daily News,* p. 23.

# Volunteer State Police

5

It's not fair to require them to go through extensive training programs when they are not paid. It's not practical.

**—Connecticut State Police Capt. Gregory Senick**
*(quoted in Waldman 2001)*

Contemporary volunteer auxiliary and reserve police represent the epitome of "community policing" by serving to bridge the gap between local community residents and police agencies. Although the dominant amount of community policing activities has been conducted at the local level by town, city, and county police agencies, there are state police agencies that routinely assign their officers to act as "resident police" in communities without an established police force (Connecticut, Vermont, etc.). Moreover, given the recent string of major school tragedies from Columbine, Colorado, to Newtown, Connecticut, many state law enforcement agencies have begun to address how they can assist communities to ensure that all children and staff are safe in school. In many ways, community policing has represented a new paradigm in policing. Community policing has a profoundly different outlook regarding police–citizen relationships than traditional methods of policing. Under the community policing concept, the police are the public, and the public are the police! Police officers are merely those who are paid to give full-time attention to the duties of every citizen (Sparrow 1988). It is extremely noteworthy that this precise understanding of police was initially proclaimed nearly 200 years ago by the father of modern policing—Sir Robert Peel. Peel recognized that the community and its police department were linked; neither was able to function properly without the other.

The development and organizational arrangements of state police forces during the early part of the twentieth century are the quintessential models of the traditional methods of policing because they resembled a military force, complete with various troops housed in barracks throughout the state under a strong central command. Moreover, with an emphasis on highway safety enforcement and the investigation of serious crimes in rural areas, very few agencies are likely to have available additional resources for community policing initiatives (the conduct of Citizen Police Academies, sponsorship of police Explorer posts, etc.) or the inclination to lobby for such activities. Therefore, it is somewhat surprising to learn that a handful of states do, in fact, have statewide auxiliary/reserve units.

This chapter first considers a selected group of traditional state police agencies that have developed into full-service state agencies responsible for statewide law enforcement services, especially on highways and in rural areas. This is followed by a closer look at those state agencies that have opted to include an auxiliary or reserve volunteer police component to supplement the strength of their existing departments. Such agencies are located in Alabama, Arizona, Connecticut, Florida, New Hampshire, Ohio, and Vermont. A section of the chapter is devoted to the rise and gradual decline of the Connecticut State Police Auxiliary program.

Throughout this book, and in this chapter, various references have been made regarding the existence of the "Volunteers in Police Service (VIPS) online directory." The directory used for these references is no longer available, having been removed at the end of March 2014 and replaced by a new set of Web pages located at: http://www.theiacp.org/VIPS. Prior to its removal, over 2,200 volunteer programs had indicated their existence by being registered and briefly described in the former online directory. Established in 2002, the former VIPS Web site was extensively used by the author. The former Web site was designed to serve as a gateway to information for law enforcement agencies and citizens interested in law enforcement volunteer programs. The new Web site and directories (domestic and international) offer hundreds of opportunities to network with other law enforcement volunteer programs, and updated contact information is provided in the new directories.

## Origins of State Police Forces

Everyday policing in the eastern settlements of colonial America largely consisted of voluntary watch groups formed by citizens and a system of slave patrols in the south. The latter patrols were used to control slave populations and have been identified by historians as the first formal police agencies in America. During the first half of the nineteenth century, a unique force was created in the region known as Texas, which was first claimed by Spain and then by Mexico after its independence. Spain encouraged immigration to Texas beginning in 1820. Spain expected the new settlers in this region to spur its economic development and to discourage any interference by such Native Americans as the Comanche and Kiowa nations. In 1821, Mexico continued the Spanish colonization plan after its independence from Spain by granting contracts to *empresarios* (a type of land agent) who would help to settle and supervise new immigrants (Henson 2013). Stephen Fuller Austin (1793–1836) was the eldest son of Moses Austin. The elder Austin had been granted various land contracts as an empresario and his son inherited these tracts. By 1834, near the end of the empresario system, Stephen Austin had helped to settle nearly 1,000 families. As the leading empresario in Texas and without an available set of established Mexican laws, Austin had administrative and judicial authority for his colony (Henson 2013).

"In 1823, only two years after Anglo-American colonization formally began in Texas, empresario Stephen F. Austin hired ten experienced frontiersmen as 'rangers' for a punitive expedition against a band of Indians" (Procter 2013). "During Austin's day, companies of men volunteered and disbanded as needed. Some served for days and others for many months. The official records show that these companies were called by many names: ranging companies, mounted gunmen, mounted volunteers, minutemen, spies, scouts, and mounted rifle companies" (Cox 2013). Late in the 1835, Texas lawmakers instituted a specific force known as a "Corps of Rangers" in order "to protect the frontier from hostile Indians. For the first time, their pay was officially set at $1.25 a day and they were to elect their own officers. They were also required to furnish their own arms, mounts, and equipment" (Cox 2013). During the war between the United States and Mexico (1846–1848), the Rangers achieved worldwide fame as scouts and as a fighting force. Later, having been organized into several companies, the Rangers were periodically called upon to contend with outlaws as well attacks from Mexican citizens and occasional threats from Indians. During various periods throughout the nineteenth century, when the Rangers did their job with such effectiveness, the need for their services was diminished, their numbers were reduced and for the most part the organization went into an inactive status. Between 1914 and 1919, "Regular rangers, along with hundreds of special rangers appointed by Texas governors, killed approximately 5,000 Hispanics...", a source of scandal and embarrassment" (Procter 2014).

In 1935, a new governor won office on a platform of better law enforcement, and the legislature established the Texas Department of Public Safety (DPS). The new agency was organized into three basic units: the Texas Rangers, the Highway Patrol, and a scientific crime laboratory and detection center known as the Headquarters Division. In 1938, with the appointment of Colonel Homer Garrison Jr. (1901–1968), as its new director, the Rangers regained much of their lost status. Over the next 30 years, "The Rangers became the plainclothesmen of the DPS: they were the detectives, and the Highway Patrol officers were the uniformed state police" (Procter 2014). Thus, the Rangers have had a long evolving history beginning in the days of Anglo settlement in Texas and are often recognized as the oldest law enforcement agency with statewide jurisdiction in North America. However, most of their earliest activities had been more military than law enforcing in nature. This tradition continued even after Texas was officially inducted into the United States on December 29, 1845, when Rangers served as scouts and as a fighting force during the war between the United States and Mexico. Two other related agencies were established in the American West primarily for border protection. The Arizona Rangers were established in 1901, and the New Mexico Mounted Police came into being in 1905 (Lyman 2005).

The first regional law enforcement effort in Arizona occurred in 1901 when the territorial governor organized the Arizona Rangers. This small force made a strong impact on the rustling and smuggling problems of the time but was disbanded in 1909, three years before Arizona achieved statehood. Twenty-two years later, because of concern regarding the growing number of accidents and unlicensed vehicles on its highways, the Arizona Highway Patrol was instituted as a branch of the Arizona Highway Department. In 1931, the initial force was limited to a superintendent, 14 patrolmen (one authorized for each county), and one desk sergeant. In 1967, the Arizona Governor's Crime Commission recommended creation of a department to "assemble state-level law enforcement activities into a single, effective governmental unit" (Arizona DPS 2013a). Two years later, on July 1, 1969, the Arizona Department of Public Safety was officially established. It consolidated the functions and responsibilities of the Arizona Highway Patrol, the Enforcement Division of the Department of Liquor Licenses and Control, and the Narcotics Division of the Arizona Department of Law. Since 1969, the department has been charged with additional responsibilities and has developed into a modern, comprehensive law enforcement agency. The department enforces state laws with primary responsibility in the areas of traffic, narcotics, organized crime/racketeering, liquor, and specific regulatory functions (Arizona DPS 2013a).

Meanwhile, in the last half of the nineteenth century, the field of American municipal policing learned about and drew upon the experience of Sir Robert Peel's London Metropolitan Police. However, political considerations trumped true reforms and consistently controlled the shaping of the American policing establishment for many years. At times, some state legislatures assumed control over big city police forces due to struggles for control over police during the late nineteenth century and even into the twentieth century (Walker 1977). For example, beginning in 1857 and for a period of 13 years, the New York State Legislature took control over the New York City force. In other states as well, legislatures intervened in the administration of municipal agencies, seeking a political advantage or because of dissatisfaction "for the way city police were or were not enforcing liquor and vice laws" (Lyman 2005, 41). However, prior to the twentieth century, the institutions that most closely resembled what would become state police were state militia forces and posses composed of citizen volunteers. Militia could be summoned by state governors, although posses were usually organized by a local official, such as a county sheriff. In time of need, sheriffs have a legal prerogative derived from older traditions to call upon the able-bodied men of their counties for assistance. In the United States, the sheriff typically is an elected office, like the office of governor.

By the early 1900s, the first state police forces were established in the eastern half of the United States to enforce the laws governing prohibition, vice, and labor disputes. Often local constables or sheriffs either could not, or would not, enforce these laws fairly. Initially, the formation of the Connecticut State Police was directly related to the problems associated with alcoholic beverage enforcement. "The roots of state law enforcement in Connecticut began in 1895 with the creation of the Law and Order League of Connecticut" (History of CSP 2013). A new state law empowered the state's governor to appoint four "agents" to enforce state liquor and vice laws, which at the time were being ignored by local authorities. The Law and Order League served until it and other versions of it were abolished in 1903. In 1903, Governor Abiram Chamberlain signed a new law establishing the creation of the Connecticut State Police and their very first responsibilities included enforcement of state liquor and gaming statutes (History of CSP 2013). In this way, the rise of the Connecticut State Police was related to concerns over illegal liquor manufacturing, its distribution, and the general public's clamor over vice enforcement (Seeley 2013).

By about the middle of the twentieth century, all of the contiguous mainland states had developed statewide law enforcement agencies.[1] (Online links to all 50 state police, state highway patrol, or public safety departments can be found at: http://www.scdps.gov/schp/links.asp. A full set of multiple links for finding information about each state police agency can also be found at: http://www.statetroopersdirectory.com/#SC.)

In the early decades of the twentieth century, the new state police agencies arose not only out of concern for improved vice and liquor law enforcement. Historically, industrial labor strife in coal and iron regions and the inadequacy of the sheriff–constable system in rural areas were contributing factors. Moreover, the rise of the automobile industry necessitated the development of highway patrol units to regulate motor vehicles and motorists (Smith 1940). Highway policing in the early years of the twentieth century was a taxing affair for troopers. "When patrolling by car and motorcycle became possible, there still was no radio system. Officers on patrol maintained contact with the barracks by telephone. When the desk officer needed to contact a patrolling trooper, he would make a phone call to one of several stores or gas stations on the man's patrol. The proprietor would raise a small flag, and the officer would call in when he saw it…. Troopers rode in all kinds of weather, and stuffed their uniforms with newspaper for insulation" (Seeley 2013).

In 1905, two years after the establishment of the Connecticut State Police, the Pennsylvania State Constabulary was created. Labor conflict appears to have been the chief catalyst for its inception. The agency focused its earliest attention on controlling strikes because business leaders believed that local police and the militia were unreliable for this purpose. "Organized labor bitterly attacked the Constabulary, denouncing its officers as 'Cossacks'" (Walker and Katz 2011, 37). A major characteristic of this force was the robust executive power granted to its superintendent who was only responsible to the governor.

Its other major characteristics included widely distributed substations for policing rural and semirural areas and its use of mounted and uniformed troops (Smith 1940). For a time, subsequent state efforts to establish similar agencies met with opposition from labor interests. For example, the legislation establishing a New York State Police force passed by only a single vote. Less controversial were those state police agencies limited to highway traffic enforcement.

An instance of the birth of a statewide highway enforcement agency took place in 1921 when the Illinois General Assembly authorized the Department of Public Works and Buildings to hire a "sufficient number of State Highway Patrol Officers to enforce the provisions of the Motor Vehicle Laws." Subsequently, the Illinois State Police was officially created in 1922. Today, it is comprised of full-time sworn personnel and civilians totaling more than 3,000 persons (Illinois State Police 2013). In 1995, the Illinois State Police had approximately 40 individuals serving as volunteers in various non-sworn roles. In 2013, 22 different local auxiliary/reserve police units were registered in the discontinued VIPS online directory for the state of Illinois, and there were more than 70 other types of local police volunteer programs listed. In recent years, however, a controversy arose regarding the unauthorized use of independent auxiliary/reserve police organizations. Most of them were operating in the Chicago metropolitan area.[2] (A 19-page copy of the Illinois Attorney General's opinion on this matter, dated December 30, 2010, can be found at http://www. ptb.state.il.us/pdf/AuxOfficersOpinion/ILAGOpinion12-31-10.pdf.)

The need for the New Jersey State Police arose when that state was making a limited effort to provide protection for its rural inhabitants. This effort was wholly dependent upon the county sheriff and his constables. Based on a political system of election and appointment, some elected officials were more competent than others. Demands for a well-trained rural police force increased in direct proportion to an increasing population and crime rate. Legislation for this purpose was first introduced in 1914 and for several years thereafter. There was opposition to this legislation from those who feared the creation of a "police state" and their possible use as strikebreakers. A wave of public sentiment surged against the proposal. However, by the beginning of the 1920s, a discernible "state police movement" had appeared in the United States and 13 states had organized such a force. Moreover, the state's chamber of commerce and the New Jersey Grange worked on behalf of the necessary legislation. The measure passed in the spring of 1921. On July 1, 1921, Herbert Norman Schwarzkopf, a graduate of the U.S. Army Military Academy at West Point, was appointed as the first superintendent. Before the year ended, 81 men successfully completed the initial three-month training program. In a severe snowstorm, they started out on horseback and motorcycle toward their posts throughout the state. Their "first modes of transportation consisted of sixty-one horses, twenty motorcycles, one car, and one truck. The horse remained the principal means of transportation throughout the twenties" (New Jersey State Police 2013). The initial success of the New Jersey State Police has been attributed to the theories adopted by Colonel Schwarzkopf who believed that the agency was not only an enforcement agency but that prevention, education, and service were equally important for the achievement of its goals (New Jersey State Police 2013).

In 2013, the state of New Jersey had about 27 local auxiliary/reserve police units registered with the former online VIPS directory and more than 50 additional types of police volunteer programs. The state police are served by about 200 non-sworn police volunteers (Volunteers in Police Service 2013). In addition, 70 volunteers serve in the New Jersey Search and Rescue (NJSAR), a volunteer emergency service organization that assists the New Jersey State Park Police. The NJSAR unit also assists with various departmental activities at the request of the park police (NJSAR 2013). Throughout most of the twentieth century, responsibilities for law enforcement in those townships without their own police departments have been carried out by the New Jersey State Police.[3]

The establishment of the New York State Police (NYSP) had a grassroots origin. Often overlooked in introductory textbooks is the fact that the NYSP was created, in large part, as a result of the lobbying efforts of two women. Although the women never actually enrolled in a volunteer police capacity, their pioneering achievement is a classic example of the importance of community-based initiatives. Their perseverance is illustrative of the type of community spirit that undoubtedly helped to motivate many persons to participate in volunteer police units between the two world wars and throughout the remainder of the twentieth century. In 1913, a construction foreman named Sam Howell was murdered during a payroll robbery in Westchester County, New York. At that time, Westchester County was a rural area with very limited police services, and Howell's murderers escaped, even though he identified them before he died. This vicious crime spurred Howell's employer, Moyca Newell, and her friend, Katherine Mayo, to initiate a movement to form a state police department to serve in rural areas. Mayo, a writer, researcher, and historian, authored a book about the value of the Pennsylvania State Police and how it could be a useful model for the state of New York.[4] In addition, New York Governor Charles Whitman urged that the shortage of National Guard recruits could be alleviated by the adoption of this act because members of the Guard would no longer be required to perform domestic police duties. In the past, these duties had taken guardsmen away from their families and regular employment, resulting in substantial inconvenience and personal financial loss. The final bill was passed in 1917. It contained the following clause to help its passage: the use of state police shall be prohibited "within the limits of any city to suppress rioting and disorder except by the direction of the Governor or upon the request of the Mayor of the city with the approval of the Governor" (Greenberg 1984). The newly formed state police was given capable leadership by its first superintendent, George F. Chandler, a former army surgeon. Although it was not his intention, Chandler's early successes with the organization of the NYSP may have motivated political figures in New York City to develop their own style of volunteer quasi-military police—the New York (City) Police Reserves. In 2013, New York State had 31 auxiliary/reserve units registered with the IACP VIPS online directory, including New York City's auxiliary police force with more than 4,000 members.

## Pennsylvania's Other State Police Force

In 1875, in the Erie, Pennsylvania, metropolitan area (in the most northwest corner of the state), an organization of nearly 1,000 members was authorized with the power of arrest and the right to carry weapons to provide policing assistance to a two-county area. This organization was known as "the State Police of Crawford and Erie Counties." It had 29 companies in the two-county area, organized along borough and township lines, and was commanded by elected captains and other officers. It was mobilized in 1877 (based on the records of the court of Crawford County).

However, its legislative origin can be traced to an 1872 statute that referred to the need to establish an organization for individuals to band together to form "a company for the recovery of stolen horses and other property, and for the detection of thieves." Residents within this region were concerned about interstate livestock rustling and requested that the state legislature permits the establishment of a public corporation to contend with the problem. "In 1872, the only police force in the Commonwealth of Pennsylvania was the Philadelphia Police Department, whose officers had statewide powers" (Neubert 1975, 1).

In the 1940s, the group had about 4,000 members and had several secretive aspects. At that time, members spoke in code and had secret handshakes, and anyone who applied for membership had to be voted in by at least 75% of the existing membership. The latter tradition was maintained till the organization was disbanded in 2005 when only 220 members remained (Simonich 2005).

This state-chartered organization was supported by donations. Local school districts were the main source of these donations because the members of the volunteer police often performed traffic control at school events. Additional traffic direction and patrol work took place at church services, community festivals and fairs, Memorial Day parades, Halloween night, and various picnics and open houses. A major concern was the provision of training for members. During the 1970s, after the passage of a state law mandating training for regular police, some efforts were made to see if a nearby college could provide such training because members would be unable to attend the full-time training programs established for municipal officers (Neubert 1975).

However, because there was also confusion over whether the new training requirements applied to such a volunteer organization, training on how and when to use force was provided by senior members, who had been schooled by companies that manufacture police equipment (Simonich 2005).

Members of the organization were recruited and deployed for a continuous period of well over a century until 2005, when the Pennsylvania General Assembly revoked its authority through the wording of the Act of Jun. 30, 2005, P.L. 29, No. 8 Cl. 44: "The General Assembly of the Commonwealth of Pennsylvania hereby enacts as follows: Section 1. The act of April 3, 1872 (1873 P.L.1061, No.1109), entitled 'An act to incorporate the State police of Crawford and Erie counties', is repealed. Section 2. This act shall take effect in 120 days." This was accomplished when officials of the Pennsylvania State Police convinced the legislature to repeal the 1872 law, dissolving the force despite the fact that the group had provided armed volunteer officers at festivals, dances, and games, sparing town governments and school districts the expense of hiring private security companies for many decades. If any organization members had to break up a fight at a festival or catch a pickpocket at a parade, their practice was to hold the individual until municipal or Pennsylvania State Police officers could arrive at the scene to take charge of the matter (Simonich 2005).

The statute repealing the volunteer Crawford/Erie police agency's charter was drafted by State Representative Ron Marsico. At the time, Marsico was concerned that the organization was "not answerable to any elected official or public body" (Simonich 2005). Marsico added that unionized members and administrators of the Pennsylvania State Police see the organization as a problem because of their spotty training and lack of any real police standards. Linette Quinn, public information coordinator of the Pennsylvania State Police, stated: "We've voiced our concerns about their existence for years" (Simonich 2005). On the other hand, Bob Merski, the Erie County sheriff, said he had worked in law enforcement for 25 years and never heard a complaint about the Crawford/Erie state police. In addition, the members of the group agreed to drop the words "state police" from their name (Simonich 2005). Nevertheless, lacking legislative support for their continued existence, the group has become only a remnant of history.

## Origins and Activities of Volunteer State Police Forces

In 1942, the Ohio State Highway Patrol Auxiliary (OSHPA) was formed when many troopers began entering the armed forces, creating a shortage of personnel for the wartime needs of patrolling highways, airports, bridges, defense plants, and military installations. At that time, membership was limited to members of the Ohio American Legion. The Legion was largely made up of World War I veterans who were unlikely to be drafted into the military

(OSHP Auxiliary Reaches 1992). The recruitment of local Legionnaires for temporary volunteer police work had occurred since the end of World War I in several American cities. Many were deputized at the time of the Boston police strike in 1919. In that same year, local American Legion members also helped to preserve the peace during labor-related strikes in Denver, Colorado, and Youngstown, Ohio. However, at other times and in different jurisdictions, Legion members assisting local law enforcement engaged in violent confrontations with striking longshoremen and steelworkers (Dale 2011).

The first official meeting for the purpose of organization and enrollment in the OSHPA was held in February 1942. By April 1942, there were 2,650 Legion members attending weekly training classes. The members of the new OSHPA were assigned to assist in emergency calls and traffic control. One of the first disasters requiring their assistance occurred on May 31, 1942, when a huge wave from Lake Erie created a great deal of property damage in North Madison. Within an hour, most of the members of the Lake County Auxiliary unit of the OSHPA were at the scene to aid in rescue and recovery efforts. By 1945, the OSHPA had reached its peak strength of nearly 5,000 members. After the war, the Auxiliary became a critical component of Ohio's civil defense preparation (OSHP Auxiliary Reaches 1992).

Today, OSHP Auxiliary members contribute thousands of hours in an assortment of functions (see Figures 5.1 through 5.3). Each member is required to log a minimum of 120 hours per year to remain active. Membership is no

**Figure 5.1** Highway Patrol Auxiliary Officer on traffic detail at Ohio State University football game. (Used with permission of the Ohio State Highway Patrol Auxiliary.)

**Figure 5.2** Highway Patrol Auxiliary Officer participating at the yearly "Shop With A Cop" event. (Used with permission of the Ohio State Highway Patrol Auxiliary.)

**Figure 5.3** Two Highway Patrol Auxiliary Officers participating at the yearly "Shop With A Cop" event. (Used with permission of the Ohio State Highway Patrol Auxiliary.)

longer limited to the members of the American Legion. The requirements to become a Highway Patrol Auxiliary in Ohio are indicated in Box 5.1.

There was a decline in active members in the OSHPA for a short period following World War II; however, as the fears related to the "Cold War" intensified, enrollment increased. During the 1950s, the OSHPA helped to conduct

**BOX 5.1    OHIO STATE HIGHWAY PATROL
AUXILIARY MEMBERSHIP REQUIREMENTS**

- U.S. citizen
- Ohio resident with valid Ohio driver license
- Good physical condition (pass a physician's exam at the applicant's expense)
- Between ages 21 and 55 (except for retired OSHP officers)
- No prior felony convictions
- Availability for training and service
- Submit to and pass a background investigation
- Ability to read and write, and convey thoughts in a clear and concise manner
- Weight proportionate to height (OSHP standard plus 10%)
- Submit to and pass a polygraph examination
- Pass written and physical tests
- Complete OSHP Auxiliary training
- Purchase a uniform
- E-mail OSPAux@dps.state.oh.us to apply

*Source:* Ohio State Highway Patrol (OSHP), http://statepatrol.ohio.gov/auxiliary.stm

nuclear disaster test alerts and other simulated exercises (e.g., evacuations). Throughout the 1950s and 1960s, the OSHPA also helped at crash scenes and with other highway traffic activities (OSHP Auxiliary Reaches 1992). In 1999, 160 men and women were serving in the OSHPA. They were engaged in a wide range of routine patrol duties. Their average age was 45, with eight years of service. Nearly half had one or more years of college. More than one-third were military veterans, and a dozen had been certified as emergency medical technicians (EMTs). About a dozen had completed the entire basic police academy (Profile of the Auxiliary 1999). Initial training requirements were 82 hours. An important state law concerning personal immunity from civil liability for damages and limitation of powers was adopted in 1998. Section 5503.11 (A) of the Ohio Revised Code specifically declares that "No member of the auxiliary unit shall have any power to arrest any person or to enforce any law of this state." A survey by Weinblatt (1993) indicated that the state of Ohio had the largest number of volunteer police officers, with more than 18,000 citizens performing a variety of police services, primarily at the local level of enforcement.

In 2011, 18 new OSHPA officers graduated from the OSHP Training Academy. It was the first auxiliary class since 2009, and the auxiliary candidates spent eight days in residence at the academy undergoing law enforcement training, which included firearms familiarization, traffic and criminal laws, self-defense, cultural sensitivity, and assisting in crash investigations (Auxiliary Officers Commissioned 2012).

Since 2008, OSHPA officers have been eligible for associate membership in the Ohio State Highway Patrol Retirees' Association (OSHPRA) if they meet the following definition: "Any person who was a member of the Ohio State Highway Patrol Auxiliary and left the Auxiliary in good standing. 'Good standing' is defined as leaving service in the Ohio State Highway Patrol or the Patrol Auxiliary under positive circumstances and not under the color of a criminal or administrative investigation for which he/she could have potentially been removed from his/her position had he/she not elected to leave" (OSHPRA Bylaws 2013, 3). (Additional information about the benefits of membership can be found at http://www.oshpretiree.org/OSHPRA_By-Laws.pdf.)

Auxiliary officers in Ohio volunteer their assistance for the annual "Buckeye Boys State Week," the largest Boys State program in the nation with a yearly attendance of 1,200 young men. Established in 1936, it is the single largest program of its type in the nation. Participants represent more than 500 high schools and also include home-schooled students. It has been held at Bowling Green State University since 1978 (American Legion 2013). Following this program, a "Junior Cadet Week" program is held at the Ohio state Highway Patrol Training Academy in Columbus, Ohio, for Boys State and Girls State graduates who are interested in learning about law enforcement.[5] In 2013, the state of Ohio had 53 auxiliary/reserve/citizen patrol units registered with the former VIPS online directory, including the Ohio Highway Patrol Auxiliary.

In 1956, the Arizona State Legislature created the Arizona Highway Patrol Reserves. In 1985, there were 100 unsalaried, fully certified reserve officers. The volunteers were assigned to each of the highway patrol's 13 regional districts on the basis of the district's needs and the residence of the volunteer. A full-time police officer provided logistical support in each district. The auxiliaries were required to serve a minimum of 16 hours per month and to obtain the same recertification that regular full-time officers needed. Basic equipment was provided as well as a prorated monthly uniform allowance. Reserve officers performed all the functions of a regular full-time highway patrol officer, except for the investigation of fatal accidents because of the extensive time commitment involved in such cases (Deitch and Thompson 1985). In 2013, throughout the state of Arizona, there were 21 auxiliary/reserve/posse units registered with the older version IACP VIPS online directory, not including its Highway Patrol Auxiliary. The current minimum requirements for selection as an Arizona reserve officer are indicated in Box 5.2.

In 2013, applicants for participation as an Arizona state police reserve officer had to pass the written examination with a minimum score of 75%. The physical fitness test was a pass/fail component of the overall selection

**BOX 5.2    ARIZONA STATE POLICE RESERVE
OFFICER MINIMUM REQUIREMENTS**

Complete an application

Be 21 years of age (or will be 21 prior to graduation from an approved
law enforcement training academy)

Possess high school diploma General Educational Development
(GED) certificate

Present birth certificate

Have a valid driver license and/or other form of identification

Pass a physical fitness test

Pass written examination

Pass extensive interview

Pass background investigation

Pass polygraph examination

Pass drug screening

Pass psychological and medical examinations

Be a U.S. citizen

*Source:* Arizona Department of Public Safety (AZDPS), http://www.
azdps.gov/careers/reserves

**BOX 5.3    ARIZONA STATE POLICE RESERVE
OFFICER MINIMUM REQUIREMENTS FOR
THE PHYSICAL FITNESS TESTS**

1.5-mile run within 16 minutes

300-meter run within 73.2 seconds

Push-ups—24 reps

Agility run in 21.8 seconds

Sit-ups—28 reps/min.

*Source:* Arizona Department of Public Safety (AZDPS), http://www.
azdps.gov/careers/reserves

process and consisted of five events: sit-ups, push-ups, 1.5-mile run, 300-
meter run, and agility run. Box 5.3 indicates each fitness event requirement.
Applicants receive either a passing or a failing score for each event. All applicants were also required to successfully complete each physical fitness test in
order to qualify for participation in the remaining components of the selection process (Arizona DPS 2013b).

An oral interview involving interpersonal skills and problem-solving
abilities was also required. In order to assist in preparation for this interview,

a Qualifications Appraisal Board (QAB) study plan is provided to each applicant. All aspects of the testing process are subject to verification based on a background investigation and polygraph examination. Finally, every Arizona reserve officer applicant has to complete a psychological evaluation to determine suitability as well as a comprehensive medical evaluation provided at no cost to the applicant (Arizona DPS 2013b).

Having been successfully screened, reserve officer candidates attend a Law Enforcement Training Academy. The training must be equivalent to that received by full-time officers (585 hours of training) and must be certified by the Arizona Peace Officer Standards and Training Board (AZPOST). The approved training academies are conducted at four different community colleges throughout the state. Classes are normally held during evenings and on weekends, and the entire training course can be completed in approximately 10–12 months[6] (Arizona DPS 2013b). The cost of the basic training academy, and certain associated equipment, is the responsibility of each reserve officer candidate. During academy attendance, the state police reserve officer candidates are designated as "reserve cadets." The Arizona DPS provides the following items to its reserve cadets and regular officers: (1) duty weapon (firearm), ammunition, holster and magazine pouch; (2) duty belt and related accessories (handcuffs and case, OC spray (oleoresin capsicum, also known as pepper spray) and case, police radio and holder); (3) reimbursement for body armor (up to $1,000); and (4) badges (wallet and breast) and police credentials. Other benefits may be available, and advanced officer training courses are available to the reserve officers. Within one year of academy graduation, all reserve officers are required to complete the field officer training program. Following completion of field training, reserve officers must contribute a minimum of 240 hours per calendar year. Continuing officer training is also required annually. All Arizona state police (full-time or reserve) are not permitted to have separate, full-authority peace officer employment/sponsorship with any other law enforcement agency, either in or outside the state of Arizona (Arizona DPS 2013b).

Arizona reserve volunteer police officers are not compensated for their services nor are they eligible for state employee benefits, except for those provided under the state's Workers' Compensation Law. They wear the same uniform and use the same equipment as full-time officers. Reserve officers purchase their own uniforms. However, they may qualify for a uniform allowance based upon satisfactory performance and by meeting the minimum work hour requirement. However, specialized equipment is provided at no cost to the officer (Arizona DPS 2013b).

In 1986, there were about 14,000 persons serving as volunteer police officers in various departments throughout the state of Florida. In Tallahassee, Florida's capital city, a reserve unit was established and members had to complete the same training as regular officers. Qualifications included citizenship;

a satisfactory background investigation; no criminal history; and two years of college credits. In addition, prospective reserves had to pass an oral interview, a polygraph exam, a medical exam, and psychological testing. Upon successful completion of the training requirements (a minimum of 360 hours in 1986), members were equipped with the same uniform and other equipment that was issued to regular officers. The volunteer police officers possessed the same police powers as regular officers (Berg and Doerner 1988). Berg and Doerner (1988) found that although some volunteer police joined for self-serving interests (maintaining or obtaining police certification), participants also derived an intrinsic sense of satisfaction through the fulfillment of their assignments.

The Florida Highway Patrol Auxiliary (FHPA) is an all-volunteer law enforcement organization dedicated to providing direct assistance and operational support to the Florida Highway Patrol and is authorized to so by Florida statutes. Founded in 1957, the FHPA has assisted the Florida Highway Patrol by patrolling the streets and highways of the state, providing timely assistance to disabled motorists, participating in vehicle equipment and license checkpoints, participating in specialized details, and responding to natural disasters and other emergency situations (About the FHPA 2013a). The total number of FHPA members is limited to five times the total number of regularly employed highway patrol officers authorized by law (sec. 321.24[3], Florida Statutes). Auxiliary trooper candidates undergo a rigorous hiring process and training similar to that of a full-time state trooper. They ride with a regular trooper to provide "second officer" backup. After additional experience and training, these volunteer police officers may be approved for "limited scope patrol" (LSP). LSP-certified officers patrol solo in a marked patrol unit to provide assistance to motorists and troopers (About the FHPA 2013a).

In Florida, the legal definition of an "auxiliary law enforcement officer" is "any person employed or appointed, with or without compensation, who aids or assists a full-time or part-time law enforcement officer and who, while under the direct supervision of a full-time or part-time law enforcement officer, has the authority to arrest and perform law enforcement functions" (sec. 943.10[8], Florida Statutes). In 2007, there were 428 members of the Florida FHPA, and 105 had 20 or more years of service. That same year, in recognition of the FHPA's service to the state of Florida, the legislature passed a new law providing the following benefits for 20-year retiring members of the FHPA: one complete uniform, the badge worn by the officer, the officer's service handgun, if one was issued as part of the officer's equipment, and an identification card marked "retired." The bill also removed the provision prohibiting compensation to individuals who volunteer for the FHPA (sec. 321.24[6]; sec.943.10[8], Florida Statutes).

While under the direct supervision of a Florida Highway Patrol Trooper, the auxiliary troopers have the authority to bear arms and the power to arrest violators. Florida law and the Florida Criminal Justice Standards and Training

Commission require that every member of the FHPA receive law enforcement training at a state-approved training center by state-certified instructors. In 2013, troopers needed to complete a minimum of 320 hours of training by approved instructors. Similar to the policies in place for Arizona basic law enforcement training, police academy programs are conducted locally at community colleges as well as from approved courses offered by the FHP. However, unlike the Arizona rule, in Florida, qualified FHPA candidates have all tuition expenses covered. In addition, Florida provides all equipment and uniforms needed for work as an auxiliary trooper (About the FHPA 2013a).

On average, it takes 12–24 months to have applications reviewed and for training to be completed to become certified as a Level II Auxiliary Trooper. Applicants must pass a basic abilities test (BAT) at a local testing center before application access is issued. In addition, there are preliminary tests for each applicant involving physical abilities, a polygraph examination, medical and eye examinations, a psychological examination, and a background investigation. Upon successful completion of the necessary academy instructional classes, FHPA officers have authority to carry a firearm, defensive spray (pepper spray), and the dart firing stun gun (known as the TASER) (About the FHPA 2013b; FHPA 2013). Law enforcement agencies use the TASER X26 and the ADVANCED TASER M26. These two devices are only available to law enforcement and are capable of recording data useful to officers in court (Tell Me About 2013).

As part of their training, qualified FHP auxiliaries ride with a full-time trooper for approximately one year. During that time, a defensive driving class and the LSP classes are taken. Forty hours of additional police vehicle instruction is then conducted by a field training officer. If all of these experiences are completed, the volunteer officer is designated a Level III Auxiliary Trooper and is authorized to drive a police vehicle to assist motorists on the freeway and to identify abandoned vehicles as well as for backing up other troopers. FHPA members must serve 24 hours per quarter or eight hours each month; however, very few, if any, volunteer police contribute only the minimum hours.

Level IV Auxiliary Trooper status may be obtained by Level III volunteers after patrolling for about one year. Auxiliary troopers so designated may complete an additional 200 hours of training and thereby qualify to respond to and investigate noncriminal crash scenes. These officers must commit to performing 16–24 or more patrol hours per week (About the FHPA 2013b).

In 2013, Florida had 111 auxiliary/reserve/citizen patrol units registered with the older version IACP VIPS directory, including the FHPA and a Florida Park Police reserve officer program. In 2011, the Florida Department of Environmental Protection's (DEP) Florida Park Police Reserve unit had 27 members. DEP Park Police reserve officers follow the same rules and training standards as full-time officers. However, reserve officers are unpaid volunteers. Upon completion of the field training officer (FTO) program, park police reserve officers may patrol alone with the same authority as a full-time officer. They are required to work at least 16 hours per month or 48 hours averaged over a three-month period. Park police reserve officers serve as a resource for augmenting the field responsibilities of regular park police officers within the Florida state park system and on other state lands. Florida state parks are some of the most beautiful in the world and may attract more than 20 million visitors each year (Florida DEP 2011).

According to the New Hampshire Revised Statutes Annotated, Chapter 106-B-19 entitled "Auxiliary State Police," "The director is authorized to recruit, train, and organize an auxiliary state police force for the purpose of providing emergency services throughout the state for peacetime or wartime emergencies or threatened emergencies and for augmenting the state police force in such manner as the director may deem appropriate. Notwithstanding other provisions the director may recruit such auxiliary force from retired state or local police." The New Hampshire State Police Auxiliary Troopers are considered part-time sworn troopers and are assigned throughout the state. They provide assistance at special events (Motorcycle Week, NASCAR, etc.) and in selected investigations as well as perform patrol work and traffic control. The minimum qualifications to become an auxiliary trooper are the same minimum qualifications to become a State Trooper I. The auxiliary troopers must also meet the same annual in-service and firearms training requirements as full-time troopers (Support Services 2013). Auxiliary troopers are required to volunteer 16 hours each month, which is usually accomplished by patrolling with a trooper and by attending firearms and in-service training. In 2006, auxiliary troopers volunteered more than 700 hours. These hours indicate that their ranks have been rather thin. In 2013, the now defunct IACP VIPS directory listings for New Hampshire had only one registered volunteer auxiliary program. However, several departments used citizen patrols.

In 2013, there were 31 Vermont auxiliary troopers assigned to the Marine/Snowmobile Division (Vermont State Police 2013b). Auxiliary troopers are paid part-time positions within the Vermont State Police. The minimum age is 19. Applicants need to reside within a 200-mile radius of departmental headquarters and must have been a resident of that geographical area for at least three years prior to applying. Living out of the residence area for educational purposes or military service was acceptable pending departmental review (Vermont State Police 2013a). All applicants must complete initial training requirements for law enforcement officers and annual training activities in order to maintain certification thereafter. (A list of the essential job functions for Vermont auxiliary troopers who are mostly assigned to the Marine Program and to the Snowmobile Enforcement Program with occasional duty to assist state troopers directing traffic at special events or in other nonroutine functions can be found at: http://vsp.vermont.gov/sites/vsp/files/Documents/VSP_Auxiliary%20Trooper%20Essential%20Job%20Functions.pdf.)

In 2013, the former VIPS online directory entry for the state of Vermont had only three programs described—none involving an auxiliary/reserve unit.

The Oregon Department of State Police was formally established in 1931 (Oregon Law 1931, Chapter 139) to serve as a rural patrol force and to provide assistance to local and county law enforcement. The Oregon State Police Reserves Board consists of retired Oregon State Police Reserves members. Board members are appointed from various regions around the state. The board meets as necessary to provide direction and oversight for the Oregon State Police Reserves program. This program has only consisted a pool of retired state police officers. (Oregon DSP 2011).

At the local level, Umpqua Community College offers a certificate of completion for the Police Reserve Academy. The academy is conducted in conjunction with the Douglas County Sheriff's Department; the Roseburg, Winston, Sutherlin, and Myrtle Creek police departments; and the Oregon State Police. This academy trains reserve officers and deputies for law enforcement agencies throughout southwest Oregon. Many full-time officers and deputies are hired from the reserve ranks. This rigorous course of study starts in mid-September and concludes in May of the following year. Classes are taught on Saturdays from 7:00 a.m. to 5:30 p.m. This is a 320-hour program designed to train police reserve officers to enter a career in law enforcement. Prospective academy students who have a letter of sponsorship from a law enforcement agency have first priority for admission into the program, and those who are not sponsored but have letters of recommendation from a law enforcement agency have second priority for admission into the program (Police Reserve Academy 2013).

The former VIPS directory entry for Oregon indicated 46 different auxiliary/reserve/citizen patrol units in 2013. For example, the city of Portland has a reserve officer program. It has the same minimum qualifications and hiring process as entry-level police officers with the exception of the college, military, or police certification requirements. Two years of service as a reserve police officer (after training and with at least of 500 hours of service rendered) satisfies the work experience requirement for entry into the full-time ranks. There are approximately 1,300 reserve officers throughout the state (Weisberg 2013). However, there was only one registered active citizen patrol group affiliated with the Oregon State Police in Florence, Oregon. The Florence Chapter of the Oregon State Police Volunteers was formed in 1994 to combat the rising number of auto break-ins. Volunteers contributed a minimum of 10 hours a month. Break-ins and thefts were reduced by more than 75% in the first year of operation. The group, which consisted of 21 members in 2013, patrols campgrounds and waysides of the central Oregon coastline providing a positive point of contact for visitors and serving as a deterrent to crime. The program is supported by grants and donations from the community and from concerned individuals. There is no state funding involved (Jarvis 2013).

South Carolina has had a system of volunteer state constables for many decades. It is unlike any of the other state auxiliary trooper or reserve units previously described. State constables are not agents of the South Carolina Law Enforcement Division (SLED), but they are regulated by that agency.[7] Depending on their specific constable commission category or class, they may be of assistance to a particular law enforcement agency. The Group III category appears to be the commission used by individuals who may be interested in a career in law enforcement or who are more settled in their respective careers and want to promote their community's safety. Generally, state constables are appointed by the South Carolina governor. Their commission type indicates whether they will be eligible upon request to assist law enforcement throughout the state. When performing such an assignment, they are not to be used to replace law enforcement in any agency. "The Chief of South Carolina Law Enforcement (SLED) advises the Governor about policies and regulations pertaining to State Constables; establishes training requirements, sets standards for conduct, prescribes limits for use of authority, determines suitability and fitness of applicants and enforces governing regulations. A South Carolina State Constable is not a stand-alone law enforcement department. It is the purpose of the Constable to assist and augment local law enforcement agency personnel efforts. A South Carolina State Constable is required under S.C. law to preserve and protect the citizens according to the laws of the state and is required to respond to any actions that result in a crime. A State Constable must protect and preserve a crime scene until a regular on-duty officer, with jurisdiction, arrives to take charge of the situation. A South Carolina State Constable is a certified law enforcement officer … may carry a concealed weapon as outlined in the regulations within the State of South Carolina only after successfully completing an approved firearms qualifications course … is not allowed to receive any compensation for services rendered; therefore Constables may not perform any private security work or private investigations. A South Carolina State Constable may not serve as a reserve police officer or any other position as a sworn law enforcement officer" (McCoy 2011).

There are a variety of reasons that will automatically disqualify individuals from holding a state constable's commission including owners or workers in the field of private security, bail bondsmen, law enforcement officers who presently are commissioned under other existing state statutes, having a criminal record, and so on. As noted previously, there exist specific standards governing issuance of any of the four categories of state constable commissions (Group I, II, III, and Advanced). For example, "The Group III state constable commission is available to qualified citizens who request such commissions for the purpose of assisting named law enforcement agencies, to employees of financial institutions whose primary job duties include investigation of criminal offenses and who have a need for inter-county authority, and to employees of utility companies deemed by the chief of SLED to be essential to public safety and security and who have a job-related need for inter-county law enforcement authority and whose primary duties include the security of utility company property and services" (SC State Constables 2012). All Group III candidates must attend an approved State Constable Basic Training School conducted by South Carolina Technical Education Colleges, complete at least 120 hours of voluntary service activity each year, and complete annual in-service training (SC State Constables 2012). Uniform costs and other expenses are the responsibility of each commissioned state constable. The cost for attending the basic training school at York Technical College, Rock Hill, South Carolina, was $560 in 2012. (The requirements for each of the various categories of state constable can be found at: http://www.sled.sc.gov/Constables.aspx?MenuID=Constables.)

The South Carolina Highway Patrol was formed in 1930 to enforce newly enacted laws governing the use of motor vehicles. It attempted to initiate an Auxiliary Trooper Program in 2006. The program was to be similar to the reserve officer program used by local law enforcement agencies, bolstering existing resources by using nonpaid volunteers to assist troopers at special events with traffic and crowd control and during times of natural disaster such as hurricanes. The auxiliary troopers were to be partnered with full-time state troopers. At that time, Russell F. Roark, former Highway Patrol Colonel, stated: "This model has worked well for local law enforcement agencies, and we are confident that it will be a plus for bolstering our presence in communities and on our roadways" (SC Highway Patrol 2006). According to Captain Jones Gamble of the South Carolina Highway Patrol, a few citizens received training, but the program was discontinued before anyone was assigned to actual duties due to budget cuts (personal communication, June 25, 2014).

In 1965, Col. C. W. Russell, a former state trooper, was appointed to direct the Alabama Department of Public Safety. Col. Russell established the Alabama State Trooper Reserve program to "serve side by side with state troopers throughout the state on routine assignments, as well as during natural disasters and other special details" (Alabama DPS 2013). In 1972, integration of the state trooper force was ordered by Judge Frank M. Johnson in what was to be known as the Paradise Case. In the federal court order, Judge Johnson ruled that public safety must hire one black trooper for each white hired until 25% of the force was black. It would be 1990 before a federal court consent decree was issued in the case.[8] As a result of another court case, height and weight standards for state trooper applicants were abolished because the requirements discriminated against women. U.S. District Judge Frank M. Johnson ordered that the standards be eliminated as part of the screening process for prospective state troopers in June 1976 (Alabama DPS 2013).

In 1978, the Alabama State Trooper Reserve program resumed functioning after more than a year's hiatus. The program was given a new start through the passage of a state law authorizing peace officer powers to active duty members. All former members who wanted to remain members were required to submit new applications. The program's new requirements included a 48-hour training course and the requirement that members work at least three shifts in every three-month period. All members would have to cover their own expenses. At the time of the announcement, Col. Meady L. Hilyer, the newly appointed director of the Alabama Department of Public Safety, stated: "Interested and qualified blacks are encouraged to apply for membership" (Reserve given service 1978, 13). In 2014, general information about the Alabama State Trooper Reserve program, a program manual, and an application were posted on the agency's Web site, but the word "closed" appeared at the top of the information site (see Alabama DPS 2014). However, there had been an effort to recruit additional members in 2009 when there were 80 reserve troopers in Alabama including three trooper reserve pilots (Kitchen 2009). At that time, applicants have been at least 21 years old and U.S. citizens. A background investigation was required, and applicants completed a training program consisting of firearms qualifications and a physical fitness test (Douglas and Jones 2009). The only specific information available at the time of the publication of this book was that the state's reserve trooper program had suspended recruitment efforts and that the active number of volunteer reserve troopers had fallen below 60. Figure 5.4 shows only a hat badge insignia. The absence of the hat might symbolize the current uncertainty surrounding the nature of this program.

**Figure 5.4** Alabama State Trooper Reserve Highway Patrol hat badge.

## The Rise and Fall of the Connecticut State Auxiliary Police

As noted previously, the Connecticut State Police was established in 1903. Its first five officers were assigned to enforce laws pertaining to intoxicating liquor and gaming violations. They received three dollars for each day of service. In 1941, concern about the need to protect the Connecticut shoreline against possible invasion was high; in a short time, the nation's entry into World War II solidified the need for an auxiliary program because there was a greatly diminished supply of men eligible for police assignments due to military call-ups. Many citizens responded for home front civil defense purposes, and before the war's end, about 1,200 auxiliary volunteers had been assigned to guard bridges, waterways, and other installations against possible sabotage. Connecticut auxiliary officers are still doing their job today but on a much smaller scale (History of CSP 2013). After the conclusions of World War II and the Korean War, many of the volunteers were absorbed by local police departments, but others were reassigned to work as volunteer troopers to help patrol highways, to assist disabled motorists, to direct traffic at accidents, to do courier work for barracks, and to back up the regular full-time troopers. These state volunteer police officers had no police arrest authority and did not respond to alarms, but they carried firearms for self-defense as they drove in marked state police cruisers (Leukhardt 1995). A state law adopted in 1951 and amended in 1963 regarding peacetime use authorized the commissioner of the Department of Public Safety "to recruit, train, and organize a volunteer police auxiliary force for the purpose of providing emergency services throughout the state" (see ch. 529, sec. 29–22, Connecticut statutes).

The year 1982 signaled the decline of both state and local auxiliary membership. In that year, a new state law required all municipal police officers to be trained and certified. The new training course consisted of 560 hours of instruction, while the basic state police auxiliary course consisted of 60 hours and two weekends of small arms training at the state police range. At first, because this law did not refer to the state auxiliary members, it impacted mostly local towns and cities. Many simply found it too expensive to try to certify their part-time volunteer officers and dissolved their units rather than risk the liability associated with having uncertified but armed and uniformed volunteers (Leukhardt 1995).

In 1986, there were about 400 auxiliary troopers, working out of the 12 state police barracks under the command of an auxiliary volunteer whose role was to be a liaison between the auxiliary force and the commanding officer of the barracks. When interviewed, Charles A. Morrison, the president of the Connecticut State Police Union, praised the auxiliary unit. "They perform a very valuable service for us and they perform a terrific assistance to regular troopers at the scene of accidents and crimes. They also free troopers for other duties" (Cavanaugh 1986, 2). Nevertheless, state police officials soon developed concerns about the need for training its auxiliary, especially because they were interested in obtaining Commission on Accreditation for Law Enforcement Agencies, Inc. (CALEA), accreditation. (The CALEA standards pertaining to volunteer police are found in Appendix A.) In 1986, when the Connecticut state police attained accreditation, the existing auxiliary force was "grandfathered in"—they could stay until their retirement (Youmans 2000). Thus it was decided that it would be best to phase out the program by not accepting new applicants, although one newspaper report indicated that hundreds of citizens were eager to join. By 1995, the trooper auxiliaries numbered 130 (Leukhardt 1995). As members reach the age of 70, they undertake administrative assignments and do not wear a uniform or carry a firearm.[9] By 2000, the auxiliaries had about 55 volunteers certified for patrol and 22 who did mostly administrative work. In addition, the minimum training hours had risen to 240 hours (Youmans 2000).

In 2003, upon the one hundredth anniversary of the Connecticut State Police, Governor John Rowland stated: "As the oldest law enforcement agency of its kind, the Connecticut State Police has survived countless societal changes and changes within its ranks—and throughout remained a steadfast bastion of security for all our citizens. Troopers and auxiliary troopers have selflessly given their lives in furtherance of this mission. It is upon the path these brave men and women have paved that the Connecticut State Police have met the challenges of the new millennium. All of the residents of our state should recognize the rich history of the Connecticut State Police and its essential role in our lives today" (Daley 2003). During its existence, 19 regular troopers and two auxiliary troopers have lost their lives while performing their duties in the Connecticut State Police (History of CSP 2013). The two volunteer troopers killed in the line of duty were Edward Truelove in 1992 and Philip Mingione in 1994 (Youmans 2000).

In 2012, the state legislative committee on public safety and security held a hearing regarding a proposed law dealing with state police staffing levels. The proposed legislation would have eliminated the mandated cap on the number of state police, which was set at 1,248. The bill also called for the elimination of the cap on the state police volunteer auxiliary force, which under current law could not exceed twice the number of state police officers. By law, the commissioner would be authorized to appoint and organize the volunteers to perform emergency services and to augment the force. The 1,248 minimum state police number had been imposed in 1998 due to an incident involving the death of a woman who had called 911 for police help but received no police response for about 20 minutes.[10] In 2012, Sgt. Andrew Matthews, an attorney and president of the state police union, spoke against the measure, fearing that an arbitrary number might be established reducing public safety. He also testified that he supported the work of the auxiliary force, which at that time consisted of 49 active patrol members and

16 performing administrative work (S.B. 32 Hearing 2012). As of May 2012, the proposal to eliminate the state police cap was considered to have "died in the Senate."

In press interviews, William Klein, the certification officer for the Police Officer Standards and Training Council (POST) in Connecticut, has indicated that the era of the auxiliary officer is ending, but in its place there has emerged a more professional and better trained police force. In addition, Jeff Matchett, president of the Connecticut Council of Police Unions, noted that if an auxiliary or part-time police officer is to carry a gun and have arrest powers, he or she must complete the same academy training as full-time police officers. In 2011, such preparation consisted of at least 818 hours of classroom and field training preceded by extensive background checks (Juliano 2011).

Nonetheless, at the local level there have been new developments in Connecticut involving volunteer police having limited authority. For example, the city of New Britain is willing to run some risk of liability and deploy volunteer auxiliary police who do not carry guns, have arrest powers and did not work regular shifts. New Britain disbanded its auxiliary force in the early 1980s but reinstituted a program in 1995 at the recommendation of its police chief and with the approval of its city council. At that time, it was noted that auxiliary officers generally fell into two categories: young people exploring law enforcement as a career and middle-aged people driven by community activism. The revival of the program was presented as a natural outgrowth of block watches and other community-based policing programs (Leukhardt 1995). However, in 2013, the now defunct VIPS online directory of registered programs indicated only four police departments having an auxiliary/reserve or citizen patrol unit. Neither New Britain nor the Connecticut state auxiliary police were listed. Yet, during 2012, seven members of the state auxiliary police unit assigned to Troop H in Hartford and their unit leader volunteered 451 days for a total of more than 4,200 hours of service. Their patrol hours were nearly four times that of any other volunteer unit. To achieve these numbers as a unit, they each had to work one 10-hour shift per week for the entire year, which is in addition to their regular full-time jobs. A unit citation was awarded attesting to their service (Auxiliary Troopers 2013b). Included among this group was Auxiliary Trooper Michael Tiernan (a member since 1965). He was named "the Connecticut State Police 2013 Auxiliary Trooper of the Year" for his many hours of dedicated service (Auxiliary Troopers 2013a). After 1995, the city of New Britain reorganized its auxiliary program, and it is now referred to as a "community service officer (CSO) Program." Members are unpaid and wear distinctive uniforms.[11] The CSO program is described "as an excellent opportunity for those interested in a career in law enforcement to gain valuable experience and for service-oriented individuals to contribute to the community" (CSO Program 2013).

## Other State Police Volunteer Initiatives

The great majority of state police agencies do not have volunteer police units who possess peace officer status, but many do use the services of civilians in closely related roles. For example, the California Highway Patrol (CHP), established in 1929 by an act of the state legislature, has a senior volunteer program that provides support for the CHP's efforts to protect travelers on county and state highways and in educating the public concerning driver safety issues. Members in the program must be at least 55 and most volunteer for a six-hour shift once a week. Statewide, in 2012, there were more than 740 senior CHP volunteers. They perform patrols to deter speeders in marked CHP vehicles bearing a removable "volunteer" sign. They also help in deploying radar trailers, work in schools, direct traffic at special events, and have administrative duties. The volunteers complete tasks that enable officers to spend more time patrolling. While on patrol, they are not armed and do not enforce the law. The use of a cruiser's siren or the making of traffic stops is not permitted. All potential members undergo a background check and must have no prior felony convictions (Scroggin 2013). There is also an active Explorer Post at the Visalia office of the California Highway Patrol (see Figures 5.5 through 5.7). Additional details about Law Enforcement Exploring are provided in Chapter 8.

Another program involving unarmed and unsworn citizens was initiated in 2013. It began as a response to the Sandy Hook Elementary School shooting in Newtown, Connecticut. The program involves Oregon State Police volunteers who patrol either on foot or in marked vehicles in neighborhoods around public schools in Lincoln County. A random schedule is used. The Oregon State Police (OSP) has used citizen volunteers in Lincoln County for

**Figure 5.5** Visalia Explorer Post 480 members engaged in training scenario. (Used with the permission of the California Highway Patrol, Visalia, California (CA).)

**Figure 5.6** Visalia Explorer Post 480 members engaged in training scenario. (Used with the permission of the California Highway Patrol.)

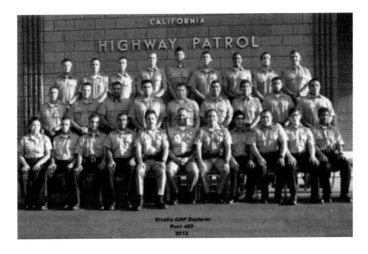

**Figure 5.7** Visalia Explorer Post 480 unit photo, ca. 2012. (Used with the permission of the California Highway Patrol.)

more than 25 years. However, this is the first time they have been specifically deployed for school safety. Volunteers qualify through background checks and training with the OSP. According to Sue Graves, the safety coordinator for Lincoln County schools, "Their role is not to intervene but to call 911 if there is a dangerous situation or if it's not an immediate danger, to call the school principal or the secretary to let them know what they're seeing so that the school principal can then take whatever action they deem is important" (Kellner 2013).

The state of Maryland has two prominent statewide volunteer police related programs: the Natural Resources Police Reserves (NRPR) and the Volunteers in Police Service (VIPS) program of the Maryland State Police. The former program was established in 1996 and the latter in 1986. In recent years, the NRPR has had about 200 members and the VIPS program has involved about 100 participants (Maryland NRP 2013; Maryland State Police VIPS 2013).

The Maryland Natural Resources Police (NRP) is a law enforcement agency with statewide jurisdiction that enforces the laws and regulations that protect Maryland's natural resources on a half million acres of land owned or controlled by the Maryland Department of Natural Resources and that ensures the enforcement of Maryland's recreational boating regulations and maritime homeland security. The NRP responds to approximately 2,400 maritime incidents a year on Maryland's Chesapeake Bay, tidal rivers, inland waters, and coastal waterways off the Atlantic Ocean (Maryland NRP 2013). Members of the NRP Reserves have assisted with radio/telephone communications, boating and hunting safety education, community and public relations, patrol with sworn NRP officers, search and rescue operations, vessel safety checks, traffic control, vehicle and vessel operations, and administrative matters (Maryland NRP Reserves 2013). In this manner, NRPR officers perform duties in the field other than law enforcement, which frees time for commissioned officers to deal with criminal matters.

The VIPS of the Maryland State Police (MSP) work in most barracks throughout the state and the human resources, forensic sciences, central records, medical, and police training divisions. In 2010, VIPS volunteers contributed more than 13,000 hours. The member of the VIPS program have been involved in fingerprinting, community service events, serving as adult advisors to Police Explorers, photographic work, role playing in live scenarios for trooper training, and a variety of administrative duties. The VIPS program also allows MSP personnel to devote more time to their direct law enforcement responsibilities (Maryland State Police VIPS 2013).

A related program involving police volunteers is conducted by the Virginia State Police (VSP). Almost any type of needed activity, except actual police work, is open to citizens over the age of 16 who can pass a background investigation. Examples of activities include computer maintenance, various administrative services (e.g., data entry, filing, typing, cataloging, and copying), radio repair and installation, telephone answering, translation, vehicle servicing, and warehousing. In 2013, the VSP advertised for volunteers to work at its sex offender registry at state police headquarters to assist with community mailings to child minding facilities, scanning documents into the registry, copying court cases, and similar activities. It also was seeking an individual with a background in insurance work for its insurance fraud and auto theft section within Division 1 Headquarters in Glen Allen, Virginia.

This volunteer would be assigned to assist with investigations and general office duties (Virginia SP 2013).

In the United States, the first Citizen Police Academy (CPA) was hosted by the Orlando (Florida) Police Department. Since that time, CPA programs have been formed by police agencies all over the country. CPAs are intended to open the lines of communication between the community and their local police and to help expand a police agency's community-based efforts. Such programs can help to alleviate some misunderstandings by providing citizens with a firsthand look at the operations, procedures, statutes, regulations, and policies that guide police in their daily duties.

In communities large and small, various state police agencies have instituted CPAs, often on an annual basis. Notable programs have been conducted by the Alaska State Troopers, Pennsylvania State Police, Kentucky State Police, Connecticut State Police, Delaware State Police, Rhode Island State Police, Utah Highway Patrol, and the Tennessee Highway Patrol. The Pennsylvania CPA has covered such topics as the history and structure of the state police, traffic law and crash investigation, executing a search warrant, defensive tactics, domestic violence issues, use of drug dogs, use of the polygraph, special emergency response teams, role of the patrol officer, criminal investigations, forensics, aviation, mounted police units, and the use of force. Ride-a-long and shooting range opportunities typically are provided. Most of the CPAs are open to a limited number of citizens above the age 18 or 21 who live or work in the jurisdiction of the agency. Many agencies also conduct background investigations of applicants (who must not have prior felony or serious misdemeanor convictions) and may even restrict participation to a select group of government, media, and community leaders. Candidates must be willing to attend weekly three-hour sessions, and the academies may last anywhere from six to ten weeks.

One typical academy is run annually by Troop P of the Pennsylvania State Police. It is open to all residents of the Troop P coverage area, which includes Bradford, Sullivan, Wyoming, and a portion of Luzerne County. The program is held on eight consecutive Wednesdays from 6 p.m. to 8 p.m. in a classroom setting. The participants receive instructions and demonstrations from various members of the Pennsylvania State Police. There is no cost to the participants. At the CPA's conclusion, a graduation is held and participants receive a certificate of participation and a class photo (Troop P Community Services Unit 2013).

## Summary

Today, opportunities to engage in "community policing" activities are available not only at local police departments but also at state police agencies. In fact, a number of state police agencies have used the services of local citizens, especially since the World War II era. Initially, these activities were devoted to civil defense functions (e.g., protecting the infrastructure vital for defense), but as threats of invasion or sabotage abated, attention and the use of volunteer police shifted to the more routine or everyday needs of public safety (highway safety, crowd control, etc.). Since the wake-up call associated with the events of 9/11, there has existed a need to rethink how best to protect America's infrastructure, major landmarks, and places involving mass gatherings (shopping malls, stadiums, etc.). Throughout the latter half of the twentieth century and continuing into the present time, volunteer police have routinely supplemented police strength at special events.

In some respects, the formation of the Texas Rangers served as a precedent for the creation of later statewide law enforcement agencies. However, its first roles centered on the protection of frontier settlements from Indians and on attacks by Mexicans who had crossed into Texas territory. In the early decades of the twentieth century, the new state police agencies were called upon for vice and liquor law enforcement, peacekeeping in coal and iron regions due to labor unrest, the provision of rural police services, and highway safety. In New York, an important justification for their establishment included less reliance on National Guard troops during emergencies. Details about the Arizona, Connecticut, Texas, Illinois, New Jersey, and New York state police agencies were presented as examples of how their origins stemmed from these specific needs. In Pennsylvania, interesting history of the volunteer state police of Crawford and Erie Counties was also examined. This organization was conceived in the 1870s to contend with livestock thieves but became a popular community resource for traffic and crowd control work during its last 50 years of existence.

In addition, information about each of the existing state volunteer police units was presented. These units and programs include the Alabama State Trooper Reserve, Arizona Highway Patrol Reserve, Connecticut State Auxiliary Police, Florida Highway Patrol Auxiliary, Florida Park Police Reserve, New Hampshire State Police Auxiliary, Oregon State Police Reserves, Ohio State Highway Patrol Auxiliary, South Carolina State Constable program, and Vermont Auxiliary Troopers.

An interesting feature of the work of the OSHP Auxiliary officers is the assistance they provide at both the annual "Buckeye Boys State Week" and "Junior Cadet Week" programs. The latter event is held for both Boys State and Girls State graduates who are interested in learning about law enforcement. After additional experience and training, FHP Auxiliary officers may be certified to patrol solo in a marked patrol unit to provide assistance to motorists and troopers. The paid part-time auxiliary troopers in Vermont are generally assigned to the marine/snowmobile division within the state police. Although their work is based on the seasons, they must complete the state's basic and annual law enforcement training requirements to remain eligible for assignments. In Oregon, many full-time officers and deputies are hired from the reserve ranks. A South Carolina State Constable's commission cannot be used for private security work. In order for the state constable program to provide maximum assistance, specific standards have been established for each of four different commission categories. The Alabama State Trooper Reserve announced the suspension of its recruitment efforts prior to the publication of this book.

The Connecticut State Auxiliary Police has been in a phasing out status since the mid-1980s. A major reason given for this decision is the state's fiscal inability to pay for the necessary enhanced training as a result of new state standards and/or CALEA requirements. However, another reason concerns an apparent disinterest in seeking qualified citizens who might be willing to pay for it themselves. It could also be due to reasons unknown by this author. In response to inquiries regarding the status of the Connecticut State Auxiliary Police program, Connecticut State Police Capt. Gregory Senick remarked: "It's not fair to require them to go through extensive training programs when they are not paid. It's not practical" (quoted in Waldman 2001). Nonetheless, many other states continue to maintain their programs and in most instances have endeavored to enhance their training and preparedness.

Moreover, volunteer programs involving unsworn positions appear to be making a comeback in a few local jurisdictions in Connecticut. For example, the city of New Britain has introduced a community service officer (CSO) program. CSOs are volunteers who receive no salary and who wear distinctive uniforms. The program is advertised as an excellent opportunity for those interested in a career in law enforcement to gain valuable experience and for service-oriented individuals to contribute to the community (CSO Program 2013). The events of September 11, 2001, and the tragedy that occurred at the Sandy Hook Elementary School in Newtown on December 15, 2012 (the nation's second-worst school shooting), surely indicate a need to develop more locally based and innovative public safety programs. In time, policy makers in Connecticut may decide to reconsider the need for their state's well-respected auxiliary trooper force.

Although the vast majority of state police agencies do not have volunteer state police units who possess peace officer status, many appear to use the services of civilians in a variety of roles ranging from citizen observer patrols to administrative assistance. In order to garner community support for their initiatives, a number of state police agencies have adopted the practice of conducting CPAs. Ride-a-long and shooting range opportunities are typically provided. Most of the CPAs are open to a limited number of applicants above the age 18 or 21 who live or work in the jurisdiction of the agency.

## Review Questions

1. The new VIPS Web site directory is divided into various categories. Identify these categories by visiting the new Web site at: http://www.theiacp.org/VIPS

2. Make a case for arguing either for or against the proposition that the Texas Rangers were America's first state police agency.

3. Provide at least three reasons for the establishment of state police in the eastern half of the United States.

4. The Crawford/Erie state police was dissolved by the legislature even though the group agreed to change its name so it could not be confused with the Pennsylvania State Police and also agreed that it would strengthen its public accountability by inviting the Erie County sheriff and district attorney to serve on its advisory board. These changes did not overcome legislative opposition to the group. Discuss whether you think that the organization could have done more to save itself.

5. Read the online copy of the Illinois Attorney General's (AG) December 30, 2010, opinion dealing with independent auxiliary police contracts. Indicate the main opinion of the AG and the reasons for it. Discuss whether you agree or disagree.

6. Look up the history and present activities of the state police organization that serves your state. Identify and discuss at least two issues associated with such activities.

7. State at least one difference and one similarity between the Ohio State Highway Patrol Auxiliary (OSHPA) and the Florida Highway Patrol Auxiliary (FHPA).

8. Berg and Doerner (1988) found that some volunteer police joined for a self-serving interest. Identify at least one example of this type of interest and discuss why or why not your example(s) should disqualify an applicant.

9. Two of the volunteer state police agencies (i.e., Florida and Connecticut) limit the total number of volunteer police based on the total number of regularly employed state police. Discuss at least two possible explanations for this limitation.

10. Some state police agencies cover all initial training expenses for volunteer police while others do not. Should such expenses be covered? Discuss.

11. The bylaws of the Ohio State Highway Patrol Retirees' Association refer to the potential need for the services of the "Retired Trooper Reserve Auxiliary." Visit the Web site of this association and review its posted bylaws in order to determine the purpose of this organization and how it differs from the OSHP Auxiliary.

12. The state legislature of Connecticut has set a state police staffing level at 1,248. There has been an unsuccessful effort to eliminate this specific staffing level. Is there any possible connection between this staffing level requirement and the phasing out of the state's auxiliary trooper program? Discuss your views.

13. New Britain's CSO program is an example of how citizen volunteers can perform non-sworn (i.e., peace officer) functions such as providing transportation to stranded motorists, patrolling school grounds, and standing by at alarms. Present arguments for and against using volunteers for these types of activities.

14. Since the tragedy that occurred at the Sandy Hook Elementary School in 2012, various new strategies have been proposed to upgrade school security including the use of volunteer school resource officers. In 2013, the state of North Carolina passed a law to permit the sheriff of each county to recruit former police officers or military police officers to act in this capacity. Give reasons for and against instituting such a program. If regular citizen volunteers were to be used in such a program, would your reasoning change?

## Notes

1. The state of Hawaii has four major police departments aligned with its four counties. Because this is an island state, these departments developed along rather partisan traditions and in relative isolation from each other. "With the creation of four counties in 1903, local police departments were developed, with each having an elected sheriff as its head. In the 1930s, counties created police commissions who had the power to appoint chiefs of police" (Hawaii DPS 2004, 8). For many years, marijuana growing and distribution has been a major underground factor in the economies of several of the state's island jurisdictions. A statewide agency would likely infringe on local law enforcement prerogatives with respect to this enterprise, which has four growing seasons in a single year. In Hawaii, every imaginable location is used to grow marijuana, from treetops to lava tubes. A county police department is the primary law enforcement agency on each island. A Department of Public Safety exists at the state level that includes Administration, Corrections, and Law Enforcement Divisions. The lattermost division is divided into two sections: Narcotics Enforcement and Sheriff. "The Narcotics Enforcement Division (NED) serves and protects the public by enforcing laws relating to controlled substances and regulated chemicals. They are responsible for the registration and control of the manufacture, distribution, prescription, and dispensing of controlled substances and precursor or essential chemicals within the State. The Sheriff Division carries out law enforcement services statewide. Its mission is to preserve the peace by protecting all persons and property within premises under the control of the Judiciary and all State facilities; providing process services and execution of court documents; handling detained persons; and providing secure transportation for persons in custody.

It also provides law enforcement services at the Honolulu International Airport" (Law Enforcement Division 2013). In Honolulu, the Sheriff Division has a very limited patrol function, primarily around the Honolulu International Airport. This role began in November 1999. The Sheriff unit also provides 24-hour services to the Civic Center complex as well as services to the Maui Memorial Hospital, Hawaii State Hospital, Waimano Training School and Hospital, and Fort Ruger at the Department of Defense. The Executive Protection staff protects the governor, lieutenant governor and, when requested, national and international dignitaries (Hawaii DPS 2004, 9). Overall, the Sheriff Division and Narcotics Enforcement Division (NED) do not appear to have the resources, trained manpower, or the support to perform the duties of a major state agency. Obviously, the establishment of a Narcotics unit was a nod to the existence of a marijuana problem. The Department of Public Safety has disclosed its problems in the narcotics enforcement field in its *Annual Report for 2004*. The report states: "Due to increases in requests for drug prevention services and investigative services needed at Hawaii's airports, prison facilities, state controlled areas on all islands and participation in federal drug taskforces, the Division needs additional personnel and resources to be able to adequately handle these current responsibilities. The Division is in critical need of a chemist and laboratory facility to conduct drug analysis that is generated from cases initiated by the department and outside agency referrals. NED is also experiencing a backlog in pharmaceutical diversion cases initiated on the neighbor islands due to a lack of presence on the islands of Maui, Kauai and Hawaii (Kona). The current law enforcement personnel complement of 12 staff members is inadequate to handle the overwhelming request for services received by the Division" (Hawaii DPS 2004, 15).

2. In 2011, the Illinois Law Enforcement Training and Standards Board, in cooperation with the U.S. Marshals Service (Northern District of Illinois), U.S. Department of Justice, and the Illinois State Police, began an investigation into nongovernmental, legally unrecognized, and unauthorized "auxiliary/reserve police organizations" offering "police assistance, services, and employees" to county and local police agencies. According to the Board, "certain illicit organizations have been successful in convincing law enforcement agencies that they are legitimate. These organizations have also attempted to create an appearance of authority through financial records and other 'legal' documents to avoid constitutional requirements establishing real law enforcement authority for the use of police powers" (Illinois Law Enforcement Training and Standards Board 2013).

3. For example, prior to 1968, when the first organized police department was established in Egg Harbor Township, the community relied heavily on the New Jersey State Police for patrol and related police duties. However, there also existed a corps of special officers that supplemented police duties within the township. In the 1960s, the uniform consisted of a blue shirt with the triangle patch on the arm sleeve. These officers wore badges issued with unique numbers, and this badge style would continue to be used for several years—including by the organized police department—before being replaced in the 1980s. Because this corps consisted of volunteers, they worked at various times on an as-needed basis (Egg Harbor Township Police 2013).

4. In 1910, Mayo "met M. Moyca Newell, a wealthy heiress. The two became life-long friends, with Newell providing the money necessary for Mayo's writing projects. The two women traveled the globe to research the facts for Mayo's reform books. Mayo began her first social reform book, *Justice For All,* in 1913 when a paymaster was murdered on Newell's estate in Bedford Hills, New York. The book was published in 1917, and was a historical look at the Pennsylvania State Police. The book was so influential that is crediting with helping to start the foundations of the New York State Police, and even Theodore Roosevelt contributed to the introduction of the book. Mayo also wrote two other books on the topic, *The Standard Bearers* (1918) and *Mounted Justice* (1922). Mayo then took on the YMCA in 1920, with the book *That Damn Y.* She followed in 1925 with *The Islands of Fear* which was published as a serial in the *New York Times.* Mayo had gone to the Philippines with Newell to research, and the book illustrated her opposition to the independence of the islands. This book set the tone for her most famous work, *Mother India.* Like her later work, the book was written in a sensationalized, almost muckraking style" (Frick 2006).

5. "Junior Cadet Week" is a joint program of the Ohio State Highway Patrol, Ohio American Legion, Buckeye Boys State, Ohio American Legion Auxiliary, Buckeye Girls State, and the Ohio State Highway Patrol Auxiliary. Each year, 20 young men at Buckeye Boys State interested in learning about law enforcement are chosen by the Ohio State Highway Patrol to spend five days following Boys State at the Ohio State Highway Patrol Academy in Columbus in an intense mini-training course on the operations of the Ohio State Highway Patrol that is called "Junior Cadet Week." During Junior Cadet Week, the 20 Boys State representatives join with 20 representatives from Buckeye Girls State who were similarly chosen plus sons and daughters of Ohio State Highway Patrol personnel. The Ohio State Highway Patrol provides the training facilities, staff, and curriculum. The OSHPA covers the cost of food and housing plus program materials for each cadet. Funding for Junior Cadet Week is provided by the Ohio State Highway Patrol. Junior Cadet Week culminates in a formal graduation ceremony attended by the superintendent of the Ohio State Highway Patrol, the Ohio American Legion department commander, the Buckeye Boys State president, the Buckeye Boys state director, the Buckeye Girls state director, and members of the OSHPA (Buckeye Boys State 2013).

6. Attendance at any of these community college academy programs is not limited to only Arizona state police "reserve cadets." Attendees can have sponsorship by other police departments or can apply under an "open enrollment" policy. The latter attendees are unsponsored (i.e., they are not affiliated with a law enforcement agency, but they desire to enroll in the academy). Such persons must complete a qualification process consisting of a background investigation, a polygraph test, and a medical examination. Such open enrollment cadets have to pay for this qualification process, which cost approximately $650 in 2013. In 2013, the approximate two-semester cost (processing and tuition) for open enrollment at the Glendale Community College law enforcement training academy was $3,780 (not including necessary personal equipment). In addition, open enrollment applicants are required to participate in a physical fitness assessment to determine their overall level of fitness. The physical fitness assessment is known as the "Cooper test" (1.5-mile run,

push-ups, sit-ups, and vertical jump), with a minimum of 40% set as the goal for the applicants to achieve (Open Enrollment 2013). Additional information about this process and printouts of various required forms (application, background questionnaire, consent, etc.) are available at: http://www.gc.maricopa.edu/justice/leo/files/oeprocess.html. At the conclusion of the academy, the recruits who are sponsored receive full peace officer certification. The open enrollment students await sponsorship or employment before full certification is achieved.

7. In the United States, there is no consistent use of the office of constable and use may vary even within a state. A constable may be an official responsible for service of process—such as summonses and subpoenas for people to appear in court in criminal and/or civil matters. Or, they may be fully empowered law enforcement officers. They may also have additional specialized duties unique to the office. In some states, a constable may be appointed by the judge of the court that he or she serves; in others, the constable is an elected or appointed position at the village, precinct, or township level of local government. In Alaska, a constable is an appointed official with limited police powers. The military police arm of the Alaska State Defense Force, a voluntary state defense group, is designated as the constabulary force of the state. This agency is empowered to act in a police capacity when called into service by the governor. Some official missions the constables have performed include port security after 9/11, disaster relief, and Alaska Pipeline patrols. In South Carolina, Group III state constables are urged to act only in instances of emergencies when police are not immediately available and when a threat to life is present. It is SLED policy that "except as necessary to preserve life, state constables should take only such actions as might be undertaken by a member of the public" (SC State Constables 2012, 7). Any handguns they carry must be concealed unless they are in a state approved uniform. South Carolina State Constable Group I can be uniformed police or investigators for a specifically designated state department (i.e., SC Department of Mental Health Public Safety, state universities, etc.). Group II are retired police in good standing that desire a state constable commission to continue to have authority and to carry a weapon as set forth by SLED. (For additional information and a state-by-state overview of the office of constable, see http://www.mobileconstable.com/constables-within-the-united-states.)

8. An immediate result of the consent decree was the promotion of 50 troopers to the rank of corporal. Promotions to other ranks soon followed. Pursuant to the consent decree, a detailed, formalized transfer and reassignment policy and expanded equal employment opportunity program were implemented as well as the development of new test summary information and evaluation procedures to establish promotional registers for each rank and the development of management training programs for sworn officers and civilians. In addition, new recruiting, testing, and hiring procedures for entry-level positions of state trooper trainees and cadets were developed and implemented, with the goal of minimal negative impact. Included was a statewide pre-sign-up publicity campaign designed to inform prospective applicants about the sign-up and testing process. During the weeklong sign-up period, an astounding number of cadet and trainee applicants—6,586, of which 39% represented minorities—made

application at 18 sites throughout the state. Applicants were required to view a videotape illustrating typical duties of a trooper and providing information about the video-driven test. They also were provided with study materials for the test, which was administered to some 3,400 applicants simultaneously in Huntsville, Montgomery, and Mobile. By the late summer of 1990, test scoring was continuing with the goal of producing a listing of the top 300–400 eligible candidates from which Public Safety planned to select for hire in early 1991 (Alabama DPS 2013).

9. Several members of the Connecticut State Police Auxiliary who have been performing administrative functions (i.e., clerical work) are well past the age of 70. For example, in 2009, auxiliary officer Alma Anderson, a New Britain native, was routinely reporting each Friday for duty at State Police Troop F Barracks. Her late husband had first become a sworn auxiliary officer in the 1950s by patrolling the waters looking for stolen boats. In 2009, she celebrated her 91st birthday and her 25th year of service with the Connecticut State Auxiliary Police Force (Vahl 2009).

10. On January 3, 1998, Heather Messenger was home with her husband, David, and her five-year-old son. When threatened by her husband, she barricaded herself in an upstairs bedroom with her son and called 911 as her husband used a cedar post to break into the bedroom, beating her to death while a state police dispatcher listened helplessly. A trooper arrived almost 20 minutes later. In 2001, a three-judge panel in Putnam Superior Court found David Messenger not guilty by reason of insanity, and he was sent to a secure psychiatric hospital for 20 years or until such time as he can prove he is no longer a danger to anyone (Summers 2001).

11. At the New Britain police Web site, the program is described under the title: "The Police Reserve: Community Service Officers." The site states that the program seeks "to recruit, train, and deploy a corps of community service officers to provide direct assistance to police officers and members of the community. Although community service officers (CSOs) do not perform law enforcement duties or have the power of arrest, they do perform functions which are currently the responsibility of sworn officers…. CSOs are deployed in pairs during the evening hours and the weekly commitment will be minimal" (CSO Program 2013). Some examples of CSO duties are providing assistance at accident scenes, completing reports in noncriminal cases, assisting in searches, providing transportation to stranded motorists, patrolling school grounds, and standing by at alarms (CSO Program 2013). Reference to the goal of patrolling school grounds may have been added as a result of the Sandy Hook Elementary School massacre, which took place in Newtown, CT, on December 14, 2012. The 911 recordings from the school massacre were released December 4, 2013, less than two weeks before the first anniversary of the tragedy, after state officials lost a fight to keep them under wraps. Prosecutors had argued that audio of seven calls placed from inside the school would cause anguish for the families of those slain and for the survivors. The recordings were released days after state law enforcement officials released a long-awaited report on the shooting and on gunman Adam Lanza, age 20. The report noted that Lanza was obsessed with school shootings and had carefully planned the rampage, but it did not uncover a clear motive (Connor 2013).

# References

About the FHPA. (2013a). Retrieved November 30, 2013 from http://www.mytrooper.org/

About the FHPA. (2013b). Retrieved November 30, 2013 from http://www.mytrooper.org/faq.htm

Alabama DPS. (2013). Department of Public Safety history: 1935–1990. Retrieved December 3, 2013 http://dps.alabama.gov/Home/wfContent.aspx?ID=0&PLH1=plhInformation-History

Alabama DPS. (2014). Alabama Reserve Program (closed). Retrieved March 1, 2014 from http://www.dps.alabama.gov/Home/wfContent.aspx?ID=70&PLH1=plhInformation-EmploymentTrooperReserveProgram

American Legion. (2013). American Legion Buckeye Boys State. Retrieved December 1, 2013 from http://www.ohiobuckeyeboysstate.com/index.html

Arizona DPS. (2013a). History. Retrieved November 30, 2013 from http://www.azdps.gov/About/History/

Arizona DPS. (2013b). Reserve officer. Retrieved November 30, 2013 from http://www.azdps.gov/careers/reserves/

Auxiliary Officers Commissioned. (2012). 18 new auxiliary officers commissioned. Applications for next class now being processed. Retrieved December 1, 2013 from http://statepatrol.ohio.gov/doc/SpareWheelSpring2012.pdf

Auxiliary Troopers. (2013a, June 6). Connecticut: Auxiliary troopers: Michael Tiernan, Troop H, Hartford. Retrieved December 5, 2013 from http://www.lexisnexis.com.libproxy.uml.edu/hottopics/lnacademic/?

Auxiliary Troopers. (2013b, June 6). Connecticut: Auxiliary troopers, Troop H, Hartford. Retrieved December 5, 2013 from http://www.lexisnexis.com.libproxy.uml.edu/hottopics/lnacademic/?

Berg, B. and W. Doerner. (1988). Volunteer police officers: An unexamined personnel dimension in law enforcement. *American Journal of Police, 7*(1), 81–89.

Buckeye Boys State. (2013). Junior cadet week. Retrieved December 1, 2013 from http://www.ohiobuckeyeboysstate.com/jr-cadet.html

Cavanaugh, J. (1986, September 28). Auxiliary state police: Peril without pay. *New York Times*, sec. 11CN, p. 2.

Connor, T. (2013). Sandy Hook shooting: 911 calls from Newtown massacre released. Retrieved December 5, 2013 from http://usnews.nbcnews.com/_news/2013/12/04/21755185-sandy-hook-shooting-911-calls-from-newtown-massacre-released

Cox, M. (2013). A brief history of the Texas Rangers. Retrieved November 30, 2013 from http://www.texasranger.org/history/BriefHistory1.htm

CSO Program. (2013). The Police Reserve: Community service officers. Retrieved December 4, 2013 from http://www.newbritainpolice.org/cso-program

Dale, E. (2011). *Criminal justice in the United States, 1789–1939.* New York: Cambridge University Press.

Daley, J. J. (2003). Preview of Andy Thibault's new book on the history of the CT State Police. Retrieved December 4, 2013 from http://www.andythibault.com/History%20of%20CT%20State%20Police.htm

Deitch, L. and L. Thompson. (1985). The reserve police officer: One alternative to the need for manpower. *The Police Chief, 52*(5), 59–61.

Douglas, A. and L. Jones. (2009, January). Join the reserve trooper program. Retrieved December 3, 2013 from http://www.fox10tv.com/news/jointhetrooperreserve-program

Egg Harbor Township Police. (2013). History of the Egg Harbor Township Police. Retrieved November 28, 2013 from http://www.ehtpd.com/about/history.html

FHPA. (2013). Florida Highway Patrol Auxiliary. Retrieved December 1, 2013 from http://fhpa.info/index.php/about-us/faq?showall = &start = 1

Florida DEP. (2011). Florida Department of Environmental Protection Division of Law Enforcement, Florida Park Police. Retrieved December 1, 2013 from http://www.policevolunteers.org/programs/index.cfm?fa = dis_pro_detail&id = 2858

Frick, K. (2006). Mayo, Katherine (Prence, Katherine). Retrieved November 29, 2013 from http://pabook.libraries.psu.edu/palitmap/bios/Mayo__Katherine.html

Greenberg, M. A. (1984). Auxiliary Police: The citizen's approach to public safety. Westport, CT: Greenwood Press.

Hawaii DPS. (2004). Retrieved January 30, 2014 from http://dps.hawaii.gov/wp-content/uploads/2012/10/PSD-AnnualReport-2004.pdf

Henson, M. S. (2013). Anglo-American colonization. In: *Handbook of Texas*. Texas State Historical Association. Retrieved November 30, 2013 from http://www.tshaonline.org/handbook/online/articles/uma01

History of CSP. (2013). Abbreviated history: A brief history of the Connecticut State Police. Retrieved December 4, 2013 from http://www.cspmuseum.org/CMSLite/default.asp?CMSLite_Page = 7&Info = History

Illinois Law Enforcement Training and Standards Board. (2013). Information on private auxiliary/reserve police organizations. Retrieved November 28, 2012 from http://www.ptb.state.il.us

Illinois State Police. (2013). History. Retrieved November 26, 2013 from http://www.isp.state.il.us/aboutisp/history.cfm

Jarvis, B. (2013). Oregon State Police Volunteers Florence Office. Retrieved December 30, 2013 from http://www.policevolunteers.org/programs/index.cfm?fa = dis_pro_detail&id = 2918

Juliano, F. (2011, March 5). Higher training standards, costs mean fewer part-time police. Retrieved December 4, 2013 from http://www.ctpost.com/local/article/Higher-training-standards-costs-mean-fewer-1043894.php#

Kellner, A. (2013, October 8). Oregon State Police Volunteers patrol Lincoln County school neighborhoods. Retrieved December 9, 2013 from http://klcc.org/post/oregon-state-police-volunteers-patrol-lincoln-county-school-neighborhoods

Kitchen, S. (2009, December 27).Troopers work to reduce road deaths amid budget worries. *Montgomery Advertiser*. Retrieved June 25, 2014 from http://www.lexisnexis.com.libproxy.uml.edu/hottopics/lnacademic/?

Law Enforcement Division. (2013). Retrieved November 27, 2013 from http://dps.hawaii.gov/about/divisions/law-enforcement-division/

Leukhardt, B. (1995, February 19). A city calls auxiliary police back to duty. Retrieved November 30, 2013 from http://articles.courant.com/1995-02-19/news/9502190210_1_auxiliary-professional-police-citizens-and-police

Lyman, M. D. (2005). *The police: An introduction* (3rd ed.). Upper Saddle River, NJ: Pearson Prentice Hall.

Maryland NRP. (2013). NRP history. Retrieved December 8, 2013 from http://www.mleo.info/maryland-natural-resources-police.html

Maryland NRP Reserves. (2013). About. General information. Retrieved December 8, 2013 from https://www.facebook.com/pages/Maryland-Natural-Resources-Police-Reserves/309503192401509?sk = info

Maryland State Police VIPS. (2013). Retrieved December 8, 2013 from http://www.policevolunteers.org/programs/index.cfm?fa = dis_pro_detail&id = 501

McCoy, D. (2011). About the South Carolina State Constables. Retrieved March 10, 2011 from http://www.police-writers.com/south_carolina_state_constables.html

Neubert, N. M. (1975). *The State Police of Crawford and Erie Counties.* Workshop in Political Theory and Policy Analysis. Police Services Study Fact Sheet No. 6. Bloomington, IN: Indiana University.

New Jersey State Police. (2013). Retrieved November 27, 2013 from http://www.njsp.org/about/20s.html

New York State Police. (1967). *The New York State Police: The first fifty years 1917–1967.* Albany, NY: New York State Police.

NJSAR. (2013). New Jersey Search and Rescue/NJ State Park Police. Retrieved November 28, 2013 from http://www.policevolunteers.org/programs/index.cfm?fa = dis_pro_detail&id = 3225

Open Enrollment. (2013). *Open enrollment.* Law Enforcement Training Academy, Glendale Community College. Retrieved December 2, 2013 from http://www.gc.maricopa.edu/justice/leo/files/oe.html

Oregon DSP. (2011, May). Oregon Department of State Police. Administrative overview. Retrieved December 3, 2013 from http://arcweb.sos.state.or.us/doc/recmgmt/sched/special/state/overview/2011statepoliceadminoverview.pdf

OSHP Auxiliary Reaches 50-Year Milestone. (1992). *Flying Wheel* (Published by the Ohio State Highway Patrol), 28(1), 12–13.

OSHPRA Bylaws. (2013). Retrieved December 8, 2013 from http://www.oshpretiree.org/OSHPRA_By-Laws.pdf

Police Reserve Academy. (2013). Umpqua Regional Police Reserve Training Program. Retrieved December 3, 2013 from http://www.umpqua.edu/police-reserve-academy

Procter, B. H. (2014). Texas Rangers, Handbook of Texas Online. Retrieved June 24, 2014 from http://www.tshaonline.org/handbook/online/articles/met04

Profile of the Auxiliary. (1999, December). Profile of the auxiliary: Who are these people? *The Spare Wheel: An Ohio State Highway Patrol Publication,* pp. 1–2.

Reserve given service. (1978, September 23). Reserve given service go-ahead. *The Tuscaloosa News,* p. 13.

S.B. 32 Hearing. (2012, February 28). Public Safety and Security Committee hearing testimony. Retrieved December 4, 2013 from http://ct-n.com/ondemand.asp?ID = 7513

SC Highway Patrol. (2006, August 18). SC Highway Patrol recruiting for auxiliary trooper program. Retrieved December 3, 2013 from http://www.scdps.gov/oea/nr2006/081806.htm

Scroggin, S. Y. (2013). Senior volunteers big benefit to Highway Patrol. Retrieved December 8, 2013 from http://www.timespressrecorder.com/articles/2012/05/04/news/news03.txt

SC State Constables. (2012). Policies and procedures: Group III. Retrieved December 3, 2013 from http://www.sled.sc.gov/Documents/Constables/PoliciesProceduresSignedByChiefKeel.pdf

Seeley, T. (2013). Connecticut State Police: An unofficial website. Retrieved November 26, 2013 from http://www.cspmail.com/

Simonich, M. (2005, March 27). Legislator hopes to dissolve 'other' state police. Retrieved December 8, 2013 from http://www.post-gazette.com/frontpage/2005/03/27/Legislator-hopes-to-dissolve-other-state-police/stories/200503270240

Smith, B. (1940). *Police systems in the United States*. New York: Harper & Brothers.

Sparrow, M. K. (1988, November). *Perspectives on policing, monograph 9: Implementing community policing*. Washington, DC: National Institute of Justice & the Program in Criminal Justice Policy & Management, John F. Kennedy School of Government, Harvard University.

Summers, S. (2001, February 18). The last word of Heather Messenger. Retrieved December 5, 2013 from http://articles.courant.com/2001-02-18/news/0102202688_1_david-messenger-barracks-state-police

Support Services. (2013). Support Services Bureau: Auxiliary troopers. Retrieved November 26, 2013 from http://www.nh.gov/safety/divisions/nhsp/ssb/auxiliary/

Tell Me About. (2013). Tell me about TASER devices. Retrieved December 5, 2013 from http://www.womenonguard.com/how_work.htm

Troop P Community Services Unit. (2013). Troop P Citizens' Police Academy. Retrieved December 10, 2013 from http://www.portal.state.pa.us/portal/server.pt/community/troop_p/4596/community_services_unit/471833

Vahl, H. (2009, December 14). Woman still serving as auxiliary state police officer at 91. Retrieved November 1, 2013 from http://positiveleo.wordpress.com/tag/connecticut-state-police/

Vermont State Police. (2013a). Auxiliary trooper application Vermont State Police. Retrieved November 30, 2013 from http://vsp.vermont.gov/sites/vsp/files/Documents/Auxiliary%20Application.pdf

Vermont State Police. (2013b). Vermont State Police FY14 budget presentation to commissioner. Retrieved November 30, 2013 from http://www.leg.state.vt.us/jfo/appropriations/fy_2014/Public%20Safety%20-%20Strategic%20program%20information.pdf

Virginia SP. (2013). Retrieved December 9, 2013 from http://www.vsp.state.va.us/Employment_Volunteers.shtm

Volunteers in Police Service. (2013). Volunteers in police service programs in New Jersey. Retrieved November 27, 2013 from http://www.citizencorps.gov/cc/listPartner.do?partner = 3&state = NJ

Waldman, L. (2001, May 29). After 40 years, auxiliary trooper retires. *The Courant*. Retrieved February 2, 2014 from http://articles.courant.com/2001-05-29/news/0105291015_1_trooper-program-auxiliary-state-police

Walker, S. (1977). *A critical history of police reform: The emergence of professionalism*. Lexington, MA: Lexington Books.

Walker, S. and C. M. Katz. (2011). *The police in America: An introduction* (7th ed.). New York: McGraw-Hill.

Weinblatt, R. (1993). *Reserve law enforcement in the United States: A National study of state, county and city standards concerning the training and numbers of non-full-time police and sheriff's personnel.* Monmouth, NJ: New Jersey Auxiliary Police Officers Association and the Center for Reserve Law Enforcement.

Weisberg, B. (2013). Ore. City shooting highlights risks faced by reserve officers. Retrieved December 6, 2013 from http://www.koin.com/news/multnomah-county/ore-city-shooting-highlights-dangers-risks-faced-by-reserve-officers#. UnmHE5opkQU.facebook

Youmans, S. (2000, July 30). *Unit begun during WWII puts volunteer troopers on patrol.* The Associated Press State & Local Wire. Retrieved December 5, 2013 from http://www.lexisnexis.com.libproxy.uml.edu/hottopics/lnacademic/?

# The Federal Government and Volunteer Policing

6

The citizen looks upon the fortune of the public as his own, and he labors for the good of the state … participates in all that is done in his country … obliged to defend whatever may be censured in it; for it is not only his country that is then attacked, it is himself.

**—Alexis de Tocqueville**
*(1835/1990, 43–44)*

## Introduction

Citizen participation related to public safety is found at all governmental levels, although the vast amount of participation takes place at the community level. This was especially the case in 1831, when Alexis de Tocqueville (1805–1859), a French nobleman, came to the United States (Figure 6.1). Ostensibly, he was commissioned to investigate the U.S. penitentiary system. Before his trip, he had been appointed a judge-auditor at the tribunal of Versailles. He traveled to the United States with his friend and fellow judge, Gustave de Beaumont. Over a nine-month period he studied the methods of local, state, and national governments as well as the everyday activities of the American people. His multivolume, *Democracy in America*, is considered to be a masterpiece concerning the nature of American democracy prior to the Civil War. He discovered, with a degree of amazement, the numerous and varied types of "associations" formed to help others and for the general good of the community. During the early days of our nation, volunteerism was a trait born of necessity because community service was rooted in westward expansion. "There was no government to solve problems on the frontier, no rich people to invest in infrastructure. If settlers wanted a church or a barn or a town they had to join hands and build one" (Kadlec 2013).

In order to maintain the promise of American democracy and to counter any trends whereby individualism might cause citizens to refrain from meeting their civic duties, Alexis de Tocqueville recommended an independent and influential judiciary, a strong executive branch, local self-government, administrative decentralization, religion, well-educated women, freedom of association, and freedom of the press. Moreover, he considered jury service to be an important civic obligation because it helps citizens to think about other people's affairs and educates them in the use of their freedom (Alexis de Tocqueville 1835/1990).

**Figure 6.1** Portrait of Alexis de Tocqueville in 1848.

Opportunities for citizen participation at the federal level became more prevalent during and after World War II. Today in the United States, citizens may do more than fulfilling such ordinary civic responsibilities as voting, calling authorities for help in emergencies, serving on juries, and participating in interest groups to influence federal policy. They can also identify, report, and enforce potential and alleged violations of various federal regulatory laws (e.g., by bringing citizen lawsuits against polluters for violations of environmental laws in the federal district courts). On an entirely unsalaried basis, citizens may also support national efforts for disaster relief by volunteering with the American Red Cross or by helping to rebuild a house in a natural disaster zone through Habitat for Humanity. In addition, opportunities to reduce the threats of terrorism by joining the U.S. Coast Guard Auxiliary (USCGA) or the Civil Air Patrol (CAP) also exist. On a temporary assignment and salaried basis, a citizen may apply to become a Federal Emergency Management Agency (FEMA) Reservist. FEMA Reservists are called upon when a national emergency is declared by the president. Interested citizens are selected and deployed on an as-needed basis. In addition, to promote the education of youth, qualified citizens can assist with such federal initiatives as Civil Air Patrol Cadets, the JROTC, and the Customs Border Protection Explorer programs. There are thousands of nonprofit organizations seeking volunteers in a variety of fields, many with local chapters. (To identify such organizations by type and location go to: http://www.volunteermatch.org or http://www.idealist.org.)

College students (undergraduate or graduate) have opportunities to serve in internships with a wide range of federal agencies. In general, requirements include U.S. citizenship or a valid work permit (for some agencies) and enrollment in an undergraduate or graduate studies program at an accredited school; there may be other requirements depending on the agency. Federal internships are often competitive because of the number of students who are interested in them. Interested students should consult their academic advisors and/or their campus office of career services.

Numerous volunteer opportunities exist at the federal level within homeland security, law enforcement, and disaster relief organizations. In addition, there are a variety of nonprofit organizations engaged in related work. It is difficult to narrow the list of agencies for inclusion in this chapter; however, the few selected include the following national (nonprofit) and federal organizations: the Metropolitan Police Reserve Corps, the CAP, the U.S. Power Squadrons (USPS), the USCGA, and the FEMA Reserves. Information about volunteer police in Puerto Rico, Guam, and the U.S. Virgin Islands is also presented. Finally, a proposal to establish a Border Patrol Auxiliary (BPA) is considered because of its relevance to national security and its potential as a provider of volunteer service opportunities (Hall et al. 2007). The chapter begins with background materials about the nature of the federal government and some historical aspects related to the federal role in public safety.

## Historical Background

The U.S. Constitution was ratified by the last of the 13 original states in 1791. The original 13 states were the successors of the 13 colonies that rebelled against British rule. The constitution created the three branches of the federal government and granted certain powers and responsibilities to each. The legislative, judicial, and executive branches have different responsibilities that have kept the branches more or less equal. The executive branch has the widest range of responsibilities and employs most of the federal workforce.

The federal system in the United States is one that is based on enumerated powers specifically granted to it in the U.S. Constitution and its statues. The Tenth Amendment to the Constitution provides that powers not delegated to the federal government or prohibited to the states by the constitution are reserved for the states. Key federal powers include the collection of taxes and duties, payment of debts, and providing for welfare and the common defense. Other federal powers include regulating commerce among multiple states and foreign nations, establishing a militia, and protecting civil rights and liberties. The idea of shared powers between states and the national government is known as "federalism," and the specific reference to this concept is found in the Tenth Amendment. Because of federalism, the designation of what is considered a local or national disaster and who should direct an emergency response can be confusing. Therefore, it is best to check a state's emergency management statute in order to determine who may declare an emergency and the powers that are provided to the state's governor, and to find out what powers are given to officials at the local level.

During the nineteenth century, there were very few federal law enforcement agencies. A notable exception is the U.S. Marshals Service, which was established in 1789.[1] The Marshals have very broad jurisdiction and authority. For more than 200 years, U.S. Marshals and their deputies have served as the instruments of civil authority used by all three branches of government and have been involved in most of the major historical episodes in America's past. For most of their history, U.S. Marshals enjoyed a surprising degree of independence in performing their duties. Quite simply, no headquarters or central administration existed to supervise the work of the Marshals until the late 1950s (Calhoun 1991; Civilian Enforcers 2013). "As our young nation expanded westward, U.S. Marshals embodied the civilian power of the Federal Government to bring law and justice to the frontier. For every new territory, marshals were appointed to impose the law on the untamed wilderness" (History 2013). Throughout much of their history, "the Marshals struggled to balance the enforcement of federal laws against the feelings of the local populace" (Calhoun 1991; Civilian Enforcers 2013). Significantly, policing has been and remains mostly a local affair. "Unlike the London police, American police systems followed the style of local and municipal governments. City governments, created in the era of the 'common man' and democratic participation, were highly decentralized.... The police were an extension of different political factions, rather than an extension of city government. Police officers were recruited and selected by political leaders in a particular ward or precinct" (Uchida 2004, 10-11).

During most of the nineteenth century, federal government jobs were held at the pleasure of the president—a person could be fired at any time. The "spoils system" meant that jobs were used to support the influence of politicians and their parties. This was changed in incremental stages by the Pendleton Civil Service Reform Act of 1883 and subsequent laws. By 1909, almost two-thirds of the U.S. federal workforce was appointed based on merit, that is, qualifications measured by tests. In contemporary times, it is a common practice to fill a variety of top level federal service positions, including some heads of diplomatic missions and executive agencies, with political appointees. The Pendleton Act required federal government employees to be selected through competitive exams and on the basis of merit; it also prevented elected officials and political appointees from firing civil servants. However, the law did not apply to state and municipal governments. Nevertheless, today, in varying degrees, most state and local government entities have competitive civil service systems that are modeled on the national system. The U.S. Civil Service Commission was created by the Pendleton Civil Service Reform Act to administer the U.S. civil service system. Effective January 1, 1978, the commission was renamed the Office of Personnel Management (OPM) under the provisions of Reorganization Plan No. 2 of 1978 (43 F.R. 36037, 92 Stat. 3783) and the Civil Service Reform Act of 1978. The OPM is also responsible for a large part of the management of security clearances.

A controversial national organization, composed entirely of volunteers, arose during wartime. The advent of World War I, as well as politics and influence, contributed to the establishment of the semisecret organization named the American Protective League (APL). The APL was formed when there was a credible threat of subversive and seditious activity within the United States. Acts of sabotage and the notorious Zimmerman Telegram had fueled these fears. During its short lifespan, the APL was engaged in ferreting out spies, saboteurs, and seditious aliens. It received recognition from the U.S. Department of Justice, the U.S. Secret Service, and other governmental departments, although it had no governmental or legal status. Its official history was published in 1919 in a book entitled *The Web: The Authorized History of The American Protective League* by Emerson Hough (Figure 6.2).

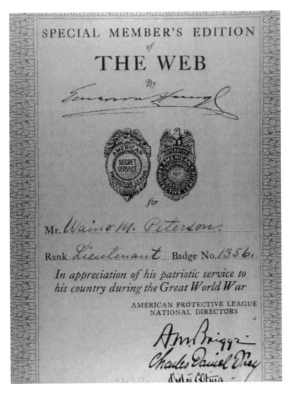

**Figure 6.2** A page from *The Web*, signed by the author in a special edition in 1919.

Perhaps as many as 200,000 or more professionals, businessmen, and wage earners who were American citizens and willing to take a special oath became members.

Unlike many nations around the world, the United States has no national police force. Currently, there are more than 1,300 federal government agencies; more than 90 of these agencies carry out one or more specialized law enforcement functions.[2] Much of the growth in federal law enforcement is due to congressional legislation. For example, in 2002, the Department of Homeland Security (DHS) was established and now has more sworn federal law enforcement agents and officers than any other department of the U.S. government. An earlier and major contributing factor toward federal policing occurred within the executive branch when the Eighteenth Amendment became effective in 1920. The Eighteenth Amendment placed a ban on the sale, distribution, and manufacture of alcoholic beverages. This prohibition lasted until its repeal by the Twenty-First Amendment in 1933. The Department of Justice enforced prohibition, along with the Customs Service, Coast Guard, and Bureau of Internal Revenue. Over time, Americans have come to expect more from federal law enforcement than ever before. Its size, jurisdiction, and responsibilities continue to grow. Some growth is clearly justified, such as the expanded role of the Federal Bureau of Investigation (FBI) in counterterrorism.[3]

Federal strategies to enhance the nation's preparedness for disaster and attack have evolved over the course of the twentieth century and into the twenty-first. Highlights from this history include the air raid warning and plane-spotting activities of the Office of Civil Defense in the 1940s, the "duck and cover" filmstrips and backyard shelters of the 1950s, and today's all hazards preparedness programs led by the DHS.[4]

Even before September 11, 2001, when al-Qaeda terrorists struck the World Trade Center in New York City and the Pentagon near Washington, D.C., killing nearly 3,000 people federal authorities and Congress enlisted local law enforcement on behalf of federal law enforcement concerns. For example, the Illegal Immigration Reform and Immigrant Responsibility Act of 1996 encouraged state and local police agencies to enter into agreements with the U.S. Attorney General to train and deputize local immigration enforcement officers. The same statute also authorized the attorney general to enlist local forces during an immigration emergency.

Since the events of September 11, various federal initiatives have been undertaken to involve the nation's local police agencies in the war on terrorism. In order to strengthen the security of the nation's transportation systems, the U.S. Transportation Security Administration (TSA) was established with the passage of The Aviation and Transportation Security Act of 2001. The statute required the TSA: (1) to be responsible for security for all modes of transportation; (2) to recruit, assess, hire, train, and deploy security officers for 450 commercial airports from Guam to Alaska in 12 months; and (3) to provide 100% screening of all checked luggage for explosives by December 31, 2002. This was a mandate for the creation of one of the largest agencies in the history of the U.S. government.

But the most controversial action after September 11 was the passage of the USA PATRIOT Act (the acronym for Uniting and Strengthening America by Providing Appropriate Tools Required to Intercept and Obstruct Terrorism Act). Less controversial have been the ongoing contributions of community-minded men and women who participate in the CAP, USCGA, Community Emergency Response Teams, and in volunteer fire units.

In 2005, Hurricane Katrina caused severe destruction along much of the Gulf Coast, devastating New Orleans. In the same year, Congress adopted the Real ID Act, which set state standards for issuing drivers' licenses to immigrants. It also required states to regulate the activities of persons who are for any reason without status. Among its provisions is the need for each state to provide electronic access to information contained in its motor vehicle database to all other states. The law has been promoted primarily as an antiterrorism measure. In addition, the Vision 100—Century of Aviation Reauthorization Act of 2003 requires air carriers providing scheduled passenger air transportation to conduct basic security training for their flight and cabin crewmembers in order to prepare them for potential threat conditions that may occur onboard an aircraft. The act further requires the TSA to develop and make available to flight and cabin crewmembers an advanced self-defense training program that includes appropriate and effective responses for defending against an attacker.

Although most states have introduced civil service testing and other basic requirements for police officer selection, the actual day-to-day operations of police departments are determined by local officials and by the discretion exercised by officers on patrol. Policing in the United States is conducted by numerous types of agencies at many different levels. Every state has its own nomenclature for agencies, and their powers, responsibilities, and funding vary from state to state. In some states, there can be several hundred local police agencies. Each agency has its own chief and manual of procedures. At a crime or disaster scene affecting large numbers of people, multiple jurisdictions involving several police agencies may be deployed. Depending on the emergency, the response can be very problematic. A case in point was the Hurricane Katrina disaster where the basic emergency channels of communication were disrupted. In such a situation, one researcher has noted that even the "moral order of the police force itself was also called into question, as many remaining officers were troubled by those who abandoned their posts after the hurricane, wondering how they could ever trust those officers again" (Sims 2007, 115). Command in such situations remains a complex and sometimes contentious issue.

Today, federal law enforcement agencies are routinely asked to assist in local law enforcement matters. In many instances, such assistance has resulted in "cross-deputization." Cross-deputization is an agreement that allows police officers to cross borders and enforce the law outside their areas of jurisdiction. Deputization agreements give tribal, federal, state, or city law enforcement officials power to enforce laws outside their own jurisdictions regardless of the identity of the perpetrator, thus simplifying the exercise of criminal jurisdiction. These agreements may include the creation of police task forces involving more than one agency. Such joint federal, regional, state, and county task forces have become an important tool to contend with crimes involving gangs, drugs, guns, and human trafficking. These highly desired agreements enable task force members to be deputized in order to cross state lines and enforce federal laws. Moreover, such agreements also become a necessity due to the need to contend with the vastly increased problems of global crime, terrorism, cyberterrorism, and cyberwarfare.

On July 29, 2010, Congress enacted a much needed criminal reform known as the Tribal Law and Order Act (TLOA) for Indian country. "TLOA encourages cross-deputization. Tribal and state law enforcement agencies in Indian country receive incentives through grants and technical assistance to enter into cooperative law enforcement agreements to combat crime in and near tribal areas. At the federal level, TLOA enhances existing law to grant deputization to expand the authority of existing officers in Indian country to enforce federal laws normally outside their jurisdiction regardless of the perpetrator's identity. This measure simplifies the exercise of criminal jurisdiction and provides greater protection of Indian country from crime through increased enforcement" (Bulzomi 2012).[5]

In 2007, in testimony before the Subcommittee on Healthy Families and Communities, Congressman John P. Sarbanes stated: "Volunteers are a large part of what makes America such a great and strong nation. Throughout this country, volunteers fill in gaps where local, state, and federal governments are unable to effectively serve people. Further, the community-minded spirit fostered by volunteer activity benefits all people by strengthening the fabric of our nation" (Dooris 2008, 42).

## Metropolitan Police Reserve Corps

The Metropolitan Police Department (MPD), founded in 1861, is the primary law enforcement agency for the District of Columbia; it is one of the ten largest local police agencies in the United States. According to its Web pages, the department uses the latest advances in evidence analysis and state-of-the-art information technology. These techniques are combined with a contemporary community policing philosophy, referred to as "customized community policing." Community policing bonds the police and residents in a working partnership designed to organize and mobilize residents, merchants, and professionals to improve the quality of life for all who live, work, and visit the nation's capital (About MPDC 2013).

From the 1920s until 1950, police officers traveled to Washington, D.C., from other jurisdictions (such as New York City and Philadelphia) to assist members of the MPD with crowd control during the Shriners convention and presidential inaugurations. Local residents also participated. They were issued a credential in the form of an auxiliary MPD badge. In time, an Auxiliary Division was created within the department. "In 1950 a number of auxiliary detectives and auxiliary detective sergeants were caught running a burglary ring. It became a major scandal since these officers were picked from the elite of Washington…. The police administration fired all of the Auxiliaries and formed the Metropolitan Police Reserves" (Blickensdorf 2014).

As in most American cities, during World War II, the police force in the nation's capital was also aided by units of civil defense. Civilian defense auxiliary police and other groups were organized in case of any attack on the nation's capital. After the war, although civil defense was no longer a top priority, it became apparent that a permanent reserve force could be of benefit to the regular police by assisting them in carrying out their everyday responsibilities (About the MPD 2013). The District of Columbia's auxiliary police that were associated with civil defense during World War II appear to be unrelated to the Auxiliary Division, which was mostly a political organization that "had more power then someone would have thought during that time period" (Blickensdorf 2014).

The Metropolitan Police Reserve Corps was established in November 1948. The organization was given greater recognition with the passage of a federal law in 1950 that gave authority to the chief of police to select, organize, train, and equip certain residents of the District and the metropolitan area in a special reserve unit known as the Metropolitan Police Reserve Corps (About the MPD 2013).

Members of the new Reserve Corps were first deployed on October 31, 1951, to guard fire alarm boxes to prevent the sounding of false alarms on Halloween night. In 1961, the Reserve Corps was called to duty and sworn in to assist with the inauguration of President John F. Kennedy. Throughout the 1960s, the Reserve Corps was frequently called upon to assist with civil demonstrations arising from national tragedies such as the assassinations of President Kennedy, his brother Senator Robert F. Kennedy, and Dr. Martin Luther King Jr. (About the MPD 2013). Figure 6.3 shows members of the Reserve Corps standing at attention outside the 6th Precinct station house.

In 1970, the chief of police prepared an order setting forth the policy, procedures, and responsibilities of the Reserve Corps. This general order was replaced in 2006 by a more comprehensive document, 26 pages in length.

**Figure 6.3** Members of the Metropolitan Police Reserve Corps standing at attention outside the 6th Precinct stationhouse in the District of Columbia, ca. 1950s.

The revised general order provided sufficient clarifications so that the Reserve Corps was better prepared to render community service and to become an integral part of the MPD (About the MPD 2013). Prospective members must successfully complete the same entrance screening required of full-time officers: a written test (national police officer entrance exam), a background suitability investigation, and medical and psychological examinations. All basic training must be substantially the same as that completed by full-time sworn officers.

The members of the corps serve in different ways, depending upon individual experience and qualifications and upon the time commitment they are able to make. For example, a Reserve Officer Level I carries out the same duties as a regular officer under the regular officer's general supervision. A Reserve Officer Level II carries out assignments under close supervision and is not authorized to carry a department-issued firearm. Some reserve officers may work indoors in a patrol district, while others will work side-by-side with patrol officers performing frontline law enforcement activities. Significantly, while on duty, Reserve Corps members are authorized to exercise the full law enforcement authority of a sworn police officer except as restricted by the 2006 General Order or by the police chief. "When not on department duty, Reserve Corps members shall possess only such police powers as granted to a private citizen" (General Order 2006, 6). Reserve officers usually begin at Level II and must have had at least one year of good standing at Level II and at least 60 college credits or 960 hours of volunteer service, or an equivalent combination of education and experience, in order to move to Level I. There are several additional requirements, and these meet or exceed the requirements, established by the Commission on Accreditation for Law Enforcement Agencies (CALEA) (General Order 2006). Reserve Corps members who successfully compete to become regular sworn police officers can be credited with training already completed as a Reserve Officer. A person with law enforcement experience can enter the force directly as a Reserve Officer Level I if various criteria are satisfied and with the approval of the chief of police (General Order 2006).

In 2009, the Reserve Corps had more than 100 members contributing at least 16 hours a month, the department's minimum volunteer commitment. According to Richard Southby, the Reserve Corps' commanding officer (with more than 20 years of service), most volunteers offer much more of their time. By his estimate, Reserve Corps members contribute about 3,000 hours a month to the department. Southby, now in retirement, is a former George Washington University faculty member and administrator. As a result of his involvement with the Reserve Corps, he helped in setting up the police science program in the College of Professional Studies at George Washington University (Morse 2009). In March 2010, the MPD began deploying the Reserve Corps in teams in order to deter crime in various targeted areas (Williams 2010).

## Civil Air Patrol

On December 1, 1941, CAP was officially established as a volunteer civilian defense organization, just one week before Japan attacked Pearl Harbor. During World War II, the CAP became famous for coastal patrol, where civilian volunteers used privately owned aircraft to spot enemy submarines along the Atlantic and Gulf Coasts. It was first placed under the control of the Office of Civilian Defense, but by April 1943, the organization was under the command of the Army Air Forces. CAP members became known as the "Minutemen" of World War II, performing many coastal patrol missions involving searching for enemy submarines and saving hundreds of crash victims (CAP History 2002). "Anti-submarine patrol for the Civil Air Patrol lasted from March 5, 1942, until August 31, 1943…. 26 CAP pilots and observers lost their lives and seven sustained serious injuries. In all, 90 aircraft were lost during that 18 months" (Burnham 1974, 28). CAP aircraft and pilots also were used for patrolling the U.S.–Mexican border to spot any unusual activities by enemy agents.

The CAP became an official auxiliary branch of the U.S. Air Force by an Act of Congress in May 1948 (Public Law 557). The Act provided that the CAP would have three major missions: aerospace education, emergency services, and a cadet program. The CAP's national headquarters is located at Maxwell Air Force Base in Montgomery, Alabama. The organization has nearly 53,000 members in 1,900 units. Applicants are screened by the FBI. Since 1986, the CAP has provided communications support to various federal and local law enforcement agencies engaged in counterdrug operations, especially in remote and sparsely populated areas. However, members cannot carry firearms or act as law enforcement officers (CAP Support to LEA 2002). Assessing natural disasters through aerial surveys and transporting vital supplies are among the many duties also performed by the CAP (Dooris 2008).

As an auxiliary of the U.S. Air Force, the CAP is organized along military lines. However, it is also classified as a nonprofit, 501(c) (3) corporation, allowing the organization to accept donations and to raise money for aircraft maintenance, fuel, and other costs and services (Dooris 2008). Its governing body is a national board whose members are elected except for the post of the senior air force advisor. The advisor's position is held by an active duty air force colonel who, in addition to serving in this critical advisory role, is also the CAP–U.S. Air Force commander. CAP is organized into eight geographic regions with a total of 52 wings. Each state, the District of Columbia, and the Commonwealth of Puerto Rico has a CAP wing. Each wing is headed by a CAP commander and has one or two retired U.S. Air Force members who perform liaison duties. The wings are subdivided into groups, squadrons, and flights depending on their size (CAP Organization 2002). In addition, there is a CAP National Staff College (NSC). The NSC offers a one-week executive management course that provides CAP officers with advanced leadership training (CAP News 2001).

The CAP provided the first direct aerial photos of the World Trade Center (WTC) disaster site in New York City. (Images can be found at http://www. Capnhq.gov.) On September 12, 2001, a day after the attack on the WTC, CAP planes began to fly over the disaster site in order to take high resolution digital images for study by the Graphic Information Program of the New York State Emergency Management Office. In addition, CAP volunteers transported cases of blood, needed medical supplies, and government officials; monitored airspace at many airports; and provided communications support to many state and local agencies (CAP News 2001).

The CAP implemented a security background check for all members in 1988. This resulted in a decrease in senior membership numbers for the next six years. CAP receives oversight from the Inspector General Program. "The CAP Inspector General Program ensures the integrity of the organization and provides CAP leadership the ability to identify and rectify program shortfalls for the purpose of bolstering efficiency.... Once every four years, the U.S. Air Force, working in conjunction with the CAP Inspector General, conducts quality assurance assessments of each of the 52 wings to streamline processes and detect and eliminate wasteful or fraudulent practices" (Dooris 2008, 47).

## U.S. Power Squadrons

The U.S. Power Squadrons (USPS) was founded in 1914 and constitutes the only other major U.S. maritime volunteer organization in addition to the Coast Guard Auxiliary (CGA). The USPS is not associated with the military; rather, it is a self-sustaining, privately funded organization composed of nearly 40,000 members organized into more than 400 squadrons across the country and in some U.S. territories. The operational unit of the USPS is the "squadron." USPS members use squadrons to conduct meetings, training, social events, and other boating-related activities. The USPS works closely with organizations such as the U.S. Coast Guard (USCG), the U.S. Coast Guard Auxiliary (USCGA), and the National Ocean Services Division of the National Oceanic and Atmospheric Administration to promote boating safety, conduct courtesy vessel safety checks, update and correct nautical charts, and to assist with other community improvement projects. The USPS offers an array of educational courses to its members, as well as the boating public, and fellowship activities afloat and ashore. Successfully completing a USPS boating safety course meets the educational requirements for boat operation in all states. "USPS is America's largest non-profit boating organization and has been honored by three U.S. presidents for its civic contributions" (About USPS 2013).

Membership in the USPS can be advantageous. For example, in 2013, the navigation law for New York State was amended. The new law requires operators of mechanically propelled vessels in New York waters (who must be over 10 years old), born on or after May 1, 1996, to be holders of a boating safety education certificate. However, there are certain exceptions, including minors between 10 and 18 accompanied by an adult certificate holder, new boat owners (within a 120-day grace period), boating safety instructors, USPS members, USCGA members, licensed captains, or on-duty emergency service, rescue, and law enforcement personnel (Peconic Bay PS 2013).

## U.S. Coast Guard Auxiliary

The USCG enforces a wide variety of laws, from halting the flow of illegal drugs, aliens, and contraband into the United States through maritime routes to preventing illegal fishing and suppressing violations of federal law in the maritime arena. Before receiving its current name in 1915, it had five predecessor agencies: the Revenue Cutter Service, the Life-Saving Service, the Lighthouse Service, the Bureau of Navigation, and the Steamboat Inspection Service.[6] Its civilian volunteer counterpart, the Coast Guard Auxiliary, was established in 1939 in response to the increasing number of recreational boating accidents.

The original name of the Coast Guard Auxiliary was the "Coast Guard Reserve." The 1939 federal law establishing it provided that members were not to hold military ranks, wear uniforms, receive military training, or "be vested with or exercise any right, privilege, power, or duty vested in or imposed upon the personnel of the Coast Guard" (Hall et al. 2007, 15). Nor were Coast Guard Reservists to be considered government employees. The Coast Guard Reserve lasted less than two years in its original form. On February 19, 1941, Congress restructured the Coast Guard Reserve, renaming the original organization the U.S. Coast Guard Auxiliary (USCGA) and establishing a new U.S. Coast Guard Reserve that would function as a source of wartime manpower, like the reserves of the other armed services (Hall et al. 2007). The CAP and the USCGA are the only military-sponsored volunteer (unsalaried) institutions in the United States (aside from ROTC and JROTC units).

The opportunities for service in the new Coast Guard Reserve included two categories—"regular reservists" and "temporary members of the reserve" (known as a "Coast Guard TR"). A Coast Guard TR was "a volunteer who served only in some designated geographic area (usually near his home or workplace) and less than full-time. Age limits for TRs were 17 and 64, and physical requirements were not stringent. Members of the Auxiliary were invited to enroll in the Reserve as TRs and bring their boats with them" (Tilley 2003, 3).

During World War II, "the character of the Auxiliary changed from an organization primarily designed to help pleasure boaters into a flexible work-force able and willing to step in wherever the USCG needed them" (Hall et al. 2007, 15). Volunteers, including movie stars such as Humphrey Bogart, as well as Arthur Fiedler, conductor of the Boston Pops Orchestra, patrolled for German U-boats. In addition, a unique Volunteer Port Security Force was established to prevent sabotage and subversive activities' on the nation's water-fronts. According to Tilley (2003, 4), "perhaps the Auxiliary's most important contribution to the war effort came in the form of the Volunteer Port Security Force.... The task of protecting the hundreds of warehouses, piers, and other facilities that kept the American shipping industry in business fell to the Coast Guard." Fortunately, the depleted forces of the Coast Guard were bolstered by its two-part Reserve system and its Auxiliary. Approximately 20,000 Reservists and Auxiliarists participated in the Volunteer Port Security Force (Tilley 2003). Generally, individuals assigned to the Port Security Force performed their unsalaried duties on shore. "As the war went on and the Coast Guard's resources were stretched thinner, Auxiliarists were called upon to fill gaps wherever active duty Coast Guardsmen left them. Auxiliarists' boats patrolled the waterfronts and inlets looking for saboteurs, enemy agents, and fires. Other Auxiliarists manned lookout and lifesaving stations near their homes, freeing regular Coast Guardsmen for sea duty. When a flood struck St. Louis in the spring of 1943, Coast Guard Auxiliarists evacuated 7,000 people and thousands of livestock. In addition, airplanes joined the Auxiliary and Auxiliarists began flying missions for the USCG (Hall et al. 2007).

(A five minute recruiting film for the Coast Guard Volunteer Port Security Force entitled "So's Your Old Man" may viewed online at: http://www. youtube.com/watch?v=x72rrOHohIC.)

One of the most challenging events in the history of the USCG was the "Mariel Boatlift." It began when Cuba suddenly announced it would permit a massive emigration through the Port of Mariel. For three weeks, a steady stream of small boats of every description, averaging 200–300 per day, made their way from Cuba to Florida. The USCG mobilized all of its resources in the area. Auxiliarists manned radios, performed search and rescue along the Florida coast, and stood watch at the stations in the Coast Guardsmen's absence (Hall et al. 2007).

Currently, the USCG is a division of the DHS. In recent years, its role in the suppression of drug trafficking has been significantly expanded. The USCG has about 35,000 active duty members and about 8,000 Reservists. More than 2,700 Reservists were called up to assist in antiterror efforts after the attacks on America's homeland on September 11, 2001. In addition, there may have been as many as 28,000 CGA members who were available for the performance of volunteer assignments during the emergency (Gilmore 2001).

Typically, many members of the Auxiliary operate their own boats to assist in marine safety programs. When so used, these craft are considered to be U.S. government property. Prior to September 11, the Auxiliary had three major missions: public education, the provision of courtesy marine inspections, and on-water operations (search and rescue, safety patrols, etc.) (Kastberg 1998).

According to Coast Guard Commander Chris Olin, Auxiliary members performed approximately 124,000 hours of volunteer duty between September 11 and December 7, 2001 (Olin 2001). By January 4, 2002, that number had reached 152,850 hours, an increase of approximately 45,040 hours over the previous year's hours in similar categories of effort (Operation Noble Eagle 2002). Hundreds of multimission waterside and shoreside patrols were conducted during this time frame (Olin 2001). Many of these patrols involved the protection of the nation's more than 360 ports, especially some 90 ports and waterway areas that had been designated as "security zones." In such zones, boat and ship traffic were prohibited. In New York City, there were eight such zones including areas near the United Nations and the WTC site. The auxiliary members augmented the work of the active duty Coast Guard personnel during the largest port security operation since World War II (Gilmore 2001).

On October 2, 2001, Viggo C. Bertelsen Jr. the volunteer national commodore of the USCGA announced that he had received a call from Admiral James M. Loy, the commandant of the Coast Guard. In the call, Loy expressed his appreciation for Auxiliary's service in providing critical assistance to the

Coast Guard's missions since the events of September 11. In particular, he said: "We couldn't have done it without you" (Bertelsen 2001).

Applicants for the CGA must be U.S. citizens at least 17 years of age. Members are eligible to take advance training courses in navigation, seamanship, communications, weather, patrols, and search and rescue procedures. The Auxiliary has members in all 50 states, Puerto Rico, the Virgin Islands, American Samoa, and Guam. Although under the authority of the commandant of the USCG, the Auxiliary is internally autonomous, operating on four organizational levels: flotilla, division, district, and national. At the national level, there are officers who are responsible, along with the commandant of the USCG, for the administration and policy making for the entire Auxiliary (Hall et al. 2007).

In the past, Auxiliarists have played limited roles in the law enforcement field; for example, providing vessels and crews for training Coast Guard members, engaging in port security, performing unobtrusive law enforcement observations, conducing safety checks by boarding recreational boats, providing transportation and platforms for Coast Guard boarding parties, rendering assistance in the validation process for Merchant Mariner credential applications, and carrying out other missions incorporated into programs such as America's Waterway Watch and Operation Patriot Readiness (Dooris 2008). However, in recent years, there have been efforts made to clarify the role of the Auxiliary in any law enforcement activities. In 2006, a policy directive was issued declaring the Auxiliary was to be restricted to the performance of only specific types of non-law enforcement missions. For example, "Auxiliary facilities may be used to conduct the newly renamed Maritime Observation Mission (MOM).... This is a non-law enforcement mission whose primary purpose is to provide increased maritime domain awareness by observing areas of interest and reporting findings to the operational commander while maintaining the safety of auxiliary personnel. Should Auxiliarists observe anything suspicious during the course of normal multi-mission patrols, they should record and report the same immediately ... but take no additional action" (Hall et al. 2007, 17). In particular, in accordance with operations policies, Auxiliarists cannot execute direct law enforcement missions, but they may support certain Coast Guard law enforcement activities. The key restriction is that no command can vest Auxiliarists with general police powers (e.g., power to search, seize, or arrest) or give them the authority to engage in any type of direct law enforcement or police action. In addition, Coast Guard Auxiliarists are prohibited from carrying weapons (Hall et al. 2007).

Dooris (2008) concluded that the USCG lacks the personnel and resources to fill critical gaps in its safety and security missions without help from its volunteer arm, the CGA. However, such a reliance has become more tenuous because Auxiliary membership has decreased by about 20% since 2003 to its current strength of 28,635. This trend is in sharp contrast to membership trends in other large volunteer groups in the United States. Furthermore, at its current strength, the Auxiliary is far from the 48,000-member goal declared, in a 1987 governmental report, as mission critical by 2000 (Dooris 2008).

The USCGA has not instituted any in-house youth program with appropriate standards for operation and, as of the present time, appears to have no interest in doing so. Nonetheless, on a limited basis, the USCGA has expanded its youth interaction by entering into participatory agreements with the Boy Scouts of America (BSA) and the U.S. Naval Sea Cadet Corps (NSCC) to provide shoreside and boating safety training opportunities to the interested youth of these organizations. However, in March 2011, the national commodore of the USCGA cautioned all subdivisions that before members undertake such training programs, "They must understand the risks involved including potential legal liability inherent in working with youth in our litigious society. Before engaging in such activities, interested members and units should first use their Chain of Leadership to obtain the consent of the District Commodore to engage in the activities; and, thereafter, consult with the District Legal Officer (DSO-LP) regarding all pertinent legal issues" (Vass 2011).

The absence of any youth division within the USCGA is in stark contrast to the youth training offered by the CAP, Police Explorers, and other organizations. The absence of a structured youth program is likely to forestall future membership of young adults in the organization.

## Proposal for a U.S. BPA

Within the DHS is the U.S. Customs and Border Protection (CBP) division, which includes the U.S. Border Patrol (USBP) and the CBP Office of Air and Marine, the largest aviation/marine force in federal law enforcement.

In 2007, Christopher Hall, a captain in the USCG, and three other senior governmental and military officers proposed the creation of a "Border Patrol Auxiliary".[7] The BPA has been proposed as a professional organization of auxiliary members working side-by-side with Border Patrol agents in support of the Border Patrol mission. To guarantee the integrity and respectability of the Border Patrol, volunteers would be screened to ensure they have the characteristics essential for maintaining the high standards of the Border Patrol.

The mission of the proposed BPA would be "to assist the U.S. Border Patrol in accomplishing the mission of detecting, interdicting and apprehending those who attempt to illegally enter or smuggle people, including terrorists, or contraband, including weapons of mass destruction, across U.S. borders between official ports of entry" (Hall et al. 2007, 37). In order to maximize the effectiveness of the BPA, a two-tiered system would be developed. The primary purpose of tier one auxiliary members would be to improve the efficiency of the Border Patrol by relieving regular Border Patrol agents from administrative and support roles, which keep them from performing direct operational missions. The primary purpose for tier two auxiliary members would be to improve the effectiveness of the Border Patrol by increasing the number of agents along the border beyond the congressionally restricted number of 18,000 Border Patrol agents.

The actual strength of the BPA would reflect the needs of the Border Patrol, but the number authorized would be at least equal to the authorized agent strength for the Border Patrol. On this point, the proposers noted that the number of USCGA members outnumbers their active duty counterparts. After completion of an appropriate training program, tier one BPA members would be required to perform a minimum of 12 hours per month or 36 hours per quarter in order to maintain proficiency in an auxiliary member's functional area. They would make up approximately 80% of the members of the BPA. Tier two auxiliary members would be the elite members of the BPA making up the remainder of the force. They would be fully trained at the Border Patrol Academy to perform side-by-side with Border Patrol agents in all aspects of border security operations. In order to maintain good standing in the force, a minimum of 16 hours per month or 48 hours per quarter would be required. In addition, the members would have to complete the same annual training as regular full-time Border Patrol agents (Hall et al. 2007). The two-tier BPA proposal parallels to some extent the two-level MPD Reserve Corps program requirements.

With regard to finding sufficient volunteers for the new BPA, the proposers pointed out that other federal agencies such as the Coast Guard Auxiliary have found them and that the BPA should have the same appeal, namely, "patriotic duty and local community impact—with little geographic overlap to create competition between them" (Hall et al. 2007, 29). However, they also indicate that recruiting tier two members would be difficult because the ideal candidates would be those persons who already possessed a law enforcement or military service background. Criminal justice college graduates would also fall into this preferred category. In addition, finding qualified tier two volunteers for service in rural areas would also be a problem. In order to address this recruitment problem, the BPA proposal would be stronger if it followed the design of the Metropolitan PD Reserve Corps, which provides specific criteria for transitioning from a Level II to a Level I Reserve Officer.

In support of their BPA proposal, Hall and his associates (2007, 44) argue that "securing the border is the first step to controlling the influx of criminal activity and illegal immigration into the United States. By creating the U.S. BPA, the Border Patrol can increase the number of qualified agents on the border, which is a proven deterrent to illegal immigrants and criminals along the border while increasing their capability and capacity across the entire spectrum of operations. All of this can be accomplished at a fraction of the cost by using volunteers. It will also expand citizen involvement in a critical area of national security. Together the nation can once again overcome a direct threat to our national security through the cooperation of governance and the people."

## The Commonwealth of Puerto Rico Auxiliary Police

The Puerto Rico Police Department (PRPD) is responsible for policing and carrying out essential public safety functions for the Commonwealth of Puerto Rico. The PRPD is the second-largest police department in the United States, second only to the New York City Police Department. The PRPD has over 17,000 police officers who serve the island's approximately 3.7 million residents (ACLU 2012, 2).

The Puerto Rico Police traces its history back to 1837, when the *La Guardia Civil de Puerto Rico* (Puerto Rico Civil Guard) was created to protect the lives and property of Puerto Ricans, who at the time were Spanish subjects. It provided police services to the entire island, although many municipalities maintained their own police force. Since taking possession of Puerto Rico in July 1898, as a result of the Spanish-American War, the United States has controlled the island as a U.S. Territory. In 1996, a substantial revision of the police organization took place by virtue of the Puerto Rico Police Act of 1996. This act included various provisions about an auxiliary police organization and indicated the following definition for an auxiliary police officer: "a volunteer citizen accredited by the police as such, subject to the norms established by the Superintendent. Through their services, they shall assist in the fight against crime and towards the welfare of the citizens. They shall receive no financial compensation whatsoever for their services" (Puerto Rico Police Act of 1996, 2012, 5).

Members of the auxiliary force have the same uniforms as regular members of the Puerto Rico Police. All pins, identification, and uniform accessories are also the same. Qualifications for membership include being an American citizen and resident of Puerto Rico The auxiliaries may render crime prevention services on routine patrol, in schools, parks, malls, urban train stations, and at other locations. They may also be assigned to provide support services at the offices of police superintendents, area command centers, districts, precincts, police detachments, and mini police stations. Auxiliary Police officers who have been trained in the proper use and safe handling of firearms and have complied with the provisions of law are authorized to use their firearms in the performance of their duties (Puerto Rico Police Act of 1996, 2012, 33–35).

## U.S. Virgin Islands Police Auxiliary Service

The U.S. Virgin Islands are located in the eastern Caribbean, approximately 1,100 miles southeast of Miami, Florida. They are 40 to 50 miles east of Puerto Rico. During the seventeenth century, the archipelago was divided into two territorial units, one English and the other Danish. Sugarcane, produced by slave labor, drove the islands' economy during the eighteenth and early nineteenth centuries. In 1917, during World War I, the United States purchased the Danish portion for $25 million, which had been in economic decline since the abolition of slavery in 1848. The United States was concerned that Germany would capture Denmark, and Denmark was afraid that the United States would simply take them if that happened. Today tourism contributes majorly to the Islands' economy; many of the tourists visit on cruise ships.

During World War I, Congress passed the National Defense Act of 1916, which required the use of the term "National Guard" for the then existing state militias and further regulated them. Congress also authorized the states to maintain Home Guards, which were reserve forces separate from the National Guards. The Secretary of War was authorized to furnish these units with rifles, ammunition, and supplies (see Vol. 40, U.S. Statutes at Large 1917, 181). In 1940, with the onset of World War II, and as a result of its federalizing the National Guard, Congress amended the National Defense Act of 1916, and authorized the states to maintain "military forces other than National Guard" (see Vol. 54, U.S. Statutes at Large 1940, 1206). This law authorized the War Department to train and arm the new military forces that would come to be known as State Guards. Many states and U.S. Territories took advantage of this law and maintained distinctive local military forces throughout the war. Congress granted U.S. citizenship to Virgin Islanders in 1927. The governor was elected by popular vote for the first time in 1970; previously he had been appointed by the U.S. president. Residents of the islands substantially enjoy the same rights as those enjoyed by mainlanders, but they may not vote in presidential elections (U.S. Virgin Islands, 2014).

As a result of the Revised Organic Act of 1954, the governor of the Virgin Islands was required to reorganize and consolidate various island governmental agencies into the executive branch. Consequently, in 1955, island police agencies were merged to form a Department of Public Safety, as an executive department. Previously, the Organic Act of 1936 had divided the U.S. Virgin Islands into two municipalities, namely the Municipality of Saint Croix and the Municipality of Saint Thomas and Saint John. Each municipality had its own law enforcement agency known as the "Police and Prison Department." The new territory-wide Department of Public Safety included both a Police Division and a Fire Division. In addition to enforcing the laws relating to public safety, the Police Division supervised a Civilian Defense Program and the activities of the Home Guard. In 1967, Civil Defense was transferred from the

Department of Public Safety to the Office of the Governor and is presently under the Office of the Adjutant General of the Virgin Islands National Guard, having been renamed the Virgin Islands Territorial Emergency Management Agency (VITEMA). In the late 1970s, responsibilities for fire prevention and control were transferred to the Office of the Governor. In 1985, as a result of these changes and other duties being removed to other executive agencies, the Department of Public Safety was renamed the U.S. Virgin Islands Police Department (VIPD). Several years earlier, the Home Guards had been renamed the Virgin Islands Police Auxiliary (Lewis 2014).

Upon acceptance into the U.S. Virgin Islands Police Department Auxiliary Program, members are required to complete a police training academy for certification (VIPD 2014a). In May 2010, ten new volunteer police recruits completed the 22-week course alongside regular police recruits (Shea 2010). Police auxiliary members must work a minimum of 24 per month, unless otherwise ordered by the Police Commissioner. The members of the police auxiliary help with civic activities and a wide range of other duties, including partnering with a patrol officer to delivering a speech at a Neighborhood Watch meeting. The members of the volunteer police in the U.S. Virgin Island can achieve various ranks from auxiliary police corporal to captain. In times of natural disaster or other emergency, auxiliary police have been called upon to serve their communities under difficult circumstances (VIPD 2014a). During the passing of Hurricane Omar in October 2008, auxiliary officers helped to maintain public safety; protected life and property; assisted with emergency evacuation and provided security at designated shelters (VIPD 2014b).

The VIPD also sponsors a police cadet program that prepares young men and women for careers in police work and in partnership with the University of the Virgin Islands provides police cadets full scholarships if they are pursuing a degree in Criminal Justice. "Cadets work alongside police officers and during official police activities, such as funerals, police week activities or other similar programs" (VIPD 2014c).

## Guam Police Department Civilian Volunteer Police Reserve

Guam, lying about 6,000 miles west of San Francisco, is an organized, unincorporated territory of the United States located in the western Pacific Ocean. After the Spanish-American War of 1898, Spain ceded Guam to the United States. It is one of five U.S. territories with an established civilian government. Guam is the southernmost and largest tropical island in the Mariana island chain and is also the largest island in Micronesia. By plane, Guam is approximately 3 hours flying distance to several major Asian cities, including Manila, Hong Kong, Tokyo, Seoul, Taipei, and Sydney.

Guam was probably explored by the Portuguese navigator Ferdinand Magellan (sailing for Spain) in 1521. The island was formally claimed by

Spain in 1565, and its people were forced into submission and conversion to Roman Catholicism beginning in 1668. For two years during World War II, the Japanese military occupied Guam until it was retaken by force in 1944. The people of Guam have been U.S. citizens since 1950. Since 1973, Guam has been represented in the U.S. Congress by a nonvoting delegate, but they do not participate in presidential elections. The people of the U.S. Virgin Islands also have a nonvoting representative in Congress. The executive branch includes a popularly elected governor, who serves a four-year term. It is home today to a relatively large U.S. military presence (Guam 2014).

Similar to the history of policing in the U.S. Virgin Islands, in 1985, Guam's Department of Public Safety was separated into two departments—the Guam Police Department and the Guam Fire Department. In 1952, the Department of Public Safety was established to replace the U.S. Navy's control over the Guam Insular Guard, a local police force dating back to 1905 (Torre 2011). Currently, the Territory of Guam has two volunteer police programs associated with its police department: the Guam Police Department's Community Assisted Policing Effort (CAPE) and the Guam Police Department's Civilian Volunteer Police Reserve composed of over 100 persons. The police reserves have peace officer authority, but the volunteers of the CAPE program are not peace officers. Regulations require that CAPE volunteers acknowledge that their services do not constitute employment for purposes of the Worker's Compensation Act and that they are not entitled to benefits under the act.

The general functions and duties of the Civilian Volunteer Police Reserve (CVPR) are to provide backup manpower for the suppression of crime, preservation of law and order, fight and control fires, and to assist in civil emergencies (Guam CVPR 2014).

In March 2012, 22 men and 11 women became members of the Guam Police Department's CVPR unit after graduating from their training academy course. Several of the volunteer police reservists had previously participated as members of the CAPE program. At the graduation event, Eddie Baza Calvo, Guam's Governor, stated: "You are putting yourself in the line of fire every day" (Taitano 2012). Indeed, in 1979, Reserve Officers Helen Lizama and Rudy Iglesias were killed when they responded to a burglary alarm at a business. They were both shot by a getaway driver as they exited their patrol car (ODMP 2014). In December 2012, an additional 25 persons completed the reserve academy that involved eight months of training (Sablan 2012). In January 2014, 29 more individuals were sworn in and among the graduates were a mother and her two children. The ceremony was held at the Sheraton Laguna Guam Resort, and the three family members took their oath of office from Guam's Lt. Governor Ray Tenorio (Reilly 2014).

In 2010, the successful recruitment, selection, and training of Guam Police Department's CVPR unit served as a role model for the passage of a law to establish a Civilian Volunteer Airport Police Reserve program within the Airport Police. The statute indicated that the authority of such new organizational personnel shall include when rendering assistance to police or fire service officers "the same powers, duties, rights (including coverage under the Worker's Compensation Act), privileges and immunities as if they were paid, full-time members of the Airport, *except* that they *shall* earn recruitment credit for services performed as volunteers" (Title 12, Chapter 1, §1112.3, Guam Code Annotated). Recruiting and training for the new Civilian Volunteer Airport Police Reserve program began in 2012.

## FEMA Reserves

For more than 200 years, disaster response and recovery efforts were left to a haphazard approach with a succession of federal agencies being given responsibilities. However, a series of damaging hurricanes and earthquakes in the 1960s and early 1970s prompted a more comprehensive approach to federal disaster assistance. In addition, new concerns about public safety arose due to the advent of nuclear power plants and the transportation of hazardous substances. Although such congressional legislations as the National Flood Insurance Act of 1986 and the Disaster Relief Act of 1974 were enacted, emergency and disaster activities were still fragmented.

Finally, in 1979, the numerous and separate disaster-related agencies and programs were merged into the FEMA by presidential executive order. Among the agencies transferred to FEMA was the Defense Department's Defense Civil Preparedness Agency. Thus, civil defense responsibilities were also shifted to FEMA. Today, FEMA (a division of the DHS) coordinates the federal government's role in preparing for, preventing, mitigating the effects of, responding to, and recovering from all domestic disasters, whether natural or man-made, including acts of terror. After the experience of Hurricane Katrina in August 2005—where a final death toll of 1,836 people has been reported, making it the third deadliest hurricane in U.S. history (FAQs, Hurricane Katrina 2013)—the Post-Katrina Emergency Reform Act of 2006 was adopted to provide improved levels of preparedness, response, and recovery by FEMA (FEMA History 2013). By comparison, according the U.S. Geological Survey, the 1906 San Francisco earthquake took more than 3,000 lives (Calvan 2005). However, "by one incontestable measure Katrina stands out among this nation's historic natural disasters. In dollars and cents Katrina was the worst. The toll is estimated at $200 billion" (Forgues-Roy 2013).

In April 2012, a major transformation of the FEMA disaster workforce was announced involving the establishment of the FEMA Reservist Program. The members of the existing disaster workforce were offered the opportunity to seek new appointments in the Reservist Program by applying for specific incident management positions within the new FEMA program.

The transformation was to be completed within a year. Most importantly, the announcement declared that the FEMA Reservist Program was a national asset and served as America's "primary resource" for disaster response and recovery, comprising up to 80% of field office positions. In addition, a wage analysis was to be conducted to align pay and pay grade distribution with the knowledge and skills associated with the duties for each of the incident management positions. Moreover, upon first deployment in a new position, mobile communication and computing equipment would be assigned and retained by the reservist for future use. Finally, a reservist ombudsman program was also announced with new positions at headquarters to advocate at a senior level on behalf of reservists (Change and Opportunity 2012).

Reservists play a very important role in meeting the needs of disaster survivors. The work of a reservist can be exhausting, frustrating, challenging, and rewarding. The hours can be long, and the conditions are sometimes difficult. In general, in order to become a FEMA Reservist, a person must want to assist others in a disaster or an emergency, be willing to commit to being professional, keep the public trust, follow all FEMA/DHS rules and regulations, and must abide by the conditions of employment. Specific qualifications include U.S. citizenship, passing a background investigation, being approved for a government-issued travel card, being able to leave home on short notice, being able to be away from home for 30 days or more, and being able to travel to any state or U.S. territory (Requirements 2013).

The desired skills for membership in the FEMA Reserves include being highly motivated, a self-starter, capable of working with little supervision, computer literate, able to prioritize tasks, customer service focused, good at working under physical and mental stress, and being able to work on an as-needed basis with a flexible work schedule (Reservist Applicants 2013).

## Summary

When America was still a very young country, Alexis de Tocqueville traveled to learn about the nation's new prison system.[8] During the course of a nine-month visit, he expanded his research, and his findings are considered an invaluable narrative about the nature of American democracy. In order for such a system to thrive, he recommended an independent and influential judiciary, a strong executive branch, local self-government, administrative decentralization, religion, well-educated women, freedom of association, and freedom of the press. Moreover, he considered jury service to be an important civic obligation because it helps citizens think about other people's affairs and educates them in the use of their freedom (Alexis de Tocqueville 1835/1990).

Alexis de Tocqueville discovered an American democracy heavily reliant on the civic activities of its citizens. Volunteers are most often engaged in community work, but they can also perform important law enforcement–related functions at the federal level. In times of peril, when most needed, civil defense volunteers and reserve or auxiliary police have been available. In particular, the CGA and CAP organizations have had long and successful histories in the field of homeland security. At the municipal level, the Reserve Corps of the MPD in Washington, D.C., represents an outstanding example of how ordinary citizens may serve as a supplemental force permitting full-time officers to handle more calls for service and other duties. The police powers that the Reserve Corps possess distinguish it from all of the other organizations discussed in this chapter.

The proliferation of local, state, and federal law enforcement agencies in the United States can result in overlapping jurisdiction. At a crime or disaster scene affecting large numbers of people, multiple jurisdictions and several police agencies may be involved. Command in such situations remains a complex and sometimes contentious issue. For example, Farber and Cen (2006) notes that Hurricane Katrina may have exposed a weakness in the federal system. Because of our federalized system, FEMA and the DHS are not in complete control. As a result of this shared power arrangement, there is no single authority to effectively prepare, respond, mitigate, and aid in recovery from disasters. The history of civil defense and homeland security in the United States has been one of frequent policy and organizational change.

The CAP was officially founded in December 1941, one week before Pearl Harbor, by citizens involved in aviation and concerned about the defense of America's coastlines. It was first placed under the control of the Office of Civilian Defense. By April 1943, the organization was under the command of the Army Air Forces. Its members became known as the "Minutemen" of World War II, performing many missions involving coastal patrol searching for enemy submarines and saving hundreds of crash victims (CAP History 2002). In 1948, a federal law was passed incorporating CAP as an official auxiliary of the newly created U.S. Air Force.

Since 1939, the USCG Auxiliary has had a history as an all-volunteer organization assisting the Coast Guard in times of war and peace. It is a proven success story that can be used as a model for any federal or state agency. Although the Auxiliary does not conduct direct law enforcement activities, Auxiliary members can man communications consoles, conduct search and rescue and safety patrols, and can provide administrative support enabling the USCG active duty forces to spend more time on maritime security and national defense. One scholar has indicated that the U.S. Coast Guard currently lacks personnel and resources and cannot fill critical gaps in its safety and security missions without help from its volunteer arm, the CGA (Dooris 2008).

This chapter also included information about volunteer police in U.S. Territories and establishing a civilian auxiliary within the Border Patrol to be known as the "U.S. Border Patrol Auxiliary." It would recruit and train two types of volunteers. Tier one auxiliary members would perform support functions. These functions would keep members from direct contact with suspects and away from the dangers involved in field operations. Tier one auxiliary members would comprise approximately 80% of the BPA. The primary purpose of these members would be to relieve Border Patrol agents from support jobs allowing them to return to performing field operations along the border. Tier two auxiliary members would be the elite members of the BPA who would attend training at the Border Patrol Academy to gain the knowledge and skills required to perform alongside Border Patrol agents in every facet of the Border Patrol mission. These members would comprise the other 20% of the BPA. Their primary mission would be to increase the number of people performing security operations along the border under the direct supervision of members of the Border Patrol. This two-tier system resembles that used by the volunteer reserve police officers in Washington, D.C., with the important distinction that its unarmed Level II officers are still available for assignments in the field. The parallel BPA volunteer is restricted to inside or clerical duties.

The USPS is a nonprofit, educational organization dedicated to making boating safer and more enjoyable by teaching classes in seamanship, navigation, and related subjects. It celebrated its hundredth anniversary in 2014.

President Carter's 1979 executive order merged many of the federal government's disaster-related responsibilities into the FEMA. In 2012, a major transformation of the FEMA disaster workforce was announced involving the establishment of the FEMA Reservist Program. The members of the existing disaster workforce were offered the opportunity to seek new appointments in the part-time salaried Reservist Program by applying for specific incident management positions within the new FEMA program. In addition, on a temporary assignment and salaried basis, citizens can apply to become a FEMA Reservist. Interested citizens who are available and qualified would be selected and deployed based on the needs of the agency.

Several ideas raised in this chapter concerned the possibility of establishing a BPA, increasing the number of Coast Guard Auxiliarists, and adding a youth program in the CGA. All three recommendations could help stem the tide of illegal border crossings, and drug smuggling, as well the overall capacity of the United States to contend with natural disasters and homeland security.

## Review Questions

1. Who was Alexis de Tocqueville, and what did he discover about the nature of American democracy in the mid-1830s?
2. Identify a charitable organization using either volunteermatch.org or idealist.org. Describe the purpose or mission of the organization.
3. Use Internet-based research tools to find at least one instance in the history of the U.S. Marshals Service that involved an effort to

balance concern for popular feelings with the needs of federal law enforcement. Discuss your findings.

4. Provide at least one example of how, prior to September 11, 2001, Congress sought to obtain the aid of local law enforcement on behalf of federal law enforcement matters.

5. The Real ID Act was enacted in 2005 at the recommendation of the 9/11 Commission to verify the authenticity of every driver's license applicant. (This statute can be accessed online at http://www.dhs.gov/xlibrary/assets/real-id-act-text.pdf.) Read the statute and list at least three of its specific provisions.

6. Implementation of the Real ID Act was delayed on several occasions. Use Internet-based research to learn the reasons for the delays in implementation. Discuss whether these delays were justified.

7. Discuss the nature and benefits of deputization agreements.

8. Distinguish between Level I and Level II members of the Metropolitan Police Reserve Corps.

9. When was the Civil Air Patrol (CAP) founded, and what role did it play during World War II?

10. Identify and describe one of the Coast Guard Auxiliary's most important contributions during World War II.

11. List at least four of the activities Coast Guard Auxiliarists have engaged in that are related to the law enforcement field.

12. During the first decade of the twenty-first century, there was a significant decline in the membership of the Coast Guard Auxiliary. Conduct online research to determine possible reasons for this decline.

13. Should there be a youth division program within the U.S. Coast Guard Auxiliary? Discuss.

14. Discuss the pros and cons for the establishment of a Border Patrol Auxiliary.

15. Identify at least three of the qualifications and three of the desired skills established for FEMA Reservists.

16. Search the Web to find a U.S. police department that is unarmed. Hint: It is a U.S. Territory. In addition, discuss the pros and cons for arming volunteer police who are directly involved in state or federal law enforcement.

## Notes

1. There is some prideful disagreement regarding the origins of federal policing and its first agencies. Some historians point to the creation of the federal judiciary and its use of marshals, while others recall the creation of the early forerunner to the U.S. Coast Guard—the Revenue Marine. Perhaps the oldest may be the Postal Inspection Service because it can trace its origins back to 1772. In that year,

the position of "surveyor" was created. Since 1737, the colonial postal system had been supervised by Postmaster General Benjamin Franklin. Franklin created the position of "surveyor" because he could no longer single-handedly regulate and audit post offices. In 1801, the title of surveyor was changed to "special agent." In 2011, there were more than 1,400 postal inspectors, about 700 postal police officers, and approximately 600 related support personnel (About the Chief 2011).

2. The jurisdiction of the majority of federal police is narrow in scope. For example, Congress and the United States Supreme Court have different police forces. There are three separate law enforcement agencies that report to Congress— Capitol Police, Government Printing Office Police, and the Library of Congress Police. If the three congressional agencies were consolidated, there would only be one chief of police, one set of hiring and training standards and policies, integrated communications systems, and therefore a reduction of bureaucracy. Since 1970, the Federal Law Enforcement Training Center (FLETC), now a component of the DHS, has been serving as America's foremost law enforcement training organization. It performs training for 90 federal agencies—63 in the executive branch, three in the legislative branch, two in the judicial branch, and 22 others (About FLETC 2011).

3. Indeed, the history of the development of the nation's federal law enforcement system has been checkered with the passage of numerous federal crimes and the establishment of a wide variety of federal agencies. This has taken place in accordance with changing congressional perceptions of "the crisis of the moment." Today, there are more than 3,000 federal crimes on the books. Many crimes, no matter how local in nature, appear to be within the reach of federal criminal jurisdiction, and the number of crimes deemed "federal" continues to increase. U.S. Postal Inspectors enforce more than 200 of these federal statutes. Their jurisdiction includes the investigation of crimes that may adversely affect U.S. mail, the postal system, or postal employees. For example, the protection of post office employees is an essential function of their responsibilities. Inspectors promptly investigate assaults and threats that occur while postal employees are performing official duties or as a result of their employment. In addition, postal inspectors invest significant resources into the investigation of mail theft by criminals.

4. For an excellent discussion of the U.S. national response system see: Davis, Lynn E., Jill Rough, Gary Cecchine, Agnes Gereben Schaefer, Laurinda L. Zeman (2007). *Hurricane Katrina Lessons for Army Planning and Operations*. Rand Corporation. Santa Monica, CA. See also the 36-page report entitled: *Civil Defense and Homeland Security: A Short History of National Preparedness Efforts* (2006, September), prepared by Department of Homeland Security: National Preparedness Task Force.

5. In general, the need for cross-deputization may have first arisen due to the overlapping jurisdictions associated with police work on Indian reservations and other tribal lands. For example, "Depending on the nature and location of the crime, and whether the offender of the victim were Indian or non-Indian, police officers of states, cities, and counties, tribes, the BIA or the FBI may be called upon when a crime occurs" (Barker and Mullen 1993, 157). The issue is made more complex due to the fact that 16 states have assumed jurisdiction for general law enforcement on various Indian reservations under the framework set forth in Public Law 280. In 1953, with the passage of Public Law 280,

"Congress transferred criminal jurisdiction in Indian country to six states. This federal law granted so-called mandatory states all criminal and civil jurisdiction over Indian land within their borders. The states affected by the legislation included California, Minnesota (except for the Red Lake Reservation), Nebraska, Oregon (excluding the Warm Springs Reservation), Wisconsin, and Alaska after it gained statehood (except for the Annette Islands Metlakatla Indians). This law effectively terminated all tribal criminal jurisdictions in the affected tribal area within these states. Public Law 280 also provides that any state (so-called optional states) wishing to assume jurisdiction over tribes within their borders may do so by state law or by amending the state constitution. Following passage of Public Law 280, 10 states chose to do so. In 1968, an amendment to Public Law 280 was passed requiring tribal consent before additional states could extend jurisdiction. Since 1968, no tribe has consented. In response to the skyrocketing crime rate and confusion with respect to jurisdiction in Indian country, Congress passed the Tribal Law and Order Act of 2010 (TLOA). It states that in cases of no referrals or declinations of criminal investigations in Indian country, "Any federal department or agency shall coordinate' with their tribal counterparts. This requirement extends to the FBI; U.S. Attorneys Offices; Drug Enforcement Agency (DEA); Bureau of Alcohol, Tobacco, Firearms, and Explosives (ATF); and others conducting investigations in tribal land" (for more details, see Bulzomi 2012).

6. The Coast Guard is an amalgamation of five formerly distinct federal services. A useful timeline that considers the establishment of those services and when they became part of what is now the U.S. Coast Guard, as well as changes in the organizational structure of the Coast Guard itself, can be found at: http://www.uscg.mil/history/faqs/when.asp.

7. The content and discussion presented here regarding the BPA are entirely based on Christopher Hall, Gregg Schauerman, Robert Ewing, and Brian Brandner, *Securing the Borders: Creation of the Border Patrol Auxiliary*, National Security Program, Kennedy School of Government, Harvard University, May 5, 2007.

8. The focus of this book is on volunteer police work, but many additional opportunities exist throughout America for contributing to public safety, especially in the fields of prisoner rehabilitation and reentry work. The services and programs offered by the Federal Bureau of Prisons, as well as state and county correctional facilities, are routinely supplemented by citizen volunteers. Many volunteers currently work within prisons as tutors, recreational aides, chaplains, and vocational instructors. Interested individuals need only to contact their closest facility to learn about volunteer positions. For more information about volunteering within the federal prison system, visit: http://www.bop.gov/jobs/volunteer.jsp.

# References

About FLETC. (2011). Retrieved August 17, 2011 from http://www.fletc.gov/about-fletc

About MPDC. (2013). Retrieved October 17, 2013 from http://mpdc.dc.gov/page/about-mpdc

About the Chief. (2011). About the chief postal inspector. Retrieved August 20, 2011 from https://postalinspectors.uspis.gov/aboutus/Chief.aspx

About the MPD. (2013). About the MPD Reserve Corps. Retrieved October 17, 2013 from http://mpdc.dc.gov/page/about-mpd-reserve-corps

About USPS. (2013). U.S. Power Squadrons. Retrieved October 16, 2013 from http://www.usps.org/newpublic2/about.html

ACLU (2012). Island of impunity: Puerto Rico's outlaw police force. Retrieved June 27, 2014 from http://www.aclu.org/files/assets/islandofimpunity_executivesummary_english_0.pdf

Barker, M. L. and Mullen, K. (1993). Cross-deputization in Indian country. *Police Studies: The International Review of Police Development, 16,* 157–166.

Bertelsen Jr., V. C. (2001). Thanks from the commandant. U.S. Coast Guard Auxiliary National Bridge Page. Retrieved January 1, 2002 from http://www.cgaux.org/cgauxweb/tbbridge.shtml

Blickensdorf, J. (2014). MPDC Auxiliary Police. Retrieved March 2, 2014 from http://www.dcmetropolicecollector.com/MPD-Reserve-Force.html

Bulzomi, M. J. (2012). Indian Country and the Tribal Law and Order Act of 2010. *FBI Law Enforcement Bulletin.* Retrieved October 15, 2013 from http://www.fbi.gov/stats-services/publications/law-enforcement-bulletin/may-2012/indian-country-and-the-tribal-law-and-order-act-of-2010

Burnham, F. A. (1974). *Hero next door.* Fallbrook, CA: Areo Publishers.

Calhoun, F. S. (1991). *The lawmen: United States marshals and their deputies: 1789–1989.* Penguin Books.

Calvan, B. C. (2005, February 27). San Francisco revises death toll for 1906 earthquake: Tally could exceed 3,400. Retrieved October 19, 2013 from http://www.boston.com/news/nation/articles/2005/02/27/san_francisco_revises_death_toll_for_1906_earthquake/?page = full

CAP History. (2002). Retrieved February 3, 2002 from http://www.capnhq.gov/nhq/pa/50-2/history.html

CAP News. (2001, September). Retrieved January 8, 2002 from http://www.capnhq.gov/nhq/capnews/01-09/news.htm

CAP Organization (2002). CAP organization. Retrieved January 8, 2002 from http://www.capnhq.gov/nhq/pa/50-2/organization.html

CAP Support to LEA. (2002). Retrieved January 8, 2002 from http://www.capnhq.gov/nhq/do/cd/leaspt.htm

Change and Opportunity. (2012). Change and opportunity in our disaster workforce. Memo to all FEMA employees from Richard Serino, Deputy Administrator, April 17, 2012. Retrieved October 9, 2013 from http://www.fema.gov/pdf/about/memo_change_opportunity_disaster_workforce_041712.pdf

Civilian Enforcers. (2013). History: Civilian enforcers. Retrieved October 14, 2013 from http://www.usmarshals.gov/history/civilian_enforcers.htm

Dooris, M. D. (2008, December). *Enhancing recruitment and retention of volunteers in the U.S. Coast Guard Auxiliary.* Master's thesis, Naval Postgraduate School, Monterey, CA.

FAQs, Hurricane Katrina. (2013). Retrieved October 19, 2013 from http://www.hurricanekatrinarelief.com/faqs.html

Farber, D. A. and Cen, J. (2006). *Disasters and the law.* New York: Aspen Publishers.

FEMA History. (2013). Retrieved October 9, 2013 from http://www.fema.gov/about-agency

Forgues-Roy, N. (2013). Was Katrina the biggest, the worst natural disaster in U.S. history? Retrieved October 19, 2013 from http://hnn.us/article/17193

General Order. (2006). General order 101.3: Organization, authority, and rules of the Metropolitan Police Department Reserve Corps, effective March 28, 2006. Retrieved October 17, 2013 from https://go.mpdconline.com/GO/GO_101_03.pdf

Gilmore, G. J. (2001, November 1). Coast guard on guard, to meet terrorism threat. *U.S. Department of Defense, American Forces Information Service.* Retrieved January 1, 2002 from http://www.defenselink.mil/news/Nov2001/n11012001_200111011.html

Guam. (2014). Territory of Guam. Retrieved July 1, 2014 from http://www.infoplease.com/country/guam.html

Guam CVPR. (2014). Civilian volunteer police reserve. Retrieved June 30, 2014 from http://www.guamcourts.org/compileroflaws/GCA/10gca/10gc066.PDF

Hall, C., Schauerman, G., Ewing, R. and Brandner, B. (2007, May 5). *Securing the borders: Creation of the Border Patrol Auxiliary.* National Security Program, Kennedy School of Government, Harvard University. Retrieved October 10, 2013 from http://www.dtic.mil/dtic/tr/fulltext/u2/a476945.pdf

History. (2013). U.S. Marshals Service. Retrieved October 14, 2013 from http://www.usmarshals.gov/history/index.html

Kadlec, D. (2013, September 19). Giving back: How retiring boomers get the rush they crave. Retrieved October 18, 2013 from http://business.time.com/2013/09/19/giving-back-how-retiring-boomers-get-the-rush-they-crave/

Kastberg, S. (1998, August 2). Watching the water. *The Times Union* (A Special Promotional Supplement), Albany, NY, p. 8.

Lewis. E. (2014). History. Retrieved June 30, 2014 from http://www.vipd.gov.vi/About_Us/History.aspx

Morse, J. (2009, May 19). Police Reserve Corps in Washington attracts a wide variety of talent. Retrieved October 17, 2013 from http://newsblaze.com/story/20090519081527tsop.nb/topstory.html

ODMP. (2014). ODMP remembers. Retrieved June 30, 2014 from http://www.odmp.org/officer/8190-reserve-officer-helen-kuulei-lizama#ixzz368UsHHsz

Olin, C. (2001, December 20). An approximate synopsis of multi-mission and overall volunteer effort as of 12/7/02. *U.S. Coast Guard Auxiliary National Bridge Page.* Retrieved January 1, 2002 from http://www.cgaux.org/cgauxweb/memtable.shtml

Operation Golden Eagle. (2002, January 4). Operation golden eagle tops 150,000 hours. Retrieved January 7, 2002 from http://www.cgaux.org/cgauxweb/memtable.shtml

Peconic Bay PS. (2013). Education – public courses. Retrieved October 16, 2013 from http://www.pbps.us/education/public/abc3.html

Puerto Rico Police Act of 1996. (2012). Puerto Rico Police Act of 1996 as amended; rev. May 9, 2012. Retrieved June 27, 2014 from http://www2.pr.gov/presupuestos/Budget_2012_2013/Aprobado2013Ingles/suppdocs/baselegal_ingles/040/040.pdf

Reilly, G. T. (2014, January 27). 29 police reserve officers graduate, total grows to 100. Retrieved June 30, 2014 from http://mvguam.com/local/news/33314-29-police-reserve-officers-graduate-total-grows-to-100.html

Requirements. (2013). Requirements to become a reservist. Retrieved October 17, 2013 from https://faq.fema.gov/app/answers/detail/a_id/1016/related/1

Reservist Applicants. (2013). Reservist applicants' desired skills. Retrieved October 17, 2013 from https://faq.fema.gov/app/answers/detail/a_id/1020/session/L3Rpb WUvMTM4MjA1MTYyNi9zaWQvQnhBYk0yRGw%3D

Sablan, J. (2012, December 31). 25 police reservists sworn in. Retrieved June 30, 2014 from http://www.guampdn.com/article/20121231/NEWS01/212310301/ 25-police-reservists-sworn-in

Shea, D. (2010, May 15). 32 new officers finish police academy. Retrieved June 30, 2014 from http://virginislandsdailynews.com/news/32-new-officers-finish-police-academy-1.790578

Sims, B. (2007). 'The day after the hurricane': Infrastructure, order, and the New Orleans Police Department's response to Hurricane Katrina. *Social Studies of Science, 37*(1), 111–118.

Taitano, Z. (2012, March 23). GPD swears in civilian volunteer police reservists. Retrieved June 30, 2014 from http://www.mvguam.com/local/news/22826-gpd-swears-in-civilian-volunteer-police-reservists.html

Tilley, J. (2003). *History of the U.S. Coast Guard Auxiliary.* Retrieved July 1, 2003 from http://www.cgaux.org/cgauxweb/news/auxhist.html

Tocqueville, A. D. (1835–1990). *Democracy in America: Volume I.* New York: Vintage Books.

Torre, M. (2011, October 28). A citizen-centric report for Guam Police Department. Retrieved June 30, 2014 from http://www.guamopa.org/docs/2010/official-citizen-centric-report/Guam%20Police%20Department%20(GPD)%20FY%20 2008-2010%20CCR.pdf

Uchida, C. D. (2004, December). The development of the American Police: An historical overview. Retrieved August 16, 2011 from http://www.globalcitizen.net/ Data/Pages/1418/Papers/2009042815114290.pdf

U.S. Virgin Islands. (2014). United States Virgin Islands. Retrieved July 1, 2014 from http://www.infoplease.com/country/us-virgin-islands.html

Vass, J. E. (2011, March 24). Youth policy. Retrieved October 17, 2003 from http:// bdept.cgaux.org/wp/wp-content/uploads/2012/11/Youth_Training_Letter.pdf

VIPD. (2014a). Police auxiliary service. Retrieved June 30, 2014 from http://www. vipd.gov.vi/Employment/Police_Auxiliary_Service.aspx

VIPD. (2014b). Police commissioner activates law enforcement personnel. Retrieved June 30, 2014 from http://www.vipd.gov.vi/Public_Interest/Press_Releases/ show_press_release_xml.aspx?id=2008-235&month=10

VIPD. (2014c). Connecting with youth. Retrieved June 30, 2014 from http://www. vipd.gov.vi/Libraries/PDF_Library/VIPD_Informant_Newsletter_v2_1_2012-2013.sflb.ashx

Williams, C. (2010, March 2). D.C. police call on reserves to boost community presence. Retrieved October 17, 2013 from http://voices.washingtonpost.com/ crime-scene/clarence-williams/dc-police-calling-on-their-res.html

# Special Issues in Volunteer Policing

# Non-Sworn Roles of Adults in Volunteer Policing

# 7

Congratulations graduates, I commend each of you for taking the time away from your schedules and families to participate in the Citizen Police Academy and for becoming a vital part of the police department!

**—Chief John M. Young Jr.**
*Kerrville (Texas) PD, The 7th CPA Graduation, October 21, 2010*

## Introduction

During America's colonial period, there was a general understanding about significant values and norms because communities were small and composed of close-knit families. Most individuals adhered to the local rules of social order because snooping neighbors and members of the local church and clergy were ever-watchful for any deviance from societal customs. For the few who transgressed and were discovered, various shaming rituals were used to encourage conformity to societal rules (Walker 1998). Moreover, newly arrived families to New England were headed by men whose authority was reinforced by the divinely ordained hierarchy in which they believed (Norton 1996, 13). This earlier form of "morality policing" has given way to today's more formal and complicated system of social controls involving an array of institutions beyond the family, clergy, and curious neighbors. The most visible of these newer social institutions consist of the components of the criminal justice system, especially the uniformed members of local police agencies and the nearly 50,000 security officers employed by the federal Transportation Security Administration (TSA). The TSA workforce was recruited to help protect America's transportation infrastructure from terrorist attacks and to ensure freedom of movement for people and commerce (TSA 2014).

In September 2011, Eric Anderson, assistant city attorney for the city of Scottsdale, Arizona, appeared before his city's Parks and Recreation Commission. He was asked to comment on the fact that budget cuts had eliminated a police patrol unit that had been assigned to cover skate parks. He replied that the city's "legal responsibilities for a skate park are the same as they are for the regular parks; generally, the City is not a guarantor of safety just like having a Police Department is not a guarantor of no crime" (City of Scottsdale 2011). Due to America's falling tax revenues arising from a declining economy, it is likely that this same scenario has taken place in many communities. According to the U.S. Department of Justice, "Police agencies are some of the hardest hit by the current economic climate. Curtailing revenues nationwide have forced local governments to make cuts in spending across the board, which includes public safety operating budgets. While budget cuts threaten the jobs of law enforcement officers, the duties and responsibilities to ensure public safety remain" (Economic Downturn 2011, 3). The Major Cities Chiefs Association found that 52% of agencies surveyed had furloughed sworn officers (McFarland 2010). Agencies have used a number of techniques to reduce their personnel costs. Layoffs, mandatory furloughs, and loss of positions through attrition have taken place as the result of these budget reductions in many police agencies. Therefore, it is not surprising that the need for alternative resources is on the agenda of many governmental agencies.

More and more agencies are turning to technology to offset the lack of human resources. For example, certain technologies such as closed-circuit televisions (CCTVs) and light-based intervention systems (LBIS) can act as force multipliers through incident intervention and crime prevention, without requiring the immediate presence of an officer (Cordero 2011). Moreover, other technological breakthroughs are being used to increase officer effectiveness and efficiency such as reducing police response times to emergency calls. For example, the tactical automatic vehicle locator (TAC-AVL) indicates to police supervisors the locations of patrol cars with a real-time map of the city, allowing them to determine whether the vehicles are in the right place at the right time. TAC-AVL enables a supervisor to see the type of call to which an officer is responding, how long the officer has been on the call, the result of the call, and whether nearby zones are understaffed (Mayer 2009).

In addition to using new technology, alternative human resources are also being used by more and more police agencies. In many agencies, responsibilities that were once performed by sworn staff have been shifted to civilian personnel, and some agencies have even engaged citizen volunteers to help alleviate the strain on police workloads. Such approaches can provide sworn staff with more time to focus on pressing and time-sensitive issues that can only be successfully managed by a law enforcement officer. Chapter 2 provides additional information concerning civilianization in police agencies.

Furthermore, in order to fulfill their public safety mission, hundreds of police agencies in the United States have turned to the general public for help. Volunteers in Police Service (VIPS) is now a major program within the International Association of Chiefs of Police (IACP). It has become a common practice among many of the nation's law enforcement agencies to have civilians volunteering their time in a variety of roles inside and outside of station houses. A list of non-sworn roles involving public safety is presented in Box 7.1. Volunteers can be recruited for each of these positions.

---

**BOX 7.1   TYPICAL CIVILIAN/NON-SWORN
LAW ENFORCEMENT POSITIONS**

Civilian Investigators
Correctional Staff
Crime Analysts
Crime Prevention/Community Outreach
Dispatchers/Call Takers
Equipment/Fleet Management
Forensic Technicians
Information Technology Specialists
Intelligence Analysts
Planners/Researchers
Property/Evidence Management
Public Information Officers
Records Management
Victim Services Providers/Advocates

*Source:* http://discoverpolicing.org/whats_like/?fa=civilian_alternatives

---

Due to ongoing technological advances in crime-fighting equipment such as in-car mobile data terminals (MDTs), computerized mapping, digital video, and wireless communication, there is a high demand for qualified information technology (IT) professionals and volunteers in police agencies.

This chapter describes a few of the non-sworn or non-peace officer roles that are currently being performed by volunteers. In addition, a brief review of a variety of adult Citizens' Police Academy (CPA) programs is presented as well as their advantages and disadvantages. Finally, a new role is described for existing members of volunteer police units as "neighborhood police academy" instructors.

## Volunteers in Police Service

One of the hundreds of programs registered at the older IACP's VIPS program Web site is administered by the Pasadena (California) Police Department (PD). Pasadena is located 10 miles northeast of downtown Los Angeles. It is a richly diverse community. About 56% of Pasadena's approximately 140,000 residents are white, 33% are Latino, 13.4% are African American, and 12.7% are Asian. The word Pasadena literally means "valley" in the Ojibwa (Chippewa) Indian language (Pasadena Facts 2014). In addition to the deployment of reserve police officers (sworn positions), the Pasadena PD has recruited citizen volunteers since 1984. The use of volunteers is viewed as an integral part of the department's efforts to use the community policing model. The Pasadena PD has attempted to integrate volunteers into the Department's overall operations. A "Volunteer Services" office coordinates the various opportunities for service with the Department (Pasadena PD 2013).

The Pasadena PD volunteers contribute their time and efforts through the following areas of service: chaplains, Citizens Assisting Pasadena Police (CAPP) patrol, equestrians, Community Response to Eradicate and Deter Identity Theft (CREDIT), Missing Persons Unit (MPU), Pawn Detail, Criminal Investigations Division's Victim Assistance, Records and Traffic sections, general volunteers, and Youth Accountability Board (YAB). The agency also sponsors a Law Enforcement Explorer unit, which includes a 22-week Explorer Academy (Pasadena PD 2013).

In 2013, the Pasadena PD had approximately 200 active volunteers. Their responsibilities included patrolling streets and parklands; providing pastoral care for officers, staff, and related family; leading volunteer programs; assisting in the investigation of identity theft and missing persons; assisting with security for the annual Tournament of Roses Parade; participating in Police Activities League (PAL) programs; providing clerical assistance; providing guidance and support to first-time juvenile offenders; and working side-by-side with sworn and non-sworn staff whenever and however needed (Pasadena PD 2013). Today, about one million people come to Pasadena to watch the Tournament of Roses. The parade was first held in 1890 (Pasadena Facts 2014).

Volunteers are integrated into most areas of Pasadena's police operations. When volunteers have completed the application process and been accepted, they can immediately begin to participate in the general volunteer program as jobs become available. Other programs may have additional training and requirements for their participants. Police volunteers may serve in more than one program upon meeting the specific criteria for the additional program.

The following brief sections describe the various volunteer areas and activities involving non-sworn Pasadena police volunteers. The information is presented to illustrate the wide range of services that volunteers can provide without the requirement of attending a lengthy and costly law enforcement training academy program.

## Volunteer Services Steering Committee

The Volunteer Services Steering Committee provides leadership in developing the department's volunteer programs and in coordinating the participants in each program. Committee members help to prepare an operations manual, volunteer handbook, and additional protocols and policies to enhance the delivery of volunteer services (Pasadena PD 2013).

# Chaplain Corp

The chaplains group is made up of ordained clergy from established and recognized faiths within the community. The chaplains serve in situations that involve death, serious injuries, suicide, and domestic violence. The chaplains console family members and offer guidance and support while leaving the officer available to focus on the police investigation. The chaplains are on a prearranged "on call" schedule and are required to respond to emergency situations upon request (Pasadena PD 2013).

# Citizens Assisting Pasadena Police

CAPP members are extra "eyes and ears" for the department. CAPP members drive designated white volunteer cars, wear department-approved uniforms, and must be able to communicate using a radio. Some of their duties are crime prevention, patrol, assisting at driving under the influence of drug (DUI) checkpoints; traffic control for requested incidents; 24-hour call out for emergencies; park safety; radar, stop sign, and red light surveys; quality of life issues; residential vacation checks; graffiti reporting; Safe Shopping Detail and Parade Watch during the holiday season; and many other activities. CAPP members are required to complete eight hours of service a month and to participate in their unit meetings and training (Pasadena PD 2013).

# Safe Shopping Detail

The Safe Shopping Detail was established to patrol shopping areas from Thanksgiving to Christmas to reduce crime during the peak holiday season. Participants are given training, and then patrols are formed by having a general volunteer accompany a CAPP member on foot patrols of key shopping areas in Pasadena (Pasadena PD 2013).

# Parade Watch

One of the department's most important activities is Parade Watch (which was established as a direct result of the terrorist attack of September 11, 2001) to enhance the overall safety of the annual Tournament of Roses Parade by using volunteers to contact all recreational vehicle owners staged along the parade route to solicit their assistance in reporting any suspicious activity or persons. Graduates of the department's CPA may sign up to participate in this annual event. Participants are given training and then go into the field in groups with active volunteers to contact all recreational vehicle drivers in the area surrounding the Rose Parade (Pasadena PD 2013).

## Volunteer Equestrian (Mounted) Unit

The Equestrian Unit provides uniformed patrol and surveillance in the Arroyo Seco Recreation Area and in the foothills of Pasadena, providing high police visibility in an area largely secluded from public view. The unit reports violations and other circumstances that may be a threat to public safety. The Volunteer Mounted (Equestrian) Unit was originally formed to assist at the Rose Bowl in patrolling parking lots during the 1984 Olympics. It was formalized and adopted by the police department in 1985 when the department recognized the need for passive patrol in the remote hiking and riding trail areas not readily accessible by patrol units. Since then, Volunteer Mounted Unit members have donated thousands of hours creating a police presence and providing an important link between the department and the community that uses the parks. Requirements for participating in this volunteer activity include riding skills, access to a serviceably sound horse and tack (ownership not required), a background check, completion of the department's CPA, and certification in first aid/cardiopulmonary resuscitation (CPR). Volunteers are required to complete 12 hours of service a month and to participate in unit meetings and training. They must also be at least 21 years old and are required to satisfactorily complete 24 hours of patrol ride-along (Pasadena Mounted Unit 2013).

## Missing Persons Unit

Volunteers in this unit assist the department's detectives by helping to conduct missing person's investigations (Pasadena PD 2013).

## Community Response to Eradicate and Deter Identity Theft

In this program, volunteers assist victims of identity theft by conducting investigations in fraud, sending letters to various financial entities, contacting outside jurisdictions, and collecting evidence (Pasadena PD 2013).

## General Volunteers

The general volunteers are individuals who desire to help the department in a variety of capacities but who prefer to work inside the department or for special events rather than going out on patrol. They are called on for clerical work, filing, staffing department and community events, participating in the Safe Shopping Detail and Parade Watch during the holiday season, participating in PAL activities, staffing the front desk, participating on disciplinary review boards (DRBs), and other activities (Pasadena PD 2013).

General volunteers may also assist with such special events as the Safe Shopping Detail over the Christmas holiday, car show, National Night Out, CPA classes, police awards luncheon, Take Your Child To Work Day, Truancy Programs, Park Watch, Traffic Rodeo, Helicopter Fly In, Neighborhood Watch events, crime prevention and service area meetings, and other special or community events. There are also opportunities to help with PAL activities and to participate on DRBs, oral boards, and promotion boards. By serving as members of these boards, citizens attend various hearings for the purpose of advising on matters concerning critical disciplinary and promotional decisions (City of Pasadena 2013).

## Youth Accountability Board

YABs are made up of adult community volunteers that hear and resolve cases involving first-time offenders deemed most amenable to rehabilitative measures. The offenders volunteer to appear before the YAB and allow it to determine their "sentences," usually in the form of contracts for restitution and community service time. In exchange for successfully completing the program, the record of the offense is eliminated. If the youth fails to complete the commitment to the board, the case is referred back for normal processing through the juvenile court system. Once a volunteer is appointed to the YAB, he/she will receive training in basic legal concepts, juvenile justice issues, theories relating to youth accountability, and issues of confidentiality and liability. Boards are usually held during evening sessions, and various time commitments are required (Pasadena PD 2013).

## Adult Police Academies

In the United States, the concept of the "Junior Police Academy" (see Chapter 8) might be considered to be the forerunner of the adult "Citizen Police Academy". However, several authors have attributed America's CPA initiatives to the efforts of the United Kingdom's Devon and Cornwall Constabulary when it created a "Police Night School" for the public in 1977. In the United States, the first adult CPA took place in 1985 when the Orlando (Florida) Police Department instituted such a program. In that same year, Missouri City, Texas, duplicated the effort. Subsequently, the practice has become a regular and featured program for educating citizens about police work throughout the nation (Ferguson 1985).

A CPA is an educational and informative program that allows citizens the opportunity to learn about the issues that face law enforcement efforts in their community. The program helps local residents better understand police work in their community, and it is also thought to promote stronger ties between communities and their respective police agencies. CPA programs do not train individuals to be reserve or auxiliary police officers, but they do produce better informed citizens. They may provide a forum in which community members and police officers are able to meet with one another to share mutual concerns. In such a setting, it is possible to forge stronger citizen–police relationships and to open new lines of communication. Information from citizens about crime problems and suspects is necessary in order to reduce crime.

Such citizen–police contacts and participation may expand community-based crime prevention efforts and offer police departments the opportunity to learn about the concerns of their communities (Breen and Johnson 2007; Brewster et al. 2005). However, it is more important for academy instructors to focus on crime prevention topics rather than public relations (Greenberg 1991).

## Pasadena CPA

In Pasadena, the CPA is an informative, 12-week classroom series that gives an inside look at Pasadena police operations while discussing the principles of community policing. Its stated purpose is to promote a greater awareness and better understanding of local law enforcement's continuously changing role in the community. Accordingly, the class covers a wide variety of subject areas including police communications, criminal law and procedures (laws of arrest), street crime enforcement, investigations, field identification, weaponless defense training, youth programs, and more. The course concludes with a graduation dinner, where students receive a certificate of completion. Requirements for participation include: 18 years of age; live, work, or own property in Pasadena; no felony convictions; and no misdemeanor convictions within one year of application (Pasadena CPA 2013).

## University of Kentucky CPA

The University of Kentucky's Police Department program is typical of many such programs. It is offered in seven or eight weekly three-hour classes, and participants take part in a formal graduation ceremony. There is no cost for participants (University of Kentucky PD 2012).

## Buffalo Grove (Illinois) CPA

The village of Buffalo Grove (10 square miles, population 41,500) is located only 30 miles outside of downtown Chicago, in its northwest suburbs. O'Hare International Airport, one of the world's busiest, is a 25-minute drive from the village. Residents there have a median household income of $88,272 (Buffalo Grove 2012b). The Buffalo Grove Police Department began its CPA in 1997. For a period of eight weekly classes, the CPA covers the use of Radio Detection and Ranging (RADAR) and Light Detection and Ranging (LIDAR) units in speed enforcement, traffic crash investigation, crime scene processing, and crimes against property and person(s), and it provides an Emergency Dispatch Center tour, firearms safety, and so forth (Buffalo Grove 2012a). The Illinois Citizens Police Academy Association has published a quarterly newsletter since March 2007 (Web site at: http://www.illinoiscpaa.org/). The Web site has links for useful brochures, alumni association bylaws, class schedules, and application and waiver forms from local CPAs.[1]

## Ponca City (Oklahoma) CPA

In Oklahoma, the city of Ponca City[2] holds an annual 13-week academy to acquaint participating citizens with all aspects of the work of its police department. Through an active alumni association, it offers CPA graduates opportunities to continue their interest and involvement in the department by volunteering in an "extra eyes" program. Such volunteers receive extra training and perform work that enables regular police officers to get back to the street more quickly, saving the taxpayers' money (City of Ponca City 2012).

## Ponca City Police Foundation Trust

Many police departments have also involved citizens in the establishment of police foundations. Such foundations are independent fundraising nonprofit corporations. The Ponca City Police Foundation Trust was organized in 2000 to financially supplement and benefit the entire community and to help keep Ponca City safe and secure. The Ponca City Police Department was the first within the state of Oklahoma to have dedicated citizens develop a police foundation on the department's behalf. Following are a few of the foundation's goals that are typical of other police foundations: assist with special equipment needs that are outside the normal department budget; provide a financial death benefit to families of active members of the police department who pass away; provide scholarship opportunities for Ponca City police officers; provide scholarship opportunities for Ponca City youth interested in pursuing a career in law enforcement; support advanced law enforcement training opportunities; support police training for members of the community as well as paid members of the police department; support the CPA and related alumni events; and support the Youth Police Academy (City of Ponca City 2012).

## Texas CPA Survey

In 1994, a survey was conducted to determine the number and nature of the citizen academies being conducted in Texas. The earliest academy implemented in Texas was in 1985. The survey indicated that, by the spring of 1994, more than 4,000 Texas citizens had attended such a program and that departmental classes were generally offered two times per year, with 27 students per class. The average academy met once each week for 11 weeks, three hours each session. The purpose, cited by 22 agencies, for conducting a program was the education of the citizens concerning the operations, policies, and procedures of the police department. Another often cited reason was the promotion of communication between the citizens and members of the police agency in an effort to improve relations. Other reasons included dispelling myths and preconceptions that the public may have concerning police work, enlisting the aid of the citizens in the prevention of crime, and promoting support of the police department and the city. Topics taught at the Texas CPAs ranged from traditional police activities such as accident investigation and crime scene investigation to newer, less traditional areas such as victim services, cults, gangs, and police stress and trauma counseling. Some agencies recommended that every police division or unit be discussed and reviewed (Blackwood 1994).

The Texas survey also gathered data about the amount spent annually by police agencies for conducting academies. This amount ranged from no departmental funds to $6,000. The agency that did not spend departmental money charged tuition. The average amount spent by agencies that did not include personnel costs was $1,600. The agencies that included personnel costs averaged $3,500 per year. These agencies reported that personnel costs consumed the largest portion of the program's budget. Several agencies used alternative sources of funding. These sources included alumni associations, citizen contributions, grants, and asset forfeitures (Blackwood 1994).

In addition, the Texas sample also revealed that police departments used a variety of methods to recruit and screen participants. The most popular method for recruitment was by word of mouth, including alumni.

Other methods for recruitment included announcements at community service clubs, neighborhood or city newsletters, flyers at the station or sub-stations, utility billing supplements, and speaking engagements by agency personnel. Requirements for attendance at the academies also varied. Some agencies allowed high school students to attend, while others had a minimum age of 21 years. A criminal history check was required by some of the agencies (Blackwood 1994). A major finding of this survey was that "all responding agencies surveyed recommended that other agencies should implement a CPA, if they haven't already done so" (Blackwood 1994, 7).

## Advantages of CPAs

In one study of the effects of a CPA on a large city in Texas, 25 graduates (experimental subjects) and 30 students entering the program (controls) were compared. Overall, compared to controls, the experimental group held more positive opinions of and demonstrated higher levels of satisfaction with the police department in all areas, including response to specific neighborhood problems, overall performance at combating and preventing crime, police image, and police services. The graduates also appeared to have a broader understanding of police work, as well as a greater appreciation and respect for officers. Furthermore, they reported significantly higher levels of involvement in crime prevention efforts than controls (Stone and Champeny 2001). Positive findings were also obtained in a study involving the attitudes of 48 attendees who completed a 12-week/36-hour program at a sheriff's department in the state of Michigan. Based on the analysis of pre- and post test responses, this study found that this particular CPA had a positive impact on the attendees' attitudes toward the police, and on their understanding of police operations, crime, and quality of life issues in their community (Breen and Johnson 2007). There were also positive outcomes in a study that compared attitudes using pre- and post tests involving citizen academies in two different cities (Brewster et al. 2005).

According to Aryani et al. (2000, 21), "Citizen police academies represent a vital part of community-oriented policing. CPAs keep the public involved by making them part of the police family … [and] provide a productive outlet for the mutual sharing of information and concerns in order to further common goals of communities and law enforcement agencies." Generally, citizen academies offer at least two additional positive benefits: (1) citizens gain a better understanding of how their police department works and (2) graduates interested in continuing their involvement in police-related activities may have the option of joining various law enforcement-related volunteer programs such as the CPA Alumni Association, Citizens on Patrol, Community Emergency Response Team, Neighborhood Watch, and VIPS.

Interested citizens bring a wealth of knowledge about their community and, particularly, the problems in their neighborhoods. In this way, agency personnel are able to learn firsthand about the concerns of citizens. Some participants may want to take a more active role in helping to reduce crime by contributing a service or by serving as a volunteer. For example, a bank executive who participated in a CPA offered to include crime prevention messages in monthly statements mailed to depositors (Seelmeyer 1987).

## Disadvantages of CPAs

Although citizen academies may have their advantages, they also have their disadvantages. For example, the programs may reach only a small number of residents. Research studies indicate that academies may be held only once or twice a year. Moreover, enrollment may be restricted to only 30 attendees at a time. In addition, the public relations aspects might be overplayed, reducing details about the ability of the criminal justice system to contend with crime and the need for private citizens to engage in array of crime prevention activities. At the same time, the planning for each academy, such as preparing the curriculum and screening applicants, might detract from the time and resources devoted to essential police work. In addition, local liability considerations may limit or eliminate high-interest activities, such as firearms instruction and ride-alongs. Although the expenditures needed to maintain a CPA are supposedly minimal, instruction may be costly if volunteer instructors are unavailable. Individual instruction may be needed for each student while on the firing range.

The Lansing (Michigan) Police Department held its first academy in the spring of 1996. Since then, they have held two CPA sessions each year. A Lansing police officer recruited the initial academy class from Neighborhood Watch coordinators, and the department has advertised subsequent classes in the local paper. Based on a review of the results of an in-house survey of Lansing's existing CPA, Bonello and Schafer (2002, P. 23) concluded: "Reaching out to citizens who are distrustful or skeptical of law enforcement and inviting them to take a closer look at police operations can prove intimidating and even unpleasant, but the rewards for doing so may be worth the effort. For agencies hoping to strengthen community alliances, the challenge for the future is to begin including a broader range of the public in their citizen police academy programs. Every department can identify groups within their community with which they have a history of misunderstandings and conflict. Departments should seek to draw academy participants from this portion of the community."

Police departments also need to maintain citizen interest when the academy ends. This is difficult unless follow-up activities are planned.

A few months after completing the academy, some participants may be disappointed if all they have to show for their efforts are a cap or T-shirt, a certificate, and memories. Departments need to develop meaningful activities after the academy has ended.

Academies could also turn into victims of their own success. Participants could become so overzealous in their concern for justice that they engage in conduct that undermines departmental policies and programs (e.g., establishing a vigilante-type neighborhood patrol organization). Another area of concern is the number of requests for crime prevention speakers and home and business security surveys that academy participation may generate. Although this is not a disadvantage per se, such requests could overburden officers by increasing their workload.

Although these disadvantages are quite real and there may always be some agency personnel who may be resistant to the idea of sharing information or enlisting the aid of citizens in the prevention of crime, the weight of the arguments appear to favor the use of citizen academies (Blackwood 1994; Breen and Johnson 2007; Brewster et al. 2005; Cohn 1996; Stone and Champeny 2001). The assistance of qualified volunteer police can help to eliminate several disadvantages of critical importance.

## Overcoming the Disadvantages of CPAs

In the United States, the existence of hundreds of CPAs demonstrates a willingness on the part of local police departments to share information with the general public. However, the weight of the evidence shows that the reach of these classes is limited. The concepts shared during academy sessions, especially those involving crime prevention methods, need to be shared with larger segments of the population. CPAs have been held for over a quarter of a century; new delivery systems should be tried, especially in more populous metropolitan areas. The primary mode of instruction has been face to face. The computer age can extend the reach of useful personal safety information and the importance for citizen cooperation.

However, achieving the support and cooperation of diverse segments of a metropolitan population will require more than an annual course or two. Hybrid academy courses involving online instruction coupled with various hands-on experiences are a better approach to reach the masses. Police codes and critical "insider" information do not have to be shared to provide an effective program. Moreover, to save the expenses associated with the personnel costs of instruction, it would be appropriate for urban and suburban police departments to use their resources to train and certify classes of citizen volunteer police instructors who would then, in turn, become qualified to offer a series of continuous free "academy style" courses to the public.

This would allow all age groups, sooner or later, to learn a variety of self-help skills. Such classes could be delivered in the traditional face to face format as well as using the hybrid model.

Moreover, because graduates of the proposed certification program are expected to become future teachers of CPAs, concern about follow-up activities should be diminished. If a "train the trainer" course for volunteer police is substituted for the existing one or two annual citizen academies in urban areas, the overall purpose of the citizen academies may be multiplied. By offering this instructional training to existing members of volunteer police units, police departments will still be able to maintain close supervision over the content that will be delivered.

The qualified volunteer police instructors will be able to extend the reach of the existing academies in such a way that a new term, such as the "neighborhood police academy," may come into usage. This term emphasizes the importance of people working together for the betterment of the community and seems to be a more accurate designation for the new and broader type of program envisioned here.

By converting various existing CPAs into "train the trainer" courses for qualifying volunteer police officers, many of the current disadvantages would be reduced. For example, the newly certified volunteer instructors would be highly motivated to concentrate on crime prevention topics and less likely to overemphasize public relations. In addition, their services can be used to develop new curriculum guides or to expand and revise current materials for diverse populations. They could also serve to augment the department's personnel resources as crime prevention speakers and home security inspectors.

Finally, volunteer police unit members who receive training for this new mission will help with VIPS program volunteer retention and recruitment because they will be participating in a highly meaningful role and will be in a position to inform others about their work as well as the numerous other roles for volunteers in police service.

## Summary

There was a time in American history when the morals of residents were policed by members of the community. Communities were smaller and family attachments strong. No one could be anonymous and punishments were swift. Society is no longer homogeneous, and America's huge metropolitan areas permit many persons to live in relative isolation unless they chose to publish aspects of their lives through social media. Responsibility for community security has shifted from the households on the block to the police station and a variety of other local, state, and federal agencies.

In times of economic decline, the resources of governmental departments become thinned and reliance on alternative resources is of vital importance. Since the attacks of September 11, 2001, there has been resurgence in a variety of existing volunteer organizations concerned with public safety. Moreover, the federal government has helped to stimulate the recruitment of volunteers through expanded Web site information, such as the VIPS program. The Pasadena PD has registered at the VIPS Web site, and a review of its programs may serve to illustrate the many types of opportunities available for neighborhood volunteer service with police agencies throughout the United States. Pasadena PD programs using volunteers include chaplains, CAPP patrol, equestrians, CREDIT, MPU, Pawn Detail, Criminal Investigations Division's Victim Assistance, Records and Traffic sections, general volunteers, and the YAB.

The Pasadena PD and hundreds of other agencies operate citizen academies concerned with law enforcement (e.g., the Federal Bureau of Investigation). The first CPA in the United States was established by the Orlando Police Department in 1985 and was modeled after a British program begun in 1977. Participants usually must pass a criminal and motor vehicle background check and must be fingerprinted. Classes are usually limited to 15–25 participants. They meet one evening a week for approximately three hours. The academies are free and last about 10 weeks. Topics cover an introduction to police operations, patrol, investigation, services, community services, special operations, road safety, criminal law and procedure, and communication. The advantages of a CPA include exposure to new perspectives and better understanding and positive and proactive contact between police and citizens. Potential limitations include possible lawsuits if a participant is killed or injured while attending, resistance among police officers or administrators, lack of resources to sponsor an academy, and the possibility that a graduate will use the information inappropriately.

Graduates of CPAs are not expected to provide any police services, but alumni groups are often established to provide information about further participation in police-related functions. If police departments are interested in reaching out to more community members, a program involving training volunteer police to instruct "neighborhood police academies" is recommended.

## Review Questions

1. Who policed the morals of colonial Americans?
2. How do police agencies cope when budgets are reduced?
3. Discuss how the Pasadena PD has attempted to integrate volunteers into its overall operations.
4. Describe two of the Pasadena PD volunteer programs.
5. State at least three purposes of Citizen Police Academies (CPAs).

6. Should community residents who have criminal backgrounds, but are now law-abiding, be eligible to attend CPAs? Discuss.
7. Search online to find at least two types of police volunteer programs involving non-sworn adults that are not listed in this chapter. Present the results of your search.
8. Search online to find out information about a CPA being offered near you. Indicate your findings.
9. List two advantages and two disadvantages of CPAs.
10. Discuss the nature of the author's recommendation regarding the establishment of "neighborhood police academies."

## Notes

1. Another association that publishes a newsletter about CPAs is the National Citizens Police Academy Association (NCPAA). The first formal election for NCPAA board members was held in Lombard, Illinois, in 1999. As of April 2012, this organization had a membership of 238 (National CPAA Directory 2012). For additional information about their history, conferences, and other activities, see: http://www.nationalcpaa.org.
2. The history of Ponca City is tied to the history of local American Indian communities, particularly its namesake, the Ponca Tribe of American Indians. They came to the area in 1877 from their traditional homelands in Nebraska and South Dakota. The experience of the Poncas reached a national audience in 1879 when Chief Standing Bear and 66 followers returned to Nebraska to bury his son. In the landmark decision *Standing Bear v. Crook*, Judge Elmer S. Dundy ruled that Indians were entitled to the rights guaranteed to citizens by the Constitution. This case had important repercussions because it opened the judicial system to Native Americans. For an outline of Ponca history see: http://www.poncacity.com/history/ponca_tribe.htm.

## References

Aryani, G. A., Garrett, T. D. and Alsabrook, C. L. (2000). The citizen police academy. *The FBI Law Enforcement Bulletin, 69*(5), 16–21.

Blackwood, B. (1994). Citizen police academies. *TELEMASP Monthly Bulletin, 1*(2), 1–8.

Bonello, E. M. and Schafer, J. A. (2002). Citizen police academies: Do they just entertain. *FBI Law Enforcement Bulletin, 71*(11), 19–23.

Breen, M. E. and Johnson, B. R. (2007). Citizen police academies: An analysis of enhanced police–community relations among citizen attendees. *The Police Journal, 80*(3), 246–266.

Brewster, J., Stoloff, M. and Sanders, N. (2005). Effectiveness of citizen police academies in changing the attitudes, beliefs, and behavior of citizen participants. *The American Journal of Criminal Justice, 30*(1), 21–34.

Buffalo Grove. (2012a). Academies. Retrieved May 18, 2012 from http://www.vbg.org/index.aspx?nid = 292

Buffalo Grove. (2012b). Demographics. Retrieved May 18, 2012 from http://www.vbg.org/index.aspx?nid = 142

City of Pasadena. (2013). Pasadena Police Department: Volunteer services. Retrieved September 25, 2013 from http://www.ci.pasadena.ca.us/police/Volunteer_Mission_Statement/

City of Ponca City. (2012). Community and volunteer involvement. Retrieved May 23, 2012 from http://www.poncacityok.gov/index.aspx?NID = 193

City of Scottsdale. (2011). City of Scottsdale, Parks and Recreation Commission, approved work study session summary minutes, September 7, 2011. Retrieved May 24, 2012 from http://www.scottsdaleaz.gov/Assets/documents/BoardAgendas/Parks/2011+Minutes/09-07-11_Approved_Work_Study_Session_Summary_Minutes.pdf

Cohn, E. G. (1996). The citizen police academy: A recipe for improving police-community relations. *Journal of Criminal Justice, 24*(3), 265–271.

Cordero, J. (2011). *Reducing the cost of quality of policing: Making community safety cost effective and sustainable.* NJLM Educational Foundation, Friends of Local Government Services, Vol. 3(1). Trenton, NJ: The Cordero Group.

Economic Downturn. (2011). *The impact of the economic downturn on American police agencies.* Washington, DC: U.S. Department of Justice, Office of Community Oriented Policing Services.

Ferguson, R. E. (1985). The citizen police academy. *FBI Law Enforcement Bulletin, 54*(9), 5–7.

Greenberg, M. A. (1991). Citizen police academies. *FBI Law Enforcement Bulletin, 60*(8), 10–13.

Mayer, A. (2009). Geospatial technology helps East Orange crack down on crime. *Geography & Public Safety, 1*(4), 8–9.

McFarland, C. (2010). *State of America's cities survey on jobs and the economy.* Washington, DC: National League of Cities, Center for Research and Innovation.

National CPAA Directory. (2012). Retrieved May 18, 2012 from http://www.nationalcpaa.org/pdf/MembersList_4_16_12.pdf

Norton, M. B. (1996). *Founding mothers and fathers: Gendered power and the forming of American society.* New York: Alfred A. Knopf.

Pasadena CPA. (2013). Citizen police academy. Retrieved September 26, 2013 from http://www.ci.pasadena.ca.us/police/citizen_police_academy/

Pasadena Facts. (2014). Retrieved January 22, 2014 from http://www.ci.pasadena.ca.us/Pasadena_Facts_and_Statistics/

Pasadena Mounted Unit. (2013). Mounted Volunteers Unit. Retrieved September 26, 2013 from http://www.ci.pasadena.ca.us/police/mounted_volunteers/

Pasadena PD. (2013). VIPS program. Retrieved September 25, 2013 from http://www.policevolunteers.org/programs/?fa = dis_pro_detail&id = 736

Seelmeyer, J. (1987). A citizen's police academy. *Law and Order, 35*(12), 26–29.

Stone, W. E. and Champeny, S. (2001). Assessing a citizen police academy. *Police Practice and Research, 2*(3), 219–241.

TSA. (2014). Careers. Retrieved March 2, 2014 from http://www.tsa.gov/careers

University of Kentucky PD. (2012). Welcome to the citizen police academy. Retrieved May 21, 2012 from http://www.uky.edu/Police/citizensacademy.html

Walker, S. A. (1998). *Popular justice: A history of American criminal justice* (2nd ed., Rev.). New York: Oxford University Press.

# Youth Involvement in Police Work

8

Effective school-to-work transition programs can combat the disillusionment of youths who are struggling to finish high school, making good on the promise that a diploma will lead to a stable and decent-paying job.

—**Jon Bright**
*(1992, 59)*

## Introduction

Since the 1960s, hundreds of U.S. police agencies have established Law Enforcement Explorer Posts. Today, "over 33,000 Explorers and 8,425 adult volunteers participate in Law Enforcement Exploring. The program highlights include: the National Law Enforcement Exploring Leadership Academies, ride-alongs, career achievement awards, National Law Enforcement Exploring Conferences, and scholarship opportunities" (Exploring 2014). The prototypes for this well-known contemporary youth program were established during the first quarter of the twentieth century when various units of "junior" or "boy police" as well as school boy safety patrols were sponsored by local police departments, public schools, and private schools. The youth photographed in Figure 8.1 were only playacting and did not belong to any "junior police" program in 1900; rather, they wore police costumes to welcome a visit by Rear Admiral William T. Sampson during a weeklong town celebration. However, when and where actual programs existed, they were highly publicized and deemed to be constructive alternatives to an unstructured street life. Such programs were organized in Chicago, Illinois; Berkeley, California; Council Bluffs, Iowa; Cincinnati, Ohio; and New York City, New York. The members of these early youth organizations received instruction in law enforcement and safety topics, thereby inaugurating the first "youth police academies." With the adoption of community policing during the last two decades of the twentieth century, programs embracing the earlier spirit of these efforts began to reemerge (LeConte 2012b). According to Pat Fuller, former chief of the Austin Independent School District (ISD) Police Department, "Our biggest problem is that the schools keep pulling our officers off of the campus to teach more classes. The students may not see it, but we do. And so do the schools—the

**Figure 8.1** Maynard, Massachusetts, Merchant's Week, May 14–19, 1900. Each day had a theme. May 16, 1900, was selected as the day to honor a visit by Rear Admiral William T. Sampson, the "Hero of Santiago" in the Spanish-American War. Boys from the town were dressed up in police uniforms to serve as members of his official escort. Other children, both boys and girls, were dressed up as marines. From left to right: Harrison Persons, Douglas Salisbury, Daniel Sullivan, James Ryan, Charles Dyson, and Raymond Veitch.[1] (Used with permission of the Maynard Historical Society.)

junior police academy (JPA) works. It supports a healthy and safe school environment, and we will continue to use it" (Fuller 2012).

The present chapter focuses on the establishment of five prominent youth programs: youth or junior police academies; junior police programs (e.g., Police Athletic Leagues, Explorers, cadets); school safety patrols; police academy magnet schools; and youth courts. In addition, the newest model for the delivery of police education and training for youth that was started in Los Angeles, the Police Orientation and Preparation Program (POPP), is also described. Short-term types of police-sponsored and/or school-based academy programs include: the crime scene investigation camp, the physical training or boot camp model involving at-risk youth, and more generalized programs of instruction with academic units of instruction. The efforts of safety patrollers are devoted to pedestrian safety near school crossings at elementary and middle schools. These safety patrol members may also be assigned to hallways and doorways at times of high levels of hallway traffic during the day. Other types of junior police programs are harder to pin down except to note that they tend to fall within a continuum beginning with the pursuit of recreational goals (e.g., Police Athletic Leagues) to those that perform a limited range of enforcement activities (e.g., crowd control).

The origins and purposes of the various programs are described. Many youth have been brought a step closer to becoming police officers or have been able to focus their studies and narrow their career goals because of their participation in these various types of programs. The topics of liability and insurance as well as youth protection from abuse are also considered. The chapter concludes with an overview of trends and recommendations regarding future developments in the field.

## Youth (Junior) Police Academies

The origin of youth (junior) police academies coincided with the advent of junior police in the first two decades of the twentieth century. By the 1930s, most of the early junior or boy police programs were transformed into Police Athletic (or Activities) Leagues (PAL). On occasion, police-related instruction was shared with youngsters. For example, one such mini "junior police academy" was instituted in the late 1940s in Birmingham, Alabama, as a regular feature of the city's recreation program. In 1949, it served 50 children aged 9–13. Various crime prevention demonstrations and investigatory procedures were presented by members of the Birmingham Police Department (Popular Activity 1949). Today, PAL is a national program with a membership exceeding 1.5 million children aged 6–18. More than 300 American law enforcement agencies in some 700 cities are running these programs (Hollywood Community 2013).

A typical example of a modern-day short-term JPA took place during a five-day period in June 2012 on the campus of Washington State Community College (WSCC) in Marietta, Ohio. Its goal was to provide students who are interested in a career in law enforcement or a related field with a hands-on view of the criminal justice system and its procedures. The only eligibility requirements involved a letter of interest and being in a grade from 9 through 12. Online publicity for the academy stated that "the Junior Police Academy is not a disciplinary, recreational, or underprivileged camp but is part of the summer camp program at WSCC" (WSCC 2012). It also indicated that a Level II Academy would be held on the campus the following week that was open to only those students entering grades 9 through 12 who had successfully completed the Level I Academy. Participants were to have the opportunity "to investigate, prepare, and present in mock court a crime that resembles a real life situation in which a 'judge' oversees the courtroom presentation and a jury decides guilt or innocence" (WSCC 2012).

Some communities, such as the village of Buffalo Grove, Illinois, offer both adult and youth academies. The village's junior academy is designed for students who are 12–15 years of age and who either live and/or attend school in Buffalo Grove. Following a national trend, this youth program was held in June after the end of the school year (Buffalo Grove 2012a). In addition to having to sign an injury liability release waiver, applicants were required to grant permission for a law enforcement records check. Participation could be denied to any applicant with a criminal arrest record (Buffalo Grove 2012b).

No doubt the popularity of such short-term academies fostered the creation of an online program known as the "JPA Content Lab." According to posted information on its home page, the site has developed its content in collaboration with an "Advisory Council, members of the law enforcement community and feedback from the cadets themselves" (LeConte 2012a). The site also indicates that "new lessons are currently being field tested in the Austin schools.... Everything here is a work in progress, not only in terms of content, but digital technology as well. We want to know what works with kids and web browsers! ... The information is current and will be updated on a regular basis. We encourage instructors to take full advantage of the program's new digital distribution by checking back from time to time for updates and new multimedia content. New units will be created based on events in the news, so instructor's can provide a timely discussion of the issues that impact youth and our communities" (LeConte 2012a). Titles from its extensive list of free online lessons can be found in Box 8.1.

JPAs can be quite varied. A popular type focuses on the world of the crime scene investigator and is organized as a camp. This format was used by the South Bend (Indiana) Police Department in their weeklong June 2011 program. The campers practiced collecting fingerprints, laying mold on tire tracks, hunting for evidence, taking pictures of mock crime scenes, and digging up DNA samples. Students watched exercises conducted by the police Special Weapons and Tactics (SWAT) team and the K-9 unit. According to South Bend Police Lt. Richard Powers, "the whole idea is to give them a taste of what we do every day in our jobs" (Ferreira 2011).

Another format involves physical training as well as an extended delivery time frame for at-risk youth. This type of academy is conducted by the city of Burlington, North Carolina. It originated in 1996 and currently involves a collaborative effort by the Burlington Police Department, Graham Police Department, Alamance County Sheriff's Department, and the Alamance Burlington School System with a mission intended to provide at-risk middle school-aged juveniles social skills that can make them more productive students and citizens. Academy participants are mentored for the following school year by personnel associated with each participating law enforcement agency (City of Burlington 2012). They are referred to as "cadets" and are selected by law enforcement staff from students recommended by the Alamance Burlington School System. The cadets undergo a structured four-week training program, focusing on

**BOX 8.1   JUNIOR POLICE ACADEMY
CONTENT LAB LESSONS**

Introductory Units:
- Introduction to the Junior Police Academy
- History of Policing
- A Quick Guide to Being a Police Officer
- You're Under Arrest
- Hazards on Patrol
- Do You Have What It Takes?
- Patrolling the Streets

Careers in Law Enforcement:
- Law Enforcement in the United States
- FBI
- Sheriff
- K-9 Unit SWAT
- School Resource Officer
- Bomb Squad
- Secret Service
- Your Place in Law Enforcement
- Civilian Support

Citizens and Law Enforcement:
- Police and the Bill of Rights
- Do We Need Police to Be Happy?

Bullying Units:
- Cyber-Bullying
- Mastering Social Skills
- Reconnecting: Social Skills in the Internet Age
- Stop and Think: Social Survival Skills
- Stop Bullying: Take a Stand!

Technology Units:
- Crime Scene Investigation (CSI)
- The Secret Language of Police
- Police and Technology

*Source:* https://sites.google.com/site/jpacourse2012/introductory-units/ll

goal setting and self-esteem, conflict resolution and mediation, violence and substance abuse prevention, principles of law and justice, and decision-making skills. The first week of the academy is a 24-hour per day program where the participants and leaders are away from home. All other weeks are conducted at the training center in Haw River, North Carolina

(City of Burlington 2012). The cadets complete a community service project and a high and low ropes confidence course. Drills and physical fitness are used to develop teamwork and to maintain discipline. There is no cost to the cadets and their families for participating in the academy. Community donations are solicited to fund the various needs (food, clothing, etc.) of the academy in the form of cash, goods, and services from businesses, charitable organizations, and private citizens. The program's personnel, facilities, and transportation costs are funded by the agencies involved (City of Burlington 2012).

Avery Montgomery graduated from the Burlington Police Department's JPA in 2006. In July 2011, he returned to the academy as a guest speaker informing the academy cadets about how the academy had helped him make positive changes in his own life. He stressed those lessons from the academy "can help in all aspects of their lives" (Bost 2011).

A more generalized program that is held away from the homes of its participants is the Cadet Lawman Academy. In June 2012, it was held for seven consecutive days in Burns Flat, Oklahoma, at a former air force base. In 2011 and 2012, more than 200 young men and women completed these academies. Candidates for the program must be residents of Oklahoma, rising seniors, and in the top half of their class scholastically. In 1973, two Oklahoma Highway Patrol lieutenants visited Kansas to observe a similar program. It involved mostly classroom work with limited hands-on activities. The Cadet Lawman Academy was started in Oklahoma in 1974 and at that time was cosponsored by the Jaycees and the Oklahoma Highway Patrol—Safety Education Division. Later sponsors includes the Oklahoma State Troopers Association, the Oklahoma Highway Patrol, and the Oklahoma Elks. The current weeklong program includes training in precision driving, traffic and boating law enforcement, firearms instruction, self-defense, and law enforcement history. Activities also include a tour of the state reformatory in Granite, Oklahoma. This is a state prison that opened in 1910 and currently holds medium-level security prisoners. The cadets also participate in other tours and practical exercises (Cadet Lawman 2012). The 41st Cadet Lawman Academy was held in Burns Flat in June 2014.

## Junior Police

The rise of junior or youth police academies followed the reemergence of another type of youth program under the sponsorship of law enforcement or school agencies—junior police. The exact origins of junior police organizations may be clouded in time, but they appear to be based on the inclusion of military training as a school activity. For example, Rowbatham (1895) discusses the Rossall Corps of 1862, believed to be the first school in England to establish such a corps among its boys. Various photos of uniformed Rossall Corps members can be found in the four-page *Boy's Own Annual* article dated 1926, written by Captain H. V. Leonard and entitled "The Earliest Public School Volunteer Corps."

Coincidentally, also in the year 1862, the U.S. Congress passed The Morrill Act, which set aside 30,000 acres of public lands for public higher education. The land was then to be sold and the money from the sale of the land was to be put in an endowment fund that would provide support for the "land-grant" colleges in each of the states. Income from the sale of these lands has endowed liberal arts, engineering, agriculture, and military (officer) training at new colleges throughout the United States. The South's secession allowed northern progressives to pass this legislation. Eventually, the schools that were created offered new opportunities for education beyond high school, legislation that members of Congress from the slave-holding states had blocked. "The land-grant has improved the lives of millions of Americans. This was not the case in the early stages. At the time the grants were established, there was a separation of races. In the South, blacks were not allowed to attend the original land-grant institutions. There was a provision for separate but equal facilities, but only Mississippi and Kentucky set up any such institutions. This situation was rectified in 1890 when the Second Morrill Act was passed and expanded the system of grants to include black institutions" (Lightcap 2013). Historically, black land-grant institutions are located in 18 states, the District of Columbia and the U.S. Virgin Islands. (The complete list can be found at: http://www.aplu.org/page.aspx?pid = 1074.)

Virginia Polytechnic Institute and State University (Virginia Tech) was founded on October 1, 1872, as the Virginia Agricultural and Mechanical College (VAMC) in Blacksburg, Virginia. As a land-grant college, military training was mandatory for all able-bodied male students, so the student body was organized into a corps of cadets. A discussion of the establishment of collegiate level Reserve Officer Training Corps (ROTC) and the Junior ROTC is found in Chapter 9.

Junior police programs share many similarities with military schools. For example, in 1925, an advertisement placed in various publications by the Association of Military Colleges and Schools of the United States[2] stated: "The military schools of the country are not conducted primarily for the purpose of making army officers, but to make men. Sound scholarship and true development of the boy physically, mentally, and morally, constitute the fundamental principle of the military school … and carries into his life-work right ideals of citizenship and service" (Figure 8.2).

> # "Why send my boy to a Military School?"
>
> THE interested parent naturally asks this question. *"He does not intend to go into the Army or Navy. Why should I educate him in a military school?"*
>
> The answer follows quickly and naturally:
>
> The military schools of the country are not conducted primarily for the purpose of making army officers, but to make men.
>
> Sound scholarship and true development of the boy physically, mentally and morally, constitute the fundamental principle of the military school. Thorough preparation for college is provided. Also strong courses for those not going to college.
>
> Military training does not supplant or detract from the soundness of the academic work, but goes hand in hand with it. It serves
>
> —to develop initiative, self-control, self-reliance;
> —to secure punctuality, orderliness, efficiency;
> —to give erect carriage and manly bearing;
> —to develop the ability to think clearly and act promptly;
> —to promote a high personal standard of honor.
>
> These are not merely the attributes of the soldier. They are acquired in the military school, but they are the necessary qualifications of the successful, respected man in business life.
>
> One of our great Presidents said:
>
> "I am always glad to see the uniform worn in connection with education. To me it has a deeper meaning than an attribute of war. It means discipline, of course, but in addition it signifies that the man is not living for himself alone, but for the social life at large."
>
> The boy trained in the military school goes forth with a disciplined mind, and carries into his life-work right ideals of citizenship and service to his fellow men.
>
> The Association of Military Colleges and Schools of the United States invites your investigation of its members when choosing a school for your boy. Schools which are members of this association have met the requirements of the United States Government and have regular Army officers detailed as instructors in Military Science and Tactics.
>
> *Published by The Association of Military Colleges and Schools of the United States*

**Figure 8.2** Military Colleges and Schools advertisement, ca. 1925.

Junior police programs also provide opportunities for fostering positive relationships among younger citizens and for promoting activities associated with good citizenship. Various formats have been used in these programs, ranging in emphasis from recreational to enforcement. An example of the recreational type is PAL. At present, in New York City, more than 60,000 youth participate in PAL activities. An enforcement type of program existed in the city of Phoenix, Arizona, in the early 1940s. Only a single traffic police officer was assigned to school crossings. Instead of adult traffic officers, the city relied on a corps of junior police. They received uniforms from local organizations, and their authority to perform traffic duty came from the Phoenix Police Department. They watched school crossings, directed traffic, handed out tickets, and performed other tasks associated with traffic control (Greenberg 2008). Today, the successor organization to the 1940s Phoenix corps of junior police is the Phoenix Police Department's Explorer Post 2906. Established in 1973, members range in age from 14 to 21 (14 years old is acceptable only if the member has graduated from the eighth grade). The Phoenix Explorers have directed off-street traffic and parking, performed crowd control at parades, helped in neighborhood clean-up drives, and display crime prevention materials at local fairs (City of Phoenix 2013).

Historically, the largest municipal junior police program was established by Captain John Sweeney in New York City. In 1914, Sweeney commanded a lower East Side police precinct and created a youth program for boys, aged 11–16.[3] They had uniforms, participated in marching drills, and carried green and white flags. Modeled after the police hierarchy, the junior police inducted boys as patrolmen and promoted them up the ranks to chief inspector. Members attended meetings twice a week where they learned marching drills, participated in track meets and baseball games, enjoyed public swimming pools, and learned first aid, safety, and personal hygiene. At its peak, the program had an enrollment of 6,000 boys. A much smaller number of young women (approximately 50) were selected entirely on the basis of merit to work alongside their male counterparts. They routinely escorted younger children across busy streets, monitored dance halls so that underage girls would not enter, and helped to keep tenement fire escapes clear of debris. By 1917, the junior police had expanded to 32 precincts. Shortly thereafter, the program collapsed when Captain Sweeney retired from the police force and no other leader emerged or was appointed to take his place (Greenberg 2008). The titles of "junior police" or "boy police" are very rarely used anymore. Today, most of these programs use the titles of "Police Explorer" or "police cadet."

## Law Enforcement Exploring

The Law Enforcement Exploring program originated within the Exploring Division of the Boy Scouts of America (BSA). As early as 1959, there were Explorer posts specializing in law enforcement in Southern California. In 1976, the Exploring Division of the BSA received a one-year grant from the Law Enforcement Assistance Administration (LEAA) to enhance and promote Law Enforcement Exploring. This grant helped to create the National Law Enforcement Exploring Committee (NLEEC) and led to the appointment of a professional member of the national BSA staff as director of Law Enforcement Exploring. A membership drive was also conducted (Law Enforcement Exploring 2011).

Since 1998, Law Enforcement Explorer programs have been a cooperative venture between Learning for Life (an affiliate of the BSA) and hundreds of police agencies throughout the United States. These programs are designed to give young men and women between the ages of 14 and 21 a chance to find out more about law enforcement careers (Greenberg 2008). In some areas of the country, Explorers may go to an Explorer academy, similar to the junior or youth police academies. These are usually held during consecutive weekends or over weeklong retreats. However, unlike many junior academies, participants are more likely to receive physical training and to learn discipline, emulating regular police academies. Of course, any training and discipline regimen is conducted in an age-appropriate and abbreviated format, and opportunities for social developmental experiences are included in the program. The typical academy always ends with a graduation ceremony where attendance certificates, additional certifications (such as cardiopulmonary resuscitation certification), and other awards are given out. However, because Explorers are participants in an ongoing youth program, their experiences are more likely to have a lasting impact. This is especially true for those Explorer Post members who have the good fortunate to attend one or more of the biennial National Law Enforcement Exploring Conferences. Explorers who attend such a major event not only have the chance to interact with their peers from around the country but to enhance their own relationships with their fellow post members. National conferences are conducted every second year and attended by thousands of Law Enforcement Explorers and adult leaders. Tuition is charged, and space is limited. Young people come together for a week of team and individual competitions, seminars, demonstrations, exhibits, recreation, and fun. The 2012 conference was held at Colorado State University in Fort Collins, and the 2014 conference was held at the Bloomington campus of Indiana University.

The concept and use of the term "Exploring" dates back to at least 1922. Steadily, Law Enforcement Explorer Posts came into being. For example, in 1969, the St. Petersburg Law Enforcement Explorer Post 280 (now Post 980) was established (Figures 8.3 and 8.4). In 1971, young women were admitted

**Figure 8.3** Police Explorers Post 980 members engaged in training simulation exercise. (Used with the permission of the St. Petersburg (Florida) Police Department.)

**Figure 8.4** Police Explorers Post 980 members. Exploring provides the chance to work directly with police officers, go on ride-alongs, receive police training, meet new friends, and feel good about helping out in the community. (Used with the permission of the St. Petersburg (Florida) Police Department.)

to posts as determined by their chartering organization, and the upper age of Exploring was raised from 17 to 20. In that same year, there were at least 14 active units in the state of Florida with a focus on law enforcement, and a statewide organization was created to plan activities and to publish a newsletter (Folsom 1971). In 1976, members of Explorer Post 280 took a first-place award in a pistol match, competing against 14 other posts (Pistol Team Wins 1976). By the 1990s, girls made up about half of the entire Explorer membership nationwide (Greenberg 2008). By 2009, there were more than 2,000 Law Enforcement Explorer Posts in the United States; these posts accounted for about 35,000 of the group's 145,000 members worldwide (Steinhauer 2009). Various short online videos featuring information about Law Enforcement Exploring are available.[4]

Law Enforcement Explorer Posts have been established from Maine to California as well as in the state of Hawaii and in U.S. territories. Due to the creativity and initiative of police chiefs and mentors, many interesting and useful projects have been developed to engage post members. For example, the Westland Police Department in Michigan has established a "Sober-Up Program." It uses a golf cart with an extra safety break; the cart is marked to look like a Westland police car complete with flashing blue and red emergency lights. Cones, street signs, and various "fatal vision goggles" were also acquired. When worn, the goggles distort the vision of the participant showing them what they would see should they become impaired or intoxicated. A program participant drives the modified golf cart through an obstacle course while wearing the goggles. In this way, the participant and spectators learn what distorted vision does to a person's ability to safely operate a vehicle. The course is run by the Westland Police Explorers, who donate their time to educate community residents, and it has been brought to various community events as well as to the students of John Glenn High School (Westland Police 2012b).

Since 1996, the New York's Broome County Sheriff's Office has sponsored a Law Enforcement Explorer program, Post No. 100. Participant ages range from 14 to 20. In 2007, there were 15 students enrolled in the program.

Its purposes are to introduce youth to law enforcement careers and to the nature of the criminal justice system as well as to promote character development, self-esteem, and citizenship training among Broome County's youth. The program strives to present experiences that are challenging, thought-provoking, and essential to the development of young people interested in law enforcement (Broome County 2007).

The Explorers from Post 100 meet once a week for two hours. During this time, they receive training and instruction on child fingerprinting, traffic enforcement, crime scene investigation, officer survival, shoot/don't shoot, the use of force, the K-9 unit, criminal procedure law, domestic violence, and other topics. The Explorers are issued uniforms purchased with funds from grants, fundraising, and donations. They learn about career opportunities in law enforcement at the local, state, federal, and military levels while analyzing criminal justice college education requirements and visiting law enforcement training academies. They have the opportunity to assist sheriff's deputies in different training exercises, such as alcohol and tobacco stings. The sheriff's detectives partner with Explorers and take them to various business establishments to attempt to purchase cigarettes or alcohol. The purpose is to check these establishments for compliance with local and state laws regarding the sale of alcohol and tobacco products to anyone underage. Explorers are under the direct supervision of the detectives to ensure that problems do not occur. In Broome County, New York, the Endicott, Johnson City, and Vestal police departments have used the sheriff's Explorers to conduct similar investigations in their communities (Broome County 2007). Chapter 2 describes a similar program involving members of the New York City Auxiliary Police Force.

In February 2007, the Post 100 Explorers defended their title in the annual "Explorer Post Mall Show" by taking first-place honors for the eighth consecutive year. Their child fingerprinting exhibit processed more than 175 children. There were K-9 demonstrations as well as defensive tactics and handcuffing procedures. The Explorers also ran a 10-minute video that they produced highlighting the different topics that are covered in the Explorer program (Broome County 2007).

In 2007, the Post 100 Explorers worked more than 85 events including a balloon rally, a winter carnival, various runs, and other community gatherings. They also assisted with the sheriff's summer camp program. Traffic control, security, and child fingerprinting are a large portion of their additional community service activities. In October 2005, the Explorers were introduced to Operation Safe Child, assisting deputies in downloading information into a database and transmitting that information to the Division of Criminal Justice Services (DCJS). This data collection enhances the ability of law enforcement to locate missing or abducted children. By working these events each year, the Explorer program has reduced police overtime expenditures. An important purpose of these hands-on efforts is to help build a better working relationship and understanding between the youth and law enforcement officers. Members can be promoted to the ranks of sergeant and lieutenant after having demonstrated their progress in the program. Several unit members have acted as instructors, teaching search and rescue procedures to local Boy Scout troops, using course outlines and training they received while in the program. These undertakings have contributed to the program's success and have helped many of Broome County's youth come together to learn about law enforcement—how it affects them individually and also their community (Broome County 2007).

Explorer posts have also been established at many fire companies and some ambulance services. An example of the latter is the Henrietta Volunteer Ambulance Service in Upstate New York. The service began in 1963 with just one ambulance and 200 calls and has expanded today to a fleet of 10 vehicles and more than 5,800 calls annually. This Explorer post offers an opportunity for students to learn about the field of emergency medicine, medical procedures, lifesaving skills, and how to react in an emergency. Qualified members are eligible to participate in observation shifts aboard an ambulance (Henrietta Ambulance 2012). A combined four-page *Waterloo Police and Fire Explorer Handbook* contains a succinct list of rules including one that states: "Any misuse of learned tactics will be immediate grounds for termination" (Waterloo Handbook 2012, 1).

In addition, the 15 fire stations of the Aurora (Colorado) Fire Department have a Fire Exploring Program. (Its detailed 36-page *Explorer Program Operations Manual* can be found at: https://www.auroragov.org/cs/groups/public/documents/digitalmedia/002200.pdf.) The city of Aurora[5] has had a Law Enforcement Explorer Post since 1980 (Figures 8.5 and 8.6). Its alumni

**Figure 8.5** Aurora Law Enforcement Explorer Post 2024 member serving food at a community service event. The Post has approximately 35 members. (Used with the permission of the Aurora (Colorado) Police Department.)

**Figure 8.6** Aurora Law Enforcement Explorer Post 2024 members at a community service event. (Used with the permission of the Aurora (Colorado) Police Department.)

include more than two dozen current members of local, state, and federal law enforcement agencies (Police Explorers 2013). Explorers who excel in the program are eligible for leadership positions in the post. Post leaders plan and organize post functions. Explorers who complete eight hours of service or training each month have the opportunity to ride with a patrol officer and experience police operations in the field firsthand. Moreover, Aurora Post 2024 members who excel in the program are eligible to receive civil service preference points when they apply to become an Aurora police officer. The Aurora Police Explorer Post is NOT a "scared straight" or "second chance" program for juveniles with behavioral problems (Aurora Explorers 2014).

## Liability and Medical Insurance for Explorer Post Members and Advisors

Two critical concerns for any agency considering the sponsorship of a Law Enforcement Explorer Post are liability and insurance. Currently, any participating organizations are covered with primary general liability insurance. (A participating organization is defined as its board of directors and/or trustees, its officers and employees, in their official and individual capacity.)

This liability policy is primary except for automobiles or watercraft owned or used by the participating organization. In such cases, the general liability policy provides excess coverage.

If an Exploring volunteer is an employee of the participating organization, he or she is provided with primary liability coverage as long as Learning for Life guidelines are followed. A nonemployee (volunteer, parent, etc.) is provided with excess coverage. Most Explorer advisors (e.g., regular police officers) are employees of the participating partner; therefore, they have primary liability coverage, which covers the organization and its employees. However, it does not cover the youth in an Explorer post.

Accident insurance is the responsibility of individual Explorer posts and its leadership. Many local Exploring councils provide accident insurance to their youth members by collecting a small fee each year. If such an accident policy is not available or not provided, arrangements for assistance should be made through the local Exploring council office (Career Exploring FAQs 2013).

An example of a local Exploring council accident coverage for Learning for Life Explorers and adult volunteer leaders is the secondary "accident and sickness insurance" policy held by the Greater St. Louis Area Council. Their policy only covers individuals registered in the council. It covers them for accidents and sickness (as well as for accidental death and dismemberment) while they are participating in any official Scouting activity or Learning for Life Exploring activity. The council purchases this coverage annually from Health Special Risk. Benefits are in excess of any other insurance covering the individual. Accident medical benefits are limited to $15,000; sickness to $7,500; ambulance to $6,000. A copy of the Health Special Risk's Memorandum of Coverage is required for out-of-council resident camps. In addition, the "Boy Scouts of America general liability policy provides coverage for a bodily injury or property damage claim that is made and arises out of an Official Scouting Activity" (Insurance Information 2011).

## Youth Protection Issues

Since October 2009, it has been a felony in Florida to commit a battery[6] on a Law Enforcement Explorer in the line of duty. When the law was initially proposed, it was touted as providing the juvenile Explorers the same legal protection that officers have while on patrol (Wilmath 2008). This law may serve as a model for other states concerned with the safety and protection of their Law Enforcement Explorers.

It is an unpleasant fact that some Explorer post mentors/advisors have been charged with and/or convicted of Explorer member abuse. Learning for Life now requires the completion of a training program before adult volunteers can be assigned to work with youth. Accordingly, the Explorer movement has posted an online series of links under the heading of "Youth Protection Training" that can be accessed at: http://exploring.learningforlife. org/services/resources/youth-protection-training.

The preface to these materials states: "Youth safety is the No. 1 concern of Learning for Life. To increase awareness of the societal problem of child abuse, including sexual abuse, and to create even greater barriers to child abuse than currently exist, Learning for Life has implemented enhanced Youth Protection policies" (Youth Protection 2013). As of June 1, 2010, all registered adult Explorer volunteers, no matter what their position entails, must complete Youth Protection training prior to beginning their volunteer service and show proof of completion of the training. This training must be retaken every two years, and all registered adults in posts participating in summer activities (law enforcement conference, etc.) are required to take the Youth Protection training prior to participating in the event. The instruction can also be provided in a live format at the request of a concerned group. Moreover, every Explorer Post is encouraged to conduct Youth Protection training with all Explorers (youth) once a year using "Youth Protection: Personal Safety Awareness AV-09DVD27" (which can be obtained from a local council office). This visual training covers the topics of sexual harassment, acquaintance rape, Internet safety, and suicide awareness. (The leader discussion guide can be found at: http://www.learningforlife.org/pubs/av/46-506.)

## Safety Patrols

By 1902, there were only about 23,000 cars in operation in the United States compared with about 17 million horses, but as many as 50 small motor clubs were already established to assist the pioneering motorists of the day. On March 4, 1902, in Chicago, nine of those clubs joined together to create a national motoring organization known as the American Automobile Association (AAA) (Figure 8.7). Within two decades, the AAA had the wisdom to adopt an existing school safety patrol program—a unique youth organization that quickly spread throughout the nation. It was distinctive because it provided a specific service—namely, pedestrian safety in and around school buildings. The Chicago Motor Club has been widely recognized as the initiator of the first patrol unit to become affiliated with the AAA. Beginning in the early 1920s, a typical patrol consisted of 4–12 boys, depending on the size of the school and the number of hazardous intersections. It was a common sight to see them stopping traffic by raising their hands or stop signs and

**Figure 8.7** AAA's fiftieth anniversary commemorative U.S. postage stamp. The AAA school safety patrol was founded in Chicago in 1920 by Charles M. Hayes, president of the Chicago Motor Club, after several children at a school crossing were killed by a speeding car. Horrified by the incident, Hayes pledged to help prevent such a tragedy from happening again. (From http://www.blogtalkradio. com/aaatalkradio/2010/04/19/aaa-school-safety-patrol-1)

then proceeding to escort students across city streets. They wore white "Sam Browne belts"[7] with badges attached to denote ranks. Some had bright colored felt armbands. During inclement weather, poncho-type capes and rain hats were added to the uniform. Patrol members were selected for service based on their good grades and leadership qualities. The AAA also introduced traffic safety education into elementary and junior high schools and pioneered driver education in high schools (AAA 2014).

In 1923, due to the rise of vehicular traffic and concern about pedestrian safety, Police Chief August Vollmer of Berkeley, California, changed the orientation of his "junior police program" from spotting crime to protecting children with the creation of the "Berkeley Traffic Police Reserve" (Greenberg 2008).

Oak Ridge Elementary School was built in 1991 on an 18-acre tract of land in Eagan, Minnesota. Its 30 classrooms on two levels serve nearly 630 students from kindergarten through the fifth grade. The classrooms are designed with one open wall in order to encourage students and staff to make better use of all the resources in the school as well as to promote "a sharing relationship between staff, students, and visitors to our school" (About Oak Ridge 2013). *The Oak Ridge School Safety Patrol Manual* declares that: "The purpose of the safety patrols is to assist in training school children in how to cross streets, to assist school children upon arrival and dismissal, and to protect them from any type of accident" (Patrol Manual 2012). Box 8.2 states several of the rules concerning students assigned to bus patrols.

In 2000, the AAA School Safety Patrols had approximately a half-million participants, and by 2013, this number was estimated to have risen to 600,000 (Chandler 2013). In recent decades, increased traffic and concern about civil liability have diminished the nature of their responsibilities. For the most part, patrols have been confined to sidewalk duty (Greenberg 2008).

Nevertheless, opportunities to engage in lifesaving acts related to school safety still exist, and patrollers have been recognized for heroic actions on a yearly basis. In 1961, U.S. Attorney General Robert F. Kennedy presented lifesaving awards to young AAA safety patrol heroes. Two years later, his brother President John F. Kennedy did the same. In 2011, the AAA honored seven elementary students for their courageous actions that saved the lives of others. The patrollers received AAA Lifesaving Medals in a ceremony at the Rayburn House Office Building. They joined an exclusive group of 399 students who, since 1949, had previously received the medal—the highest honor that can be bestowed on a patroller. Typical actions included stepping into oncoming traffic to pull a fellow student from the path of a distracted driver or preventing an adult from entering a crosswalk as a vehicle approached. Former patrol members include Presidents Jimmy Carter and Bill Clinton, Vice President Joe Biden, as well as several Supreme Court justices, U.S. senators, governors, and U.S. Olympic gold medalists (AAA Honors 2011).

## BOX 8.2    BUS PATROL RULES

The bus driver is the person responsible for the safety of both the bus and passengers.

Bus patrols are aides to help with student safety.

The bus driver will establish rules and expectations for his or her bus.

The bus driver is the person in charge of *everything* that happens on his or her bus.

They are the only person on the bus that assigns students to specific seats.

The bus driver will decide how he/she will rotate the duties of front, middle, and back patrol duties.

### FRONT PATROL

1. Sits in a front seat and assists with flagging students across the street using proper flagging techniques.
2. Is the first person on and last person off the bus.

### MIDDLE PATROL

1. Makes sure all students are seated before the bus starts moving.
2. Assists in keeping the aisle clear.
3. Assists in keeping the bus safe.

### BACK PATROL

1. Makes sure all students are seated before the bus starts moving.
2. Assists in keeping the aisle clear.
3. Assists with the use of the emergency door when necessary.
4. Assists in keeping the bus safe.

*Source:* Patrol Manual, 2012, The Oak Ridge school safety patrol manual, available at: http://learn.district196.org/pluginfile.php?file =%2F156989%2Fmod_resource%2Fcontent%2F0%2FSafety_Patrol_Manual_2012.pdf

In 1935, a large newspaper photo spread featured the junior police force of Ponca City, Oklahoma. Today, Ponca City has a population of about 25,000, of which more than 2,000 are Native Americans. The Ponca City Police Department sponsors a youth police academy and a citizens police academy. It also provides extra hospitality for foreign visitors. In a citizen exchange program sponsored by the U.S. Chamber of Commerce, a citizen of Zimbabwe attended a session of the citizen police academy (CPA) followed by a tour of the police department (Police Host 2012).

**Figure 8.8** Safety patrol members from the St. Hyacinth and St. John the Baptist Schools, Westbrook, Maine, October 27, 1939. (Used with the permission of the Westbrook Historical Society, Westbrook, ME.)

The length of time students served depended on the schools. Some schools selected students to serve for a full year and others changed students on a monthly basis. The job of the safety patrol was to regulate the safe movement of children in the immediate vicinity of a school. At some schools, the duties of the safety patrol also included raising and lowering the flag each day. As school-age leaders in traffic safety, patrols helped teach students about traffic safety on a peer-to-peer basis. They also served as role models to the younger children who looked up to them.

In 1939, some members of the School Boy Patrol at the St. Hyacinth Parish School and St. John the Baptist School in Westbrook, Maine, were responsible for escorting children nearly half a mile in order to assist them in crossing busy streets (Figure 8.8). Today, due to their numbers, safety patrollers are the most visible of the police-related youth organizations. Although escorting youth safely from one street corner to the next is no longer a routine activity, various school districts still permit them to maintain the peace on school buses and to assist younger children getting on and off school buses. In addition, in some schools, selected students continue to help maintain decorum along school hallways and in remote corridors.

## Police Academy Magnet Schools

The Los Angeles Police Academy Magnet School Program was established in 1997 as a cooperative effort of the Los Angeles Police Department (LAPD), the Los Angeles Unified School District (LAUSD), and various corporate sponsors. The program was originally implemented at two high schools and later expanded to five more. In 2001, the Mulholland Middle School was added to the program. In 2005, the five schools participating in the program included Monroe, Dorsey, Wilson, San Pedro, and Reseda high schools. The Luther Burbank Middle School's Police Academy Magnet program was begun in 2009. A California Partnership Academy Grant is a major funding source for the daily operation of the Los Angeles Police Academy Magnet School Program. Approximately $40,000 is raised annually, and college scholarships are awarded to deserving graduating senior cadets (LA PAM 2005).

Reseda High School's Police Academy Magnet began in the fall of 1998. The Reseda High School program is designed to be a career pathway to educate students about law enforcement through a rigid course of study involving intense physical training and compulsory community service. An LAPD officer is assigned full-time to teach, counsel, and mentor the students through their police academy experience.

The founder of the Los Angeles Unified School District Board (LAUSD) Police Academy Magnet Schools is Roberta Weintraub (Figure 8.9), an experienced member and past president of the LAUSD. She was concerned about the need for community residents to serve as police officers. In 1995, she enlisted the support of the mayor of Los Angeles, the superintendent of the LAUSD, and the LAPD police chief to establish the Police Academy Magnet Schools. The curriculum emphasizes thematic academics, discipline, community service, physical fitness, and moral and ethical studies (PAMS Founder 2013). Joel Schaeffer was the first Reseda Police Academy Magnet coordinator. He coached football at Reseda High for 23 years and taught in the LAUSD for 40 years. The school named its field after him (Sondheimer 2013). Currently, there are four high schools and two middle schools participating, with approximately 1,200 students. Alise Cayen has been the Police Academy Magnet coordinator at Reseda High School since 2005. She is the person in charge of organizing and producing the PAMS annual commencement ceremony (Alise Cayen, personal communication, January 28, 2014).

Another unique youth program was also inaugurated in Southern California. For more than 50 years, the LAPD has had a distinctive cadet preparation program for youth between 13 and 20 years of age. These LAPD cadet candidates must first complete a 144-hour program that meets on

**Figure 8.9** Roberta Weintraub, founder and executive director, Los Angeles Police Academy Magnet Schools.

Saturdays for 18 consecutive weeks. The program is designed to quality them for future participation as an LAPD cadet. (Information about this academy is available at: http://www.lapdcadets.com/about/academy.)

The PAMS concept has spread to other regions. For example, the School for Law Studies, Law Enforcement, Homeland Security and Forensic Sciences was recently established within the Miami-Dade County Public Schools in collaboration with the city of Miami and the Miami Police Department. Students that are accepted into the program have access to forensic science labs, courtroom labs, and computer simulation centers. It is expected that students will have the opportunity to attend dual enrollment programs with Florida International University, the University of Miami, and Miami-Dade Community College (Miami PD 2013).

The Sacramento Police Department has had success with its Criminal Justice Magnet Academy program, which reported an enrollment of 467 at its four high schools during the 2011–2012 school year (Annual Report 2013). Participants are required to perform 50 hours of community service per year, to maintain a specific grooming standard, to wear a provided academy uniform once a week, and to represent the academy in a positive way at all times. The students are also required to maintain an 80% attendance rate and to earn 90% of their credit requirements to qualify (Sacramento PD 2013). According to its *2011–12 Annual Report*, "the Criminal Justice Academy is a partnership between high schools, and public and private organizations that focus on providing knowledge and skills-based education relevant to the work environment high school students may encounter upon graduation. The Criminal Justice Academy offers a school-within-a-school framework, taking students as a group from their freshman year through their senior year. The program is a paramilitary type of academy modeled after the Sacramento Police Department's Police Academy" (Annual Report 2013, 4). In addition, there are opportunities to hold leadership positions such as commanders, captains, lieutenants, sergeants, and corporals. These appointments permit the academy cadets "to learn the complex nature of leadership and the dynamics of human relations. The Sacramento Police Foundation sponsors an annual summer Leadership Camp where cadets learn about integrity, honor, and pride" (Annual Report 2013, 10).

## Police Orientation and Preparation Program

Roberta Weintraub, the PAMS founder, has also developed another unique program. Her newest model for the delivery of police education and training for youth is the POPP. It is an exploratory educational experience that places career-bound, law enforcement students in an established LAPD training environment. Currently, classes are held at the LAPD's Ahmanson Recruit Training Center. POPP recruits twelfth-graders and community college students who may satisfy high school diploma requirements and earn four college certificates leading toward an associate's degree in administration of justice. A team of LAPD staff and officers, LAUSD coordinators and consultants, and Los Angeles Community College deans and instructors contribute to the program. For high school students, the program can help them complete the first year of community college by the time they graduate from high school. The program also spans the time from high school to career entry by immersing students in a focused effort. A tutoring service is provided by private funding. All new students must complete a four-week "pre-academy" course, which includes nutrition and physical training, English, and study skill courses, all taught by qualified police officers and high school or college instructors. The program's goals include: providing a rigorous, two-year college curriculum administered by professors that provides high school seniors and college freshman cadets with 15 college units per semester; affording cadets job opportunities in the public and private sector while in school; and offering a curricular foundation that enables cadets to obtain an associate's degree and/or transfer to a four-year university before applying for a wide range of public safety occupations. According to Weintraub, POPP ultimately offers a path to middle-class jobs for children of lower-income families and creates a "home-grown" police force that is made up of members of Los Angeles communities (Torok 2013). (The POPP handbook can be downloaded from the link found at: http://poppartc.com/requirements.)

## Youth Courts

The modern youth court concept began in the early 1970s, when a small number of local communities began to experiment with a formalized structure of peer justice. From 1993 to 2008, the number of local youth and teen courts in which volunteer youth help "sentence" their peers has grown from 75 to more than 1,000, according to a report from the Global Issues Resource Center. Approximately 112,000 juvenile cases have been referred to local youth and teen courts. In addition, more than 133,000 volunteers, including youth and adults, have volunteered to help with the disposition of these juvenile cases (Peterson and Beres 2008).

Youth courts are also known as teen courts, peer courts, or student courts. They are juvenile justice programs in which young people are "sentenced" by their peers. Youth courts are established and administered in a wide variety of ways, but most youth courts are used as an alternative sentencing option for first-time offenders aged 11–17 who are charged with misdemeanor nonviolent offenses. In the majority of youth courts, the offender has acknowledged his or her guilt and participates in a youth court voluntarily, rather than going through the more formal, traditional juvenile justice procedures.

---

**BOX 8.3   YOUTH COURT MODELS**

The *Adult Judge Model* employs an adult judge to rule on courtroom procedure and to clarify legal terminology. Youth volunteers serve as defense and prosecuting attorneys and as jurors. Young people may also serve as bailiffs and clerks. This is the most common model.

The *Youth Judge Model* is similar to the Adult Judge Model except that a juvenile serves as the judge, usually after a term of service as a youth court attorney.

The *Peer Jury Model* employs a panel of teen jurors who question the youth offender directly. No defense or prosecuting attorney is employed. The judge is usually an adult volunteer.

The *Tribunal Model* has no peer jury. Instead, the prosecuting and defense attorneys present cases to a juvenile judge who determines the sentence.

---

Youth courts differ from other juvenile justice programs because they involve other young people in the process, especially in determining the offender's sanction. For example, a peer jury may assign an offender to a combination of community service, conflict resolution training, restitution, youth court jury duty, and/or educational workshops. Depending on the model used, young people may serve as jurors, prosecuting attorneys, defense attorneys, bailiffs, clerks, and even judges.

Because youth courts are developed in local communities and by local communities, there is no cookie-cutter approach to the structure of these programs. However, Box 8.3 indicates some common models that youth courts employ.

Regardless of the model employed, most youth courts are based in the juvenile justice system or in a community setting. The most common agencies operating or administering youth court programs are juvenile courts and private nonprofit organizations (29% each). The next most common agencies are law enforcement agencies and juvenile probation departments (17% each). Schools are the operating agencies for about 10% of youth courts, while a variety of other agencies (e.g., city government, the administrative office of the court) are less commonly the operating agency (Peterson and Beres 2008).

## Future Directions

There is documentation available indicating that the Police Academy Magnet Schools are achieving their primary goal of increasing the number of high school students who enter college. However, there is much less evidence about the success or long-term value of holding intermittent and relatively brief youth academies. According to Bright (1992, 40), "Young people make a significant contribution to the crime problem both as offenders and victims, and they should be the principal focus of any crime prevention strategy." It is hard to imagine how programs of short duration (e.g., a weeklong summer youth academy) can have desirable and lasting effects when the problems encountered by youth are often compounded by family breakdown, poor schools and housing, the proliferation of drugs and guns, limited employment opportunities, and the social and physical decline of neighborhoods. The four-week Burlington Police Department's JPA appears to be an exception. Although short duration youth academies may or may not have a lasting effect for participants, the practice of having in-house officers, such as school district police officers, to offer such programs on a routine basis should be expanded and evaluated. As Chief Fuller noted: "When an officer stands before a class and presents material that he understands and loves, students respect that. When a student raises his hand and shows genuine curiosity about a profession that he sees depicted a thousand times a day on radio and television, officers return that respect" (Fuller 2012). The Police Academy Magnet Schools appear to represent the optimum type of police-oriented youth program.

Comparable to like the magnet schools, most Explorer posts and Junior ROTC units insist that, to remain affiliated, participants must maintain strict requirements related to their character and academic performance. Consequently, the inclusion of a Law Enforcement Explorer program can strengthen any department's or school district's efforts to resist and prevent crime and disorder among youth. Such programs may also lead to a more congenial relationship between the youth of a community and the police. Police agencies should develop these programs as an integral agency function, and they should draw on the knowledge and skills of current and retired police officers as well as qualified community members. College students over 21 can be recruited to serve as volunteer post advisors under faculty supervision. Through involvement with such programs, youthful participants are bound to become more career focused, empowered, and more concerned about lifelong learning. In addition, police officers, teachers, and adult volunteers will have the satisfaction of knowing that they are participating in a meaningful and needed activity.

For the sake of maintaining interest and enthusiasm for the Explorer movement, individual Explorer units have offered programs beyond the usual activities of training lectures, crowd control, clerical work, dispatch work, ride-alongs, and such community projects as clean-up drives.[8] Occasionally, newsworthy activities have been reported. For example, in May 2009, a controversy erupted when the *New York Times* reported that Explorer programs were engaging in "training thousands of young people in skills used to confront terrorism, illegal immigration and escalating border violence" (Steinhauer 2009). The report indicated that during a simulation exercise, an Explorer group used compressed-air guns, known as Airsoft guns, that fire tiny plastic pellets[9] (Steinhauer 2009). It remains to be seen whether this activity will become widespread. Upon the publication of this particular news report, hundreds of comments were posted on the *New York Times'* online commentary Web site regarding the type of training being provided; the vast majority of these were unfavorable.[10]

The official Web site for the Law Enforcement Explorer program is found at: http://exploring.learningforlife.org/services/career-exploring/law-enforcement. The site provides recent updates about the program. For example, at its October 2010 meeting, the National Law Enforcement Exploring Committee (NLEEC)[11] approved voluntary training certification for Law Enforcement Exploring, effective on January 1, 2011. Each agency or organization that has its basic or advanced training program for Law Enforcement Explorers certified will receive paperwork from the national office signed by the national director for Law Enforcement Exploring and the chairperson of the subcommittee for training certification that designates this fact. Each course presented in a basic or advanced training program must have a written lesson plan that includes a variety of basic information such as the title of the lesson, number of instructional hours, learning objectives, testing procedures, and so on. Such documentation could prove invaluable when seeking high school or college credits (Law Enforcement Training 2012). It is interesting to speculate that the advent of individual Explorer training certification might someday serve as the model or catalyst for the establishment of a national individual police officer training certification (see Lindsay and Greenberg 2013). This type of police training standard would greatly enhance the development of police professionalism. Box 8.4 provides a list of additional recommended activities or projects for Explorer posts.

Larson et al. (2009, 2) concluded that "some of the current methods used to involve citizens in the policing of their communities are: Community Oriented Policing, Problem Oriented Policing, Police Reserves, and Volunteer Citizen Patrol. All of these methods should be used together for services to be delivered in the most effective way." In addition, carefully screened and trained youth should be used to enhance the delivery of a wide array of selected public safety activities. However, in many communities, financing for such services are often lacking, or they are given scant support.

## BOX 8.4   NEW ROLES FOR POLICE EXPLORER POSTS

- Assist with new citation approach for juvenile delinquency/status offenses
- Conduct seminars on law and security (active shooter, identity theft, etc.)
- Revitalize School Resource Officer (SRO) and anti-bullying programs
- Monitor/investigate reports of elder abuse
- Provide crime victim services
- Help to coordinate neighborhood watch programs
- Staff storefront locations
- Operate bookmobiles for homebound residents
- Engage in cemetery inspections
- Assist with animal cruelty investigations
- Serve as tutors/assistant coaches in community centers and on playgrounds
- Encourage leaders in minority communities to attend CPAs

## Summary

Throughout the nation, there exist a variety of police-sponsored and/or school-based programs involving youth. Generally, these programs are being supervised by police officers, retired military personnel, and/or teachers. This chapter reviewed several types: youth police academies; recreational (e.g., PAL); limited enforcement (e.g., Explorers); magnet school (LA Police Academy Magnet Schools, Sacramento PD Criminal Justice Academy, etc.); and school safety (e.g., AAA Safety Patrollers). The short-term youth police academies are typically held for a week during the summer, and their popularity has contributed to the creation of the "JPA Content Lab," an online program with posted lessons that can be easily accessed by all students, teachers, parents, and counselors.

A new and promising program to bridge the gap between high school and career entry was also described—the POPP. It was founded by Robert a Weintraub, who also founded the LA Police Academy Magnet Schools. In 2011, Weintraub commented about her new initiative: "Here is a high school/college degree program that provides students with an educational program that includes extensive physical training, discipline, plus real and simulated experiences that will enhance a law enforcement career decision" (Weintraub 2011).

During their heyday, the early junior police programs provided opportunities for fostering positive relationships between younger citizens and the police as well as opportunities for practicing values associated with good citizenship. In some cities, these units evolved into Police Athletic Leagues (PAL). Many of these traditions are now being carried out by thousands of members of numerous Law Enforcement Explorer Posts, safety patrollers, and by military-related organizations such as the Junior ROTC. In this way, the early junior police who participated in community projects have served as pathfinders for those contemporary local police agencies and federal services interested in community policing by assisting youth. In some ways, the coincidence of new police-related Explorer units in the 1960s along with the inadequate and oftentimes uncivil response of police during the social upheavals of that period may have encouraged the reforms that took place in later years, such as the "community policing movement" that began in the late 1970s. The former demonstrated the importance of citizen participation in police work, while the latter demonstrated how the absence of citizen participation can lead to citizen abuse. Today, two of the signature policies of "community policing" are having regular officers leave their cars in order to encourage positive contacts with businesses and community residents and seeking possible partnerships with community groups as often as possible.

Short-term youth (junior) police academies have varying emphases. A few basic types of police-sponsored and/or school-based academy programs include: the crime scene investigation camp (e.g., South Bend, Indiana); the physical training or boot camp model involving at-risk youth (e.g., Burlington, as seen in Figure 8.10); and more generalized programs of instruction with academic units of instruction (e.g., the Oklahoma's Cadet Lawman Academy). Programs for at-risk youth tend to exceed the duration of the other types of programs.

**Figure 8.10** A past graduating class from the Burlington (North Carolina) Police Department Junior Police Academy. The academy is a nationally recognized at-risk youth program developed in 1996. (Used with the permission of the Burlington Police Department.)

Currently, more than 33,000 Explorers and more than 8,400 adult volunteers participate in Law Enforcement Exploring in the United States. The program highlights include: the National Law Enforcement Exploring Leadership academies, ride-alongs, career achievement awards, National Law Enforcement Exploring conferences, and scholarship opportunities (Westland Police 2012a; AAA 2014). The types and duration of training provided to Law Enforcement Explorers varies from post to post and ranges from a simple orientation class to extensive multilevel academic and practical application-based instructional programs. In some instances, such training has been accepted for high school and/or college academic credit. On at least one occasion, unfavorable publicity was engendered by militaristic role-playing activities. In order to remove some of the uncertainty and inconsistency with respect to such training, a new national training certification program was established in 2011. Its goals are to provide validation and recognition for those Law Enforcement Posts or organizations that provide training programs that meet or exceed minimum standards with respect to curriculum development and content, performance evaluation procedure, record management, and instructor qualifications. Like the CALEA certification program, this youth program certification is voluntary.

The Broome County Sheriff's Law Enforcement Explorer Post Web pages claim that it is one of the most successful Exploring posts in its local area, noting that their curriculum and course outlines have been used as guides by other Explorer posts. It attributes its success rate to continual adult leadership and programs that encourage youth development (Broome County 2007). Continued requests for unit Explorers are indicative of the success of the program. Ultimately, however, the availability of local resources, the integrity of a unit's advisors, and the decisions made by the leadership of the sponsoring agency will determine the quality and effectiveness of a particular youth program.

Throughout the twentieth century, many communities have experimented with programs involving youth in the performance of limited types of police work (e.g., crowd control). In addition, youth in both urban and rural settings have engaged in important roles in the field of pedestrian safety. The AAA safety patrollers were the most ubiquitous of these organizations because they were routinely assigned to traffic and crossing guard duty at the streets adjacent to their elementary and middle schools. They also helped to keep order on school buses, assisted younger children getting on and off school buses, and maintained decorum along school hallways. In several towns and cities, some members of the first wave of junior police groups actually engaged in a limited amount of routine street patrol. The junior police members were trained to perform their assignments by local police agencies. Heroic actions by the safety patrollers still take place when a pedestrian's safety is at risk. One source has estimated that some 600,000 individuals participate in such patrols in 32,000 elementary or middle schools (see Chandler 2013).

The early twentieth-century creation of junior police forces in Berkeley and in New York City and their modern-day Explorer counterparts exemplify the basic aspect of community policing by bringing communities and police closer together. Moreover, by providing additional personnel, they may fill gaps in the public safety net. In some ways, the early junior police who participated in community projects may have served as the pathfinders for those contemporary police who have been, once again, assigned to walk foot patrols around business and residential areas and to ride bicycles so that community problems might be better identified and resolved.

According to John Ellison, a former police chief in West Linn, Oregon, "The promises of community policing are many. They include—strengthening the capacity of communities to resist and prevent crime and social disorder; creating a more harmonious relationship between the police and the public, including some power sharing with respect to police policy making and tactical priorities; restructuring police service delivery by linking it with other municipal services; and reforming the police organization model by creating larger and more complex roles for individual officers" (2006, 12).

Progress in police work with youth involving Explorer posts, JPAs, magnet schools, as well as Drug Abuse Resistance Education (D.A.R.E.), Gang Resistance Education and Training (G.R.E.A.T.), and PAL programs[12] is continuing. These programs demonstrate that frontline full-time police officers, as well as non-sworn adult police volunteers, can play significant roles as educators and mentors of youth. In the late 1990s, the first Police Academy Magnet Schools began to appear. Due to their multiyear nature, they appear to represent a value-added approach to the existing mix of police-oriented youth programs.

Youth programs should be broadened to include other municipal agencies (e.g., schools, hospitals, emergency services, and so on). In addition, many school districts have begun to recognize the value of having students engage in peer mediation, student courts, conflict resolution, teen courts, and similar programs. "Youth courts empower youth to be active participants in community problem solving, and they foster important values, attitudes, and beliefs related to the implementation and execution of the justice system" (Peterson and Beres 2008, 6). It is interesting to note that for several decades in the twentieth century, most efforts aimed at the protection of school children were carried out solely by the students themselves under the watchful eyes of their teachers. Today, this type of activity rarely occurs due to the violent nature of many inner-city schools and concerns over school district liability. Nevertheless, if after appropriate screening and training today's school-age youth were offered more opportunities for undertaking such duties, perhaps they might be better prepared to face life's greater challenges, and our schools might be safer. The selection and training of youth for participation in teen courts in hundreds of communities is a positive step forward because they offer a positive alternative to traditional juvenile justice and school disciplinary procedures.

The following chapter will address several semi-military/homeland security programs involving youth at the federal level, such as Junior ROTC, Civil Air Patrol cadets, and Explorer units sponsored by federal law enforcement agencies. A few federal internship programs are also examined as well as the new Federal Emergency Management Agency (FEMA) Corps.

## Review Questions

1. List at least five topics that might be included in a typical short-term junior police academy. Select one topic from this list and explain who might be best qualified to serve as the topic's instructor.
2. Identify several types of activities engaged in by Broome County (New York) Explorer Post members and discuss the appropriateness of having police Explorers participate in alcohol and tobacco stings.
3. Discuss the types of insurance coverage available to individual Explorer posts, their members, and their leadership.
4. The successor organization to the 1940s Phoenix corps of junior police is the police department's Explorer Post 2906. Provide arguments for and against the idea of permitting Post 2906 Explorers to serve as sworn traffic enforcement officers, a practice in which junior police were permitted to participate in the past.
5. Many of the junior police programs discussed in this chapter have or have had a rank structure similar to that of the regular police hierarchy. Provide arguments for and against the use of such a rank structure.
6. Discuss a few of the benefits and possible drawbacks of participating in a Law Enforcement Exploring Program as an adult volunteer or as a student participant.
7. Describe the Westland (MI) Police Department's Explorer Post "Sober-Up Program."
8. Search online to find an article describing a recent incident that led to the AAA Lifesaving Medal being awarded. Summarize these facts. Do you consider the actions worthy of such a medal? Explain your views.
9. Do you believe that it should be a more serious crime to assault a Police Explorer than to assault a person who has no such affiliation? Explain your views.

10. For a number of decades prior to World War II and a few years there-after, it was a common sight to observe safety patrol boys and girls stopping traffic in order to escort students across streets near school buildings. Is there any need to reinstitute this practice? If so, who might object? Explain your views.

11. Discuss the pros and cons of organizing short-duration (e.g., a week-long summer youth academy) versus longer-term police-affiliated youth programs, such as a police magnet school.

12. Examine the list of proposed new roles for Police Explorers found in Box 8.4. Do you believe that these roles should or can be performed by qualified Police Explorers? Explain your views.

# Notes

1. As part of "Merchants Week," boys dressed as police were on hand to escort Rear Admiral William T. Sampson (the "Hero of Santiago") when he visited Maynard, MA, on May 16, 1900. He was presented with a shuttle from the Assabet Mills. (The original photo is in the Maynard Historical Society Archives and is reproduced here with permission of the Society.)

2. The Association of Military Colleges and Schools of the United States (AMCSUS), formed in 1914, is a nonprofit service organization that, since its founding, has served as an advocate for military colleges and schools and has acted as a liaison with the Departments of Defense and Education. Currently there are nine military colleges and universities, five military junior colleges, 25 military preparatory (institute) schools, and one associate member school in the association (AMCSUS 2012).

3. It is important to note that many police agencies maintain adult auxiliary or reserve police programs that involve sworn duties as well as Law Enforcement Explorer units that function in a non-sworn capacity; such dual programs can be found, for example, in the Manchester Township (NJ) Police Department. Another key difference is that the initial age of membership can be as low as 14 for an Explorer, but auxiliaries are usually 18 or older.

4. Two four-minute slide show videos produced in 2009 and featuring a total of 44 different photographs of police Explorer posts can be viewed online at: http://www.youtube.com/watch?v=WqKGPsbPXsA and at http://www.youtube.com/watch?v=1aTfi3Jik-g. A useful nine-minute video that provides a good over-view of the variety of activities in which Explorers engage can be found at: http://www.youtube.com/watch?v=CBYd4hR62A0.

5. Known as the "Gateway to the Rockies," Aurora sits at an elevation of 5,435 feet and is adjacent to Denver International Airport. Aurora is about 13 miles from Littleton, CO—the site of the April 1999 Columbine High School massacre. In July 2012, James Holmes opened fire in a crowded Aurora movie theater. Holmes has pleaded not guilty by reason of insanity to multiple charges of murder and attempted murder. He is accused of killing 12 people and injuring 70 during a midnight showing of the feature film *The Dark Knight Rises*.

6. Chapter 784.03 of the Florida Statutes defines felony battery as occurring when a person, "Actually and intentionally touches or strikes another person against the will of the other; or intentionally causes bodily harm to another person."

7. "The telltale sign of the safety patrol is the neon belts. The design, with its waist and diagonal shoulder straps, is named for a 19th century British army officer who used the belt to carry his sword. The design has remained but the colors have changed—from white to neon orange to a fluorescent green that the AAA calls 'lectric green'" (Chandler 2013).

8. For example, the Pinellas Park (FL) police and Explorers have volunteered their time to eradicate graffiti from buildings, walls, and fences. On one occasion, they painted over illicit art at 30 locations to eliminate gang-related and so-called "tagger" graffiti. Tagger art is graffiti usually done by nongang individuals (Michalski 2009).

9. The news article focused on the Explorer program in Imperial County, a needy county in Southern California where the local economy appears to be based largely on the criminal justice system. In addition to the sheriff and local police departments, there are two state prisons and a large Border Patrol and immigration enforcement presence (see Steinhauer 2009).

10. One commentator, who was serving on the executive board of the National Capital Area Council, Boy Scouts of America, wrote: "Please readers, understand that there are those of us in the leadership of the Scouting Movement who are as appalled as you are. And we're Scouting's majority by a long mile. Your beef is with the local law enforcement Explorer Post leaders in Imperial County, California, not with the BSA. If you care to study the history and the peculiar sociology of Scouting a little more closely, you will discover that precisely this concern—an encroachment of paramilitary indoctrination—has been eschewed by the Scouts in Britain and the USA ever since Scouting's foundation a hundred years ago" (Pocalyko 2009).

11. The National Association of Law Enforcement Explorers functioned as the principal organization for Law Enforcement Exploring until the formation of the National Law Enforcement Exploring Committee (NLEEC) in 1976. The NLEEC provides advice and guidance on the Exploring program. The committee comprises the directors of several federal law enforcement agencies, various sheriffs and chiefs of police, the provost marshal of the U.S. Army, representatives from allied organizations, and individuals from the private sector who support law enforcement. A national youth representative and a vice national youth representative also serve on the NLEEC (Law Enforcement Exploring 2011).

12. In New York City, PAL evolved from the establishment of junior police, play-street movement, and the Twilight Athletic League (PAL 2012). Founded 1983 in Los Angeles, the Drug Abuse Resistance Education (D.A.R.E.) program is currently a police officer-led series of classroom lessons taught from kindergarten through twelfth grade. "It is now being implemented in 75 percent of our nation's school districts and in more than 43 countries around the world" (DARE 2012). Established in 1991, Gang Resistance Education and Training (G.R.E.A.T.) is also police-instructed, but its curricula for elementary and middle schools focus on youth crime, gang, and violence prevention.

The Federal Law Enforcement Training Center (FLETC) sponsors regional advanced training for G.R.E.A.T. instructors who have taught G.R.E.A.T. for at least one year (GREAT 2012).

# References

AAA. (2014). History: A century of service. Retrieved March 3, 2014 from http://newsroom.aaa.com/about-aaa/history/

AAA Honors. (2011). AAA honors seven elementary school students on Capitol Hill with 2011 lifesaving medal for the heroic actions. Retrieved October 2, 2013 from http://newsroom.aaa.com/tag/school-safety-patrol/

About Oak Ridge. (2013). About Oak Ridge elementary. Retrieved October 4, 2013 from http://www.district196.org/or/AboutUs.html

AMCSUS. (2012). Our mission and purposes. Retrieved June 1, 2012 from http://www.amcsus.org/page.cfm?p = 12

Annual Report. (2013). Sacramento Police Department, Criminal Justice Academy, 2011–2012 annual report. Retrieved October 3, 2013 from http://www.sacpd.org/pdf/youth/youthar12.pdf

Aurora Explorers. (2014). What type of activities and benefits are available to explorers? Retrieved January 24, 2014 from http://www.auroraexplorers.com/Postoverview.html

Bost, C. (2011, July 12). Junior police academy returns a better man. Retrieved May 21, 2012 from http://www.thetimesnews.com/common/printer/view.php?db = burlington&id = 45828

Bright, J. (1992). *Crime prevention in America: A British perspective*. Chicago, IL: Office of International Criminal Justice/The University of Illinois at Chicago.

Broome County. (2007). Broome County Sheriff 2007 annual report. Retrieved September 28, 2013 from http://www.gobroomecounty.com/files/sheriff/pdfs/OfficeOfSheriffAnnualReport.pdf

Buffalo Grove. (2012a). Academies. Retrieved May 18, 2012 from http://www.vbg.org/index.aspx?nid = 292

Buffalo Grove. (2012b). Participant liability waiver and hold harmless agreement. Retrieved May 18, 2012 from http://www.vbg.org/DocumentCenter/Home/View/88

Cadet Lawman. (2012). Cadet Lawman Academy. Retrieved May 22, 2012 from http://www.cadetlawman.com/

Career Exploring FAQs. (2013). Retrieved September 27, 2013 from http://exploring.learningforlife.org/contact-us/exploring-faqs/

Chandler, M. A. (2013, September 9). How much do you know about the school safety patrol? Retrieved October 3, 2013 from http://articles.washingtonpost.com/2013-09-09/local/41890468_1_dangerous-student-practices-safety-patrol-patrol-badges

City of Burlington. (2012). Junior police academy. Retrieved May 21, 2012 from http://www.ci.burlington.nc.us/index.aspx?NID = 526

City of Phoenix. (2013). Law enforcement explorer program. Retrieved September 25, 2013 from http://phoenix.gov/police/explor1.html

DARE. (2012). About DARE. Retrieved May 24, 2012 from http://www.dare.com/home/about_dare.asp

Ellison, J. (2006). Community policing: Implementation issues. *FBI Law Enforcement Bulletin, 75*(4), 12.

Exploring. (2014). Law enforcement career exploring. Retrieved March 3, 2014 from http://exploring.learningforlife.org/services/career-exploring/law-enforcement/

Ferreira, C. (2011). Real-world CSI for South Bend teens. Retrieved May 18, 2012 from http://articles.wsbt.com/2011-06-17/south-bend-teens_29672542

Folsom, A. (1971). Youth form state-wide law enforcement organization. *Law and Order, 19*(12), 121, 128.

Fuller, P. (2012). The junior police academy works. Retrieved May 21, 2012 from http://www.juniorpoliceacademy.org/jpa-works/

GREAT. (2012). Welcome to the G.R.E.A.T. web site. Retrieved May 24, 2012 from http://www.great-online.org/

Greenberg, M. A. (2008, April). A short history of junior police. *The Police Chief, 75*(4), 172–180.

Henrietta Ambulance. (2012). Explorer post. Retrieved May 23, 2012 from http://henriettaambulance.org/explorer-post/

Hollywood Community. (2013). Hollywood Community Police Activities League (PAL) program. Retrieved September 24, 2013 from http://www.lapdonline.org/hollywood_community_police_station/content_basic_ view/23690

Insurance Information. (2011). Insurance information for volunteers. Retrieved October 2, 2013 from http://www.stlbsa.org/volunteers/pages/insurance-information-for-volunteers.aspx

LA PAM. (2005). Los Angeles Police Academy Magnet School Program. Retrieved October 3, 2013 from http://www.lacp.org/2005-Articles-Main/YouthPrograms/Report2-MagnetSchools.html

Larson, J., Lewis, V., Day, K. and Kelso, C. (2009). Reducing the cost of crime through reserve police officers and volunteer citizen patrol. *Research in Business and Economics Journal, (3)*, 1–8. Retrieved May 29, 2012 from http://www.aabri.com/manuscripts/09316.pdf

Law Enforcement Exploring. (2011, July). Law enforcement exploring: Program and resource guide for adult leaders. Retrieved May 24, 2012 from https://c183757.ssl.cf1.rackcdn.com/wp-content/documents/LEE_Program%20and%20Resource%20Guide_0811.pdf

Law Enforcement Training. (2012). Law enforcement training certification. Retrieved May 23, 2012 from https://c183757.ssl.cf1.rackcdn.com/lawenforcement/Law-Enforcement-Exploring-Training-Certification.pdf

LeConte, K. (2012a). JPA content lab. Retrieved May 18, 2012 from https://sites.google.com/site/jpacourse2012/home

LeConte, K. (2012b). Message from JPA Program Director Kelly LeConte. Retrieved May 21, 2012 from http://www.juniorpoliceacademy.org/what-is-jpa/

Lightcap, B. (2013). *The Morrill act of 1862.* Retrieved October 2, 2013 from http://www3.nd.edu/~rbarger/www7/morrill.html

Lindsay, V. and Greenberg, M.A. (2013). The evolution of the need for establishing a national certification program for criminology/criminal justice majors. *Journal of the Institute and International Studies*, No. 13, 129–139.

Miami PD. (2013). Training center – Magnet high school. Retrieved October 3, 2013 from http://www.miami-police.org/magnet_program.html

Michalski, T. (2009, April 23). Police, explorers conduct 'paint out'. Retrieved May 24, 2012 from http://www.tbnweekly.com/pubs/pinellas_park_beacon/content_articles/042309_par-06.txt

PAL. (2012). Police athletic league of New York City: History. Retrieved May 24, 2012 from http://www.palnyc.org/800-PAL-4KIDS/History.aspx

PAMS Founder. (2013). Retrieved October 3, 2013 from http://resedapoliceacademy-magnet.com/pams-founder/

Patrol Manual. (2012). The Oak Ridge school safety patrol manual. Retrieved October 4, 2013 from http://learn.district196.org/pluginfile.php?file =%2F156989%2Fmod_resource%2Fcontent%2F0%2FSafety_Patrol_Manual_2012.pdf

Peterson, S. B. and Beres, J. (2008). *The first report to the nation on youth courts and teen courts.* Cleveland, OH: Global Issues Resource Center.

Pistol Team Wins. (1976, February 27). Pistol teams wins in pistol match. *St. Petersburg Independent*, p. 5-B.

Pocalyko, M. (2009, May 14). Online post no.423. Retrieved October 6, 2013 from http://community.nytimes.com/comments/www.nytimes.com/2009/05/14/us/14explorers.html?sort = oldest

Police Explorers. (2013). Aurora Police Department explorer post 2024. Retrieved September 28, 2013 from https://www.auroragov.org/LivingHere/YouthResources/PoliceExplorers/index.htm

Police Host. (2012). Police host exchange visitor. *City News*, p. 4.

Popular Activity. (1949). *Popular activity of the Birmingham recreation program is the Junior Police Academy …. (photo caption).* Free Press, Birmingham, UK, p. 10.

Rowbatham, J. F. (1895). *The history of Rossall School* (1st ed.), Manchester, UK: John Heywood.

Sacramento PD. (2013). Criminal Justice Magnet Academy. Retrieved October 3, 2013 from http://www.sacpd.org/getinvolved/student/magnet/

Sondheimer, E. (2013, January 14). Football: Ex-Reseda coach Joel Schaeffer dies. Retrieved October 3, 2013 from http://latimesblogs.latimes.com/varsitytimes-insider/2013/01/football-ex-reseda-coach-joel-schaeffer-dies.html

Steinhauer, J. (2009, May 14). Scouts train to fight terrorists, and more. *New York Times*, p. A1.

Torok, R. (2013, May 1). Turning teens into police officers. Retrieved January 25, 2014 from http://www.jewishjournal.com/los_angeles/item/turning_teens_into_police_officers

Waterloo Handbook. (2012). Waterloo Police, S.A.E.S.A. Explorers handbook. Retrieved May 23, 2012 from http://www.docstoc.com/docs/23703765/Waterloo-Police-Explorers-Handbook

Weintraub, R. (2011, July 14). A Note from our founder, Roberta Weintraub. Retrieved January 25, 2014 from http://poppartc.com/2011/07/a-note-from-our-founder-roberta-weintraub/

Westland Police. (2012a). About us: Westland police explorers. Retrieved May 26, 2012 from http://www.westlandpoliceexplorers.com/index.php?option = com_content&view = article&id = 47&Itemid = 53

Westland Police. (2012b). The sober up program. Retrieved May 26, 2012 from http://www.westlandpoliceexplorers.com/index.php?option=com_content&view=article&id=52&Itemid=58

Wilmath, K. (2008, December 24). Police explorer's bravery inspires bill. *Tampa Bay Times*. Retrieved May 24, 2012 from http://www.tampabay.com/news/article947749.ece

WSCC. (2012). Junior Police Academy. Retrieved May 18, 2012 http://www.wscc.edu/programs-and-certificates/public-service/public-safety-academies/junior-police-academy.html

Youth Protection. (2013). Youth protection training. Retrieved September 27, 2013 from http://exploring.learningforlife.org/services/resources/youth-protection-training/

# Youth Involvement in Public Safety and Security at the Federal Level

# 9

We cannot always build the future for our youth, but we can build our youth for the future.

**—Franklin Delano Roosevelt**
*Address at the University of Pennsylvania, September 20, 1940*

## Introduction

Adult volunteer participation in law enforcement is found at all governmental levels, but it is mostly a local endeavor. At the federal level, there exist a variety of obvious roles such as: voting in national elections, calling emergency federal "hotlines," serving on federal juries, and participating in interest groups to influence federal policy. Other roles also exist. For example, citizen participation in identifying and reporting potential and alleged violations of various federal regulatory laws, such as bringing citizen lawsuits in the federal district courts against polluters for violations of environmental laws. The Internal Revenue Service has had a citizen reward program for many years. Also known as the "whistle-blower program," it offers informants rewards of up to 30% of any fines and unpaid taxes recouped by the government. Other federal agencies have similar programs, and awards can be in the million-dollar range (see Kocieniewski 2012). However, citizen participation also includes mainstream organizations concerned with public safety, disaster relief, and homeland security, such as the Federal Emergency Management Agency (FEMA), the U.S. Coast Guard Auxiliary, and the Civil Air Patrol.

Of course, young people under the age of 18 cannot vote or sit on juries and are unlikely to possess the type of information necessary to benefit from the various bounty programs conducted by federal agencies. Nevertheless, as we have seen in Chapter 8, youth and young adults still have other significant opportunities to contribute to the field of law enforcement at the local level. Moreover, there exist several national and federal programs for involving youth in the field of public safety and security. The most well-known examples are: Senior (college level) Reserve Officers' Training Corps (ROTC) units, Junior ROTC units, U.S. Navy Sea Cadets,[1] and the Civil Air Patrol Cadet Program.

Although numerous operational similarities exist, it would be a mistake to assume that the current mix of federal law enforcement related youth programs has been simply modeled after the local and state Police Explorer programs of the past half century (discussed in Chapter 8) because other factors must be considered. For example, for nearly 100 years, the federal government has been directly involved in youth education and occupational preparation, primarily due to the need for preparedness in the area of national defense. During the 1920s and 1930s, aside from the Civilian Conservation Corps (CCC),[2] the most well-known (but now forgotten) example of such a program was the Citizens' Military Training Camp (CMTC) program introduced by Major General Leonard Wood in 1913.

Today, the most manifest and enduring examples of federal law enforcement or military-related youth initiatives are: Senior (college level) ROTC units, Junior ROTC units, U.S. Navy Sea Cadets, and the Civil Air Patrol Cadet Program. In 2012, a partnership between FEMA (a division within the U.S. Department of Homeland Security) and the Corporation for National and Community Service (CNCS) formed the FEMA Corps for young people aged 18–24. In addition, a frequently asked question at the FEMA Web site is whether young people under 18 can participate in the Community Emergency Response Team (CERT) program. This is considered a local decision. Someone under 18 should be with a parent or have permission to attend. Some communities have reached out specifically to young people. Florida's Winter Springs High School offers the training to high school students. CERT is a great way to address the community service requirements for high school students, and it provides students with useful skills. According to the FEMA Web page, CERT also fits nicely with training given to Boy and Girl Scouts and to the Civil Air patrol.

In addition to the foregoing list of organizations, there are a variety of federal Law Enforcement Explorer Leadership academies as well as more than two dozen Explorer Posts sponsored by the U.S. Customs and Border Protection service. A few features of the civilian military training camps of past generations have appeared again in these modern-day programs. Apparently, each arose out of concern for the future well-being of youth. Several programs also address the need to prepare thousands of young people for future careers related to homeland security. This chapter considers many of the leading federal initiatives for youth in public safety activities as well as information regarding the availability of federal internship opportunities.

## The Citizens' Military Training Camps

Military training camps for civilians were established just prior to World War I. In 1913, under the direction of Major General Leonard Wood, two "vacation camps" were held for students from educational institutions in

Monterey, California, and Gettysburg, Pennsylvania. The men who attended these camps paid their own expenses. Four camps were held in 1914, and five camps were offered in 1915. A 1916 amendment to the National Defense Act led to the establishment of 12 camps, with the federal government covering the expenses associated with each camp. By 1921, the camp programs gained a permanent status when the CMTC program was created under the 1920 National Defense Act (Citizens' Military Training 2013). It could be considered a "youth" program because participants could be as young as 17. The CMTC program ended in 1941. The purpose of CMTCs was to train young men (approximately 17–30 years old) of good character for 30 day summer periods of time in order to promote citizenship, patriotism, and Americanism, as well as to benefit the young men individually and to instill in them a sense of obligation to the country through physical, athletic, and military training. Those interested filed an application, which included a medical fitness statement and a certificate of good moral character signed by a prominent citizen such as a member of the clergy, a current or former officer of the armed forces, or a schoolteacher (War Department 1925).

Initially, the program consisted of three training levels (Red, White, and Blue), and in 1923, an advanced Red level course was added. In time, the courses were simply identified as: Basic, Red, White, and Blue. There was no obligation to join the regular service, but opportunities did exist to do so. The government paid all expenses including transportation to and from the camps, as well as paying for all food, clothing, housing, and medical care (War Department 1925).

Instruction was given over a four-year period with each course conducted for a month during the summer. The usual age of participation in the first or basic course was between 17 and 24. By 1924, the total number of civilian trainees had passed the 30,000 level (Citizens' Military Training 2013). National Guard, organized reserves and, later, ROTC personnel could also take the advanced training levels in order to increase their rank (War Department 1925).

Camp Meade (renamed Fort Meade in 1929) belonged to the III Corps area. It was named for Maj. Gen. George Gordon Meade, whose victory at the Battle of Gettysburg proved a major factor in turning the tide of the Civil War in favor of the North. The largest number of CMTC participants in the III Corps area, which included men from Pennsylvania, Maryland, Virginia, and the District of Columbia, trained at Camp Meade, Maryland. In 1923, about 4,000 attended Camp Meade, and the number remained high in 1940 at approximately 3,000. Participants at Camp Meade had facilities such as a theater, swimming pool, and library (War Department 1925). The Army Tank School was originally located at Fort Meade after World War I. It became a training center during

World War II, its ranges and other facilities used by more than 200 units and approximately 3.5 million men between 1942 and 1946 (Fort Meade History 2013).

## College Level ROTC Units

Members of college level ROTC units engage in most of the same activities as regular college students. For example, they earn a four-year academic degree and learn to think and reason at the college level. However, at the same time, they learn leadership skills and have experiences that will qualify them to become commissioned officers in the particular military unit (e.g., Army, Air Force, Navy, and Marines) located on their campus. ROTC is taken for elective credit and, depending upon the student's major, may count as a minor in military science. The modern Army Reserve Officers' Training Corps was created by the National Defense Act of 1916. This program commissioned its first class of lieutenants after World War I. The concept behind ROTC, however, had its roots in military training that began taking place in civilian colleges and universities as early as 1819 with the founding of the American Literary, Scientific and Military Academy at Norwich, Vermont (today's Norwich University). Thereafter, various other military schools were established, including the civilian land-grant colleges, which came after the Civil War and required military training to be part of their curriculum (History of ROTC 2013). In 1887, the Marian Military Institute (MMI) was established in Alabama. The school evolved over the years and it traces its organization in the year 1842. It is considered the oldest military junior college in the nation. An ROTC program was introduced at MMI in 1916.

The Naval Reserve Officer Training Corps (NROTC) at the Berkeley campus of the University of California is among the oldest ROTC units in the country. One of the original six ROTC units created, NROTC Berkeley was originally headed by Chester W. Nimitz, the famous World War II fleet admiral. Since then, NROTC Berkeley has been training college students in the disciplines of leadership, physical fitness, and military sciences. Over the years, the addition of such institutional affiliates as the California Maritime Academy, University of California Davis, and Stanford University has increased the number of officers the unit has commissioned into the Navy and Marine Corps. Today, the unit has four officers, two civilian staff members, and 60–70 midshipmen (NROTC Berkeley 2013).

Currently, ROTC college programs are offered at more than 1,000 colleges and universities across the United States. Unlike other service branches, the Coast Guard has a different format for preparing officer candidates who are still undergraduate college students at certain approved colleges and institutions. The age qualification ranges from 19 through 27. It is called the College

Student Pre-Commissioning Initiative (CSPI) program.[3] Following college graduation, CSPI students attend the 17-week officer candidate school (OCS) in New London, Connecticut. Upon successful completion of OCS, graduates receive a commission as an ensign (O-1) and an assignment in one of the Coast Guard missions, including (but not limited to) marine safety and prevention, contingency planning, law enforcement and incident management, vessel navigation and safety, search and rescue coordination, and icebreaking. Information about this program is available at: http://www.ocoastguard.com/cspi.

## FEMA Corps

In 2012, the Department of Homeland Security's FEMA and the CNCS partnered to establish the FEMA Corps. The unit is limited to a maximum of 1,600 members within the AmeriCorps National Civilian Community Corps (NCCC), and its activities are solely devoted to disaster preparedness, response, and recovery (FEMA Corps 2013). A relatively new program, its goals include: the enhancement of the federal government's disaster capabilities; increasing the reliability and diversity of the disaster workforce; promoting an ethic of service; expanding education and economic opportunity for young people; and achieving significant cost savings. On a yearly basis, the program is expected to see a savings of approximately $60 million (FEMA Corps 2013).

FEMA Corps is a full-time residential service program for individuals aged 18–24. FEMA Corps members are assigned to one of five NCCC campuses (located in Denver, Colorado; Sacramento, California; Perry Point, Maryland; Vicksburg, Mississippi; and Vinton, Iowa). This program has been established to augment FEMA's existing workforce. FEMA also has a cadre of reservists that FEMA continues to call upon (FAQs 2013). Volunteers work directly with disaster survivors, support disaster recovery centers, and share disaster preparedness and mitigation information with the public (FEMA Corps 2013).

FEMA Corps members serve full-time for a 10-month term with an option to extend for a second year. Members serve in teams of 8–12 persons and are assigned to projects throughout the region served by their campus; they also travel to complete service projects throughout those regions. To be considered for FEMA Corps, candidates must first apply to AmeriCorps NCCC. The program is open to all U.S. citizens between the ages of 18 and 24. Members are given a living allowance of approximately $4,000 for 10 months of service; housing; meals; limited medical benefits; if needed, up to $400 a month for child care; and member uniforms, and members become eligible for the Segal AmeriCorps Education Award upon successful completion of the program (FEMA Corps 2013).

## Junior ROTC Units

In a variety of ways, the Junior ROTC units resemble the style of the junior police organizations, magnet schools, junior police academies, and military training camps previously reviewed. The Army Junior Reserve Officers' Training Corps (JROTC) also came into being with the passage of the National Defense Act of 1916. Under the provisions of this federal law, high schools were able to obtain a loan of federal military equipment, and students were able to receive instruction from active duty military personnel. In 1964, the ROTC Revitalization Act opened up JROTC to the other military services and replaced most of the active duty instructors with retirees who worked for and were cost shared by the schools. Title 10 of the U.S. Code declares that "the purpose of Junior Reserve Officers' Training Corps is to instill in students in United States secondary educational institutions the value of citizenship, service to the United States, personal responsibility, and a sense of accomplishment" (U.S. Army 2014). Leavenworth High School in Kansas claims the distinction of having the first official JROTC program in the United States. The school's official JROTC program has been in existence since 1917; however, it had a military science and tactics program as far back as 1897 (Lewis 2012).

In 1996, there were more than 2,400 JROTC programs nationwide. By 1999, the number of programs exceeded 2,600 with more than 400,000 participants (Hanser and Robyn 2000). In Hawaii, 29 public and private schools had JROTC programs in 1996. Kamehameha School established the first JROTC unit in Hawaii in 1916, followed by Punahou School in 1918. McKinley was Hawaii's first public school unit (in 1921) followed by Roosevelt (in 1938). Common curriculum topics include military history, science, and current affairs. Students can also participate on the rifle and drill teams; attend military balls; be part of the adventure training team, color guard, and honor guard; attend summer camps and field trips; and complete various community service projects. Activities are selected for self-esteem and leadership development (Kakesako 1996). See Box 9.1 for a list of JROTC program objectives compiled by the Jackson Public Schools in Mississippi.

Francis Lewis High School is located in Queens, one of the five boroughs comprising New York City. It is the city's second largest high school and arguably one of the nation's most diverse. With nearly 4,600 students enrolled, the school has nearly double the capacity for which it was designed more than 40 years ago. There are so many students that two school day sessions are held, with the first starting just after 7 a.m. and the second ending just before 7 p.m. There are no lockers due to lack of space; students must carry necessary books and materials throughout the day. With almost 700 cadets, Francis Lewis High School's JROTC program,

**BOX 9.1    OBJECTIVES OF JROTC PROGRAMS**

Awareness of the rights and responsibilities of citizenship

Preparation to be good leaders; willingness to show initiative and take charge

Ability to think logically and communicate effectively with others, orally and in writing

Commitment to improving physical fitness

Commitment to living drug free

Improved self-discipline and positive self-motivation

Awareness of the historical perspective of the military services

Awareness of the importance of teamwork

Development of core character traits and values for successful living

Greater self-awareness of strengths and weaknesses

Awareness of the problem solving/decision-making process for resolving issues

Fostering adaptability and confidence

Preparation for successful living upon graduation from high school

*Source:* http://www.jackson.k12.ms.us/content.aspx?url=/page/447

begun in 1994, is the largest in the country and recently won a national drill team competition. According to retired First Sgt. Richard Gogarty, Francis Lewis' senior army instructor: "The biggest mistake I ever made was underestimating kids…. You let them run with something, and they'll get it done" (Arel 2009). Most Francis Lewis cadets will go on to college. In fact, since 2003, 20 of them have been accepted to the U.S. Military Academy at West Point. Besides drill teams, the program also has male and female Raider squads (a sport similar to Ranger Challenge in Senior ROTC), an honor guard, a drum corps, and a choir. On any given day, some 300 students stay after school to participate in JROTC extracurricular activities. But for the overwhelming majority of students, their ROTC experience ends with graduation. This is because many are not American citizens; due to their alien status, they are not eligible to receive Senior ROTC scholarships (Arel 2009).

Junior RTOC cadets also get involved in community activities and may, on a rare occasion, earn a small salary due to a grant opportunity. For example, students in Aztec High School's Army JROTC program in Farmington, New Mexico, have begun using a $75,000 grant from the New Mexico Youth Conservation Corps to maintain and improve the nearby

Aztec Ruins National Monument while also learning skills and earning pay. Cadets work to replace pipes, build fences, grow gardens, remove invasive species, help with archaeological digs, and complete any other projects needed to preserve the monument. Selected students who participate in the program earn $2,000 to $3,000 as employees of the National Park Service (NMJROTC Unit 2012).

## Civil Air Patrol Cadets

Another federal program that predates the establishment of Law Enforcement Explorers posts is the Civil Air Patrol Cadet Program. Civil Air Patrol came into being in December 1941 as a civilian arm of the Army Air Force. It provided valuable war-related services, from hunting for German submarines off the coast to locating downed military pilots. It also supervised an extensive cadet program that provided military and aviation training to teenagers (see Figure 9.1 photo). The Civil Air Patrol guarded our coastlines against enemy infiltrators and U-boat attacks. After World War II, the Civil Air Patrol's contributions were recognized when Congress made this organization an official civilian auxiliary of the U.S. Air Force.

Although there are many youth-oriented programs in the United States today, Civil Air Patrol's cadet program is unique in that it uses aviation as its cornerstone. Thousands of young people aged 12 through 21 are introduced to aviation through Civil Air Patrol's cadet program. Young people are allowed to progress at their own pace through a 16-step program including aerospace education, leadership training, physical fitness, and moral leadership. Cadets compete for academic scholarships to further their studies in fields such as engineering, science, aircraft mechanics, aerospace medicine, meteorology, as well as many others. Those cadets who earn cadet officer status may enter the air force as an airman first class (E3) rather than an airman basic (E1) (CAP 2012). There are approximately 24,000 cadets of whom about 20% are female (see Cadets 2010).

**Figure 9.1** Civil Air Patrol Cadet Walter Spangenberg, a high school student, is seen in this photo at Stevens Airport in Frederick, Maryland, ca. 1943. (Courtesy of Library of Congress, Prints and Photographic Div.)

**Figure 9.2** CBP Explorers from Post 4701 (JFK Airport, New York, New York) and Post 4601 (Newark, New Jersey) pose at the New York City Marathon on November 1, 2009.

## Customs and Border Protection Explorer Posts

Today, more than 700 Explorers serve in Customs and Border Protection (CBP), a branch of the U.S. Department of Homeland Security. CBP appears to be the largest Law Enforcement Explorer Program in the federal government, having 28 posts, primarily in Texas, Arizona, and California at various ports of entry and at Border Patrol sectors. Routine activities include assisting with passenger processing and crowd control at airports and seaports, observing and assisting with surveillance operations, observing vessel searches, and taking field trips (CBP Explorer Program 2007). Some CBP Explorers have also participated as "crash victims" at simulated crash scenes during first responder drills (CBP Explorer Program 2008).

Some federally sponsored Explorers have engaged in other unusual activities. For example, the CBP Post 4701 (JFK Airport, New York, New York) and CBP Post 4601 (Newark, New Jersey) helped provide security at the start of the 2009 New York City Marathon (as seen in Figure 9.2). The New York City Marathon had more than 40,000 runners from all over the world. The Explorers' job was to control the starting line until the 26.2-mile race began. To start their job, the Explorers arrived at the runner's check-in area in Ft. Wadsworth, Staten Island, at 4:30 a.m. Their first assignment was to keep all runners in their designated areas prior to relocation at the starting area. The runners are started in staggered groups with the elite runners in the first group. The Explorers formed a human chain across the starting line to hold the runners in place. Five seconds before the start, members of the chain must run to the sides of the road in order to get out of the way of the runners (CBP Explorer Program 2009).

## National Law Enforcement Exploring Leadership Academy

The idea for the creation of federal leadership academies for Law Enforcement Explorers was first conceived by a Federal Bureau of Investigation (FBI) supervisory special agent who developed a curriculum for the program. The first National Law Enforcement Exploring Leadership Academy was conducted in

1985 at the FBI Academy in Quantico, Virginia. This FBI-sponsored National Law Enforcement Exploring Leadership Academy served as the model for similar local, regional, state, and federal agency sponsored Explorer academies. The National Law Enforcement Exploring Leadership Academy is considered a leading program. It is offered on a biennial schedule, hosted by various federal law enforcement agencies. The academy offers selected Explorers the opportunity to learn leadership skills (team building, how to motivate others, etc.). The academies also include historical, ceremonial, and recreational activities. In addition, the U.S. Drug Enforcement Administration (DEA), FBI, U.S. Marshals Service, and the Secret Service have hosted academies in the Washington, DC area, and the U.S. Military Police has hosted an academy in Ft. Leonard Wood, Missouri. The week-long federal academies are conducted during the summer when a National Law Enforcement Explorer Conference is not being held. The first biennial National Academy was held in 1979 at Michigan State University. Information about the leadership academies is posted on the Law Enforcement Exploring section of the Learning for Life Web site approximately one year prior to the event (Law Enforcement Exploring 2011, 13).

In July 2005, the DEA conducted a Law Enforcement Explorer Leadership Program at the DEA Training Academy in Quantico. Thirty Law Enforcement Explorers, aged 15–20, who had expressed serious interest in pursuing a career in federal law enforcement, attended the program. Training took place in the classroom and in the field using practical and team-building training scenarios. The students also experienced a "day in the life" of a DEA special agent, which included instruction in firearms, physical fitness, defensive tactics, and a team-building obstacle course. At the conclusion of the program, the Explorers received a graduation certificate and a video detailing their week-long experiences (DEA 2014). In order to attend a leadership program, youth usually submit an application consisting of all high school and college transcripts, letters of recommendation, and a detailed essay.

Currently attending college, Samantha Faro-Petersen of Winthrop, Massachusetts, is representative of the type of student selected to attend one of these academies. In 2011, she attended the National Law Enforcement Explorer FBI Leadership Academy after graduating from Pope John XXIII High School. In March 2012, she was selected as the "Explorer of the Year" at Winthrop Police Explorer Post 99. As a lieutenant at the post, she organized the biweekly meetings and helped to run the post's activities, including assisting with fundraising efforts for trips to the national conference (Domelowicz 2012).

## FBI Field Office Initiatives for Youth

The Criminal Justice Information Services (CJIS) Division of the FBI includes an extensive "Community Outreach Program." It is a nationwide initiative that connects local FBI offices with their communities. The program employs civilian community outreach specialists who coordinate programs and lead teams of volunteers from the FBI that provide meaningful services to communities throughout the nation. The overall program is designed to improve the FBI's understanding of the communities they serve and the threats these communities face. A large number of its outreach activities involve youth and school presentations. Programs have been presented on a variety of topics, including Hardest Working Student Award, Junior Special Agent Program, Student's Academy, Stranger Danger, Internet Safety, Cultural Awareness, K-9 Demonstration, and the Students Who Achieve Today (SWAT) Team.

The "Stranger Danger" presentation educates area youth about staying safe and provides practical information to prevent abduction, child abuse, and Internet stalking. In West Virginia, for "Cultural Awareness" purposes, FBI staff present a February Black History Month program to area schools. The program includes a choir of FBI employees who sing traditional and historical African American music. Choir members discuss the songs with the children to further cultivate cultural awareness. The "Student's Academy" is a 12-week course that gives students at high schools an inside view of the FBI. The "SWAT Team" serves as a catalyst to involve area high school students in projects such as child identification fingerprinting, producing public service announcements, creating drug and alcohol awareness posters, distributing child identification kits, and serving as ushers or escorts at FBI ceremonies (FBI, Community Outreach 2013).

The "Junior Special Agent Program" provides a biweekly overview of FBI and CJIS Division programs for fourth- and fifth-grade students that include lessons on civic duty. Students who complete the program are presented with a Junior Special Agent badge and credentials by the assistant director of the CJIS Division during a graduation ceremony. In 2012, more than 150 fourth- and fifth-grade students at Harms Elementary School in southwest Detroit completed the "FBI Junior Special Agent Program." Andrew G. Arena, Special Agent-in-Charge of the Detroit Division, said to the students: "You can be whatever you want to be. I'm from this neighborhood and this is what I've achieved" (Detroit Public Schools 2012). During the training sessions, the students learned about how law enforcement works and how they can make a difference in the community. Topics included bullying avoidance, self-defense, physical fitness, and the duties of the FBI (Detroit Public Schools 2012).

Other FBI initiatives involving youth have included additional educational programs. For example, in July 2013, a one-day FBI Baltimore Field Office Teen Academy Program for high school students aged 14–18 was offered to provide a firsthand look at law enforcement as a career choice. The competitively selected students learned about major investigations and participated in a variety of "hands-on" exercises that illustrated the duties and responsibilities of the FBI. Prospective attendees had to be residents of Delaware or Maryland, have a grade point average (GPA) of at least 2.5, provide a school reference, answer an essay question, and submit a completed application form (Teen Academy 2013).

An earlier illustration of FBI community outreach involved the FBI's Challenge Program held at the Police Fire Academy of Santa Teresa High School in San Jose, California. Goals of the program included reducing the risk of youth involvement in gang activities and drug abuse. The High School Police Fire Academy was established in 1988 as a "magnet" program to draw students from all areas of San Jose who expressed an interest in a public safety career. The FBI Challenge Program began in February 1994 as a supplement to the existing high school academy program. Staff members from the Police Fire Academy and the FBI developed an instructional program designed to motivate, encourage, and challenge students to excel, not only academically but also in their personal lives. FBI volunteers conducted presentations to help the students better understand the FBI's law enforcement role. They served as positive role models in discouraging student involvement in youth gangs and illicit drugs. Twice monthly training sessions (50 minutes in duration) covered a variety of topics including the history of the FBI and its jurisdiction, the importance of completing high school and staying out of trouble, positive alternatives to gangs and drug use, the uses and importance of fingerprints for law enforcement, the training required for agents, how to take fingerprints, the FBI's role in child abduction cases, and cultural diversity in law enforcement. The students at the Police Fire Academy are known as "cadets" and perform more than 5,000 hours of community service each year, involving such activities as event security, graffiti cleanup, park trail building and cleanup, assistance at domestic violence and child abuse conferences, recycling, and so on. (Smith and Stapleton 1995).

There at least two FBI-sponsored Explorer Posts. Post 2060 is affiliated with the New York field Office. The Edwin C. Shanahan Memorial Post 1920 is sponsored by the Chicago field office as a community outreach activity but is not a part of the FBI. The post is named to honor the memory of Special Agent Shanahan who was born and raised in Chicago and began his service with the FBI in 1920. Five years later, he became the first FBI agent in the United States to be killed in the line of duty. It is a registered 501(c)(3) organization and Illinois nonprofit charitable organization, assisting youths in their communities. Activities in the post are carried out in collaboration with local law enforcement agencies to give students hands-on exercises. Post goals involve instilling self-confidence and developing leadership abilities among the participating students. The post educates the students in learning segments. Seven learning sessions were completed in the first semester that began in August 2012. Six additional sessions are taught in the second semester, leading up to graduation. Topics of instruction include an introduction to the FBI selection process, the history and organization of the FBI, legal principles, basics of investigations, counterintelligence, evidence response and collection, interviewing and interrogations, and weapons familiarization. FBI personnel volunteer their time to conduct all sessions and are assisted by the post's layperson board of directors (Chicago FBI Explorers 2014).

## Youth Programs in American Territories

The United States possesses five major overseas areas namely, Puerto Rico, the U.S. Virgin Islands in the Caribbean, American Samoa, Guam, and the Northern Mariana Islands in the Pacific (see Figure 9.3). Those born in the major territories and commonwealths, except for American Samoa, possess U.S. citizenship. American citizens residing in the territories and commonwealths have many of the same rights and responsibilities as citizens residing in the United States; however, they are generally exempt from federal income tax, may not vote for president, and have only nonvoting representation

**Figure 9.3** In 2009, the United States Mint released proof quarter images depicting themes honoring the District of Columbia and five U.S. territories—Guam, American Samoa, U.S. Virgin Islands, the Commonwealth of Puerto Rico, and the Northern Mariana Islands.

in the U.S. Congress. American Samoa, Guam, and the Virgin Islands are all territories of the United States. Washington, D.C., and the Northern Mariana Islands are commonwealths. Puerto Rico was once a territory but is now a commonwealth. American Samoans are considered U.S. nationals not citizens. They can elect one nonvoting delegate to the U.S. House of Representatives, who is permitted to cast votes on amendments to a bill but not on its final passage. The 580,000 U.S. citizens living in Washington, D.C., have one nonvoting delegate in Congress, but they can vote for president due to the ratification of the 23rd Amendment of the U.S. Constitution, sending three members to the Electoral College (Rubin 2014).

Two CBP Explorer Posts from the Caribbean participated in the week-long 2006 National Law Enforcement Exploring Leadership Academy conference held at Northern Arizona University in Flagstaff, Arizona. The two participating posts were San Juan Post 818 and U.S. Virgin Islands Post 5101. CBPs Puerto Rico Explorers Post 818 sent 18 Explorers and U.S. Virgin Islands Post 5101 sent seven Explorers to participate in the hostage negotiation, emergency field first aid, pistol, bomb search, crime prevention, shoot/don't shoot, and white-collar crime competitions. Members of CBP Explorer Posts in Puerto Rico and the U.S. Virgin Islands have attended 10 National Law Enforcement Explorer Conferences since 1988. There have been at least seven Explorer Posts in Puerto Rico. At least two of these posts had themes other than border protection; for example, the Ponce, Puerto Rico, post focused on fire and emergency services. Explorer Post 156 in Carolina, Puerto Rico, was the first military aviation Exploring Post in the United States (Explorer Posts 2006).

## Federal Internships for College Students

There are also numerous internship opportunities throughout the federal government. However, many of the positions involve stiff competition and require early application. These are mainly available to college students at the undergraduate and graduate levels. (To access internship opportunities and information within the federal government for undergraduate, graduate, and law students, visit the links indicated at the federal government Web page: http://answers.usa.gov/system/templates/selfservice/USAGov/#!portal/1012/article/3800/Government20Internships.)

There are a variety of agencies offering internship opportunities, including the Consumer Product Safety Commission, the Department of Homeland Security, the Smithsonian Institution, the Peace Corps, the Internal Revenue Service, the Department of Justice, and the Administrative Office of the U.S. Courts. The Administrative Office of the U.S. Courts supports the mission of the federal courts to provide equal justice under the law. It accepts interns throughout the year in many of its program offices and recruits students with career goals and interests in court administration and management, information technology, human resources, budget and finance, law, criminal justice, legislative and public affairs, and education and training.

The mission of the DEA is to identify, target, investigate, disrupt, and dismantle the international, national, state, and local drug trafficking organizations that are having the most significant impact in the United States. They are committed to investigating and prosecuting major drug law violators in the United States and all over the world. The DEA currently accepts college students in volunteer (nonpaid) internships throughout the year in many of their domestic offices, which are located throughout the United States. Student volunteers may work up to six months with the DEA to gain experience in clerical and administrative support positions that involve activities such as organizing nondrug evidence, answering telephones, or performing research projects. Students are required to be enrolled at least half-time in college and in good academic standing in order to participate in the program (Watt 2010).

The special agents of the U.S. Naval Crime Investigative Service (NCIS) "are among the most adept and resourceful law enforcement professionals anywhere. Never restricted to a narrow specialty, even relatively junior agents are expected to handle a wide variety of criminal, counterterrorism, and counterintelligence matters with equal skill. Special Agents travel the globe and may even be stationed aboard ship" (Careers at NCIS 2013). The NCIS encourages college juniors, seniors, and graduate students who are interested in a criminal justice career to apply for an internship with an NCIS field office. The NCIS internship is an unpaid, hands-on opportunity, designed to provide education-related work assignments for students. The NCIS seeks individuals who possess strong academic credentials, outstanding character, and a high degree of motivation. Those candidates who exhibit excellent research, analytical, and communication skills are considered, regardless of academic major. Internship candidates who reside in or who attend the universities located within the respective field office geographic area of operations are afforded priority consideration in the selection process (NCIS Honors 2013). A 50-page guide to the NCIS Honors Intern Program with descriptions of dozens of field office opportunities is available online at: http://www.ncis.navy.mil/Careers/Interns/Pages/default.aspx.

The mission of NCIS is to investigate and defeat criminal, terrorist, and foreign intelligence threats to the United States Navy and Marine Corps— ashore, afloat, and in cyberspace. It is the federal law enforcement agency charged with conducting investigations of felony-level offenses affecting the Navy and Marine Corps—that is, crimes punishable by confinement for more than one year. The NCIS is comprised of some 2,400 personnel in more than 40 countries around the globe. The organization is roughly 90% civilian, and its cadre of federal agents—about half its total personnel—is 98% civilian (NCIS Honors 2013).

For many years, the FBI has sponsored a robust summer intern program for high-achieving college students; in 2014, however, budgetary restrictions affected the FBI's ability to staff the internship programs. Consequently, in 2014, the Bureau suspended the FBI Honors Internship Program, the FBI Volunteer Internship Program, and the Cyber Internship Program. Interested students will need to keep informed about the availability of these and all federal internship opportunities by periodically examining agency Web sites (see FBI Internships 2013). A selected list of potential internship opportunities with federal intelligence agencies and law enforcement agencies is included in Appendix D.

## Summary

The present chapter has described a range of federal initiatives for involving youth in public safety and security. In particular, Junior and Senior ROTC units offer valuable leadership skills training and may qualify individuals to become commissioned officers in a branch of the armed forces. In addition, the Civil Air Patrol Cadet Program also includes opportunities for educational and career advancement. Opportunities for participation in the new FEMA Corps exist that can provide service members with one or more years of hands-on experience in the field of emergency management. Various living allowances and educational stipends are paid to FEMA Corps and senior ROTC participants.

In addition, college students at the undergraduate and graduate levels can apply for a wide variety of federal agency internships. However, many of the positions involve stiff competition and require early application. For example, the NCIS encourages college juniors, seniors, and graduate students who are interested in a criminal justice career to apply for an internship with an NCIS field office.

Although the concept of "community policing" is generally associated with local law enforcement, the broad reach of federal criminal statutes and their enforcement extends into local communities. Thus, federal law enforcement agencies have every reason to be concerned about community youth and to establish and maintain youth programs. Federal agencies and agents who work with youths are promoting public safety and the quality of community life.

At the federal level, the achievement of the promises of community policing may be enhanced through junior police units such as Police Explorers and related public safety programs. By involving young people, any federal department strengthens its abilities to resist and prevent crime and disorder. The mere addition of such a program supports more congenial relationships among the youths of a community, the local police, and special agents federal. All law enforcement agencies should develop these programs as an integral agency function, and they should draw on the knowledge and skills of individual federal officers and agents. Through involvement with such programs, individual officers are bound to become more committed, empowered, and analytical within their own professional careers. However, due to major concerns about the threat posed by terrorists, there is a potential for federal law enforcement agencies to exploit their community outreach programs for intelligence gathering purposes.

## Review Questions

1. Identify at least four youth programs at the federal level that are concerned with public safety and security.
2. State the purpose of the Citizens' Military Training Camp (CMTC) program. Search online to identify any similar program that might still be in existence.
3. List the areas of study and training involved in the NROTC Berkeley program.
4. Indicate three roles performed by FEMA Corps members.
5. List at least five JROTC program objectives compiled by the Jackson Public Schools in Mississippi and discuss their relevance for building self-esteem and leadership skills.
6. Many students in the Army JROTC program at Francis Lewis High School (Queens, New York) are not American citizens; due to their alien status, they are not eligible to receive Senior ROTC scholarships after they graduate. Discuss the pros and cons of this policy.
7. The FBI has conducted a variety of community outreach programs involving youth. Discuss why the FBI considers these to be important initiatives.
8. The American Civil Liberties Union (ACLU) has commented that on some occasions "it appears FBI agents are improperly exploiting the goodwill established through its community outreach programs as a method of gaining access to community members for investigative purposes" (see German 2013). Conduct online research to ascertain the validity or invalidity of this commentary.
9. Search online to find at least one federal agency that interests you. Describe the nature and qualifications of any internships available for college students.

## Notes

1. Sea Cadet organizations exist in most of the maritime nations of the world. In 1958, at the request of the U.S. Navy, the Navy League of the United States established the Naval Sea Cadet Corps (NSCC) for American youth aged 13–17. The program is designed for youth who have a desire to learn about the Navy, Marine Corps, Coast Guard, and Merchant Marines. "Sea Cadets are authorized by the Secretary of the Navy to wear Navy uniforms appropriately marked with the Sea Cadet Corps insignia. The objectives of the Sea Cadet program are to introduce youth to naval life, to develop in them a sense of pride, patriotism, courage, self-reliance, and to maintain an environment free of drugs and gangs" (Sea Cadets 2013). In addition, a junior version of the Sea Cadet program is also conducted for youth in the age range of 11–14. This is also a Navy League program. It is designed to introduce young people to maritime and military life and to prepare them for later entrance into the NSCC (Navy League 2013).

2. Formed in March 1933, the Civilian Conservation Corps, was one of the first New Deal programs. It was a public works project intended to promote environmental conservation and to build good citizens through vigorous, disciplined outdoor labor. President Franklin Roosevelt believed that this civilian "tree army" would relieve the rural unemployed and keep youth "off the city street corners." The CCC operated under the supervision of the U.S. Army. Camp commanders had disciplinary powers and corpsmen were required to address superiors as "sir." By September 1935, more than 500,000 young men had lived in CCC camps, most staying from six months to a year. In all, nearly three million young men participated in the CCC and more than 800 parks were built (see Foner and Garraty 1991).

3. CSPI is a scholarship and leadership training program for future Coast Guard officers. Enrolled students must adhere to high standards of performance and conduct in order to maintain their scholarship status. In this way, the program is similar to ROTC. However, unlike the typical ROTC program, CSPI students are actually active duty enlisted members of the Coast Guard with full pay and benefits—until completion of OCS, when they receive a commission as an officer. An important requirement is sophomore or junior undergraduate status or having been accepted for enrollment in a bachelor degree program at an accredited college or university designated as a minority institution. Links to the institutions that satisfy this educational requirement are found at: http://www.gocoastguard.com/find-your-career/officer-opportunities/programs/college-student-pre-commissioning-initiative-(scholarship-program).

## References

Arel, S. (2009). Big-city JROTC is model program. Retrieved May 22, 2012 from http://armyrotc.wordpress.com/2009/12/02/big-city-jrotc-is-model-program/

Cadets. (2010, April 8). Cadets by the numbers. Retrieved May 24, 2012 from http://www.capmembers.com/file.cfm/media/blogs/documents/Stats_C091196AC47C8.pdf

CAP. (2012). Cadet programs. Retrieved May 24, 2012 from http://www.gocivilairpatrol. com/about/civil_air_patrols_three_primary_missions/cadet_p rograms.cfm

Careers at NCIS. (2013). Retrieved October 10, 2013 from http://www.ncis.navy.mil/ Careers/Pages/default.aspx

CBP Explorer Program. (2007, September 21). Be an explorer. Retrieved May 24, 2012 from http://www.cbp.gov/xp/cgov/careers/explorer_program/explorer.xml

CBP Explorer Program. (2008, October 28). CBP explorers and officers survive disaster drill 'plane crash'. Retrieved May 24, 2012 from http://www.cbp.gov/xp/ cgov/careers/explorer_program/expl_news/drill_plane_crash.xml

CBP Explorer Program. (2009, November 16). Explorers help to provide security at the start of the 2009 New York City Marathon. Retrieved May 24, 2012 from http://www.cbp.gov/xp/cgov/careers/explorer_program/expl_news/ny_marathon.xml

Chicago FBI Explorers. (2014). Chicago FBI Explorers: About. Retrieved March 4, 2014 from http://www.facebook.com/Chicagoexplorerpost1920/info

Citizens' Military Training. (2013). Citizens' Military Training Camp. Retrieved October 7, 2013 from http://1-22infantry.org/history/cmtcpartone.htm

DEA (2014). Law enforcement explorers. Retrieved June 27, 2014 from http://www. justice.gov/dea/ops/Training/Community.shtml

Detroit Public Schools. (2012, February 3). FBI hosts graduation ceremony for 'FBI junior special agents' -1st program of its kind in Southwest Detroit. Retrieved September 24, 2013 from http://detroitk12.org/content/2012/02/03/fbi-hosts-graduation-ceremony-for-f bi-junior-special-agents1st-program-of-its-kind-in-southwest-detroit/

Domelowicz, J. (2012, March 16). Three-year veteran Faro-Petersen named 2011 Explorer of the Year. *Winthrop Transcript*. Retrieved May 24, 2012 from http:// www.winthroptra nscript.com/2012/03/16/three-year-veteran-faro-petersen-named-2011-explorer-of-the- year/

Explorer Posts. (2006, July 6). Explorers Posts 818 and 5101 represent the Caribbean. Retrieved October 8, 2013 from http://cbp.gov/archived/xp/cgov/newsroom/ news_releases/archives/2006_news_releases/ 072006/07062006.xml.html

FAQs. (2013). Frequently asked questions (FAQs). Retrieved October 9, 2013 from http://www.nationalservice.gov/about/frequently-asked-questions-faqs#12454

FBI, Community Outreach. (2013). Retrieved October 10, 2013 from http://www.fbi. gov/about- us/cjis/community-outreach

FBI Internships. (2013). Retrieved October 12, 2013 from http://www.fbijobs.gov/ 2.asp

FEMA Corps. (2013). Retrieved October 9, 2013 from http://www.nationalservice. gov/programs/americorps/fema-corps

Foner, E. and Garraty, J. A. (1991). *The reader's companion to American history*. New York: Houghton Mifflin Harcourt.

Fort Meade History. (2013). Retrieved October 7, 2013 from http://www.ftmeade. army.mil/pages/history/history.html

German, M. (2013, February 15). Is the FBI's community outreach program a Trojan horse? Retrieved October 10, 2013 from http://www.aclu.org/blog/ national-security/fbis- community-outreach-program-trojan-horse

Hanser, L. M. and Robyn, A. E. (2000). *Implementing high school JROTC career academies*. Santa Monica, CA: RAND.

History of ROTC. (2013). History of ROTC beginning. Retrieved October 2, 2013 from http://www.hsu.edu/interior4.aspx?id = 2996

Kakesako, G. K. (1996). Snap and polish. Retrieved May 22, 2012 from http://archives.starbulletin.com/96/12/10/news/story1.html

Kocieniewski, D. (2012, September 12). Whistle-blower awarded $104 million by I.R.S. *New York Times*, p. A1.

Law Enforcement Exploring. (2011, July). Law Enforcement Exploring: Program and resource guide for adult leaders. Retrieved May 24, 2012 from http://c183757.ssl.cf1.rackcdn.com/wp- content/documents/LEE_Program%20and%20Resource%20Guide_0811.pdf

Lewis, P. (2012). Our history: The first JROTC unit. Retrieved May 22, 2012 from http://www.usd453.org/gen/usd453_generated_pages/Our_History__The_First_JROTC_ Unit_m1208.html

Navy League. (2013). Navy League Cadets – Age 11–14. Retrieved September 24, 2013 from http://www.seacadets.org/public/programs/nlcc/

NCIS Honors. (2013). NCIS Honors Intern Program. Retrieved October 9, 2013 from http://www.ncis.navy.mil/Careers/Interns/Documents/NCIS%20Honors%20Intern%20Program%20June%202013.pdf

N.M. JROTC Unit. (2012, February). N.M. JROTC unit lands $75,000 grant for spring project. *The Cadet, 3*(1), 2.

NROTC Berkeley (2013). Naval Reserve Officers Training Corps, UC Berkeley. Retrieved October 9, 2013 from http://navyrotc.berkeley.edu/

Rubin, J. (2014). Can American Samoans vote? Retrieved January 23, 2014 from http://www.slate.com/articles/news_and_politics/explainer/2008/01/canamerican_samoan svote.html

Sea Cadets. (2013) Sea Cadets – Ages 13 – 17. Retrieved September 30, 2013 from http://www.seacadets.org/public/programs/nscc/

Smith, W. E. and Stapleton, M. E. (1995). FBI challenge program: Inspiring youth to a law enforcement career. *FBI Law Enforcement Bulletin, 64*(9), 1–5.

Teen Academy. (2013). Baltimore FBI Field Office Teen Academy flyer. Retrieved September 24, 2013 from http://www.youth202.org/sites/default/files/Teen%20Academy%20brochure%20new.pdf

U.S. Army. (2014). U.S. Army Junior ROTC: History. Retrieved June 27, 2014 from http://www.cadetcommand.army.mil/jrotc-history.aspx

War Department. (1925). Album of photographs of Citizen Military Training Camp, Camp Meade, Maryland, 1925 – 1925, scope and content. Retrieved October 7, 2013 from http://research.archives.gov/description/542449

Watt, M. (2010). Internship opportunities within the federal government. Retrieved October 8, 2013 from http://gwired.gwu.edu/career/merlin-cgi/p/downloadFile/d/24559/n/off/other/1/name/FedInternship_Opportunities_20101pdf/

# Legal Issues and Volunteer Police

# 10

The police are the public and the public are the police; the police being only members of the public who are paid to give full time attention to duties which are incumbent on every citizen in the interests of community welfare and existence.

**—Sir Robert Peel**

During his service as home secretary, Sir Robert Peel (1788–1850) introduced a number of important reforms to British criminal law. His changes to the penal code system resulted in fewer crimes carrying a death penalty sentence and the provision of educational programs for inmates. In the criminal justice field, he is most often remembered as the "founder of modern policing" (Nazemi 2013). In 1829, Peel was successful in establishing the Metropolitan Police of London. His achievement helped him become prime minister of England in 1835. The initial force had over a thousand officers and was studied throughout the century as a new approach to crime fighting. In time, after the passing of the County Police Act in 1839, its style was duplicated in the London Boroughs and then into the counties and towns.

Many characteristics of Peel's police were adopted in the United States. Peel proclaimed that "The police are the public and the public are the police." (Commissioner Bratton's Blog 2014) One of the major tenets of this understanding was the recognition that police must secure the willing cooperation of the public in voluntary observation of the law, and a vital way to accomplish this support was by constantly demonstrating absolute impartiality in the enforcement of the law and in the delivery of services. These tenets form an important part of modern-day police efforts. Both sworn volunteer police (i.e., those possessing peace officer status) and non-sworn police volunteers may best contribute to the safety of the public by following Peel's tenets. Peel established the Metropolitan Police based on several major principles or tenets. In many communities throughout the world, these principles are cited as the basic foundation for current law enforcement organizations and community policing (see Box 10.1).

Police officers and their volunteer counterparts or aides not only need to be familiar with Peel's tenets but also with many other regulations and laws. There are a huge number of principles, rules, court decisions, and statutes that program administrators and volunteer police and police volunteers need to know. Some changes in state law can be expected from time to time.

## BOX 10.1 PEEL'S PRINCIPLES FOR POLICING

1. The basic mission for which the police exist is to prevent crime and disorder.
2. The ability of the police to perform their duties is dependent upon public approval of police actions.
3. Police must secure the willing cooperation of the public in voluntary observance of the law to be able to secure and maintain the respect of the public.
4. The degree of cooperation of the public that can be secured diminishes proportionately to the necessity of the use of physical force.
5. Police seek and preserve public favor not by catering to the public opinion but by constantly demonstrating absolute impartial service to the law.
6. Police use physical force to the extent necessary to secure observance of the law or to restore order only when the exercise of persuasion, advice, and warning is found to be insufficient.
7. Police, at all times, should maintain a relationship with the public that gives reality to the historic tradition that the police are the public and the public are the police; the police being only members of the public who are paid to give full-time attention to duties which are incumbent on every citizen in the interests of community welfare and existence.
8. Police should always direct their action strictly toward their functions and never appear to usurp the powers of the judiciary.
9. The test of police efficiency is the absence of crime and disorder, not the visible evidence of police action in dealing with it.

*Source:* http://lacp.org/2009-Articles-Main/062609-Peels9Principals-SandyNazemi.htm

For example, in 2012, a new state law in Oregon became effective relating to the status of reserve police officers. The law includes reserve officers within the definitions of "peace officer" and "police officer" for certain purposes (see House Bill 3153, 76th oregon legislative assembly—2011 Regular Session). In Illinois, a rule change by the Law Enforcement and Standards Training Board was implemented in 2006. It requires that all municipal governments (and law enforcement agencies) that exercise their option to create an auxiliary police unit in the state of Illinois shall provide the Illinois Law Enforcement and Standards Training Board with a copy of their local ordinance. Moreover, the rules requires that the "Ordinance shall explicitly indicate whether auxiliary officers are designated as having conservator of the peace powers. In the case of municipalities which create auxiliary police units by ordinance, but explicitly state (within the ordinance) that officers are not to exercise 'conservator of the peace' powers, then all auxiliary officers so designated shall be required to complete the 40-Hour Mandatory Firearms Training Course before being permitted to carry a firearm.... Auxiliary police officers with conservator of the peace powers will be directed to attend the 400-Hour Basic Law Enforcement Officer Training Course at a certified State academy" (Statement of Policy 2006).

This chapter highlights several legal concepts and laws that are crucial for the achievement of the basic police mission of preventing crime and disorder as well as the successful fulfillment of the numerous tasks associated with being a volunteer law enforcement officer. It deals, especially, with those liability issues that may arise when private citizens take on volunteer policing roles. The Federal Emergency Management Agency's (FEMA) *The Citizen Corps Volunteer Liability Guide* is briefly reviewed. The materials in this chapter and those available in the *Volunteer Liability Guide* are offered for general information purposes only. They do not constitute legal advice, and the user is encouraged to seek out state-specific counsel from a qualified attorney before taking any action.

## Overview of the Law

The U.S. government, the governments of each of the 50 states, and their many subdivisions have established rights and responsibilities through a system of laws. Laws are considered a system because they come from more than one source and they work together. A basic understanding of this system helps one understand the laws that may affect volunteer police liability. The components of the legal system include the following:

- Constitutions outline the principles of a government and provide a foundation for its exercise of powers. Federal and state governments have constitutions.
- Statutes are codes of laws that are enacted by the elected members of the legislatures of federal, state, territorial, tribal, and local governments.
- Regulations are rules adopted by government agencies to implement statutes.
- Common law or case law is a body of legal principles derived from the decisions of federal and state courts in individual lawsuits, which factor into deciding the outcome of later cases.

All of these components of the law affect one another, and they all affect emergency or police volunteers. Courts interpret constitutions, statutes, and regulations when deciding cases before them. Legislatures that do not like a court decision may pass a statute that could produce different results in future cases. Agencies revise regulations to conform to new statutes or to comply with court decisions. Complete research of a legal issue looks at all these components of the law and how they interact (FEMA 2014).

## Status and Authority

There are about 15,000 municipal or local police departments and about another 3,500 county, state, and federal law enforcement agencies in the United States. The municipal agencies may also include a variety of specialized groups such as school and transit police forces. No other nation in the world has ever had as many different types of police departments as the United States; a fact that means no two police agencies in America are structured alike or function in the same way (Inciardi 2000). Therefore, agency responsibilities, patrol policies, technology, departmental rules, and a wide range of other practices will vary from agency to agency and from state to state. The same pattern holds true for volunteer police units.

The city of Waltham, Massachusetts, is 8.5 miles from Boston and occupies about 13 square miles. The city is home to Brandeis University and Bentley University, which have a combined full-time enrollment of approximately 10,000 students (Waltham, MA, 2013).

Its population is about 62,000. Approximately 45% of the adult population who are over the age 25 has a bachelor's degree or higher. The median household income is about $68,000, and about 10% of the population is below the poverty level (U.S. Census Data 2013). The area is known for its cotton mills and famous pocket watches. It is safer than 48% of the cities in the United States (Crime Rates 2013), and in 2011 had 174 full-time police department employees, of whom 147 were police officers.

Early in 2011, the following notice concerning auxiliary police appeared at the bottom of the city of Waltham's Web page: "February 1, 2011—Effective immediately the Waltham Police Department will not be accepting applications for the position of Auxiliary Police Officer. There will be NO First Tuesday of the Month Recruiting Meeting until further notice. Please check back with this website periodically" (Auxiliary Police Department 2011). What had happened to cause this announcement?

The events leading to the unit's demobilization were a shoplifting arrest and a 2011 lawsuit by the alleged shoplifter for use of excessive force, false arrest, and false imprisonment. The suit was filed against two Waltham City police officers and one auxiliary officer. Eventually, the lawsuit was settled.

At the time, however, an issue arose over the liability coverage for the city's auxiliary police force when the private firm handling legal matters for the Waltham Police Department refused to represent the volunteer auxiliary officer. Subsequently, the police chief ordered the suspension of all activities by the 14-member auxiliary police force.

All is now well. The auxiliary unit is functioning as in the past, and the city maintains an attractive Web site to encourage recruitment. Waltham reinstated its volunteer force in the fall of 2013 after obtaining a new insurance policy for its auxiliary program and after amending its local ordinances, which had not previously included the term "auxiliary police officers" (Sherman 2013; see Figure 10.1). Waltham's auxiliaries are not designated as peace officers, and they are not permitted to carry firearms (Sherman 2013). Throughout the year, they patrol and provide traffic support for road and bicycle races, parades, and other community events. Training requirements include the completion of the 120-hour Massachusetts Reserve Intermittent Police Academy within two years of appointment. This training takes place at the Waltham Police Department. Officers receive annual training and certification in cardiopulmonary resuscitation (CPR), the Red Cross First Responder course, handcuffing, use of force, defensive tactics, the use of over-the-counter pepper spray, and expandable batons (Waltham Auxiliary Police 2013).

A related case involved the reserve police force in Fort Worth, Texas. The city suspended the program in March 2011 when questions arose about whether the city council had properly approved each reserve officer.

**Figure 10.1** Russ Malone administering oath of office to eight Waltham (Massachusetts) Auxiliary Police Officers in 2013. The Waltham Auxiliary Police Department is a non-sworn, unarmed, volunteer organization of men and women between the ages of 21 and 70 that are committed to the safety and well-being of the citizens of Waltham. (Courtesy of Robert G. Logan, photographer, and used with permission of Russ Malone, City Clerk and Clerk of the Waltham City Council.)

Another question arose regarding whether a city with civil service for police could maintain a reserve force. The Texas attorney general determined that the city could maintain a reserve force that does not take a civil service examination. The opinion states that "The statute authorizing reserve police forces presumes the coexistence of reserve and 'regular police'" and "We have not found, nor has any briefing submitted to this office purported to find, any Texas case that has stated or implied that reserves must comply with civil service requirements" (Opinion No. GA-0893, November 22, 2011). Subsequently, a new general order for police reserves was drafted, and the reserves were permitted to resume operations. The reserve program has been made a part of the patrol division, rather than in a separate division. In addition, a no-rank system was devised, other than probationary reserve officers and reserve officers. Fort Worth reserve officers can work a minimum of 15 hours a month and up to 20 hours per week. A minimum of 560 hours training is required to become a reserve officer (Reserve LEO News 2013).

Fort Worth police reserve officers are sworn law enforcement officers and must become certified by the Texas Commission on Law Enforcement Officer Standards and Education. This is accomplished through course attendance from 6 p.m. to 10 p.m. Monday through Thursday for a period of 20 weeks. While on duty, these volunteer police possess the same authority as peace officers. They are usually assigned to the patrol division and assist regular patrol officers in the performance of their duties. A normal work assignment usually is six hours, once a week. Requirements for membership include a high school diploma or General Educational Development (GED) certificate and 12 semester hours of college; 21 years of age at time of certification; weight standards based on an individual's percentage of body fat; vision correctable to 20/20 with no color vision deficiency; and a valid Texas driver's license. Moreover, applicants must pass a physical fitness test, a medical exam, an extensive background check, a polygraph examination, and a psychological examination. Before acceptance, all applicant credentials are reviewed by the Police Personnel Review Board (Fort Worth Police 2013). The original draft of the new 2012 General Order for Fort Worth police reserves includes the following statement about carrying a service firearm: "Reserve officers may carry their department-issued service weapon only for the period of time the Reservist is actually on duty and discharging the official functions of a duly constituted peace officer as authorized by the Chief of Police. When off-duty, Reserve Officers are encouraged to report breaches of the peace or on-view felonies for response by an on-duty officer. Reserve Officers should be mindful that any law enforcement action taken by them while off duty may be considered by a court of law to be action taken by a civilian" (Fort Worth Police Department, General Order, Section 217.06 D).

The temporary suspensions of the volunteer police units in Waltham and Fort Worth involved very basic issues regarding the nature of their legal status and authority. An important related concept is "jurisdiction." Jurisdiction generally refers to a specific geographical area. In the field of criminal justice, it has a wider meaning—the right or authority of a justice agency to act in regard to a particular subject matter, territory, or person. A city's police may not patrol or answer calls for service outside the city's boundaries unless cooperative agreements with those other jurisdictions have been developed or assistance has been requested by a neighboring agency due to a specific incident. In addition, various states specifically authorize municipal police officers to exercise police powers outside the territorial limits of their municipality under specified circumstances such as fresh pursuit or when summoned by another officer. Thus, absent such special agreements, or under circumstances identified by statutes, a local law enforcement officer possesses no more authority to act than a private citizen when acting outside his or her jurisdiction (Florida Attorney General 1989). Police who are appointed by statewide agencies typically possess statewide jurisdiction. Several states have statewide volunteer police units. For a discussion concerning these units, see Chapter 5.

## Sovereign Immunity and the Public Duty Doctrine

Historically, the doctrine of sovereign immunity shielded municipalities from tort liability. The source of the doctrine is thought to be rooted in the English theory that "The king can do no wrong." This has been interpreted to mean that the sovereign, be it national, state, or local, was completely immune from all tort liability unless the sovereign gave consent. As far back as the thirteenth century, "Applications to the king in council or in person were occasionally made and redress afforded" and "it was possible to obtain relief against a sheriff and bailiff in the administrative court known as the exchequer..." (Borchard 1926, 21). In addition, "Edward I (1239–1307), the so-called English Justinian, introduced a regular course of procedure for bringing claims against the king" (Borchard 1926, 23). As a general rule, the doctrine of sovereign immunity prohibits all suits against the United States unless it has given consent (e.g., see *Cohens v. Virginia*, 19 U.S. 264 [1821]; *Library of Congress v. Shaw*, 478 U.S. 310 [1986]; *Block v. North Dakota*, 461 U.S. 273 [1983].)

Although the doctrine of sovereign immunity has been abolished in many jurisdictions, courts are still very reluctant to impose liability on a municipality for its failure to provide adequate police protection. The general rule in such cases is that a municipality owes police protection to the general public but owes no duty to any particular individual (e.g., see *Brutomesso v. Las Vegas Metro. Police Dept.*, 591 P. 2d 254, 1979; *Doe v. Hendricks*, 590 P.2d 647, 1979; *Schuster v. City of New York*, 154 N.E.2d 534, 1958).

Absent a "special duty" to a particular individual, a municipality is not liable for its failure to provide adequate police protection (see also *Riss v. City of New York*, 22 N.Y. 2d 579, 240 N.E.2d 860, 1968).

In the West Virginia Supreme Court of Appeals case of *Gloria Allen v. Greenbrier County Sheriff's Dept. and Greenbrier County Commission* (decided June 28, 2013), the court affirmed the granting of summary judgment for respondents stating that the public duty doctrine barred a petitioner's negligence claim. In discussing the public duty doctrine, the court stated that "The duty to... provide police protection runs ordinarily to all citizens and is to protect the safety and well-being of the public at large; therefore, absent a special duty to the plaintiff(s), no liability attaches to a municipal... police department's failure to provide adequate... police protection" (see the 1999 opinion in *Rhodes v. Putnam County. Sheriff's Dept.*, 530 S.E.2d 452, 455, 1999; quoting the 1991 opinion in *Randall v. Fairmont City Police Dept.*, 412 S.E.2d 737, 747–748).

In West Virginia, the four requirements necessary to establish such a "special duty" or "special relationship" exception are codified in W. Va. Code § 29–12–5 as follows: "(1) An assumption by the state governmental entity, through promises or actions, of an affirmative duty to act on behalf of the party who was injured; (2) knowledge on the part of the state governmental entity's agents that inaction could lead to harm; (3) some form of direct contact between the state governmental entity's agents and the injured party; and (4) that party's justifiable reliance on the state governmental entity's affirmative undertaking."

All members of the public and those who volunteer to assist the police need to know about the principle called the "public duty doctrine." A community's understanding of this doctrine should serve to reinforce the selfless nature of police work as well as the remarkable civic benefits conferred by those persons who would undertake police responsibilities without monetary compensation. Surely, the average police officer and volunteer considers every person as well as the public at large to be worthy of his or her response. It would be quite an unusual case for such officers to refrain from helping others by proclaiming otherwise. Nevertheless, there is a public duty doctrine, which holds that the government and its representatives have no duty to any specific person (absent a special relationship) but have duties to the public at large.

There have been other cases where the courts have affirmed this principle. One of the first cases to address this issue was *South v. Maryland*, 59 U.S. 396 (1856). In this case, the Supreme Court found that a sheriff or public officer could only be found personally liable if they failed to provide protection to someone they had entered into a special agreement to protect. But they found no recorded case in American or English law where an officer was subject to personal liability for failure to protect an individual from injury to their property or person. From this case the "public duty doctrine" was formed. In *Warren v. District of Columbia,* (444 A.2d. 1, D.C. Ct. of Ap. 1981), the District of Columbia Court of Appeals, in a four to three vote, stated that official police personnel and the government employing them owe no duty to victims of criminal acts and thus are not liable for a failure to provide adequate police protection unless a special relationship exists.

In the case of *Castle Rock v. Gonzales,* 545 U.S. 748 (2005), the U.S. Supreme Court found that Jessica Gonzales did not have a constitutional right to police protection even in the presence of a restraining order. By a vote of seven to two, the court ruled that Gonzales had no right to sue her town under 42 U.S.C. § 1983 and her local police department for failing to protect her and her children from her estranged husband. Her husband murdered the woman's three children. In the hours before her children were found dead in her husband's car, Gonzales had contacted the police department on five occasions to ask for assistance.

In a related case, *DeShaney v. Winnebago County Dept. of Social Service, et al.,* 489 U.S. 189 (1989), the petitioner sued respondents claiming that their failure to act to protect him deprived him of his liberty in violation of the due process clause of the Fourteenth Amendment to the U.S. Constitution. By a vote of six to three, the U.S. Supreme Court held that a state government agency's failure to prevent child abuse by a custodial parent did not violate the child's right to liberty under the due process clause of the Fourteenth Amendment. In this case, the petitioner was Joshua DeShaney. He was beaten and permanently injured by his father, with whom he lived as a result of a divorce decree. Respondents were social workers and other local officials who received complaints that petitioner was being abused by his father; they had reason to believe that this was happening but nonetheless did not act to remove the petitioner from his father's custody. The opinion, by Chief Justice William Rehnquist, held that the due process clause protects against state action only and because it was Randy DeShaney, the child's father, who abused Joshua, the Winnebago County Department of Social Services (DSS), a state actor, was not responsible. Rehnquist's opinion stated that although the DSS's failure to act may have made it liable for a tort under Wisconsin state law, the Fourteenth Amendment does not transform every tort by a state actor into a violation of constitutional rights. The court left open the possibility that the act of creating a Department of Social Services to investigate and respond to allegations of child abuse may have meant that Winnebago County assumed a duty to prevent what Randy DeShaney did to Joshua DeShaney, and that any failure to fulfill that duty may have constituted a tort.[1]

## Torts and Negligence Law

No one desires to be the respondent in a lawsuit. Volunteer police who have devoted months undergoing training and who have had years of service want to be assured that all of this effort will not be squandered due to a legal action. Volunteers and their supervisors can diminish this risk by undergoing proper training in accordance with their assigned positions and state standards. With regard to emergency situations, established plans such as the incident command system[2] should be used. At every training opportunity, volunteers need to understand the scope of their duties and how these should best be carried out in a variety of situations. When in the field, long detailed documentation would not be expected in emergencies, but maintaining a journal or notes could prove helpful in the event of a lawsuit. Moreover, awareness of basic tort law principles may help concerned volunteers avoid the types of conduct that could result in a legal action.

A "tort" is an action that harms another. It is often referred to as a "civil wrong" for which a lawsuit can be started. It occurs when a person acts, or fails to act, without right and as a result another is harmed. Torts involve civil actions for personal injuries or property damage rather than a criminal action or a contractual claim.

The law of torts can be found in statutes, court decisions, and constitutional provisions; it applies to government entities, individual citizens, and businesses. It protects individual and business interests from harm and provides a means for those harmed by another to seek compensation for their loss.

Tort liability claims also provide a basis for distributing losses to those who are responsible for the harm. Tort law provides a systematic means for analyzing and resolving liability claims, while protecting the interests of the person injured and the governmental jurisdiction. Torts encompass a very broad area of the law including such categories of law as intentional acts that harm others, negligence, and strict liability cases. Intentional acts that harm others include trespass, assault and battery, intentional infliction of emotional distress, defamation, and invasion of privacy. Negligence involves unintentional acts or omissions that cause harm to another. A person has a duty to exercise that degree of care, skill, and diligence that a reasonable or prudent person would exercise under similar circumstances. This rule, as applied to governmental entities, must be understood in terms of the essential elements of negligence. The elements include the duty owed to conform to a defined standard of care, a breach of that duty, damages, and causation.[3] Strict liability is liability without fault and relates to situations where one is held responsible for the consequences of his/her actions or omissions, regardless of fault or exercise of due care. Strict liability was first applied in cases involving abnormally dangerous activities such as blasting but has achieved significantly broader application in the law of product liability and workers' compensation (Oleck 1982).

## Immunity and Indemnification in Claims of Negligence

When authorized volunteers respond in a disaster emergency, immunity may be available to them. For example, the use of auxiliary police units in New York State "has been … found to be proper for such activities as patrolling the streets [and] unprotected public parks in … the late hours…" (Collins 1981, 629). While performing such activities, the individual member and the municipality are immune from liability for torts committed during the performance of authorized drills (Collins 1981). The key factor to ensuring that volunteers are protected during disasters for possible negligent actions is that they are formally appointed by the emergency management agency or other governmental entity. The volunteer thus becomes a "public actor" rather than a private citizen offering aid. In addition to formally appointing or authorizing the volunteer, the public agency should provide training and guidance to volunteers so as to minimize harm to citizens. A failure to formally appoint the volunteer to assist in a disaster response means that the various forms of "governmental immunity" do not apply to the actions of the volunteer and other standards of care may apply. This protection, however, does not apply where the actor intentionally harms another. In addition, governmental immunity does not apply to criminal conduct.

Governmental immunity is a special form of immunity recognized for some activities of public agencies in more than a dozen states. These laws make a distinction between governmental functions, which are traditionally performed by the government, and those functions that are proprietary in nature or that are performed traditionally by the private sector. Under the governmental function theory, core governmental functions—such as public safety, firefighting, police activities, health and building inspections, as well as the collection of taxes—are mandated responsibilities that can be performed only by governmental units. Because of the unique role that these essential governmental functions have in the community, public agencies and employees enjoy immunity from claims of negligence under state law. Each state that recognizes governmental immunity defines what is a governmental function (Pine, n.d; Pine 2013).

Proprietary functions, however, have no special immunity attached to the activity. Proprietary activities may be performed by either a public or private organization. Public actors or volunteers do not enjoy immunity when performing proprietary activities (Pine, n.d; Pine 2013).

Other state immunity statutes may be beneficial to volunteers who respond in disasters as long as they are acting on behalf of the public authority. A critical element of these provisions involves the defining of an "emergency." If the emergency activity is not included in the definition of "emergency," then the immunity provision does not apply. These immunity provisions extend protection to negligent acts but not to actions for gross negligence or intentional or willful actions intended to harm another. Gross negligence is more than mere thoughtlessness, inattention, or a mere mistake resulting from inexperience or confusion.

The concept of "indemnification" involves protection against personal financial loss for the actions of governmental employees and volunteers. Official representatives of a governmental unit (volunteers) who are named individually in a tort action are generally entitled to protection against personal financial loss or indemnification. (In the present discussion, "indemnification" refers to the payment of any settlement or judgment for a negligent act.) This may apply to both attorney's fees and judgments that might be awarded. Almost all states recognize that the governmental unit is liable for the negligent acts or omissions of its agents (volunteers) or employees who are acting within the scope of their duties as public employees. The employee in this context includes not only paid staff but also volunteers. Elected officials who receive no pay and volunteers would be included in this definition of employee. The liability for the employee's actions is passed on to the governmental unit as employer, under a theory generally known as "vicarious liability." However, most state indemnification statutes provide that, where the employee (or volunteer) acted with malice or the employee's actions were outside the scope of the job, no defense is provided nor shall any judgment be paid (Pine, n.d; Pine 2013).

## The Volunteer Protection Act 42 USCA §§ 14501-14505 (1997)

Beginning in the mid-1980s, suits against volunteers grew in number and attracted the attention of national media. At about the same time, the insurance picture for volunteers and nonprofit organizations darkened. Premiums rose dramatically, coverage exclusions increased, and several types of coverage became unavailable. Due to substantially higher insurance premiums, some nonprofit organizations cut back on services (Public Entity Risk Institute 1999).

In response, Congress enacted the Volunteer Protection Act of 1997 (VPA) in order to encourage volunteerism by reducing the possibility of litigation brought against volunteers. The federal statute sought to make available statutory immunity to increase the labor pool for voluntary organizations.

In particular, punitive damages may not be awarded against a volunteer acting within the scope of his/her responsibilities to a nonprofit organization, even when harm is caused due to an act or omission of the volunteer on behalf of the organization or entity. A variety of conditions qualify this immunity.[4] For example, the immunity does not attach to the volunteer's organization. The VPA does not exempt volunteers from liability for any harm caused while driving a motor vehicle. This exclusion is important because research indicates that half the claims involving emergency response organizations arise from vehicle accidents (Pine, n.d; Pine 2013).

The VPA only applies to 501(c)(3) organizations and governmental entities. In addition, the VPA does not prevent a nonprofit from bringing an action against a volunteer. Despite the existence of the VPA, many volunteers remain *fully liable* for any harm they cause, and all volunteers remain liable for some actions (Public Entity Risk Institute 1999). In general, the limitations on the liability of a volunteer under this act do not apply to any misconduct that: (a) constitutes a crime of violence (as that term is defined in section 16 of title 18, United States Code) or act of international terrorism (as that term is defined in section 2331 of title 18) for which the defendant has been convicted in any court; (b) constitutes a hate crime (as that term is used in the Hate Crime Statistics Act (28 U.S.C. 534 note); (c) involves a sexual offense, as defined by applicable state law, for which the defendant has been convicted in any court; (d) involves misconduct for which the defendant has been found to have violated a federal or state civil rights law; or (e) where the defendant was under the influence (as determined pursuant to applicable state law) of intoxicating alcohol or any drug at the time of the misconduct.

Volunteer immunity laws may provide volunteers with some protection, but they are not complete solutions. Many persons in the nonprofit sector mistakenly believe that volunteer protection statutes provide volunteers (including directors and officers) with complete protection from civil liability. A second mistaken belief is that volunteer immunity laws provide protection from liability for the nonprofit entity. Belief in either of these myths could lead to potentially disastrous consequences. For this reason, volunteer immunity laws should be understood by both the volunteer and the organization. Other risk management mechanisms, including insurance, should be in place to fill the gaps and to provide peace of mind. The bottom line appears to be that if certain conditions are satisfied, volunteers may be protected from claims of negligence, but they are not protected against claims of gross negligence. Thus, if a lawsuit contains an allegation of gross negligence against a volunteer, the volunteer must defend against the action and will typically incur defense costs in doing so.

The frequency of employment practices claims, which include claims of discrimination, harassment, retaliation, and wrongful termination, has grown substantially since the early 1990s. In fact, employment practices claims are the most common type of claims brought against nonprofits. The cause of these allegations may be the result of the actions of an organization's volunteers or its employees. Volunteer administrators, managers, supervisors, and board members cannot rely on federal and state volunteer immunity laws for protection against these lawsuits because such statutes do not provide immunity from federal civil rights laws, which are the basis of most employment practices claims (CNA 2011).

## Liability in New York State: A Case Study

Volunteer police authority and liability issues can vary from state to state. During the 1950s, in counties and cities throughout New York, units of auxiliary police were organized under the various local community civil defense units, which were each headed by a local volunteer director. Currently, there are approximately 60 volunteer police units in New York. "Today, auxiliary police officers wear uniforms almost identical to regular police, drive police cars which look almost identical to regular police cars and which are equipped with the same emergency lights, sirens, and police radios. Auxiliary police officers usually carry police batons (a potentially deadly weapon) and handcuffs. ... departments have begun to outfit auxiliary police officers with bullet resistant vests. Some police departments permit auxiliary police officers to carry mace and guns when they receive the same training as regular police officers.... In some counties, auxiliary police perform duties such as issuing summonses for handicap parking violations, checking vacation homes, participating in emergency rescues, riding as second man in patrol cars, and performing administrative work for police departments" (Franckel 2013).

Auxiliary police were organized in New York State pursuant to the New York State Defense Emergency Act 1951 (the Act) and NYS CPL 2.10:26 (designation of peace officer) and CPL 2.20 (powers of peace officers), which came about as a result of the federal Civil Defense Act of 1950. At the time, there was substantial federal and state concern about a nuclear attack by the Soviet Union. A comprehensive plan was needed to ensure the safety and survival of the citizens of New York in the event of an anticipated or actual nuclear attack.

The Act defines auxiliary police, auxiliary firemen, bomb squads, radiological units, rescue squads, emergency medical units, monitoring and decontamination squads, and all other similar forces having duties and responsibilities in connection with civil defense as "volunteer agencies." The Act imposes, upon virtually every county in the state, the obligation to recruit, train, equip, and discharge auxiliary police officers. The Act also provides worker's compensation coverage and immunity (see Article 9 § 113) for negligent acts only when auxiliary police officers are performing duties "relating to civil defense, including but not limited to activities pursuant thereto, in preparation for anticipated attack, during attack, or following attack or false warning thereof, or in connection with an authorized drill or test."

In regard to the authorized scope of auxiliary police duties, these volunteer police were given the authority to perform duties only during specifically limited instances related to the fear of an enemy attack. The Act states that the "local legislative body of any county, town, city, or village may by resolution confer or authorize the conferring upon members of the auxiliary police the powers of peace officers, subject to such restrictions as such body shall impose, and subject to the provisions of subdivision twenty-six of section 2.10 and section 2.20 of the criminal procedure law" (see Article 8 § 105). CPL § 2.10:26 provides the restrictions that auxiliary police officers shall have the power of peace officers set forth in CPL § 2.20 only during a period of imminent or actual attack by enemy forces and during drills authorized under § 29-b of Article 2-B of the executive law, providing for the use of civil defense forces in disasters. In addition, other than directing traffic during official drills (see Criminal Procedure Law, § 2.10:26), there is no statutory authority that permits auxiliary police officers to conduct specific activities. Nevertheless, at present, "Auxiliary Police are trained and extensively utilized by police departments for a myriad of activities far outside of the original intent, scope, and authorization of the New York State Defense Emergency Act" (Franckel 2013).

The expansion of duties was acknowledged in *Fitzgibbon v. County of Nassau, et al.*, 541 N.Y.S.2d 845 147 A.D.2d 40 (N.Y.A.D. 2 Dept., 1989): "It is clear that the contemporary functions of auxiliary police units have evolved beyond those contemplated by the framers of the Act ... there is little question that auxiliary police units have been principally deployed in order to assist law enforcement personnel in combating the threat of crime from within, and less so as the statutorily envisaged civilian reserve to be mobilized in preparation for the perceived threat of external invasion or natural disaster." In addition, in *People v. Rosario*, 78 N.Y.2d 583, 585 N.E.2d 766, 578 N.Y.S.2d 454 (1991), the New State Court of Appeals (the state's highest court) ruled that the "fellow officer" rule (which entitles police officers and police agencies to pass along probable cause from one police officer to another) applied to auxiliary police.[5] Under the rule, a police officer is entitled to assume the reliability of information obtained from a radio bulletin, telephone, or teletype alert and to make a warrantless arrest based upon that information, when the source of the information is a "fellow police officer" or police department. If the probable cause existed prior to being transmitted to the arresting officer, then the arresting officer has probable cause to make the arrest.

However, there is a serious risk of liability exposure for acts of negligence in New York State. In *Fitzgibbon v. County of Nassau, et al.,* (1989), the plaintiff David Fitzgibbon Jr. was crossing a street in Massapequa Park, Nassau County, at approximately 11:00 p.m., when he was struck and injured by a marked RMP (radio motor patrol car) owned by the defendant Nassau Auxiliary Police Unit 316 and operated by the defendant Auxiliary Police Officer (APO) Frank Dennis Jr. APO Dennis was in uniform and on patrol at the time of the accident. The plaintiff alleged that APO Dennis operated the patrol car in a negligent manner and that he had done so with the "consent and permission" of the defendant, the county of Nassau. The defendants moved for summary judgment to dismiss the plaintiff's complaint, arguing that the New York State Defense Emergency Act conferred complete immunity with regard to any claim premised upon APO Dennis's alleged negligence because the functions performed were part of a statutory civil defense "drill" or training exercise to which the immunity provision of the Act applied. It was also alleged that the defendant county of Nassau was negligent in its supervision of Officer Dennis and vicariously liable for his conduct under the doctrine of *respondeat superior*. Interestingly, in an effort to avoid liability, the defendant Nassau County also argued that it did not direct, maintain, or control the auxiliary unit's activities and, accordingly, was not responsible to the plaintiff under the doctrine. The Supreme Court (the lower trial court) denied the respective motions of the defendants, thereby precluding the granting of summary judgment to dismiss the plaintiff's complaint. The court also found that questions of fact existed with respect to the county's vicarious liability for Dennis's alleged negligence. The defendants appealed this decision to the appellate division, which upheld the decision, ruling that APO Dennis's patrol was a routine patrol and not a "drill" or training exercise entitling the defendants, including APO Dennis, to immunity. The justices of the appellate division finalized their decision by stating "It must be concluded that the activities in question are not among those to which the shield of immunity was intended to apply."[6]

Thus, in New York State (absent any local immunity law), contemporary volunteer auxiliary police officers appear to perform their routine patrols beyond the scope of the state's Emergency Defense Law as well as the federal VPA. The lack of legal authority creates a myriad of legal issues, one of which is liability for negligent acts. In New York State, lack of appropriate legal authority could also result in loss of eligibility for the workers' compensation benefits (see Franckel 2013).

It is important that volunteer police in all jurisdictions of the United States carefully review the scope of their authority in relation to the duties they perform, so that in the event of alleged negligent actions they can obtain the benefits associated with the applicable state and federal immunity and indemnification statutes.

# The Law Enforcement Officers Safety Act of 2004

This federal statute and its subsequent amendments concern a peace officer's ability to carry a concealed weapon off-duty throughout the United States. In this regard, it supersedes most state law, local ordinances, and local policy restricting carrying off-duty. However, it does not exempt such officers from federal laws, which regulate firearms on aircraft and federal property. Moreover, all officers must still obey local prohibitions or restrictions against the carrying of concealed weapons on (1) private property if the owner imposes such restrictions and (2) state or public property, such as courthouses or a public park. In addition, an officer is still subject to his or her employing agency's policies and conditions of employment. The agency can develop a policy to dictate what the standards are for employees of that agency that carry firearms (e.g., qualification standards). An agency, it appears, is not free to develop a policy about how it will implement the provisions of this act relative to other law enforcement officers (California Attorney General 2013). Useful information about the Law Enforcement Officers Safety Act (LEOSA) for persons who are about to retire or who are retired can be found at: http://www.dhs.gov/xlibrary/assets/foia/mgmt_instruction_257_01_001_law_enforcement_officers_safety_act.pdf.

LEOSA and its amendments have generated much commentary, and case law is developing on this topic. Despite its 2010 amendments, LEOSA and related laws remain an issue subject to interpretation. When an individual is considering membership in a particular volunteer police unit, it is quite appropriate to inquire if the sponsoring agency meets the standards that will qualify its volunteer police members for the benefits of this law. According to an opinion of the attorney general of the state of California, all active reserve officers will be authorized to carry, "If they meet the criteria of the Act (active). Retired reserves are not likely to qualify—they need to have non-forfeitable retirement rights. Most don't" (California Attorney General 2013).

In order to be considered a qualified law enforcement officer for the benefits of this act to apply, the following criteria must be met. The officer must be "an employee of a governmental agency who (1) is authorized by law to engage in or supervise the prevention, detection, investigation, or prosecution of, or the incarceration of any person for any violation of law, and has statutory powers of arrest; (2) is authorized by the agency to carry a firearm; (3) is not the subject of any disciplinary action by the agency; (4) meets standards, if any, established by the agency which require the employee to regularly qualify in the use of a firearm; (5) is not under the influence of alcohol or another intoxicating or hallucinatory drug or substance; and (6) is not prohibited by Federal law from receiving a firearm" (see title 18, United States Code, § 926B).

As long as individuals meet the criteria set forth in LEOSA, they will be protected from the carry permit requirements of other jurisdictions. This consideration occurred in a courtroom, when for the first time, a New York City trial judge was asked to consider the applicability of LEOSA. It involved the arrest of an elected part-time constable from Pennsylvania, conceded to be a constable by the prosecution, who was arrested in New York City for carrying a concealed firearm without a license. The issue in this case was whether by virtue of his status as a law enforcement officer, the defendant was entitled to carry his weapon across state lines without having a gun permit. A hearing was held to determine the merits of the defendant's motion to dismiss the case. The sole witness was the defendant. The court's opinion reviewed the elements of the LEOSA requirements and determined that the defendant satisfied the necessary criteria. He therefore came within the protections of LEOSA, and the grand jury indictment was dismissed ending the case unless the prosecution should appeal. The 14-page decision by New York County Supreme Court Justice Arnold A. Zweibel in the case of *People v. Rodriguez* (2006) can be found at: http://www.handgunlaw.us/documents/agopinions/NYCtLEOSARulingPeoplevsRodriguez.PDF.

In 2011, after several similar cases of U.S. Coast Guard (USCG) officers getting into conflicts with this law, the Coast Guard issued its own LEOSA policy. The new Coast Guard policy defines who is a qualified law enforcement officer with respect to only certain uniformed active duty, reserve Coast Guard members, and special agents of the Coast Guard Investigative Service (CGIS). The policy specifically states that "Civilian members of the USCG and members of the Auxiliary are not covered by the LEOSA unless they are CGIS special agents or otherwise meet the LEOSA definition of 'qualified law enforcement officer.'" Perhaps, some of the problems in the past could have been cleared up if that policy had already been in existence. (The full text of the USCG policy is available at: http://www.uscg.mil/announcements/alcoast/549-10_alcoast.txt.)

In view of the current restrictions placed on the activities of Coast Guard Auxiliary members, it is not surprising that the Coast Guard LEOSA policy has excluded members of the Coast Guard Auxiliary. However, eligibility under LEOSA is still possible for those volunteer police who have law enforcement responsibilities and who satisfy all of its other provisions, such as possessing the appropriate identification.

Within the 2013 National Defense Authorization Act, an amendment was added to the required LEOSA identification (ID) card language. The amendment mandates that qualified law enforcement officers must carry a photographic ID that "identifies the employee as a police or law enforcement officer of the agency," and that qualified retired law enforcement officers carry a photographic ID "that identifies the person has having been employed as a police or law enforcement officer." The LEOSA does "not bestow either an explicit right to obtain the required photographic ID or a federal remedy for an agency's failure to issue one" (Baranowski 2013). Thus, to be in full compliance with the amended Act, concerned individuals will be dependent upon their agency's cooperation with respect to the issuance of the necessary ID.

A person carrying an ID card designating them as an "auxiliary or reserve police officer" does not automatically mean that they are a qualified law enforcement officer in their jurisdiction or for the purposes of LEOSA. In some jurisdictions, a police or sheriff's department may have an auxiliary or reserve program, but their assignments may be quite limited to directing traffic at fairs, helping with searches for lost children, lending a hand at disasters, and so on (e.g., see aforementioned information about Waltham's auxiliary police). In various jurisdictions, volunteers may be qualified to carry firearms, but they do not have arrest authority. On the contrary, there are many departments that have authorized volunteers to serve as part-time peace officers or police officers and that offer them the same or equivalent training as full-time paid officers (e.g., see Fort Worth reserve police information presented earlier).

Any person interested in volunteer police work should ascertain the nature of their authority and legal status because state laws will vary in their definitions of such terms as auxiliary or reserve (see Chapter 4). Furthermore, active and retired qualified law enforcement officers (including members of reserve police units) should fully educate themselves on the firearm laws of any jurisdiction in which they are traveling and should strive to always be in compliance with the various laws because their knowledge is what will ultimately protect them. Finally, police administrators and other officials concerned with public safety and volunteer programs need to think realistically and carefully about the activities to be included in their programs. They need to design preservice training that considers real-life situations. The lives of citizens could be placed unnecessarily at risk by poorly conceived strategies.

## Volunteer Liability Guide

*The Citizen Corps Volunteer Liability Guide* (CCVLG) is a FEMA publication available online at: http://www.ready.gov/guides. It provides an overview of liability concerns and suggests approaches to address these concerns. Liability refers to the legal responsibility for one's acts or omissions and includes such matters as legally imposed payment of damages for personal injury or property damage, penalties for practicing a profession or trade without the required license or permit, compensation for lost income and medical expenses of an injured volunteer, and damages for breach of contract. The topic of liability is a significant concern and a potential barrier to volunteer involvement in volunteer policing and other programs involving the delivery of emergency services. To offer guidance in this area, FEMA funded the nonprofit Public Entity Risk Institute (PERI) to develop the 100-page guide. The following three paragraphs contain excerpts from this guide to illustrate its contents.

Liability and liability protection for emergency volunteers (volunteers in preparedness planning, emergency response, and disaster mitigation and recovery) are usually matters of state law. These laws differ significantly: some states provide much better emergency volunteer liability protection than others. In addition to appearing inequitable, these differences create a barrier to interstate mutual aid. Organizations that manage volunteers are reluctant to respond to a disaster in another state if their volunteers' licenses will not be recognized, or if they will have less liability protection and fewer Workers' Compensation benefits than are offered in their home state. The complexity, uncertainty, and lack of parity between states leaves many advocating a comprehensive federal solution, but Congress has not acted, despite a flurry of bills introduced in Congress in 2005 and 2006. (FEMA 2014, 3)

State statutes, case law, and regulations all affect emergency volunteer liability protection. Most states' statutes and regulations are available online, but finding them can be difficult for someone unfamiliar with legal research. States organize their statutes and regulations differently, so there is no single place to look. A statute's or regulation's meaning is also affected by case law, which can be difficult to find and interpret. Bringing these diverse sources of law together with confidence usually requires a legal professional. (FEMA 2014, 6)

The three types of liability are civil liability, injury benefits for emergency volunteers, and penalties for breach of licensing and certification requirements.... There are four major types of civil liability (also known as tort liability): a) negligent acts or omissions; b) intentional acts; c) liability for the acts of others; and d) strict liability. (FEMA 2014, 10)

The CCVLG consists of the following resources: *Citizen Corps Volunteer Liability Manual*; Glossary of Terms; Volunteer Liability Checklists; Links to State Statutory and Legislative Web sites; How-To Guide on Finding Bills and Statutes Online; References, and Additional Resources. About half of this manual or guideline consists of its appendices. They include the following: a glossary of terms that are used in the manual and are important to the understanding of liability issues; volunteer liability checklists that contain a series of questions to lead the reader through an investigation of the protection provided to emergency volunteers in their states; links to state statutory, legislative, and emergency management agency websites; a description of how to search for state laws online; additional resources of potential interest to users of the CCVLG; and examples of approaches used in different states. (FEMA 2014)

# Commission on Accreditation for Law Enforcement Agencies Standards

The Commission on Accreditation for Law Enforcement Agencies, Inc. (CALEA®), was established in 1979 by the International Association of Chiefs of Police, the National Organization of Black Law Enforcement Executives, the National Sheriffs' Association, and the Police Executive Research Forum as an independent accrediting authority. Accreditation by this organization is a highly prized recognition of law enforcement professional excellence. To achieve "accredited" status, an agency must comply with hundreds of "best practice" standards established by CALEA for the operation of police organizations. CALEA sends an assessment team to examine all aspects of a department's policies and procedures, management, operations, and support services. Participation in the CALEA process is voluntary, but it is important because it can provide some assurance that the accredited police department is rated highly by its peers based on compliance with national standards and that it will be maintaining compliance with the identified standards by reporting annually to CALEA. As of 2008, fewer than 4% of law enforcement agencies had completed this process (Fresno Police Department 2008).

"Agencies that seek accreditation are required to comply only with those standards that are specifically applicable to them. Applicability is based on two factors: an agency's size and the functions it performs. Applicable standards are categorized as mandatory or other-than-mandatory. Agencies must comply with all applicable mandatory standards and at least 80% of applicable other-than-mandatory standards. If an agency cannot comply with a standard because of legislation, labor agreements, court orders, or case law, waivers can be sought from the Commission" (CALEA 2013).

In Kansas, the Ottawa Police Department's quest to achieve national accreditation had the unexpected consequence of causing the disbanding of its four-officer reserve unit in 2013. As part of the accreditation process, CALEA standards specify that every member of the reserve force must complete the same training as a full-time certified police officer. Certification requires 576 hours of training at the Kansas Law Enforcement Training Center in Hutchinson, in addition to 40 hours of annual training to maintain certification. All officers who wear a department's uniform, carry a gun, and are authorized to make arrests must undergo the same training, regardless of whether the officer is full-time or reserve. The reserve officers declined to pursue the more than 500 hours of academy training due to the time commitment that would have been required. An arrangement was made to have the four reserve officers join the county's sheriff's reserves unit and one reserve officer pursued that option (Carder 2013).

As previously discussed at some length in Chapter 5, CALEA standards greatly impacted the volunteer police program within the Connecticut State Police. In response to the nation's entry into World War II, the Connecticut State Police organized an auxiliary program and assigned their 1,200 volunteers to guard bridges and installations vital to defense against possible sabotage. Auxiliary officers are still doing their job today but as a much smaller unit. No one has been added to state trooper auxiliary ranks since 1988. The stated reasons for this freeze on recruitment was that the new training adopted by both the state and CALEA had now reached more than 800 hours, making it unlikely that volunteers would be able to attend and that the state authorities would bear the cost of this training. Nevertheless, when the new training hours became mandatory, existing auxiliary trooper members were permitted to remain. In 1995, there was a list of 900 people waiting for openings, and the force had been reduced to 130 members. At that time, auxiliary troopers patrolled highways and helped disabled motorists, directed traffic at accidents, did courier work for barracks, and backed up troopers. They had no arrest powers and did not respond to alarms. They did carry firearms but only for self-defense as they drove in marked state cruisers (Leukhardt 1995). Today there are less than 50 auxiliary troopers in the program; as they "retire," they are not replaced, and eventually, the program will cease to exist. When volunteers turn 70, they have the option of serving as administrative aides. They do not wear a uniform or carry a gun.[7]

World War II also spurred such Connecticut municipalities as Milford, New Britain, Hartford, New Haven, Bridgeport, Waterbury, and Stamford to create similar programs. However, when state training requirements were passed in 1982 for anyone doing police work, these units were disbanded. The new state law required all municipal police officers to be trained and certified. At that time, the cost of running a 560-hour police academy was deemed to be excessive for the purpose of only certifying their part-time officers. Before the new laws, many auxiliary officers carried guns and could make arrests. The Milford force had part-time members until the mid-1990s, but the stringent certification standards and the expense of providing that training led to its demise. Because most of the volunteers had other full-time jobs, making them complete a police academy program did not seem practical. An alternative was devised to spread the volunteer police training over time—namely, three nights a week over three years. Most of those trained men and women have since retired, and the few remaining are often retired police officers who have kept up their certification (Juliano 2011).

In Connecticut, there is no distinction between full-time and part-time officers with regard to their certification. "Certification is the formal acknowledgement that a police officer has met the minimum, entry level requirements and basic training requirements of the Council and is thus authorized to exercise the authority of a police officer. Certification is awarded after the minimum entry level requirements have been met and basic training requirements have been completed, and is valid for a period not to exceed 3 years" (Klein 2013). According to William E. Klein, the certification officer for the Police Officer Standards and Training Council (POST) in Connecticut, although the era of the auxiliary cop is ending, in its place has emerged a more professional and better trained police force (Juliano 2011).

This trend is also illustrated by new training requirements in the state of Illinois. Due to insurance coverage needs, on December 31, 2011, Illinois instituted a 400-hour mandatory basic law enforcement training course for volunteer police that matched what regular officers attended. Milan (Illinois) Police Chief Mark Beckwith said that these new training rules for auxiliary police forced the disbanding of his city's auxiliary unit. This unit was active for 42 years and worked unselfishly during times of floods, windstorms, snowstorms, parades, concerts, and city events. "The unit was truly community policing in every sense of the word," according to Beckwith (Geyer 2012).

In the foregoing jurisdictions and in many others, higher training standards have affected the status of volunteer police units. Many units have simply folded, while others have attempted to offer long periods of part-time instruction in order to keep their members in compliance with the new higher standards. However, if existing state laws permit, a wide range of organizations have sought to preserve their units by making clear distinctions between levels or types of volunteer service. For example, in Wenham, auxiliary and reserve police units were reorganized in 2006 in consideration of the accreditation standards (Waters 2008). In New Britain (Connecticut), a new designation for volunteer police without arrest authority was created—community service officer (CSO). (It is also known as "the Police Reserve program.") The CSOs do not perform law enforcement duties nor do they have the power of arrest, but they do perform functions that are also the responsibility of sworn officers. Some examples of CSO duties are: assistance at accident scenes; completing reports in noncriminal cases; assisting in searches; providing transportation to stranded motorists; patrolling school grounds; and standing by at alarms. As with other types of volunteer police units, CSOs enable police officers to have more time to devote to law enforcement and public safety matters. The CSOs are deployed in pairs during the evening hours, and the volunteers receive no salary. Their uniforms are distinctive in order not be confused with those of regular officers, and volunteer safety is a paramount concern. At its Web page, the online posted materials end with these civic-minded words: "This program is an excellent opportunity for those interested in a career in law enforcement to gain valuable experience and for service-oriented individuals to contribute to the community" (Wardell 2013).

Thus, the higher training standards can be either a hindrance or a stimulus for organizing volunteer police units. Much will depend upon the discretion of police administrators and other public officials tasked with police oversight responsibilities. Moreover, there is a wide range of new activities for volunteer police to engage in (e.g., see Chapters 11 and 12). The reader is also referred to this book's Epilogue for suggestions about how to approach the need to upgrade or institute a volunteer police unit. The CALEA standards for volunteer police are set forth in Appendix A.

## Summary

In colonial America, a constable-watch system was imported from England. In this approach to policing, the people were, in fact, the police. Watch participation was a compulsory duty for the community's male population. However, over time it became a common practice for wealthier and disinterested citizens to pay for a watch replacement, which led to overall poor policing. The system broke down when Boston and other cities deployed the most elderly citizens and occasionally sentenced minor offenders to serve on the watch. The success of the new approach to policing begun in London in 1829 eliminated the constable-watch system in England and later in the United States. Irrespective of the disappointing practices of a bygone era, citizens who are recruited and trained by police agencies for volunteer positions in contemporary society embody the highest ideals of civic participation and concern for community safety.

Police officers and their volunteer counterparts or aides should familiarize themselves with police history including the classic tenets composed by Sir Robert Peel, who organized London's Metropolitan Police. His list of law enforcement standards is highly applicable today. In addition, there exist a huge number of legal principles to be concerned about. These include local ordinances, peace officer standards and training requirements, departmental rules and regulations, case law, and state and federal statutes.

Many of these legal principles are not well known; for example, as a general rule, the government owes a duty to protect their citizens as a whole but to individuals only if a special relationship can be proven. According to the rule set forth by the U.S. Supreme Court in the 1989 *DeShaney* case, nothing in the language of the Fourteenth Amendment's due process clause requires a state to protect the life, liberty, and property of its citizens against invasion by private actors. The clause is phrased as a limitation on the state's power to act, not as a guarantee of certain minimal levels of safety and security. In order to supplement the governmental agents assigned to protect the public, volunteers are a vital resource, especially in emergency situations. Properly managed, they can play critical roles in crisis situations, and they can do much to prevent crises from taking place.

Some municipalities have had problems arise concerning liability coverage and the legal status of their volunteer police. For more than three decades, Waltham's auxiliary police had been providing safety at a host of civic functions such as parades and festivals, but the entire force was demobilized for more than a year after the attorney representing the police agency refused to represent an auxiliary member sued for false arrest. In the city of Fort Worth, the volunteer force was suspended due to concern about whether proper documentation existed indicating that reserve appointments had been approved by the city council. Although these forces were eventually reinstated, other communities may no longer be accepting applications for volunteer police positions because of uncertainties over liability and related matters. In recent years, the advent of CALEA standards has led to the permanent disbanding of various volunteer units.

Any number of legal issues may arise in connection with the utilization of volunteer resources. In order to bring an action for the negligence of a governmental entity, such as a governmental employee (or authorized volunteer), it must be proved that there was a breach of a specific duty involving the exercise of a degree of care, skill, and diligence that a reasonable or prudent person would have exercised under similar circumstances. Additional elements, such as damages and causation must also be shown.

The concept of "indemnification" involves protection against personal financial loss for the actions of governmental employees and volunteers. However, the governmental entity may not be liable for an employee's (or volunteer's) actions if the employee acted outside the scope of his or her duties, acted with an intent to harm (malice) or the intent to harm another, or if the actions were with reckless disregard for the rights of others. Role-playing exercises and drills help to reveal the gray areas where employees and volunteers do not understand their jobs. The risks of civil liability can be reduced by proper training.

The Volunteer Protection Act of 1997 (VPA) sought to reduce the personal liability of volunteers so long as certain conditions were satisfied. The statute provides that no volunteer of a nonprofit organization or governmental entity shall be liable for harm caused by an act or omission of the volunteer on behalf of the organization or entity if the volunteer was acting within the scope of the volunteer's responsibilities in the nonprofit organization or governmental entity at the time of the act of omission; if appropriate or required, the volunteer was properly licensed, certified, or authorized by the appropriate authorities for the activities or practice in the State; the harm was not caused by willful or criminal misconduct or gross negligence, and so forth; or the harm was not caused by the volunteer operating a motor vehicle, vessel, aircraft, or other vehicle for which the state requires the operator or the owner of the vehicle, craft, or vessel to possess an operator's license or maintain insurance. Clearly, the successful deployment of volunteers in today's world requires an appropriate combination of volunteer oversight, government protections, risk management processes and procedures (e.g., completion of necessary training programs and certifications), and insurance coverage. FEMA's CCVLG provides an overview of liability concerns and suggests approaches to address these concerns. It also deals with the methods and procedures for risk assessment.

The Law Enforcement Officers Safety Act of 2004 (LEOSA) is important because with certain limitations and conditions, LEOSA exempts qualified active or retired law enforcement officers ("retirees") from most state and local laws that prohibit the carriage of concealed firearms. However, many potential candidates for its benefits, both regular and reserve police, may not yet be familiar with the law. Despite its 2010 and 2013 amendments, understanding LEOSA and related laws seems to be subject to some interpretation. Active and retired law enforcement officers should fully educate themselves on the firearm laws of any jurisdiction in which they are traveling and should strive to always be in compliance with the various laws because their knowledge is what will ultimately protect them. Volunteer and regular law enforcement officers carry concealed firearms for one major purpose—the protection of human life. Given the nature of our litigious society, off-duty officers or retirees should be especially concerned about the potential or actual use of their firearms. A shooting incident becomes a lot more complicated if a court determines that an individual was in illegal possession of the weapon used in the case.

## Review Questions

1. One of Sir Robert Peel's principles is that the police should demonstrate "absolute impartial service to the law." In 2013, a federal court ruled that the New York City Police Department's stop-and-frisk policy violated the civil rights of minorities. Find out more information about stop and frisk and discuss whether such laws or their exercise violate this principle.

2. In Illinois, auxiliary police officers with "conservator of the peace powers" are required to attend the 400-hour Basic Law Enforcement Officer Training Course at a certified state academy. Waltham, Massachusetts, requires a 120-hour training program for its auxiliary members, and in Fort Worth, a minimum of 560 hours training is required to become a reserve officer. What, if any, justifications can be given for the disparity in these training requirements?

3. Both the Fort Worth and Waltham volunteer police were suspended. Do you believe these suspensions were warranted? Discuss your reasoning.

4. Explain why jurisdiction is important for both regular and volunteer police.

5. Explain the "public duty doctrine" and discuss why it may be of great interest to the general public as well as volunteer police.

6. Find *Castle Rock v. Gonzales*, 545 U.S. 748 (2005) online and carefully review the court's opinion. If you were a member of the court, explain how you would have voted and state your reasons.

7. Provide at least three examples of torts.

8. Define "negligence."

9. Identify at least one factor to ensure that volunteers are protected for possible negligent actions during their response in disasters.

10. Congress enacted the Volunteer Protection Act of 1997 (VPA) in order to encourage volunteerism by reducing the possibility of litigation brought against volunteers. List at least three conditions that will render VPA benefits inapplicable to a volunteer.

11. Discuss the significance of the opinion by New York County Supreme Court Justice Arnold A. Zweibel in the case of *People v. Rodriguez* (2006).

12. Discuss how CALEA and higher state training standards have affected volunteer police units.

13. Dr. Peter Moskos received his PhD in Sociology from Harvard University. He is a former Baltimore City police officer and currently is an associate professor at John Jay College of Criminal Justice. Professor Moskos has stated that Sir Robert Peel is often mistakenly credited with having authored the "Nine Principles of Policing." Who should be credited? For more information, go to: http://www.copinthehood.com/2011/09/principles-that-never-were.html

## Notes

1. The 1989 *DeShaney* decision remains a subject of contention. It has prompted a large literature, including at least one book (Lynne Curry's *The DeShaney Case: Child Abuse, Family Rights and the Dilemma of State Intervention*, University of Kansas Press 2007) and many law review articles. Lower courts have cited it hundreds of times. No doubt the severity of Joshua DeShaney's injuries when he was four years old prompted this interest. Joshua was beaten so severely that he fell into a life-threatening coma. Emergency brain surgery revealed a series of hemorrhages caused by traumatic injuries to the head inflicted over a long period of time. Joshua did not die, but he suffered brain damage so severe that he was expected to spend the rest of his life confined to an institution for the profoundly retarded. Randy DeShaney was subsequently tried and convicted of child abuse. For information about Curry's book see: http://www.kansaspress.ku.edu/curdes.html.

2. Training materials for the incident command system (ICS) are provided by FEMA. The system is a standardized on-scene all-hazards concept that allows users to adopt an integrated organizational structure to match the complexities and demands of single or multiple incidents without being hindered by jurisdictional boundaries. The system helps ensure the safety of responders and others, achieve tactical objectives, and efficiently use resources. ICS is used by all levels of government—federal, state, tribal, and local—as well as by many nongovernmental organizations and the private sector. FEMA's Emergency Management Institute (EMI) offers more than 40 independent study courses concerned with ICS and related topics. These are self-paced, no-cost courses designed for people who have emergency management responsibilities and for the general public. (To obtain more information go to: http://www.fema.gov/incident-command-system.)

3. A duty maybe based upon a specific statute, judicial decisions, or found in a governmental rule. Such a duty requires a person to use a reasonable degree of attention, perception, memory, knowledge, intelligence, and judgment in his or her actions. Statutory duties include traffic codes, motor vehicle maintenance codes, workplace safety requirements, park construction and maintenance standards, environmental regulations, or inspection requirements. A "duty breach" is a failure to conform to that standard of care or a failure to carry out the duty. "Damages" refers to the actual loss or damage to the injured party. The "causation" element of negligence is the requirement that there must be a connection between the acts of the governmental employee, official, or agency body and injury to a third party, and the loss must be related to the act of the government representative. All negligence cases have these elements in common, and absence of proof of any one element will defeat a finding of liability (Pine, n.d.).

4. The VPA provides protection to nonprofit and government volunteers if: (1) the volunteer was acting within the scope of his or her responsibility; (2) the volunteer was properly licensed, certified, or authorized to engage in the activity or practice; (3) the harm was not caused by willful, criminal, or reckless misconduct, gross negligence, or conscious, flagrant indifference to the rights or safety of the individual harmed by the volunteer; and (4) the harm was not caused by the operation of a motor vehicle, aircraft, or other vehicle for which an operator's license or insurance is required by the state.

5. In *People v. Rosario*, a New York City Auxiliary Police Officer, while on routine patrol, received a radio transmission about a murder suspect and, upon spotting the murder suspect, advised a regular police officer who then made the arrest. The arrest, made by a regular police officer, was based upon information obtained from an auxiliary police officer who obtained the information from a radio transmission from the New York City Police Department. It should be noted that New York City Auxiliary Police use the same police radios as the regular police and receive the same radio transmissions. The New York State Court of Appeals ruled that the auxiliary police officer received extensive training, which was sufficient to pass along probable cause under the "fellow officer" rule and decided that the lack of peace officer status did not prevent the rule from applying to a New York City Auxiliary Police Officer.

6. Auxiliary police officers in Nassau County now have the protection of the Nassau County Charter § 2105(b) page 160, which provides: "Volunteer workers

shall be county employees for the purpose of receiving benefits pursuant to the workers' compensation law and shall be indemnified, defended, and held harmless by the county against any claim, demand, suit, or judgment for property damages, personal injury, including death, and any other liability which may be assessed against volunteer workers by reason of alleged negligence or other act committed by volunteer workers who were acting in the discharge of their duties within the scope of their employment or authorized volunteer duties." According to Franckel (2013), auxiliary police officers working in Nassau County, while on a function not authorized by New York's Defense Emergency Act, should currently have the protection of the Nassau County charter as a volunteer worker (barring the county filing for bankruptcy).

7. Since 1922, 21 troopers and auxiliary troopers of the Connecticut State Police Department have died for the state of Connecticut and its citizens during the performance of their duties. On May 25, 1994, Auxiliary Trooper Phillip A. Mingione of Milford was struck and killed on I-91 in the town of North Haven. Auxiliary Mingione had stopped and was standing outside his vehicle when a passing motorist lost control of her car and struck Auxiliary Mingione. On November 13, 1992, Auxiliary Trooper Edward W. Truelove stopped for a disabled motorist in the truck climbing lane of I-84 in Cheshire. After directing the driver and passenger to safety on the far side of the guardrail, Auxiliary Truelove radioed for a tow truck and attempted to safeguard the scene with his strobe lights. Several minutes later, an interstate truck driver drove into the rear end of the cruiser and Auxiliary Truelove was killed in the crash. If not for his concern about the occupants of the broken down car and his orders to move off the roadway, they too might have died (CSPAAA 2014).

# References

Auxiliary Police Department. (2011). Recruiting. Retrieved October 26, 2013 http://www.city.waltham.ma.us/auxiliary-police-department

Baranowski, J. (2013). LEOSA welcomes the military by requiring new identification card language for all. Retrieved October 26, 2013 http://le.nra.org/leosa/leosa-welcomes-the- military.aspx

Borchard, E. M. (1926). Governmental responsibility in tort, IV. *Yale Law Journal, 36*(1), 1–41.

CALEA. (2013). Law enforcement program: The standards. Retrieved November 1, 2013 from http://www.calea.org/content/law-enforcement-program-standards

California Attorney General. (2013). HR 218 – Law Enforcement Officers Safety Act (LEOSA)—Issues. Retrieved October 26, 2013 from http://ag.ca.gov/firearms/forms/pdf/leosiss.pdf

Carder, D. (2013, October 30). Police disband reserve force. Retrieved October 31, 2013 from http://ottawaherald.com/news/103113reserve

CNA. (2011). The myth of volunteer immunity. Retrieved October 22, 2013 from https://www.cnapro.com/pdf/Myths%20of%20Volunteer%20Immunity%2012-11.pdf

Collins, H. C. (1981). Municipal liability for torts committed by volunteer anticrime groups. *Fordham Urban Law Journal, 10*(4), 595–631.

Commissioner Bratton's Blog. (2014, March 6). Peel's nine principles of policing. Retrieved June 27, 2014 from http://www.nyc.gov/html/nypd/html/administration/commissioners_corner.shtml

Crime rates. (2013). Crime rates for Waltham, MA. Retrieved October 26, 2013 from http://www.neighborhoodscout.com/ma/waltham/crime/

CSPAAA. (2014). Honor Roll Photos. Retrieved June 27, 2014 from https://www.cspaaa.com/honor_roll/list.asp

DeShaney v. Winnebago County Department of Social Services, 489 US 189, 109 S. Ct. 998, 103 L. Ed. 2d 249 - Supreme Court, 1989.

FEMA. (2014). *Citizen corps volunteer liability guide.* Washington, DC: Community Preparedness Division, Federal Emergency Management Agency.

Florida Attorney General. (1989, September 15). Florida Attorney General advisory legal opinion – AGO 89-62: Officer's duty to provide aid to ill or injured. Retrieved October 29, 2013 from http://www.myfloridalegal.com/ago.nsf/Opinions/85E4F114E318503185256570006E05B3

Fort Worth Police. (2013). Reserve division. Retrieved October 28, 2013 from http://www.fortworthpd.com/divisions/reserve-division.aspx

Franckel, P. L. (2013). Auxiliary police authority and liability for negligence. Retrieved October 1, 2013 from http://www.hurt911.org/articles/auxiliary_police_liability.html

Fresno Police Department. (2008). CALEA accreditation. Retrieved October 31, 2013 from http://www.fresno.gov/Government/DepartmentDirectory/Police/AboutFresnoPD/CALEAAccreditation.htm

Geyer, T. (2012, January 8). Illinois rules force many cities to drop auxiliary police units. Retrieved October 31, 2013 from http://qctimes.com/news/local/illinois-rules-force-many-cities-to-drop-auxiliary-police-units/article_59f88ec8-3a7a-11e1-983f-0019bb2963f4.html

Inciardi, J. (2000). *Elements of criminal justice* (2nd ed.). New York (NY): Oxford University Press.

Juliano, F. (2011, March 5). Higher training standards, costs mean fewer part-time police. Retrieved November 1, 2013 from http://www.ctpost.com/local/article/Higher-training-standards-costs-mean-fewer-1043894.php#

Klein, W. E. (2013). *Frequently asked questions.* Police Officer Standards and Training Council. Retrieved November 1, 2013 from http://www.ct.gov/post/cwp/view.asp?a = 2058&q = 291946

Leukhardt, B. (1995, February 19). A city calls auxiliary police back to duty. Retrieved November 1, 2013 from http://articles.courant.com/1995-02-19/news/9502190210_1_auxiliary-professional-police-citizens-and-police

Nazemi, S. (2013). Sir Robert Peel's nine principals of policing. Retrieved October 20, 2013 from http://lacp.org/2009-Articles-Main/062609-Peels9Principals-Sandy-Nazemi.htm

Oleck, H. L. (1982). *Oleck's tort law practice manual.* Englewood Cliffs, NJ: Prentice-Hall.

Opinion No. GA-0893. (2011, November 22). Texas Attorney General Opinion No. GA-0893 Re: Whether a city that has adopted civil service rules for its police officers under chapter 143 of the Local Government Code may authorize a reserve police force. Retrieved October 28, 2013 from https://www.oag.state.tx.us/opinions/opinions/50abbott/op/2011/htm/ga-0893.htm

Pine, J. C. (n.d.). *Catastrophe readiness and response course; Session 5: Political and legal issues'*. Emergency Management Institute, FEMA, pp. 27–33. Forthcoming. Retrieved October 21, 2013 from www.training.fema.gov/.../catastrophe/Session%205%20Legal%20Issues...

Pine, J. C. (2013). Political and legal issues. In R. Bissell (Ed.), *Preparedness and response for catastrophic disasters* (pp. 77–108). Boca Raton, FL: CRC Press, Taylor and Francis Group.

Public Entity Risk Institute. (1999). Understanding the volunteer protection act. Retrieved October 22, 2013 from http://www.riskinstitute.org/peri/index.php?option = com_bookmarks&task = detail&id = 584

Reserve LEO News. (2013). Fort worth to resume reserve police officer program. Retrieved October 26, 2013 from http://www.vleoa.org/

Sherman, E. (2013, June 22). Waltham auxiliary police officers could return. Retrieved October 26, 2013 from http://www.wickedlocal.com/waltham/news/x1220217363/Waltham-auxiliary-police-officers-could-return

Statement of Policy. (2006, October 11). *Statement of policy auxiliary police officers*. Illinois Law Enforcement and Standards Training Board. Retrieved October 26, 2013 from http://www.ptb.state.il.us/pdf/auxiliary.pdf

U.S. Census Data. (2013). Waltham, MA. Retrieved October 26, 2013 from http://quickfacts.census.gov/qfd/states/25/2572600.html

Waltham Auxiliary Police. (2013). The Waltham Auxiliary Police Department is currently seeking qualified applicants. Retrieved October 26, 2013 from http://www.city.waltham.ma.us/police-department/pages/auxiliary-police

Waltham, MA. (2013). Retrieved October 26, 2012 from http://www.city-data.com/city/Waltham-Massachusetts.html

Wardell, J. (2013). CSO program. Retrieved November 1, 2013 from http://www.newbritainpolice.org/cso-program

Waters, W. (2008, March 15). Wenham police department to be restructured. Retrieved October 31, 2013 from http://www.wickedlocal.com/hamilton/news/x563308331

# Volunteer Police and the Prevention of Human Trafficking

# 11

> It ought to concern every person, because it is a debasement of our common humanity. It ought to concern every community, because it tears at our social fabric. It ought to concern every business, because it distorts markets. It ought to concern every nation, because it endangers public health and fuels violence and organized crime. I'm talking about the injustice, the outrage, of human trafficking, which must be called by its true name—modern slavery.
>
> **—President Barack Obama**[1]

In the 1990s, Kathleen Barry (1995) estimated that the number of women and children trafficked worldwide for prostitution was approaching the numbers associated with the African slave trade of the 1700s. Approximately 150 years ago, the Thirteenth Amendment of the U.S. Constitution was adopted, banning slavery and involuntary servitude. Nevertheless, according to combined figures from the U.S. Justice, Labor, and State Departments, more than 100,000 people are presently being forced into servitude in the United States. Every year, human traffickers generate billions of dollars in profits by victimizing millions of people worldwide. Human trafficking is considered to be one of the fastest growing criminal industries in the world (Polaris Project 2013d).

This chapter considers the important role that volunteer police and other concerned individuals may play in the prevention of human trafficking and worker exploitation. It indicates the various types of existing human slavery (contract, chattel, etc.) and describes a citizen's role in the prevention of human trafficking. Victims of trafficking often do not speak the language of their new country and may in fact be illegal immigrants who fear deportation. Minors are especially vulnerable to exploitation and several states have begun to recognize this problem through the passage of "Safe Harbor" legislation. For example, in 2008, New York enacted the Safe Harbor for Exploited Children Act, which recognizes that children in prostitution are not criminals or delinquents but victims of child sex trafficking and child sexual abuse that need specialized services. In addition, in 2010, the Texas Supreme Court declared that child victims of prostitution should be provided counseling, rehabilitation, and services instead of being placed in a detention system that is ill-suited to their needs.[2]

The U.S. Department of State's Office to Monitor and Combat Trafficking in Persons is the country's leading agency with respect to a worldwide effort to reduce human trafficking. The Trafficking Victims Protection Act of 2000[3] (TVPA) is the nation's primary statute for combating this phenomenon, which has a variety of forms including forced labor, sex trafficking, bonded labor, debt bondage, involuntary domestic servitude, forced child labor, child soldiers, and child sex trafficking. "The Office has responsibility for bilateral and multilateral diplomacy, targeted foreign assistance, and public engagement on this issue of modern slavery and partners with foreign governments and civil society to develop and implement effective counter-trafficking strategies" (U.S. Department of State 2013a). Under the Trafficking Victims Protection Act of 2000, the phrases "trafficking in persons" or "human trafficking" have been used as umbrella terms for activities involved when one person obtains or holds another person in compelled service. Human trafficking is the acquisition of people by improper means such as force, fraud, or deception, with the aim of exploiting them (UNODC 2013b).

The United Nations Office on Drugs and Crime (UNODC) undertakes regional and transnational initiatives that seek to strengthen the rule of law, stability, and development. It targets the world's most vulnerable regions where the convergence of drugs, crime, corruption, and terrorism threatens regional and global security. It also tries to cope with organized crime and human trafficking, including the smuggling of migrants. Smuggling of migrants involves the procurement, for financial or other material benefit, of illegal entry for a person into a country of which that person is not a national or resident (UNODC 2013b). Such crimes are high on the international agenda because they pose major threats to security, which undermines human progress and challenges democracy. Virtually every country in the world is affected by these crimes. The challenge for all countries is to target the criminals who exploit desperate people and to protect and assist victims of trafficking and smuggled migrants, many of whom endure unimaginable hardships in their quest for a better life (UNODC 2013b).

The UNODC recognizes that the resources available to deal with these threats are minute compared to the suffering these threats instill (UNODC 2010). According to Yury Fedotov, the UNODC's executive director, human trafficking is a crime with millions of victims that stretches around the globe, although much of it remains hidden. "We are dealing with a crime of the 21st Century: adaptive, cynical, sophisticated; existing in developed and developing countries alike.... We need more sharing of best practices, greater mutual legal assistance, more joint operations across borders, national strategies on human trafficking linked to regional and international approaches, as well as the cooperation of key stakeholders such as civil society, the private sector and the media" (UNODC 2013a).

In 2014, as the February date for America's biggest sports event—the Super Bowl—was approaching, New Jersey's law enforcers redoubled their efforts to reduce the threat of sex trafficking. Many believe the state's sprawling highway system, its proximity to New York City, and its diverse population make it an attractive base of operations for traffickers. Consequently, New Jersey officials have trained law enforcement personnel, hospitality workers (e.g., hotel and nightclub employees), high school students, airport employees, and others in identifying the signs of trafficking. Local houses of worship are notifying congregants of warning signs, and truckers are being trained to look for people—mostly women but also men—who may be held against their will. To be prosecuted, sex trafficking must involve—unlike prostitution—not only a buyer and seller of sex but also a pimp or trafficker controlling the transaction, according to the New Jersey Attorney General's Office. In Arizona, where the 2015 Super Bowl will take place, Senator John McCain's wife, Cindy, has been speaking out, calling the Super Bowl the "largest human-trafficking venue on the planet" (Zezima 2014).

This chapter considers the definitions, cases, and types of human trafficking. It also addresses whether volunteer police in the United States should be considered stakeholders in the global fight against human trafficking and modern-day slavery. Arguments justifying this point of view can be based on the potential and significant roles volunteer police may undertake—for example, obtaining the cooperation of ordinary citizens, addressing the needs of victims, enforcing the laws designed to halt trafficking, protecting human rights, and providing other essential resources for the prevention of human trafficking and related crimes. In addition, various kinds of initiatives designed to facilitate the work of existing local volunteer police organizations are considered. The importance of federal assistance in harnessing the energies and talents of volunteer police is addressed as well as the form such assistance might take. Appendix E provides a brief annotated list of books and online videos concerning human trafficking.

## Definitions

The U.S. government considers trafficking in persons to include all of the criminal conduct involved in forced labor and sex trafficking, essentially the conduct involved in reducing or holding someone in compelled service. Under the Trafficking Victims Protection Act of 2000 and its amendments and consistent with the United Nations *Protocol to Prevent, Suppress, and Punish Trafficking in Persons, Especially Women and Children* (hereinafter referred to as the Palermo Protocol),[4] individuals may be trafficking victims regardless of whether they once consented, participated in a crime as a direct result of being trafficked, were transported into the exploitative situation, or were simply born into a state of servitude. Despite a term that seems to connote movement, at the heart of the phenomenon of trafficking in persons are the many forms of enslavement, not the activities involved in international transportation (U.S. Department of State 2013b).[5]

Within the United Nations, the Office of the High Commissioner for Human Rights (OHCHR) is mandated to promote and protect the enjoyment and full realization by all people of all rights established in the Charter of the United Nations and in international human rights laws and treaties. A 2002 report entitled *Recommended Principles and Guidelines on Human Rights and Human Trafficking* was prepared by the OHCHR. The report was developed in order to provide practical, rights-based policy guidance on the prevention of trafficking and on the protection of victims of trafficking. The OHCHR report recommended that nations and—where appropriate— intergovernmental and nongovernmental organizations consider adopting and consistently using the internationally agreed upon definition of trafficking contained in the Palermo Protocol.

Under Article 3(a), the Palermo Protocol defines trafficking in persons as: "The recruitment, transportation, transfer, harboring, or receipt of persons, by means of the threat or use of force or other forms of coercion, of abduction, of fraud, of deception, of the abuse of power or of a position of vulnerability or of the giving or receiving of payments or benefits to achieve the consent of a person having control over another person for the purpose of exploitation. Exploitation shall include, at a minimum, the exploitation of the prostitution of others or other forms of sexual exploitation, forced labor or services, slavery or practices similar to slavery, servitude, or the removal of organs." Article 3(b) states the consent of a victim of trafficking in persons to the intended exploitation set forth in subparagraph (a) of this article shall be irrelevant where any of the means set forth in subparagraph (a) have been used. Article 3(c) of the Protocol further states that the recruitment, transportation, transfer, harboring, or receipt of a child for the purpose of exploitation shall be considered "trafficking in persons" even if this does not involve any of the means set forth here.

Article 3(b) indicates that the consent of the victim is irrelevant. It should be understood that the consent of the victim at any stage of the trafficking process is irrelevant. Just as legally a person cannot consent to slavery; neither can a victim consent to trafficking. "Exploitation, rather than coercion, is the operative concept in this definition. A definition of trafficking, based on a human rights framework, should protect all who are trafficked, drawing no distinctions between deserving and undeserving victims of trafficking, that is those who can prove they were forced and those who cannot. Any definition based on the victim's consent places the burden of proof on the victim and offers a loophole for traffickers to use the alleged consent of the victim in their own defense" (Hynes and Raymond 2002, 198–199).

## The Polaris Project: Hotline, Advocacy, Services, Training

Founded in February 2002 by two Brown University graduates, Katherine Chon and Derek Ellerman, the "Polaris Project is a leading organization in the global fight against human trafficking and modern-day slavery. Named after the North Star 'Polaris' that guided slaves to freedom along the Underground Railroad, Polaris Project is transforming the way that individuals and communities respond to human trafficking, in the United States and globally. By successfully pushing for stronger federal and state laws, operating the National Human Trafficking Resource Center hotline (1–888–373–7888), conducting trainings, and providing vital services to victims of trafficking, Polaris Project creates long-term solutions that move our society closer to a world without slavery" (Polaris Project 2013a). Law enforcement officers, service providers, and other key first responders have used the Polaris Project for valuable training on how to recognize the signs of trafficking.[6]

Human trafficking is a form of modern-day slavery where people profit from the control and exploitation of others. As defined under U.S. federal law, victims of human trafficking include children involved in the sex trade, adults aged 18 or over who are coerced or deceived into commercial sex acts, and anyone forced into different forms of "labor or services," such as domestic workers held in a home, or farm workers forced to labor against their will. The factors that each of these situations has in common are elements of force, fraud, or coercion that are used to control people. This ability to control may then be used to induce someone into commercial sex acts, labor, or services. Numerous people in the field have summed up the concept of human trafficking as "compelled service" (Polaris Project 2013d).

Labor trafficking occurs in diverse contexts that encompass all forms of labor or services. Common places where forced labor has been found in the United States range from domestic servitude and small-scale "mom and pop" labor operations to more large-scale operations such as farms and factories. Certain brokers that supply labor to multinational corporations have also been identified as an emerging type of labor traffickers. Sex trafficking includes commercial sexual exploitation of children (CSEC), as well as every instance where an adult is in the sex trade as the result of force, fraud, or coercion. Sex trafficking occurs in street prostitution, online escort services, residential brothels, and brothels disguised as massage businesses. Under U.S. and international law, commercially sexually exploited children found in the sex trade are considered to be victims of trafficking, even if no force or coercion is present. Victims of human trafficking in the United States include American citizens or foreign nationals, adults or minors, and men or women. Foreign-born victims in the United States may be either documented or undocumented (Polaris Project 2013d).

**Figure 11.1** National Human Trafficking Resource Center hotline call specialists are available 24 hours a day, 7 days a week, 365 days a year to take reports from anywhere in the country related to potential trafficking victims, suspicious behaviors, and/or locations where trafficking is suspected to occur. All reports are confidential. Interpreters are available. (From http://www.polarisproject.org/what-we-do/national-human-trafficking-hotline/report-a-tip)

Because human trafficking is considered to be one of the fastest growing criminal industries, the U.S. government and academic researchers are currently working on an annual estimate of the total number of trafficked persons in the United States. With 100,000 children estimated to be in the sex trade in the United States each year, it is clear that the total number of human trafficking victims in this country reaches into the hundreds of thousands when estimates of both adults and minors as well as sex and labor trafficking are aggregated (Polaris Project 2013d). The Polaris Project focuses on the day-to-day needs of the victims of human trafficking as well as the creation of long-term solutions that affect systemic and social change. For both of these purposes, in 2012, Polaris Project launched Vision 2020 to expand their impact on a global scale. One aspect of this initiative is to build on the work of the National Human Trafficking Resource Center (NHTRC) hotline (Figure 11.1) by identifying and connecting globally with human trafficking hotlines in order to develop a more coordinated and data-driven response to modern-day slavery. In addition, training and technical assistance may be offered to support the creation and expansion of hotlines in target countries (Polaris Project 2013c).

## Trafficking in Persons Worker Exploitation Task Force

Within the U.S. Department of Justice, the Trafficking in Persons Worker Exploitation Task Force (TPWETF) seeks to prevent trafficking in persons and worker exploitation throughout the United States and to investigate and prosecute cases when such violations occur. The Task Force is chaired by the Assistant Attorney General for Civil Rights and the Solicitor of Labor. Other Department of Justice participants in this national effort include: the Federal Bureau of Investigation (FBI), the Immigration and Naturalization Service (INS), the Executive Office for United States Attorneys, the Justice Department's Criminal Division, and the Office of Victims of Crime and the Violence against Women Office. The TPWETF also works in coordination with the Department of Labor, the Department of State, the Equal Employment Opportunity Commission, and various U.S. Attorneys' offices across the country (U.S. Department of Justice 2013).

The Criminal Section of the Civil Rights Division has primary enforcement responsibility for America's involuntary servitude and peonage statutes and plays an active role as a leading member of the TPWETF. The Criminal Section's attorneys conduct grand jury investigations and prosecute cases. The section works closely with the FBI, the INS, and the 94 U.S. Attorneys Offices to ensure that allegations of trafficking and slavery are investigated. Since the creation of the TPWETF, the number of open slavery investigations in the section has tripled (U.S. Department of Justice 2013). The rise in such cases may be due to an increase in the smuggling of immigrants. When immigrants enter the United States illegally, they have an increased risk of being exploited by criminals because they may be indebted to them. A Rutgers University study of 300 smuggled Chinese immigrants found that many of them had been tortured before paying off their debts (Gordy 2000). The Criminal Section also works with victim/witness coordinators from the FBI, INS, U.S. Attorneys' Offices, and the Executive Office for United States Attorneys to assist victims of trafficking in receiving health care, housing, and other protections. Since 2000, the TPWETF has operated a Complaint Line at 1–888–428–7581 (weekdays, 9 a.m. to 5 p.m. EST) for anyone to report suspected instances of trafficking or worker exploitation. A TPWETF Complaint Line call is toll-free and offers foreign language translation services in most languages as well as text telephone (TTY) (U.S. Department of Justice 2013). TTY is also sometimes called a telecommunication device for the deaf or TDD. However, TTY is the more widely accepted term as it is used by many people not just people who are deaf (see http://www.abouttty.com).

## Cases and Types of Human Trafficking

Slavery can be found in almost every country. Its various forms can include contract slavery (the individual initially agrees to engage in work but discovers upon arrival usually in a foreign land that they are powerless to leave); debt bondage (where an individual ostensibly works to pay off a debt, but in reality, the obligation is not permitted to end); and chattel slavery (where an individual is kept in permanent servitude as a result of being captured, born, or sold into it) (Bales 1999). According to Bales (1999, 26), "Much modern slavery is hidden behind a mask of fraudulent labor contracts." For example, it has been estimated that there may be as many as 1,000 domestic slaves in London. The discovery of such cases is often hampered because a contract for hire can be produced to delay the detection of the reality of the situation by honest officials or to provide a justification for dishonest ones to simply walk away. Many of these workers will be told how and what they must answer if questioned by the officials of the host country (Bales 1999).

In 1999, a conviction for "conspiring to enslave" 14 women was obtained by the U.S. Justice Department. The women had been forced to work as prostitutes in a network of nine brothels in several southern states (see the story of Rosa later in this chapter). In 1993, a conviction was obtained in a case involving U.S. citizens who were employed as migrant laborers but were forced to sleep in a single room and work in the fields patrolled by a guard armed with a machete.

In 2001, Got, a four-year-old Thai boy, was detained by immigration officials in California. He had been rented by his heroin-addicted mother to serve as a decoy for a ring engaged in the smuggling of prostitutes from Thailand to the United States. At the time of his detention, doctors discovered that he suffered from a serious case of chicken pox complicated by his HIV-positive status. Got was hospitalized and officials began deportation proceedings for his return to Thailand "where it was likely that his use as a disguise for illegal entry by Thai prostitutes would continue" (Barone 2003, 580). Fortunately, his deportation was stopped and he was issued a temporary visa (T visa) in accordance with the terms of a new federal statute—The Trafficking Victims Protection Act of 2000.

Another example of modern-day slavery concerns the case of Mende Nazer who was kidnapped when she was 12 years old from her home in the Nuba Mountains region of Sudan. Until her escape eight years later, Nazer tended to the needs of the family she was sold to. She washed their clothes, cooked their meals, cleaned their home, and cared for their children. When she did not comply with the wishes of the family, they beat her. At the time of her escape, she was living in London, having been passed along to another family. It has been estimated that more than 11,000 southern Sudanese have been abducted during the past two decades (Winter 2004).

A fourth illustration of a modern-day form of slavery involves Rosa, a 13-year-old girl who came to the United States from Mexico. She had been promised employment in a Texas restaurant but instead was taken to a rural area in Florida where she was compelled to work in a brothel after being gang raped. After six months in captivity, she was able to escape with two other young girls (Lederer 2004). The story of Rosa and information about the latest governmental efforts to combat trafficking can be found at the U.S. Department of State's Web site (http://www.state.gov). The story of Rosa is presented in detail at: http://2001-2009.state.gov/g/tip/rls/rm/2005/48309. htm Each of the foregoing cases involved various aspects of contract, chattel, and debt bondage.

In another instance, Russian women were recruited and imported into the United States as folk dancers. Instead, they were forced to work as exotic dancers. The women were not free to leave their employment, were threatened with violence if they attempted to escape, and had their travel documents and return airline tickets confiscated by their employer. The women were forced to turn over their earnings to their captors. This case began as a contract arrangement but quickly became a case involving deceit and coercion. Debt bondage was used in another case when Mexican farm workers were smuggled into the United States, then held, and forced to work for their captors to pay off their smuggling fees. Fees were usually $5,000 or more, and the victims were held by threats of violence. According to the victims, they were smuggled into the United States in a van; during the three-day trip, they were not allowed to leave the van for bathroom breaks or for food. The youngest victim was 13 years of age (U.S. Department of Justice 2013). Human trafficking can be said to exist, whether or not victims initially went voluntarily or consented, because it is what happens to victims along the pipeline of activity through force, fraud, and coercion that signifies cases of modern-day slavery (Lederer 2004; LILYA 4-EVER 2004).

The training information provided by New Jersey officials in preparation for the 2014 Super Bowl noted that human trafficking may involve a local woman forced into sex work by a man she initially thought had romantic intentions or a woman from another country whose family is threatened. The indications may be a woman who appears not to be in control, who looks frightened, and who may exhibit signs of physical abuse. Victims are often runaways, the impoverished, abuse victims, or those living in the country illegally (Zezima 2014). Box 11.1 provides a summary of a 2010 United Nations report on human trafficking.

## Trafficking Victims Protection Act of 2000

The Trafficking Victims Protection Act of 2000 (TVPA) has three purposes: (1) to prevent trafficking; (2) to punish traffickers; and (3) to protect victims. The statute provides for a T visa (capped at 5,000 per year for victims of trafficking) and the alternative U visa for victims of certain crimes. However, these visas are contingent on the applicant agreeing to provide investigative

**BOX 11.1   GLOBAL REPORT ON TRAFFICKING
IN PERSONS: KEY FINDINGS**

- The most commonly reported purpose of human trafficking is sexual exploitation (79%), followed by forced labor (18%), but many types of trafficking may be underreported, in part because they are largely "invisible"—including forced or bonded labor, domestic servitude and forced marriage, organ removal, and exploitation of children for begging, the sex trade, and warfare.
- Women comprise by far the largest portion of trafficking victims (80%–84%).
- The number of convictions of traffickers is increasing but not proportionately to the growing awareness (and, probably, size) of the problem.
- Most trade in humans occurs at the national or regional level, though interregional trafficking is also common.
- A growing number of countries are taking steps to address human trafficking, but there are still many, especially in Africa, that lack the necessary legal instruments to do so.

*Source:* UNODC, 2010, UNODC: Promoting health, security and justice, 2010 annual report. Available at: http://www.unodc.org/documents/frontpage/UNODC_Annual_Report_2010_LowRes.pdf

and prosecutorial assistance against the traffickers or other alleged criminals. The purpose of the U visa is to give victims of certain crimes temporary legal status and work eligibility in the United States for up to four years.[7] The U visa is a nonimmigrant visa, and only 10,000 U visas may be issued every fiscal year. Family members may also be included on the petition including spouses, children, unmarried sisters and brothers under 18, mothers, fathers, as well as stepparents and adoptive parents. An approved T or U visa petition will automatically grant the applicant work eligibility in the United States (U-Visa 2013). An essential difference with respect to these two types of visas is that U visas are awarded to people who have suffered substantial physical or mental abuse as a result of having been a victim of specified criminal activity.[8]

The TVPA also created an interagency Task Force on Trafficking in Persons (see earlier) to study and combat trafficking as well as increased penalties for those found guilty of trafficking. The law also created the Office to Combat and Monitor Trafficking in Persons in order to assist victims in the United States and in foreign countries through the provision of necessary services (shelter, medical care, etc.). This office is required to prepare an annual report about the status of trafficking in persons throughout the world. The statute was adopted in response to the need for reforms to deal with the problem of human trafficking. For example, one study found many drawbacks in the prosecution of involuntary servitude cases. "The cases are complicated and difficult to put together, they fall into the purview of a number of agencies, and it's not always clear who has responsibility.... Victims frequently wind up treated like criminals themselves, detained and deported to the countries from which they were seeking to escape in the first place" (Fighting the Slave Trade 2000, 25). In 1988, the "involuntary servitude" statutes had been narrowly defined by the U.S. Supreme Court (see, e.g., *U.S. v. Kominski* 487 U.S. 931). The court's legal definition did not extend to modern-day traffickers' practices of using blackmail, coercion, and fraud.

## Volunteer Police Roles

Since World War II, many opportunities have existed to foster a public safety role for concerned citizens. The present era is no exception. Concerned individuals as well as volunteer police can directly contribute to the ideal contained in Article I of the *Universal Declaration of Human Rights* (1948) that "Human beings are born free and equal in dignity and rights."

Federal and state governments can do more to help victims and to deter traffickers. In particular, the federal government could implement a series of initiatives designed to facilitate the work of existing local volunteer police units and several related agencies on the federal level. For example, the federal government can establish volunteer police units in order to assist various federal agencies with the use of new hotlines and the enforcement of the laws designed to protect foreign workers from exploitation. It would be quite worthwhile for the federal government to appoint a representative from the volunteer police community to become a member of the TPWETF. This individual could make recommendations about how to harness the energies and talents of the more than 200,000 volunteer police in the United States (U.S. Department of Justice 2011).

Since 2004, the International Association of Chiefs of Police (IACP) has seen a vast increase in the number of volunteers that are being used by law enforcement agencies to perform police duties (U.S. Department of Justice 2011, 25). Figure 11.2 illustrates this trend. Many U.S. police agencies have some type of volunteer worker. They may be police reserves, auxiliaries, administrative aides, Community Emergency Response Team (CERT) members, or serving in other capacties.[9] These units comprise an important part of today's world of law enforcement and should be considered an essential resource in the protection of human rights and in the enforcement of laws concerned with the prevention of human trafficking. A critical need in this

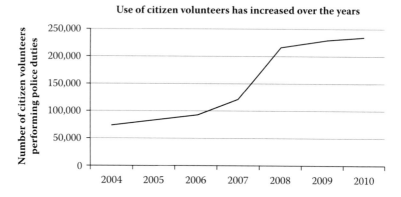

**Figure 11.2** Police volunteer numbers and trends. (From U.S. Department of Justice, The impact of the economic downturn on American police agencies, U.S. Department of Justice, Office of Community Oriented Policing Services, Washington, DC, 2011.)

regard involves appropriate training. This could be done through the establishment of an auxiliary police training division at one or more of the national or regional law enforcement training centers. The centers could teach leadership development, appropriate reporting techniques, how to handle drug and smuggling offenders, crime prevention, and surveillance skills. The course of study could also be made available to the volunteer members of the National Park Service, Civil Air Patrol, U.S. Coast Guard Auxiliary, and other groups with more limited policing responsibilities. Thus, volunteers in the field of policing could be sent for extra training in much the same way as the National FBI Academy provides extra training for local police officials.

Financial support for the supervision and in-service training of local volunteer police units could be augmented by the federal government. A program could be established through congressional action modeled on the Defense Department's original "Troops to Teachers Program." This program has helped to place several thousand veterans from all branches of the armed forces into positions within local school districts. Significantly, for each veteran who qualified by October 1, 1995, school districts received an incentive grant of up to $50,000 to help pay their salaries during a five-year period. More than 31,000 persons retire each year from the military, many of them relatively young (Hewitt and Siew 1998). Just as some of them have become schoolteachers, others could draw upon their military training and help to train and supervise new volunteer police personnel.

Police and volunteer police could also be joined by other community professionals and members of concerned groups and organizations. Generally, these additional human resources: (1) will know the nature of the human trafficking problem and working together may develop new ways to help reduce this problem; (2) may help to disseminate information regarding the purpose of the

T and U visas for victims of human trafficking and related crimes; and (3) help to inform the public about the existence of the Worker Exploitation Task Force Complaint Line. Moreover, the proliferation of nongovernmental organizations (NGOs) dedicated to the protection of human rights (e.g., Amnesty International and Human Rights Watch) may also provide concerned citizens with opportunities to counter the trade in humans. Some have referred to recent developments as a "rights revolution" (Ignatieff 2000; Power 2001; Sellars 2002). However, as Cmiel (2004, 131) indicates "more human rights NGOs do not necessarily mean that fewer people are being detained or tortured."

The principal congressional sponsor of the Trafficking Victims Protection Act of 2000 was Christopher H. Smith of New Jersey. In a speech delivered on the floor of the U.S. House of Representatives in 2001, Congressman Smith concluded: "What we need to make this law work are 'true believers' who will spare no effort to mobilize the resources and the prestige of the United States government to implement this important Act and shut down this terrible industry, which routinely and grossly violates the most fundamental human rights of the world's most vulnerable people" (Smith 2001). "New Jersey has a huge trafficking problem," said Smith, co-chairman of the House anti-human trafficking caucus. "One Super Bowl after another after another has shown itself to be one of the largest events in the world where the cruelty of human trafficking goes on for several weeks" (in Zezima 2014). No single agency can solve this complex social problem, which has numerous global aspects. A combined community-police effort is needed to address this difficult problem.

## Volunteer Crime Prevention Specialists

In recent decades, the field of crime prevention has become a specialization among police departments. Police officers attend additional training in this field to earn qualifications from a variety of associations and state governments.[10] Volunteer police are also welcome to attend these training programs. In general, crime prevention is a field that recognizes that public safety must no longer remain the exclusive domain of the criminal justice system; rather, it should be pursued through a network of other state institutions and nongovernmental organizations. Most importantly, the prevention of crime requires the proactive participation of communities and individual citizens, in partnership with police, other government agencies, local businesses, neighborhood groups, schools, and any other partner with a stake in the community.

In 1972, the National Crime Prevention Institute (NCPI) defined "crime prevention" as "the anticipation, recognition, and appraisal of a crime risk and the initiative of some action to remove it." (NCPI 1978, 1). In 1990, the National Crime Prevention Council[11] developed a supplemental and more practically oriented definition: "Crime prevention is a pattern of attitudes and behaviors directed at reducing the threat of crime and enhancing the sense of safety and security, to positively influence the quality of life in our society, and to develop environments where crime cannot flourish." One rationale underlying crime prevention is that "the cops, courts, and corrections approach" has been unable to cope with the actual quantity of crime. Furthermore, this punitive approach fails to address the opportunities and the root causes that give rise to criminal behavior.

An important aspect of crime prevention is teaching about its definitions and then putting together an appropriate response based on the problem to be addressed. Education appears to be an important tool to prevent some forms of trafficking. If children and adults are aware of the stories that traffickers tell, and recognize the patterns of traffickers, this might decrease some trafficking. A counter-trafficking program in Romania works with school-age children, educating the children on the risks of trafficking. It appears to be having some success. However, educating people on the risks of trafficking helps only in situations where children are not initially taken by force (Brusca 2011). The huge but rather demobilized force of U.S. volunteer police should become more knowledgeable about the problem, and specialists should be trained from among their ranks to educate the general public about anti-trafficking laws, the state of their enforcement, and the patterns of traffickers. America's lead in this regard could spur other police departments throughout the world to include their volunteer police in a similar effort. In this way, more forces might be mobilized to decrease the success of traffickers.

Albemarle is a 726-square-mile county located in the state of Virginia. As of 2012, Albemarle County's population was about 102,000. Its county seat is Charlottesville, and its police force celebrated its thirtieth anniversary in 2012. Col. Steven Sellers, Albemarle County's police chief, says human trafficking can involve many forms of extortion. Sex trafficking, which falls under the umbrella of human trafficking, can be tied to underage sex acts, child pornography, and—most commonly—prostitution. Both types are occurring in Albemarle County, according to Col. Sellers, and the victims are primarily foreign nationals. Human trafficking is one of the least understood crimes, and Col. Sellers has indicated that more police training is needed to better distinguish it from other issues (Newsplex.com 2013). "In order for traffickers to be caught and prosecuted, the victims must be found, but the extreme fear among the victims makes this crime much more difficult to uncover. Many times a person is held for years before they either escape, die, or are let go. Consequently, the traffickers have many years to continue in the buying and selling of individuals. This issue is even more pronounced for children, who just by the nature of their age are at a disadvantage. The opportunity to be heard or rescued is diminished as often a child is either constantly held captive, is escorted by an adult at all times or is coerced into not speaking up" (Brusca 2011, 15).

Targeting human trafficking is a challenge for officers because it can be a quick moving underground business, but Col. Sellers recognizes that the problem needs to be a priority for police departments (Newsplex.com 2013). Moreover, law enforcement agencies are often the first responders at trafficking situations (Clawson et al. 2006; Wilson et al. 2006) and are more likely to encounter perpetrators of human trafficking than federal agencies (De Baca and Tisi 2002). "Another difficulty is getting victims to come forward against their traffickers. There is the fear of retaliation, the fear of being punished for the crimes committed while enslaved, or the fear of being ostracized after telling their story" (Brusca 2011, 17).

Coincidentally, Chief Sellers is in the process of establishing an auxiliary force.[12] In addition to having selected volunteers serve as specialists in the field of crime prevention, volunteer police can play significant roles in manning key checkpoints (e.g., rest stops) along major highways and at transportation hubs to distribute informational flyers for travelers to be alert for possible traffickers and their victims. Depending on their level of training, they could also be called upon to assist in aided cases as well as crimes in progress.

## Nongovernmental Prevention Efforts

The Salvation Army was founded in London, England, in 1865, by the husband and wife team of Catherine and William Booth. The Booths went against Victorian conventions and took their ministry to the streets of London's east side where they reached out to the destitute and desperate. Their efforts included direct interventions to help women and girls involved in organized sexual exploitation. The Salvation Army has opened homes to protect and shelter them.[13] In 2010, Anne's House became the first long-term, residential program in the Chicago area for young women and girls who were victims of sex trafficking. The program offers comprehensive residential services to sex trafficking victims and was established to address the limited number of shelters and services available for this unique population (Anne's House 2013).

In the United Kingdom, the Salvation Army's effort to help women and girls in prostitution has included the opening of many rescue homes. In a different era, it also has played a volunteer role in the field of law enforcement. The Salvation Army participated in the planning and execution of an undercover investigation into the trafficking of young girls for prostitution. A detailed account of this role was published in July 1885 by the *Pall Mall Gazette* in a series of articles called "The Maiden Tribute of Modern Babylon." The series created enough fervor to foment public opinion in support of the Criminal Law Amendment Act of 1885, a measure passed in the United Kingdom that raised the age of consent from 13 to 16 (although reformers sought 18). The Salvation Army's advocacy efforts were a major catalyst in the bill's passage. More than a century later, in the United States and abroad, the Salvation Army is part of a revived movement for the abolition of sex trafficking and other forms of commercial sexual exploitation (Salvation Army 2013b).

The Department of Homeland Security (DHS) has teamed up with Western Union to combat human trafficking. Western Union has agreed to provide multilingual training and awareness materials to select Western Union locations in the southwest border region and other areas across the United States. Working with the DHS, Western Union plans to use training and awareness materials developed by the DHS Blue Campaign to educate agents who regularly interact with the public on potential indicators of human trafficking and on how to identify victims. In the past, Western Union and the Western Union Foundation have worked with and supported several U.S. global organizations combating human trafficking (Pankratz 2013).

Redlight Traffic is a 501(c)(3) organization under the Seattle Kiwanis Memorial Fund established in 1947. In 2013, Redlight Traffic launched a first-of-its-kind app for iPhones and Androids that funnels citizens' anonymous tips on suspected prostitution activities to law enforcement through a secure Web site that can only be accessed by police officers. The aims of the new app include teaching citizens how to identify signs of sex trafficking; giving citizens an easy way to do something about the problem; and providing law enforcement with data that can potentially help officers rescue victims and build criminal cases against pimps and men who pay for sex. Through the app, citizens will be able to report their suspicions, upload photos and GPS locations, and provide information on a business, vehicle, or person—whether that person is a suspected prostitute, pimp, or buyer. Officers are then able to search and review individual reports and view a map of all reported incidents in an area (Green 2013). (More information is available from: http://www.redlighttraffic.org/app.)

Banks and credit card companies can play a crucial role in shutting down human traffickers by flagging the electronic fingerprints they leave behind, according to Manhattan District Attorney (DA) Cyrus Vance. An estimated 14,000 to 17,000 people are smuggled into the United States each year and forced to work as domestic servants, laborers, or in the sex trade, according to estimates from the DA's office. Human trafficking is a global business worth $32 billion a year, according to the U.S. State Department. The International Labor Organization estimates that nearly 21 million people worldwide are victims of slavery or forced labor. Almost half are thought to be trafficked, either across borders or within their own countries. The Manhattan DA's office and the Thomson Reuters Foundation are coordinating the efforts of a working group set up by the banks. U.S. and European financial institutions already have a regulatory duty to report suspected illegal activity, but there have been few efforts to leverage methods used to spot money laundering, extremist violence, and other crimes to hone in on human trafficking. The first bank to do so was JPMorgan Chase, and it has developed a model for monitoring transactions and partnering with law enforcement (McGurty 2013).

## Summary

Under the TVPA, the phrases "trafficking in persons" or "human trafficking" have been used as umbrella terms for activities involved when one person obtains or holds another person in compelled service. The TVPA describes this compelled service using a number of different terms: involuntary servitude, slavery, debt bondage, and forced labor. The TVPA uses definitions drawn from and correlated with the United Nations *Protocol to Prevent, Suppress, and Punish Trafficking in Persons, Especially Women and Children* (the Palermo Protocol).

The document entitled *Recommended Principles and Guidelines on Human Rights and Human Trafficking* published in 2002 by the OHCHR was developed in order to provide practical, rights-based policy guidance on the prevention of trafficking and on the protection of victims of trafficking. The purpose of the OHCHR is to promote and facilitate the integration of a human rights perspective into national, regional, and international anti-trafficking laws, policies, and interventions. The *Principles and Guidelines* serve as a framework and reference point for the work of OHCHR on this issue. The term "trafficking," as used in the *Principles and Guidelines,* is taken from the Palermo Protocol and refers to the recruitment, transportation, transfer, harboring, or receipt of persons, by means of the threat or use of force or other forms of coercion, of abduction, of fraud, of deception, of the abuse of power, or of a position of vulnerability or of the giving or receiving of payments or benefits to achieve the consent of a person having control over another person, for the purpose of exploitation. Exploitation includes, at a minimum, the exploitation of the prostitution of others or other forms of sexual exploitation, forced labor or services, slavery or practices similar to slavery, servitude, or the removal of organs. This critical definition comes from the *Protocol to Prevent, Suppress and Punish Trafficking in Persons, Especially Women and Children, Supplementing the United Nations Convention against Transnational Organized Crime*, Article 3(a), also known as the Palermo Protocol.

The Polaris Project is a leading organization in the global fight against human trafficking and modern-day slavery. Its activities involve operating a national hotline, legislative advocacy, victim services, and trainings on how to recognize the signs of trafficking. Under U.S. and international law, commercially sexually exploited children found in the sex trade are considered to be victims of trafficking, even if no force or coercion is present. Victims of human trafficking in the United States include U.S. citizens or foreign nationals, adults or minors, and men or women. Foreign-born victims in the United States may be either documented or undocumented. Every year, human traffickers generate billions of dollars in profits by victimizing millions of people around the world and in the United States. Human trafficking is considered to be one of the fastest growing criminal industries in the world. Law enforcement officers, service providers, and other key first responders have been able to benefit from the training provided by the Polaris Project on how to recognize the signs of trafficking (Polaris Project 2013d).

Efforts to curtail the exploitation of individuals have also been undertaken by a variety of nongovernmental organizations including the Salvation Army, Western Union, the Redlight Traffic organization, and the Thomson Reuters Foundation. For example, working with DHS, Western Union plans to use training and awareness materials developed by the DHS Blue Campaign to educate agents who regularly interact with the public on potential indicators of human trafficking and on how to identify victims.

Federal and state governments can do more to help victims and deter traffickers. In particular, the federal government could implement a series of initiatives designed to facilitate the work of existing local volunteer police units and related agencies on the federal level. For example, the federal government can establish volunteer police training courses to instruct qualified volunteers about how best to protect foreign workers from exploitation. A critical need exists for volunteer police to have appropriate training so that they can be assigned to engage in such activities as speaking to groups about the signs of trafficking; educating people who may be at risk of victimization; addressing the needs of victims; enforcing the variety of laws concerned with human trafficking; and protecting human rights. There is also a need to mobilize volunteer police for law enforcement supporting roles at the time of large sporting events such as the Super Bowl. The existence of more than 200,000 police volunteers makes them important stakeholders in the field of public safety.

## Review Questions

1. List at least five types of human trafficking.
2. Identify stakeholders who could work together in order to address the problem of human trafficking.
3. Do you consider volunteer police to be important stakeholders in efforts to cope with human trafficking? Discuss.
4. The definition of human trafficking established by the Palermo Protocol indicates that victim consent to trafficking must be

considered irrelevant. Discuss why this clause was included in this international agreement to prevent and suppress human trafficking.

5. Provide at least three ways that the Polaris Project seeks to create long-term solutions in the global fight against human trafficking and modern-day slavery.

6. Indicate at least three of the venues where sex trafficking may take place.

7. State two functions of the Trafficking in Persons Worker Exploitation Task Force.

8. List the three purposes of the Trafficking Victims Protection Act of 2000.

9. What agreement with the U.S. government do victims seeking either T or U visas have to make as part of the visa application process?

10. Identify two initiatives involving volunteer police that might be undertaken by the federal government to deter and suppress human trafficking.

11. Do you believe volunteer police force members would be interested in serving as crime prevention specialists to educate the public about human trafficking deterrence and enforcement? Discuss.

12. Explain why it may be difficult to identify and find victims of human trafficking.

13. Chief Sellers is in the process of establishing an auxiliary police force. What arguments would you make to him about the advantages and disadvantages of using his new volunteer police unit to combat human trafficking?

14. Present three of the benefits or aims of the Redlight Traffic new app program.

15. There are scant statistics and much debate over how much sex trafficking increases during a Super Bowl or other large sporting event, but it has been enough of a concern to prompt New Jersey and previous Super Bowl host cities to pay attention to it. What assignments, if any, do you think volunteer police could undertake to reduce any sex trafficking activity at the time of the Super Bowl?

## Notes

1. Source of President Obama's quote: U.S. State Department, Office to Monitor and Combat Trafficking in Persons Web page. Retrieved December 29, 2013, http://www.state.gov/j/tip/index.htm.

2. In 2010, the Texas Supreme Court ruled that children involved in prostitution are victims not criminals (see In Matter of B.W., June 18, 2010, No. 08-1044). In this case, a 13-year-old girl flagged down the car of an undercover officer and offered to engage in oral sex for $20. She was arrested for prostitution.

The trial court (Family Court) found her guilty of a Class B misdemeanor of prostitution, and she received a sentence of 18 months' probation. The Court of Appeals affirmed the judgment, and the case was appealed. The Supreme Court of Texas reversed the Court of Appeals by a 6–3 decision. The court cited a variety of reason for its decision including the finding that because a 13-year-old child cannot consent to sex as a matter of law, the 13-year-old in this case cannot be prosecuted as a prostitute. The Supreme Court argued that children below the age of 14 cannot understand the significance of agreeing to sex and, therefore, could not satisfy the "knowing" requirement of the statute. The Court cited longstanding common law, Texas statutes, and numerous cases. "The notion that an underage child cannot legally consent to sex is of longstanding origin and derives from common law." The court also reasoned that treating child prostitutes as victims rather than criminals will also undermine the ability of pimps to play on the child's fear of police, removing a powerful tool pimps use to assert control. (The full text of the opinion can be found online at: http://caselaw.findlaw.com/tx-supreme-court/1527849.html.)

3. The Trafficking Victims Protection Act of 2000 (TVPA) was created to combat traffickers through punishment and also to protect trafficking victims. Its protections include new types of visas for victims of trafficking (T visas) and violence (U visas), which allow victims to stay in the United States from three years to permanent residency in exchange for investigative and prosecutorial assistance against traffickers. "Through the TVPA, new crimes were created around trafficking, which will make prosecution possible. Protection for victims comes through the visas, prevention of trafficking comes through establishing programs for increasing job skills, increasing education for children, and offering grants to international organizations who employ women" (Brusca 2011, 16).

4. The Palermo Protocol is an international treaty developed in Palermo, Italy, by member states of the United Nations in December 2000 for the purpose of undertaking a comprehensive international approach to prevent and combat trafficking in persons, especially women and children, including measures to prevent such trafficking, to punish the traffickers, and to protect the victims of such trafficking and the internationally recognized human rights of such victims. It supplements the United Nations Convention against Transnational Organized Crime and it is to be interpreted together with this Convention. The protocol entered into force on December 25, 2003, and by the end of 2009, 117 states had signed and 133 states were party to the protocol. In addition, a second agreement was also developed entitled the *Protocol Against Smuggling of Migrants by Land, Sea, and Air.* An online copy of the first Protocol can be found at: http://www.osce.org/odihr/19223. It is 12 pages in length. Ten years after the Palermo Protocol's adoption, Brusca (2011) addressed its strengths and weaknesses. "Even with the Palermo Protocol and the states' domestic anti-trafficking laws in place, only one to two percent of trafficked individuals are rescued. When the trafficked person is a child, the chance for rescue before extensive damage has been done is slim due to the vulnerable nature of a child" (Brusca 2011, 9–10).

5. The term "traffickers" is used in the 2002 OHCHR report entitled *Recommended Principles and Guidelines on Human Rights and Human Trafficking.* It is used to refer to recruiters; transporters; those who exercise control over trafficked persons;

those who transfer and/or maintain trafficked persons in exploitative situations; those involved in related crimes; and those who profit either directly or indirectly from trafficking, its component acts, and related offences (OHCHR 2002).

6. The organization's founders, Katherine Chon and Derek Ellerman, read a newspaper article describing the horrific conditions of a brothel located near their college apartments. The brothel had been disguised as a massage business. But inside the building, police officers had found six Asian women with cigarette burns on their arms being held in a situation of debt bondage. "This was like slavery," were the words of the officer who handled the investigation. Together, they developed a vision for an organization where everyday people could come together to overcome the contemporary forms of slavery. The day after graduation, they packed up a U-Haul truck and relocated to Washington, D.C., to launch the Polaris Project's first office on Capitol Hill. Their strategy "was grounded in an analysis of human trafficking as a market-based phenomenon driven by two primary factors: low-risk and high-profit. They believed then, as they do today, that modern-day slavery can be eliminated by reaching a tipping point where human trafficking becomes a high-risk, low-profit endeavor.... Early on, they launched an innovative victim outreach program to uncover trafficking locations, directly target trafficking networks, identify victims and connect them to services. As the organization grew, staff members worked with coalition partners to help pass landmark bills through Congress and groundbreaking legislation in 48 states that protect victims and punish perpetrators. In 2007, Polaris Project expanded the National Human Trafficking Resource Center to operate as a national anti-slavery lifeline" (Polaris Project 2013b).

7. However, extensions are available upon documentation by a certifying agency that the foreign national's presence in the United States is required to assist in the investigation or prosecution of the qualifying criminal activity. Certifying agencies can be federal, state, or local law enforcement agencies, prosecutors, judges, or other authorities that investigate or prosecute criminal activity. Other agencies such as child protective services, the Equal Employment Opportunity Commission, and the Department of Labor also qualify as certifying agencies because they have criminal investigative jurisdiction within their respective areas of expertise. Moreover, an individual who has held U nonimmigrant status might eventually apply for a Green Card (permanent residence). For this to occur, the individual must have been physically present in the United States for a continuous period of at least three years since the date of admission as a U nonimmigrant and the individual must not have unreasonably refused to provide assistance to law enforcement since receiving a U nonimmigrant visa (U.S. Citizen and Immigration Services 2013).

8. Qualifying criminal activity is defined as being an activity involving one or more activities that violate U.S. criminal law, including blackmail, domestic violence, extortion, false imprisonment, rape, torture, and other related crimes (U.S. Citizen and Immigration Services 2013).

9. Bartels (2014, 8) has determined that volunteers in policing carry out the following types of administrative roles: "Working on the police newsletter, answering phones, acting as a greeter at the front desk, assisting with photography, performing data entry, or being assigned as a clerk in the records department

or property room." Such administrative duties were carried out by volunteers in 152 out of a sample of 300 police departments. The sample was randomly generated at: http://www.random.org from a list of 22,446 registered programs provided by the Volunteers in Policing program (Bartels 2014).

10. Crime prevention practitioner certifications are awarded by a variety of governmental and organizational entities and include the National Crime Prevention Association's National Crime Prevention Specialist certification; Florida Office of the Attorney General's Crime Prevention Practitioner designation; New York State Crime Prevention Coalition's Crime Prevention Specialist certification; Ohio Crime Prevention Association's Certified Crime Prevention Specialist program; Texas Crime Prevention Association's Certified Crime Prevention Specialist program; Virginia Department of Criminal Justice Services Crime Prevention Specialist designation; ASIS International's Certified Protection Practitioner (CPP) program; International Society of Crime Prevention Practitioner's Crime Prevention Specialist certification; and Fox Valley Technical College's Crime Prevention Professional, Practitioner, or Specialist programs.

11. A very useful PowerPoint (PPT) presentation (44 slides) on the subject of crime prevention, which includes the definitions provided here, can be found at: http://www.slideshare.net/NCPC/crime-prevention-history-and-theory-presentation. The PPT's content can be adapted for a variety of community groups. It is a production of the National Crime Prevention Council. The council has also placed several other PPT programs on the Internet. In the late 1970s, the leaders of 19 organizations began to work together and developed the National Citizens' Crime Prevention Campaign. This effort was expanded into an additional entity known as the Crime Prevention Coalition of America. In 1982, the coalition group founded the National Crime Prevention Council (NCPC) to manage the campaign, administer the coalition, and promote crime prevention through trainings, technical assistance, and publications (NCPC 2013).

12. The Albemarle County Police Department has a VIPS program that contributed more than 1,700 hours to the department in 2012. Volunteers in the house check program supplement officers by providing safety checks on vacant homes. Two police chaplains have also been integrated into the department's wellness program, providing services for the mind, body, and spirit. Future plans involve gaining authorization from the board of supervisors to formally establish an auxiliary police officer (APO) program. APOs are certified police officers who volunteer their time to support the mission of the agency. APOs undergo the same rigorous appointment and training standards as paid police officers. "APOs will be tasked with assisting in traffic safety efforts, crime prevention tasks, select enforcement assignments, and administrative tasks. The APO program will support the department's efforts to build capacity", and the citizen involvement will help to "enhance the safety of the community" (ACPD 2012, p. 20).

13. By 1887, rescue homes were introduced to America. The first was opened in New York. Within seven years, 15 homes were operating across the United States. These homes were primarily for destitute women. Many who came were young expectant mothers. A Salvation Army Web site states: "It should be understood that The Salvation Army never served as an adoption agency. Mothers were referred to an adoption agency of their choice and worked with

these agencies independently of The Salvation Army Booth Maternity Homes" (Salvation Army 2013a). In recent times, there has been criticism of the past practices of these homes in Canada. In particular, the question of whether forced adoptions had taken place was raised. In response, the Salvation Army has indicated that these "homes were operational during a time when there was a tremendous social stigma attached to being an unwed mother" and began an internal review of the subject (Carlson 2012). On the contrary, during recent years, the Salvation Army has established an "Initiative against Sexual Trafficking" (IAST) to educate persons desiring to become better informed about human trafficking and the current efforts to contend with such exploitation and the dehumanization of human beings. Information can be found at: http://iast.net.

# References

ACPD. (2012). *Albemarle County Police Department 2012 annual report.* Retrieved December 30, 2013 from http://www.albemarle.org/upload/images/forms_center/departments/Police/forms/2012% 20Annual%20Report%20.pdf

Anne's House. (2013). Anne's House: A residential program for trafficking victims. Retrieved December 30, 2013 from http://s147851.gridserver.com/annes-house-a-residential-program-for-trafficking-victims/

Bales, K. (1999). *Disposable people: New slavery in the global economy.* Berkeley: University of California Press.

Barone, T. (2003). Note & Comment: The Trafficking Victims Protection Act of 2000: Defining the problem and creating a solution. *Temple International and Comparative Law Journal, 17*(Fall), 579–594.

Barry, K. (1995). *The prostitution of sexuality: The global exploitation of women.* New York: New York University Press.

Bartels, E. C. (2014). *Volunteer police in the United States: Programs, challenges, and legal aspects.* Heidelberg, Germany: Springer.

Brusca, C. S. (2011, Summer). Palermo Protocol: The first ten years after adoption. *Global Security Studies, 2*(3), 1–20.

Carlson, K. B. (2012, March 13). Coerced adoption: Salvation Army launches review of maternity homes that housed unwed mothers. Retrieved January 3, 2014 from http://news.nationalpost.com/2012/03/13/coerced-adoption-salvation-army-launches-review-of-maternity-homes-that-housed-unwed-mothers/

Clawson, H. J., Dutch, N. and Cummings, M. (2006, October). *Law Enforcement Response to Human Trafficking and Implications for Victims: Current Practices and Lessons Learned.* Fairfax, VA: Caliber, An ICF International Company. Retrieved June 28, 2014 from https://www.ncjrs.gov/pdffiles1/nij/grants/216547.pdf

Cmiel, K. (2004). Review essay: The recent history of human rights. *American Historical Review, 109*(1), 117–135.

De Baca, L. and Tisi, A. (2002, August). Working together to stop modern day slavery. *Police Chief, 69*(8), 78–80.

Fighting the Slave Trade. (2000, April 17). *The Washington Post National Weekly Edition* p. 25.

Gordy, M. (2000, February 20). A call to fight forced labor. *Parade*, pp. 4–5.

Green, S. J. (2013, October 30). Sex-trafficking app to tip off police. *Seattle Times*. Retrieved from http://seattletimes.com/html/localnews/2022158566_sextraffickingapp2xml.html

Hewitt, B. and Siew, W. (1998, November 23). In the trenches. *People Weekly, 50*(19), 143–144.

Hynes, H. P. and Raymond, J. G. (2002). Put in harm's way: The neglected health consequences of sex trafficking in the United States. In J. Silliman and A. Bhattacharjee (Eds.), *Policing the national body: Sex, race, and criminalization* (pp. 197–229). Cambridge, MA: South End.

Ignatieff, M. (2000). *The rights revolution*. Toronto: Anansi Press.

Lederer, L. (2004). Trafficking in persons: A modern-day form of slavery. Retrieved February 29, 2004 from http://www.state.gov/g/tip/rls/rm/2002/14325.htm

LILYA 4-EVER. (2004). LILYA 4-EVER: A film by Lukas Moodysson examining the tragic realities and horrors of trafficking in humans. Presentation at the Secretary's Open Forum, Washington, DC. Retrieved February 29, 2004 from http://www. State.gov/s/p/of/proc/22337pf.htm

McGurty, F. (2013, April 25). Banks can help to stop human trafficking. Retrieved January 2, 2013 from http://www.reuters.com/article/2013/04/25/us-banks-trafficking-idUSBRE93O1FU20130425

NCPC. (2013). History. Retrieved December 30, 2013 from http://www.ncpc.org/about/history

NCPI. (1978). *The practice of crime prevention, Volume 1: Understanding crime*. Lexington, KY: The National Crime Prevention Institute Press.

Newsplex.com. (2013, November 4). Police: Human sex trafficking a growing problem. Retrieved December 27, 2013 from http://www.newsplex.com/home/headlines/230611621.html

OHCHR. (2002). *Recommended principles and guidelines on human rights and human trafficking*. Retrieved December 29, 2013 from http://www.ohchr.org/Documents/Publications/Traffickingen.pdf

Pankratz, H. (2013, November 6). Western Union and Homeland Security team up to combat human trafficking. *Denver Post*. Retrieved December 27, 2013 from http://www.denverpost.com/breakingnews/ci_24469238/western-union-amp-homeland-security-team-up-combat

Polaris Project. (2013a). About Polaris Project. Retrieved December 30, 2013 from http://www.polarisproject.org/about-us/overview

Polaris Project. (2013b). Founding story. Retrieved December 30, 2013 from http://www.polarisproject.org/about-us/overview/founding-story

Polaris Project. (2013c). Global programs. Retrieved December 30, 2013 from http://www.polarisproject.org/what-we-do/global-programs

Polaris Project. (2013d). Human trafficking. Retrieved December 28, 2013 from http://www.polarisproject.org/human-trafficking/overview

Power, J. (2001). *Like water on stone: The story of Amnesty International*. Boston, MA: Allen Lane.

Salvation Army. (2013a). Additional services: Salvation Army maternity homes: History. Retrieved January 3, 2014 from http://www.use.salvationarmy.org/use/www_usn20.nsf/vw-text-dynamic-arrays/F74D62E42552DA77852579A3007B4147

Salvation Army. (2013b). Combating human trafficking. Retrieved December 30, 2013 from http://salvationarmyusa.org/usn/combating-human-trafficking

Sellars, K. (2002). *The rise and rise of human rights*. Stroud, Gloucestershire, UK: Sutton Publishing.

Smith, C. H. (2001). Fighting the scourge of trafficking in women and children. *Congressional Record, 147*(163): 2179–2180.

UNODC. (2010). UNODC: Promoting health, security and justice. 2010 annual report. Retrieved December 27, 2013 from http://www.unodc.org/documents/frontpage/UNODC_Annual_Report_2010_LowRes.pdf

UNODC. (2013a). General Assembly reviews efforts to combat human trafficking. Retrieved December 27, 2013 from http://www.unodc.org/unodc/en/frontpage/2013/May/general-assembly-reviews-efforts-to-combat-human-trafficking.html?ref = fs1

UNODC. (2013b). UNODC on human trafficking and migrant smuggling. Retrieved December 27, 2013 form http://www.unodc.org/unodc/en/human-trafficking/index.html?ref = menuside

U.S. Citizen and Immigration Services. (2013). Questions & Answers: Victims of criminal activity, U nonimmigrant status. Retrieved December 30, 2013 from http://www.uscis.gov/humanitarian/victims-human-trafficking-other-crimes/victims-criminal-activity-u-nonimmigrant-status/questions-answers-victims-criminal-activity-u-nonimmigrant-status

U.S. Department of Justice. (2011, October). *The impact of the economic downturn on American police agencies*. Washington, DC: U.S. Department of Justice, Office of Community Oriented Policing Services.

U.S. Department of Justice. (2013). Civil Rights Division: Trafficking in Persons and Worker Exploitation Task Force. Retrieved December 31, 2013 from http://www.parentsinaction.net/english/Complaints/Human_Trafficking_Complaint_USDOJ.htm

U.S. Department of State. (2013a). Office to Monitor and Combat Trafficking in Persons. Retrieved December 19, 2013 from http://www.state.gov/j/tip/index.htm

U.S. Department of State. (2013b). What is modern slavery? Retrieved December 29, 2013 from http://www.state.gov/j/tip/what/

U-Visa. (2013). U Visa for immigrants who are victims of crimes. Retrieved December 31, 2013 from http://www.usimmigrationsupport.org/visa-u.html

Wilson, D., Walsh, W. and Kleuber, S. (2006, May). Trafficking in human beings: Training and services among US law enforcement agencies. *Police Practice and Research, 7*(2), 149–160.

Winter, J. (2004). BBC News: My life as a modern-day slave. Retrieved February 29, 2004 from http://newsvote.bbc.co.uk/mpapps/pagetools/print/news.bbc.uk/2/hi/africa/3430305.stm

Zezima, K. (2014, January 6). NJ works to curb sex trafficking before super bowl. Retrieved January 7, 2014 from http://www.philly.com/philly/news/new_jersey/20140106_ap_9c1854ad76b74a4996aba69147ac3e6b.html?c=r

# The Future of Volunteer Police

# 12

How wonderful it is that nobody need wait a single moment before starting to improve the world.

**—Anne Frank Haimowitz 2014**

## Background

The opening quote is attributed to Anne Frank, a victim of the Holocaust. Her famous diary was first published in Dutch in 1947 under the title *Het Achterhuis* (*The Secret House*) by her father, Otto Frank, who survived the concentration camps. Her diary provides an account of a teenager living in hiding with seven others in fear for their lives in occupied Holland during World War II. Anne Frank died in 1945, just before her sixteenth birthday, in the Bergen-Belsen concentration camp (BBC News 2014). President John F. Kennedy discussed Anne Frank in a 1961 speech. He said: "Of all the multitudes who throughout history have spoken for human dignity in times of great suffering and loss, no voice is more compelling than that of Anne Frank" (David 2013). Information about various Holocaust memorials and historic sites in Amsterdam can be found at: http://www.kennesaw.edu/holocaustmemorials/amsterdam.shtml.

The present work has consistently urged the use of volunteer police for the betterment of society, but as we consider the future of volunteer policing, it is prudent to consider the past. The Nazis, for a time, deployed volunteer police. After Adolf Hitler was appointed chancellor of Germany in 1933, he called upon elements of the Nazi party to act as auxiliary police. The *Schutzstaffel* or SS, initially Hitler's bodyguards, and the *Sturmabteilung* or SA, the street fighters or storm troopers of the Nazi party, were extended official police authority, further increasing the power of the Nazi party in German society (SS Police State 2014). Thus, as we look toward the future, a word of caution is in order. Volunteer police have not always been used to enhance democratic principles or righteous purposes.

In the United States, the merit selection of local and state police took hold during the first third of the twentieth century up until this time and in various eras, American law and order was kept by a variety of local residents, including: clergymen; militia members; vigilantes; temporarily mobilized posse members; self-appointed or compulsory serving slave patrollers and watch members (especially, during the 1700s to 1865); elected mayors, sheriffs, constables, and justices of the peace; private detectives and guards; and police and correctional officers who were often selected as a result of simple payoffs and the existence of the "spoils system." The "spoils system" arose during the administration of President Andrew Jackson (1829–1837). It was widely used for the selection of paid governmental employees until laws were passed for the establishment of civil service commissions for the merit selection of governmental employees at the federal, state, and local levels. Throughout the nineteenth century, appointments to police ranks were dependent upon "loyalty to the party that was most victorious in the most recent election." For example, New York City's police officers "were subject to immediate removal upon the failure of their party to win reelection" (Johnson et al. 2008, 221).

In the 1800s and early 1900s, there also existed a wide range of voluntary organizations including anti-horse thief protection societies, law and order leagues, and ethnically based welfare agencies. Later, in some communities, this diverse mix was supplemented by part-time peace officers known as "auxiliary or reserve police." World War II, as well as the Korean and Cold War eras, gave rise to a new generation of volunteer police groups under the banner of "civil defense auxiliary police." A large part of this book has considered the activities of volunteer police that have taken place during the post–World War II era.[1]

This chapter reviews a few of the current or emerging trends for citizens willing to undertake the duties of part-time volunteer police in the United States. Several new roles are just emerging and were selected because of their potential for reducing crime and disorder. For example, volunteer police can be called upon to help with school safety, homelessness, and the prevention of human trafficking (see Chapter 11). They can also assist with crime prevention educational programs like Drug Abuse Resistance Education (D.A.R.E.), Gang Resistance Education and Training (G.R.E.A.T.), or conflict resolution classes (see VIPS in a School Setting 2010). New state training guidelines require volunteer police who are peace officers to complete many more hours of training. In some jurisdictions, this has led to the phasing out of volunteer police units. In addition, due to the limited availability of municipal financial resources, more and more states are encouraging local police candidates to pay for their own police training.

## Current Trends in Volunteer Policing

Since the early 1980s, when the concept of community policing began to spread, the role of volunteers in policing has been expanding. Today, it is not unusual to find community residents volunteering their time to work as sworn or non-sworn uniformed auxiliary or reserve officers; police administrative assistants; amateur radio operators; search and rescue team members; mounted patrol members; chaplains; computer specialists; crime lab assistants; crime prevention aides; maintenance assistants; translators; citizen patrol members; youth service workers; and in investigatory support assignments. Reserve police are "becoming widely accepted in tactical units across the country.... Reserves who are physicians, nurses, or trained EMS personnel in their full-time positions volunteer to serve on tactical units" (Wolf and Russo 2005, 27). In the formation of their tactical teams, various police departments have called upon such medical and EMS career personnel to join as part-time law enforcement officers. Throughout the United States and in many countries within the British Commonwealth, volunteers have become an integral part of community support for the police because they provide additional resources without extra costs.

The role of volunteer police chaplains is particularly important because they have been involved in, but not limited to, counseling peace officers and their families; counseling members of other city departments and their families; visiting sick or injured employees; responding to major incidents and cases involving serious injury to an employee or community member; providing assistance to victims and their families; speaking to civic and public groups; participating in patrols; performing crisis intervention; and providing input on community issues and problems.

Unarmed, but uniformed, citizens who engage in citizen patrol units often in vehicles with an amber light bar and marked with the words "volunteer patrol" have become quite popular in many towns in the Sun Belt, particularly within the states of Florida, Arizona, and California. Their duties have included neighborhood watch patrol; vacation house checks; document delivery; transportation details; traffic control; school patrol; assisting with DUI/license check points; and parking enforcement. Their police vehicles are equipped with a radio for communications with police dispatchers. Retirees from northern states oftentimes fill the volunteer ranks of these southern citizen patrol units. Since the 1960s, the Sun Belt (as seen in Figure 12.1) has been one of the most important growth regions in the United States (Briney 2009).

**Figure 12.1** This map provides an outline of the states most commonly included in the definition of the Sun Belt, which stretches from South Carolina and Florida in the East to California in the West.

In communities throughout America, volunteers have also participated in various mounted units. They assist in areas where crowd control is important, but they are also available for ceremonial functions in color guard formation. Communities may have both reserve and/or unsworn civilian mounted units. In previous chapters, information about such units in New York City and Maryland has been highlighted. The city of Arcadia, California, is an upper-middle class community of approximately 60,000 people who live in an area located 20 miles east of Los Angeles. At one time, it had both a sworn reserve established in 1997 and a civilian mounted volunteer patrol program established in 2003. However, within a few years, the latter unit was disbanded. Its regular (salaried) mounted and reserve officers patrol a horse trail that runs the entire length of the city and the Santa Anita Race Track. The track is considered by many to be the finest facility of its type in the country (City of Arcadia 2013b). Recently, the city of Arcadia decided that all of its reserve police officers would become paid part-time employees (City of Arcadia 2013a).

Another important trend in the field of volunteer police has been the establishment of Law Enforcement Explorer Posts for youth in the 14–20 age group. Exploring as a youth movement can be traced to the 1920s and posts specifically associated with police departments began to emerge in the 1960s and 1970s under the direction of the Boy Scouts of America.[2] They are very common today, and their activities have kept pace with new technologies. Local, regional, and national junior police academy programs have been organized. Merit selection may be used by some of these academies because of limited space and personnel resources. In general, post participants must maintain good moral character and at least average grade work. When not engaged in training exercises, many Law Enforcement Explorers have opportunities to practice their skills by providing security, crowd, and traffic control at community events. The youth involved in such career exploration posts must register with the Learning for Life Corporation. Law Enforcement Exploring programs are based on five areas of emphasis: career opportunities, life skills, citizenship, character education, and leadership experience. (For more information, go to: http://www.learningforlife.org.)

Individual Explorer posts can specialize in a variety of career skills. The Learning for Life Web site states that "at a time when drugs and gangs are ravaging many of our schools and communities, Learning for Life programs can be a catalyst to help stop this trend."

Police departments and school districts have also initiated other types of youth programs including peer mediation, student courts, conflict resolution, and antibullying programs. It is interesting to note that for several decades in the twentieth century, most efforts aimed at the protection of schoolchildren traveling by foot to and from school and within school corridors were carried out by the students themselves under the watchful eyes of their teachers. Today, this type of activity rarely occurs due to concerns over school district liability. Perhaps, if after appropriate screening and training, today's school-age children (especially, those over age 14) were offered more opportunities for undertaking such duties, they might be better prepared to face life's greater challenges and our schools might be safer.

In 2013, the International Association of Chiefs of Police (IACP) conducted a study of those programs that had registered with the Volunteers in Police Service (VIPS) program. The study was supported by a grant awarded by the Bureau of Justice Assistance (BJA) within the U.S. Department of Justice. Program managers of established VIPS programs were asked to gather and share information on promising approaches, programmatic challenges, and resource needs. Responses were collected from 226 of these law enforcement volunteer program managers.

When asked if their agency had expanded or limited the duties volunteers can perform as a result of fiscal issues, 31% of respondents in the IACP study indicated that they had expanded volunteer duties. This was an increase over the 2009 VIPS Program Analysis when just 20% indicated an increase in volunteer duties. The most common volunteer activities were administrative duties (71%); community outreach/crime prevention (65%); citizen patrols (63%); emergency preparedness/response (48%); chaplain services (45%); and volunteer program administration (42%). The use of volunteers in investigations increased from 16% in 2009 to 27% in 2013. Other advanced and skill-based volunteer duties respondents reported included: research, technology, translation/interpretation, code or parking enforcement, crime analysis, fleet maintenance, and subpoena or warrant services (VIPS Program Analysis 2013).

## Violence Prevention in School Settings

According to the Centers for Disease Control and Prevention, "Violence is a serious public health problem in the United States. From infants to the elderly, it affects people in all stages of life. In 2010, over 16,250 people were victims of homicide and over 38,360 took their own life" (Violence Prevention 2013). In the United States, an estimated 50 million students are enrolled in pre-kindergarten through twelfth grade. Another 15 million students attend colleges and universities across the country. School violence is youth violence (bullying, fighting, weapon use, punching, slapping, kicking, etc.) that occurs on school property, on the way to or from school or school-sponsored events or during a school-sponsored event (About School Violence 2013). This section highlights recommendations and reasons for the use of volunteer police in school settings.

In 2013, the state of Utah reached a high plateau that was unusual for a small state with just 2.86 million residents. In that year, more than a half million people were holding a Utah permit to carry concealed firearms, but the largest share of those permits went to people who were living outside of Utah. The split was 62% to 38%. The main reason appeared to be that Utah's permit was recognized by more states than other permits, allowing for easier interstate travel by Utah permit holders with guns (Davidson 2013)—perhaps a fortunate opportunity for all these individuals. On the contrary, the proliferation of guns and permit holders could be a potential threat for many others. The availability of guns may be especially threatening to those children living in neighborhoods where they "can't attend class without fear of being recruited by gangs; where they can't enjoy afterschool activities without putting their lives at risk" (Rice 2013).

However, according to James Alan Fox, murders including guns are not increasing, at least with respect to mass killings in America. Much more common than public shootings are "family annihilations, where a guy kills his wife, children, and himself" (Welch and Hoyer 2013). Fox is a professor of criminology at Northeastern University and coeditor of the book, *Extreme Killing: Understanding Serial and Mass Murder*.[3] Nevertheless, incidents of deadly violence continue to take place in public and private spaces. Shoppers in malls, workers in offices, and especially schoolchildren in their schools are the potential victims. Gun control measures have been stalled on the federal level. Gun control advocates are now trying to build political support at the local level to compete with the National Rifle Association. For example, one organization, Moms Demand Action for Gun Sense in America, mounted a successful campaign during the summer of 2013 to pressure Starbucks into banning guns from its cafés and was hoping to have similar support from McDonald's (Epstein 2013). These advocates are prepared to take one little step at a time.

The need for better solutions for violent crime control is of paramount importance. It is likely that advocates for more law enforcement, self-defense measures, and/or stricter gun regulation will continue their discussions for years to come. While this debate rages, school districts and police agencies are forming new partnerships to ensure safer schools. Moreover, there is a growing recognition that school safety is a shared responsibility among schools, law enforcement, and the community. This understanding has led to a role for volunteer police.

This role is addressed in several sections of a resource document published by the VIPS program. The VIPS program is a partnership between the IACP and the BJA within the Office of Justice Programs, U.S. Department of Justice. The 19-page document provides information specific to law enforcement volunteer efforts in elementary, middle, and high school settings. In concise words, the guide states: "Community volunteers play important roles in implementing and maintaining school-based public safety programs. Their presence in and around schools enhances public safety and allows law enforcement agencies to focus on policing and enforcement functions. Volunteer tasks may include monitoring crosswalks while students are on their way to and from school, registering and tracking school visitors, patrolling school building and grounds during and after school hours, and assisting at special events. Parents, school neighbors, and students can volunteer to accomplish these tasks and build stronger relationships between law enforcement and the school community" (VIPS in a School Setting 2010). Moreover, it recommends that "Reserve police officers are a valuable resource to the community and the police department and are increasingly being called upon to help bolster safety and security in schools. Reserve or auxiliary police officers are highly trained community volunteers who often wear the same uniform and perform the same duties as regular police officers but are unpaid and work part-time. Reserves undergo thorough background checks and most are required to attend an accredited law enforcement academy to obtain proper police certification.... Volunteer officers may respond to calls for service regarding accidents, emergencies, crimes, threats, altercations, and/or requests for aid within the schools.... They can also assist with crime prevention educational programs like D.A.R.E. (Drug Abuse Resistance Education), G.R.E.A.T. (Gang Resistance Education And Training), or conflict resolution classes" (VIPS in a School Setting 2010). The IACP VIPS program has posted numerous resources for establishing police volunteer units on school campuses.[4]

In 2004, an unsworn local VIPS program volunteer teamed up with a school resource officer (SRO) at a Modesto, California, elementary school. The elementary school was in a low-income, high minority, and highly transient neighborhood. They initiated a truancy intervention program patterned after the local sheriff's department's program. The goal of the program was to increase daily attendance and reduce tardiness through parental contact. Working one morning a week, armed with a telephone, a list of absentees, and two thermometers with disposable mouthpieces, they visited the various homes of the absent students. The parents of many of the children were surprised to find a representative from the police department standing at their door asking why their child was not at school. The surprises only continued for those parents who claimed their child had a fever, and the thermometer reading showed 98.6. Other excuses ranged from a lack of clothing, to lice infection, to not being able to get up on time. As a direct result of their efforts, unexcused absences as well as excused absences were decreased by a third (Volunteer Profiles 2013).

Since the Sandy Hook Elementary School massacre in Newtown, Connecticut, in December 2012, many school districts and state governments have been searching for ways to protect their students. One of the most popular decisions has been to hire more SROs. Nationwide, there are about 10,000 such officers assigned to schools from kindergarten through twelfth grade. In 2013, the U.S. Department of Justice awarded $46.5 million to fund 370 additional SROs. SROs are selected from the ranks of local and state police agencies and are assigned to work at local schools on a full-time schedule. However, paid officers may only be one option. In 2013, the North Carolina State Legislature created a Volunteer School Safety Resource Program.[5] The idea was being looked into by officials with the Winston-Salem/Forsyth County Schools. Only individuals with prior law enforcement or military experience would be eligible to volunteer for the program, and they would be required to update or renew their law enforcement training and be certified by the state's Criminal Justice Education and Training Standards Commission as having met the educational and firearms proficiency standards (Herron 2013).

However, in a response to the North Carolina initiative, one commentator noted that there is evidence that in certain instances SROs might escalate adolescent behavior into criminal behavior and that paid SROs do not receive enough training. Consequently, there is no reason to believe that volunteer officers will be better trained than their salaried counterparts (Hill 2013). An SRO carries out some of the functions of a guidance counselor or social worker, such as mentoring or advising, but with arresting authority and a license to carry a weapon in schools. In a national assessment of SRO programs, SROs reported that they spend approximately 20 hours per week on law enforcement activities, 10 hours on advising and mentoring, 5 hours on teaching (e.g., G.R.E.A.T. or D.A.R.E. programming), and another 6 or 7 hours on other activities (Finn and McDevitt 2005). It appears that academic research is limited related to the effectiveness of SROs or law enforcement at keeping schools safe. In Alabama, a study during the 1994–1996 school years indicated that the presence of SROs decreased school violence and disciplinary actions between school years (Johnson 1999). In November 2011, the Justice Policy Institute issued a 43-page report about SROs and recommended that they and other law enforcement officers be removed from schools stating: "School safety can be addressed without on-site SROs. And although there is some evidence that SROs can play a positive role as counselors and mentors in schools, these roles can be better filled by people primarily trained in these areas" (Petteruti 2011, 31).[6]

In addition, junior police programs should be enlisted in new efforts to reduce bullying. Bullying has progressed from attacks in the hallway or on a bus to attacks that can occur anytime due to texting, e-mails, YouTube, and social media such as Facebook, Twitter, LinkedIn, and so forth. A variety of measures concerning school safety have already been implemented to reduce bullying and harassment in schools, but if additional human resources were made available, perhaps more students might benefit.[7] As previously indicated in Chapter 8, supervisors of youth programs should be carefully vetted to reduce any risk of abuse.

## Active Shooter and Carjacking Response and Prevention

Law enforcement agencies should take full advantage of such programs as auxiliary/reserve police and Law Enforcement Explorer Posts to fulfill the need for supplemental human resources. Qualified members of these volunteer police programs can be certified to conduct a variety of programs to educate the public with respect to personal safety. In an age of widespread availability of firearms, the promotion of personal safety in public spaces is akin to learning how to swim. Instruction is needed for basic survival. Two areas of critical concern are carjacking and the active shooter.

Carjacking involves stealing a car by force. It is a very serious and sometimes traumatic form of auto theft. It is also a crime of opportunity that can threaten an individual's personal safety. Most local and state criminal codes do not define "carjacking." It is reported as either auto theft or armed robbery. This means that no solid statistics exist on time, place, and victims. Though a carjacking can occur at any time, a sizable share appears to take place during the late night hours (LAPD 2013). The U.S. Department of State's Bureau of Diplomatic Security has declared that "Carjacking has become one of the most prevalent crimes in many parts of the world. Most carjacking occurs for the sole purpose of taking the car; it is a crime without a political agenda and does not specifically target Americans" (U.S. Department of State 2002). Individuals can learn to protect themselves by becoming familiar with the methods, ruses, and locations commonly used by carjackers. (The Bureau of Diplomatic Security has produced a two-page flyer on avoiding carjacking that is available at: http://www.state.gov/documents/organization/19697.pdf.)

Explorer post members can be enlisted to place carjacking prevention fliers or brochures in the waiting rooms of auto dealer service departments, repair shops, and gas stations. An active Law Enforcement Explorer Post was established in 1999 at the California Highway Patrol (CHP) office in Visalia. The Explorer program has provided young men and women with an opportunity to see the inner workings of the CHP and to make lifelong friendships. Through the program, participants attend weekly meetings and training sessions, work in the CHP office, ride along with patrol officers, participate in community events, and attend Explorer competitions that are held throughout the state. Activities have included participating in a DUI checkpoint by working the line and standing with officers as they talked with drivers and handing out DUI checkpoint information. When individuals were arrested and had to have their vehicles towed, Explorers assisted in filling out vehicle storage forms and citations. Periodically, Visalia Explorers also assist the agency with its "active shooter" training. Explorers play the role of both victims and suspects and engage officers in "paintball" type shooting scenarios (CHP 2013).

Although an active shooter incident is unpredictable and is usually a rapidly evolving event, procedures have been developed to enhance public safety. (See the video produced by the city of Houston at: http://www.youtube.com/user/RunHideFight.) Qualified volunteer police officers and senior volunteer police and Explorers can deliver presentations designed to increase chances of survival in an active shooter event.

## Professionalism and Volunteer Police: Training and Accreditation

Volunteer police unit members, especially those of the sworn (i.e., peace officer) category, must comply with the most current training standards and other qualifications established by their state's Peace Officer Standards and Training (POST) Commission. This has been a matter of serious concern among regular police agencies and their volunteer police participants. Noncompliance with such standards can result in the termination of the concerned auxiliary and reserve volunteer member. However, it is the existence of a second set of standards that has resulted in the disbanding of one or more volunteer police units. The additional standards were developed by the Commission on Accreditation for Law Enforcement Agencies, Inc. (CALEA). Those police agencies interested in achieving recognition through national accreditation must comply with CALEA. CALEA, created in 1979, is a private, nonprofit organization that serves as the main accreditation source for law enforcement agencies across the United States. Significantly, CALEA has separate standards regarding auxiliaries and reserves. Appendix A provides a copy of the latest available standards. For example, CALEA Standard 16.4.1 requires that agencies seeking the commission's national accreditation must have a written directive that establishes and describes the agency's auxiliary program that includes a statement that auxiliaries are not sworn officers and a description of the duties of auxiliaries, including their role and scope in authority. Standard 16.4.3 states that "If auxiliaries wear uniforms, the uniforms clearly distinguish them from sworn officers." As part of the accreditation process, the CALEA standards also specify that every member of a volunteer or paid reserve force must complete the same training as a full-time certified police officer. Only 4% of the 18,000 non-federal law enforcement agencies in the United States have earned CALEA accreditation (Carder 2013).

In several jurisdictions (Kansas City, Connecticut State Police, etc.), new training standards and accreditation issues have been used as the principal justifications for phasing out the use of existing volunteer police units. Police administrators have stated that they either do not have the financial resources to provide the volunteer training and/or doubt that volunteers will be willing to devote themselves to the longer training requirements. The Ottawa (Kansas) Police Department has an authorized strength of 27 full-time paid officers, and it had a reserve unit consisting of four volunteer police officers. The reserve officers assisted with staffing special events, working during certain holidays and when other staffing needs arose. Uniforms, some equipment, and training were provided (City of Ottawa 2013). However, according to Dennis Butler, the Ottawa police chief, the standards set forth for CALEA accreditation caused the elimination of Ottawa's reserve force when the reserve officers declined to pursue the same training as full-time certified police officers (more than 500 hours of academy training). Chief Butler remarked: "They have other careers and other jobs, and it just didn't make sense for them, given their situations. They provided us with a tremendous amount of support.... We certainly appreciate all they have done for the department" (Carder 2013). Nevertheless, the discontinuance of this reserve unit still left opportunities for the public to participate in the police department's unsworn VIPS program.

Although only a relatively small number of agencies have achieved CALEA recognition and the process for accreditation can take as long as three years to complete, the CALEA standards can provide a benchmark for agencies to aspire to whether or not they are ready to begin the application process. The standards pertaining to auxiliaries and reserves appear to represent a reasonable attempt to assure quality. Surely, police agencies that strive to follow them are moving higher on a scale of professionalism. Clearly, when followed, the standards also raise the status of the concerned volunteer police groups. Carte and Carte (1975) have authored a book about the history of August Vollmer, the principal architect of the professional model of policing. The authors identified at least six attributes in Vollmer's model of police professionalism: (1) rigorous training; (2) dedication; (3) use of the latest science and technology; (4) community involvement; (5) high standards of conduct; and (6) separation from politics.

The development of accreditation standards is an important benefit for the American public. According to these professional standards, if police agencies desire to have their police volunteers assume full police duties, they must train them in the same manner as regular police. This type of training is greatly needed not only for the improvements it can mean for the delivery of police services but also because it can aid and equip the next generation of police officers with a foundation they would not otherwise have had. Across the country, many young adults are joining reserve or auxiliary forces as well as Law Enforcement Explorer posts to learn about police careers. They are sharing their experiences via the social media and other online services. At the same time, agency contact persons are registering with the VIPS program online directory and posting information about their volunteers on their own agency Web sites. These efforts are contributing to a greater public awareness about volunteer police opportunities and helping to foster the selection of new members. In these ways, agencies are better able to draw upon the vast talents and energies of the American citizenry and helping to promote such basic democratic attributes as consensus building, community participation in government, and equality of opportunity.

## Immigration and Border Security

In 2013, there was widespread agreement in the United States that America's immigration system was broken. Too many employers were hiring undocumented workers, and it was estimated that 11 million people were living in the United States without appropriate documentation. President Obama proposed a plan that would continue efforts to secure America's borders as well as provide undocumented immigrants with a legal way to earn citizenship. His plan included requiring background checks, paying taxes and a penalty, going to the back of the line, and learning English. His plan was also designed to stop businesses from exploiting the system by knowingly hiring undocumented workers by establishing a reliable way to verify that their employees possess the necessary legal immigration status. An aspect of his enforcement approach was the goal of improving partnerships with border communities and law enforcement as well as creating tough criminal penalties for trafficking in passports and immigration documents and schemes to defraud (White House 2013).

The second largest unit of volunteer police in America is made up of the various posses administered by the Maricopa County (Arizona) Sheriff's Office. It has approximately 3,000 members and its activities and initiatives are routinely touted by the county's long-serving sheriff—Joe Arpaio. In November 2010, in a special ceremony, he swore in 56 new posse members added to address the issue of illegal aliens. The event was highly publicized because the actor Lou Ferrigno was among the new volunteers. Posse members also include the actors Steven Seagal and Peter Lupus. According to Sheriff Arpaio: "Law enforcement budgets are being cut and agencies are losing personnel and yet the battle to stop illegal immigration must continue. Arizona is the busiest port of entry for people being smuggled in from Mexico, Latin and South America. So asking for the public's help in this endeavor makes sense, especially given the success the posses have experienced over the years" (Seper 2010).

During the 2010 swearing-in ceremony, Sheriff Arpaio candidly remarked that he did not expect that the trio of actors would be available for duty anytime soon. He noted that both Seagal and Ferrigno were busy actors and also held other volunteer police positions. At that time, Seagal had been a volunteer deputy with the Jefferson Parish County Sheriff's Office in Louisiana for more than 20 years, and Ferrigno was serving as a reserve deputy with the Los Angeles County Sheriff's Office.[8] Arpaio stated: "But they can be instrumental in heightening public awareness of the immigration issue and encouraging others to join the posse's effort to help reduce the flow of illegal immigrants into our communities" (Seper 2010).

Three years later, following the tragedy at Sandy Hook Elementary School, Sheriff Arpaio began sending his county's armed volunteer posse members to patrol the schools in Phoenix after receiving instruction provided by Steven Seagal. A training simulation exercise involving three armed intruders (portrayed by law enforcement officers) was held, and Seagal conducted training on hand-to-hand defense techniques, drawing upon his martial arts experience (Chasmar 2013).

Although the protection of schoolchildren requires a high level of vigilance and preparation, dealing with the problem of undocumented immigrants within the United States need not always have to be a punitive undertaking. Volunteer police can be recruited to assist persons who may be in need of English language proficiency as well as information about the customs and norms of the United States. An important aspect of this educational program would be to inform immigrants who may be undocumented that they can seek help from law enforcement, emergency shelters, as well as obtain legal assistance without the fear of deportation. This assistance may be needed because of elder abuse, child abuse, domestic violence, sexual assault, human trafficking, or other violent crimes. In order to receive such assistance, victims must cooperate with the prosecution (see the Violence Against Women Act of 1994 and its 2000 and 2005 amendments). Volunteer police of the unsworn variety might be appropriate for this task. Such multilingual volunteers can be recruited for this purpose, thereby helping to establish a more positive relationship between the police and this vulnerable segment of the population.

It may be that the U.S. border is the weakest link in the nation's chain of security. If that is the case, civilians with expertise in the areas of security training, tactics, and planning should be welcomed. Southern border states are particularly at risk because of their proximity to the notorious drug cartels and gangs operating in Central and South America. Members of the general public, all police officers, and police volunteers should be aware of the U.S. State Department's Consular Information Program, which informs the public of conditions abroad that may affect their safety and security. (Country specific information, travel alerts, and travel warnings are vital parts of this program and can be found online at: http://travel.state.gov/content/passports/english/alertswarnings.html.) Alerts concern short-term events that travelers should know about, such as an outbreak of H1N1 or evidence of an elevated risk of terrorist attacks. When these short-term events are over, the alert is cancelled. Warnings are issued to urge travelers that they should very carefully reconsider plans to travel to a particular country. Examples of reasons for issuing such a warning might include unstable government, civil war, ongoing intense crime or violence, or frequent terrorist attacks (U.S. Department of State 2013b). A travel warning is also issued when the U.S. government's ability to assist American citizens is constrained due to the closure of an embassy or a consulate or because of a drawdown of its staff. As of December 17, 2013, there were 34 countries included on the travel warning list. In the Western Hemisphere, the countries included Mexico, El Salvador, Honduras, Colombia, and Venezuela (U.S. Department of State 2013a). In the posted travel warning regarding the security situation in Mexico, information on security conditions is provided for specific regions of Mexico. This particularization is provided because millions of U.S. citizens safely visit Mexico each year for study, tourism, and business, including more than 150,000 who cross the border every day. Nevertheless, the warning states that "Carjacking and highway robbery are serious problems in many parts of the border region, and U.S. citizens have been murdered in such incidents" (U.S. State Department 2013c).

Chapter 6 provides details about a proposal for the establishment of a U.S. Border Patrol Auxiliary (BPA). The plan concerns a professional organization of auxiliary members working side-by-side with Border Patrol agents in support of the Border Patrol's mission. This volunteer police force would be screened to ensure they have the traits essential to maintain the high standards of the U.S. Border Patrol. The proponents of the plan have emphasized that the first step to controlling the influx of criminal activity and illegal immigration into the United States involves a secure border. Because the Border Patrol is a proven deterrent to illegal immigrants and criminals along the border, the deployment of the auxiliary force can serve as a force-multiplier that increases the agency's operational capability throughout the full range of its responsibilities (see Hall et al. 2007). Significantly, the use of a federal volunteer unit should also mean that there will be less need to rely on local police volunteers, such as Sheriff Arpaio's posse members.

## Homelessness and Volunteer Police[9]

Like many undocumented aliens, the homeless population is especially vulnerable to becoming crime victims. Homeless teens may engage in sex for items they need to survive. Homelessness can involve a continuous cycle of response by law enforcement personnel. In wintertime, it can be a life-and-death matter as police try to deal with complaints about transients camping near buildings and in parks. Moreover, the problem can be compounded when interest groups raise concerns about the rights of those transients who want to be left alone or to be who they are. Some police agencies have resorted to transporting the homeless out of their area, a practice known as "dumping." According to the National Coalition for the Homeless (2009), families with children are among the fastest growing segments of the homeless population. Moreover, approximately half of all women and children experiencing homelessness are fleeing domestic violence. Volunteer police can play a strategic role in dealing with the homeless population. Because their volunteer ranks often consist of middle-aged adults, they represent a cross-section of the occupations found in a community. These roots place them in a unique position to engage in the necessary collaboration and pooling of resources essential for working with the homeless.

According to San Bernardino (California) Police Chief Robert Handy, "It's difficult to keep up with ... we deal with chronic homelessness and offer them services but many don't want services. They want that lifestyle. There's a lot of mental illness or criminal backgrounds with the homeless" (Nolan and Emerson 2013a). Chief Handy also commented that his resources were limited in contending with the city's homeless population (Nolan and Emerson 2013a). Although limited, city resources and social services across San Bernardino County are available to the homeless and the working poor, who need a range of services, from transitional housing to food banks. However, Tom Hernandez, the county's homeless services program manager, estimated that more than 30% of homeless people are not aware of the services that are available to them. "Criminal backgrounds, mental illness and substance abuse, relationship issues, physical and developmental disabilities, the economic downturn, all find a part in the different stories of homelessness" (Nolan and Emerson 2013b).

Police Chief Gregory Veitch (Saratoga Springs, New York) has stated: "Police officers do not, however, have the legal authority to require an individual to receive any services offered through government programs, nonprofit organizations, or private entities. The challenge of dealing with the homeless population in any locality is a community issue and one that the local police department has only a small part in addressing" (Veitch 2013). In recent years, Saratoga Springs and other U.S. cities have established Code Blue alert programs, but only after the deaths of homeless persons were discovered due to weather-related conditions.[10] Volunteer police along with clergy and social service professionals can form teams in an emergency effort to shelter homeless persons during cold and stormy nights.

Homelessness is an extremely complex social problem that impacts the quality of life in every community. There are no easy solutions. Many homeless are on the street because of substance abuse, mental illness, or both.

Sometimes the disorder issues associated with homelessness are criminal in nature but difficult to enforce. Volunteer police can be qualified and trained to assist communities in providing better service to this "at-risk" population. They can participate and even lead "homeless outreach teams." Such a team has been established in San Diego and consists of police officers, county health and human services specialists, and psychiatric clinicians from a private nonprofit organization (San Diego PD 2013). In addition, to working as part of these teams, volunteer police can also be assigned to meet with individuals or groups that are experiencing problems dealing with the homeless. Various police agencies have posted information that is relevant for this purpose; for example, the Monterey police and San Diego Police Department have prepared a useful set of tips that can be discussed with concerned persons. In addition, specialized units of volunteer police could be recruited and trained to serve as "community center resource officers." Such auxiliary police units could be used to assist existing staff with security at local homeless shelters, soup kitchens, and daytime neighborhood drop-in centers. Perhaps with such additional personnel, these centers could also provide empowerment classes and other structured programming for homeless persons and families.

It is important to note that homelessness does not always indicate a police problem. There have been instances when people in such circumstances have aided the police. In September 2013, for example, Glen James, a panhandler and shelter resident, discovered a backpack at the South Bay shopping plaza in Boston. The bag had $2,400 in cash and nearly $40,000 in traveler's checks along with a passport and personal papers belonging to a student from China. James immediately flagged down police, who in short order returned the bag to its owner. For his actions, James received a citation at Boston police headquarters, where Police Commissioner Edward F. Davis praised his "extraordinary show of character and honesty" (Schworm 2013). Moreover, there have been instances when members of the homeless population have gone to the aid of overpowered police officers. This occurred in San Francisco in 2013 when Ryan Raso was the only person in a small crowd who rescued a female police officer who was being choked and beaten by a suspect. At that moment, the suspect, a larger woman, was reaching for the officer's service firearm. In 2012, Charles Alexander, a former gang leader and homeless man, "saved a Dallas police officer who was being pummeled by a suspect said to be high on drugs" (Dicker 2013).

## Reserve Officers Training Corps Police Cadets

In 1908, the first police academy was opened in Berkeley, California, when August Vollmer realized that many officers lacked the skills necessary to solve crimes. For the greater part of the twentieth century, the emphasis on police training has not been on academic work but rather on physical training and experience. However, a college education is beginning to emerge as one of the most valuable assets a police officer can have, especially if there is an interest in promotion and advancement (Armstrong and Polk 2002). Warren (1999) indicates that it is important for law enforcement agencies to partner with organizations such as colleges and professional organizations in order to ensure a quality training program. He points out that there is also an increased need for training that is focused on police ethics, cultural diversity, and methods of stress adaptation.

In the United Kingdom, due to economic conditions, there has been a shifting of some police training responsibilities from the police service to colleges and universities as well as recommendations to do a lot more in this regard (Neyroud 2011). It is a way of shifting the cost of training onto individuals rather than onto the government. However, "this trend is in full swing in many U.S. states, where individuals pay their own way to attend the basic police academy and then go in search of police employment" (Cordner and Shain 2011, 282). At some college campuses, this training takes place in a separate facility or in a section of a building somewhat removed from the academic department. Some colleges will grant academic credit for the completion of basic police schools or academies in the form of elective credits that may be applied for a current or future degree.[11] Significantly, the offering of any such academic credit is discouraged by the degree certification requirements of the Academy of Criminal Justice Sciences.[12] Perhaps a more integrated and rigorous approach to police education might be more acceptable to future planners who are charged with judging the quality of academic programs. A model for this approach is addressed here.

ROTC stands for "Reserve Officer Training Corps." Most branches of the U.S. armed forces sponsor both junior and senior level ROTC programs at selected American high schools and colleges. An adaptation of this program would involve a college undergraduate undertaking police training while still a student and then graduating with a college degree and a certification as a sworn volunteer police officer. Such a program would require an agreement between the participating colleges and the sponsoring law enforcement agencies. It is not an entirely new idea. In the early 1970s, Indiana University developed an on-the-job paid student cadet program to enhance the quality of its university security force. It was a three-year program that led to cadets having full police authority including the carrying of firearms. At the end of the students' junior year, the program required completion of an eight-week summer session involving advanced police training (Delaney 1973). Over the years, police departments in various cities have embraced the idea of recruiting paid cadets who must maintain satisfactory grades and complete their degree programs to remain in good standing. For several decades, the New York City Police Department has had a cadet program for city residents with at least 45 credits and a 2.0 Grade Point Average (GPA). The program provides tuition assistance (up to $20,000), an hourly wage, flexible work hours during the school year, and full-time summer employment. Students must earn a minimum of 12 credits each semester and be enrolled in a four-year degree program at an accredited college within New York City, Nassau, or Westchester counties (NYPD Cadets 2013).

The proposed program would not detract from any of the requirements of an undergraduate degree program or limit student activities but would be an enhancement to any program by giving it a distinctive career focus. The proposed program would be offered as an optional choice (track) within an existing bachelor's degree program. Additional benefits would include improving academic competence and performance (especially communication skills) and increasing the leadership abilities of participants.

A key focus of the program would be fostering the development of very useful career-building skills and experiences. Students would serve a two- to three-year internship with the sponsoring law enforcement agency and participate in a variety of community public safety events as reserve cadets. They would be required to pass background checks, appear in uniform, and have their own command structure. Each of these elements is a fundamental requirement in most public safety agencies.

The field service (cadet) aspects of the program would be supervised by members of the sponsoring agency. This would include the necessary instruction for becoming "certified reserve officers." An office for the personnel involved in the program would be maintained on the college campus. Good academic standing would be a prerequisite for continuous participation. Students in the program would learn to work as a team and develop an *esprit de corps*—two essential attributes for criminal justice career success.

In essence, the program would have many "ROTC" features, the main difference being that its "commissioned" graduates would have had actual volunteer police reserve experience. Having developed a solid record of work in the field of public safety along with good references, students would be much more employable. Moreover, they would have a much better understanding of the occupation and be prepared to deal with the stresses of police work.

One program that comes close to this model exists at the University of Central Florida (UCF) in association with the Orange County Sheriff's Office. It is career track internship program in which college seniors majoring in criminal justice are given the opportunity "to participate in two semesters of job-shadowing with deputies in varying roles with the agency, including road patrol, aviation, marine patrol, communications, evidence, and court services.... Interns in this program, called Law Enforcement Officer Training Corps Cadets, report to a reserve officer, who in turn reports to a full-time sheriff's office volunteer services commander and to human resources personnel for background information. One large advantage to this program is that the curriculum devised by the reserve officer internship coordinator is designed with the university program in mind. This is possible because the reserve officer is a criminal justice faculty member of the university, and attempts to create the necessary link between the practice and theory that students report to be missing in other types of internship experiences" (Wolf and Russo 2005). Although the UCF program is unlike the proposed program because it does not include a requirement that the college students engage in the extensive training necessary to become reserve or regular police officers by the time of their graduation from college, students in the UCF program have the option of attending a law enforcement academy after graduation. Most of the students who complete the UCF program and the academy go into full-time law enforcement positions with either the sheriff's office or a local police agency and some become reserves[13] (personal communication from Ross Wolf, January 2, 2013).

There are a number of college programs in the United States where credit for police academy attendance is incorporated into a four-year degree program in criminal justice, enabling graduates to become eligible for police employment upon graduation. For example, at Alvernia University in Reading, Pennsylvania, criminal justice majors may graduate with a Reading Police Academy certification. The academy is located on the university's campus. The basic training course as prescribed by Pennsylvania Act 120 is designed to provide students with the initial skills necessary to begin their police careers. The Act 120 course is required training for all Pennsylvania municipal police officers. Two types of students attend the academy. The first are newly hired police officers enrolled to satisfy the requirements of Act 120. The second are preservice students who have not yet been hired by a police department. The preservice students are taking the course in the hopes of enhancing their chances of police employment. To be accepted into the academy, applicants must pass physical fitness tests, a criminal background check, and a psychological exam. The course consists of 820 hours and is completed in a 20-week program. Alvernia students have the option of attending the Reading Police Academy and are eligible to apply for the academy during their junior year in order to attend during the first semester of their senior year. The students start the academy in July and are in training at the academy until December. This allows them to obtain Act 120 certification as part of their four-year degree without extended time or expense (Reading Police Academy 2013).

East Texas Baptist University (ETBU)[14] is located in Marshall, Texas, a city of 25,000, 150 miles east of Dallas. Students at ETBU can complete a four-year university degree and be eligible to test for a basic Texas peace officer's license without the need for additional police academy training. The ETBU program was approved by the Texas Commission on Law Enforcement (TCOLE) in December 2013 to serve as an academic alternative peace officer basic training provider. In the past, students who graduated from ETBU with either a bachelor of science or bachelor of arts degree in criminal justice had to continue their training for licensure by attending a certified law enforcement academy elsewhere. The criminal justice program at ETBU had to demonstrate the ability and the commitment to meet all of the standards for law enforcement training and education within the state of Texas. The program was designed to exceed state requirements in several areas, including classroom contact hours, internship requirements, and physical fitness and skills training. Prior to acceptance into the program, students must pass the same background, medical, and psychological exams required for any officer entering a department or training program (ETBU 2013a). Significantly, the completion of this program will also make students eligible for part-time paid or unpaid reserve officer appointments. However, neither the Alvernia University nor the ETBU program mentions the possibility of a reserve police officer opportunity in their online posted materials.

The merging of police training with the curriculums of college and university degree programs appears to be a possible trend in the making, but it must be cautioned that "Higher education can be quite an intransigent institution in its own right, so one should not approach it naively when looking for better models for police education and training" (Cordner and Shain 2011, 283).

## Prerogatives of Police Chiefs

Over the course of the history of volunteer policing in America, critical decisions regarding the creation or continuation of volunteer police units have taken place due to the actions initiated by police leaders. For example, in 1918, the reorganization of the New York City's Home Defense League into regiments and brigades of a mobile reserve police force to aid the regular police in disasters or other emergencies was initially proposed by New York City's Police Commissioner Enright. In 1942, New York City's Mayor La Guardia established an auxiliary police program that he entitled "the City Patrol Corps." In 1976, Sanford D. Garelik, the head of the New York City Transit Authority Police Force, created the city's first volunteer auxiliary transit police unit to reduce crime in the subways. In 1988, the Columbus (Ohio) Auxiliary Police Force became the "Columbus Police Reserve" at the behest of Police Chief James G. Jackson and other city leaders (Greenberg 2005). In 2013, the Albemarle County (Virginia) Auxiliary Police unit was initiated by the county's police chief. Conversely, such units have also been abolished by police administrators. In the early 1990s, the city of New Brunswick (New Jersey) ended its auxiliary program but revised it in 2012 (Kratovil and del Rosario 2012). The Chattanooga (Tennessee) Police Department abolished its reserve program in 2000 when the department applied for accreditation from CALEA. The announced reasons for its termination had to do with the finances and time frames needed for satisfying the new standards for training of volunteer police officers if accreditation guidelines were to be met (Gregory 2007).

Using volunteers to help supplement sworn staff is a possible way for law enforcement agencies to continue to enhance public safety. Volunteer police can provide communities with another layer of protection and are an ideal way to enhance civic engagement for uplifting the quality of life. However, the encouragement of partnerships between the public and police are often tied to the decisions made by key law enforcement officials. In a 2003 study conducted at Eastern Michigan University, Madison Heights Police Department Sgt. Stephen Worton concluded: "As a continuation of the community policing programs of the early to mid-1990s, police volunteerism leads to a furthering of trust between a law enforcement agency and the community it serves. The drawbacks of police volunteers are minor: liability can be minimized by proper selection and training, and negative perceptions from sworn officers will eventually diminish as volunteers prove their worth and continue to express their respect for their police officers. Agencies both large and small, rural and urban, are well served by volunteers" (Worton 2003, 21).

## The Need for an American Institute of Volunteer Police

This work has covered a large number of citizen-based and police-sponsored initiatives in the field of volunteer policing. However, although there are some national and state-level membership associations involving active and/ or retired volunteer police,[15] there are very few scholars engaged in volunteer police research and there is no government-sponsored entity to encourage the research necessary to discern the full potential of the volunteer police movement in the United States.

The existence of the IACP VIPS Web-based directory and related resources was a huge beginning, but more effort is needed. The IACP VIPS program, which had relied on voluntary registration, included listings and brief descriptions of auxiliary and reserve police units; citizen patrols; search and rescue units; Community Emergency Response Team (CERT) units; mounted posses; Law Enforcement Explorer Posts; local, state, and federal citizen police academy alumni associations; volunteer and unsworn police administrative units; and so forth. However, it is quite another task to determine through carefully designed studies how such volunteers are actually contributing to greater public safety and to make recommendations for their success in the future.

The establishment of an American Institute of Volunteer Police can greatly enhance the future of volunteer police by considering new initiatives for their deployment as well as the quality of their education and training.

In addition, such an institute can examine how citizen participation in the field of law enforcement affects the practices and development of community policing, human rights, and the rule of law. In the field of public safety, the stakes are often high because a life or lives will depend upon the initial performance of first responders.

## Summary

Volunteer police are serving throughout the United States. Many are in sworn positions with full law enforcement authority, but a large segment also engage in administrative roles, search and rescue units, medical teams, and citizen patrols. Citizen patrols composed of seniors are quite common in the nation's Sun Belt region. Moreover, since the events of September 11, there appears to have been a spurt in the establishment of Law Enforcement Explorer Posts, especially with respect to their sponsorship by federal agencies. Chapter 9 reviewed the variety of programs for youth initiated by federal agencies.

In 2013, a new state law authorizing volunteer safety resource officer programs in North Carolina public schools was passed. It came as a direct response to the fears generated about school safety after the Sandy Hook Elementary School tragedy and in consideration of older incidents. Under the law, a local school board can enter into an agreement with a sheriff or police chief to provide security at schools by assigning volunteer school safety resource officers. The law requires that volunteer SROs have prior experience as law enforcement officers or as military police officers. The volunteers can make arrests and carry weapons on school property when carrying out official duties. The law provides immunity from liability claims for good-faith actions taken by the volunteers while performing their duties. Also under the law, volunteer SROs must receive training on social and cognitive development of elementary, middle, and high school children; meet selection standards established by the sheriff or police chief; work under supervision of the sheriff, police chief, or their designee; and meet the same educational and firearms proficiency standards required of special deputy sheriffs or special law enforcement officers. North Carolina's new law was among the many actions taken nationwide by state and local governments to address school safety.

In addition, it would be worthwhile for any community to consider having volunteer police work on "truancy intervention teams." Such an initiative was undertaken in 2004, when an unsworn VIPS program volunteer teamed up with a SRO at a Modesto, California, elementary school. A VIPS program recommendation is that reserve police officers can be a valuable resource for school safety and security. They can also assist with crime prevention educational programs.

In Arizona, after the Sandy Hook Elementary School massacre, Maricopa County Sheriff Joe Arpaio directed members of his volunteer police posse (the second largest in the United States) to begin patrols of Phoenix area schools. In past years, he has recruited posses to not only contend with illegal immigration concerns but also reduce the dangers of drug cartel violence spilling across southern border states. In order to accomplish such demanding assignments, the importance of the CALEA standards for auxiliaries and reserves assume prominence. According to these professional standards, if police agencies desire to have their volunteers undertake more complex police duties, they must train them in the same manner as regular police.

Several additional ideas regarding the mobilization of volunteer police were discussed in this chapter. These concerned carjacking, active shooter incidents, immigration, border security, and homelessness. Such future recommendations included the creation of a "Border Patrol Auxiliary" (BPA) to protect the integrity of America's borders. BPA volunteers would be selected and screened to ensure they have the characteristics essential to maintain the high standards of the U.S. Border Patrol. Other recommendations involved having qualified volunteer police: (1) deliver presentations designed to increase chances of survival in an active shooter event or carjacking; (2) assist immigrants in need of English language proficiency and knowledge about America's laws and customs; and (3) lead "homeless outreach teams." In particular, volunteer police can reduce the stress of undocumented immigrant crime victims about deportation matters, and they can participate—along with clergy and social service professionals—to form teams in an emergency effort to shelter homeless persons during cold and stormy nights.

Looking toward the future, two other recommendations were discussed for the advancement of police professionalism: (1) using an ROTC style undergraduate education model to encourage careers in law enforcement and (2) establishing an American Institute of Volunteer Police to encourage the research necessary to bring to fruition the full potential of the volunteer police movement.

The activities proposed here are designed to reduce and deter crime. When there exists only limited resources to supplement ongoing efforts or to initiate new programs, the use of qualified volunteer police should be considered. Each of these new possibilities requires imagination—a characteristic that Drucker (1990, 113) warns can become suppressed in volunteer organizations: "Non-profits are prone to become inward-looking. People are so convinced that they are doing the right thing, and are so committed to their cause, that they see the institution as an end in itself. But that's a bureaucracy. Soon people in the organization no longer ask: Does it service our mission? They ask: Does it fit our rules? And that not only inhibits performance, it destroys vision and dedication." Governmental organizations are prone to the same type of inertia; perhaps, they tend to stagnate even more.

In 2013, the IACP asked program managers of established VIPS programs to gather and share information about their programs and needs. A key finding of their study was that volunteers continue to take on additional duties in law enforcement volunteer programs. Recruiting new volunteer police and qualifying existing members to perform new missions should always require that some level of research be performed. A wise police chief demands evidence of success before initiating a new program. This can be satisfied through the use of Herman Goldstein's "scanning, analysis, response, and assessment" (S.A.R.A) model[16] and case studies of existing volunteer organizations and programs. A major goal of this book has been to explore the current and past operations of such initiatives and to reveal existing trends and the potential for future undertakings.

Ultimately, the present work has attempted to answer the question: Who are American volunteer police? They are the men, the women, and even the children who have committed their extra time to the delivery of services associated with public safety. They represent all racial, ethnic, and religious segments of American society. As long as their ranks are strong and they adhere to democratic principles of equality and fairness, there should be sufficient resources and elasticity to cope with the social control and criminal justice issues of the future.

## Review Questions

1. Identify at least four types of school violence.
2. Describe how a volunteer police officer might assist in a truancy prevention program.
3. Discuss the advantages and disadvantages of having a volunteer school resource officer program.
4. State how volunteer police and Law Enforcement Explorers can help prevent carjacking and reduce the risks associated with an active shooter incident.
5. Identify the CALEA standard that may have the greatest impact on the longevity of various volunteer police units and explain why this is so.
6. There are at least six attributes in August Vollmer's model of police professionalism. Discuss how the establishment of a volunteer police program may help foster two or more of these attributes.
7. The documentary film *Bully* has been shown in schools across America in an effort to stop the problem at its source. A 40-page guide for using this film is available at: http://www.facinghistory.org/for-educators/educator-resources. Read at least the first few pages of this guide and identify from the information presented how some

young students may respond when viewing this film. To access this resource a login is required.

8. Read page 34 of the study guide for the film *Bully*. Based on its content, discuss how Lee Hirsch, the film's director, was able to obtain permission to film inside schools, particularly in Sioux City.

9. In January 2013, after Sheriff Arpaio announced his intent to have Steven Seagal serve as a self-defense instructor, the Arizona House Minority Leader called the plan to use movie actor Seagal as an instructor "ludicrous." Discuss the pros and cons of involving celebrities in efforts to control and prevent crime.

10. Discuss how the use of volunteer police to aid the homeless may diminish the police practice known as "dumping."

11. Discuss the pros and cons of using an ROTC college cadet model to provide volunteer and/or regular police education and training.

12. Explain how the Alvernia University and East Texas Baptist University police track degree programs differ from the University of Central Florida's Law Enforcement Officer Training Corps program.

13. Can you think of any areas or needs in the field of public safety that volunteer police can fulfill? Describe these areas and indicate the type of education and training that might be needed to fulfill such roles.

14. Based on your understanding of the nature of volunteer police programs, provide at least three advantages and three disadvantages for relying on a volunteer program to augment police services.

## Notes

1. Readers are encouraged to review the following works concerning volunteer police history in order to obtain a fuller understanding of the rise of contemporary volunteer police units in the United States: Greenberg (1984, 2005); and Bartels (2013). Greenberg (1984) explores the origins of the two major types of citizen volunteer police—auxiliary and reserve. The first section of this work is devoted to the early origins of policing and the remainder presents a case study of the use of volunteer police in New York City. Greenberg (2005) builds upon the former work by chronicling the nature and purpose of volunteer police units in America since 1620. In particular, the history of volunteer policing (using a robust definition of the concept) is interwoven with the nation's past in order to consider the possibilities for a safer and more secure future. It also includes details regarding homeland security efforts and various citizen emergency response groups, such as the Civil Air Patrol, U.S. Coast Guard Auxiliary, Community Emergency Response Teams, and fire units. In 44 pages, Bartels (2013) covers an overview of volunteer police in the United States, including training programs, requirements, and qualifications; the nature and implications of the "Stand Your Ground" law and the "Good Samaritan" law; cases of police volunteers killed or seriously injured on duty; and a comparative analysis of volunteer programs worldwide.

2. For an informative review of the history and activities of junior police, see Chapters 8 and 9. An informative 10-minute promotional video for the July 14–19, 2014, National Law Enforcement Exploring Conference held at Indiana University is posted at: http://www.youtube.com/watch?v=9DwqiXKOaj0&feature=c4-overview&list=UUkpz2qX3Oiag3pvI-0WL9iQ.

3. In 2012, a second edition of this work co-edited by James Alan Fox and Jack Levin was published by Sage. It is filled with contemporary and classic case studies illustrating the many violent expressions of power, revenge, terror, greed, and loyalty. The book examines the theories of criminal behavior and applies them to many well-known and lesser-known multiple homicide cases from around the world. The work considers the commonalities and variations among multiple murders; addresses the characteristics of killers and their victims; and, in the concluding chapter, discusses the special concerns of multiple murder victims and their survivors.

4. On March 31, 2014, IACP closed down the former VIPS website, http://www.policevolunteers.org, and transitioned VIPS resources to a newly redesigned IACP website whose homepage is http://www.theiacp.org/VIPS. Perhaps, the most valuable set of resources ever compiled involving the management of citizen participation in police work can now be found at http://www.theiacp.org/VIPSResources. This IACP Web page provides links to hundreds of useful planning documents. These posted materials can readily be adapted for establishing specialized volunteer police units to assist school districts. For example, there are links to: the 10-page Baltimore County (MD) Police Department "Auxiliary Unit Standard Operating Procedures"; the 11-page General Order regarding the operation of the Waynesboro (VA) Police Reserve Unit; and the 21-page procedures and guidelines of the Longview (WA) Auxiliary/Reserve Police Program. These specific resource links are found under the "Policies and Procedures" section on the Web page. Of course, there exist many other valuable online resources dealing with crime prevention, such as *Best Practices of Youth Violence Prevention: A Sourcebook for Community Action*, a study by Thornton et al. (2002). Their research examines the effectiveness of specific violence prevention practices in four key areas: parents and families; home visiting; social and conflict resolution skills; and mentoring. It is a June 2002 publication of the National Center for Injury Prevention and Control of the Centers for Disease Control and Prevention, Atlanta, GA. It can be downloaded in English or Spanish using the various links found at: http://www.cdc.gov/violenceprevention/pub/yv_bestpractices.html.

5. The law creating the Volunteer School Safety Resource Program is entitled the "Gold Star Officer Program/School Volunteer." The North Carolina statute: (1) defines volunteer school safety resource officer as a person who volunteers as a school safety resource officer in a program developed by a sheriff or chief of police; (2) provides that school safety resource officers may carry a weapon on school property providing that they are engaged in official duties; (3) provides that a local board of education may enter an agreement with the sheriff or chief of police to provide security at schools by assigning volunteer school safety resource officers; (4) authorizes sheriffs or chiefs of police to establish volunteer school safety resource officer programs by recruiting nonsalaried special deputies or special law enforcement officers to serve as school safety resource officers

in public schools; (5) requires that volunteers in the program must have prior experience as either a law enforcement officer or as a military police officer; (6) requires that a program volunteer must receive training on research into the social and cognitive development of elementary, middle and high school children; (7) requires that the volunteer must meet the selection standards and any additional criteria established by the sheriff or chief of police; (8) provides that a volunteer must report to the sheriff or chief of police and work under the direction and supervision of the sheriff or chief of police or their designee; (9) requires that a volunteer must update or renew their law enforcement training and be certified by the North Carolina Sheriffs' Education and Training Standards Commission or the North Carolina Criminal Justice Education and Training Standards Commission as meeting the educational and firearms proficiency standards required of persons serving as a special deputy sheriff or special law enforcement officer but is not required to meet the physical standards required for certification but must have a standard medical exam to ensure a volunteer is in good health; (10) authorizes a volunteer to have the power of arrest while performing the duties of a volunteer school safety resource officer; (11) provides that there is no liability on the part of and no cause of action may arise against a volunteer school safety resource officer, the Sheriff or Chief of Police or employees supervising, or the public school system or its employees for any good-faith action during the performance of their duties; and (12) provides that the assets of the State and Local Governmental Law-Enforcement Officers' Separate Insurance Plan may be used to pay the employer health insurance contributions on behalf of state law enforcement officers" (North Carolina Sheriffs'Association 2013, 3–4). Numbers were added for clarification purposes.

6. Among the alternatives to a police presence in schools, the Justice Policy Institute recommends the creation of "graduated responses to student behavior that take into account the circumstances of the case … to limit the referrals to the juvenile justice system, suspensions and expulsions by establishing a rubric and system for meting out discipline. This could also include developing an agreed upon discipline code that makes it clear what is an arrestable offense and what is not. Ideally, jurisdictions should aim for zero referrals from schools to the justice system" (Petteruti 2011, 32).

7. In 2010, a study conducted by http://bullying.org showed that: 15% of students have missed school out of fear of being bullied; 71% of students reported bullying as an ongoing problem at their school; and 54% of students have witnessed physical abuse take place at the hand of another student (Coster 2012). The documentary film entitled *Bully* premiered in 2012. It was directed by Lee Hirsch and filming began in the fall of 2009, shortly after two 11-year-old boys—one from Massachusetts and one from Georgia—committed suicide following prolonged harassment at school. Hirsch spent the rest of that academic year in a handful of schools across the country, following five students and families. He wanted to understand how bullying is handled and how it is approached within the walls of the school building. Among the victims featured are a 12-year-old boy who sustains regular taunts, jabs, and punches from classmates; a 16-year-old one-time basketball star who became a town outcast after coming out as a lesbian; and a 14-year-old girl jailed for wielding a gun on her school bus to protect herself from bullying. The film also follows two families dealing with the

aftermath of teen suicide (Rappaport 2012). *Bully* has been shown in schools across America in an effort to stop the problem at its source. Recently, the Ohio School District screened the film for all 9,000 of its students as a teaching tool to reach out to both bullies and their victims (Coster 2012). A guide for using this film is available at: http://safeschools.facinghistory.org. In order to view this guide, a brief online registration form must be completed.

8. Actor Steven Seagal's volunteer experiences as a Jefferson Parish Sheriff's Office deputy were filmed in the reality series "Steven Seagal: Lawman" on the A&E cable network. Steven Seagal, who has played no-nonsense tough guys in dozens of movies, has also been sworn in as a sheriff's deputy in Doña Ana County in Southern New Mexico. This took place in January 2013 when Seagal was 60 years old and more than a year after Seagal was named a part-time deputy in sparsely populated Hudspeth County in West Texas. Hudspeth County, which is east of El Paso, is best known for the drug busts of Willie Nelson, Snoop Dogg, and other celebrities at a Border Patrol checkpoint in Sierra Blanca. At the time of Seagal's swearing-in, a Doña Ana County sheriff's spokeswoman said that Seagal is a reserve officer. According to New Mexico law, he can carry out police work only while with a commissioned peace officer. She said Seagal is expected to take part in border security training in the coming months (Borunda 2013).

9. According to the Stewart B. McKinney Act, 42 U.S.C. § 11301, et seq. (1994), a person is considered homeless who "lacks a fixed, regular, and adequate night-time residence; and … has a primary night time residency that is: (A) a supervised publicly or privately operated shelter designed to provide temporary living accommodations … (B) An institution that provides a temporary residence for individuals intended to be institutionalized, or (C) a public or private place not designed for, or ordinarily used as, a regular sleeping accommodation for human beings." The term "homeless individual" does not include any individual imprisoned or otherwise detained pursuant to an act of Congress or a state law.

10. In many communities, authorities may declare a "Code Blue" alert during periods of extreme cold weather. The response to such an alert is to trigger a multiagency effort to reduce hypothermia deaths during the winter months by protecting the homeless, seniors, and other vulnerable populations. Typically, first-responders, trained volunteers, and one-to-one mentors form a team to spread the word about the Code Blue program. The success of such an initiative depends upon transporting, housing, and communicating with those in need of shelter. Volunteer police can perform each of these roles. They can be invaluable extra hands by assisting in the community centers and temporary shelters that will be occupied for the duration of Code Blue emergencies. According to Bridgeton, New Jersey's mayor, Albert B. Kelly, "We really need volunteers just to be present to help some of our most vulnerable citizens … the work itself is not hard, but it's work that is good and decent and worthy of our best efforts" (Kov 2013). Center directors are less likely to get "burned out" or overwhelmed by working multiple overnight shifts to keep their centers open if volunteers, such as auxiliary or reserve police, are available for center work. In the city of Baltimore, officials announce a Code Blue day for the following weather-related events: when temperatures are expected to be below 25° with winds of 15 miles per hour or higher; when temperatures are less than 20°; or during other periods of intense winter weather (Scharper 2010).

11. A few examples of state-approved law enforcement academies housed on various college campuses that may be open to qualified members of the public include Stark State College in North Canton, OH; Yuba College in Marysville, CA; Alvernia University in Reading, PA; and Niagara University in Lewiston, NY.

12. To be certified by the Academy of Criminal Justice Sciences (ACJS), the institution must provide evidence demonstrating that the program is in compliance with all requirements of the certification standards. The standards were adopted in 2005. Standard D.3 of the "Certification Standards for College/University Criminal Justice Baccalaureate Degree Programs" states: "Only credit from institutions that are accredited by their regional higher education accrediting body is accepted for transfer into an undergraduate criminal justice program. No academic credit is awarded by the criminal justice program for life experience or for military, police academy, or other professional training." For further information, contact: ACJS Academic Review Committee Chair, Dr. Gerald Bayens. e-mail: gerald.bayens@washburn.edu.

13. At the time of the preparation of this book, Dr. Ross Wolf, associate professor of criminal justice and associate dean for academic affairs and technology at the College of Health and Public Affairs, University of Central Florida (UCF), was serving as a reserve chief in the Orange County Sheriff's Office Reserves and as the coordinator for the Law Enforcement Officer Training Corps for that agency. The training and qualifications to become a reserve deputy are the same as that of a full-time deputy. Many former members of the reserve unit have become full-time sheriff's office employees. Wolf has traveled to Hong Kong and Singapore to conduct research on volunteer policing and to share his knowledge of American volunteer law enforcement. UCF students have studied volunteer policing in England during study abroad programs. (Dr. Ross Wolf can be contacted via e-mail at: ross.wolf@ocfl.net.)

14. East Texas Baptist University (ETBU), affiliated with the Baptist General Convention of Texas, is a private, Christian university of liberal arts and sciences. ETBU was founded as the College of Marshall in 1912. It became East Texas Baptist College in 1944. ETBU is accredited by the Southern Association of Colleges and Schools Commission on Colleges to award baccalaureate and master's degrees. Enrollment is approximately 1,200 students and more than 85% of full-time faculty members have earned doctorates or terminal degrees (ETBU 2013b).

15. The following information about several national and statewide volunteer police associations is entirely based on their respective Web site postings. *The Reserve Law Officers Association of America* was founded in 1970 to serve the needs of volunteer peace officers. It is a tax exempt nonprofit fraternal organization, and it offers insurance for line of duty injuries. *The Volunteer Law Enforcement Officer Alliance* strives to assist in the formation, expansion, and training of state, county, and city volunteer law enforcement units and to promote awareness of the role of the volunteer officer in providing for the safety of the citizens of their communities. Membership also includes an insurance plan while performing any and all law enforcement, emergency response, and criminal justice duties while working in any full-time, part-time, auxiliary, and reserve volunteer capacity. It was incorporated, as a not for profit corporation, in the state of Florida in 2009. *The Massachusetts Volunteer Law Enforcement Officer Association* (MA-VLEOA)

seeks to promote the ideals, goals, general welfare, and professionalism of the volunteer law enforcement officers of the Commonwealth of Massachusetts. The MA-VLEOA has established a scholarship to honor the memory of Massachusetts Institute of Technology Officer Sean Collier who was murdered in the line of duty on April 18, 2013. Officer Collier started his law enforcement career as an auxiliary officer in Somerville, MA. The Sean Collier Scholarship will provide reserve academy tuition assistance to members of the MA-VLEOA. *The California Reserve Peace Officers Association* (CRPOA) membership is open to anyone who is involved in or supportive of law enforcement. CRPOA serves the entire law enforcement community through organizational networking, education, legal services, and medical benefits. Annual training conferences are held. It works closely with the California State Legislature on bills where volunteers are involved. *The New York State Association of Auxiliary Police, Inc.* (NYSAAP), is a type A not for profit trade association incorporated in 1973 as the New York State Auxiliary Police Association, Inc. In 2001, it was reorganized under its current name to represent members of uniformed volunteers in law enforcement, primarily auxiliary police in New York State. It works closely with the New York State Legislature on bills concerning volunteer police work and benefits.

16. Herman Goldstein's S.A.R.A. model involves scanning, analysis, response, and assessment. The first step is to identify the problem and scan the community so that you understand the underlying dynamics that can inform your response. The next step is to analyze the pressure points where intervention can make a positive difference. In the response phase, all the data collected from the previous steps can be used to build in a series of assessments that can allow you to make course corrections along the way.

# References

About School Violence. (2013). Retrieved December 16, 2013 from http://www.cdc.gov/violenceprevention/youthviolence/schoolviolence/index.html

Armstrong, D. and Polk, O. E. (2002). College for cops: The fast track for success. *Journal of the Institute of Justice and International Studies, 17*(5), 24–26.

Bartels, E. C. (2013). *Volunteer police in the United States: Programs, challenges, and legal aspects.* Heidelberg, Germany: Springer.

BBC News. (2014). 1952: Anne Frank published in English. Retrieved March 4, 2014 from http://news.bbc.co.uk/onthisday/hi/dates/stories/april/30/newsid_3715000/3715435.stm

Borunda, D. (2013, January 24). Actor Steven Seagal sworn in as Doña Ana County sheriff's deputy. *El Paso Times.* Retrieved December 19, 2013 from http://www.elpasotimes.com/newupdated/ci_22435057/actor-steven-seagal-sworn-do-ana-county-sheriffs

Briney, A. (2009). Sunbelt. Retrieved December 15, 2013 from http://geography.about.com/od/specificplacesofinterest/a/sunbelt.htm

Carder, D. (2013, October 30). Police disband reserve force. *Ottawa Herald.* Retrieved October 31, 2013 from http://ottawaherald.com/news/103113reserve

Carte, G. and Carte, E. (1975). *Police reform in the United States: The era of August Vollmer,* 1905–1932. Berkeley, CA: University of California Press.

Chasmar, J. (2013, February 10). Sheriff Joe Arpaio, actor Steven Seagal train posses to guard schools. *The Washington Times*. Retrieved December 19, 2013 from http://www.washingtontimes.com/news/2013/feb/10/sheriff-joe-arpaio-actor-steven-seagal-train-posse/

CHP. (2013). Visalia Explorer Post 480. Retrieved December 24, 2013 http://www.chp.ca.gov/recruiting/explorers_visalia.html

City of Arcadia. (2013a) City of Arcadia, CA: Volunteer programs. Retrieved December 15, 2013 from http://www.ci.arcadia.ca.us/home/index.asp?page = 1560

City of Arcadia. (2013b). Information on the Arcadia Mounted Enforcement Team. Retrieved December 15, 2013 from http://www.ci.arcadia.ca.us/home/index.asp?page = 1612

City of Ottawa. (2013). Police programs. Retrieved December 18, 2013 from http://www.ottawaks.gov/Departments/Police/Programs/tabid/146/Default.aspx

Cordner, G. and Shain, C. (2011, August). Editorial: The changing landscape of police education and training. *Police Practice & Research, 12*(4), 281–285.

Coster, J. (2012, May 22). Increase in bullying affecting youth. Retrieved May 26, 2012 from http://my.hsj.org/Schools/Newspaper/tabid/100/view/frontpage/articleid/528821/newspaperid/3334/Increase_in_bullying_affecting_youth.aspx

David, J. A. (2013, April 1). C.S. Lewis Daily: A tribute to Anne Frank. Retrieved March 4, 2014 from http://johnadavid.wordpress.com/2013/04/01/c-s-lewis-daily-a-tribute-to-anne-frank/

Davidson, L. (2013, December 7). Permits for concealed guns: Utah hits 500K. *The Salt Lake Tribune*. Retrieved December 16, 2013 from http://www.sltrib.com/sltrib/politics/57214669-90/utah-permits-permit-gun.html.csp?page = 2

Delaney, M. J. (1973). *Indiana University Police Academy Cadet Program evaluation: Police technical assistance report*. Arlington, VA: Westinghouse Justice Institute.

Dicker, R. (2013, September 3). Ryan Raso, homeless man, saves female police office. *The Huffington Post*. Retrieved December 20, 2013 from http://www.huffingtonpost.com/2013/09/03/ryan-raso-homeless-man_n_3860450.html

Drucker, P. F. (1990). *Managing the nonprofit organization: Principles and practices*. New York, NY: HarperCollins.

Epstein, R. J. (2013). Gun control battle moves to main street. Retrieved December 16, 2013 from http://www.politico.com/story/2013/12/gun-control-efforts-101153.html?hp = f1

ETBU. (2013a). ETBU gets approval for peace officer training. Retrieved December 22, 2013 from http://www.marshallnewsmessenger.com/news/etbu-gets-approval-for-peace-officer-training/article_9f2ba857-d034-5122-8d05-78a3f191a1f6.html

ETBU. (2013b). History. Retrieved December 22, 2013 from http://www.etbu.edu/about/glance/

Finn, P. and McDevitt, J. (2005). *National assessment of school resource officer programs: Final project report*. Washington, DC: National Institute of Justice.

Greenberg, M. A. (1984). *Auxiliary police: The citizens approach to public safety*. Westport, CT: Greenwood Press.

Greenberg, M. A. (2005). *Citizens defending America: From colonial times to the age of terrorism*. Pittsburgh, PA: University of Pittsburgh Press.

Gregory, L. (2007, October 14). Backups in reserve. *Chattanooga Times Free Press.* Retrieved January 19, 2014 from http://www.timesfreepress.com/news/2007/oct/14/Backups-in-reserve/

Haimowitz, M. (2014). We didn't wait a single moment. Retrieved June 28, 2014 from http://jewishpalmbeach.org/community/feature/we_didnt_wait_a_single_moment/

Hall, C., Schauerman, G., Ewing, R. and Brandner, B. (2007, May 5). *Securing the borders: Creation of the Border Patrol Auxiliary.* Master's thesis. National Security Program, Kennedy School of Government, Harvard University. Retrieved October 10. 2013 from http://www.dtic.mil/dtic/tr/fulltext/u2/a476945.pdf

Herron, A. (2013, August 23). Armed volunteers could find place in local schools. *Winston- Salem Journal.* Retrieved December 12, 2013 from http://www.journalnow.com/news/local/article_62e5a9f2-0c57-11e3-8a16-001a4bcf6878.html?mode = jqm

Hill, C. (2013, July 14). The problem of volunteer school resource officers. Retrieved December 12, 2013 from http://pulse.ncpolicywatch.org/2013/07/24/the-problem-of-volunteer-school-resource-officers/

Johnson, H. A., Travers, N. T. and Jones, M. (2008). *History of criminal justice* (4th ed.). Newark, NJ: LexisNexis Group.

Johnson, I. M. (1999). School violence: The effectiveness of a school resource officer program in a southern city. *Journal of Criminal Justice, 27,* 173–192.

Kov, D. J. (2013, December 17). Bridgeton's Code Blue program shaping up. Retrieved December 22, 2013 from http://www.thedailyjournal.com/article/20131217/NEWS01/312170013/B-ton-s-Code-Blue-program-shaping-up

Kratovil, C. and del Rosario, A. (2012, July 28). City resurrects auxiliary police program with 7 volunteers. Retrieved January 19, 2014 from http://newbrunswicktoday.com/article/city-resurrects-auxiliary-police-program-7-volunteers

LAPD. (2013). Carjacking. Retrieved December 17, 2013 from http://www.lapdonline.org/crime_prevention/content_basic_view/1368

National Coalition for the Homeless. (2009, July). Who is homeless? Retrieved December 19, 2013 from http://www.nationalhomeless.org/factsheets/who.html

Neyroud, P. (2011). *Review of police leadership and training.* London: Home Office.

Nolan, M. and Emerson, S. (2013a, August 18). Dealing with the homeless: Lessons in success, failure. Retrieved December 18, 2013 from http://www.sbsun.com/social- affairs/20130818/dealing-with-the-homeless-lessons-in-success-failure

Nolan, M. and Emerson, S. (2013b, August 17). San Bernardino County poised to help the homeless. Retrieved December 18, 2013 from http://www.sbsun.com/social-affairs/20130817/san-bernardino-county-poised-to-help-the-homeless

North Carolina Sheriffs' Association. (2013, July 22). Special Legislative Report. *Weekly Legislative Report.* Retrieved December 12, 2013 from http://www.ncsheriffs.org/Weekly%20Legislative%20Report/2013/NCSA%20Weekly%20Legislative%20Report-2013.07.22.pdf

NYPD Cadets. (2013). Retrieved December 26, 2013 from http://www.nypdcadets.com/

Petteruti, A. (2011, November). *Education under arrest: The case against police in schools.* Washington, DC: Justice Policy Institute.

Rappaport, J. (2012). Interview with Director Lee Hirsch: Bullying impacts who we are as a nation. Retrieved May 22, 2012 from http://safeschools.facinghistory.org/content/interview-director-lee-hirsch-bullying-impacts-who-we-are-nation

Reading Police Academy. (2013). Retrieved December 23, 2013 from http://www.readingpa.gov/content/reading-police-academy

Rice, C. (2013, December 3). Beyond Newtown: The larger tragedy of guns and kids. Retrieved December 16, 2013 from http://www.thecrimereport.org/archive/2013-12-beyond- newtown-the-larger-tragedy-of-guns-and-kids

San Diego PD. (2013). Prevention tips: Dealing with homeless people. Retrieved December 18, 2013 from http://www.sandiego.gov/police/services/prevention/tips/homeless.shtml

Scharper, J. (2010, December 14). City declares 'Code Blue' conditions. *The Baltimore Sun*. Retrieved December 22, 2013 from http://articles.baltimoresun.com/keyword/code-blue

Schworm, P. (2013, September 16). Police honor homeless man's good deed. *The Boston Globe*. Retrieved December 19, 2013 from http://www.bostonglobe.com/metro/2013/09/16/glen-james-homeless-man-who-returned-bag-cash-honored-boston-police/yUZjfKiELlXDURjhQwQ23O/story.html

Seper, J. (2010, November 17). Arizona sheriff Arpaio forms armed 'immigration posse' with Hollywood actors. *The Washington Times*. Retrieved December 18, 2013 from http://www.washingtontimes.com/news/2010/nov/17/arizona-sheriff-arpaio-forms-armed-immigration-pos/

SS Police State. (2014). SS and SA become auxiliary police units. Retrieved March 4, 2014 from http://www.ushmm.org/outreach/en/article.php?ModuleId = 10007675

Thornton, T. N., Craft, C. A., Dahlberg, L. L., Lynch, B. S. and Baer, K. (2002). *Best practices of youth violence prevention: A sourcebook for community action (Rev.)*. Atlanta, GA: Centers for Disease Control and Prevention, National Center for Injury Prevention and Control.

U.S. Department of State. (2002). Carjacking: Don't be a victim. Retrieved December 17, 2013 from http://www.state.gov/m/ds/rls/rpt/19782.htm

U.S. Department of State. (2013a). Current travel warnings. Retrieved December 19, 2013 from http://travel.state.gov/travel/cis_pa_tw/tw/tw_1764.html

U.S. Department of State. (2013b). International travel. Retrieved December 19, 2013 from http://travel.state.gov/travel/

U.S. Department of State. (2013c). Travel warning: Mexico, July 12, 2013. Retrieved December 19, 2013 from http://travel.state.gov/travel/cis_pa_tw/tw/tw_6033.html

Veitch, G. (2013, December 12). Letter to the editor. *Saratoga Wire*. Retrieved December 18, 2013 from http://www.saratogawire.com/article/1780/131216-police-homeless/

Violence Prevention. (2013). Retrieved December 16, 2013 from http://www.cdc.gov/ViolencePrevention/

VIPS Program Analysis. (2013). 2013 Volunteers in Police Service program analysis of registered volunteer law enforcement programs. Retrieved January 18, 2014 from http://www.policevolunteers.org/files/2013_Analysis_Results_Report.pdf

Volunteer Profiles. (2013). Herb Hamby: Modesto, California, Police Department. Retrieved December 12, 2013 from http://www.policevolunteers.org/vips_action/?fa = volunteer_profiles

Warren, G. A. (1999). *Police academy training for 21st century law enforcement*. Dover, DE: Delaware Law Enforcement Institute.

Welch, W. M. and Hoyer, M. (2013, December 15). 30 mass killings, 137 victims: A typical year. *USA Today*. Retrieved December 16, 2013 from http://www.usa-today.com/story/news/nation/2013/12/15/mass-killings-main/3821897/

White House. (2013). Immigration: Creating an immigration system for the 21st century. Retrieved December 18, 2013 from http://www.whitehouse.gov/issues/immigration

Wolf, R. and Russo, C. (2005). Utilizing reserves: Getting the most from your volunteers. *Campus Law Enforcement Journal, 35*(3), 24–28.

Worton, S. (2003, September). *Volunteers in police work: A study of the benefits to law enforcement agencies. An applied research project submitted as part of the School of Police Staff and Command Program.* Eastern Michigan University. Retrieved January 20, 2014 from http://www.emich.edu/cerns/downloads/papers/PoliceStaff/Police%20Personnel%20(e.g.,%20%20Selection,%20%20Promotion)/Volunteers%20in%20Police%20Work.pdf

# Epilogue

Readers of this book may want to know more about volunteer policing, how to improve an existing program, or even how to start a volunteer police unit. The acquisition and study of some basic reading materials are essential, including the following works: Everett M. King's *The Auxiliary Police Unit* (Charles C. Thomas, 1960), 215 pages; Elizabeth C. Bartels' *Volunteer Police in the United States* (Springer, 2014), 44 pages; Ross Wolf and Carol Jones' Volunteer Police: Choosing to serve (CRC Press, 2015); and the Federal Emergency Management Agency's *The Citizen Corps Volunteer Liability Guide,* 100 pages.

King's book, although quite outdated, presents a well-ordered guide covering nearly every aspect of organizing a functional unit and is invaluable for an administrator planning such an institution. A special order, 230-page paperback edition of this work became available in May 2012. (It is published by Literary Licensing, LLC.) Bartels' book is available in both e-book and softcover formats. It can serve as an overview of the challenges facing volunteer policing units. It also contains examples of international volunteer police programs to provide recommendations and best practices. FEMA's guide provides an overview of liability concerns and suggests approaches to address these concerns. It is a free publication available at: http://www.ready.gov/guides. The material in this guide is offered for general information purposes only. It does not provide legal advice, and the user is encouraged to seek out state-specific counsel from a qualified attorney before taking any action. Chapter 10 contains additional information about the guide.

In 1993, Richard Weinblatt's 250-page book—*Reserve Law Enforcement in the United States: A National Study of State, County, and City Standards Concerning the Training & Numbers of Non-full-time Police and Sheriff's Personnel was published.* It provides an overview of the numbers, training standards, and rules governing full-time, part-time, and volunteer law enforcement officers in the United States based on research conducted prior to 1993. Dr. Weinblatt is the dean of the School of Public and Social Services and the School of Education at Ivy Tech Community College based in Indianapolis. Additional information about his background and publications is available at: http://www.thecopdoc.com/index.html.

The next step in preparation for a new volunteer police program or for updating an existing program is to engage in networking with other concerned persons. The annual training conference of the California Reserve

Peace Officers Association (CRPOA) is highly recommended. In August 2013, the CRPOA held a four-day training conference in San Jose with more than 300 reserve officers and coordinators in attendance. Topics covered included building searches, understanding street gangs, identity theft, crimes against children, search and seizure, and officer safety. The conference also included an eight-hour Reserve Coordinator Introduction class for newer reserve coordinators that was followed the next day by a four-hour Reserve Coordinator Update class for experienced coordinators. Nearly 50 attendees participated in the two classes, which provided information and discussions on reserve training, reserve levels, selection standards, training requirements, and recruitment. The CRPOA's 2014 annual conference was held in San Diego. CRPOA's training programs are open to volunteers in policing, search and rescue members, and reserve and full-time peace officers. The knowledge gained by conference attendance is useful to persons not only from California but from other states as well (C. Adams, personal communication, January 29, 2014).

Finally, concerned readers should routinely refer to the newly revised Web pages of the IACP VIPS program which can be found at http://www.theiacp.org/VIPS. The site contains hundreds of useful documents dealing with the management of citizens who have volunteered to participate in crime prevention programs, such as volunteer police. This important Web resource includes examples of volunteer program manuals; position descriptions; and screening, waiver, and confidentiality forms. Many of these documents should be of special interest to new program developers as well as the coordinators and members of existing units of volunteer police.

# Appendix A:
# The Commission on Accreditation for Law Enforcement Agencies Reserve and Auxiliary Police Standards

Appendix A contains sections 16.3 and 16.4 from the *Standards for Law Enforcement Agencies* along with the manual's definition of "reserve" and "auxiliary." The Commission on Accreditation for Law Enforcement Agencies, Inc. (CALEA®), is the registered copyright holder and publisher of this information. The material is from *Standards for Law Enforcement Agencies*, ©2006, update 5.17 from August 2013. All rights are reserved. Permission has been granted to reprint these standards and definitions.

## Reserve

A sworn officer, armed or unarmed, who works less than full time, with or without compensation, and who, by their assigned function or as implied by their uniform, performs duties associated with those of a police officer.

## Auxiliary

A non-sworn, unarmed, uniformed or non-uniformed, affiliate whose duties contribute to the mission of the agency in a support capacity. Included are police volunteers, law enforcement cadets, law enforcement explorers, senior citizen groups, and other volunteers. Excluded are part-time paid employees of the agency and reserve officers.

### 16.3.1 Program Description

A written directive establishes and describes the agency's reserve officer program.

> **Commentary:** Terminology describing reserve officers can vary from jurisdiction to jurisdiction and for the purpose of this manual,

the glossary term will be used. Reserve officers generally assist full-time sworn personnel in the day-to-day delivery of law enforcement services and for emergencies, consistent with applicable law. To accomplish these tasks, they may require law enforcement powers equivalent to those of full-time officers. The directive should describe the duties and responsibilities of reserve officers, define their authority and discretion in carrying out their duties, including any limitations or restrictions to this authority, and delineate the amount of supervision they are to receive.

**Commission Interpretation (November 16, 2001).** The Commission acknowledges that some agencies utilize reserve officers who do not meet the definition of an "employee." For example, some agencies utilize volunteer reserve officers and the absence of wages or salary excludes them from the definition. For the purpose of this Standards Manual, all reserve officers shall be considered "employees" when applying standards dealing with performance evaluations. Procedures and forms used for evaluating the performance of the agency's reserve officers may be the same as those used for full-time sworn officers or they may differ significantly, based on distinctions made in the role, scope of authority, or responsibilities of the reserve officer.

## 16.3.2 Selection Criteria

Excluding the educational requirements for reserve officers, the selection criteria for reserves relating to knowledge, skills, and abilities are the same as that for full-time officers.

> **Commentary:** Experience, physical condition, and other job-related selection criteria applicable to full-time officers apply equally to reserves. The process of selection may be different from that of full-time officers, but the criteria are the same, with the exception of educational requirements which are addressed in 16.3.9. —Change Notice 5.7 (November 20, 2009)

## 16.3.3 Entry Level Training

The agency requires all sworn reserve officers to complete a recruit academy training program comparable to that required in standard 33.4.1, prior to any routine assignment in any capacity in which the reserve officer is allowed to carry a weapon or is in a position to make an arrest, except as part of a formal field training program required in standard 33.4.3. If the agency restricts or prohibits reserves from performing specific functions, topics related to those functions may be omitted from the curriculum.

> **Commentary:** The intent of this standard is to ensure that reserve officers receive training equal to that required of full-time officers in those areas of assigned duties and responsibilities. The training should be the same as that received by full-time officers or an equivalent, parallel course that meets the requirements of standard 33.4.1. The subject matter in the training program should over topics related to assigned duties and responsibilities to the same extent that full-time officers are trained to perform like functions. Training hours and schedule may vary to accommodate the reserve schedule and the course duration may be extended.
>
> If a comparable recruit-training program for reserves exists in the state, successful completion of this program may fulfill the requirements of this standard.

> **Commission Interpretation (March 14, 2008):** If the reserve officer state certification training does not include critical task training identified by CALEA for the responsibilities performed by the reserve officer, such training must be delivered. Those critical tasks include: Community Interaction; Introduction to Basic Law; Post Crime Considerations; Introduction to Traffic; Field Activities; Use of Force; First Aid for Criminal Justice Officers; Law Enforcement Vehicle Operations; and Personnel. Further information regarding critical tasks may be found on the CALEA website.

## 16.3.4 Uniforms and Equipment

Uniforms and equipment for reserve officers are the same as those for full-time officers who perform such functions.

> **Commentary:** Equipment and uniforms for reserve officers, except for insignia, patches, or badges, should not be distinguishable from those of full-time officers. However, quantity of uniforms and equipment may be reduced to reflect the level of activity of reserve officers. The purchase of equipment/uniforms may be the responsibility of the reserve officer.

## 16.3.5 In-Service Training

Reserve officers receive in-service training equivalent to that statutorily required for full time officers performing such functions.

> **Commentary:** None.

### 16.3.6  Use of Force Training & Firearms Proficiency

Reserve officers are trained in use of force policy(ies) and tested for weapons proficiency with the same frequency as full-time officers in accordance with standard 1.3.11.

> **Commentary:** Reserve officers' schedules may not permit participation in regularly scheduled weapons training. They should qualify either as a part of the regularly scheduled program or in a special reserve qualifications program. Qualifying standards and scores for reserve officers should be Identical to those for regular officers.

### 16.3.7  Bonding/Liability Protection

Reserve officers are bonded and/or provided with public liability protection equal to that provided to full-time officers.

> **Commentary:** The protection attached to the functions of full-time officers should be provided to reserve officers.

### 16.3.8  Performance Evaluations

A written directive requires performance evaluations for reserve officers be conducted in accordance with the standards in (Chapter 35 Performance Evaluation).

> **Commentary:** None.

### 16.3.9  Educational Requirements

Reserve officers possess high school equivalency diplomas and meet all state educational requirements at the time of sworn appointment.

> **Commentary:** Education is an important attribute for both full-time officers and reserve officers. Careful consideration should be given to the function and responsibilities of reserve officers before establishing educational criteria that differ from that of full-time officers. —Change Notice 5.7 (November 20, 2009)

### 16.4.1  Program Description

A written directive establishes and describes the agency's auxiliary program, to include:

> *a. a statement that auxiliaries are not sworn officers; and*
> *b. a description of the duties of auxiliaries, including their role and scope of authority.*

**Commentary:** Auxiliaries are not commissioned as law enforcement officers and do not have the authority to make a full custody arrest. Auxiliaries may be assigned to law enforcement–related community service functions. They can also be used as a resource in emergencies and large-scale special events. Generally, they receive significantly less training than sworn officers or full-time employees. However, if the agency chooses to involve them in various activities to assist in the day-to-day delivery of law enforcement services, it should ensure that their duties do not require the status of a sworn officer, their level of training is adjusted according to the scope of their authority, and that unauthorized weapons or equipment are not carried in the performance of their duties.

## 16.4.2 Training

Auxiliaries receive training in those authorized and assigned duties.

**Commentary:** Auxiliaries may provide services to support any law enforcement duties not requiring sworn officer status. However, if the agency chooses to use them, auxiliaries should receive training appropriate to the duties anticipated.

## 16.4.3 Uniforms

If auxiliaries wear uniforms, the uniforms clearly distinguish them from sworn officers.

**Commentary:** To have an auxiliary appear to be a regularly sworn officer can be hazardous to the auxiliary, confusing to the public, and a potential detriment to the image of the agency. Unless the auxiliary is clearly distinguishable from the sworn officer, members of the community may expect assistance in situations for which the auxiliary is not trained or empowered to act. Purchase of the uniform may be the responsibility of the auxiliary, **compliance may be OBSERVED.**

# Appendix B: Modern Era National Service Time Line

| | |
|---|---|
| 1960s | **Retired Senior Volunteer Program (RSVP); Foster Grandparent Program; Senior Companion Program** <br> Demonstration projects launched for these three programs to demonstrate the effectiveness of the service model and to engage older Americans in a range of service activities. |
| 1964 | **VISTA (Volunteers in Service to America)** <br> Created by President Lyndon B. Johnson as a part of the "War on Poverty." |
| 1970s | **Senior Service Programs + Peace Corps + VISTA = The ACTION Agency** |
| 1973 | **Domestic Volunteer Service Act of 1973** <br> RSVP, Foster Grandparent Program, and Senior Companion Program become authorized through this act. |
| 1989 | **Points of Light Foundation** <br> President George H.W. Bush creates the Office of National Service in the White House and the Points of Light Foundation to foster volunteering. |
| 1990 | **National and Community Service Act of 1990** <br> Signed by President Bush, the legislation authorizes grants to schools to support service-learning through Serve America and demonstration grants. Learn and Serve America is created. |
| 1992 | **AmeriCorps National Civilian Community Corps (NCCC) created** |
| 1993 | **Corporation for National and Community Service created** <br> AmeriCorps created; Senior Corps incorporates the three senior-focused programs: Foster Grandparents, Senior Companions, and RSVP. |
| 1994 | **King Holiday and Service Act of 1994** <br> Congress establishes MLK Day as a national day of service. |
| 2002 | **2002 State of the Union Address** <br> After 9/11, President George W. Bush asks all Americans to devote two years or 4,000 hours to volunteer service during their lifetimes. |
| 2006 | **President's Higher Education Community Service Honor Roll** <br> Launched by CNCS to honor the nation's top college and universities for their commitment to community service, civic engagement, and service learning. |
| 2007 | **First Annual AmeriCorps Week** <br> Officially launched in May 2007. |
| 2009 | **Edward M. Kennedy Serve America Act signed** <br> April 21, 2009: President Barack Obama signs bipartisan law to expand and strengthen national service programs. |
| 2009 | **First Annual September 11th Day of Service and Remembrance** |

*Continued*

| | |
|---|---|
| **2010** | **Social Innovation Fund launched** |
| | Ensures that high-impact nonprofits are able to attract the resources they need to grow and improve the economic, education, and health prospects of low-income communities. |
| **2011** | **5-Year Strategic Plan** |
| | The plan details specific objectives, strategies, and performance measures, which determine how CNCS will evaluate success over the next five years. |
| **2012** | **FEMA Corps launched** |
| | An innovative new partnership designed to strengthen the nation's ability to respond to and recover from disasters while expanding career opportunities for young people. |

*Source:*  http://www.nationalservice.gov/about/who-we-are/our-history/national-service-timeline

# Appendix C: Preventing Terrorist Attacks

## How You Can Help

This is a message that bears repeating, no matter where you live in the world: Your assistance is needed in preventing terrorist acts.

It is a fact that certain kinds of activities can indicate terrorist plans that are in the works, especially when they occur at or near high-profile sites or places where large numbers of people gather—such as government buildings, military facilities, utilities, bus or train stations, and major public events. If you see or know about suspicious activities, such as the ones listed below, please report them immediately to the proper authorities. In the United States, that means your closest Joint Terrorist Task Force, located in an FBI field office. In other countries, that means your closest law enforcement/counterterrorism agency.

**Surveillance:** Are you aware of anyone video recording or monitoring activities, taking notes, using cameras, maps, binoculars, and so on, near key facilities/events?

**Suspicious Questioning:** Are you aware of anyone attempting to gain information in person, by phone, mail, email, and so on, regarding a key facility or people who work there?

**Tests of Security:** Are you aware of any attempts to penetrate or test physical security or procedures at a key facility/event?

**Acquiring Supplies:** Are you aware of anyone attempting to improperly acquire explosives, weapons, ammunition, dangerous chemicals, uniforms, badges, flight manuals, access cards or identification for a key facility/event or to legally obtain items under suspicious circumstances that could be used in a terrorist attack?

**Suspicious Persons:** Are you aware of anyone who does not appear to belong in the workplace, neighborhood, business establishment, or near a key facility/event?

**"Dry Runs":** Have you observed any behavior that appears to be preparation for a terrorist act, such as mapping out routes, playing out scenarios with other people, monitoring key facilities/events, timing traffic lights or traffic flow, or other suspicious activities?

**Deploying Assets:** Have you observed abandoned vehicles, stockpiling of suspicious materials, or persons being deployed near a key facility/event?

If you answered yes to any of the above ... if you have observed any suspicious activity that may relate to terrorism ... again, please contact the Joint Terrorist Task Force or law enforcement/counterterrorism agency closest to you immediately. Your tip could save the lives of innocent people, just like you and yours.

*Source:* https://www.fbi.gov/about-us/investigate/terrorism/help-prevent-terrorist-attacks

# Appendix D: Selected Government Internship Opportunities with Federal Government Intelligence Agencies and Law Enforcement Agencies

| Agency Name | Opportunity | Web Sites |
|---|---|---|
| **Central Intelligence Agency** www.cia.gov | Undergraduate student internships or undergraduate co-ops, and graduate studies programs are available. | https://www.cia.gov/careers/student-opportunities/index.html |
| **Department of Energy, Office of Intelligence and Counterintelligence** www.energy.gov | **The DOE Scholars Program:** For students or recent college graduates. | http://orise.orau.gov/doescholars |
| **Department of Homeland Security, Intelligence and Analysis** www.dhs.gov | **Secretary's Honors Program (SHP):** For exceptional recent graduates. | http://www.dhs.gov/secretarys-honors-program |
| | **CBP Explorer Program:** For young men and women aged 14 through 21 who assist the border patrol law enforcement mission. | http://www.cbp.gov/careers/outreach-programs/youth/explorer-program |
| | **Student Internship and Training Opportunities and Job Opportunities for Recent Graduates** | http://www.dhs.gov/student-opportunities-0 http://www.dhs.gov/job-opportunities-recent-graduates |
| | **DHS Education Programs:** A 10-week summer research experience for undergraduate students majoring in DHS-related science, technology, engineering and mathematics (HS-STEM) disciplines. | http://www.orau.gov/dhseducation/ |

*Continued*

| Agency Name | Opportunity | Web Sites |
|---|---|---|
| **Department of State, Intelligence and Research** www.state.gov | **Student Programs:** U.S. Department of State Internship Program and Pathways Programs. The U.S. Department of State offers two programs: one for high school, undergraduates; and another for graduate and postgraduate students who are interested in working in a foreign affairs environment. | http://careers.state.gov/ intern |
| **Department of Treasury, Office of Intelligence and Analysis** www.treasury.gov | **Pathways Programs:** Developed by the Office of Personnel Management (OPM) to reform the student hiring programs across the government. There are three main hiring options: Internship Program, Recent Graduate Program, and the Presidential Management Fellows (PMF) Program | http://www.treasury.gov/ careers/Pages/ pathways-programs.aspx |
| **Defense Intelligence Agency** www.dia.mil | **Academic Semester Internship Program:** For full-time undergraduate seniors and graduate students **Cooperative Education Program:** Opportunity to gain valuable work experience. **National Intelligence Scholars Program:** For the most well-qualified college graduates. | http://www.dia.mil/careers/ students/ |
| **Drug Enforcement Administration** www.justice.gov/dea | Students must be able to meet all DEA employment requirements. For information on student employment opportunities, call 202-307-4088. | http://www.justice.gov/dea/ careers/student-entry-level. shtml |
| **Federal Bureau of Investigation** www.fbi.gov | **Honors Internship Program:** FBI paid student internship opportunity. | https://www.fbijobs.gov/231. asp |
| | **Volunteer Internship Program** (non paid): For undergraduates (junior or senior), graduates, or post doctorate students. | https://www.fbijobs.gov/239. asp |
| | **Laboratory Division's Visiting Scientist Program:** Students, postgraduates, and university faculty are eligible to apply for this FBI program. | https://www.fbijobs.gov/242. asp |

*Continued*

| Agency Name | Opportunity | Web Sites |
|---|---|---|
| **National Security Agency** www.nsa.gov | **NSA internships:** Various types including co-op, scholarships, and work study for undergraduates and graduate students. | http://www.nsa.gov/careers/ opportunities_4_u/students/ undergraduate/index.shtml http://www.nsa.gov/careers/ opportunities_4_u/students/ graduate/index.shtml |

*Source:* Adapted from http://www.umuc.edu/students/support/careerservices/jobsearch/ internships/upload/Federal-Government-Student-Internship.pdf

# Appendix E: Human Trafficking—A Brief Annotated Bibliography

## Books

Aronowitz, A. A. (2013). *Human Trafficking, Human Misery*. Lanham, MD: Scarecrow Press. 304 pp. Paperback book.

> The book takes a victim-oriented approach to examine the criminals and criminal organizations that traffic in and exploit their victims. The author focuses on the different groups of victims and the various forms of and markets for trafficking, many of which remain overlooked including organ trafficking, child soldiers, mail-order brides, and adoption, as well as the use of the Internet in trafficking.

Bales, K. and Soodalter, R. (2009). *The Slave Next Door: Human Trafficking and Slavery in America Today*. Berkeley, CA: University of California Press. 320 pp. Hardcover book.

> This work contains information about modern-day slaves, slaveholders, and traffickers as well as from experts, counselors, law enforcement officers, rescue and support groups, and others. It explores what private citizens can do to subdue this horrific crime.

DeStefano, A. M. (2008). *The War on Human Trafficking: U.S. Policy Assessed*. New Brunswick, NJ: Rutgers University Press. 208 pp. Paperback book.

> This book considers cases involving the forced labor of immigrants and details the events leading up to the creation of the Trafficking Victims Protection Act of 2000, the federal law that first addressed the phenomenon of human trafficking. The author assesses the effectiveness of the 2000 law and its progeny, showing the difficulties encountered by federal prosecutors in building criminal cases against traffickers.

Gallagher, A. T. (2012). *The International Law of Human Trafficking*. Cambridge, UK: Cambridge University Press. 596 pp. Paperback book.

> This book by a leading international legal authority on the issue presents the key norms of international human rights law, transnational criminal law, refugee law, and international criminal law, in the process identifying and explaining the major legal obligations of states with respect to preventing trafficking, protecting and supporting victims, and prosecuting perpetrators.

Powell, C. and Burroughs, D. (2011). *Not in My Town: Exposing and Ending Human Trafficking and Modern Day Slavery*. Birmingham, AL: New Hope Publishers. 192 pp. Paperback book.

    This work includes a DVD dealing with human trafficking, sex exploitation, forced labor, and agricultural slavers. Cases from U.S. cities as well as from Amsterdam, India, Cambodia, and other regions are reviewed. (To hear an 18-minute interview with coauthor Charles Powell, go to: http://www. newhopedigital.com/2012/09/charles-powell-not-in-my-town.)

Simon, R. J. and Hepburn, S. (2013). *Human Trafficking Around the World: Hidden in Plain Sight*. New York: Columbia University Press. 552 pp. Paperback book.

    The authors recount the lives of victims during and after their experience with trafficking, and they follow the activities of traffickers before capture and their outcomes after sentencing. Each chapter centers on the trafficking practices and anti-trafficking measures of a single country, 24 in all. This study points out those most vulnerable in each nation and the specific cultural, economic, environmental, and geopolitical factors that contribute to each nation's trafficking issues. The authors set forth clear policy recommendations to combat trafficking.

# Videos

*Human Trafficking in the U.S.* (2013, September 23). 2 hrs. 49 min.

    This C-SPAN coverage is of a hearing held before the U.S. Senate Committee on Homeland Security and Government Affairs. Federal, state, local, and tribal officials testified on their efforts to combat human trafficking within the United States. The State Department reported that nearly 20,000 people were trafficked to the United States for prostitution, domestic servitude, and other related crimes. Among the issues addressed in the hearing were the causes of human trafficking, identifying victims, intervention and treatment of victims, and the impact on local communities. (View online at: http:// www.c-spanvideo.org/program/Traffickingint.)

*Affected for Life* (2014). 24 min. approx.

    Produced by the United Nations Office on Drugs and Crime (UNODC), this is a training and awareness-raising video on human trafficking. The film is targeted at prosecutors, judges, law enforcement officers, and other specialized audiences, and it illustrates the elements and different forms of human trafficking. The film is available in full-length with abbreviated versions in Arabic, English, French, Russian, and Spanish. The UNODC has enlisted the help of prominent personalities from the worlds of art, music, film, sports, and literature to highlight key issues and to draw attention to UNODC activities in the fight against illicit drugs and international crime. These goodwill ambassadors include Mira Sorvino (actress), Nicolas Cage (actor), Ross Bleckner (artist), Christopher Kennedy Lawford (activist), and Shahid Afridi (cricket star/athlete). (View online at: http://www.unodc.org/ unodc/en/human-trafficking/video-and-audio-on-human-trafficking-and-migrant-smuggling.html?ref = menuside#training_film.)

*Victim, Survivor, Leader: Empowering CSE and Trafficked Youth* (2013, October 16).
39 min. approx.

Rachel Lloyd, who has spent 15 years as the CEO of Girls Educational and Mentoring Services (GEMS), discusses direct services to survivors of commercial sexual exploitation and trafficking. Her talk highlights GEMS' groundbreaking "Victim, Survivor, Leader model," and she explores the stages of healing for victims of trafficking and the core principles for providing services at each stage. Lloyd is a nationally recognized expert on the issue of child sex trafficking in the United States and played a key role in the successful passage of New York State's groundbreaking Safe Harbor Act for Sexually Exploited Youth, the first law in the country to end the prosecution of child victims of sex trafficking. Her trailblazing advocacy is the subject of the critically acclaimed documentary *Very Young Girls* (Showtime 2007) and her memoir *Girls Like Us* (Harper Collins 2011). (View online at: http://www.youtube.com/watch?v=jGy9MxEOxX0.)

# Index

# Inhaled Delivery Systems for the Treatment of Asthma and COPD

Inhaled therapies form the cornerstone for treatment of patients with asthma and COPD. Evolving technology has resulted in availability of a wide range of devices for delivery of inhaled drugs. The four different delivery systems – pressurized metered-dose inhalers, slow mist inhalers, dry powder inhalers, and nebulizers – are unique in design and require distinct inhalational instructions for correct use. This book provides current information about inhalation devices, including their advantages and disadvantages, with guidance for optimal techniques of use. The book emphasizes appropriate selection of inhalation devices based on patient and health care professional factors, as well as device attributes that allow selection of the right medication in the right inhalation device at the right time for the right patient.

**Key features:**

- Addresses the objective of precision medicine – the right medication in the right inhaler device at the right time.

- Inputs by international thought leaders who have published widely on inhaled medications and/or inhaled delivery systems for clinicians, trainees, and respiratory therapists.

- Discusses the development of audio-based systems and smart inhalers for patient monitoring.

T0139074

# Inhaled Delivery Systems for the Treatment of Asthma and COPD

Edited By

## Donald A. Mahler, MD
Emeritus Professor of Medicine
Geisel School of Medicine at Dartmouth
Hanover, New Hampshire, USA

Director of Respiratory Services
Valley Regional Hospital
Claremont, New Hampshire, USA

## Rajiv Dhand, MD
Professor and Wahid T. Hanna MD Endowed Chair
Department of Medicine
Associate Dean of Clinical Affairs
University of Tennessee Graduate School of Medicine
Knoxville, Tennessee, USA

CRC Press
Taylor & Francis Group
Boca Raton London New York

CRC Press is an imprint of the
Taylor & Francis Group, an **informa** business

CRC Press
Boca Raton and London

First edition published 2023
by CRC Press
6000 Broken Sound Parkway NW, Suite 300, Boca Raton, FL 33487-2742

and by CRC Press
4 Park Square, Milton Park, Abingdon, Oxon, OX14 4RN

*CRC Press is an imprint of Taylor & Francis Group, LLC*

© 2023 selection and editorial matter, Donald A. Mahler and Rajiv Dhand; individual chapters, the contributors

### Library of Congress Cataloging-in-Publication Data

Names: Mahler, Donald A., editor. | Dhand, Rajiv, editor.
Title: Inhaled delivery systems for the treatment of asthma and COPD /
edited by Donald A. Mahler, Rajiv Dhand.
Description: First edition. | Boca Raton : CRC Press, 2023. | Includes bibliographical
references and index.
Identifiers: LCCN 2023000038 (print) | LCCN 2023000039 (ebook) |
ISBN 9781032215730 (paperback) | ISBN 9781032215747 (hardback) |
ISBN 9781003269014 (ebook)
Subjects: MESH: Asthma--drug therapy | Pulmonary Disease, Chronic Obstructive--drug
therapy | Administration, Inhalation | Respiratory Therapy--methods | Nebulizers and
Vaporizers | Aerosols
Classification: LCC RC591 (print) | LCC RC591 (ebook) | NLM WF 648 |
DDC 616.2/38061--dc23/eng/20230505
LC record available at https://lccn.loc.gov/2023000038
LC ebook record available at https://lccn.loc.gov/2023000039

ISBN: 978-1-032-21574-7 (hbk)
ISBN: 978-1-032-21573-0 (pbk)
ISBN: 978-1-003-26901-4 (ebk)

DOI: 10.1201/9781003269014

Typeset in Palatino
by KnowledgeWorks Global Ltd.

# Table of Contents

## Foreword

Inhalation is the preferred route of administration of nearly all medications for the treatment of asthma and COPD via various hand-held devices or nebulizer systems. While hand-held devices are commonly used because of their relative simplicity and convenience, technical challenges to their correct use are frequently not met, resulting in ineffective delivery of these medications to the lungs, thus undermining their clinical benefit. Nebulizer systems for medication delivery, while less convenient than hand-held devices, are most often used in the hospital and emergency room settings and serve as valuable alternatives to hand-held devices in outpatients who are unable to master the technical challenges to their effective use. Asthma and COPD affect hundreds of millions of people worldwide, and COPD is the third leading cause of death globally, underscoring the vital importance of effective delivery of inhaled medications.

Drs. Donald A. Mahler and Rajiv Dhand, two widely recognized and highly respected authorities on inhaled delivery systems with whom I have had the distinct privilege to serve in various committees and conferences related to aerosol therapy, have assembled an international group of distinguished experts to contribute to their book a total of 14 chapters covering a wide range of key topics relevant to inhaled delivery systems for treating asthma and COPD, in addition to other respiratory diseases (cystic fibrosis, bronchiectasis, and pulmonary hypertension) responsive to a variety of medications deliverable by the inhaled route.

Their book is an up-to-date and comprehensive review of the mechanics and technical aspects of differing inhaled delivery systems, the requirements for their optimal use by both adult and pediatric patients, their relative advantages and disadvantages depending on host characteristics, their use in different clinical settings and for the treatment of different respiratory disorders, the ongoing development of "smart" inhalers utilizing advanced digital technology to optimize delivery technique, patient adherence, and the physician-patient relationship, and practical issues regarding cost and patient access in the current regulatory environment. As such, the book serves as a uniquely valuable resource for a variety of health care professionals, as well as inhalational device manufacturers.

*Donald P. Tashkin, MD, FCCP, ATSF*
*Distinguished Emeritus Professor of Medicine*
*Division of Pulmonary and Critical Care Medicine, Clinical Immunology & Allergy*
*David Geffen School of Medicine at UCLA*

# About the Editors

**Donald A. Mahler (MD, FCCP)** is Emeritus Professor of Medicine at Geisel School of Medicine at Dartmouth in Hanover, New Hampshire. He currently works as a pulmonary physician at Valley Regional Hospital in Claremont, New Hampshire, where he is Director of Respiratory Services.

His research interests include the evaluation/treatment of dyspnea and clinical outcomes in COPD. Under the mentorship of the late Alvin Feinstein, MD, Dr. Mahler developed and established the psychometric properties of the interviewer-administered baseline and transition dyspnea indexes (BDI/TDI), which have been translated into over 80 languages. The BDI/TDI have been used as an outcome measure in phase 3 clinical trials involving medications approved by the Food and Drug Administration and/or the European Medicines Agency for treatment of patients with COPD. These include Serevent®, Spriva®, Advair®, Brovana®, Tudorza®, Daliresp®, Arcapta®, Ultibro®, Anoro®, Striverdi®, Stiolto®, Utibron®, and Yupelri®.

In collaboration with the late John C. Baird, PhD, the interviewer administered BDI/TDI were converted into self-administered and computerized (SAC) versions, enabling patients to provide a direct rating of breathlessness during daily activities. The SAC versions have been translated into 12 languages and have been included as an outcome measure in phase 3 and 4 clinical trials evaluating therapies for patients with interstitial lung disease and COPD.

Dr. Mahler has authored/co-authored over 180 original research articles and over 100 editorials, book chapters, and non-peer-reviewed articles. In addition, he has written/edited four books on dyspnea.

In June 2014, he created the website, https://www.donaldmahler.com, with the vision "to positively affect the daily lives of those with COPD and their families." In February 2015, Dr. Mahler authored *COPD: Answers to Your Questions* (Two Harbors Press) to address the common questions posed by those with COPD, family members, and their caregivers. In January 2022, he wrote *COPD: Answers to Your Most Pressing Questions about Chronic Obstructive Pulmonary Disease* (Johns Hopkins University Press).

**Dr. Rajiv Dhand** (MD, FCCP, FACP, FAARC, FRSM, ATSF) serves as Professor of Medicine with tenure, the Wahid T. Hanna MD Endowed Chair of the Department of Medicine, Service Chief of the Medical Service and Associate Dean of Clinical Affairs at the University of Tennessee, Graduate School of Medicine in Knoxville, TN. Previously, he served as Division Director of Pulmonary, Critical Care, and Environmental Medicine at the University of Missouri. He is a Past President of the International Society of Aerosols in Medicine (ISAM).

Dr. Dhand is a skilled pulmonologist who is internationally recognized for his work on inhaled therapies. He helped to establish the scientific basis for the use of metered-dose inhalers in mechanically ventilated patients. He was an invited member of several Task Forces that developed Guidelines on Aerosolization of Medication that were published in *CHEST*, *European Respiratory Journal*, and *Journal of Aerosol Medicine and Pulmonary Drug Delivery*.

Dr. Dhand served as a principal investigator on many clinical trials over the past 20 years, principally related to bronchodilator therapy in patients with chronic obstructive pulmonary disease (COPD). His experience includes studies in experimental, translational, and clinical research and he is the recipient of several research grants during his career.

Dr. Dhand has been awarded Fellowships of the American College of Physicians, American College of Chest Physicians, American Thoracic Society, Royal Society of Medicine, American Association of Respiratory Care, and International Society of Aerosols in Medicine. He is Editor-in-Chief of the *ISAM Textbook of Aerosol Medicine*. Dr. Dhand has held multiple editorial appointments including *CHEST, Journal of Aerosol Medicine and Pulmonary Drug Delivery, Respiratory Care*, and *International Journal of COPD*. He is the Respiratory Section editor for *Advances in Therapy* and US Editor-in-Chief of *Pulmonary Therapy* Journal. He has published over 170 articles in peer-reviewed journals and has lectured at a host of national and international venues. He remains actively engaged in clinical practice as well as teaching and training medical students, internal medicine residents, and pulmonary/critical care medicine fellows.

# Contributors

**Israel Amirav**
Professor
Pediatric Pulmonology Unit
Dana-Dwek Children's Hospital
Tel Aviv Medical Center
Tel Aviv University
Tel Aviv, Israel

**Isaac N. Biney**
Assistant Professor
Division of Pulmonary and Critical
    Care Medicine
Graduate School of Medicine
Knoxville, Tennessee

**Rajiv Dhand**
Professor of Medicine
Wahid T. Hanna MD Endowed
    Chair of Medicine
Associate Dean of Clinical Affairs
Graduate School of Medicine
Knoxville, Tennessee

**Myrna B. Dolovich**
Professor of Medicine (Part-time)
McMaster University
Head, Firestone Research Aerosol Lab
Affiliate, Research Institute of St Joes
St Joseph's Hospital, Hamilton
Ontario, Canada

**Alexander G. Duarte**
Professor
Pulmonary, Critical Care and Sleep
    Medicine
University of Texas Medical Branch
Galveston, Texas

**Mahmoud M. Ibrahim**
Pulmonary, Critical Care and Sleep
    Medicine
University of Texas Medical Branch
Galveston, Texas

**Jie Li**
Department of Cardiopulmonary
    Sciences
Division of Respiratory Care
Rush University
Chicago, Illinois

**Bruce K. Rubin**
Distinguished Professor of Pediatrics
    and Biomedical Engineering
Virginia Eminent Scholar in
    Pediatrics
Virginia Commonwealth University
    School of Medicine
Richmond, Virginia

**Francisco J. Soto**
Associate Professor of Medicine
Director, Pulmonary Vascular
    Disease
Division of Pulmonary and Critical
    Care Medicine
Graduate School of Medicine
Knoxville, Tennessee

**Paul D. Terry**
Professor
Department of Medicine
Graduate School of Medicine
Knoxville, Tennessee

# Introduction

*Donald A. Mahler and Rajiv Dhand*

Inhaled therapies are the cornerstone of treatment for individuals with asthma and COPD. To be effective, patients need to inhale the medication deep into the lower respiratory tract to activate receptors that dilate airways or reduce airway inflammation. Although both the specific molecule(s) and the delivery system are important for effective therapy, the major focus by professional respiratory organizations and pharmaceutical companies has been on development and promotion of specific molecule(s). Unfortunately, there has been limited guidance on the selection of the most appropriate inhaled delivery system for the individual patient. The four different delivery systems – pressurized metered-dose inhalers, slow mist inhalers, dry powder inhalers, and nebulizers – are unique in design and require distinct inhalational instructions for correct use by patients.

The purpose of writing this book is to address an important, but neglected topic: What should health care professionals consider when selecting an inhaled delivery system for an individual with asthma or COPD? A new resource is needed for several reasons:

1. Increased awareness of the high prevalence of incorrect inhalational technique among users.

2. The unique features of the four different inhaled delivery systems.

3. Emerging evidence that various patient factors (e.g., age, sex, cognitive function, manual dexterity, and peak inspiratory flow) affect optimal use of the inhaled delivery system.

4. The development of audio-based and digital systems for monitoring correct inhaler technique.

This book addresses the objective of precision medicine – selecting the right medication *in the right inhalation device* at the right time. The 14 chapters provide guidance for health care professionals to match an inhaled delivery system with the individual patient who has asthma and/or COPD. Moreover, this information enhances understanding about the appropriate use and care of inhaled delivery systems. Finally, we hope that the contents of the book provide a springboard for addressing new research questions.

# 1 Principles of Inhaled Therapy

*Omar S. Usmani and Federico Lavorini*

CONTENTS

## INTRODUCTION

Delivering drugs using the inhalation route to the lungs is the foundation of the everyday clinical management of patients with airway diseases (1–3). The inhaled route, as opposed to systemic drug administration, allows key therapeutic benefits. Targeting the drugs to the site of action in the lungs achieves a quicker onset of action, a reduction in the dose of drug used, and an improved therapeutic ratio (efficacy to adverse event ratio). The global pandemic has seen a seismic need for us to understand aerosol science, for example, infectious aerosols and therapeutic aerosols (4). In this chapter we discuss the physiochemical factors that control the transport, delivery, and deposition of inhaled drug within the lungs.

## MECHANISMS OF DRUG DEPOSITION IN THE LUNGS

Inhaled drug deposition is an active process that requires the inspired therapeutic particles to be maximally retained within the airways of the lungs and minimize loss of drug in the exhaled air (5, 6). The chief mechanisms that control inhaled medical aerosol deposition within the airways are inertial impaction, sedimentation, and diffusion (Figure 1.1) (7, 8).

These physical mechanisms act concurrently on the inhaled drug particles as they follow the airstream on their trajectory within the respiratory tract and collectively contribute to the deposition of aerosolized drug within the lungs. The relative proportions and extent to which each mechanism contributes and predominates are dependent on the physicochemical properties of the drug particle, the pathology and geometry of the local airways, the airstream parameters, and the inhalation maneuver and pattern of breathing of the patient

### Inertial Impaction

Inertial impaction of inhaled drug particles occurs when the forward momentum of an individual drug particle causes it to maintain its original path and direction of flow in the airstream leading it to impact on the surrounding airway wall, in a region of the respiratory tract where there is a change in the bulk direction of the airstream. Inertial impaction predominantly occurs with inhaled drug particles at airway bifurcations in larger branches of the airways

DOI: 10.1201/9781003269014-1

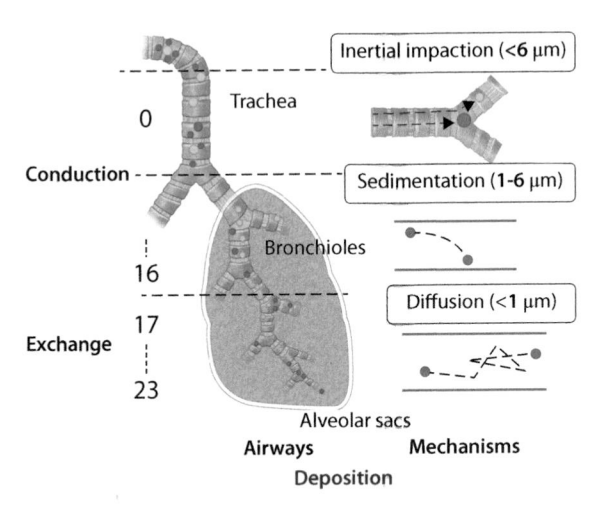

**Figure 1.1** Mechanisms of aerosol deposition in the airways.

in the respiratory tract where the velocities of airflow are high and where rapid and fast changes occur in the path and direction of the airstream (Figure 1.1).

Impaction of inhaled drug particles within the lungs is beneficial. However, inertial impaction is also the prime determinant of drug depositing within the oropharynx that can lead to unwanted local adverse effects and through oral bioavailability, depending upon the pharmacokinetic behavior and metabolism of the drug systemic adverse effects. The ballistic high-velocity nature of the aerosol spray emitted from inhaler devices, such as some pressurized metered-dose inhalers (pMDIs), or inhaled with intense inspiratory force and flows by the patients, as is needed with some dry powder inhalers (DPIs), can lead to significant proportions of the emitted drug particles impacting within the oropharynx and minimal amounts, in some cases less than 20%, reaching the lungs (9–11).

Inhaler devices have evolved to slow down the emitted aerosol spray and plume velocity, such as newer pMDIs with refined drug formulations (12), the slow mist inhaler (SMI) (13), and DPIs requiring gentler inhalation flows (14) that can decrease oropharyngeal impaction. In clinical practice, valve-holding chambers (VHCs) and spacers are sometimes used and attached to pMDIs that allow an extension to the inhaler mouthpiece, and by increasing the distance the aerosol spray has to travel, VHCs slow down the velocity of the aerosol spray, which has a two-fold effect (15, 16). First, VHCs allow time for the aerosol propellant to evaporate and this results in smaller drug particles that have greater potential to reach the lower respiratory tract compared to large inhaled drug particles (17), and secondly the ballistic impact of the aerosolized drug within the oropharyngeal cavity is reduced (15). The slow mist inhaler emits an aerosol spray that is slow and steady with a longer duration compared to pMDIs containing a greater fraction of fine particles (18, 19). Inertial impaction and gravitational sedimentation are the main mechanisms that influence the deposition of large, fast-moving inhaled particles of drug between 1μm and 10μm.

### Gravitational Sedimentation

Gravitational sedimentation of inhaled drug particles within the lungs occurs under the action of gravity and causes deposition within the airways when

the gravitational force acting on a drug particle overcomes the total force of air resistance. Sedimentation occurs where the velocity of the airstream is low allowing the available time for the inhaled drug particles to settle within the airway (residence time), being most efficient in the branching small airways where the distance to deposit on the airway walls is smaller compared to the larger airways (Figure 1.1). The breath-hold pause instruction often given to patients after inhalation of the aerosol enhances the action of sedimentation on inhaled drug particles in achieving greater airway deposition (20).

### Diffusion

Diffusion is the random collision of gas molecules of air present in the airways with very small particles, in this case inhaled drug particles, which displaces and pushes the aerosolized drug particles about within the airways, in an irregular and erratic manner (5). As a consequence of diffusion, a drug particle in stationary air continues to move around in a random manner, even in the absence of gravity, and this can lead the inhaled drug particles to contact and deposit on the surrounding airway wall. Diffusion predominantly occurs in the distal small airways and alveoli, where airflow velocities are at their lowest, the residence time within the airways is long, and the distance an inhaled particle has to travel before hitting the airway wall is short (Figure 1.1). Diffusion is the main deposition determinant of slow-moving, small submicron (<1 μm) particles.

## FACTORS AFFECTING DEPOSITION

Many factors can influence the deposition of inhaled aerosolized drug particles within the airways and they can generally be divided into aerosol characteristics and patient variables (Table 1.1).

## Table 1.1: Factors Affecting Airways Deposition of Inhaled Medical Aerosols

| Aerosol Factors | Patient Factors |
|---|---|
| Drug particle characteristics: | Inhalation maneuver: |
| • particle density<br>• particle electrostatics<br>• particle shape<br>• particle size and fraction | • breathing frequency<br>• breath-hold pause<br>• chin lift<br>• degree of lung inflation<br>• exhalation to end tidal breath before inhalation<br>• inhaled aerosol volume<br>• inspiratory flow<br>• nose vs. mouth breathing |
| Drug formulation: | Airway features: |
| • hygroscopicity<br>• surfactant<br>• molecule charge | • adult vs. pediatric<br>• airways disease type<br>• diameter and obstruction<br>• severity of disease |
| Aerosol generation system: | Healthcare features: |
| • inhaler device type<br>• maintenance of device | • competency of healthcare to teach, train and instruct patient<br>• inhaler regimen<br>• patient adherence<br>• patient technique |

## Aerosol Properties

Of the physicochemical aerosol properties, drug particle size, or mass median aerodynamic diameter (MMAD) for therapeutic aerosols, is the most significant factor that determines the overall amount of inhaled drug particles depositing within the lungs and also the distribution of aerosolized drug within the airway regions. The branching airway system of the respiratory tract acts primarily as a defense mechanism analogous to a series of filters sequentially removing harmful airborne particulate matter from the inspired airstream. Inhaled drug particles therefore need to overcome the barriers to achieve effective drug deposition. Generally, inhaled particles >100 microns in size are usually trapped in the upper airway nasal cavity, where those >10 micron typically deposit in the oropharyngeal region, and particles between 2 and 6 microns deposit in the conducting airways. Extra fine inhaled drug particles, defined as those less than 2.1 microns (21), have the best potential to reach the small airways and distal lung region.

It is clear that modulating the particle size of inhaled drug can optimize drug delivery to the lungs and the clinical benefit experienced by the patients in terms of impact on their disease (22–24). Indeed, this will depend upon the drug class and pharmacological action of the drug and also the lung region it is thought best to target the drug with respect to receptors for the drug (25, 26). In a landmark *in vivo* study investigating the effect of inhaled drug particle size in patients with asthma using short-acting beta-agonist, the authors observed aerosolized particles of 6- and 3-micron MMAD of monodisperse aerosol achieved a good bronchodilator response as assessed with the forced expiratory volume in one second ($FEV_1$), whereas the 1.5-micron MMAD aerosols achieved less airways bronchodilation with $FEV_1$ (10). However, overall the smaller particles achieved greater total lung deposition of drug compared to the larger particles. The authors explained this paradox by noting that the larger particles achieved a better bronchodilator response as the short-acting beta-2 agonist particles were preferentially depositing in the proximal large conducting airways where the beta-2 receptors were associated with a greater density of airway smooth muscle and the endpoint used to asses bronchodilator response, the $FEV_1$, was relatively more selective for eliciting a response in this lung region compared to the smaller aerosols depositing in the distal smaller conducting airways (10, 27, 28). Indeed, $FEV_1$ in spirometry is a marker of large airways (29). Since this study, the importance of targeting drug to the small conducting airways has been established, where small-airway dysfunction can be accurately assessed, occurs in obstructive airways diseases of asthma and COPD, and contributes to patient symptom burden and patient outcomes (24, 25). Importantly, inhaler formulations have been engineered to allow commercial devices that can be prescribed to patients that target drug to the large and also small airways, the whole airway tree, and have been shown to improve clinical outcomes compared to large particle therapy (23). In vitro studies have shown that small particles can be exhaled, with values documented as high as 70%; however, these used modes and breathing conditions that did not replicate the human lung and particles that were not therapeutic aerosols. Subsequent in vivo studies using inhaled drug particle show that small therapeutic drug particles are minimally exhaled 4–6% and in similar proportions to large drug particles exhaled 1–3%.

Other physicochemical properties that have been engineered to enhance deposition of inhaled drug particles have been altering the shape of the particles (30), utilizing electrostatic charge on particles (31), using low-density gases, such as helium (32), and changing aerosol properties with low-density large porous

particles (33). Particle size may not remain constant as a generated aerosol moves through a delivery system and the respiratory tract. Volatile aerosols may become smaller through evaporation droplets of pure water that evaporate rapidly even under conditions of 100% humidity because of increased pressure inside a small droplet caused by surface tension. For example, a 1-micron droplet of water will evaporate within 0.5 s at room ambient temperature, even under saturated conditions. A 10-micron droplet will evaporate within approximately 1 min (34). It has been shown that the humid airway environment may cause water-soluble hygroscopic drug particles to increase their size causing aerosolized particles to deposit more proximally compared to inert non-hygroscopic particles, yet this phenomenon of "hygroscopic growth" has been shown only using non-pharmacological aerosols in vitro experimentally and in healthy subjects in vivo, but not with therapeutic drug particles in actual patients with respiratory disease (35, 36).

Recent pharmaceutical engineering and developments in drug chemistry have focused on the formulation in pMDIs with respect to their propellants. The Montreal Protocol Treaty in 1989 established the need to eradicate the use of chlorofluorocarbons (CFCs) as propellants in the formulation in pMDIs to protect the ozone layer in the stratosphere, with consequent reformulation of pMDIs with non-ozone depleting propellants, such as hydrofluoroalkanes (HFAs) (37, 38). Reproducible delivery of inhaled drug had to be shown and also clinical outcomes, so some pMDI incorporated improved actuator design, new compatible elastomeric valve components, and changes in the orifice geometry (39, 40). The Kigali amendment of 2019 extends the coverage to HFA and there is innovation in low global warming potential propellants to replace the existing HFA propellants in pMDIs.

### Patient Variables

The way each subject breathes also affects drug deposition in the airways. Respiratory frequency, tidal volume, and lung volume will affect the residence time of aerosols in the lungs, and hence the probability of deposition by gravitational and diffusional forces. Changing lung volume will also alter the dimensions of the airways and parenchyma. High level of ventilation during exercise and breath-holding represents extremes of breathing patterns which give rise to markedly different deposition patterns. The results of experiments measuring the effect of breathing pattern on the distribution of aerosol deposition indicate that a) total deposition decreases as breathing frequency increases; b) slow, deep breathing produces uniform deposition throughout the lung, but with little aerosol collection in the large airways; c) rapid, shallow ventilation results in enhanced large-airway deposition and marked heterogeneity in deposition distribution; and d) slow, shallow breathing at high end-expiratory volumes enhanced small-airway deposition (41). In clinics, the most important patient variable affecting inhaled aerosol deposition in the lungs is the breathing maneuver, which influences deposition efficiency and therapeutic efficacy of the inhaled drug particles. For pMDIs and the SMI a slow and steady inhalation over 5 seconds is optimal (42), and patients should be instructed to inhale "slowly, steadily, naturally, deeply and comfortably" [Usmani, personal communication]. It has been shown that a fast, rapid, and quick inhalation decreases aerosol in the lungs and increases oropharyngeal impaction (43). Actuation of pMDIs at the start of the inhalation maneuver during low lung volumes has been shown to enhance the deposition of inhaled drug within the lungs (44). It is important that prior to inhalation from any device that patients lift their chin up, in order to open the airway (45) and

also exhale to end tidal functional residual capacity in order to have enough inhaled volume to carry the drug particles in the inspiratory airstream (46). A greater inhaled volume on inspiration allows more aerosolized particles to be effectively deposited within the lungs and carried toward the peripheral airways (47). Instruction to patients to exhale the aerosol via the nose and not the mouth may be beneficial [Usmani, personal communication], where data show the dose of nasal corticosteroid may be significantly reduced in asthma patients with rhinitis (48). In contrast to pMDIs, DPIs are dependent upon the patient's inspiratory flow to operate and require quicker, faster inspiratory inhalation flows to generate sufficient peak inspiratory flow (PIF) and optimally de-aggregate the powdered drug from its carrier molecule and effectively aerosolize the powder into respirable inhaled particles in order to achieve adequate lung deposition (49). The internal resistance of a DPI, and hence the flow required to overcome this resistance, varies with different DPI designs (50). Of note, findings from observational studies (51, 52) suggest that 32–47% of inpatients admitted for exacerbations of COPD demonstrated a suboptimal PIF (<60 L/min) prior to discharge; suboptimal PIF was also reported in 19–78% of stable outpatients with COPD. Taken together, these findings suggest that many patients do not generate sufficient inspiratory force to overcome the resistance of prescribed DPIs. Several independent predictors for suboptimal PIF have been identified, including patient effort, female gender, shorter height, and older age (53, 54).

With the conventional nebulizers the ideal breathing maneuver is relaxed tidal breathing by the patient, and where some new nebulizer devices assess the patient's breathing maneuver and pulse to deliver aerosolized drug only during the inhalation phase leading to a more efficient system and less drug wastage. As discussed, at the end of the inhalation maneuver the breath-hold pause enhances the deposition of inhaled drug in the lungs, with the required airway residence time for the aerosolized particles to make contact with the airway walls through the deposition mechanisms of gravitational sedimentation and diffusion (44).

The configuration of the lungs and airways is important since the efficiency of deposition depends, in part, upon the diameters of the airways, their angles of branching, and the average distances to alveolar walls. Furthermore, along with the inspiratory flow, airway anatomy specifies the local velocity of the airstream, and thus whether the flow is laminar or turbulent. There are inter-intra-species differences in lung morphometry; even within the same individual, the dimensions of the respiratory tract vary with changing lung volume, with aging, and with pathological processes. A highly significant change in the effective anatomy of the respiratory tract occurs when there is a switch between nose and mouth breathing or when the nose is bypassed by a tracheostomy or by an endotracheal tube. The nose has a major role as a collector of inhaled aerosol particles. The combination of a small cross-section for airflow, sharp curves, and interior nasal hairs helps maximize particle impaction. The loss of filtering capacity of the nose may be involved in the exercise-induced asthma. With rising levels of exercise and increasing ventilation, the high-resistance nasal pathway will be abandoned in favor of the low-resistance oral pathway, thus increasing the exposure to more aerosol particles particularly large particles, such as pollen particles. Respiratory diseases markedly influence the distribution of inspired particles. Bronchoconstriction will lead to diversion of flow to non-obstructive airways. With advancing diseases, the remaining healthy airways may be exposed increasingly to inspired particles. Narrowing by inflammation or mucus can increase linear velocities of airflow, enhance

inertial deposition, and cause more central deposition patterns. In very sick patients, there may be increases in aerosol deposition which are associated with flow limitation (9, 55). As discussed, the caliber of the patient's airways can affect the lung deposition of inhaled drug, where patients with asthma have less inhaled aerosol deposition in the lungs compared to healthy subjects (9, 55) and following induced bronchoconstriction of the airways (56). However, recently, it has been shown that by altering the pharmaceutical formulation and using drug of smaller particle size may overcome the airway narrowing present in asthma and COPD leading to levels of lung deposition as observed in healthy subjects (57, 58).

Evidence is accumulating that healthcare professionals give inadequate device demonstration to patients as they themselves lack knowledge and instruction in inhaler devices (59). As a consequence, patients are taught incorrectly, or not taught at all, and errors in inhalation technique have been shown to have a direct consequence on worsening disease control and exacerbations in patients, and lead to a greater health economic burden (60). Demonstrating inhaler technique to a patient is an essential part of the management of patients with respiratory disease in outpatients and on the ward as an inpatient and improve disease outcomes (61, 62). Patients should have their inhaler technique checked at every opportunity as it has been shown that correct inhaler technique decreases over time (63). Decreased cognition in elderly patients (64) and relatively poor strength in their hands (65) may lead to an incorrect inhaler technique and focused attention will be needed here with the patient and their caregivers. Simplifying inhaler regimens with the same inhaler device type for concomitant inhaled medications in patients with asthma or COPD can lead to improved clinical outcomes and reduced health care use (66).

## FUTURE DIRECTIONS

There is a need for ongoing innovation in inhaled delivery systems to be able to keep up with the rapid advances being seen in in drug discovery, particularly in biopharmaceutics and pharmacogenomics. Inhaled drug delivery systems must be designed in order to achieve better control of aerosolized drug delivered to the airways to be effective in the management of local disease and airway pathology and also for the treatment of systemic disease (67). Indeed, inhaled drug delivery to the lungs is increasingly being investigated as a route for the systemic delivery of therapeutic drug (68). The large surface area of the lungs and vascular supply, particularly the alveolar region, may allow inhaled drug to be effectively absorbed and large molecule peptides and proteins that are unable to be absorbed through the gastrointestinal tract or undergo high metabolic hepatic breakdown may also benefit from the inhalation route in order to achieve a systemic effect. There are clear therapeutic benefits for patients with decreased adverse drug effects and practical advantages of avoidance with needles compared to parenteral therapy.

## REFERENCES

1. Lavorini F, Buttini F, Usmani OS. 100 years of drug delivery to the lungs. Handb Exp Pharmacol 2019;260:143–159.
2. Lavorini F, Fontana GA, Usmani OS. New inhaler devices - the good, the bad and the ugly. Respiration 2014;88(1):3–15. DOI:10.1159/000363390
3. Yernault JC. Inhalation therapy: An historical perspective. Eur Respir Rev 1994;4:65–67.

4. Mitchell JP, Berlinski A, Canisius S, et al. Urgent appeal from International Society for Aerosols in Medicine (ISAM) during COVID-19: Clinical decision makers and governmental agencies should consider the inhaled route of administration: A statement from the ISAM Regulatory and Standardization Issues Networking Group. J Aerosol Med Pulm Drug Deliv 2020;33(4):235–238.

5. Darquenne C. Deposition mechanisms. J Aerosol Med Pulm Drug Deliv 2020;33(4):181–185.

6. Verbanck S, Kalsi HS, Biddiscombe MF, et al. Inspiratory and expiratory aerosol deposition in the upper airway. Inhal Toxicol 2011;23(2):104–111.

7. Agnew JE. Physical properties and mechanisms of deposition of aerosols. In: Clarke SW, Pavia D, editors. Aerosols and the lung. London: Butterworths; 1994. p. 49–70.

8. Yu J, Chien YW. Pulmonary drug delivery: Physiologic and mechanistic aspects. Crit Rev Ther Drug Carrier Syst 1997;14:395–453.

9. Melchor R, Biddiscombe MF, Mak VH, et al. Lung deposition patterns of directly labelled salbutamol in normal subjects and in patients with reversible airflow obstruction. Thorax 1993;48:506–511.

10. Usmani OS, Biddiscombe MF, Barnes PJ. Regional lung deposition and bronchodilator response as a function of β2-agonist particle size. Am J Respir Crit Care Med 2005;172:1497–1504.

11. Iwanaga T, Tohda Y, Nakamura S, et al. The Respimat® Soft Mist inhaler: Implications of drug delivery characteristics for patients. Clin Drug Investig 2019;39(11):1021–1030.

12. Johal B, Murphy S, Tuohy J, et al. Plume characteristics of two HFA-driven inhaled corticosteroid/long-acting beta2-agonist combination pressurized metered-dose inhalers. Adv Ther 2015;32(6):567–579.

13. Dreher M, Price D, Gardev A, et al. Patient perceptions of the re-usable Respimatt® Soft Mist™ inhaler in current users and those switching to the device: A real-world, non-interventional COPD study. Chron Respir Dis 2021;18:1479973120986228.

14. Corradi M, Chrystyn H, Cosio BG, et al. NEXThaler, an innovative dry powder inhaler delivering an extrafine fixed combination of beclometasone and formoterol to treat large and small airways in asthma. Expert Opin Drug Deliv 2014;11(9):1497–1506.

15. Vincken W, Levy ML, Scullion J, et al. Spacer devices for inhaled therapy: Why use them, and how? ERJ Open Res 2018;4(2):00065-2018.

16. Lavorini F, Barreto C, van Boven JFM, et al. Spacers and valved holding chambers-the risk of switching to different chambers. J Allergy Clin Immunol Pract 2020;8(5):1569–1573.

17. Verbanck S, Biddiscombe MF, Usmani OS. Inhaled aerosol dose distribution between proximal bronchi and lung periphery. Eur J Pharm Biopharm 2020;152:18–22.

18. Hochrainer D, Hölz H, Kreher C, et al. Comparison of the aerosol velocity and spray duration of Respimat Soft Mist inhaler and pressurized metered dose inhalers. J Aerosol Med 2005;18:273–282.

19. Dhand R. Aerosol plumes: Slow and steady wins the race. J Aerosol Med 2005;18(3):261–263.

20. Sonnenberg AH, Taylor E, Mondoñedo JR, et al. Breath hold facilitates targeted deposition of aerosolized droplets in a 3D printed bifurcating airway tree. Ann Biomed Eng 2021;49(2):812–821.

21. Hillyer EV, Price DB, Chrystyn H, et al. Harmonizing the nomenclature for therapeutic aerosol particle size: A proposal. J Aerosol Med Pulm Drug Deliv 2018;31(2):111–113.
22. Sonnappa S, McQueen B, Postma DS, et al. Extrafine versus fine inhaled corticosteroids in relation to asthma control: A systematic review and meta-analysis of observational real-life studies. J Allergy Clin Immunol Pract 2018;6(3):907–915.e7.
23. Usmani OS. Treating the small airways. Respiration 2012;84(6):441–453.
24. Usmani OS, Dhand R, Lavorini F, et al. Why we should target small airways disease in our management of chronic obstructive pulmonary disease. Mayo Clin Proc 2021;96(9):2448–2463.
25. Usmani OS, Han MK, Kaminsky DA, et al. Seven pillars of small airways disease in asthma and COPD: Supporting opportunities for novel therapies. Chest 2021;160(1):114–134.
26. Usmani OS. Small-airway disease in asthma: Pharmacological considerations. Curr Opin Pulm Med 2015;21(1):55–67.
27. Usmani OS, Biddiscombe MF, Nightingale JA, et al. Effects of bronchodilator particle size in asthmatic patients using monodisperse aerosols. J Appl Physiol 2003;95(5):2106–2112.
28. Biddiscombe MF, Barnes PJ, Usmani OS. Generating monodisperse pharmacological aerosols using a spinning top aerosol generator. J Aerosol Med 2006;19:245–253.
29. Usmani OS. Calling time on spirometry: Unlocking the silent zone in acute rejection after lung transplantation. Am J Respir Crit Care Med 2020;201(12):1468–1470.
30. Hassan MS, Lau RW. Effect of particle shape on dry particle inhalation: Study of flowability, aerosolization, and deposition properties. AAPS PharmSciTech 2009;10(4):1252–1262.
31. Xi J, Si X, Longest W. Electrostatic charge effects on pharmaceutical aerosol deposition in human nasal-laryngeal airways. Pharmaceutics 2014;6(1):26–35.
32. Peterson JB, Prisk GK, Darquenne C. Aerosol deposition in the human lung periphery is increased by reduced-density gas breathing. J Aerosol Med Pulm Drug Deliv 2008;21(2):159–168.
33. Edwards DA, Ben-Jebria A, Langer R. Recent advances in pulmonary drug delivery using large, porous inhaled particles. J Appl Physiol 1998;85:379–385.
34. Mercer TT. Aerosol technology in hazard evaluation. New York (NY): Academic Press; 1973.
35. Finlay WH, Stapleton KW, Chan HK, et al. Regional deposition of inhaled hygroscopic aerosols: In vivo SPECT compared with mathematical modeling. J Appl Physiol 1996;81:374–383.
36. Chan HK, Eberl S, Daviskas E, et al. Changes in lung deposition of aerosols due to hygroscopic growth: A fast SPECT study. J Aerosol Med 2002;15:307–311.
37. Dolovich M. New delivery systems and propellants. Can Respir J 1999;6:290–295.
38. Zeidler M, Corren J. Hydrofluoroalkane formulations of inhaled corticosteroids for the treatment of asthma. Treat Respir Med 2004;3:35–44.
39. Lewis D. Metered-dose inhalers: Actuators old and new. Expert Opin Drug Deliv 2007;4:235–245.

40. Acerbi D, Brambilla G, Kottakis I. Advances in asthma and COPD management: Delivering CFC-free inhaled therapy using Modulite technology. Pulm Pharmacol Ther 2007;20:290–303.

41. Byron PR. Respiratory drug delivery. Boca Raton (FL): CRC Press; 1990. p. 1–38.

42. Laube BL, Janssens HM, de Jongh FH, et al. What the pulmonary specialist should know about the new inhalation therapies. Eur Respir J 2011;37(6):1308–1331.

43. Newman SP, Pavia D, Clarke SW. How should a pressurized beta-adrenergic bronchodilator be inhaled? Eur J Respir Dis 1981;62:3–21.

44. Newman SP, Pavia D, Clarke SW. Improving the bronchial deposition of pressurized aerosols. Chest 1981;80:909–911.

45. Horiguchi T, Kondo R. Determination of the preferred tongue position for optimal inhaler use. J Allergy Clin Immunol Pract 2018;6(3):1039–1041.e3.

46. Ohar JA, Ferguson GT, Mahler DA, et al. Measuring peak inspiratory flow in patients with chronic obstructive pulmonary disease. Int J Chron Obstruct Pulmon Dis 2022;17:79–92.

47. Pavia D, Thomson M, Shannon HS. Aerosol inhalation and depth of deposition in the human lung. The effect of airway obstruction and tidal volume inhaled. Arch Environ Health 1977;32:131–137.

48. Shaikh WA. Exhaling a budesonide inhaler through the nose results in a significant reduction in dose requirement of budesonide nasal spray in patients having asthma with rhinitis. J Investig Allergol Clin Immunol 1999;9(1):45–49.

49. Buttini F, Quarta E, Allegrini C, et al. Understanding the importance of capsules in dry powder inhalers. Pharmaceutics 2021;13(11):1936.

50. Levy ML, Carroll W, Izquierdo Alonso JL, et al. Understanding dry powder inhalers: Key technical and patient preference attributes. Adv Ther 2019;36(10):2547–2557.

51. Ghosh S, Pleasants RA, Ohar JA, et al. Prevalence and factors associated with suboptimal peak inspiratory flow rates in COPD. Int J Chron Obstruct Pulmon Dis 2019;14:585–595.

52. Mahler DA. Peak inspiratory flow rate as a criterion for dry powder inhaler use in chronic obstructive pulmonary disease. Ann Am Thorac Soc 2017;14(7):1103–1107.

53. Duarte AG, Tung L, Zhang W, et al. Spirometry measurement of peak inspiratory flow identifies suboptimal use of dry powder inhalers in ambulatory patients with COPD. Chronic Obstr Pulm Dis 2019;6(3):246–255.

54. Malmberg LP, Rytila P, Happonen P, et al. Inspiratory flows through dry powder inhaler in chronic obstructive pulmonary disease: Age and gender rather than severity matters. Int J Chron Obstruct Pulmon Dis 2010;5:257–262.

55. Kim CS, Kang TC. Comparative measurement of lung deposition of inhaled fine particles in normal subjects and patients with obstructive airway disease. Am Rev Respir Dis 1997;155:899–905.

56. Svartengren M, Anderson M, Philipson K, et al. Individual differences in regional deposition of 6-micron particles in humans with induced bronchoconstriction. Exp Lung Res 1989;15:139–149.

57. De Backer W, Devolder A, Poli G, et al. Lung deposition of BDP/formoterol HFA pMDI in healthy volunteers, asthmatic, and COPD patients. J Aerosol Med Pulm Drug Deliv 2010;23(3):137–148.

58. Virchow JC, Poli G, Herpich C, et al. Lung deposition of the dry powder fixed combination beclometasone dipropionate plus formoterol fumarate using NEXThaler® device in healthy subjects, asthmatic patients, and COPD patients. J Aerosol Med Pulm Drug Deliv 2018;31(5):269–280.
59. Plaza V, Giner J, Rodrigo GJ, et al. Errors in the use of inhalers by health care professionals: A systematic review. J Allergy Clin Immunol Pract 2018;6(3):987–995.
60. Usmani OS, Lavorini F, Marshall J, et al. Critical inhaler errors in asthma and COPD: A systematic review of impact on health outcomes. Respir Res 2018;19(1):10.
61. van Beerendonk I, Mesters I, Mudde AN, et al. Assessment of the inhalation technique in outpatients with asthma or chronic obstructive pulmonary disease using a metered-dose inhaler or dry powder device. J Asthma 1998;35:273–279.
62. Capstick TG, Azeez NF, Deakin G, et al. Ward based inhaler technique service reduces exacerbations of asthma and COPD. Respir Med 2021;187:106583.
63. Klijn SL, Hiligsmann M, Evers SMAA, et al. Effectiveness and success factors of educational inhaler technique interventions in asthma & COPD patients: A systematic review. NPJ Prim Care Respir Med 2017;27(1):24.
64. Allen SC. Competence thresholds for the use of inhalers in people with dementia. Age Ageing 1997;26:83–86.
65. Armitage JM, Williams SJ. Inhaler technique in the elderly. Age Ageing 1988;17:275–278.
66. Usmani OS, Hickey AJ, Guranlioglu D, et al. The impact of inhaler device regimen in patients with asthma or COPD. J Allergy Clin Immunol Pract 2021;9(8):3033–3040.e1.
67. Biddiscombe MF, Usmani OS. Is there room for further innovation in inhaled therapy for airways disease? Breathe (Sheff) 2018;14(3):216–224.
68. Gonda I. Systemic delivery of drugs to humans via inhalation. J Aerosol Med 2006;19:47–53.

# 2 Goals of Pharmacotherapy for Asthma and COPD

*Donald A. Mahler and Marc Miravitlles*

## CONTENTS

## INTRODUCTION

The goals of inhaled therapy for patients with asthma and chronic obstructive pulmonary disease (COPD) have evolved from enhancing lung function to improving clinical outcomes. This paradigm shift was largely a result of two factors: 1) an emphasis on patient experiences and symptoms related to their airway disease and exacerbations and 2) the development of instruments and scales to quantify symptoms, especially dyspnea, quality of life, exercise capacity, and exacerbations. Currently, patient advocacy organizations, investigators, thought leaders, professional organizations, and pharmaceutical companies prioritize these patient-reported outcomes (PROs).

Evidence from phases II, III, and IV clinical trials has demonstrated that various inhaled therapies improve PROs in those with asthma and COPD. Such information has enabled expert panels and global leaders to provide specific pharmacologic recommendations targeted to achieve the goals of therapy for these airway diseases. Ideally, the stated goals from national and international experts/organizations assist health care professionals (HCPs) in addressing three decisions required when prescribing inhaled therapy (Figure 2.1): 1) Do I select a short-acting and/or one or more long-acting bronchodilators? 2) What class(es) of medication is/are appropriate or best for the individual patient–beta-agonist, muscarinic antagonist, and/or corticosteroids? 3) Which delivery system is appropriate or best for the individual patient?

The following information reviews the stated goals of pharmacotherapy by major organizations and/or countries for individuals with asthma and COPD. Although the overall goals of pharmacotherapy apply regardless of the delivery system (inhaled, injected, intravenous, or swallowed), the inhaled approach is preferred for individuals with asthma and COPD.

## ASTHMA

The Global Initiative for Asthma (GINA) is the most widely recognized professional source for prescribing therapies for individuals with asthma (1). In addition, Expert Panel Reports of the United States National Asthma Education and Prevention Program provide guidelines for the diagnosis and management of children and adults with asthma (2). Asthma experts sponsored by the Japanese Society of Allergology published guidelines for adults with

DOI: 10.1201/9781003269014-2

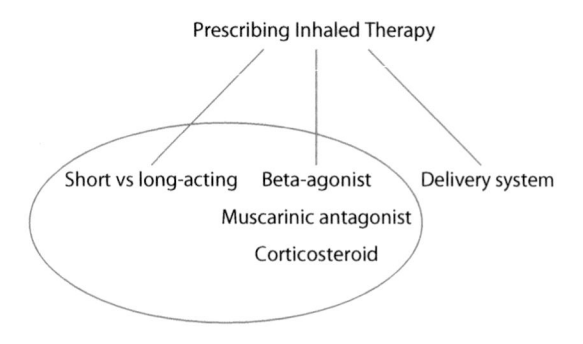

**Figure 2.1** When prescribing inhaled therapy, health care professionals (HCPs) must make three decisions—two involve selecting the medication(s) (circled), while the other relates to selecting the delivery system.

asthma living in Japan (3). Furthermore, the Department of Veterans Affairs partnered with the Department of the Defense in the United States to develop a clinical practice guideline for the primary care management of asthma (4). Information on recommended goals for the treatment of asthma found in these four documents is presented below in alphabetical order and is summarized in Table 2.1.

### Department of Veterans Affairs/Department of Defense

In 2019, a panel of multidisciplinary experts published a clinical practice guideline based on a systematic review of clinical and epidemiological evidence related to asthma (4). The guideline is intended for the "primary care management of asthma" with the main goal being "Asthma Control." Specific criteria are listed for assessing whether a patient's asthma is "Controlled" or "Not Controlled" based on two components: Impairment and Risk (Table 2.1). Impairment is assessed by daytime symptoms, night time awakening, interference with normal activities, short-acting beta-agonist (SABA) use, and the Asthma Control Test. Risk is assessed by the number of exacerbations requiring oral systemic corticosteroids and treatment-related adverse effects.

### Expert Panel Report 3 of the National Asthma Education and Prevention Program

In 1989, the National Asthma Education and Prevention Program was created to address asthma issues in the United States. Three Expert Panel Reports have been published – in 1991, 2002, and 2007. According to the Expert Panel Report 3, the goal of therapy is "Control of asthma," based on two components: Reduce impairment and Reduce risk. Specific items for these components are listed in Table 2.1. In 2020, a focused update on six priority topics was published based on systematic reviews using the Population, Intervention, Comparator, and Outcomes (PICO) format (2).

### GINA

GINA was established following a workshop in 1993 organized by the National Heart, Lung, and Blood Institute and the World Health Organization. GINA

## Table 2.1: **Goals of Pharmacotherapy in Asthma**

| Source (Alphabetical Order) | Goals |
| --- | --- |
| Department of Veterans Affairs and Department of Defense (4) | Asthma control<br><br>*Impairment*<br><ul><li>Daytime symptoms</li><li>Nighttime awakening</li><li>Interference with normal activities</li><li>SABA use for symptom control</li><li>Asthma control test score</li></ul>*Risk*<br><ul><li>Exacerbation requiring oral steroids</li><li>treatment-related adverse effects</li></ul> |
| Expert Panel Report 3 of the National Asthma Education and Prevention Program (2) | Control of asthma<br><br>*Reduce Impairment*<br><ul><li>Prevent symptoms</li><li>Infrequent use of inhaled SABA</li><li>Maintain (near) normal pulmonary function</li><li>Maintain normal activity levels</li><li>Meet patient/family expectations of asthma</li></ul>*Reduce risk*<br><ul><li>Prevent recurrent exacerbations</li><li>Prevent loss of lung function</li><li>Provide optimal pharmacotherapy</li></ul> |
| Global Initiative for Asthma (1) | Asthma control<br>*Symptom control*<br><ul><li>Daytime asthma symptoms</li><li>Night waking due to asthma</li><li>SABA reliever for symptoms more than twice/week</li><li>Any activity limitation due to asthma</li></ul>*Risk factors for poor asthma outcomes*<br><ul><li>Various factors listed in document</li></ul> |
| Japanese Guidelines for Adult Asthma (3) | Asthma control<br><ul><li>Asthma symptoms (in daytime or at night)</li><li>Use of reliever</li><li>Limitations of activities, including exercise</li><li>Lung function</li><li>Diurnal (weekly) variation in PEF</li><li>Exacerbation</li></ul> |

*Abbreviations:* PEF = peak expiratory flow; SABA = short-acting beta-agonist.

has published a "Global Strategy for Asthma Management and Prevention," that has been updated annually since 2002 (1). The GINA Science Committee currently consists of 16 experts from 11 different countries. The committee used a 2009 definition of asthma control, "The extent to which the features of asthma are apparent or have reduced or eliminated by controller treatment" (5). Asthma control is considered over the past four weeks based on two domains: symptom control and risk of adverse outcomes, particularly exacerbations (1). The document proposed that the level of asthma symptom control be classified as, "Well controlled," "Partly controlled," and "Uncontrolled," based on specific items for asthma listed in Table 2.1.

### Japanese Guidelines for Adult Asthma

In 2020, 12 asthma experts representing the Japanese Society of Allergology updated a Japanese guideline for adult asthma published three years earlier (3). The new guideline noted that the prevalence of asthma in Japan had increased from 1% to 10% or higher in children and to 6% to 10% in adults since the 1960s. The stated aims of asthma treatment are "Symptom control" and "Avoidance of future risks." Based on six specific items for asthma control listed in Table 2.1, asthma can be assessed as "Well controlled," "Insufficiently controlled," and "Poorly controlled."

### COPD

The Global Initiative for Obstructive Lung Disease (GOLD) is the most recognized source for prescribing inhaled therapies for individuals with COPD (6). The GOLD program was initiated in 1998 with the first report being issued in 2001. Subsequent revisions have been made based on levels of evidence with yearly updates since the fourth major revision in 2017. In addition, the American Thoracic Society and Canadian Thoracic Society have each published clinical practice guidelines on pharmacotherapy for patients with COPD (7, 8). Experts on COPD in Spain have updated published guidelines on pharmacologic management (9). Information on recommended goals for the treatment of COPD in these four documents is presented in alphabetical order below and is summarized in Table 2.2.

### American Thoracic Society

In 2020, the American Thoracic Society (7) published a clinical practice guideline to address specific clinically important questions regarding pharmacologic management of COPD. The introduction stated that the aims of pharmacologic treatment of COPD are to 1) improve quality of life; 2) control symptoms; and 3) reduce the frequency of exacerbations. Six clinical questions were posed using the PICO format. The expert panel used the Grading of Recommendations Assessment, Development, and Evaluation (GRADE) approach for each clinical question. Two questions examined therapy for "patients with COPD who complained of dyspnea or exercise intolerance," whereas a third question addressed "patients who experience advanced refractory dyspnea."

### Canadian Thoracic Society

In 2019, a panel of six respirologists, three clinicians/epidemiologists, two primary care physicians, and one pharmacist in Canada updated a clinical practice guideline from a position statement that was published in 2017 (8).

## Table 2.2: Goals of Pharmacotherapy in COPD

| Source (Alphabetical Order) | Goals |
|---|---|
| American Thoracic Society (7) | Improve quality of life<br>Control symptoms<br>Reduce the frequency of exacerbations |
| Canadian Thoracic Society (8) | Improve shortness of breath<br>Improve exercise tolerance<br>Improve physical activity<br>Prevent exacerbations |
| Global Initiative for Chronic Obstructive Lung Disease (6) | *Reduce symptoms*<br>• Relieve symptoms<br>• Improve exercise<br>• Improve health status<br>*Reduce risk of exacerbations*<br>• Prevent disease progression<br>• Prevent and treat exacerbations<br>• Reduce mortality |
| Spanish COPD Guideline (9) | Alleviate symptoms<br>Reduce frequency/severity of exacerbations<br>Improve quality of life<br>Extend survival |

The authors proposed that their guideline was "a step toward personalized therapy based on increasing individual characterization." The approach to pharmacotherapy aligns treatment decisions with "symptom burden" and the "risk of future exacerbations" as shown in Table 2.3.

The recommended goals of therapy are detailed in two PICO questions. PICO 1 addressed optimal use of inhaled and oral pharmacologic maintenance therapies for "symptom burden." with the expressed intent to "improve shortness of breath, exercise tolerance, physical activity, and health statues." PICO 2 addressed "preventing acute exacerbations in stable COPD patients."

### GOLD

The GOLD Scientific Committee consists of 18 experts from nine countries. The document provides two major goals for treatment of stable COPD: 1) reduce

## Table 2.3: Approach to Pharmacotherapy Proposed by the Canadian Thoracic Society (8)

| | Mild | Moderate and Severe | |
|---|---|---|---|
| *Symptom burden* | | | |
| Dyspnea (mMRC scale) | 1 | $\geq 2$ | |
| CAT | $< 10$ | $\geq 10$ | |
| *Risk of Exacerbation* | | *Low* | *High* |
| (# in past year) | | Low: $\leq 1$ not requiring ED visit or hospitalization<br>High = > 2 treated with antibiotic and/or corticosteroid or >1 requiring ED visit or hospitalization | |

*Abbreviations:* CAT = COPD assessment test; ED = Emergency Department; mMRC = modified Medical Research Council scale.

symptoms and 2) reduce risk. There are three specific outcomes for each goal as shown in Table 2.2 (6). Initial pharmacological treatment is recommended based on categorizing each patient into one of four quadrants (A, B, C, and D) according to low or high symptoms as measured on the modified Medical Research Council scale or the COPD Assessment Test (CAT) and low or high risk of exacerbations according to the number and type of events in the past year.

After initial therapy is prescribed, a management cycle of [Review → Assess → Adjust → Review] is recommended to evaluate whether treatment goals have been obtained. If not, then the HCP should consider the predominant treatment trait— dyspnea or exacerbations—to decide on any changes in pharmacologic treatment.

### Spanish COPD Guideline

In 2021, the Spanish COPD guideline (GesEPOC) for the pharmacological treatment of stable patients with COPD were updated (9). First published in 2012, the current GesEPOC is the fourth update. The document stated that it was the first clinical guideline on COPD to propose treatment based on clinical phenotypes (9). According to the authors, the guideline offers a more individualized approach to COPD treatment tailored according to the clinical characteristics of patients and their level of complexity. The 2021 guideline assesses five new PICO questions using GRADE methodology (9).

Once a diagnosis of COPD is made, patients are stratified as being either *low or high risk* based on three criteria as described in Table 2.4. Initial pharmacological treatment is guided by symptoms in low-risk patients and by clinical phenotype in high-risk individuals. The document states that there is greater need for therapy in the higher risk level.

This guideline introduces the concept of control of COPD as an objective of treatment for the first time (10). Control of COPD consists of two components: clinical impact (how much the disease interferes with the daily life of patients) and clinical stability (the lack of impairment over time and the absence of exacerbations) (10). The variables used to measure impact and stability are shown in Table 2.4. A patient is considered to be controlled when the disease has a low impact and stable.

### Table 2.4: Risk Stratification and Control Criteria Proposed in the 2021 Spanish COPD Guideline (9)

| Clinical Evaluation | With Adjustment for FEV$_1$% | |
|---|---|---|
| Low clinical impact (At least three of the four criteria should be fulfilled) | | |
| | FEV$_1 \geq 50\%$ | FEV$_1 \leq 49\%$ |
| • Dyspnea | 0–1 | 0–2 |
| • Rescue medication | ≤3 times/week | |
| • Sputum color | White or absent | |
| • Physical activity | ≥30 min/day | |
| Clinical stability (Both criteria should be fulfilled) | | |
| • Subjective perception | Same or better | |
| • Exacerbations in the last three months | None | |
| Control | Low impact + Stability | |

*Abbreviation:* FEV$_1$ = forced expiratory volume in one second.

## DISCUSSION

"Asthma Control" is the primary goal of pharmacotherapy for individuals with asthma as described in four recently published documents (Table 2.1). *Impairment/symptoms* and the *risk of future exacerbations* are the two major components that reflect whether a person's asthma is controlled or not. Both the Department of Veterans Affairs/Department of Defense (4) and the Expert Panel Report 3 (2) use *impairment* to include symptoms, ability to perform normal activities, and use of an inhaled short-acting beta-agonist (SABA) bronchodilator and the heading *risk* to include exacerbations. GINA (4) lists *symptom control* to capture the same items as those included with *impairment*. The Japanese Guidelines (3) enumerate symptoms, use of reliever inhaler, and exacerbations as three of six items that reflect "Asthma Control."

*Symptom relief* and *reducing the risk of future exacerbations* are the major goals of pharmacotherapy for individuals with COPD as described in the four recently published documents (Table 2.2). Improvement in quality of life is included in the American Thoracic Society document (7) as well as in the Spanish Guideline (9) as a specific objective, whereas improved health status is listed under the heading "Reduce Symptoms" in the GOLD Strategy (6). Improvements in exercise tolerance and physical activity are additional goals proposed by the Canadian Thoracic Society (8), while "Improve exercise" is included under the heading "Reduce symptoms" in the GOLD strategy (6). Both the GOLD strategy (6) and the Spanish Guideline (9) propose that "Reduce mortality/extend survival" are further aims of therapy for patients with COPD.

Although the overall goals of pharmacotherapy are remarkably similar for patients with asthma and COPD, the conceptual approach is generally different. Whereas "disease control" is the dominant theme of pharmacotherapy for asthma, only the Spanish COPD guideline recommends this concept for individuals with COPD (9). In 2014, Soler-Cataluña *et al.* (10) first proposed "clinical control in COPD" defined as "The long-term persistence of a situation of low clinical impact." Subsequently, prospective studies demonstrated that lack of control of COPD, as defined in the Spanish guideline (9), is very sensitive to clinical changes in patients (11) and is a very good predictor of poor outcomes, including exacerbations, hospital admissions, or mortality (12). Furthermore, the concept of "disease control" in COPD is supported by the findings of an online survey in which 445 individuals with COPD indicated that "symptom control" was the top information priority when searching the internet about their condition (13).

Despite the general difference in approach noted above, specific objectives of pharmacotherapy are consistent for both asthma and COPD—relief of symptoms and reducing the risk of a future exacerbation (Tables 2.1 and 2.2). Certainly, dyspnea, or breathing difficulty, is the most common symptom experienced by patients with airway obstruction. Coughing is another frequent complaint in both asthma and COPD and may be the presenting symptom in either condition. Exacerbations are a major burden for patients with asthma and COPD that contribute to morbidity and, at times, mortality and add substantially to health care costs. Thus, reducing the risk of a future exacerbation is a shared goal for both asthma and COPD.

Numerous inhaled medications have been shown to be beneficial by improving symptoms and by reducing the risk of an exacerbation in patients with asthma and COPD (1, 6). To be effective, the medication must be inhaled deep into the lower respiratory tract to act on airway receptors. Selecting one or more medications in an appropriate inhaled delivery system and then

instructing patients with asthma and COPD on correct inhaler technique are critical to achieve the goals of pharmacotherapy (14).

## REFERENCES

1. Reddel HK, Bacharier LB, Bateman ED, et al. Global initiative for asthma strategy 2021: Executive summary and rationale for key changes. Am J Respir Crit Care Med 2022;205:17–35.
2. Expert Panel Working Group of the National Heart, Lung, and Blood Institute (NHLBI) administered and coordinated National Asthma Education and Prevention Program Coordinating Committee. 2020 focused updates to the asthma management guidelines: A Report from the National Asthma Education and Prevention Program Coordinating Committee Expert Panel Working Group. J Allergy Clin Immunol 2020;146:1217–1270.
3. Nakamura Y, Tamaoki J, Nagase H, et al. Japanese guidelines for adult asthma 2020. Allergol Int 2020;69:519–548.
4. VA/DoD clinical practice guideline for the primary care management of asthma. https://www.healthquality.va.gov/guidelines/cd/asthma. Accessed 21 Sept 2022.
5. Reddel HK, Taylor DR, Bateman ED, et al. An official American Thoracic Society/European Thoracic Society statement: Asthma control and exacerbations: Standardizing endpoints for clinical asthma trials and clinical practice. Am J Respir Crit Care Med 2009; 180:59–99.
6. Global initiative for Chronic Obstructive Lung Disease. Global strategy for the diagnosis, management, and prevention of chronic obstructive pulmonary disease. 2022 report. https://goldcopd.org/2022-gold-reports-2. Accessed 21 Sept 2022.
7. Nici L, Mammen MJ, Charbek E, et al. Pharmacologic management of chronic obstgructive pulmonary disease. An official American Thoracic Society clinical practice guideline. Am J Respir Crit Care Med 2020;201;e56–e69.
8. Bourbeau J, Bhutani MN, Hernandez P, et al. Canadian Thoracic Society clinical practice guideline on pharmacotherapy in patients with COPD – 2019 update of evidence. Can J Respir Crit Care Sleep Med 2019;3:210–232.
9. Miravitlles M, Calle M, Molina J, et al. Spanish COPD guidelines (GesEPOC) 2021: Updated pharmacological treatment of stable COPD. Arch Bronchoneumol 2021;58:69–81.
10. Soler-Cataluña JJ, Alcazar-Navarrete B, Miravitlles M, et al. The concept of control of COPD in clinical practice. Int J Chronic Obstr Pulm Dis 2014;9:1397–1405.
11. Soler-Cataluña JJ, Alcazar B, Marzo M, et al. Evaluation of changes in control status in COPD: An opportunity for early intervention. Chest 2020;157:1138–1146.
12. Miravitlles M, Sliwinski P, Rhee CK, et al. Changes in control status of COPD over time and their consequences: A prospective international study. Arch Bronconeumol 2021;57(2):122–129.
13. Mahler DA, Cerasoli F, Della L, et al. Internet health behaviors of patients with chronic obstructive pulmonary disease and assessment of two disease websites. Chronic Obstr Pulm Dis 2018;5:158–166.
14. Usmani OS, Hickey AJ, Guranlioglu D, et al. The impact of inhaler device regimen in patients with asthma or COPD. J Allergy Clin Immunol Pract 2021;9:3033–3040.

# 3 Pressurized Metered-Dose Inhalers (pMDI)

*Donna D. Gardner and Sandra G. Adams*

CONTENTS

## INTRODUCTION

One of the most important aspects of living with an obstructive lung disease such as asthma or chronic obstructive pulmonary disease (COPD) is empowering patients to manage their disease every day with correct and consistent use of the prescribed inhaled medications. The most common device used to administer aerosolized medication day-to-day for acute symptom relief and for maintenance treatment is the pressurized metered-dose inhaler (pMDI). Similar to all inhalers, the pMDI requires proper inhaler technique in order to ensure effective medication delivery deep into the lungs. The pMDI requires patients to inhale slowly and to appropriately coordinate their breathing with inhaler actuation to ensure effective medication delivery (1). Incorrect use of the pMDI is a significant barrier to appropriately treating and managing asthma and/or COPD. Correct use of the pMDI is essential.

## WHAT IS A pMDI AND WHAT DOES IT LOOK LIKE?

A pMDI is a multi-dose device that generates an aerosol to deliver medication to the airways. The concept is about 65 years old, with a Meshberg metering valve device that was originally designed for dispensing perfume using a glass container. Since the introduction of this original device to the market, the pMDI has evolved to

DOI: 10.1201/9781003269014-3

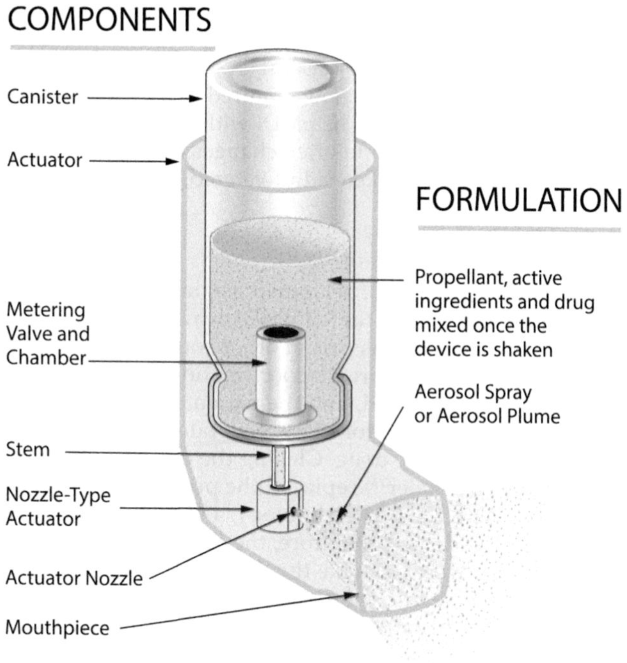

## COMPONENTS

Canister

Actuator

### FORMULATION

Propellant, active
ingredients and drug
mixed once the
device is shaken

Metering
Valve and
Chamber

Aerosol Spray
or Aerosol Plume

Stem

Nozzle-Type
Actuator

Actuator Nozzle

Mouthpiece

**Figure 3.1** Illustrated are components of the metered-dose inhaler depicting a suspension of the propellant, active ingredients, and drug after being shaken (pink with blue dots), as well as the components of the canister and actuator as labeled.

provide effective delivery of inhaled medication to the lungs (Figure 3.1). The active medication(s) and the propellant are sealed in the pMDI aluminum canister which rests within a plastic actuator. A closed pressurized reservoir within the canister protects the ingredients from degradation, contamination, moisture, and light. When the device is shaken appropriately, the medication is suspended or dissolved in the propellant. Pressing/actuating the canister allows a known, predefined volume of propellant and micronized drug to be released from the metering valve and chamber (2, 3). The propellant drives the drug through the actuator nozzle and into the air. The propellant droplets evaporate immediately, resulting in an aerosol spray or an aerosol plume, which is ready for inhalation through the mouthpiece (4).

The current pMDIs contain hydrofluoroalkane (HFA) propellants. The HFAs deliver an aerosol plume with a low-impact force, yet have a smaller delivery orifice, resulting in a slowly delivered aerosol plume. These factors facilitate inhalation deep into the lungs and produce less mouth and throat irritation when the pMDIs are used correctly. The HFA carries the drug in solution. The dose may feel and taste different than the "old" pMDIs, which used chlorofluorocarbons (CFCs) and were discontinued by an international agreement under the Montreal Protocol. The HFA pMDI aerosol contains a wide range of particle sizes (0.5–10 μm) (5). Despite these small particle sizes, less than 30% of the dose reaches the lower respiratory tract even if the inhalation technique is flawless (6, 7). This is because a significant portion (more than 70%) of the medication deposits in the

back of the throat (oropharynx) (6, 7). A slower inhalation reduces deposition of the drug in the oropharynx and deep breathing facilitates deeper deposition in the lungs where the medication is most useful (5).

All pMDIs in the United States are now required to have a dose counter, like the ones pictured in Figure 3.2. The pMDI with dose counter indicates the number of puffs left in the device and often changes color when nearing the last few doses. When the last puff is taken/administered, it is important to throw the device away.

## BREATH-ACTUATED INHALER (BAI)

The breath-actuated inhaler (BAI), beclomethasone dipropionate (QVAR) Redihaler™, is the only breath-actuated pMDI available in the United States. Other medications are available as BAI in other countries. These BAI devices overcome the need for the hand-breath coordination. The dose is ready for inhalation when the cap is opened, and the patient breathes in through the mouthpiece. The patient's inspiratory flow generated by inhalation triggers the release of a unit-dose of the drug. Closing the cap prepares the device for the next dose. The Redihaler™ replaced the previous beclomethasone (QVAR) formulation. With the BAI technology, a very low inspiratory flow is required to trigger the device; therefore, the BAI should not be shaken or primed. If the patient were to shake the device, there is a chance the device will actuate the dose into the air because of the sensitivity of the trigger mechanism. In addition, this device should not be used with a valved holding chamber or spacer. This breath-actuated inhaler technology improves particle stability, provides a consistent dose, and has more efficient lung deposition. Finally, this device may be useful for patients who have difficulty using a traditional pMDI due to reduced strength in the hands, debilitating diseases, or cognitive issues that make hand-breath actuation and coordination challenging (1).

## WHAT MEDICATIONS ARE AVAILABLE IN pMDIs?

Currently, there are various short-acting and long-acting individual and/or combinations of the three different classes or types of medications: short-acting beta-agonist (SABA), short-acting muscarinic antagonists (SAMA, or anticholinergic agents), inhaled corticosteroids (ICSs), and combination medications that include a long-acting beta-agonist (LABA) and ICS, LABA and long-acting muscarinic antagonist (LAMA), ICS, LABA, and LAMA (see Figure 3.2), and ICS and SABA (not pictured).

## HOW TO USE THE pMDI

Educating patients using the actual device (from the patient or in placebo form) and the "teach back" or "return demonstration" technique is essential to ensure that patients have the appropriate knowledge and skills to successfully manage their obstructive lung disease. Effective education empowers patients to manage their disease and increases their awareness of the danger signs indicating clinical deterioration or exacerbation (8). The healthcare professional (HCP) must regularly assess and reassess medication adherence and inhaler technique at each patient encounter in order to optimize disease management and control (8, 9). Furthermore, with advances in digital monitoring technology and communication, the use of telemedicine and education can be woven into the care of patients using the pMDI (see Chapter 7). Digital monitoring systems with text messages or reminder systems can improve adherence to medication use.

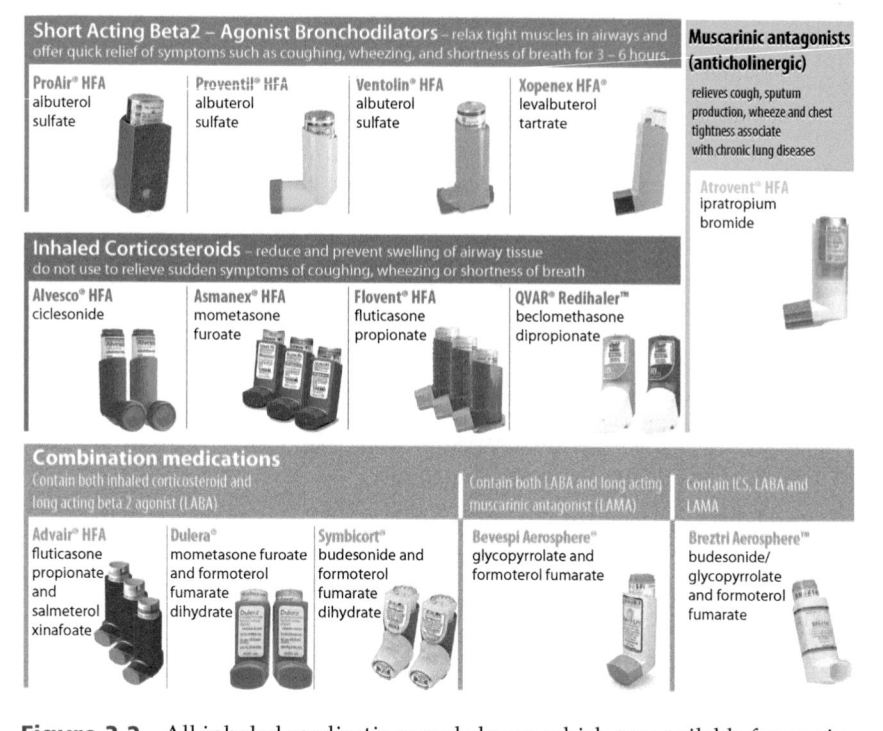

**Figure 3.2** All inhaled medications and classes which are available for use in the metered-dose inhaler throughout the United States are depicted.

## CLOSED-LIP TECHNIQUE

The pMDIs can be inhaled using the "closed lip" technique or with a valved holding chamber (sometimes referred to as a "spacer"). When using the "closed lip" technique, firing (or actuating) the device too early or too late may completely undermine delivery. Early firing, even by 0.5 seconds, before the onset of inspiration can reduce deposition of aerosol in the lung by 34% (10). However, waiting until after the first half of inspiration to fire the device typically reduces lung deposition by 41% (10).

The pMDI should be inhaled slowly and steadily following a maximal expiration. The inhaler should be actuated just *after* the onset of inspiration if using the "closed lip" technique. The total inhalation should take about 3–5 seconds. Finally, the breath should be held for about 6–10 seconds after full inhalation.

## CLOSED-LIP TECHNIQUE: STEPS TO PROPERLY USE THE pMDI

1. Take the cap or dustcover off the inhaler mouthpiece and look inside the mouthpiece to make sure nothing is inside the mouthpiece (like a gum wrapper or coin that might be accidentally inhaled into the airways).

2. Shake the inhaler for approximately 5 seconds (see manufacturer's instructions for each device because this may not be necessary for some HFA pMDIs).

3. Before the first use and if not used for a period of time, *prime* the pMDI by holding the mouthpiece away from you and pushing the top of the canister down, releasing one puff of medication into the air. Repeat these steps if needed, according to the manufacturer's instructions.

23

## TO USE THE pMDI

1. Sit or stand up straight.
2. Check the dose counter to make sure there are doses available.
3. Remove the cap or dustcover off the inhaler mouthpiece and look inside the mouthpiece to make sure nothing is inside the mouthpiece (like a gum wrapper or coin) that might be accidentally inhaled into the airways.
4. Hold the pMDI upright with the mouthpiece at the bottom and the canister on top.
5. Shake the device for at least 5 seconds *before* each use.
6. Face away from the device, breathe out to empty your lungs.
7. Place the pMDI mouthpiece between your lips and teeth.
8. Seal your lips tightly around the mouthpiece.
9. Start breathing slowly in and immediately push down on the top of the inhaler *once*, to release the medication or aerosol spray.
10. Continue breathing in very slowly for 3–5 seconds or until your lungs are full of air.
11. Remove the inhaler from your lips and hold your breath for up to 10 seconds or as long as possible.
12. Breathe out slowly, away from the device.
13. Wait for 20–60 seconds if another puff of medicine is needed and then repeat the steps above, starting with step 8. Shake the device for 5 seconds before each use.
14. When finished using the pMDI, always replace the cap or dustcover.

To reduce the risk of thrush if the pMDI contains an inhaled corticosteroid, rinse your mouth and gargle with water and SPIT the water OUT—Do NOT swallow this water—to reduce the risk of thrush.

See the video for reference: https://youtu.be/2_dLTUtKlWE

Note: The pMDI plastic holder should be cleaned with a damp cloth or with "swishing" in water to prevent occlusion of the canister nozzle. Do NOT place the canister in water.

## OPEN-MOUTH TECHNIQUE

The open-mouth technique for MDI inhalation is no longer recommended by many experts (11). The amount of force and velocity with which the medication came out of the older CFC formulations was high, resulting in significant deposition of the medication in the mouth. Therefore, with the old CFC formulations, actuating the MDI while holding it approximately two finger breadths away from the lips made sense and helped reduce the unwanted oropharyngeal deposition. Now, the HFA formulations have completely replaced the CFC formulations. Therefore, the open-mouth technique is no longer felt to be useful or needed since the HFA formulation comes out of the MDI with less force and velocity, resulting in more medicine reaching the lungs and less being deposited in the oropharynx.

## VALVED HOLDING CHAMBERS (VHCs) AND SPACER DEVICES WITH pMDIs

Valved holding chambers (VHCs) and spacer devices have been developed in order to eliminate problems with coordination. The chambers reduce the velocity of the aerosol being delivered and generally increase the medication delivery to the peripheral airways. Because the VHC has a one-way valve, it is not necessary to begin the breath prior to actuating the pMDI, thereby removing the need for hand-breath coordination. Similar to the closed-lip technique, a slow inspiration through the VHC after actuation of the pMDI is required to deliver the medicine deep into the lungs. Finally, a breath-hold lasting 6–10 seconds is still expected when using the pMDI with VHC.

## THE VALVED HOLDING CHAMBER AND SPACER DEVICES WITH pMDI: STEPS FOR PROPER USE

1. Take the cap or dustcover off the inhaler mouthpiece and look inside the mouthpiece to make sure nothing is inside (like a gum wrapper or coin) that might be accidentally inhaled into the airways.

2. Shake the inhaler for approximately 5 seconds (see manufacturer's instructions for each device).

3. Before the first use and if not used for a period of time, *prime* the pMDI by holding the mouthpiece away from you and push the top of the canister down, releasing one puff of medication into the air. Repeat these steps if needed, according to the manufacturer's instructions.

## TO USE THE pMDI WITH VHC

1. Sit or stand up straight.

2. Check the dose counter on the canister to make sure there is a dose available.

3. Take the cap or dustcover off the inhaler mouthpiece and the VHC mouthpiece. Look inside the mouthpieces to make sure nothing is inside the mouthpiece (like a gum wrapper or coin) that might be accidentally inhaled into the airways.

4. Hold the pMDI upright with the mouthpiece at the bottom and the canister on top.

5. Shake the inhaler for approximately 5 seconds (see manufacturer's instructions for each device).

6. Place the mouthpiece of the pMDI into the rubber-sealed end of the VHC.

7. Turn away from the pMDI and VHC and breathe out to empty your lungs.

8. Place the VHC mouthpiece between your lips and teeth.

9. Seal your lips tightly around the VHC mouthpiece.

10. Press down on the top of the pMDI *once* to actuate the medication and release the aerosol spray.

11. Start breathing in slowly over 3–5 seconds until your lungs are full of air.

12. Remove the VHC mouthpiece from your lips.

13. Hold your breath for up to 10 seconds or as long as possible.

14. Breathe out slowly, away from the device.

15. Wait for 20–60 seconds if another puff of medicine is needed and then repeat the steps above, beginning with Step 8. Shake the inhaler for approximately 5 seconds.

16. When finished with using the pMDI, always replace the cap or dustcover.

To reduce the risk of thrush if the pMDI contains an inhaled corticosteroid, rinse your mouth, gargle with water, and SPIT the water OUT—Do NOT swallow this water.

See the VIDEO for reference: https://youtu.be/03EeVhhUajc

## TO USE A BREATH-ACTUATED INHALER (BAI)

1. Make sure the cap or dustcover is closed over the mouthpiece.

2. Look at the dose counter to see there is a dose available.

3. Sit or stand up straight.

4. Hold the inhaler upright.

5. Remove the cap or dustcover from the BAI mouthpiece until you hear a "click" sound. This indicates the dose is loaded and ready for you to inhale.

6. Turn away from the mouthpiece of the inhaler and breathe out to empty your lungs.

7. Place the mouthpiece between your lips and make a tight seal (make sure fingers do not cover the "airvents" on top of the canister).

8. Breathe in deeply through the mouth. As you inhale, the BAI will release a puff of medicine.

9. Remove the device from your mouth.

10. Hold your breath for up to 10 seconds or as long as you are able.

11. Slowly exhale.

12. Close the cap or dust cover firmly over the mouthpiece and make sure it "clicks" to close the cap tightly.

13. If a second dose is needed, wait for 20–60 seconds, then repeat the steps, beginning with Step 4. Hold the inhaler upright.

See the VIDEO for reference: https://youtu.be/wxF2aXfW_DE

*Note*: The BAI should never be primed, shaken, or used with a VHC or spacer. This device may be an alternative for patients with arthritis if they are not able to actuate the traditional pMDI. The BAI is approved for children aged 4 years and older.

## WHEN TO USE A pMDI

The pMDI may be used for rescue/as a quick relief medication or as a maintenance/controller medication or both, depending on the medication in the device. Medications classified as short-acting beta 2 agonist (SABA) bronchodilators and the short-acting muscarinic antagonists (SAMA) (Figure 3.2) are used as a quick relief medication when the patient is experiencing signs and symptoms associated with obstructive lung diseases, such as wheezing, cough, shortness of breath, and/or chest tightness. The medications classified as

inhaled corticosteroids (ICSs) are used as maintenance/controller medications and have been recently recommended to be used as a quick relief medication (to replace the SABA) when combined with either formoterol or albuterol for patients with asthma (8, 12). After using any medication with an inhaled corticosteroid, it is important to remind the patient to rinse and gargle with water and spit to reduce the risk of oral thrush. *Candida* is a fungus that often causes thrush. This fungus is a normal type of flora that lives in our mouths. When the ICS particles are deposited in the mouth and on the tongue, the immune system within the oropharynx weakens and allows the fungus to grow and spread throughout the mouth, which is called oral thrush. The lesions of thrush are often sore and usually appear as small white patches on the inner cheeks, tongue, roof of mouth, and throat. Some patients report having a "cotton-like" dryness in their mouth and some lose their sense of taste. Others with thrush experience pain while eating or swallowing and may have cracking or redness at the corners of the mouth. Therefore, to markedly reduce the risk of thrush, it is imperative to rinse and gargle with water and spit out the water to remove the deposited medication from the mouth and throat. However, if a patient develops thrush, treatment with antifungal lozenges, liquid, or pills is usually very effective.

## ADVANTAGES OF THE pMDI

### The Patient

Advantages of using a pMDI include the following: it is portable, lightweight, compact, and requires short treatment time. The pMDI does not require a high inspiratory flow, the medication dose is the same with each actuation, and many combinations of medications are available within one device. Furthermore, the advantages of using a pMDI with a VHC include significantly improved patient coordination, higher lung deposition of medication, and reduced deposition of medication in the oropharynx and mouth. In addition, the required inspiratory effort to inhale the medication is lower when a VHC is used. Similar to the pMDI, the BAI's advantages include being portable, lightweight, compact, and requiring short treatment time. The BAI also has multiple doses and a combination of medications in one device. One major advantage of the BAI over the pMDI is that the BAI does not require the coordination of inhalation and actuation.

### The Healthcare Professional

The advantages of the pMDI from the point of view of the HCP include those mentioned in the patient advantages above. In addition, various combinations of medications are available in the pMDI formulation, allowing for improved likelihood that the preferred classes of medications will be available on insurance plans and hospital formularies.

## DISADVANTAGES AND COMMON ERRORS WHEN USING THE pMDI

### The Patient

The disadvantages of the pMDI include the hand-breath coordination needed when using this device in order to successfully inhale the medication deep into the lungs and that the medication may deposit in the back of the mouth/throat instead of being delivered to the airways deep within the lungs.

Also, to actuate the device, the patient must push down on the canister, which may be difficult for some with significant hand arthritis. Some common errors when using pMDI occur in many patients with hand/finger pain, who may turn

the device upside down to actuate with their thumb. However, the device will not work when upside down because the propellants are gravity dependent and only work when the device is upright.

There is frequently confusion in the use of pMDI due to the plethora of devices on the market and the similar appearance of devices, such as the Respiclick and Digihaler, which are dry powder inhalers but appear like the pMDI and BAI devices. Patients may not properly understand how to use the pMDI, including how to prepare and handle the device before each dose. Other common mistakes including breathing in too quickly, which is associated with depositing more medicine in the oropharynx rather than deep in the lungs. In addition, if the medication is used without a VHC, critical errors often result in ineffective delivery of medication into the lungs. These major errors include the following: Actuating the canister too early (before starting the inhalation), stopping/ceasing inspiration upon release of the medication aerosol, and actuating the device too late in the inhalation cycle. In addition, if the breath-hold does not occur, the drug may be expelled and not delivered to the airways. Any error in any step may lead to inadequate drug delivery to the lung (13). Several studies have shown that patients with COPD and asthma commonly misuse the pMDI in real life (10, 14–16).

Furthermore, the disadvantages of using the pMDI with VHC or spacer are that it is not as portable as the pMDI alone, the VHC requires regular cleaning, and there are additional costs associated with purchasing the VHC. Lastly, the BAI has some disadvantages as well, which include accidental release of the medication into the air if the patient inadvertently shakes the device with the cap open and that there may be some confusion with the BAI because people are not familiar with this device.

### The Healthcare Professionals

There is confusion in the use of the pMDI among HCP due to the plethora of devices on the market, and the HCP may not properly understand all the steps required to properly use the inhaler. Mastering pMDI use involves preparing and handling the device as well as ensuring optimal inhaler technique. A single error in any step of the inhaler technique may lead to suboptimal drug delivery to the lung (13). Even when patients are given detailed instructions and are appropriately able to demonstrate the technique back to the educator (called return demonstration), the intricacies and the number of steps required may result in one or more critical inhaler technique errors. In addition, frequently, any given patient's inhaler technique deteriorates over time, and requires reassessing inhaler technique at every encounter and reviewing the proper steps, whether in person or via a telehealth visit.

### CONCLUSIONS

Successful management of the symptoms and complications of obstructive lung diseases requires teamwork between the healthcare professionals and the patients in order to improve health outcomes. Adherence and proper use of inhaled medications for obstructive lung diseases via traditional pMDI and breath-actuated pMDI require careful and repeated instruction, assessment, and reassessment at every patient-HCP encounter. HCPs need to exhibit vigilance to detect errors in inhaler technique, whether subtle or obvious, that may reduce drug delivery and overall effectiveness of the inhaled medications in patients with obstructive lung diseases.

## REFERENCES

1. Usmani O. Choosing the right inhaler for your asthma or COPD patient. Ther Clin Risk Manag 2019;15:461–472.
2. Salvi S, Shevade M, Aggarwal A, et al. A practical guide on the use of inhaler devices for asthma and COPD. J Assoc Physicians India 2014;15:326–338.
3. Tena A, Clara P. Deposition of inhaled particles in the lungs. Arch Bronchoneumol 2012;48(7):240–246.
4. Chierici V, Cavalieri L, Piraino A, et al. Consequences of not-shaking and shake-fire delays on the emitted dose of some commercial solution and suspension pressurized metered dose inhalers. Expert Opin Drug Deliv 2020;17(107):1025–1039.
5. Sanchis J, Corrigan C, Levy M, et al. Inhaler devices from theory to practice. Respir Med 2013;107:495–502.
6. Newman S, Weisz A, Clarke S. Improvement of drug delivery with a breath actuated pressurised aerosol for patients with poor inhaler technique. Thorax 1991;46(10):712–726.
7. Leach C, Colice G. A pilot study to assess lung deposition of HFA-beclomethasone and CFC-beclomethasone from a pressurized metered dose inhaler with and without add-on spacers and using varying breathhold times. J Aerosol Med Pulm Drug Deliv 2010;23(6):355–361.
8. Reddel HK, Bacharier LB, Bateman ED, et al. Global initiative for asthma strategy 2021 - Executive summary and rationale for key changes. Am J Respir Crit Care Med 2022;205(1):17–35.
9. Global Initiative for Chronic Obstructive Lung Disease. Global strategy for the diagnosis, management, and prevention of chronic obstructive pulmonary disease. 2023 report. [cited 2022 Dec 21]. Available from: https://goldcopd.org/2023-gold-report-2
10. Kaplan A, Price D. Matching inhaler devices with patients: The role of the primary care physician. Can Respir J 2018;2018:9473051.
11. Labiris NR, Dolovich MB. Pulmonary drug delivery. Part II: The role of inhalant delivery devices and drug formulations in therapeutic effectiveness of aerosolized medications. Br J Clin Pharmacol 2003;56(6):600–612.
12. Papi A, Chipps BE, Beasley R, et al. Albuterol-budesonide fixed-dose combination rescue inhaler for asthma. N Engl J Med 2022;386:2071–2083.
13. Usmani O, Lavorini F, Marshall J, et al. Critical inhaler errors in asthma and COPD: A systematic review of impact on health outcomes. Respir Res 2018;19(10):1–20.
14. Lavorini F, Usmani O. Correct inhalation technique is critical in achieving good asthma control. Prim Care Respir J 2013;22(4):385–386.
15. Sanchis J, Gich I, Pedersen S, et al. Systematic review of errors in inhaler use. Has patient technique improved over time? Chest 2016;105(2):394–406.
16. Molimard M, Raherison C, Lignot S, et al. Chronic obstructive pulmonary disease exacerbation and inhaler device handling: Real-life assessment of 2935 patients. Eur Respir J 2017;49:1601794.

# 4 Spacers and Valved Holding Chambers

*Rajiv Dhand and Myrna B. Dolovich*

## CONTENTS

## INTRODUCTION

Pressurized metered-dose inhalers (pMDIs) became commercially available in 1956 and patients with asthma and chronic obstructive pulmonary disease (COPD) rapidly adopted them as the preferred modality for personalized treatment (1) and they remain immensely popular to this day (2). The unique attributes of convenience of use, perceived ease of use of pMDIs, and portability are major factors for their widespread use among patients. However, soon after the introduction of pMDIs two significant problems became apparent, namely, the inability of many patients to synchronize their inhalation with actuation of the pMDI and the high velocity of the emitted aerosol spray that resulted in high oropharyngeal deposition of drug (3, 4). Several devices were developed to overcome these twin problems, including complex breath-activated devices which initiated drug delivery only when the patient developed adequate negative inspiratory pressure to simple tubes (5, 6) and chambers (7, 8) that added space between the patient's mouth and the pMDI.

The introduction of spacers and valved holding chambers (VHCs) in the 1980s as accessory devices for pMDI delivery of aerosolized drugs proved to be of major benefit for many adult and pediatric patients. Coordinating actuation of the pMDI to release the dose of medication with inhalation of the fast-moving aerosol cloud emitted was challenging for the majority of adult and all pediatric users of pMDI treatments for asthma (9); the attachment of a spacer or VHC to the pMDI allowed patients to manage these two maneuvers, thereby obtaining their aerosolized medication more easily. The design, properties, and function of a number of spacers and VHCs will be discussed in this chapter, describing the differences between products and the many factors and outcome measures that should be considered when choosing a spacer/VHC for patients.

Spacer devices, also known as "add-on devices," "extension devices'" "accessory devices," or "valved holding chambers," are available in a variety of dimensions and design features (Figure 4.1). The drug emitted by a pMDI forms an aerosol cloud

DOI: 10.1201/9781003269014-4

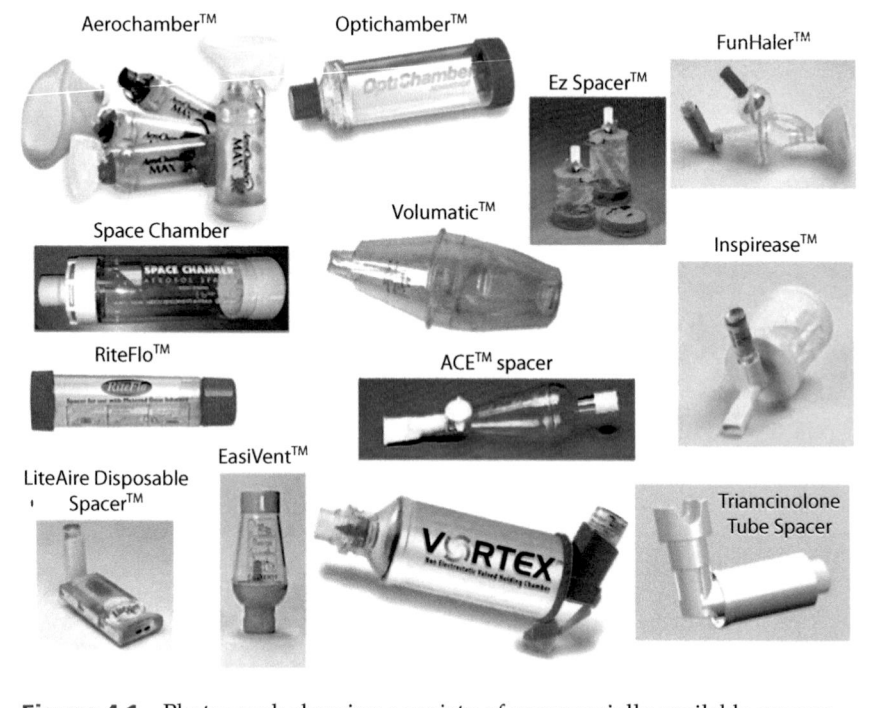

**Figure 4.1** Photograph showing a variety of commercially available spacers and VHCs for attachment with pMDIs. Spacers and VHCs have several designs and are available in a variety of sizes (see text for details).

within the spacer. A VHC has a one-way valve to hold the aerosol in the chamber after pMDI actuation for a finite time and permits airflow into, but not out of, the patient's mouth (Figure 4.2). In the "reverse-flow" design, the pMDI placed close to the mouth is actuated in a direction away from the patient into a spacer from which the patient inhales, thereby doubling the length that the aerosol travels (10). Spacers reduce oral deposition while VHCs can reduce both oral deposition and the need for precise synchronization between actuation and inhalation (Table 4.1).

## HOW SPACERS/VHCs WORK

Spacers and VHCs have several effects on the aerosol produced by pMDIs (Figure 4.2). First, the high velocity of the drug aerosol emitted from the pMDI actuator is reduced due to the impaction and loss of large particles to the chamber walls, along with losses resulting from the increased distance/time between actuation and inhalation by the patient. Second, the deposition of drug in the oropharynx is reduced because larger particles, which have the greatest inertia at high velocity and which are most likely to deposit in the mouth or throat, impact, or sediment due to gravity within the spacer. The residual aerosol or "respirable" portion of the original aerosolized drug, contained in smaller particles <5μm in diameter, remains available for inhalation and deposition in the lung. Finally, the use of a VHC holds the remaining aerosol within the chamber for a finite time after pMDI actuation, reducing the need for precise coordination between actuation of the pMDI and inhalation of the remaining aerosol. Some VHCs incorporate an audible feedback signal to warn against too rapid an inspiratory flow; in other devices this signal is used as a guide to promote the optimal inhalation flow rate

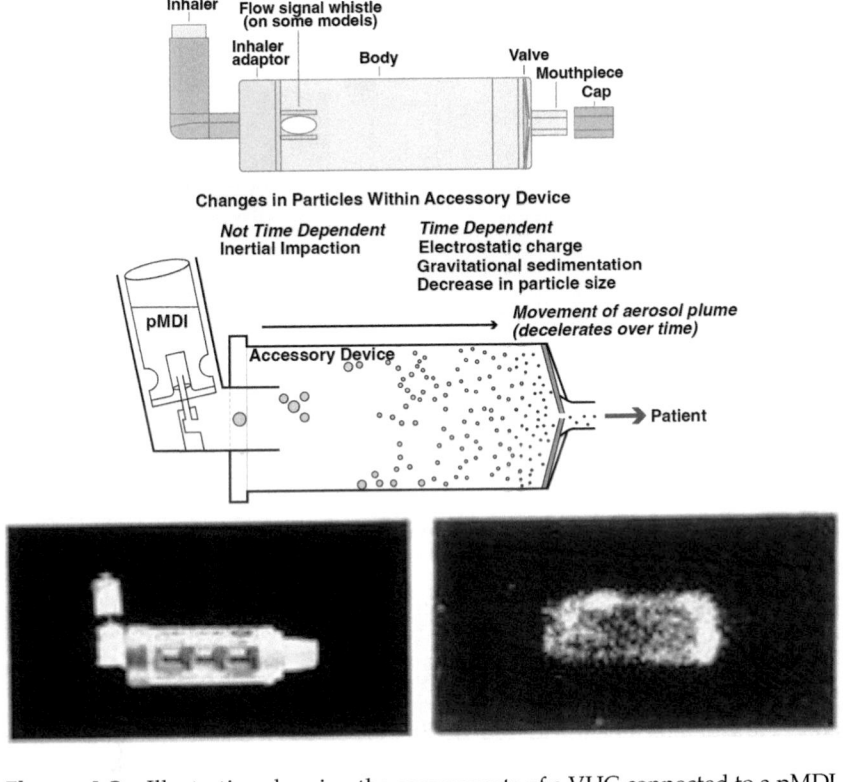

**Figure 4.2** Illustration showing the components of a VHC connected to a pMDI (top panel). In the AeroChamber, the reed that signals flow is incorporated into the outer ring of the rubber backpiece. The changes in the aerosol plume produced by the pMDI as it traverses the chamber of the VHC are shown (middle panel). The aerosol plume released from the pMDI travels at varying velocities, dependent on the formulation (propellants, excipients, and drug) (11). At high velocities, the plume impacts on the valve and may fold back on itself, traveling to the back of the VHC. This movement likely results in particle deposition on the VHCs inner surface, reducing the available aerosol for inhalation as well as altering the particle size of the available aerosol (12). As inhalation begins, the aerosol plume again reverses direction, moving toward the mouth with a decreased forward velocity. During this finite time, partial evaporation of the propellant(s) continues, increasing the fine particle fraction of the available aerosol and further decreasing the overall particle size of the aerosol. Two images (lower panel) show the AeroChamber™ VHC, with a pMDI inserted into the rubber backpiece on the left and on the right, a gamma camera scan post one actuation from a radioactive bronchodilator aerosol. The high concentration of "hot spots" on the inspiratory valve (white area) represents particles from the pMDI that would otherwise impact in the oropharynx and larynx. (Modified from M Dolovich. Physical principles underlying aerosol therapy. Journal of Aerosol Medicine 1989; 2(2): 171–186. Reproduced with permission.)

## Table 4.1: Spacers/VHCs: Function and Effect

| Effect of Spacer/VHC | Clinical Impact |
| --- | --- |
| Reduces need for coordination between inhalation and actuation | Beneficial for 20–50% of patients using pMDIs who have difficulty with coordinating inhalation with actuation (13) |
| Selective removal of larger particles by impaction on spacer walls | Reduction in size of the aerosol particles exiting the spacer/VHC leading to more uniform deposition of aerosol in the healthy lung (14, 15) |
| Decreased spray velocity and reduced oropharyngeal deposition | Reduced local and systemic side-effects (e.g., tremor, oral thrush) (4, 16) |
| Feedback signal to guide optimal inhalation flow | Increase in lung deposition as a proportion of nominal dose (8, 17–19) |

*Abbreviations:* pMDI = pressurized metered-dose inhaler; VHC = valved holding chamber.

with pMDI use. The use of spacers also reduces the bad taste associated with oral deposition of some drugs (triamcinolone acetonide, flunisolide) and propellants and mitigates the "cold-Freon effect" in some patients (20).

## AEROSOL DELIVERY TO THE LUNG

Reduction in the forward velocity of the aerosol as it traverses the spacer/VHC coupled with the decrease in particle size of the aerosol reduces drug deposition in the oropharynx by several folds (4, 17). Dolovich and co-workers (21) reported the clinical evaluation of a VHC that was the early version of the AeroChamber, a 145-mL cylinder which incorporated a rubberized opening into which the pMDIs mouthpiece actuator (or "boot") could fit regardless of pMDI actuator shape. Using a [99m]technetium radiolabeled pMDI aerosol they showed a reduction in throat deposition, from 65% with the pMDI alone to 6.5% with the AeroChamber in bronchitic subjects (21). Notably, *peripheral* lung deposition of aerosol improved and there was more uniform lung deposition with use of the VHC in the healthy subjects, but not in those with chronic bronchitis, underscoring the influence of airways obstruction on aerosol deposition in the lung. Moreover, in the COPD subjects, lung deposition was almost identical for the pMDI alone (17.4%) versus the pMDI with holding chamber (18.0%) when the values were corrected for tissue adsorption of radioactivity (21).

Newman and co-workers, employing radiolabeled aerosol and a 750-mL spacer device with a one-way inhalation valve (Nebuhaler, Astra Pharmaceuticals), corroborated the dramatic reduction in aerosol losses in the throat from ~80% with the pMDI alone, but they noted a corresponding increase in aerosol loss in the chamber (~56%) (8). In that study (8), there was a significant increase in the fraction of the total dose to the lungs with a valved large volume spacer (20.9%) compared to a pMDI alone (8.7%). Besides the device characteristics, other factors, such as the age-specific breathing pattern and airway morphology, also influence lung deposition of aerosol from spacer devices (19).

## FACTORS INFLUENCING DRUG DELIVERY FROM SPACERS AND VHCs

The design of spacers and VHCs employ 3 basic concepts—the open tube (OT) design, the reservoir or holding chamber (HC) design, and the reverse-flow (RF) design, in which the pMDI, placed close to the mouth—is fired in the direction away from the patient (10, 22, 23).

Some spacers integrate flow restrictors to control the patient's inspiratory flow and incorporate mechanisms to coordinate inhalation with pMDI actuation (e.g., Optihaler, Healthscan Products, Cedar Grove, NJ). Other spacers/VHCs provide

## Table 4.2: Factors Influencing Performance of Spacers and VHCs

| pMDI related | Spacer/VHC related | Patient related |
|---|---|---|
| Volume of aerosol cloud | Dimensions (size, shape) | Age |
| Concentration of aerosol | Presence of valves (inspiratory, expiratory) | Tidal volume |
| Aerosol velocity | Materials (plastic, metal, non-conducting polymers) | Inspiratory flow |
| Metering valve dimension | Flow indicators | Coordination with actuation; dose of API inhaled |
| Excipients in formulation | pMDI actuator design | Breath-hold |
| Formulation (e.g., type of propellant, vapor pressure) | Vents for air entrainment | Presence of airway obstruction |
| | Durability of device | Use of facemask or mouthpiece |

*Abbreviations:* API = active pharmaceutical ingredient; pMDI = pressurized metered-dose inhaler; VHC = valved holding chamber.

an audible warning when the patient inhales too fast (e.g., Aerosol Cloud Enhancer, DHD Diemolding Healthcare Division, Canastota, NJ; AeroChamber, Monaghan Medical Corporation, Plattsburgh, NY; Inspirease, Schering Corporation, Kenilworth, NJ). Collapsible plastic bags are used to increase the volume of some spacers but can degrade if alcohol is an excipient in the formulation. However, several issues associated with pMDIs are not resolved simply by adding a spacer/VHC because a pMDI and spacer/VHC combination creates a unique device whose performance is influenced by a variety of factors (Table 4.2).

Several different spacer/VHCs, based on the three concepts mentioned above and with volumes ranging from 15 to 750 ml, are currently available (Table 4.3). Figure 4.1 illustrates some devices that are currently commercially available.

## Table 4.3: Volume of Some Commonly Employed Spacers/VHCs

| Type of spacer/VHC | Trade Name | Volume (ml) |
|---|---|---|
| **Open Tube Spacers** | Microspacer | 15 |
| | Azmacort | 113 |
| | Ellipse | 230 |
| **Holding Chambers** | OptiChamber | 140 |
| | AeroChamber | 145 |
| | Vortex | 180[a] |
| | Rondo | 270 |
| | Babyhaler | 350 |
| | Nebuhaler | 700 |
| | Volumatic | 750 |
| **Reverse-Flow Design** | Optihaler | 70 |
| | Ace | 170 |
| | Inspirease | 700 |

*Abbreviations:* VHC = valved holding chamber.

[a] Approximate volume based on the dimensions of the chamber.

The impaction of particles is related to their mass, velocity, and distance traveled on release from the pMDI. Therefore, particles emerging from the pMDI actuator at a higher velocity have an increased tendency to impact on the inner surface of the spacer. This factor is especially important for small volume spacers, as drug losses on the walls of such spacers lead to a significant reduction in total drug output from the spacer (24, 25).

Early studies demonstrated that more aerosolized drug would likely be available for deposition in the lung when using longer and wider tubes attached to pMDIs (5). However, the portability of a larger, wider spacer becomes an issue for ambulatory patients. In a VHC, the amount of "respirable" aerosol was shown to increase with some formulations (7, 26). Usually, a spacer/VHC increases the fine particle fractions (FPFs) of the aerosol released into the device and this may translate into a greater fine particle mass of drug available for inhalation (27, 28), if the emitted dose is higher with a larger VHC design. However, a higher efficiency of drug delivery, especially with inhaled corticosteroids, needs to be balanced with the potential to cause greater side effects (29–32), and this outcome may not be looked upon favorably by regulatory agencies.

The portability and ease of use of an accessory device could influence patients' compliance with treatment. Except for the Inspirease, spacers/VHCs employed in ambulatory patients are non-collapsible; thus, pMDI and accessory spacers/VHCs are larger and heavier than the pMDI alone. Corr and colleagues found that spacers with a chamber volume of 145 ml width 9 cm, and length of 11 cm had a high efficiency for delivering aerosol from a pMDI (7). Likewise, drug output from accessory devices with a volume between 145 and 250 mL was found to be comparable to that from the pMDI alone (25). Accessory devices with volumes of ~ 700 ml improve pulmonary deposition of aerosol (8), but their large size makes them cumbersome for patients to carry. Although devices with smaller chamber volumes (≤120 mL) are more portable, they have the potential to significantly reduce drug delivery (25). Thus, accessory devices with intermediate volumes (~150 mL) appear to provide the best combination of performance and portability.

Patients should be instructed to release one actuation of the pMDI into the spacer or holding chamber per inhalation as inhalation after actuation of multiple doses into the spacer markedly reduces total drug available due to increased wall loses (33–35). In a large volume spacer/VHC, particles are evenly distributed throughout inhalation because the aerosol cloud becomes static before inhalation. In contrast, the aerosol cloud remains turbulent in small-volume spacers, and they may deliver an initial burst of concentrated aerosol followed by comparatively aerosol-free air (36) that could drive the aerosol further down the bronchial tree. In a large volume spacer, a single actuation of the pMDI may not deliver all the drug particles during one inhalation compared with a smaller volume spacer (37).

The low-resistance, one-way valve situated behind the mouthpiece (Figure 4.2) in VHCs retains the aerosol for a finite time within the device until the patient inhales and allows VHCs to be used with tidal breathing as well as with a single, deep inspiration. The inhalation valve must withstand the initial pressure from pMDI actuation yet have a sufficiently low resistance to open readily on inhalation, especially when using a VHC for infants and children (38–40). In VHCs, drug losses due to sedimentation occur during the interval between actuation and inhalation, while losses due to impaction are flow dependent and occur non-uniformly, mostly in the distal part of the spacer/VHC (41), and on the inhalation valve upon pMDI actuation.

Some VHCs also incorporate an exhalation valve. The exhalation valve should be a low resistance valve to allow comfortable exhalation, but with sufficient resistance to prevent re-entry of the aerosol into the VHC. A large dead space

between inspiratory and expiratory valves could reduce mean dose delivery (42, 43). The last part of each inhalation is trapped between the inspiratory and expiratory valve and may be lost with exhalation. This dead space in the delivery system constitutes an increasing fraction of the tidal volume in infants and children below the age of 4 years and tends to produce an inverse relationship between age and the dose of drug delivered (43, 44).

Valves may become jammed if soiled or damaged and require cleaning or replacement of the device if that doesn't resolve the issue. The valve material may degrade over a year of use due to the propellants in the pMDI formulation, losing its ability to respond to inspiratory and expiratory pressures.

## ELECTROSTATIC CHARGE

Aerosols emitted from pMDIs have an intrinsic electrostatic charge (45) which varies with different formulations (46–48). VHCs made from non-conducting polymers also acquire surface electrostatic charge during manufacture, packaging, and storage (49). Deposition of aerosol particles on the walls of electrostatic spacers due to electrostatic attraction reduces the drug dose and half-life of the aerosol in the spacer (33, 50).

O'Callaghan and colleagues (33) and Barry and O'Callaghan (50) first reported that drug output was more than two-fold higher when the spacer was coated with a thin film of an antistatic spray before actuation of the pMDI compared to the non-coated device. The antistatic lining also negated the reduction in drug output which occurred when there was a 20-sec delay between actuation of the pMDI and a simulated patient breath. Similarly, improvement in albuterol output delivered by a volumatic spacer in which the static charge was decreased was reported by Dewsbury and colleagues (51). Priming the spacer with multiple doses from a pMDI can also increase drug deposition in the lungs (52), but it could reduce the number of doses available for therapy. Electrostatic charge is reduced by build-up of a thin layer of drug and surfactant that are components of the aerosol spray. This coating is washed off by rinsing the spacer and drug output diminishes until the protective coating builds up again (33–35). Priming is not recommended for those HFA pMDIs that do not contain surfactant; priming the spacer may have a variable effect on drug output and is wasteful of medication (53).

Electrostatic charge on the inner walls of plastic spacers can significantly influence drug output (33, 50). Washing a plastic spacer, newly removed from its packaging and drip drying, can decrease the electrostatic charge in the unused spacer. But drying must occur before the initial use, which is not always convenient for patients. Drying the spacer by wiping it with a cloth will increase the electrostatic charge and is not recommended. The electrostatic charge, and the drug output, will vary over time because of priming of the spacer with use and additional variations introduced by periodically washing the spacer that is needed for hygienic reasons and to prevent build-up of powder on the inspiratory valve from altering the properties of the valve. Thus, washing and subsequent priming of the spacer could result in repeated variations in the amount of drug output from the spacer (54).

The effects of electrostatic charge can be overcome by either lightly coating the internal surface of the VHC or spacer with an antistatic spray, or spraying it with an antistatic lining, washing with a dilute solution (1:5,000) of household detergent and air drying for 24 hours, or by using a metallic spacer (55, 56). The material used to coat the spacer should be non-toxic if inhaled by the patient and approved by the Food and Drug Administration for human use. If a non-static spacer is used, the potential for higher dose delivery may require dose modifications of some drugs, such as inhaled corticosteroids, that produce significant local or systemic side effects (29–32).

Use of a non-static spacer could have several benefits:

- Increased drug output, this effect could be particularly beneficial for expensive medications (demonstrated with several drugs and spacers). After detergent washing, drug output from intermediate volume (145 ml) spacers/VHCs was shown to be equivalent to large volume spacers (750 ml) in both in-vitro and in-vivo studies (29, 55–58). Similarly, after application of an anti-static coating, differences in drug output between large volume and intermediate volume spacers were less evident with HFA-pMDIs compared to the CFC formulations (15, 59, 60). These observations could be explained by the reduced velocity of the aerosol plume emitted by the HFA-pMDIs compared to CFC-pMDIs, thus resulting in fewer wall losses (61).

- Protection of aerosol dose when there is a delay between actuation and inhalation (as in infants and children).

- Greater uniformity in drug output over time (not shown conclusively).

- Enhanced therapeutic effects (62). The response to albuterol administered with a pMDI during periods of nocturnal bronchospasm was reported to increase mean percentage predicted $FEV_1$ values more with an antistatic spacer than with a non-conducting spacer (63). Likewise, in a real-world retrospective study a cohort using an antistatic spacer reported a decrease in the annualized rate of moderate to severe exacerbations, prolonged time to first moderate to severe exacerbation and reduced incidence of visits to the Emergency Department and hospitalizations compared to those using any non-antistatic spacer over a period of 1 year (64).

However, the use of non-static spacers could also be associated with certain adverse effects:

- Higher drug output has the potential for greater local/systemic side effects (29–32)

- The coefficient of variation in the drug output from the spacer may not decrease, i.e., the drug output per dose showed significant variation even in coated spacers (42, 43).

## SWITCHING pMDIs AND SPACERS ALTERS DRUG DELIVERY

The addition of spacers and VHCs to pMDIs contributes to variability in delivery of drug in both children and adults (14, 25, 28, 65–69). The combination of a pMDI with an accessory device has unique characteristics because different pMDIs have different vapor pressures, aerosol velocities, and aerosol volumes (70). Various spacers/VHCs are not interchangeable with different pMDIs because different spacers/VHCs have variable effects on total drug output, fine particle dose, and dose protection against incoordination and actuation (25, 71–73). Significant variations in drug output occur when the drug canister is removed from its native actuator and then coupled with a third-party actuator built into the spacer (74). The dimensions of the valve stem in the universal actuator are usually larger than that of the native mouthpiece actuator of the pMDI. This issue is mainly a problem for spacers integrated into ventilator circuits but is also relevant for portable, reverse-flow spacers and VHCs. Beyond the variability in aerosol characteristics introduced by using a spacer/VHC, it is worth considering that clinical outcomes associated with use of these devices are influenced by other factors, including patient preference, technique of use, and adherence to treatment (75). A systematic review highlighted the high frequency of incorrect inhaler use reported over a

span of 40 years. Surprisingly, incorrect use of pMDIs persisted with addition of inhalation chambers and adults committed errors with pMDIs and chambers more frequently than children (76). In view of these findings, real-world studies are needed to evaluate the clinical use and benefit and the cost-effectiveness of using spacers/VHCs with pMDIs in patients with asthma and COPD.

## USE OF SPACERS/VHCs IN CHILDREN

There are two main problems related to spacer use in children (77). Because of the low tidal volume, it takes several breaths for a child to clear the aerosol from the chamber and during this time, aerosol passively disappears from the reservoir by sedimentation due to gravity. Second, the inspiratory valve used in holding chambers must operate at low inspiratory flow rates observed in children and ensure unidirectional air flow from the holding chamber with exhalation outside the device. Otherwise, the aerosol retained in the holding chamber may be blown away during exhalation.

A single slow and deep breath followed by a breath-hold is ideal (22, 78). If the patient is unable to take a deep breath, tidal breathing through the device may be similarly effective in children (79). Other investigators have suggested that tidal breathing may not be as effective as a deep inspiration (18). If tidal breathing is employed, the pMDI should be activated at the beginning of a tidal inhalation (80). In very young children with low tidal volumes, fewer breaths are needed to clear the aerosol from a smaller volume compared to a large volume spacer/VHC. Physicians should consider the spacer volume/tidal volume ratio when selecting an appropriate device for their young patients. Too high a spacer volume/tidal volume ratio limits the amount of drug a child might inhale from the spacer and reduces efficacy of the therapy. Three-to-five tidal breaths are usually recommended before significant losses of useful aerosol are incurred.

VHCs can be used to administer pMDI medications to neonates and very young children with appropriately fitting facemasks (81, 82). Snug but comfortable fit of the mask to the cheeks is important to avoid leakage of aerosol-laden air around the facemask edges (81) and minimization of facemask dead space (83) is critical to avoid re-breathing through the mask, thereby not drawing aerosol from the VHC (77).

## RECOMMENDATIONS FOR USE

The use of spacers/VHCs is recommended by several national and international guidelines, especially for children using inhaled corticosteroids with pMDIs (84, 85). However, these guidelines are less frequently implemented in clinical practice. For example, surveys show that less than 50% of patients with asthma and COPD have spacers/VHCs and many patients presenting to an emergency room with exacerbations of asthma or COPD have not used these devices (86–88). Use of spacers/VHCs may be more common among patients who have a primary care physician or those who have been hospitalized for an acute exacerbation of asthma or COPD (88). Moreover, a significant proportion of patients exhibit errors in the use of pMDIs and spacers (89). Infants, children below the age of 3 years, the elderly and frail individuals who are unable to coordinate inhalation with actuation of the pMDI, those with compromised comprehension or manual dexterity, and those experiencing acute attacks of asthma or COPD could benefit from use of spacers/VHCs with their pMDIs (90–95). In young children (ages 2 months to 5 years) a low-cost home-made modified 500-mL plastic bottle spacer was shown to be as effective as a commercially available spacer for treatment of acute airway obstruction as measured by improvements in clinical score and pulmonary function (96). Most elderly patients can use pMDIs and spacers

## Table 4.4: **Technique for Using a Spacer/VHC**

1. Sit or stand up straight with the chin up and neck slightly extended
2. Shake the pMDI and remove its cap
3. If using a VHC check that the valve(s) is moving appropriately
4. Fit the pMDI into the spacer/VHC with the canister up and hold it in an upright position
5. Keep the pMDI-spacer/VHC assembly in a horizontal position on one hand holding the pMDI with the other hand supporting the mouthpiece end of the spacer/VHC
6. Breathe out as far as comfortable
7. Place the mouthpiece of the spacer/VHC between the teeth and seal the lips around it. If a facemask is used, place it gently but firmly over the nose and lips to make a tight seal
8. Start a slow breath in and immediately press the inhaler once. Continue to breathe in slowly for 3–4 seconds until the lungs are full
9. Hold the breath for 10 seconds or for as long as is comfortable
10. While holding the breath take the spacer/VHC out of the mouth (or lower the mask)
11. Exhale into room air. Do not exhale into the spacer/VHC
12. Repeat the sequence of steps 2–11 for additional doses
13. Take the pMDI out of the spacer/VHC, and replace the cap on the pMDI and the mouthpiece of the spacer/VHC
14. Rinse the mouth and gargle after inhalation of a corticosteroid

*Abbreviations:* pMDI = pressurized metered-dose inhaler; VHC = valved holding chamber.

effectively (97). The addition of a large facemask can facilitate aerosol delivery in the elderly patient, particularly if keeping the spacer/VHC mouthpiece in the mouth proves difficult. However, adult patients of all ages who exhibit appropriate technique of pMDI use may not derive greater bronchodilation from the use of a pMDI and spacer/VHC compared to a pMDI alone (98, 99).

Use of spacers/VHCs in ambulatory patients adds to the cost of treatment compared with pMDIs alone and the increased permutations of the delivery device could be confusing for some patients. Significant variability in drug output occurs with pMDI and different spacers/VHCs and some pMDI and spacer/VHC combinations may reduce drug delivery (23, 24, 36, 58, 72, 99, 100).

## COMPARISON OF EFFICACY OF pMDIs AND SPACERS/VHCs WITH DRY POWDER INHALERS (DPIs) AND NEBULIZERS

pMDIs and VHCs are convenient for administering bronchodilators to infants and children, and to adults during acute exacerbations of asthma or COPD. Several systematic reviews and meta-analyses have concluded that administration of bronchodilators with a pMDI and VHC combination is equally effective as a nebulizer or a DPI in both children and adults with acute asthma (101). A lower incidence of side effects with the pMDI and VHC in patients with acute asthma receiving bronchodilator therapy may be an added advantage (102–106).

## INHALATION TECHNIQUE FOR SPACERS/VHCs

The recommended technique for using a spacer/VHC is summarized in Table 4.4.

■ Multiple doses must never be actuated into the spacer/VHC. Each actuation should be followed by inhalation of the aerosol (33).

■ Multiple actuations into the spacer/VHC before inhalation create turbulence and significantly reduce the respirable fraction of the aerosol (24, 33, 35, 50).

- There should be minimal delay between actuation of the pMDI and breathing in through the spacer/VHC. Too long a delay ($\geq$ 10 sec) significantly reduces the dose available for inhalation (24, 25, 33, 50, 107, 108).

- Coordination between inhaling and actuation of the pMDI is required even while using a spacer/VHC. Actuation of the pMDI without inhaling or during exhalation may further reduce drug delivery (25).

- A single slow and deep inhalation followed by a breath-hold is optimal (22, 78).

- Spacers/VHCs are not generic devices and should not be used interchangeably with other pMDIs (70).

## MAINTENANCE OF SPACERS/VHCs

Manufacturers of spacers/VHCs provide guidance for maintenance. Clearly, poor maintenance of spacers/VHCs could influence the efficiency of aerosol delivery (71).

Spacers/VHCs must be washed before their first use and cleaned periodically because they can be contaminated with microorganisms. Bacterial contamination of spacers appears to be fairly common. Contamination with *Pseudomonas aeruginosa, Staphylococcus aureus,* and *Klebsiella pneumoniae* was reported in 35% of spacers/VHCs used by children with asthma (109). Hence, it is recommended that patients should wash their spacers before first use and frequently thereafter (preferably weekly) according to the procedure outlined in Table 4.5. The spacer/VHC should not be washed in the dishwasher. Lukewarm tap water with a few drops of household detergent is recommended for cleaning (56). According to the manufacturer's instructions, the spacers/VHCs life is between 6 and 12 months and they should be replaced periodically, at least annually.

## CONCLUSION

The appropriate use of spacers/VHCs to deliver pMDI aerosols can confer significant benefits for some patients, especially infants, children, the elderly, and those with acute exacerbations of asthma or COPD. The use of spacers/VHCs is more forgiving of errors related to actuation-inhalation incoordination. However, patients and clinicians need careful instructions about the nuances in correct use of spacers/VHCs to optimize treatment with these devices.

## Table 4.5: Washing and Cleaning Instructions for Spacers and VHCs

- Disassemble the spacer/VHC after the last dose of the day
- Immerse in lukewarm water containing a few drops of household detergent
- Shake the parts in water and let it soak for 15 minutes
- Rinse the soapy water off the parts, including the mouthpiece with lukewarm water
- Do not rinse or rub the inside surfaces of the parts
- Place all the parts on a dry paper towel and air dry
- Reassemble the parts and ensure that the valve functions properly
- Wash the spacer/VHC frequently (preferably weekly)
- After each cleaning and drying and prior to use, prime the spacer/VHC by actuating 1 or 2 puffs from the pMDI into the spacer/VHC without inhaling the aerosol. Conducting metal spacers do not need priming
- Spacers should not be wrapped in a cloth for storage

*Abbreviations:* pMDI = pressurized metered-dose inhaler; VHC = valved holding chamber.

## REFERENCES

1. Stein SW, Thiel CG. The history of therapeutic aerosols: A chronological review. J Aerosol Med Pulm Drug Deliv 2017;30:20–41. DOI:10.1089/jamp.2016.1297
2. Pritchard JN. The climate is changing for metered-dose inhalers and action is needed. Drug Des Devel Ther 2020;14:3043–3055.
3. Newman S. Respiratory drug delivery: The essential theory and practice. Richmond (VA): Respiratory Drug Delivery Online; 2009. p. 177–216. Chapter 6, Pressurized metered dose inhalers.
4. Kim CS, Eldridge A, Sackner MA. Oropharyngeal deposition and delivery aspects of metered-dose inhaler aerosols. Am Rev Respir Dis 1987;135:157–164.
5. Morén F. Drug deposition of pressurized inhalation aerosols I. Influence of actuator tube design. Int J Pharm 1978;1:205–212.
6. Newman SP, Millar AB, Lennard-Jones TR, et al. Pressurised aerosol deposition in the human lung with and without an "open" spacer device. Thorax 1989;44:706–710.
7. Corr D, Dolovich M, McCormack D, et al. Design and characteristics of a portable breath-actuated particle size selective medical aerosol inhaler. J Aerosol Sci 1982;13:1–7.
8. Newman SP, Millar AB, Lennard-Jones TR, et al. Improvement of pressurised aerosol deposition with Nebuhaler spacer device. Thorax 1984;39(12):935–941.
9. Epstein SW, Manning CPR, Ashley MJ, et al. Survey of the clinical use of pressurized aerosol inhalers. Can Med Assoc J 1979;120:813–816.
10. Dolovich M. Inhalation technique and inhalation devices. In: Pauwels R, O'Byrne P, editors. Lung biology in health and disease. New York (NY): Marcel Dekker, Inc.; 1997. p. 229–255. Chapter 10, Beta2-agonists in asthma treatment.
11. Liu X, Doub WH, Guo C. Evaluation of metered dose inhaler spray velocities using Phase Doppler Anemometry (PDA). Int J Pharm 2012;423:235–239.
12. Sarkar S, Peri SP, Chaudhury B. Investigation of multiphase multicomponent aerosol flow dictating pMDI-spacer interactions. Int J Pharm 2017;529:264–274.
13. Konig P. Spacer devices used with metered dose inhalers: Breakthrough or gimmick? Chest 1985;88:276–284.
14. Dalby RN, Somaraju S, Chavan VS, et al. Evaluation of aerosol drug output from the OptiChamber and AeroChamber spacers in a model system. J Asthma 1998;35:173–177.
15. Mitchell JP, Nagel MW, Rau JL. Performance of large-volume versus small-volume holding chambers with chlorofluorocarbon-albuterol and hydrofluoroalkane-albuterol sulfate. Respir Care 1999;44:38–44.
16. Salzman GA, Pyszczynski DR. Oropharyngeal candidiasis in patients treated with beclomethasone dipropionate delivered by metered-dose inhaler alone and with AeroChamber. J Allergy Clin Immunol 1988;81:424–428.
17. Newman SP, Moren F, Pavia D, et al. Deposition of pressurized suspension aerosol inhaled through extension devices. Am Rev Respir Dis 1981;124:317–320.
18. Roller CM, Zhang G, Troedsen RG, et al. Spacer inhalation technique and deposition of extrafine aerosol in asthmatic children. Eur Respir J 2007;29:299–306.

19. Dolovich MB. Influence of inspiratory flow rate, particle size, and airway caliber on aerosolized drug delivery to the lung. Respir Care 2000;45(6):597–608.
20. Lavorini F, Fontana GA. Targeting drugs to the airways: The role of spacer devices. Expert Opin Drug Deliv 2009;6:91–102.
21. Dolovich M, Ruffin R, Corr D, et al. Clinical evaluation of a simple demand inhalation MDI aerosol delivery device. Chest 1983;83(1):36–41.
22. Nikander K, Nicholls C, Denyer J, et al. The evolution of spacers and valved-holding chambers. J Aerosol Med Pulm Drug Deliv 2014;27:S4–S23.
23. Vincken W, Levy ML, Scullion J, et al. Spacer devices for inhaled therapy: Why use them and how? ERJ Open Res 2018;4:00065-2018. DOI:10.1183/23120541.00065-2018
24. O'Callaghan C, Barry P. Spacer devices in the treatment of asthma. BMJ 1997;314:1061.
25. Wilkes W, Fink J, Dhand R. Selecting an accessory device with a metered-dose inhaler: Variable influence of accessory devices on fine particle dose, throat deposition, and drug delivery with asynchronous actuation from a metered-dose inhaler. J Aerosol Med 2001;14(3):351–360.
26. Dolovich M. Lung dose, distribution, and clinical response to therapeutic aerosols. Aerosol Sci Technol 1993;18(3):230–240.
27. Dolovich M. Characterization of medical aerosols: Physical and clinical requirements for new inhalers. Aerosol Sci Technol 1995;22(4):392–399.
28. Finlay WH, Zuberbuhler P. In vitro comparison of salbutamol hydrofluoroalkane (Airomir) metered dose inhaler aerosols inhaled during pediatric tidal breathing from five valved holding chambers. J Aerosol Med 1999;12:285–291.
29. Nair A, Menzies D, Hopkinson P, et al. In vivo comparison of the relative systemic bioavailability of fluticasone propionate from three anti-static spacers and a metered dose inhaler. Br J Clin Pharmacol 2009;67:191–198.
30. Gillen M, Forte P, Svensson JO, et al. Effect of a spacer on total systemic and lung bioavailability in healthy volunteers and in vitro performance of the Symbicort® (budesonide/formoterol) pressurized metered dose inhaler. Pulm Pharmacol Ther 2018;52:7–17. DOI:10.1016/j.pupt.2018.08.001
31. Singh D, Collarini S, Poli G, et al. Effect of AeroChamber Plus™ on the lung and systemic bioavailability of beclometasone dipropionate/formoterol pMDI. Br J Clin Pharmacol 2011;72:932–939.
32. Dorinsky P, DePetrillo P, DeAngelis K, et al. Relative bioavailability of budesonide/glycopyrrolate/formoterol fumarate metered dose inhaler administered with and without a spacer: Results of a phase I, randomized, crossover trial in healthy adults. Clin Ther 2020;42(4):634–648. DOI:10.1016/j.clinthera.2020.02.012
33. O'Callaghan C, Lych J, Cant M, et al. Improvement in sodium cromoglycate delivery from a spacer device by use of an antistatic lining, immediate inhalation, and avoiding multiple actuation of drugs. Thorax 1993;46:603–606.
34. Clark DJ, Lipworth BJ. Effect of multiple actuations, delayed inhalation and antistatic treatment on the bioavailability of salbutamol via a spacer device. Thorax 1996;51:981–984.
35. Rau JL, Restrepo RD, Deshpande V. Inhalation of single vs multiple metered-dose bronchodilator actuations from reservoir devices: An in vitro study. Chest 1996;109:969–974.

36. Verbanck S, Vervaet C, Schuermans D, et al. Aerosol profile extracted from spacers as a determinant of actual dose. Pharm Res 2004;21(12):2213–2218. DOI:10.1007/s11095-004-7673-7.

37. Dubus JC, Dolovich M. Emitted doses of salbutamol pressurized metered-dose inhaler from five different plastic spacer devices. Fundam Clin Pharmacol 2000;14:219–224.

38. Holzner PM, Muller BW. An in vitro evaluation of various spacer devices for metered-dose inhalers using the Twin Impinger. Int J Pharm 1994;106:69–75.

39. Bisgaard H. Delivery of inhaled medication to children. J Asthma 1997;34(6):443–467.

40. Fink JB. Metered-dose inhalers, dry powder inhalers, and transitions. Respir Care 2000;45(6):623–635.

41. Ogrodnik N, Azzi V, Sprigge E, et al. Nonuniform deposition of pressurized metered-dose aerosol in spacer devices. J Aerosol Med Pulm Drug Deliv 2016;29:490–500.

42. Bisgaard H. A metal aerosol holding chamber devised for young children with asthma. Eur Respir J 1995;8(5):856–860.

43. Bisgaard H, Anhøj J, Klug B, et al. A non-electrostatic spacer for aerosol delivery. Arch Dis Child 1995;73(3):226–230.

44. Berg E, Madsen J, Bisgaard H. In vitro performance of three combinations of spacers and pressurized metered-dose inhalers for treatment of children. Eur Respir J 1998;12:472–476.

45. Kwok PCL, Chan H-K. Electrostatic charge in pharmaceutical systems. 2nd ed. New York (NY): Taylor & Francis Group, 2005. p. 1–14. (Encyclopedia of pharmaceutical technology).

46. Peart J, Magyar C, Byron PR. Aerosol electrostatics: Metered-dose inhalers (MDIs). In: Dalby RN, Byron PR, Farr SJ, editors. Respiratory drug delivery-VI. Buffalo Grove (IL): Interpharm Press; 1998. p. 227–233.

47. Glover W, Chan H-K. Electrostatic charge characterization of pharmaceutical aerosols using electrical low-pressure impaction (ELPI). J Aerosol Sci 2004;35(6):755–764.

48. Keil JC, Kotian R, Peart J. Using and interpreting aerosol electrostatic data from the electrical low pressure impactor. In: Dalby RN, Byron PR, Peart J, et al., editors. Respiratory drug delivery-X. River Grove (IL): Davis Horwood International Publishing; 2006. p. 267–277.

49. Bisgaard H, Anhoj J, Wildhaber JH. Spacer devices. In: Bisgaard H, O'Callaghan C, Smaldone GC, editors. Drug delivery to the lung. New York (NY): Marcel Dekker Inc.; 2002. p. 389–420.

50. Barry PW, O'Callaghan C. The effect of delay, multiple actuations and spacer static charge on the in vitro delivery of budesonide from the Nebuhaler. Br J Clin Pharmacol 1995;40:76–78.

51. Dewsbury NJ, Kenyon CJ, Newman SP. The effect of handling techniques on electrostatic charge on spacer devices: A correlation with in vitro particle size analysis. Int J Pharm 1996;137:261–264.

52. Kenyon CJ, Thorsson L, Borgstrom L, et al. The effects of static charge in spacer devices on glucocorticosteroid aerosol deposition in asthmatic patients. Eur Respir J 1998;11:606–610.

53. Peart J, Kulphaisal P, Orban JC. Relevance of electrostatics in respiratory drug delivery. Business Briefing: Pharmagenerics. 2003. Available from: http://www.touchbriefings.com/pdf/890/PT04_peart.pdf.

54. Janssens HM, Devadason SG, Hop WCJ, et al. Variability of aerosol delivery via spacer devices in young asthmatic children in daily life. Eur Respir J 1999;13:787–791.

55. Wildhaber JH, Devadason SG, Hayden MJ, et al. Electrostatic charge on plastic spacer devices influences the delivery of salbutamol. Eur Respir J 1996;9:1943–1946.

56. Pierart F, Wildhaber JH, Vrancken I, et al. Washing plastic spacers in household detergent reduces electrostatic charge and greatly improves delivery. Eur Respir J 1999;13:673–678.

57. Wildhaber JH, Devadason SG, Eber E, et al. Effect of electrostatic charge, flow, delay and multiple actuations on the in vitro delivery of salbutamol from different small volume spacers for infants. Thorax 1996;51(10):985–988.

58. Rau JL, Coppolo DP, Nagel MW, et al. The importance of nonelectrostatic materials in holding chambers for delivery of hydrofluoroalkane albuterol. Respir Care 2006;51(5):503–510.

59. Barry PW, O'Callaghan C. In vitro comparison of the amount of salbutamol available for inhalation from different formulations used with different spacer devices. Eur Respir J 1997;10(6):1345–1348. DOI:10.1183/09031936.9710061345

60. Dolovich M. Aerosols. In: Barnes PJ, Grunstein MM, Leff AR, et al., editors. Asthma. Philadelphia (NY): Lippincott-Raven; 1997. p. 1349–1366. Chapter 93.

61. Dolovich MB, Dhand R. Aerosol drug delivery: Developments in device design and clinical use. Lancet 2011;377(9770):1032–1045.

62. Levy ML, Hardwell A, McKnight E, et al. Asthma patients' inability to use a pressurised metered-dose inhaler (pMDI) correctly correlates with poor asthma control as defined by the global initiative for asthma (GINA) strategy: A retrospective analysis. Prim Care Respir J 2013;22:406–411.

63. Prabhakaran S, Shuster J, Chesrown S, et al. Response to albuterol MDI delivered through an anti-static chamber during nocturnal bronchospasm. Respir Care 2012;57(8):1291–1296.

64. Burudpakdee C, Kushnarev V, Coppolo D, et al. A retrospective study of the effectiveness of the AeroChamber Plus® Flow-Vu® antistatic valved holding chamber for asthma control. Pulm Ther 2017;3(2):283–296.

65. Ahrens R, Lux C, Bahl T, et al. Choosing the metered-dose inhaler spacer or holding chamber that matches the patient's need: Evidence that the specific drug being delivered is an important consideration. J Allergy and Clin Immunol 1995;96(2, Suppl 1):288–294.

66. Kenyon CJ, Dewsbury NJ, Newman SP. Differences in aerodynamic particle size distributions of innovator and generic beclomethasone dipropionate aerosols used with and without a large volume spacer. Thorax 1995;50:846–850.

67. Miller MR, Bright P. Differences in output from corticosteroid inhalers used with a volumatic spacer. Eur Respir J 1995;8:1637–1638.

68. Barry PW, O'Callaghan C. Inhalational drug delivery from seven different spacer devices. Thorax 1996;51:835–840.

69. Nagel MW, Wiersema KJ, Bates SL, et al. Performance of large- and small-volume valved holding chambers with a new combination long-term bronchodilator/anti-inflammatory formulation delivered by pressurized metered dose inhaler. J Aerosol Med 2002;15:427–433.

70. Lavorini F, Barreto C, van Boven JFM, et al. Spacers and valved holding chambers-the risk of switching to different chambers. J Allergy Clin Immunol Pract 2020;8(5):1569–1573.

71. Mitchell JP, Nagel MW. Valved holding chambers (VHCs) for use with pressurised metered-dose inhalers (pMDIs): A review of causes of inconsistent medication delivery. Prim Care Respir J 2007;16(4):207–214.

72. Williams RO III, Patel AM, Barron MK, et al. Investigation of some commercially available spacer devices for the delivery of glucocorticoid steroids from a pMDI. Drug Dev Ind Pharm 2001;27(5):401–412.

73. Dissanayake S, Nagel M, Falaschetti E, et al. Are valved holding chambers (VHCs) interchangeable? An in vitro evaluation of VHC equivalence. Pulm Pharmacol Ther 2018;48:179–184.

74. Childers AG, Cummings RH, Kaufman BD, et al. Comparative study of dose delivery and cascade impaction performance of four metered-dose inhaler and spacer combinations. Curr Ther Res 1996;57:75–87.

75. Brennan VK, Osman LM, Graham H, et al. True device compliance: The need to consider both competence and contrivance. Respir Med 2005;99:97–102.

76. Sanchis J, Gich I, Pedersen S. Aerosol Drug Management Improvement Team (ADMIT). Systematic review of errors in inhaler use: Has patient technique improved over time? Chest 2016;150(2):394–406. DOI:10.1016/j.chest.2016.03.041

77. Janssens HM, Tiddens HA. Aerosol therapy: The special needs of young children. Paediatr Respir Rev 2006;7(Suppl 1):S83–S85.

78. Newman SP, Pavia D, Garland N, et al. Effects of various inhalation modes on the deposition of radioactive pressurized aerosols. Eur J Respir Dis 1982;63(Suppl. 119):57–65.

79. Stephen D, Vatsa M, Lodha R, et al. A randomized controlled trial of 2 inhalation methods when using a pressurized metered dose inhaler with valved holding chamber. Respir Care 2015;60:1743–1748.

80. Berlinski A, von Hollen D, Hatley RHM, et al. Drug delivery in asthmatic children following coordinated and uncoordinated inhalation maneuvers: A randomized crossover trial. J Aerosol Med Pulm Drug Deliv 2017;30:182–189.

81. Janssens HM, Tiddens HAWM. Facemasks and aerosol delivery by metered dose inhaler-valved holding chamber in young children: A tight seal makes the difference. J Aerosol Med 2007;20(Suppl 1):S59–S65.

82. Smaldone GC, Sangwan S, Shah A. Facemask design, facial deposition, and delivered dose of nebulized aerosols. J Aerosol Med 2007;20(Suppl 1):S66–S77.

83. Shah SA, Berlinski AB, Rubin BK. Force-dependent static dead space of face masks used with holding chambers. Respir Care 2006;51(2):140–144.

84. Global Initiative for Asthma (GINA). 2022. [cited 2022 Jun 30]. Available from: https://ginasthma.org/wp-content/uploads/2022/05/GINA-Main-Report-2022-FINAL-22-05-03-WMS.pdf

85. UK National Institute for Clinical Excellence. Guidance on the use of inhaler systems(devices) in children under the age of 5 with chronic asthma. Technology Appraisal guidance No. 10 2000 [cited 2022 June 30]. Available from: http://www.nice.org.uk

86. Fitzgerald JM, Chan CK, Holroyde MC, et al. The CASE survey: Patient and physician perceptions regarding asthma medication use and associated oropharyngeal symptoms. Can Respir J 2008;15:27–32.

87. Hilton S. An audit of inhaler technique among asthma patients of 34 general practitioners. Br J Gen Pract 1990;40:505–506.

88. Guss D, Barash IA, Castillo EM. Characteristics of spacer device use by patients with asthma and COPD. J Emerg Med 2008;35:357–361.

89. Bryant L, Bang C, Chew C, et al. Adequacy of inhaler technique used by people with asthma or chronic obstructive pulmonary disease. J Prim Health Care 2013;5:191–198.

90. Pool JB, Greenough A, Gleeson JG, et al. Inhaled bronchodilator treatment via the Nebuhaler in young asthmatic patients. Arch Dis Child 1988;63:288–291.

91. Rau JL. Practical problems with aerosol therapy in COPD. Respir Care 2006;51:158–172.

92. Kerem E, Levison H, Schuh S, et al. Comparison with nebs in acute asthma in children. Efficacy of albuterol administered by nebulizer versus spacer device in children with acute asthma. J Pediatr 1993;123:313–317.

93. Parkin PC, Saunders NR, Diamond SA, et al. Randomized trial spacer vs. nebulizer for acute asthma. Arch Dis Child 1995;72:239–240.

94. Robertson CF, Norden MA, Fitzgerald DA, et al. Treatment of acute asthma: Salbutamol via jet nebulizer vs. spacer and metered dose inhaler. J Paediatr Child Health 1998;34:142–146.

95. Mandelberg A, Tsehori S, Houri S, et al. Is nebulized aerosol treatment necessary in the pediatric emergency department? Chest 2000;117:1309–1313.

96. Zar HJ, Streun S, Levin M, et al. Randomised controlled trial of the efficacy of a metered dose inhaler with bottle spacer for bronchodilator treatment in acute lower airway obstruction. Arch Dis Child 2007;92(2):142–146. DOI:10.1136/adc.2006.101642

97. Ho SF, OMahony MS, Steward JA, et al. Inhaler technique in older people in the community. Age Ageing 2004;33(2):185–188. DOI:10.1093/ageing/afh062

98. Lee H, Evans HE. Evaluation of inhalation aids of metered-dose inhalers in asthmatic children. Chest 1987;91:366–369.

99. Demirkan K, Tolley E, Mastin T, et al. Salmeterol administration by metered-dose inhaler alone vs metered-dose inhaler plus valved holding chamber. Chest 2000;117:1314–1318.

100. Lakamp RE, Berry TM, Prosser TR, et al. Compatibility of spacers with metered-dose inhalers. Am J Health Syst Pharm 2001;58(7):585–591.

101. Dolovich MB, Ahrens RC, Hess DR, et al. Device selection and outcomes of aerosol therapy: Evidence-based guidelines: American College of Chest Physicians/American College of Asthma, Allergy, and Immunology. Chest 2005;127(1):335–371.

102. Rodrigo C, Rodrigo G. Salbutamol treatment of acute severe asthma in the ED: MDI versus hand held nebulizer. Am J Emerg Med 1998;16:637–642.

103. Cates CJ, Welsh EJ, Rowe BH. Holding chambers (spacers) versus nebulisers for beta-agonist treatment of acute asthma. Cochrane Database Syst Rev 2013;9:CD000052.

104. van Geffen WH, Douma WR, Slebos DJ, et al. Bronchodilators delivered by nebuliser versus pMDI with spacer or DPI for exacerbations of COPD. Cochrane Database Syst Rev 2016;2016(8):CD011826. DOI:10.1002/14651858.CD011826.pub2

105. Idris AH, McDermott MF, Raucci JC, et al. Emergency department treatment of severe asthma. Metered-dose inhaler plus holding chamber is equivalent in effectiveness to nebulizer. Chest 1993;103:665–672.

106. Raimondi AC, Schottlender J, Lombardi D, et al. Treatment of acute severe asthma with inhaled albuterol delivered via jet nebulizer, metered dose inhaler with spacer, or dry powder. Chest 1997;112:24–28.
107. Slator L, von Hollen D, Sandell D, et al. In vitro comparison of the effect of inhalation delay and flow rate on the emitted dose from three valved holding chambers. J Aerosol Med Pulm Drug Deliv 2014;27(Suppl. 1):S37–S43.
108. Chambers FE, Brown S, Ludzik AJ. Comparative in vitro performance of valved holding chambers with a budesonide/formoterol pressurized metered-dose inhaler. Allergy Asthma Proc 2009;30(4):424–432. DOI:10.2500/aap.2009.30.3252
109. Cohen HA, Cohen Z, Pomeranz AS, et al. Bacterial contamination of spacer devices used by asthmatic children. J Asthma 2005;42:169–172.

# 5 Slow Mist Inhalers

*P. N. Richard Dekhuijzen, Matteo Bonini, and Federico Lavorini*

## CONTENTS

## INTRODUCTION

Slow mist inhalers (SMIs) have been part of the spectrum of inhalation devices since 2003. They are considered to be a separate class of inhaler devices, besides pMDIs, DPIs, and nebulizers.

## WHAT IS AN SMI?

In essence, the SMI is classified as a pocket-sized device that can generate a single-breath aerosol from a propellant-free liquid drug solution (1). SMIs deliver the drug solution using mechanical energy produced by a spring, generating a fine, slow-moving mist over a longer period compared to other devices (1.2–1.5 s versus 0.15–0.35 s). This allows patients more time to synchronize actuation and breathing, possibly reducing the errors due to poor coordination. The slow-moving mist also reduces the requirements for a high inspiratory effort by the patient. Of relevance, SMIs offer advanced technology containing a high small-particle fraction, resulting in low drug deposition in the oropharynx and high total lung deposition (>50%), effectively targeting the site of disease (2). However, patients using SMIs may require additional support in the assembly and proper priming procedures (3). Like pMDIs, SMIs can also be combined with spacers, although the combination is yet to be fully evaluated. In addition, the Respimat inhaler with a T-piece adapter can be safely used to deliver medications in mechanically ventilated tracheostomized patients (4).

The only SMI currently available is the Soft Mist Inhaler Respimat, developed by Boehringer Ingelheim. This device contains different bronchodilators as separate entities and in combinations. Other SMIs are in development, e.g., by Merxin (5).

DOI: 10.1201/9781003269014-5

## HOW DOES A SMI WORK?

The Respimat SMI uses a nozzle system (the Uniblock) to aerosolize a metered dose of drug solution into tiny particles suitable for inhalation (6). A schematic overview of the Respimat and its components is shown in Figure 5.1 (7). The Respimat SMI generates an aerosol independently of the patient's inhalation effort, with a slow velocity and prolonged duration, which may facilitate the coordination of actuation and inhalation. Since the aerosol generated by the Respimat SMI has a high fine-particle fraction delivered at a slow velocity, lung deposition is maximized and

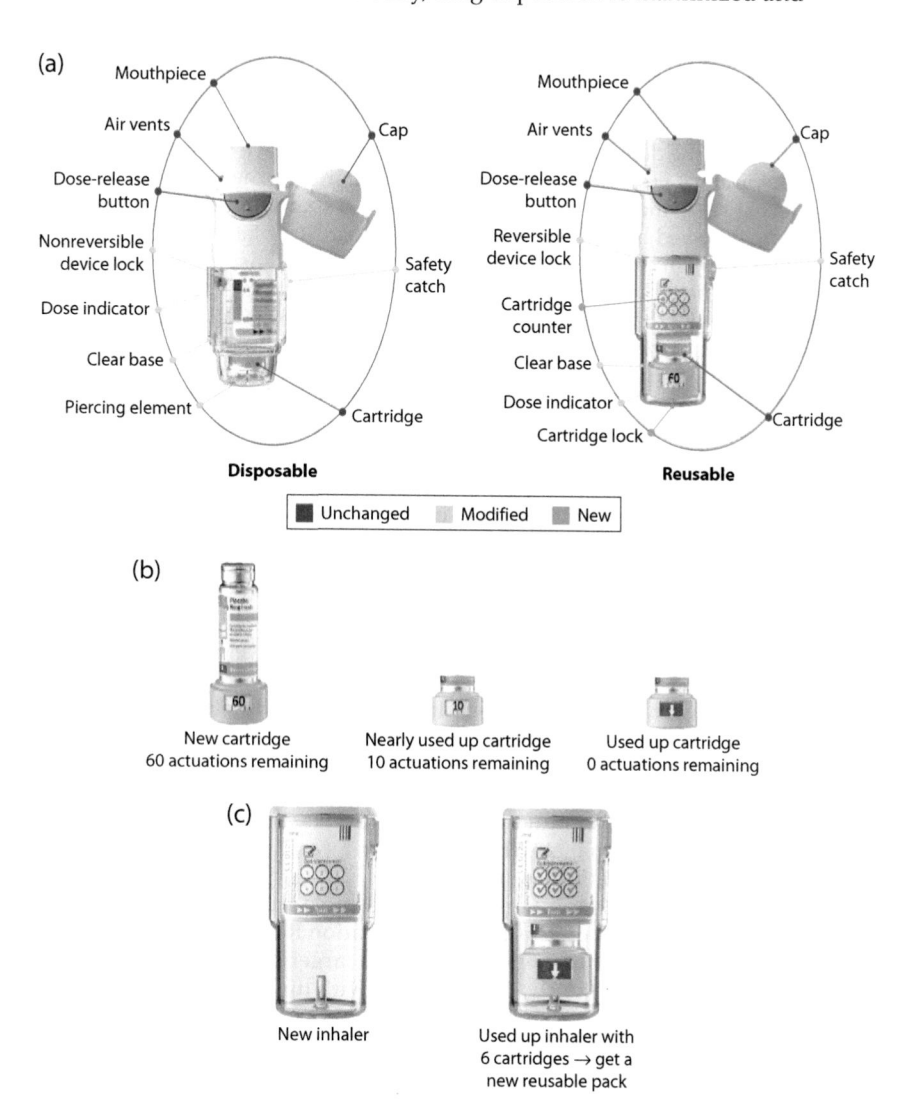

**Figure 5.1** Schematic drawing of the reusable Respimat SMI (7).

oropharyngeal deposition minimized, even at low inhalation flows. More than 60% of the drug dose released by the Respimat SMI falls within a fine-particle dose of <5.0 μm, which enhances drug delivery to the smaller bronchi and bronchioles (8).

The Respimat SMI has a favorable lung deposition profile in patients with asthma or COPD. In six patients with asthma, drug deposition to the whole lung and the peripheral airways using the Respimat SMI (57.1% and 39.7%, respectively) was higher than when using MDIs or DPIs (whole lung deposition 20.0–44.3%; peripheral airway deposition 11.3–29.2%). The deposition fractions for the Respimat SMI in the upper, central, and peripheral airways were in the ranges of 41.3–44.3%, 13.8–22.6%, and 34.6–42.4%, respectively (8).

Mechanisms to release drug differ significantly among inhaler types. Patients have to generate a certain inspiratory flow through DPIs to disperse the drug and get it out of the device and into the lungs. So, users have to generate a certain inspiratory flow rate to overcome the resistance in the DPI. In case of high internal resistance, patients have to generate a sharp and fast (2–3 seconds) inspiration, followed by a breath hold of 5–10 seconds (the latter is the case for all inhaler types). In case of lower internal resistance, the inspiration through the device may be less powerful. In case of a pMDI, the drug is released after actuation of the device, irrespective of the inspiratory flow. Clearly, however, there must be an inspiratory maneuver in order to get the released drug into the airways. The inspiratory flow through the SMI, however, may be low, e.g., 30 liters/min. The release of drugs from an SMI is initiated by actuating the device. Again, lung deposition occurs only when the patient inhales simultaneously, but the inhalation may be at low flow rates as with pMDIs. A significant advantage of the SMI is the low plume velocity which enables the patient to inhale the dose even more easily. In vivo studies have confirmed that lung deposition after inhaling through an SMI of pMDI is higher than through a DPI (9).

This improved deposition in the lungs combined with reduced oropharyngeal deposition is caused by the slower aerosol velocity of the Respimat SMI relative to other inhalers. The aerosol spray velocity of the Respimat SMI (0.84 and 0.72 m/s at 80 and 100 mm from the end of the nozzle, respectively) is lower than that of seven different pMDIs; the slowest MpDI spray velocity was 2.47 and 1.71 m/s at 80 and 100 mm from the end of the nozzle, respectively (10). Similarly, the Respimat SMI produces an aerosol cloud that moves much more slowly than aerosol clouds from pMDIs (mean velocity 100 mm from the nozzle: Respimat SMI, 0.8 m/s; MDIs, 2.0–8.4 m/s). The soft mist produced by the Respimat SMI had a longer mean duration (1.5 s) than that produced by MDIs (0.15–0.36 s) (11).

Recently, an improved second-generation Respimat reusable inhaler was released. In more detail, this second-generation Respimat inhaler is characterized by an easier device assembly, a larger dose indicator window, and, more importantly, it is reusable, with up to six cartridges with an intuitive cartridge-exchange mechanism (7). The updated design was intended to improve the usability and environmental impact of the Respimat inhaler while preserving the pharmaceutical performance and basic functions of the disposable Respimat inhaler. The reusable version of the Respimat has improved usability, with no effect on the efficiency of drug delivery, aerosol particle size, or required inhalation method across multiple cartridge use. Furthermore, studies assessing patients' satisfaction

and preferences indicate that the new reusable version of Respimat has consistently been shown to be well accepted by patients with asthma and COPD with a high degree of patients' satisfaction.

There could also be potential environmental benefits of reusable inhalers. The carbon footprint of an item, individual, or organization, is one of the most important and quantifiable environmental impacts, assessed by the amount of greenhouse gases (often expressed in terms of $CO_2$ equivalents) generated throughout the lifecycle. At variance with pMDIs that contain hydrofluorocarbon (HFC) propellants (HFC-134a and HFC-227ea), which are potent greenhouse gases, SMIs such as the Respimat do not require propellants since the energy to dispense an aqueous solution as a mist of particles is provided by a spring. Hänsel et al. compared the carbon footprints of Respimat versus pMDIs for several drug combinations, including Respimat reusable and disposable (12). They found that switching from an HFC pMDI to a disposable Respimat resulted in an approximate 95% reduction in the lifecycle carbon footprint. Compared with the disposable device over one month, use of the Respimat reusable over three months would further reduce the monthly carbon footprint to 0.34 kg $CO_2$ eq (corresponding to a 57% reduction), or 0.23 kg $CO_2$ eq if used over 6 months (a 71% reduction).

## WHICH MEDICATIONS ARE AVAILABLE IN AN SMI?

The Respimat SMI device contains different bronchodilators (Table 5.1): short-acting beta-2-agonists (fenoterol), ultralong-acting beta-2-agonists (olodaterol), short-acting anticholinergics (ipratropium bromide), two combinations of a short-acting anticholinergic and a short-acting beta-2-agonist (ipratropium plus salbutamol, and ipratropium plus fenoterol), ultralong-acting anticholinergics (tiotropium), and the combination of an ultralong-acting anticholinergic and an ultralong-acting beta-2-agonist (tiotropium plus olodaterol). Inhaled corticosteroids are not available in this device.

## HOW SHOULD SMIs BE USED?

The instructions on how to use an SMI are available in several languages. The English version is available at https://www.medical.respimat.com/ie/HCP/how-to-use#:˜:text=Point%20the%20inhaler%20to%20the%20back%20of%20the,10%20 seconds%20or%20for%20as%20long%20as%20comfortable (13).

For daily use, there are three steps: turn, open, and press.

### Table 5.1: Medications Available in SMIs

| | |
|---|---|
| Short-acting beta-2-agonists | Fenoterol |
| Ultralong-acting beta-2-agonists | Olodaterol |
| Short-acting anticholinergics | Ipratropium bromide |
| Short-acting anticholinergic combined with a short-acting beta-2-agonist | Ipratropium plus salbutamol<br>Ipratropium plus fenoterol |
| Ultralong-acting anticholinergics | Tiotropium |
| Ultralong-acting anticholinergic combined with an ultralong-acting beta-2-agonist | Tiotropium plus olodaterol |

*Abbreviation:* SMI = slow mist inhalers.

**51**

TURN

- Keep the cap closed.
- **TURN** the clear base in the direction of the arrows on the label until it clicks (half a turn).

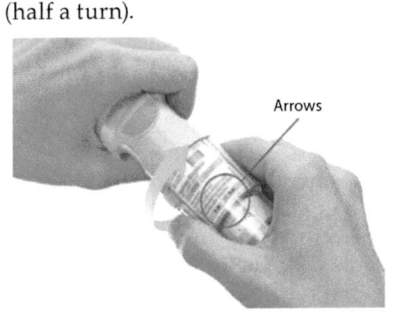

OPEN

- **OPEN** the cap until it snaps fully open.

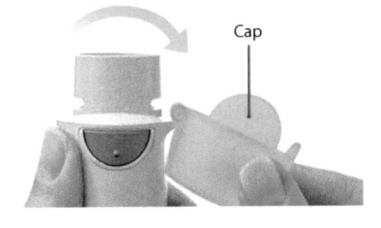

PRESS

- Breathe out slowly and fully.
- Close the lips around the mouthpiece without covering the air vents. Point the inhaler to the back of the throat.
- While taking a slow, deep breath through the mouth, **PRESS** the dose-release button and continue to breathe in slowly for as long as comfortable.
- Hold the breath for 10 seconds or for as long as comfortable.
- Repeat **TURN, OPEN, PRESS** for a total of 2 puffs.
- Close the cap until the inhaler is used again.

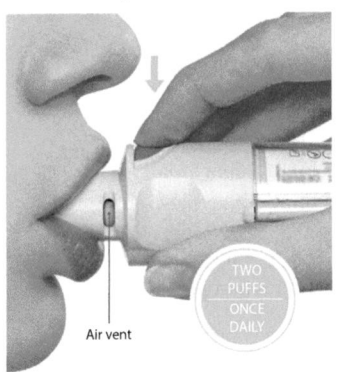

## IS THE SMI USED AS RESCUE THERAPY?

The SMIs containing short-acting beta-2-agonists and/or short-acting anticholinergics can be used as rescue therapy.

## IS THE SMI USED AS MAINTENANCE THERAPY?

The SMIs containing long-acting beta-2-agonists and/or long-acting anticholinergics can be used as maintenance therapy.

## ADVANTAGES OF SMIs FOR PATIENTS AND HCPs

Several studies and reviews have shown that poor inhalation technique may severely impact the clinical efficacy of medications, resulting in impaired disease control, worsening quality of life, increased exacerbation and mortality risk, increased hospitalization, and, in turn, increased health care expenditure. Factors like ease of use will influence actual use, patient preferences, and adherence (1, 14, 15).

Some characteristics of the Respimat device may support its ease of use. Patients only need to generate a low inspiratory flow rate through the device to get the medication into the airways. The low velocity of the plume and the long plume duration enable the patient to inhale an optimal portion of the delivered dose. And finally, the high fine-particle fraction ensures a high deposition throughout the entire lung. Patients may appreciate the lack of propellants that might contribute to the carbon footprint, and the availability of a reusable device (up to five times, by replacing an empty canister with a new one) (1).

Patients may rank their experiences and appreciation of an inhaler using the Patient Satisfaction and Preference Questionnaire (PASAPQ). The Respimat SMI scored high in the performance and convenience domains (16).

In a comparative analysis of adherence with seven different types of inhalers, the Respimat SMI was associated with the lowest risk of underuse (5.5%), defined as taking < 50% of the doses prescribed, in patients with COPD (1). MDIs were associated with a higher rate of overuse (taking > 125% of doses) and a lower rate of optimal use (= 75% and = 125%) compared with Respimat SMI in this analysis (17).

Comparative studies have been performed with SMIs, pMDIs, and DPIs. Comparing SMIs and pMDIs, patients (n = 201) significantly favored the Respimat SMI, with 81% reporting a preference for Respimat SMI compared to a pMDI (18). Compared to DPIs, the total satisfaction score in 153 patients with asthma was higher for the Respimat SMI (85.5) than for DPI (76.9), and the majority of patients preferred the Respimat SMI (74%) to DPI (17%) (19).

## DISADVANTAGES OF SMIs FOR PATIENTS AND HCPs

Possible disadvantages of the Respimat SMI are that the device needs some basic assembly and priming before the first use. Some patients, especially those with manual dexterity impairment, may have difficulty putting the cartridge into the base, following the Turn-Open-Press procedure, and then priming the device. Children may also find it difficult to produce adequate airflow to correctly operate some inhalers. In a study in children (aged < 5 years) with respiratory disease, 83% of 4-year-olds achieved adequate inhalation using the Respimat SMI unaided or with parental help, and 100% of 3- to 4-year-olds achieved adequate inhalation with the addition of a valved holding chamber (20). Another disadvantage of the currently available SMIs is that they do not contain ICS, either as a single agent or in combination with a long-acting beta-2-agonist or together with a beta-2-agonist and a long-acting anticholinergic.

## COMMON ERRORS WHEN USING SMIs

In a recent meta-analysis, the mistakes when using an SMI, as reported in eleven studies, were analyzed (21). Among the eleven studies with step-by-step data, the most common errors were failure to (1) exhale completely and away from the device (47.8% (95% CI: 33.6–62.0)); (2) hold the breath for up to 10 seconds (30.6% (95% CI: 17.5–43.7)); (3) take a slow, deep breath while pressing the dose-release button (27.9% (95% CI: 14.5–41.2)); (4) hold the inhaler upright (22.6% (95% CI: 6.2–39.0)); and (5) turn the base toward the arrows until it clicked (17.6% (95% CI: 3.0–32.2)). Device use errors occurred in about 6 of 10 patients who used SMIs. Data on errors after addressing these issues by repeated training are not available to the best of our knowledge.

## CONCLUSIONS

The currently available SMI (Respimat) has a number of features that may support patients in its correct use. These characteristics include the low inspiratory flow needed to inhale the drug properly, the low velocity and long plume duration, and the high fine-particle fraction. In clinical studies, these features appear to translate into a positive appreciation of its ease of use.

## REFERENCES

1. Iwanaga T, Tohda Y, Nakamura S, Suga Y. The Respimat Soft Mist Inhaler: implications of drug delivery characteristics for patients. Clin Drug Investig 2019;39:1021–1030.
2. Bonini M, Usmani OS. Demystifying inhaler use in chronic obstructive airways disease. Barc Respir Netw Rev 2018;4(4):304–318.
3. Baiardini I, Braido F, Bonini M, et al. Why do doctors and patients not follow guidelines? Curr Opin Allergy Clin Immunol 2009;9:228–233.
4. Mehri R, Alatrash A, Ogrodnik N, et al. In vitro measurements of Spiriva Respimat dose delivery in mechanically ventilated tracheostomy patients. J Aerosol Med Pulm Drug Deliv 2021;34:242–250.
5. MRX004. [cited 2022 Mar 26]. Available from: https://www.merxin.com/products/mrx004
6. Wachtel H, Kattenbeck S, Dunne S, et al. The Respimat development story: Patient-centered innovation. Pulm Ther 2017;3:19–30.
7. Dhand R, Eicher J, Hänsel M, et al. Improving usability and maintaining performance: Human-factor and aerosol-performance studies evaluating the new reusable Respimat inhaler. Int J Chron Obstruct Pulmon Dis 2019;14:509–523.
8. Perriello EA, Sobieraj DM. The Respimat Soft Mist Inhaler, a novel inhaled drug delivery device. Conn Med 2016;80:359–364.
9. Iwanaga T, Kozuka T, Nakanishi J, et al. Aerosol deposition of inhaled corticosteroids/long-acting $\beta_2$-agonists in the peripheral airways of patients with asthma using functional respiratory imaging, a novel imaging technology. Pulm Ther 2017;3:219–231.
10. Hochrainer D, Holz H, Kreher C, et al. Comparison of the aerosol velocity and spray duration of Respimat Soft Mist inhaler and pressurized metered dose inhalers. J Aerosol Med 2005;18:273–282.
11. Tamura G. Comparison of the aerosol velocity of Respimat Soft Mist inhaler and seven pressurized metered dose inhalers. Allergol Int 2015;64:390–392.

12. Hänsel M, Bambach T, Wachtel H. Reduced environmental impact of the reusable Respimat® Soft Mist™ Inhaler compared with pressurised metered-dose Inhalers. Adv Ther 2019;36:2487–2492.
13. How to use the Respimat device. [cited 2022 Mar 26]. Available from: https://www.medical.respimat.com/ie/HCP/how-to-use#:˜:text=Point%20 the%20inhaler%20to%20the%20back%20of%20the,10%20seconds%20or%20 for%20as%20long%20as%20comfortable
14. Bourbeau J, Bartlett SJ. Patient adherence in COPD. Thorax 2008;63:831–838.
15. Small M, Anderson P, Vickers A, et al. Importance of inhaler-device satisfaction in asthma treatment: Real-world observations of physician-observed compliance and clinical/patient reported outcomes. Adv Ther 2011;28:202–212.
16. Davis KH, Su J, González JM, et al. Quantifying the importance of inhaler attributes corresponding to items in the patient satisfaction and preference questionnaire in patients using Combivent Respimat. Health Qual Life Outcomes 2017;15:201.
17. Koehorst-ter Huurne K, Movig K, van der Valk P, et al. The influence of type of inhalation device on adherence of COPD patients to inhaled medication. Expert Opin Drug Deliv 2016;13:469–475.
18. Schurmann W, Schmidtmann S, Moroni P, et al. Respimat Soft Mist inhaler versus hydrofluoroalkane metered dose inhaler: Patient preference and satisfaction. Treat Respir Med 2005;4:53–61.
19. Hodder R, Reese PR, Slaton T. Asthma patients prefer Respimat® Soft Mist™ Inhaler to Turbuhaler. Int J Chron Obstruct Pulmon Dis 2009;4:225–232.
20. Kamin W, Frank M, Kattenbeck S, et al. A handling study to assess use of the Respimat Soft Mist Inhaler in children under 5 years old. J Aerosol Med Pulm Drug Deliv 2015;28:372–381.
21. Navaie M, Dembek C, Cho-Reyes S, et al. Device errors with soft mist inhalers: A global systematic review and meta-analysis. Chronic Respir Dis 2020;17:1–13.

# 6 Dry Powder Inhalers

*Donald A. Mahler and Roy A. Pleasants*

CONTENTS

## WHAT IS A DRY POWDER INHALER?

A dry powder inhaler (DPI) is a hand-held device that contains a powder medication that can be inhaled by an individual into the lower respiratory tract. The first DPI introduced was Intal Spinhaler® (sodium cromoglycate) by Fisons in the United Kingdom in 1967 and in the United States in 1970, to prevent both immediate and late antigen-induced asthmatic reactions (1). The developers found that sodium cromoglycate needed to be attached to lactose as a carrier particle to achieve effective delivery of the medication with the Spinhaler®, a feature that remains a critical aspect of DPI formulation (1). The next DPI introduced was the Rotohaler® in 1977 by Allen & Hanburys for the delivery of albuterol (1).

Although the Spinhaler® and Rotohaler® are relatively inefficient devices for drug delivery to the lung, the development process provided a background for the subsequent proliferation of DPIs following the signing of the Montreal Protocol in 1987 (see Chapter 1). The intent of his global agreement was to protect the ozone layer by phasing out the production and consumption of ozone-depleting substances such as chlorofluorocarbons (CFCs) which were used as a propellant in pressurized metered-dose inhalers (pMDI) (2).

There are three basic types of DPIs (Figure 6.1). 1) A single-unit device in which a capsule is inserted into a cavity within the DPI and is then punctured by a piercing apparatus before dosing; Aerolizer®, Breezhaler®, and HandiHaler® are examples. 2) A multi-unit device which contains a number or series of blisters; as found in the Accuhaler®/Diskus®, Ellipta®, and Genuair®/Pressair® DPIs. 3) A reservoir device which contains a bulk amount of drug powder with an internal mechanism to provide/deliver a single dose upon actuation. Examples of reservoir DPI are the Digihaler®, Easyhaler®, and Turbohaler®/Turbuhaler® (3).

Most DPIs are dispensed in sealed foil packaging with a desiccant to protect the drug formulation from environmental moisture. Both high humidity as well as the patient's exhalation into the mouthpiece of the DPI can reduce the amount of respirable drug emitted, due to the clumping of the powder and consequently

DOI: 10.1201/9781003269014-6

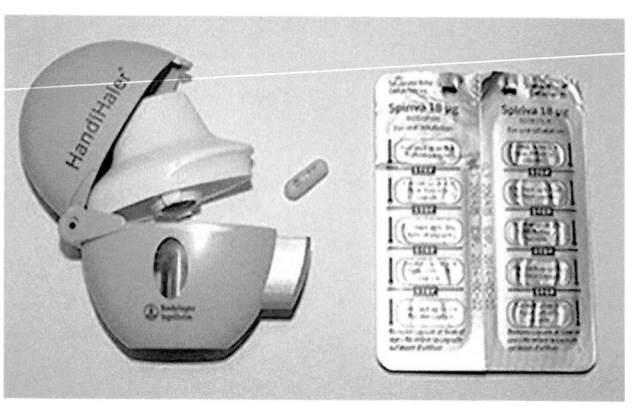

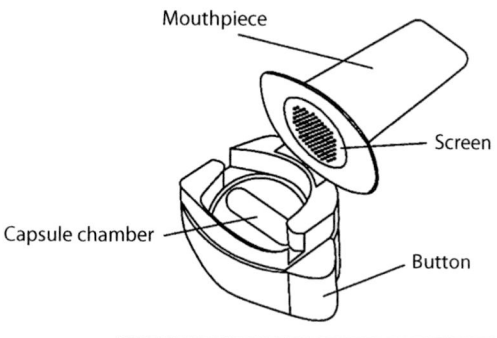

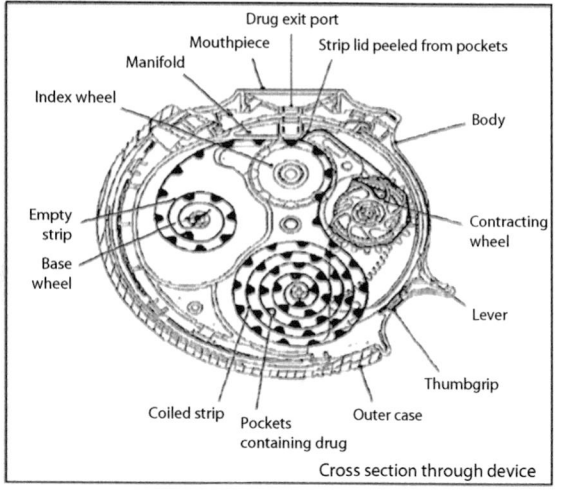

**Figure 6.1** HandiHaler® (a) and Breezhaler® (b) are examples of single-unit devices in which a capsule is inserted into a cavity. (c) The Diskus® is a multi-unit-dose dry powder inhaler that contains a number of blisters. Internal components of the Diskus® are shown on the right. (d) The Turbuhaler® is a reservoir dry powder inhaler that contains a bulk amount of drug powder with an internal mechanism to deliver a single dose upon actuation.

*(Continued)*

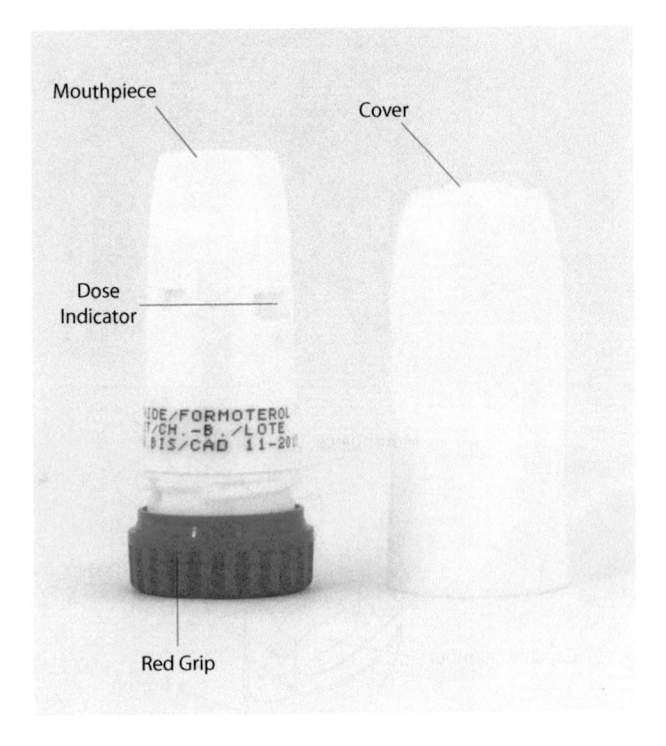

Mouthpiece

Cover

Dose
Indicator

Red Grip

**Figure 6.1** (*Continued*)

reduced dispersal of fine particles (4). DPIs should be stored in a dry location with average relative humidity below 40–45% (5).

## HOW DOES A DPI WORK?

Most dry powder formulations consist of a mixture of micronized drug less than five microns (µm) in mass median aerodynamic diameter attached to larger carrier particles (usually lactose) which act as bulking agents and improve the flowability of the powder. An alternative formulation is that of micronized drug particles as agglomerates in a packet or pellet. DPIs are activated when the patient inhales through the device, creating turbulent energy that aerosolizes, disaggregates, and disperses the powder formulation into respirable particles (3) (Figure 6.2). As the drug leaves the metering cup inside the DPI during the first few milliseconds, the beginning of inhalation should be "fast." If this does not occur, drug particles remain too large and are deposited in the mouth (6).

### Peak Inspiratory Flow

The generation of turbulent energy within DPIs is determined by the individual's peak inspiratory flow (PIF) and the internal resistance (r) of the DPI (3) (Table 6.1). The PIFr can be measured using an inspiratory flow meter and is defined as the maximum airflow generated during inhalation through the simulated resistance of a DPI (7). In vitro studies using lung models have established both minimal and optimal PIF values that have been extrapolated for clinical application (8–10).

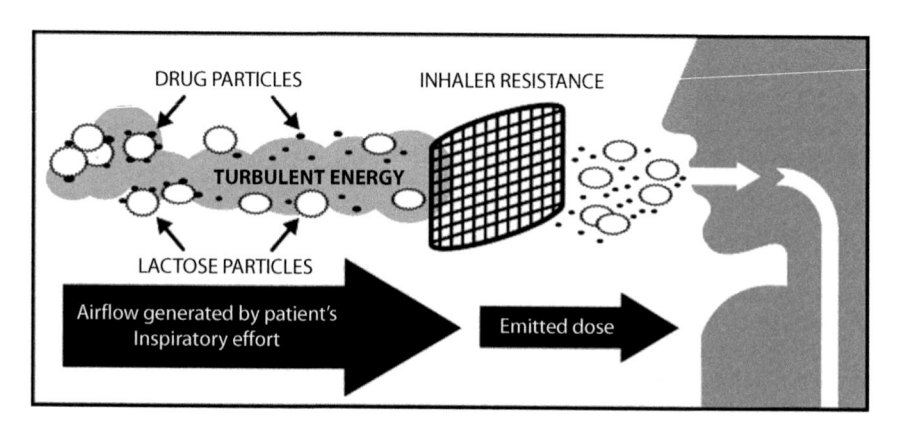

**Figure 6.2** For most dry powder formulations, the drug particles are attached to a lactose carrier which acts as a bulking agent and improves the flowability of the powder. By inhaling through the device, the patient creates turbulent energy that disaggregates and disperses the powder formulation into respirable particles. Turbulent energy is determined by the patient's peak inspiratory flow and the internal resistance of the dry powder inhaler (DPI).

### Minimal PIFr

A minimal PIFr is required for each DPI to *initiate* disaggregation of the powder, with 30 liters/minute recommended for low-to-medium high-resistance DPIs and 20 liters/minute for high-resistance DPIs (10, 12). If PIFr is below this minimal value, disaggregation of the powder formulation is ineffective. This leads to a reduced fine-particle dose emitted from the device and results in the patient receiving little or no therapeutic effect (3).

### Optimal PIFr

In vitro studies using lung models show that drug delivery and the fine-particle dose (< 5 μm in diameter) are enhanced with increasing inspiratory flows (8, 9). An optimal PIFr is determined when a plateau occurs in the emitted dose and fine-particle dose despite higher inspiratory flows (8). There is a general

### Table 6.1: Dry Powder Inhalers According to Their Internal Resistance

| Internal Resistance | Dry Powder Inhaler |
|---|---|
| Low | Breezhaler® |
| Medium–low | Accuhaler®/Diskus®, Diskhaler®, and Ellipta® |
| Medium | Clickhaler®, Genuair®/Pressair®, InHub®, Digihaler®/RespiClick®/Spiromax® and Turbuhaler® (Symbicort) |
| Medium–high | Easyhaler® (combination), Flexhaler®/Turbohaler®/Turbuhaler® (Pulmicort), NEXThaler®, and Twisthaler® |
| High | Easyhaler® (monotherapy) and HandiHaler® |

*Note:* Dry powder inhalers are listed in alphabetical order within the five resistance groupings according to Clerk Clement International Limited (7). For InHub, the airflow resistance is 0.035 kPa$^{0.5}$ liters/minute, placing it in the medium-resistance category (11).

consensus that an optimal PIFr $\geq$ 60 liters/minute applies to most low-to-medium high-resistance DPIs and $\geq$ 30 liters/minute for high-resistance DPIs (3, 12, 13). Moreover, PIFr can be considered a predictive therapeutic biomarker to assess whether an individual patient is unlikely to achieve optimal drug delivery and clinical benefit when using a DPI (14).

## WHAT DRY POWDER INHALERS AND MEDICATIONS ARE AVAILABLE?

Dry powder inhaler devices and medications approved for the treatment of asthma and/or COPD are listed in Table 6.2. All classes of dry powder devices/medications are available except for short-acting muscarinic antagonist (SAMA) bronchodilators. These include short- (SABA) and long-acting beta-agonist (LABA) bronchodilators, long-acting muscarinic antagonist (LAMA) bronchodilators, inhaled corticosteroids (ICS), LABA/LAMA combinations, ICS/LABA combinations, and an ICS/LABA/LAMA combination.

## HOW SHOULD A DPI BE USED?

In general, information for a DPI ("Instructions for Use" in the United States and "Patient Information Leaflet" in Europe) describes that after preparing the inhaler device (e.g., pressing the lever or opening the cover and placing the capsule in the device), the patient should hold the inhaler away from the mouth and then breathe out completely, making sure not to exhale directly into the mouthpiece. The individual then inserts the mouthpiece into the mouth and closes the lips. Inhalation instructions are provided by each pharmaceutical company and are different for each DPI (15).

In 2009, Magnussen et al. (16) examined the effects of two different inhalation instructions on PIF measured through the HandiHaler® device. These investigators found that PIF was approximately 13 liters/minute higher when patients with COPD performed a "fast, forceful" inhalation compared with a "slow, deep" effort (16). In 2011, a joint task force of the European Respiratory Society and the International Society for Aerosols in Medicine provided recommendations for patients to inhale "forcefully from the beginning of inhalation" when using a DPI (3). A simple instruction for patients is to inhale "hard and fast" (17). For DPIs that contain capsules, it is recommended that patients repeat the inhalation to ensure receiving the full dose (3). After complete inhalation, the patient should hold the breath for "as long as possible" or for up to 10 seconds to enable the fine particles to deposit deep into the lower respiratory tract (3).

Mechanical and electromechanical devices have been developed for DPIs to help guide patients to achieve adequate inhalations. The In Check DIAL® is a portable inspiratory flow meter that has been used to measure PIFr to assess whether the patient can generate optimal turbulent energy within the DPI (7). Two specific DPIs incorporate a mechanism that requires a threshold inspiratory flow to allow the release of the powder medication from the device. Genuair®/Pressair® (AstraZeneca, Wilmington, DE) is a medium-resistance DPI that requires a minimum inspiratory flow of 40 liters/minute to allow the trigger mechanism to provide acoustic and optical signals that the individual patient has inhaled the medication successfully (16, 18). The NEXThaler® (Chiesi, Parma, Italy) is a medium-high-resistance DPI with a breath actuation mechanism that limits dose release until the pressure drop across the device is approximately 1.8 kPa (19). This guarantees that the dose is released only when the individual achieves a threshold inspiratory flow of at least 35 liters/minute (19). In addition, DPIs can have built-in (Teva Digihaler®) or attachable (Hailie®,

## Table 6.2: Dry Powder Inhaler Devices and Medications Approved for the Treatment of Asthma and/or COPD

| Inhaler Device | Medication (Generic) | Frequency of Use |
|---|---|---|
| | **Short-acting beta-agonist** | |
| Clickhaler | Albuterol | 4–6 hours PRN[a] |
| Digihaler/RespiClick/ Spiromax | Albuterol | 4–6 hours PRN[a] |
| Turbuhaler | Terbutaline | 4–6 hours PRN[a] |
| | **Long-acting beta-agonist (LABA)** | |
| Accuhaler/Diskus | Salmeterol | Twice daily |
| Breezhaler | Indacaterol | Once daily |
| Diskhaler | Salmeterol | Twice daily |
| | **Long-acting muscarinic antagonist (LAMA)** | |
| Breezhaler | Glycopyrronium | Once daily |
| Ellipta | Umeclidinium | Once daily |
| Genuair/Pressair | Aclidinium | Twice daily |
| HandiHaler | Tiotropium | Once daily |
| | **Inhaled corticosteroid (ICS)** | |
| Clickhaler | Budesonide | Twice daily |
| Digihaler/RespiClick/ Spiromax | Fluticasone propionate | Twice daily |
| Easyhaler | Budesonide | Twice daily |
| Flexhaler/Turbuhaler | Budesonide | Twice daily |
| Twisthaler | Mometasone furoate | Twice daily |
| | **LABA/LAMA** | |
| Breezhaler | Indacaterol and glycopyrronium | Once daily |
| Ellipta | Vilanterol and umeclidinium | Once daily |
| Genuair/Pressair | Formoterol and aclidinium | Twice daily |
| | **ICS/LABA** | |
| Accuhaler/Diskus | Fluticasone propionate and salmeterol | Twice daily |
| Digihaler/RespiClick/ Spiromax | Fluticasone propionate and salmeterol | Twice daily |
| Easyhaler | Fluticasone propionate and salmeterol | Twice daily |
| Ellipta | Fluticasone furoate and vilanterol | Once daily |
| InHub | Fluticasone propionate and salmeterol | Twice daily |
| NEXThaler | Beclomethasone and formoterol | Twice daily |
| Turbuhaler | Budesonide and formoterol | Twice daily |
| | **ICS/LABA/LAMA** | |
| Ellipta | Fluticasone furoate, vilanterol, and umeclidinium | Once daily |

[a] Pro re nata or as needed.

Adherium Ltd, Auckland, New Zealand) sensors that measure inspiratory flow along with inspiratory volume and provide digital information/feedback.

## IS A DPI USED AS RELIEVER/RESCUE THERAPY?

Both albuterol and terbutaline are available in DPIs that can be used "as needed" to relieve symptoms in those with asthma and COPD (Table 6.2). However, since 2019, the Global Initiative for Asthma (GINA) has recommended against SABA-only treatment of asthma, as the use of one or more SABA canisters per month is associated with an increased risk of exacerbations and mortality (20). To control symptoms and to reduce the risk of serious exacerbations, GINA recommends that "All adults and adolescents with asthma should be treated with ICS-containing therapy: either regularly every day or, in mild asthma, with ICS-formoterol taken as needed for symptom relief" (21).

The 2021 GINA strategy proposed two treatment tracks for asthma (21). For *Track 1*, low-dose ICS-formoterol is recommended as a reliever because it reduces the risk of severe exacerbations compared with using a SABA reliever with/without a maintenance controller (21). Both beclomethasone-formoterol (NEXThaler®) and budesonide-formoterol (Turbuhaler®) are the available DPIs for such use (Table 6.2). For *Track 2*, SABA as the reliever is proposed as an alternative approach along with daily ICS maintenance therapy (21).

For COPD, the 2022 Global Initiative for Obstructive Lung Disease (GOLD) recommends that "Rescue short-acting bronchodilators should be prescribed for all patients for immediate symptom relief" (22). For initial pharmacotherapy for patients with low symptoms and a low risk of exacerbations (Group A), the GOLD strategy proposes either a short-acting or a long-acting bronchodilator (22).

## IS A DPI USED AS MAINTENANCE THERAPY?

DPIs are used widely, as once- or twice-daily maintenance therapy, for patients with asthma and COPD. For patients with asthma, GINA has recommended that patients take ICS-formoterol as daily maintenance treatment and as needed for symptom relief in steps 3–5 of *Track 1* (21). Both beclomethasone-formoterol (NEXThaler®) and budesonide-formoterol (Turbuhaler®) are available DPIs for maintenance and reliever therapy, respectively (Table 6.2). For *Track 2*, step 2, low-dose maintenance ICS therapy is recommended by GINA, of which budesonide (Clickhaler®, Easyhaler®, Flexhaler®/Turbuhaler®), fluticasone propionate (Digihaler®/RespiClick®/Spiromax®), and mometasone furoate (Twisthaler®) are available (21) (Table 6.2). For steps 3–5 in *Track 2*, ICS-LABA maintenance treatment is recommended with beclomethasone-formoterol (NEXThaler®) and budesonide-formoterol (Turbuhaler®), available as DPIs (Table 6.2). For step 5 in both *Tracks 1 and 2*, add-on LAMA therapy has been proposed by GINA (21). Available dry powder LAMAs include Breezhaler®, Ellipta®, Genuair®/Pressair®, and HandiHaler® devices (Table 6.2).

For patients with COPD, monotherapy with LABA or LAMA as well as a combination LABA/LAMA has been recommended for the treatment of symptomatic patients (22–25). The DPI options for this COPD phenotype include three LABAs, four LAMAs, and three LABA/LAMA combination bronchodilators (Table 6.2). The ICS/LABA and ICS/LABA/LAMA combinations have been recommended for patients who have high symptoms and/or are considered at increased risk for an exacerbation (22, 23, 25). Seven ICS/LABA combination DPIs are available, while there is one ICS/LABA/LAMA dry powder inhaler (Ellipta®) (Table 6.2). Furthermore, Bourbeau et al. (24) have suggested ICS/LABA/LAMA "triple therapy" for patients with persistent dyspnea and poor health status.

## ADVANTAGES OF A DPI

### For Patients

A major advantage for patients is that DPIs are breath-actuated such that hand-breath coordination is not required. In contrast, actuation of a pMDI (i.e., press down on the canister) and a slow mist inhaler (SMI) (i.e., press a button) needs to be coordinated with inhalation for optimal deposition of the medication into the lower respiratory tract (see Chapters 3 and 5).

### For Patients and HCPs

As noted in Table 6.2, two or more different medications and/or combinations are available in the same DPI: Accuhaler®/Diskus®, Breezhaler®, Digihaler®/RespiClick®/Spiromax®, Easyhaler®, Ellipta®, Genuair®/Pressair®, and Turbohaler®/Turbuhaler®. This availability provides inhaler familiarity and continuity for both patients and HCPs, making it easier to "step up" or "step down" therapy. Moreover, HCPs can instruct patients on the same exhalation/inhalation technique for using a particular DPI after the device has been prepared.

### For the Environment

DPIs do not contain a propellant, and their minimal carbon footprint is mainly attributed to raw materials and manufacturing. Although hydrofluoroalkanes were developed as an alternative propellant for pMDIs, they are greenhouse gases and are planned to be phased down under the Kigali Amendment to the Montreal Protocol (see Chapter 1). Due to environmental concerns, some countries have promoted switching from pMDIs to DPIs and slow mist inhalers (SMIs) as part of a sustainable strategy (26).

## DISADVANTAGES OF A DPI

### For Patients

Some patients with asthma and COPD are unable to completely disaggregate the powder within the DPI due to an inability to inspire forcefully. This can be assessed by a suboptimal PIFr. Characteristics of patients with a suboptimal PIFr include older age, female sex, short stature, and Black race (10, 27, 28); these four patient characteristics are variables that also predict lower lung function. In addition, a reduced inspiratory capacity as percent predicted, a marker of lung hyperinflation that adversely affects inspiratory muscle strength, and maximal inspiratory pressure are additional predictors of suboptimal PIFr (10, 29).

How common is a suboptimal PIFr? Haughney et al. (27) reported that 6.3% of 994 adults with asthma had a PIFr < 30 liters/min against a high-resistance DPI. For stable outpatients with COPD, the reported prevalence of a PIFr < 60 liters/minute for low-to-medium high-resistance DPIs ranges from 19% to 84% (14). For a high-resistance DPI, Al-Showair et al. (30) reported a 57% prevalence of a PIFr < 30 liters/minute measured directly through the HandiHaler® (Boehringer Ingelheim Pharma GmbH & Co; Ingelheim, Germany) in 163 outpatients with COPD. In patients hospitalized for a COPD exacerbation with PIFr measured prior to discharge, the reported prevalence of a suboptimal PIFr is 32% to 68% for a medium-low resistance DPI and 21% for a high-resistance DPI (14, 31, 32). The wide prevalence ranges for suboptimal PIFr likely reflect differences in patient populations as well as timing and methods of measuring PIFr.

As most dry powder formulations are attached to a lactose carrier, some HCPs advise patients with lactose intolerance not to use lactose-containing DPIs to minimize the risk of a hypersensitivity reaction (33). User life is

the time interval from the removal of the inhaler from its packing until the manufacturer can no longer assure drug stability (> 80% of the respirable drug must be available at the end of the user life). For DPIs, user life ranges from four months (formoterol/budesonide Easyhaler®) to three years (formoterol/budesonide Turbohaler®) (34). User-life information is provided in the "Instructions for Use" in the United States and "Patient Information Leaflet" in Europe.

### For HCPs

Some HCPs may not appreciate that patients should inhale "hard and fast" when using a DPI. Ideally, HCPs will query the patient about the expected symptomatic benefit (i.e., Are you able to breathe easier?) with a dry powder bronchodilator. If the patient reports little or no improvement, it is important for the HCP to ask the patient to describe and/or demonstrate the inhalation technique. If possible, the HCP should measure PIF against the simulated resistance of a particular DPI to assess whether the patient is likely or unlikely to benefit (14).

## PATIENT ERRORS USING A DPI

Numerous investigators as well as systematic reviews have described technique errors in DPI use in patients with asthma and COPD. In 2008, Lavorini et al. (35) identified 27 articles on the incorrect use of DPIs in the management of adult patients with asthma or COPD. The most frequent error—"No exhalation before inhalation"—was consistently observed with eight different DPIs. The second most frequent error—"No breath hold"—was observed with five of seven different DPIs (35). Certainly, errors were expected given the observation by the authors that as many as 25% of patients in these studies never received verbal instructions on the DPI technique (35).

In 2016, Sanchis et al. (36) analyzed inhaler errors in 130 groups of patients who were involved in 21,497 tests with DPIs between 1975 and 2014. Of these, 44% [confidence interval (CI), 34–54%] had acceptable inhalation technique, while 23% (CI, 18–29%) had poor technique (36). Analyses also included 52 study groups in which full information on error frequencies for all five essential steps for DPIs was available (Table 6.3). Failure to "breathe out completely" was the

### Table 6.3: Frequencies of Errors for Five Essential Steps for DPI Use Involving Adults with Either Asthma or COPD[a]

| Step | Action | Error Percentage |
|------|--------|------------------|
| 1 | Prepare the device: uncap, load the device | 25 |
| 2 | Turn away from the inhaler and breathe out completely | 45 |
| 3 | Place teeth and lips around the mouthpiece to form a seal | 8 |
| 4 | Breathe in with a single brisk, deep inhalation | 16 |
| 5 | Hold the breath for 5 to 10 seconds or as long as possible | 35 |

[a] Results based on 52 study groups of patients (36).

most common error that occurred in an average of 45% (CI, 40–51%) of patients (36). The next most frequent error was "failure to breath-hold" in 35% (CI, 31–39%) of individuals (36). If a DPI is shaken, tilted, or dropped after the dose is loaded, delivery can be reduced (37).

Although general information on errors with DPIs is important, data on specific DPIs are clinically useful. In 2017, Price et al. (38) reported that "Insufficient inspiratory effort" was the most common critical error in 3,660 patients with asthma, which was associated with "uncontrolled asthma" in those using the Turbuhaler® (adjusted odds ratio = 1.30) and Diskus® (adjusted odds ratio = 1.56) devices, along with an increased exacerbation rate. In addition, Jang et al. (39) reported critical handling errors with four different DPIs (41% for the Breezhaler®, 12.5% for the Diskus®, 27.8% for the Ellipta®, and 44.4% for the Genuair®) in a prospective study of 261 Korean patients with COPD.

## CONCLUSIONS

All three types of DPIs—single-unit, multi-unit, and reservoir—are used throughout the world for the treatment of patients with asthma and COPD. Dry powder medications are available as both reliever/rescue and maintenance therapies. The patient should inhale forcefully, or "hard and fast," to create turbulent energy within the DPI to disaggregate (i.e., pull off) the medication from the lactose carrier and then break the powder formulation into small, respirable particles. The turbulent energy generated by the patient is determined by the patient's PIFr and the internal resistance of the specific DPI. Generally, optimal values for PIFr are ≥ 60 liters/minute for low-to-medium high-resistance DPIs and ≥ 30 liters/minute for high-resistance devices.

A major advantage of DPIs is breath actuation as no hand-breath coordination is required, as with pMDIs and SMIs. In addition, two or more different medications and/or combinations are available in many of the same DPIs, providing device familiarity and continuity for patients and HCPs. As some patients with asthma and COPD have a suboptimal PIFr, they may be unable to completely disaggregate the powder within the device. This can result in a reduced dose delivered into the lower respiratory tract and affect efficacy. Common patient errors using a DPI are failure to breathe out completely before inhaling and failure to breath-hold after complete inhalation.

## REFERENCES

1. Stein SW, Thiel CG. The history of therapeutic aerosols: A chronological review. J Aerosol Med Pulm Drug Deliv 2017;30:20–41.
2. The Montreal Protocol on substances that deplete the ozone layer. [cited 2022 Apr 27]. Available from: https://www.state.gov/key-topics-office-of-environmental-quality-and-transboundary-issues/the-montreal-protocol-on-substances-that-deplete-the-ozone-layer/
3. Laube BL, Janssens HM, de Jongh FHC, et al. What the pulmonary specialist should know about the new inhalational therapies. Eur Respir J 2011;37:1308–1331.
4. Maggi L, Bruni R, Conte U. Influence of the moisture on the performance of a new dry powder inhaler. Int J Pharm 1999;177:83–91.

5. USP 32. General notices and requirements: Applying to standards, tests, assays, and other specifications of the United States Pharmacopeia. [cited 2022 Mar 7]. Available from: https://www.usp.org/sites/default/files/usp_pd/EN/USPNF/generalNoticesandRequirementsFinal.pdf

6. Everard ML, Devadason SG, LeSouef PN. Flow early in the inspiratory manoever affects the aerosol particle size distribution from a Turbuhaler. Respir Med 1997;91:624–628.

7. Sanders MJ. Guiding inspiratory flow development of the In-Check DIAL G16, a tool for improving Inhaler technique. Pulm Med 2017;2017:1495867.

8. Yokoyama H, Yamamura Y, Ozeki T, et al. Analysis of relationship between peak inspiratory flow rate and amount of drug delivered to lungs following inhalation of fluticasone propionate with a Diskhaler. Biol Pharm Bull 2007;30:162–164.

9. Abdelrahim ME, Assi KH, Chrystyn H. Dose emission and aerodynamic characterization of the terbutaline sulfate dose emitted from a Turbuhaler at low inhalation flow. Pharm Dev Technol 2013;18:944–949.

10. Mahler DA. The role of inspiratory flow in selection and use of inhaled therapy for patients with chronic obstructive pulmonary disease. Respir Med 2020;161:105857.

11. Cooper A, Parker J, Berry M, et al. Wixela Inhub: Dosing performance *in vitro* and inhaled flow rates in healthy subjects and patients compared with Advair Diskus. J Aerosol Med Pulm Drug Deliv 2020;33:323–341.

12. Haidl P, Heindl S, Siemon K, et al. Inhalation device requirements for patients' inhalational maneuvers. Respir Med 2016;118:65–75.

13. Ghosh S, Ohar JA, Drummond MB. Peak inspiratory flow rate in chronic obstructive pulmonary disease: Implications for dry powder inhalers. J Aerosol Med Pulm Drug Deliv 2017;30:381–387.

14. Mahler DA, Halpin DMG. Peak inspiratory flow as a predictive therapeutic biomarker in COPD. Chest 2021;160:491–498.

15. Mahler DA. Peak inspiratory flow rate as a criterion for dry powder inhaler use in chronic obstructive pulmonary disease. Ann Am Thorac Soc 2017;14:1103–1107.

16. Magnussen H, Watz H, Zimmermann I, et al. Peak inspiratory flow through the Genuair® Inhaler in patients with moderate or severe COPD. Respir Med 2009;103:1832–1837.

17. Mahler DA. COPD: Answers to your most pressing questions about chronic obstructive pulmonary disease. Baltimore (MD): Johns Hopkins University Press; 2022. p. 78.

18. Chrystyn H, Niederlaender C. The Genuair® inhaler: A novel, multidose dry powder. Int J Clin Pract 2012;3:309–317.

19. Corradi M, Chrystyn H, Cosio BG, et al. NEXThaler, an innovative dry powder inhaler delivering an extrafine fixed combination of beclomethasone and formoterol to treat large and small airways in asthma. Expert Opin Drug Deliv 2014;11:1497–1506.

20. Reddel HK, FitzGerald JM, Bateman ED, et al. GINA 2019: A fundamental change in asthma management: Treatment of asthma with short-acting bronchodilators alone is no longer recommended for adults and adolescents. Eur Respir J 2019;53:1901046.

21. Reddel HK, Bacharier LB, Bateman ED, et al. Global initiative for asthma strategy 2021: Executive summary and rationale for key changes. Am J Respir Crit Care Med 2022;205:17–35.

22. Global Initiative for Chronic Obstructive Lung Disease. Global strategy for the diagnosis, management, and prevention of chronic obstructive pulmonary disease. 2022 report. [cited 2022 Sept 21]. Available from: https://goldcopd.org/2022-gold-reports-2

23. Nici L, Mammen MJ, Charbek E, et al. Pharmacologic management of chronic obstructive pulmonary disease. An official American Thoracic Society clinical practice guideline. Am J Respir Crit Care Med 2020;201:e56–e69.

24. Bourbeau J, Bhutani MN, Hernandez P, et al. Canadian Thoracic Society clinical practice guideline on pharmacotherapy in patients with COPD – 2019 update of evidence. Can J Respir Crit Care Sleep Med 2019;3(9):1–23. DOI:10.1080/24745332.2019.1668652

25. Miravitlles M, Calle M, Molina J, et al. Spanish COPD guidelines (GesEPOC) 2021: Updated pharmacological treatment of stable COPD. Arch Bronchoneumol 2022;58:69–81.

26. British Thoracic Society. Environment and lung health position statement, 2020. [updated 2022 10 Feb; cited 2022 Mar 7]. Available from: https://www.brit-thoracic.org.uk/aboutus/goverance-documents-and-policies/position-statements/

27. Haughney J, Lee AJ, McKnight E, et al. Peak inspiratory flow measured at different inhaler resistances in patients with asthma. J Allergy Clin Immunol Pract 2021;9:890–896.

28. Mahler DA, Niu X, Deering KL, et al. Prospective evaluation of exacerbations associated with suboptimal peak inspiratory flow among stable outpatients with COPD. Int J Chron Obstruct Pulmon Dis 2022;17:559–568.

29. Van der Palen J. Peak inspiratory flow through Diskus and Turbuhaler, measured by means of a peak inspiratory flow meter (In-Chck DIAL®). Respir Med 2003;97:285–289.

30. Al-Showair RAM, Tarsin WY, Assi KH, et al. Can all patients with COPD use the correct inhalation flow with all inhalers and does training help? Respir Med 2007;101:2395–2401.

31. Clark B, Wells BJ, Saha AK, et al. Low peak inspiratory flow rates are common among COPD inpatients and are associated with increased healthcare resource utilization: A retrospective cohort study. Int J Chron Obstruct Pulmon Dis 2022;17:1483–1494.

32. Mahler DA, Demirel S, Hollander R, et al. High prevalence of suboptimal peak inspiratory flow in hospitalized patients with COPD: A real-world study. Chronic Obstr Pulm Dis 2022;17:559–568.

33. Robles J, Motheral L. Hypersensitivity reaction after inhalation of a lactose-containing dry powder inhaler. J Pediatr Pharmacol Ther 2014;19:206–211.

34. Pleasants RA, Tilley SL, Hickey AJ, et al. User-life of ICS/LABA inhaler devices should be considered when prescribed as relievers. Eur Respir J 2021;57:2003921.

35. Lavorini F, Magnan A, Dubus JC, et al. Effect of incorrect use of dry powder inhalers on management of patients with asthma and COPD. Respir Med 2008;102:593–604.

36. Sanchis J, Gich I, Pedersen S. Systematic review of errors in inhaler use: Has patient technique improved over time? Chest 2016;150:394–406.

37. Kondo T, Tanigaki T, Yokoyama H, et al. Impact of holding position during inhalation on drug release from a reservoir-, blister-, and capsule-type dry powder inhaler. J Asthma 2017;54:792–737.
38. Price DB, Roman-Rodriguez M, McQueen RB, et al. Inhaler errors in the CRITIKAL study: Type, frequency, and association with asthma outcomes. J Allergy Clin Immunol Pract 2017;5:1071–1081.
39. Jang JG, Chung JH, Shin KC, et al. Comparative study of inhaler device handling technique and risk factors for critical inhaler errors in Korean COPD patients. Int J Chron Obstruct Pulmon Dis 2021;16:1051–1059.

# 7 Digital Inhalers for the Management of Obstructive Lung Diseases

*Roy A. Pleasants and Stephen L. Tilley*

## CONTENTS

## INTRODUCTION

Nonadherence and improper inhaler technique are major contributors to poor outcomes in patients with asthma and chronic obstructive pulmonary disease (COPD) (1–4). Reasons for such behaviors are multifactorial, including self-treatment of a variable, symptom-based disease. It is well documented that physician assessment is little better than chance (3, 4) at judging patient's adherence with inhalers, and self- and parental reports often overestimate treatments actually taken (5). Inhaler technique is frequently suboptimal and even when properly taught, patients need retraining (2, 6).

To address these problems, inhalers have been reengineered with digital sensors to detect proper use by patients (7). Attachable or embedded electromechanical sensors record and wirelessly transmit data showing when and how patients use their inhalers. When applied to patient care, they are termed digital inhaler health solutions. These devices came to the market about 10 years ago to improve medication adherence (8). Most clinical studies report that using digital inhalers improves care in COPD and asthma patients, adolescents, and older patients. With the rapid expansion of telehealth in the outpatient setting, ongoing gaps in inhaler use, costs associated with uncontrolled obstructive lung diseases, and organizations and payers increasingly supportive of digital telehealth, it is projected the global digital inhaler market will be in the billions of US dollars before 2030 (9).

In this chapter, we present an overview of the different components and applications of the digital inhaler health solution. This includes the devices, platform components, clinical evidence, privacy and security issues, and finally the patient and physician interfaces in applying this to care.

## DIGITAL INHALER PLATFORM

Figure 7.1 shows a digital platform consisting of inhaler(s) with sensors, the patient, smartphone and dedicated app, the healthcare professional (HCP), and their dashboard portal (8). Remote patient monitoring (RPM) occurs

DOI: 10.1201/9781003269014-7

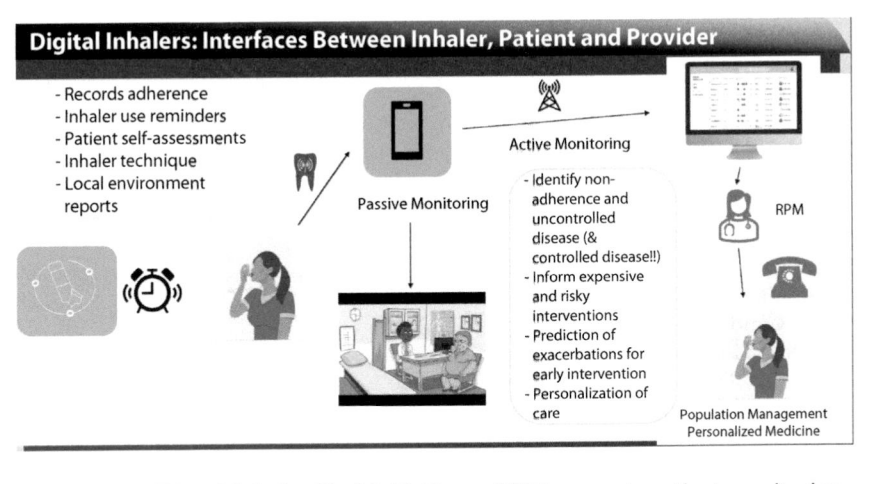

**Figure 7.1** Digital Inhaler Health Platform. RPM = remote patient monitoring.

when the HCP accesses digital data through their dashboard portal to help guide care. When the HCP has real-time access to the patient's inhaler use, it is termed active RPM. With passive RPM, the same data are still recorded and ultimately available. Alternating between active and passive monitoring of inhaler use might be employed. Depending on the specific digital inhaler product, the clinician can review the patient's adherence, assess the inhaler technique, evaluate recorded patient-reported outcomes (PRO), and generate reports for review and documentation. Integration into the electronic health record will ultimately connect inhaler data with other aspects of care more readily.

## Description of Devices

Table 7.1 describes common, available digital inhalers. Electronic sensors are either attached (CapMedic®, Hallie®, INCA, Propeller Health, Amiko Respiro®) or embedded in the inhaler (Respiro RSX01, Teva Digihaler®). With each inhaler actuation, an electronic sensor time stamps and records use, stores these data for a finite time, and transmits the data when a paired mobile device is in close proximity. Sensors rely on pressure changes, audio, or vibration for such measurements (8, 10). A radar sensor transmits data via Bluetooth® technology. While devices can record each actuation, they do not ensure the patient receives a therapeutic dose, such as when pressing the attached sensor without inhaling, or if the product is compromised, such as past-expiry.

To help guide inhaler technique, inspiratory-capable (IC) sensors for pressurized metered dose inhaler (pMDI) and dry powder inhalers (DPI) can measure flows (Capmedic®, Digihaler®, Adherium Hailie® for Symbicort® pMDI, and Amiko Respiro®) and others detect proper shaking or upright position for pMDIs (Capmedic®, Hallie®). With Digihaler®, the patient can see whether they achieved the proper inspiration categorically, while with CapMedic®, flashing lights and audio coach the patient. The patient and clinician may consider this feedback on technique as a value-added function, rather than solely monitoring adherence. Notably, sensors that detect shaking are available for pMDIs (Hailie®, Capmedic®), but no sensor warns about shaking DPIs, known to decrease dose delivery (11).

# Table 7.1: Currently Available Digital Inhaler Devices

| Digital Inhaler Name Manufacturer | Description Sensors | Inhaler Compatibility | Clinician Interface | Patient Interface | Photos of Devices and Inhalers |
|---|---|---|---|---|---|
| Capmedic® Cognita Labs, LLC Houston, TX | Records each actuation Companion digital device to measure PEF and FEV1 | Most pMDIs in US including Ventolin®, Proair®, Symbicort®, Advair®, Flovent®, Dulera®, Atrovent®) | Portal dashboard reporting patient's inhaler use and lung function when measured by a companion spirometer (FEV1, PEF) | Track medication use and inhaler technique on app Vocally coaches for correct inhaler use based on inhaler shaking, orientation, coordination, duration of inhalation, and breath-hold | 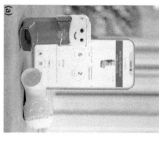 |
| Hailie® Adherium LLC, Auckland, NZ | Records each actuation Attachable sensors Depending on device, detects actuation by pressure, temperature, acoustics | Compatible with most pMDIs and DPIs including Diskus®, Turbuhaler®, Handihaler®, Symbicort® pMDI, Ventolin®, Proair®, Dulera®, Atrovent® pMDI), Bevespi® MDI | Portal dashboard reporting patient's inhaler use and lung function when measured by a companion spirometer (PEF) | Smartphone dashboard Audible, scheduled alerts from sensor Patient can input PEF if measured by companion device |  |

(Continued)

## Table 7.1: Currently Available Digital Inhaler Devices (Continued)

| Digital Inhaler Name Manufacturer | Description Sensors | Inhaler Compatibility | Clinician Interface | Patient Interface | Photos of Devices and Inhalers |
|---|---|---|---|---|---|
| Respiro®<br>Amiko<br>Milan, Italy | Records each actuation and inhalational flow for DPI and pMDI<br>Attachable, electromechanical sensors<br>Built-in sensors for RSX01 | Compatible with most pMDIs and DPIs including Accuhaler®, Turbuhaler®, Handihaler® | Portal dashboard reporting patient's inhaler use and inhalational flows<br>Reports with trends of inhaler use and clinical data entered by a patient | Smartphone dashboard<br>Audible, scheduled alerts from the sensor and/or smartphone | 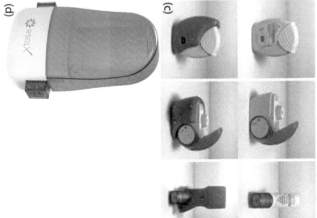 |

(Continued)

# Table 7.1: Currently Available Digital Inhaler Devices (Continued)

| Digital Inhaler Name Manufacturer | Description Sensors | Inhaler Compatibility | Clinician Interface | Patient Interface | Photos of Devices and Inhalers |
|---|---|---|---|---|---|
| Propeller sensors Propeller Health, Madison WI, Respironics | Attachable, electromechanical sensors | Compatible with most pMDIs (e.g., Ventolin®, Symbicort® pMDI); SMIs (Respimat®), and DPIs (Diskus®, Turbuhaler®, Handihaler®, Ellipta®) | Portal dashboard reporting, patient's inhaler use Reports trends of inhaler use and clinical data entered by a patient Environmental daily reports | Smartphone dashboard Audible, scheduled alerts from the attached sensor Alerts on worsening Environmental reports | (e) |
| Digihaler® Teva Pharm Tel Aviv, Israel | Records each actuation and inhalational flow Embedded sensors measuring pressure changes in airflow | US Proair Digihaler® (albuterol) Armonair Digihaler® (Fluticasone) Airduo Digihaler® (Fluticasone/ Salmeterol) Europe Symbicort Digihaler® (Under development) | Portal dashboard reporting, patient's inhaler use and inhalational flows (aids inhaler technique and provides a physiologic measure) Reports with trends of inhaler use and clinical data entered by a patient | Smartphone dashboard Audible, scheduled alerts from sensor App alerts on worsening, refills Local environmental reports | (f) |

*Abbreviations:* DPI = dry powder inhaler; FEV1 = forced expiratory volume in 1 second; PEF = peak expiratory flow; pMDI = pressurized metered dose inhaler; SMI = soft mist inhaler.

(Continued)

## Regulatory Approval

The US Food and Drug Administration (FDA) and European Medicines Agency (EMA) provide guidance to manufacturers of attachable devices and inhalers with embedded sensors (12–15). In Europe, software specifically developed for the diagnosis or treatment of disease falls under the medical device directive. The FDA provides specific guidance on premarket submissions of software combined/contained in medical devices. Prior to marketing, attachable digital inhaler sensors must meet regulatory standards for devices (510K in the US), and if built directly into the inhaler, both drug and device regulations apply (combination product). In addition to device approval, associated software must go through regulatory review and approval (16). In the US, the Digital Health Center of Excellence, part of the Center for Devices and Radiological Health, serves as a resource for regulatory advice and support to the FDA (17). The FDA also regulates medical apps, defined as apps intended to be used as "accessory to a regulated medical device" or having the ability to "transform a mobile platform into a regulated medical device." Apps that do not satisfy this definition are designated health apps and are not regulated as such.

Attachable sensors do not have to demonstrate clinical efficacy; rather, device safety is the priority, including not interfering with inhaler operation, medication delivery, or obstructing the dose counter or label. Both the built-in and attachable electronic monitoring devices for digital inhalers are considered low risk (Class II, US FDA). The Digihaler®, a combination product, was approved as a New Drug Application and device through the Center for Devices and Radiologic Health (18). For Digihaler®, several other federal agencies were involved in the review process for the app including cybersecurity and patient-facing materials.

## PRIVACY AND CYBERSECURITY

Privacy and security are a concern for patients and HCPs due to sharing of sensitive personal and health data on smartphones and the internet (19–21). The American College of Physicians advocates that protected health information be secure from improper access or use, and supports an environment of trust while improving care (22). Factors affecting an individual's willingness to share personal health data include the user's motive, perceived benefits, and the sensitivity of the information (20). Healthcare systems considering digital inhalers will want to address any cybersecurity issues and likely require an in-depth review prior to implementation. Remote digital device monitoring in cardiac diseases and diabetes may serve as models.

Digital inhaler device manufacturers must adhere to privacy standards set forth by regulators such as the US FDA and EMA. Cybersecurity with medical devices undergoes rigorous regulatory assessment, and multiple agencies are involved. US Federal regulations, called quality system regulations, require that medical device manufacturers address risks during development and post-marketing (17). In the US, all transfer of data is encrypted and secured according to standards set by the National Institute of Standards and Technology and Security Operations Center.

User Agreements on the mobile app inform patients about data aggregation and de-identification and may include sharing for public health and scientific research. The Privacy Policy explains how personal and health information is collected, stored, disclosed, and transferred when any element of digital services is used. These must meet the Health Insurance, Portability, and Accountability Act (HIPAA) regulations, whether by a covered entity (HCP) or non-covered entity (20). The minimum data required are name, smartphone number, mailing

address, and email address in order to e-consent. Additional health (e.g., HCP info) and personal information (medications, triggers) is required to use all platform elements. Parental or guardian consent is required for minors.

### Patient and Provider Interfaces

After enrolling in the digital inhaler platform, patients can use their mobile app to review inhaler use over time and receive inhaler technique feedback if available. Depending on the capabilities of the app, additional interface occurs, such as patients to record patient-reported outcomes (PROs) or reviewing local environment reports. All devices provide audible and/or visual alerts to remind patients to use their maintenance inhalers; this function can be activated and deactivated. Patients may also receive messages such as the need to resync and alerts to contact their HCP with excess short-acting β-2 agonist (SABA) use. Digital inhalers that assist with inhaler technique provide feedback on the smartphone dashboard, and sometimes visually or from sensors. In terms of usability and perceived value, digital inhalers have been well received by asthmatics and COPD patients enrolled in clinical studies (20, 23–25).

HCP can use the dashboard portal to review enrollee's data to monitor inhaler use for clinical care, assess the need for follow-up (depending on the predefined digital inhaler strategy), and generate reports for documentation and billing. The frequency of review and the HCP's response are based on the clinical plan discussed with the patient.

Attrition occurs with digital inhaler use, by as much as 40% of patients in the first 6 months (26) and 55% in 1 year (27). Reasons include device malfunction, loss of interest, concerns about intrusiveness, and perhaps because patients do not want to share their growing non-adherence. One study in adults found a small percentage (5.3%) of devices malfunctioned with use (28), while pediatric studies reported higher rates of snap-on device loss or damage (29, 30).

### CLINICAL EVIDENCE

Studies in asthma and COPD support the use of digital inhalers in the outpatient setting among adults and children to improve adherence and clinical outcomes (24, 27, 29, 31–35). Importantly, these studies provide a greater understanding of patient behaviors using inhalers and more objective evidence of the role of adherence on patient outcomes. Table 7.2 describes peer-reviewed, randomized, prospective studies of digital inhalers, assessing the impact on outcomes, adherence with controllers and relievers, need for acute care visits, and PROs. Table 7.3 shows studies evaluating the use of digital inhalers to predict exacerbations.

### Identifying Rescue and Maintenance Inhaler Patterns

Digital inhaler studies have better-characterized inhaler usage patterns with relievers and controllers (36, 37) than shown with databases or patient self-report. Assessment of SABA use is recommended in current guidelines as a measure of disease control for asthma and COPD (38–40), as overuse of SABA is related to increased morbidity and mortality (5, 41). In a prospective study of 58 COPD patients using digital inhalers, four SABA use patterns were found: 1) frequent use, regular pattern, 2) frequent use, no pattern, 3) infrequent users, and 4) infrequent, but intense use (36). Groups 2 and 3 were the most common use patterns and rescue inhaler use compelled by symptoms. Frequent inhaler use with no pattern was associated with more symptoms compared with frequent use with a regular daily pattern. A prospective study in 32 COPD

**Table 7.2: Studies of Digital Inhalers Reporting Clinical Outcomes**

| Study Design Duration | Setting Study Population Study Group(s) | Digital Device Drug(s) | Patient and Clinician Interface with EMD and Apps | Primary Outcome | Secondary Outcome |
|---|---|---|---|---|---|
| Chan (2015) RCT 6 months | Pediatric Specialty; Children with asthma aged 6–15 yr on ICS (n=220) with recent exacerbation requiring ED; EMD+BF vs Usual care | Adherium SmartTrack®; ICS pMDI; Albuterol pMDI | Patient adherence reminders by device | Medication adherence: 84% with EMD vs 30% in the control group ($p<0.0001$); No difference in school absenteeism | ↑asthma score with EMD; Improvement in comorbidity score ($p=0.008$); Child ACT ($p<0.001$) improved in EMD+BF; Lower SABA use in EMD+BF($p=0.002$); No effect on FEV1 |
| Mosnaim (2020) R, single-blinded 14 weeks | Allergy clinic; Adults with uncontrolled asthma (n=100); EMD + BF vs Usual care with passive EMD | Propeller Health ICS and SABA pMDI | Yes | ↑ in SABA-free days = 19% for EMD+ BF vs 6% in the control group (passive EMD) | ↑ ICS adherence over 14 weeks = −2% EMD+BF vs −17% in control group |
| Merchant (2016) RCT, parallel arms 12 months | Allergy clinic; Children and adults with asthma > 5 years old (n=495); EMD + BF vs Usual care | Propeller Health Albuterol pMDI | Clinician access to dashboard; Personalized feedback to the patient via mobile phone app | ↑ SABA free days in EMD+BF vs usual care group +17% vs +21%, $p<0.01$) | ↑ in ACT with EMD+BF vs control group (+6.2 vs +4.6 $p<0.01$) |

(Continued)

**Table 7.2:** **Studies of Digital Inhalers Reporting Clinical Outcomes (Continued)**

| Study Design Duration | Setting Study Population Study Group(s) | Digital Device Drug(s) | Patient and Clinician Interface with EMD and Apps | Primary Outcome | Secondary Outcome |
|---|---|---|---|---|---|
| Foster (2014) RCT 6 months | Primary Care Adults with mod/severe asthma based on ACT (n=143) EMD + BF vs Adherence discussion only vs Usual care 6 months | Adherium Smarttrack® ICS/LABA (Accuhaler®) Albuterol pMDI | Patient Inhaler reminders with Clinician dashboard prompting patient contact with suboptimal inhaler adherence | No difference in ACT among three groups | Adherence in EMD+BF = 74%, usual care = 46%; discussion only group = 46% ↓ exacerbation rates with inhaler reminders (11% vs 28%) No difference in other PRO or FEV1 among three groups |
| O'Dwyer (2016) RCT, parallel | Pharmacies were unit of randomization Community pharmacists assisted with digital inhalers | INCA® ICS/LABA Accuhaler® | EMD + BF | ↑Adherence 60.8% in EMD + BF + Inhaler instruction vs 44.2% in Inhaler instruction only vs 33.2% in usual care | SGRQ (−6.1) in EMD + BF group at 2 and 6 months Inhaler training group had improvement at 2 months, but not at 6 months |
| Morton (2017) RCT, Open-label | Pediatric asthma 6–16 years old (n=77) Intervention group (EMD with controller reminders and review of adherence at clinic visits 1 year | Adherium Smartinhaler(R), Smartturbo(R) ICS pMDI and ICS DPI SABA pMDI | Passive recording of EMD use Adherence reviewed at clinic visits with HCP | No difference in ACQ(p=0.35) | Adherence improved in intervention group 70% vs 49% (p=0.001) ↓ exacerbations in intervention group (p=0.008) and hospitalizations (p<0.001) No difference in SABA use, FEV1, or PAQLQ or asthma severity |

(Continued)

**Table 7.2: Studies of Digital Inhalers Reporting Clinical Outcomes (Continued)**

| Study Design Duration | Setting Study Population Study Group(s) | Digital Device Drug(s) | Patient and Clinician Interface with EMD and Apps | Primary Outcome | Secondary Outcome |
|---|---|---|---|---|---|
| Sulaiman (2018) RCT | Pulmonary Clinic Adults with severe asthma and exacerbations in last year (n=360) Control (Intensive education = technique and adherence) vs Intervention (Intensive education + BF from EMD) 3 months | INCA (Seretide®) | BF via monthly nurse visits in Intervention Group vs 63% in control group (p<0.01) | 73% of adherence (frequency of use, correct technique) in EMD+BF vs | PEF at 3 months NSS between groups ACT or AQLQ NSS between groups |
| Gregoriano (2019) Single-blind RCT | Pulmonary clinic Adult asthma and COPD with exacerbation in the last year (n=149) 6 months | Smartinhaler® Albuterol pMDI Controllers DPI | EMD with Clinician dashboard + BF. (Patient inhaler alerts, Clinician assessments) vs Passive EMD | No effect on time to first exacerbation (HR 0.65, 95% CI 0.21–2.07, p=0.024) | Trend in decreased exacerbation frequency (RR=0.61, CI=0.35–1.03, p=0.07) Days adherent > in intervention group (pMDI 82±14% vs 60±30%, p=0.01) And DPI controllers (90±10% vs 80±21%, p=0.01) No effects on SGRQ |
| Jochmann 2021 Open-label, Proof of Concept study | Pediatric Pulmonary Clinic Pediatric Asthma (n=35) previously enrolled in passive digital inhaler study, 6 months | Smartinhaler® ICS | Patients enrolled in prior passive EMD study switched to either active monitoring or continued on passive EMD Dashboard not employed | No effect on adherence (78% vs 83%, p=0.304) Improvement in PROs with active intervention | Not specified Difficulties with 10 inhalers unable to download smartphone data. Seven subjects lost their digital sensor |

*(Continued)*

**Table 7.2: Studies of Digital Inhalers Reporting Clinical Outcomes (Continued)**

| Study Design Duration | Setting Study Population Study Group(s) | Digital Device Drug(s) | Patient and Clinician Interface with EMD and Apps | Primary Outcome | Secondary Outcome |
|---|---|---|---|---|---|
| Criner 2021 Phase 4, Randomized, open-label trial | Eight research sites in US including pulmonary clinics Mod-severe COPD (n=138) 6 months | Smartinhaler® ICS/LABA | Patients randomized to passive EMD with daily sensors reminders vs passive EMD with no reminders Dashboard not employed | Adherence improved 17% of devices not connected at with reminders 28 days, because devices were (77.6% vs 60.2%; uploaded and synced by p<0.001) patients without direct supervision | None reported |
| Moore 2021 Open-label, parallel-group RCT | Multi-national clinic study Uncontrolled adult asthma (n=437) 6 months | ICS/LABA SABA | Randomized to five groups based on data feedback from device and/or prescriber Dashboard applied in active feedback by prescriber group | Mean(SD) adherence 82.2% (16.8) in the maintenance to participants and HCPs arm vs 70.8(27.3)% in the control Difference of 12.0% SS(95% CI: 5.2–18.8%; p<0.001) Adherence also significantly greater in other arms vs Control | Mean SABA-free days (months 4–6) significantly greater in those who received data on rescue use vs control ACT scores improved in all study arms – NSS between groups |

*Abbreviations:* ACQ = Asthma Control Questionnaire; Asthma ACT = Asthma Control Test; AQLQ = Asthma Quality of Life Questionnaire; BF = biofeedback; COPD = chronic obstructive pulmonary disease; DPI = dry powder inhaler; EMD = electronic monitoring device; FEV1 = forced expiratory volume in 1 second; HCP = healthcare professional; ICS = inhaled corticosteroid; LABA = long-acting β-2 agonist; NSS = not statistically significant; PEF = peak expiratory flow; pMDI = pressurized metered dose inhaler; PAQLQ = Pediatric Asthma Quality of Life Questionnaire; PRO = patient-reported outcome; RCT = randomized clinical trial; SABA = short-acting β-2 agonist; SD, standard deviation; SGRQ = St George Respiratory Questionnaire; SMI = slow mist inhaler.

**Table 7.3: Use of Digital Inhalers to Predict Acute Events in Asthma and COPD Patients**

| Author (Year) Design | Study Population Study Group(s) Duration | Digital Device Drug(s) | Outcome Measures | Outcome |
|---|---|---|---|---|
| Killane (2016) RCT, parallel group | Adults with asthma (n = 184) EMD + Inhaler teaching vs Inhaler teaching only 3 months | INCA ICS/LABA – Accuhaler® Clinician assessment of medication adherence by EMD recordings at monthly study visits Clinician feedback to subject at study visits regarding adherence | Exacerbation risk | < 80% adherence by EMD predictive of AECOPD |
| Pleasants (2019) Prospective open-label | Adults with asthma (n = 360) on ICS/LABA with exacerbation in prior year Passive EMD 24 weeks | Teva Digihaler® Albuterol | Clinical, $\beta$-2 agonist use, and inspiratory flow measures to predict exacerbations using machine learning modeling | PIF and inhalation volume measured by Digihaler decline with exacerbations Albuterol use increases with exacerbations. |
| Snyder (2020) Prospective open-label | COPD with a history of exacerbation (n = 336) 24 weeks | Teva Digihaler® Albuterol DPI | Clinical, B-agonist use, and inspiratory flow measures to predict exacerbations | PIF and inhalation volume measured by Digihaler decline with exacerbations Albuterol use increases with exacerbations |
| Sumino (2018) Prospective observational | COPD (n = 35) 12 weeks | Propeller Albuterol pMDI Passive EMD without dashboard | Exacerbation risk based on albuterol use compared to baseline | Odds ratio of an exacerbation 1.54 (1.21–1.97 with ↑ albuterol use > 100% |
| Patel (2013) RCT, secondary analysis using nested cohort | Severe asthma (n = 303) 24 weeks | Adherium Albuterol pMDI and ICS/FOR DPI Passive EMD without dashboard | Albuterol use to predict exacerbations | Each associated with an increased risk of future severe exacerbation Higher mean daily albuterol use (OR 1.24) Higher days of albuterol use (OR 1.15) Higher maximal 24-h use (OR 1.09) |

patients found that the majority (73%) of SABA over-users were on guideline-concordant therapies, while 27% of the over-users were not (37).

SABA use is known to increase around exacerbations, but now we have more objective evidence. One digital inhaler study reported that increased SABA use from baseline (100%), rather than the number of puffs, was most predictive of an ensuing exacerbation in asthma and COPD (25). In a study employing albuterol Digihaler®, increased SABA use was observed about 5 days prior to receipt of systemic corticosteroids in adult asthmatics (mean 2.2–4.0 puffs/day), then declined to baseline over a similar timeframe (42). In a similar study on COPD, albuterol use changed around exacerbations to a lesser extent (mean 3.3–4.3 puffs/day) (43). A downside of digital inhalers is the inability to document nebulizer use; a third of COPD patients use nebulizers acutely or chronically (44).

Characterizing maintenance inhaler use may identify patients for whom interventions for non-adherence would improve outcomes; as well as patients who are controlled, but non-adherent. Studies using digital inhalers have objectively identified different patterns of maintenance adherence (30, 45–48). Employing a digital inhaler that records use and inhaler technique, four adherence patterns in COPD were identified: 1) regular use, good technique, 2) regular use, frequent critical inhaler error, 3) irregular use, good technique, and 4) irregular use, frequent critical errors (49). In a study of pediatric asthmatics monitored for a median of 92 days, the median (range) monitored adherence was 74% (21–99%). They identified four groups: 1) good adherence during monitoring with improved control, 24%; 2) good adherence with poor control, 18% (severe therapy-resistant asthma); 3) poor adherence with good control, 26%; and 4) poor adherence with poor control, 32% (30).

## Controller Adherence in the Clinical Setting

Adherence to inhaled medications in asthma and COPD is the lowest among common chronic diseases, in part related to symptom variability and quick response to bronchodilators (3). Based on pharmacy claims data, regular use of daily maintenance medications is often <50% in patients with asthma (50) and COPD (51). Clinicians commonly overestimate adherence to inhaled therapies. In one study, digital records of adherence were more accurate than relying on a dose counter (52). Studies in asthma and COPD (4, 53, 54) support the regular use of maintenance inhalers (termed adherent and controlled), and this is the basis for clinicians to promote the daily use of controllers. On the other hand, the definition of optimal adherence continues to change in asthma, whereas the needed use of ICS or ICS/FOR is increasingly being shown to be as effective as regular use in some asthmatics (55).

Most studies demonstrate that digital inhaler use improves medication adherence, defined by decreased rescue inhaler use and regular use of controllers (27, 31–35, 56, 57). Compared to passive adherence monitoring, the effect is greater in patients with biofeedback through reminder alerts and active clinician monitoring (Table 7.2) (31–34, 56). A randomized control trial in 437 uncontrolled adult asthmatics evaluated the effect of direct biofeedback over 24 weeks on inhaler adherence. The study found that in the group with biofeedback using a smartphone app, adherence to DPI increased by 82%, compared to 69% in a control group with passive monitoring (31). Two studies reported improved adherence using the dashboard throughout the study to provide feedback (33, 58). Another study in 100 uncontrolled adult asthmatics found over a period of 14 weeks that ICS adherence declined less with the use of digital inhalers (2%) than in the control group (17%) who did not receive reminders or feedback on medication use (32). Other studies found more substantial improvements in

controller adherence with digital inhalers (28, 33, 56–58), but baseline adherence was poor. These data indicate that patients already adherent with controllers are less likely to benefit from digital inhalers that simply document adherence.

### Role in Exacerbations

In addition to reducing exacerbations by improving controller adherence and greater patient engagement, digital inhalers may help identify clinical worsening. In two prospective, observational studies with IC-albuterol Digihaler®, a post-hoc machine learning model using inhaler use frequency and inhalation measures was able to predict an ensuing exacerbation (receiver operating curve - asthma 0.79 and COPD 0.81) (42, 43). Albuterol use increased most evidently 5 days prior to the exacerbation; the same pattern was found in asthmatics using digitalized budesonide/formoterol DPI as needed (Maintenance and Reliever Therapy) (59).

A potential role of IC-digital inhalers could be the ability to provide ambulatory lung function measures, specifically peak inspiratory flow (PIF) and inhaled volume (Vin), analogous to peak expiratory flow monitoring. Studies using spirometry or a portable inspiratory device (InCheckDial®) show PIF (60, 61, 62) and Vin are bronchodilator responsive (62–64) and change with clinical worsening in asthma and COPD (59, 65, 66). Using the IC-albuterol Digihaler®, studies in asthma and COPD showed both the mean Vin and PIF decreased during outpatient exacerbations, the former to a greater extent (asthma 18% vs 12%, COPD 16% vs 9%, respectively) (42, 43). For the IC-Digihaler®, the recommended full expiration followed by a full inspiration yields a maximum inspiratory flow and Vin. For pMDIs, the recommended slow and forceful exhalation followed by a deep slow inhalation through the inhaler yields Vin. The sensors are accurate if used properly (67–69).

### Inhaler Adherence in Clinical Drug Trials

Digital inhalers should be considered for use in drug trials to quantify inhaler use and lessen the impact of non-adherence on results (70, 71). In an analysis of 87 randomized clinical trials of add-on therapy in severe asthma, none had objective evidence of inhaler adherence (72). Patient self-report of adherence is prone to overestimation due to social desirability bias (5). Mechanical dose-counters on inhalers are often used to measure adherence in trials but overestimate actual use compared with adherence measurements by digital inhalers (52).

## APPLYING DIGITAL INHALERS TO CLINICAL PRACTICE
### Patient Selection

To employ digital inhalers, the HCP should first determine if there are any barriers such as cost or side effects that limit use of the medication to be digitalized. Importantly, the HCP should determine if RPM is reimbursable since not all US payers consider these codes billable. They should determine if and how the patient uses a nebulizer to understand how a digital inhaler fits into the patient's inhaled medications. Although not necessary, ideally the patient must possess and know how to operate a smartphone. Table 7.4 shows representative patient types that may benefit from a digital inhaler health solution. Benefits from using digital inhalers arise principally from improved adherence to maintenance inhalers, while monitoring rescue inhalers serves as a surrogate for uncontrolled disease. Optimizing the inhaler technique could help any of the proposed patient types but should be done in conjunction with adherence monitoring.

## Table 7.4: **Patients Who May Benefit from a Digital Inhaler Health Solution**

Uncontrolled asthma or COPD in outpatient setting despite optimal prescriptions
Considering addition of costly interventions such as biologics or procedures
Considering risky interventions such as biopsy or costly radiology for alternative
 diagnosis
Post-acute care for exacerbation such as post-ED for asthma or post-hospital for COPD
Patient with suspected or known poor inhaler technique with suboptimal disease control
Use of ICS/FOR Maintenance and Reliever Therapy (MART) for asthma

### Prescribing and Dispensing Devices

While not all inhaler sensors require a prescription, the HCP will initiate the process for patients to obtain the device. For attachable sensors, will agree contractually to purchase the devices including access to the cloud server. Attachable digital sensors can be dispensed at the clinician's site or sent by postal delivery to the patient. Digital inhalers with built-in sensors require a prescription; therefore, HCP should follow formulary procedures such as prior authorization and other dispensing requirements.

### Informing and Enrolling the Patient

Digital inhalers will impact the patient, the HCP, and patient–HCP interactions. Typically, it will be the prescriber who will decide on the need for a digital inhaler, followed by a discussion with the patient. The intent of digital inhalers is to increase patient self-care and provide objective evidence of inhaler use, so the discussion should proceed on that basis. The patient should receive an overview of the devices and mobile app functions, how this may benefit their care, security and privacy issues, costs, goals, and the monitoring plan. Clinical responsibility for reviewing and acting on potentially continuous data streams needs to be very clear and documented on how the prescriber and patient will employ digital inhalers. A written action plan may be appropriate. Telling the patient to seek medical care as they normally would is a reasonable strategy, rather than relying on the prescriber to identify acute worsening prospectively. However, in the post-acute care period, desired monitoring may be daily. There is a paucity of data on whether such a model improves outcomes, only that inhaler use is suboptimal in this setting (47).

Enrolling a patient in a digital health solution is best done in-person or by video telehealth, where the provider can assist and instruct the patient. In one study of COPD patients, a significant number (17%) of technical failures occurred if patients attempted to complete enrollment on their own (35). The devices are easy to attach, it is the operation that may be complex. For prescription combination digital inhalers, a trained dispensing pharmacist could assist the patient with app download, device syncing, and operation.

After receiving the sensor, the patient downloads the manufacturer's companion app onto their smartphone, and they are required to e-consent to User and Privacy agreements. The agreements describe in detail how the data will be collected, transmitted, and utilized. The patient will not be able to use all platform functions without the use of a cloud server through their smartphone. An alternative for the patient without a smartphone or patients choosing not to share their data wirelessly is to bring their digital inhaler to in-person clinic visits and having the data uploaded. Some Adherium devices also have a USB port for download (Hailie Connect®).

## PATIENT MONITORING

While the use of digital inhalers to provide reminder alerts and technique feedback has benefits, it must be acknowledged that changes in patient behavior may be limited for a variety of reasons. Rather, the greatest value of digital inhalers will be in understanding the patient's behavior and adapting treatments thereof.

The strategy and time interval for digital monitoring are part of the personalization of patient care. Based on current evidence, the time period needed to correctly assess maintenance inhaler adherence likely needs to be at least 3 months (73). The HCP's investment in time and resources should be considered. While one study of stable patients reported that 1 week of monitoring defined maintenance adherence (36), most studies followed patients for many months. In some studies, it was found that adherence improved, then declined over time, often becoming evident at about 3–6 months (31). Also not accounted for in these studies was seasonal variation in disease control.

Payers may influence the frequency of monitoring. In the US, the Committee on Medicare and Medicaid Services criteria for RPM permits billing as often as once monthly and must contain digitally collected data for 16 days/month. While feedback from the mobile app and digital inhaler is important for the patient to remain engaged, HCP feedback is necessary, and waiting too long will lead to dropouts.

## CONCLUSIONS

Available for more than two decades, digital inhalers and associated health platforms remain new to many clinicians and healthcare organizations. A digital inhaler is described by whether it is an attachable device or a drug and device product combination, and whether it has the capability to guide inhaler technique by detecting inspiratory flow or shaking. When used as intended, digital inhaler data can be a powerful tool to engage patients in active discussions about their actual medication-taking behaviors, attitudes toward their prescribed treatments, and beliefs about their disease.

Most studies demonstrate that digital inhalers enhance medication management by improving adherence and clinical outcomes. Additional data are needed to show if devices improve inhaler technique and in whom and how long they should be employed. Digital inhalers represent a great opportunity to help solve some key problems with inhaler use.

## ABBREVIATIONS

**COPD**   chronic obstructive pulmonary disease
**DPI**   dry powder inhaler
**EMA**   European Medicines Authority
**FDA**   Food and Drug Administration
**HCP**   healthcare professional
**HIPAA**   Health Insurance, Portability, and Accountability Act
**IC**   inspiratory capable
**PIF**   peak inspiratory flow
**pMDI**   pressurized metered dose inhaler
**PRO**   patient-reported outcome
**RPM**   remote patient monitoring
**SABA**   short-acting $\beta$-2 agonist
**Vin**   inhaled volume

## REFERENCES

1. Chongmelaxme B, Chaiyakunapruk N, Dilokthornsakul P. Association between adherence and severe asthma exacerbation: A systematic review and meta-analysis. J Am Pharm Assoc 2020;60:669–685.
2. Price DB, Román-Rodríguez M, McQueen RB, et al. Inhaler errors in the CRITIKAL study: Type, frequency, and association with asthma outcomes. J Allergy Clin Immunol Pract 2017;5:1071–1081.
3. George M, Bender B. New insights to improve treatment adherence in asthma and COPD. Patient Prefer Adherence 2019;1:1325–1334.
4. George M. Adherence in asthma and COPD: New strategies for an old problem. Respir Care 2018;63:818–831.
5. Patel M, Perrin K, Pritchard A, et al. Accuracy of patient self-report as a measure of inhaled asthma medication use. Respirology 2013;3:546–552.
6. Pleasants RA, Hess DR. Aerosol delivery devices for obstructive lung diseases. Respir Care 2018;63:708–733.
7. Blakey JD, Bender BG, Dima AL, et al. Digital technologies and adherence in respiratory diseases: The road ahead. Eur Respir J 2018;52:1801147.
8. Chan AHY, Pleasants RA, Dhand R, et al. Digital inhalers for asthma or chronic obstructive pulmonary disease: A scientific perspective. Pulm Ther 2021;7:345–376.
9. Global digital dose inhalers market to reach $4.9 billion by 2026 – Benzinga. https://www.strategyr.com/market-report-digital-dose-inhalers-forecasts-global-industry-analysts-inc.asp
10. Mehta PP. Dry powder inhalers: A concise summary of the electronic monitoring devices. Ther Deliv 2021;1:1–6.
11. Janson C, Loof T, Telg G, et al. Impact of inhalation flow, inhalation volume and critical handling errors on delivered budesonide/formoterol dose in different inhalers: An in vitro study. Pulm Ther 2017;3:243–253.
12. Xiroudaki S, Schoubben A, Giovagnoli S, et al. Dry powder inhalers in the digitalization era: Current status and future perspectives. Pharmaceutics 2021;13:1455.
13. Dimitrova EK. Quality requirements for drug-device combinations. Available from: https://www.ema.europa.eu/en/quality-requirements-drug-device-combinations
14. Combination Products. [cited 2022 Apr 1]. Available from: https://www.fda.gov/media/114537/download
15. Guidance for the content of premarket submissions for software contained in medical devices. [cited 2022 Apr 1]. Available from: https://www.fda.gov/regulatory-information/search-fda-guidance-documents...
16. Policy for device software functions and mobile medical applications guidance for industry and food and drug administration staff. 2019. [cited 2022 Apr 1]. Available from: https://www.fda.gov/media/80958/download
17. Digital Health Center of Excellence | FDA. [cited 2022 Apr 1]. https://www.fda.gov/medical-devices/digital-health-center-excellence
18. https://www.fda.gov/about-fda/fda-organization/center-devices-and-radiological-health
19. Taitsman JK, Grimm CM, Argawal S. Protecting patient privacy and data security. N Engl J Med 2013;368:977–979.
20. Kim KK, Sankar P, Wilson MD, et al. Factors affecting willingness to share electronic health data among California consumers. BMC Med Ethics 2017;18:25.

21. Campbell JI, Eyal N, Musiimenta A, et al. Ethical questions in medical electronic adherence monitoring. J Gen Intern Med 2016;31(3):338–342.
22. Rockwern B, Johnson D, Sulmasy LS. Health information privacy, protection, and use in the expanding digital health ecosystem: A position paper of the American College of Physicians. Ann Intern Med 2021;174:994–998.
23. Foster JM, Smith L, Usherwood T, et al. The reliability and patient acceptability of the SmartTrack device: A new electronic monitor and reminder device for metered dose inhalers. J Asthma 2012;49:657–662.
24. Merchant R, Inamdar R, Henderson K, et al. Digital health intervention for asthma: Patient-reported value and usability. JMIR Mhealth Uhealth 2018;6(6):e133.
25. Sumino K, Locke ER, Magzamen S, et al. Use of a remote inhaler monitoring device to measure change in inhaler use with chronic obstructive pulmonary disease exacerbations. J Aerosol Med Pulm Drug Deliv 2018;31:191–198.
26. Chen J, Kaye L, Tuffli M, et al. Passive monitoring of short-acting beta-agonist use via digital platform in patient with chronic obstructive pulmonary disease: Quality improvement retrospective analysis. J Med Inform Res 2019;3:e13286.
27. Merchant RK, Inamdar R, Quade RC. Effectiveness of population health management using the propeller health asthma platform: A randomized clinical trial. J Allergy Clin Immunol Pract 2016;4:455–463.
28. Morton RW, Elphick HE, Rigby AS, et al. STAAR: A randomised controlled trial of electronic adherence monitoring with reminder alarms and feedback to improve clinical outcomes for children with asthma. Thorax 2017;72:347–354.
29. Lee J, Tay TR, Radhakrishna N, et al. Nonadherence in the era of severe asthma biologics and thermoplasty. Eur Respir J 2018;51:1701836.
30. Jochmann A, Artusio L, Jamalzadeh A, et al. Electronic monitoring of adherence to inhaled corticosteroids: An essential tool in identifying severe asthma in children. Eur Respir J 2017;50:1700910.
31. Moore A, Preece A, Sharma R, et al. A randomised controlled trial of the effect of a connected inhaler system on medication adherence in uncontrolled asthmatic patients. Eur Respir J 2021;57:2003103.
32. Mosnaim GS, Stempel DA, Gonzalez C, et al. The impact of patient self-monitoring via electronic medication monitor and mobile app plus remote clinician feedback on adherence to inhaled corticosteroids: A randomized controlled trial. J Allergy Clin Immunol Pract 2020;20:1586–1594.
33. O'Dwyer S, Greene G, MacHale E, et al. Personalized biofeedback on inhaler adherence and technique by community pharmacists: A cluster randomized clinical trial. J Allergy Clin Immunol Pract 2020;8(2):635–644.
34. Sulaiman I, Greene G, MacHale E, et al. A randomised clinical trial of feedback on inhaler adherence and technique in patients with severe uncontrolled asthma. Eur Respir J 2018;51:1701126.
35. Criner GJ, Cole T, Hahn KA, et al. The impact of budesonide/formoterol pMDI medication reminders on adherence in chronic obstructive pulmonary disease (COPD) patients: Results of a randomized, phase 4, clinical study. Int J Chron Obstruct Pulmon Dis 2021;16:563–577.
36. Bowler R, Allinder M, Jacobson S, et al. Real-world use of rescue inhaler sensors, electronic symptom questionnaires and physical activity monitors in COPD. BMJ Open Respir Res 2019;6(1):e000350.

37. Fan VS, Gylys-Colwell I, Locke E, et al. Overuse of short-acting betaagonist bronchodilators in COPD during periods of clinical stability. Respir Med 2016;116:100–106.
38. https://ginasthma.org/
39. Cloutier MM, Dixon AE, Krishnan JA, et al. Managing asthma in adolescents and adults: 2020 asthma guideline update from the National Asthma Education and Prevention Program. JAMA 2020;324:2301–2317.
40. https://goldcopd.org/2022-gold-reports-2
41. Patel M, Pilcher J, Reddel HK, et al. Metrics of salbutamol use as predictors of future adverse outcomes in asthma. Clin Exp Allergy 2013;43:1144–1151.
42. Pleasants R, Safioti G, Reich M, et al. Rescue medication use and inhalation patterns during asthma exacerbations recorded by Digihaler. Ann Allergy Asthma Immunol 2019;123:S14–S17.
43. Snyder LD, Safioti G, Reich M, et al. Objective assessment of rescue medication use and inhalation characteristics of COPD patients recorded by the electronic ProAir Digihaler. Am J Respir Crit Care Med 2020;201:A4305.
44. Tashkin DP. A review of nebulized drug delivery in COPD. Int J Chron Obstruct Pulmon Dis 2016;11:2585–2596.
45. Lacasse Y, Archibald H, Ernst P, et al. Patterns and determinants of compliance with inhaled steroids in adults with asthma. Can Respir J 2005;12:211–217.
46. Tibble H, Chan A, Mitchell EA, et al. A data-driven typology of asthma medication adherence using cluster analysis. Sci Rep 2020;10(1):1–8.
47. Sulaiman I, Cushen B, Greene G, et al. Objective assessment of adherence to inhalers by patients with chronic obstructive pulmonary disease. Am J Respir Crit Care Med 2017;195:1333–1343.
48. De Keyser HEH, Kaye L, Anderson WC, et al. Electronic medication monitors help determine adherence subgroups in asthma. Respir Med 2020;164:105914.
49. Sulaiman I, Seheult J, MacHale E, et al. Irregular and ineffective: A quantitative observational study of the time and technique of inhaler use. J Allergy Clin Immunol Pract 2016;4:900–909.
50. Normansell R, Kew KM, Stovold E. Interventions to improve adherence to inhaled steroids for asthma. Cochrane Database Syst Rev 2017;4:CD012226.
51. Mueller S, Wilke T, Bechtel B, et al. Non-persistence and non-adherence to long-acting COPD medication therapy: A retrospective cohort study based on a large German claims dataset. Respir Med 2017;122:1–11.
52. Killane I, Sulaiman I, MacHale E, et al. Predicting asthma exacerbations employing remotely monitored adherence. Healthc Technol Lett 2016;3:51–55.
53. Vestbo J, Anderson, Calverley JP, et al. Adherence to inhaled therapy, mortality and hospital admission in COPD. Thorax 2009;64:939–943.
54. Dekhuijzen R, Lavorini F, Usmani OS, et al. Addressing the impact and unmet needs of nonadherence in asthma and chronic obstructive pulmonary disease: Where do we go from here? J Allergy Clin Immunol Pract 2018;6:785–793.
55. Jackson DJ, Bacharier LB. Inhaled corticosteroids for the prevention of asthma exacerbations. Ann Allergy Asthma Immunol 2021;127:524–529.
56. Chan AH, Stewart AW, Harrison J, et al. The effect of an electronic monitoring device with audiovisual reminder function on adherence to inhaled corticosteroids and school attendance in children with asthma: A randomised controlled trial. Lancet Respir Med 2015;3:210–219.

57. Foster JM, Usherwood T, Smith L, et al. Inhaler reminders improve adherence with controller treatment in primary care patients with asthma. J Allergy Clin Immunol 2014;134:1260–1268.

58. Gregoriano C, Dieterle T, Breitenstein AL, et al. Does a tailored intervention to promote adherence in patients with chronic lung disease affect exacerbations? A randomized controlled trial. Respir Res 2019;20:273.

59. Patel M, Pilcher J, Pritchard A, et al. Efficacy and safety of maintenance and reliever combination budesonide–formoterol inhaler in patients with asthma at risk of severe exacerbations: A randomised controlled trial. Lancet Respir Med 2013;1:32–42.

60. Broeders MEAC, Molema J, Hop WCJ, et al. The course of inhalation profiles during an exacerbation of obstructive lung disease. Respir Med 2004;98:1173–1179.

61. Taube C, Kanniess F, Grönke L, et al. Reproducibility of forced inspiratory and expiratory volumes after bronchodilation in patients with COPD or asthma. Respir Med 2003;97:568–577.

62. O'Donnell DE, Forkert L, Webb KA. Evaluation of bronchodilator responses in patients with "irreversible" emphysema. Eur Respir J 2001;18:914–920.

63. Bass H. The flow volume loop: Normal standards and abnormalities in chronic obstructive pulmonary disease. Chest 1973;63:171–175.

64. Wells RE. Mechanics of respiration in bronchial asthma. Am J Med 1959;384–393.

65. Chrystyn H, Soussi M, Tarsin W, et al. Inhalation characteristics when patients use a dry powder inhaler (DPI) are related to their lung function when they are stable and when recovering from an acute exacerbations. Am J Respir Crit Care Med 2020;201:A3939.

66. Watz H, Tetzlaff K, Magnussen H, et al. Spirometric changes during exacerbations of COPD: A post hoc analysis of the WISDOM trial. Respir Res 2018;19:251.

67. Chrystyn H, Saralaya D, Shenoy A, et al. Investigating the accuracy of the Digihaler, a new electronic multidose dry-powder inhaler, in measuring inhalation parameters. J Aerosol Med Pulm Drug Deliv 2022;35:166–177. DOI:10.1089/jamp.2021.0031

68. D'Arcy S, MacHale E, Seheult J, et al. A method to assess adherence in inhaler use through analysis of acoustic recordings of inhaler events. PLoS One 2014;9(6):e98701.

69. Rogueda P, Grinovero M, Ponti L, et al. Telehealth ready: Performance of the Amiko Respiro Sense connected technology with Merxin DPIs. Drug Delivery to the Lungs (DDL2018).

70. Pilcher J, Shirtcliffe P, Patel M, et al. Three-month validation of a turbuhaler electronic monitoring device: Implications for asthma clinical trial use. BMJ Open Respir Res 2015;2:e000097.

71. Patel M, Pilcher J, Chan A, et al. Six-month in vitro validation of a metered-dose inhaler electronic monitoring device: Implications for asthma clinical trial use. J Allergy Clin Immunol 2012;130:1420–1422.

72. Mokoka MC, McDonnell MJ, MacHale E, et al. Inadequate assessment of adherence to maintenance medication leads to loss of power and increased costs in trials of severe asthma therapy: Results from a systematic literature review and modelling study. Eur Respir J.2019;53(5):1802161.

73. Jochmann A, Artusio L, Usemann J, et al. A 3-month period of electronic monitoring can provide important information to the healthcare team to assess adherence and improve asthma control. ERJ Open Res 2021;7.

# 8 Nebulizers

*Paul D. Terry and Rajiv Dhand*

## CONTENTS

## INTRODUCTION

Nebulizers convert liquid medicines into a fine mist for inhalation, typically to treat a variety of airway disorders, such as asthma, chronic obstructive pulmonary disease (COPD), and cystic fibrosis (CF). Nebulizers are commonly used for rescue therapy to provide rapid short-term relief of acute respiratory conditions, such as acute exacerbations of asthma, COPD, and acute bronchospasm. When first developed in the mid-nineteenth century, nebulizers used hand-held pumps to force a liquid against a plate or baffle, nebulizing (or "atomizing") it for inhalation through a tube or mask. For example, "the Pulverisateur," invented in France in 1858, was a large, heavy, and cumbersome device that used a bicycle-style pump to draw solution from a glass reservoir and force it through a small nozzle into an impaction plate to produce an inhalable mist (1). The first electric nebulizers, invented in Europe in the early 1930s, used compressed air to nebulize a variety of medicines thought to improve asthma symptoms (2). An early example was the "Pneumostat," invented in Germany in the early 1930s, a large, noisy, nine-pound device that was affordable to own only to the very wealthy (1). Over time, incremental improvements were made in nebulizers to maximize drug penetration into the lungs. Today's nebulizers are small, light, quiet, and are often battery-operated, making them increasingly portable and convenient to use.

Three types of nebulizer designs are commonly used in clinical practice, namely, jet or pneumatic nebulizers, ultrasonic nebulizers, and vibrating mesh nebulizers.

DOI: 10.1201/9781003269014-8

## JET NEBULIZERS

Jet, or pneumatic, nebulizers use compressed air or oxygen to draw liquid from a reservoir and nebulize it into droplets against internal baffles (Figure 8.1). By forcing air through a constricted outlet to increase its velocity, the nebulizer creates a vacuum that pulls medicine up a capillary tube into the "jet stream," hence the name. Most modern jet nebulizers are powered by high-pressure air or oxygen provided by a tabletop compressor, compressed gas cylinder, or 50-psi wall outlet. Patients typically receive nebulizer therapy through small-volume nebulizer units (capacity 5–20 mL), but some receive large-volume nebulizer therapy (capacity up to 200 mL) for longer-term treatment, or "In-line" therapy when operated in a ventilator circuit.

Typical nebulizer equipment consists of a pressurized gas source, a flowmeter, oxygen tubing, a medicine cup, a mouthpiece or mask, a normal saline solution, and the prescribed medication. The treatment time for jet nebulizers ranges between 10 and 25 minutes (3), depending on the airflow rate used to drive the nebulizer. The driving pressure or the flow rate of compressed air applied to the jet affects aerosol output and particle size from jet nebulizers. The higher the pressure or flow rate, the greater the output over time in terms of the total solution aerosolized, and the smaller the particle size (3). A gas flow of 6 to 8 L/min is usually selected to optimize drug delivery (4). The mass median aerodynamic diameter (MMAD) of aerosols produced by jet

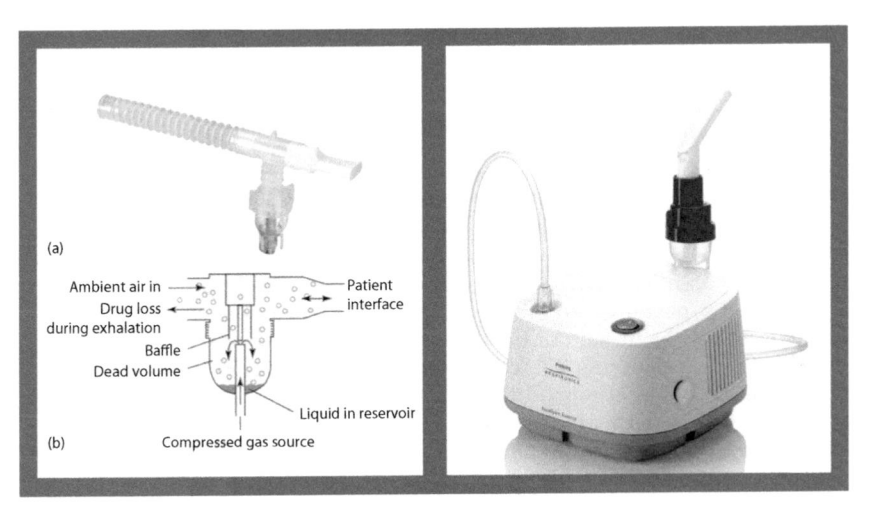

**Figure 8.1** The left panel shows components of a jet nebulizer (a). In (b), the operation of jet nebulizers is shown. Compressed gas is delivered through a jet, and the expansion of the jet creates a negative pressure that entrains the solution to be aerosolized into the gas stream. The solution is sheared into a liquid film that is unstable and breaks into droplets because of surface tension forces. A baffle is placed in the aerosol stream and the larger particles impact the baffle and are returned to the nebulizer reservoir, whereas the smaller particles are carried by the airstream to the patient. The right panel shows the components of a jet nebulizer for home use including a nebulizer, mouthpiece (or facemask), connecting tubing, and compressor unit.

nebulizers varies but should be between 1 and 4 µm to optimize deposition in the lower respiratory tract. The density of the gas powering the nebulizer also affects nebulizer performance. In the rare situation that the nebulizer is powered with heliox (helium:oxygen 80:20), the gas flow to the nebulizer is increased by at least 50% to 9–15 L/min to compensate for the lower density of the gas (5).

Jet nebulizers are not inherently efficient for drug delivery to the lung. Significant amounts of aerosolized medicine can be trapped within the nebulizer, in the connecting T-piece and in the mouthpiece or face mask. As a result of the continuous aerosol output during treatment, much of the medicine can also be lost to the atmosphere during exhalation (3). The high flow of gas through a jet nebulizer evaporates solvent during nebulization and adiabatic expansion of the gas cools the output air and concentrates the solution in the nebulizer cup. The rate of evaporation depends on the volume of fluid placed in the reservoir. Nebulizer output can cool by >10°C below ambient temperature during treatment and the concentration of the reservoir solution can increase by up to 30% (6, 7). With a reservoir fill volume of 3 to 5 mL, compared with the 2 mL in the unit dose "nebules," a greater total amount of drug is aerosolized and delivered to the patient, albeit with a longer treatment time (3, 8). At the end of nebulization, when no further aerosol is produced, ~0.5–1.5 mL of the concentrated solution remains in the nebulizer reservoir as a *dead volume* containing drug that is unavailable to the patient (3, 8). Some common terms are used to describe the "dose" of the drug delivered by nebulizers (Table 8.1).

Jet nebulizers are the most employed nebulizers in clinical practice because they are reliable, durable, and economical, but they are not inherently a quiet or highly efficient design and are not always conveniently small. Jet nebulizers have inherent advantages and disadvantages, and variances in nebulizer performance are a function not only of their design but also of the source of energy (compressed gas or electrical compressor), gas flow and pressure, connecting tubing, interface used (spacer, and mouthpiece or mask), and the patient's breathing pattern (9). The interplay of these factors results in significant variations in nebulizer performance not only among different brands but also between nebulizers of the same brand (10–12). Other factors that influence nebulizer performance include the viscosity, density, and surface tension of the solution to be nebulized. Increasing the viscosity of the solution, such as with increasing concentrations of some medications, could decrease the nebulizer output rate as well as droplet size (13, 14). In contrast, reducing the surface tension increases nebulizer output (15). When suspensions, instead of solutions, are nebulized in a jet nebulizer, the aerosol droplets are larger compared to those with solution formulations (16).

Technological improvements that have accrued in jet nebulizers over time include conventional constant-output models with a corrugated tube acting as a reservoir, which increases efficiency by mitigating drug loss, particularly during exhalation (12). In jet nebulizers with a collection bag, aerosol generated during expiration is stored in the collection bag and is available to the patient with the next inspiration. A one-way valve located between the mouthpiece and the nebulizer separates fresh gas from exhaled gas (12). To further address the aerosol delivery inefficiencies, newer designs, such as breath-enhanced jet nebulizers, release more aerosol during inhalation, whereas breath-actuated jet nebulizers sense the patient's inspiratory flow and deliver aerosol only on inspiration, with consequent less wastage of drug

## Table 8.1: Nebulizer Dose, Lung Aerosol Deposition, and Drug Effects

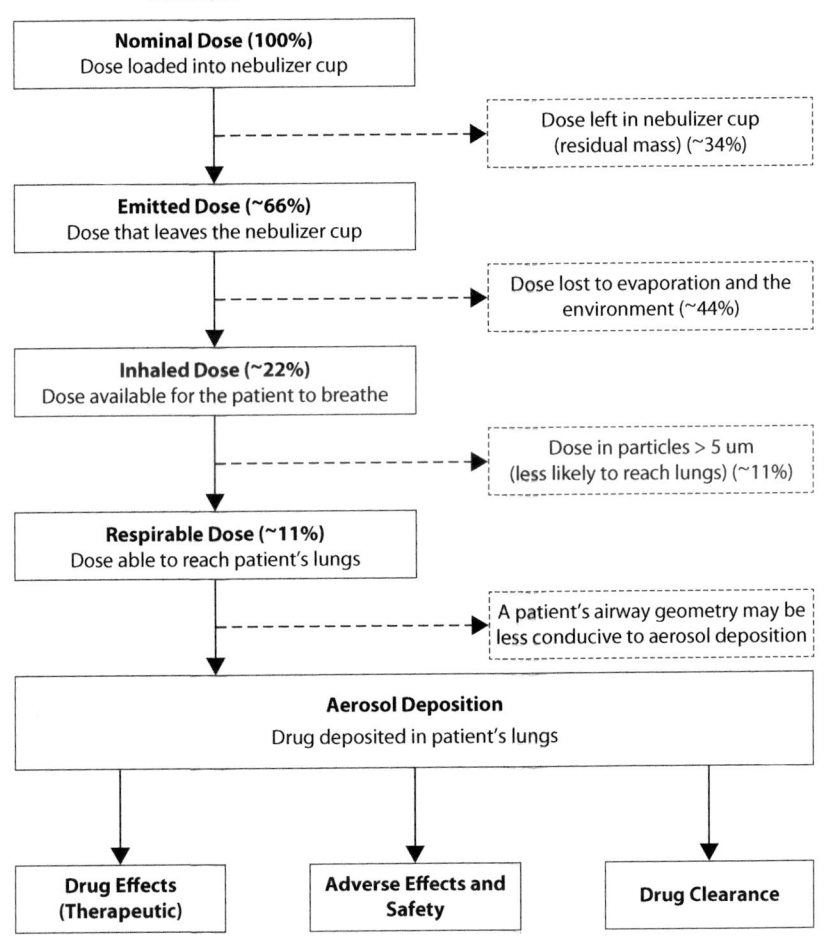

(Figure 8.2). In breath-enhanced nebulizers, for example, the PARI LC Plus (Starnberg, Germany), additional airflow is routed through the nebulizer during inspiration to enhance aerosol generation, and in some designs, one-way valves are provided to reduce aerosol output during exhalation (17–19). In a dosimetric nebulizer, either manual interruption of airflow, as in the Pari LL, or by a spring-loaded valve, as in the AeroEclipse, prevents aerosol generation during exhalation. The AeroEclipse has a higher output than a breath-enhanced nebulizer (PARI LCD, Starnberg, Germany) (20).

Large-volume nebulizers, such as the high-output extended aerosol respiratory therapy (HEART) nebulizer (Cardinal Health, Dublin, OH, US), Air Life Misty Finity (Vyaire, Chicago, IL, US), Flo-Mist (Smiths Medical, Minneapolis, MN, US) and HOPE nebulizer (B&B Medical Technologies, Carlsbad, CA, US) have reservoirs larger than 200 mL and are designed for continuous aerosol delivery (see below).

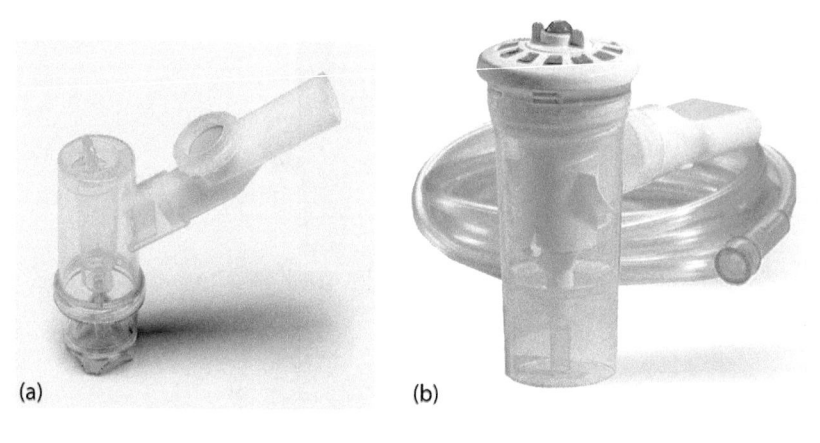

(a)                                    (b)

**Figure 8.2**   Examples of breath-enhanced (a) and breath-actuated nebulizers (b). In the breath-enhanced nebulizer (Nebutech, Salter Labs, Hudson, NH, US), the patient breathes through the nebulizer during inspiration, thereby increasing airflow and enhancing nebulizer output. During exhalation, a one-way valve directs away from the nebulizer chamber and aerosol output is decreased. In the breath-actuated nebulizer (AeroEclipse, Monaghan, Plattsburgh, NY, US), a breath-actuated valve allows airflow only during inhalation so that no aerosol is produced during exhalation and aerosol loss is minimized.

## ULTRASONIC NEBULIZERS

Ultrasonic atomization, first used in humidifiers, was adapted for nebulizer use in the mid-1960s, an innovation that allowed the production of finer aerosols than were typical of jet nebulizers at that time, in smaller, quieter devices, and with shorter durations of treatment (Figure 8.3) (2, 21). These devices transmit sound waves generated by vibrating a piezoelectric crystal at high frequency (~1–3 MHz) to the surface of the drug solution, generating aerosol that is typically more consistent in size than that produced by jet nebulizers (22–24). The size of the particles generated by ultrasonic nebulizers is inversely proportional to the vibration frequency of the piezo crystal. The surface tension and density of the solution also influence droplet size (25). Compared with jet nebulizers, most ultrasonic nebulizers have a faster rate of nebulization, require a shorter operation time, and have a larger aerosol particle size (26). The particle size and aerosol density produced by ultrasonic nebulizers also depend on the gas flow carrying the aerosol particles from the nebulizer to the patient. The increase in solution concentration during ultrasonic nebulizer operation is less pronounced than with jet nebulizers (27). Unlike jet nebulizers, the solution temperature increases by 10°C to 15°C after 10 minutes of ultrasonic nebulization (27), and this could denature thermolabile therapeutic agents.

The cost and bulk of ultrasonic nebulizers, their tendency for mechanical malfunction, and their relative inefficiency in nebulizing drug suspensions (28), liposomes (29), or more viscous solutions, are major limitations to their use. Hence, ultrasonic nebulizers are less commonly used than other nebulizer designs. Several small-volume ultrasonic nebulizers (Beetle Neb, Drive Medical, Chicago, IL, US; Lumiscope, Just Nebulizers, Fulton, MD, US; Minibreeze, Mabis DMI, Ontario, Canada) in which drug solutions, including bronchodilators,

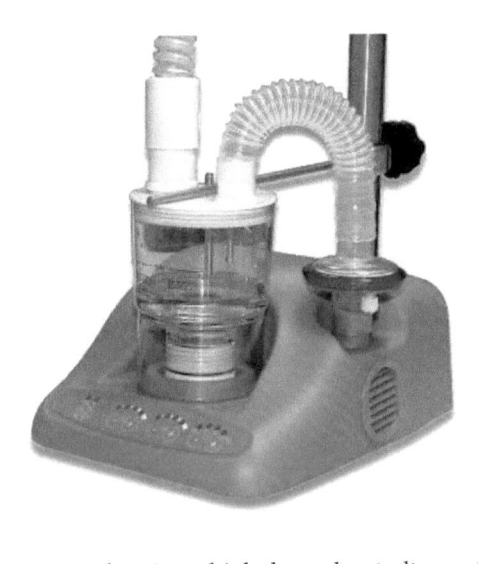

**Figure 8.3**  Illustration showing a high throughput ultrasonic nebulizer that can be used for humidification or inhalation therapy (DeVilbiss ultrasonic nebulizer, Somerset, PA). The unit can be wall mounted with a rail clamp or placed on a movable stand for greater flexibility. The integrated timer features settings of 0/15/30/45 or 60 minutes.

anti-inflammatory agents, and antibiotics, are placed directly into the manifold on top of the transducer, have been marketed to improve portability. These devices use the patient's inspiratory airflow to carry the aerosol from the nebulizer.

## VIBRATING MESH NEBULIZERS

Mesh technology emerged in nebulizer devices in the 1980s and 1990s (30, 31). Like ultrasonic nebulizers, active mesh nebulizers, such as the Aerogen (Galway, Ireland) or eFlow nebulizers (PARI, Starnberg, Germany), use energy from a vibrating piezoelectric element to mechanically pump the solution through a vibrating membrane ("mesh") at the top of the liquid reservoir (Figure 8.4) (32). A dome-shaped aperture plate is attached to a plate that is connected to a piezo-ceramic element surrounding the aperture plate. When energy is applied to the piezoelectric element, the aperture plate vibrates at ~130 kHz. The up and down movement of the plate, by about 1 μm, creates a micro-pumping action, whereby short filaments of the solution liquid pass through 1000–7000 laser-drilled holes in the aperture plate and break up into droplets that are overall finer, and more consistent in particle size than those produced by ultrasonic nebulizers. The size of the droplets depends on several factors, including the shape and size of the holes in the mesh, and the surface tension and viscosity of the solution. In contrast with jet nebulizers, vibrating mesh nebulizers have smaller residual volumes (ranging from 0.1 to 0.4 mL); the nebulizer drug output is higher, and the exit velocity of the aerosol is lower (<4 m/s).

In passive vibrating mesh nebulizers, such as the MicroAir U100 (Omron, Kyoto, Japan) or I-neb (Philips Respironics, Murrysville, PA, US), the mesh

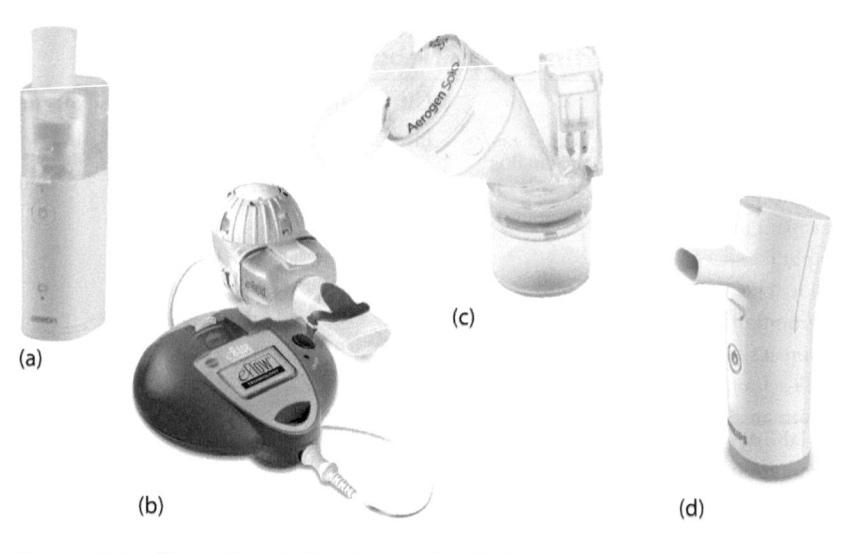

**Figure 8.4** Examples of vibrating mesh nebulizers, including the Omron NE-U100 portable MicroAir (a); PARI eFlow (b), Aerogen Solo (c), and Philips Innospire Go (d).

is separated from an ultrasonic horn by the solution to be nebulized. A piezoelectric transducer vibrates the horn and the vibrations of the horn push the solution through the mesh (32).

Mesh nebulizers have shorter treatment times of ~5–7 minutes, with less undesired heating or waste of the liquid than previous designs, all in smaller, more portable, quieter, battery-operated devices (12, 31) (Table 8.2). For example, the InnoSpire Go mesh nebulizer (Figure 8.4) delivers treatment in a small, light (111 g), quiet (<35 dB), upright design that can be filled and used up to 30 times from a single charge of the internal battery, without removable parts that require manipulation. Thus, mesh nebulizers may be preferred over compressor-driven jet nebulizers for their convenience, ease of use, and treatment satisfaction (33). Moreover, suspension formulations, such as budesonide, and various antibiotics can be delivered by mesh nebulizers, although viscous drugs and suspensions can clog the mesh's pores (12, 30). For these reasons, vibrating mesh nebulizers are convenient for use in outpatients and during the mechanical ventilation of hospitalized patients (34). The higher efficiency of the vibrating mesh nebulizers to deliver drugs to the lungs could result in greater systemic side effects, hence the nominal dose of the drug may need to be adjusted according to the efficiency of the delivery system (34).

The vibrating mesh technology has been adapted for volumetric nebulization, whereby the drug solution is dripped from a tube feed and pump system directly onto the surface of the mesh. The rate of nebulization is determined by the output of the solution by the syringe pump, and the infusion rate should not exceed the maximum output rate of the mesh. Some mesh nebulizers can aerosolize single drops (~15 µL) of various formulations.

Despite its advantages, vibrating mesh technology is expensive to manufacture and comes with a significantly increased cost for the consumer, particularly compared with jet nebulizers (Table 8.2). Mesh nebulizers must also

**Table 8.2: Comparison of Characteristics of Jet, Ultrasonic, and Vibrating Mesh Nebulizers**

| Features | Jet | Ultrasonic | Vibrating Mesh |
|---|---|---|---|
| Power source | Compressed gas/electrical mains | Electrical mains | Batteries/electrical mains |
| Portability | Limited | Limited | Portable |
| Treatment time | Long | Intermediate | Short |
| Output rate | Low | Higher | Highest |
| Residual volume | 0.5–1.5 mL | Variable but low | ≤ 0.2 mL |
| **Environmental Contamination** | | | |
| *Continuous use* | High | High | High |
| *Breath-activated* | Low | Low | Low |
| **Performance Variability** | High | Intermediate | Low |
| **Formulation Characteristics** | | | |
| *Concentration* | Increases | Variable | No change |
| *Temperature* | Decreases | Increases | Minimal change |
| *Suspensions* | Low efficiency | Poor efficiency | Variable |
| *Denaturation* | Possible[a] | Probable[a] | Possible[a] |
| **Cleaning** | Required | Required | Required |
| | Single-patient use | Multiple-patient use | Single-patient use |
| **Cost** | Very low | High | High |

[a] Denaturation of DNA occurs with all the nebulizers.

be cleaned regularly to prevent buildup and blockage of the mesh apertures, especially when drug suspensions are aerosolized.

## ADAPTIVE AEROSOL DELIVERY (AAD)

The products of new technologies include "intelligent" nebulizers such as the I-neb Adaptive Aerosol Delivery (AAD) System for the delivery of prostacyclin (12). The I-neb AAD System continuously adapts to changes in the patient's breathing pattern and pulses aerosol only during the inspiratory part of the breathing cycle (35). This eliminates the waste of aerosol during exhalation and provides precise aerosol dose delivery from a unique metering chamber design. Through the vibrating mesh technology, the metering chamber design, and the AAD Disc function, the aerosol output rate and metered dose can be tailored to the demands of the specific drug to be delivered. In the I-neb AAD System, aerosol delivery is guided through two algorithms, one for the Tidal Breathing Mode (TBM), and one for slow and deep inhalations, the Target Inhalation Mode (TIM). The aim of TIM is to reduce the treatment time by increasing the total inhalation time per minute and to increase lung deposition by reducing impaction in the upper airways through slow and deep inhalations. A key feature of the AAD technology is the patient feedback mechanisms that guide the patient on delivery performance and signal completion of the dose. These feedback signals, which include visual, audible, and tactile forms, appear to promote a high level of compliance with the use of the I-neb AAD System (Philips Respironics, Murrysville, PA) (35).

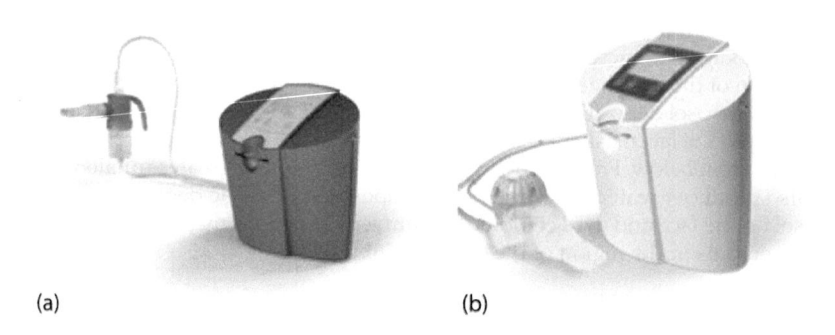

(a)  (b)

**Figure 8.5**   The AKITA jet nebulizer system (left panel) and the AKITA 2 system (right panel) are shown (Vectura Delivery Devices, Cambridge, UK). The AKITA 2 system uses the PARI APIXNEB vibrating mesh nebulizer.

## AKITA SYSTEM

The AKITA device (Vectura Delivery Devices, Cambridge, UK) applies positive pressure delivered with a computer-controlled compressor to control the entire inhalation maneuver of the patient (Figure 8.5). It has been used with both conventional jet nebulizers and vibrating mesh nebulizers. The AKITA system improves delivery efficiency (36), with up to 60% drug deposition in the lung periphery of patients with COPD, and >80% pulmonary deposition in CF patients (37). The device stores the patient's pulmonary function on a smart card that is programmed to generate aerosol during specific phases of inspiration. Aerosol generation during early inspiration targets more peripheral airways, whereas central airways could be targeted by aerosol generation during the later phases of inspiration (38). The AKITA 2 system uses the PARI APIXNEB vibrating mesh nebulizer (Figure 8.5), and its use in patients with asthma for targeting small airways with high-dose inhaled corticosteroids reduced the number of exacerbations requiring oral corticosteroids over one year of treatment (39).

## SMALL PARTICLE AEROSOL GENERATOR (SPAG)

The small particle aerosol generator (SPAG; ICN Pharmaceuticals, Costa Mesa, CA), a large-volume, pneumatically powered nebulizer, is used to aerosolize Ribavirin. It employs a drying chamber with its own flow control to produce an extra fine aerosol (MMAD 1.2–1.4 µm) with a relatively high output. In mechanically ventilated infants with severe Respiratory Syncytial Virus (RSV) infection, aerosol administration of Ribavirin with SPAG reduced the duration of ventilation, oxygen support, and hospital stay (40).

## EFFECT OF FORMULATION

The presence of a preservative in a drug solution and admixture with other drugs affect nebulizer output and aerosol characteristics (15, 41, 42). Drug mixtures need to be physically and chemically compatible (43–46).

## MOUTHPIECE VERSUS FACEMASK DELIVERY

Aerosol deposition in nasal passages significantly reduces drug delivery to the lung (47–49) and could reduce bronchodilator efficacy when the nebulizer is employed with a facemask versus a mouthpiece (50). Facemasks may be necessary for the treatment of acutely dyspneic or uncooperative patients. For

optimal efficacy, the facemask should produce a tight seal (51–53) to avoid aerosol leakage and increased aerosol deposition around the eyes (54). The orientation of the nebulizer with respect to the facemask also influences the pattern of aerosol deposition. In "Front-loaded" masks, the nebulizer is inserted directly into the facemask, whereas in "Bottom-loaded" masks the aerosol enters the mask from below. Front-loaded masks provide not only greater inhaled mass but also produce greater facial and ocular deposition (55). The deposition of aerosol on the face and eyes could be minimized by using a mask with vents, as well as cutouts in the region of the eyes (55, 56).

## CONTINUOUS AEROSOL DELIVERY

In patients with acute severe asthma, short-acting bronchodilators (e.g., albuterol 5–15 mg/h) (57) are often given continuously. Large-volume nebulizers or the HEART nebulizer are commonly used for continuous aerosol delivery because they can provide consistent drug output for 4–8 h, respectively (58–60). A Cochrane Review found that patients with acute asthma derive modest benefits from continuous bronchodilator therapy in the Emergency Room setting (61). Solutions in large-volume nebulizers may become increasingly concentrated over several hours of use and patients need close monitoring for signs of drug toxicity (59).

## NEBULIZER USE IN THE TIME OF COVID-19

Aerosol that does not deposit in the lung during a patient's inhalation can exit a nebulizer into the ambient environment during exhalation. Therefore, there is concern about the potential risk for transmission of severe acute respiratory syndrome coronavirus 2 (SARS-CoV-2) through aerosolized respiratory droplets during the treatment of patients with coronavirus disease 19 (COVID-19) (62). Due to concerns that aerosol generated by the nebulizer might carry the virus to the surrounding environment, several clinical societies made recommendations against the use of nebulizers during the COVID-19 pandemic (63, 64). However, there is currently no conclusive evidence supporting an increased risk of viral transmission during nebulization in COVID-19 patients, or for patients to switch to treatment via hand-held inhalers for the reason of preventing infection. Jain and coworkers performed a pilot clinical study using scintigraphy to investigate the dispersion pattern of technetium (Tc)-radiolabeled exhaled droplets during nebulization with a jet nebulizer and compressor (65). The authors reported that nebulizer use did not affect the dispersion of respiratory aerosols during tidal breathing. These results suggest that nebulization *per se* has a clinically insignificant role in the dispersion of exhaled aerosols. Consistent with this view, guidelines from other expert groups, such as The National Institute for Health and Care Excellence (NICE) in the UK, The New and Emerging Respiratory Virus Threats Advisory Group (NERVTAG) (66–68), and The Centers for Disease Control and Prevention (CDC) in the US (69), have not advised against the use of nebulizers during the COVID pandemic.

There are several ways to mitigate even a small risk of virus transmission during nebulizer therapy. The type of nebulizer device, type of interface, flow rate, and patient characteristics can affect fugitive emissions during nebulizer treatment. For example, McGrath et al. (70) used a simulation model to show higher fugitive aerosol concentrations with tracheostomy interfaces compared with those from nasal cannula when using pediatric, but not adult, breathing profiles. The study also found that as the flow rate increased, fugitive emissions and MMAD of the aerosol both decreased. Another simulation by Avari et al. (71)

compared viral dispersion (nebulized bacteriophages) from several respiratory support methods, finding the highest air concentrations with the use of high-flow nasal oxygen and nasal prongs, and the lowest concentrations with the use of invasive ventilation and helmet ventilation with a positive end-expiratory pressure (PEEP) valve. Li and colleagues provide guidance for reducing fugitive aerosol emissions from nebulizers in clinical practice (72). They conducted a study on nine healthy volunteers who were given saline with a small-volume nebulizer (SVN) or vibrating mesh nebulizer (VMN). They found that SVN produced higher fugitive aerosol concentrations than VMN, whereas facemasks generated higher aerosol concentrations than mouthpieces. Adding an exhalation filter to the mouthpiece or a scavenger to the facemask reduced fugitive aerosol concentrations for both SVN and VMN (72).

Notwithstanding the nebulizer type used, the medication loading process needs to be performed using an aseptic technique to prevent contamination of the reservoir and reduce the risk of bio-aerosol dispersion. A mouthpiece should be preferred over a facemask to improve treatment efficiency and reduce fugitive emissions (70). Furthermore, placing a filter on the nebulizer's outlet reduces exposure of health care personnel (HCP) to aerosol medications (72–74). An exhalation filter attached to a jet nebulizer reduced exhaled aerosol droplets between 0.06 and 0.1 μm in size by 98% (75). Thus, the emission of exhaled aerosol droplets from jet or mesh nebulizers could be effectively reduced by use of a mouthpiece and a filter attached to the exhalation port of the nebulizer. In hospital settings, the use of appropriate Personal Protective Equipment (PPE) by HCP, including N-95 mask, face shield, gloves, and gown, as well as powered air-purifying respirators (PAPRs) if needed, can also reduce transmission of infectious agents during nebulizer use (76).

## INSTRUCTIONS FOR GENERAL NEBULIZER USE

What follows are basic guidelines for nebulizer use. However, consumers should always carefully read and understand the manufacturer's instructions. Nebulizers could be operated by a gas source of 50 psi from a wall source or compressed gas from a cylinder. When nebulizers are used at home, they are generally operated by gas flow from a compressor that provides a lower pressure. Nebulizers used for home care must be matched to an appropriate compressor to ensure optimal particle sizes and adequate drug output in the emitted aerosol (77).

- Wash hands with soap and water before preparing the nebulizer for use.
- Place the machine on a hard surface. Check to see if the air filter in the compressor is clean. If it is dirty, rinse it using cold water and let it air dry. Plug in the machine.
- With premixed medicine, open the medicine container and place the medication in the nebulizer cup. If medicines need to be mixed, place the correct amounts into the container using a dropper or syringe.
- Add sterile normal saline if needed.
- Connect the medicine container to the machine using the tubing. Connect the mask or mouthpiece to the top of the container.
- Place the mouthpiece between your teeth. Close your lips around it. When using a mask, place the mask on your face.

- Turn on the machine. Keep the medicine container in an upright position. Breathe in and out slowly and deeply through your mouth until the mist is gone.

- The treatment is over when all the medicine is gone or there is no more mist coming out. The treatment should be stopped when the nebulizer begins to sputter (78). The entire treatment may take up to 20 minutes.

## GENERAL NEBULIZER CLEANING

### Jet Nebulizers

To start, remove the tubing and set it aside. Never place the compressor under water.

#### After Each Use

i. Disassemble the nebulizer and discard any remaining solution from the medication cup.

ii. Rinse each piece under warm running water for 30 seconds.

iii. Tap out excess water and lay pieces on a lint-free cloth to dry.

iv. Store the plastic tubing and medication chamber in a plastic bag between uses.

#### At the End of Each Day

i. Disassemble the nebulizer and discard any remaining solution from the medication cup.

ii. Leave each piece submerged in a bowl of warm, soapy water for 30 minutes.

iii. Rinse each piece under warm water for 30 seconds.

iv. Tap out excess water and lay pieces on a lint-free cloth to dry.

v. Change the nebulizer daily when appropriate for infectious disease control, such as with COVID-19.

#### Disinfect Every 3 Days

i. Disassemble nebulizer.

ii. Place all pieces in a large bowl with two parts of sterile water and one part of white vinegar, fully submerged, for 30–60 minutes, or with a dilute solution of a quaternary ammonium compound, such as benzalkonium chloride, for 10 minutes, or per the manufacturer's instructions.

iii. Rinse each piece under warm water for 30 seconds.

iv. Tap out excess water and lay pieces on a lint-free cloth and dry overnight.

v. Clean the outside surface of the nebulizer with cloth soaked with 70% alcohol.

#### Longer Term

Most compressors have an air filter that needs to be replaced every 6 months and/or per the manufacturer's instructions.

## Table 8.3: Cleaning Instructions for Four Commonly Used Vibrating Mesh Nebulizers

| Mesh Nebulizer | Link to Cleaning Instructions |
| --- | --- |
| InnoSpire Go (Philips) | https://www.healthstore.philips.com/cleaning |
| Aerogen Solo / Aerogen Pro (Aerogen) | https://www.aerogen.com/wp-content/uploads/2017/05/30-914-Rev-D-Aerogen-USB-Controller-IM-US-WEB.pdf (pp. 25-29) |
| Pari eFlow Nebulizer System (Pari) | https://www.manualslib.com/manual/1618550/Pari-Eflow-Rapid-178g1005.html?page=46 |
| Akita Jet Nebulizer (Vectura) | https://www.manualslib.com/manual/1732099/Vectura-Akita-Jet.html?page=12#manual |

### Vibrating Mesh Nebulizers

Cleaning instructions for vibrating mesh nebulizers are generally similar to those for jet nebulizers but can be more idiosyncratic depending on the brand. Most models require disassembly, rinsing, and cleaning of individual parts after each use, disinfection daily (which may include boiling or use of disinfection solution), and unclogging the aerosol head as needed. However, some require additional nebulization of cleaning or disinfection solution or distilled water; in this regard, some models have their own self-cleaning program. Here, we provide website links to cleaning instructions for a few commonly used vibrating mesh nebulizers (Table 8.3).

Multi-dose drug solutions for use in nebulizers have the potential to become contaminated. This can be prevented by refrigerating the solutions and discarding the syringes every 24 h (79, 80).

## ADVANTAGES AND DISADVANTAGES OF NEBULIZERS

Nebulizers have several advantages and disadvantages when compared with other inhalation devices, namely pressurized metered dose inhalers (pMDIs), dry powder inhalers (DPIs), and soft mist inhalers (SMIs) (81) (Table 8.4). Some advantages of nebulizers are related to the technique and training required to use the device, convenience, capacity to deliver a higher drug dose, ability to aerosolize solutions and suspensions, including medications that are not available for aerosolization with inhalers, and several other considerations (Table 8.4).

### Technique and Ease of Use

Nebulizers can be used by patients of any age and are commonly used to deliver medicine to children. Because the nebulizer treatments last several minutes and there is no need for training on a specific breathing pattern, nebulizers are more forgiving of faulty technique compared to inhalers. Indeed, inhaler use, particularly in elderly patients, is subject to several critical and non-critical errors that result in inadequate symptom relief for patients (82, 83). However, nebulizers are not free of potential problems with their use. For example, basic nebulizer inhalation technique, such as sitting in an upright position during therapy, may not be practiced by all patients (84).

**Table 8.4: Advantages and Disadvantages of Each Type of Aerosol-Generating Device or System Clinically Available**

| Type | Advantages | Disadvantages |
|---|---|---|
| **Small-Volume Jet Nebulizer** | Patient coordination not required | Lack of portability |
| | Effective with tidal breathing | Pressurized gas source required |
| | High dose possible | Lengthy treatment time |
| | Dose modification possible | Device cleaning required |
| | No HFA release | Contamination possible |
| | Can be used with supplemental oxygen | Not all medications available in solution form |
| | Can deliver combination therapies if compatible | Does not aerosolize suspensions well |
| | Able to deliver solutions of drugs (e.g., dornase alfa) not available in other devices | Device preparation required |
| | | Performance variability |
| | | Expensive when compressor is added in |
| **Ultrasonic Nebulizer** | Patient coordination not required | Expensive |
| | High dose possible | Need for electrical power source (wall outlet or batteries) |
| | Dose modification possible | Contamination possible |
| | No HFA release | Not all medications available in solution form |
| | Small dead volume | Device preparation required before treatment |
| | Quiet | Does not nebulize suspensions well |
| | Newer designs small and portable | Possible drug degradation |
| | Faster delivery than jet nebulizer | Potential for airway irritation with some drugs |
| **Vibrating Mesh** | No drug loss during exhalation (breath-actuated devices) | Frequent malfunctions |
| | Small and portable | Relatively expensive |
| | Quiet operation | Difficulty delivering viscous drugs and suspensions |
| | Reduced treatment times | Can be difficult to clean |
| | Increased output volume and efficiency | |
| | Consistent fine-particle generation | |
| | Higher drug deposition in the lungs | |
| | Output rate adjustable | |
| | Can work with low drug volumes | |
| | Low residual volumes | |
| | Not likely to overheat drug solutions | |

*(Continued)*

## Table 8.4: Advantages and Disadvantages of Each Type of Aerosol-Generating Device or System Clinically Available (Continued)

| Type | Advantages | Disadvantages |
|---|---|---|
| **Pressurized MDI** | Portable and compact | Coordination of breathing and actuation needed |
| | Treatment time is short | Device actuation required |
| | No drug preparation required | High pharyngeal deposition |
| | No contamination of contents | Upper limit to unit dose content |
| | Dose-dose reproducibility high | Potential for abuse |
| | Some can be used with breath-actuated mouthpiece | |
| | | Not all medications are available |
| | | Many use HFA propellants in the United States |
| **Holding Chamber, Reverse-Flow Spacer, or Spacer** | Reduces the need for patient coordination | Inhalation can be more complex for some patients |
| | Reduces pharyngeal deposition | Can reduce the dose available if not used properly |
| | | More expensive than MDI alone |
| | | Less portable than MDI alone |
| | | Integrated actuator devices may alter aerosol properties compared to native actuator |
| **DPI** | Breath-actuated | Requires moderate to high inspiratory flow |
| | Less patient coordination required | Some units are single dose |
| | Propellant not required | Can result in high pharyngeal deposition |
| | Small and portable | Not all medications available |
| | Short treatment time | |
| | Dose counters in most newer designs | |
| **SMI** | Compact | Not breath actuated |
| | Small and Portable | Not currently available in many countries |
| | Multi-dose device | Not all medications are available |
| | Less coordination needed vs. pMDI | |
| | Short treatment time | |
| | High lung deposition | |

*Abbreviations:* DPI = dry powder inhaler; pMDI = pressurized metered dose inhalers; SMI = soft mist inhaler; HFA = hydrofluoroalkane

*Source:* Modified from Dolovich et al. (81).

103

Although many patients in need of maintenance therapy for chronic lung disease can use pMDIs (with or without a spacer) or DPIs, certain patients will most likely benefit from administration by nebulizer (85, 86). These include:

- Patients with cognitive impairment, e.g., Alzheimer's dementia, intellectual disability, or altered consciousness, which preclude effective use of handheld inhalers.

- Patients with impaired manual dexterity due to arthritis, Parkinsonism, or stroke.

- Patients who have severe pain or muscle weakness due to neuromuscular disease.

- Patients who are unable to use pMDIs or DPIs in an optimal manner despite adequate instruction and training, such as those patients who are generally debilitated after hospitalization or by chronic illness and are unable to coordinate their breathing with a pMDI, or patients who cannot generate adequate inspiratory flow for effective aerosol delivery from a DPI.

- Patients with inadequate symptom relief with appropriate use of pMDIs/DPIs.

- Patients who do not comply with the use of pMDIs and DPIs or who prefer nebulizers.

- Patients who need respiratory medications that are not available in pMDI or DPI formulations; in the United States, for example, some antibiotics, mucolytics, and prostaglandins are not available in hand-held inhalers.

- Patients who are unable to afford therapy with pMDIs or DPIs.

## Other Considerations

Other potential disadvantages of nebulizers are their relatively poor efficiency, high residual volume of 0.5–1.5 mL, and a significant amount of aerosol wasted during exhalation with continuous operation. Limited access to accessories, the use of damaged parts, and patients engaging in self-repairs, are other problems associated with nebulizer use (84). Another limitation of nebulizers, which has now been resolved, was the lack of availability of long-acting muscarinic antagonists (LAMAs) in solution. The approval of glycopyrrolate (Lonhala, Sunovion) in 2018 and revefenacin (Yupelri, Mylan/Theravance) in 2019 has overcome this limitation.

## EVOLVING PERSPECTIVES ON MAINTENANCE TREATMENT WITH NEBULIZERS

Most patients with stable COPD are prescribed maintenance therapy via inhaler, due to the perceived convenience of inhalers compared with nebulizers. In fact, until recently, nebulizers were not generally recommended for maintenance therapy for COPD. For example, in the first (2001) annual report of the Global Initiative for Chronic Obstructive Lung Disease (GOLD), and all subsequent Reports until 2010, GOLD stated that "Nebulizers are not recommended for regular treatment because they are more expensive and require appropriate maintenance" (87). In 2010, GOLD no longer stated that nebulizers were inappropriate for patients with stable COPD, but recommendations for their use were still cautious. The evolution toward accepting nebulizers as a standard inhalation delivery device in patients with stable COPD continued, and caveats regarding such use were removed from the GOLD Reports in 2017 (87).

For many years, inhalers and nebulizers were considered to be equally effective when used optimally, and it was considered that most patients could be trained to use their inhalers appropriately. However, the scientific evidence underlying this assumption is weak (88). Moreover, recent investigations, especially those that include patient perceptions as an outcome measure, suggest that nebulizers may provide more satisfactory symptom relief for some users (Table 8.5). These results are not surprising given the potential for suboptimal inhaler use by patients. Indeed, poor inhaler technique compromises symptom relief in up to 94% of patients with COPD (86). Inhaler use training could reduce such errors, yet even extensive training may not mitigate patients' misuse of inhalers. For example, in the survey conducted by Hanania et al. (89), 79% of patients with COPD reported at least one physical or cognitive impairment that

**Table 8.5:** **Surveys of patient-reported symptom control, quality of life, and device preference with nebulizers vs. inhalers**

| First Author, Year | Study Type | Sample Size | Study Findings |
|---|---|---|---|
| Barta, 2002 (90) | Patient survey (via postal questionnaire) | 82 with COPD | Nebulized treatment at home helped patients feel comfortable and more in charge of their own symptom control; compliance was generally excellent |
| Sharafkhaneh, 2013 (91) | Telephone survey of randomly selected patients and caregivers | 400 patients with COPD and 400 caregivers | Most patients and caregivers (~80%) preferred therapy with nebulizers vs. inhalers for controlling symptoms and improving quality of life |
| Dhand, 2018 (92) | Online survey using the Harris Poll Online panel | 254 patients with COPD | 54% of patients with COPD preferred nebulizers to other inhalation devices |
| Hanania, 2018 (89) | Web-based, descriptive, cross-sectional US-based survey | 499 with self-reported COPD | Most (35%) patients reported no device preference, whereas 33% preferred pMDIs, 12% preferred nebulizers, 10% preferred SMIs, and 9% preferred DPIs. Patients with more severe symptoms (mMRC score ≥ 2) were most likely to report using a nebulizer. |

*Abbreviations:* COPD = chronic obstructive pulmonary disease; DPI = dry powder inhaler; pMDIs = pressurized metered dose inhalers.
*Source:* From Terry and Dhand (88).

could limit their ability to correctly manipulate an inhaler device, including arthritis, poor eyesight, poor hearing, memory problems, tremor, difficulty with fine motor activities, depression, or anxiety, and more than half of the respondents had multiple limitations. Consequently, even assuming inhaler-nebulizer equivalence with perfect use, most patients with COPD may not achieve optimal benefits from inhalers due to co-morbid physical and cognitive limitations that cannot be improved by device training alone.

In summary, nebulizers remain a cornerstone of respiratory drug delivery. Compared with pMDIs or DPIs, nebulizers are more forgiving of faulty technique, can deliver larger doses and a wider range of medications and formulations, and appear to provide greater symptomatic benefit in studies of patient-reported outcomes. The use of nebulizers in the ambulatory setting has been facilitated by modern technologies and designs that have increased their portability and reduced their noise, size, and treatment times. Nonetheless, nebulizers still vary in terms of design and interface, cost, nebulization and delivery efficiency, output rate, drug degradation, "smart" or "intelligent" design features, and overall performance. Consideration of these factors is needed to optimize nebulizer use based on the patient's individual needs and preferences.

## REFERENCES

1. American Association for Respiratory Care: Virtual Museum: Aerosol delivery devices. [cited 2022 Feb 23] https://museum.aarc.org/galleries/aerosol-delivery-devices/
2. Anderson PJ. History of aerosol therapy: Liquid nebulization to MDIs to DPIs. Respir Care 2005;50:1139–1150.
3. Burks AW. Aerosols and aerosol drug delivery systems. In: Burks AW, Holgate ST, O'Hehir R, et al. editors. Middleton's allergy: Principles and practice. Amsterdam: Elsevier; 2020.
4. Hess D, Fisher D, Williams P, et al. Medication nebulizer performance. Effects of diluent volume, nebulizer flow, and nebulizer brand. Chest 1996;110:498–505.
5. Hess DR, Acosta FL, Ritz RH, et al. The effect of heliox on nebulizer function using a beta-agonist bronchodilator. Chest 1999;115:184–189.
6. Phipps PR, Gonda I. Droplets produced by medical nebulizers. Some factors affecting their size and solute concentration. Chest 1990;97:1327–1332.
7. Stapleton KW, Finlay WH. Determining solution concentration within aerosol droplets output by jet nebulizers. J Aerosol Sci 1995;26:137–145.
8. Broaddus VC. Aerosols and drug delivery. In: Broaddus VC, Ernst J, King TE Jr, et al. editors. Murray & Nadel's textbook of respiratory medicine. Vol 1, 7th ed. Amsterdam: Elsevier; 2022.
9. Rau JL. Design principles of liquid nebulization devices currently in use. Respir Care 2002;47:1257–1275; discussion 1275–1278.
10. Alvine GF, Rogers P, Fitzsimmons KM, et al. Disposable jet nebulizers. How reliable are they? Chest 1992;101:316–319.
11. Waldrep JC, Keyhani K, Black M, et al. Operating characteristics of 18 different continuous-flow jet nebulizers with beclomethasone dipropionate liposome aerosol. Chest 1994;105:106–110.
12. Ari A. Jet, ultrasonic, and mesh nebulizers: An evaluation of nebulizers for better clinical outcomes. Eurasian J Pulmonol 2014;16:1–7.
13. McCallion ONM, Taylor KMG, Thomas M, et al. Nebulization of fluids of different physicochemical properties with air-jet and ultrasonic nebulizers. Pharm Res 1995;12:1682–1688.

14. McCallion ONM, Taylor KMG, Thomas M, et al. The influence of surface tension on aerosols produced by medical nebulisers. Int J Pharm 1996;129:123–136.

15. MacNeish CF, Meisner D, Thibert R, et al. A comparison of pulmonary availability between Ventolin (albuterol) nebules and Ventolin (albuterol) Respirator Solution. Chest 1997;111:204–208. DOI:10.1378/chest.111.1.204

16. Ferron GA, Gebhart J. Estimation of the lung deposition of aerosol particles produced with medical nebulizers. J Aerosol Sci 1988;19:1083–1086.

17. Devadason SG, Everard M, Linto JM, et al. Comparison of drug delivery from conventional versus "Venturi" nebulizers. Eur Respir J 1997;10(11):2479–2483.

18. Ho SL, Kwong WT, O'Drowsky L, et al. Evaluation of four breath-enhanced nebulizers for home use. J Aerosol Med 2001;14(4):467–475.

19. Leung K, Louca E, Coates AL. Comparison of breath-enhanced to breath-actuated nebulizers for rate, consistency, and efficiency. Chest 2004;126(5):1619–1627.

20. Rau JL, Arzu A, Restrepo RD. Performance comparison of nebulizer designs: Constant output, breath-enhanced, and dosimetric. Respir Care 2004;49:174–179.

21. Dessanges JF. A history of nebulization. J Aerosol Med 2001;14:65–71.

22. Mercer TT. Production of therapeutic aerosols: Principles and techniques. Chest 1981;80:813–818.

23. Lentz YK, Anchordoquy TJ, Langsfeld CS. Rationale for the selection of an aerosol delivery system for gene delivery. J Aerosol Med 2006;19:372–384.

24. Harvey CJ, O'Doherty MJ, Page CJ, et al. Comparison of jet and ultrasonic nebulizer pulmonary aerosol deposition during mechanical ventilation. Eur Respir J 1997;10:905–909.

25. Mercer TT, Tillery MI, Chow HY. Operating characteristics of some compressed-air nebulizers. Am Ind Hyg Assoc J 1968;29:66–78.

26. Niven RW, Ip AY, Mittelman S, et al. Some factors associated with the ultrasonic nebulization of proteins. Pharm Res 1995;12:53–59.

27. Steckel H, Eskandar F. Factors affecting aerosol performance during nebulization with jet and ultrasonic nebulizers. Eur J Pharm Sci 2003;19:443–455.

28. Nikander K, Turpeinen M, Wollmer P. The conventional ultrasonic nebulizer proved inefficient in nebulizing a suspension. J Aerosol Med 1999;12:47–53.

29. Leung KKM, Bridges PA, Taylor KMG. The stability of liposomes to ultrasonic nebulization. Int J Pharm 1996;145:95–102.

30. Vecellio L. The mesh nebuliser: A recent technical innovation for aerosol delivery. Breathe 2006;2:252–260.

31. Pritchard JN, Hatley RHM, Denyer J, et al. Mesh nebulizers have become the first choice for new nebulized pharmaceutical drug developments. Ther Deliv 2018;9:121–136.

32. Dhand R. Nebulizers that use a vibrating mesh or plate with multiple apertures to generate aerosol. Respir Care 2002;47:1406–1416.

33. Nickerson C, Von Hollen D, Garbin S, et al. Preference and quality of life of adult chronic obstructive lung disease (COPD) patients when using a novel mesh nebulizer compared to traditional jet nebulizer (TJN). Eur Respir J 2020;56:640. DOI:10.1183/13993003.congress-2020.640

34. Dhand R. How should aerosols be delivered during invasive mechanical ventilation. Respir Care 2017;62:1343–1367.

35. Denyer J, Dyche T. The adaptive aerosol delivery (AAD) technology: Past, present, and future. J Aerosol Med Pulm Drug Deliv 2010;23(Suppl 1):S1–S10.
36. Brand P, Beckmann H, Maas-Enriquez M, et al. Peripheral deposition of alpha1-protease inhibitor using commercial inhalation devices. Eur Respir J 2003;22:263–267.
37. Griese M, Ramakers J, Krasselt A, et al. Improvement of alveolar glutathione and lung function but not oxidative state in cystic fibrosis. Am J Respir Crit Care Med 2004;169:822–828.
38. Ruffin RE, Dolovich MB, Wolff RK, et al. The effects of preferential deposition of histamine in the human airway. Am Rev Respir Dis 1978;117(3):485–492.
39. van den Bosch WB, Kloosterman SF, Andrinopoulou ER, et al. Small airways targeted treatment with smart nebulizer technology could improve severe asthma in children: A retrospective analysis. J Asthma 2022;59:2223–2233. DOI:10.1080/02770903.2021.1996597
40. Smith DW, Frankel LR, Mathers LH, et al. A controlled trial of aerosolized ribavarin in infants receiving mechanical ventilation for severe respiratory syncytial virus infection. N Engl J Med 1991;325:24–29.
41. Coates AL, MacNeish CF, Meisner D, et al. The choice of jet nebulizer, nebulizing flow, and addition of albuterol affects the output of tobramycin aerosols. Chest 1997;111(5):1206–1212.
42. Berlinski A, Waldrep JC. Nebulized drug admixtures: Effect on aerosol characteristics and albuterol output. J Aerosol Med 2006;19(4):484–490.
43. Burchett DK, Darko W, Zahra J, et al. Mixing and compatibility guide for commonly used aerosolized medications. Am J Health Syst Pharm 2010;67(3):227–230. DOI:10.2146/ajhp080261
44. McKenzie JE, Cruz-Rivera M. Compatibility of budesonide inhalation suspension with four nebulizing solutions. Ann Pharmacother 2004;38(6):967–972.
45. Akapo S, Gupta J, Martinez E, et al. Compatibility and aerosol characteristics of formoterol fumarate mixed with other nebulizing solutions. Ann Pharmacother 2008;42:1416–1424.
46. Kamin W, Erdnüss F, Krämer I. Inhalation solutions–which ones may be mixed? Physico-chemical compatibility of drug solutions in nebulizers–update 2013. J Cyst Fibros 2014;13(3):243–250. DOI:10.1016/j.jcf.2013.09.006
47. Everard ML, Hardy JG, Milner AD. Comparison of nebulized aerosol deposition in the lungs of healthy adults following oral and nasal inhalation. Thorax 1993;48(10):1045–1046.
48. Chua HL, Collis GG, Newbury AM, et al. The influence of age on aerosol deposition in children with cystic fibrosis. Eur Respir J 1994;7:2185–2191.
49. Nikander K, Agertoft L, Pedersen S. Breath-synchronized nebulization diminishes the impact of patient-device interfaces (face mask or mouthpiece) on the inhaled mass of nebulized budesonide. J Asthma 2000;37(5):451–459.
50. Kishida M, Suzuki I, Kabayama H, et al. Mouthpiece versus face mask for delivery of nebulized salbutamol in exacerbated childhood asthma. J Asthma 2002;39(4):337–339.
51. Sangwan S, Gurses BK, Smaldone GC. Face masks and facial deposition of aerosols. Pediatr Pulmonol 2004;37(5):447–452.
52. Hayden JT, Smith N, Woolf DA, et al. A randomised crossover trial of face mask efficacy. Arch Dis Child 2004;89(1):72–73.

53. Erzinger S, Schueepp KG, Brooks-Wildhaber J, et al. Face masks and aerosol delivery in vivo. J Aerosol Med 2007;20(Suppl 1):S78–S84.
54. Bisquerra RA, Botz GH, Nates JL. Ipratropium-bromide-induced acute anisocoria in the intensive care setting due to ill-fitting face masks. Respir Care 2005;50(12):1662–1664.
55. Smaldone GC, Sangwan S, Shah A. Face mask design, facial deposition, and delivered dose of nebulized aerosols. J Aerosol Med 2007;20(Suppl 1):S66–S77.
56. Smaldone GC. Advances in aerosols: Adult respiratory disease. J Aerosol Med 2006;19:36–46.
57. Peters SG. Continuous bronchodilator therapy. Chest 2007;131(1):286–289.
58. Berlinski A, Waldrep JC. Four hours of continuous albuterol nebulization. Chest 1998;114(3):847–853.
59. Raabe OG, Wong TM, Wong GB, et al. Continuous nebulization therapy for asthma with aerosols of beta2 agonists. Ann Allergy Asthma Immunol 1998;80(6):499–508.
60. Kelly HW, Keim KA, McWilliams BC. Comparison of two methods of delivering continuously nebulized albuterol. Ann Pharmacother 2003;37(1):23–26.
61. Camargo CA Jr, Spooner CH, Rowe BH. Continuous versus intermittent beta-agonists in the treatment of acute asthma. Cochrane Database Syst Rev 2003;(4):CD001115.
62. Lavorini F, Usmani OS, Dhand R. Aerosol delivery systems for treating obstructive airway diseases during the SARS-CoV-2 pandemic. Intern Emerg Med 2021;16:2035–2039.
63. Halpin DMG, Criner GJ, Papi A, et al. The 2020 GOLD science committee report on COVID-19 and chronic obstructive pulmonary disease. Am J Respir Crit Care Med 2021;203(1):24–36.
64. Respiratory Care Committee of Chinese Thoracic Society. Expert consensus on preventing nosocomial transmission during respiratory care for critically ill patients infected by 2019 novel coronavirus pneumonia. Zhonghua Jie He Hu Xi Za Zhi 2020;43(4):288–296.
65. Jain GK, Chandra L, Dhand R. Clinical evaluation of dispersion and disposition of exhaled droplets during nebulization using 3-D gamma scintigraphy. Paper presented at NAPCON 2020 (virtual). 22nd Joint National Conference of National College of Chest Physicians (India) and Indian Chest Society. January 27–31, 2021. New Delhi, India.
66. Fink JB, Ehrmann S, Li J, et al. Reducing aerosol-related risk of transmission in the era of COVID-19: An interim guidance endorsed by the International Society of Aerosols in Medicine. J Aerosol Med Pulm Drug Deliv 2020;33(6):300–304. DOI:10.1089/jamp.2020.1615
67. Hui DS, Chan MT, Chow B. Aerosol dispersion during various respiratory therapies: A risk assessment model of nosocomial infection to health care workers. Hong Kong Med J 2014;20(Suppl 4):9–13.
68. National Institute for Health and Care Excellence, COVID-19 rapid guideline: Severe asthma (NICE guideline [NG166]). 2020. Available from: https://www.nice.org.uk/guidance/ng166
69. CDC. Interim US Guidance for risk assessment and public health management of healthcare personnel with potential exposure in a healthcare setting to patients with coronavirus disease 2019 (COVID-19). [cited 2020 Apr 15]. Available from: https://www.cdc.gov/coronavirus/2019-ncov/hcp/guidance-risk-assessment-hcp.html

70. McGrath JA, O'Toole C, Bennett G, et al. Investigation of fugitive aerosols released into the environment during high-flow therapy. Pharmaceutics 2019;11:254.
71. Avari H, Hiebert RJ, Ryzynski AA, et al. Quantitative assessment of viral dispersion associated with respiratory support devices in a simulated critical care environment. Am J Respir Crit Care Med 2021;203:1112–1118.
72. Harnois LJ, Alolaiwat AA, Jing G, et al. Efficacy of various mitigation devices in reducing fugitive emissions from nebulizers. Respir Care 2022;67(4):394–403.
73. McGrath JA, O'Sullivan A, Bennett G, et al. Investigation of the quantity of exhaled aerosols released into the environment during nebulisation. Pharmaceutics 2019;11(2):75.
74. Wittgen BP, Kunst PW, Perkins WR, et al. Assessing a system to capture stray aerosol during inhalation of nebulized liposomal cisplatin. J Aerosol Med 2006;19:385–391.
75. Schuschnig U, Ledermuller R, Gramann J. Efficacy of the PARI filter-valve set to prevent environmental contamination with aerosol during nebulizer therapy. 2020. Preprint. https://www.researchgate.net/publication/342987954
76. Liu M, Cheng S-Z, Xu K-W, et al. Use of personal protective equipment against coronavirus disease 2019 by healthcare professionals in Wuhan, China: Cross sectional study. BMJ 2020;369:m2195. DOI:10.1136/bmj.m2195
77. Smith EC, Denyer J, Kendrick AH. Comparison of twenty three nebulizer/compressor combinations for domiciliary use. Eur Respir J 1995;8:1214.
78. Malone RA, Hollie MC, Glynn-Barnhart A, et al. Optimal duration of nebulized albuterol therapy. Chest 1993;104:1114–1118.
79. Rau JL, Restrepo RD. Nebulized bronchodilator formulations: Unit-dose or multi-dose? Respir Care 2003;48:926–939.
80. Bell J, Alexander L, Carson J, et al. Nebuliser hygiene in cystic fibrosis: Evidence-based recommendations. Breathe (Sheff) 2020;16:190328. DOI:10.1183/20734735.0328-2019
81. Dolovich MB, Ahrens RC, Hess DR, et al. Device selection and outcomes of aerosol therapy: Evidence-based guidelines: American College of Chest Physicians/American College of Asthma, Allergy, and Immunology. Chest 2005;127:335–371.
82. Melani AS, Bonavia M, Cilenti V, et al. Inhaler mishandling remains common in real life and is associated with reduced disease control. Respir Med 2011;105:930–938.
83. Duarte AG, Tung L, Zhang W, et al. Spirometry measurement of peak inspiratory flow identifies suboptimal use of dry powder inhalers in ambulatory patients with COPD. Chronic Obstr Pulm Dis 2019;6:246–255.
84. Alhaddad B, Smith FJ, Robertson T, et al. Patients' practices and experiences of using nebuliser therapy in the management of COPD at home. BMJ Open Respir Res 2015;2:e000076. DOI:10.1136/bmjresp-2014-000076
85. Dhand R, Dolovich M, Chipps B, et al. The role of nebulized therapy in the management of COPD: Evidence and recommendations. COPD 2012;9:58–72.
86. Usmani OS. Choosing the right inhaler for your asthma or COPD patient. Ther Clin Risk Manag 2019;15:461–472.
87. Terry P, Dhand R. Inhalation therapy for stable COPD: 20 years of GOLD reports. Adv Ther 2020;37:1812–1828.

88. Terry P, Dhand R. Maintenance therapy with nebulizers in patients with stable COPD: Need for reevaluation. Pulm Ther 2020;6:177–192.

89. Hanania NA, Braman S, Adams SG, et al. The role of inhalation delivery devices in COPD: Perspectives of patients and health care providers. Chronic Obstr Pulm Dis 2018;5:111–123.

90. Barta SK, Crawford A, Roberts CM. Survey of patients' views of domiciliary nebuliser treatment for chronic lung disease. Respir Med 2002;96:375–381.

91. Sharafkhaneh A, Wolf RA, Goodnight S, et al. Perceptions and attitudes toward the use of nebulized therapy for COPD: Patient and caregiver perspectives. COPD 2013;10:482–492.

92. Dhand R, Mahler DA, Carlin BW, et al. Results of a patient survey regarding COPD knowledge, treatment experiences, and practices with inhalation devices. Respir Care 2018;63:833–839.

# 9 Inhalation Therapy in Infants and Children

*Bruce K. Rubin and Israel Amirav*

## CONTENTS

## INTRODUCTION

In this chapter, we first describe why infants/small children are different with respect to their anatomy/physiology and their behavior. We will then review the available aerosol-generating devices and conclude with suggestions to improve clinical outcomes of aerosol therapy in this age group.

### Anatomy/Physiology/Behavior

Infants and children younger than three years of age present unique challenges to aerosol delivery. Small children have anatomical limitations, as well as emotional challenges, and barriers to compliance. The devices used for aerosol delivery in infants and younger children were originally designed for adults. Less is known about the anatomic, physiological, and behavioral issues related to use of aerosol devices that are specific to infants. For example, if a baby is fighting the nebulizer face mask and crying, parents might substitute "blow by" treatment in which the mask is removed from the nebulizer tubes and the open end of the tube is held close to the infant's face, a technique that is no longer recommended because of its very low efficiency in delivering aerosol to the lungs (1). Alternatively, parents might tighten the grip on the mask, thinking that this will result in improved delivery. If the therapy fails, this may lead physicians to falsely assume that an increased drug dosage is required.

In terms of their anatomy, infants have a pharynx that is much higher in the upper respiratory tract, near the base of the tongue (Figure 9.1). They are largely nose breathers, and their larynx and supraglottic region are less rigid, and subsequently more susceptible to obstruction or collapse, particularly on inspiration. The epiglottis, which is relatively narrow and floppy, is located nearer the palate. This may explain why infants preferentially breathe through their nose (2).

Nose breathing serves as a barrier to aerosol delivery since the nose and nasopharynx have high resistance to flow. It has been shown that infants' noses are efficient in filtering air, which decreases the inhalation of toxins, as well as inhaled therapies (3). Infants also have faster growth of lung parenchyma relative to airway growth, which leads to increased airway conductance (4). The implications of this remain largely unexplored, but a greater proportion of aerosol particles may reach the lung parenchyma because they travel a shorter distance. Because of their diameter, infants' lungs are more susceptible to obstruction of airways with airway disease. Another consideration is airflow.

DOI: 10.1201/9781003269014-9

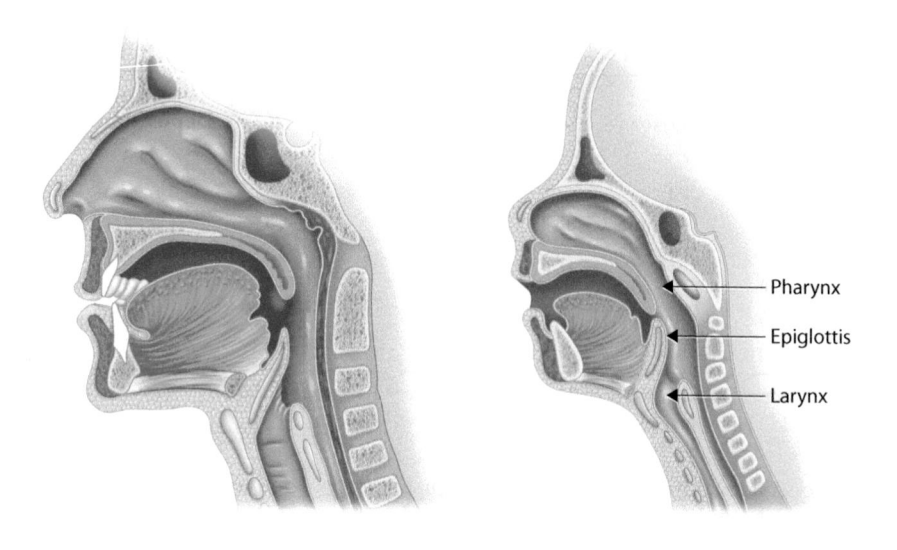

**Figure 9.1**  The upper airway of adults (left) compared with that of infants (right): pharynx and supraglottic region: Less rigid; epiglottis: Narrow, floppy, and closer to palate; larynx: Higher and very close to the base of the tongue.

Infants have a faster inspiratory airflow but with lower volumes than older children, leading to aerosol delivery to the more proximal airways upon inhalation.

Infants breathe more rapidly and with a smaller tidal volume, decreasing lung deposition. This breathing pattern, compounded with nose breathing, results in more aerosol particles getting trapped in the upper respiratory tract. We have recently compared nasal and oral delivery of aerosol in anatomically correct replicas of infants' faces containing both nasal and oral upper airways (5). Three CT-derived upper respiratory tract replicas representing infants/toddlers aged 5, 14, and 20 months were studied and aerosol delivery (using a lung mechanical simulator) to the "lower respiratory tract" (LRT) by either the oral or nasal route for each of the replicas was measured at the "tracheal" opening. Nasal delivery to the LRT exceeded oral delivery in the 5- and 14-month models and was equivalent in the 20-month model. Differences between nasal and oral delivery diminished with age/size and were unrelated to tidal volumes (5).

*In vivo* studies employing aerosolized radiolabeled particles to measure lung deposition in infants with various pulmonary diseases are few, but the results are strikingly similar regardless of disease state (Table 9.1).

These *in vivo* studies have demonstrated that lung deposition of radiolabeled aerosols is no more than 2% for age 12 months and under, but by the age of about 3 years, it has increased to about 5%. Compared to children over age 8 and adults who may deposit 20–40% of the mouth dose below the larynx, these deposition values appear to be minute. However, since the infant's airway surface area is relatively small, it turns out that these "adult doses," although markedly attenuated, provide a similar clinical response without increased adverse effects.

Children generally do not know how to adequately inhale through a mouthpiece until about 3–4 years of age. Because of this, a face mask that is

**Table 9.1: Lung Deposition of Aerosol Therapeutics Given to Infants and Young Children with Different Diseases/ Disorders**

| Author | Disease | Age (Mean, m) | n | Lung Deposition (%) |
|--------|---------|---------------|---|---------------------|
| Chua (6) | CF | 9 | 12 | **1.3** |
| Mallol (7) | CF | 12 | 5 | 2 |
| Tal (8) | Asthma, CF, BPD | 21 | 15 | 2 |
| Fok (9) | BPD | 3 | 13 | **1.7** |
| Amirav (10) | Bronchiolitis | 8 | 12 | **1.5** |
| Amirav (11) | Asthma | 6 | 12 | **1.7** |
| Amirav (12) | Healthy | 9 | 10 | **1.6** |

*Abbreviations:* BPD = bronchopulmonary dysplasia; CF = cystic fibrosis.
*Note:* Bold values are outcome of interest.

comfortable and has a tight seal may improve aerosol delivery (13). Even a 1-cm gap between the mask and the face led to a 50% reduction in aerosol delivery with a small-volume nebulizer (14). A tight-fitting seal is most important when it comes to aerosol delivery through pressurized metered dose inhalers (pMDIs) with valved holding chambers (VHCs) because drug delivery occurs only when the infant or child inhales through the device. With jet nebulizers, a poor seal results in the escape of drug and admixture with outside air, and with the new breath-actuated nebulizers, a tight seal is required for drug delivery. Unfortunately, current facemask designs do not consider the distinct anatomical and physiological needs of infants and young children. A study involving the NebuChamber mask demonstrated a 30% higher efficiency of airway delivery with an improved design and a tighter seal (15). It is important to note that in both this study and another (16), it was shown that dose variability increased with decreased cooperation by the children. This suggests that a tight-fitting mask design is a less important factor than child compliance.

Crying during aerosol delivery is a complex issue. Crying is characterized by a long exhalation, followed by a short inspiratory gasp. This increases the chances that the drug will remain in the upper respiratory tract, since the drug is only available during the short inhalation phase, and not during exhalation. Additionally, crying is accompanied by agitation, which makes a poor mask seal more likely. Infants cry in reaction to being "smothered" by an uncomfortable facemask, and the caregiver may then create a tighter, more forceful seal, exacerbating the discomfort. This leads to struggling, and a further compromised seal. Crying has been shown to be a primary cause of poor face-to-mask seal, and while crying is a common occurrence during aerosol delivery, it is not inevitable. It has been suggested that allowing children to play with the facemask before delivery makes the child less likely to cry. Parents should be coached on techniques to relax the child and ease them into the therapy. Such techniques include having the child hold the facemask up to their parents or favorite stuffed animal or rewarding the child for proper use of the device.

There are studies that demonstrate a clear positive correlation between the level of infant distress and deposition of aerosol in the upper respiratory tract, which leads to swallowing and gastrointestinal tract deposition and absorption (17).

## AEROSOL-GENERATING DEVICES

### Pneumatic or Small Volume Jet Nebulizers (SVNs)

Jet nebulizers are sometimes used for children because of the misconception that children are unable to effectively use a pMDI even with a VHC (18). Although the response to medications given by a pMDI with holding chamber can be similar to that achieved by a nebulizer, because the use of the pMDI is much faster, more portable, less expensive than individually administered nebulizer doses, does not require cleaning, there is less pharyngeal deposition and less swallowed drug, and greater adherence with therapy when using a pMDI and chamber, a jet nebulizer should be used when the medication is only available as a nebulizer solution (e.g. dornase alfa, hypertonic saline).

### Large-Volume Nebulizer

The large-volume pneumatic nebulizer (LVN) has a reservoir volume greater than 100 mL and can be used to administer a solution over a prolonged period. LVNs work on the same principles as small-volume nebulizers, with the exception that the residual volume is greater and the effects of evaporation over time are more profound. When using the LVN to administer a solution containing medications, such as bronchodilators, the medication becomes increasingly concentrated over time because of preferential evaporation of the diluent (19).

### Ultrasonic Nebulizers (USN)

USN produce ultrasonic waves directly into the solution, which produces aerosol on the surface of the liquid. USNs are capable of higher aerosol outputs (0.5–7 mL/minute) and higher aerosol densities than most conventional jet nebulizers. Particle size is affected by the frequency of the waves, while output is affected by the amplitude of the signal. Frequency is usually device-specific and is not user-adjustable. Unlike jet nebulizers, the temperature of the solution placed in a USN increases during use. As the temperature increases, the drug concentration may also rise, increasing the likelihood of undesired side effects. In addition, some drugs may be adversely affected by the increased operating temperature (20). Pulmonary deposition of drugs delivered by currently available ultrasonic nebulizers is so poor that these cannot be recommended for the administration of asthma medications (21).

Several other hazards are associated with using an USN. Over hydration may occur when using a USN for prolonged treatment of a neonate, small child, or other patient with fluid and electrolyte imbalances. The high-density aerosols from USNs have been associated with bronchospasm, increased airway resistance, and irritability in a substantial proportion of the population (22).

### Vibrating Mesh Nebulizers (VMN)

A relatively recent advance in nebulizer therapy is the vibrating mesh nebulizer (VMN). In this device, a piezo element vibrates a mesh or horn in contact with drug. As the liquid passes through multiple holes in the mesh, the vibrating action generates medicated aerosol. Because the mesh is uniform by design, this can be tailored to specific medications and the resulting aerosol usually has a smaller and more uniform particle size (mass median aerodynamic diameter; MMAD and geometric standard deviation; GSD) than jet nebulizers. The VMN devices are small, more portable than pneumatic jet nebulizers, generally battery or AC powered, and are silent and fast. There is also the ability to give a higher dose of drug to the patient. Because of these properties, the VMN is an attractive alternative delivery device for children (23).

However, VMN devices are more expensive to purchase, cannot be effectively used with very viscous drugs or drug suspensions, drug-carrier complexes (e.g. liposomes) may be disrupted, and pores in the mesh can be clogged, for example if a patient chooses to administer hyperosmolar saline through their VMN. The mesh is difficult to clear and can also be clogged with soap residue.

### Pressurized Metered Dose Inhalers (pMDIs)

The pMDI is the most commonly prescribed method of aerosol delivery. More formulations of aerosol drugs are currently available for use by pMDI than for use with other aerosol delivery systems. Properly used, pMDIs are at least as effective as nebulizers for drug delivery (24). For this reason, pMDIs are often the preferred method for delivering bronchodilators to both spontaneously breathing and intubated patients.

pMDI actuation into a VHC decreases impaction losses by reducing the velocity of the aerosol plume and allowing time for evaporation of the propellants before impacting on a surface. The dose of medication with the pMDI is much smaller than with the nebulizer.

Effective use of the pMDI is technique dependent (25). Common hand-breath coordination problems include actuating the pMDI before or after the breath. Some patients, especially infants, young children, the elderly, and patients in acute distress may not be able to use a pMDI. These problems reduce aerosol delivery to the lung but can be corrected by using a VHC (*vide infra*). Good patient instruction should include demonstration, practice, and confirmation of patient performance. Repeated instruction improves performance; but should occur several times.

### Spacers and Valved Holding Chambers

Spacers and VHCs are accessory devices, that when used properly can decrease oropharyngeal deposition of drug and improve hand-breath coordination. A spacer device is an open-ended straight tube or bag that provides space for the pMDI plume to expand and slow, and soluble particles become smaller before entering the airway. A VHC incorporates a one-way valve that permits the aerosol to be drawn from the chamber during inhalation, diverting the exhaled gas to the atmosphere, not disturbing any remaining aerosol suspended in the chamber. Patients with small tidal volumes can generally empty the aerosol from the chamber with 3–6 successive breaths. For use with infants, VHCs should have minimal dead space, and a valve that will open or close with the pressures and flow generated by the patient (26).

The use of a VHC should be encouraged at all ages and especially for young children. These accessory devices can reduce the need to coordinate the breath with actuation, reduce oral deposition, increase respirable particles, and improve lower respiratory tract deposition. These devices lead to a 10- to 15-fold reduction in the pharyngeal dose of aerosol from the pMDI (26, 27).

The belief that a nebulizer is better than a pMDI if the patient is not able to inhale with optimal technique using the inspiratory hold is not supported by research. In fact, if the patient cannot perform an optimal maneuver using a pMDI, they will be unable to perform an effective inhalation using a nebulizer. Although optimal technique is always preferred, it is often difficult to attain with an infant, small child, or severely dyspneic patient. In such cases, the alternative to optimal deposition may be to increase the pMDI or nebulizer dosage.

## Respimat[(R)] Soft Mist Inhaler (SMI)

The SMI was developed over 20 years ago but has been in commercial use for only the past decade, primarily to deliver tiotropium. The device is uniquely powered by spring compression, thus requiring no electricity to operate. The SMI produces an aerosol over 1.2 seconds at a velocity of about 10 M/s; much less that a pMDI and hence the name "soft mist." The slower aerosol velocity improves coordination, and the SMI is generally easier to use than the pMDI used without a VHC. Drug delivery to the lung of adults is highly efficient; in the range of 40%. However, actuation and inhalation still need to be coordinated and this can be a problem for young children (28). Coordination with a SMI could be improved with the use of a holding chamber in children (29). As well, the medication dose chamber in a SMI is relatively small at 11–14 µL, limiting the amount of medication that can be administered with each inhalation.

## Dry Powder Inhalers

DPIs are alternatives to pMDIs in older children and adults. Because of portability and rapid ease of use, many patients prefer a DPI. Dose adjustment may be needed when the same drug is administered by a DPI instead of by pMDI and many medications are not available as a DPI. The internal geometry of the DPI device influences the resistance offered to inspiration and the inspiratory flow required to produce an aerosol (30). Because DPIs are mostly dependent on inspiratory pressure drop to generate the aerosol (31), very young children (<6 years old) cannot use DPIs effectively. Breath coordination is also an issue with DPIs. Exhalation into a DPI blows out the powder from the device and reduces drug delivery. Moreover, the humidity in the exhaled air may influence subsequent aerosol generation from the DPI, especially when a very cold device interacts with a warm breath.

DPIs are breath-actuated, and they reduce the problem of coordinating inspiration with actuation that complicates the use of pMDIs. The technique of using DPIs differs in important respects from the technique employed to inhale drugs from a pMDI. Although DPIs are easier to use than pMDIs, up to 25% of patients may use DPIs improperly (32).

## NEW STRATEGIES AND DELIVERY DESIGNS

One novel delivery method involves using a hood, which reduces infant crying during therapy. Since this method does not involve placing a mask over the child's face, infants are often more compliant, with a similar clinical benefit and lung deposition. There is a renewed interest in the use of similar hoods as those originally described by us (17) during the Covid-19 pandemic, though the purpose of using the hoods was more to protect caregivers during aerosol therapy rather than to facilitate treatment of patients (33).

Another advance in the field is the development of the SootherMask, which is a face mask that attaches to the VHC (34). It is a soft and flexible mask that has a slot for the child's pacifier. The mask accepts most pacifiers and provides rapid and efficient delivery of pMDI aerosol treatment to children during normal breathing while they suck on the pacifier. It was developed based on anthropometric analysis of the infant's facial structure, and thus, is better aligned to the infant's face, achieves a seal with minimal force, and minimizes dead space.

## FINAL RECOMMENDATIONS FOR DEVICE SELECTION

The administered dose of aerosolized medication should be the same for all ages. Although more drug deposits in the airway of adults and older children because there is a greater airway surface, there is no age-associated dose adjustment needed independent of the delivery system. Whenever possible,

patients should employ only one type of aerosol-generating device for inhalation therapy. The technique of using each device is different, and repeated instruction is necessary to ensure that the patient uses the device appropriately. The use of several devices for inhalation can be confusing for patients and may decrease their adherence to therapy.

Sadly, many clinicians, including physicians, nurses, and pharmacists do not know the correct technique for using pMDIs or DPIs and thus cannot teach this to their patients. Often it is the respiratory therapist or certified asthma educator who is the best educator (35).

## REFERENCES

1. Rubin B. Bye-bye, blow by. Respir Care 2007;52(8):981.
2. Becquemin MH, Swift DL, Bouchikhi A, et al. Particle deposition and resistance in the noses of adults and children. Eur Respir J 1991;4:694–702.
3. Schwab JA, Zenkel M. Filtration of particulates in the human nose. Laryngoscope 1998;108:120–124.
4. Stocks J, Godfrey S. Specific airway conductance in relation to postconceptional age during infancy. J Appl Physiol Respir Environ Exerc Physiol 1977;43(1):144–154. DOI:10.1152/jappl.1977.43.1.144
5. Amirav I, Borojeni A, Halamish A, et al. Nasal versus oral aerosol delivery to the "lungs" in infants and toddlers. Pediatr Pulmonol 2015;50:276–283.
6. Chua HL, Collis GG, Newbury AM, et al. The influence of age on aerosol deposition in children with cystic fibrosis. Eur Respir J 1994;7:2185–2191.
7. Mallol J, Rattray S, Walker G, et al. Aerosol deposition in infants with cystic fibrosis. Pediatr Pulmonol 1996;21:276–281.
8. Tal A, Golan H, Grauer N, et al. Deposition pattern of radiolabeled salbutamol inhaled from a metered-dose inhaler by means of a spacer with mask in young children with airway obstruction. J Pediatr 1996;128:479–484.
9. Fok TF, Monkman S, Dolovich M, et al. Efficiency of aerosol medication delivery from a metered dose inhaler versus jet nebulizer in infants with bronchopulmonary dysplasia. Pediatr Pulmonol 1996;21:301–309.
10. Amirav I, Balanov I, Gorenberg M, et al. Beta agonist aerosol distribution in RSV bronchiolitis in infants. J Nucl Med 2002;43:487–491.
11. Amirav I, Luder A, Chleechel A, et al. Lung aerosol deposition in suckling infants. Arch Dis Child 2012;97(6):497–501.
12. Amirav I, Newhouse M, Luder A, et al. Feasibility of aerosol drug delivery to sleeping infants: A prospective observational study. BMJ Open 2014;4(3):e004124. DOI:10.1136/bmjopen-2013-004124
13. Amirav I, Newhouse MT. Aerosol therapy with valved holding chambers in young children: Importance of facemask seal. Pediatrics 2001;108:389–394.
14. Everard ML, Clark AR, Milner AD. Drug delivery from holding chambers with attached facemask. Arch Dis Child 1992;67(5):580–585.
15. Amirav I, Mansour Y, Mandelberg A, et al. Redesigned face mask improves "real life" aerosol delivery for nebuchamber. Pediatr Pulmonol 2004;37(2):172–177.
16. Esposito-Festen JE, Ates B, Van Vliet FJ, et al. Effect of a facemask leak on aerosol delivery from a pMDI-spacer system. J Aerosol Med 2004;17(1):1–6.
17. Amirav I, Balanov I, Gorenberg M, et al. Nebulizer hood compared to mask in wheezy infants: Aerosol therapy without tears. Arch Dis Child 2003;88:719–723.

18. Newhouse MT, Dolovich MB. Aerosol therapy: Nebulizer vs metered dose inhaler. Chest 1987;91:799–800.
19. Berlinski A, Willis JR, Leisenring T. In-vitro comparison of 4 large-volume nebulizers in 8 hours of continuous nebulization. Respir Care 2010;55(12):1671–1679.
20. Fink JB, Dhand R. Aerosol therapy. In: Fink JB, Hunt G, editors. Clinical practice in respiratory care. Philadelphia (PA): Lippincott Raven; 1998.
21. Nakanishi AK, Lamb BM, Foster C, et al. Ultrasonic nebulization of albuterol is no more effective than jet nebulization for the treatment of acute asthma in children. Chest 1997;111(6):1505–1508. DOI:10.1378/chest.111.6.1505
22. Boucher RGM, Kreuter J. Fundamentals of the ultrasonic atomization of medicated solutions. Ann Allergy 1968;26:59.
23. Moody GB, Luckett PM, Shockley CM, et al. Clinical efficacy of vibrating mesh and jet nebulizers with different interfaces in pediatric subjects with asthma. Respir Care 2020;65(10):1451–1463. DOI:10.4187/respcare.07538
24. Rubin BK, Fink JB. Optimizing aerosol delivery by pressurized metered dose inhalers. Respir Care 2005;50:1191–1197.
25. Fink JB, Rubin BK. Problems with inhaler use: A call for improved clinician and patient education. Respir Care 2005;50:1360–1375.
26. Nikander K, Nicholls C, Denyer J, et al. The evolution of spacers and valved holding chambers. J Aerosol Med Pulm Drug Deliv 2014;27(S1):S1–S4.
27. Rubin BK, Fink JB. Treatment delivery systems. Chapter 34 In: Castro M, Kraft M, editors. Clinical asthma. Philadelphia, PA: Elsevier-Mosby; 2008. p. 303–312.
28. Kamin W, Frank M, Kattenbeck S, et al. A handling study to assess use of the Respimat® Soft Mist™ inhaler in children under 5 years old. J Aerosol Med Pulm Drug Deliv 2015;28(5):372–381. DOI:10.1089/jamp.2014.1159
29. Wachtel H, Nagel M, Engel M, et al. In vitro and clinical characterization of the valved holding chamber AeroChamber Plus ® Flow-Vu® for administrating tiotropium Respimat® in 1-5-year-old children with persistent asthmatic symptoms. Respir Med 2018;137:181–190. DOI:10.1016/j.rmed.2018.03.010
30. Bisgaard H, Ifversen M, Klug B, et al. Inspiratory flow rate through the Diskus/Accuhaler inhaler and Turbuhaler inhaler in children with asthma. J Aerosol Med 1995;8:100.
31. Clark AR, Weers JG, Dhand R. The confusing world of dry powder inhalers: It is all about inspiratory pressures, not inspiratory flow rates. J Aerosol Med Pulm Drug Deliv 2020;33(1):1–11. DOI:10.1089/jamp.2019.1556
32. Kesten S, Elias M, Cartier A, et al. Patient handling of a multidose dry powder inhalation device for albuterol. Chest 1994;105:1077–1081.
33. Shaw KM, Lang AL, Lozano R, et al. Intensive care unit isolation hood decreases risk of aerosolization during noninvasive ventilation with COVID-19. Can J Anesth 2020;67, 1481–1483. DOI:10.1007/s12630-020-01721-5
34. Amirav I, Luder AS, Halamish A, et al. Design of aerosol face masks for children using computerized 3D face analysis. J Aerosol Med Pulm Drug Deliv 2014;27(4):272–278.
35. Hanania NA, Wittman R, Kesten S, et al. Medical personnel's knowledge of and ability to use inhaling devices: Metered-dose inhalers, spacing chambers, and breath-actuated dry powder inhalers. Chest 1994;105:111–116.

# 10 Selection of Inhaler Delivery System for Adult Outpatients

*David M. G. Halpin and P. N. Richard Dekhuijzen*

## CONTENTS

## INTRODUCTION

Consideration of the delivery system is essential when prescribing inhaled therapy for asthma or COPD to adult outpatients. Often a number of inhaler devices containing drugs of the appropriate class are available for prescription, and while there is evidence of the efficacy of the device and the drugs it contains in a population of patients, there is no evidence of which therapies are best suited to individual patients. In these circumstances, prescribers must still decide which therapy and inhaler delivery system to recommend. National and international guidelines do not make recommendations on how to select the optimal inhaler for a patient despite emphasizing the importance of a patient being able to use their device correctly (1–3). In part, this is because much of the time there isn't a single "best" choice and all devices can produce similar outcomes in patients when using the correct technique for inhalation (4).

Selecting the delivery system is likely to be influenced by clinicians' knowledge and personal beliefs about the actual and perceived benefits and disadvantages of particular drug and inhaler combinations. It will also be influenced by whether the patient is already taking inhaled therapy and whether they can use their current device correctly. The final choice should be made jointly by the prescriber and the patient taking into account all of these factors and is likely to differ from one patient to the next. Taking account of patients' goals and preferences in this way has been shown to improve outcomes for patients with asthma and is likely also to do so for patients with COPD (5, 6).

Worldwide, there are currently at least 33 different inhaled therapies containing different bronchodilators (both short- and long-acting) and inhaled corticosteroids (ICS), alone or in combinations. In addition, at least 22 different inhaler devices are available (1, 7). In many cases, a range of drugs is available in each device; in other cases, only one drug is available in a particular device. For simplification, devices can be grouped into four main types: pressurized metered-dose inhalers (pMDI), slow mist inhalers (SMI), dry powder inhalers (DPI), and nebulizers; however, not all devices within a group have similar properties and these differences must be taken into account as part of the decision making process.

DOI: 10.1201/9781003269014-10

The multiple permutations of medications and delivery systems, as well as clinicans' and patients' preferences and beliefs make it challenging to follow a precision medicine approach and choose an appropriate medication in a delivery system that matches individual patient factors. In practice, it appears many clinicians do not address this challenge, with for example 89% of physicians reporting that medication class was more important than device type in one recent survey (8). Such attitudes undoubtedly contribute to the poor adherence and persistence with inhaled therapy that has been prevalent since inhalers were introduced in the 1960s (9).

In this chapter, we review the evidence that should inform the selection. We review the features of the different inhalers that may affect selection and patient factors that affect their ability to use specific inhalers correctly, as well as evidence about clinicians' and patients' beliefs that may influence the choice of device. We also review algorithms that have been proposed to help with the selection of a device for an individual patient and present a synthesis of these together with our recommendations on how to select a delivery system when treating adult outpatients with asthma or COPD.

## INHALED DELIVERY SYSTEMS

The characteristics, advantages, and limitations of the four broad types of delivery systems have been summarized extensively (10–14) (and chapters in this book). Not all drugs are available in each of the four device types, but most classes of therapy are, and often specific drugs and combinations are available in more than one device.

Characteristics of the different devices that may affect their selection are summarized in Tables 10.1 and 10.2. Devices differ in their size and portability. They also differ in the number of steps required to prepare them (15), in the force needed to load or actuate them (16), in the time taken to deliver the drug, and in the need for cleaning and maintenance, as well as in the inspiratory maneuver required to use them effectively (10). The number of steps has an impact on the ease of use and the likelihood that patients use the inhaler correctly (17). There are also quite significant differences in the carbon footprint of devices, reflecting whether or not they contain a propellant gas, what they are made from, how they are manufactured, and whether they can be reused or recycled. This is also an important consideration now for patients and payers in some countries (18, 19).

Devices differ in the proportion of drug delivered to the oropharynx and the large and small airways and this may influence clinicians' and patients' selection and use of a delivery system. Higher oropharyngeal deposition of corticosteroids increases the risk of local side effects which adversely affect adherence and persistence with therapy (26). The extent to which devices deliver drug particles to the peripheral airways compared to central airways has been claimed to affect the efficacy of therapy (27) but this is controversial (28). There is evidence that extra-fine particles act at the level of large- to moderate-caliber airways to produce most of their beneficial effect (29), and centrally deposited particles also affect peripheral airway function (30), suggesting central deposition is no less effective than peripheral deposition. However, it is possible that extra-fine formulations of ICS have greater effects on small airways than non-extra-fine formulations as a result of higher peripheral deposition (31), although it is possible that the differences are simply due to an overall increase in pulmonary deposition rather than greater delivery to small airways (32).

The availability of smart inhalers which incorporate sensors that detect the date and time of use, inspiratory flow, and inspired volume may also affect

## Table 10.1: Summary of Device Features that May Affect Selection

| Device Attributes | pMDI | SMI | DPI | Nebulizer |
|---|---|---|---|---|
| Portable | Yes | Yes | Yes | Jet - limited Ultrasonic - some |
| Need for loading | No | Initial insertion of cartridge - not for each dose | Some | Placing solution in chamber |
| Need for preparation before each dose | No If breath-actuated - yes | Yes | Yes | Yes |
| Manual force required for actuation (16) | High | Low | Medium to low | Very low |
| Need for coordination of actuation & inhalation | Yes If breath-actuated - no If spacer used - no | Minimal | No | No |
| Inspiratory maneuver | Slow and steady | Slow and steady | Hard and fast | Tidal breathing |
| Inspiratory effort required | Low | Low | Medium to high | Low |
| Carbon footprint | High | 1/20th pMDI | 1/10th pMDI | N/A |
| Oropharyngeal deposition | Low/medium | Low | Medium | Low |
| Time taken to deliver drug | Quick | Quick | Quick | Jet - slow Ultrasonic - quick |
| Regular cleaning recommended | Yes | No | No | Yes |

*Source:* Data from (11–13, 15, 16, 21–25). Reprinted with Permission of the American Thoracic Society. Copyright © 2022 American Thoracic Society. All Rights Reserved. Halpin and Mahler (20). Annals of the American Thoracic Society Is an Official Journal of the American Thoracic Society).

*Abbreviations:* DPI = dry powder inhaler; PIFr = peak Inspiratory flow against simulated resistance; pMDI = pressurized metered-dose inhaler; SMI = slow mist inhaler.

device selection. These allow the identification of problems and feedback in real time (33) and can provide HCPs with objective data on adherence and technique (34, 35). They can be used as part of disease management programs to facilitate self-management (36) and may improve outcomes (37).

## PATIENT FACTORS

A number of patient factors are relevant to inhaler device selection (Table 10.2). Patient's cognitive ability, their manual dexterity and coordination skills, the inspiratory flow that they can achieve, and their attitudes and beliefs are important factors when selecting a device. Poor inhaler technique and errors using devices are more common with advancing age (38), but this is likely to be

## Table 10.2: **Summary of Factors Affecting Device Selection**

| Device Attributes | Patient Factors | Clinician Factors |
|---|---|---|
| Molecule/drug class | Ability to perform | Knowledge of availability |
| Type of delivery system (pMDI, | conscious inhalation | of devices |
| DPI, SMI, nebulizer) | Cognitive ability | Familiarity with devices |
| Size | Manual dexterity | Personal preferences |
| Need for loading | Coordination | Availability of samples |
| Need for priming | Ability to perform correct | Formulary availability |
| Inspiratory maneuver required | inspiratory maneuver | Ease of teaching |
| Inspiratory effort required | PIFr | Desire to maintain |
| Carbon footprint | Familiarity with device | continuity of device |
| Ease of use | Attitudes and beliefs | |
| Pulmonary deposition | | |
| Time taken to deliver drug | | |
| Need for cleaning | | |
| Smart features | | |
| Cost | | |

*Abbreviations:* DPI = dry powder inhaler; PIFr = peak Inspiratory flow against simulated resistance; pMDI = pressurized metered-dose inhaler; SMI = slow mist inhaler.

mainly due to confounders such as cognitive impairment or reduced manual dexterity. When these factors have been independently assessed, older age alone has not been found to affect pMDI or DPI use (39, 40).

Cognitive impairment is not a common problem in patients with asthma but is found in 32–57% of COPD patients (41, 42). Adequate cognition is required to understand the instructions and perform the steps for preparing and using a handheld device or a nebulizer. Many patients with COPD and some with asthma have comorbidities that affect manual dexterity or grip strength, such as arthritis, neuromuscular or cerebral vascular disease. pMDIs require sufficient strength to actuate the inhaler, and although breath-actuated devices are triggered by inhalation they still require priming, which requires a degree of strength (16). Patients with poor dexterity may struggle to load a DPI, particularly if capsules require extraction from foil, insertion into the device, or puncturing prior to administration (16). Tremor may result in shaking of the device and loss of the dose (43). Loading of nebulizers and priming of SMIs can be performed in advance by a relative or carer if the patient is unable to perform these steps.

Adequate coordination is necessary to ensure the correct timing and sequence of exhaling completely, actuating the inhaler if necessary, inhaling in the correct manner, and then breath holding. With pMDIs, if the aerosol bolus is released too late in the respiratory maneuver, or if inspiration ceases on release of the aerosol, the lung deposition will be poor (44). Many patients lack coordination for the split-second timing required between beginning a slow inhalation and activation of a pMDI (45). SMIs are more tolerant of delay in inhalation as the plume duration is long (46), but premature inhalation will reduce drug delivery. Coordination is not needed for DPIs and nebulizers.

Inspiratory flow, flow acceleration, and inhaled volume are important factors for patients to successfully inhale drug particles from handheld devices into the lower respiratory tract (10). The recommended inspiratory flow is 30–60 L/min for a pMDI and 15–30 L/min for an SMI (47). Each DPI has a unique internal resistance and patients must create turbulent energy within the device during inhalation to disaggregate the powder into fine particles. Peak inspiratory flow (PIF), defined as the maximal airflow during a forced inspiratory maneuver,

against the simulated resistance (r) of a specific DPI is a biomarker that can be used to assess whether a patient can achieve optimal drug deposition with that device (47). The minimal and optimal PIFr values required for effective use of DPIs differ between devices depending on their internal resistance. In general, for low to medium high-resistance DPIs, a minimal PIFr of 30 L/min and an optimal PIFr ≥ 60 L/min have been proposed (10, 48, 49). For a high-resistance DPI, a minimal PIFr of 20 L/min and an optimal PIFr ≥ 30 L/min have been proposed (49). Most patients with asthma can generate a sufficient PIFr to use all types of DPI (50), whereas in stable outpatient, with COPD, the prevalence of suboptimal PIFr (< 60 L/min) across low to medium high-resistance DPIs varied from 19% to 84% (51). Advanced age, female sex, and reduced inspiratory capacity (IC) but not FEV1 are the most consistent patient characteristics associated with a lower PIFr (51). In patients with COPD, age reduces PIFr independently of the severity of the disease (51, 52).

As well as physiological and physical factors, patients' beliefs and preferences must be taken into account when selecting an inhaled therapy (53). A key issue is familiarity with a device, and selecting a therapy in a device which the patient is already using may be the best strategy, provided they are using it correctly. Patients who are prescribed their preferred inhalation device have higher treatment satisfaction, fewer device use errors, better adherence, and lower health resource utilization and costs (54–57). A meta-analysis of patients' preferences regarding inhaler characteristics found that the common preferences were for small inhaler devices that were portable, durable, perceived as easy to use, and fast in medication administration (58). However, inhaler selection should take account of the individual patient's own preferences. Satisfaction with an inhaler device also affects compliance and persistence with inhaled therapy (59, 60).

## CLINICIAN FACTORS

Clinicians' knowledge of the existence of different delivery systems, their familiarity with them, and their confidence about instructing patients on how to use them affect device selection (Table 10.2), but often their choice is based on habit (61). In some cases, selection is limited by availability of specific devices due to contractual or formulary limitations. New devices may take some time to appear on formularies and many formularies deliberately limit the number of different devices that are listed. Formularies may also deliberately restrict devices to specific classes such as pMDIs on the basis of cost and clinicians may be forced to prescribe a sub-optimal device for a specific patient. In some countries, particularly the USA, physicians are commonly provided with free samples of inhalers to give to their patients (62). Although allowing immediate initiation of therapy and demonstration of correct use of the device, the availability of samples will influence the choice of device. Continuing to prescribe a device which the patient is familiar with, and can use correctly, is important. In a Delphi analysis, most clinicians agreed that devices were not readily interchangeable, even if active substances and dosages were kept the same (63).

HCPs views on the desirable characteristics of devices and their ranking of importance differ significantly from those of patients (64), and nurses placed little importance on whether inhalers needed fine motor skills or hand strength (65). Ignoring these factors can clearly lead to inappropriate device selection.

Patients commonly make errors using devices (9, 66–68) and ease of teaching and assessment of correct inhaler technique are important attributes for clinicians when selecting an inhaler device (63). Many clinicians have limited

knowledge about how to use inhalers, even those that have been in use for many years, with nearly 85% of HCPs unable to demonstrate the correct technique (69). Poor understanding of the correct use of devices also impacts the HCPs' ability to identify whether patients can use them properly, compromising appropriate device selection. Patient inhaler user technique is usually assessed by observing the patient using the device, sometimes using a checklist (70); however, this depends on the clinician knowing how the device should be used and recognizing critical errors. Observation of inhaler technique in a clinical setting may show that a patient knows how to use an inhaler, but gives no information about whether they do so on a regular basis (71).

## SELECTING DEVICES FOR MAINTENANCE THERAPY COMPARED TO RELIEVER THERAPY

A different approach to selecting an inhaler device may needed when prescribing a once- or twice-daily maintenance therapy as compared to a reliever therapy which may be needed at any time of day as well as away from a patient's home. The size and portability of the delivery system are particularly important considerations when prescribing reliever medication.

## INHALER-NAÏVE PATIENTS VERSUS THOSE ALREADY ON INHALED THERAPY

A different approach to selecting an inhaler device is needed when prescribing a device to a patient for the first time compared to prescribing a device to a patient who is already taking inhaled therapy. When selecting a device for the first time, the device should be selected on the basis of the characteristics discussed above using the approach outlined below. When adding or changing therapy in patients already using a device, if they have a good technique and are happy with the device, continuity of device should be the main determinant of the delivery system for the new therapy. COPD patients prescribed one or more additional inhaler devices requiring inhalation techniques similar to their previous device(s) showed better outcomes than those who were prescribed devices requiring different techniques (72), and switching of devices without a clinical justification has been associated with poorer outcomes (73). At follow-up review, a new delivery system may be needed if a new drug is required either as an alternative or as an addition and it is only available in a different device, or if the patient is unable or unwilling to use their current delivery system. When selecting a new delivery system in this setting, the characteristics discussed above using the approach outlined below should again be used to guide selection.

## SELECTING A DELIVERY SYSTEM

A number of proposals on factors that should be considered when selecting an inhaler device have been published. However, until recently, there has been no attempt to analyze or reconcile these different perspectives. A systematic review of published algorithms for inhaler selection in outpatients with COPD identified nine different algorithms or hierarchical recommendations to guide clinicians with device selection in stable patients with COPD (4, 12, 13, 15, 18, 19, 51, 74, 75). The inclusion of the device, patient, and clinician factors discussed above and the order in which they were considered varied considerably between the different algorithms (Table 10.3) (20). The algorithm proposed by Janknegt et al. (15) is unique in that after three decision steps based on the patient's inhalation maneuver and inhalation strength, the device is then chosen according to a ranking of attributes including continuity of device, numbers

## Table 10.3: Attributes and Factors Included in Published Algorithms for Inhaler Selection in Patients with COPD

| | Patient Factors | | | | | | | | | Device Attributes | | | | | | | | | | HCP Factors | | | | | |
|---|---|---|---|---|---|---|---|---|---|---|---|---|---|---|---|---|---|---|---|---|---|---|---|---|---|
| | Age | Ability to perform conscious inhalation | Cognitive ability | Manual dexterity | Coordination | Ability to perform correct inspiratory manoeuvre | Inspiratory flow/PIFr | Familiarity with device | Personal preferences | Molecule/drug class | Type (pMDI, DPI, SMI, neb) | Size, robustness, and need for loading | Inspiratory effort required | Carbon footprint | Ease of use | Pulmonary deposition | Time taken to deliver drug | Smart features | Cost | Habit/preference | Knowledge | Availability of samples | Formulary | Ease of teaching | Continuity of device |
| Dekhuijzen (74, 77) | 1 | | 3 | | | | 2 | | | | | | | | | | | | | | | | | | |
| Dolovich (4) | 2= | | | | 2= | | | | 8= | | 4* | | | | 4* | | | | | | | | 3 | 5 | 4* |
| Janknegt (15) | 1 | | 1 | 2 | 3 | | | | | | | | | 6= | 6= | | | | | 8= | | | | | |
| Mahler (51) | 1 | | 2 | 2 | | | | | | 1 | 7 | | | | 6= | | 6= | | 4 | 8= | | | 3 | 4* | 5 |
| Suarez-Barcelo † (13) | | | | | | | | | | | | | | | | | | | | | | | | | |
| Usmani ‡ (12) | | | 2= | 2= | | | | | | | | | | | | | | | | | | | | | |
| Usmani ‡ (19) | | | 1= | 1= | 1 | 3 | 3 | | | 2= | 3= | 3= | | | 3= | | 3= | | 2= | | | | 4 | 2= | |
| Virchow (18) | | 1# | | | 2 | | 3 | | 3 | 3 | | | | 2 | | | 2 | | | | | | | 4 | 1 |
| Voshaar/ Chapman (75, 76) | | | | | | | | | | | | | | | | | | | | | | | | | |

*Source:* Reprinted with Permission of the American Thoracic Society. Copyright © 2022 American Thoracic Society. All Rights Reserved. Halpin and Mahler (20) Annals of the American Thoracic Society Is an Official Journal of the American Thoracic Society.

*Note:* *Continuity of Device, Numbers of Steps Per Inhalation, Risk of (critical) Errors, Hygiene Aspects, a Feedback Mechanism, and Risk of Inhalation with an Empty Inhaler Were Incorporated in a System of Objectified Judgement Matrix. Numbers refer to rank order in which factors are considered by the respective authors.

† These Recommendations Are Specifically for Long-Term Care Settings. ‡ These Recommendations Are Specific for Elderly Patients.
# Ability to Perform Conscious Inhalation Is Included as the First Factor to Consider in the Original Algorithm Published by Voshaar et al. (75) but It Is Not Included in the English Version Published by Chapman et al. (76).
"=" = attributes given equal ranking in algorithm; DPI = dry powder inhaler; HCP = heath care professional; PIFr = peak inspiratory flow against simulated resistance; pMDI = pressurized metered-dose inhaler; SMI = soft mist inhaler.

## Table 10.4: **Questions to Guide Selection of Inhaler Delivery System**

Patient Factors

- Can the patient perform a specific inspiratory effort? (incorporates cognitive and respiratory muscle functions)
- Can the patient handle/use the device? (considers manual dexterity and hand strength)
- If a DPI is considered: Can the patient generate an optimal peak inspiratory flow? (measured against the simulated resistance of the specific DPI)

Device Attribute

- Is the molecule(s)/drug class available in the device?

HCP Factor

- Is the patient currently on inhaled therapy and able to use their current device correctly, and if so, can new therapy be prescribed in the same device?

*Source:* Originally published in: Halpin and Mahler with Permission.
*Abbreviation:* DPI = dry powder inhaler.

of steps per inhalation, risk of errors, hygiene aspects, a feedback mechanism, and risk of inhalation with an empty inhaler. These factors were incorporated in an objectified judgement matrix which ranks inhalers, but the decision is not patient specific.

Given the numerous medication-device options available for the treatment of asthma and COPD, there is a clear need for practical information to assist HCPs in selecting an inhaler delivery system. A systematic approach to inhaler selection seems better than the current "gestalt" by clinicians, but no rigorous assessment of any of the published algorithms has been performed. The systematic review of algorithms for inhaler selection in COPD found that patient factors were considered most frequently in the algorithms (19 times) compared with device attributes (10 times) and HCP factors (7 times). On the basis of the frequency of their appearance in the algorithms, five specific attributes/factors were identified as key factors for device selection: ability to perform the required inspiratory maneuver and handle the device correctly, sufficient inspiratory flow for dry powder inhalers, availability of molecule(s) in the device, and continuity of device (Table 10.4) (20).

When recommending an inhaled therapy, the first question to consider is whether or not the patient is already using an inhaler device, and if so, whether they are using it correctly (Figure 10.1). If the answer to both of these questions is yes, then continuity of device should be the overriding principle guiding the choice of the new therapy. If a patient is not currently taking an inhaled therapy, if there are problems with their ability to use their current device, or if a change of drug requires the use of a different device because the new treatment is not available in the same device, then a stepwise approach to selecting the optimum device is required.

Selecting a device that contains the required drug or class of drug seems the next most logical step and availability of the device in a formulary must be the next consideration. HCPs must then make a provisional choice of device taking into account their own beliefs and habits as well as those of the patient. This should include patient's preferences on size and portability, need for loading, strength required, time taken to deliver the drug, efficiency of drug deposition, ability of the HCP to teach its correct use, cost, and carbon footprint.

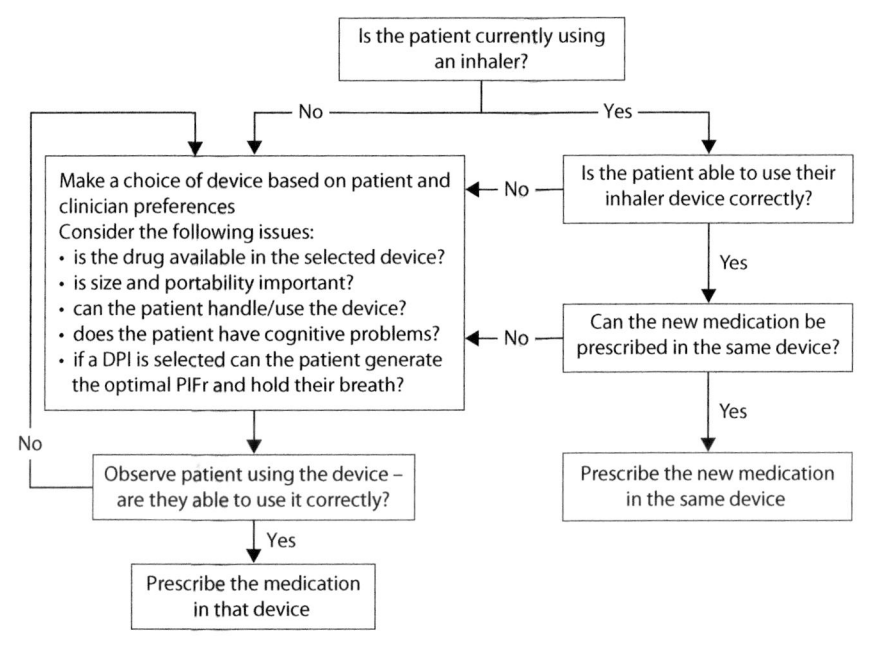

**Figure 10.1** Recommended approach to selecting an inhaler delivery system. DPI = dry powder inhaler; PIFr = peak inspiratory flow against simulated resistance.

If the provisional choice is a pMDI, many clinicians recommend that a valved holding chamber (spacer) should always be used to minimize the difficulties patients have with coordination and performing the optimal inspiratory maneuver for a pMDI, as well as increasing pulmonary and reducing oropharyngeal deposition. This is particularly important for corticosteroid-containing pMDIs (10) but is also relevant to optimize the delivery of bronchodilators. Currently available spacers range in volume from <50–750 mL (78) but spacers with volumes from 150 to 250 mL have been shown to be as effective as those with larger volumes (79) and are more portable. Retrospective analysis of primary care records in the UK found significantly more patients prescribed ICS via a pMDI and a spacer were controlled compared with those on pMDIs alone (80); however, a similar but larger analysis with matching of patient characteristics found no evidence that prescribing spacer devices was associated with improved asthma outcomes or reduced oropharyngeal candidiasis (81). If there is any doubt that the patient will not be able to use a pMDI correctly, they should be prescribed a spacer; however, there is evidence that incorrect use of pMDIs is more common in older patients if they use a spacer (82). It has been suggested that each pairing of a pMDI device plus spacer should be considered as a unique delivery system and that once a spacer has been chosen, like the device itself, it should not be changed without good reason (83).

The selection of a provisional device should also take account of the patient's cognitive ability and manual dexterity. For those with impaired cognition, Dekhuijzen et al. (53, 74, 77) recommend two options for an inhaler delivery system: a pMD onI + spacer or nebulizer therapy. Similarly, Suarez-Barcelo et al. (13) suggest pMDI + spacer, SMI, and nebulizer as options for those with "moderate/severe cognitive impairment." For individuals with poor manual

dexterity, Mahler (51) proposed nebulizer therapy as the preferred delivery system, while Suarez-Barcelo et al. (13) suggested a nebulizer be "a device to consider" along with pMDI + spacer or SMI for those with "insufficient dexterity." Selecting the provisional device could be assisted by using a decision aid (84, 85).

Once a provisional device has been selected, the patient's ability to use the device correctly should be assessed. This includes checking that they load and prime the device correctly, adequately coordinate inhalation with actuation, and perform the correct inspiratory maneuver. If the provisional device is a DPI, clinicians should objectively assess the patient's ability to generate sufficient inspiratory flow by measuring their PIFr. If the patient has a suboptimal PIF as defined by < 60 L/minute, or < 30 L/minute for a high-resistance DPI, Voshaar, Dekhuijzen, Suarez-Barcelo, Mahler and Janknegt, (13, 15, 51, 74, 75, 77) all propose that a pMDI, SMI, or a nebulizer be prescribed instead. As well as assessing the PIFr, clinicians should check that the patient is able to hold their breath for at least 5 seconds after performing the inhalation, as some patients may be able to generate the desired PIFr, but they then find it hard to hold their breath as a result of the excessive use of all the respiratory muscles and the discomfort of breathing.

If the patient can use the provisional device satisfactorily then this should be the device that is prescribed, but if they cannot, an alternative provisional device should be selected and the patient's ability to use this device is correctly assessed. This iterative approach should continue until a device that can be used correctly is identified.

## CONCLUSION

A systematic approach which takes account of device characteristics and patient and clinician factors should be used to select the optimum delivery system for each patient.

## REFERENCES

1. Global Initiative for Chronic Obstructive Lung Disease (GOLD). Global strategy for the diagnosis, management, and prevention of chronic obstructive pulmonary disease. 2021 Report. [cited 2021 Jan 11]. Available from: http://www.goldcopd.org/
2. Nici L, Mammen MJ, Charbek E, et al. Pharmacologic management of chronic obstructive pulmonary disease. An Official American Thoracic Society Clinical Practice Guideline. Am J Respir Crit Care Med 2020;201(9):e56–e69.
3. Global Initiative for Asthma. Global strategy for asthma management and prevention. (updated 2019). 2019. Available from: http://www.ginasthma.org
4. Dolovich MB, Ahrens RC, Hess DR, et al. Device selection and outcomes of aerosol therapy: Evidence-based guidelines: American College of Chest Physicians/American College of Asthma, Allergy, and Immunology. Chest 2005;127(1):335–371.
5. Wilson SR, Strub P, Buist AS, et al. Shared treatment decision making improves adherence and outcomes in poorly controlled asthma. Am J Respir Crit Care Med 2010;181(6):566–577.
6. Inhaler Error Steering Committee, Price D, Bosnic-Anticevich S, et al. Inhaler competence in asthma: Common errors, barriers to use and recommended solutions. Respir Med 2013;107(1):37–46.

7. Capstick T, Atack K. The leeds inhaler device guide. 2018. [cited 2021 April]. Available from: http://www.cpwy.org/doc/2003.pdf

8. Hanania NA, Braman S, Adams SG, et al. The role of inhalation delivery devices in COPD: Perspectives of patients and health care providers. Chronic Obstr Pulm Dis 2018;5(2):111–123.

9. Sanchis J, Gich I, Pedersen S. Systematic review of errors in inhaler use: Has patient technique improved over time? Chest 2016;150(2):394–406.

10. Laube BL, Janssens HM, de Jongh FH, et al. What the pulmonary specialist should know about the new inhalation therapies. Eur Respir J 2011;37(6):1308–1331.

11. Sanchis J, Corrigan C, Levy ML, et al. Inhaler devices - from theory to practice. Respir Med 2013;107(4):495–502.

12. Usmani OS. Choosing the right inhaler for your asthma or COPD patient. Ther Clin Risk Manag 2019;15:461–472.

13. Suarez-Barcelo M, Micca JL, Clackum S, et al. Chronic obstructive pulmonary disease in the long-term care setting: Current practices, challenges, and unmet needs. Curr Opin Pulm Med 2017;23(Suppl 1):S1–S28.

14. Capstick TG, Clifton IJ. Inhaler technique and training in people with chronic obstructive pulmonary disease and asthma. Expert Rev Respir Med 2012;6(1):91–101; quiz 2–3.

15. Janknegt R, Kooistra J, Metting E, et al. Rational selection of inhalation devices in the treatment of chronic obstructive pulmonary disease by means of the System of Objectified Judgement Analysis (SOJA). Eur J Hosp Pharm 2021;28(2):e4.

16. Ciciliani A-M, Langguth P, Wachtel H. Handling forces for the use of different inhaler devices. Int J Pharm 2019;560:315–321.

17. Klijn SL, Hiligsmann M, Evers S, et al. Effectiveness and success factors of educational inhaler technique interventions in asthma & COPD patients: A systematic review. NPJ Prim Care Respir Med 2017;27(1):24.

18. Virchow JC, Crompton GK, Dal Negro R, et al. Importance of inhaler devices in the management of airway disease. Respir Med 2008;102(1):10–19.

19. Usmani O, Capstick T, Saleem A, et al. Inhaler choice guideline. 2020. Available from: https://www.guidelines.co.uk/respiratory/inhaler-choice-guideline/455503.article

20. Halpin DMG, Mahler DA. A systematic review of published algorithms for selecting an inhaled delivery system in COPD. Ann Am Thorac Soc 2022;19(7):1213–1220.

21. Dhand R, Dolovich M, Chipps B, et al. The role of nebulized therapy in the management of COPD: Evidence and recommendations. COPD 2012;9(1):58–72.

22. Panigone S, Sandri F, Ferri R, et al. Environmental impact of inhalers for respiratory diseases: Decreasing the carbon footprint while preserving patient-tailored treatment. BMJ Open Respir Res 2020;7(1):e000571.

23. Hänsel M, Bambach T, Wachtel H. Reduced environmental impact of the reusable Respimat® Soft Mist™ inhaler compared with pressurised metered-dose inhalers. Adv Ther 2019;36(9):2487–2492.

24. Fink JB, Colice GL, Hodder R. Inhaler devices for patients with COPD. COPD 2013;10(4):523–535.

25. Dolovich MB, Dhand R. Aerosol drug delivery: Developments in device design and clinical use. Lancet 2011;377(9770):1032–1045.

26. Molimard M, Le Gros V, Robinson P, et al. Prevalence and associated factors of oropharyngeal side effects in users of inhaled corticosteroids in a real-life setting. J Aerosol Med Pulm Drug Deliv 2010;23(2):91–95.

27. Postma DS, Roche N, Colice G, et al. Comparing the effectiveness of small-particle versus large-particle inhaled corticosteroid in COPD. Int J Chron Obstruct Pulmon Dis 2014;9:1163–1186.

28. Lavorini F, Pedersen S, Usmani OS. Dilemmas, confusion, and misconceptions related to small airways directed therapy. Chest 2017;151(6):1345–1355.

29. Boulet LP. Comparative improvement of asthma symptoms and expiratory flows after corticosteroid treatment: A method to assess the effect of corticosteroids on large vs. small airways? Respir Med 2006;100(3):496–502.

30. Timmins SC, Diba C, Schoeffel RE, et al. Changes in oscillatory impedance and nitrogen washout with combination fluticasone/salmeterol therapy in COPD. Respir Med 2014;108(2):344–350.

31. Goldin JG, Tashkin DP, Kleerup EC, et al. Comparative effects of hydrofluoroalkane and chlorofluorocarbon beclomethasone dipropionate inhalation on small airways: Assessment with functional helical thin-section computed tomography. J Allergy Clin Immunol 1999;104(6):S258–S267.

32. Busse WW, Brazinsky S, Jacobson K, et al. Efficacy response of inhaled beclomethasone dipropionate in asthma is proportional to dose and is improved by formulation with a new propellant. J Allergy Clin Immunol 1999;104(6):1215–1222.

33. Carpenter DM, Roberts CA, Sage AJ, et al. A review of electronic devices to assess inhaler technique. Curr Allergy Asthma Rep 2017;17(3):17.

34. Chan AH, Harrison J, Black PN, et al. Using electronic monitoring devices to measure inhaler adherence: A practical guide for clinicians. J Allergy Clin Immunol Pract 2015;3(3):335–349 e1-5.

35. Bowler R, Allinder M, Jacobson S, et al. Real-world use of rescue inhaler sensors, electronic symptom questionnaires and physical activity monitors in COPD. BMJ Open Respir Res 2019;6(1):e000350.

36. Halpin D, Banks L, Martello A. Working together to go 'beyond the pill': Building a virtuous network of collaborators. BMJ Innov 2016;2(1):1.

37. Price D, Jones R, Pfister P, et al. Maximizing adherence and gaining new information for your chronic obstructive pulmonary disease (MAGNIFY COPD): Study protocol for the pragmatic, cluster randomized trial evaluating the impact of dual bronchodilator with add-on sensor and electronic monitoring on clinical outcomes. Pragmat Obs Res 2021;12:25–35.

38. Barbara S, Kritikos V, Bosnic-Anticevich S. Inhaler technique: Does age matter? A systematic review. Eur Respir Rev 2017;26(146):170055.

39. Gray SL, Williams DM, Pulliam CC, et al. Characteristics predicting incorrect metered-dose inhaler technique in older subjects. Arch Intern Med 1996;156(9):984–988.

40. Maricoto T, Santos D, Carvalho C, et al. Assessment of poor inhaler technique in older patients with asthma or COPD: A predictive tool for clinical risk and inhaler performance. Drugs Aging 2020;37(8):605–616.

41. Yohannes AM, Chen W, Moga AM, et al. Cognitive impairment in chronic obstructive pulmonary disease and chronic heart failure: A systematic review and meta-analysis of observational studies. J Am Med Dir Assoc 2017;18(5):451 e1–e11.

42. Cleutjens FA, Franssen FM, Spruit MA, et al. Domain-specific cognitive impairment in patients with COPD and control subjects. Int J Chron Obstruct Pulmon Dis 2017;12:1–11.

43. Barrons R, Pegram A, Borries A. Inhaler device selection: Special considerations in elderly patients with chronic obstructive pulmonary disease. Am J Health Syst Pharm 2011;68(13):1221–1232.

44. Newman SP, Pavia D, Clarke SW. How should a pressurized beta-adrenergic bronchodilator be inhaled? Eur J Respir Dis 1981;62(1):3–21.

45. McFadden ER, Jr. Improper patient techniques with metered dose inhalers: Clinical consequences and solutions to misuse. J Allergy Clin Immunol 1995;96(2):278–283.

46. Keating GM. Tiotropium Respimat((R)) Soft Mist inhaler: A review of its use in chronic obstructive pulmonary disease. Drugs 2014;74(15):1801–1816.

47. Mahler DA, Halpin DMG. Peak inspiratory flow as a predictive therapeutic biomarker in COPD. Chest 2021;160(2):491–498.

48. Ghosh S, Ohar JA, Drummond MB. Peak inspiratory flow rate in chronic obstructive pulmonary disease: Implications for dry powder inhalers. J Aerosol Med Pulm Drug Deliv 2017;30:381–387.

49. Haidl P, Heindl S, Siemon K, et al. Inhalation device requirements for patients' inhalation maneuvers. Respir Med 2016;118:65–75.

50. Haughney J, Lee AJ, McKnight E, et al. Peak inspiratory flow measured at different inhaler resistances in patients with asthma. J Allergy Clin Immunol Pract 2021;9(2):890–896.

51. Mahler DA. The role of inspiratory flow in selection and use of inhaled therapy for patients with chronic obstructive pulmonary disease. Respir Med 2020;161:105857.

52. Jarvis S, Ind PW, Shiner RJ. Inhaled therapy in elderly COPD patients: Time for re-evaluation? Age Ageing 2007;36(2):213–218.

53. Dekhuijzen PN, Lavorini F, Usmani OS. Patients' perspectives and preferences in the choice of inhalers: The case for Respimat(®) or HandiHaler(®). Patient Prefer Adherence 2016;10:1561–1572.

54. Chorao P, Pereira AM, Fonseca JA. Inhaler devices in asthma and COPD–an assessment of inhaler technique and patient preferences. Respir Med 2014;108(7):968–975.

55. Oliveira MVC, Pizzichini E, da Costa CH, et al. Evaluation of the preference, satisfaction and correct use of Breezhaler((R)) and Respimat((R)) inhalers in patients with chronic obstructive pulmonary disease - INHALATOR study. Respir Med 2018;144:61–67.

56. Dahl R, Kaplan A. A systematic review of comparative studies of tiotropium Respimat(R) and tiotropium HandiHaler(R) in patients with chronic obstructive pulmonary disease: Does inhaler choice matter? BMC Pulm Med 2016;16(1):135.

57. Chrystyn H, Small M, Milligan G, et al. Impact of patients' satisfaction with their inhalers on treatment compliance and health status in COPD. Respir Med 2014;108(2):358–365.

58. Navaie M, Dembek C, Cho-Reyes S, et al. Inhaler device feature preferences among patients with obstructive lung diseases: A systematic review and meta-analysis. Medicine 2020;99(25):e20718.

59. Schurmann W, Schmidtmann S, Moroni P, et al. Respimat Soft Mist inhaler versus hydrofluoroalkane metered dose inhaler: Patient preference and satisfaction. Treat Respir Med 2005;4(1):53–61.

60. Barbosa CD, Balp MM, Kulich K, et al. A literature review to explore the link between treatment satisfaction and adherence, compliance, and persistence. Patient Prefer Adherence 2012;6:39–48.
61. Halpin DMG. Understanding irrationality: The key to changing behaviours and improving management of respiratory diseases? Lancet Respir Med 2018;6(10):737–739.
62. Brown JD, Doshi PA, Talbert JC. Utilization of free medication samples in the United States in a nationally representative sample: 2009–2013. Res Social Adm Pharm 2017;13(1):193–200.
63. Ninane V, Brusselle GG, Louis R, et al. Usage of inhalation devices in asthma and chronic obstructive pulmonary disease: A Delphi consensus statement. Expert Opin Drug Deliv 2014;11(3):313–323.
64. Roche N, Scheuch G, Pritchard JN, et al. Patient focus and regulatory considerations for inhalation device design: Report from the 2015 IPAC-RS/ISAM workshop. J Aerosol Med Pulm Drug Deliv 2017;30(1):1–13.
65. Bogelund M, Hagelund L, Asmussen MB. COPD-treating nurses' preferences for inhaler attributes - a discrete choice experiment. Curr Med Res Opin 2017;33(1):71–75.
66. Melani AS, Bonavia M, Cilenti V, et al. Inhaler mishandling remains common in real life and is associated with reduced disease control. Respir Med 2011;105(6):930–938.
67. Molimard M, Raherison C, Lignot S, et al. Chronic obstructive pulmonary disease exacerbation and inhaler device handling: Real-life assessment of 2935 patients. Eur Respir J 2017;49(2):1601794.
68. Alhaddad B, Smith FJ, Robertson T, et al. Patients' practices and experiences of using nebuliser therapy in the management of COPD at home. BMJ Open Respir Res 2015;2(1):e000076.
69. Plaza V, Giner J, Rodrigo GJ, et al. Errors in the use of inhalers by health care professionals: A systematic review. J Allergy Clin Immunol Pract 2018;6(3):987–995.
70. Batterink J, Dahri K, Aulakh A, et al. Evaluation of the use of inhaled medications by hospital inpatients with chronic obstructive pulmonary disease. Can J Hosp Pharm 2012;65(2):111–118.
71. Pritchard JN, Nicholls C. Emerging technologies for electronic monitoring of adherence, inhaler competence, and true adherence. J Aerosol Med Pulm Drug Deliv 2015;28(2):69–81.
72. Bosnic-Anticevich S, Chrystyn H, Costello RW, et al. The use of multiple respiratory inhalers requiring different inhalation techniques has an adverse effect on COPD outcomes. Int J Chron Obstruct Pulmon Dis 2017;12:59–71.
73. Thomas M, Price D, Chrystyn H, et al. Inhaled corticosteroids for asthma: Impact of practice level device switching on asthma control. BMC Pulm Med 2009;9:1.
74. Dekhuijzen PN. [Inhaler therapy for adults with obstructive lung diseases: Powder or aerosol?]. Ned Tijdschr Geneeskd 1998;142(24):1369–1374. Dutch
75. Voshaar T, App EM, Berdel D, et al. [Recommendations for the choice of inhalatory systems for drug prescription]. Pneumologie 2001;55(12):579–586. German.
76. Chapman KR, Voshaar TH, Virchow JC. Inhaler choice in primary practice. Eur Respir Rev 2005;14:117–122.

77. Dekhuijzen PN, Vincken W, Virchow JC, et al. Prescription of inhalers in asthma and COPD: Towards a rational, rapid and effective approach. Respir Med 2013;107(12):1817–1821.
78. Newman SP. Spacer devices for metered dose inhalers. Clin Pharmacokinet 2004;43(6):349–360.
79. Mitchell JP, Nagel MW. Valved holding chambers (VHCs) for use with pressurised metered-dose inhalers (pMDIs): A review of causes of inconsistent medication delivery. Prim Care Respir J 2007;16(4):207–214.
80. Levy ML, Hardwell A, McKnight E, et al. Asthma patients' inability to use a pressurised metered-dose inhaler (pMDI) correctly correlates with poor asthma control as defined by the global initiative for asthma (GINA) strategy: A retrospective analysis. Prim Care Respir J 2013;22(4):406–411.
81. Guilbert TW, Colice G, Grigg J, et al. Real-life outcomes for patients with asthma prescribed spacers for use with either extrafine- or fine-particle inhaled corticosteroids. J Allergy Clin Immunol Pract 2017;5(4):1040–1049, e4.
82. Ho SF, OMahony MS, Steward JA, et al. Inhaler technique in older people in the community. Age Ageing 2004;33(2):185–188.
83. McIvor RA, Devlin HM, Kaplan A. Optimizing the delivery of inhaled medication for respiratory patients: The role of valved holding chambers. Can Respir J 2018;2018:5076259.
84. Gagné ME, Légaré F, Moisan J, et al. Development of a patient decision aid on inhaled corticosteroids use for adults with asthma. J Asthma 2016;53(9):964–974.
85. Stacey D, Légaré F, Lewis K, et al. Decision aids for people facing health treatment or screening decisions. Cochrane Database Syst Rev 2017;4(4):CD001431.

# 11 Inhalation Therapy in the Intensive Care Unit

*Jie Li and Rajiv Dhand*

## CONTENTS

## INTRODUCTION

More than five million patients are admitted annually to U.S. Intensive Care Units (ICUs) (1). Many patients admitted to ICUs require intensive or invasive monitoring, support of airway, breathing, or circulation, and stabilization of acute or life-threatening medical problems. ICU patients often require respiratory support, such as oxygen (low and high flow) by mask or nasal cannula, and ventilatory support, such as noninvasive ventilation (NIV), or invasive mechanical ventilation (IMV), to help them breathe and maintain oxygenation. Inhaled therapies, especially bronchodilators, corticosteroids, and antibiotics, are commonly prescribed in patients receiving care in the ICU (2, 3). Many patients who require aerosol therapy in the ICU setting have chronic respiratory problems and have been receiving aerosolized medications prior to admission. Devices employed in ambulatory patients, including pressurized metered-dose inhalers (pMDIs), dry powder inhalers (DPIs), soft mist inhalers (SMIs), and small-volume nebulizers (SVNs), are not designed and approved for aerosol administration in patients receiving respiratory support by IMV, NIV, or high-flow nasal cannula (HFNC). Thus, the challenge of administering aerosolized therapies is to adapt these aerosol-generating devices to the equipment employed for patients requiring various modes of respiratory support in the ICU.

Clinicians taking care of patients requiring respiratory support with IMV, NIV, or HFNC in the ICU have the choice to either interrupt these therapies and administer aerosols with the techniques employed in ambulatory patients, or to integrate these aerosol-generators into the respiratory support equipment and provide effective targeted dosing to the lung, with minimal disruption of respiratory and ventilatory support (4, 5). Discontinuing the respiratory support may cause precipitous drops in oxygenation, alveolar collapse, increased work of breathing, cardiovascular instability, and dyspnea. Given the harm of interrupting respiratory support to administer conventional inhalation therapy for these patients in the ICU, aerosolized medications need to be delivered in conjunction with respiratory support. However, simply plugging an aerosol device into an oxygen or ventilator circuit is not straightforward and may impact delivery efficiency as well as patient safety. For example, an SVN connected to a ventilator circuit for intubated patients delivered <25% of the lung dose achieved in spontaneously breathing non-intubated patients (6). For medications whose actions are dependent on an adequate lung dose for effects, such as

**Ventilator-related**
- Ventilation mode
- Tidal volume
- Respiratory rate
- Duty cycle
- Inspiratory waveform
- Breath-triggering mechanism

**Device-related–pMDI**
- Type of spacer or adapter
- Position of spacer in circuit
- Timing of pMDI actuation
- Type of pMDI

**Drug-related**
- Dose
- Formulation
- Aerosol particle size
- Targeted site for delivery
- Duration of action

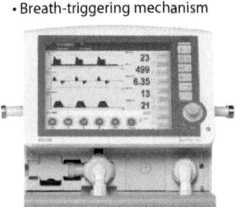

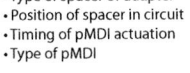

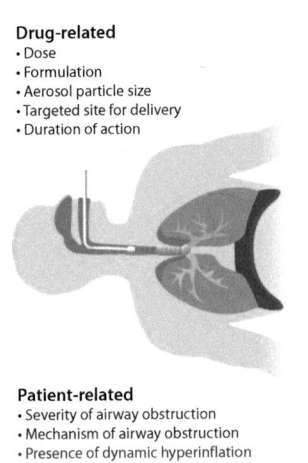

Patient Wye

Clear Chamber
AeroChamber* H.C.
MIDI Actuator

AeroChamber*
H.C. M.V.
Connector

Inspiratory
Limb

**Device-related–Nebulizer**
- Type of nebulizer
- Fill volume
- Gas flow rate
- Cycling: inspiration vs. continuous
- Duration of nebulization
- Position in circuit

**Circuit-related**
- Endotracheal or tracheostomy tube
- Humidity of inhaled gas
- Density of inhaled gas
- Leak in circuit
- Bias flow

**Patient-related**
- Severity of airway obstruction
- Mechanism of airway obstruction
- Presence of dynamic hyperinflation
- Patient-ventilator synchrony

**Figure 11.1** Factors influencing aerosol delivery in patients receiving invasive mechanical ventilation. pMDI = pressurized metered-dose inhaler.

antibiotics, surfactants, and muco-active agents, a goal of aerosol administration to patients in the ICU is to achieve or exceed the target dose levels achieved with the drug label in the ambulatory patient (7).

Aerosol devices are not designed for use in a pressurized environment, and inserting them into pressurized circuits may cause leaks, reduce circuit pressure, and negatively impact gas volumes delivered to patients. The optimal techniques for aerosol therapy in patients in the ICU differ from those employed in ambulatory patients and require appropriate device selection, placement, operation, and dose administration (volume or frequency of drug delivery) (8).

## AEROSOL GENERATORS AND THEIR CONFIGURATION FOR ICU PATIENTS

Considerable research, from bench to bedside, has focused on identifying factors impacting aerosol delivery during IMV(Figure 11.1), NIV (Figure 11.2), and HFNC (9–11). Variables associated with aerosol therapy during mechanical ventilation, first presented by Dhand and Tobin (12), have become a blueprint for assessing aerosol administration for a broader range of respiratory support. Aerosol delivery effectiveness is influenced by not only patient characteristics, such as the inhalation technique and severity of airway disease, but also the characteristics of aerosol devices integrated into respiratory support devices, their placement in the circuit, and the interface of these devices to patients (12, 13). As such, the features of aerosol devices that are commonly employed for aerosol delivery in the ICU, as well as a host of factors influencing aerosol delivery via each type of respiratory support (IMV, NIV, and HFNC), will be reviewed (Table 11.1), and considerations for optimal aerosol delivery will be summarized in this chapter (Table 11.2).

### Devices Employed for Aerosol Delivery in the ICU

Nebulizers are the most utilized aerosol devices in the ICU. The advantages of nebulizers include little to no requirement for coordination of breathing patterns or inspiratory effort, the ability to deliver a wide range of liquid medications,

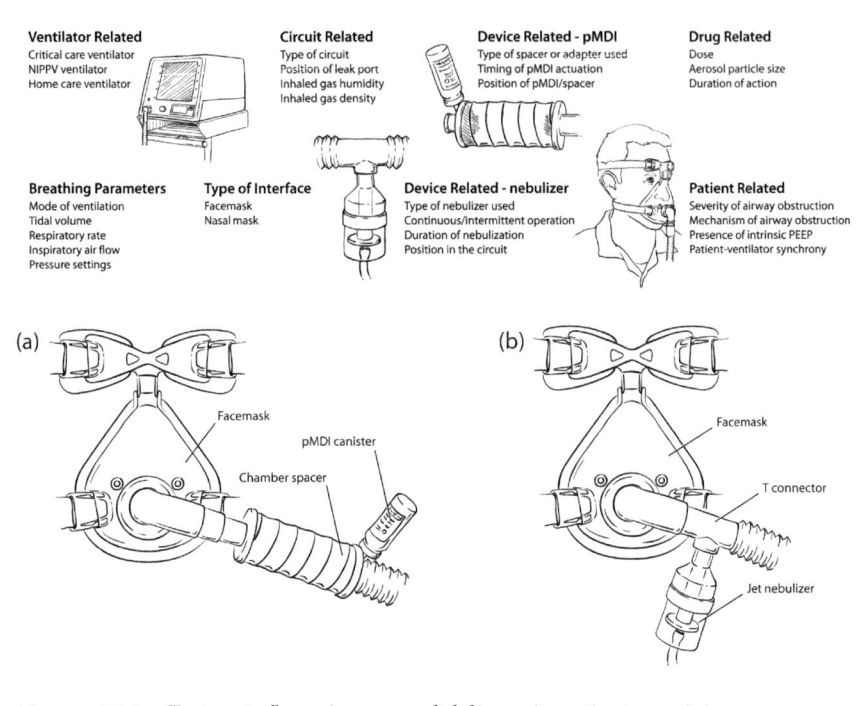

**Figure 11.2** Factors influencing aerosol delivery in patients receiving noninvasive ventilation (top panel). The connection of pMDIs and nebulizers with facemasks is shown in the Bottom panel. pMDI = pressurized metered-dose inhaler. *Abbreviations*: NIPPV = non invasive positive pressure ventilation; PEEP = positive end- expiratory pressure; pMDI = pressurized metered-dose inhaler.

and the relative ease of adjusting the administered dose placed in the reservoir (14). Nebulizers can be attached to a ventilator circuit with commonly available T-adapters. The spring-loaded T-adapter obviates the need for disconnecting the circuit for each nebulizer treatment (Figure 11.3).

A pMDI consisting of a canister and mouthpiece actuator is open to the atmosphere and cannot be directly used in a pressurized circuit. When a pMDI is used in-line with a pressurized circuit, the drug canister is removed from the actuator and used with a third-party spacer or adapter (Figure 11.3). When a pMDI is actuated, large particles containing propellants, preservatives, and medication, are emitted at high velocity and become smaller and slower as they traverse the first 10 cm. The use of a reservoir device allows propellants to evaporate, reduces particle size, slows down the velocity of the aerosol particles, and decreases impactive deposition as the aerosol passes into the circuit (14). Synchronizing pMDI actuation with the start of inspiration is critical for efficient drug delivery during ventilation, as random actuation greatly reduces the inhaled dose (15).

The SMI uses mechanical energy to create low-velocity and small particle size aerosols of 10 µl of liquid solutions in a single actuation lasting 1.2 seconds. Again, the SMI is designed to be open to the atmosphere and requires a third-party adapter to be used in ventilator circuits. There is great variability between different adapters. A reservoir may be used but is not critical for the use of SMI in which emitted particles are smaller than the pMDI. Because each actuation emits aerosol for 1.2 seconds (14), inspiratory time should match the duration of

**Table 11.1: Variables that Affect Aerosol Delivery and Deposition during Various Modes of Respiratory Support in the ICU**

| Variables | | HFNC | NIV | IMV |
|---|---|---|---|---|
| Differences | Interfaces | Size of nasal cannula, connection tightness of nasal cannula | Vented vs non-vented mask, nasal mask vs full face mask vs total face mask vs helmet | The size of artificial airway, endotracheal tube vs tracheostomy |
| | Settings | Gas flows | Modes, pressure settings | Mode, ventilation parameters including tidal volume, respiratory rate, duty cycle, trigger mechanism, and inspiratory flow waveform |
| | Others | Open mouth vs close mouth breathing | Leak; single limb vs dual limb ventilator | Patient-ventilator synchrony |
| Common | Patient related | Severity and mechanism of airway obstruction, presence of dynamic hyperinflation | | |
| | Aerosol device related | pMDI: type and volume of third-party spacer or adapter, the position of the spacer in the circuit, timing of actuation. Nebulizer: type and placement of nebulizer, fill volume, inspiration synchronized vs continuous, duration of nebulization, driving gas flow | | |
| | Circuit related | Humidification, circuit leak | | |
| | Drug related | Dose, formulation, aerosol particle size, targeted site for delivery, duration of action | | |

*Abbreviations:* HFNC = high-flow nasal cannula; IMV = invasive mechanical ventilation; NIV = noninvasive ventilation; pMDI = pressurized metered dose inhaler.

aerosol emission, and gas flow from the ventilator should be synchronized with SMI actuation.

DPIs are passive devices that require patients to generate an inspiration flow, usually >30 L/min, to draw the powder from the reservoir (14). In the ICU environment, the DPI cannot be integrated into a circuit, and there are no approved commercially available methods for DPI administration during ventilator support. In addition, the powders can be greatly affected by humidity, which causes the powder to clump and reduces the dispersion of the drug into respirable particles (16).

### Configuration of Inhalation Devices in ICU Patients

The configuration of medical aerosol inhalation devices for patients in ICUs depends on the medication, device availability with those drugs, the respiratory support device being used (Table 11.3), and whether the patient could tolerate interruption of respiratory support.

**Table 11.2: Optimization of Aerosol Delivery during Various Modes of Respiratory Support in the ICU**

| | | HFNC | NIV | IMV |
|---|---|---|---|---|
| Interface | | Large size of nasal cannula and tightly connect it to patient nasal prongs | Non-vented mask is preferred | Changing artificial airway size or type for the sole purpose of improving aerosol delivery is not recommended |
| Aerosol device | | VMN or pMDI with spacer are preferred, pMDI needs to be actuated at the beginning of inspiration | | |
| Aerosol device position | VMN | At the inlet of humidifier | Between mask and exhalation valve in the single-limb ventilator and between mask and Y-piece in the dual-limb ventilator | At the inlet of humidifier |
| | pMDI and spacer | Close to nasal cannula | | Close to Y-piece in the inspiratory limb |
| Humidification | | No need to turn off humidifier | Humidification does not affect aerosol delivery | Turning off humidifier for routine aerosol therapy is not recommended |
| Settings | | Titrate flow down during aerosol delivery | Changing the mode or settings for the sole purpose of improving aerosol delivery is not recommended | |

*Abbreviations:* HFNC = high-flow nasal cannula; IMV = invasive mechanical ventilation; NIV = noninvasive ventilation; pMDI = pressurized metered dose inhaler; VMN = vibrating mesh nebulizer.

If patients are placed on invasive mechanical ventilation, interruption of ventilation is not recommended for aerosol administration. The aerosol device must be placed in-line with the ventilator. Besides nebulizers, pMDIs can be placed in-line with a spacer or adapter to deliver aerosolized medication (Figure 11.3). On the other hand, some patients receiving NIV or HFNC may tolerate interruption of therapy for short intervals to provide aerosol delivery, such as individual actuation of pMDIs or SMIs. Interruption for 10–15 minutes to provide nebulizer treatments may not be as well tolerated. In patients requiring consistent NIV or HFNC, an interruption of respiratory support could have greater adverse effects than the potential benefit of aerosol administration. Fortunately, using optimal techniques to administer aerosols via NIV or HFNC can produce similar inhaled doses and clinical effects as conventional aerosol devices (10, 11). Thus, interrupting NIV or HFNC for the sole purpose of improving aerosol delivery efficiency creates undue risk for patients. Nevertheless, an assessment of risks vs benefits should guide the decision whether to interrupt NIV or HFNC to administer conventional nebulization via mouthpiece or facemask, or to place a nebulizer in-line with NIV or HFNC.

Some aerosolized medications have a short half-life, requiring continuous administration, such as inhaled epoprostenol for patients with severe

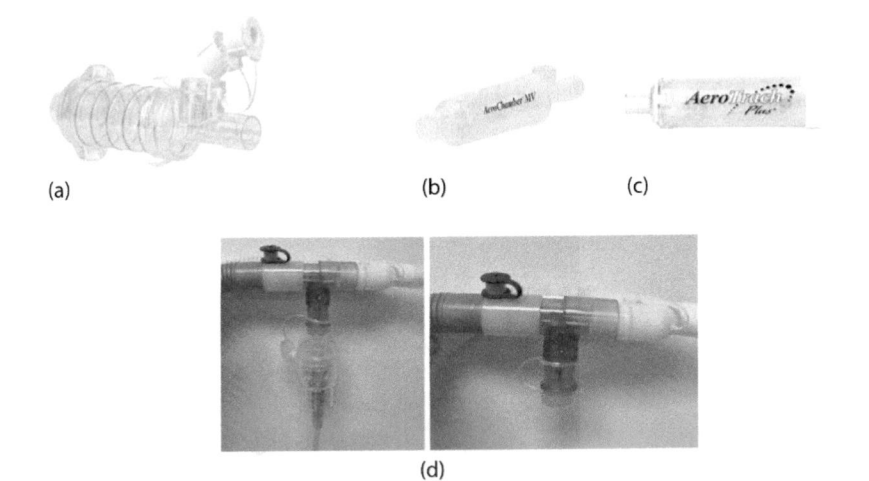

(a)  (b)  (c)

(d)

**Figure 11.3**   Adapters used to connect pressurized metered-dose inhalers (pMDIs) and nebulizers in-line in ventilator circuits. Reservoir chambers used to connect pMDIs in mechanically ventilated patients are shown (top panel, a and b). A special adapter is employed to connect pMDIs to tracheostomy tubes (c). A jet nebulizer is placed in-line with the ventilator circuit via a spring-loaded T-adapter (d, left). When the nebulization is completed, the jet nebulizer is removed from the ventilator circuit, leaving the T-adapter in-line with the Port capped (d, right).

**Table 11.3:  Characteristics of Aerosol Delivery in Ambulatory and ICU Patients**

| Characteristics | Ambulatory | HFNC | NIV | IMV |
|---|---|---|---|---|
| Inhalation pathway | Oro-nasal | Nasal | Oro-nasal | Artificial airway |
| Aerosol carrier type | Patient inspiratory flow | Patient inspiratory flow + HFNC flow (10–60 L/min) | Patient inspiratory flow + ventilator delivery flow (30–60 L/min) and leak flow (10–30 L/min) | Patient inspiratory flow + ventilator delivery flow (30–60 L/min) or ventilator delivery flow (30–60 L/min) only |
| Aerosol carrier waveform | Sinusoidal | Sinusoidal + square | Sinusoidal + Descending | Sinusoidal + Descending or square or descending |
| Total flow | 20–40 L/min | 30–100 L/min | 60–150 L/min | 30–100 L/min |
| Aerosol surrounding temperature and humidity | Ambient | 37 °C, 100% | 31–34 °C, up to 100% | 37 °C, 100% |
| Aerosol storage | Oro-nasal pharynx | Oro-nasal pharynx + HFNC circuit | Oro-nasal pharynx + non-vented mask | Ventilator circuit |

*Abbreviations:* HFNC = high-flow nasal cannula; IMV = invasive mechanical ventilation; NIV = noninvasive ventilation.

hypoxemia or pulmonary hypertension, and nebulizers need to be placed in-line with respiratory support (17, 18). For other medications, placement of a nebulizer in-line with respiratory support is also commonly employed when higher than labeled doses are needed to provide relief, such as inhaled albuterol for patients with acute severe asthma (19).

## FACTORS INFLUENCING OPTIMAL AEROSOL DELIVERY VIA RESPIRATORY SUPPORT DEVICES

### Invasive Mechanical Ventilation

#### Aerosol Device

Nebulizers and pMDI with spacer could be placed in-line with an invasive mechanical ventilator. Jet nebulizers (JNs) and vibrating mesh nebulizers (VMNs) are the commonly utilized nebulizers during IMV (2, 9). JN can be operated continuously with an external gas source or intermittently with inspiration synchronized with gas flow from the ventilator. The former requires a driving gas from an external gas source, usually at a gas flow of 6–8 L/min, the introduction of the external gas flow into the ventilator system impacts ventilator settings, for example, it increases tidal volume delivery and alters the fraction of inspired oxygen ($F_IO_2$) to patients (9). More importantly, it interferes with the ventilator's ability to sense patient effort and makes the ventilator difficult to trigger (20). For patients with muscle weakness or severe air-trapping, the continuous JN may worsen patient-ventilator trigger asynchrony. If continuous JN is used, close monitoring of patient triggering is needed with adjustment of ventilator settings and alarms as needed and return to pre-treatment settings after completion of the nebulizer treatment. In contrast, for inspiration-synchronized JN, the driving gas flow is typically from the set volume of gas delivered to the patient. Thus, it does not affect ventilator function. Continuous aerosol causes waste during the exhalation phase; however, inspiration-synchronized nebulization does not substantially improve nebulizer efficiency and it prolongs the duration of each treatment by up to 3-fold compared to continuous operation (21).

VMNs and pMDIs are not driven by gas flow, thus, neither device affects ventilator sensors or the set ventilatory parameters. The inhaled drug dose with VMN is reported to be 2–3-fold higher than with JN (22–24) and similar to pMDI and spacer (24–26). The higher efficiency of VMNs is mainly due to a higher total output because of their low residual volume (<0.1 mL), in contrast to 0.5–1.2 mL residual volume for JNs.

#### Nebulizer Placement

To optimize delivery efficiency, researchers placed various nebulizers at different positions of the ventilator circuit, including between circuit and airway, in the inspiratory limb 15–80 cm from the airway, and near the ventilator (inlet and outlet of the humidifier) (22, 23, 27). With bias flow, VMN was most efficient when placed close to the ventilator (23), as bias flow carries the continuously produced aerosol into the inspiratory limb toward the patient between inspirations, resulting in a reservoir effect with a 50–80% increase in delivered dose (23). When there is no bias flow and the VMN is placed near the ventilator, a bolus of aerosol from the continuous VMN collects in the humidifier and nearby tubing, but a tidal volume of 500 mL is insufficient to carry the bolus of aerosol to the patient through the 6-foot long tubing in the inspiratory limb of the circuit (22). This explains why in the absence of bias flow the inhaled dose is higher with VMN placed close to Y-piece than at the humidifier. With

a continuously operating JN, the driving gas flow carries the aerosol. In this setting, the JN output acts like the bias flow so that it is more efficient in a position closer to the humidifier without bias flow, but as bias flow is added to the circuit there is greater aerosol washout, and the inhaled dose is reduced with JN at this position.

Interestingly, when the JN is placed at the inspiratory limb close to Y-piece, the inhaled dose with the JN operated in inspiration-synchronized mode is 2–3-fold higher than that with operation in the continuous mode (28). However, when the nebulizer is placed at the inlet of the humidifier, no significant differences in the inhaled doses are found between the two modes of operation of JNs (21). Zhang et al. (27) reported that placing an inspiration-synchronized JN at a distance of 80 cm from the Y-piece in the inspiratory limb resulted in a higher inhaled dose than placing it at the inlet of the humidifier or between the endotracheal tube and Y-piece. However, the inspiratory limb of the ventilator heated wire circuit is usually 150–160 cm long and disconnecting such circuits to place an aerosol device is not feasible.

### Reservoir Volume and Placement for pMDI

pMDIs cannot be directly placed in-line with the ventilator circuit, they are connected via a reservoir device or adapter with two open ports (Figure 11.3). The inhaled dose is significantly lower with a reservoir volume less than 150 mL than that with a reservoir volume higher than 150 mL (24, 26, 29). The pMDI and the reservoir chamber need to be placed at the Y-piece of the inspiratory limb. Notably, with an adapter that has a very small volume (20–30 mL), the aerosol efficiency was found to be low at regular tidal volume settings (29). With adapters that had a 90-degree right-angled bend, aerosol delivery was even lower (26).

### Humidification

During invasive ventilation, administration of dry gases may irritate the airway, and cause dryness of the airway mucosa leading to mucociliary dysfunction, mucus plugging, and atelectasis. Accordingly, providing heat and humidification of the inspired gases is essential in a patient with an artificial airway (30). Active humidifiers heat the water in the chamber, which heats and humidifies dry air when it passes over the chamber. In contrast, passive humidifiers, called heat-moisture exchangers (HMEs), are placed between the ventilator circuit and the airway to capture heat and humidity from exhaled gases, which are in turn used to heat and humidify the inhaled gases. As most HMEs filter aerosol particles, they must be removed or bypassed during aerosol delivery. Alternatively, the nebulizer can be placed between the HME and patient, but exhaled aerosols can build up on the HME and increase the resistance to airflow imparted by the HME over time.

Most medical aerosols are hygroscopic and grow larger when passing into the gas with high absolute humidity. This can occur in a heated ventilator circuit, or as inhaled aerosol encounters the exhaled heat and humidity in the airway. Consequently, the inhaled dose is reduced by ~50% in heated circuits compared to dry circuits (22, 31, 32). However, turning off the active heater to deliver aerosol within 10 minutes does not improve aerosol delivery efficiency (33), as the circuits are not completely dry and cooled down in this short interval. Interestingly, when using models which exhale heat and humidity, the placement of an aerosol device near the patient shows little to no change in delivery efficiency with the dry vs wet circuits (34). As such, it is not recommended to turn off the active heater for the sole purpose of improving aerosol delivery. For antibiotics or other cost-prohibitive medications,

considering that it may take a long period for a humidifier and circuits to cool down, using an HME rather than an active heater for humidification might be a practical solution; nebulizers can bypass the HME or be placed between the HME and the patient (35).

In summary, the use of VMN or pMDI with a spacer is preferred for optimal aerosol delivery in patients with chronic obstructive pulmonary disease (COPD) and asthma during invasive ventilation and a JN is a less efficient alternative. When a VMN is utilized, it is recommended to place the VMN at the inlet of the humidifier in the presence of bias flow, or in the inspiratory limb close to the Y-piece in the absence of bias flow in the circuit. When a pMDI is utilized, a spacer with a minimum volume of 150 mL placed in the inspiratory limb close to the Y-piece is recommended. If an HME is used, it must be removed or bypassed during aerosol delivery. If the patient uses an active heater for humidification, it is not recommended to turn off the heater for routine aerosol therapy.

## Evaluation of Treatment Effects

The inhaled dose during invasive ventilation varies, due to patient characteristics such as the severity of airway obstruction, lung function, breathing efforts, etc., and the aforementioned factors influencing aerosol delivery (Figure 11.1). Assessment of treatment effects could help to titrate the nominal dose for individual patients. For example, when a bronchodilator is utilized, the bronchodilator responses can be assessed via the changes in the airway resistance and intrinsic positive end-expiratory pressure (PEEPi) for patients with COPD and asthma (13). For other inhaled medications such as corticosteroids or antibiotics, which do not generate immediate airway responses, the measurement of bronchoalveolar lavage or systemic levels can help to provide guidance regarding the optimal drug dose (36). In patients receiving mechanical ventilation, the upper airway is bypassed by an artificial airway so that the systemic levels of the aerosolized medication reflect the dose deposited in the lower airway. Thus, the concentrations of the aerosolized medication in the urine or blood could be used to evaluate the aerosol delivery efficiency and serve as guides to determine the appropriate nominal dose.

## Tracheostomy/laryngectomy Patients without Invasive Mechanical Ventilation

Clinically, some patients in the ICU may not require ventilator support but still need to maintain an open airway, such as a tracheostomy. When they require aerosol therapy, although their upper airway is intact, using conventional aerosol therapy with a mask or mouthpiece has low aerosol delivery efficiency (37), as most of the tidal volume is delivered via the tracheostomy rather than the upper airway. Additionally, the tracheostomy tube creates a barrier for aerosol inhalation via the upper airway. If the patients have a cuffed tracheostomy tube or have undergone a laryngectomy, which completely bypasses the upper airway, patients could only breathe in and out via the tracheostomy or laryngectomy. In such patients, aerosol delivery is achieved via tracheostomy or laryngectomy (Figure 11.4).

In patients with a tracheostomy collar, JN can be used via an extension tubing to maintain the nebulizer cup in a vertical position (Figure 11.4a) or with a T-piece (Figure 11.4b). For patients requiring humidification, JN or VMN can be placed in-line with the humidification circuit (Figure 11.4c and d) without interrupting humidification. Notably, placing the nebulizer close to the patient (Figure 11.4e and f) in the humidification setup generated a lower inhaled dose than directly placing the nebulizer with an extension tubing (Figure 11.4a and b) (34). When a pMDI is used, an open-ended spacer is needed to connect the pMDI

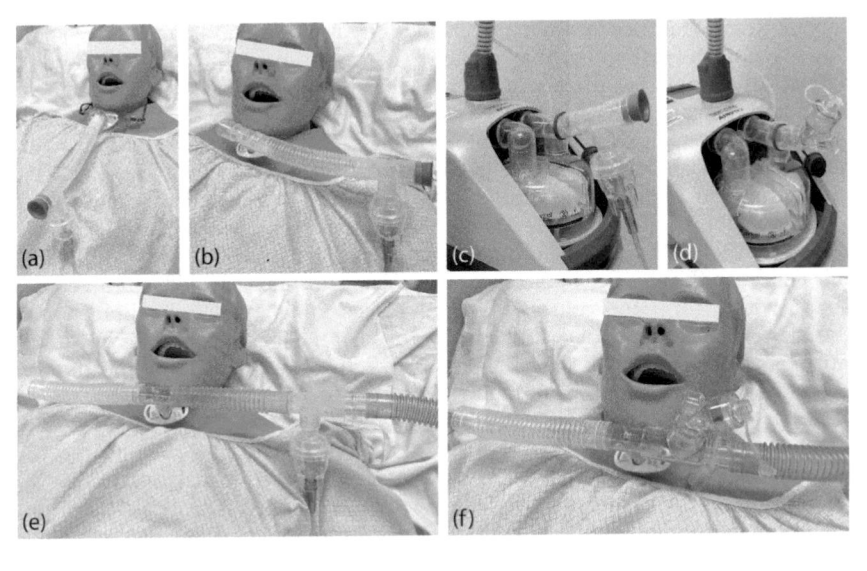

**Figure 11.4** Schematic showing nebulizer setups for patients with a tracheostomy demonstrated on a mannikin. A jet nebulizer is connected to a tracheostomy collar via an extension tubing (panel a) or via a T-piece (panel b), with the other end capped. When heated humidification is provided, a jet nebulizer (panel c) or a vibrating mesh nebulizer (panel d) is placed at the humidifier. When cool aerosol is provided via T-piece, a jet nebulizer (panel e) or a vibrating mesh nebulizer (panel f) is placed close to the T-piece.

with the tracheostomy or laryngectomy tube (Figure 11.3). A pMDI should be actuated at the beginning of inspiration, and patients are allowed to breathe in and out via the spacer several times. A manual resuscitator connected with the spacer has been employed to deliver breaths for patients during aerosol delivery. However, an in vitro study found that the inhaled mass with the assistance of manual ventilation was similar to that achieved with spontaneous breathing via various aerosol devices that were placed in-line with the tracheostomy (38).

### Non-invasive Ventilation

Unlike IMV, NIV uses a mask or helmet rather than an endotracheal or tracheostomy tube to access the airway. As masks tend to leak, compensation for changing levels of leaks is required, implying that gas flows are higher and more turbulent than those during IMV (Table 11.3). Two types of ventilators are employed for NIV. A single-limb bi-level ventilator driven by a turbine is most commonly utilized, and this ventilator adjusts flow through a fixed orifice exhalation valve placed between the circuit and mask to compensate for the mask leak. More recently, dual-limb conventional critical care ventilators have been equipped with modules to provide NIV.

#### Aerosol Device Type and Placement

Only continuous JN, VMN, or pMDI with spacer could be placed in-line with single-limb ventilators to deliver aerosolized medication (Figures 11.2 and 11.5). Due to the negligible residual volume, VMNs have a higher delivery efficiency than JNs (39, 40). Aerosol devices placed between the mask and the exhalation valve provide higher aerosol delivery efficiency than placement close to the ventilator

(41–43). Placing the aerosol device closer to the ventilator allows the aerosol to be flushed through and leak from the exhalation valve, while placing the aerosol device between the mask and the exhalation valve reduces such losses. The addition of a 15 cm extension tubing between the VMN and the exhalation valve further enhances aerosol delivery (41), due to the reservoir effect of the extension tubing. However, the added volume of the tubing could increase the dead space, which may be detrimental for patients with asthma or COPD. When dual-limb ventilators are used for NIV, there is no fixed leak in the circuit but air leaks from face masks continue to be a factor in reducing the efficiency of aerosol delivery.

### NIV Interface

NIV can be connected to patients via a nasal mask, a full face mask, a total face mask, or a helmet. Full face masks are the most commonly used interfaces and two types are commonly employed: vented masks with the exhalation port incorporated (only used with a single-limb circuit) or non-vented masks. The use of vented masks greatly reduces aerosol delivery efficiency (42, 43) and they are not recommended. Only non-vented masks should be employed during aerosol delivery via NIV.

### Ventilator Type

VMNs placed in optimal positions in the single-limb ventilator and dual-limb ventilator achieve similar efficacy of inhaled dose delivery (43). The optimal position in a single-limb circuit is 15 cm away from the exhalation valve and close to the mask, whereas in a dual-limb circuit placement of the VMN is optimal in the inspiratory limb at a distance of 15 cm from the Y-piece.

### Humidification

In contrast to IMV, turning off humidification during aerosol delivery via NIV does not improve aerosol delivery (44), probably because NIV employs gases with a lower temperature and absolute humidity than IMV.

In summary, to optimize aerosol delivery via NIV, the use of a VMN or a pMDI with a spacer provides more efficient aerosol delivery than a JN. Aerosol devices should be placed between the non-vented mask and the exhalation valve in the single-limb ventilator or 15 cm away from the Y-piece in the inspiratory limb of the dual-limb ventilator. A pMDI should be actuated at the beginning of inspiration. Vented masks should be avoided during aerosol delivery. Turning off the humidifier does not improve aerosol delivery during NIV.

### High-flow Nasal Cannula

High-flow nasal cannula provides heated and humidified gas for patients, with the gas flow set higher than the patient's peak inspiratory flow during tidal breathing. Oxygen therapy with HFNC is now being increasingly utilized for patients with COPD because high-flow gas washes out the dead space in the upper airway, thereby reducing $PaCO_2$ and the work of breathing (45). HFNC is an ideal platform to continuously deliver aerosolized medication to patients (46). Unlike NIV, HFNC can be used continuously for days, even weeks, as the probability of skin breakdown or discomfort from the continuous use of HFNC is much lower than that with a tightly fitted mask. Moreover, HFNC flows are lower and more laminar than flows employed during NIV (**Table 11.3**).

Transnasal pulmonary aerosol delivery via HFNC has become popular in ICUs worldwide and key factors influencing the efficiency of drug delivery have been explored in multiple in vitro and in vivo studies (5, 47–51). Notably, aerosol administration with JN and a mask or mouthpiece while HFNC is in use decreases the inhaled dose compared to aerosol administered through the

HFNC (47), thus, the concurrent use of a nebulizer with a mask/mouthpiece during HFNC treatment should be avoided (11).

## Nebulizer Types

During aerosol administration via HFNC, VMNs deliver several-fold higher drug doses than JNs (48, 49). Additionally, JNs require external-driven gas (usual gas flow of 6–8 L/min), which limits their use in patients who need HFNC gas flow less than 8 L/min, such as in small children. The use of JN in-line with HFNC alters the gas flow, humidity, and $F_IO_2$, which might cause malfunction for some HFNC devices, such as Airvo2 (Fisher & Paykel, Auckland, New Zealand). In contrast, VMNs are preferred for aerosol delivery via HFNC because they are driven by electricity and no external gas flow is needed for their operation.

## Nebulizer Placement

In adults and older children, the inhaled drug dose is higher with the nebulizer placed at the humidifier than when it is placed close to the nasal cannula, especially at low flow settings (49–51). Aerosol particles leaving the nasal prongs are <2.1 μm in diameter, as larger particles generated by aerosol devices rain out either in the humidifier, circuit, or nasal prongs where the condensation can occlude gas flow. More of the aerosol emitted by a VMN placed before or after the humidifier chamber during exhalation is available to be inhaled in the next inspiration, reducing the waste of aerosol. In contrast, nebulizer placement close to the cannula has a more limited reservoir for collecting aerosol between inspirations.

## Gas Flow Settings

By definition, HFNC gas flows are typically set to meet or exceed a patient's tidal peak inspiratory flow, so as to reduce air entrainment and also generate a certain level of positive airway pressure (52). Unfortunately, gas flow higher than a patient's tidal peak inspiratory flow during aerosol administration reduces inhaled drug dose by increasing waste of aerosol. With medium gas flows (15–30 L/min for adults and 0.5–1.0 L/min/kg for young children), in vitro models report higher inhaled drug dose with distressed breathing than with quiet relaxed breathing (49–51, 53, 54). Setting the HFNC gas flow lower than the patient's tidal peak inspiratory flow benefits transnasal aerosol delivery. In fact, HFNC flow set at 50% of the patient's tidal peak inspiratory flow was shown to be more comfortable and to provide higher pulmonary drug delivery compared to higher HFNC flows (55, 56).

Tidal peak inspiratory flow varies in different patients and there is no commercially available device to provide a breath-by-breath measurement of patient's tidal peak inspiratory flow. Most adult patients with acute respiratory failure do not spontaneously generate peak flows above 40 L/min during tidal breathing (52). For patients with acute hypoxemic respiratory failure, a pragmatic solution is to titrate down gas flow with high $F_IO_2$ to provide acceptable target oxygen saturations prior to aerosol administration. Empirically titrating the HFNC flow down to 20–25 L/min for adult patients with acute respiratory failure or 15–20 L/min for adult patients who are not in acute respiratory distress, or 0.5 L/min/kg for young children could provide efficient aerosol delivery with HFNC (11).

Assessment of patient responses to inhaled medication, such as improvement of oxygenation or pulmonary arterial pressure for inhaled epoprostenol (17), or the increment of forced expiratory volume in one second ($FEV_1$) for inhaled albuterol can provide confidence on appropriate dosing (56, 57). Notably, when the flow is titrated down during aerosol delivery, HFNC benefits such as

constant $F_IO_2$ or reduction of work of breathing would be compromised, thus closely monitoring the patient responses is warranted. If needed, a concentrated drug solution could be used to shorten the duration of low flow settings for aerosol delivery (58).

In summary, a VMN placed at the inlet of the humidifier is preferred for aerosol delivery via HFNC. HFNC gas flows need to be titrated down to a tolerable low flow during aerosol delivery for optimal nebulizer efficiency.

## FUGITIVE AEROSOLS AND MITIGATION STRATEGIES

Nebulizers generate a significant amount of fugitive aerosols, even for patients who do not have airborne diseases. Reducing the second-hand inhalation of fugitive aerosols would be beneficial for healthcare workers. Invasive ventilation is a closed system and filters should be placed at the outlet of the ventilator, whether or not aerosol is being administered. During nebulization, the fugitive aerosols leaked from the invasive ventilator would be minimal, depending on the type of filter used. Placing a filter at the expiratory port of the ventilator reduces fugitive aerosols and also protects the expiratory flow sensor (35). Notably, the filter may become obstructed with aerosols over time, increasing the expiratory resistance, thus it needs to be frequently changed especially during continuous nebulization. For NIV, when a nebulizer is placed between the mask and the exhalation port in the single-limb ventilator, a filter needs to be placed between the nebulizer and exhalation valve (Figure 11.5) or at the exhalation port (59). For HFNC, placing a procedure mask over the patient's face reduces fugitive aerosols, with and without medical aerosol administration (60).

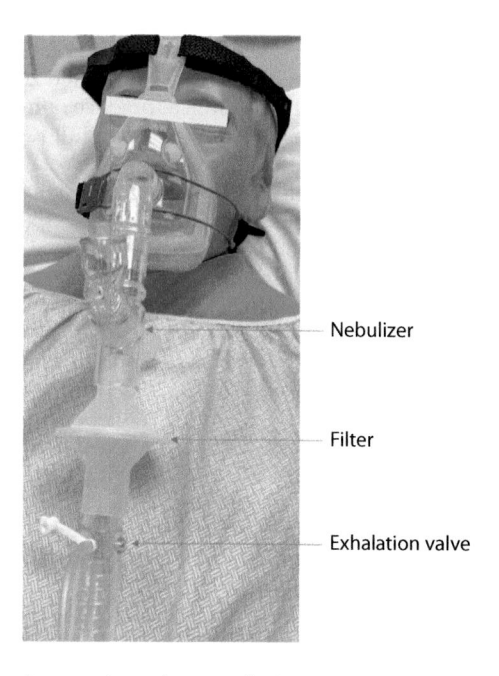

Nebulizer

Filter

Exhalation valve

**Figure 11.5** During noninvasive ventilation using a single-limb circuit, a vibrating mesh nebulizer is placed between the exhalation valve and the mask. A filter is placed between the nebulizer and the exhalation valve to reduce the release of fugitive aerosols into the room environment.

## CONCLUSION

Compared to ambulatory patients, aerosol therapy for patients in the ICU needing respiratory support is challenging, due to a host of factors influencing drug delivery. In addition to patient characteristics and the features of the aerosol generators, the configuration of the respiratory support devices, such as device settings, placement of the aerosol generator, and humidification, influence aerosol delivery, resulting in variable inhaled doses. Understanding these factors can help to optimize aerosol delivery for patients in the ICU. Close monitoring of patient responses and adjustment of respiratory support device settings and nominal doses are also necessary. With careful attention to techniques of administration, aerosolized therapies are effective for patients in the ICU.

## REFERENCES

1. Society of Critical Care Medicine (SCCM). SCCM | Critical Care Statistics. [cited 2022 July 19]. Available from: https://sccm.org/Communications/Critical-Care-Statistics
2. Reva Research Network, AT@ICU Study Group, Ehrmann S, et al. Aerosol therapy in intensive and intermediate care units: Prospective observation of 2808 critically ill patients. Intensive Care Med 2016;42(2):192–201. DOI:10.1007/s00134-015-4114-5
3. Lyu S, Li J, Wu M, et al. The use of aerosolized medications in adult intensive care unit patients: A prospective, multicenter, observational, cohort study. J Aerosol Med Pulm Drug Deliv 2021;34(6):383–391. DOI:10.1089/jamp.2021.0004
4. Lyu S, Li J, Yang L, et al. The utilization of aerosol therapy in mechanical ventilation patients: A prospective multicenter observational cohort study and a review of the current evidence. Ann Transl Med 2020;8(17):14.
5. Li J, Tu M, Yang L, et al. Worldwide clinical practice of high-flow nasal cannula and concomitant aerosol therapy in the adult ICU setting. Respir Care 2021;66(9):1416–1424. DOI:10.4187/respcare.08996
6. MacIntyre NR, Silver RM, Miller CW, et al. Aerosol delivery in intubated, mechanically ventilated patients. Crit Care Med 1985;13(2):81–84. DOI:10.1097/00003246-198502000-00005
7. Wong FJ, Dudney T, Dhand R. Aerosolized antibiotics for treatment of pneumonia in mechanically ventilated subjects. Respir Care 2019;64(8): 962–979. DOI:10.4187/respcare.07024
8. Dhand R. Inhalation therapy in invasive and noninvasive mechanical ventilation. Curr Opin Crit Care 2007;13(1):27–38. DOI:10.1097/MCC.0b013e328012e022
9. Dugernier J, Ehrmann S, Sottiaux T, et al. Aerosol delivery during invasive mechanical ventilation: A systematic review. Crit Care 2017;21(1):264. DOI:10.1186/s13054-017-1844-5
10. Dhand R. Aerosol therapy in patients receiving noninvasive positive pressure ventilation. J Aerosol Med Pulm Drug Deliv 2012;25(2):63–78. DOI:10.1089/jamp.2011.0929
11. Li J, Fink JB, MacLoughlin R, et al. A narrative review on trans-nasal pulmonary aerosol delivery. Crit Care 2020;24(1):506. DOI:10.1186/s13054-020-03206-9
12. Dhand R, Tobin MJ. Bronchodilator delivery with metered-dose inhalers in mechanically-ventilated patients. Eur Respir J 1996;9(3):585–595. DOI:10.1183/09031936.96.09030585

13. Dhand R, Tobin MJ. Inhaled bronchodilator therapy in mechanically ventilated patients. Am J Respir Crit Care Med 1997;156(1):3–10. DOI:10.1164/ajrccm.156.1.9610025
14. Pleasants RA, Hess DR. Aerosol delivery devices for obstructive lung diseases. Respir Care 2018;63(6):708–733. DOI:10.4187/respcare.06290
15. Diot P, Morra L, Smaldone GC. Albuterol delivery in a model of mechanical ventilation. Comparison of metered-dose inhaler and nebulizer efficiency. Am J Respir Crit Care Med 1995;152(4 Pt 1):1391–1394. DOI:10.1164/ajrccm.152.4.7551401
16. Dhand R. Inhalation therapy with metered-dose inhalers and dry powder inhalers in mechanically ventilated patients. Respir Care 2005;50(10): 1331–1334; discussion 1344–1345.
17. Li J, Gurnani PK, Roberts KM, et al. The clinical impact of flow titration on epoprostenol delivery via high flow nasal cannula for ICU patients with pulmonary hypertension or right ventricular dysfunction: A retrospective cohort comparison study. J Clin Med 2020;9(2):464. DOI:10.3390/jcm9020464
18. Chen SH, Chen LK, Teng TH, et al. Comparison of inhaled nitric oxide with aerosolized prostacyclin or analogues for the postoperative management of pulmonary hypertension: A systematic review and meta-analysis. Ann Med 2020;52(3–4):120–130. DOI:10.1080/07853890.2020.1746826
19. Rodrigo GJ, Rodrigo C. Continuous vs intermittent beta-agonists in the treatment of acute adult asthma: A systematic review with meta-analysis. Chest 2002;122(1):160–165. DOI:10.1378/chest.122.1.160
20. Beaty CD, Ritz RH, Benson MS. Continuous in-line nebulizers complicate pressure support ventilation. Chest 1989;96(6):1360–1363. DOI:10.1378/chest.96.6.1360
21. Wan GH, Lin HL, Fink JB, et al. In vitro evaluation of aerosol delivery by different nebulization modes in pediatric and adult mechanical ventilators. Respir Care 2014;59(10):1494–1500. DOI:10.4187/respcare.02999
22. Ari A, Areabi H, Fink JB. Evaluation of aerosol generator devices at 3 locations in humidified and non-humidified circuits during adult mechanical ventilation. Respir Care 2010;55(7):837–844.
23. Ari A, Atalay OT, Harwood R, et al. Influence of nebulizer type, position, and bias flow on aerosol drug delivery in simulated pediatric and adult lung models during mechanical ventilation. Respir Care 2010;55(7):845–851.
24. Naughton PJ, Joyce M, Mac Giolla Eain M, et al. Evaluation of aerosol drug delivery options during adult mechanical ventilation in the COVID-19 era. Pharmaceutics 2021;13(10):1574. DOI:10.3390/pharmaceutics13101574
25. Ari A, Harwood RJ, Sheard MM, et al. Pressurized metered-dose inhalers versus nebulizers in the treatment of mechanically ventilated subjects with artificial airways: An in vitro study. Respir Care 2015;60(11):1570–1574. DOI:10.4187/respcare.04125
26. Marik P, Hogan J, Krikorian J. A comparison of bronchodilator therapy delivered by nebulization and metered-dose inhaler in mechanically ventilated patients. Chest 1999;115(6):1653–1657. DOI:10.1378/chest.115.6.1653
27. Zhang C, Mi J, Zhang Z, et al. The clinical practice and best aerosol delivery location in intubated and mechanically ventilated patients: A randomized clinical trial. Biomed Res Int 2021;2021:6671671. DOI:10.1155/2021/6671671

28. Miller DD, Amin MM, Palmer LB, et al. Aerosol delivery and modern mechanical ventilation: In vitro/in vivo evaluation. Am J Respir Crit Care Med 2003;168(10):1205–1209. DOI:10.1164/rccm.200210-1167OC

29. Boukhettala N, Porée T, Diot P, et al. In vitro performance of spacers for aerosol delivery during adult mechanical ventilation. J Aerosol Med Pulm Drug Deliv 2015;28(2):130–136. DOI:10.1089/jamp.2013.1091

30. American Association for Respiratory Care, Restrepo RD, Walsh BK. Humidification during invasive and noninvasive mechanical ventilation: 2012. Respir Care 2012;57(5):782–788. DOI:10.4187/respcare.01766

31. Fink JB, Dhand R, Grychowski J, et al. Reconciling in vitro and in vivo measurements of aerosol delivery from a metered-dose inhaler during mechanical ventilation and defining efficiency-enhancing factors. Am J Respir Crit Care Med 1999;159(1):63–68. DOI:10.1164/ajrccm.159.1.9803119

32. Fink JB, Dhand R, Duarte AG, et al. Aerosol delivery from a metered-dose inhaler during mechanical ventilation. An in vitro model. Am J Respir Crit Care Med 1996;154(2 Pt 1):382–387. DOI:10.1164/ajrccm.154.2.8756810

33. Lin HL, Fink JB, Zhou Y, et al. Influence of moisture accumulation in inline spacer on delivery of aerosol using metered-dose inhaler during mechanical ventilation. Respir Care 2009;54(10):1336–1341.

34. Ari A, Harwood R, Sheard M, et al. Quantifying aerosol delivery in simulated spontaneously breathing patients with tracheostomy using different humidification systems with or without exhaled humidity. Respir Care 2016;61(5):600–606. DOI:10.4187/respcare.04127

35. Rello J, Rouby JJ, Sole-Lleonart C, et al. Key considerations on nebulization of antimicrobial agents to mechanically ventilated patients. Clin Microbiol Infect 2017;23(9):640–646. DOI:10.1016/j.cmi.2017.03.018

36. Luyt CE, Eldon MA, Stass H, et al. Pharmacokinetics and tolerability of amikacin administered as BAY41-6551 aerosol in mechanically ventilated patients with Gram-negative pneumonia and acute renal failure. J Aerosol Med Pulm Drug Deliv 2011;24(4):183–190. DOI:10.1089/jamp.2010.0860

37. Bugis AA, Sheard MM, Fink JB, et al. Comparison of aerosol delivery by face mask and tracheostomy collar. Respir Care 2015;60(9):1220–1226.

38. Alhamad BR, Fink JB, Harwood RJ, et al. Effect of aerosol devices and administration techniques on drug delivery in a simulated spontaneously breathing pediatric tracheostomy model. Respir Care 2015;60(7):1026–1032.

39. Galindo-Filho VC, Ramos ME, Rattes CSF, et al. Radioaerosol pulmonary deposition using mesh and jet nebulizers during noninvasive ventilation in healthy subjects. Respir Care 2015;60(9):1238–1246. DOI:10.4187/respcare.03667

40. Galindo-Filho VC, Alcoforado L, Rattes C, et al. A mesh nebulizer is more effective than jet nebulizer to nebulize bronchodilators during non-invasive ventilation of subjects with COPD: A randomized controlled trial with radiolabeled aerosols. Respir Med 2019;153:60–67. DOI:10.1016/j.rmed.2019.05.016

41. Michotte JB, Jossen E, Roeseler J, et al. In vitro comparison of five nebulizers during noninvasive ventilation: Analysis of inhaled and lost doses. J Aerosol Med Pulm Drug Deliv 2014;27(6):430–440. DOI:10.1089/jamp.2013.1070

42. Tan W, Dai B, Lu CL, et al. The effect of different interfaces on the aerosol delivery with vibrating mesh nebulizer during noninvasive positive pressure ventilation. J Aerosol Med Pulm Drug Deliv 2021;34(6):366–373. DOI:10.1089/jamp.2020.1623

43. Tan W, Dai B, Xu DY, et al. In-vitro comparison of single limb and dual limb circuit for aerosol delivery via noninvasive ventilation. Respir Care 2022;67(7):807–813.

44. Saeed H, Elberry AA, Eldin AS, et al. Effect of nebulizer designs on aerosol delivery during non-invasive mechanical ventilation: A modeling study of in vitro data. Pulm Ther 2017;3(1):233–241. DOI:10.1007/s41030-017-0033-7

45. Huang X, Du Y, Ma Z, et al. High-flow nasal cannula oxygen versus conventional oxygen for hypercapnic chronic obstructive pulmonary disease: A meta-analysis of randomized controlled trials. Clin Respir J 2021;15(4):437–444. DOI:10.1111/crj.13317

46. Levy SD, Alladina JW, Hibbert KA, et al. High-flow oxygen therapy and other inhaled therapies in intensive care units. Lancet 2016;387(10030): 1867–1878. DOI:10.1016/S0140-6736(16)30245-8

47. Bennett G, Joyce M, Fernández EF, et al. Comparison of aerosol delivery across combinations of drug delivery interfaces with and without concurrent high-flow nasal therapy. Intensive Care Med Exp 2019;7(1):20. DOI:10.1186/s40635-019-0245-2

48. Dugernier J, Hesse M, Jumetz T, et al. Aerosol delivery with two nebulizers through high-flow nasal cannula: A randomized cross-over single-photon emission computed tomography-computed tomography study. J Aerosol Med Pulm Drug Deliv 2017;30(5):349–358. DOI:10.1089/jamp.2017.1366

49. Li J, Williams L, Fink JB. The impact of high-flow nasal cannula device, nebulizer type, and placement on trans-nasal aerosol drug delivery. Respir Care 2022;67(1):1–8. DOI:10.4187/respcare.09133

50. Li J, Wu W, Fink JB. In vitro comparison between inspiration synchronized and continuous vibrating mesh nebulizer during trans-nasal aerosol delivery. Intensive Care Med Exp 2020;8(1):6. DOI:10.1186/s40635-020-0293-7

51. Li J, Gong L, Ari A, et al. Decrease the flow setting to improve trans-nasal pulmonary aerosol delivery via "high-flow nasal cannula" to infants and toddlers. Pediatr Pulmonol 2019;54(6):914–921. DOI:10.1002/ppul.24274

52. Li J, Scott JB, Fink JB, et al. Optimizing high-flow nasal cannula flow settings in adult hypoxemic patients based on peak inspiratory flow during tidal breathing. Ann Intensive Care 2021;11(1):164. DOI:10.1186/s13613-021-00949-8

53. Réminiac F, Vecellio L, Heuzé-Vourc'h N, et al. Aerosol therapy in adults receiving high flow nasal cannula oxygen therapy. J Aerosol Med Pulm Drug Deliv 2016;29(2):134–141. DOI:10.1089/jamp.2015.1219

54. Dailey PA, Harwood R, Walsh K, et al. Aerosol delivery through adult high flow nasal cannula with heliox and oxygen. Respir Care 2017;62(9): 1186–1192. DOI:10.4187/respcare.05127

55. Li J, Gong L, Fink JB. The ratio of nasal cannula gas flow to patient inspiratory flow on trans-nasal pulmonary aerosol delivery for adults: An in vitro study. Pharmaceutics 2019;11(5):225. DOI:10.3390/pharmaceutics11050225

56. Li J, Chen Y, Ehrmann S, et al. Bronchodilator delivery via high-flow nasal cannula: A randomized controlled trial to compare the effects of gas flows. Pharmaceutics 2021;13(10):1655. DOI:10.3390/pharmaceutics13101655

57. Li J, Zhao M, Hadeer M, et al. Dose response to transnasal pulmonary administration of bronchodilator aerosols via nasal high-flow therapy in adults with stable chronic obstructive pulmonary disease and asthma. Respiration 2019;98(5):401–409. DOI:10.1159/000501564

58. Li J, Wu W, Fink JB. In vitro comparison of unit dose vs infusion pump administration of albuterol via high-flow nasal cannula in toddlers. Pediatr Pulmonol 2020;55(2):322–329. DOI:10.1002/ppul.24589
59. Kaur R, Weiss TT, Perez A, et al. Practical strategies to reduce nosocomial transmission to healthcare professionals providing respiratory care to patients with COVID-19. Crit Care 2020;24(1):571. DOI:10.1186/s13054-020-03231-8
60. Li J, Alolaiwat AA, Harnois LJ, et al. Mitigating fugitive aerosols during aerosol delivery via high-flow nasal cannula devices. Respir Care 2022;67(4):404–414. DOI:10.4187/respcare.09589

# 12 Inhaled Therapy for Other Respiratory Diseases

## Cystic Fibrosis and Non-Cystic Fibrosis Bronchiectasis

*Mahmoud Ibrahim, MD and Alexander G. Duarte, MD*

## CONTENTS

## INTRODUCTION

Once regarded as an orphan disease, bronchiectasis is now recognized more frequently due to greater clinician awareness, increased chest tomography (CT) availability, and genetic testing (1). Bronchiectasis may be classified as related to cystic fibrosis (CF) or non-cystic fibrosis. Bronchiectasis related to CF arises from genetic mutations in the cystic fibrosis transmembrane conductance regulator (CFTR) gene that give rise to defective airway epithelial ion transport and altered mucociliary clearance. In contrast, non-CF bronchiectasis (NCFB) represents a diverse set of conditions associated with altered mucociliary clearance, airway inflammation, and airway infections not associated with CFTR gene mutations.

In management of CF and NCFB, inhalation therapy is a preferred method of drug delivery as medication that directly deposits on the airway provides therapeutic benefits with reduced systemic side effects. Therapies to prevent, relieve, and treat airway narrowing, secretion accumulation, inflammation, and microbial infections associated with bronchiectasis include bronchodilators, corticosteroids, mucolytics, and antimicrobials. Moreover, many professional society guidelines recommend various inhalation therapies as a prominent form of drug administration in patients with bronchiectasis (2, 3).

## BRONCHODILATORS

Bronchodilators are frequently prescribed for dyspnea relief and the US Bronchiectasis Research Registry found that 61% of patients with non-CF bronchiectasis were prescribed a bronchodilator (4). Yet, evidence-based data to indicate that bronchodilators are effective at a population level are lacking. A systematic review examined the effectiveness of short-acting β-agonists or anticholinergics in children and adults with bronchiectasis were unable to identify adequately designed trials (5). Evidence to support the use of long-acting bronchodilators to improve lung function, mucociliary clearance, or dyspnea relief in patients with bronchiectasis is even less robust (6). For the individual patient, short-acting β-agonists and/or short-acting antimuscarinics

DOI: 10.1201/9781003269014-12

may provide dyspnea relief and aid in the clearance of secretions. They may also mitigate excessive coughing associated with mucolytic therapy-associated bronchospasm (7). As for the delivery device, preference should be guided by convenience, ease of administration, and availability. Pressurized metered dose inhaler (pMDI) delivery of short-acting β-agonists or soft mist inhaler delivery of combined short-acting β-agonists and/or short-acting antimuscarinics is acceptable. Jet nebulizer delivery of short-acting bronchodilators is a common method that may be more convenient for a given patient but additional research is needed to assess clinical efficacy, patient preference, and outcomes with nebulizer delivery using adaptive aerosol delivery or vibrating mesh technology (8).

## CORTICOSTEROIDS

As bronchiectasis is associated with neutrophilic airway inflammation, clinicians may feel compelled to prescribe inhaled corticosteroids, although this therapy is primarily effective in eosinophilic airway disease. However, inhaled corticosteroids are prescribed to 44% of patients with CF and 39% of patients with non-CF bronchiectasis (4, 9). Yet, a US consensus group that examined findings from 8 clinical trials involving 419 subjects with CF did not find supporting evidence of benefits from the use of inhaled corticosteroids regarding lung function, quality of life, and exacerbation rates (10). Similarly, the European Society of CF recommendations indicates that inhaled corticosteroids have no proven efficacy, outside of the treatment of concomitant asthma (11). For adults with NCFB, a review of the short-term effects of inhaled corticosteroid administration found no improvement in pulmonary function tests, exacerbations rates, or health-related outcomes (2, 12). Studies included inhaled corticosteroids delivered via pMDI (13, 14). Of note, concerns about inhaled corticosteroids increasing airway bacterial density and association with an increased risk for pneumonia and nontuberculous mycobacterial (NTM) lung infections limit their use in bronchiectasis (15, 16). In summary, the risks seem to outweigh the benefits of inhaled corticosteroid use in patients with bronchiectasis.

## MUCOLYTICS

In patients with bronchiectasis, mucus hyperconcentration and airway mucus stasis result in ciliary dysfunction that contribute to airway inflammation and lung infections. Consequently, therapeutic agents that decrease mucus concentration through rehydration of airway surface liquid can decrease mucus viscosity and facilitate clearance of secretions. In patients with CF, hypertonic saline reduces IL-8 levels in sputum and bronchoalveolar lavage fluid, consistent with an anti-inflammatory effect (9). Moreover, hypertonic saline administration via Pari LC plus jet nebulizer to children and adults with CF over 48 weeks yielded significant improvements in lung function and reduced exacerbations (17). A Cochrane review found improved outcomes in patients receiving inhaled hypertonic saline (7%) compared to control subjects (18). In patients with NCFB, administration of jet nebulized 7% saline over 3 months improved lung function and health-related quality of life and decreased antibiotic use compared to nebulized saline (0.9%) (19). The comparison of 6% and 0.9% saline administration by mesh nebulizer to 40 subjects with NCFB over 12 months yielded improved lung function and quality of life (20). Thus, nebulized saline is a safe and effective mucolytic agent, but the optimal solution tonicity and

type of nebulizer that are needed for optimal efficacy in NCFB require further investigation.

Administration of dry powder mannitol (Pharmaxis, Sydney, Australia) by Orbital delivery device to rehydrate the airways of patients with CF revealed improvements in lung function (21, 22). Dry powder inhaled mannitol (400 mg twice daily) is approved for use in adults with CF, as an add-on therapy to standard practice, in the EU, UK, and Australia. In 2020, dry powder mannitol received FDA approval as an add-on maintenance therapy for adults with CF (23). In contrast, in patients with NCFB, a 52-week international trial assessed dry powder mannitol in 461 subjects and found no significant difference in exacerbation rates between the study and control groups (23). In addition, a systematic review of patients with NCFB found no significant improvements in lung function, quality of life, exacerbation rates, and health care utilization with mannitol administered as a dry powder inhaler (24, 25). Another class of mucolytics is N-acetylcysteine and other thiol derivatives that break disulfide bonds leading to reduced mucus viscosity. A Cochrane Review identified clinical trials of nebulized thiol derivatives and, while they were generally well tolerated, no significant benefit was observed in patients with CF (26).

Dornase alfa (Pulmozyme, Genentech, San Francisco, CA, USA) is a purified solution of the recombinant enzyme, human DNase, which reduces mucus viscosity by cleaving airway extracellular DNA released from neutrophils. A systematic review examined 19 trials involving infants to adults with CF and the authors reported improvements in lung function and reduced exacerbation rates (27). For effective lower airway deposition, dornase alfa is administered via regulatory agency-approved devices including Pari eRapid (vibrating mesh) and jet nebulizer and compressor systems; Pari-Proneb, Pari Baby, Pulmo-Aide, Mobilaire, and Porta-Neb (9). In contrast, nebulized dornase alfa has not been shown to be effective in patients with NCFB. A multicenter study compared twice daily dornase alfa and placebo over 6 months in 349 adults with NCFB and found that the use of dornase alfa was associated with more frequent exacerbations and a greater decline in $FEV_1$ (28). Thus, while there are clinical similarities among patients with bronchiectasis, extrapolation of clinical trial data from the CF population to the non-CF population is not recommended.

## ANTIBIOTICS

Since 1945, several antibiotics have been administered by inhalation for the treatment of chronic airway infections (Table 12.1) (29). In the last decade of the

## Table 12.1: Approved Antibiotic Formulation and Delivery Devices

| Drug | Brand Name | Manufacturer | Formulation | Device |
|------|-----------|-------------|-------------|--------|
| Aztreonam | Cayston | Gilead | Solution | Mesh nebulizer |
| Colistin | Colobreathe | Forest Labs | Powder | Turbospin |
| Colistin | ColoMycin | Xellia | Solution | Jet and mesh nebulizer |
| Tobramycin | TOBI | Novartis | Solution | Jet nebulizer |
| Tobramycin | TOBI | Novartis | Powder | T-326 inhaler |
| Tobramycin | Bramitob/Bethkis Tobramycin USP | Chiesi, Teva | Solution | Jet nebulizer |

## Table 12.2: Inhaled Antibiotics for the Treatment of Cystic Fibrosis Bronchiectasis

| Author & Publication Year | Drug Dose & Frequency | Delivery Device | Subjects (N) | Primary Outcomes | Results |
|---|---|---|---|---|---|
| Ramsey, 1999 | Tobramycin 300 mg bid Administered on 28-day cycle | PARI LC PLUS jet nebulizer & Pulmo-Aide compressor | 520 | Lung function (FEV1) and density of *Pseudomonas aeruginosa* in sputum | At 6 months, nebulized tobramycin improved lung function, reduced hospitalizations and reduced sputum density of *Pseudomonas* |
| Konstan, 2010 | Tobramycin powder 112 mg bid compared to tobramycin 300 mg bid | T-326 Inhaler: Dry powder inhaler PARI LC PLUS jet nebulizer & Pulmo-Aide compressor | 553 | Safety & efficacy: Lung function (FEV1), density of *Pseudomonas*, antibiotic use, administration time between nebulized tobramycin and DPI | At 24 weeks, DPI tobramycin had comparable safety and efficacy profile to nebulized tobramycin. DPI treatment time was less (5.6 min vs 19.7 min) |
| McCoy, 2008 | Aztreonam lysine 75 mg bid – tid Administered on 28-day cycle | Pari LC PLUS jet nebulizer | 246 | Clinical worsening: time to need for additional anti-pseudomonal antibiotics for exacerbations | At 84 days of follow up, nebulized aztreonam delayed need for antibiotic therapy, improved lung function, symptoms and reduced sputum density of *Pseudomonas* |
| Schuster, 2012 | Micronised Colistimethate 1,662,500 IU bid compared to tobramycin 300 mg bid | Dry powder inhaler Pari LC PLUS jet nebulizer with suitable compresser | 380 | Lung function (FEV1) from baseline at 24 weeks, adverse events, medication compliance | DPI colistimethate was non-inferior compared to nebulized tobramycin solution Cough and abnormal taste more frequent with colistimethate DPI |

*Abbreviations:* FEV1 = forced expiratory volume in 1 second; DPI = dry powder inhaler.

# Table 12.3: A Closer Look at Inhaled Delivery Systems

| Device Name | Description | Instructions for Use |
|---|---|---|
| TOBI Podhaler | • Dry powder inhaler<br>• Manufactured by BGP Products Operation GmbH (Vitaris), Steinhausen, Switzerland | • Store capsules in blister cards; remove only immediately before use<br>• Wash and dry hands<br>• Unscrew the lid and body of mouthpiece in counterclockwise direction<br>• Place one capsule in chamber at top of podhaler device<br>• Put mouthpiece back on and screw tightly in clockwise fashion<br>• Press the blue button all the way down one time only<br>• Breathe out all the way. Place mouth over mouthpiece with tight seal. Inhale deeply with single breath. Hold for 10 seconds, and exhale slowly<br>• Repeat second inhalation using same capsule<br>• Confirm used capsule is pierced and empty. Toss it away<br>• Repeat three more times until full dose is taken<br>• Wipe mouthpiece with clean cloth<br>• Place lid back on and store at room temperature between 68 and 77 degrees Fahrenheit |
| Turbospin | • Dry powder inhaler<br>• Manufactured by Forest Laboratories, New York, NY, USA | • Remove the cap and unscrew the mouthpiece<br>• Insert capsule into chamber with widest end first<br>• Put mouthpiece back on and screw tightly<br>• To pierce the capsule, hold mouthpiece upright and gently push the piston upwards until the visible line is reached. This locks the capsule in place<br>• Continue pushing the piston as far as it will go and then release. Do this only once<br>• Breathe out all the way. Place mouth over mouthpiece with tight seal. Inhale deeply with single breath. Hold for 10 seconds, and exhale slowly<br>• Repeat second inhalation using same capsule<br>• Check capsule has been emptied. Rinse mouth with water<br>• Unscrew mouthpiece, then remove and discard empty capsule |
| PARI eFlow | • Electronic nebulizer<br>• Manufactured by PARI Innovative Manufacturers, Midlothian, VA, USA | • Pour medication into reservoir as prescribed. Do not overfill<br>• Attach medication cap; it will snap audibly into place<br>• Press cap down gently and twist it clockwise<br>• Link nebulizer handset to control unit with connecting cord<br>• Place mouth over mouthpiece. Press on/off button on the control unit to start generating the aerosol<br>• The green LED lights up and emits a tone<br>• Sit in an upright and relaxed position. Breathe in and out as deeply and calmly as possible through the mouthpiece<br>• Keep the mouthpiece in your mouth even when exhaling. Avoid breathing through your nose<br>• Always hold the handset horizontally<br>• When completed, clean and disinfect the system after each use |

twentieth century, clinical trials that examined the effect of inhaled antibiotics for the treatment of chronic *Pseudomonas* colonization in patients with CF showed promising results (Table 12.2) (30). An initial trial examined tobramycin delivery via ultrasonic nebulizer to stable patients with CF and reported improved lung function, reduced exacerbations, and decreased sputum density of *Pseudomonas* (31). A subsequent multicenter trial assessed the efficacy and safety of nebulized tobramycin over 6 months and demonstrated clinical benefits (Table 12.2) (32). Following these reports, FDA approval was granted for chronic maintenance therapy with inhaled tobramycin to patients with CF > 6 years of age. Inhaled tobramycin is formulated for use with a specific nebulizer/compressor PARI-LC PLUS jet nebulizer and DeVilbiss Pulmo-Aide compressor. The Pari-LC is a breath-enhanced nebulizer designed to provide more aerosolized medication during inhalation than on exhalation, an internal valve closes to route air out via the expiratory valve in the mouthpiece. This process results in greater aerosol containment in the nebulizer chamber leading to greater inhaled aerosol mass and reduction in loss to the ambient surroundings (33). A dry powder formulation of tobramycin is commercially available (TOBI Podhaler) that is well tolerated and reduces delivery time with similar clinical efficacy compared with the nebulized formulation (Table 12.3) (9).

Inhaled aztreonam was approved for CF patients with chronic *Pseudomonas* infection. Approval was based on clinical trials demonstrating improvements in lung function, symptoms and decreased density of Pseudomonas in sputum (Table 12.2) (34, 35). Aztreonam is delivered by vibrating mesh nebulization (75 mg) on a 28-day on, 28-day off cycle. Thrice daily dosing (75 mg) with a 28-day cycle is the optimal schedule (35, 36). Currently, inhaled aztreonam is approved for patients with CF ≥ 6 years of age and chronic *Pseudomonas* airway colonization. Inhaled colistimethate, a polymyxin version of colistin, is available as a solution for nebulization. In Europe, it is first-line therapy for the treatment of CF with chronic *Pseudomonas* infection. A dry powder formulation (Colobreathe) is available for use in Europe that delivers an emitted dose of 125 mg from a Turbospin device (Table 12.3; Figure 12.1).

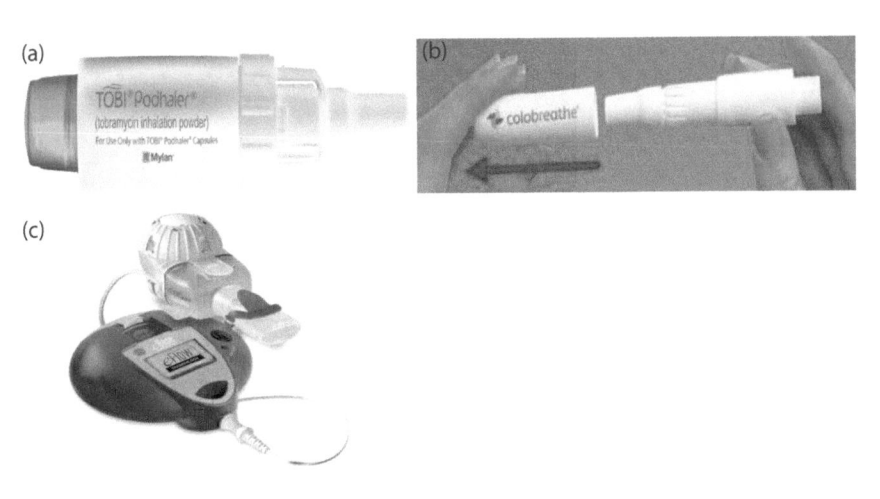

**Figure 12.1** Devices employed for delivery of inhaled antibiotics: (a) TOBI Podhaler, dry powder inhaler; (b) Turbospin, dry powder inhaler; (c) Pari eFlow, electronic nebulizer.

## Table 12.4: Inhaled Antibiotics for the Treatment of Non-cystic Fibrosis Bronchiectasis

| Author and Publication Year | Drug Dose and Frequency | Delivery Device | Subjects (N) | Primary Outcome | Results |
|---|---|---|---|---|---|
| Barker, 2000 | 300 mg tobramycin bid | PARI LC PLUS jet nebulizer and a Pulmo-Aide compressor | 74 | Pseudomonas aeruginosa sputum density, lung function | Significant reduction in sputum Pseudomonas aeruginosa but no difference in lung function in nebulized tobramycin compared to placebo group |
| Barker, 2014 | 75 mg aztreonam lysin tid Administered on 28-day cycle | Pari LC PLUS jet nebulizer | AIRBX1: 266 AIRBX2: 274 | Quality of Life-Bronchiectasis Respiratory Symptom scores and exacerbations | In two phase 3 trials (AIRBX1 & AIRBX2), nebulized aztreonam did not provide significant clinical benefit compared to placebo group |
| De Soyza, 2018 | Ciprofloxacin dry powder inhaler 32.5 mg bid Administered on 14 or 28-day cycles | Dry powder inhaler | 416 | Time to first exacerbation and frequency of exacerbations | At 48 weeks, dry powder inhaler ciprofloxacin 14 days on/off cycle significantly delayed time to first exacerbation & reduced exacerbations compared to placebo; dry powder inhaler 28 days not different to placebo |
| Aksamit, 2018 | Ciprofloxacin dry powder inhaler 32.5 mg bid Administered on 14 or 28-day cycles | Dry powder inhaler | 521 | Time to first exacerbation and frequency of exacerbations | At 48 weeks, 14- and 28-day dry powder inhaler ciprofloxacin cycles showed a trend for increased time to first exacerbation compared to placebo Neither treatment arm showed statistical significance in endpoints |
| Haworth, 2019 | Liposomal ciprofloxacin 135 mg, ciprofloxacin 54 mg | PARI LC Sprint jet nebulizer | ORBIT3: 290 ORBIT4: 308 | Time to first exacerbation | At 48 weeks, nebulized liposomal ciprofloxacin led to longer median time to first exacerbation compared to placebo in ORBIT-4 group but not in ORBIT-3 or pooled analysis |
| Haworth, 2014 | Colistin 1 million IU | I-neb adaptive mesh nebulizer | 144 | Time to first exacerbation | Primary endpoint not reached Colistin increased time to first exacerbation but did not reach statistical significance compared to placebo |

*Abbreviations:* IU = International units; tid = three times daily.

**Table 12.5: Compatibility of Solutions/Suspensions Used Simultaneously with Jet Nebulizers**

| | Albuterol | Budesonide | Dornase Alfa | Ipratropium | Sodium Chloride (5.8%) | Tobramycin |
|---|---|---|---|---|---|---|
| Albuterol | | NR | NR | C | NR | C |
| Budesonide | C | | NR | C | C | C |
| Dornase alfa | NR | NR | | NR | NR | NR |
| Ipratropium | C | C | NR | | NR | C |
| Sodium chloride (5.8%) | NR | C | NR | NR | | NR |
| Tobramycin | C | C | NR | NR | NR | |

*Abbreviations:* C = compatible; NR = not recommended.

*Note:* (a) All solutions should be prepared from formulations without preservatives, (b) physical and chemical compatibilities do not predict the effects on aerosol aerodynamic behavior, (c) decreases in temperature can occur with nebulizers and investigations on compatibility are limited, (d) combining solutions can increase total chamber volume with diminished drug delivery. Modified from Burchett DK. Am J Health-Syst Pharm 2010 (45), Kamin W. J Cystic Fibrosis 2014 (46).

Clinical trials examining inhaled antibiotics in patients with NCFB have not demonstrated significant improvements in lung function, symptoms, or exacerbations (Table 12.4). Early clinical trials demonstrated reductions in airway bacterial density (37–39). Multicenter trials comparing clinical outcomes of dry powder and nebulized liposomal ciprofloxacin in patients with NCFB did not achieve their primary endpoints (Table 12.4) (40–42). A comprehensive meta-analysis reported a decrease in bacterial density and a small but statistically significant decrease in exacerbation rates without an improvement in quality of life (43). Concerns about the diversity of underlying causes of bronchiectasis, variation in exacerbation rate, and study design appear to influence the findings in the non-CF population. Currently, the European Respiratory Society and British Thoracic Society recommend inhaled antibiotics (colistin or gentamicin) for patients with ≥ 3 exacerbations/year with chronic *P. aeruginosa* airway infection (2, 44).

## COMBINATIONS OF NEBULIZER SOLUTIONS

Inhalation therapy by jet nebulization can be time-consuming lasting 10 to 15 minutes per medication. To reduce drug delivery time, patients may combine drug solutions in a nebulizer chamber to shorten administration time. However, certain drug solutions should not be combined as this can lead to incompatibilities that may alter drug efficacy. Clinicians should be aware of these drug compatibilities and Table 12.5 provides guidance regarding the compatibility of various drug solutions for nebulization (45, 46).

## CONCLUSION

Inhaled therapies are commonly employed in patients with bronchiectasis and have shown beneficial effects in patients with CF bronchiectasis. However, similar improvements in clinical outcomes with inhaled therapies have not been reported in patients with non-cystic fibrosis bronchiectasis.

## REFERENCES

1. Imam JS, Duarte AG. Non-CF bronchiectasis: Orphan disease no longer. Respir Med 2020;166(105940):105940.
2. Polverino E, Goeminne PC, McDonnell MJ, et al. European Respiratory Society guidelines for the management of adult bronchiectasis. Eur Respir J 2017;50(3):1700629.
3. Cystic Fibrosis Foundation. Chronic medications to maintain lung health clinical care guidelines. [cited 2022 Jun 3]. Available from: https://www.cff.org/chronic-medications-maintain-lung-health-clinical-care-guidelines
4. Aksamit TR, O'Donnell AE, Barker A, et al. Adult patients with bronchiectasis: A first look at the US Bronchiectasis Research Registry. Chest 2017;151(5):982–992. DOI:10.1016/j.chest.2016.10.055
5. Franco F, Sheikh A, Greenstone M. Short acting beta-2 agonists for bronchiectasis. Cochrane Database Syst Rev 2003;(3):CD003572.
6. Martínez-García M, Oscullo G, García-Ortega A, et al. Rationale and clinical use of bronchodilators in adults with bronchiectasis. Drugs 2022;82(1):1–13.
7. Restrepo RD. Inhaled adrenergics and anticholinergics in obstructive lung disease: Do they enhance mucociliary clearance? Respir Care 2007;52(9):1159–1173; discussion 1173–1175.
8. Daniels T, Mills N, Whitaker P. Nebuliser systems for drug delivery in cystic fibrosis. Cochrane Database Syst Rev 2013;(4):CD007639.

9. Anderson PJ. Cystic fibrosis and bronchiectasis. In: Dhand R, editor. ISAM Textbook of Aerosol Medicine. Knoxville (TN): International Society for Aerosols in Medicine; 2016. p. e755–e780. ISBN 978-0-9963711-0-0.

10. Mogayzel PJ Jr, Naureckas ET, Robinson KA, et al. Cystic fibrosis pulmonary guidelines. Chronic medications for maintenance of lung health. Am J Respir Crit Care Med 2013;187(7):680–689. DOI:10.1164/rccm.201207-1160oe

11. Smyth AR, Bell SC, Bojcin S, et al. European cystic fibrosis society standards of care: Best practice guidelines. J Cyst Fibros 2014;13(Suppl 1):S23–S42.

12. Kapur N, Petsky HL, Bell S, et al. Inhaled corticosteroids for bronchiectasis. Cochrane Database Syst Rev 2018;5(5):CD000996.

13. Elborn JS, Johnston B, Allen F, et al. Inhaled steroids in patients with bronchiectasis. Respir Med 1992;86(2):121–124.

14. Hernando R, Drobnic ME, Cruz MJ, et al. Budesonide efficacy and safety in patients with bronchiectasis not due to cystic fibrosis. Int J Clin Pharm 2012;34(4):644–650.

15. Tsang KW, Ho PL, Lam WK, et al. Inhaled fluticasone reduces sputum inflammatory indices in severe bronchiectasis. Am J Respir Crit Care Med 1998;158(3):723–727.

16. Liu VX, Winthrop KL, Lu Y, et al. Association between inhaled corticosteroid use and pulmonary nontuberculous mycobacterial infection. Ann Am Thorac Soc 2018;15(10):1169–1176. DOI:10.1513/AnnalsATS.201804-245OC

17. Elkins MR, Robinson M, Rose BR, et al. A controlled trial of long-term inhaled hypertonic saline in patients with cystic fibrosis. N Engl J Med 2006;354(3):229–240. DOI:10.1056/NEJMoa043900

18. Wark P, McDonald VM. Nebulised hypertonic saline for cystic fibrosis. Cochrane Database Syst Rev 2009;(2):CD001506.

19. Kellett F, Robert NM. Nebulised 7% hypertonic saline improves lung function and quality of life in bronchiectasis. Respir Med 2011;105(12):1831–1835.

20. Nicolson CHH, Stirling RG, Borg BM, et al. The long term effect of inhaled hypertonic saline 6% in non-cystic fibrosis bronchiectasis. Respir Med 2012;106(5):661–667.

21. Nevitt SJ, Thornton J, Murray CS, et al. Inhaled mannitol for cystic fibrosis. Cochrane Database Syst Rev 2020;5(5):CD008649.

22. De Boeck K, Haarman E, Hull J, et al. Inhaled dry powder mannitol in children with cystic fibrosis: A randomised efficacy and safety trial. J Cyst Fibros 2017;16(3):380–387.

23. Bronchitol (mannitol) inhalation powder [Internet]. Fda.gov. [cited 2022 Jun 3]. Available from: https://www.accessdata.fda.gov/drugsatfda_docs/label/2020/202049s000lbl.pdf

24. Bilton D, Tino G, Barker AF, et al. Inhaled mannitol for non-cystic fibrosis bronchiectasis: A randomised, controlled trial. Thorax 2014;69(12):1073–1079.

25. Tarrant BJ, Le Maitre C, Romero L, et al. Mucoactive agents for chronic, non-cystic fibrosis lung disease: A systematic review and meta-analysis. Respirology 2017;22(6):1084–1092.

26. Tam J, Nash EF, Ratjen F, et al. Nebulized and oral thiol derivatives for pulmonary disease in cystic fibrosis. Cochrane Database Syst Rev 2013;2013(7):CD007168. DOI:10.1002/14651858.CD007168.pub3

27. Yang C, Montgomery M. Dornase alfa for cystic fibrosis. Cochrane Database Syst Rev 2021;3(3):CD001127. DOI:10.1002/14651858.CD001127.pub5

28. O'Donnell AE, Barker AF, Ilowite JS, et al. Treatment of idiopathic bronchiectasis with aerosolized recombinant human DNase i. rhDNase study group. Chest 1998;113(5):1329–1334.

29. Garthwaite B, Barach AL, Levenson E, et al. Penicillin aerosol therapy in bronchiectasis, lung abscess and chronic bronchitis [Internet]. Amjmed.com. 1947 [cited 2022 Jun 3]. Available from: https://www.amjmed.com/article/0002-9343(47)90158-7/fulltext

30. Quon BS, Goss CH, Ramsey BW. Inhaled antibiotics for lower airway infections. Ann Am Thorac Soc 2014;11(3):425–434.

31. Ramsey BW, Dorkin HL, Eisenberg JD, et al. Efficacy of aerosolized tobramycin in patients with cystic fibrosis. N Engl J Med 1993;328(24):1740–1746. DOI:10.1056/NEJM199306173282403

32. Ramsey BW, Pepe MS, Quan JM, et al. Intermittent administration of inhaled tobramycin in patients with cystic fibrosis. Cystic Fibrosis Inhaled Tobramycin Study Group. N Engl J Med 1999;340(1):23–30. DOI:10.1056/NEJM199901073400104

33. Fink JB, Stapleton KW. Nebulizers. In: Dhand R, editor, ISAM textbook of aerosol medicine. Knoxville (TN): International Society for Aerosols in Medicine;2016. p. e617–e655. ISBN 978-0-9963711-0-0.

34. McCoy KS, Quittner AL, Oermann CM, et al. Inhaled aztreonam lysine for chronic airway *Pseudomonas aeruginosa* in cystic fibrosis. Am J Respir Crit Care Med 2008;178(9):921–928.

35. Retsch-Bogart GZ, Quittner AL, Gibson RL, et al. Efficacy and safety of inhaled aztreonam lysine for airway pseudomonas in cystic fibrosis. Chest 2009;135(5):1223–1232.

36. Oermann CM, Retsch-Bogart GZ, Quittner AL, et al. An 18-month study of the safety and efficacy of repeated courses of inhaled aztreonam lysine in cystic fibrosis. Pediatr Pulmonol 2010;45(11):1121–1134.

37. Barker AF, Couch L, Fiel SB, et al. Tobramycin solution for inhalation reduces sputum *Pseudomonas aeruginosa* density in bronchiectasis. Am J Respir Crit Care Med 2000;162(2 Pt 1):481–485.

38. Murray MP, Govan JRW, Doherty CJ, et al. A randomized controlled trial of nebulized gentamicin in non-cystic fibrosis bronchiectasis. Am J Respir Crit Care Med 2011;183(4):491–499.

39. Barker AF, O'Donnell AE, Flume P, et al. Aztreonam for inhalation solution in patients with non-cystic fibrosis bronchiectasis (AIR-BX1 and AIR-BX2): Two randomised double-blind, placebo-controlled phase 3 trials. Lancet Respir Med 2014;2(9):738–749.

40. De Soyza A, Aksamit T, Bandel T-J, et al. RESPIRE 1: A phase III placebo-controlled randomised trial of ciprofloxacin dry powder for inhalation in non-cystic fibrosis bronchiectasis. Eur Respir J 2018;51(1):1702052.

41. Aksamit T, De Soyza A, Bandel T-J, et al. RESPIRE 2: A phase III placebo-controlled randomised trial of ciprofloxacin dry powder for inhalation in non-cystic fibrosis bronchiectasis. Eur Respir J 2018;51(1):1702053.

42. Haworth CS, Bilton D, Chalmers JD, et al. Inhaled liposomal ciprofloxacin in patients with non-cystic fibrosis bronchiectasis and chronic lung infection with *Pseudomonas aeruginosa* (ORBIT-3 and ORBIT-4): Two phase 3, randomised controlled trials. Lancet Respir Med 2019;7(3):213–226.

43. Laska IF, Crichton ML, Shoemark A, et al. The efficacy and safety of inhaled antibiotics for the treatment of bronchiectasis in adults: A systematic review and meta-analysis. Lancet Respir Med 2019;7(10):855–869.
44. Hill AT, Sullivan AL, Chalmers JD, et al. British Thoracic Society Guideline for bronchiectasis in adults. Thorax 2019;74(Suppl 1):1–69.
45. Burchett DK, Darko W, Zahra J, et al. Mixing and compatibility guide for commonly used aerosolized medications [Internet]. Unboundmedicine. com. 2010 [cited 2022 Jun 3]. Available from: https://www. unboundmedicine.com/medline/citation/20101066/full_citation/Mixing_ and_compatibility_guide_for_commonly_used_aerosolized_medications_
46. Kamin W, Erdnüss F, Krämer I. Inhalation solutions–which ones may be mixed? Physico-chemical compatibility of drug solutions in nebulizers– update 2013. J Cyst Fibros 2014;13(3):243–250.

# 13 Inhaled Therapy for Other Respiratory Diseases

## *Pulmonary Hypertension*

*Isaac N. Biney and Francisco J. Soto*

## CONTENTS

## INTRODUCTION

The 6th World Symposium on Pulmonary Hypertension (PH) organized by the World Health Organization defines PH as mean pulmonary artery pressure (mPAP) >20 mmHg measured during right heart catheterization (1). PH is classified into five groups: Group 1, pulmonary arterial hypertension (PAH); group 2, PH due to left heart disease; Group 3, PH related to lung disease and/or hypoxia; group 4, PH due to pulmonary artery obstructions; and group 5, PH with unclear or multifactorial mechanisms (1). In addition to mPAP >20 mmHg, group 1 PAH definition requires a pulmonary capillary wedge pressure ≤15 mmHg and pulmonary vascular resistance (PVR) ≥3 Wood units.

Available PH-specific therapies lead to vasodilation and inhibition of smooth muscle cell proliferation (2) and target one of three pathways central to endothelial function (Figure 13.1): prostacyclin, nitric oxide, and endothelin pathways (3). The Food and Drug Administration (FDA) has approved ten drugs for use in PH. Four of these are available for administration via the inhalational route (4) (Table 13.1). PH-specific therapies are currently indicated for group 1, group 4, and more recently, for a subset of group 3 secondary to interstitial lung disease (ILD) (5).

## ADVANTAGES AND LIMITATIONS OF INHALED THERAPIES FOR PULMONARY HYPERTENSION

Delivering the drug directly to the site of disease allows for high local concentrations, reduces the risk of systemic side effects (6), and potentially decreases cost of treatment (7). Drug delivery to well-ventilated regions enhances blood flow and improves gas exchange (8). Inhaled route limitations include irritant effects on the airways (7), unpredictable breathing patterns affecting the exact dose of drug delivered (4), short half-life of the available therapies requiring frequent inhalations and longer inhalation time, and cumbersome use and maintenance of the delivery systems (9).

DOI: 10.1201/9781003269014-13

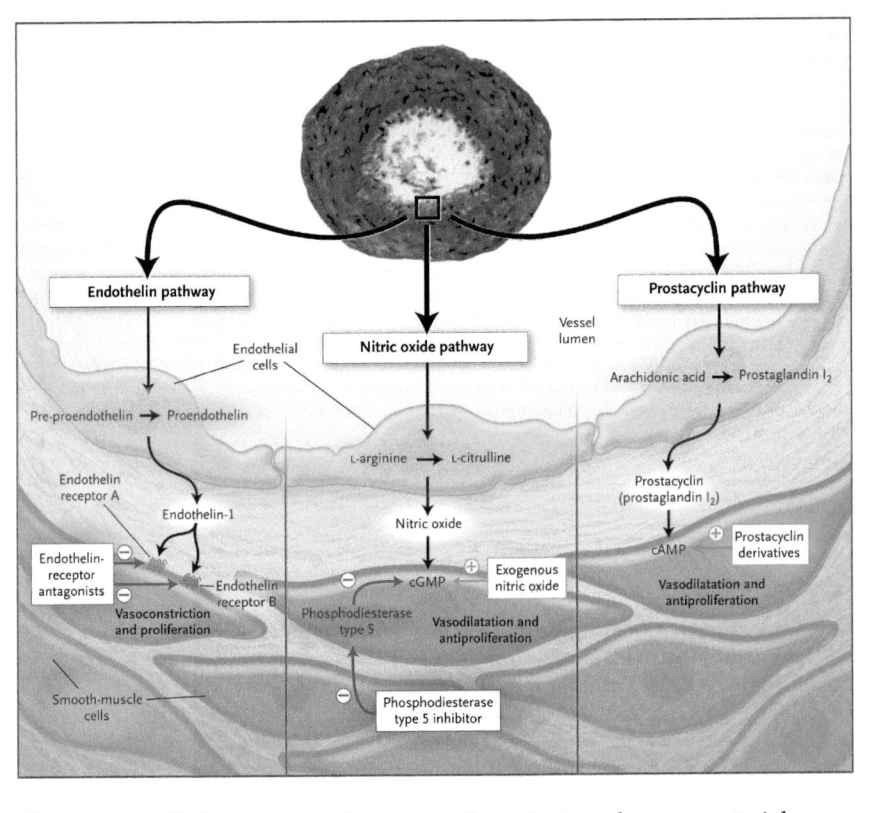

**Figure 13.1**   Pathway targets for current therapies in pulmonary arterial hypertension (PAH). The three major pathways involved in the pathophysiology of PAH; The prostacyclin pathway, nitric oxide pathway, and endothelin pathway are shown. The transverse section of a small pulmonary artery in a patient with PAH is shown at the top of the figure with intimal proliferation and medial hypertrophy. There is decreased production of prostacyclin and endogenous nitric oxide and increased production of endothelin-1. (From the New England Journal of Medicine, Marc Humbert, Olivier Sitbon, Gérald Simonneau, Treatment of Pulmonary Arterial Hypertension, volume 351, pages 1425–1436. Copyright © 2022 Massachusetts Medical Society. Reprinted with permission from Massachusetts Medical Society.)

## PATHWAYS

### Prostacyclin Pathway

Prostacyclin is a prostaglandin synthesized by vascular endothelial cells. It binds to receptors stimulating the production of cyclic adenosine monophosphate, promoting pulmonary artery vasodilation, and inhibiting vascular smooth muscle cell proliferation and platelet aggregation (10). Three prostacyclin analogs are available for inhaled delivery: iloprost (Ventavis®), treprostinil (Tyvaso®), and epoprostenol (Flolan®, Veletri®) (11).

### *Iloprost*

Iloprost was the first prostacyclin analog approved for inhalation use (12). It is indicated for the treatment of group 1 PAH (13, 14). It requires 6–9 inhalations

**Table 13.1: Formulation, Delivery Device, Dose, and Indications of Currently Available Inhaled Therapies for Pulmonary Hypertension**

| Drug | Brand Name (Manufacture) | Formulation | Delivery Device | Dose | Indication |
|---|---|---|---|---|---|
| Iloprost | Ventavis (Actelion Pharmaceuticals | Aerosol | I-neb AAD system | 2.5 or 5 µg/dose 6–9 times/day | Group 1 PAH |
| Treprostinil | Tyvaso (United Therapeutics) Tyvaso DPI | Aerosol Dry powder | Opti-neb (Tyvaso inhalation system) Dry powder inhaler | 3–12 puffs (18–72 µg)/dose 4 times/day 1 puff (16–64 µg)/dose 4 times/day | Group 1 PAH Group 3 PAH related to ILD |
| Epoprostenol | Flolan (GlaxoSmith Kline) Veletri (Actelion Pharmaceuticals) | Aerosol Aerosol | Vibrating mesh nebulizer Vibrating mesh nebulizer | 10–50 ng/kg/min | Vasoreactivity testing[a] PH in critically ill patients[a] |
| Nitric oxide | N/A Vero biotech | Gas | Cylinder-based systems Genosyl DS Disposable cassette | 5–40 ppm 1–80 ppm | Vasoreactivity testing[a] PH in critically ill patients[a] |

[a] Off-label application.

*Abbreviations:* AAD = adaptive aerosol delivery, DPI = dry powder inhaler, DS = delivery system, ILD = interstitial lung disease, PAH = pulmonary arterial hypertension, PH = pulmonary hypertension.

a day of either 2.5 or 5 µg dose per treatment to maintain therapeutic levels (4) given its 20–30-minute half-life (15).

*Efficacy*

Iloprost approval for PAH was based on a study showing improvement in a combined endpoint of at least one New York Heart Association class and at least a 10% increase in 6-minute walk distance (6MWD) (16).

*Delivery Devices*

In the United States (US) and the European Union (EU), inhaled iloprost is administered using the I-neb adaptive aerosol delivery (AAD) system (Phillips Respironics Ltd., UK) (13, 17). This device is a small, portable, light, and quiet delivery system coupling a vibrating mesh nebulizer platform with AAD technology (Figure 13.2A). The I-neb AAD system delivers a precise dose by pulsing the aerosol during the first 50–80% of the inhalation and adapting the delivery to the patient's breathing pattern (18). Synchronization with inspiration helps avoid waste during exhalation and allows the dose delivered to be reasonably predicted (19). The performance of the I-neb AAD system has been confirmed by *in vitro* studies in which the measured delivered doses of the 2.5 and 5 µg metered iloprost doses were 2.8 and 4.9 µg, respectively (20). The I-neb device provides visual, auditory, and tactile

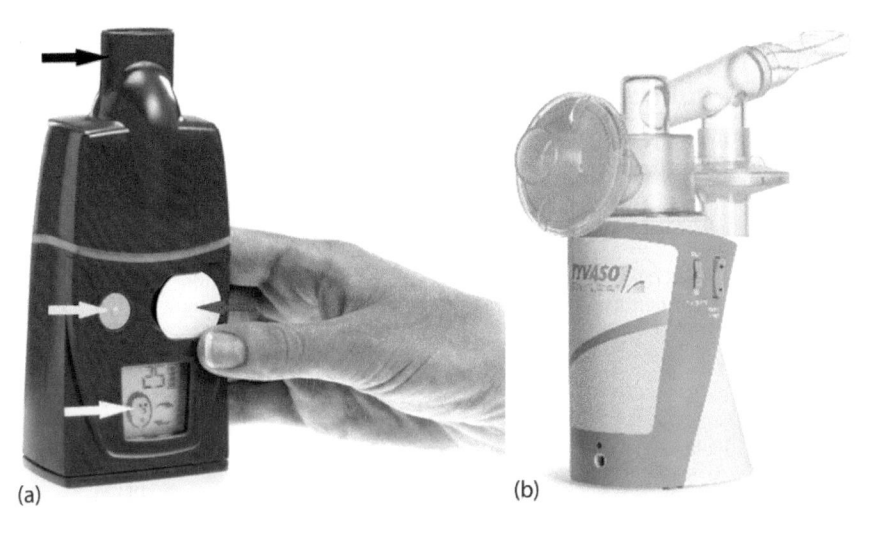

**Figure 13.2** (a, b) The I-neb adaptive aerosol delivery system (a) showing the on button (yellow arrow), display screen (white arrow), dosing disc (red arrow), and the mouthpiece (black arrow). (Republished with permission of Daedalus Enterprises Inc., from inhaled therapies for pulmonary hypertension, Hill et al., Respiratory Care, volume 60, issue 6, ©2015), and the TYVASO inhalation system. (b) The run/program switch allows the patient to set the number of breaths and deliver the dose. The volume/breaths toggle button increases or decreases the volume of the prompts or the number of breaths to be delivered when the switch is set to run or program, respectively. (Used with permission. ©2022 United Therapeutics Corporation.)

feedback after each inhalation and after the programmed dose is completed. Moreover, it can also monitor patient adherence (19). Disadvantages of the I-neb device include the time for each treatment (up to 10 minutes) and the need for thorough cleaning after each use to maintain the function of the vibrating mesh (21, 22). Instructions for using the I-neb are shown in Table 13.2.

BREELIB™ (Vectura Group plc Chippenham, UK) is a recently introduced nebulizer. Iloprost delivery with BREELIB™ was well tolerated in a recent study of PAH patients with the delivery of 5 µg of iloprost in a median duration of 2.6 minutes (21). The BREELIB™ has a vibrating mesh aerosol generator that offers a breath-triggered aerosol bolus followed by aerosol-free air. The speed of inhalation is restricted by a mechanical flow-limitation valve and feedback is provided when the target inhalation volume is reached. This ensures the delivery of an exact and reproducible dose (22). It was approved in the EU in 2016. Recent data confirmed its ability to provide an acute hemodynamic response with delivery of iloprost (23).

### Treprostinil

Treprostinil can be administered via subcutaneous, intravenous (IV), inhaled, and oral routes (24). Inhaled treprostinil (iTRE) is indicated for the treatment of group 1 PAH and group 3 ILD-related PH (14, 25). It is administered four times daily and is the most stable of the prostacyclin analogues, with hemodynamic effects observed beyond 3 hours post-inhalation (26).

## Table 13.2: Instructions for Using the I-neb Adaptive Aerosol Delivery (AAD) System and the Tyvaso Inhalation System

| Device | Instructions |
|---|---|
| I-neb AAD system | 1. Charge the battery for 3–6 hours<br>2. Insert the prescribed dosing disc<br>3. Assemble the device<br>4. Turn on the device and wait until the start-up screen appears which will show the dose about to be taken<br>5. Hold the I-neb horizontally with the display screen facing down<br>6. Seal your lips around the mouthpiece and breathe in and out through your mouth<br>7. After a few breaths, the device will start delivering a medication, this will be felt as a vibration with each breath<br>8. Continue to breathe through the device until the buzzer is heard which indicates treatment is complete<br>9. Removing the mouthpiece from the mouth will pause the treatment |
| Tyvaso inhalation system | 1. The prescribed number of breaths should be set<br>2. Load the medication cup and assemble the device<br>3. Power on the device, if the internal battery is too low to deliver the full treatment, plug in the device<br>4. Hold the device upright, the display screen should be visible, and avoid covering the bottom of the device so the audio speaker is not blocked<br>5. Push the start button, when prompted, exhale to prepare to inhale<br>6. When prompted to inhale, place lips securely around the mouthpiece and inhale for 3 seconds. When the lights stop flashing, remove the lips from the mouthpiece and exhale normally<br>7. Repeat for each remaining breath |

*Abbreviation:* AAD = adaptive aerosol delivery

### Efficacy

iTRE approval for group 1 PAH was based on a trial showing improvement in 6MWD, pro-brain natriuretic peptide and quality of life (27). Approval for use in group 3, ILD-related PH was based on a recent study showing improvement in 6MWD (28).

### Delivery Devices

iTRE is administered with the Tyvaso inhalation system (Figure 13.2B), the Opti-Neb-ir Model ON-100/7 (Nebu-Tec, Elsenfeld, Germany) (29). This is a hand-held ultrasonic, pulsed delivery device delivering approximately 6 µg of treprostinil per breath (24). The medication is initiated at a dose of 3 breaths (18 µg) four times daily. The maintenance goal is 9–12 breaths (54–72 µg) per dose (30), delivered in 2–3 minutes (31). The system's display screen indicates the programmed number of breaths and breaths left in the current dose, prompts the patient to inhale and exhale, and informs when the treatment session is complete. It requires daily assembly and cleaning, and its maintenance can be burdensome (31). Instructions for using the Tyvaso inhalation system are shown in Table 13.2.

iTRE is also available in a dry powder inhalation (DPI) formulation (32, 33). The FDA recently approved the Tyvaso DPI (United Therapeutics/MannKind Corporation, US) which was shown to be safe and well tolerated (34). The cartridges come in four different strengths (16, 32, 48, and 64 µg) which allows

dose titration. The cartridge is inserted into the device and the dose is delivered in one inhalation (35). Another DPI formulation is the LIQ861 (Liquidia, North Carolina, US), an investigational DPI using PRINT® technology to enhance deep-lung delivery and enable drug administration in 1–2 breaths (31, 36, 37) that is currently awaiting FDA approval.

## Epoprostenol

Epoprostenol was the first FDA-approved prostacyclin for PAH, based on a trial demonstrating improved exercise tolerance, hemodynamics, and survival compared to conventional therapy (7, 38). Epoprostenol is the least stable of the prostacyclins. Its half-life is 3–5 minutes and is administered by continuous IV infusion (39, 40). The IV formulation can be aerosolized and used therapeutically off-label. However, it requires continuous nebulization due to its short half-life, making it impractical for long-term use (4, 7).

### *Drug Delivery and Efficacy*

Vibrating mesh nebulizers are used to administer inhaled epoprostenol (iEPO), with no delivery system specifically designed for this purpose (41, 42). Jet nebulizers have been used but their inherent properties affect dose delivery (43). In mechanically ventilated patients, the vibrating mesh nebulizer is placed within the inspiratory limb, or at the humidifier inlet or outlet. Placement at the humidifier inlet/outlet results in higher drug deposition. Placement at the inlet prevents variability of drug deposition with tidal volume (Figure 13.3) (41). iEPO can also be delivered to patients on non-invasive positive pressure ventilation (NIPPV) and on high-flow nasal cannula (HFNC). The nebulizer is connected to the distal end of the NIPPV circuit and on the dry side of the

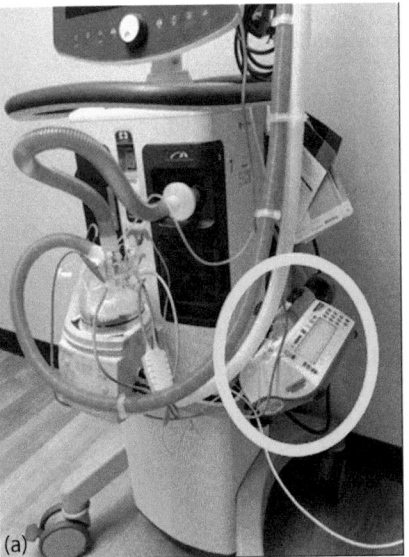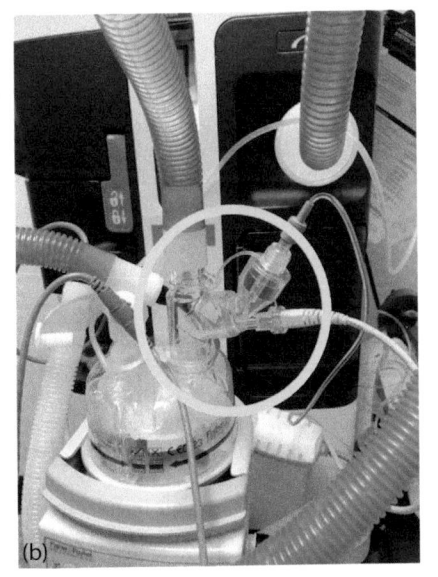

**Figure 13.3** (a, b) Medfusion 3500 syringe pump (aqua circle 3a) used to deliver epoprostenol solution using a vibrating mesh nebulizer (aqua circle 3b) placed at the humidifier inlet (dry side) in a mechanical ventilation circuit.

HFNC humidifier (44, 45). If delivered with HFNC, the inhaled dose is higher when gas flow is set below the patient's inspiratory flow (46).

iEPO has been shown to consistently reduce pulmonary arterial pressures (PAP) in patients undergoing cardiac surgery, heart and lung transplantation, and patients with nonspecific critical illnesses. The clinical significance of these findings is unknown (47). In critically ill patients, continuous administration of epoprostenol allows for dose titration (48).

## Nitric Oxide Pathway

Nitric oxide (NO) is a highly diffusible gas produced by vascular endothelial cells. It binds to and activates soluble guanylate cyclase resulting in vasodilation. It also inhibits platelet aggregation and has antiproliferative and anti-inflammatory effects (4). Given its very short half-life (seconds), it can be delivered by inhalation to exert local effects on the pulmonary vasculature with little or no systemic absorption (49).

## Inhaled Nitric Oxide

Inhaled NO (iNO) is only approved for the treatment of PAH in newborns in both the US and EU. In adults, iNO is used off-label for vasoreactivity testing during the hemodynamic assessment of PAH patients (1).

### Drug Delivery and Efficacy

iNO is used in cardiac surgery and in heart or lung transplantation, decreasing PAP and PVR with effects similar to iEPO (50). Small uncontrolled studies have examined the long-term use of iNO in pediatric and adult patients, but no large, randomized trials are available (51–55). Drawbacks to the use of iNO include its cost and rebound PH crises from abrupt discontinuation (7).

Most available iNO delivery systems are cylinder-based with pressurized NO buffered with an inert gas. They can deliver iNO continuously or in a pulsed fashion synced with respiration (56). iNO can be administered to mechanically ventilated patients and to spontaneously breathing patients by either face mask or nasal prongs (7, 56). The concentration of nitrogen dioxide ($NO_2$), a toxic metabolite, is monitored to ensure safe levels are maintained. The FDA has recently approved the Genosyl delivery system (Vero Biotech, Atlanta, Georgia: https://www.vero-biotech.com/) a portable device that generates NO from $NO_2$ using an ascorbic acid cartridge (56).

## CONCLUSION

Drug administration by the inhalational route for PAH offers unique advantages by delivering medication directly to the pulmonary vasculature. Iloprost and treprostinil are approved for the management of PAH currently delivered by nebulization. Time required for treatment administration and maintenance of the delivery device are major drawbacks of the currently available systems. The recent introduction of a DPI formulation of treprostinil may help mitigate some of the challenges. Epoprostenol and nitric oxide are used off-label in the inpatient setting but the need for continuous administration is a major limitation for chronic management of PAH.

## ABBREVIATIONS

**FDA**    Food and Drug Administration
**HFNC**    High-flow nasal cannula
**iEPO**    Inhaled epoprostenol
**ILD**    Interstitial lung disease

| iNO | Inhaled nitric oxide |
|---|---|
| iTRE | Inhaled treprostinil |
| IV | Intravenous |
| mPAP | Mean pulmonary artery pressure |
| NIPPV | Non-invasive positive pressure ventilation |
| NO | Nitric oxide |
| PAH | Pulmonary arterial hypertension |
| PH | Pulmonary hypertension |
| PVR | Pulmonary vascular resistance |
| US | United States |
| WU | Wood units |

## REFERENCES

1. Simonneau G, Montani D, Celermajer DS. et al. Haemodynamic definitions and updated clinical classification of pulmonary hypertension. Eur Respir J 2019;53(1):1801913.
2. Sommer N, Ghofrani HA, Pak O. et al. Current and future treatments of pulmonary arterial hypertension. Br J Pharmacol 2021;178(1):6–30.
3. Galiè N, Channuck RN, Frantz RP. et al. Risk stratification and medical therapy of pulmonary arterial hypertension. Eur Respir J 2019;53(1):1801889.
4. Keshavarz A, Kadry H, Alobaida A. et al. Newer approaches and novel drugs for inhalational therapy for pulmonary arterial hypertension. Expert Opin Drug Deliv 2020;17(4):439–461.
5. Saunders H, Helgeson SA, Abdelrahim A. et al. Comparing diagnosis and treatment of pulmonary hypertension patients at a pulmonary hypertension center versus community centers. Diseases 2022;10(1):5.
6. Labiris NR, Dolovich MB. Pulmonary drug delivery. Part I: Physiological factors affecting therapeutic effectiveness of aerosolized medications. Br J Clin Pharmacol 2003;56(6):588–599.
7. Hill NS, Preston IR, Roberts KE. Inhaled therapies for pulmonary hypertension. Respir Care 2015;60(6):794–802; discussion 802–805.
8. Baradia D, Khatri N, Trehan S. et al. Inhalation therapy to treat pulmonary arterial hypertension. Pharm Pat Anal 2012;1(5):577–588.
9. Gessler T. Inhalation of repurposed drugs to treat pulmonary hypertension. Adv Drug Deliv Rev 2018;133:34–44.
10. Mandras S, Kovacs G, Olschewski H. et al. Combination therapy in pulmonary arterial hypertension-targeting the nitric oxide and prostacyclin pathways. J Cardiovasc Pharmacol Ther 2021;26(5):453–462.
11. Liu K, Wang H, Yu SJ. et al. Inhaled pulmonary vasodilators: A narrative review. Ann Transl Med 2021;9(7):597.
12. McLaughlin VV, Palevsky HI. Parenteral and inhaled prostanoid therapy in the treatment of pulmonary arterial hypertension. Clin Chest Med 2013;34(4):825–840.
13. Ventavis [package insert]. San Francisco (CA): Actelion Pharmaceuticals US, Inc.; 2019.
14. Galiè N, Humbert M, Vachiery JL. et al. 2015 ESC/ERS guidelines for the diagnosis and treatment of pulmonary hypertension: The joint task force for the diagnosis and treatment of pulmonary hypertension of the European Society of Cardiology (ESC) and the European Respiratory

Society (ERS): Endorsed by: Association for European Paediatric and Congenital Cardiology (AEPC), International Society for Heart and Lung Transplantation (ISHLT). Eur Respir J 2015;46(4): 903–975.

15. Hoeper MM, Schwarze M, Ehlerding S. et al. Long-term treatment of primary pulmonary hypertension with aerosolized iloprost, a prostacyclin analogue. N Engl J Med 2000;342(25):1866–1870.

16. Olschewski H, Simonneau G, Galie N. et al. Inhaled iloprost for severe pulmonary hypertension. N Engl J Med 2002;347(5):322–329.

17. Ventavis [package insert]. Madrid (Spain): Poligono Industrial Santa Rosa; 2021.

18. Hardaker LE, Hatley RH. In vitro characterization of the I-neb Adaptive Aerosol Delivery (AAD) system. J Aerosol Med Pulm Drug Deliv 2010;23(Suppl 1):S11–S20.

19. Dhand R. Intelligent nebulizers in the age of the Internet: The I-neb Adaptive Aerosol Delivery (AAD) system. J Aerosol Med Pulm Drug Deliv 2010;23(Suppl 1):iii–v.

20. Van Dyke RE, Nikander K. Delivery of iloprost inhalation solution with the HaloLite, Prodose, and I-neb Adaptive Aerosol Delivery systems: An in vitro study. Respir Care 2007;52(2):184–190.

21. Gessler T, Ghofrani HA, Held M. et al. The safety and pharmacokinetics of rapid iloprost aerosol delivery via the BREELIB nebulizer in pulmonary arterial hypertension. Pulm Circ 2017;7(2): 505–513.

22. Gessler T. Iloprost delivered via the BREELIB(TM) nebulizer: A review of the clinical evidence for efficacy and safety. Ther Adv Respir Dis 2019;13:1753466619835497.

23. Richter MJ, Wan J, Ghofrani HA. et al. Acute response to rapid iloprost inhalation using the Breelib™ nebulizer in pulmonary arterial hypertension: The Breelib™ acute study. Pulm Circ 2019;9(3):2045894019875342.

24. Kumar P, Thudium E, Laliberte K. et al. A comprehensive review of treprostinil pharmacokinetics via four routes of administration. Clin Pharmacokinet 2016;55(12):1495–1505.

25. Tyvaso [package insert]. Research Triangle Park (NC): United Therapeutics Corp.; 2021.

26. Voswinckel R, Enke B, Reichenberger F. et al. Favorable effects of inhaled treprostinil in severe pulmonary hypertension: Results from randomized controlled pilot studies. J Am Coll Cardiol 2006;48(8):1672–1681.

27. McLaughlin VV, Benza RL, Rubin LJ. et al. Addition of inhaled treprostinil to oral therapy for pulmonary arterial hypertension: A randomized controlled clinical trial. J Am Coll Cardiol 2010;55(18):1915–1922.

28. Waxman A, Restrepo-Jaramillo R, Thenappan T. et al. Inhaled treprostinil in pulmonary hypertension due to interstitial lung disease. N Engl J Med 2021;384(4):325–334.

29. Channick RN, Voswinckel R, Rubin LJ. Inhaled treprostinil: A therapeutic review. Drug Des Devel Ther 2012;6:19–28.

30. Soto FJ, Kravitz JN, Dhand R. Inhaled treprostinil in group 3 pulmonary hypertension. N Engl J Med 2021;384(19):1869–1870.

31. Roscigno RF, Vaughn T, Parsley E. et al. Comparative bioavailability of inhaled treprostinil administered as LIQ861 and Tyvaso® in healthy subjects. Vascul Pharmacol 2021;138: 106840.

32. Voswinckel R, Reichenberger F, Gall H. et al. Metered dose inhaler delivery of treprostinil for the treatment of pulmonary hypertension. Pulm Pharmacol Ther 2009;22(1):50–56.

33. Feldman J, Habib N, Fann J. et al. Treprostinil in the treatment of pulmonary arterial hypertension. Future Cardiol 2020;16(6):547–558.

34. Spikes L, Bajwa AA, Burger CD. et al. BREEZE: Open-label, clinical study to evaluate the safety and tolerability of a treprostinil dry powder inhaler in patients with pulmonary arterial hypertension currently using Tyvaso. Eur Respir J 2021;58(Suppl 65):PA1928.

35. Tyvaso DPI [package insert]. Research Triangle Park (NC): United Therapeutics/MannKind Corporation; 2022.

36. Hill NS, Feldman JP, Sahay S. et al. INSPIRE: A phase 3 open-label, multicenter study to evaluate the safety and tolerability of LIQ861 in pulmonary arterial hypertension (PAH) (Investigation of the safety and pharmacology of dry powder inhalation of treprostinil NCT03399604). J Heart Lung Transp 2019;38(11):S11.

37. Roscigno R, Vaughn T, Anderson S. et al. Pharmacokinetics and tolerability of LIQ861, a novel dry-powder formulation of treprostinil. Pulm Circ 2020;10(4):2045894020971509.

38. Barst RJ, Rubin LJ, Long WA. et al. A comparison of continuous intravenous epoprostenol (prostacyclin) with conventional therapy for primary pulmonary hypertension. N Engl J Med 1996;334(5):296–301.

39. Velitri [package insert]. San Francisco (CA): Actelion Pharmaceuticals US Inc.; 2021.

40. Flolan [package insert]. Research Triangle Park (NC): GlaxoSmithKline; 2021.

41. Anderson AC, Dubosky MN, Fiorino KA. et al. The effect of nebulizer position on aerosolized epoprostenol delivery in an adult lung model. Respir Care 2017;62(11):1387–1395.

42. Li J, Augustynovich AE, Gurnani PK, et al. In-vitro and in-vivo comparisons of high versus low concentrations of inhaled epoprostenol to adult intubated patients. Respir Res 2021;22(1):231.

43. Siobal M. Aerosolized prostacyclins. Respir Care 2004;49(6):640–652.

44. Ammar MA, Sasidhar M, Lam SW. Inhaled epoprostenol through noninvasive routes of ventilator support systems. Ann Pharmacother 2018;52(12):1173–1181.

45. Li J, Harnois LJ, Markos B. et al. Epoprostenol delivered via high flow nasal cannula for ICU subjects with severe hypoxemia comorbid with pulmonary hypertension or right heart dysfunction. Pharmaceutics 2019;11(6):281.

46. Li J, Gurnani PK, Roberts KM. et al. The clinical impact of flow titration on epoprostenol delivery via high flow nasal cannula for ICU patients with pulmonary hypertension or right ventricular dysfunction: A retrospective cohort comparison study. J Clin Med 2020;9(2):464.

47. Buckley MS, Feldman JP. Inhaled epoprostenol for the treatment of pulmonary arterial hypertension in critically ill adults. Pharmacotherapy 2010;30(7):728–740.

48. Muzevich KM, Chohan H, Grinnan DC. Management of pulmonary vasodilator therapy in patients with pulmonary arterial hypertension during critical illness. Crit Care 2014;18(5):523.

49. Abman SH. Inhaled nitric oxide for the treatment of pulmonary arterial hypertension. Handb Exp Pharmacol 2013;218:257–276.

50. Rao V, Ghadimi K, Keeyapaj W. et al. Inhaled nitric oxide (iNO) and inhaled epoprostenol (iPGI(2)) use in cardiothoracic surgical patients: Is there sufficient evidence for evidence-based recommendations? J Cardiothorac Vasc Anesth 2018;32(3):1452–1457.
51. Ivy DD, Parker D, Doran A. et al. Acute hemodynamic effects and home therapy using a novel pulsed nasal nitric oxide delivery system in children and young adults with pulmonary hypertension. Am J Cardiol 2003;92(7):886–890.
52. Pérez-Peñate GM, Juliá-Serdà G, Ojeda-Betancort N. et al. Long-term inhaled nitric oxide plus phosphodiesterase 5 inhibitors for severe pulmonary hypertension. J Heart Lung Transplant 2008;27(12):1326–1332.
53. Barst RJ, Channick R, Ivy D. et al. Clinical perspectives with long-term pulsed inhaled nitric oxide for the treatment of pulmonary arterial hypertension. Pulm Circ 2012;2(2):139–147.
54. Channick RN, Newhart JW, Johnson FW. et al. Pulsed delivery of inhaled nitric oxide to patients with primary pulmonary hypertension: An ambulatory delivery system and initial clinical tests. Chest 1996;109(6):1545–1549.
55. Preston IR, Klinger JR, Landzberg MJ, et al. Vasoresponsiveness of sarcoidosis-associated pulmonary hypertension. Chest 2001;120(3):866–872.
56. Gianni S, Carroll RW, Kacmarek RM. et al. Inhaled nitric oxide delivery systems for mechanically ventilated and nonintubated patients: A review. Respir Care 2021;66(6):1021–1028.

# 14 Regulatory Considerations Related to Inhaled Delivery Systems

*Lydia I. Gilbert-McClain*

## CONTENTS

## INTRODUCTION

The development of inhalation drugs for asthma and COPD has many advantages from both a safety and efficacy perspective. The inhaled route of administration allows for target delivery of the therapeutic to the site of action with the advantage of conferring efficacy while limiting systemic exposure and adverse effects. The advent of inhaled corticosteroids for the management of asthma is a clear example of the advantages of the inhaled route of delivery versus the systemic route of administration. Corticosteroids were first used to treat asthma in the 1950s (1). As a chronic inflammatory condition, the benefits of corticosteroids for the management of asthma are without question; however, the adverse effects of prolonged use of systemic corticosteroids were a limiting factor for its regular use in the maintenance treatment of asthma. The advent of corticosteroid drug products delivered via the inhaled route has the benefit of delivering effective therapies at significantly lower doses with resultant reduced systemic exposure and side effects. These advantages allowed for the use of corticosteroids for the maintenance treatment across the spectrum of asthma severity (mild to severe disease).

Efficacy of inhaled corticosteroids (ICS) for asthma was first reported in an article published in the Lancet in 1972 in which the author described inhaled beclomethasone having efficacy for the treatment of asthma with lesser adverse effects than systemic corticosteroids (2). In 1976, the first inhaled corticosteroid Vanceril (beclomethasone dipropionate, SCHERING) [now discontinued] was approved by the United States Food and Drug Administration (FDA) (3). Numerous single-ingredient ICS products have since been approved as well as fixed-dosed combination products of inhaled corticosteroids in combination with long-acting inhaled bronchodilators.

Since the first introduction of metered-dose inhalers in the late 1950s, many orally inhaled products including single-ingredient and fixed-dose combination products have been approved for asthma and COPD in a number of different devices and various formulations. As with all new

DOI: 10.1201/9781003269014-14

drugs, the demonstration of adequate evidence of efficacy and safety is necessary to support the approval of a new drug product by the FDA and the statutory requirements for drug development and approval are set forth in the Code of Federal Regulations (4). Because inhalation products incorporate a device, they are drug-device combination products, and both components, the device and the drug formulation constitute the drug product. Evidence of efficacy and safety must support not only the drug formulation but the efficacy and safety of the entire product. This means that the drug development program for each inhalation product is expected to generate data that provide information regarding all aspects of the product's clinical performance.

In this chapter, the regulatory considerations that impact the efficacy and safety of inhalation products are discussed. Regulatory issues for the development of generic products are not discussed in this chapter. Development of the generics of these complex dosage forms has unique considerations that are not the focus of this chapter. The FDA publishes product-specific guidance to provide recommendations to drug companies developing generics of orally inhaled products. The reader is referred to the FDA website on Product-Specific Guidance for further information on generic drug development (5).

## DEVICE CONSIDERATIONS: DATA REQUIREMENTS

Consistent with its mission of promoting public health by providing safe and effective medicines for the American people, consumers can be assured that all inhaled products approved for marketing have undergone rigorous testing such that the product has met the statutory requirements to assure the safety and efficacy of the product for its intended use as described in the labeling for the product. Because device changes can have a significant impact on the safety and efficacy of drug-device combination products, as a general rule, drug developers use the product intended for marketing in their clinical studies and this would include not just their pivotal studies but the early dose-ranging studies. Several factors, including the drug substance, (i.e., the active pharmaceutical ingredient), the excipients (if any), and formulation and device characteristics may impact overall product performance and as a result the efficacy and safety of the product.

Device performance and formulation attributes for pressurized metered-dose inhalers (pMDIs) and dry powder inhalers (DPIs) are described in an FDA guidance document that provides information on the data necessary to support the performance of the drug product including the formulation and the device components. Among the many Chemistry, Manufacturing, and Controls (CMC) considerations needed to ensure the safety and efficacy of the product is the assurance that the drug product performance is such that the product delivers the correct therapeutic doses of drug substances consistently throughout the proposed shelf life of the product (6).

Several considerations influence the amount of data drug developers need to provide to demonstrate the adequate performance of their drug product. Factors such as the extent of previous regulatory experience with the active pharmaceutical ingredient(s) (API (s)), novel excipients in the formulation, and the device being used in the drug product can significantly impact the quantity of data needed to be generated to support a new drug product. For example, when a manufacturer develops a new drug product that incorporates a previously approved device, and that contains an active

pharmaceutical ingredient already approved in an inhalation product the amount of data needed to be generated would generally be less. An example of this concept can be seen with the DPI single-ingredient, fixed-dose dual-ingredient, and fixed-dose triple-ingredient ELLIPTA products developed by GlaxoSmithKline. The ELLIPTA device is designed with two foil blister strips. Each blister strip contains the dry powder formulation [the single-ingredient products containing the active ingredient on each strip, the dual-ingredient products containing one active ingredient on each strip, and the triple ingredient product containing two of the active ingredients on one strip and the other active ingredient on one strip]. Delivery of the dose from the device involves the opening/turning of the inhalation mouthpiece which makes the dose ready for oral inhalation allowing the patient to receive the aerosolized formulation (7).

The first of these products approved was BREO ELLIPTA (fluticasone furoate and vilanterol inhalation powder, GlaxoSmithKline, Research Triangle Park, NC) a fixed-dose combination of an ICS (fluticasone furoate) and a long-acting beta-agonist (vilanterol). With the subsequent approval of the other ELLIPTA products, the FDA CMC reviews acknowledged the prior products' approval in the same device, and where appropriate the presence of a previously approved active ingredient. For example, with the FDA CMC regulatory considerations for the approval of ANORO ELLIPTA (umeclidinium bromide and vilanterol inhalation powder), the FDA CMC reviewer acknowledges the prior approval of vilanterol as part of the BREO ELLIPTA new drug application (8).

Another consideration that impacts the quantity of data needed with respect to device issues is that clinical tolerability data from any specific formulation or device may not be directly inferred from another. SPIRIVA® HANDIHALER® (tiotropium bromide inhalation powder, Boehringer Ingelheim Pharmaceuticals, Inc. Ridgefield, CT) was approved in 2004 for COPD. A new formulation of tiotropium bromide SPIRIVA® RESPIMAT® was subsequently developed for COPD and approved in 2014. Although the same active ingredient was present in both of these products, this change in formulation and device necessitated that the drug developer provide new data to support the tolerability of the new formulation, and the performance of the new device, as part of the overall evaluation of the safety and efficacy of the new product for the intended population.

The development of a new drug product that incorporates a new device not previously approved would need more extensive clinical data to support the safety of the product and in particular the robustness of the device. For conditions like asthma and COPD, where typically these therapies are used chronically, assurance of device functionality over repetitive use is essential. Further, approval of a product with a new device that had never been marketed previously raises questions about how the device would function in patients' hands overall. While clinical trials have limitations in addressing all the potential concerns that could ensue with a brand-new device, regulators are intentional about evaluating device robustness and patient-related issues that may pose a problem when new products are placed on the market. The goal of dedicated patient acceptance studies, and human factors engineering throughout the development program, is to ensure a high likelihood of success so that the interface between approved drug products and consumers would be as smooth as possible. Most of these evaluations to assess device robustness and functionality in patients' hands take place as part of the pivotal clinical

trials and long-term safety trials where the effects of the formulation with chronic use can be evaluated, and device performance over the life of the device can be observed over a number of life cycles in a larger number of patients.

For example, the approval of the first RESPIMAT product COMBIVENT® RESPIMAT® (Ipratropium bromide and albuterol, Boehringer Ingelheim Pharmaceuticals, Inc., Ridgefield, CT) inhalation spray, the FDA required long-term safety data to evaluate the performance of the device over time. The approval of Combivent® Respimat® was introducing a brand-new inhalation device into the marketplace for which there was no prior real-world experience. The RESPIMAT® product comprises of two parts: a cartridge containing the formulation in solution and the inhalation device (the Respimat inhaler). The cartridge must first be inserted into the inhaler in order to use the product. Once inserted into the inhaler the cartridge is not removed. The device uses mechanical energy to generate a slow-moving aerosol cloud of medication from a metered volume of the drug solution. Prior to first use, the inhaler must be primed by actuating the inhaler toward the ground until an aerosol cloud is visible and then repeating the process three more times (9).

In the initial new drug application (NDA) submission, the product manufacturer provided data from two pivotal studies of 12-week treatment duration to support the efficacy and safety of the product. The active ingredients of the product ipratropium bromide and albuterol are well-known bronchodilators previously approved in other inhalation dosage forms as single-ingredient and combination products and the safety profile of these moieties is well established. As such, absent a new device, 12-week studies ordinarily may have been sufficient to support efficacy and safety. However, from the FDA's assessment, data from 12-week duration studies were insufficient to assess the long-term performance of a brand-new device. The application was not approved in the initial cycle due to inadequate long-term safety data and the lack of patients' use and handling information for the new drug delivery platform (10). In contrast to Combivent inhalation aerosol, [a standard press and breathe pMDI] that had been on the market for a long time and was a familiar device for patients, the new Respimat product was introducing a device for which there was no prior real-world experience. The Combivent Respimat product was intended to be a replacement product for the then-marketed Combivent inhalation aerosol (a pMDI product propelled by chlorofluorocarbons) and intended for long-term use. The FDA requested data to evaluate the long-term device robustness and performance and patient usability and acceptability as a requirement to support approval (11, 12). The company conducted a 48-week long-term safety and patient acceptability study that focused on the evaluation of device performance and patient acceptability of the Respimat product compared to the Combivent pMDI and albuterol and ipratropium bromide pMDI products (12).

An example of product changes that led to patient complaints was seen with the introduction of the more environment-friendly albuterol pMDIs propelled by hydrofluoroalkanes (HFA) to replace pMDIs propelled by the ozone-depleting chlorofluorocarbons (CFCs). Initially, many patients complained that the medication was not getting into their lungs and voiced concerns regarding the efficacy of these products as well as complaints regarding the taste and "feel" of the products (13). Differences between pMDIs propelled by CFC and pMDIs propelled by HFA contributed to these initial complaints as the spray from HFA-propelled pMDIs felt softer than the spray from CFC pMDIs. Subsequently,

FDA posted a "Frequently Asked Questions" page on its website to address complaints about the transition from CFC-propelled albuterol inhalers to HFA-propelled albuterol inhalers. The data from clinical trials with these products confirmed the efficacy of the HFA albuterol inhalers (14). Regular cleaning of the actuator and mouthpiece of HFA inhalers to prevent clogging of the inhaler orifice as well as being mindful of the priming instructions for these inhalers were differences that consumers had to adapt to with the transition to HFA-propelled pMDI inhalers. The labels for these HFA products note the importance of proper washing in that the inhaler may cease to deliver the medication if not thoroughly cleaned and dried (15).

## FORMULATION CONSIDERATIONS

Patients with asthma and COPD characteristically have underlying airway hyperreactivity and may be particularly sensitive to minor changes in a formulation or device. Consequently, paradoxical bronchospasm is a potential safety concern with inhaled products in this population. The Full Prescribing Information for all orally inhaled products for asthma and COPD include a general warning statement about the potential for paradoxical bronchospasm. Impurities in the formulation must be tightly controlled. For pMDIs, potential sources of impurities can be from compounds that leach from elastomeric or plastic components, or coatings of the container and closure system as a result of direct contact with the formulation. FDA through years of experience with these products has acquired a wealth of knowledge regarding such potential impurities (16) and FDA guidance documents provide recommendations for the evaluation of leachables [and extractables] and for setting limits for levels of such impurities in drug product formulations (6).

Although DPIs are more complex device/container closure systems than pMDIs, the potential for leachables is significantly reduced because the drug product formulation in the DPI is [by definition] a dry powder and, unlike pMDIs, does not contain solvent systems such as organic propellants and co-solvents which can facilitate leaching. Dry powder formulations, usually contain the API blended with lactose as an excipient which acts [among other things] to provide stability to the formulation, improve the flowability of the powder during manufacturing, and as a bulking agent in powder uptake from the device during inhalation and aerosolization. Particles of the API stick to the larger carrier particles of lactose by physical forces of interaction and are separated from the carrier when the device is actuated and the powder is inhaled (17).

Lactose may contain milk proteins, and this is stated in the Description section of the Full Prescribing Information for DPI products containing lactose. The presence of milk proteins may be a potential safety issue for people with significant milk allergies. Following the initial approval of Advair Diskus (fluticasone propionate and salmeterol inhalation powder, GlaxoSmithKline, Research Triangle Park, NC) in 2000, there were post-marketing reports of hypersensitivity reactions following administration of Advair Diskus in patients with severe milk protein allergy and the Full Prescribing Information was subsequently updated with a Contraindication and a Warning about this safety issue (18). A case report of a severe hypersensitivity reaction in a child with milk protein allergy following the administration of Advair Diskus was published in 2014 in the Journal of Pediatric Pharmacology Therapeutics (19). This experience is not unique to Advair Diskus and similar Warning and Contraindication statements can be found in other lactose-containing DPI products e.g., ASMANEX® TWISTHAER® (mometasone furoate inhalation powder, Merck & Co., INC, Whitehouse Station, NJ 08889, US) (20).

## DEVICE-RELATED MEDICATION ERRORS

Unlike pMDI devices in which the dose is metered when the patient activates the device and breathes in, DPIs are available as multidose metered devices (e.g., ASMANEX TWISTHALER), single-dose devices (e.g., SPIRIVA® Handihaler®), and multiple unit dose devices (e.g., BREO ELLIPTA) (see Chapter 6). SPIRIVA® Handihaler® is comprised of the inhalation device (the Handihaler®) and the formulation (i.e., tiotropium blended with lactose monohydrate) in single-dose capsules. In order to use the product, the patient must insert a single-dose capsule into the Handihaler with each use.

Following the approval of Spiriva® Handihaler® [in 2004], there were complaints regarding patients' mishandling of the capsules and mistakenly swallowing them rather than using them in the accompanying inhaler devices. Similar complaints with another single-dose DPI product [no longer marketed] Foradil® Aerolizer™ (formoterol fumarate inhalation powder, Novartis Pharmaceuticals Corporation, East Hanover, New Jersey) were reported. The FDA issued a public health advisory recommending that healthcare providers advise patients on the proper use of the capsules and that swallowing them was ineffective (21) and updated the label for SPIRIVA® HANDIHALER® with additional clarifying language and warnings that the capsules must not be swallowed (22).

## COMBINATION PRODUCTS: DEVICE CONSIDERATIONS

Fixed-dose combination products of inhaled corticosteroids and long-acting beta-agonists (ICS/LABA), fixed-dose combinations of different classes of bronchodilators: long-acting anticholinergics, and long-acting beta-agonists (LAMA/LABA) and fixed-dose combination products of inhaled corticosteroids, long-acting anticholinergics, and long-acting beta-agonists (ICS/LAMA/LABA) have been approved in a number of different devices and formulations including pressurized metered dose inhalers, dry powder inhalers in various prototypes, and more recently, a slow mist inhaler platform. Fixed-dose combination products provide the convenience of having two or more medications that a patient would otherwise be taking in two separate inhalers combined in a single inhaler. These combinations have been considered an improvement in the therapeutic armamentarium for asthma and COPD because reducing the number of inhalers simplifies treatment regimens. Such simplification of medication administration for patients has been shown in clinical studies to improve patient compliance and reduce healthcare resource utilization (23, 24).

From a regulatory perspective, there must be assurance, however, that not only these combinations are safe and effective, but that they provide a benefit over the individual active ingredients. Thus, the development of these products must satisfy the regulatory requirement that each active ingredient in the combination makes a contribution to the claimed effects of the combination product and that the combination is safe and effective for a significant patient population requiring such concurrent therapy as defined in the labeling for the drug (25).

For these fixed-dose combination products, device considerations involve [among other things] that drug developers provide data showing a lack of pharmaceutical interaction of the individual ingredients within the device. Typically, such information would ordinarily be provided with data that demonstrate that there is pharmaceutical comparability between the single ingredients as delivered by the combination and the corresponding single-ingredient drug products. In general, this would be achieved using

the same device for the monotherapy and combination drug products and using formulations for the monotherapy products that have qualitative and quantitative comparability to that used for the combination drug products. In addition, demonstrating that the *in vitro* dose delivery and aerodynamic particle size distribution for each of the individual active ingredients are comparable across the monotherapy and combination products are necessary to provide assurance that the dose of each ingredient delivered from the combination product is the same as the dose delivered from the single-ingredient products.

Using exactly the same device and formulation (except for active ingredients) significantly reduces the complexities in demonstrating comparability. However, device sameness may not always be achievable for comparability. Device and/or formulation differences between the comparators can complicate the development of these combination products because it makes the demonstration of comparability [while surmountable] more challenging. For example, with the development of DULERA® (mometasone furoate and formoterol fumarate dihydrate, Merck & Co., Inc., Whitehouse Station, NJ, US) inhalation aerosol an ICS/LABA pMDI propelled with HFA-227, the formoterol monotherapy used in the clinical trials was different from the formoterol in the combination product (Dulera) in that the formoterol monotherapy product used HFA-134a as the propellant, and had lactose in the formulation as an excipient. Additionally, the inhaler device for the formoterol monotherapy product had a different valve than the combination product. Comparability between the formoterol single monotherapy product and Dulera was able to be established through various *in vitro* evaluations of drug-delivery characteristics (26).

Lack of pharmaceutical comparability between the combination product and the monotherapy comparators presents additional complexities to the development of fixed-dose combination products. In the clinical studies for the development of Symbicort® (budesonide and formoterol dihydrate, AstraZeneca Pharmaceuticals LP, Wilmington, DE) inhalation aerosol, a pharmaceutically different formoterol monotherapy comparator was used in the clinical studies. Symbicort is an inhalation aerosol formulation propelled by HFA-227. However, the formoterol single-ingredient comparator used in the clinical trials was the Oxis Turbohaler (formoterol fumarate dihydrate, AstraZeneca, UK Limited) a dry powder formulation of formoterol. A pharmacodynamic approach comparing bronchodilatory effects of various doses of formoterol administered via the Oxis Turbohaler or from Symbicort on a constant background of a fixed dose of budesonide was used to ensure that the formoterol delivered either from the dry powder formulation (Oxis Turbohaler) or from the inhalation aerosol (Symbicort) produced comparable bronchodilation (27, 28).

Ensuring pharmaceutical comparability between single- and corresponding dual-combination products can have the advantage of streamlining the drug development program for combination products that contain more than two active ingredients. For example, with the initial approval of TRELEGY ELLIPTA (fluticasone furoate, umeclidinium, and vilanterol inhalation powder, GlaxoSmithKline, Research Triangle Park, NC, US) the FDA accepted the data generated from clinical trials completed with the dual-combination product, BREO ELLIPTA (fluticasone furoate and vilanterol inhalation powder, GlaxoSmithKline, Research Triangle Park, NC) and the single-ingredient product INCRUSE ELLIPTA (umeclidinium inhalation powder, GlaxoSmithKline, Research Triangle Park, NC, US) to support the efficacy of TRELEGY ELLIPTA to improve lung function in COPD. This streamlined approach to achieve approval of the triple-combination product was made possible because the product developers provided data to support the

pharmaceutical sameness or comparability of the triple-combination product compared with the dual-combination products of the ICS/LABA (BREO ELLIPTA), the LAMA/LABA (ANORO ELLIPTA), and single-ingredient LAMA (INCRUSE ELLIPTA) and ICS (ARNUITY ELLIPTA) products (29).

The full prescribing information for TRELEGY ELLIPTA notes that "comparative *in vitro* data for drug delivery and aerodynamic particle size distribution of the delivered drugs fluticasone furoate, umeclidinium, and vilanterol demonstrated that there were no pharmaceutical interactions, and each drug was delivered in a comparable manner whether administered via a single ELLIPTA inhaler or from separate inhalers" (30).

## DOSING CONSIDERATIONS

As is expected for all new products, establishing the appropriate dose and dosing regimen is of critical importance for orally inhaled products for asthma and COPD. The objective of dose-ranging studies is to select both an appropriate nominal dose and a dosing frequency that would ensure adequate efficacy and safety of the product for the proposed indication in that patient population. Less frequent dosing is one of the ways to simplify treatment regimens and potentially improve compliance with chronic dosing. As such, drug products with long-lasting efficacy that can be dosed once daily instead of multiple times per day are an attractive option for patients on chronic inhaler therapy. Establishing efficacy with once-daily dosing regimens, however, must be achieved without compromising safety or efficacy and dose exploration is always a critical part of this process. Once-daily dosing may not always provide better efficacy compared to a multiple-dose treatment regimen. Flovent Diskus (fluticasone propionate inhalation powder, GlaxoSmithKline) is an orally inhaled corticosteroid approved with a twice-daily dosing regimen. In clinical studies, efficacy for the same nominal dose administered as a once-daily dosing regimen compared to a twice-daily dosing regimen was numerically and statistically inferior to the same nominal dose given twice daily (31).

Sometimes, multiple clinical trials may be needed to select an appropriate nominal dose and dosing frequency that would provide an acceptable risk/benefit profile for the product. The development of TUDORZA™ PRESSAIR (aclidinium bromide inhalation powder, AstraZeneca Pharmaceuticals LP, Wilmington, DE) a long-acting anticholinergic bronchodilator, is an example of how these two elements of dosing (the nominal dose and dosing frequency) factor into determining efficacy and safety. Initial pivotal studies using a dose of 200 µg of aclidinium administered once daily showed that the trough $FEV_1$ (the primary endpoint) was statistically superior to placebo; however, the effect size was only 60 mL. The FDA raised concerns over the significance of this effect given its modest size compared to the $FEV_1$ response seen for other bronchodilators approved for COPD. The drug developer subsequently conducted additional dose exploration and pivotal studies using higher doses, and a twice-daily dosing regimen. A dose of 400 µg administered twice daily demonstrated acceptable bronchodilator efficacy and the product was approved at a dose of 400 µg administered twice daily (32).

When a new product contains an active moiety that had been previously approved for oral inhalation, dosing information from the approved product may be useful to help guide the initial dose selection for the new product. For example, with the development of Spiriva Respimat for COPD, the general clinical pharmacology and biopharmaceutics for tiotropium bromide had already been evaluated with the development of the SPIRIVA Handihaler product, and the appropriate dosing interval of once-daily dosing for tiotropium

## Table 14.1: Comparative Pharmacokinetics: Spiriva Respimat vs. Spiriva Handihaler

| | Spiriva Respimat 5 µg | Spiriva Respimat 10 µg | Spiriva Handihaler 18 µg |
|---|---|---|---|
| **Study 249** | 26.1 | 64.6 | 20.2 |
| AUC 0–6 ss, pg.h/mL | 63.5 | 148 | 52.2 |
| AUC 0–24 ss, pg.h/mL | 561 | 1230 | 428 |
| Urinary Excretion 0–12 h, ng | | | |

*Source:* United States Food and Drug Administration. Application no. 021936 summary review (33).

*Abbreviation:* ss = steady state.

bromide for COPD had been established. Therefore, dosing considerations for the Respimat product were for selection of the nominal dose. An assessment of the systemic exposure of tiotropium delivered from Spiriva Respimat compared with the systemic exposure of tiotropium delivered from the previously approved Spiriva Handihaler product was a key safety consideration. Because these products are locally acting, pharmacokinetic comparisons provide support for the nominal dose selection from the perspective of systemic safety; however, dedicated clinical trials were conducted to establish efficacy and further evaluate safety.

As shown in Table 14.1, data from one of the pharmacokinetic studies demonstrate that the systemic exposure of tiotropium 5 µg from the Respimat is a closer match to the systemic exposure of tiotropium 18 µg from Spiriva Handihaler compared to tiotropium 10 µg from the Respimat. Pivotal clinical efficacy and safety trials supported the 5 µg dose (2 inhalations of 2.5 µg per spray once daily) for COPD which is the approved dose (33).

## HUMAN FACTORS

Device considerations for orally inhaled products also include human factors testing. That is, the evaluation that the device itself will be safe and effective for the intended users, uses, and use environments (34). Depending on the complexity of the device, human factors testing may also include specific patient use studies. The FDA has published guidance on the type of human factors studies and related clinical study considerations that should be taken into account with respect to combination products (35). Dedicated patient use studies were conducted with the Respimat platform to evaluate the use of the device in patients' hands prior to approval. Currently, there are four bronchodilator Respimat products on the market: Combivent Respimat (ipratropium bromide and albuterol), Spiriva Respimat (tiotropium bromide), Striverdi Respimat (olodaterol hydrochloride), and Stiolto Respimat (olodaterol hydrochloride and tiotropium bromide). For the approval of the first Respimat product (Combivent), the manufacturer completed human factors testing and patient handling studies, so these studies did not need to be repeated for subsequent products. The Respimat inhaler is the same device for all the products, but the cartridge containing the medication in solution is different for each product. While the Respimat platform is quite complex (compared to other orally inhaled platforms), this innovation allows for several advantages from the patient's perspective. Once assembled, the product is easy to use as the need for breath coordination (as needed for pMDIs) is not a factor. However, it was noted in patient handling studies that initial assembly of the product (i.e., inserting

the cartridge into the base of the inhaler) could be problematic for some older patients or patients with joint problems of the hand and assistance may be needed with initial assembly (33). The fine particle aerosol mist generated with this platform results in a higher fine particle size allowing for more product to deposit in the lower airways. Aerosol is generated from this propellant-free product when the base is turned 180 degrees and the release button is pressed. A metered volume of the solution is expressed through a nozzle creating a fine mist (36) (see Chapter 5).

## DOSE COUNTING MECHANISMS

Dose counting mechanisms are an integral part of DPI devices; however, the same is not the case with pMDIs. Knowing when to replace a pMDI was a challenge until a dose-counting mechanism was incorporated into the device. Prior to this advancement, unreliable methods such as manually counting doses, and testing whether the inhaler would float in water were some of the measures used by consumers to decide when to replace their inhalers. Such unreliable methods were problematic both from a safety and efficacy standpoint particularly with respect to short-acting bronchodilator inhalers used for quick relief of acute symptoms of airflow obstruction (37). Since the publication of the FDA guidance on dose counters (38), all pMDIs are now developed with a counting mechanism so that patients can confidently know when it is time to replace their inhalers. This is particularly helpful for short-acting bronchodilator products that are not typically used on a regular daily basis.

## PEDIATRIC CONSIDERATIONS

Orally inhaled asthma products for pediatric patients include all of the general considerations previously discussed for drug-device combination products as well as issues specifically related to pediatric patients. Since systemic drug exposure to orally inhaled products cannot predict efficacy or define all aspects of the safety of these products, clinical trials are needed to evaluate safety and efficacy in the pediatric population. In general, dedicated pediatric studies are conducted in patients under 12 years of age, whereas patients 12 years of age and older are included (with some exceptions) in adult asthma studies. Separate evaluations across various age ranges in these pediatric studies are necessary because it cannot be assumed that efficacy in one age range would translate to efficacy across all pediatric age ranges. For example, available data from some short-acting bronchodilator studies show a lack of efficacy in children less than 4 years of age. A clinical trial conducted with XOPENEX HFA (levalbuterol tartrate, Sunovion Pharmaceuticals Inc., Marlborough, MA) in children less than 4 years of age showed no statistically significant difference between XOPENEX HFA and placebo. There was also an increased incidence of asthma-related adverse reactions compared to placebo in that study (39). Clinical trials with Ventolin HFA (albuterol sulfate inhalation aerosol, GlaxoSmithKline, Research Triangle Park, NC) in children under 4 years of age did not establish efficacy (40). The full prescribing information for Proventil HFA (albuterol sulfate, Merck & Co., Inc.; Whitehouse Station, NJ, US) and PROAIR-HFA (albuterol sulfate, Teva Respiratory LLC, Frazer, PA, US) do not describe any studies conducted in children under 4 years of age and state that safety and efficacy in pediatric patients under 4 years of age have not been established (41, 42).

A concern with pMDIs and pediatric patients is inhaler technique, and spacer devices are often used to address this issue. *In vitro* characterization studies must be conducted with spacers to ensure adequate drug delivery when they are used with pMDIs because inhalation times and other factors

may impact drug delivery. For instance, the use of QVAR® inhalation aerosol (beclomethasone dipropionate HFA, Teva Respiratory LLC, Frazer, PA, US) with a spacer in children less than 5 years of age is not recommended because *in vitro* studies showed that the amount of medication delivered through the spacer decreased rapidly with increasing wait times of 5–10 seconds. The QVAR label recommends that if QVAR is used with a spacer device it is important to inhale immediately (43).

## CONCLUSIONS

Orally inhaled products are the cornerstone of the therapeutic management of asthma and COPD. These products are complex dosage forms, and both the drug formulation and device components can impact the safety and efficacy of these products. Both components (formulation and device) are fully evaluated during development and undergo extensive testing to assure safety and efficacy prior to being placed on the market. Consumers can be assured that approval of these products for marketing only occurs after satisfactory fulfillment of all regulatory requirements with adherence to the highest scientific standards.

**Disclaimer:** Dr. Gilbert-McClain serves as a regulatory consultant to the pharmaceutical industry providing clinical and regulatory advice regarding their drug development programs. Confidentiality agreements preclude naming these companies. Dr Gilbert-McClain worked at the Food and Drug Administration in the review division that regulates the development of drugs for asthma and COPD but does not represent the agency and all information discussed in this chapter is in the public domain and the opinions expressed are her own.

## REFERENCES

1. Alangari AA. Corticosteroids in the treatment of acute asthma. Ann Thorac Med 2014;9(4):187–192.
2. Clark TJ. Effect of beclomethasone dipropionate delivered by aerosol in patients with asthma. Lancet 1972;1:1361–1364.
3. United States Food and Drug Administration. Vanceril. Application no. 017573. Approval. [cited 2022 Feb 15]. Available from: https://www.accessdata.fda.gov/scripts/cder/daf/index.cfm?event=overview.process&ApplNo=01753
4. Code of Federal Regulations 21 CFR §312 (IND regulations) and 21 CFR §314 (NDA regulations). https://www.ecfr.gov/current/title-21/chapter-I/subchapter-D
5. [cited 2022 Mar 23]. Available from: https://www.fda.gov/drugs/guidances-drugs/product-specific-guidances-generic-drug-development
6. Guidance for Industry: Metered Dose inhaler (MDI) and Dry Powder Inhaler (DPI) Drug Products. Chemistry, Manufacturing, and Controls Documentation. Draft Guidance. [cited 2022 Feb 16]. Available from: https://www.fda.gov/media/70851/download
7. United States Food and Drug Administration. Application no. 204275. Full prescribing information. [cited 2022 Mar 23]. Available from: https://www.accessdata.fda.gov/drugsatfda_docs/label/2019/204275s017lbl.pdf

8. United States Food and Drug Administration. Application no. 204275. CMC reviews.[cited 2022 Jan 20]. Available from: https://www.accessdata.foda.gov/drugsatfda_docs/nda/2013/204275Orig1s000ChemR.pdf accessed 1/20/2022 https://www.accessdata.fda.gov/drugsatfda_docs/nda/2013/203975Orig1s000ChemR.pdf

9. United States Food and Drug Administration. Combivent® Respimat® Full Prescribing Information. [cited 2022 Jan 10]. Available from: https://www.accessdata.fda.gov/drugsatfda_docs/label/2011/021742000lbl.pdf

10. United States Food and Drug Administration. Application no. 021747. Summary Review. [cited 2022 Feb 20]. Available from: https://www.accessdata.fda.gov/drugsatfda_docs/nda/2011/021747Orig1s000SumR.pdf

11. United States Food and Drug Administration. Application no. 021747. FDA action letter. [cited 2022 Feb 23]. Available from: https://www.accessdata.fda.ogv/drugsatfda_docs/nda/2011/021747Orig1s000Other ActionLtrs.pdf

12. United States Food and Drug Administration. Application no. 021747. FDA Review: Administrative Documents (s) & Correspondence. [cited 2022 Feb 23]. Available from: https://www.accessdata.fda.gov/drugsatfda_docs/nda/2011/021747Orig1s000AdminCorres.pdf

13. Fiore K. Doctors hear gripes about HFA inhalers. MedPage Today. [updated 2009 Mar 11; cited 2022 Feb 23]. Available from: https://www.medpagetoday.com/allergyimmunology/asthma/13227

14. United States Food and Drug Administration. Frequently asked questions. Transition from CFC propelled albuterol inhalers to HFA albuterol inhalers: Questions and Answers. [cited 2022 Feb 23]. Available from: https://www.fda.gov/drugs/questions-answers/transition-cfc-propelled-albuterol-inhalers-hfa-propelled-albuterol-inhalers-questions-and-answers

15. United States Food and Drug Administration. Xopenex HFA. Full prescribing information. [cited 2022 Mar 23]. Available from: https://www.accessdata.fda.gov/drugatfda_dcos/label/2017/021730s039labl/pdf

16. Schroeder AC. Leachables and extractables in OINDP: An FDA perspective. Presented at the PQRI Leachables and extractables Workshop, Bethesda, Maryland, December 5–6, 2005. [cited 2022 Jan 12]. Available from: https://pqri.org/wp-content/uploads/2015/08/pdf/AlanSchroederDay1.pdf

17. Pilcer G, Wauthoz N, Amighi K. Lactose characteristics and the generation of the aerosol. Adv Drug Deliv Rev 2012;64(3):233–256.

18. United States Food and Drug Administration. Full prescribing information Advair Diskus 2008. [cited 2022 Mar 24]. Available from: https://www.accessdata.foda.goc/drugsatfda_docs/label/2008/021077s029lbl.pdf

19. Robles J, Motheral L. Hypersensitivity reaction after inhalation of a lactose-containing dry powder inhaler. J Pediatr Pharmacol Ther 2014;19(3):206–211.

20. United States Food and Drug Administration. Full prescribing information for Asmanex Twisthaler. [cited 2022 Mar 24]. Available from: https://www.accesdata.fda.gov/drugsatfda_docs/label/2021/021067s032lbl.pdf

21. FDA warns on Mistaken Ingestion of Inhaled Spiriva and Foradil Capsules. Medical News. Physician's First Watch. NEJM Journal Watch. [cited 2008 Mar 3]. Available from: https://www.jwatch.org/fw200803030000001/2008/03/03/fda-warns-mistaken-ingestion-inhaled-spiriva-and

22. United States Food and Drug Administration. Spiriva Handihaler. Approval letter 021395s033ltr. [cited 2022 Feb 2]. Available from: https://www.accessdata.fda.gov/drugsatfda_docs/appletter/2011/021395s033ltr.pdf

23. Yu AP, Guerin A, de Leon DP, et al. Clinical and economic outcomes of multiple versus single long-acting inhalers in COPD. Respir Med 2011;105(12):1861–1871. DOI:10.1016/j.rmed.2011.07.001

24. Marceau C, Lemiere C, Berbiche D, et al. Persistence, adherence, and effectiveness of combination therapy among adult patients with asthma. J Allergy Clin Immunol 2006;118(3):574–581. DOI:10.1016/j.jaci.2006.06.034

25. Code of Federal Regulations 21CFR 300.50. [cited 2022 Mar 25]. Available from: https://www.ecfr.gov/current/title-21/chapter-1/subchapter-D/part-300/subpart-B/section-300.50

26. United States Food and Drug Administration. Application no. 022518Orig1s000 summary review. [cited 2022 Mar 28]. Available from: https://www.accessdata.fda.gov/drugsatfda_docs/nda/2010/022518Orig1s000SumR.pdf

27. United States Food and Drug Administration. Application no. 021929 office director memo. [cited 2022 Mar 28]. Available from: https://www.accessdata.fda.gov/drugsatfda_docs/nda/2006/021929s000_ODMemo.pdf

28. Miller CJ, Senn S, Mezzanotte WS. Bronchodilation of formoterol administered with budesonide: Device and formulation effects. Contemp Clin Trials 2008;29(2):114–124.

29. United States Food and Drug Administration. Application no. 209482. Summary review. [cited 2022 Feb 2]. Available from: https://www.accessdata.fda.gov/drugsatfda_docs/nda/2017/209482Orig1s000SumR.pdf

30. United States Food and Drug Administration. Trelegy Ellipta. Full Prescribing information. [cited 2022 Mar 30]. Available from: https://accessdata.fda.gov/drugsatfda_docs/label/2017/209482s000lbl.pdf

31. Purucker ME, Rosebraugh CJ, Zhou F, et al. Inhaled fluticasone propionate by diskus in the treatment of asthma: A comparison of the efficacy of the same nominal dose given either once or twice daily. Chest 2003;124(4):1584–1593.

32. United States Food and Drug Administration. Application no. 202450. Summary review. [cited 2022 Mar 22]. Available from: https://www.accessdata.fda.gov/drugsatfda_docs/nda/2012/202450Orig1s000SumR.pdf

33. United States Food and Drug Administration. Application no. 021936. Summary review. [cited 2022 Mar 22]. Available from: https://www.accessdata.fda.gov/drugsatfda_docs/nda/2014/021936Orig1s000SumR.pdf

34. United States Food and Drug Administration. Guidance for industry and Food and Drug Administration Staff. Applying human factors and usability engineering to medical devices. [updated 2016 Feb; cited 2022 Mar 29]. Available from: https://www.fda.gov/media/80481/download

35. United States Food and Drug Administration. Draft Guidance for industry and FDA Staff. Human Factors Studies and Related Clinical Study Considerations in Combination Product Design and Development. [updated 2016 Feb; cited 2022 Mar 29]. Available from: https://www.fda.gov/media/96018/download

36. United States Food and Drug Administration. Application no. 021936. Response to Device Consult Request. Other Reviews. [cited 2022 Mar 29]. Available from: https://www.accessdata.fda.gov/drugsatfda_docs/nda/2014/021936Orig1s000OtherR.pdf

37. Sander N, Fusco-Walkert SJ, Harder JM, et al. Dose counting and the use of pressurized metered-dose inhalers: Running on empty. Ann Allergy Asthma Immunol 2006;97(1):34–38.
38. United States Food and Drug Administration. Guidance for industry. Integration of dose-counting mechanisms into MDI drug products. [cited 2003 Mar 2]. Available from: https://www.fda.gov/media/71073/download
39. United States Food and Drug Administration. Xopenex HFA. Full Prescribing Information. [cited 2022 Mar 30]. Available from: https://www.accessdata.fda.gov/drugsatfda_docs/label/2017/021730s039lbl.pdf
40. United States Food and Drug Administration. Ventolin HFA. Full Prescribing information. [cited 2022 Mar 30]. Available from: https://www.accessdata.fda.gov/drugsatfda_docs/label/2021/020983s041lbl.pdf
41. United States Food and Drug Administration. Proventil HFA. Full Prescribing information. [cited 2022 Mar 30]. Available from: https://www.accessdata.fda.gov/drugsatfda_docs/label/2017/020503s054lbl.pdf
42. United States Food and Drug Administration. ProAir HFA. Full Prescribing Information. [cited 2022 Mar 30]. Available from: https://www.accessdata.fda.gov/drugsatfda_docs/label/2019/021457s036lbl.pdf
43. United States Food and Drug Administration. QVAR inhalation aerosol. Full Prescribing information. [cited 2022 Mar 10]. Available from: https://www.accessdata.fda.gov/drugsatfda_docs/label/2017/020911s030lbl.pdf

# Index

Note: Locators in *italics* represent figures and **bold** indicate tables in the text.

# Section II   Classical Initial Decisions

## Section III   Product Launch

# List of Abbreviations

| | |
|---|---|
| **3Fs** | Friends, family, and fools |
| **4Cs** | Consumer, cost, communication, and convenience |
| **4Ps** | Product, price, promotion, and place |
| **ACA** | Affordable Healthcare Act |
| **AOR** | Authorized Organization Representative |
| **ARRA** | American Recovery and Reinvestment Act |
| **B2B** | Business to Business |
| **BRIC** | Brazil, Russia, India, and China |
| **BTC** | Beta Test Coordinator |
| **CCR** | Central Contractor Registry |
| **CDC** | Certified Development Company |
| **CDRH** | Center for Devices and Radiological Health |
| **CEO** | Chief executive officer |
| **CER** | Comparative effectiveness research |
| **CFR** | Code of Federal Regulations |
| **cGMP** | Current good manufacturing practice |
| **CI** | Competitive intelligence |
| **CMO** | Contract Manufacturing Organization |
| **CMS** | Centers for Medicare and Medicaid Services |
| **CPI** | Consumer Price Index |
| **CRO** | Contract Research Organization |
| **DoD** | Department of Defense |
| **DUNS** | Data Universal Numbering System |
| **E-Biz POC** | E-Business point of contact |
| **EGC** | Emerging growth company |
| **EHR** | Electronic health record |
| **EIN** | Employer identification number |
| **eRA** | Electronic Research Administration |
| **EU** | European Union |
| **FDA** | Food and Drug Administration |
| **GDP** | Gross domestic product |
| **GE** | General Electric |
| **GPO** | Group purchasing organization |
| **GUI** | Graphical user interface |
| **HHS** | Department of Health and Human Services |
| **HIT** | Health information technologies |
| **IDE** | Investigation Device Exemption |
| **IND** | Investigational New Drug |
| **IP** | Intellectual property |
| **IPO** | Initial public offering |

| | |
|---|---|
| **JV** | Joint venture |
| **KISS** | Keep it simple, stupid |
| **KM** | Knowledge management |
| **KPI** | Key performance indicator |
| **M&A** | Mergers and acquisitions |
| **MCPI** | Medical Consumer Price Index |
| **MRI** | Magnetic resonance imaging |
| **NAICS** | North American Industry Classification System |
| **NB** | Notified body |
| **NDA** | New drug application |
| **NIH** | National Institutes of Health |
| **NBA** | National Bankers Association |
| **NSF** | National Science Foundation |
| **OECD** | Organisation for Economic Co-Operation and Development |
| **ONC** | Office of the National Coordinator for Health Information Technology |
| **OOPD** | Office of Orphan Products Development |
| **PI** | Principal investigator |
| **PMDL** | Pharmaceutical and Medical Device Law |
| **PMA** | Premarket approval |
| **PMN** | Premarket notification |
| **R&D** | Research and development |
| **ROI** | Return on investment |
| **SBA** | Small Business Administration |
| **SBIC** | Small Business Investment Company |
| **SCORE** | Service Corps of Retired Executives |
| **SIA** | Strategic international alliance |
| **SME** | Small and medium-sized enterprise |
| **SO** | Signing official |
| **STTR** | Small business technology transfer |
| **SWOT** | Strengths, Weaknesses, Opportunities, and Threats |
| **VC** | Venture capital |
| **VHRD** | Virtual human resource development |

# Section I

# Development on a Shoestring

# 1

## Risk Is a Four-Letter Word

Do you have a solution to a problem, or do you have a solution looking for a problem?

## 1.1 Introduction

**Commercialization** is profiting from innovation through the sale of or incorporation of a specific technology, for example, high-temperature superconductivity, into products, processes, or services. Commercialization emphasizes activities including product/process development, manufacturing, and marketing, as well as any supporting research. Commercialization, not innovation or invention *per se*, is primarily driven by firms' expectations of securing a competitive advantage in the marketplace [1]. Innovation delivers the benefits of a new method, idea, product, or procedure to customers or clients, whereas commercialization monetizes innovative ideas. For most start-ups, commercializing innovative ideas allows founders and shareholders to reap the financial benefits.

Commercializing a knowledge-based product or service requires a realistic, methodical approach combined with a great deal of perseverance. In this book, we use the terms *technology commercialization* and *technology transfer* as (1) transforming research into practical applications with commercial potential, (2) seeking patent protection for those innovations, and (3) licensing to industry participants via contractual agreements. Commercialization includes extensive market research, competitive analysis, value proposition development, and business plan development.

This book is intended to serve as a high-level guide to key questions and critical issues that will confront you, the founding entrepreneur, as you begin your quest to commercialize your knowledge-based innovations emanating from your laboratory.

### 1.1.1 Invention and Innovation

*Invention* and *innovation* are commonly used in overlapping ways to refer to developing new technology and incorporating it into new products, processes, and services. Confusion often arises from subtle differences in the meaning of each term; hence, for our purposes, these two terms will be defined as follows:

*Invention:* devising or fabricating a novel device, process, or service. Invention is the conception of a new product, process, or service, but not putting it into use. Although inventions can be protected by patents, many are not, and most patents are never exploited commercially.

*Innovation:* the development and application of a new product, process, or service, and assumes novelty in the device or in its application. Thus, innovation encompasses either using an existing product in a new application or developing a new device for an existing application. Innovation includes activities that support dissemination and application of an invention, such as scientific, technical, and market research; product, process, or service development; and manufacturing and marketing.

## 1.2 Commercializing Knowledge-Based Products

Developing, distributing, and commercializing knowledge-based, scientific, and advanced high-technology products reflect a growing worldwide trend toward high-technology industries, including wireless communications, information technology, pharmaceuticals, life sciences, nanotechnology, and education. Commercializing knowledge-based products is a complex undertaking—Figure 1.1 depicts the process of going "from your brain to your bank account."

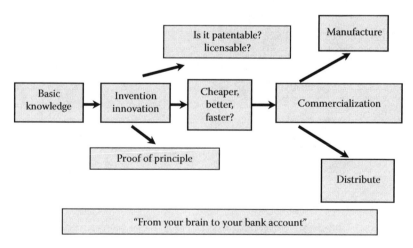

**FIGURE 1.1**
Commercialization of knowledge-based technology.

**TABLE 1.1**

Famous Solutions for Common Problems

| Product Name | Description | Problem ("Need") |
|---|---|---|
| Ronco power spray guns | Gun that washes cars in less than 5 min | Waxing/washing cars simultaneously |
| Chop-O-Matic | Kitchen appliance to quickly cut onions, potatoes, etc. | Teary eyes<br>Time-consuming tasks |
| Dial-O-Matic | Slice a potato so thin you can read a newspaper | Cutting food ultrathin |
| Veg-O-Matic | Slices, dices, and juliennes to perfection | Lower kitchen skills for specialized recipes |
| Feather-touch knife | So sharp it can shave the eyebrows off a NJ mosquito | Incredibly sharp table knives |
| Ginsu knife | So sharp it can cut a cow in half. And that's no bull | Ruggedly sharp large knives |

*Source:* Modified from Popeil, R. *The Salesman of the Century.* Delacorte Press, New York, 1995.

Ron Popeil, the so-called Salesman of the Century, became famous for mass marketing household products on television. Although Table 1.1 lists consumer products, notice that each item is targeted toward solving a specific problem, that is, the "need."

Although you begin your quest as the great specialist with a vision for an innovative product and its associated need, you must become the great generalist and communicator once you have started your company and hired your team (as seen in Figure 1.2). In addition, you must familiarize

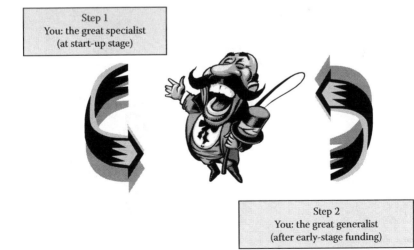

**FIGURE 1.2**
The great secret.

yourself with a myriad of specialties including manufacturing, marketing and sales, legal, accounting, finance, and human relations, as shown in Figure 1.2.

### 1.2.1 Establishing Your Communications Platform

Furthermore, much like Ron Popeil, you must become your company's greatest communicator (i.e., salesman). Who better than you to lead your team to commercial success and its attendant financial rewards (as shown in Figure 1.3)?

In a start-up company, your ability to communicate is the heart and soul of attaining fair value. While a business plan is essential, your emotion and deep commitment to the enterprise's success cannot be conveyed to a potential investor from a business plan or a PowerPoint slide deck. Your communication skills will instill confidence and trust, thereby adding needed credibility to everything written down on paper.

Positioning within the marketplace and communicating value to both investors and customers are critical. Irrespective of whether your company is a start-up or a more mature endeavor, you can achieve these goals in four sequential steps [2]:

Step 1. Develop your investment proposition

Step 2. Identify and target your investor and customer audience

Step 3. Develop your communications platform

Step 4. Maintain constant communications with the marketplace

Team

Commercialization

**FIGURE 1.3**
You: the great communicator.

## 1.3 Risk in a Start-Up Environment

The word *risk* is derived from the Latin *riscare*, "to dare" or "run into danger." Risk is omni-present and involves many disciplines including probability, statistics, psychology, and history. In entrepreneurial terms, *risk* is uncertainty around financial and operating results. In a start-up environment, risk is the possibility of losing a portion of the invested capital, at best delivering less-than-projected results, and at worst threatening the viability of the new enterprise.

Peter Drucker, the management guru, identified four business risks [3,4]:

1. Risk inherent to the business
2. Risk one can afford to take
3. Risk one cannot afford to take
4. Risk one cannot afford not to take

Start-ups face unique risks, and the reality is that only certain innovations may be suitable for the creation of a start-up company. Along with the invention team, management should analyze several factors to determine whether a start-up is the most appropriate path to commercialization.

1. **Demand:** Potential for the core technology to provide a solid platform for multiple markets or product opportunities
2. **Competition:** Identification of other companies that address similar needs or offer similar solutions
3. **Licensing:** Likelihood of interest from existing companies in licensing your technology
4. **Early-Stage Funding:** Availability of capital to build and grow your business, together with the interest, capabilities, and track record of likely investors
5. **Commitment:** Level of commitment and personal involvement of the inventors
6. **Support:** Presence of a true business champion for both your technology and your new venture

Most successful knowledge-based businesses are started by people who already have several years of relevant technical experience. A profound understanding of the technology involved, of customer behavior, and of market dynamics are critical to grow an innovative idea into the minimal level of sales to become financially viable (also known as breakeven or escape sales velocity).

For example, before founding Intel, Gordon Moore and Robert Royce already had several years' experience at Fairchild Semiconductors. Conversely,

**TABLE 1.2**

Examples of Crucial Start-Up Risks

| Within the Organization (Internal) | In the Marketplace (External) |
|---|---|
| Key executive/managerial positions cannot be filled | Sales are only 50% of prediction |
| A key member of staff, such as the head of R&D, leaves abruptly | Inability to obtain patent protection |
| Prototype delays | Costs spiral out of control |
| Failure to obtain regulatory approvals | Distributor partner breaches agreement |

**TABLE 1.3**

Your Risk Mitigation Table

| Risk Category | Issues to be Answered by Team |
|---|---|
| 1. Technological | Does the new technology really work? |
| 2. Financial | Can you raise enough capital? |
| 3. Market | Is the market size large enough? |
| 4. Regulatory | Can you meet FDA, EPA, OSHA, ISO, SEC, IRS, etc. regulations? |
| 5. Operational | Is adequate management in place? |
| 6. Force majeure | Are you prepared for natural disasters, fire, floods, hurricanes, etc.? Can you afford adequate business insurance? |

there are examples (albeit fewer) of revolutionary concepts that have been invested and commercialized by visionaries with no experience whatsoever. Steve Jobs and Steve Wozniak quit their university studies to found Apple, and Fred Smith developed FedEx's concept of "on-time delivery" while still a graduate student in business school. Table 1.2 presents four crucial internal and external risks to consider when deciding whether or not to start a company.

As a start-up founder, your most important goal is to mitigate business risks. Develop a "risk mitigation table" and work to minimize each risk's likelihood and impact. Generally, for knowledge-based entrepreneurial companies, there are six major sources of risk, as shown in Table 1.3.

## 1.4 Your Innovation and Opportunity Recognition

Were you aware that Thomas Edison did NOT invent the light bulb? Not only did 22 inventors have the idea before Edison did, but 22 researchers actually invented incandescent electric lamps before Edison did. Edison did not steal their ideas, but instead improved on their idea by first understanding the market. He realized that a lower-priced and longer-lasting light bulb was necessary if light bulbs were to enter mainstream use, so he and his dream team created the incandescent light bulb, and the rest is history. The

1. Unique selling proposition. "Unique" defined from the customer's viewpoint, not R&D or design departments. Superiority is derived from design, features, attributes, specification, and positioning.
2. Strong market orientation that prevails throughout the entire new product project.
3. Pre-development strategy that includes market and technical studies, market research, business analysis, prototype production, etc.
4. Unambiguous and early product definition. Including target market definition, concept and benefits, positioning strategy, product failures, and prioritized attributes.
5. Clearly specified budgets (including materials, capital equipment, and staff).

**FIGURE 1.4**
Top five reasons for new product successes.

moral of the story is that (s)he who had the idea first doesn't necessarily win. In fact, if your idea is so good, there is a good chance that many others have thought of it before you. The winner takes the idea to market first (first mover advantage), continues development based on customer feedback, and then commercializes and scales the business to achieve escape velocity.

Your innovative idea must appeal to potential investors. You must develop a roadmap, not an advertising leaflet or a technical description, which answers the following two questions: (1) What is the customer benefit? (2) What market problem "pain" does your idea alleviate?

Commercial success is generated from satisfied customers, not from amazing products. Customers buy a product to satisfy a need or to solve a problem—perhaps by reducing effort, increasing pleasure, enhancing their self-image, and so on. Thus, the first characteristic of a successful business idea is that it clearly articulates the need it will satisfy or problem it will solve, and whether it will be delivered as a product or as a service. Marketing specialists often refer to a product or service's distinctiveness as its "Unique Selling Proposition." Figure 1.4 summarizes the top five reasons for new product successes.

## 1.5 What Is the Level of Market Pain?

*What market problem are you trying to solve?* A business idea only has real economic value if people want your product or service and are willing to pay for it at a price that is profitable to you. Furthermore, a successful business idea has a clearly identifiable market need and a target customer group(s).

*How will it make money for you and your investors?* Most products generate revenue directly from sales. In some cases, however, the "revenue mechanism"

- Meets a screaming market need
- Highly innovative or disruptive
- Unique product/service
- Focused to mitigate risks
- Promises high long-term profitability

**FIGURE 1.5**
The five characteristics of a killer idea.

can be more complicated: for example, the product is given away free of charge to the consumer but is paid for by advertisers. Last, a successful business idea clearly articulates how and when money will be made.

To merit the consideration of professional investors, any business idea must meet the "five killer criteria" shown in Figure 1.5. Although investors live with the risk of losing their money, they will limit this risk as much as possible, so a single issue may halt their pursuing a business idea.

## 1.6 Presenting Your Business Idea

The way you present your business idea to an investor will be the acid test of your efforts. Investors will notice and show interest based on content and your professional qualifications. Remember that most venture capitalists, whose time is limited, receive up to 40 business ideas *every week*.

Therefore, your first goal is clarity. Investors will typically not have familiarity with your product's technology or the jargon of your trade, and are unlikely to take the time to understand confusing terms or concepts. Your second goal is conciseness of content and expression. If an investor shows interest, there will be ample opportunity at a later time for detailed descriptions and exhaustive financial calculations.

Developing business ideas is only one aspect of starting a business. Your ideas must be screened and evaluated to determine those that warrant further investigation. Should your product or service be deployed by an existing company, or should a new company be launched?

Entrepreneurs must provide compelling answers to questions such as

- What is the size of the market served by this product?
- Are there competitive products already in this market?
- How does your product compare to and differentiates from competing products?
- Who are your current competitors?

Many concepts may be feasible under the right conditions, and the feasibility tests listed in Table 1.4 will help you determine those conditions.

**TABLE 1.4**

Assessing Your Business Risks and Market Pain

| | Strong | Weak |
|---|---|---|

*Your industry*

What are the demographics, trends, patterns of change, and life cycle stage of your selected industry?

Are there low or high barriers to entry? If so, what are they?

What is the development status of your innovative technology?

What are typical profit margins in your industry?

What is the status of your target industry? Expanding? Contracting?

*Your target market*

Is there a market large enough to make your concept feasible and worth the time and effort to create a new product/service?

*Customers*

What are the current and expected demographics of your target market?

What is your customer profile? Who is your customer?

Have you contacted some of your largest customers?

Who are your competitors and how do you differentiate yourself?

*Product/service*

What are the features and benefits of the product or service?

What are the product development tasks and what is the timeline for completion?

Is there potential for intellectual property rights (copyrights, patents, etc.)

How is your product or service differentiated from others in the market?

*Finance*

What are your start-up capital requirements?

What are your working capital requirements?

What are your fixed cost requirements?

How long will it take to achieve positive cash flow?

What is the break-even point for your start-up business?

*Distribution channels*

What are potential distribution channels and which customers will be served by them?

Are there ways to innovate in the distribution channel?

*Your start-up team*

Can an appropriate start-up team be put together to execute your concept?

What executive and technical expertise does your team possess?

What are the team gaps and how do you plan to fill them?

*Note:* Entrepreneurs are willing to work 80 hours a week to avoid working 40 hours a week.

## 1.7 Sizing Your Intended Market

Technology entrepreneurs face a unique problem of sizing their intended market since they typically develop their business from a research and development (R&D) perspective, often ignoring the intricacies of new or emerging markets. It is difficult to determine the rate at which a new technology will be accepted and the rate at which your innovation may replace existing approaches to solving the same problem.

The rate of market acceptance depends on factors such as

- New legislation and enforcement of existing legislation
- Number of competitors
- Approval from governmental entities (if required)
- Product pricing
- Training required to use the technology
- Capital invested in alternative approaches
- Other synergistic technologies

Factors that affect the rate at which an emerging market adopts your technology create financial risk, and investors are often reluctant to provide significant financing while the market risk is high. Instead, they wait until preliminary customer acceptance is demonstrated before making significant investments. As such, targeting a very large intended market is crucial to attracting investors.

The *market buildup method* is commonly used to size your intended market. Market buildup is a market forecasting technique that involves identifying the set of potential buyers within a particular market and learning their product preferences or choices. Forecasting demand in an emerging market provides companies with a sense of whether the product or service would attract a sufficiently large number of buyers to be financially viable.

Your emerging market demand is the total product volume (1) as a function of a customer group, (2) in a geographical area, (3) during a particular period, (4) in a specified marketing environment, and (5) under a defined marketing program.

## 1.8 Before You Start...

A good idea does not necessarily result in a good product. And a good product does not necessarily result in a successful company. The first

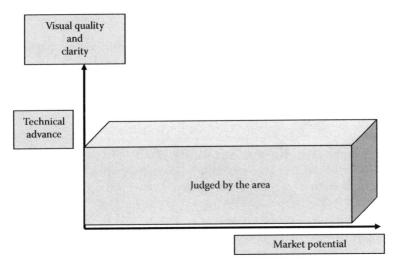

**FIGURE 1.6**
Presenting your ideas convincingly.

milestone in starting a high-growth company is to develop a convincing product that solves a market problem. To do so, you must consider your idea from the investor's perspective, that is, to clearly and concisely demonstrate how customers benefit from your idea, how you will deliver the product or service and in which markets, and how and when money will be made. Last, you must present your idea in a convincing fashion, as shown in Figure 1.6.

In general, most entrepreneurs are "technology driven," whereas investors are "market driven." While technology driven focuses on the scientific or technical merits of the idea, market driven is the profit potential versus the financial risks of the start-up organization. Thus, there is a clear dichotomy between entrepreneurial and investment cultures, with the former focused on cutting-edge innovations and the latter focused on market needs. The entrepreneur must bridge this cultural gap by ensuring that his or her technology addresses a "crying market need."

### 1.8.1 Your Business Planning and Commercialization Channels

Many technology entrepreneurs view business planning as a necessary evil, an admission "ticket" to the commercialization game, but business planning is actually the business counterpart of scientific theory construction, and is the process by which "conjecture is turned into certitude" and "intuition is replaced by facts" [5]. Business planning is the precursor of commercialization, and your business plan and commercialization channels must be clearly communicated to all your stakeholders. There are three broad channels for commercializing your technology:

1. Selling or assigning ownership of the technology to an existing company
2. Licensing the technology to an existing company
3. Starting a new company

   Choosing the right channel is critical. Key variables to making this decision include the nature of the technology itself, the industry it will be applied to, and the objectives of the inventor. Many will consider starting a new company for the following reasons:

- Market potential for the opportunity is worth the added risk.
- Maximizing the value of the technology.
- Desire to work with an experienced business person who can lead the company.
- Existing contacts to create a business team and access to other support and resources.
- Prior attempts to license the technology have been unsuccessful.

### 1.8.2 Key Initial Considerations

Creating a successful new company is difficult, and success is often heavily influenced by factors outside your control. The stark reality is that a very large proportion of start-ups fail. Although creating a new company to commercialize your technology holds the highest risk, it can also lead to the highest reward. Following are items to consider when deciding whether to start a new company:

1. Is your invention a disruptive technology? If not, how would it be categorized?
2. How soon can a commercial product come to market?
3. What is the level of risk associated with this start-up?
4. Does the technology have clear applications and a definable market?
5. Who owns the intellectual property?
6. What will be your role in the new company: full-time employee, advisory board member, executive, or consultant?
7. What are the goals for the company? Is it to grow the company and position it for an acquisition or a possible initial public offering? Or, is it to build a small, yet sustainable business?

8. Will capital from private investment companies be needed? If so, will the company eventually be sold or go public? Private investors rely on these exit strategies to get a return on their investments.

9. What is the current valuation of the company? Valuations are based on several factors, including stage of development, proof-of-concept lab data, whether there is a working prototype, if there are any paying customers.

10. Have you spoken to potential customers? Valuable information includes what customers care most about, needs most critical to address, current solutions (if any) to their problems, and how much they are willing to expend on a solution.

Finally, the following legal steps are necessary before you start:

- Select the legal form for the business (sole proprietorship, corporation, partnership, or Limited Liability Company).
- Apply for federal and state employer tax identification numbers (if needed).
- Obtain the proper licenses that apply to your business.
- Apply for workers' compensation and other insurance through private insurance carriers.
- Register a trade name if applicable.
- Apply for any trade name registration, registration, trademarks, copyrights, or patents necessary to protect your assets.
- Engage and consult qualified advisors in law and taxes as needed.

Legal counsel may greatly enhance the decision-making process when starting a company. An attorney with experience in small business entity formation and equity considerations can be a reliable and trusted advisor.

## 1.9 After You Start...

Firms may encounter difficulties bringing new technology to market at any of several points during the commercialization process. Often, the most difficult stage is converting a prototype into a salable product. In the pharmaceutical industry, for example, a new drug must undergo costly and time-consuming clinical trials with no guarantee of a successful outcome. In electronics, scaling up production using state-of-the-art manufacturing facilities can cost in excess of several hundred million dollars with significant uncertainty as to the time required to achieve full-scale production with acceptable yields.

Small firms face daunting financial constraints in the cost-prohibitive stages of commercialization. Because venture capital and contributions from wealthy individuals (often called angels) are rarely sufficient to these commitments, small firms frequently ally with partners that provide the necessary working capital. As compensation for contributing working capital, these partners may demand patent licenses, equity, and/or other forms of remuneration. Such arrangements are more likely to succeed when the small firm and its partner(s) are in the same line of business. For instance, several large pharmaceutical companies have provided support to small biotechnology firms in return for a license to the new drug. Large companies, by contrast, can manufacture and market a new drug through existing distribution channels with no need to establish a partnership [1].

As shown in Figure 1.7, inadequate capitalization is the most prevalent cause of new product failures, but there are others to consider.

The following legal steps are necessary after you start:

- File returns for both state and federal taxes.
- Comply with all state and federal requirements for withholding and payment of payroll taxes on behalf of employees (if any).
- Comply with all state/federal sales and use tax regulations, as applicable.
- Pay local property taxes, as applicable.
- Obtain a US Employee Identification Number, if needed (IRS Form SS-4).
- Protect the intellectual property that is the foundation of the new company.

1. Inadequate capitalization—biggest reason small companies fail
2. Target market—large enough to be profitable
3. Poor product quality/performance—product does not meet customer needs
4. Insignificant differentiation—product is not a major improvement on competitive offerings
5. Poor execution of marketing mix—wrong price, wrong distribution, wrong product launch

**FIGURE 1.7**
Top five reasons for new product failures.

Also, continue to refine and practice your 1-min "elevator pitch," and network with other entrepreneurs and representatives in the industry.

### 1.9.1 Your Product Pipeline

Investors are attracted to innovative discoveries that could lead to multiple products or product lines (so-called platform technologies). A platform technology is a technology that could lead to multiple additional products and is the basis of a product pipeline. Investors often ask, "Is it a product or a company?" Single product ideas ("one-pony shows") are viewed as inherently more risky.

A new enterprise can certainly be formed around a single product, but the enterprise will be less attractive to institutional investors unless the product represents a huge, untapped market opportunity.

Determining a company's initial product is often very difficult—especially for platform technologies with many different applications. In some cases, the inventor might want to consider licensing the platform technology for further development to an established company, rather than creating a start-up with multiple products.

## 1.10 How to Think Like an Executive

To become a successful executive, you will require traits to operate, influence, and lead a commercialization team. This book will assist you in

- Identifying your knowledge boundaries—and how to expand your horizons
- Preparing for uncertainty and the unexpected
- Focusing on results, not activities
- Hiring people smarter than you
- Becoming the great communicator
- Demonstrating your ability to not only invent but also lead

Successful innovation and commercialization of your product depend on more than a strong scientific and technological base. Commercialization is based on reasoned judgments about future profitability from investments in product design and development, manufacturing, marketing, sales, and distribution. Figure 1.8 presents the commercialization process from an executive perspective, that is, by focusing on major milestones.

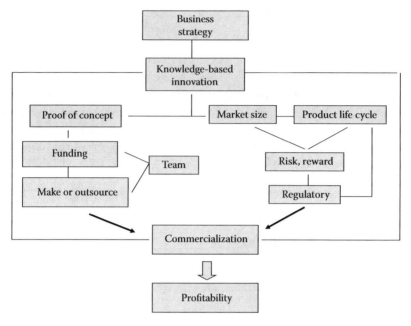

**FIGURE 1.8**
Commercialization from an executive's perspective.

## 1.11 Five Pillars of Small Businesses Success

Some 40 million businesses are started each year, yet a paltry 350,000 break out of the pack, grow, and ultimately become profitable. So how can a small business owner overcome common pitfalls and achieve success? Whether you're already in business or preparing to start a business, it takes hard work, tenacity, and drive. Here are the five pillars that make a small business successful [6].

1. **People**

   For your small business to succeed, you need a fantastic team. Surround yourself with people who are much smarter than you and who complement your knowledge and skills. Your company can accomplish amazing things with leadership, and a team that is inspired is hardworking and believes in the mission. Success in business requires passion about a problem that fills a crying need in the marketplace.

2. **Plan**

   Just about everyone in the business world agrees that having a plan is important. A business plan is akin to a PhD thesis, but in contrast to a thesis, a business plan may start slow and then grow over time. Your business plan must answer three key questions:

- Who are your target customers?
- What problems are you trying to solve for them?
- What are the most effective marketing and promotional strategies?

3. **Process**

Dr. W. Edwards Deming, the father of Statistical Quality Control said, "85 percent of the reasons for failure to meet customer expectations are related to deficiencies in systems and processes ... rather than the employee." It's crucial that you have a full and clear understanding of your company's processes and have the right systems in place.

As a start-up, implementation is everything—you must assign responsibilities and accountability, set goals, and track performance.

4. **Product**

Does your product solve a problem? Does the product exist yet? Is there something in the marketplace that your product addresses in a different way? Is there a true demand for your product?

5. **Profit**

Profitability is the ultimate measure of business success, so a critical component of running a successful business is understanding your company's finances. "If you want to be successful in business, you need to become proficient at handling certain numbers. You need to be able to read and understand your financial dashboard" [7].

In summary, starting and running a successful business can be a fulfilling and rewarding experience. As a small business owner, you should never stop learning, innovating, planning, and growing. Leaders spend 5% of their time on the problem and 95% of their time on the solution.

## References

1. Office of Technology Assessment, 1995.
2. Corbin, J. *Investor Relations: The Art of Communicating Value*. Aspatore, Inc., 2004.
3. Drucker, P.F. *Innovations and Entrepreneurship*, HarperBusiness, reissue edition, 2006.
4. Drucker, P.F. *Managing for Results*, HarperBusiness, reissue edition, 2006.
5. Servo, J.C. *Business Planning for Scientists and Engineers*. Fourth Edition, p. 5. Dawinbreaker, 2005.
6. Carbajo, M. https://www.sba.gov/blogs/5-pillars-small-businesses-success.
7. Fotopulos, D. *Accounting for the Numberphobic: A Survival Guide for Small Business Owners*. AMA, New York, 2015.

# 2

---

## *The Innovation Imperative*

---

When a great executive meets up with a bad business, it is usually the business whose reputation remains intact.

**Warren Buffett**

---

### 2.1 Introduction

Innovation is a buzzword that means many different things to different people, so defining terms is in order. **Innovation**, derived from the Latin *innovatio*, to renew or to change, is the application of knowledge in a novel way for economic benefit. **Innovation activities** are all scientific, technological, organizational, financial, and commercial steps undertaken to implement an innovation, but may also include research and development (R&D) not directly related to a particular innovation.

"Innovation is the ability to see change as opportunity, not a threat," as Steve Jobs famously quipped. The minimum requirement for an innovation is that the product, process, marketing, method, or organizational method must be new (or significantly improved) to the firm [1]. Innovation can thus be viewed as three distinct activities, as seen in the following:

1. The acquisition of new knowledge through leading-edge research
2. The application of new knowledge to create products and services
3. The introduction of advanced-technology products and services into the marketplace

The process starts with an invention, and then progresses to innovation, and finally to commercialization, as discussed in the subsequent paragraphs.

---

### 2.2 Invention, Innovation, and Commercialization

**Invention** is the creation of new products or processes through new knowledge or from a combination of existing knowledge. **Innovation** is the initial

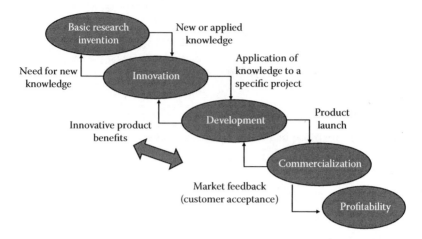

**FIGURE 2.1**
The five recognized steps from invention to profitability.

commercialization of invention by producing or selling a new product, service, or process. As discussed in Chapter 1, **commercialization** is the process of turning the invention, concept, or innovation into a product or service that can be sold in the marketplace.

Most technological innovation consists of certain predictable incremental steps in knowledge-based industries. Generally, there are five recognized steps from basic research innovation to profitability as graphically shown in Figure 2.1.

Innovation encompasses an **entire process** from opportunity identification, ideation, or invention to development, prototyping, production marketing, and sales. Conversely, entrepreneurship is focused solely on commercialization [2].

### 2.2.1 Types of Innovation

According to Professor Clayton M. Christensen of Harvard Business School in his book, *The Innovator's Dilemma* [3], innovations are either (1) sustaining or (2) disruptive, as shown in Figure 2.2.

1. **Sustaining**
   - Continuous
   - Discontinuous
2. **Disruptive**
   - Improve products in an unexpected fashion
   - Lower price
   - Enabling technologies

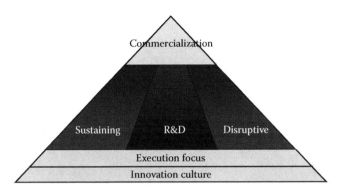

**FIGURE 2.2**
Ideal types of start-up innovations.

**Sustaining innovations** improve the performance attributes that are most valued by mainstream customers when choosing a product. For example, the data storage capacity of a USB flash drive increased from 8 MB in 2000 to 8 GB by 2007. The two types of sustaining innovation are *incremental innovation* and *radical innovation*. **Incremental innovation** is created during the ordinary course of business by companies producing and selling established products. Most of the time, an innovator is an employee of the company and often has a personal interest (e.g., a bonus or a promotion) as motivation [4]. Incremental innovation frequently occurs within large established organizations and is typically performed by "intrapreneurs."

**Radical innovation** creates new value and entirely new competencies within an industry. Importantly, radical innovation may lead to abandoning an existing practice or product. For example, the introduction of minimally invasive coronary stents has nearly eliminated the practice of open-heart procedures for coronary artery bypass surgeries.

Sometimes, though, performance improvements progress beyond market demand for such improvements. In their efforts to provide better products than their competitors, companies may "overshoot" the consumers' appreciation or willingness to pay for improved performance or technological sophistication.

**Disruptive innovations**, sometimes referred to as breakthrough innovations, destroy the competencies of incumbent firms in an industry. Breakthrough innovations are generally considered "out-of-the-blue" solutions that cannot be compared to any existing practices or techniques. These innovations employ enabling technologies (a technology that can be applied to drive radical change) and create new markets. Most breakthroughs are developed by R&D groups that often have not thought specifically about a particular commercial market application.

Conventional wisdom says "listen to the market," but breakthroughs often come from research laboratories, universities, or other entities that do not have ready touchpoints with customers. These technologies are introduced to the marketplace with the expectation they will be adopted by the consumer [5]. Some examples of disruptive innovations include digitized medical records, super-strong glass that keeps mobile device screens from breaking, and mobile payments via smartphones.

## 2.2.2 Disruptive Technologies

Clayton M. Christensen and Joseph Bower coined the term *disruptive technologies* in their 1995 article "Disruptive Technologies: Catching the Wave" [6]. Currently, "disruptive" is used in business and technology literature to describe innovations that improve a product or service in ways that the market does not expect, typically by lowering price or orienting toward a different set of consumers.

Disruptive innovations create a new (and unexpected) market by applying a different set of values. This is summarized in Table 2.1.

### 2.2.2.1 Disruptive High-Tech Innovations

The brisk pace of technology innovations—including mobile devices and apps, social networking, and the cloud—heralds unprecedented opportunities for start-ups in the dynamic high-tech field. Innovations are transforming a variety of sectors in unforeseen ways in this "connected" era. Leaders such as Amazon, Facebook, Google, and Microsoft are joined by upstarts from many countries in the world.

### 2.2.2.2 Porter's Model

Published in 1980, Michael E. Porter's *Competitive Strategy: Techniques for Analyzing Industries and Competitors* lays out a model called "Five Forces," which has since become a widely used and recognized tool for analyzing industrial structure, competition, and the strategic options of players. In the

**TABLE 2.1**

Disruptive Technology Examples

| Old Technology | New Technology |
| --- | --- |
| Slide rules | Handheld calculators |
| Chemical photography | Digital photography |
| Movie theaters | VCR rentals |
| Vinyl records | CDs |
| Typewriters | Computer word processors |
| Open-chest coronary bypass surgery | Catheter-based coronary stents |
| Exploratory gastro-enteric surgery | Capsule endoscopy (pill that you swallow and transmits continuous images via telemetry) |

context of disruptive technologies. Porter's Five Forces model can be used to determine to what extent and in what ways a disruptive trend has unfolded (ex-post) or is likely to manifest its impact (ex-ante) [7].

The model is based on the insight that a successful corporate strategy might seize the opportunities and guard against the threats of the organization's external environment. Porter identifies five competitive forces (bargaining power of suppliers, threat of new entrants, bargaining power of buyers, threat of substitute products, and rivalry among competitors; see Table 2.2) that shape every industry and every market, and focuses on the activities and influences of a company's main external actors (customers, suppliers, existing competitors, and new entrants) and on the characteristics of the goods or services that are bought and sold. These forces determine the intensity of competition and hence the profitability and attractiveness of an industry. The objective of corporate strategy should be to modify these competitive forces in a way that improves the competitive position of the organization by influencing or exploiting particular characteristics of its industry.

An innovation is classified as "disruptive" (or at least as having disruptive potential) if it has or may have a **major impact on at least one** of the five competitive forces. For example, one disruptive impact of the Internet in consumer markets is the significant increase in transparency of prices across sellers, thus increasing the bargaining power of consumers. In media markets, the Internet has become a substitute for classified advertising in newspapers. Table 2.2 provides some examples to illustrate how new technologies or other innovations (also including changes in the regulatory framework,

**TABLE 2.2**

Disruptive Innovations and Their Impact on Competition (Porter's "Five-Forces" Framework)

| Competitive Force | Disruptive Innovation Examples |
|---|---|
| Rivalry in the market | Internet: sales of used cars are increasingly initiated on specialized Internet platforms |
| Threat of new entrants | Digital photography enabled electronics companies to enter the camera market |
| | Online intermediaries taking commission from existing service providers (e.g., hotel reservation services, best price finders) |
| | Online retailers competing with conventional retail stores |
| Bargaining power of customers | Internet has increased price transparency in consumer goods |
| | Changes in the regulatory framework/liberalization of markets, allowing customers to select providers (utilities, telecoms) |
| Bargaining power of suppliers | Electronic components requiring rare earth elements (dependence on raw material providers) |
| | Substitution of products/services |
| | Internet: substation of classified advertising |
| | Computers replacing typewriting machines |

which can also be framed as a disruptive innovation) have had impacts on their respective competitive forces.

### 2.2.3  Classifications of Innovations

Every year, *BusinessWeek* publishes its popular "50 Most Innovative Companies" [8]. *BusinessWeek* classifies Apple as a product innovator, Google as a customer experience innovator, and IBM as a process innovator. These classifications can help us answer questions such as, "What are we innovating around?" and "How many levers are we turning?" [9]. According to this classification scheme, there are four types of innovation:

- **Process innovation:** Process innovation updates internal business processes to improve efficiency. For example, a hypothetical coffee shop called Coffee Express uses a new and faster machine to make cappuccino for customers. Toyota is considered the role model of process innovation through continuous improvement ("kaizen").
- **Product/offering innovation:** Product/offering innovation provides a new product or service to existing customers. For example, 3M began offering Post-It® Notes to customers of its existing office supply lineup.
- **Customer experience innovation:** Customer experience innovation involves improving the customer's shopping experience, which might include enhancing the visual appeal of a retail location or enhancing the website to provide additional product information of recommendations for complementary products. Visual merchandizing is an example from the retail industry.
- **Business model innovation:** Business model innovation is a reconfiguration of one or more of the following: target customer base, degree of insourcing or outsourcing production or inputs to the production process, or product pricing model.

In established organizations, each type of innovation happens in a different department. For example, the delivery or product departments drive process innovation, while new product development, business development, or portfolio management departments develop product/offering innovations. Brand managers are typically responsible for customer experience innovations, and business model innovations are developed within strategy departments.

### 2.2.4  Oslo Classification of Innovations

The Organisation for Economic Co-operation and Development of the European Union published "Proposed Guidelines for Collecting and Interpreting Technological Innovation Data," known as the Oslo Manual.

According to the Oslo Manual [10], innovations can be divided into the following four distinct classes:

1. **Product innovation:** introduction of a new product or significant improvements to an existing product related to its inherent characteristics or intended uses. Product innovation includes advancements in technical specifications, components/materials, incorporated software, user friendliness, or other functional characteristics. Product innovations can utilize new knowledge or technologies or can be based on new uses or combinations of existing knowledge or technologies.

2. **Process innovation:** implementation of a new or significantly improved production or delivery method, including significant changes in techniques, equipment, or software. A process innovation can be designed to decrease unit costs of production or delivery, to increase quality, or to produce or deliver new or significantly improved products.

3. **Marketing innovation:** implementation of a new marketing method involving significant changes in product design or packaging, product placement, promotion, or pricing. Marketing innovations are aimed at better addressing customer needs, opening up new markets or newly positioning a firm's product on the market, with the objective of increasing the firm's sales.

4. **Organizational innovation:** implementation of a new organizational method in the firm's business practices, workplace organization, or external relations. Organizational innovations can be designed to increase a firm's performance by reducing administrative or transaction costs, improving workplace satisfaction (and thus labor productivity), gaining access to nontradable assets (such as noncodified external knowledge), or reducing costs of supplies.

In a start-up organization, the entrepreneur and the team must decide which innovation classification best fits their organizational goals.

### 2.2.5 An Innovation Culture

An **innovation culture** is focused on (1) discovering hidden opportunities and (2) commercially exploiting proprietary technologies. Harvard business strategy guru Gary Hamel stated that "pursuing incremental improvements while rivals re-invent the industry is like fiddling while Rome burns" [11].

Developing a culture of innovation is one of the key drivers of success—or failure—of a start-up organization. A good, well-aligned culture can propel a start-up to success, but the wrong culture will stifle its ability to adapt to a fast-changing world. So how do you evaluate your corporate culture? And what steps can you take to create a strong corporate culture that will best support your organization's activities? As founder, you must decide what type of organization culture to establish.

**Organizational culture** is the collective behavior of people in an organization and the meanings that the people attach to their actions. Culture includes organization values, visions, norms, working language, systems, symbols, beliefs, and habits. It is also the pattern of such collective behaviors and assumptions taught to new organizational members as a way of teaching these new members to perceive, think, and feel. Organizational culture affects the way people and groups interact with each other, with clients, and with stakeholders [12].

Deal and Kennedy [13] defined organizational culture as *the way things get done around here* and created a model of culture based on four different types of organizations. Each organizational type quickly defines the feedback received by the organization, the way members are rewarded, and the acceptable level of risks:

1. **Work hard, play hard**
   - Rapid feedback/reward and low risk
   - Stress from quantity of work expected rather than uncertainty
   - High-speed action coupled with high-speed recreation
   - Examples: restaurants, software companies, and ladies' shoe manufacturers

2. **Tough-guy macho**
   - Rapid feedback/reward and high risk
   - Stress from high risk and potential loss/gain of reward
   - Focus on the present rather than the longer term
   - Examples: police, surgeons, politicians, and sports figures

3. **Process culture**
   - Slow feedback/reward and low risk
   - Low stress, plodding work, comfort, and security
   - Stress from internal politics and stupidity of the system
   - Bureaucracies and other means to maintain status quo
   - Focus on security of the past extending into the future
   - Examples: banks, insurance companies, teaching hospitals, and universities

4. **You-bet-your-company culture**
   - Slow feedback/reward and high risk
   - Stress from high risk and delay before knowing if actions have paid off

- Focus on executing business plans and strategies
- Examples: aircraft manufacturers, oil companies, and start-ups

### 2.2.6 Mechanisms of Innovation

Technology can enable and drive innovation, but to truly capitalize on technology's potential and unleash an organization's creative energy, technology know-how must be combined with business and marketing insights. Entrepreneurs should view consistent business and technology integration as crucial to innovation. Some mechanisms of innovation include the following:

- Novelty in product or service (differentiation; offering something no one else does)
- Novelty in process (offering products in a new way)
- Complexity (offer something that others find difficult to master)
- Timing (first mover advantage, fast follower)
- Add/extend competitive factors (e.g., price, quality, choice)
- Robust design (contribute a technology platform on which other variations can build)
- Reconfiguring the parts (building more effective business networks)

### 2.2.7 Most Iconic Failure-to-Innovate

What's wrong with this picture? In 2002, Kodak, defeated by the digital photography revolution, filed for Chapter 11 bankruptcy *despite* the early invention of a digital camera by a Kodak engineer, Steven Sasson, in 1975 [14]. Sadly, the digital camera was only one of countless technological innovations that Kodak failed to successfully commercialize.

Immensely successful companies can become myopic and product oriented instead of focusing on consumers' needs. Kodak's story of failure has roots firmly planted in its successes, which made the company stagnant and resistant to change. Its insular corporate culture led executives to believe that its strength was in its brand and marketing, and the company tragically underestimated the threat of an innovative technology such as digital photography [15].

Kodak's history shows that innovation alone is insufficient; companies must also have a clear business strategy that can adapt to changing times. Without such a strategy, disruptive innovations can sink a company's fortunes—even when the innovations are their own.

It wasn't always that way at Kodak. When Kodak's founder George Eastman [16] first began using his patented emulsion-coating machine to mass produce dry plates for photography in 1880, he was the one being disruptive. For more than a century thereafter, Kodak dominated the world of film and popular photography. In 1976, Kodak commanded 90% of film sales and 85% of camera sales in the United States [17], surpassing $10 billion in sales in 1981.

In 2015, the digital photography market—cameras, lenses, printers, and complementary products—was valued at more than $70 billion. Photography services account for several hundred billion more in revenues, and opportunities for providing these services digitally have become big business [18].

Just 25 years ago, very few people foresaw the opportunity for digital photography, and even fewer could have predicted digital photography's impact on related markets. Even fewer would have predicted the rise of the micro-stock photography market and the proliferation of and growth in Internet photo-sharing sites. While perhaps the impact on the photo processing market could have been predicted, most were surprised by how rapidly digital photography has displaced film. When digital cameras were introduced, customizing merchandise with personal photographs was in its infancy, with few firms offering customized products to customers who mailed in photographs.

Before the advent of the digital camera, photography-related markets included cameras, interchangeable lenses, film, film processing equipment, photo printers, scanners, and some storage products. However, the introduction of the digital camera disrupted all these markets. Overall, these markets are substantially larger than in the past since a far greater number of people who are involved with digital photography (e.g., using smartphones) than ever used traditional silver halide photography.

## 2.3 What Gets Measured Gets Attention… and What Gets Attention Gets Done

The sad truth is that 80%–90% of all innovations fail to produce the desired financial results [19]. Why? Following are the 10 most common reasons for innovation failures:

- Failure to meet needs of the market
- Poor launch timing
- Negative market conditions
- Ineffective or inconsistent branding
- Technical or design problems
- Overestimation of market size
- Poor positioning and segmentation

- Inadequate or nonexistent distribution
- Inappropriate metrics to measure success
- Insufficient differentiation from existing products

In today's business world, innovation is the mantra of success. For start-ups, the big winners are those that match new, marketable ideas with customers' needs before anyone else can. It takes flexibility, creativity, and exceptional planning. But measuring innovation is tricky, since such metrics are a combination of art and science. We throw around terms such as *creativity*, *breakthroughs*, *sustaining innovation*, and *disruptive innovation*, without any sense of how to shape, track, and measure the innovation process.

Why don't more companies measure innovation? Because innovation is a nebulous term, definitions differ, and expectations vary [20]. Following are some ways to think about developing metrics.

1. **Garbage in, garbage out. Nothing in, nothing out.**

   If you believe in the age old adage "garbage in, garbage out," then the scope of the problem becomes painfully poignant. Nothing in, nothing out. If you don't measure innovation, how do you know if you are getting it? You don't know, at least not in any systematic way.

   The most innovative organizations carefully consider what goes *into* the innovation process, but also consider what should come *out* of it. They focus on different types of measurements and include both quantitative aspects of the business (e.g., financial results, number of new products brought to market) and qualitative elements (e.g., leadership behaviors).

2. **Articulate the end game: Define the outputs.**

   Many companies zero in on the basics of the financial bottom line—top line revenue and overall profitability—when gauging success. Many also focus on their "net promoter score" (a customer loyalty metric) [21]. These high-altitude metrics are indeed important, but they have limited value when measuring—and driving—innovation. Why? Because these metrics are difficult to interpret within the context of innovation and organizational initiatives, and thus do not inspire action around clearly identifiable operating goals.

3. **Fuel the innovation engine: Identify the inputs.**

   Innovation also involves setting specific goals around ways of *fueling* innovation—things you do internally to help you hit your targets [22].

4. **Create your own metrics.**

   GE (General Electric) takes a customized approach. Over the past decade, employees have filed more than 20,000 patents, many of which have paved the way for the company to assume a leadership position in sustainable energy development and the "industrial Internet." GE's emphasis on protecting intellectual property runs deep in the company's culture and started when GE's founder established its R&D function in the early 1900s. GE has viewed patents as an essential "input" to innovation and has developed metrics around patent awards.

## 2.3.1 Key Performance Indicators

What are the primary challenges faced by start-ups to measuring innovation effectively? According to the research firm Arthur D. Little [23], there are three challenges: (1) use of key performance indicators (KPIs), (2) benchmarking, and (3) deployment.

### 2.3.1.1 Use of KPIs

First, innovation performance is difficult to measure and interpret. Most companies have some form of KPI system to show performance and help manage innovation. However, few companies believe that their KPIs are the right ones; nearly 72% of companies rate their innovation performance indicators as weak.

Next, many companies are unable to systematically obtain credible data for peer companies or even from their own organization, resulting in unending internal debates over data robustness and credibility. Ultimately, these debates engender a gradual loss of confidence in their KPI system altogether.

Furthermore, companies face difficulties interpreting when employing metrics such as market share, gross margins, or time to market. Although these metrics are computationally straightforward, they are less than helpful in differentiating between cause and effect. For example, if your average time to market is 14 months, should your market share decrease because your execution is simply too slow compared to competitors', or should your market share increase since you are only considering incremental low-return innovations?

### 2.3.1.2 Benchmarking

Even useful KPIs are challenging to translate into meaningful improvements. Where KPIs are measured and interpreted, companies struggle with setting shared priorities for improvement. For example, an R&D manager may correctly conclude from benchmarks that the company should innovate more in partnership with its suppliers, but may have trouble finding common ground with a procurement officer who has to meet yearly savings targets. And even when there is a consensus about priority improvements, are you focusing on what matters most for the company as a whole?

### 2.3.1.3 Deployment

Incidental improvements rarely mature into a system and culture of continuous improvement. Regularly changing priorities (and KPIs) often hinder companies in tracking innovation performance and trends over time, and demonstrating the success of the implemented improvement actions. Senior leadership support for actions can also be lost because the business case is rarely proven, often despite improvements in innovation performance.

## 2.4 What Gets Rewarded Gets Done Even Faster

Advancements in science and technology directly or indirectly create the overwhelming majority of newly created jobs. Furthermore, at least half of US GDP (gross domestic product) growth in recent decades has been attributed to technological innovation.

Manufacturing in the United States plays an outsized role in supporting and driving American innovation, and increasingly our ability to manufacture undergirds our future abilities to innovate and to create high-paying jobs [24].

- Manufacturing represents 12% of US GDP but contributes 60% of US R&D employees, 75% of US private sector R&D, and most patents issued in the United States [25].

- US manufacturers develop innovations at more than twice the rate of their counterparts in service industries and other US economic sectors. Thirty percent of US manufacturers reported an innovation between 2010 and 2014 compared to only 13% for nonmanufacturing businesses [26]. High-tech manufacturers report even higher rates of product and process innovation.

- For many technologies, the capabilities gained in production are intertwined with new learning and knowledge-based activities of research, development, and design. The iterative innovation cycle between engineering and production on the shop floor is responsible for a range of breakthrough technologies and has prompted many firms to reconnect production with development and design [27].

- Manufacturing output has increased 30% since the end of the 2009 recession, growing at roughly twice the pace of the economy overall. The years 2009 to 2015 mark the longest period since 1965 during which manufacturing outpaced overall US economic output [28].

- Since February 2010, the United States has added 725,000 manufacturing jobs, expanding employment in this sector at the most rapid pace in nearly two decades [29]. Manufacturing also supports millions of additional jobs throughout its supply chain and in local communities [30].

- Global executives in every industry and geography ranked the US #1 destination for business investment because of its highly productive workforce, sizeable and transparent markets, low-cost energy, and historic lead in innovation [31].

- The United States' renewed competitiveness in manufacturing is luring production back onto its shores. Nearly 54% of US-based manufacturers surveyed have returned manufacturing to the United States, a phenomenon known as reshoring.

However, not all industries were born equal regarding product or process innovations. There are wide disparities among industries in average percentages of companies reporting at least one innovation in a given year. For example, the electrical appliances industry reports 53% per year while all other industries average 13%. Manufacturers of communications equipment, aircraft and spacecraft, pharmaceuticals, and computers report rates of innovation at least double the US manufacturing sector average [32]. Additional statistics on innovation across industries are shown in Figure 2.3.

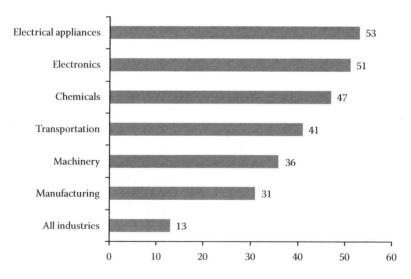

**FIGURE 2.3**
Companies introducing a new product or process innovation (2008–2010, in percentage). (From National Science Foundation, National Center for Science and Engineering Statistics. *Science and Engineering Indicators.* Arlington, VA (NSB 14-01), February 2014.)

**TABLE 2.3**

Core Competencies of Innovation

| Behavior Patterns | Knowledge, Skills, and Abilities |
|---|---|
| 1. Creativity | • Generating ideas<br>• Critical thinking<br>• Synthesis/reorganization<br>• Creative problem solving |
| 2. Enterprising | • Identifying problems<br>• Seeking improvement<br>• Gathering information<br>• Independent thinking<br>• Technological savvy |
| 3. Integrating perspectives | • Openness to ideas<br>• Research orientation<br>• Collaboration<br>• Engaging in non-work-related interests |
| 4. Forecasting | • Perceiving systems<br>• Evaluating long-term consequences<br>• Visioning<br>• Managing the future |
| 5. Managing change | • Sensitivity to situations<br>• Challenging the status quo<br>• Intelligent risk taking<br>• Reinforcing change |

## 2.5 Your Innovation Core Competencies

To build a culture of innovation, founders must foster and develop "innovation competencies." Innovation competencies are a group of behavior patterns that result from a critical mass of knowledge, skills, and abilities, combined with motivation and persistence. These competencies form a necessary basis for exceptional executive performance [33].

Table 2.3 presents five core competencies necessary to support a culture of innovation.

## 2.6 Five Discovery Skills of Innovative Leaders

In the *Innovator's DNA*, Christensen et al. list five behaviors (discovery skills) that characterize innovative leaders [34]:

1. Associational thinking
2. Questioning

3. Observing

4. Networking

5. Experimenting

Christensen denotes these attributes as "discovery skills," all of which focus on identifying new opportunities as a critical element of the front end of the innovation process.

In addition to these important idea-generating qualities, other skills are equally important to navigate the entire innovation process given its inherently high level of ambiguity and uncertainty. Accordingly, the five personal leadership competencies essential for success in today's environment are as follows:

1. **A Leapfrogging Mind-Set.** Leading disruptive innovation requires a mind-set focused on *leapfrogging*, that is, creating or doing something radically new or different that produces significant progress. Leaders with an unyielding commitment to creating breakthroughs secure an advantage by focusing all efforts on adding value to the market.

2. **Boundary Pushing.** Pushing boundaries occurs on both the personal level and the strategic level. Leaders who live abroad, work across different functions, and surround themselves with diverse team members continually expand their mind-sets and creative problem-solving abilities. At the strategic level, leaders continually push the limits of their teams, organizations, and partners.

3. **Data-Intuition Integration.** Most leaders demand hard data when making important decisions, but in times of disruption, robust data rarely exist. Leaders must use whatever information they can obtain from any and all sources inside and outside the organization—but then be comfortable using their intuition and experience to fill the gaps.

4. **Adaptive Planning.** Leading disruptive innovation requires managing incredible levels of uncertainty. Adaptive planning creates a feedback loop between action and outcomes, whereby the organizations continually examine results to successively modify and optimize assumptions and approaches. Outcomes, both positive and adverse, provide insights to more effectively calibrate to the needs of the market.

5. **Savoring Surprise.** Disruptive innovation is laden with surprise— unexpected technological advancements, competitive moves, customer feedback, political and regulatory shifts, and other unforeseen events. Most companies strive to avoid surprises, but leaders who

recognize that surprises are inevitable (and natural in business, and life) are better able to actually use surprise as a strategic tool. These leaders are more agile and more likely to capitalize on the unforeseen or unexpected.

To summarize, leaders who want to make a significant difference for themselves and their organizations need to embrace new skills in today's increasingly disruptive competitive environment. While new behaviors are important, so are new mind-sets. Leading disruptive innovation requires a new set of assumptions, many of which require humility, that is, the recognition that we do not (and cannot) have all the answers, and that disruptive innovation is all about finding clarity while embracing uncertainty.

Innovation does not necessarily proceed linearly from basic scientific research to product development; instead, it is an iterative process of both matching market needs to technological capabilities and conducting research to fill gaps in knowledge. Such iterations occur in all phases of the innovation process, including product conception, product design, manufacturing, and marketing. Commercial success depends as much on establishing and protecting a proprietary advantage in the marketplace as on generating scientific and technical advances [35].

## 2.7 The Process of Innovation

The process of innovation varies dramatically across industries and product lines. In some industries such as pharmaceuticals, innovation depends heavily on scientific breakthroughs, while in others (e.g., electronics), innovation is driven by product and process design. In addition, innovation takes on different characteristics throughout product and industry life cycles. Nascent industries exhibit high levels of product innovation as firms settle on the primary characteristics and architectures of their new offerings; later phases are characterized more by process innovation, as firms improve manufacturing for existing product lines.

Technological innovation is developing and utilizing new products and processes, and demands novelty in the product/process/service and/or application. Innovation therefore includes not only development of entirely new products, processes, and services that create new applications but also development of new products, processes, and services for use in existing applications. Examples include integrated circuits replacing vacuum tubes in electronic applications and manufacturers of flat panel displays adapted semiconductor manufacturing equipment to their needs.

Innovation is more than just invention—innovation must lead to new products, processes, and services that are not obvious to someone skilled in the field and that represent clear departures from prior practice. Innovation requires an invention entering the ordinary course of business in an industry. Many inventions are never put into practice; some cannot meet users' cost or performance requirements, while others lack technologically feasibility.

## 2.8 Innovation in Different Industries

No single model accurately depicts the process of innovation; innovation occurs differently in different industries and in product lines as firms develop products and processes that meet market needs. In the pharmaceutical industry, for example, innovation is closely coupled to scientific discoveries and follows a fairly linear pathway through manufacturing and marketing. Nonetheless, firms often commence activities with longer lead times earlier than when these activities would otherwise be undertaken, for example, constructing manufacturing facilities while the drug is undergoing clinical trials.

Many obstacles impede the innovation process in pharmaceuticals. For example, existing products are often protected by strong patent protection, markets are quite easily identified and quantified, and third-party payment systems (e.g., insurance companies, health maintenance organizations) relax some cost constraints on new products.

In contrast, innovation in the semiconductor industry is driven primarily from new product design and improvements in manufacturing technology rather than from advances in basic science. Commercial success in the semiconductor industry is more elusive, as product life cycles tend to be short (typically not longer than 3 years) and consumers are highly sensitive to cost.

The aircraft industry's innovation is highly concentrated in a few producers that act as integrators of components from a broad range of suppliers. Furthermore, aircraft product cycles are several decades long, and manufacturers work closely with users to define product specifications and costs.

As the aforementioned examples suggest, innovators face different obstacles in developing and marketing new products, processes, and services, and must proceed through a different set of steps to successfully bring a new invention to market. Not only do differences in industry structure and the nature of markets impose different constraints on the innovation process, but science, technology, and innovation in different industries are linked in different ways. Innovators follow many different pathways through the innovation process, and facilitating innovation and the commercialization of emerging technologies necessarily takes different forms.

## 2.9 Creating Your Own Innovation Culture

Innovative technology is the cornerstone of value creation, enabling the previously impossible. Start-up entrepreneurs must develop their own "innovation culture" that is capable of achieving success. Research has identified the 10 most desirable characteristics in the innovator-leader, as follows:

1. Initiative
2. Assertiveness
3. Achievement
4. Efficiency
5. High quality
6. Systematic planning
7. Monitoring
8. Commitment
9. Relationships
10. Creativity

A culture of innovation can be the start-up's primary source of competitive advantage, but to create this culture, you cannot merely hold a couple of meetings and pay lip service. You must execute. Some companies, such as Apple, are always innovating popular products, while most others are merely spectators in a contact sport. Innovation gives start-ups their strength, staying power, and value.

The most successful start-ups strike the optimal balance between breakthrough innovations and incremental innovations. Admittedly, when one thinks of innovation, *bold* as opposed to *incremental* more readily comes to mind. Bold conjures up a mental image of people in white coats bent over laboratory benches conducting scientifically or technologically challenging research. Ultimately, the balance between incremental and breakthrough innovations depends on the growth objectives of the start-up. The company will need to pursue a greater percentage of breakthrough innovations to achieve a higher targeted growth rate, provided finances permit. Incremental innovations, meanwhile, protect the market share of pipeline products and complement the breakthrough innovation portfolio.

Ultimately, the portfolio balance between incremental and breakthrough innovations will depend on your growth objectives. The higher your targeted growth rate, the higher the percentage of breakthrough innovations you will need to pursue, risk appetite permitting. Incremental innovations, meanwhile, help protect market share and margins of existing products and services and in that way complement your company's breakthrough innovation. This is visually summarized in Figure 2.4.

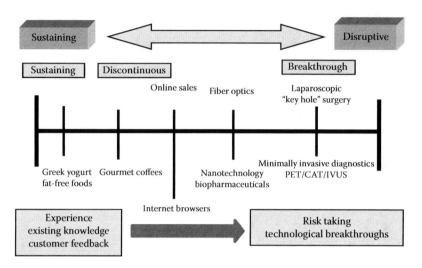

**FIGURE 2.4**
The innovation continuum.

Innovative start-ups command a price premium in the financial markets. The price premium may be observed in initial valuation or may become apparent during subsequent financing rounds.

## References

1. Tiwari, R. Defining Innovation. February 2002, http://www.global-innovation .net.
2. Solow, R. Heavy Thinker, *Review of Prophet of Innovation: Joseph Schumpeter and Creative Destruction*, by Thomas K. McCraw. The New Republic, May 21, 2007.
3. Christensen, C. The innovator's dilemma, *Harvard Business Review*, 1997.
4. Wikipedia, http://en.wikipedia.org/wiki/Innovation.
5. Wikipedia, http://www.go4funding.com/Articles/Types-Of-Innovations.aspx.
6. Christensen, C.M. and Bower, J.L. Disruptive technologies: Catching the wave, *Harvard Business Review*, January–February 1995.
7. INNO-Grips—Global Review of Innovation Policy Studies. http://www.pro inno-europe.eu/innogrips2.
8. http://www.businessweek.com/magazine/toc/10_17/B4175innovative_com panies.htm
9. Catalign Innovation Consulting, http://www.catalign.in/2009/11/4-types-of -innovations-businessweek.html.
10. Oslo Manual: Guidelines for Collecting and Interpreting Innovation Data, 3rd Edition, October 2005.
11. Hamel, G. Strategy as revolution. *Harvard Business Review*, July–August 1996.

12. Wikipedia, http://en.wikipedia.org/wiki/Organizational_culture.

13. Deal, T.E. and Kennedy A.A. *Corporate Cultures*, Perseus Book Publishing LLC, HarperCollins Publishing, New York, 1982.

14. What's wrong with this picture? Kodak's 30-year slide into bankruptcy, http://knowledge.wharton.upenn.edu/article/whats-wrong-with-this-picture -kodaks-30-year-slide-into-bankruptcy/.

15. http://www.forbes.com/sites/avidan/2012/01/23/kodak-failed-by-asking-the -wrong-marketing-question/

16. http://en.m.wikipedia.org/wiki/Eastman_Kodak

17. Kılıç, E., Hatem, M., Lofty, R., with the collaboration of O. Amat, Barcelona School of Management, Universitat Pompeu Fabra, 2013. Eastman Kodak Co., http://www.econ.upf.edu/docs/case_studies/61en.pdf.

18. Digital Photography: Global MarketsPR Newswire, http://s.tt/1d19c.

19. Andreoli, S. http://www.forbes.com/sites/steveandriole/2015/02/20/why-inno vation-almost-always-fails/.

20. Kaplan, S. http://www.fastcodesign.com/3031788/how-to-measure-innovation -to-get-real-results.

21. http://en.wikipedia.org/wiki/Net_Promoter

22. http://www.quintiles.com/~/media/library/fact%20sheets/re-ignite-product -development-and-sales-data-insights.pdf

23. Kolk, M., Kyte, P, van Oene, F., and Jacobs, J. Innovation: Measuring it to man- age it. Arthur D. Little, Prism/1/2012, http://www.adlittle.com/downloads /tx_adlprism/Prism_01-12_Innovation.pdf.

24. Making in America: U.S. manufacturing entrepreneurship and innovation. June 2014, http://www.whitehouse.gov/sites/default/files/docs/manufacturing _and_innovation_report.pdf.

25. Bureau of Economic Analysis, Department of Commerce.

26. National Science Foundation, Science and Engineering Indicators.

27. MIT Production in the Innovation Economy Commission. *Production in the Innovation Economy*, 2013.

28. Bureau of Economic Analysis, Department of Commerce, NIPA tables.

29. Bureau of Labor Statistics, Department of Labor, Current Employment Statistics Survey.

30. McKinsey Global Institute. *Manufacturing the Future*, November 2012.

31. AT Kearney. Foreign Direct Investment Confidence Index, 2014.

32. National Science Foundation, National Center for Science and Engineering Statistics. Science and Engineering Indicators, 2014.

33. Innovation Competency Model, http://www.innovationinpractice.com/inno vation_in_practice/2011/04/innovation-competency-model.html.

34. Dyer J., Gregersen, H., and Christensen H.W. The Innovator's DNA: Mastering the Five Skills of Disruptive Innovators. *Harvard Business School Publishing, July 19, 2011.*

35. U.S. Congress Office of Technology Assessment. *Innovation and Commerciali- zation of Emerging Technology*, OTA-BP-ITC-165. US Government Printing Office, Washington, DC, September 1995.

# 3

# *Development on a Shoestring (Bootstrapping)*

A Rolex does not keep time any better than a Timex.

## 3.1 Introduction

Start-ups are not a small version of a large company. A start-up is a temporary organization designed to search for a repeatable and scalable business model ... that someday aspires to grow up to become a real company! A start-up is an organization dedicated to innovation under conditions of extreme financial constraints. Large companies have the luxury of allocating budgets to new products and can weather market uncertainties.

So where do start-ups get their initial financial resources? The answer is many start-ups are financed on a "shoestring" or "bootstrapping" basis. **Shoestringing** or **bootstrapping** is the *internal generation* of initial financing, using primarily your own personal resources, and sometimes complemented by various forms of equity investments or loans from family, friends, and relatives.

Bootstrapping is entrepreneurship in its purest form. It is the transformation of inventive value into financial capital. The overwhelming majority of entrepreneurial companies are financed through this "highly creative" process, as well as formal sources of private equity [1]. Interestingly, academic research has suggested that bootstrapping techniques can minimize risk because of the absence of outside venture capital (VC) investors [2]. When everybody says "no"—from the banker to the private investor—the tough small business owners turn to themselves ... they raise money from within by bootstrapping [3].

Because bootstrappers have no choice except to be resourceful, they may have an ironic advantage over other individuals who hail from more resource-rich environments in terms of developing their managerial and entrepreneurial skill sets. To a certain extent, being deprived of resources forces the entrepreneur to find other inventive ways to make do (or make do without) [4].

Entrepreneurial bootstrapping is more celebrated, studied, and desirable than ever before. Business school students flock to courses on entrepreneurship. Managers, fearful of losing their perch on the corporate ladder, yearn to step off on their own. Policymakers pin their hopes for job creation and economic growth on start-ups rather than on the once-preeminent corporate giants.

## 3.2  Cutting Corners and Pinching Pennies

Of course, not every entrepreneur bootstraps. The legendary Mitch Kapor raised nearly $5 million of VC in 1982 (a small fortune in those days), enabling Lotus to launch the 1–2–3 spreadsheet. Lotus 1–2–3 was the software industry's most successful advertising campaign. Significant initial capital is indeed a must in industries such as biotechnology or supercomputers where tens of millions of dollars have to be spent on research and development before any revenue is realized. Bootstrapping follows a predictable two-stage sequence, as depicted in Figure 3.1.

Many start-ups rely on bootstrapping, which is easier said than done. History shows that successful bootstrappers follow these principles:

- Place great emphasis on critical prelaunch preparations. Conduct enormous amounts of research: library research, bookstore research, Internet research, and especially field research (the nonscholarly translation of field research: network, network, network, with prospective

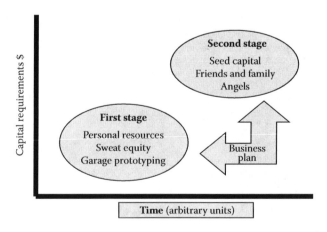

**FIGURE 3.1**
Stages of bootstrapping financing.

- Establish low administrative salaries from the start. You can always go up.
- Remember: every dollar spent on administration takes a dollar away from producing sales.
- Overhead or profits: your choice.
- Do not overhire: make everyone multitask.

**FIGURE 3.2**
Overhead bootstrapping.

suppliers, customers, advisory board members, and other potential friends of the business).

- Crawl before you walk. Learn to barter. Think outside the box—like the editor who trades her proofreading services in exchange for an ad for her business in a local trade publication.

- Forget appearances. A Taj Majal–style headquarters will only serve you after you are successful, not before. Start your business out of your home.

- Negotiate terms carefully. Negotiate terms for purchases from vendors and sales to customers. When possible, arrange the purchase–sales sequence in a way that customers finance the purchase of inventory through prepayment terms.

- Advertise a product that could be produced, if response to the ad justifies its production.

- Develop business communications and media skills. Be worthy of media attention (i.e., be newsworthy) as a result of a unique product, company history, team, or even aspiration.

- Be extra careful of your overhead expenses, as summarized in Figure 3.2.

## 3.3 Bootstrapping Start-Ups via Sweat Equity

An early-stage technology company will almost certainly need some kind of financial support to successfully get started. The key problem is that most institutional funding organizations (e.g., banks and most conventional investors) will be accustomed to investing in very different propositions. Table 3.1 summarizes the different investing propositions between institutions and start-ups.

While you may get some support from the bank, you will almost certainly have to put up some sort of personal security against the loan. Be very wary

**TABLE 3.1**

Investing Propositions versus Start-Up Characteristics

| Banks and Some Investors Prefer These Characteristics | Technology Start-Up Business Have These Characteristics |
|---|---|
| • Stable cash flow forecasts | • Fluctuating cash needs |
| • Business track record | • Business inexperience |
| • Steady growth forecasts | • High growth rate |
| • An easy-to-understand market | • New markets/complicated technology |
| • High fixed asset ratio | • Low fixed assets ratio |

of this; remember that setting up a business and commercializing research is extremely high risk. If you are unable to pay off your debts, the banks will collect on their security.

At first, most entrepreneurs spend their own money, technical resources, and time in the yet-to-be formed company. At this point, the company is in the "dream" or "idea" stage and the entrepreneur is accumulating "sweat equity."

According to Investopedia, sweat equity "is the contribution to an innovative project or startup enterprise in the form of effort and toil." Sweat equity is the ownership interest, or increase in value, that is created as a direct result of hard work by the owner(s) and is the preferred mode of building equity for cash-strapped entrepreneurs in their start-up ventures, since they may be unable to contribute much financial capital to their enterprise. In the context of real estate, sweat equity refers to value-enhancing improvements made by homeowners themselves to their properties. The term is probably derived from the fact that such equity is considered to be generated from the "sweat of one's brow" [5].

For example, consider an entrepreneur who spends a year in her start-up. After a year of developing the business and getting it off the ground, she sells a 25% stake to an angel investor for $500,000. The sale gives the business a valuation of $2 million (i.e., $500,000/0.25), of which the entrepreneur's share (sweat equity) is $1.5 million.

Bootstrapping diminishes your dependence on banks and other forms of financing. Some typical examples are as follows:

- Negotiating extended terms with vendors
- Negotiating advance payments from customers
- Working from home until the business is established
- Keeping inventories at a minimum
- Leasing equipment (usually from the manufacturer)

### 3.3.1 Bootstrapping Best Practices

Lahm and Little [6], in their excellent study entitled "Bootstrapping Business Start-ups: A Review of Current Business Practices," identified and discussed two methods that broadly address bootstrapping. These two methods include the acquisition and control of resources (both tangible and intangible) and the efficient uses of those resources to finance the enterprise for growth. These authors provide a list of 13 practical suggestions for bootstrapping business start-ups, as shown below:

1. Start-up entrepreneurs with little capital should be advised to strongly consider a business model that entails compensation before the delivery of a product or service (e.g., consulting, mail order, or niche-oriented Internet businesses that do not require a glitzy website).

2. An emphasis on prelaunch preparations, perhaps several years in advance, may be wise.

3. More education and training are needed for would-be entrepreneurs such that they are more familiar with traditional sources of capital and nontraditional sources. Bootstrapping should be a course unto itself in university-level entrepreneurship programs.

4. Stockpile nonperishable business assets over a long period. Businesses that have resulted from a hobby often start out with many of the necessary tools, contacts, sources, and skills on the part of the owner to be well equipped from their inception.

5. Conduct enormous amounts of research: library research, bookstore research, Internet research, and especially field research (the non-scholarly translation of field research: network, network, network, with prospective suppliers, customers, advisory board members, and other potential friends of the business).

6. Consider an agency or brokerage-type business: connect a party who needs to sell with a party who needs to buy.

7. Get quotes. Provide a vendor with a general idea of a needed end result for a manufactured product (or a service) and ask for design specifications, pricing, projected delivery schedules, and terms (be sincere as a prospective customer).

8. Negotiate terms carefully. Negotiate terms for purchases from vendors and sales to customers. When possible, arrange the purchase–sales sequence in a way that customers finance the purchase of inventory through prepayment terms.

9. Choose a location wisely. Consider the "image" needs of the business, but also seek economic development dollars (or stakeholders) and co-location opportunities in neighbors with synergistic potential. Do not choose a location because it is close to home and convenient for the owner. It must be convenient for the customer, for the logistical needs of the business, and in a nurturing environment.

10. Advertise a product that could be produced, if response to the ad justifies its production.

11. Develop business communications and media skills. Be worthy of media attention (i.e., be newsworthy) as a result of a unique product, company history, team, or even aspiration.

12. Be generous. People are willing to follow a leader who understands their needs and fulfills those needs.

13. Sell in volume at wholesale, rather than one unit at a time.

### 3.3.2 Savings, Investments, and Salable Assets

This is always the preferred place to start. Theoretically, all you are doing is transferring your assets from one investment (your savings account) to another (your new business). But understand that you are increasing your risk by a quantum leap, although you are also increasing your opportunity for future rewards.

### 3.3.3 Your Family and Friends Network

Beyond sweat equity, most tech start-ups raise their first capital from friends and family. Friends and family financings are always the easiest to complete, often taking less than 2 months from start to finish. Friends and family rounds usually raise $25,000 to $150,000 in total [7].

Friends and family investors share the following characteristics:

- They do not need to be "Not accredited"
- May be "unsophisticated" in finance
- Invest their own capital
- Investing in a friend (you), not necessarily in the business
- Passive investors (do not demand board seats or managerial posts)

### 3.3.4 Life Insurance

If you own life insurance policies with a cash value, you probably shouldn't, because term life insurance is a far better deal. Consider cashing in such policies and putting that money to far better use—your business. Remember, however, that you may owe some income tax on accumulated interest (in excess of the premiums you paid) from your life insurance policy.

Ask yourself whether you really need life insurance at all. If you have no financial dependents, you won't need it to replace your income if you pass away. If you do need life insurance, however, secure good term life coverage before you cancel or cash in your current policy. Otherwise, your dependents will be in trouble if you pass away after you have canceled your current policy but before you have secured new coverage.

### 3.3.5 Credit Cards

Credit cards provide expensive money, perhaps, but easy money as well. No personal guarantees here, no bankers looking over your shoulder; just sign your name and get on with the business at hand. In the increasingly competitive credit-card market, interest rates on some cards are around 10%, so be sure to shop around rather than simply accumulating a balance on whatever platinum-hued card currently happens to be in your wallet or pitched through an ad, and when you carry a balance from month to month, always make your credit-card payments on time unless you enjoy paying even higher interest rates—in many cases upward of 20%.

### 3.3.6 Home Equity

Proceed with extreme care when borrowing against home equity. A misstep could cost you the roof over your family's head. Do not even consider this option until you have thoroughly reviewed your overall personal financial situation.

### 3.3.7 Financing with a Business Plan

Lenders and professional investors read a business plan as much to find out about the preparer as to understand the business. They look for thoroughness, professionalism, and attention to detail in the plan, in addition to the presentation of a credible scenario for running a successful business. After all, thoroughness, professionalism, and attention to detail are the same traits they want to see in the person responsible for managing the money they invest in or lend to the business. What better early indication of these characteristics than your business plan?

The sophisticated investor has learned from experience—horses don't win races; jockeys do. The jockey is you, the business owner, and the business plan is the first official indication of the kind of race your horse is going to run.

Business plans take a lot of time and focus to prepare well and are not to be confused with an afternoon jaunt at the beach. Similar to successfully locating the right financing and finding the right mentor, developing a successful business plan separates the potential doers from the dreamers.

By and large, only the truly committed take the trouble to prepare a business plan. You find some exceptions, of course; some potential small business owners have enough of their act together to carry a good business plan in their head, and, yes, some of those business owners have gone on to achieve great success. But these same business owners may have accomplished even greater success and avoided some early mistakes if they had taken the time to record and refine their ideas in a tangible business plan. The depth of your early commitment to writing a business plan directly correlates to your chances for success, and a well-thought-out business plan demonstrates your depth of commitment to end up at the helm of a successful small business.

Occasionally, investors will fund a start-up business strictly on the basis of a compelling business plan. In this case, the investors will be putting all their trust in you, the entrepreneur, to execute the business plan as presented.

### 3.3.8 Fundraising Importance of Patents

Patents enable entrepreneurs to acquire financial capital under the most favorable terms in earlier founding rounds [8]. Firms having larger patent portfolios enjoy a greater likelihood of sourcing initial capital, and of achieving liquidity through an initial public offering. Given the lengthy government certification process, it provides an early reliable "due diligence" signal for investors by which the quality of their investment can be better quantified [9].

Given the fundraising importance of patent protection, the entrepreneur/investor must guard against making innocent mistakes that may prevent their ability to obtain a patent. An inventor has 1 year from the date of "first public disclosure" of the invention to file a patent application in the US Patent Office. **First public disclosures** are many, and surprisingly they include the following:

- Disclosures at presentations and poster sessions
- Prior public uses or demonstrations
- Prior conversations with potential partners
- Prior publications or interviews
- Prior sales of prototypes at beta sites

Also, keep in mind that if the US application is filed after the public disclosure, the inventor is not able to file for patent protection in many countries. There is only a 6-month "grace" period in Japan, Korea, and Russia There is a 1-year grace period in Canada, Australia, and Mexico.

Also understand that the loss of foreign patent rights greatly diminishes the financial value of intellectual property in the eyes of investors. For that reason, and for your maximum protection, consider filing a patent application before embarking on any public disclosure.

- Is the patent in a subject area that is earning significant profits?
- Are there currently patent litigation cases in process in the subject area?

- Does the invention allow for reduced costs or increased performance?
- Are there any competitors that could directly benefit from your invention?
- Are there blocking or dominating patents in this area?
- Do you have freedom to operate?
- Do you have an inventorship/ownership policy in place?

In summary, a patent can help your company be more "investable." Fundamentally, investors will analyze the risks and potential rewards of a single investment. Owning one or more patents can reduce the risk of the company by strengthening the competitive advantage and providing an additional marketable asset.

## 3.4 Outsourcing for Your Capital Needs

Outsourcing institutions—banks, the Small Business Administration (SBA), Small Business Investment Companies (SBICs), angel investors, and venture capitalists—are *not* primary resources for start-up capital.

This is because most of these outsourcers are looking for either significant collateral and operating history (banks and the SBA) or a business in an industry with uncommon opportunities for return on investment (venture capitalists). Meanwhile, angels are the most versatile of the outsourcing resources, but they're also the most difficult to find. We discuss each of these resources in this section [10].

Outsourcers, with the possible exception of SBICs, have a well-deserved role in the financing world; that role just doesn't happen to be at the start-up stage. After your business has matured and has a track record, the outsourcers may become a part of the financing game for your business.

The first thing to discover when considering which outsourcer to use is whether they're loaning you money (banks, SBA, and others) or investing their money (venture capitalists, some angels, and the like). Or, stated another way, will they be creditors or will they be part owners?

Outsourcing resources fall into two general categories: banks and nonbanks. Most banks don't make start-up loans to small business owners unless an owner's collateral is such that it will cover 100% of the loan. Examples of such collateral include real estate (including home equity) and stocks and bonds.

A bank's primary role in the small business lending arena is funding growth, for example, financing the expansion of a small business that has a track record. Most banks can offer a wide variety of creative loan packages designed to finance the existing small business. These loans include the financing possibilities discussed in the subsequent sections.

### 3.4.1 Asset-Based Financing

Asset-based financing is a general term describing the situation whereby a lender accepts as collateral the assets of a company in exchange for a loan. Most asset-based loans are collateralized against either *accounts receivable* (money owed by customers for products or services sold but not yet paid for), inventory, or equipment. Accounts receivable is the favorite of the three because it can be converted into cash more quickly (theoretically within 30 days, if these are terms you are offering). Banks advance funds only on a percentage of receivables or inventory, the typical percentages being 75% of receivables and 50%, or less, of inventory.

For example, using these percentages, if your business has $30,000 in receivables due from customers and $50,000 in inventory, the bank may loan you 75% of $30,000 (which is equal to $22,500) and 50% of $50,000 (which is equal to $25,000). The total of the two ($47,500) would then be available for you to use as working capital. These percentages vary based on the industry and the quality of the receivables and the inventory.

### 3.4.2 Banking on Banks

The old joke goes: "A bank will always loan you money, as soon as you prove you don't need it." Contrary to the popular opinion that bankers enjoy turning down prospective borrowers, bankers are in business to lend money. Every time bankers sit down in front of a prospective borrower, they hope that what they're about to see is a deal that will work. After all, *no loans* means no investment income for the bank, and no investment income means no marble columns—and without marble columns, what would hold up their gold-inlaid ceilings?

Make no mistake about it, banks are in business to lend money and make profits, which banks do by playing the spread—charging you more to use their money than they're paying somebody else (namely, depositors) to get it.

Banks tend to shy away from small companies experiencing rapid sales growth, a temporary decline, or a seasonal slump. In addition, firms that are already highly leveraged (a high debt-to-equity ratio) will usually have a hard time getting more bank funding.

Banks rely on four key requirements to lend you money. These key requirements are summarized in Figure 3.3.

If you have decided to seek a bank loan, the following terms are generally required to qualify:

- A written business plan or loan proposal
- Investment of your own money (usually 10% to 30% of the loan amount)

- You know your business and your market niche
- Credible forecast covering the load period
- You will be able to repay the loan:
  - Risks are minimized
  - Financial ratios are conservative and attainable
  - Hard assets are available as collateral
  - Personal loan guarantee
- Current revenues

**FIGURE 3.3**
What bankers want to see.

- Enough assets to collateralize the loan (usually one to two times the loan)
- Good character and personal credit
- Personal guarantee (your personal assets will be at risk)
- Obtaining a loan for 100% of capital needs is usually not possible
- Lenders usually require borrowers to have some personal or other source of cash to cover at least 25% or more of the total need
- Loans usually must be for business equipment, inventories, and operating expenses. Loans to cover loss of income are not available

### 3.4.3 Line of Credit

A line of credit involves the bank's setting aside designated funds for the business to draw against the ebb and flow of cash as needs dictate. As line-of-credit funds are used, the credit line is reduced; conversely, when payments are made, the line is replenished.

An advantage of line-of-credit financing is that no interest is accrued unless the funds are actually used. Ironically, the best time to arrange for your business's line of credit is when your business is doing well and you need the money the least. Why? Because that's when getting approval from the banker for the line of credit will be easiest, and you'll qualify for the best loan terms.

Don't make the mistake of overlooking a line of credit just because you don't presently need money. (Remember, a "line" doesn't cost anything if you don't draw against it.) Establish your credit line when things are going well. Sooner or later, if you're like most small businesses, you'll need the cash.

### 3.4.4 Letter of Credit

A **letter of credit** is a guarantee from the bank that a specific obligation of the business will be honored. Letters of credit are most often used to buy products unseen from overseas vendors. The bank generates its income in these situations by charging fees for making the guarantee.

## 3.5 Getting Money from Nonbanks

Banks don't have a lock on the small business lending market. Investment brokerage firms and major business conglomerates are also important players in the small business lending market. Most nonbank lenders find their niche by specializing in a specific category of loan, such as leasing or asset-based financing.

Leasing companies (where you can lease your business's equipment or furniture and fixtures), for example, are the most common nonbank financing resource, with 25% of small businesses availing themselves of some sort of leasing financing. *Leasing* is basically a rental—you pay a monthly fee for the use of an item, and at the end of the lease term, you return the item to the company that leased it to you. A compilation of nonbank resources follows in this section.

### 3.5.1 The Small Business Administration

An SBA loan is a loan made by a local lender (bank or nonbank) that is, in turn, guaranteed by a federal agency called the Small Business Administration (SBA). The SBA provides its backup guarantee as an inducement for banks to make loans that otherwise may be too risky from a banker's perspective.

Only in rare cases does the SBA actually provide the money itself. SBA loans usually provide longer repayment terms and lower down-payment requirements than conventional bank loans. They're available to most for-profit small businesses that don't exceed the SBA's parameters on size (which can vary depending on the industry). SBA loans can be used for a number of reasons, including (in infrequent cases) start-up monies if you have sufficient collateral in long-term assets.

Getting an SBA loan is not easy; to the contrary, the agency is extremely selective about whom it approves. Consider the primary criteria the SBA looks for when considering guaranteeing a loan:

- The owner must have invested at least 30% of the required capital and must be willing to guarantee the balance of the loan.
- The owner must be active in the management of the business.
- All principals must have a clean credit history.
- The business must project adequate cash flow to pay off the loan, and the debt/net worth ratio must fall within the SBA's approved guidelines.
- The SBA does not lend money. It provides guarantees to a bank that if a person does not repay a loan, the SBA will pay a major percentage of the loan back to the bank.

- All banks can make SBA-guaranteed loans but most have restrictions on what types of loans they are willing to make.
- The SBA only wants to guarantee loans to people who are likely to repay the loan.
- All SBA loans are made to individuals for a business. The individual is personally liable to repay the loan.

SBA loans have a reputation for being cumbersome and subject to enormous red tape. This reputation had been deserved in years past, but technology has made inroads everywhere, even in the government. The SBA's LowDoc Program (short for "low documentation"), for loans under $100,000, promises to process loan requests in less than 48 h and requires the borrower to fill out only a one-page application form. Other documentation you can be expected to furnish when applying for an SBA loan in excess of $100,000 includes (1) a personal financial statement, (2) 3 years of tax returns, and (3) 3 years of financial projections (Pro Forma Statements).

The SBA offers a wide variety of educational materials and seminars for both current and aspiring small business owners. It also provides financial assistance through loans and loan-guarantee programs. In recent years, these programs have become significantly more user-friendly, and today, the SBA is an excellent resource for the capital-seeking small business owner who has trouble attracting funding through the conventional private-sector sources.

**The SBA, however, does not have any grant programs to start a business.** Beware of the common myth that there is a lot of "free government grant money" for start-ups.

To find a local bank or nonbank institution that works with the SBA, look in the Yellow Pages for SBA Approved Lending Sources or call the SBA at 800-827-5722. If you're on the Internet, see www.sba.gov for more information about SBA loans that may work for you.

### 3.5.2 Small Business Investment Companies

SBICs are privately owned, quasi–venture capital firms organized under the auspices of the SBA. SBICs either lend money to, or invest money in, small businesses primarily within their local area. Categorized as *Federal Licensees* (meaning the federal government has given the SBIC its stamp of approval), SBICs either fund start-ups or provide operating funds with which to expand existing businesses. Through their relationship with the SBA, they're also able to offer particularly favorable terms and conditions to *disadvantaged businesses* (businesses owned by women and minorities).

Hundreds of SBICs operate around the country. To find out more about them, call the SBA at 800-827-5722, check out the SBA's website (www.sba .gov), or contact a nearby Small Business Development Center.

### 3.5.3 Certified Development Companies

Another program of the SBA, the Certified Development Company (CDC) program (also known as the 504 Loan Program), provides long-term (10- and 20-year) fixed-rate loans for small businesses. This program focuses on financing fixed assets, such as real estate (land and buildings). CDCs work with a local lender; typical financing may include 50% from the local lender, 40% from the CDC, and 10% down from the small business being helped. The asset being purchased acts as its own internal collateral. Several hundred CDCs exist nationwide. For the CDC nearest you, call the SBA at 800-827-5722 or visit the SBA's website (www.sba.gov) and inquire about the 504 Loan Program.

### 3.5.4 Your State's Economic Development Department

Many states have an Economic Development Department (sometimes a stand-alone governmental agency, possibly housed within the state's Department of Commerce) that offers a variety of loan programs to statewide businesses. The programs offered are usually modeled after SBA loans but can often offer better terms and conditions than the SBA, especially for those businesses that employ many employees. Such state departments will also generally offer *microloan* programs designed to assist small business start-ups.

### 3.5.5 Minority Funding Resources

The resources for low-income and minority funding (which, in many cases, is defined to include women-owned businesses) are many. Look to the following for starters:

a. The National Bankers Association (NBA) in Washington, DC, represents minority-owned banks that target loans to minority-owned businesses. For the nearest member bank in your area, call the NBA at 202-588-5432 or visit its website at www.natianalbankers.org.

b. Most states have an agency that provides one-stop assistance on financial services for small businesses. Check the library or the phone book for such an agency in your state and then ask about state-operated minority funding resources.

c. At the federal level, the SBA can help direct callers to local organizations that can, in turn, help locate low-income and minority funding opportunities. Call the SBA at 800-827-5722 for the resource nearest you or surf its website at www.sba.gov.

d. The U.S. Commerce Department's Minority Business Development Agency funds Business Development Centers nationwide whose function is, in part, to help minority-owned start-up businesses. Call 888-324-1551 for more information or visit its website at www. mbda .gov.

### 3.5.6 Exploring Your Ownership Options

In theory, all businesses have three ownership options:

- Privately held, with the founder being the only shareholder
- Privately held, sharing ownership with partners or other shareholders
- Publicly held, meaning that shares in your company are available to the investing public via the stock market

In reality, of course, most businesses only have the first two of these options—going for it alone or having partners or minority shareholders. Few businesses have the management, resources, and appeal needed to go public, either at the start-up stage or in the course of the business's growth.

There is no right or wrong answer as to which of the three options you should use, but there is a right or wrong way to determine which works best for you. At the heart of making that decision is … you guessed it… you! You are the primary ingredient that will determine which of the three options will work best for your business. Your criteria to use in making this decision should include the kind of person you are, the way you communicate, the way you delegate, and the manner in which you work with people.

The kind of business you intend to start also can be a factor. If, for example, you intend to start a high-tech manufacturing business, you may find that the key employees you want will demand some ownership as part of their compensation packages. On the other hand, if you intend to go into the consulting business, sole ownership is the likely ticket for you.

### 3.5.7 Service Corps of Retired Executives

The Service Corps of Retired Executives (SCORE) has helped create more than 56,000 new businesses and allowed more than 107,000 businesses increase revenue.

Federally funded, SCORE consists of more than 10,000 volunteers in hundreds of cities across the United States who provide free counseling, mentoring, and advice to prospective or existing small businesses. SCORE volunteers provide the specific advice and resources you need through customized, one-on-one or team mentoring.

SCORE, an excellent concept to be sure, can be a tad on the hit-or-miss side, however, because the majority of SCORE's volunteers are ex–large-company employees. Thus, not all of them have known what it's like to have been there as their own small business takes off. If you happen to be assigned to the right volunteer, however, SCORE can be the best deal in town—occasionally even providing you with a much needed mentor. SCORE is definitely a service worth trying, especially to pose online questions to counselors or to contact the office nearest you (website at www.score.org, or call 800-634-0245).

### 3.5.8 Consider Looking for a Partner with Deep Pockets

This is one of the most overlooked sources of money. Many small businesses resist this approach because they want to own 100% of the business. However, it is better to own 50% of a growing successful business than 100% of a business that never gets off the ground. Funding sources can come from any one of these "other" deep pocket sources:

- A specialized supplier
- A strategic partner
- A venture capitalist
- A private equity dealer
- A private offering
- A private investor
- An "angel" investor

### 3.5.9 Finding a Guarantor or Loan Co-Borrower

This works well when a family member or close friend is reluctant to give you cash up front but they think you have a good idea for a business and a good chance to succeed. They may be willing to either guarantee a loan or co-sign for a loan. Before going out looking for money, remember three tips described below:

1. **When you need a loan, establish a personal relationship.** Loans are about trust, and trust starts with familiarity. Invite your lender to your place of business. Impress the lender with your product samples or services. Take advantage of their experience and contacts by asking for help on nonbanking issues. Ask him to join your informal business advisory board. You may even learn more about your business from your lender.
2. **Know your numbers cold.** Every business loan has terms and conditions. Be sure you understand them. Learn about a balance sheet, a profit and loss statement, and cash flow projections.
3. **Sweeten the deal.** What lenders want even more than your loan are new customers. Ask about the lender's other products and services. If you are pleased with the lender's products and services, refer family

and friends to do business with the lender company, but whatever you do

- Don't fool yourself. Know your weaknesses.
- Know your financial break-even point. If you are bad with numbers, hire a good bookkeeper or accountant.
- Do not bankrupt your business because you are too proud to admit that you need help.
- Know what you should say when you meet with a lender.
- Thoroughly describe your background, experience, and education.
- Stick to the facts. Be truthful with the lender. Confidence in your ability and integrity is very important.
- State exactly how much money you require. Never ask "how much can I get?"
- Outline what you plan to do with the money. Using the cash to replace lost income is not a valid reason for a loan.
- Define how the business will generate the cash flow required to pay back the bank loan.
- Tell the lender how much of your own money you are investing in the business. Most lenders require your share to be 25%–30%, which includes investments you have already made.
- Bottom line, "When in doubt, tell the truth."

### 3.5.10 Small Business Investment Company

Congress created the SBIC program in 1958 to fill the gap between the availability of VC and the needs of small businesses in start-up and growth situations. SBICs, licensed and regulated by the SBA, are privately owned and managed investment firms that use their own capital, plus funds borrowed at favorable rates with an SBA guarantee, to make VC investments in small businesses. Virtually all SBICs are profit-motivated businesses.

They provide equity capital, long-term loans, debt-equity investments, and management assistance to qualifying small businesses. The only small businesses that cannot qualify for SBIC assistance are other SBICs, finance and investment companies, finance-type leasing companies, companies with less than one-half of their assets and operations in the United States, passive or casual businesses (those not engaged in regular and continuous business operation), and companies that will use the proceeds to acquire farm land.

There are two types of SBICs—regular SBICs and specialized SBICs, also known as 301(d) SBICs. Specialized SBICs invest in small businesses owned by entrepreneurs who are socially or economically disadvantaged. The SBIC Program makes funding available to all types of manufacturing and service industries. The cost of money on SBIC loans and debt securities issued by small concerns is regulated by the SBA in the interest of the small business concerns and is limited to the applicable state regulations governing such loans and debt securities, or by SBA regulations, whichever is lower.

Loans made to and debt securities purchased from small concerns should have minimum terms of 5 years. Many investment companies seek out small businesses with new products or services because of the strong growth potential of such firms. Some SBICs specialize in the field in which their management has special knowledge or competency. Most, however, consider a wide variety of investment opportunities. Information on local SBICs can be obtained by contacting the Small Business Answer Desk at 1-800-U-ASK-SBA or by visiting the SBA Home Page on the Internet at http://www.sbaonline .sba.gov. Contact: U.S. Small Business Administration Office of Financial Assistance 409 Third Street, SW, Washington, DC, 20416.

## 3.6 Controlling Your Initial Start-Up Expenses

There's a fine line between starting your business on a shoestring and watching it fail because of a lack of resources. You don't want to invest lavishly at first, yet you want to look professional in the eyes of your potential customers. The paradox and the challenge are to maintain the image of a solid, successful company without letting your expenses lead to uncompetitive pricing and failure [11].

The trick is to determine the point at which your business runs both effectively and efficiently. This is a key issue for any start-up that can determine whether you'll be able to survive. The good news is, if you master the art of trimming expenses early in the game, you'll develop good habits that'll serve you well as your company grows.

The first thing to do is cut your initial budget to the bare minimum. Chances are your business will start slow, so doing things for a dime that would otherwise cost a dollar is a great discipline. Here are some tips to keep early costs under control.

### 3.6.1 Four Tips for Reducing Your Start-Up Costs

One of the biggest concerns for new entrepreneurs is start-up costs. Even if you are not renting an office or laboratory space for your business, there are still other bills to be paid before you start seeing a profit. While most business owners plan for these expenses, many don't anticipate just how many extra costs they'll encounter along the way. If you're starting a business on a budget, follow the four tips shown in Table 3.2 to minimize your expenses and maximize your bottom line [12].

**TABLE 3.2**

Minimize Your Expenses and Maximize Your Bottom Line

| Tips | How Best to Proceed |
|---|---|
| 1. Create a realistic budget | ..... and stick to it "come hell or high water" |
| 2. Be flexible | When you developed your business plan, you probably also had a vision of the things you wanted for your business: all the latest equipment, a full-time staff, and your own private office. Every entrepreneur hopes that they will be able to make these business dreams come true, but the reality is that you'll sometimes have to sacrifice them to keep your company running. |
| 3. Go inexpensive, but not cheap | Many small business owners who spend a lot of money up front on services like marketing and Web design end up regretting it in the long run. There are countless cost-effective tools available for small business owners who want to save money by taking care of their own branding and website development. However, "free" isn't always the right answer. |
| 4. Evaluate and reevaluate | If you've followed all of these steps to save money in the early stages of your start-up, the best way to continue saving as your business grows is to continually revisit and revise your budget. Seek financial advice from accountants and fellow small business owners and then go over your expenses and try to cut back where you can. |

### 3.6.2 Controlling Labor Costs

Controlling labor costs is probably the most formidable challenge you will face. Don't learn the hard way, for example, that turnover wreaks havoc on your profits. When it's time to hire, do it carefully and intelligently, and if an employee's performance is not up to your standards, do not be too quick to fire him or her. Work with the individual to improve job performance.

While competitive compensation is essential to attracting good people, it doesn't have to all be in the form of salary. Remember the tip about turning your fixed costs into variable ones? It works in compensation as well. Supplement a small salary with the potential for healthy bonuses based on your company's earnings.

Give your employees perks, such as flexible work hours. Train them adequately for their responsibilities, and take the time to give them timely feedback and direction. Be passionate about your company and about your employees.

Refrain from hiring too much staff and expanding too quickly. With each new employee, there will be associated expenses that you may not be ready to underwrite. A better choice might be to outsource noncore competencies. You may outsource functions such as payroll, accounts payable, accounts receivables, periodic financial statements, taxes, legal, advertising, and so on [13].

### 3.6.3 Controlling Your Sales Performance

You have only three ways to increase your business's financial performance:

- Increasing sales (in which case, those increased sales may or may not have a positive impact on profitability)
- Increasing prices (in which case, the entire amount of the increase will have a positive impact on profitability, assuming that you don't lose customers because of the price increase)
- Decreasing expenses (in which case, the entire decrease will have a positive impact on profitability, assuming that you don't lose business because the expense reduction has a negative impact on your product or service quality)

In other words, you'll find a one-to-one leverage factor at work on your bottom-line profits when you increase prices or cut expenses. This is why the successful small business owner always looks to the expense and pricing categories first when in a profitability crunch: Results can be instantaneous, and the impact is usually dollar on dollar.

Whether starting a new company or running an existing one, you must always remember that controlling expenses is a cultural issue, and cultural issues begin at the top. This means that many of your employees are going to emulate you. If you have overstuffed chairs in your office and idle secretaries in your foyer, your employees are likewise going to demonstrate a penchant for spending unnecessary money. We're talking about the old practice of leading by example.

Whenever we walk into a business's lobby or reception area and we're greeted by the gurgle of cascading waterfalls and the sight of bronze sculptures, we're reminded again of Sam Walton and Wal-Mart. Linoleum floors and metal desks were the order of the day at Wal-Mart's frugal corporate headquarters in Bentonville, Arkansas. No wonder they could underprice and outperform such longtime competitors such as Sears, Montgomery Ward, and J.C. Penney, whose overhead included the cost of maintaining plush corporate offices in the towering skyscrapers of Chicago and Dallas.

### 3.6.4 Controlling Fixed and Variable Expenses

Two kinds of expenses need controlling: fixed and variable. *Fixed expenses* don't fluctuate with sales; they're usually negotiated in the start-up stage and then left to their own devices until the original negotiations lapse and it's time to renegotiate them. Such periods may be anywhere from 1 year to 5 years.

Effective control of these fixed expenses, which include such categories as insurance, rent, and equipment leases, requires the small business owner's skillful negotiation, because after they're established, renegotiation time probably won't come around for a while. That cost is then fixed, and you can do little about it.

*Variable expenses* are those expenses that fluctuate with sales—as sales go up, variable expenses go up as well (and vice versa). You can delegate the determination of the prices to be paid for variable expenses, as long as you remember that the responsibility for controlling them, in the early stages of a business anyway, should always rest with you (the owner). You should approve all purchase orders and sign all checks that relate to variable expenses.

As your company grows, you may choose to delegate the responsibility for controlling expenses to other responsible individuals inside the company, or you may still choose to maintain control by signing the checks and questioning the invoices that support those checks.

A key to controlling expenses is keeping your employees cost-conscious: If the employees know that you or other key managers are cost-conscious and will question unreasonable or unnecessary expenses, then they, too, will be motivated to contain them. Incentives are also an often-used tool for cutting costs—give your employees a reason (bonus, perks, recognition) to look for unnecessary costs, and they're sure to find them.

Always be aware that the 80–20 rule is alive and well when it comes to managing your expenses. In this case, the 80–20 rule says that 80% of your wasted expense dollars can be found in 20% of your expense categories. For businesses that have a number of employees, the wages and salary account is usually the largest expense category and, thus, the most often abused.

We don't mean to say that expenses shouldn't be challenged in every category. Quick and easy dollars can usually be found by rooting around in such expense accounts as utilities, travel, insurance, and, of course, the compost heap of them all, the "miscellaneous" expense account.

Effective expense control isn't only a profitability issue; it is also an important element for controlling cash flow. Because lack of cash is usually the number one warning signal of a small business's impending failure, how better to begin building a solid foundation than by controlling your company's expenses?

### 3.6.5 Controlling Your Budgeting Process

Start-up businesses of all sizes need accurate budgets to help balance financial accounts and create business goals. You can design a weekly, monthly, quarterly, or annual budget. A start-up business should develop at least one general budget that captures projected expenses and sales revenues. Without a solid budget, a new business might spend more than it earns and become insolvent [14].

One critical mistake many start-up entrepreneurs make is underestimating the budgeting process [15]. The traditional budgeting process proceeds as follows:

- Set goals that will enable you to grow.
- Break the goals down so that there is clear ownership and accountability for each goal by a specific team.
- Refine goals into measurable targets.
- Figure out how many new people are required to hit the targets.
- Estimate the cost of the effort.
- Benchmark against the industry.
- Make global optimizations.
- Execute.

This all sounds very mechanical and automatic, but your budget is your roadmap for the future. Do it right the first time around!

### 3.6.6 The Golden Rule

For many small businesses, the cost of getting started and keeping the business going for the first few months is quite high while income is unusually low. Budgeting for those initial costs will tell you how much capital you will need to have available to you upfront before it is sensible to start spending it all. The budgeting rule is not only to have a reasonably reliable figure but also to know how you came up with it for your budgeting process [16].

Budgeting (also known as *forecasting*) is the periodic (usually annual) review of past financial information with the purpose of forecasting future financial conditions. If you've completed your business plan, you, in effect, prepared your first budget when you forecasted your profit and loss statement for the upcoming year.

The only difference in preparing a budget for your ongoing business is that you'll now enjoy the advantage of having yesterday's figures to work with. The process of budgeting is one that should apply not only to your business but also to your personal finances, especially if you have trouble saving money.

In your small business, you have two ways to budget expenses from year to year. The first—the easy way—is to assume a percentage increase for each expense category, both variable and fixed. For example, say that you decide that your telephone expense (a variable expense) will increase by 5% next year, your rent (a fixed expense) will remain the same, and your advertising and promotion (a variable expense) will increase by 10%. Whoosh! A few multiplications later, and you have budgeted these expenses for the course of a year.

### 3.6.6.1 *Zero-Based Budgeting*

Zero-based budgeting, on the other hand, makes the assumption that last year's expenses were zero and begins the budgeting process from that point. For example, the zero-based formula assumes that your supplies' expense account begins at zero; thus, you must first determine who consumed what supplies last year, who will be consuming them this year, and how much will be consumed. Then, you must determine what price you'll pay for this year's supplies.

In this manner, zero-based budgeting forces you to annually manage your consumption at the same time that you're annually reviewing your costs. The effect of zero-based budgeting is that you'll no longer include prior years' mistakes in the current year's budgets. For example, when budgeting telephone expenses for the year, instead of increasing it by a flat percentage, zero-based budgeting demands that you make sure that your prior year's bill was the lowest it could be. This assumption forces you to determine who's using your phones for what kind of activity and also to reprice your rates with telephone carriers. Instead of forecasting a 5% increase, you may well end up projecting a 5% decrease. The zero-based method also assumes that you'll check out prices with vendors other than those that you're presently using.

Far too many small businesses don't budget expenses at all. Furthermore, of those small business owners who do, few use zero-based budgeting, despite its many advantages. Not budgeting is truly one of the most expensive mistakes you can make as a small business owner. Sure, zero-based budgeting may take more of your time, but it can pay big dividends in controlling your bottom-line profitability.

Remember that cash is king. The most critical piece is your cash flow management. You need a system that will give you an accurate picture of your bank account balance right now, as well as at various points in the future. Will you make payroll on the 30th? Will you make rent on the first? When in the next 2 months should you buy those fancy 3D printers or expensive analytical equipment [17]?

## 3.7 Minimizing Start-Up Risk with Part-Time Ventures

Some people believe that starting your own business is the riskiest of all small business options. However, if you're starting a business that specifically uses your skills and expertise, the risk may not be nearly as great as you think.

Besides, risk is relative: Those who are employed by someone else are taking a risk, too—a risk that their employer will continue to offer them the opportunity to remain employed.

One way to minimize the risk of starting a full-time business is to work into a part-time one. Suppose for a moment that you're a computer trouble-shooter at a large company and making $75,000 per year. You're consider-ing establishing your own computer consulting service and would be happy making a comparable amount of money. If you find through your research that others performing the services you intend to provide are charging $80 per hour, you'll need to actually spend about 20 h/week consulting (assum-ing that you work 50 weeks per year).

Because you can run your consulting business from your home (which can generate small tax breaks) and you can do it without purchasing costly new equipment, your expenses should be minimal. (Note: We have ignored your employer's benefits here, which, of course, have value, too.) Rather than leaving your day job and diving into your new business without the safety of a regular paycheck, you have the option of starting to moonlight as a con-sultant. Over the course of a year or two, if you can average 10 h/week of consulting, you're halfway to your goal.

Then, after you leave your job and can focus all your energies on your business, getting to 20 h/week of billable work won't be such a stretch. Many businesses, by virtue of leveraging their owner's existing skills and expertise, can be started with low start-up costs. You can begin building the framework of your company using *sweat equity* (the time and energy you invest in your business, as opposed to the capital) in the early, part-time years. As long as you know your competition and can offer your customers a valued service at a reasonable cost, the principal risk with your time business is that you will not do a good job marketing what you have to offer.

### 3.7.1 Buying an Existing Business

In the event that you do not have a specific idea for a business you want to start, but you have exhibited considerable business management skills, consider buying an established business. Although buying someone else's business can, in some cases, be riskier than starting your own, at least you know exactly what you're getting into right from the start. The good news, however, is that you often don't have to waste time and energy creating an infrastructure—it's already in place, which allows you, the buyer, to dive right into the business, without having to waste time on the peripherals.

Buying an existing business often requires that you invest more money at the outset, in the form of a down payment to buy the business. Thus, if you don't have the ability to run the business and it performs poorly, you have a lot more to lose financially.

### 3.7.2 Evaluating Buying a Business

In the American legal system, an accused is presumed innocent until proven guilty beyond a reasonable doubt. When you're purchasing a business, however, you should assume, until proven otherwise, that the selling business owner is guilty of making the business appear better than reality.

We don't want to sound cynical, but more than a few owners out there try to make their businesses look more profitable, more financially healthy, and more desirable than they really are. The reason is quite simple: Business sellers generally seek to maximize the price their business will command. Thus, don't trust only your gut when evaluating a business, because you could be fooled.

Buying a business can be tricky because the business brokerage market rarely favors the buyer. The following list presents some of the obstacles you're likely to encounter when buying a business:

- The necessary confidentiality of transactions: You can't publicly investigate a lot of the background information.
- Few listings: A paucity of businesses for sale means that the seller is in control. For good businesses that are fairly priced, there are usually plenty of potential buyers waiting in the wings.
- Unpublished prices of previous sales: There are no benchmarks. No templates to follow.
- Emotional circumstances surrounding the sale: People can get more emotional about selling their business than they do about selling real estate. Blood, sweat, retirement, and, yes, egos, are involved. Emotions run high, on both sides.

Buying a business is a long, detail-ridden, and stressful procedure. Don't rush it; be sure to cover your bases. We hit all the key points of consideration in this chapter.

### 3.7.3 Kicking Their Tires

Before you make an offer to buy a small business, you're going to want to do some digging into the company to minimize your chances of mistakenly buying a problematic business or overpaying for a good business. This process is known as *due diligence*, and it is every bit as important as hiring an attorney or signing the purchase agreement.

Smart buyers build plenty of contingencies into a purchase offer for a small business, just as they do when buying a home or other real estate. If your financing doesn't come through or you find some dirty laundry in the business (and you're not buying a laundromat), contingencies allow you to back out of the deal legally. However, knowing that you'll draft all purchase offers with plenty of contingencies shouldn't encourage you to make a purchase offer casually. Making an offer and doing the necessary research and homework are costly, in both time and money.

Before making an offer for a business, you'll want reasonably clear answers to the important due diligence questions discussed in the following sections.

### 3.7.4 Due Diligence on Owners and Key Employees

A business is usually only as good or bad as the owners and key employees running it. Ethical, business-savvy owners and key employees generally run successful businesses worthy of buying. Unscrupulous, marginally competent, or incompetent business owners and key employees are indicative of businesses that you should avoid.

Just as you wouldn't (we hope) hire employees without reviewing their resumes, interviewing them, and checking employment references, you shouldn't make an offer to buy a business until you do similar homework on the owners and key employees of the business for sale. Here's a short list of information we suggest gathering as well as suggestions on how to find it:

**Business background:** Request and review the owner's and key employees' resumes, remembering that some people may fabricate or puff up information on that piece of paper. Are the backgrounds impressive and filled with relevant business experience? Just as you should do when hiring an employee, check resumes to make sure that the information they provide is correct. Glaring omissions or inaccuracies send a strong negative message as to the kind of people you're dealing with.

**Personal reputations in the business community:** The geographic and work/professional communities to which we belong are quite small. Any business that has been up and running for a number of years has had interactions with many people and other companies.

Take the time to talk to others who may have had experience dealing with the business for sale (vendors, Chamber of Commerce, Better Business Bureau, and so on) and ask them their thoughts on the company's owners and key employees. Of course, we shouldn't need to remind you that you can't always accept the statements of others at face value. You have to consider the merits, or lack thereof, of the source.

**Credit history:** If you were a banker, we hope you wouldn't lend money to anyone without first assessing their credit risk. At a minimum, you should review the seller's credit history to see how successful they've been at paying off, on time, money they've borrowed. Even though you won't be lending money to the business seller you're speaking with, we recommend that you check his credit records. A problematic credit record could uncover business problems the owner had that he may be less than forthcoming in revealing. The major agencies that compile and sell personal credit histories and small business information are Experian (www.experian.com), Equifax (www.equifax.com), Transunion (www.transunion.com), and Dun & Bradstreet (800-234-3867; www.dnb.com).

**Key customers:** The people who can usually give you the best indication of the value of a business for sale are its current customers. Through your own research on the business or from the current owner, get a list of the company's top 5 to 10 customers and ask them the following questions:

- In general, how is the company perceived by its customers?
- Does it deliver on time?
- How do its products or services compare to its competitors' offerings?
- Does it have a culture of integrity?
- What does the company do best?
- What does it need to improve?

**Key employees:** If the employees of the business for sale are aware of the prospects of the impending sale, be sure to interview them and get their insider's take on the condition of the business. You also want to know whether they intend to remain as employees under the new ownership.

### 3.7.5 Why Is the Owner Selling?

After you locate a potentially attractive business for sale, the serious work begins. First, try to discover the reason the owner is selling. Small business owners may be selling for a reason that shouldn't matter to you (they've reached the age and financial status where they simply want to retire), or they may be selling for reasons that should matter to you (the business is a never-ending headache to run, it isn't very profitable, or competition is changing the competitive landscape).

If an owner wants to sell for some negative reason, that shouldn't necessarily sour you on buying the business. If the business has a low level of profitability, it isn't necessarily a lemon—quite possibly the current owner hasn't taken the proper steps (such as cost management, effective marketing, and so on) to boost its profitability. You may well be able to overcome hurdles the current owner can't. But before you make a purchase offer and then follow through on that offer, you absolutely, positively should understand many aspects of the business including, first and foremost, why the current owner wants out.

The list below describes how to discover why the current owner is selling (where appropriate, get the current owner's permission to speak with certain people):

**Chat with the owner.** This isn't a terribly creative, Sherlock Holmes–type method, and yes, we know that many sellers aren't going to be completely candid about why they are selling, but you never know.

Besides, you can verify the answer you get from the owner against what other sources tell you about the owner's motivations to sell.

**Talk with the business owner's advisors.** As we explain throughout this chapter, in the course of evaluating the worth of a business, you should be speaking with various advisors, including those you hire yourself. Don't overlook, however, the wealth of information and background that the current owner's advisors have. These advisors may include lawyers, accountants, bankers, and the business's own board of advisors or directors.

**Confer with industry sources.** Most industries are closely knit groups of companies, each one knowing, in general, what's going on with the other businesses in the same industry. Most importantly, the vendor salespeople or manufacturers' representatives who call on the industry can be a terrific source for information. Sure, they may not be completely candid, but your job is to read between the lines of what they have to say. (They generally won't out-and-out lie to you either. They're aware that you could be their next customer.)

**Seek out customers.** (Carefully!). The business's current customers usually do not know that a business is for sale, but they can provide you with the information you need to determine whether the current owner is selling from strength or from weakness.

**Discuss with key employees.** Some employees probably know the real answer as to why the business is for sale. Your job: Find out what they know. In your discussions with and investigations about the current owner, also reflect upon these final, critical questions: How important is the current owner to the success of the business? What will happen when he or she is no longer around? Will the business under new management lose key employees, key customers, and so on?

### 3.7.6 Understanding the Company's Culture

When you buy a small business, you're adopting someone else's child. Depending on the strength of its already-formed personality and how it meshes with yours, you may or may not be successful in molding that business into your image.

Eight out of 10 dentists recommend Crest. Eight out of 10 acquisitions fail to meet expectations. Why? A clash of cultures. Ninety-two percent of the survey respondents said that their deals would "have substantially benefitted from a greater cultural understanding prior to the merger." Seventy percent conceded that "too little" effort focuses on culture during integration [18].

Is your expectation compatible with their "culture"? Culture can be defined as "how we do things around here in order to succeed" [19]. To prevent future headaches, ensure that your "culture" is in line with theirs [20]. Part of the problem may be that, especially when integrating companies are in the same or similar businesses, the acquirer tends to assume they are "just like me" and dismiss the need for deep cultural analysis.

Likewise, when the acquirer and acquiree in a deal get along with each other, they tend to assume that their companies will get along equally well. No two companies are cultural twins, and companies seldom get along with each other as easily as their executives might. In fact, the survey establishes that the issue of culture comes down to two fundamental problems: understanding both cultures and providing the right amount and type of leadership.

For understandable reasons, leaders discount the impact of corporate culture when they acquire. They have other factors to consider at the time of the acquisition—market opportunities, operational and business process synergies, financial analysis, and potential profits. These factors are obviously important. In addition, "culture" is not only an amorphous concept, it is believed to be immeasurable and inherently unmanageable. Most leaders probably just assume that culture will "iron itself out" over time. However, organizational culture is too important to be left up to hope and natural evolution.

## 3.8 The JOBS Act and Crowdfunding

In an effort to jump-start the entrepreneurial economy, the JOBS (Jumpstart Our Business Startups) Act created a new provision in the Securities Act of 1933 Section 4(6) that allows Emerging Growth Companies (EGCs) to raise up to $1 million in any 12-month period by selling securities through authorized intermediaries, subject to certain limitations on the matter of the offering and by limiting the amount any person is permitted to invest.

**Emerging Growth Companies** are a new category of issuer. EGCs are those with (1) less than $1 billion total annual gross revenues in their most recent fiscal year and (2) have not had a registered public offering before December 8, 2012 [21].

The JOBS Act (signed into law April 6, 2012) facilitates financing across the spectrum from seed capital to public offerings. Below are some of the most important aspects and implications:

- Permitting "crowdfunding."
- Easing restrictions on fundraising from accredited investors.
- Easing mandatory reporting triggers under the SEC Act.
- Increasing the amount of money companies may raise in "mini-IPOs."

- Reducing many burdens on EGCs going public.
- Providing more capital to entrepreneurs and EGCs, creating jobs, and providing opportunities for nonaccredited investors to invest in both community-based businesses and entrepreneurial companies.
- For the last several years, the number of VC financings in the US has continued to drop—approximately 3500 VC led deals; VCs are raising less capital and continue to finance only larger opportunities with significant IRR potential and with exits of greater than $50 million.
- Although angel statistics are difficult to obtain, they funded nearly as much as VCs.
- Fewer than 10% of all accredited investors in the United States invest in private financings. Except as friends or family, nonaccredited investors have no exposure to private financings.
- There are 25,000,000 ECGs in the United States; many are looking for funding and banks aren't lending, and identifying investors is extremely difficult given securities laws.

### 3.8.1  The JOBS Act at a Glance

The JOBS Act seeks to accomplish this goal by, among other measures, relaxing certain provisions of the Sarbanes–Oxley and Dodd–Frank Acts insofar as those provisions apply to a class of newly public companies dubbed "Emerging Growth Companies." A primary goal of the legislation is to facilitate the ability of growing companies to raise capital, as shown below:

- Removes the prohibition on general solicitation in connection with transactions dealing with Rule 508 or Rule 144A, provided that sales are limited to qualifying investors.
- Allows the thresholds that trigger registration of a security under Section 12(g), including a different threshold for banks and bank holding companies.
- Provides, to a new category of ECGs, relief from requirements and other restrictions applicable to IPOs (initial public offerings) and, on a transitional basis for up to 5 years, relief from certain reporting requirements.
- Adds a crowdfunding exemption and authorizes the SC to increase the amount permitted to be raised in a Regulation A offering to $50 million in any 12-month period.
- Modifications to Rule 506 will provide substantial freedom for issuers to promote their offerings to a wider group of investors.
- Anyone who can convince the investing public that they have a good business idea can become an entrepreneur.

- Modeled in part on campaign donations, since politicians have been collecting small donations from the general public for decades.
- Another route for business funding (since VCs reject 98% of business plans).

### 3.8.2 Title III of the US JOBS Act

- The Act limits both the aggregate value of securities that an issuer may offer through a crowdfunding intermediary and the amount that an individual can invest.
- An issuer may sell up to an aggregate of $1,000,000 of its securities during any 12-month period.
- Investors with an annual income or net worth of up to $40,000 will only be permitted to invest $2000 and above $40,000 and less than $100,000 investors shall be entitled to invest 5% of their annual income or net worth in any 12-month period.
- Investors with an annual income or net worth greater than $100,000 will be permitted to invest 10% of their annual income or net worth.
- Investors are limited to investing $100,000 in crowdfunding issues in a 12-month period.
- Investors who purchase securities in a crowdfunding transaction are restricted from transferring those securities for a period of 1 year. This restriction is subject to certain exceptions, including transfers (i) to the issuer, (ii) to an accredited investor, (iii) pursuant to an offering registered with the SEC, (iv) or to the investor's family members.

### 3.8.3 Equal Access and Disclosure

Equal access to and disclosure of material information is a core principle of federal and state securities regulations. It is essential for investors to have the necessary information to appreciate the potential risks and rewards of an investment. The JOBS Act requires issuers to provide investors with a description of the following:

- *Company:* the issuer and its members, including the name, legal status, physical address, and the names of the directors and officers holding more than 20% of the shares of the issuer.
- *Offering:* the anticipated business plan of the issuer, the target offering amount, the deadline to reach the target offering amount, and the price to the public of the securities.
- *Structure:* the ownership and capital structure of the issuer, including terms of the securities of the issuer being offered.

- *Valuation:* how the securities being offered are being valued, and examples of methods for how such securities may be valued by the issuer in the future, including during subsequent corporate actions.
- *Risks:* the risks to purchasers of the securities relating to minority ownership in the issuer, the risks associated with corporate actions, including additional issuances of shares, a sale of the issuer or of assets of the issuer, or transactions with related parties.
- The intermediary crowdfunding portals are also required to make available to the SEC and to potential investors any information provided by the issuer no later than 21 days before the first day on which securities are sold to any investor.

### 3.8.4 Crowdfunding

Crowdfunding refers to the funding of an EGC by selling small amounts of equity to many investors. This form of crowdfunding has recently received attention from policymakers in the United States with direct mention in the JOBS Act; legislation that allows for a wider pool of small investors with fewer restrictions [22].

With the passing of the Act, the word of the day seems to be crowdfunding. While this concept has arguably been around a long time, it is still formally recognized as a new industry to many consumers, particularly those outside the United States.

**Crowdfunding** is, by definition, "the practice of funding a project or venture by raising many small amounts of money from a large number of people, typically via the Internet."

Crowdfunding has its origins in the concept of crowdsourcing, which is the broader concept of an individual reaching a goal by receiving and leveraging small contributions from many parties. Crowdfunding is the application of this concept to the collection of funds through small contributions from many parties in order to finance a particular project or venture [23].

Theoretically, crowdfunding allows EGCs to sell securities to anyone, without being compelled to produce the onerous amounts of information currently required by existing federal law. A number of US organizations have been founded to provide education and advocacy related to equity-based crowdfunding as enabled by the JOBS Act. They include the following:

- National Crowdfunding Association
- Crowdfunding Professional Association
- CrowdFund Intermediary Regulatory Advocates

Crowdfunding is not available to non-US companies, public companies, or investment companies, including companies exempt by Section 3(b) or 3(c) of the Investment Company Act of 1940. In addition, securities sold in a crowd-funding deal may not be transferred for 1 year from the date of purchase, except in limited circumstances.

### 3.8.5 Issuer Requirements

EGCs seeking to raise capital under Section 4(6) [24] are required to provide certain information to potential investors, such as

- The company
- Its business
- Officers and directors
- Major stockholders (greater than 20%)
- Terms of the offering securities being offered for sale

Importantly, the JOBS Act requires that EGCs must provide more detailed financial disclosures for larger offerings. Thus, if the aggregate amount of the offering is $100,000 or less, the issuer must only provide tax returns for the company's most recently completed fiscal year, and financial statements certified by the company's chief executive officer.

In contrast, if the aggregate amount is $100,000 to $500,000, the issuer must provide financial statements reviewed by an independent public accountant. If the aggregate amount being offered exceed $500,000, the issuer must provide audited financial statements.

### 3.8.6 Intermediary Requirements

The JOBS Act requires that crowdfunded offerings be conducted through authorized third-party "intermediaries" [25]. Intermediaries, crowdfunding brokers, and funding portals have significant duties under the JOBS Act to provide information to investors, reduce the risk of fraud, and, where required under the Act, ensure that investors and issuers satisfy the requirements outlined in Title III of the JOBS Act.

The JOBS Act requires these intermediaries to, among other things:

- Provide disclosures that the SEC determines appropriate by rule, including regarding the risks of the transaction and investor education materials
- Ensure that each investor (1) reviews investor education materials; (2) positively affirms that the investor understands that the investor is risking the loss of the entire investment, and that the investor could bear such a loss; and (3) answers questions that demonstrate that the investor understands the level of risk generally applicable

to investments in start-ups, emerging businesses, and small issuers and the risk of illiquidity

- Take steps to protect the privacy of information collected from investors
- Take such measures to reduce the risk of fraud with respect to such transactions, as established by the SEC, by rule, including obtaining a background and securities enforcement regulatory history check on each officer, director, and person holding more than 20% of the outstanding equity of every issuer whose securities are offered by such person
- Make available to investors and the SEC, at least 21 days before any sale, any disclosures provided by the issuer
- Ensure that all offering proceeds are only provided to the issuer when the aggregate capital raised from all investors is equal to or greater than a target offering amount, and allow all investors to cancel their commitments to invest
- Make efforts to ensure that no investor in a 12-month period has purchased crowdfunded securities that, in the aggregate, from all issuers, exceed the investment limits set forth in Title III, Section 4A of the JOBS Act; plus any other requirements that the SEC determines are appropriate.

### 3.8.7 Funding Portals

Title III of the JOBS Act adds a new Section 3(h) to the Exchange Act that requires the SEC to exempt, conditionally or unconditionally, an intermediary operating a funding portal from the requirement to register with the SEC as a broker.

The intermediary, though, would need to register with the SEC as a funding portal and would be subject to the SEC's examination, enforcement, and rulemaking authority. The funding portal also must become a member of a national securities association that is registered under Section 15A of the Exchange Act.

A funding portal is defined as a crowdfunding intermediary that does not (i) offer investment advice or recommendations; (ii) solicit purchases, sales, or offers to buy securities offered or displayed on its website or portal; (iii) compensate employees, agents, or others persons for such solicitation or based on the sale of securities displayed or referenced on its website or portal; (iv) hold, manage, possess, or otherwise handle investor funds or securities; or (v) engage in such other activities as the SEC, by rule, determines appropriate.

The JOBS Act directs the SEC to adopt rules to implement Title III within 270 days of enactment of the Act. The president signed the JOBS Act into law on April 5, 2012.

### 3.8.8 Restrictions on Funding Portals

The JOBS Act imposes several restrictions on the activities of a registered funding portal. A funding portal is *not* permitted to

- Provide investment advice or make recommendations
- Solicit purchases, sales, or offers to buy the securities offered or displayed on its website or portal
- Compensate employees, agents, or other persons for such solicitation or based on the sale of securities displayed or referenced on its website or portal
- Hold, manage, possess, or otherwise handle investor funds or securities
- Engage in any other activities the SEC determines to prohibit in its crowdfunding rulemaking

In addition, each funding portal and each crowdfunding broker is prohibited from

- Compensating promoters, finders, or lead generators for providing the intermediary with the personal identifying information of any potential investor
- Allowing its directors, officers, or partners (or any person occupying a similar status or performing a similar function) to have a financial interest in any issuer using the services of the intermediary

### 3.8.9 Crowdfunding Sites for Social Entrepreneurs

If money is the only thing stopping you from doing something good in the world, stop waiting and start doing some good! Nothing better symbolizes entrepreneurship than fundraising. Social entrepreneurs are no different. Today, there are a host of online resources for crowdfunding that social entrepreneurs can use to fund their projects, films, books, and social ventures. The following list presents the crowdfunding go-to sites:

- Kickstarter.com: Kickstarter is the 800-pound gorilla in crowdfunding, originally designed and built for creative arts; many technology entrepreneurs now use the site, some reporting to have raised millions of dollars. The Kickstarter funding model is an all-or-nothing model. You set a goal for your raise; if your raise exceeds the goal, you keep all the money; otherwise, your supporters don't pay and you don't get anything. This protects supporters from some of the risk of your running out of money before your project is completed.
- StartSomeGood.com: StartSomeGood is great for early-stage social good projects that are not (yet) 501(c)(3) registered nonprofits.

StartSomeGood uses a unique "tipping point" model for fundraising, allowing you to set a funding goal and a lower "tipping point" at which your project can minimally proceed and where you will collect the money you raise.

- Indiegogo.com: Indiegogo allows you to raise money for absolutely anything, using an optional "keep what you raise" model with higher fees or pay less to use an all-or-nothing funding approach.

- Rockethub.com: Rockethub is also a broad platform targeting "artists, scientists, entrepreneurs, and philanthropists" on their site, using a keep-what-you-raise model that rewards you for hitting your funding goal (or penalizes you for failing to hit it).

All of these sites are making great things happen for real people every day, advancing the arts, entrepreneurship, and philanthropy in myriad ways. Check them and others all out and then decide which one is the best for your needs.

## References

1. Freear, J., Sohl, J.E., and Wetzel, W. Angels: Personal investors in the venture capital market. *Entrepreneurship and Regional Development*, 7, 85–94, 1995.
2. Carter, N.M., Brush, C., Gatewood, E., Greene, P., and Hart, M. Does enhancing women's financial sophistication promote entrepreneurial success? Paper presented at the Promoting Female Entrepreneurship: Implications for Education, Training and Policy Conference, Dundalk Institute of Technology, Ireland, 20, November 2002.
3. McCune, J.C. Bootstrapping: Cutting corners and pinching pennies to finance your business, *Bankrate.com*, Internet, 1999, http://www.bankrate.com/brm/news/biz/Cashflow_banking/19991101.asp.
4. Bhide, A. Bootstrap finance: The art of start-ups. *Harvard Business Review*, 70 (November–December), 109–117, 1992.
5. http://www.investopedia.com/terms/s/sweatequity.asp
6. Lahm, R.J. and Little, H.T., Jr. *Bootstrapping Business Start-Ups: A Review of Current Business Practices*. 2005 Conference on Emerging Issues in Business and Technology, http://paws.wcu.edu/RJLahm/teaching/entrepreneurship/Bootstrapping_Lahm.pdf.
7. http://www.angelblog.net/Startup_Funding_the_Friends_and_Family_Round.html
8. Hsu, D. and Ziedonis, R.H. Patents as Quality Signals for Entrepreneurial Ventures. Copenhagen, DRUID Summer Conference, Denmark, June 2007, http://www2.druid.dk/conferences/viewpaper.php?id=1717&cf=9.
9. Spence, M. Job market signaling. *Quarterly Journal of Economics*, 87, 355–374, 1973.

10. Tyson, E. and Schell, J. *Small Business for Dummies*, Wiley Publishing, Inc., Hoboken, NJ, 2008.
11. Sugars, B. Keeping Your Costs Down, http://www.entrepreneur.com/article /177116.
12. Fallon, N. Business News Daily, www.businessnewsdaily.com/5358-startup -budget-tips.html.
13. http://earlygrowthfinancialservices.com/where-is-your-startup-overspending/
14. http://smallbusiness.chron.com/budget-startup-business-1351.html
15. http://www.businessinsider.com/ben-horowitz-budget-process-kills-startups -2014-7
16. http://search.aol.com/aol/search?s_it=topsearchbox.search&v_t=wscreen -smallbusiness-w&q=budgeting+startups+++pdf
17. http://jeffmagnusson.com/agile-budgeting-cash-is-king/
18. Perspectives on merger integration. McKinsey, http://www.mckinsey.com/~/media /mckinsey/dotcom/client_service/Organization/PDFs/775084%20Merger%20 Management%20Article%20Compendium.ashx.
19. Schneider, W.F. Merger or acquisition failing? http://www.cdg-corp.com /documents/WES%20M%20&%20A%20article.pdf.
20. http://knowledge.senndelaney.com/docs/thought_papers/pdf/SennDelaney _cultureclash_UK.pdf
21. http://ww2.cfo.com/growth-companies/2013/10/the-jobs-act-crowdfunding -and-emerging-businesses/
22. http://www.forbes.com/sites/tanyaprive/2012/11/27/what-is-crowdfunding -and-how-does-it-benefit-the-economy/
23. http://en.wikipedia.org/wiki/Crowdfunding
24. http://en.wikipedia.org/wiki/Jumpstart_Our_Business_Startups_Act
25. http://www.sec.gov/divisions/marketreg/tmjobsact-crowdfundingintermedi ariesfaq.htm

# 4

## Funding a Knowledge-Intensive Business

### 4.1 Introduction

Starting your own knowledge-intensive business is definitely not for everyone; it can be a highly stressful way to earn a living. On the positive side, you have total control over your life; there's no boss telling you what to do and when to do it. You are the master, or mistress, of your own destiny, and you will be doing what you like, when you like to do it, and how you like to do it.

However, there is a dark side; you will work longer hours and there is no guarantee that, magically, money will appear in your bank account biweekly, or monthly. That security of income suddenly disappears, as dozens of other things require paying before you can take your wage.

The majority of would-be entrepreneurs underestimate the amount of money they need to start a business. Here is a list of some of the *initial* costs you will encounter [1]:

1. All the documents, and professional help—licenses, permits, incorporation, legal fees, accountancy fees, partnership agreements, and more

2. Equipment (manufacturing, computers, printers, cash registers, alarms, chairs, desks, phones, the list goes on)

3. Inventory: goods, or raw materials, work-in-process

4. Insurance—liability, life, building, umbrella policies, and so on

5. Rent, down payments, and any leasehold improvements

6. Air conditioning, gas, oil, water, telephone, Internet, and so on

7. Staff payroll, taxes, benefits, training

8. Delivery, warehousing, courier, postage, and so on

9. Marketing costs: business cards, stationery, advertising, website, mailing lists, online, travel, accommodation, entertainment, conferences, and so on

10. Professional association memberships

In many cases, the above list will only represent the starting point of all the money you will need to fund your start-up, and all that is even before you start to pay yourself. Remember, you are unlikely to start your business one day and be able to pay all your expenses from profit the next. Cash flow is a critical component of survival, so it is vital that you have sufficient capital to bridge the gap between the day you start your business and the time your business not only can sustain itself but also make a profit. Consider the following list of undercapitalized start-ups that made it big:

- Starbucks was started by three guys in 1971 who invested $1350 each. 2015 brand value: $132 billion.
- UPS was started by a couple of teenagers who possessed one bicycle between them and $100. 2015 brand value: $40 billion.
- Apple—It's 1976, two guys make a sale, buy a bunch of parts bought on credit and deliver some computers. 2015 brand value: $200 billion.
- Gillette started in 1903 with 25 cents. 2015 brand value: $22 billion.
- Nike, in 1963, launched with $1000. 2015 brand value: $20 billion.
- Hewlett Packard started in 1938 in a garage with the princely sum of $538 dollars. 2015 brand value: $40 billion.

## 4.2 Starting Your Start-Up

Your start-up's demand for cash depends on the costs associated with developing and marketing your product. Entrepreneurs creating a sweat equity company in their garage and initially funded by personal savings do not need to seek, or solicit, investment capital.

In contrast, the entrepreneur who plans to start a new biopharmaceutical company must spend countless hours trying to secure large amounts of investment capital. Once the initial capital is secured, founders will immediately start planning when and how to secure the next "round" of financing.

Start-up firms are voracious in their appetite for cash, and raising money is a never-ending process, being at the mercy of the investment community. The decision to form a modest investment company or an equity investment company is largely dependent on your timeline to market launch.

While your innate desire to preserve ownership and operational control of the venture via a modest investment company is understandable, many commercial opportunities require extensive partnering, in both investment and strategy.

Most start-ups go through a predictable series of steps, before raising capital. Figure 4.1 summarizes the typical history of a start-up.

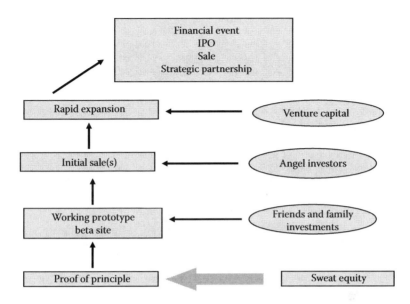

**FIGURE 4.1**
Typical historical development.

## 4.3 When Is the Best Time to Start Your Start-Up?

Entrepreneurs get so excited about forming a company that they often lose sight of the hard road ahead. It is easy to overlook the fundamentals of building a successful business. While there is no mathematical formula for determining the best time to start a new company, raising enough capital to cover the first year of operations is a good rule of thumb.

The "best" time has less to do with the stage of research than with the ability to raise capital. Innovative discoveries are generally quite far from being products and have increased chances of failure during development. The pathway from concept to product entails substantial risk. Therefore, the more embryonic the discovery, the higher the risk.

Investors prefer companies that are advanced in product development. For knowledge-intensive products, such as drugs or high technology, companies with mid-stage human clinical trials or those with successful beta tests of their software are desired.

Investors can be stratified according to their comfort levels with risks at each of the stages of the commercialization process. Those at the early (highest-risk) end are often called "seed" investors, and those at the later (lower-risk) stages are called "mezzanine" investors. It is important for entrepreneurs to clearly understand the risk profile associated with commercializing their product, since it enables them to better assess the investment climate.

## 4.4 Start-Up Fundraising Principles

*Dig your water hole before you are thirsty.*

The amount of money you plan to raise should be sufficient to accomplish key milestones that will either (1) make your start-up self-sufficient or (2) enable you to raise additional capital at *a higher valuation*. Higher valuations enable management to keep a greater percentage of the company, in anticipation of future financing rounds.

Like it or not, the entrepreneur needs to prepare for an exhaustive due diligence process. Due diligence is the analysis and evaluation conducted by firms considering an investment in your company and focuses primarily on (1) your management team, (2) the market opportunity, and (3) your technology, including intellectual property protection, usually in that order.

You should prepare a list of references and accomplishments of key management team members (including your scientific advisory board members) and your technology. Furthermore, have your patent firm prepare a status report on your patents, including a "freedom to operate" opinion, so you can verify that your products are proprietary and that you are not encumbered by the patents of others.

In summary, what do you need to attract investors?

- A great business model
- A great business plan
- A great management team
- Proprietary technology
- A growing market segment

## 4.5 Types of Financing for Start-Ups

So you think you are ready to commercialize your innovation? Congratulations! Now you need start-up financing—that initial infusion of money needed to turn the idea into something tangible. And that is where it becomes very tricky.

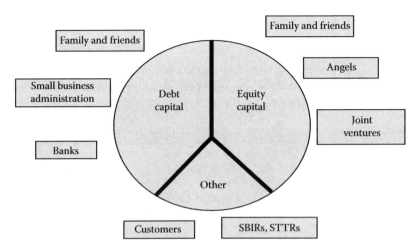

**FIGURE 4.2**
Types of financing for start-ups.

When you are just starting out, you are not yet at the point where a traditional lender or investor would be interested in you. So that leaves you with selling cherished assets, borrowing against your home, maxing out credit cards, dipping into a 401(k), and asking loved ones for loans. There is a lot of risk involved, including the risk of bankruptcy with your personal finances and soured relationships with friends and family [2].

The type of investors that you should seek for your start-up will depend on (1) the type of company that is being built, (2) the stage of development, and (3) the projected capital needs. The type of financing available to you will depend on

- The amount you need and how it will be used
- Your personal financial condition
- Your available collateral
- Your ability to manage a business
- Your determination, presentation skills, and ability to negotiate

Basically, start-ups can raise capital by three mechanisms: (1) equity, (2) debt, or (3) other, as shown in Figure 4.2.

### 4.5.1 Equity Financing Process

Equity financing is the process of raising capital through the sale of shares in an enterprise. Equity financing essentially refers to the sale of an ownership interest to raise funds for business purposes. With equity financing, a company gives investors shares in the company's ownership in exchange for capital. There is no promise to repay the investment like in a loan arrangement, nor is there an interest component.

There is, however, a cost to equity capital. In order for investors to agree to invest in the company, they expect to earn an "acceptable return" that justifies the risk of the investment.

That "acceptable return" varies over time and across industries as investors compare the potential upside, the potential risks, and the risk–reward profile of investment opportunities other than the given company. If the company fails to meet these return expectations, investors can share their ownership interest and move capital elsewhere, reducing the value of the company and hampering future efforts to raise capital [3].

Equity financing spans a wide range of activities in scale and scope, from a few thousand dollars raised by an entrepreneur from friends and family, to giant initial public offerings (IPOs) running into the billions by household names such as Google and Facebook.

While the term is generally associated with financings by public companies listed on an exchange, equity financing includes financings by private companies as well. Equity financing is clearly distinct from debt financing, which refers to funds borrowed by a business [4].

Equity financing involves not just the sale of common equity but also the sale of other equity or quasi-equity instruments such as preferred stock, convertible preferred stock, and equity units that include common shares and warrants.

A start-up that grows into a successful company will likely require several rounds of equity financing as it evolves. Since a start-up typically attracts different types of investors at various stages of its evolution, it may use different equity instruments for its financing needs.

For example, friends and family as well as angel investors—who are generally the first investors in a start-up—are inclined to favor convertible preferred shares rather than common equity in exchange for funding new companies, since the former have greater upside potential and some downside protection. Once the company has grown large enough to consider going public, it may consider selling common equity to institutional and retail investors. Later on, if it needs additional capital, the company may opt for secondary equity financings such as a rights offering or an offering of equity units that includes warrants as a "sweetener."

The characteristics of equity financing for start-ups is summarized in Table 4.1.

### 4.5.2 Debt Financing

In contrast, debt financing is when a company takes out a loan or issues a bond to raise capital. While there can be much complexity in the details of large corporate debt deals, the fundamentals are largely similar to common

**TABLE 4.1**

Equity Financing for Start-Ups

| Investor Types | Characteristics |
| --- | --- |
| Friends and family<br>Typical round: $10 to $100,000 | Not necessarily "accredited" individuals<br>"Passive" investment<br>Personally interested in the technology |
| Angels<br>Typical round: $50 to $500,000<br>Increasingly as angel groups | Accredited individuals<br>Expertise and personal investments<br>Bets on the jokey, not the horse |
| Venture Capital<br>Typical round: $1 million to $5 million<br>Looks for an "exit" | Professional investors<br>LLP, General Partnerships<br>Follow-on investments |

household debts already familiar with individuals. Companies can accept long-term financing to purchase facilities, equipment, or other long-term assets, similar to a family that takes out a mortgage loan to purchase a house or a loan to buy a car.

Debt is borrowing money from an outside source with your promise to repay the principal, in addition to an agreed-upon level of interest. Although the term tends to have a negative connotation, start-up companies often turn to debt to finance their operations. In fact, even the healthiest of corporate balance sheets will include some level of debt. In finance, debt is also referred to as "leverage." The most popular source for debt financing is the bank, but debt can also be issued by a private company or even a friend or family member [5].

*We can now define debt financing as: A method of financing in which a company receives a loan and gives its promise to repay the loan* [6].

Debt financing includes both secured and unsecured loans. Security involves a form of collateral as an assurance the loan will be repaid. If the debtor defaults on the loan, that collateral is forfeited to satisfy payment of the debt. Most lenders will ask for some sort of security on a loan. Few, if any, will lend you money based on your name or idea alone.

In addition to secured or unsecured loans, most debt will be subject to a repayment period. There are three types of repayment terms:

1. **Short-term loans** are typically paid back within 6 to 18 months.

2. **Intermediate-term loans** are paid back within 3 years.

3. **Long-term loans** are paid back from the cash flow of the business in 5 years or less.

The most common source of debt financing for start-ups often isn't a commercial lending institution, but family and friends. When borrowing money from your relatives or friends, have your attorney draw up legal papers dictating the terms of the loan. Why? Too many entrepreneurs borrow money

**TABLE 4.2**

Summary Differences between Debt and Equity Financing

| Debt (Bank Loan) | Equity (Angels, Venture Capital) |
| --- | --- |
| Emphasis on collateral and cash flow | Return on investment |
| Repayment starts immediately after funding | Deferred repayment |
| Debt return based on ability to pay | Repayment based on financial performance |
| Lowest risk for lender | Highest risk for investor |
| Lowest cost if business is successful | Higher cost if business is successful |
| No ownership dilution | Heavy ownership dilution |
| Focused on short-term expansion | Focused on long-term business prospects |
| Monitoring relationship | May demand board seats, plus upper management participation |
| Boilerplate documents | Complex documentation |

from family and friends on an informal basis. The terms of the loan have been verbalized but not written down in a contract.

Lending money can be tricky for people who can't view the transaction at arm's length; if they don't feel you're running your business correctly, they might step in and interfere with your operations. In some cases, you can't prevent this, even with a written contract, because many state laws guarantee voting rights to an individual who has invested money in a business. This can create and has created a lot of hard feelings. Make sure to check with your attorney before accepting any loans from friends or family.

Table 4.2 summarizes the most common differences between debt and equity financing available to entrepreneurs.

## 4.6 Alternative Financing Opportunities

Most businesses don't start with bank loans or venture capital. Most actually start their organizations financed with a combination of personal resources, "bootstrapping," and help from family and friends. Only a small number of start-ups begin with a bank loan, and even less start with a venture capital infusion.

If you have little cash or personal assets and bad personal credit, bank loans are not an immediate option. Your first step may be to recruit an equity partner ("angel") or a cosigner. Creative and determined entrepreneurs routinely start businesses without bank loans.

### 4.6.1 Sweat Equity and Friends, Family, and Fools (3Fs)

Usually, the founders each put a great deal of time ("sweat equity"), plus some of their personal funds into the enterprise during its early years to help with initial expenses. More committed entrepreneurs, especially those without co-founders, may invest a considerable amount of their own money into the company, frequently using credit cards and home equity loans.

Also, entrepreneurs may tap their friends and families ("friends, family, and fools") as early angels to provide initial funding. Soliciting money from family and friends can be emotionally draining. It is wise to be clear upfront about your goals and intentions. A written agreement or contract will be useful.

### 4.6.2 Nonprofit Foundation Grants

Nonprofit foundations are often good starting places to seek funding if your mission and goals are compatible with the missions and goals of the nonprofit foundation.

Occurring more frequently in healthcare, certain nonprofit foundations may be interested in sponsoring "orphan drug" development, new cancer therapies, fighting exotic tropical diseases, and so on. For example, the Food and Drug Administration (FDA) Office of Orphan Products Development (OOPD) provides incentives for sponsors to develop products for rare diseases. The program has successfully enabled the development and marketing of more than 2800 orphan designations, and more than 400 drugs and biologic products for rare diseases have been granted FDA approval since 1983 [7].

The Humanitarian Use Device Program has been the first step in approval of more than 150 Humanitarian Device Exemption approvals [8]. Orphan status is applied to drugs and biologics that are defined as those intended for the safe and effective treatment, diagnosis, or prevention of rare diseases/disorders that affect fewer than 200,000 people in the United States, or that affect more than 200,000 persons but are not expected to recover the costs of developing and marketing a treatment drug.

The Humanitarian Use Device program designates a device that is intended to benefit patients by treating or diagnosing a disease or condition that affects fewer than 4000 individuals in the United States per year as per 21 CFR 814.3(n).

The OOPD administers two extramural grant programs. The Orphan Products Grants Program provides funding for clinical research that tests the safety and efficacy of drugs, biologics, medical devices, and medical foods in rare diseases or conditions. The Pediatric Device Consortia Grant Program provides funding to develop nonprofit consortia to facilitate pediatric medical device development.

There are a few other factors that positively influence the economics of orphan drug development: timelines are typically shorter [9], the FDA is often more flexible with approvals because of the lack of alternative treatments [10], and approved orphan drugs often require less marketing, have a faster uptake, and are generally well reimbursed.

All these considerations have made orphan drug development strategies increasingly popular with big pharma and venture capital investors—and, thus, with biotech entrepreneurs—but what financial rewards have start-up orphan drug companies actually reaped, and how likely is it that your company will draw interest from big-pocketed buyers?

Although a rare disease is defined as one that affects fewer than 200,000 people in the United States, the number of such conditions totals approximately 7000 and collectively they affect nearly 30 million Americans, or one in 10 of the population. According to the FDA, one-third of all new drug approvals over the last 5 years have been for rare diseases. In 2013, the Pharmaceutical Research and Manufacturers of America claimed that there are more than 450 new medicines for rare diseases in clinical-stage development or undergoing FDA review, including 85 for genetic disorders [11].

### 4.6.3 SBIR and STTR Grants

Small Business Innovation Research (SBIR) and Small Business Technology Transfer (STTR) are federal grant programs that fund research in companies with fewer than 500 employees. See Chapter 5 for more details.

These programs recognize that much of the United States' innovation occurs within the small business sector, and they aim to accelerate further innovation in specific areas of research. More than 2 billion dollars in grants are awarded each year by agencies of the federal government under published solicitations.

SBIR/STTR Awards have three phases:

- Phase I (up to $150,000), in which new concepts undergo "proof of principle"
- Phase II (up to $1 million), in which successful Phase I projects are developed into products
- Phase IIb (up to $3 million) in which the Phase II projects are moved close to commercialization

SBIR/STTR awards are made to the small business, but a portion of the funds may be subcontracted to a university, or another research entity laboratory, which can be a great source for managing proof-of-concept projects without having to pay for expensive infrastructure such as instrumentation in a private sector laboratory (up to 33% for SBIR and 60% for STTR during Phase I).

#### 4.6.3.1 Academic Start-Ups

SBIR/STTR awards are attractive to academic start-ups for two reasons: They play to the grant-writing strengths of academic researchers and the entrepreneurial founder. These are outright grants, not equity investments (e.g., you don't have to give a piece of the company away to get the money). The major downside to the awards is that there can be a significant lag between Phase I and Phase II awards, and it may be difficult to keep research teams together (i.e., meet payroll, and keep the lights on) while the Phase II application is pending.

Many academics have been tempted to use the SBIR/STTR programs to extend their academic research instead of using the funds to build a company and develop products.

### 4.6.3.2 Expert Review Panels

Expert panels are utilized to review the grant applications for both technical and commercial merit. Applications that are academically focused are generally not accepted, but used in their intended manner, SBIR/STTR awards are an excellent way to fund early research in a start-up and the Phase II awards are robust. Still, a company trying to build its entire portfolio of products from SBIR/STTR grants without other investments is not likely to secure sufficient resources.

## 4.7 Obtaining Small Business Financing

Benjamin Franklin, Thomas Edison, Wilbur and Orville Wright—the annals of American history are filled with numerous people who created something new that changed an entire industry and even our way of life. Most people know the "famous" inventors, but many other folks invent something that becomes a business success.

Every year, *Inc.* magazine publishes its list of "The 500 Fastest Growing Companies in America." This list includes tomorrow's potential goliaths of the business world. Such companies as Apple, Microsoft, Timberland, Oracle, and Twitter have graced and then graduated from the list since its inception.

| Industry | Number of *Inc.* 500 Companies Listed (2014) |
|---|---|
| Telecommunications and wireless | 65 |
| IT Services | 50 |
| Software | 48 |
| Financial Services | 41 |
| Government Services | 38 |
| Health | 38 |
| Energy | 35 |
| Pharmaceuticals and biotechnology | 29 |

Clearly, if your start-up is any of the fastest-growing industries, you stand a better chance of getting equity financed by any of the resources that are listed in the subsequent paragraphs.

### 4.7.1 Angels: Investors with a Heart

Angels are individuals—usually ex-entrepreneurs who are experienced enough to understand and live with the financial risks they take—with money available to lend or invest. The angels' motives may vary: Most seek to increase their net worth, some want to help (mentor) aspiring entrepreneurs, while some simply crave a "piece of the action."

Angels typically invest capital in seed, start-up, and early-stage companies. Angels are often successful, excited entrepreneurs themselves, or retired executives who wish to "give back" their time and expertise. Angels invest their own money; that is, they are *not* money managers, and generally prefer to invest in local companies, looking to make a reasonable return on investment.

According to a 2010 report distributed by the Angel Capital Education Foundation, total start-up funding from venture capital funds, state funds, and angel investors totals approximately $20.8 billion annually. Surprisingly, friends and family contributed nearly three times that amount of capital to thousands of start-ups each year. With approximately $60 billion in start-up funding from friends and family, entrepreneurs must consider this important option as they seek to launch new businesses [12].

Angels are an *accredited investor* (an SEC definition) that includes

- **Financial position**
  - Net worth: $1 million
  - Annual personal income: $200,000
  - Family income: $300,000
- **Assumptions**
  - Knowledgeable—capable of performing own due diligence
  - Can afford to lose the entire investment
- **Implications**
  - Giving up regulated disclosure, but many are now part of Angel groups

### 4.7.2 Angels Classification

Angels come in many forms: Some fly in flocks (i.e., belong to angel organizations or investment groups), some work solo, some look for a piece of the company's ownership (equity), and others prefer lending (debt). Almost all angels demand personal involvement in your business, however, and in many cases, the know-how an angel can bring to the table is worth more than the capital itself.

Angels are like the highway patrol—the time that you need them the most is the time they are the most difficult to find. Movements are afoot, however, to make the identity of angels more accessible. According to the Yellow Pages Publishers Association, "angels" will soon be a Yellow Pages heading in most telephone books (along with "psychic life readings" and "body piercing").

The SBA spawned Active Capital (activecapital.org), and you'll discover a mix-and-match format designed to bring together aspiring small-business start-ups and "accredited small-business investors." The "accredited small-business investor" must have a net worth in excess of $1 million or an individual annual income in excess of $200,000 (or $300,000 joint income).

Angel investors are individuals who invest their own personal money in a fledgling enterprise. An angel investor is usually someone who has led the launch and development of successful companies, followed by a financially profitable exit. Angel investors often form groups so potential investments can be better evaluated.

Each angel typically invests between $25,000 and $100,000. If a group pools their capital, the total amount of investment can reach more than $1 million dollars. Angel investors usually come in at an earlier stage than venture capital financing.

Equity investors receive stock in the company, with the amount dependent on the value ("valuation") of the company in proportion to how much they have invested. The cash value placed on a new company ("pre-money valuation") is somewhat arbitrary and subject to negotiation, with entrepreneurs usually thinking high valuations and investors a much lower valuation.

It is inevitable that after multiple rounds of equity investment, the investors will own a majority of the shares of the company. Academics often view this outcome as "losing control" of their company (often called "Founder's syndrome" or "founderitis"), but without external investments, the company would not be able to move forward (unless you have a rich uncle).

The Founder's syndrome [13] is a difficulty faced by many organizations where one or more founders maintain disproportionate power and influence after the effective initial establishment of the project, leading to a wide range of problems for both the organization and those involved. The passion and charisma of the founder or founders, which were such an important reason for the successful establishment of the organization, become a limiting and destructive force, rather than the creative and productive force they were in the early stages [14].

Do YOU have Founder's syndrome [15]? If you answer "Yes" to most of the following questions, you may suffer from an incurable case of founderitis:

1. When you leave, will you feel skeptical that things might be managed differently?
2. Are you staying because it's "best" for the organization if you stay?

3. Do you identify with the organization as being a part of who you are?

4. Do you fear the organization will change its mission contrary to your original mission and vision?

5. Can you separate organizational issues from your personal viewpoint of the issues?

6. Do you relate to the organization as belonging to you by saying, "My organization"?

7. Do you feel as though you are indispensable and irreplaceable?

8. Do you want to stay involved long after you depart to avoid feeling a sense of great personal loss?

If you want to find an angel in your own backyard, your state or city may have an angel-matching program. Ask local bankers, accountants, financial advisors, or lawyers for their input on how to find a local angel-matching program; call your local Chamber of Commerce; or contact your state's Department of Commerce.

### 4.7.3 Venture Capital

Venture capital firms and organizations offer cash in exchange for equity in later-stage companies, so they are, in effect, an organized version of angel investing. According to Wikipedia, venture capital (VC) is financial capital provided to early-stage, high-potential, high-risk, high-growth start-up companies. A venture capital fund makes money by owning equity in the companies it invests in, which usually have novel technologies or business models in high-technology industries (e.g., biotechnology, IT, or software).

The typical venture capital investment occurs after the seed funding round, and the angel round(s), frequently referred to as a growth funding round (a.k.a. Series A round). The VC seeks to generate returns through an eventual realization event, such as an IPO or a trade sale of the company [16]. Venture capital is a subset of private equity.

One of the first steps toward a professionally managed venture capital industry was the passage of the Small Business Investment Act of 1958; this Act officially permitted the US Small Business Administration (SBA) to license private small business investment companies (SBICs) to help finance and manage small entrepreneurial businesses in the United States.

Before World War II, money orders (originally known as "development capital") were primarily the exclusive domain of wealthy individuals and families. Modern private equity investments began to emerge after World War II with the founding of the first two venture capital firms in 1946, American Research and Development Corporation (ARDC) and J.H. Whitney & Company.

ARDC was founded by Georges Doriot [17], the "father of venture capitalism" (and former dean of Harvard Business School and founder of INSEAD) [18], with Ralph Flanders and Karl Compton (former president of MIT), to encourage private sector investments in businesses run by soldiers returning from World War II. ARDC was the first institutional private equity investment firm that raised capital from sources other than wealthy families, although it had several notable investment successes as well. ARDC is credited with the first trick when its 1957 investment of $70,000 in Digital Equipment Corporation would be valued at more than $355 million after the company's IPO in 1968 (representing a return of more than 1200 times on its investment and an annualized rate of return of 101%) [19].

### 4.7.4 Venture Capital Financing

As opposed to more conservative sources of capital, which look closely at a business's past performance and its collateral before handing out cash, venture capital firms focus primarily on future prospects when looking at a business plan. Thus, venture capital is useful for a few sophisticated businesses in higher risk, higher-reward industries. Venture capital firms look for the possibility of hefty annual returns (30% or more) on their investments in order to offset the losses that are sure to occur within their high-risk portfolios.

Unfortunately, very few start-ups are in a position to take advantage of venture capital financing. The typical venture capital firm funds only 2% of the deals under consideration. Moreover, that 2% has to meet a wide range of investment criteria, such as highly attractive niches, sophisticated management, and potential for high return—criteria that the typical small business start-up cannot begin to meet. Do not be disappointed at not qualifying for venture capital funding. Venture capital is usually reserved for fast-growing "start-ups" that have a proven track record of business successes.

### 4.7.5 Venture Capital Firms

Venture capitalists (VCs) are professional investors and money managers who manage and invest a pool of money from high net worth individuals and institutional investors who are looking for higher returns on their investments than the average stock market returns.

There are thousands of venture firms in the United States, and each firm usually specializes in a particular industry. There are more VCs focused on high tech than life sciences, simply because an exit in a life science is usually much longer, and riskier.

VCs provide significant value to a start-up company that goes beyond monetary value. Many VCs were themselves former executives who launched and managed successful companies and they can provide valuable advice and guidance. In addition, when a VC signs up to invest in your enterprise, you are automatically getting their entire network of friends. VCs have impressive networks of associates that can help start-ups solve business-related problems.

### 4.7.6 Venture Capital's Management Fees

VCs make money by charging a management fee of the managed funds they raise from accredited wealthy individuals and institutional investors. It is in a VC firm's best interest to make money for their own investors, because their reputation is on the line. In turn, their reputation is based on their investment track records. If managers have below average success rates, investors are likely to choose a different money manager.

Equally important as selecting the right CEO (chief executive officer) is the proper choice of the right investors. Investors play a critical role in shaping the company, providing network, management, and so on. The quality of your seed investors will play a key role in attracting future investments.

Sometimes, the entrepreneur is in such desperate need for funding that he or she accepts investments from inexperienced investors. These investors often have unrealistic expectations, little industry-specific network and little credibility with follow-on investors. Few start-ups can survive inexperienced seed investors.

---

## 4.8 Persuasive Business Presentations

*Leadership is the art of communication.*

As a budding entrepreneur, you might as well get used to this: As an entrepreneur, you will be giving presentations till the cows come home, and persuasive presentations will become your trademark.

A **persuasive presentation** (speech) aims to get your audience to accept your business premise by prompting them to act, think, or feel in a desired manner, without coercion or force. Figure 4.3 presents the four cornerstones of persuasive presentations.

**Pathos** refers to presenting your reasons to believe in something, overcoming risks, natural apprehensions, perceived problems, and so on. **Ethos** refers to your personal technical competence, goodwill, and dynamism to be trusted with investor's moneys. **Logos** are your set of rational, logical, and validated proofs. Last, **Mythos** are the combined force of ethical values, industry beliefs, and national culture that may prompt investments in you and your company.

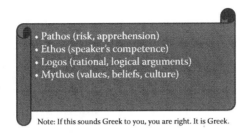

**FIGURE 4.3**
The four cornerstones of persuasive presentations.

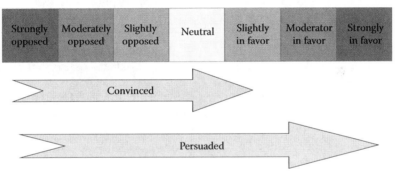

**FIGURE 4.4**
Degrees of convincing and persuading.

Persuasive speech is the most complicated form of verbal communication. It involves moving your audience to accept your premise from a position of deep skepticism/opposition to strongly/enthusiastically embracing your proposed solution based on its perceived benefits [20]. The entire sequence is shown in Figure 4.4.

## 4.8.1 Rookie Mistakes

There is an old adage that goes: "Your presentation is 20% *what* you say, and 80% *how* you say it." Most rookie entrepreneurs tend to ignore their demeanor when making presentations, believing that their data "speaks for itself."

Another hurdle is the fact that most people become tongue-tied when placed in front of an audience. Most of us "freeze" when asked to give an important presentation. Did you hear the joke about the survey that asked aspiring entrepreneurs what are their three greatest fears in life? Their answer is seen below:

1. Fear of dying
2. Fear of speaking in public
3. Fear of dying while speaking in public

Figure 4.5 presents a tongue-in-cheek list of do's and don'ts for entrepreneurs.

### 4.8.2 Your Elevator Pitch

> I only had one superstition. I made sure to touch all the bases when I hit a homerun.
>
> **Babe Ruth**

The **elevator pitch** derives its name from an apocryphal story: after submitting a "teaser" document to a VC, and after waiting many weeks to hear something from the VC, suddenly you get an unexpected phone call from the Managing Partner. "I am in the elevator going to a meeting. Tell me why I should fund your company now." The Partner has just asked you to three questions: Why me? Why you? Why now?

Guess what? You only have one chance of getting funded. Thus, an elevator pitch must be a concise, carefully planned, and well-practiced description about your company that anyone should be able to understand in the time it would take to ride up three floors in an elevator. Like Babe Ruth, your pitch needs to touch these bases:

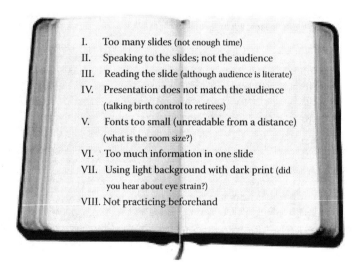

I.     Too many slides (not enough time)

II.    Speaking to the slides; not the audience

III.   Reading the slide (although audience is literate)

IV.   Presentation does not match the audience (talking birth control to retirees)

V.    Fonts too small (unreadable from a distance) (what is the room size?)

VI.   Too much information in one slide

VII.  Using light background with dark print (did you hear about eye strain?)

VIII. Not practicing beforehand

**FIGURE 4.5**
How to screw up your presentation in eight easy steps.

- A burning market need and your proposed solution to the burning need
- Your team and how they are uniquely qualified to manage the company
- How you will make money for your investors
- Memorable tagline/pitch **closing**

### 4.8.2.1 Elevator Pitch Must-Haves

Your pitch should have a riveting **opening**; that is, it should grab the interest of your recipient. Your pitch should show **passion**—if you are not excited about your idea, no one else will be.

**Brief descriptions.** After your pitch be prepared to answer questions briefly. You must prepare a brief description of how the business is different from the competition, a brief description of how you will make money, a brief description of the resources you need from investors, and a brief description of the returns/payback the investor can expect.

**Last three bits of advice:** (1) Always use the KISS (Keep It Simple, Stupid) principle. (2) Do not use Techno-Latin, a language that only you understand. (3) Highlight marketing advantages, not merely technical benefits.

## 4.9 The Knowledge-Intensive Industry

The knowledge-intensive industry is vast, feverishly paced, and extremely competitive. For companies in this field, one thing is certain—today's new product is tomorrow's commodity. That is the main risk of a high-tech venture, and that is one of the challenges of a high-tech enterprise.

The term *knowledge-intensive industry* derives from the recognition of the role of knowledge and technology in economic growth. Knowledge, as embodied in human beings (as "human capital") and in technology, has been central to the economic development of many advanced countries.

The science-based system, essentially public research laboratories and institutes of higher education, carries out key functions in the knowledge-based economy, including knowledge production, transmission, and transfer.

Modern economies are more strongly dependent on the production, distribution, and use of knowledge than ever before. Output and employment are expanding fastest in high-technology industries, such as computers, electronics, biotechnology, nanotechnology, and aerospace. Knowledge-intensive service sectors, such as education, communications, and information, are growing even faster.

## 4.10 Employment in a Knowledge-Intensive Economy

Employment in a knowledge-intensive economy is characterized by increasing demand for more highly skilled workers. Knowledge-intensive and high-technology economies tend to be the most dynamic in terms of output and employment growth. Changes in technology, and particularly the advent of information technologies, are making educated and skilled labor more valuable, and unskilled labor much less so.

Government policies will need more stress on upgrading human capital through promoting access to a range of skills, and especially the capacity to learn; enhancing the *knowledge distribution power* of the economy through collaborative networks and the diffusion of technology; and providing the enabling conditions for organizational change at the firm level to maximize the benefits of technology for productivity.

## 4.11 Knowledge Codification

In order to facilitate economic analysis, distinctions can be made between different kinds of knowledge that are important in the knowledge-based economy: know-what, know-why, know-how, and know-who. Knowledge is a much broader concept than information, which is generally the "know-what" and "know-why" components of knowledge. These are also the types of knowledge that come closest to being market commodities or economic resources to be fitted into economic production functions. Other types of knowledge—particularly know-how and know-who—are more "tacit knowledge" and are more difficult to codify and measure [21].

- **Know-what** refers to knowledge about facts. How many people live in New York? What are the ingredients in pancakes? and When was the battle of Waterloo? are examples of this kind of knowledge. Here, knowledge is close to what is normally called information— it can be broken down into bits. In some complex areas, experts must have a lot of this kind of knowledge in order to fulfill their jobs. Practitioners of law and medicine belong to this category.

- **Know-why** refers to scientific knowledge of the principles and laws of nature. This kind of knowledge underlies technological development and product and process advances in most industries. The production and reproduction of know-why is often organized in specialized organizations, such as research laboratories and universities. To get access to this kind of knowledge, firms have to interact with these organizations either through recruiting scientifically trained labor or directly through contacts and joint activities.

- **Know-how** refers to skills or the capability to do something. Businessmen judging market prospects for a new product or a personnel manager selecting and training staff have to use their know-how. The same is true for the skilled worker operating complicated machine tools. Know-how is typically a kind of knowledge developed and kept within the border of an individual firm. One of the most important reasons for the formation of industrial networks is the need for firms to be able to share and combine elements of know-how.

- **Know-who** involves information about who knows what and who knows how to do what. It involves the formation of special social relationships that make it possible to get access to experts and use their knowledge efficiently. It is significant in economies where skills are widely dispersed because of a highly developed division of labor among organizations and experts. For the modern manager and organization, it is important to use this kind of knowledge in response to the acceleration in the rate of change. The know-who kind of knowledge is internal to the organization to a higher degree than any other kind of knowledge.

Learning to master the four kinds of knowledge takes place through different channels. While know-what and know-why can be obtained through reading books, attending lectures, and accessing databases, the other two kinds of knowledge are rooted primarily in practical experience. Know-how will typically be learned in situations where an apprentice follows a master and relies upon him as the authority. Know-who is learned in social practice and sometimes in specialized educational environments. It also develops in day-to-day dealings with customers, subcontractors, and independent institutes. One reason why firms engage in basic research is to acquire access to networks of academic experts crucial for their innovative capability. Know-who is socially embedded knowledge that cannot easily be transferred through formal channels of information.

## 4.12 Information Technology

The development of information technology may be regarded as a response to the need for handling the know-what and know-why portions of knowledge more effectively. Conversely, the existence of information technology and communications infrastructures gives a strong impetus to the process of codifying certain types of knowledge. All knowledge that can be codified and reduced to information can now be transmitted over long distances with very limited costs. It is the increasing codification of some elements of knowledge that have led the current era to be characterized as "the information society"—a society where a majority of workers will soon be producing, handling, and distributing information or codified knowledge.

The digital revolution has intensified the move toward knowledge codification and altered the share of codified versus tacit knowledge in the knowledge stock of the economy. Electronic networks now connect a vast array of public and private information sources, including digitized reference volumes, books, scientific journals, libraries of working papers, images, video clips, sound and voice recordings, graphical displays, and electronic mail. These information resources, connected through various communications networks, represent the components of an emerging, universally accessible digital library.

Because of codification, knowledge is acquiring more of the properties of a commodity. Market transactions are facilitated by codification, and diffusion of knowledge is accelerated. In addition, codification is reducing the importance of additional investments to acquire further knowledge. It is creating bridges between fields and areas of competence and reducing the "dispersion" of knowledge.

These developments promise an acceleration of the rate of growth of stocks of accessible knowledge, with positive implications for economic growth. They also imply increased change in the knowledge stock owing to higher rates of scrapping and obsolescence, which will put greater burdens on the economy's adjustment abilities.

High-tech entrepreneurs face that risk—and that challenge—with imagination, innovation, and insight, but, unfortunately, many do not—and cannot—bring the same creativity and competence to the management of their companies' business affairs.

As a result, promising high-tech companies often fail, not for lack of ideas, but for the same reasons companies in any and every industry can, and do—lack of capital when they need it most; a naive understanding of the marketplace; poor forecasts of development and production costs; mismanaged growth; inadequate tax planning; the wrong advisers, at the wrong time.

## References

1. *Starting a Business 101 (Canadian Edition)*, Blue Beetle Books, http://www.small businesssuccess.ca/ebooks/meridian/pdfs/eBook-Starting-a-Business-101.pdf.
2. http://www.entrepreneur.com/article/52718

3. http://www.fool.com/knowledge-center/2015/10/24/the-key-differences-between-debt-and-equity-financ.aspx
4. http://www.investopedia.com/terms/e/equityfinancing.asp
5. http://entrepreneurs.about.com/od/financing/a/debtfinancing.htm
6. http://www.entrepreneur.com/encyclopedia/debt-financing
7. http://www.accessdata.fda.gov/scripts/opdlisting/oopd/
8. http://www.fda.gov/ForIndustry/DevelopingProductsforRareDiseases Conditions/ucm2005525.htm
9. Meekings, K.N., Williams, C.S., and Arrowsmith, J.E. Orphan drug development: An economically viable strategy for biopharma R&D. *Drug Discov. Today,* 17, 660–664, 2012.
10. Sasinowski, F.J. Quantum of effectiveness evidence in FDA's approval of orphan drugs. *Drug Inf. J.,* 46, 238–263, 2012.
11. http://www.pharmatimes.com/article/13-10 09/US_biopharma_452_drugs_for _rare_diseases_now_in_R_D.aspx
12. http://blog.startupprofessionals.com/2010/08/friends-and-family-largest -startup.html
13. McNamara, C. Founder's Syndrome: How Corporations Suffer—And Can Recover, http://managementhelp.org/misc/founders.htm.
14. https://en.wikipedia.org/wiki/Founder's_syndrome
15. http://www.leadingtransitions.com/pdfs/Leadership%20Guide.pdf
16. http://en.wikipedia.org/wiki/Venture_capital
17. WGBH Public Broadcasting Service. Who made America?—Georges Doriot.
18. Ante, S.E. *Creative Capital: Georges Doriot and the Birth of Venture Capital.* Harvard Business School Press, Cambridge, MA, 2008. ISBN 1-4221-0122-3.
19. Venture Impact: The Economic Importance of Venture Backed Companies to the U.S. Economy. NVCA.org. Retrieved 2013.
20. Lucas, S.E. Speaking to persuade. Chapter 15, http://www.jdcc.edu/includes /download.php?action=2023&download_file_id=5274&action=2023&table _num=.
21. Smith, E.A. The role of tacit and explicit knowledge in the workplace, http:// www.basicknowledge101.com/pdf/KM_roles.pdf.

# 5

## SBIR/STTR Grants

## 5.1 Introduction

A **grant**, also known as a *cooperative agreement*, is a monetary award given by a *grantor* to a *grantee*. A *grant request* is an advance promise of what you or your organization (the grantee) proposes to do when the grantor fulfills your request for funding. The most distinguishing characteristic between a grant and a cooperative agreement is the degree of federal participation or involvement during the performance of the work activities. When a federal agency program officer participates in funded project activities, it is called a cooperative agreement. When the grant applicant is the sole implementer of project activities, it is called a grant.

What kind of entrepreneur applies for a grant? A person who is in need of cash flow and who is willing to roll up his sleeves, dig deep for hard-to-find information, and speak boldly and proudly about their technology, identifying current funding needs and explaining their commercialization capabilities.

What does it take to get started? First and foremost, you need to learn from knowledge and experience—part of which is presented in this chapter. Also, you should deeply desire to make a difference in the lives of others. Whether it's a grant-funded intervention or prevention or a contract bid award for delivering an excellent quality of goods or services, you should be ready to give it your full attention. It is akin to a full-blown PhD dissertation.

Some grant awards come with no strings attached, but many others require you to use the funds in a certain way. Grantors with strings attached to their funds are almost always government grantmaking agencies (local, state, and federal public sector funders). Grantors with literally no strings attached are referred to as *private sector funders*. These usually include corporate and foundation grantmakers.

What can a grant pay for? A grant award can be used for whatever the funder agency wants to fund. This means that reading the funding guidelines is critical when it comes to improving your chances for success. Remember that not following instructions to the letter is an automatic reason for rejection.

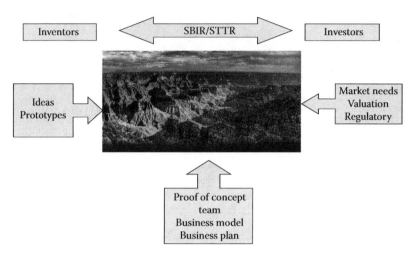

**FIGURE 5.1**
Bridging the "valley of death."

From an entrepreneurial perspective, Small Business Innovation Research (SBIR)/Small Business Technology Transfer (STTR) grants are frequently used to "bridge the valley of death," as depicted in Figure 5.1.

## 5.2 The World of SBIR/STTR Grants

The SBIR/STTR grants program's wonderfully patriotic mission is "Supporting scientific excellence and technological innovation through the investment of federal research funds in critical American priorities to build a strong national economy one small business at a time" [1].

In the words of program founder Roland Tibbetts: "to provide funding for some of the best early-stage innovation ideas—ideas that, however promising, are still too high risk for private investors, including venture capital firms" [2]. For the purposes of the SBIR/STTR programs, the term *small business* is defined as a for-profit business with fewer than 500 employees, owned by one or more *individuals* who are citizens of, or permanent resident aliens in, the United States of America [3].

Funds are obtained by allocating a certain percentage of the total extramural (research and development [R&D]) budgets of the 11 federal agencies with extramural research budgets in excess of $100 million. Approximately $2.5 billion is awarded through this program each year.

The United States Department of Defense (DoD) is the largest agency in this program, with approximately $1 billion in SBIR grants annually. More than half the awards from the DoD are to firms with fewer than 25 people and a third are to firms of fewer than 10. A fifth are minority or women-owned businesses. Historically, a quarter of the companies receiving grants are receiving them for the first time.

As of September 2015, SBIR programs are in place at the following agencies:

- Department of Agriculture
- Department of Commerce (National Institute of Standards and Technology and National Oceanic and Atmospheric Administration)
- Department of Defense
- Department of Education
- Department of Energy
- Department of Health and Human Services (National Institutes of Health [NIH])
- Department of Homeland Security
- Department of Transportation
- Environmental Protection Agency
- National Aeronautics and Space Administration
- National Science Foundation (NSF)

## 5.3 Before You Write Your Application

Theoretically, one would identify an unmet public health need or problem and then develop a product that significantly affects the problem. In the real world, companies develop a technology and then search for a problem where their technology can create a product. Young companies often have difficulty deciding on which problem to focus on. A grant application that does not focus on a narrow unmet public health need is unlikely to fare well in review.

You need a clear vision of the product you will make with your technology before you begin writing a grant application. It is probably not good business strategy to let NIH Funding Opportunity Announcements influence your choice of problem or product. Instead, deciding on your product and its development pathway requires both market research and strategic planning.

You need to know the size of the public health problem, current solutions and their drawbacks, and ongoing research efforts and progress. For your product or technology, you need to know its market advantages and be able to list the milestones necessary to develop the product for sale, the estimated time and costs for each milestone, and your exit strategy along the development pathway.

---

## 5.4 Purposes and Goals of SBIR/STTR Grants

The SBIR program is one of the largest examples of US government public–private partnerships. A premise of the SBIR program is that small businesses are an important front for new ideas, but that they likely will need some support in their early stages as they translate these ideas into innovative products and services for the market. Founded in 1982, the SBIR program is designed to encourage small business to develop new processes and products and to provide quality research in support of the many missions of the US government.

Today's knowledge-based economy is driven in large part by the nation's capacity to innovate. One of the defining features of the US economy is a high level of entrepreneurial activity. Entrepreneurs in the United States see opportunities and are willing and able to take on risk to bring new welfare-enhancing, wealth-generating technologies to the market. Yet, while innovation in areas such as genomics, bioinformatics, and nanotechnology presents new opportunities, converting these ideas into innovations for the market involves substantial challenges [4].

The American capacity for innovation can be strengthened by addressing the challenges faced by entrepreneurs. Public–private partnerships are one means to help entrepreneurs bring new ideas to market [5]. According to the Small Business Innovation Development Act of 1982 P.L. 106-554 signed December 21, 2000, the purposes and goals of the SBIR grant program are as follows:

- To stimulate technological innovation
- To use small business to meet federal R&D needs
- To foster and encourage participation by minorities and disadvantaged persons in technological innovation
- To increase private-sector commercialization innovations derived from federal R&D

The aims of the STTR program, Small Business Research and Development Enhancement Act of 1992 P.L. 107-50 are as follows:

- To stimulate and foster scientific/technological innovation through cooperative R&D carried out between small business concerns and research institutions (typically universities)
- Foster technology transfer between small business concerns and research institutions

The STTR program is a set-aside program designed to facilitate cooperative R&D between small business concerns and US research institutions—with immediate potential for commercialization. The STTR program provides an opportunity for small businesses to partner with academic institutions to develop products with biomedical applications (e.g., assays, research tools, medical devices, biomarkers, therapeutics, and software development).

Since the STTR program is a collaborative research effort between a small business and a research institution, this partnership can offer the following benefits:

- Enhanced credibility, which can increase the chances of winning an STTR award.
- Additional opportunity for proposal review before submission.
- Opportunity for research ideas to develop within the research institution.
- At some research institutions, the researcher can take a leave of absence to work on an SBIR/STTR project.
- SBIR applications have historically outnumbered STTR applications by more than eightfold, causing the success rate for SBIR applicants to be lower than that for STTR applicants.

## 5.5 Detailed Program Description

The SBIR and STTR grants are programs intended to help eligible small businesses conduct advanced R&D. Funding takes the form of contracts or grants. The recipient programs must have high potential for commercialization and must meet specific US Government R&D needs. Programs provide billions of dollars of research support to translate innovative ideas into useful commercial products.

However, these programs are highly competitive and applications to various governmental agencies (e.g., NIH, NSF, DoD, etc.) differ greatly, with success rates generally below 20% for Phase I applications. The SBIR/STTR helps government agencies to conduct innovative R/R&D that results in product, process, or service that will

- Improve human health
- Speed process of discovery
- Reduce cost of medical care/cost of research
- Improve research tools and technology

Phase I
    Feasibility study
    $100K–150K   12 months

Phase II
    Full R&D
    2-year award $500K–$1 million

Phase III
    Commercialization stage
    Use of non-grant funds

**FIGURE 5.2**
Three phases program.

## 5.6 Eligibility Requirements

Generally, businesses with fewer than 500 employees are eligible to receive an SBIR award. Phase I of the Agency's SBIR program determines the technical feasibility and quality of performance of the proposed innovation. Phase II awards are based on the results of Phase I and the technical merit and commercial potential of the innovation. Phase II may not complete the total R&D needed for commercialization, as shown in Figure 5.2.

Below is a summary of some of the most important eligibility requirements:

- Organized for-profit US business.
- At least 51% United States–owned and independently operated.
- Small business located in the United States.
- P.I.'s primary employment with a small business during a project or fewer employees.
- Eligibility is determined at time of award.
- No appendices allowed in Phase I.
- The PI *is* required to have expertise to oversee project scientifically and technically.
- Applications *may be* submitted to different agencies for similar work.
- Awards may *not* be accepted from different agencies for duplicative projects.

## 5.7 SBIR/STTR Are Sequential Programs

The SBIR/STTR program is a highly competitive three-phase program that reserves a specific percentage of federal R&D development funding for

**TABLE 5.1**

Three Sequential Multiphase Programs

| Phases | Comments |
|---|---|
| SBIR Phase I Median Award $210K/year (FY2014) | Awards to approximately 10% of applications (FY2014) |
| STTR Phase I Median Award $230K/year (FY2014) | Fast-Track—Combined Phase I/II application |
| Competing Phase II (renewal) | For FDA-related products |
| | Awards up to $1M per year for 2 to 3 years |
| Phase III | Remaining steps of commercialization |
| | Not funded by government. Funded by other sources |

award to small businesses in partnership with nonprofit research institutions to move ideas from the laboratory to the marketplace, to foster high-tech economic development, and to address the technological needs of the federal government.

By including qualified small businesses in the nation's R&D effort, SBIR awards are intended to stimulate innovative new technologies to help agencies meet their missions in many areas including health, the environment, and national defense. SBIR and STTR grants are sequential multiphase programs [6], as summarized in Table 5.1.

## 5.8 Format for Grant Application Package

The format for government grant requests varies from agency to agency, but some common threads exist in the highly detailed, structured, stylized regimen that is commonly referred to as an *application package*. These common threads include a standard cover, certification and assurances forms, narrative sections, and the budget narrative and forms. Of course, all types of government grant applications require mandatory attachments or appendices, such as financial statements and résumés of project staff.

Always follow the pagination, order of information, and review criteria guidelines. All government grants are awarded on the basis of your meeting their specific review criteria, which are written and published in each funding agency's grant application guidelines. The review criteria tell you what the peer reviewers will read and rate when they receive your grant application.

As you read through the application guidelines, highlight all narrative writing requirements and look for sections that tell you how the grant reviewers will rate or evaluate each section of the narrative. By formatting and writing to meet the review criteria, you can edge out the competition and increase your funding success rate.

### 5.8.1 Applicant Organization and Qualifications

Any funding source you approach will have questions about your legal name and organizational structure. Although the wording may vary slightly from one application to another, the cover documents and narratives of grant applications and cooperative agreements all ask for the same basic information. Understanding exactly what the application is asking for and knowing how to reply in the right language are critical. Keep in mind that any discrepancy in your application will be grounds for rejection.

The following list summarizes the common requirements by government funding sources [7]:

- **Legal name of the organization applying:** Be sure to list your organization's *legal* name here.
- **Type of applicant:** Check the box that best describes your organization's forming structure. For example, you can choose from state agency, county, municipal, township, interstate, intermunicipal, special district, independent school district, public college or university, Indian Tribe, individual, private, profit-making organization, and other (which you have to specify).
- **Eligibility:** Is your organization a type of applicant that isn't eligible? Search for a partner (government agency or nonprofit) that can be the lead grant applicant or RFP (request for proposal) responder. Doing so will get dollars into the front door of your organization or business because you'll be incorporated into the funding request as a subcontracting partner. So get ready to negotiate your services and products during the planning and writing period. That way, you'll have monies earmarked for you in the funding request's budget narrative and detail.

If an organization is waiting on nonprofit designation, it's common to partner with an established nonprofit to act as the fiscal agent. (An *established nonprofit* is one that has been around for more than 3 years.)

- **Year founded:** Enter the year that your organization incorporated or was created.
- **Current operating budget:** Supply the applicant organization's operating budget total for the current fiscal year.

When it comes to money, supply information that portrays the truth and nothing but the truth!

- **Employer identification number and DUNS Number:** This portion of the form asks for the seven-digit EIN (employer identification number) assigned to your organization by the Internal Revenue Service. The EIN is also called a *taxpayer reporting number.*

In addition to the EIN, federal grantmaking agencies require that all grant applicants have a nine-digit DUNS (Data Universal Numbering System) Number, an identification number that makes it easier for others to recognize and learn about your organization. You can register for a unique DUNS Number at the Dunn & Bradstreet website, www.dnb.com/US/duns_update.

The DUNS Number is a unique nine-digit identification sequence that provides unique identifiers of single business entities while linking corporate family structures together.

- **Organization's fiscal year:** Indicate the 12-month time frame that your organization considers to be its operating, or fiscal, year. The fiscal year is defined by the organization's bylaws and can correspond with the calendar year or some other period, such as July 1 to June 30.
- **Congressional districts:** On a federal grant application, you need to list all the congressional districts in which your organization is located and your grant-funded services will be implemented. You can get this information by calling the public library or surfing the Internet to locate your legislator's website—which will contain their district numbers.
- **Contact person information:** Name the primary contact in your organization for grant or cooperative agreement negotiations, questions, and written correspondence. Make your contact person an individual who helped write the grant and who's quick enough on their feet to answer tough technical questions from the funder, especially by phone.
- **Address:** Provide the current street and mailing address for the applicant organization.
- **Telephone/fax/e-mail information:** List the contact person's telephone and fax numbers (with area code) as well as an e-mail address.

## 5.9 The Famous (Infamous?) Grants.gov

Why do so many entrepreneurs fail to apply for government grants? The answer is that they fear the inherent complexities of federal grant applications. Federal grants are the most difficult grants for which to apply—far more difficult than foundation, corporate, or state and local government grants. Federal grants are known for their short deadlines, technically worded writing and review criteria, and quadrillions of intimidating forms. Grants.gov (which is found online at www.grants.gov) attempts to facilitate the process.

When the federal government first launched Grants.gov, it was as if every grant writer's worst fears had come true. Technology was taking over the submission process, and it wasn't readily accepted or wanted. The process would be seamless and straightforward—at least that's what the feds told everyone. But there were many glitches along the way while the online e-grant submission website was being perfected. Today, it's still a work in progress, but it is the way it must be done.

Grants.gov is a central storehouse for information on more than 1000 grant programs. It provides access to approximately $400 billion in annual awards. As you can see, there are plenty of grant programs and billions of dollars available. Even in slow economy years, grants are still awarded, and the payments keep coming, rain or shine, if you have been awarded a grant.

Throughout the Grants.gov website, you'll find tidbits of valuable information that help first-time grant writers familiarize themselves with the basic questions, such as "What is a grant?" and "Who's eligible for one?" Some of the eligible applicant categories for federal grants are the following:

- Government organizations
- Education organizations
- Public housing organizations
- Nonprofit organizations
- For-profit organizations
- Small businesses
- Individuals

### 5.9.1 Grants.gov Home Page

The Grants.gov home page is your gateway to everything you need to know to find federal grants, apply for federal grants, and follow-up on federal grant applications submitted.

The Grants.gov home page looks straightforward at first glance, but in reality it can be very tortuous. Many novice grant writers are intimidated by the federal grant writing process. They fear the technical instructions, lengthy writing requirements, and many forms with "I don't have a clue" types of information fields. Even the most fearless grant writer—one who can master the federal grant application research and writing process—is further aghast at the online grants. It may be best to engage a knowledgeable consultant to help with the submission.

### 5.9.2 Getting Registered to Apply

In order to apply for a grant from Grants.gov, you or your organization must complete the (not so easy) Grants.gov registration process. You can register as an organization or as an individual. I explain both ways in the following sections.

The registration process can take between three to five business days. It can even take as long as 2 weeks if all the steps aren't completed on a timely basis. In order to get your organization registered to submit grant applications on the Grants.gov system, you need to follow these steps:

1. **Get a Dun & Bradstreet number (DUNS Number).**

   You can do this online at www.dnb.com/US/dunsupdate. In fact, there's a link to this website on Grants.gov. This registration is free and gives you a common tracking number for doing business with the government (federal, state, and local).

2. **Register with the Central Contractor Registry (also known as the CCR).**

   What is the CCR? It's a secondary website that collects all your organization's contact information. The information requested is similar to what you submit in your annual IRS tax return, such as name of organization, address, contact person, and contact person's information including Social Security number. You'll also be asked to upload your banking information (the bank's tracking number and the organization's bank account number). This info is used to facilitate electronic banking transfers between the government and your organization.

3. **Create a username and password with the Grants.gov credential provider.**

   You'll receive a user name and password from a third-party credential provider contracted by the government. At that point, you'll be routed back to Grants.gov to complete your registration with the access point information.

4. **Grants.gov and eRA Commons: Required *early* registration for SBIR newcomers.**

   If your company is applying for an NIH SBIR grant for the first time, it must register with *both* NIH eRA Commons and Grants.gov. (eRA stands for Electronic Research Administration.) The NIH does not award grants to unregistered applicants. Unfortunately, registration cannot be done at the last minute. eRA Commons and Grants. gov require your company to register at least 4 weeks prior to the grant submission due date. To be safe, prepare to spend approximately 5 weeks [8].

A university is required to register in eRA Commons to electronically submit a grant application. Only individuals with legal signing authority at the university (e.g., dean)—known as signing officials (SOs)—can register their organizations. Once the organization is registered, the SO can register or affiliate the principal investigator (PI) in Commons.

More than 13,000 organizations are already registered in Commons. To see if your organization is already registered, check this Quick Query: Commons Registered Organizations. If your organization is not listed, SOs can register their institutions at the Register Grantee Organization link on the eRA Commons home page. The following are the three basic tasks:

1. Register the applicant organization in eRA Commons
2. Create a new PI account
3. Create new user accounts

### 5.9.3 Obtaining AOR Authorization

This step sounds terribly difficult, but it isn't! The E-Business Point of Contact (or E-Biz POC) at your organization must respond to the registration e-mail from Grants.gov and login at Grants.gov to authorize you as an Authorized Organization Representative (AOR). Your E-Biz POC is the executive director or person who manages finances at your organization.

Only the AOR can log on and conduct business or grant-related transactions with the federal government. At any time, you can track your AOR authorization status by logging in with your username and password that you obtained in Step 3 above.

## 5.10 The Bayh–Dole Act, or the Cavalry to the Rescue

The **Bayh–Dole Act** or **Patent and Trademark Law Amendments Act** (Pub. L. 96-517, December 12, 1980) is United States legislation dealing with intellectual property arising from federal government–funded research. Sponsored by two senators, Birch Bayh of Indiana and Bob Dole of Kansas, the Act was enacted by the US Congress on December 12, 1980, is codified at 94 Stat. 3015 and in 35 U.S.C. § 200–212, and is implemented by 37 C.F.R. 401.

The key change made by Bayh–Dole was in ownership of inventions made with federal funding. Before the Bayh–Dole Act, federal research funding contracts and grants obligated inventors (wherever they worked) to assign inventions they made using federal funding to the federal government [9]. Bayh–Dole permits a university, small business, or nonprofit institution to elect to pursue ownership of an invention in preference to the government [10].

If an organization (such as a grantee) elects to retain title to a subject invention for which it has obtained assignment, the organization is obligated to do the following:

- Grant to the government a nonexclusive, nontransferable, irrevocable, paid-up license to practice or have practiced for or on behalf of the United States the subject invention throughout the world.
- File its initial patent application within 1 year after its election to retain title.
- Notify the government if it will not continue prosecution of an application or will let a patent lapse.
- Convey to the federal agency, upon written request, title to any subject invention if the organization fails to file, does not continue a prosecution, or will allow a patent to lapse.
- In each patent, include a statement that identifies the contract under which the invention was made and notice of the government's rights in the invention.
- Report on the utilization of subject inventions.
- Require in exclusive licenses to use or sell in the United States that products will be manufactured substantially in the United States.
- Agree to allow the government to "march in" and require licenses to be granted, or to grant licenses, in certain circumstances, such as if the organization has not taken effective steps to achieve practical application of the invention.

Certain additional requirements apply to nonprofit organizations only. Nonprofits must also

- Assign rights to a subject invention only to an organization having as a primary function the management of inventions, unless approved by the federal agency
- Share royalties with the inventor
- Use the balance of royalties after expenses for scientific research or education
- Make efforts to attract, and give preference to, small business licensees

### 5.10.1 Intellectual Property Control Resulting from Federal Funding

The Bayh–Dole Act gave US universities, small businesses, and nonprofits intellectual property control of their inventions that resulted from federal government–funded research.

The Bayh–Dole Act is a significant 20th-century piece of legislation in the field of intellectual property in the United States. Perhaps the most important contribution of Bayh–Dole is that it reversed the presumption of title, permitting a university, small business, or nonprofit institution to elect to pursue ownership of an invention.

### 5.10.2 "March-In" Rights under the Act

Entrepreneurs need to be aware that your ownership of federally sponsored intellectual property rights has some limits. The Code of Federal Regulations (CFR) TITLE 35, PART II, CHAPTER 18, § 203 "March-in rights" states:

a. With respect to any subject invention in which a small business firm or nonprofit organization has acquired title under this chapter, the Federal agency under whose **funding agreement the subject invention** was made **shall have the right,** in accordance with such procedures as are provided in regulations promulgated hereunder to **require the contractor**, an assignee or exclusive licensee of a subject invention to grant a nonexclusive, partially exclusive, or exclusive license in any field of use to a responsible applicant or applicants, upon terms that are reasonable under the circumstances, and if the contractor, assignee, or exclusive licensee refuses such request, to grant such a license itself, if the Federal agency determines that such—

1. action is necessary because the contractor or assignee has not taken, or is not expected to take within a reasonable time, effective steps to achieve practical application of the subject invention in such field of use;

2. action is necessary to alleviate health or safety needs which are not reasonably satisfied by the contractor, assignee, or their licensees;

3. action is necessary to meet requirements for public use specified by Federal regulations and such requirements are not reasonably satisfied by the contractor, assignee, or licensees; or

4. action is necessary because the agreement required by section 204 has not been obtained or waived or because a licensee of the exclusive right to use or sell any subject invention in the United States is in breach of its agreement obtained pursuant to section 204.

b. A determination pursuant to this section or section 202 (b)(4) shall not be subject to the Contract Disputes Act (41 U.S.C. § 601 et seq.). An administrative appeals procedure shall be established by regulations promulgated in accordance with section 206. Additionally, any contractor, inventor, assignee, or exclusive licensee adversely affected by a determination under this section may, at any time within sixty days after the determination is issued, file a petition in the United States Court of Federal Claims, which shall have jurisdiction to determine the appeal on the record and to affirm, reverse, remand or modify, as appropriate, the determination of the Federal agency. In cases described in paragraphs (1) and (3) of subsection (a), the agency's determination shall be held in abeyance pending the exhaustion of appeals or petitions filed under the preceding sentence.

## 5.11 Recommendations for Killer Proposals

How do you ensure that your grant proposal looks more like science, and less like science fiction? Science fiction will not be funded by the government.

The following sections will discuss some of the most important principles we recommend to maximize your chances of getting your proposal funded.

### 5.11.1 Focus on a Market Need, Not on Your Technology

Developing a core technology that can be used to create many different products may be an outstanding business strategy, but a deadly approach for an SBIR/STTR application.

Your best grant writing strategy is to *focus* on a specific need for a specific health problem. For example, imagine that your technology enables inexpensive rapid genetic tests for susceptibility to cancer, heart disease, infectious diseases, or other health problems. Your application would probably be assigned to the National Human Genome Research Institute based on this technology but would the Genome program staff be supportive? Would scientific reviewers be supportive? How would business reviewers evaluate the product when it is not clear what specific health problem your product will test?

Conversely, consider instead an application focused on applying your genetic testing technology to a specific type of breast cancer. The application would be assigned to the National Cancer Institute. Cancer reviewers are likely to be enthusiastic about an innovative product that affects their area. Business reviewers are likely to be enthusiastic about the potential sales of an innovative product addressing a major health problem.

Because you focused on a single use, you could submit additional SBIR/ STTR applications for other uses based on the same core technology. I strongly suggest you direct your applications to different review groups and different institutes. For example, an application on cardiac screening could be directed to the National Heart, Lung, and Blood Institute and one on asthma could be directed to the National Institute of Allergy and Infectious Diseases. In each application, it is critical to focus on the public health significance of the product in that specific area, plus the financial impact of the product in the market and to your company.

Examples of focusing on a single area include the following:

- Neuropharmacology
- Respiratory sciences
- Cardiovascular sciences

### 5.11.2 Specific Aims (Significance, Innovation, and Approach)

Begin your Specific Aims section with a paragraph briefly describing the problem and why it is significant. Then, briefly describe the current status of solutions and unmet public health needs. Check the IC's web pages for background information that may help you. Describe your product in the next paragraph. Hypothesize why your product is an innovative solution to the problem.

Present your Specific Aims in bullet format. Describe two to four measurable Specific Aims for Phase I research and, for each, the criteria by which success will be judged. Make your Specific Aims "end points" as opposed to a "best effort." Your Specific Aims may be milestones, or, if appropriate, each of your Specific Aims may be subdivided into milestones.

A review committee should easily be able to determine if your Specific Aims have been achieved and agree that successfully accomplishing them justifies Phase II funding. Propose a timeline for achieving your Specific Aims in table or graphic format. Do not propose more work than reviewers would think reasonable to achieve in Phase I. Estimate the additional time and funding necessary to bring your product to market after the completion of Phase I.

### 5.11.3 Significance (A Major, Unsolved Public Health Problem)

Describe the significance of the public health problem. My advice is to appeal to reviewers by focusing on a single disease even if your technology has multiple applications. Describe the number and composition of the population affected. Give references to supporting statistical data. Provide background on the current solutions to the problem, their limitations, and the discoveries needed. Show reviewers you know the field by the breadth of your knowledge of both published and unpublished work by others, some of whom could be your reviewers.

### 5.11.4 Innovation (Your Specific Product)

Describe why your product is innovative. Does it work better, faster, or at lower cost than what is currently available? What are its public health implications? Estimate your product's potential financial projections. How are you protecting your intellectual property? Explain why the Phase I milestones outlined in Specific Aims will justify a Phase II award. Describe milestones projected for Phase II and the progress necessary for your company to either sell the product or license the further development to another organization. Spend considerable effort on this section because it greatly affects your score.

### 5.11.5 Preliminary Studies (Why Your Approach Is Likely to Succeed)

Although the SBIR/STTR solicitation states that "Preliminary data are not required," do not be misled. Most applications include good preliminary data. Review committees are likely to have greater enthusiasm for proposals with highly encouraging preliminary data. Poorly presented or poorly interpreted preliminary data will likely result in your proposal not being "competitive." You can kiss a "noncompetitive" proposal goodbye.

Include preliminary studies that support the feasibility of your project. They may consist of your own publications and those of others, as well as unpublished data from your laboratory. To improve your "Investigator" score, emphasize work you have accomplished that indicates you can direct the proposed research and achieve your Specific Aims. Interpret results critically and evaluate alternative meanings but do not overinterpret. You can be assured that critical members of the review committee will look for explanations other than the ones you propose.

The Preliminary Studies section of your Research Plan should convince reviewers that your approach could work. Reviewers may also use your work described in this section to assess the investigator criterion. Be aware that the Phase I progress report in your Phase II application will list the milestones proposed and achieved in Phase I.

### 5.11.6 Research Design (What You Will Call Success)

The Research Design section of your Research Plan should spell out in detail what you are going to do, how you are going to do it, and your criteria for success. Reviewers will use this section to evaluate your approach and innovation. Make it easy for reviewers by organizing this section by Specific Aims and include a timeline in table or diagram format to quickly convey your entire project to reviewers.

Give a rationale for each set of experiments. Convince reviewers that your methods are appropriate to your Specific Aims. If your methods are innovative, show how you have changed existing or proven methods while avoiding technical problems. Also, do not forget to provide supporting data and references.

Describe the kinds of results you expect and how they will support continuation of your project. Present other possible outcomes and contingency plans. Define the criteria for evaluating the success or failure of each set of experiments. If possible, include statistical analysis as reviewers are impressed by statistics.

Describe hazards anticipated and precautions you propose. Spell out your sources of important reagents and equipment, as well as details of any use of animals or human subjects. Be sure to follow NIH guidelines. Explain how credible collaborators will participate in your proposed research. Your research proposal should include letters that describe collaborators' agreements with you, including their expert role on the project and hours to be committed.

### 5.11.7 Project Summary/Abstract (Your Chance to Blow Your Own Horn)

Your title and project summary/abstract are very important components of your application because all reviewers read them and they contain information relating to all five review criteria. Compose your abstract last because your plans may change as you write other components. Hone your abstract to summarize everything in your application in the 30 lines allowed. Include no proprietary information because your abstract will become public if you receive an award.

Write a few sentences each on the public health problem, issues with current solutions, how your product would address unmet needs, a summary of your approach, collaborators and unique resources, Phase I Specific Aims, and how anticipated results will justify Phase II and further product development. Conclude with the additional time and funding necessary to bring your product to market after the completion of Phase I.

The required Project Narrative is a description in three sentences or less of the relevance of your project to public health.

### 5.11.8 Final Words of Wisdom

Rudolph [11], in his "How to write a winning SBIR grant application in 3 easy lessons," recommends the use of the following procedure:

- Follow the guidelines for each section.
- Provide enough detail so that reviewers fully understand what you plan to do, how you will do it, how you will *know* that you have done it, and the importance of doing it.

- Make the proposal easy to read—white space between paragraphs, descriptive subject headers every paragraph or two, figures and charts to illustrate your points.

- Read the review criteria (in the *Application Guide*) and clearly address each major point. Reviewers use a checklist—make it easy for them to find the information they need to evaluate your proposal.

- Make sure the budget, budget justification, and all other sections match and support the proposed work.

- Get strong letters of support from collaborators, business partners, and prospective customers.

- Ask somebody else to proofread the proposal and criticize it before you can consider it as final. Two heads are better than one.

### 5.11.9  Practical Answers to Frequently Asked Questions

The following are practical answers to frequently asked questions about the SBIR and STTR grant programs [12]:

- PI's role

    The PI plans and directs the project and plays a central role in leading the technical aspects of the project. The PI will usually serve as the primary contact for the federal agency's SBIR/STTR program and works to ensure that the project is concurrent with the guidelines of that federal agency's SBIR or STTR program.

    Under SBIR program requirements, all PIs must be primarily employed (more than 50%) by the small business at the start and during the performance period of the grant.

    Under STTR program guidelines, the PIs do not need to be primarily employed by the small business that is submitting the proposal. However, the PI is still required to have a formal appointment with or commitment to the small business that is submitting the proposal. As in SBIR projects, PIs involved in STTR projects are responsible for the overall scientific and technical direction of the project. Each agency has specific requirements on the percentage of work effort that the PI should contribute to the STTR project. It is important to carefully examine STTR agency solicitations for information about the required PI work effort.

- Fast-track applications

    The Fast-Track mechanism for SBIR and STTR applications allows for an expedited decision-making and award process specifically aimed at scientifically meritorious applications with high potential for commercialization. In the Fast-Track review process, both Phase

I and Phase II proposals are submitted and reviewed together. The Fast-Track application must contain a product development plan (commercialization plan) that addresses specific topics.

- Multiple participating agencies

    Your proposal can be tailored to match the interests, priorities, and unique requirements of specific agencies. (Since each agency has different needs and areas of emphasis, it is important to custom tailor each proposal to fit the agency.)

    Caution: The agencies do require that you disclose in each proposal whether you are submitting a "similar or related idea" to other agencies. It is important to disclose not only how multiple proposal submissions may be similar but also how they are different. If there are substantial and important differences between the proposals that are submitted to multiple agencies, and more than one agency wants to give you an award, it is possible to accept multiple awards, as long as the agencies agree.

    However, if the proposals are duplicative, and multiple agencies are interested in giving your company an SBIR/STTR award, then you can legally only accept one offer.

- Submitting the same proposal multiple times

    The agencies differ considerably on how they view multiple proposals on one topic in their solicitation. They may have different rules about submitting the same idea in multiple proposals, and whether an idea can be submitted for consideration under both SBIR and STTR programs. It is important to read the specific agency's solicitation guidelines carefully before submitting your proposal multiple times to the same agency.

- Solicitation process for grant proposals

    Each of the participating federal agencies lists solicitations that address specific research topics one to four times per year. These federal agencies won't accept unsolicited proposals that do not correlate with their proposed research topics of interest.

    Research topics for some agencies are more focused than others. For example, the DoD can be very specific in their solicited research topics. Research topics for the NIH and the NSF tend to be more general in scope, which often allows SBIR applicants to submit proposals that serve their particular research areas of interest while still meeting the overall science and technology areas outlined by such agencies.

    Each agency releases its solicitation lists at different times during the year. A schedule of each federal agency's annual SBIR program solicitation dates can be found at the SBIR.gov website. Through the SBIR.gov website, prospective applicants can filter their searches by agency and keywords. An alternative resource that can be used to track seasonal solicitation dates by agency is SBIR Gateway's Phase I Solicitation Finder located at www.zyn.com/sbir/scomp.htm.

- Differences between a solicitation and a presolicitation announcement

  SBIR solicitations are specific requests for proposals released by the federal agencies participating in the program, which may result in the award of Phase I SBIR funding agreements.

  SBIR presolicitation announcements, released by SBA, contain pertinent data on SBIR solicitations such as research topic areas that are about to be released by the participating federal agencies.

- Goals of the federal agencies that participate in the SBIR program

  The DoD uses SBIR as a procurement solution to mission requirements; they are interested in obtaining solutions that result from the SBIR applicant's R&D efforts. The NIH and NSF use SBIR grants for general societal benefit; they normally are not viewed as the end customer for the technology that is created with SBIR awards. The Department of Energy uses SBIR as both a procurement tool to meet mission requirements and for general societal benefit.

- Reviewers of grant proposals

  Depending on agency, SBIR/STTR proposals may undergo an internal review, an external review, or a review that incorporates both internal and external reviewers. With internal reviews, agency members review the SBIR proposal. External reviews involve a review by people outside of the agency, such as university personnel or other experts in the field.

  The DoD, the Department of Advanced Research Projects Agency, and the Department of Transportation all use an internal review process. NASA uses both internal reviewers and at least two independent reviewers. The NIH uses dual review systems composed of an external peer review panel, an advisory panel, and an internal review group. The NSF uses ad hoc external review panels. US Department of Agriculture proposals are reviewed by a separate review panel for each topic area; proposals are subsequently reviewed by an ad hoc review panel.

- Ensuring that your proposal meets a reviewer's expectations

  SBIR/STTR applications are evaluated on the basis of the following core review criteria:
  - Exceptional Technical Merit
  - Team Qualifications
  - Value to Agency

- High Potential for Commercialization
- Cost/Cost Realism

Each SBIR agency has different priorities in terms of these evaluation criteria. For specific agency SBIR and STTR review criteria, consult SBIR program information on agency websites and contact agency SBIR/STTR program leaders.

- Dwell time from proposal to award notification

After the close of SBIR/STTR solicitations, the amount of time that lapses before award winners are notified can vary between 3 and 6 months, depending on the agency. Information about the SBIR/STTR award selection and notification time frame can typically be found in the agency solicitation or on the SBIR/STTR program section of the agency website. Links to the SBIR home pages of SBIR agencies can be found at SBIR.gov or on the SBIR Gateway website at www.zyn.com/sbir.

- What are your chances of getting funded?

The good news: Your Uncle Sam has deep pockets. The bad news: Your Uncle has very short arms. The success rate for Phase I applications is between 10% and 15% [13].

**The award rate** describes the chance of an individual application being funded and is the number that more closely reflects institute and center paylines (which can vary rather significantly from one institute or center to another).

$$\text{AWARD RATE} = \frac{\text{Number of awards in a fiscal year}}{\text{Applications reviewed (\textbf{including resubmissions} in that fiscal year)}}$$

**The funding rate** reflects the number of investigators who seek and obtain funding. Each principal investigator (PI)* is counted once, whether they submit one or more applications or receive one or more awards in a fiscal year.

$$\text{FUNDING RATE} = \frac{\text{Number of unique PIs* receiving funding in a fiscal year}}{\text{Number of unique PIs* with applications reviewed in that fiscal year}}$$

*includes those on multiple PI applications

The **success rate** describes the likelihood of a project or an idea getting funded, rather than of the success of the individual application submission.

$$\text{SUCCESS RATE} = \frac{\text{Number of awards in a fiscal year}}{\text{Applications reviewed (\textbf{excluding resubmissions} in that fiscal year)}}$$

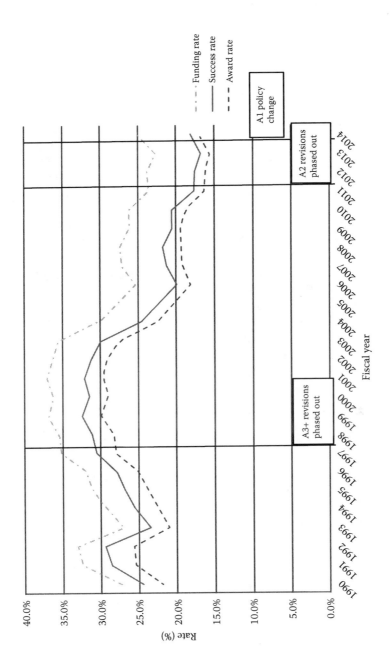

**FIGURE 5.3**

Award, success, and funding rates for research project grants (fiscal years 1990–2014). Excludes awards made with American Recovery and Reinvestiment Act (ARRA) funds, and ARRA-solicited applications.

Being awarded a grant is becoming increasingly harder. The government's own statistics show the history of awards as well as success and funding rates from 1990 to 2014. This is graphically shown in Figure 5.3 (not in constant dollars).

- The intriguing "Omnibus" Solicitation

    The Omnibus, or Omnibus Solicitation, is a long (more than 100 pages) report in which each NIH institute and center describes its high priorities for SBIR funding. It is published annually, usually in January, and it's free.

    Why do they call it the Omnibus? Because nobody wants to call it by its full title, a definite a double mouthful: "Omnibus Solicitation of the National Institutes of Health, Centers for Disease Control and Prevention, Food and Drug Administration, and Administration for Children and Families for Small Business Innovation Research (SBIR) and Small Business Technology Transfer (STTR) Grant Applications: NIH, CDC, FDA, and ACF Program Descriptions and Research Topics."

    The reason to read the Omnibus is that NIH institutes and centers are *not* peas in the same SBIR pod. In practice, for example, SBIR funding limits are different among NIH institutes. Some seem willing to make much higher SBIR Phase I and Phase II grant awards than others. Others offer million-dollar post-Phase II SBIR grants for certain projects (generally drug and medical device research). The Omnibus tells which do and which don't.

- Annual SBIR/STTR informational conferences

    Every year, funding agencies host daylong SBIR conference to help newcomers learn more about SBIR funding possibilities. Attending a conference isn't essential by any means to winning SBIRs, but they usually have several good presentations by grantees who have won multiple SBIRs, and they're good occasions to buttonhole grant officials to ask questions. Every year, the conferences are held in a different city.

---

## References

1. Small Business Innovation Research (SBIR) and Small Business Technology Transfer (STTR) Programs at the NIDCR. Nidcr.nih.gov. 2011-03-25. Retrieved 2011-06-02.
2. http://www.gpo.gov/fdsys/pkg/CHRG-111hhrg48735/pdf/CHRG-111hhrg48735.pdf
3. http://en.m.wikipedia.org/wiki/Small_Business_Innovation_Research

4. Venture Funding and the NIH SBIR Program. Committee for Capitalizing on Science, Technology, and Innovation, *An Assessment of the Small Business Innovation Research Program*; Charles W. Wessner, ed., National Research Council, http://www.nap.edu/download.php?record_id=12543#.

5. National Research Council, *Government-Industry Partnerships for the Development of New Technologies: Summary Report*, Charles W. Wessner, ed. The National Academies Press, Washington, DC, 2002.

6. http://qb3.org/sites/qb3.org/files/pictures/docs/Milman%20Presentation %202011-09-20.pdf

7. Browing, B.A. http://www.dummies.com/store/product/Grant-Writing-For -Dummies-5th-Edition.productCd-1118834666,navId-322436.html.

8. http://sciencesherpa.com/guide-to-nih-sbir-grant-tips-and-resources/

9. Stevens, A. The enactment of Bayh–Dole. *Journal of Technology Transfer*, 29, 93–99, 2004.

10. Emerging energy and intellectual property—The often unappreciated risks and hurdles of government regulations and standard setting organizations. *The National Law Review*. Husch Blackwell. 2012-05-22. Retrieved 2012-07-02.

11. http://rudolphbiomed.com/2011/07/how-to-write-a-winning-sbir-grant -application-in-3-%E2%80%9Ceasy%E2%80%9D-steps/

12. http://asbtdc.org/sbir-faq/

13. Rockey, S. http://nexus.od.nih.gov/all/2015/06/29/what-are-the-chances-of -getting-funded/?utm_source=nexus&utm_medium=email&utm_content =nihupdate&utm_campaign=jun.

# 6

# Marketing and Marketing Research on a Shoestring

Advertising is what you pay for, publicity is what you pray for.

## 6.1 Introduction

**What is marketing?** The concept of marketing is confusing to many people. Is marketing sales, public relations, branding, or advertising? The simple answer is that marketing is a mix of all of these things. Marketing encompasses everything you do to put your product or service in front of your *potential* customers [1].

We do not emphasize the word *potential* without reason. One thing that many companies and business owners do wrong in their marketing efforts is to think of the entire world (universe) as their potential client base. This is an inappropriate way to go about marketing your company or yourself [2].

Last, it is important to recognize that, in marketing, there are two major forms of advertising and promotion; there is one that is directed to individuals (Business to Consumer) and one that is directed to businesses (Business to Business [B2B]).

Business to Consumer is when a company wants to sell a product or a service directly to a consumer (an individual person). B2B, on the other hand, is when a company wants to sell a product or service to another company [3].

**Marketing research** is any organized effort to gather information about target markets or customers. It is a very important component of business strategy [4]. Marketing research is a key factor in maintaining competitiveness over competitors. Marketing research provides critical information to identify and analyze the market need, market size, and your competition.

Information is power. Marketing research, which includes social and opinion research, is the systematic gathering and interpretation of information about individuals or organizations using statistical and analytical methods and techniques of the applied social sciences to gain insight or support decision-making.

Start-ups and small, underfunded companies are often stuck in a chicken-or-egg type dilemma when it comes to marketing research: They need good marketing research information in order to make key decisions to grow the company; however, they need money to do the research to get good market information to make the fundamental decisions to commercialize products and make them profitable.

It is a common dilemma that confounds many start-up founders. They have great ideas, great products, and great people. They need actionable marketing information in order to move their companies forward, but they lack the resources to obtain that information. Fortunately, start-ups and small, resource-poor companies can obtain good, usable marketing information inexpensively through a number of unconventional methods and sources discussed in this chapter.

## 6.2 A Small Business Is Not a Little Big Business

In their article in the *Harvard Business Review,* Welsh and White remind us that a small business is not a little big business [5]. An entrepreneur is not a multinational conglomerate but a struggling, underfinanced, and understaffed individual. To survive, an entrepreneur must apply principles different from those of a president of a large and established corporation.

The authors argue that the traditional assumption among mangers has been that small businesses can use essentially the same managerial principles "as the big boys," only on a suitably reduced scale. The basic assumption is that small businesses are like big businesses except that small companies have lower sales, smaller assets, and fewer employees.

Nothing could be further from the truth. Smallness creates what the authors call a special condition referred to as **resource poverty**. Resource poverty distinguishes small firms from their larger counterparts and thus requires critically different management styles and strategies. This can be summarized as shown in Table 6.1.

**TABLE 6.1**

"Resource Poverty" Applicable to Small Companies

| Strategies | Disadvantage(s) Compared to Established Businesses |
| --- | --- |
| Executive salaries | Represents a much larger percentage of overall costs |
| Human resources | Difficulty in attracting expensive but necessary talent |
| | Salaries versus stock options "skin in the game" |
| Business activities | Cannot afford large personnel expenditures in accounting, finance, marketing, sales, promotions, etc. |
| | Product launch expenses |
| External environment | Government regulations, industry standards |
| | Seasonal sales variations |
| | Insurance and banking needs |
| | Stakeholder demands |
| Internal environment | Cash flow management |
| | Reaching break-even point |

As we can see from Table 6.1, small businesses do not have the resources compared to big businesses, so how can they operate and survive? The owners of small businesses need to wear many hats and have multiple skill sets. From finance to accounting, from marketing to human resources, from operations to negotiations, the small business person needs to understand all the elements of doing business.

Thus, where and how does the small business owner have the time to fulfill all these fundamental needs and functions, while at the same time creating the necessary innovations? Churchill and Lewis [6] identified eight factors, four related to the enterprise and four related to the owner, as follows:

A. Company-related factors:
1. Financial resources, including cash and borrowing power
2. Personnel resources, relating to numbers, depth, and quality
3. Systems resources, relating to information, planning, and control
4. Business resources, relating to customer relations, market share, supplier relations, manufacturing, technology, and company position in its industry

B. Owner-related factors:
1. Personal goals and business goals
2. Operational abilities relating to marketing, inventing, producing, and distribution
3. Managerial ability and willingness to delegate responsibility
4. Strategic abilities in matching strengths and weaknesses of the company

Also, the entrepreneur's salary in a small business represents a much larger fraction of revenues than in a big company, often such a large fraction that little is left over to pay additional managers or to reward investors. Similarly, small businesses cannot usually afford to pay for the kind of accounting and bookkeeping services they need, nor can new employees be adequately tested and trained in advance.

### 6.2.1 Difference between Marketing, Advertising, and Public Relations

*Marketing, advertising, public relations*—what do all those terms even mean? Although we could break these terms down into stodgy textbook definitions, we think noted humorist and marketing professional S.H. Simmons [7,8] put it in a more relatable context by analyzing these related fields through the prism of wooing a foxy lady:

> *If a young man tells his date she is intelligent, looks lovely, and is a great conversationalist, he's saying the right things to the right person and that is*

*marketing. If the young man tells his date how handsome, smart, and success-ful he is, that is **advertising**. If someone else tells the young woman how hand-some, smart, and successful her date is, that's **public relations**.*

According to Chron [9], marketing is the overall process of communicating and delivering products to a target audience through the marketing mix of product, price, place, and promotion. Promotion is a combination of commu-nication activities that include advertising and public relations. Deciding on what resources to apply to each of these promotion areas is a result of other factors identified in an overall marketing plan.

Advertising is a means of communication to a target audience using mostly paid media such as television, radio, the Internet, and print publications. Successful advertising programs include themes that communicate company mission, branding, and services, as well as specific product information. The media for advertising are chosen based on what market research has identified as the most successful way of reaching a target audience and the financial resources that can be applied to advertising based on the marketing budget.

Public relations is a communication method used by businesses to convey a positive image to a target audience and the general pub-lic. Public relations methods can include press releases, community involvement, and speaking at public forums on issues important to a target audience. Small companies with small advertising budgets can use public relations as an inexpensive medium to establish the company name and communicate a brand image. Successful public relations programs highlight company accomplishments and posi-tive contributions to community.

To summarize: Advertising is paid media, public relations is earned media. This means you convince reporters or editors to write a positive story about you or your client, your candidate, brand, or issue. It appears in the editorial section of the magazine, newspaper, TV station, or website, rather than the "paid media" section where advertising messages appear. Hence, your story has more credibility because it was independently verified by a trusted third party, rather than purchased [10].

## 6.3 Marketing Research Fundamentals

Marketing research is the best way of getting an overview of consumers' wants, needs, and beliefs. The research can be used to determine how a product should be marketed. Peter Drucker [11] eloquently argued that marketing research is the "quintessence of the marketing effort."

There are two major types of marketing research. Primary research is subdivided into quantitative/qualitative research and secondary research.

- **Primary research.** This is research you compile yourself or hire someone to gather for you.
- **Secondary research.** This type of research is already compiled and organized for you. Examples of secondary information include reports and studies by government agencies, trade associations, or other businesses within your industry. Most of the research you gather will most likely be secondary.

Regardless of whether you perform primary or secondary marketing research, the following are the critical factors that should be investigated:

- **Market information.** Through marketing information you can uncover the prices of different products in the market, as well as the supply-and-demand situation. Market researchers have a wider role than previously recognized by helping their clients to understand social, technical, and even legal aspects of markets.
- **Market segmentation.** Market segmentation is the division of the market or population into subgroups with similar motivations. It is widely used for segmenting on geographic differences, personality differences, demographic differences, technographic differences, use of product differences, psychographic differences, and gender differences. For B2B segmentation, firmographics is commonly used.
- **Market trends.** Market trends are the upward or downward movement of a specific market, during a period. Determining the market size may be more difficult if one is starting with a new innovation. In this case, you will have to derive the figures from the number of potential customers, or customer segments.
- **SWOT analysis.** SWOT is a written analysis of the Strengths, Weaknesses, Opportunities, and Threats to a business entity. Not only should a SWOT be used in the creation stage of the company, it could also be used throughout the life of the company. A SWOT may also be written up for the competition to understand how to develop the marketing and product mixes.
- **Marketing effectiveness.** Marketing effectiveness is the quality of how marketers go to market with the goal of optimizing their spending to achieve good results for both the short term and the long term. It is also related to Marketing ROI (return on investment)

and Return on Marketing Investment [12]. Marketing effectiveness includes the following:

- Customer analysis
- Choice modeling
- Competitor analysis
- Risk analysis
- Product research
- Advertising the research findings
- Marketing mix modeling
- Simulated test marketing
- Clearly identifying your target market
- Determining your target market potential
- Preparing, communicating, and delivering satisfaction to your customers

## 6.4 Marketing Research for Business/Planning

### Needs, wants, and demands

Companies can't give job security. Only customers can.

**Jack Welch**
*CEO General Electric*

Marketing theory divides human necessities into three basic parts: needs, wants, and demands. **Needs** comprise some of the most basic and fundamental necessities of life such as food, shelter, protection, good health, and so on. These needs are not created by marketing, since they already exist in society.

**Wants** are desires for things that satisfy deeper requests, such as gourmet foods, sports cars, vacations to exotic locales, and so on. Advanced societies are continually reshaping wants by societal forces such as schools, families, business corporations, healthcare alternatives, and so on. Entrepreneurial companies are very active in satisfying consumer wants with innovative solutions and approaches. Needs are few; wants are many. Remember the old adage that "People don't know what they want, only what they know."

**Demands** are wants for specific high-quality, high-priced products/ services that deliver superior performance. Entrepreneurial firms shine in this marketing sphere. Most of the innovations carry a hefty price tag, thus satisfying the demands of affluent customers, who are willing and able to

**FIGURE 6.1**
Marketing program tools.

buy these offerings. If we use the 80/20 rule, 20% of customers purchase 80% of the demand offerings.

Start-ups can market and promote their products by utilizing the marketing program tools shown in Figure 6.1.

## 6.5 Acquiring Marketing Research Information

You can use various methods of market research to find out information about markets, target markets and their needs, competitors, market trends, and customer satisfaction with products and services. Your businesses can learn a great deal about your customers, their needs, how to meet those needs, and how your business is doing to meet those needs.

### 6.5.1 Primary Research Information

Acquire your marketing research information from all of the following sources:

- Set your marketing budget.
- Determine what information you needed.
- Set a timeline for your research.

- Analyze the secondary research material you located.
- Locate, read, and learn existing information about the target market, industry, competition, and product/service.
- Find all relevant facts.
- Organize a lot of critical information that was missing.
- Conduct primary research.
- Design research tools, who you would talk to and what you would ask them.
- Analyze the results of the primary research and secondary research data.
- Integrate this information into the business plan by adjusting the marketing strategy (pricing, advertising, product/service alterations) to give credibility to your sales projections.

*Did you use any of the following tools to conduct your primary research?*

- Telephone surveys
- Interviews
- Focus groups
- Mailed questionnaires

*Did you find out the answers to any of these questions from your primary market research?*

- Is there a need for your product?
- What price will your customers pay?
- How often do they buy a product or service like yours?
- How do they buy it now?
- What makes them want to buy it?
- What company do they usually buy it from?
- What do they like about the product or service?
- What don't they like about it?

*Did you include the following information on your competitors thru competitive analysis?*

- A list of all key competitors
- Location
- Years in business

- Product/service sold
- Pricing schedule
- Hours of operation
- Customer profile
- A description of their marketing strategies
- Size of company
- Marketing/promotional strategy
- Your observations
- An analysis of their strengths and weaknesses
- A strategy on how you will deal with these competitors

*Where did you get the information on your competitors?*

- I hit the pavement and visited my competition personally, and I observed their setup, customers, staff, and professionalism.
- I collected any material I could find from them.
- I asked their customers (primary research).
- I used secondary sources such as the Yellow Pages, trade associations, and newspapers to gather information.
- I looked at their website.

*What steps did you take to conduct a strategic competitive analysis? Did you*

- Develop a thorough list of all the competition you will face in the industry.
- Search for direct competitors who offer products or services that are essentially the same as yours.
- Search for indirect competitors who are businesses that offer products or services that can be substituted for yours.
- Identify each competitor's strengths.
- Identify each competitor's weaknesses.
- Identify your top three competitive advantages.
- Identify your top three weaknesses.
- Develop a strategy for dealing with competitors.
- Work out some best-case/worst-case scenarios on paper.
- Make sure your pricing, positioning, and marketing strategies are flexible enough to deal with these situations.

### 6.5.2 Secondary Research Information

The vast majority of research you can find will be secondary research. While large companies spend huge amounts of money on market research, the good news is that plenty of information is available for free to entrepreneurs on a tight budget. The best places to start? Your local library and the Internet [13].

Secondary data are outside information assembled by government agencies, industry and trade associations, labor unions, media sources, chambers of commerce, and so on, and found in the form of pamphlets, newsletters, trade and other magazines, newspapers, and so on. It is termed secondary data because the information has been gathered by another, or secondary, source. The benefits of this are obvious—time and money are saved because you don't have to develop survey methods or do the interviewing.

Secondary sources are divided into three main categories:

1. **Public.** Public sources are the most economical, as they're usually free, and can offer a lot of good information. These sources are most typically governmental departments, business departments of public libraries, and so on.

2. **Commercial.** Commercial sources are equally valuable, but usually involve costs such as subscription and association fees. However, you spend far less than you would if you hired a research team to collect the data firsthand. Commercial sources typically consist of research and trade associations, organizations like SCORE (Service Corps of Retired Executives) and Dun & Bradstreet, banks and other financial institutions, publicly traded corporations, and so on.

3. **Educational.** Educational institutions are frequently overlooked as viable information sources, yet there is more research conducted in colleges, universities, and polytechnic institutes than virtually any sector of the business community.

Government statistics are among the most plentiful and wide-ranging public sources of information. Start with the Census Bureau's helpful *Hidden Treasures—Census Bureau Data and Where to Find It!* In seconds, you'll find out where to find federal and state information. Other government publications that are helpful include the following:

- *Statistical and Metropolitan Area Data Book.* Offers statistics for metropolitan areas, central cities and counties
- *Statistical Abstract of the United States.* Data books with statistics from numerous sources, government to private
- *U.S. Global Outlook.* Traces the growth of 200 industries and gives 5-year forecasts for each

Don't neglect to contact specific government agencies such as the Small Business Administration. They sponsor several helpful programs such as SCORE and Small Business Development Centers, which can provide you with free counseling and a wealth of business information. The Department of Commerce not only publishes helpful books like the *U.S. Global Outlook* but also produces an array of products with information regarding both domestic industries and foreign markets through its International Trade Administration branch. The above items are available from the US Government Printing Office.

One of the best public sources is the business section of public libraries. The services provided vary from city to city, but usually include a wide range of government and market statistics, a large collection of directories including information on domestic and foreign businesses, as well as a wide selection of magazines, newspapers, and newsletters.

Almost every county government publishes population density and distribution figures in accessible census tracts. These tracts will show you the number of people living in specific areas, such as precincts, water districts, or even 10-block neighborhoods. Other public sources include city chambers of commerce or business development departments, which encourage new businesses in their communities. They will supply you (usually for free) with information on population trends, community income characteristics, payrolls, industrial development, and so on.

Among the best commercial sources of information are research and trade associations. Information gathered by trade associations is usually confined to a certain industry and available only to association members, with a membership fee frequently required. However, the research gathered by the larger associations is usually thorough, accurate, and worth the cost of membership. Two excellent resources to help you locate a trade association that reports on the business you're researching are *Encyclopedia of Associations* (Gale Research) and *Business Information Sources* (University of California Press) and can usually be found at your local library.

Research associations are often independent but are sometimes affiliated with trade associations. They often limit their activities to conducting and applying research in industrial development, but some have become full-service information sources with a wide range of supplementary publications such as directories.

Educational institutions are very good sources of research. Research there ranges from faculty-based projects often published under professors' bylines to student projects, theses, and assignments. Copies of student research projects may be available for free with faculty permission. Consulting services are available either for free or at a cost negotiated with the appropriate faculty members. This can be an excellent way to generate research at little or no cost, using students who welcome the professional experience either as interns or for special credit.

Look in the *Encyclopedia of Associations* (Gale Cengage Learning), found in most libraries, to find associations relevant to your industry. You may also want to investigate your customers' trade associations for information that can help you market to them. Most trade associations provide information free of charge.

*Did you use any of the following tools in your secondary research?*

- Census information
- Trade associations
- Chamber of Commerce
- Market profiles
- Libraries
- Lifestyles profiles
- Local magazines/newspapers
- Going on line

### 6.5.2.1 Marketing Research Online

You may already be conducting online market research for your business—but you may not know it. Some of the easiest to use and most common tools are located right at your fingertips. Web searches, online questionnaires, customer feedback forms—they all help you gather information about your market, your customers, and your future business prospects.

The advent of the Internet has presented small businesses with a wealth of additional resources to use in conducting free or low-cost market research. The following pages will describe the different types of tools to conduct online market research, go over the general categories of market research, and advise you on how to create the best online searches and questionnaires [14].

These days, entrepreneurs can conduct much of their market research without ever leaving their computers, thanks to the universe of online services and information. Start with the major consumer online services, which offer access to business databases. Here are a few to get you started [15]:

- *KnowThis.com* is a marketing virtual library that includes a tab on the site called "Weblinks." The tab contains links to a wide variety of market research web resources.
- *BizMiners.com* lets you choose national market research reports for 16,000 industries in 300 US markets, local research reports for 16,000 industries in 250 metro markets, or financial profiles for 10,000 US industries. The reports are available online for a nominal cost.
- *MarketResearch.com* has more than 250,000 research reports from hundreds of sources consolidated into one accessible collection that's

updated daily. No subscription fee is required, and you pay only for the parts of the report you need with its "Buy by the Section" feature. After paying, the information is delivered online to your personal library on the site.

## 6.6 Your Start-Up Marketing Plan

Without marketing, no one will ever know that your business exists—and if customers do not know you are in business, you will not record any sales. When your marketing efforts are working, however, and customers are streaming through the door, an effective customer service policy will keep them coming back for more. So now it is time to create the plans that will draw customers to your business again and again.

A marketing plan consists of the strategies and devices you are going to use to effectively communicate to your target audience. A customer service plan focuses on your customer's requirements and the ways of filling those requirements. The two must work in concert.

Descriptions of your market and its segments, the competition, and prospective customers should be in your business plan. This is the start of your marketing plan. On the basis of this information, you can begin choosing the communication channels to use to get the word out about your business: social media, blogs, e-mail newsletters, Web banners, pay-per-click ads, radio, TV, billboards, direct mail, fliers, print ads, seminars, technical conferences, live presentations to audiences, webinars, and other venues. Then, prioritize your tactics and begin with the ones that your research has shown to be the most effective for your audience.

For your customer service plan, think about what it'll take to develop relationships with your customers that can be mutually beneficial for years to come. Since repeat customers are the backbone of every successful business, in your customer service plan, you'll want to outline just how you're going to provide complete customer satisfaction. Consider money-back guarantees, buying incentives, and the resolution of customer complaints. Determine what your customer service policy will say, how you'll train your employees to attend to the needs of your customers and how to reward repeat customers. Remember, this is just the beginning: Your program should evolve as the business grows.

To begin attracting your first customers, it's helpful to create a profile of the end user of your product or service. Now's the time to get in the habit of "talking up" your business—telling everyone you know about it. Ask for referrals from colleagues, suppliers, former employers, and other associates. You can improve the quality of your referrals by being specific in your request. For example, an insurance broker developed a successful referral network by asking existing clients if they knew anyone who was "in a two-income professional family with young children," rather than just asking if they knew anyone who needed insurance.

Consider offering free consultations or an introductory price to first-time buyers. Consider joining forces with a complementary business to get them to help you spread the word about your new venture. For example, a carpet cleaner might offer incentives to a housecleaning service if they'd recommend them to their regular customers. Once you've done work for a few satisfied customers, ask them for a testimonial letter to use in your promotions.

## 6.7 Guerrilla Marketing

The term *guerilla marketing* is often used to describe the most inexpensive, small-scale, and short-term marketing techniques. It can be defined as marketing that uses creativity and effort to maximize sales impact at the lowest cost. It is a low-budget approach to marketing that relies on ingenuity, cleverness, and surprise rather than traditional techniques [7].

The concept of guerrilla marketing was invented as an unconventional system of promotions that relies on time, energy, and imagination rather than a traditional big marketing budget. Typically, (1) guerrilla marketing campaigns are unexpected and unconventional, (2) they are potentially interactive, and (3) specific customers are targeted in unexpected places. The objective of guerrilla marketing is to create a unique, engaging, and thought-provoking concept to generate buzz, and consequently turn viral.

One way of differentiating your "resource poor" start-up company inexpensively is to use a marketing concept known as guerrilla marketing. This concept was introduced by Jay Conrad Levinson [16] with the intention of helping small companies make big marketing splashes but only using a very limited budget.

Levinson teaches that marketing encompasses everything you do to promote your business, from the moment of conception to the point at which customers buy your product or service and begin to patronize your business on a regular basis. The key words to remember are *everything* and *regular* basis.

The meaning is clear: Marketing includes the name of your company, the determination of whether you will be selling directly or through distributors, your method of manufacturing, the location of your business headquarters, your advertising method, your sales training, your sales presentation, your telephone inquiries, web address effectiveness, your customer-based problem solving ability, your expected growth plan, and your follow-up. If you gather from this that marketing is a complex process, you are right. If you do not see guerrilla marketing as an iterative, circular process, it will be a straight line that leads directly to the nearest bankruptcy court.

According to Hutter and Hoffmann [17], three aspects distinguish guerrilla marketing from traditional marketing, namely, (1) surprise, (2) diffusion, and (3) low cost effect. A guerrilla marketing campaign should be surprising to your competition, meaning it should not follow the traditional marketing norms. Guerrilla marketers create and execute seven "strategies" as follows:

1. Purpose of your strategy
2. How you will achieve this purpose, focusing on the benefits to the consumer
3. Define your target market (or markets)
4. Define the guerrilla marketing weapons you will employ
5. Clearly focus on your niche market
6. Explain your identity (see below)
7. Calculate your budget, expressed as a percentage of your expected gross revenues

Take a moment to understand the crucial difference between your *image* and your *identity*. Image implies something artificial, contrived, and not genuine. Conversely, identity describes what your business is really all about.

### 6.7.1 Guerilla Marketing Tactics

Never *assume* that a large market exists for your wonderful new product. Create it! Guerrilla marketing is as different from conventional marketing as guerrilla warfare is from conventional warfare. Below are some tactics that are easy to understand, easy to implement, and outrageously inexpensive:

- Organize technical demonstrations
- Develop a sales script (your elevator speech)
- Sell at every opportunity
- Sponsor memorable events
- Speak at many technical occasions
- Ask for referrals from colleagues
- Create samples (touchy-feelies)
- Create specification sheets
- Create an unforgettable award
- Collect testimonials
- Get a journalist to write about your company/technology
- Show great interest in customer needs
- Create and distribute timely white papers

- Create a widely circulated newsletter
- Cooperate with other businesses
- Exhibit at important trade shows
- Get yourself published. Write an e-book.
- Join and participate
- Organize community hospital-oriented projects.
- Fake publicity stunts
- Attention-getting press releases

## 6.7.2 Apple's Guerrilla Marketing

By any measure, Apple is unquestionably one of the world's most successful retailers. Even though Apple never sold directly to consumers before it opened the first store in a mall in Tyson's Corner, Virginia, Apple has achieved some incredible bragging rights for its retail channel [18].

Apple operates more than 380 retail stores that employ more than 40,000 people and plays host to more than a million visitors every day. Apple's retail operations are on track to generate more than $20 billion in 2012. Amazingly, Apple's stores average more than $7000 per square foot, which is more than twice the former gold standard, Tiffany & Company. It is estimated that Apple's Fifth Avenue store generates more than $35,000 per square foot, making it the highest grossing retailer in New York City—ever! Apple stores are now the highest-performing stores in retail history.

### 6.7.2.1 Humble Beginnings

It wasn't always that way. Apple experienced massive failures in the 1990s when selling its products through retailers such as Sears and CompUSA. Its computers were muscled out of view and its brand so weakened that many retailers refused to properly market or stock Apple's computers. Even though Apple entered the retail business largely as a defensive move to gain more control of the customer experience, the climate then was anything but welcoming. Gateway was operating direct-to-consumer retail stores and failing fast. Apple had to learn how to do retail its products differently.

Less than 2 years after Apple opened its retail stores, Gateway declared bankruptcy, shut down all of its shops and laid off more than 2500 workers. Three years later, CompUSA shuttered its 23-year-old chain of stores. Thus, while there was little expectation and no guarantee that Apple might succeed selling its own computers in this challenging retail climate, amazingly, somehow it managed to survive.

### 6.7.2.2 Unconventional Thinking

But how did Apple survive the disappearance of its two retail distributors? Consider the following questions:

- How did a company with no experience in retail become the fastest in US history to reach annual sales of $1 billion during the worst financial crisis in modern times?
- How did a company with only four products become the most profitable retailer in history while creating an experience that is now the standard by which all others are measured?
- Why did a company that was losing money decide to enter the retail market against the recommendations of every expert and where all retail businesses were going out of business?
- How did Apple entice millions of people to visit their stores and pay full price when all their products are readily available at other retailers and even tax-free online at Amazon.com?

Clearly the answer to these questions is that Apple had to think differently about retail and make their stores more than just a place people go to buy things. They had to devise a way to enrich the lives of the people who shop at the Apple stores and do more than simply deliver a transactional experience. In short, they had to reinvent retail.

Did you know that Apple rarely invents anything new? Entire books are written about how Steve Jobs borrowed ideas for Apple from other places like Xerox and Sony, famously embracing the motto "Good artists borrow. Great artists steal." Apple clearly didn't invent the PC, the MP3 player, downloadable music, or the mobile phone. The Mac, iPod, iTunes, and iPhone were all successful because Apple had ample time to improve upon existing designs and functionality. As a consequence of being late to these markets, Apple was forced to adopt a stunningly different (guerrilla) marketing strategy than anyone else. And that is guerrilla marketing at its best!

## 6.8 Your Marketing Plan

Firms that are successful in marketing invariably start with a marketing plan. Large companies have plans with hundreds of pages; small companies can get by with a half-dozen sheets. Put your marketing plan in a three-ring binder. Refer to it at least quarterly, but better yet monthly. Leave a tab for putting in monthly reports on sales/manufacturing; this will allow you to track your performance as you follow the plan [19].

The guerrilla plan should cover 1 year. For small companies, this is often the best way to think about marketing. Things change, people leave, markets evolve, customers come and go. Later on, we suggest creating a section of your plan that addresses the medium-term future—2 to 4 years down the road. But the bulk of your plan should focus on the coming year.

You should allow yourself a couple of months to write the plan, even if it's only a few pages long. Developing the plan is the "heavy lifting" of marketing. While executing the plan has its challenges, deciding what to do and how to do it is marketing's greatest challenge. Most marketing plans kick off with the first of the year or with the opening of your fiscal year if it's different.

Who should see your plan? The answer: All the players in your company. Firms typically keep their marketing plans very, very private for one of two very different reasons: Either they're too skimpy and management would be embarrassed to have them see the light of day, or they're solid and packed with information… which would make them extremely valuable to the competition.

You cannot do a marketing plan without getting many people involved. No matter what your size, get feedback from all parts of your company: finance, manufacturing, personnel, supply, and so on—in addition to marketing itself. This is especially important because it will take all aspects of your company to make your marketing plan work. Your key people can provide realistic input on what's achievable and how your goals can be reached, and they can share any insights they have on any potential, as-yet-unrealized marketing opportunities, adding another dimension to your plan. If you're essentially a one-person management operation, you'll have to wear all your hats at one time—but at least the meetings will be short!

What's the relationship between your marketing plan and your business plan or vision statement? Your business plan spells out what your business is about—what you do and don't do, and what your ultimate goals are. It encompasses more than marketing; it can include discussions of locations, staffing, financing, strategic alliances, and so on. It includes "the vision thing," the resounding words that spell out the glorious purpose of your company in stirring language. Your business plan is the US Constitution of your business: If you want to do something that's outside the business plan, you need to either change your mind or change the plan. Your company's business plan provides the environment in which your marketing plan must flourish. The two documents must be consistent.

### 6.8.1 The Benefits of a Marketing Plan

Based on marketing research, a marketing plan, on the other hand, is replete with meaning. It provides you with several major benefits. Let's review them.

- **Rallying point:** Your marketing plan gives your troops something to rally behind. You want them to feel confident that the captain of the vessel has the charts in order, knows how to run the ship, and has a port of destination in mind. Companies often undervalue the impact of a "marketing plan" on their own people, who want to feel part of a team engaged in an exciting and complicated joint endeavor. If you want your employees to feel committed to your company, it's important to share with them your vision of where the company is headed in the years to come. People don't always understand financial projections, but they can get excited about a well-written and well-thought-out marketing plan. You should consider releasing your marketing plan—perhaps in an abridged version—companywide. Do it with some fanfare and generate some excitement for the adventures to come. Your workers will appreciate being involved.

- **Chart to success:** We all know that plans are imperfect things. How can you possibly know what's going to happen 12 months or 5 years from now? Isn't putting together a marketing plan an exercise in futility... a waste of time better spent meeting with customers or fine-tuning production? Yes, possibly, but only in the narrowest sense. If you don't plan, you're doomed, and an inaccurate plan is far better than no plan at all. To stay with our sea captain analogy, it's better to be 5° or even 10° off your destination port than to have no destination in mind at all. The point of sailing, after all, is to get somewhere, and without a marketing plan, you'll wander the seas aimlessly, sometimes finding dry land but more often than not floundering in a vast ocean. Sea captains without a chart are rarely remembered for discovering anything but the ocean floor.

- **Company operational instructions:** Your child's first bike and your new VCR came with a set of instructions, and your company is far more complicated to put together and run than either of them. Your marketing plan is a step-by-step guide for your company's success. It's more important than a vision statement. To put together a genuine marketing plan, you have to assess your company from top to bottom and make sure all the pieces are working together in the best way. What do you want to do with this enterprise you call the company in the coming year? Consider it a to-do list on a grand scale. It assigns specific tasks for the year.

- **Captured thinking:** You don't allow your financial people to keep their numbers in their heads. Financial reports are the lifeblood of the numbers side of any business, no matter what size. It should be no different with marketing. Your written document lays out your game plan. If people leave, if new people arrive, if memories falter, if events bring pressure to alter the givens, the information in the written marketing plan stays intact to remind you of what you'd agreed on.

- **Top-level reflection:** In the daily hurly-burly of competitive business, it's hard to turn your attention to the big picture, especially those parts that aren't directly related to the daily operations. You need to take time periodically to really think about your business—whether it's providing you and your employees with what you want, whether there aren't some innovative wrinkles you can add, whether you're getting all you can out of your products, your sales staff, and your markets. Writing your marketing plan is the best time to do this high-level thinking. Some companies send their top marketing people away to a retreat. Others go to the home of a principal. Some do marketing plan development at a local motel, away from phones and fax machines, so they can devote themselves solely to thinking hard and drawing the most accurate sketches they can of the immediate future of the business.

Ideally, after writing marketing plans for a few years, you can sit back and review a series of them, year after year, and check the progress of your company. Of course, sometimes it is hard to make time to review the marketing history (there is that annoying real world to deal with), but looking back can provide an unparalleled objective view of what you've been doing with your business life over a number of years.

### 6.8.2 Researching Your Market

Whether you're just starting out or if you've been in business for years, you should always stay up-to-date with your market information. Below, we discuss the best methods for finding your relevant data [20].

The purpose of market research is to provide relevant data that will help solve the marketing problems a business will encounter. This is absolutely necessary in the start-up phase. Conducting thorough market surveys is the foundation of any successful business. In fact, strategies such as market segmentation (identifying specific segments within a market) and product differentiation (creating an identity for your product or service that separates it from your competitors') would be impossible to develop without market research.

Your market research should be designed to answer two major questions: (1) what are your target market needs, and (2) your proposed solutions to answer those needs, as depicted in Figure 6.2.

Whether you're conducting market research using the historical, experimental, observational, or survey method, you'll be gathering two types of data. The first will be "primary" information that you will compile yourself or hire someone to gather. Most information, however, will be "secondary," or already compiled and organized for you. Reports and studies done by government agencies, trade associations, or other businesses within your

**FIGURE 6.2**
Marketing research. (Modified after Naresh K. Malhotra. *Marketing Research: An Applied Orientation*, Pearson Education, Upper Saddle River, NJ, 2000.)

industry are examples of the latter. Search for them, and take advantage of them.

When conducting market research on a shoestring, there are basically two types of information that can be gathered: exploratory and specific. Exploratory research is open-ended in nature, helps you define a specific problem, and usually involves detailed, unstructured interviews in which lengthy answers are solicited from a small group of respondents. Specific research is broader in scope and is used to solve a problem that exploratory research has identified. Interviews are structured and formal in approach. Of the two, specific research is more expensive.

There are basically three avenues you can take: (1) direct mail, (2) phone surveys, and (3) personal interviews. These are discussed below.

### Direct Mail

If you choose a direct-mail questionnaire, be sure to do the following in order to increase your response rate:

- Make sure your questions are short and to the point.
- Make sure questionnaires are addressed to specific individuals and they're of interest to the respondent.
- Limit the questionnaire's length to two pages.
- Enclose a professionally prepared cover letter that adequately explains what you need.
- Send a reminder approximately 2 weeks after the initial mailing. Include a postage-paid self-addressed envelope.

Unfortunately, even if you employ the above tactics, response to direct mail is always low, and is sometimes less than 5%.

### Phone Surveys

Phone surveys are generally the most cost-effective, considering overall response rates; they cost approximately one-third as much as personal interviews, which have, on average, a response rate that is only 10%. The following are some phone survey guidelines:

- At the beginning of the conversation, your interviewer should confirm the name of the respondent if calling a home, or give the appropriate name to the switchboard operator if calling a business.

- Pauses should be avoided, as respondent interest can quickly drop.

- Make sure that a follow-up call is possible if additional information is required.

- Make sure that interviewers don't divulge details about the poll until the respondent is reached.

As mentioned, phone interviews are cost-effective but speed is another big advantage. Some of the more experienced interviewers can get through up to 10 interviews an hour (however, speed for speed's sake is not the goal of any of these surveys), but five to six interviews per hour is more typical. Phone interviews also allow you to cover a wide geographical range relatively inexpensively. Phone costs can be reduced by taking advantage of cheaper rates during certain hours.

### Personal Interviews

There are two main types of personal interviews:

1. **The group survey.** Used mostly by big business, group interviews can be useful as brainstorming tools resulting in product modifications and new product ideas. They also give you insight into buying preferences and purchasing decisions among certain populations.

2. **The depth interview.** One-on-one interviews where the interviewer is guided by a small checklist and basic common sense. Depth interviews are either focused or nondirective. Nondirective interviews encourage respondents to address certain topics with minimal questioning. The respondent, in essence, leads the interview. The focused interview, on the other hand, is based on a preset checklist. The choice and timing of questions, however, are left to the interviewer, depending on how the interview goes.

When considering which type of survey to use, keep the following cost factors in mind:

- **Mail.** Most of the costs here concern the printing of questionnaires, envelopes, postage, the cover letter, time taken in the analysis and presentation, the cost of researcher time, and any incentives used.
- **Telephone.** The main costs here are the interviewer's fee, phone charges, preparation of the questionnaire, cost of researcher time, and the analysis and presentation of the results of the questioning.
- **Personal interviews.** Costs include the printing of questionnaires and prompt cards if needed, the incentives used, the interviewer's fee and expenses, cost of researcher time, and analysis and presentation.
- **Group discussions.** Your main costs here are the interviewer's fees and expenses in recruiting and assembling the groups, renting the conference room or other facility, researcher time, any incentives used, analysis and presentation, and the cost of recording media such as tapes, if any are used.

## 6.9 Competitive Intelligence

The Society of Competitive Intelligence Professionals defines Competitive Intelligence as "the process of ethically collecting, analyzing, and disseminating accurate, relevant, specific, timely, foresighted, and actionable intelligence regarding the implications of the business environment, competitors and the organization itself."

Competitive intelligence (CI) is the selection, collection, interpretation, and distribution of publicly held information that is strategically important to a firm. A substantial amount of this information is publicly accessible via the World Wide Web, periodic company SEC filings, the patent literature, company promotional campaigns, and so on.

The knowledge-intensive world is ruled by hypercompetition. Hypercompetition is a rapid and dynamic competition characterized by unsustainable advantage. It is the condition of rapid escalation of competition based on price-quality positioning, competition to protect or invade established product or geographic markets, and competition based on vast scientific knowledge, deep pockets, and the creation of even deeper pocketed alliances [21].

The knowledge base for managing in this hypercompetitive environment is called Competitive Intelligence. CI is a process that provides you insights into what might happen in the near future. This process requires that we go from data to information to intelligence. Here is a basic example:

Data → Prices for our products have dropped by 5%

Information → New offshore facilities enjoy significantly lower labor costs

Intelligence → Our key competitor is about to acquire a facility in China that will...

The differences between data, information, and intelligence can be subtle, but very real:

Data → Unconnected pieces of information: Nice to know, but so what!

Information → Increased knowledge derived by understanding the relationships of data: Interesting, but how does it relate to what I do! The knowledge-intensive business world is driven by hypercompetition.

Intelligence → Organizing the information to fully appreciate the implications and impact on the organization: Oh really, then we better do something!

A formalized CI program should

- Anticipate changes in the marketplace
- Anticipate actions of competitors
- Discover new or potential competitors
- Learn from the successes and failures of others
- Increase the range and quality of acquisition targets
- Learn about new technologies, products, and processes that affect your business
- Learn about political, legislative, or regulatory changes that can affect your business
- Enter new businesses
- Look at your own business practices with an open mind
- Help implement the latest management tools

### 6.9.1 CI Is a Top Management Function

CI is not for everyone. In fact, most companies do not use CI. Despite the fact that most executives rely on the flow of information for decision-making, only a handful of companies have a fully functional, integrated CI process in place. Why is that? Perhaps the most important reason is attitudinal: the way executives think about CI [22]. Have you ever heard some of the comments listed below? Or perhaps you have said them yourself!

- CI is spying; it is unethical. I don't want any part of it.
- It was not part of my school curriculum. It must not be important.
- CI is a cost center. We do not have a budget for it.
- How do I quantify CI's cost/benefit ratio?
- Nothing happens in this industry that I don't know already.
- If I don't know it, is it not worth knowing.
- We tried it before, and it didn't work.
- I am too busy to review all this garbage.

CI requires authorization by the highest echelons of management. CI is a top management function. It can provide vital analysis of competitor capabilities, plans, intentions, and limitations. It spotlights industry structure and trends. It may also reveal political, economic, and social forces affecting your company.

The CI life cycle is iterative, consisting of four major functions: (1) planning and direction, (2) information collection, (3) analysis and forecast, and finally (4) information and dissemination, as shown in Figure 6.3.

CI is particularly useful in industries with long development and approval cycles, such as the pharmaceutical and biotechnology industries. These industries are faced with long research and development times—sometimes 10 to 15 years for innovative drugs—coupled with uncertain and hugely

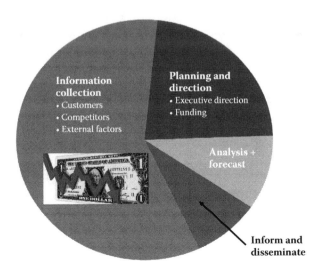

**FIGURE 6.3**
The CI life cycle.

expensive clinical trials. This allows continual tracking of a drug's progress by competitors through the public FDA approval process.

Thus, pharmaceutical/biotechnology companies utilize CI during the years of drug development to help determine if a new drug development should be continued, or dropped. Likewise, it allows companies to monitor a competitor's activities and decide whether to initiate their own drug development for a specific indication.

### 6.9.2 CI Should Be Actionable

CI differs from data and information since it requires some form of analysis. The purpose of this analysis is to derive some meaning from the piles of data and information that bury everyone. By going through analysis and filtering, we can refine it enough so that someone can act on it and understand their options, giving them an opportunity to make forward-looking decisions.

Note that **Information** is factual. It is numbers, statistics, bits of data, and interesting stories that seem important. **Intelligence**, on the other hand, is an *actionable* list of data that have been analyzed, filtered, and distilled. This is what we call intelligence know-how.

Thus, when you present CI to your staff, they should draw a conclusion and make an important decision quickly. Therefore, CI should put conclusions and recommendations up front with supporting research behind the analysis. CI should not simply present the facts, declaring what we found, but instead make a statement, saying this is what we believe is about to happen.

CI involves the use of public sources to develop data on your competition, competitors, and the market environment. It can then transform those data into actionable policies (intelligence). In this context, "public" means all the information you can legally and ethically identify, obtain, locate, deduce, and access [23].

CI is also known by several other names: competitor intelligence, business intelligence, strategic intelligence, marketing intelligence, competitive technical intelligence, technology intelligence, and technical intelligence, depending on what specific information is being targeted [24].

The development of CI usually proceeds in a five-phase predetermined cycle, as seen below:

1. **Establish your needs.** Clearly identify the information needed on the competition, or the competitive environment.
2. **Collect data.** Assemble raw data, using legal and ethical means, from public sources.
3. **Analyze the data.** Convert data into useful information.
4. **Communicate intelligence.** Convey the finished intelligence to the decision-maker(s) for their use.
5. **Actionable intelligence.** Provide strategic direction to decision-maker(s) in a timely manner.

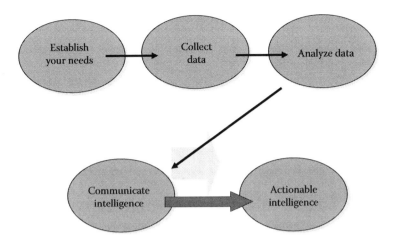

**FIGURE 6.4**
Five-phase intelligence cycle.

These phases are visually summarized in Figure 6.4.

### 6.9.3 Market Intelligence

Market intelligence is focused on the very current activities in the marketplace. You can look at it as the qualitative side of the quantitative data research you have conducted in many retail markets. The primary beneficiaries of market intelligence are usually the marketing department, market research, and the sales force. To a lesser degree, market intelligence serves those in market planning by providing retrospective data on the success and failure of their own sales efforts.

Market intelligence's focus is on sales, pricing, payment, and financing terms, as well as on promotions being offered and their effectiveness. Market intelligence's time horizon typically runs from 3 to 6 months back to no more than 6 months in the future. Sometimes, however, the horizon is actually measured in terms of weeks, or even days, rather than months.

## References

1. http://www.moderndaymarketing.co.uk/SpecialReportWebOpt.pdf
2. Heasman, L. Modern Day Marketing, http://www.moderndaymarketing.co.uk/SpecialReportWebOpt.pdf.
3. Gummesson, E. and Polese, F. B2B is not an island! *Journal of Business & Industrial Marketing*, 24(5), 337–350, 2009.

4. https://en.wikipedia.org/wiki/Market_research
5. Welsh, J.A. and White, J.F. A small business is not a little big business. *Harvard Business Review*, 50(4), 9172, https://hbr.org/1981/07/a-small-business-is-not-a -little-big-business/ar/4.
6. Churchill, N.C. and Lewis, V.L. The Five Stages of Small Business Growth Harvard Business Review, Reprint 83301, Boston. May–June 1983.
7. Margolis, J. and Garrigan, P. Guerrilla Marketing for Dummies, p. 12, Wiley Publishing Inc., Hoboken, NJ, 2008.
8. Heuring, E. and Heuring, J. Brief History of the Simmons Hardware Company, 2010. http://www.thckk.org/history/simmons-hdwe.pdf.
9. http://smallbusiness.chron.com/difference-between-marketing-advertising -public-relations-sales-promotion-22873.html
10. Forbes/entrepreneurs, July 8, 2014. http://www.forbes.com/sites/robertwynne /2014/07/08/the-real-difference-between-pr-and-advertising-credibility/.
11. Drucker, P.F. *Management: Tasks, Responsibilities, Practices.* Harper & Row, Australia, p. 864, 1974. ISBN 0-06-011092-9.
12. https://en.wikipedia.org/wiki/Marketing_effectiveness
13. http://www.entrepreneur.com/article/217388
14. http://www.inc.com/guides/biz_online/online-market-research.html
15. https://bookstore.entrepreneur.com/product/start-your-own-business-6th -edition/
16. Levinson, J.C. *Guerrilla Marketing.* Houghton Mifflin Company, New York, 1933.
17. Hutter, K. and Hoffmann, S. Guerrilla marketing: The nature of the concept and propositions for further research. *Asian Journal of Marketing*, 1–16, 2011.
18. Chazin, S. The secrets of Apple's retail success, http://www.marketingapple .com/Apple_Retail_Success.pdf.
19. How to create a marketing plan. Entrepreneur, www.entrepreneur.com /article/43018.
20. http://www.entrepreneur.com/article/43024
21. http://en.wikipedia.org/wiki/Hypercompetition
22. Kahaner, L. *Competitive Intelligence.* Touchstone Books, Rockefeller Center, New York, 1996.
23. McGonagle, J.J. and Vella, C.M. *Bottom Line Competitive Intelligence.* Quorum Books, Westport, CT, 2002.
24. What is competitive intelligence and why should you care about it? Chapter 2, http://search.aol.com/aol/search?enabled_terms=&s_it=wscreen-smallbusiness -w&q=competitive+intelligence+++pdf.

# 7

## Establishing Your Dream Team

### 7.1 Introduction

It is well established that teams outperform individuals, especially when performance requires multiple skills, judgments, and experiences. One of your first tasks is to establish a "dream team" of specialists as a cohesive organization.

**Organizations** generally consist of groups of people who work together for the achievement of common goals. A **team** comprises any group of people linked in a common purpose. However, a group in itself does not necessarily constitute a team. Teams are especially appropriate for conducting tasks that are high in complexity and have many interdependent subtasks, such as the development and commercialization of knowledge-intensive products. Last, **teamwork and team building** are an organized effort to improve your overall team effectiveness.

There are five reasons why your dream team is particularly important during the start-up phase:

1. Complex tasks—the necessary allocation of tasks is only possible with a team that displays complementary skills.
2. New sorts of problems continually arise—a well-functioning team, well deployed, will find the optimal solution.
3. External investors—are betting their money in you and your team.
4. Shared vision—it is ultimately the people behind the idea who will make it successful.
5. Shared burden—the team has the advantage that the whole burden is shared across the team; if one member drops out, the whole enterprise does not collapse.

Building your start-up is a process that requires a wide variety of talents that are rarely all found in a single person. Because your idea is innovative, there are no standard solutions for the problems that will arise. A group of people with complementary skills will always solve problems better than any individual ever could.

## 7.2 Hiring Your Dream Team

More than anything else, the hiring of your dream team will decide the ultimate fate of your company. In the author's experience, at the board level (during our formative years), we spent more time dealing with "people issues" than any other subject.

For their technical team, entrepreneurs should select people whose talents are recognizably complementary to their own weaknesses. To select the optimal executive team, you start by objectively understanding yourself, what you know, and what your weakest areas of expertise are. This is easier said than done, since self-criticism is as rare as rain in the desert, particularly after you have climbed to the top of the ladder by talent, perseverance, and guts, as shown in Figure 7.1.

In hiring your technical team, you will need to initially decide between a heterogeneous or a homogenous group [1].

- The members of a *heterogeneous executive team* are diverse in terms of their abilities and experiences.

- In contrast, the members of a homogeneous executive team are similar to one another in terms of their abilities and experiences.

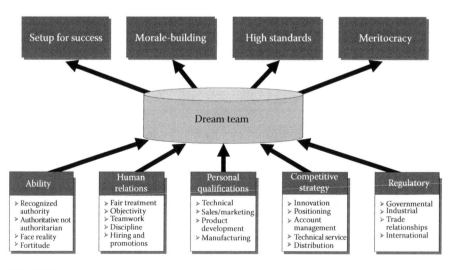

**FIGURE 7.1**
Your dream team. Select executives with complementary skills to yours.

Heterogeneous teams are traditionally favored by investors because (1) the shared intense effort is required by a start-up; (2) the loss of one member is less likely to result in start-up abandonment; (3) the team concept allows expertise across major functional areas: marketing, finance, operations, sales, and so on; and (4) a skilled team lends credibility to the start-up and lowers risks to investors [2].

### 7.2.1 Teamwork Not Titles

A real team is a small number of people with complementary skills, committed to a common vision. The vision includes (1) a common purpose, (2) an agreed approach, (3) performance standards, and (4) realistic goals for which they hold themselves mutually accountable [3]. Goals at the executive team level are assigned based on individual skills (specialization), regardless of formal titles.

### 7.2.2 Team Discipline

The technical team must be goal oriented. Goals specify in advance what each member must accomplish and periodically evaluate the degree to which members have met those goals. This is illustrated in Figure 7.2.

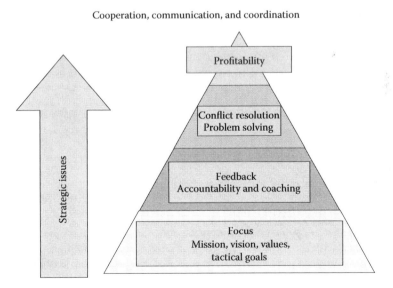

**FIGURE 7.2**
Dream team goals. Be crystal clear about your goals to reach profitability.

| Activities (inputs) | Outcomes (outputs) |
| --- | --- |
| Market research | Repeat sales |
| Meetings, conferences | Cost reductions |
| Development plans | Product launches |
| B2B proposals | Product extensions |
| Reengineering | Increased market share |
| Competitive intelligence | Winning competitive contracts |

**FIGURE 7.3**
Activities versus outcomes. Concentrate on outcomes (and be specific).

### 7.2.3 Focus on Outcomes, Not Activities

*What gets measured gets done.*

In most large companies, the vast majority of objectives is really nothing more than activity-based goals. In his 1999 book, Douglas K. Smith laid out a guide for evaluating and realigning goals to achieve specific outcomes. *Activities are not objectives. Activities are how we achieve the objectives, the outcome-based goals* [4].

It is not enough to say: "This week I will visit a minimum of four customers." That is **activity**. It should be: "This week, out of the four customers, I will get a large purchase order from at least one." That is **outcome**. Figure 7.3 illustrates some important differences between activities and outcomes.

## 7.3 Teamwork and Team Building

Tuckman and Jensen [5] (Four-Phase Model) identified a life cycle of stages through which most teams experience, namely, forming, storming, norming, performing, and adjourning. According to this view, the team begins with the forming stage, where members are just beginning to associate themselves with the team. At this stage, the team lacks a clear vision, purpose, and structure, whereas in the storming stage, members realize the complexity of the problem and might get polarized into subgroups. In the norming stage, team members form lasting relationships with other colleagues and the team clearly defines the specific expectations from individual members in terms of both actions and behaviors. The fourth stage of team development is the

**TABLE 7.1**

Tuckman and Jensen Teambuilding Model

| Stage | Characteristics |
|-------|-----------------|
| 1. Forming | • Excessive caution<br>• Uncertainty of goals and procedures<br>• Avoidance of conflict<br>• Search for direction |
| 2. Storming | • Interpersonal conflict<br>• Power struggles<br>• Criticisms of fellow members<br>• Challenges to goals<br>• Questioning previous decisions |
| 3. Norming | • Cohesion<br>• Mutual support<br>• Willingness to consider conflicting alternatives<br>• Sharing knowledge |
| 4. Performing | • Full involvement<br>• Acceptance of other views<br>• Voluntary efforts<br>• Warm relationships and fusion<br>• Group creativity at maximum |
| 5. Adjourning | • Acceptance of team breakup<br>• Sadness in the face of team success<br>• Team asked to "stand down" and disperse |

performance stage, where the team is set to perform the task after which the team lapses into an adjourning stage where it does not possess the kind of energy demonstrated in the performance stage [6]. This is illustrated in Table 7.1.

## 7.4 Intellectual Capital Management

Savvy founders realize that start-up market value multiples associated with its intangible assets (staff, patents, trademarks, trade secrets, brandings, etc.) are often many times higher than the multiples associated with the cash flows generated from its tangible assets in isolation [7].

The challenge facing start-ups is to implement business practices and systems to manage, leverage, and exploit these intellectual assets, compared to traditional accounting approaches.

Intellectual capital management is composed of several related "assets" as defined below:

- Human Capital—the people element of an organization. It includes owners, employees, contractors, suppliers, and those who collectively bring to the organization their individual abilities (i.e., know-how,

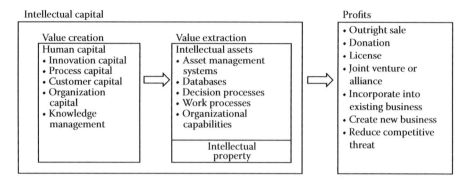

**FIGURE 7.4**
Intellectual capital overview.

experience, skills, creativity). Human capital is one of the two major elements comprising intellectual capital.

- Intellectual Assets—the tangible or physical description of specific knowledge to which an organization may assert ownership rights (i.e., documents, databases, processes, inventions, programs). Intellectual assets are the other major element comprising intellectual capital.

- Intellectual Property—the subset of intellectual assets for which legal protection has been obtained (i.e., patents, trademarks, copyrights, trade secrets).

- Intellectual Capital—the collective elements of human capital and intellectual assets... the "knowledge" of an organization that can be converted into profit.

Intellectual capital management, then, is the processes and structures used to undertake the two activities of "value creation" and "value extraction" from any organization and, with the concepts above, could be generally conceived of as shown in Figure 7.4.

## 7.4.1 Human Capital

**Human capital** is the composite of knowledge, habits, and social and personality attributes, including creativity, embodied in the ability to perform labor so as to produce economic value for an organization [8].

It is a measure of the economic value of your staff's skill set. This measure builds on the basic production input of labor measure where all labor is thought to be equal. The concept of human capital recognizes that not all labor is equal and that the quality of employees can be improved by investing in them. The education, experience, and abilities of your staff have an economic value for employers [9].

Economist Theodore Schultz [10] invented the term in the 1960s to reflect the value of our human capacities. He believed that human capital was like any other type of capital; it could be invested in through education, training, and enhanced benefits that will lead to an improvement in the quality and level of production, thus increasing enterprise value.

Human capital is an intangible asset—it is not owned by the firm that employs it and is generally not fungible. Specifically, individuals arrive at 9 a.m. and leave at 5 p.m. (in the conventional office model), taking most of their knowledge and relationships with them in their heads.

Human capital, when viewed from a time perspective, consumes time in one of key activities:

1. Technical knowledge (activities involving one employee)
2. Collaboration (activities involving more than one employee)
3. Processes (activities specifically focused on the knowledge and collaborative activities generated by organizational structure—such as silo impacts, internal politics, etc.)
4. Absence (annual leave, sick leave, holidays, etc.)

Despite the lack of formal ownership, start-ups can gain from high levels of training, in part because it creates a corporate culture or vocabulary teams use to create cohesion.

Studies of human capital proliferated in the 1980s after US manufacturers realized that Japanese firms often bested them on price and quality in large part because of their human relations policies, such as teamwork production methods, employee involvement in decision-making, job rotation, and pay for performance [11].

One of the first studies to consider investment outcomes found positive correlations to return on assets and return on investment among 495 business units drawn from a sample of private-sector US employers and a suite of alternative pay systems, including profit-sharing, gain sharing, employee stock options, employee stock ownership plans, and production incentive or bonus plans [12].

## 7.4.2 Knowledge Management

Knowledge management (KM) [13] is the process of capturing, developing, sharing, and effectively using organizational knowledge to enhance enterprise value. It refers to a multidisciplinary approach to achieving organizational objectives by making the best use of knowledge [14].

In our context, knowledge refers to the theoretical or practical understanding of a subject. It can be implicit (as with practical skill or expertise) or explicit (as with the theoretical understanding of a subject).

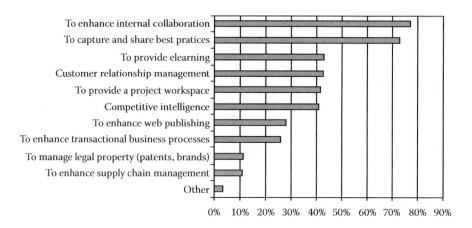

**FIGURE 7.5**
Objective for knowledge management efforts. (Source: IDC, 2002.)

KM efforts typically focus on organizational objectives such as improved performance, competitive advantage, innovation, the sharing of lessons learned, integration, and continuous improvement of the organization [15].

Knowledge teams are multidisciplinary, cross-functional, and hubs of knowledge to the entire organization. Knowledge teams provide start-ups with two keys: (1) share existing knowledge ("knowing what you know") and (2) provide knowledge for innovation ("creating and converting").

A 2002 IDC report [16] cited various objectives for KM efforts as seen in Figure 7.5.

KM efforts overlap with organizational learning and may be distinguished from that by a greater focus on the management of knowledge as a strategic asset and a focus on encouraging the sharing of knowledge. It is an enabler of organizational learning [17]. In summary, the KM cycle [18] can be illustrated in Figure 7.6.

### 7.4.3 Your Seven Knowledge Levers

Companies are increasingly recognizing the contribution of knowledge to their bottom line if effectively managed. But what are the key levers of a knowledge-based strategy that realize these benefits [19]? This section outlines seven such levers that can be used to create value for your knowledge-based business:

- Customer knowledge—*the most vital knowledge*
- Knowledge in products—*"smarts" add value*

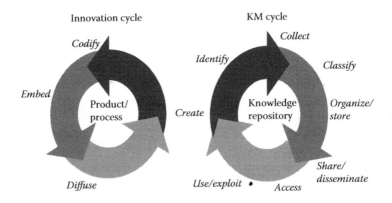

**FIGURE 7.6**
Knowledge cycle.

- Knowledge in processes
- Know-how when needed most—*sharing best practices*
- Organizational memory—*do we know what we know?*
- Knowledge in relationships—*who you know*
- Knowledge assets—*intellectual capital*

*Customer Knowledge.* Meeting or, even better, exceeding customer's expectations is a key strategic benefit. Customers provide useful feedback on products and services and how their needs are evolving. They are the major source of ideas for improved products and services. Most companies know a lot less about their customers and their markets than they claim. Too much reliance is placed on traditional market research and customer satisfactions surveys that tell them little of the real customers' concerns, desires, wishes, and desires. You need a deep intuitive understanding of customers' latent and unidentified needs.

*Knowledge in Products and Services.* "Intelligent" or "smart" products can command premium prices and be more beneficial to users. One example is the "intelligent" oil drill that bends and weaves its way to extract more oil than ever from the pockets of oil in underground formations. Customization also adds value and creates a more personalized offering. Hotel chains or car rental companies, for example, can make suitable rooms or cars available by knowing the customer's preferences. In creating new products, companies use a lot of knowledge, gleaned from market research and prototype testing. Yet only a fraction of the knowledge generated makes it into the final product. Smart organizations will create opportunities out of this knowledge.

*Knowledge in Processes.* In many companies, there are often differences in performance levels of 3:1 or more between different groups performing the same process. The detail and knowledge used is different. If this knowledge of best practice can be diffused and learned, then overall performance will improve. Every business process contains embedded knowledge. It is the result of thinking and codifying what was formerly a series of ad hoc tasks into something that is systematic and routine. The processes are also surrounded by the skills and knowledge of the person applying them and the experts who developed them. Making this knowledge more widely accessible is part of exploiting this lever.

*Know-How When Needed Most.* "Our most valuable asset is people," according to many academic reports, although the actual way people are treated and managed often belies this claim. The challenge is to turn individual know-how into organizational knowledge. Many organizations apply this lever through a "learning organization" program that stimulates personal development and organizational learning. Another aspect of this lever is to understand what motivates knowledge workers and reward them accordingly.

*Organizational Memory.* Much knowledge flow in organizations is transitory. It occurs in conversations, meetings, and e-mails. This strategic lever is a way of addressing the issue of knowing "what we know" or once knew. It helps avoid repeating the mistakes of the past, and in drawing lessons from similar situations elsewhere. Organization memory exists in many forms—processes, databases, artifacts, documents, but above all the minds of people. Sometimes overlooked are archives owned by outsiders, such as researchers, customers, or former employees. They may have retained detail that your own company lost as people left.

*Knowledge in Relationships.* Such depth of knowledge is not easily replaced overnight. Companies have many relationship webs involving customers, suppliers, employees, business partners, shareholders, and so on. These relationships involve sharing knowledge and understanding—not just of needs and factual information but also of deeper knowledge such as behaviors, motivations, personal characteristics, ambitions, and feelings. Such knowledge is often highly personal, but is easily lost during restructuring.

*Knowledge Assets.* Knowledge is one of the intangible assets of a company that do not appear in its balance sheet. The core of this lever is the adage "what you can measure you can manage." Many economists have argued that knowledge is now a critical resource that needs such an approach. However, most business managers have not turned this concept into practice. While accountants and auditors pore over detailed figures about every piece of physical plant and machinery, the major contributor to the value of their business, intellectual capital, gets scant attention. It so happens that changes in intellectual capital are usually lead indicators of future financial performance—an important reason for taking their measurement and management seriously.

### 7.4.4 Intellectual Property Management

Historically, intellectual property (IP) has been approached from three different perspectives—research and development (R&D), legal, and business. Because of the legal complexities, IP has largely been the purview of legal counsel, where focus is typically on legal registrations of patents and trademarks and providing support to R&D or business units. R&D departments generally measure IP performance by the number of inventions and by product support and enhancement.

## 7.5 Accountants and Lawyers

Remember that accountants and lawyers are cost centers. Necessary, indispensable, and crucial, but cost centers nevertheless. The founder must carefully select the proper accounting/legal team. By proper, I mean professionals who are familiar with the special circumstances surrounding start-ups. Engage only those individuals that are "specialized" in the intricacies of start-ups.

### 7.5.1 Accountants

Neither accountants nor lawyers academically "specialize" in start-ups, but in practice, the representation of start-ups becomes a *de facto* specialization for both professions. For example, a small business accountant will (1) help you with your business plan, (2) set up an inexpensive accounting system such as QuickBooks, and (3) patiently guide you through the intricacies of accounting jargon and Generally Accepted Accounting Practices. You will need all of this for your initial funding, plus all the necessary periodic reports to your investors.

### 7.5.2 Lawyers

The small business lawyer will help you navigate the process of incorporation and represent your small business during legal negotiations. Perhaps the lawyer will agree to be paid in installments tied to specific milestones. Bob Loblow, a small business lawyer, blogs that lawyers should be selected based on three criteria: local, right sized, and start-up focused [20].

The Walker Corporate Law Group listed the "Top 10 reasons why entrepreneurs hate lawyers" [21]:

- #10—"Because they don't communicate clearly or concisely"
- #9—"Because they don't keep me informed"

- #8—"Because they are constantly over-lawyering"
- #7—"Because they have poor listening skills"
- #6—"Because inexperienced lawyers are doing most of the work"
- #5—"Because they spend too much time on insignificant issues"
- #4—"Because they don't genuinely care about me or my matter"
- #3—"Because their fees are through the roof"
- #2—"Because they are unresponsive"
- #1—"Because they are deal-killers"

## 7.6 Managing Managers

*Be a coach, not a referee.*

As founder, one of your most pressing goals should be to make sure that your managers have all the tools necessary to perform their jobs well. Managers need to understand not only the "what" but also the "why" behind your business plan. Give them a sincere sense of ownership in the organization and its future. Figure 7.7 summarizes the complex issue of managing managers.

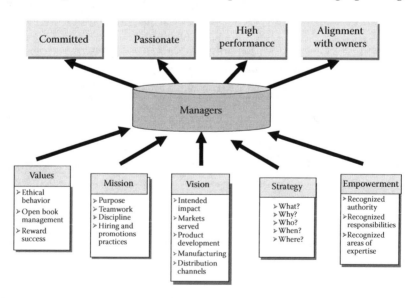

**FIGURE 7.7**
Managing managers.

### 7.6.1 How Is Managing Managers Different from Managing Projects?

*We must all row in the same direction.*

You will find that effective mangers need to know less about "how" and more about "why." Managers should be evaluated primarily on team-based financial success, rather than products, schedules, or activities. Their opinions should carry extra weight along with responsibility and corresponding authority.

### 7.6.2 A Roadmap for Managing Managers Effectively

*Don't bring me problems; bring me solutions.*

Bruce McGraw listed the following important leadership skills for senior managers [22]:

- Set the vision. It is essential that you communicate the long-term goals of your department or organization to your managers clearly and often. A shared vision provides the touchstone to help your managers make decisions and solve problems.

- Network with other managers and technical resources to get things done across your organization.

- Set straightforward, measureable objectives for each manager and project under your authority. Have short-term and long-term goals for each person who reports to you and reinforce those goals in monthly or quarterly meetings.

- Talent management—hiring, giving effective feedback, and developing talent for the project work.

- Demonstrating accountability and holding team members and project managers accountable.

- Influencing others—up (your leaders), across (your peers), and down (your project managers and team).

- Facilitate problem solving. It may be tempting to jump in and solve a problem yourself. You have been there and solved that problem successfully before. However, your managers need to learn and they need to put their own stamp on projects.

- Do not micromanage. Let me say that again—do not micromanage. Rather, offer advice and ask leading questions to help clarify a situation and your subordinate manager's options. You are also in a better position than before to break down barriers to solving problems by using your position and influence.

- Be a role model. Social learning theory, also called social cognitive theory, supports the idea that people learn new behaviors and change existing ones based not just on their experience but also on their observations of significant others, such as senior managers. Your values, priorities, and even your mode of dress may be copied.

## 7.7 The Firing Line

Regardless of how careful you are in hiring your dream team, it may be necessary to dismiss an important team member. No matter the reason, whether poor work performance, inability to act as a team member, or an economic downturn, firing someone is very unpleasant for you and the executive.

As founder, even if the firing is well deserved, in actuality, terminating an executive is never easy considering the disruptions suffered by both the employee and your own team. It is frequently highly emotional, confrontational, and may even carry legal consequences if the employee has not been given enough chances to correct their weaknesses before being dismissed [23].

### 7.7.1 At-Will Employment versus Employment Contracts

At-will employment is generally described as follows: "Any hiring is presumed to be 'at will'; that is, the employer is free to discharge individuals 'for good cause, or bad cause, or no cause at all,' and the employee is equally free to quit, strike, or otherwise cease work" [24].

At-will employment [25] is a term of art used in US labor law for contractual relationships in which an employee can be dismissed by an employer for any reason (i.e., without having to establish "just cause" for termination) and without warning [26]. When an employee is acknowledged as being hired "at will," courts generally deny the employee any claim for loss resulting from the dismissal. The rule is justified by its proponents on the basis that an employee may be similarly entitled to leave his or her job without reason or warning [27].

### 7.7.2 Employment Contracts for Key Employees

The doctrine of at-will employment can be overridden by a written contract or civil service statutes (in the case of government employees). As many as 34% of all US employees apparently enjoy the protection of some kind of "just cause" or objectively reasonable requirement for termination that takes them out of the pure "at-will" category, including the 7.5% of unionized private-sector workers, the 0.8% of nonunion private-sector workers protected by union contracts, the 15% of nonunion private-sector workers with individual express contracts that override the at-will doctrine, and the 16% of the total workforce who enjoy civil service protections as public-sector employees [28].

A written employment contract is a document that you and your employee sign, specifying the terms of your relationship. You don't enter into a written contract with every employee you hire. In fact, written employment contracts are generally the exception, rather than the rule. In some situations, however, it makes good sense to ask a key employee to sign a contract. According to the NOLO legal encyclopedia [29], the employment contract can address many aspects of the employment relationship, such as

- Duration of the job (1 year, 2 years, or indefinitely)
- Information about the employee's responsibilities
- The benefits (such as health insurance, vacation leave, disability leave, etc.) the employee will receive
- Grounds for termination
- Limitations on the employee's ability to compete with your business once the employee leaves
- Protection of your trade secrets, client lists, and other sensitive information
- Your ownership of the employee's work product (e.g., if the employee writes books or develops patentable inventions)
- A method for resolving any disputes that arise about the agreement

### 7.7.3 How to Fire an Employee Correctly

If you have a problem with an employee, you have two choices: (1) try to coach them and work with them to improve their performance, or (2) fire them. Firing an employee can be costly and cause your employee a great deal of emotional and financial difficulties. Done the wrong way, firing someone can also open you or your organization to liability and lawsuits. Unfortunately, however, there are situations where terminating an employee is your best and only option [30].

The following 10 steps are considered appropriate when dealing with troublesome employees:

1. **Set your expectations clearly and concisely.** Discuss with your employees any behavior that could be grounds for termination.
2. **Conduct regular performance appraisals.** Communicate regularly how you view their performance, and how to improve any deficiencies.
3. **Act quickly and decisively when problems are noticed.** Quickly communicate performance problems as soon as you are aware of them, and coach your employee on how to improve their behavior, and what needs to be rectified [31].

4. **Humanely consider personal factors.** Health problems, death in the family, divorce or other relationship trauma, moving stress, and financial troubles are all part of life and can understandably cause otherwise valuable employees to temporarily lose focus.

5. **Focus on the problem and keep copious records.** Have the problem employee sign a document outlining the conversation to cover yourself and the company. It should specifically state that the employee is not admitting fault, but has been told that job performance is not satisfactory and may result in termination.

6. **Termination meeting.** State your case and the reason(s) for termination. You've given the employee ample time to correct any failings, and that hasn't happened.

7. **Aftermath of termination.** You don't need to delineate your reasons— if they need reiteration, they can be stated in a letter. In this case, the less you say the better.

8. **Separation legal details.** Explain the severance package you are offering, if any. If necessary, remind them of any legally binding agreements the employee has signed, such as an agreement not to disclose company secrets. If you are asking the terminated employee to sign legal documents, allow him or her a few days to take the documents home and review them.

9. **Offer assistance.** If the employee worked in good faith, but simply lacked the skills necessary for the job or the right temperament for your company, you may offer to provide a recommendation regarding his or her reliability, attitude, teamwork, and whatever parts of the job were successfully performed.

10. **Separate the person from the problem.** Keep it professional, and not personal. It will help the employee's self-esteem and ability to secure other employment.

## References

1. Building a New Venture Team. Chapter 6, http://foba.lakeheadu.ca/hartviksen /3215/Management%20Team.ppt.
2. Allen, K.R. *Launching New Ventures: An Entrepreneurial Approach.* ISBN-10: 053848179X.
3. Katzenbach, J.R. *Teams at the Top.* Harvard Business School Press, McKinsey & Company, Inc., 1998.
4. Smith, D.K. *Make Success Measurable!* John Wiley & Sons, Inc., 1999.
5. Tuckman, B.W., Developmental Sequence in Small Groups, http://openvce.net /sites/default/files/Tuckman1965DevelopmentalSequence.pdf.

6. Smith, M.K. and Bruce W. Tuckman—Forming, storming, norming and performing in groups, the encyclopedia of informal education, www.infed.org /thinkers/tuckman.htm.

7. http://www.nortonrosefulbright.com/files/the-management-of-intellectual -capital-pdf-329kb-99687.pdf

8. https://en.wikipedia.org/wiki/Human_capital

9. http://www.investopedia.com/terms/h/humancapital.asp#ixzz3hTs35Ct3

10. Schultz, T.W. Investment in Human Capital, *The American Economic Review*, 51:1, 1–17, 1961.

11. Task Force on Human Capital Management. 2003. Accounting for People Report. UK Department for Trade and Industry, http://webarchive.national archives.gov.uk/20090609003228/http://www.berr.gov.uk/files/file38839.pdf.

12. Mitchell, D. and Lawler, E. *Alternative Pay Systems, Firm Performance and Productivity*. Center for Effective Organization Publication G 89-6 (149). School of Business Administration, University of Southern California, 1989.

13. https://en.wikipedia.org/wiki/Knowledge_management

14. http://web.archive.org/web/20070319233812/http://www.unc.edu/~sunnyliu /inls258/Introduction_to_Knowledge_Management.html

15. Gupta, J. and Sharma, S. *Creating Knowledge Based Organizations*. Idea Group Publishing, Boston, 2004. ISBN 1-59140-163-1.

16. http://www.providersedge.com/docs/km_articles/IDC_KM_Study_April _2002.pdf

17. Nonaka, I. The knowledge creating company. *Harvard Business Review*, 69(6), 96–104, 1991.

18. http://www.umsl.edu/~lacitym/evekmbif7.ppt

19. Seven Ways to Create Value through Knowledge, May 2002, http://www.skyrme .com/kshop/kmseven_p4.pdf.

20. Loblow, B. http://www.bothsidesofthetable.com/2010/01/21/how-to-work-with -lawyers-at-a-startup/.

21. Walker, S.E., Top 10 reasons why entrepreneurs hate lawyers, http://venture hacks.com/articles/hate-lawyers.

22. McGraw, B. Managing Managers Requires Good Leadership Skills, May 12, 2011, http://fearnoproject.com/2011/05/12/managing-managers-requires-good -leadership-skills/.

23. Muenz, R. The Firing Line. *Lab Manager*, December 2014, http://www.labmanager .com/leadership-and-staffing/2014/11/the-firing-line#.VOJDYz-DiqQ.

24. Rothstein, M.A., Knapp, A.S., and Liebman, L. *Cases and Materials on Employment Law*. Foundation Press, New York, p. 738, 1987.

25. http://en.wikipedia.org/wiki/At-will_employment

26. Shepherd, J. *Firing at Will: A Manager's Guide*. Apress Media, 3–4, 2011.

27. Epstein, R. *In Defense of the Contract at Will*, 57 U. Chi. L. Rev. 947, 1984.

28. Verkerke, J.H. Discharge, in Dau-Schmidt, K.G., Harris, S.D. and Lobel, O., eds., *Labor and Employment Law and Economics*, vol. 2 of *Encyclopedia of Law and Economics*, 2nd ed., pp. 447–479. Northampton: Edward Elgar Publishing, 448, 2009.

29. http://www.nolo.com/legal-encyclopedia/written-employment-contracts -pros-cons-30193.html

30. How to fire an employee. Wikipedia, http://www.wikihow.com/Fire-an-Employee.

31. Cliff, E. The right way to fire someone. *Entrepreneur*, September 2006, http:// www.entrepreneur.com/article/166644.

# 8

## Strategic Planning for Start-Ups

Plans are nothing. Planning is everything.

**Dwight D. Eisenhower**

## 8.1 Introduction

Strategic planning is a tool for organizing the present on the basis of the projections of the desired future. That is, a strategic plan is a roadmap to lead an organization from where it is now to where it would like to be in 5 or 10 years.

It is necessary to have a strategic plan for your chapter or division. In order to develop a comprehensive plan for your chapter or division that would include both long-range and strategic elements, we suggest the methods and mechanisms outlined in this manual.

Your plan must

Be simple to follow.

Be written logically and purposefully.

Be clear to everyone.

Be based on the real current situation.

Have enough time allowed to give it a time to settle. It should not be rushed.

Over the past decades, you may have witnessed an explosion in the use of management tools and techniques—everything from Six Sigma to benchmarking. Keeping up with the latest and greatest, as well as deciding which tools to put to work, is a key part of every leader's job. But it's tough to pick the winners from the losers.

As new management tools appear every year, others seem to drop off the radar screen. Unfortunately, there is no official scorekeeper for management tools. Thus, choosing and using "fad management" tools can become a risky and potentially expensive gamble, leaving many business leaders stymied and confused [1].

Since 1993, Bain & Company, a leading management consulting company, launched a multiyear research project to get the facts about management tools and trends. The objective of the study was to provide managers with information to identify and integrate tools that improve bottom-line results as well as understand their strategic challenges and priorities.

Bain systematically assembled a database that now includes nearly 8000 businesses from more than 70 countries in North America, Europe, Asia, Africa, the Middle East, and Latin America. The *Bain & Company's 2005 Management Tools* survey received responses from a broad range of international executives. To qualify for inclusion in the study, a tool had to be relevant to senior management, topical as evidenced by coverage in the business press, and measurable. Bain focused on the most discussed management tools as shown in Table 8.1.

Would you like to know the surprising results? Out of all the management tools surveyed, 79% of respondents preferred strategic planning, followed closely by customer relationship management at 75%. In fact, strategic planning is a long-time favorite tool, having been used by more than half of companies in every survey since Bain started this project. Not surprisingly, the most popular tools are the ones that create the highest returns and results-oriented ratings [2]. See Table 8.2 for more details.

**TABLE 8.1**

Most Frequently Discussed Management Tools

| | |
|---|---|
| 1. Activity-based management | 14. Mission and vision statements |
| 2. Balanced scorecard | 15. Offshoring |
| 3. Benchmarking | 16. Open market innovation |
| 4. Business process reengineering | 17. Outsourcing |
| 5. Change management programs | 18. Price optimization models |
| 6. Core competencies | 19. Radio frequency identification (RFID) |
| 7. Customer relationship management (CRM) | 20. Scenario and contingency planning |
| 8. Customer segmentation | 21. Six sigma |
| 9. Economic value added analysis | 22. Strategic alliances |
| 10. Growth strategies | 23. Strategic planning |
| 11. Knowledge management | 24. Supply chain management |
| 12. Loyalty management | 25. Total quality management |
| 13. Mass customization | |

*Source:* Modified after Bain & Company (2005). http://www.bain.com/management_tools /Management_Tools_and_Trends_2005.pdf.

**TABLE 8.2**

Top Five Management Tools Ranked by Usage Rate

| Management Tool Name | Usage (%) |
|---|---|
| Strategic management | 79 |
| Customer relationship management | 75 |
| Benchmarking | 73 |
| Outsourcing | 73 |
| Customer segmentation | 72 |

*Source:* Modified after Bain & Company (2005). http://www.bain.com/management_tools /Management_Tools_and_Trends_2005.pdf.

## 8.2 Strategic Planning for Start-Ups

**Strategic planning** is the process used by an organization to visualize its desired future and develop the necessary steps and operations to achieve those aims. It directs managers to determine how they will be expected to behave. In order to determine the direction of the organization, it is necessary to understand its current position and the possible avenues through which it can pursue a particular course of action. Generally, strategic planning deals with at least one of three key questions [3]:

1. "What do we do?"
2. "For whom do we do it?"
3. "How do we excel?"

The key components of "strategic planning" include an understanding of the firm's vision, mission, values, and strategies [4]. (Often a "Vision Statement" and a "Mission Statement" may encapsulate the vision and mission.)

- **Vision:** Outlines what the organization wants to be, or how it wants the world in which it operates to be (an "idealized" view of the world). It is a long-term view and concentrates on the future. It can be emotive and is a source of inspiration. For example, a charity working with the poor might have a vision statement which reads "A World Without Disease."

- **Mission:** Defines the fundamental purpose of an organization or an enterprise, succinctly describing why it exists and what it does to achieve its vision. For example, the charity above might have a mission statement as "providing jobs for the homeless and unemployed."

- **Values:** Beliefs that are shared among the stakeholders of an organization. Values drive an organization's culture and priorities and provide a framework in which decisions are made. For example, "Knowledge and skills are the keys to success" or "Give a man bread and feed him for a day, but teach him to farm and feed him for life." These example maxims may set the priorities of self-sufficiency over shelter.

- **Strategy:** Strategy, narrowly defined, means "the art of the general"— a combination of the ends (goals) for which the firm is striving and the means (policies) by which it is seeking to get there. A strategy is sometimes called a roadmap—which is the path chosen to plow toward your end vision. The most important part of implementing the strategy is ensuring that the company goes in the right direction, which is toward the end vision.

Unlike operational planning—which stresses how to get things done—and long-range planning—which primarily focuses on translating goals and objectives into current budgets and work programs—strategic planning is concerned with identifying barriers and issues to overcome. Managers are more likely to act on the assumption that current trends will continue into the future (steady-state management), while entrepreneurs need to anticipate new trends and possible surprises that represent both opportunities and threats.

## 8.3 Your Value Chain Analysis

The term **value chain** was first used by Michael Porter in *Competitive Advantage: Creating and Sustaining Superior Performance* [5]. The value chain analysis describes the activities that an organization must undertake and links them to its competitive strength and position.

The value chain concept revolves around the notion that an organization is more than just an agglomeration of machinery, equipment, facilities, technology, and human resources. Only when these support activities are aligned with primary activities will customers be persuaded to buy its products or services. The combination of all these factors becomes the source of competitive advantage. This is illustrated in Figure 8.1.

Notice the important distinction between primary and support activities. **Primary activities** are those directly involved with the creation or delivery of your product or service. **Support activities** help improve effectiveness or efficiency of the operation. **Profit margin** is the ability of the organization to

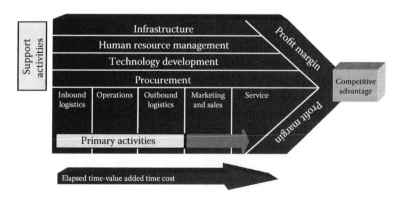

**FIGURE 8.1**
Porter's value chain. (Source: Modified after Porter 1985.)

successfully deliver a product/service at a price that is higher than the combined costs of all the activities in the value chain. The numerical difference between price and cost is your profit margin.

You should perform your competitive advantage analysis within your value chain by

- Analyzing which costs are related to every single activity
- Determining the optimal price of your product/service to your customer
- Identifying potential cost advantages you may have over your competitors
- Analyzing how your product/service potentially adds value (lower cost, higher performance, user-friendly, just-in-time delivery, etc.) to your customer's value chain

## 8.4 Your Value Proposition

Killing two stones with one bird.

A **value proposition** is a promise of worth to be delivered and a belief from the customer that profit will be experienced. A value proposition can apply to an entire organization, or parts thereof, or customer accounts, or products or services. Creating a value proposition is a part of business strategy [6]. Developing a value proposition is based on a review and analysis of the benefits, costs, and value that an organization can deliver to its customers, prospective customers, and other constituent groups within and outside the organization. It is also a positioning of value, where Value = Benefits − Uncertainty (includes economic risk) [7].

Why should anyone buy anything from you? What do you have to offer? New products are "new" and therefore untested; generally, they cannot attract customers. The value proposition is best quantified by the value equation as shown in Figure 8.2 [8].

In order to attract their customers, entrepreneurs need to develop a compelling value proposition. As seen in Figure 8.2, a customer would be persuaded to buy your new product/service if (a) the benefits outweigh his costs/risks and (b) it solves a major serious problem. Figure 8.3 presents a stepwise process for establishing your value proposition.

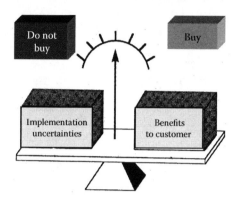

**FIGURE 8.2**
Value equation. (Modified after Rackham, *Spin Selling*, McGraw-Hill Book Co © 1998.)

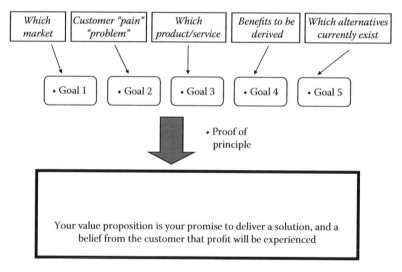

**FIGURE 8.3**
Value proposition.

Examples of value propositions (also called company slogans):

| | |
|---|---|
| Coke | The pause that refreshes |
| FedEx | The world on time |
| E. F. Hutton | When E. F. Hutton speaks, people listen |
| American Express | Don't leave home without it |
| Lexus | The passionate pursuit of perfection |
| IBM | Global solutions for a small planet |
| Apple | The power to be your best |
| DeBeers | A diamond is forever |
| Visa | It is everywhere you want it to be |
| Intel | Intel inside |
| AT&T | Reach out and touch someone |
| BMW | The ultimate driving machine |
| FOX | Fair and balanced |
| CNN | The most trusted name in news |
| Clairol | Only her hairdresser knows for sure |

## 8.5 SWOT Analysis

A **SWOT** analysis is a strategic planning tool used to evaluate the **S**trengths, **W**eaknesses, **O**pportunities, and **T**hreats involved in a project or in a business venture. It involves specifying the objective of the business venture or project and identifying the internal and external factors that are favorable and unfavorable to achieving that objective. The technique is credited to Albert Humphrey [9], who led a research project at Stanford University in the 1960s and 1970s using data from Fortune 500 companies.

- **Strengths:** attributes of the organization helpful to achieving the objective
- **Weaknesses:** attributes of the organization harmful to achieving the objective
- **Opportunities:** *external* conditions helpful to achieving the objective
- **Threats:** *external* conditions harmful to achieving the objective

A generic SWOT analysis is presented in Figure 8.4.
Your SWOT analysis should be conducted as follows:

- **Step 1.** The present. List all your current strengths and weaknesses.
- **Step 2.** The future. List all future opportunities and strengths.

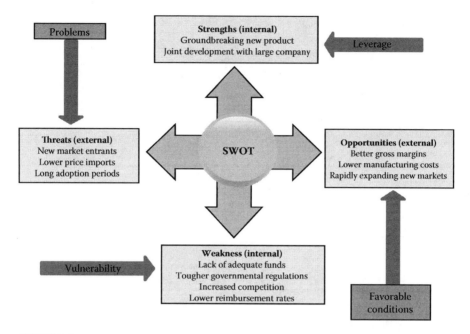

**FIGURE 8.4**
Generic SWOT analysis.

- **Step 3.** Your action plan. Address all four areas individually.
- **Step 4.** Develop an operational plan, complete with specific tasks and dates of completion.

## 8.6 Recognizing Growth Stages

Small business success doesn't just happen. Some fairly predictable but not very orderly (chaotic) stages characterize its evolution. Most entrepreneurs caught up in the day-to-day goings on in a business don't recognize these stages until they've passed, though. Time to open your eyes. The following sections describe the three stages of business evolution.

### 8.6.1 The Start-Up Years

The start-up years are the years when survival motivates your thoughts and actions. Everything that happens within the business is dominated by you; words such as *delegation*, *team*, and *consensus* generally are not yet part of the business's vocabulary. These are the hands-on years. For some owners, they're the most enjoyable years of the business; for all owners, they're an integral part of the learning process.

The work during this time is exceptionally hard—often the physically and emotionally draining kind of hard. The hours are long and sometimes tedious, but by the end of the day, you can see, touch, and feel the progress you've made. The gratification is instantaneous. The duration of this first stage can vary greatly. Some businesses may fly through the start-up stage in less than a year, but most spend anywhere from 1 to 3 years growing out of the stage. Others—oftentimes those in the more competitive niches—spend as many as five or more years in the start-up stage.

You'll know you've graduated from the start-up stage when profitability and orderliness become a dependable part of your business. The hectic days of worrying about survival are replaced by the logical, orderly days of planning for success.

### 8.6.2 The Growth Years

The growth years are the years when your business achieves some sense of order, stability, and profitability. Your evolving business has survived the mistakes, confusion, and chaos of the start-up years, and now optimism, camaraderie, and cooperation should play an important role in the organization.

Key employees surface, efficient administrative systems and controls become part of the business's daily operating procedures, and the need to depend on you for everything disappears.

The business of doing business remains fun for most small business owners in this stage, because increasing sales translate into increasing profits every small business owner's dream. The balance sheet puts some flesh on its scraggly bones as you generate cash as a result of profitability. You learn to delegate many of those unpleasant tasks that you performed in the past.

Survival is no longer your primary motivator. At last, the daily choices that you make can be dictated by lifestyle goals instead of survival. We have further good news: This stage can last a long time if the growth is gradual and remains under control, and if you manage the business and its expanding population of employees properly.

### 8.6.3 The Transition Years

The third stage, the transition years, can also be called the restructuring stage or the diversification stage. This is the stage when something basic to the success of the growth years has changed or gone wrong. As a result, in order for the business to survive, a strategic change in direction, or transition, is required.

Many factors can bring about the transition period, but the following are the most common:

- Relentless growth: This is because relentless sales growth requires relentless improvement in the business's employees, systems, procedures, and infrastructure—and many businesses simply can't keep up with such pressures.

- Shrinkage of sales and the disappearance of profits, or even prolonged periods of stagnation: This is the opposite of growth. The causes for this shrinkage or stagnation can come from anywhere and everywhere, and they often include such uncontrollable factors as new competitors, a changing economy, new technology, and changes in consumer demand.

## 8.7 How to Think Like an Executive

You decided to start your own company because you are a specialist in some technical field. Your technical expertise allowed you to innovate a new product that you want to commercialize as soon as possible.

You were the acknowledged specialist as a researcher/inventor. Surprisingly, as an owner, you must now become the great generalist. Being a generalist means knowing your specialty, but also knowing (and appreciating) about all the other specialties needed to build a successful company. Now, you must think like an executive, not like a specialist, a researcher, or an inventor.

### 8.7.1 The Great Irony

There is only one generalist job in a start-up and that is the job of the owner/inventor. However, there is no generalist path that gets you there. Ironically, it takes a specialist path to prepare you for the generalist's top job (i.e., the executive).

First, you must be a specialist in some advanced technical field, such as medical science, pharmacology, engineering, life sciences, computer science, telecommunications, and the like. As an owner/inventor, you must be able to become an orchestra conductor, not just a great instrument player, and still perform a brilliant job in your specialty. This is graphically depicted in Figure 8.5.

### 8.7.2 Your Team Depends on You

Your team members want to know the mission, vision, direction, and status of the company on a periodic basis, and that can only come from the communications ability of the owner/inventor. As top dog, you must be the ultimate communicator, coach, counselor, pacifier, and arbiter, particularly during conflicts, as shown in Figure 8.6.

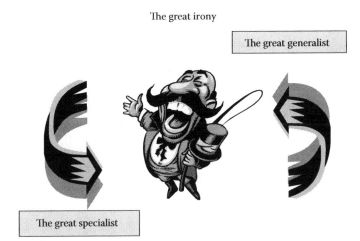

**FIGURE 8.5**
You, as the greatest generalist.

**FIGURE 8.6**
You, the great communicator.

Each team member wants to know how they fit into the overall organizational structure, and what is their future as the organization grows. You must provide the tools, resources, and empowerment to your team to allow them to do their specialized jobs.

### 8.7.3 Sole Proprietorship or Partnership?

Sole ownership is always the least conflictive and most popular of the options for starting a company, assuming that you have access to the necessary funds to launch your business, industry knowledge, and energy to make a go of the business by yourself. Sure, the leverage and financial benefits that partners and shareholders bring to the table can be worth their weight in potential opportunities, but decision-making in shared ownership situations requires consensus, and consensus can take a lot of time. Besides, consensus doesn't always represent your own personal best interests, and when your name is on the dotted line, your personal best interests should be at or near the top of the reasons for making decisions.

### 8.7.3.1 Being the Sole Owner

Being the sole owner has the following advantages:

- It's generally easier, quicker, and less expensive. No lawyers are required to write partnership agreements and assist in determining answers to all the questions that partnership agreements require.
- The profits (or losses) are totally yours.
- You have no need to seek consensus. Your way is the only way.
- You don't waste time catering to the often-aggravating demands of shareholders, minority or otherwise. There's no possibility of shareholder lawsuits.

Being the sole owner also has the following disadvantages:

- You have no one to share the risk with you.
- Your limited skills will have to make do until you can hire someone with complementary skills.
- Single ownership can be lonely. Many times, you'll wish you had someone with whom to share the problems and stress. You may be able to do this with trusted, senior employees. Of course, if you have good friends or a strong marriage partner, these people can be a source of much needed support.

Still confused as to whether you want to do it alone or share ownership? Answer the following questions to help with the decision.

### 8.7.3.2 Partnership?

Do you absolutely, positively need a partner? To provide cash? Knowledge? If you do, that settles the issue; if you don't, continue with the following questions:

- Are you capable of working with partners or shareholders? Will you have a problem sharing the decisions and the profits as well as the risks?
- Does your business fit the multiple ownership profile? In other words, does this business have room for two partners, and is it a business that has the growth potential to support two partners? Will a partner have an important role in the organization? Would his or her complementary skills enhance the business's chance for success?

- What are the legal requirements of multiple ownership? Can you live within these legal parameters?

- What do you have in common with other business owners who have opted for multiple ownership? Where do you see conflicts? Ask your banker, accountant, or attorney for the names of other business owners who have opted for multiple ownership. Interview those owners. Get their feedback on the list of pluses and minuses.

- What's the likelihood of finding a partner with complementary skills and a personality compatible with yours? This ability depends on how wired into the business community you are and the line of work you're going into. If you have a lot of business contacts and know exactly what you want, finding a partner may be easy. More typically, it isn't.

If you opt for multiple ownership, you'll live with the decision for a long, long time. If you elect sole ownership at the start, however, you can always seek partners later if you feel that you need them for the business success that you desire.

Partners make sense when they can bring needed capital to the business along with complementary management skills. Unfortunately, partners also present the opportunity for turmoil, and, especially in the early stages of a business's growth, turmoil takes time, burns energy, and costs money—all of which most small-business founders lack.

A partnership in the right hands will outperform a sole proprietorship in the right hands, any day. Having *minority shareholders* (any and all shareholders who collectively own less than 50%) can also make sense, especially after the business is out of the blocks and has accumulated value.

However, minority shareholders can be a pain; they have legal rights that often run counter to the wishes of the majority. Because majority shareholders are ceded the right to make the final decisions, courts have determined that minority shareholders must have an avenue of appeal. Thus, minority shareholders, particularly in our litigious society, sometimes look to the courts whenever they feel their rights of ownership are being violated. Unfortunately, shareholder suits are a sign of the times.

Occasionally, especially where venture capital financing is involved, the founder of the business may find himself or herself working for majority shareholders. Fortunately, this situation rarely occurs because the typical small business founder has already proven that taking orders from others is not exactly one of his or her inherent strengths. We've found that, on the infrequent occasions when this situation does occur, more often than not the founder of the company is the first one to get the boot when the going gets tough, as the chief financiers step in to protect their investment. That's why we strongly recommend that you find a way to retain majority control.

### 8.7.3.3 Getting a Business Partner

Here's a fact that not everyone knows: According to studies, partnerships outperform sole proprietorships by a wide margin. We're not talking rocket science here; this statement is nothing more than a simple fact of life: two heads are better than one!

Sometimes, one plus one equals significantly more than two if the partners can blend their skills and talents. In other words, synergy. (Google, Apple Computer, and Hewlett Packard are examples of companies that began as partnerships.)

So, why may a partnership make sense to you? Here are some reasons:

Although you're probably aware of your own strengths, your human nature lets you more easily overlook your weaknesses. Ask those who know you well—family, friends, and current or previous coworkers—what complementary skills you should seek in a business partner. Consider the following advantages:

- Additional capital: Two savings accounts are better than one.
- Greater problem-solving capacity.
- More flexibility: One partner goes on vacation or gets sick, the other one minds the store.
- Ease of formation: Legally speaking, partnerships are easier and less expensive to form than corporations.
- Less risk: Profits aren't the only thing partnerships share.

How do you find a partner (or partners)? The same way you locate a key employee, a consultant, or a mentor. Clearly identify your need (in this case, the skills you're looking for) and then network your available resources.

When forming a partnership, you're beginning what you hope will be a long-term relationship—a long-term relationship that oftentimes rivals marriage in terms of complexity. If you're smart, you can determine a way to test the chemistry of the partnership before you get too far involved, and cannot get out.

Want to read a business partner joke? Here is one for you [10]:

> A very successful businessman had a meeting with his new son-in-law. "I love my daughter, and now I welcome you into the family," said the man. "To show you how much we care for you, I'm making you a 50–50 partner in my business. All you have to do is go to the factory every day and learn the operations."
> 
> The son-in-law interrupted, "I hate factories. I can't stand the noise."

"I see," replied the father-in-law. "Well then you'll work in the office and take charge of some of the operations."

"I hate office work," said the son-on-law. "I can't stand being stuck behind a desk all day."

"Wait a minute," said the father-in-law. "I just made you a half-owner of a highly profitable corporation, but you don't like factories and won't work in a office. What am I going to do with you?"

"Easy," said the young man. "Buy me out!!!"

## 8.8 Competitive Intelligence

According to Jane Hodges in *MoneyWatch* [11], there is nothing unethical about CI. Most of the time, it simply involves gathering together pieces of a puzzle that are available to anyone—if they have the time and the determination to find them.

But because the search can be tedious, it is tempting to look for shortcuts to get the needed information, especially when time is tight. When that happens, legal and ethical lines may be crossed. Table 8.3 lists some of the most common tactics that may get you into trouble.

Modern CI is often divided into four different, but overlapping, types: (1) strategic, (2) competitor, (3) tactical, and (4) technical.

**TABLE 8.3**

Competitive Intelligence Tactics to Avoid

| Tactics | Description |
|---|---|
| Pretext | Approaching a source under false identity or deceptive pretense |
| Dumpster mining (diving) | Surreptitiously gathering discarded key documents through garbage or empty raw material pails on dumpsters |
| CDA, NDA bypassing | Encouraging a source to violate terms of a noncompete or nondisclosure agreement (NDA) they signed with their employer |
| Acquiring trade secrets | Finding the proprietary advantage to a competitor's success, specifically when it's a closely guarded secret, such as stealing formulas or software proprietary codes |
| Paying sources for proprietary information | Giving cash to someone who can tell you what you want to know about a competitor |
| Enticement recruitment | Deliberately targeting competitor's key employees with the purpose of obtaining trade secrets |
| Computer hacking | Penetrating competitor's computer systems to gain access to proprietary information on pricing, business plans, customer lists, etc. |

### 8.8.1 Strategic Intelligence

Strategic intelligence is CI supporting strategic, as distinguished from tactical decision-making. This means providing higher levels intelligence on the competitive, economic regulatory, and political environment in which you firm operates now and in which it will operate in the future.

*Who and What Does Strategic Intelligence Help?*
Strategic intelligence is typically used by senior managers and executives who make and then execute overall corporate strategy. Its most common applications are in the development of the following:

- Long-term (3- to 5-year) strategic plans
- Capital investment plans
- Political risk assessments
- Merger and acquisition, joint venture, and corporate alliance policies and plans
- Research and development planning

*What Does Strategic Intelligence Focus on?*
Strategic intelligence usually focuses on the overall strategic environment. A firm's direct competitive environment and its direct competitors are, of course, included in that focus. It should also include its indirect competitors. In addition, strategic intelligence should develop CI on the long-run changes caused by, as well as affecting, all of the forces driving industry competition, including the following:

- Suppliers
- Customers
- Substitute products or service
- Potential competitors

You conduct strategic CI analysis when you must focus on many critical factors, such as technology trends, regulatory developments, and even political risks that, in turn, affect these forces. Strategic intelligence's focus is less on the present than it is on the past, and is primarily on the future. The time horizon of interest typically runs from 2 years in the past to 5 or even 10 years in the future.

- In terms of an interest in the past, you will be collecting and analyzing data so that your firm can evaluate the actual success (or failure) of its own strategies and of those of your competitors. This, in turn permits you to better weigh options for the future. You are looking to the past to learn what may happen in the future.

- With respect to the future, you are seeking a view of your firm's total environment: competitive, regulatory and political. As with radar, you are looking for warnings of impending problems, and alerts to upcoming opportunities—always in time to take needed action.

*Who and What Does Competitor Intelligence Help?*
Competitor intelligence is most often used by strategic planning operations or by operating managers within strategic business units. It may also be useful to product managers, as well as to those involved with product development, new business development, and mergers and acquisitions.

*What Does Competitor Intelligence Focus on?*
Competitor intelligence usually helps you answer a wide variety of key business questions, including ones such as these:

- Who are our competitors right now?
- Who are our potential competitors?
- How do our competitors see themselves? How do they see us?
- What are the track records of the key people at our competitors? What are their personalities? What is the environment in their own company? What difference do these people make in terms of our ability to predict how these competitors will react to our competitive strategy?
- How and where are our competitors marketing their products/ services? What new directions will they probably take?
- What markets or geographic areas will (or won't) be tapped by our competitors in the future?
- How have our competitors responded to the short- and long-term trends in our industry in the past? How are they likely to respond to them in the future?
- What patents or innovative technology have our competitors or potential competitors recently obtained or developed? What do those changes and innovations mean to us?
- What are our competitors' overall plans and goals for the next 1–2 years in the markets where they currently compete with us? What are their plans and goals for their other firms and how will those affect the way they run their business competing with us?
- Competitor intelligence's time horizon typically runs from 6 to 12 months in the past to 1–2 years in the future.

*Who and What Does Technical Intelligence Help?*

Technical intelligence is particularly useful if you are involved with your firm's research and development activities. Using basic CI techniques, those practicing technical intelligence now often can determine the following:

- Competitors' current manufacturing methods and processes
- A competitor's access to, use of, and dependence on, outside technology, as well as its need for new technology
- Key patents and proprietary technology being used by, being developed by, or being acquired by competitors
- Types and levels of research and development conducted by competitors, as well as estimates of their current and future expenditures for research and development
- The size and capabilities of competitors' research staff

## 8.8.2 Business Intelligence

"Business intelligence" is a particularly difficult term to deal with. At one time, this term was actually used by some CI professionals to describe CI in a very broad way, and to describe only intelligence provided in support of corporate strategy by others. Now, its use seems to have been fully co-opted by those involved with data management and data warehousing. There, it can refer to

- The software used to manage vast amounts of data
- The process of managing that data, also called data mining
- The output of either of the first two

In summary, virtually all of the reported applications and successes of business intelligence deal with processes that are internally oriented, from process control to logistics, and from sales forecasting to quality control. The most that can be said of its relationship to intelligence is that data mining and related techniques are useful tools for some early analysis and sorting tasks that would be impossible for human analysts.

## 8.8.3 Ten Commandments of CI

In 1988, Fuld and Company [12] published its "Ten Commandments of Legal and Ethical Intelligence Gathering":

1. Thou shall not lie when representing thyself.
2. Thou shall observe thy company's legal guidelines.

3. Thou shall not tape record a conversation.

4. Thos shall not bribe.

5. Thou shall not plant eavesdropping devices.

6. Thou shall not mislead anyone in an interview.

7. Thou shall neither obtain nor give price information to thy competitor.

8. Thou shall not swap misinformation.

9. Thou shall not steal a trade secret.

10. Thou shall not knowingly press someone if it may jeopardize that person's job or reputation.

## References

1. Olsen, E. *Strategic Planning for Dummies*. Wiley Publishing Inc., Hoboken, NJ, 2007.
2. http://www.bain.com/management_tools/Management_Tools_and_Trends_2005.pdf
3. Renger, R. and Titcomb, A. A three step approach to teaching logic models. *American Journal of Evaluation*, 23(4), 493–503, 2002.
4. Wikipedia, https://en.wikipedia.org/wiki/Strategic_planning
5. Porter, M.E. *Competitive Advantage: Creating and Sustaining Superior Performance*. The Free Press, 1985.
6. Value proposition, http://en.wikipedia.org/wiki/Value_proposition
7. Kaplan, R.S. and Norton, D.P. Strategy maps: Converting intangible assets into tangible outcomes. *Harvard Business Press*, 2004. ISBN 978-1-59139-134-0. Retrieved September 21, 2011.
8. Rackham, N., McGraw-Hill Book Co., Toronto, ON, 1988.
9. Humphrey, A. SWOT Analysis for Management Consulting. *SRI Alumni Newsletter* (SRI International), 2005.
10. http://www.notboring.com/jokes/work/5.htm
11. Hodges, J. Thou shall not steal your competitors secrets. *Moneywatch*, March 28, 2007, http://www.cbsnews.com/news/thou-shalt-not-steal-thy-competitors-secrets.
12. http://cdn2.hubspot.net/hub/17073/file-13332891-pdf/resource-center/fuld-and-company-new-competitor-intelligence-excerpt.pdf

# 9

## Virtual Organizations

### 9.1 Introduction

The adoption of the Internet for business use has led toward the emergence of "virtual" organizations. The five primary motives of enterprises to "go virtual" are summarized as follows:

- Reduced costs and enhanced productivity
- Increased satisfaction, closer teamwork, greater flexibility, and the retention of valued employees
- Decentralization of control, with increased flexible working patterns
- Empowerment of the workforce, improved decision making, and increased outsourcing
- Paradigm shift from hierarchical organizational structures to flatter organizations

If you founded a traditional company, then everyone on your team would work out of the same office, you would install a water cooler, a fruit smoothie stand, and a snack station where your employees could catch up on the latest gossip. You would recognize each person by first name, and you would ask about each other's kids, pets, hobbies, and other goings-on. You'd host annual picnics and holiday parties.

When your business is virtual, that whole "bonding" thing gets a little more complicated.

There are no water coolers to gather around. You rarely if ever see your employees in person, and you probably don't know their spouses' names, let alone the names of their kids and pets, or what they do in their free time. There are no annual picnics or holiday parties, because you all live in different cities and/or countries. Figure 9.1 presents an example of a virtual organization.

As a business owner managing a virtual team, your challenge is to look past physical distance and still create a cohesive and conscious virtual

Example of a "virtual" organization

- The technology completed by a virtual team
- The authors are in California and New York
- The prototype is made in Massachusetts
- The pilot production is made in China
- The proof of concept is performed in Ohio
- Deadlines are coordinated by the team leader in Massachusetts

**FIGURE 9.1**
Virtual organizations have no boundaries.

| Traditional | Virtual |
|---|---|
| • Employee recruitment and utilization at one location only | • Employee recruitment in any geographical location |
| • Communications and brainstorming are face to face and frequent | • Communication via telephone, e-mail, videoconferencing, social networking, etc. |
| • Fixed work hours | • Flexible work hours |
| • Work limited to work place | • Work performed from any suitable location |

**FIGURE 9.2**
Traditional versus virtual companies.

culture—a company culture tailored to the needs of your virtual business and remote employees.

Figure 9.2 summarizes some of the most glaring differences between traditional and virtual companies.

## 9.2 Is a Virtual (Boundaryless) Company in Your Future?

Virtual or boundaryless companies are those in which the boundaries, including vertical, horizontal, external, and geographic boundaries, are dynamic. Table 9.1 shows the most important characteristics of virtual companies.

Virtual organizations are not for everyone. Going virtual sounds easy and straightforward, but before deciding to "go virtual," you must consider the advantages and disadvantages shown in Table 9.2.

### 9.2.1 Functional (Bricks and Mortar) or Virtual?

Functional or traditional organizational structures employ a familiar power dynamic: Somebody leads, others follow, with extra managers selected to

**TABLE 9.1**

Characteristics of Virtual Companies

| Management | Divisional Structure |
|---|---|
| Simplest, highly informal | Organized around products, projects, or markets |
| Coordination of tasks by direct supervision | Executives help determine product–market and financial objectives |
| Few rules and regulations, informal evaluation and reward system | Largely autonomous and self-directed Requires "self-starters" |
| Collaborative work is usually conducted virtually rather than face to face | 80% of work time spent communicating, and 20% of work is accomplished independently |
| Project manager could be located in the United States, while the developers are in Asia | Changes the traditional concept of the "office" and "bricks-and-mortar" |

**TABLE 9.2**

Going Virtual Pros and Cons

| Advantages | Disadvantages |
|---|---|
| Shifts employees focus from activities to results | Reduces personal contact with decision makers, isolating crucial communications |
| Reduces real estate expenses | Disperses employees, making personal communication difficult |
| Provides access to global markets and presents a local face to global clients | Potential intercultural or policy clashes between teams |
| Allows employees a more flexible schedule | Blurs the separation between work and personal life |
| Opportunity to hold meetings and establish presence despite distance or location | Specialized equipment is not accessible to multiple users |
| Work environment without geographical boundaries | Requires technology such as telephones, Internet tools, computers |
| Maximum personal autonomy | No daily face-to-face contact with co-workers or supervisors |

help run things smoothly, efficiently, and predictably. Many companies still use this structure of top boss, middle management, and employees because it provides control and stability. Functional structures divide technical activities into semiautonomous groups composed of highly specialized individuals, as shown in Figure 9.3.

In contrast to functional structures, virtual companies perform most of their business transactions through the Internet and e-commerce, typically do not have headquarters or an office space, and operate with a very small staff. Most aspects of their business, including research and development, marketing, and sales, are typically outsourced. Staff interactions are conducted by telecommunications, and the primary managerial role of the virtual company is to monitor and manage the outsourced activities.

- Structure provides a means of balancing two conflicting forces
  - Need for the division of tasks into meaningful groupings
  - Need to integrate the groupings for efficiency and effectiveness

**FIGURE 9.3**
Traditional forms of organizational structure.

By minimizing their infrastructure ("bricks and mortar"), the virtual company keeps its operating costs to a minimum. A simple definition of globalization is the interweaving of markets, technology, information systems, and telecommunications networks in a way that is shrinking the world from a size medium to a size small, according to Thomas L. Friedman, author of *The World Is Flat: A Brief History of the Twenty-First Century*, which is an international bestselling book that analyzes globalization, primarily in the early 21st century.

A "**virtual**" business employs electronic means to transact business as opposed to a traditional brick-and-mortar business that relies on face-to-face transactions with physical documents and physical buildings. By minimizing their infrastructure (bricks and mortar), the virtual company keeps its operating costs to a minimum.

### 9.2.2 Networking Technologies

Web 2.0 networking technologies—wikis, blogs, YouTube, Skype, Facebook, MySpace, Twitter, Dig, and the like—were fringe technologies or did not exist a decade ago. Now, they are mainstream, and businesses worldwide are rapidly adopting them. Video communications are beginning to replace time-consuming, time-intensive business travel, and instantaneous communications regardless of distance are on the horizon.

Common communication tools utilized when working virtually:

- Conference calls
- OnSync
- WebEx
- Highrise
- eBuddy
- Google Docs
- MPK20
- Facetime
- GoToMeeting

## 9.3 Virtual Management

The term *virtual management* is quite recent and was brought about by the rise of the Internet, globalization, outsourcing, telecommuting, and virtual teams. Its management is frequently composed of widely dispersed groups and individuals who rarely, if ever, meet face to face [1]. Traditional forms of organizational structures historically provided management with a ready-made means to balancing two conflicting forces, as shown in Figure 9.4.

Due to developments in information technology within the workplace, along with a need to compete globally and address competitive demands, organizations have embraced virtual management structures. Virtual teams are typically composed of team members who are not located face to face, and their communication is mediated through information and communication technologies (e.g., video conferencing, e-mail, and intranets). Virtual teams represent an important emerging organizational structure that facilitates collaboration between team members located almost anywhere in the world. It is estimated that 41 million corporate employees globally will spend at least 1 day a week as a virtual worker and 100 million will work from home at least 1 day a month.

The implementation of a virtual team structure has been shown to produce many benefits including reduced real estate expenses, increased productivity, access to global markets, and environmental benefits owing to a reduction in airline flights. Virtual teams are also becoming increasingly popular with workers who want to work at home, which can increase employee engagement. Furthermore, as a result of using appropriate communication media, a virtual team is not limited to members from the same physical location or organization. As such, team members can be assembled according to the skills and backgrounds required, from anywhere in the world, enabling the organization to become more flexible and to compete globally.

The virtual management could be introduced as a part of the virtual human resource development (VHRD) [2]. The VHRD model is an approach

- Functional structure
  - An organizational form in which the major functions of the firm, such as production, marketing, R&D, and accounting, are grouped internally.

**FIGURE 9.4**
Traditional companies follow a "functional structure."

of utilizing the captured knowledge and information inside the enterprise environment (top management, external expertise, knowledge worker, workforce), and leveraging this knowledge to a dynamic e-content for developing and enhancing the human capital competitive advantage. This model focuses on rendering the human capital with the skills needed and driving their performance to face any future situation and solve it, by capturing the knowledge object during the interaction activities between the users and reuse it in producing a dynamic e-content for the training and development purpose and in the same adding value for the enterprise competitive advantage.

As with face-to-face teams, management of virtual teams is a crucial component in the effectiveness of the team. However, compared to leaders of face-to-face teams, virtual team leaders face the following difficulties: (a) logistical problems, including coordinating work across different time zones and physical distances; (b) interpersonal issues, including an ability to establish effective working relationships in the absence of frequent face-to-face communication; and (c) technological difficulties, including appropriate technology and ease of use. In global virtual teams, there is the added dimension of cultural differences that affect a virtual team's functioning.

## 9.4 Virtual Management Factors

An extensive study conducted by Jury [3] examined what factors increase leader effectiveness in virtual teams. This study identified five factors that are essential for effective leadership of virtual teams:

1. Time savings and increased productivity
2. Extended market opportunity on global scale
3. Accessing wider talent pool
4. Increased job satisfaction
5. Organizational flexibility and cost savings

There are numerous features of a virtual team environment that may affect the development of follower trust and the team members have to trust that the leader is allocating work fairly and evaluating team members equally.

Virtual team leaders need to spend more time than conventional team counterparts being explicit about expectations, because the patterns of behavior and dynamics of interaction are unfamiliar. Moreover, even in information-rich virtual teams using video conferencing, it is hard to replicate the rapid exchange of information and cues available in face-to-face discussions. In order to develop role clarity within virtual teams, leaders should focus on developing (a) clear objectives and goals for tasks, (b) comprehensive milestones for deliverables, and (c) communication channels for seeking feedback on unclear role guidance.

While technology choice is important for the development of role clarity, virtual team leaders should be aware that information overload may result in situations when a leader has provided too much information to a team member [4]. Virtual team leaders need to become virtually present in order to closely monitor team members and notice any changes that might affect their ability to undertake their tasks.

Because of the distributed nature of virtual teams, team members have less awareness of the wider situation of the team or dynamics of the overall team environment. Consequently, as situations change in a virtual team environment, such as adjustments to task requirements, modification of milestones, or changes to the goals of the team, it is important that leaders monitor followers to ensure that they are aware of these changes and make amendments as required.

Finally, when examining virtual teams, it is crucial to consider that they differ in terms of their virtuality. Virtuality refers to a continuum of how "virtual" a team is [5]. There are three predominant factors that contribute to virtuality, namely, (a) the richness of communication media; (b) distance between team members, in both time zones and geographical dispersion; and (c) organizational and cultural diversity.

## 9.5 Virtual Team

A virtual team (also known as a geographically dispersed team, distributed team, or remote team) [6] is a group of individuals who work across time, space, and organizational boundaries with links strengthened by webs of communication technology, or teleworking [7]. Powell, Piccoli, and Ives define virtual teams in their literature review article as "groups of geographically, organizationally and/or time dispersed workers brought together by information and telecommunication technologies to accomplish one or more organizational tasks" [8].

Members of virtual teams communicate electronically and may never meet face to face. Virtual teams are made possible by a proliferation of fiber-optic technology that has significantly increased the scope of off-site communication. Virtual teams allow companies to procure the best talent without geographical restrictions. According to Hambley et al., "virtual teams require new ways of working across boundaries through systems, processes, technology, and people, which requires effective leadership... despite the widespread increase in virtual teamwork, there has been relatively little focus on the role of virtual team leaders" [9].

In addition, you must add the "hidden costs" associated with hiring in-house personnel, that is, health and insurance benefits, taxes, payroll, office furnishings, equipment, training, and so on. Adding these expenses to a traditional staffer's salary actually increases the final monetary outlay by 2 to 2 1/2 times. This does not include the portion of the day the in-house staff is usually nonproductive owing to breaks, lunch, inefficiency, lack of work assignments, and so on.

Are *global teams, virtual transnational teams,* or *multicultural teams* different names for the same work unit? To be considered virtual, a team must have the following three attributes:

- It is a functioning team—individuals who are interdependent in their tasks, share responsibility for outcomes, see themselves as an intact social unit embedded in one or more social systems, and collectively manage their relationships across organizational boundaries [10].
- The members of the team are geographically dispersed.
- The team relies on technology-mediated communications rather than face-to-face interaction to accomplish their tasks.

The advent of virtual workers—employees whose primary work location is in a nontraditional location—has increased 50% over the last 10 years. Access to high-speed Internet connections, software solutions that enable remote collaboration, and improved telephone conferencing systems all allow employees to work seamlessly with colleagues around the world [11].

---

## 9.6 Strategies for Virtual Organization Success

According to Thompson and Caputo [12], reducing real estate costs and maintenance fees will lower operating expenses and increase profit margins. However, no organizational transition is without risk. Having a human capital management strategy for recently staffed or newly transitioned virtual workers is critical to ensuring a successful immediate and long-term return on investment.

Effective implementation is based on key elements, including the selection, management, and engagement of virtual workers, sound HR policies, and communication and change management support. Effective elements in implementing a virtual workforce include the following:

- Determining readiness for a virtual workforce
- Identifying jobs that lend themselves to work virtually

- Selecting employees who can work remotely
- Managing the virtual workforce
- Ensuring that virtual workers are engaged
- Establishing policies for the virtual work environment
- Developing a change management and communication strategy

## 9.7 Determining Your Readiness for a Virtual Workforce

Founders must consider a number of factors before instituting or expanding virtual work programs. Failing to adequately plan for the transition can introduce a significant amount of risk and hidden cost that can eat away at the program's anticipated return on investment. The following questions can help determine if an organization is ready for a virtual work program:

- Does the senior management team vocally support virtual work?
- Can we measure and manage virtual workers' engagement?
- Have virtual work–specific HR policies been established?
- Is there a space reduction or hoteling plan in place?
- Is there a plan for measuring virtual worker performance?
- Have we detailed the changing structure and tasks of virtual jobs?
- Is there a communication plan in place?
- Can managers be trained on how to manage virtual workers?

## 9.8 Overcoming the Inherent Difficulties

Teams by their very nature are interdependent [13]. Although they specify responsibilities and hire members with complementary skills, the ultimate purpose of teams is to coordinate work toward a common goal. Teams must have a shared understanding of the goals and the processes that will help them achieve that goal. In virtual teams, separated by geographical distance (and time zone differences), the process of developing a shared understanding is more challenging.

Figure 9.5 summarizes the pros and cons of virtual organizations, from a managerial perspective.

| Pros | Cons |
|------|------|
| • Enables cost sharing and skills | • Potential loss of operational control |
| • Creates a "best of everything" | • Loss of control over emerging technology |
| • Encourages knowledge sharing | • Requires difficult-to-acquire managerial skills |
| • Accelerates organizational learning | • Potential loss of control over a critical supplier |
| • Smaller capital commitment | |

**FIGURE 9.5**
Pros and cons of virtual organizations.

While the traditional teams, also known as conventional or colocated teams, consist of individuals working in close physical proximity, the term "virtual teams" refers to a group of individuals who are separated by physical distance while united by a shared goal. Generally, the virtual teams consist of talent across geographies, cultures, languages, and different time zones [14].

The "group dynamics" experienced by the members of virtual teams are complex, since members of virtual teams rely solely on electronic communication and collaboration technology to facilitate interactions among them. For a virtual team, the challenges experienced by a traditional team increase manifoldly. Below are the major differences between traditional and virtual teams:

- **Selection of team members.** Virtual team members are frequently selected based on their functional skills, but performing in a virtual team environment is not easy for everyone. However, lack of direct human interactions and social focus in a virtual setting might lead to isolation and seclusion.

- **Organization structure.** Compared to the traditional teams, virtual teams support flatter organization structure with blurred lines of authorities and hierarchies. This is required to survive in hypercompetitive market, deliver results faster, and encourage creativity—which are the primary objectives for forming a virtual team.

- **Leadership style.** In virtual team setting, managers cannot physically control the day-to-day activities and monitor each team member's activities; therefore, they need to delegate a little more as compared to traditional teams. The command-and-control military leadership style is giving way to the more democratic and coaching style of today.

- **Knowledge exchange and decision taking.** Often in traditional teams, information is exchanged and discussed during informal discussions. But in case of virtual teams, members have very limited or no informal access to information. Hence, there is a need for more frequent updates on project status and to build a shared database to provide all the important information to the team. Considering the time zone differences in global virtual teams, it becomes difficult to schedule meetings.

- **Relationship building.** When traditional team members meet face-to-face in the workplace every day, they develop close social ties with each other. They develop rapport with each other when they interact, discuss, and reach a consensus. In a virtual team, the interactions tend to be more task-focused. Further, lack of verbal cues and gestures (body language) in virtual settings complicates communication.

- **Psychological "social contract."** A psychological social contract refers to an unwritten relationship between an employer and its staff concerning mutual expectations and work outcomes. Misunderstanding or gaps in communication result in violation of the unspoken psychological "social contract" with negative effects on the team's effectiveness. Virtual teams experience difficulties in building trust, cohesion, and commitment among their members.

In summary, members of virtual teams (1) must rely heavily on mediating technologies for their day-to-day communications, (2) do not share the same work context, and (3) are not geographically proximate. These three factors conspire to inhibit knowledge sharing and shared understanding on virtual teams.

## References

1. http://en.wikipedia.org/wiki/Virtual_management
2. Hanandi, M. and Grimaldi, M. Internal organizational and collaborative knowledge management: A virtual HRD model based on Web 2.0. *The International Journal of Advanced Computer Science & Applications*, 1(4), 11–19, 2010.
3. Jury, A.W. Leadership Effectiveness within Virtual Teams: Investigating Mediating and Moderating Mechanisms. PhD Thesis, School of Psychology, The University of Queensland, 2008.
4. Jury, A.W. Key themes for effective virtual team leaders. Illuminations. Australian Psychological Society, 5–7, 2008.
5. Kirkman, B.L., Rosen, B., Gibson, C.B., Tesluk, P.E., and McPherson, S.O. Five challenges to virtual team success: Lessons from Sabre Inc. *Academy of Management Executive*, 16(3), 67–79, 2002.
6. http://blog.hubstaff.com/5-steps-to-becoming-a-better-virtual-employee-an-employers-perspective/

7. Jones, C. *Teleworking: The Quiet Revolution (2005 Update)*. Gartner, Stamford, CT, 2005.

8. Powell, A., Piccoli, G., and Ives, B. Virtual teams: A review of current literature and directions for future research. *Database for Advances in Information Systems*, 35(1), 6–36, 2004.

9. Hambley, L.A., O'Neill, T., and Kline, T. Virtual team leadership: Perspectives from the field. *International Journal of E-Collaboration*, 3(1), 40–63, 2007.

10. Hackman, J.R. The design of work teams. In J.W. Lorsch, ed., *Handbook of Organizational Behavior*. Prentice Hall, Upper Saddle River, NJ, 1987.

11. McLennen, K.J. *The Virtual World of Work: How to Gain Competitive Advantage through the Virtual Workplace*. Information Age Publishing, Inc., Charlotte, NC, 2008.

12. Thompson, C. and Caputo, P. *Reality of Virtual Work: Is Your Organization Ready?* Aon Consulting, http://www.aon.com/attachments/virtual_worker_whitepaper.pdf.

13. Gibson, C.B. and Cohen, S.G. Virtual Teams that Work, http://www.communicationcache.com/uploads/1/0/8/8/10887248/virtual_teams_that_work_creating_conditions_for_virtual_team_effectiveness.pdf.

14. MSG Management Study Guide. Virtual teams vs traditional teams, http://managementstudyguide.com/virtual-teams-and-traditional-teams.html.

# Section II

# Classical Initial Decisions

# 10

## Make-versus-Buy Decision

### 10.1 Introduction

Here is the multimillion dollar question: Should start-ups perform manufacturing operations on their own or should they buy them from an outsourcing provider? Current global competition forces companies to reevaluate their existing processes, technologies, and services in order to focus on core strategic activities.

Love it or hate it, outsourcing is now a permanent feature of business. As companies search for faster and more efficient ways of manufacturing increasingly more complex products, outsourcing noncore functions to lower-cost specialists can be an alluring prospect. Outsourcing is now increasingly used as a competitive weapon in today's economy. Outsourcing contract manufacturers can often do the job quicker, cheaper, and better.

This has resulted in an increasing awareness of the importance of the make-versus-buy decision, the dilemma start-ups face when deciding between keeping manufacturing services in-house or purchasing them from an outside provider (outsourcing contract manufacturing) [1]. Let us consider the fundamentals of outsourcing:

- Outsourcing contract manufacturing involves the transfer of the management and day-to-day execution of an entire business function to an external service provider.
- The client organization and the supplier enter into a legally binding agreement that defines the transferred services and terms.
- Under the agreement, the supplier acquires the means of production in the form of a transfer of intellectual property, know-how, people, assets, and other resources from the client.
- The client agrees to procure the services from the supplier for the term of the contract.

This chapter provides you with a make-or-buy decision process methodology that any founder can implement—whatever the size or industrial type of your organization. The make-or-buy methodology is one of your most critical strategic decisions within outsourcing contract manufacturing and should be taken in a structured and consistent manner.

A practical guide to this decision is a step-by-step guide to addressing make-or-buy decisions in a consistent and structured manner. The high-level steps are as follows:

- Evaluate whether outsourcing is right for your company.
- Determine exactly what functions to outsource and your performance expectations.
- Use a well-defined professional selection process to evaluate and select which provider(s) are right for the job.

## 10.2 Determining Your Core Competency

Core competency is the collection of skills and technologies that enables a company to provide a differentiated benefit to their customers. For example, Table 10.1 presents a summary of the core competencies of three well-known companies.

If the manufacturing process you are considering is a critical component of your company's business or dependent on highly valuable intellectual property, it is probably not a good candidate for outsourcing. After all, if the manufacturing process itself is your key differentiator, you'll want to maintain control of that crucial proprietary information.

On the other hand, if the manufacturing process is not a significant component of your business model today, there is probably no benefit to keeping manufacturing in-house. If your strengths are product marketing and commercialization, for example, you may want to find a contract manufacturer that can take over the manufacturing so that you can focus on what you do best—ideally, helping you save production time and costs in the process.

**TABLE 10.1**

Core Competencies

| Company | Benefit | Core Competency |
|---------|---------|-----------------|
| Sony | Pocketability | Miniaturization and portability |
| Federal Express | On-time delivery | Dependability and logistics management |
| Apple | Ease of use; intuitive operations; high-quality graphics; portability | Wireless communications Device mobility Cutting-edge technology |

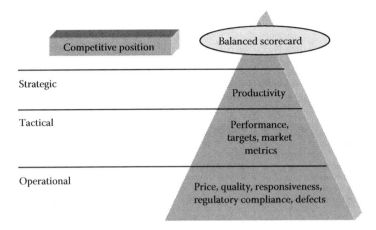

**FIGURE 10.1**
Outsourcing goals and objectives.

The 21st century is proving to be a crucial time for the knowledge-based industry. There has been a great deal of transformation in outsourcing caused by the continued drive of start-ups to cut commercialization time and focus on core competencies.

Logistics and supply chain management have often been among the first functions to be outsourced. This has moved beyond the warehousing and trucking functions and spread to ancillary services. Usually, companies decide to outsource some or all of their manufacturing functions in order to reduce costs, make more effective use of the working capital, and focus their energies creating differentiation and promoting revenue growth.

Your outsourcing goals and objectives are strategic, tactical, and operational, as summarized in Figure 10.1.

To maximize these goals and objectives, a review of make-or-buy decision must be one of your first initial decisions. The make-or-buy decision is the act of making a strategic choice between producing a product internally or buying it externally. Making the right choice can be the key factor in sustaining your company's competitive advantage and is one of the most important tasks of a successful management. This is the subject of subsequent paragraphs.

## 10.3 Deciding to Make or Buy (Outsourcing)

*Sourcing* is the act of transferring work from one internal party to another. *Outsourcing* is the act of transferring work to an external party. Whether or not to outsource is the fundamental decision of whether to make or buy.

How do you determine which products to outsource and which ones to manufacture in-house? Each business and owner is different, of course, but you need to answer these questions before making the decision:

- Can I better manage my available cash if I outsource? The answer here will primarily depend on how much cash you have. For example, by outsourcing the manufacturing process, you avoid the costs associated with maintaining an inventory of raw materials and hiring manufacturing employees.

- What do I do best? Because your time is finite, why spend a lot of time doing the things you don't do well when you can outsource those duties, thereby leaving you with more time to do the things you do well?

- Will the cost of the outsourcing tasks include a product whose quality is better than what I can produce myself at that same cost? The answer to this question is often yes, given the fact that the best outsourcing sources are almost always specialists in their specific areas of expertise.

The decision to make or buy extends beyond manufacturing, encompassing human resources, information technology, maintenance, regulatory requirements, and other fundamental business functions. According to Booz & Company [2], the dynamics of make-or-buy decisions is built on three key pillars—business strategy, risks, and economic factors. Table 10.2 presents the three key pillars in the make-or-buy decision.

### 10.3.1 Reasons for Outsourcing

Outsourcing decisions are those strategic decisions that change the operations strategy of your organization in both manufacturing and services. Your most important step in any outsourcing decision is to clearly define the

**TABLE 10.2**

Three Key Pillars in the Make-or-Buy Decision

| Pillars | Make (In-house) | Buy (Outsource) |
|---|---|---|
| Business strategy | High differentiation | Suppliers willing and able to meet requirements |
| Risks | Few alternate sources<br>Quick response times | Low switching costs<br>No sensitive intellectual property involved |
| Economic factors | Efficacy; reliability; high quality; manufacturing expertise | Lower costs; higher quality; regulated facilities; no investment required |

scope of the operations that you are considering for outsourcing. Below are some of the most important strategic decisions you will face:

**Improved quality:** Achieve a step change in quality through contracting out the service with a new service level agreement.

**Predictability:** Services will be provided via a legally binding contract with financial penalties and legal redress. This is not the case with internal services.

**Specialized skill sets:** If the manufacturing process demands specialized expertise or a new technology that does not currently exist within your organization, you may want to seek out an outside resource that has the skills and experience needed to make your product successful.

**Production capacity:** Often, the lack of sufficient production capacity is the single driver of the decision to outsource manufacturing. In those cases, making the move to contract with a partner that has the needed physical space is a no-brainer.

**Ramping up:** There is a potentially dramatic difference between in-house manufacturing and outsourcing when it comes to ramping up people and processes. If your staff does not currently possess the capabilities needed to manufacture the component or product, you'll need to consider the cost and time involved in integrating a new team into your organization.

**Technological changes:** When inevitable technology advances happen, a part becomes obsolete or feedback from the field necessitates a change in a product or component, and the company that developed the original design will be able to turn around changes more quickly. In this case, working with a contract manufacturer with design and manufacturing capabilities offers real benefits. It reduces risks when you transfer from design to manufacturing and the time and costs involved when the need for updates arises.

**Operational expertise:** Access to operational best practice that would be too difficult or time-consuming to develop in-house.

**Knowledge:** Access to intellectual property and wider experience and knowledge.

**Cost savings:** The lowering of the overall cost of the service to the business. This will involve reducing the scope, defining quality levels, repricing, renegotiation, and cost restructuring. Access to lower-cost economies through offshoring is generated by the wage gap between industrialized and developing nations.

**Cost restructuring:** Operating leverage is a measure that compares fixed costs to variable costs. Outsourcing changes the balance of this ratio by offering a move from fixed to variable cost and also by making variable costs more predictable.

**Reduced time to market:** The acceleration of the development or production of a product through the additional capability brought by the supplier.

**Staffing issues:** Access to a larger talent pool and a sustainable source of skills.

**Capacity management:** An improved method of capacity management of services and technology where the risk in providing the excess capacity is borne by the supplier.

**Risk management:** An approach to risk management for some types of risks is to partner with an outsourcer who is better able to provide the mitigation.

**Catalyst for change:** An organization can use an outsourcing agreement as a catalyst for major step change that cannot be achieved alone. The outsourcing partner becomes a change agent in the process.

**Commodification:** The trend of standardizing business processes can be served by a contract manufacturer. Outsourcing allows a wide range of businesses access to services previously only available to large corporations.

To summarize, Figure 10.2 presents a go/no-go algorithm for outsourcing your product.

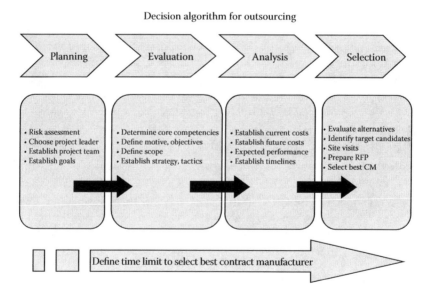

Decision algorithm for outsourcing

**FIGURE 10.2**
Go/no-go algorithm for outsourcing.

## 10.4 Partnerships with Suppliers

After you have determined the core activities of your business and laid out the necessary infrastructure, you will have to decide who will best carry out the individual stages. Activities outside the chosen focus should be assigned to third parties. Also, supporting activities within the new company need not necessarily be performed by the company. For each individual activity, the same basic question should be asked:

"Do it ourselves or have someone else do it?"—or in business jargon: "Make or buy"?

Partnerships with suppliers, for example, often cannot be dissolved from one day to the next, and many partners are hard to replace if they drop out. When making your "make or buy" decisions, you should rely mainly on the following criteria.

### 10.4.1 Strategic Significance

Your ability to render a specific service better than the competition was a major factor in your decision to start a company in the first place. This service is of "strategic" significance to your company and should be kept under your strict control. A technology company would never let go of research and development (R&D), and a manufacturer of consumer goods will never hand over marketing to a third party.

### 10.4.2 Best Supplier

Any entrepreneurial activity requires specific skills that may not be available within the management team. Your management team must therefore consider whether, in specific instances, it makes sense for the company to carry out a particular task itself. Should the company want to acquire the necessary skills, or would it be more advantageous to assign the task to a specialized supplier? For example, a team developing some electronic equipment may have mastered the electronics, but it lacks the necessary manufacturing capability—so it would do better "buying" this task. Their experience often enables specialist higher production volume.

### 10.4.3 Commercial Availability

Before you can make a decision to buy, you need to find out whether the product or service is available on the market in the desired form or with the necessary specification. Whenever possible, negotiate with several suppliers: you generally end up with better terms, and you will also find out more about whatever you are purchasing. You can also often help a supplier improve an offer. If you cannot find a supplier for what you need, you may be able to find a partner who is prepared to develop the necessary skills.

### 10.4.4 Outsourcing Partnerships

Most companies have business relationships with other companies—as a purchaser, as a supplier, or as an equal business partner. These relationships vary in their quality and intensity, from a loose, more or less coincidental relationship (a company buys its chemical supplies from a distributor with the cheapest prices) to a strategic alliance that results in intensive cooperation and mutual dependency (e.g., Microsoft and Intel in the 1980s). Exchanging ideas and people with a partner and jointly developing products or components can prove to be very fruitful.

For any start-up company, the question of how to work together with other companies is particularly relevant. Every type of cooperation (loose or close partnership) has advantages and disadvantages as discussed below:

- Loose, casual partnerships represent no great obligation for either side. Both partners can end the partnership quickly and simply; both, however, also live in the knowledge that supply or demand can dry up quickly. Furthermore, a supplier will not take much notice of a customer's particular requirements, as he will not be able to sell individually adapted products to his other customers. Loose relationships are thus typical for mass-market products, undemanding services, and standard components, for which replacement suppliers and purchasers are easily found.

- Close partnerships are characterized by a degree of tight interdependence between the partners; they are typical for highly specialized products and services, or for large volumes. In such situations, it is usually difficult for both sides to change partners at short notice, to obtain large quantities of specialized components quickly from another supplier, or to find a market for such components. The advantage for both sides is the security of a firm relationship and the possibility of concentrating on one's own strength, while also profiting from the partner's particular strengths.

For any partnership to develop into a successful business relationship, three important elements need to be in place:

1. **"Win–win situation"**: both sides must get fair shares of the advantages of the situation; without an incentive for both sides, the partnership is not viable in the long term.

2. **Balance between risks and investments:** partnerships involve risks, and often not enough attention is paid to these risks, particularly when business is good. A supplier with an exclusive contract can find himself in a difficult situation, for example, if his customer suddenly cuts back production and purchases fewer components. This is even more the case if the supplier has purchased special production tools that cannot easily be used for other customers' orders. Conversely, a customer can find himself in serious difficulties if a supplier cannot deliver (on account of bankruptcy, fire, strike, etc.). Risks and their possible financial consequences need to be taken into account in advance and, if necessary, considered in the contract.

3. **Dissolution:** just as in human relationships, tensions can arise in business relationships. Make sure that in any partnership, the conditions under which the partnership may be dissolved or one partner may withdraw are clearly defined from the start. While working on the business plan, start thinking about who you will cooperate later, and what form this cooperation will take. Partnerships offer your new company the chance to profit from the strengths of established companies and to concentrate on building up your own strengths. In this way, you can usually grow faster than you could on your own.

## 10.5 Contract Manufacturers in the Medical Device Industry

The global medical device contract manufacturing (outsourcing) market is expected to reach $50.37 billion by 2020, according to a new study by Grand View Research, Inc. [3]. Key findings in the report include the following:

- Class II medical device emerged as the largest application segment of the market in 2013. Presence of high sales volume coupled with relatively less stringent device approval regulations (as compared to class III medical devices) are some factors accounting for high outsourcing rates in this segment.

- North America was the leading regional market in 2013. Increasing prevalence of chronic diseases in the region and the consequent growth in demand for medical devices are some factors contributing to the region's large market share. Presence of stringent government regulations and healthcare-related cost-curbing endeavors are also expected to enhance the demand for outsourcing.

- Asia Pacific is expected to present this market with lucrative future growth opportunities. Growth of this region as a manufacturing hub offering lower labor and infrastructure costs is expected to fuel future market growth.

- The medical device outsourcing market is consolidated in nature and is marked by the presence of numerous mergers and acquisitions. Some key players of this market include Shandong Weigao Co. Ltd., Sterigenics International Inc., Hamilton Company, Shinva Medical Instruments Co., Inteprod LLC, Mitutoyo Corporation, Kinetics Climax, Inc., CFI Medical, Omnica Corporation, Infinity Plastics Group, Teleflex Medical OEM, Daiichi Jitsugyo Co. Ltd, ProMed Molded Products Inc., and GE.

According to Cirtec Medical Systems [4], contract manufacturers have played a significant role in the medical device industry for decades, and that role will be expanding in the years to come—some analysts expect the volume of devices built by contract manufacturers to double in the next 5 years. There are many reasons for using a contract manufacturer, but several stand out in today's industry:

- Downward price pressure, a continuing trend in foreign markets, and an increasing trend in the US market
- Limited venture capital funding
- Increasingly complex device designs leading to a need for increasingly complex manufacturing technologies

For a medical device start-up company, they key benefit of using a contract manufacturer is often efficient use of limited funds; with a strong manufacturing partner, a small company can minimize or even eliminate the need for direct capital investment, and the contract manufacturer can help speed the manufacturing because of their experience and expertise with Food and Drug Administration (FDA)–approved products.

For more moderate-size companies, contract manufacturing provides an opportunity for the company to focus on their core technology by outsourcing the day-to-day concerns of manufacturing, without employing large numbers of specialized technologists.

### 10.5.1 Medical Device Contract Manufacturing Challenges

The benefits of working with contract manufacturers are myriad, but there can also be difficulties. Some of the more common issues in the medical device industry include the following:

- Identifying a partner with a robust quality system. Some contract manufacturers have made the transition to medical devices after getting their start in telecommunications or other less regulated industries.

The quality system and quality culture may be insufficient, particularly for manufacturing FDA Class II and Class III devices.

- Finding a manufacturer with both breadth/depth in manufacturing techniques for fabrication of complex devices. The industry is seeing a surge in development of mechanically and electrically intricate, minimally invasive surgical devices, high-risk implantable devices, and miniaturized monitoring devices among other complex designs. To build these types of devices, a manufacturer must be competent in more than basic electro-mechanical assembly.

- Selecting a supplier who can support your entire product life cycle. Contract manufacturers often have a specialty—they may work primarily in a high-mix/small-volume mode or in a low-mix/high-volume mode. This may mean that as your product transitions from small development and clinical volumes to higher commercial volumes, you will need to move to a new manufacturer. This kind of change can be costly, risky, and distracting to your in-house resources, and can create regulatory delays for your product launch.

- Obtaining the right resources to support your project. Many contract manufacturers work primarily in a "build to print" mode. While this helps you achieve the primary goal of getting your device fabricated, it won't help you improve your device design for manufacturability, reduce the cost of your manufacturing process, or lean out your supply chain.

### 10.5.2 Selecting Your Ideal Medical Device Contract Manufacturer

How can you avoid these common pitfalls and develop a relationship that provides all the benefits that contract manufacturing can offer? There are some important steps that will help keep you on the path to contract manufacturing success:

Step 1: Understand the quality system requirements for your product and research potential suppliers to find a match.

- Determine the regulatory path and classification for your device. Look for manufacturers with experience working with devices of that class.

- Will the contract manufacturer deliver you a finished device, or will you perform final operations at your facility or a third party? If the device will be finished by the contract manufacturer, limit your search to suppliers who are appropriately registered with the FDA.

- How will your quality system mesh with the system at your supplier? Your contract manufacturer should have a robust method for documenting and executing quality system interfaces.

- How will you approach process risk management and qualification? A manufacturer with existing procedures for these activities could streamline your project.

Step 2: Identify a manufacturing partner with the right combination of capability and expertise for your device.

- Understand the key manufacturing processes required for fabricating your device. This might include extrusion, mechanical joining, plating or coating, overmolding or adhesives work, sealing, complex packaging, or other processes.

- Determine which key processes require high value capital equipment. Focus your search for a contract manufacturer on companies with the appropriate high value equipment already in place. This is particularly important for processes that should be completed in a cleanroom environment.

- Identify key processes that require customized process parameter development. Look for contract manufacturers with demonstrated expertise developing and qualifying those types of processes.

- Will your device include a power source? Seek a manufacturer with experience handling and shipping power sources safely; in some cases, the manufacturer may need to be specially certified for shipping.

- How will your device be tested for safety and functionality? Complex designs may require a variety of test techniques, including power up and power supply recharge testing, air and water ingress testing, mechanical strength testing, electrical function testing, pressure response testing, or package seal testing. The contract manufacturer you select should have sufficient expertise to help you determine which tests should be performed and implement those tests.

Step 3: Outline your product life cycle both in time and in manufacturing volumes. Use that outline to determine a suitable manufacturing partner.

- What range of volumes do you expect to build over the life of your product? Look for a supplier with the facilities and the organizational structure to support you through clinical trials, initial production, and the ramp of commercial manufacturing.

- How will you ensure continuity in the team throughout the product life cycle? An ideal contract manufacturer will have a history of customer service and will provide a consistent point of contact through your entire product life cycle.

Step 4: Determine your strategy for in-house resources and identify a contract manufacturer who will complement your team.

- A full-service contract manufacturing can provide design for manufacturability input for your product, helping to increase yields and decrease costs.

- If your product design isn't fully mature, a contract manufacturer with prototyping and design capabilities can be a tremendous asset to your team. This is particularly true for design aspects outside the core technology of your product, which may be a distraction to your in-house team.

- Will your product require custom test systems as part of the manufacturing process? If so, a supplier with test engineering capabilities could be ideal.

- How will your supply chain be managed? You may benefit from a contract manufacturer with the engineering and materials management personnel to provide supplier development and materials management. Early-stage companies may further benefit from a contract manufacturer with a strong Approved Vendor List to help build an initial supply chain.

## 10.6 Outsourcing in the Biopharmaceutical Industry

The biopharmaceutical industry is among the world's industrial wonders. The pharmaceutical industry is looking at an emerging market expansion and growth potential of 12% year on year, and the biologics market is expected to grow to $41 billion by 2014 [5].

However, biopharmaceutical companies are under enormous economic pressure and are facing unprecedented challenges. Current market and economic realities compel the industry to reduce fixed costs, improve efficiency, and maximize their limited resources on core competencies. Consider the following statistics:

- An anticipated loss of sales of approximately $80 billion in 2010–2015 resulting from expiring patent portfolios
- Shrinking profit margins and increasingly heavy competition
- Growing regulatory pressure owing to highly publicized exploding healthcare costs
- Recurring threats of litigation over real or perceived drug side effects

- Shifting demographic trends in both western and emerging markets, driving the demand for "smarter" pharmaceuticals to treat chronic diseases
- Growing threats to intellectual property from Third World countries
- Weak pipelines for new drugs in many of the largest firms
- Skyrocketing development and regulatory expenses

These are just some of the challenges the global pharmaceutical industry is facing today. The challenge of accelerating pharmaceutical product development while controlling costs creates a difficult balancing act for industry executives. For example, R&D spending declined in the last 4 out of 5 years, primarily attributed to the following [6]:

- Patent expirations on blockbuster drugs
- Declining R&D productivity
- Consequences of global attempts to reduce healthcare expenditures

### 10.6.1 Clinical Development Outsourcing

A Parexel Strategic Partnerships 2013 report included in-depth interviews with senior-level executives from global biopharmaceutical companies representing 39% of the industry's total R&D expenditure. The interviews included both quantitative and qualitative questions to better understand the current state of clinical development outsourcing and future trends in Strategic Partnerships [7].

Key findings from the Parexel report include the following:

- Industry executives who have already implemented Strategic Partnerships recognize the value, believing that these integrated relationships positively affect CRO (Contract Research Organization)–sponsor relationships as well as their operations.
- The operational efficiencies and impact seen by implementing Strategic Partnerships will continue to drive clinical development outsourcing.
- Biopharmaceutical executives most often equate Strategic Partnerships with oversight, governance, and the level of mutual partnership investment, rather than the volume of work, an important consideration for smaller and mid-sized companies.
- Executives believe that showcasing consistent value and measuring results are critical for the future success of this more integrated model.
- Strategic Partnerships will continue to evolve away from the traditional transactional model toward more integrated relationships

that drive value through increased alignment and efficiencies. The next generation of Strategic Partnerships must involve a greater alignment of commercial terms and a true collaboration of the best talent from the CRO and sponsor, according to biopharmaceutical executives.

- The hallmark of an optimized Strategic Partnerships model will be the measurable success of collaboratively bringing a compound to market faster.

### 10.6.2 Factors Driving Outsourcing in Biopharma

The global biopharma outsourcing market is expected to reach $40.7 billion by 2015, according to a recent report by Global Industry Analysts, Inc. [8].

There are a number of factors driving the executives' decisions to increase their investment in outsourcing. Two of the leading factors include the ability to access capabilities not found internally and the ability to reduce fixed costs and minimize utilization of internal resources. Executives felt that outsourcing provides sponsors with flexibility, helping to manage the volatility and unpredictability of the pipeline. Outsourcing allows for the sponsor to utilize internal resources more effectively while the outsourcing partner handles the peaks and troughs in activities as seen in Figure 10.3.

Biopharmaceutical manufacturers increasingly consider outsourcing as a viable option for cutting their organization's costs, especially as industry service suppliers offer a broader array of potential activities. Biopharma

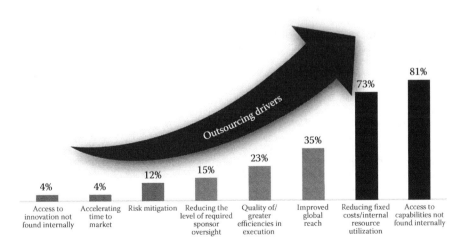

**FIGURE 10.3**
Outsourcing drivers in the biopharmaceutical industry. (Source: Parexel Strategic Partnerships 2013.)

companies report that they are contracting out more and different jobs and manufacturing operations in an effort to reduce costs, according to BioPlan Associates' *12th Annual Report and Survey of Biopharmaceutical Manufacturing Capacity and Production* [9].

It is worth noting that the BioPlan study is international in scope, and in years past, there have been significant geographic differences in potential destinations. In the 2014 study, for example, European companies considered China and the United States as likely destinations, whereas US companies preferred Singapore and Germany.

Preliminary data show that China is again the most attractive of the emerging destinations. In fact, many see it as a likely outsourcing destination during the next 5 years, most likely because of perceived cost advantages and expectations for developing quality initiatives. Among the BRIC countries (Brazil, Russia, India, and China), China continues to lead the pack, followed by India.

Contract Manufacturing Organizations (CMOs) and CROs based on emerging markets will continue to capture market share, albeit slowly. These CMOs continue to face domestic regulatory and legal hurdles and are far from obtaining approvals for US and EU markets. Perceived cost-effectiveness offered by CMOs in these markets may be eroding as other supply chain costs are figured in, and whatever advantages could be gained from cost-competitiveness also appear to be declining, judging by BioPlan's recent survey results that suggest that cost-effectiveness is waning as a selection attribute.

Nevertheless, the internationalization of biomanufacturing outsourcing markets can be expected to grow. BRIC and other developing countries have yet to pose a significant threat to US and European dominance. However, simply based on the weight of their emerging populations, their growing economic power, and demand for better, cheaper domestic biologics, it is likely that their growing bioprocessing competence will result in cGMP (current good manufacturing practice) production and export of biologics to US and EU markets in the future [10].

### 10.6.3 Performance Metrics Used in Pharma Partnerships

According to Alkermes Contract Pharma Services [11], the following initiatives are part of its service offering:

- Inspection Ready Status and Continuous Quality Improvement strategies that are reinforced by an extensive self-inspection program and a Corrective and Preventive Action database.
- Operational Excellence initiatives where a process improvement culture is enthusiastically encouraged within our manufacturing facilities, with a focus on reducing variability and eliminating waste.

- Problem solving throughout the organization is approached in a collaborative and professional manner by focusing on the specific (and often unique) needs of our partner projects, empowering employees, and optimizing existing activities in our development, scale-up, and manufacturing processes.

- A systematic training program that has created highly skilled problem solvers (black belts, green belts, and yellow belts) who can anticipate, overcome, and improve workflow challenges of partner products.

- Highly qualified chemists and scientific staff who operate in fully equipped, best-in-class facilities that include the following: raw materials, in-process and finished product release testing laboratories, microbiology laboratories, bioanalytical laboratories, stability incubators and testing facilities, method development laboratories, and method validation laboratories

- Dedicated project management staff and resources including secure intranet portal access for partners.

### 10.6.4 Outsourcing Drug Manufacturing

According to Taylor Wessing [12], for many pharma companies conducting preclinical and clinical development programs, it is often necessary, and usually cost-effective, to outsource manufacturing of the investigational drug to a CMO.

Outsourcing of investigational drugs gives rise to a number of commercial and legal issues that need to be carefully managed to limit the risks to the company concerned. Let us examine some of the risks, the problems that can arise, and the strategies that can be employed to minimize the potential exposure.

#### 10.6.4.1 Contract Manufacturing Agreements

Many of the leading CMOs are major pharma companies, and they can afford to be relatively inflexible, particularly with start-up pharmaceutical or biotech companies, when negotiating the terms of their contracts.

- Limits on liability. Understandably, CMOs will normally seek to limit their obligations to their customers to producing a drug to comply with the specification and in accordance with cGMP. While CMOs will not (by law) be able to exclude their liability for death or personal injury as a result of their negligence, it is common for the CMO to exclude liability to their customers for indirect, special, or consequential losses or for any loss of profits, revenue, business opportunity, or goodwill.

- Delivery dates. Particularly in the early stages of manufacturing, or where there is any development component to the manufacturing services, CMOs will be very reluctant to agree to fixed delivery dates for finished product. This is likely to be in direct conflict with the need of the company to manage preclinical and clinical development timelines and related costs, and there are limits to how this can be addressed. Nevertheless, it is usually possible to negotiate at least some provisions in relation to flexibility on timing of slots and forecasting that can mitigate the risks.

- The impact of partnering. The limited availability of funding for start-up biotech companies means that there is a necessity to partner programs earlier and earlier in development, and outsourcing risks can be accentuated where the biotech company has partnered the relevant program with a pharmaceutical company. An increasingly common occurrence in partnering agreements is for the pharmaceutical company to provide financial support to the biotech to enable it to take forward the preclinical and clinical development of a program to a point at which an option to commercialize the drug may be exercised and the program is then transferred. It is essential when determining the level of financial contribution from the partner that there is sufficient flexibility to deal with certain additional costs that can unfortunately arise given the risks inherent in the manufacturing process.

- Adverse events. From a legal perspective, additional problems can arise if adverse events occur in a trial or the trial drug is found to have a latent defect. It may be by no means immediately clear whether the fault lies in an innate property of the drug itself, a problem with raw materials supplied to the CMO, the manufacturing of the product, the storage or transportation of the drug, or its administration. Where the biotech company is an intermediary, there will always be a risk that it becomes embroiled in the process of determining the cause, which can result in additional costs at the very least and potentially defense of any claims that are issued by or on behalf of the trial subjects or the sponsor of the trial.

- Auditing provisions. It is important that any agreement with a CMO contains strong auditing provisions, a common formulation being a right to a minimum number of audits or inspections each year as well as unlimited additional rights in the event of a quality issue. Additional rights should also be sought to attend any audit or inspection by relevant regulatory authorities relating the drug covered by the agreement where this is permitted by the regulator. A notification of inspection provision will therefore be required, and it is useful to provide that any licensee of the drug program should also be permitted to attend as this is likely to be a requirement of any partner.

- Transfer to a new manufacturer. As development progresses from preclinical studies through clinical trials to commercialization, there is often a need to scale up the manufacturing process and frequently a need to change manufacturers as a result. When a new CMO is selected, particularly in relation to biologicals, the standard form agreements of many CMOs often contain provisions that have the effect of potentially limiting the ability of the customer to transfer manufacturing to a new manufacturer. Such a need to transfer may arise for any number of reasons including a failure of the original CMO to produce drug product to specification, delays in supply, an inability of the original CMO to supply greater volumes, insolvency, a need to be able to dual source, or quite frequently the desire of a partner to bring the manufacture of the product in-house.

- Transfer of proprietary processes. CMOs have an understandable commercial imperative to retain a manufacturing and supply mandate and will frequently argue that they need to be protected against the transfer of their proprietary process to another manufacturer. This may well be reasonable if they have a patented manufacturing process or some confidential process know-how that is essential to the manufacture of the drug. Frequently, however, it is the company that is providing the process, having developed it itself or transferring it from the previous manufacturer, and in fact, it is merely that the new manufacturer does not want to share its confidential background know-how with its competitors. The consequence of this is that a barrier to transfer is potentially created and it is worth examining in some detail how such a barrier can be overcome.

- Who developed the manufacturing process? Clearly, if the company is transferring the process to the CMO, there can be no technology proprietary to the CMO that is essential to the manufacture of the drug, and it should be possible as a condition of transfer to them that they will facilitate the subsequent transfer to another manufacturer if necessary or required. Of course, if the new manufacturer is intended to contribute considerably to the scale up of the manufacturing process or has otherwise substantially contributed to the development of the process, it may seek to negotiate financial compensation in the event of its loss of the manufacturing mandate, at least in circumstances where it is not in default.

- In practice, the prospective manufacturer may be relatively relaxed about a subsequent transfer of the manufacturing process to a customer's pharma partner compared with the potential transfer of its process to a rival CMO.

- Foreground intellectual property. What intellectual property is needed by the new manufacturer? Although CMOs will generally readily assign rights in all foreground intellectual property relating to the product, or exclusively relating to the manufacture of the product, they may well wish to retain rights to other more general foreground intellectual property in relation to the manufacturing, including the manufacturing documentation, to the extent that they are applicable to the manufacture of other products, as this will also be some compensation for the potential loss of the manufacturing mandate.

  From the company's perspective, the ideal position would be to own all foreground intellectual property, which it has arguably paid for through the service fees. In practice, if this is resisted, it may be sufficient for the customer's ability to transfer manufacturing to another manufacturer to be granted an exclusive or even just a nonexclusive freedom-to-operate license in relation to the product, or closely related class of products, which it can sublicense on to the new manufacturer along with a copy of the manufacturing documentation.

- Freedom to operate. For security, however, it would also be desirable to obtain a freedom-to-operate license under the manufacturer's background process intellectual property solely to the extent necessary for the exploitation of the foreground intellectual property. While this may well not be strictly necessary, on the basis that any subsequent manufacturer is likely to have its own existing proprietary process that it would adapt for the purposes of manufacturing the product, rather than seeking to copy the basic process and equipment of the preceding manufacturer, a freedom-to-operate license in the absence of an obligation to provide details of any proprietary process know-how is nevertheless valuable as it removes the risk of a later allegation of infringement.

- It may also be essential for the licensee to obtain copies of the manufacturing documentation. Although actual copies of this documentation may not need to be passed to a subsequent manufacturer, a full understanding of the contents may be essential to an effective transfer.

- Transferability of process. How will the transfer practically take place? It is one thing to have a license of proprietary know-how and a right to a copy of documentation, but in the event that the relationship breaks down or the manufacturing agreement is terminated as a result of breach by the manufacturer or the manufacturers insolvency, it will be essential for the customer to be able to transfer the process as quickly as possible to another manufacturer in order to minimize the impact on development and commercialization. This will be much more easily achieved if any necessary proprietary know-how and documentation is placed in escrow for automatic release in the event of breach or insolvency.

### 10.6.4.2 Pharma Outsourcing Conclusions

Outsourcing drug manufacture is often an essential part of preclinical and clinical development programs but should not be entered into lightly, and it is always worthwhile to conduct a full investigation into, and understanding of, the capabilities, reputation, and resources of a potential CMO. The performance of the CMO is likely to be a key element in the commercialization success of a drug, and companies should consider avoiding CMOs whose conditions are advantageous in the short term, but have the effect of practically preventing the company from moving manufacturing to another manufacturer in the future.

As the development of a drug moves from preclinical development toward approval, however, the financial risks arising from problems in respect of manufacturing increase substantially, and it is essential to put in place agreements (even at the preclinical stage of manufacturing) that minimize the potential exposure. This applies both when the company is contracting with a CMO and when it is acting as an intermediary in the supply chain.

Even where a CMO insists on imposing its own terms and conditions, a company that fully understands these terms and the potential areas of risk may be able to negotiate better terms or otherwise seek to lessen those risks.

## 10.7 Due Diligence: Questions to Ask Any Contract Manufacturer

When you outsource the production of your product or component to a CM, you can focus on your core capabilities. That's the idea, but not all CMs were born alike. Table 10.3 presents a few questions that may help you determine whether the potential partner is right for you [13].

**TABLE 10.3**

Due Diligence Questions for Contract Manufacturers

| Questions to Ask | Significance |
|---|---|
| Do you have best-in-class production systems in place? | A simple "yes" is not a sufficient answer. You want assurances that the CM will deliver the quality you expect, so make sure the CM has adopted quality standards and can provide documentation and test data.<br><br>Best-in-class is not simply that you ARE measuring, but HOW you are measuring yourself to a high standard. |
| Do you have quality management systems in place? | • ISO 9001 certification requires a CM to focus on continuous improvement in customer service and satisfaction.<br>• ISO 13485 is a specific quality management system for the design and manufacture of medical devices.<br>• AS 9100 is a specific quality management system for the aerospace industry.<br>The CM must have a strong record with no certification disruptions or black marks for performance. |
| Can you help with regulatory compliance issues? | The CM should not only understand the regulations and standards that your product needs to meet but also be willing to provide labeling guidance and manage regulatory filings that may be necessary. |
| Do you operate with an open book? | The CM should provide information about their production processes and costs (material, labor, and overhead) so that there are no surprises later. |
| What's your inventory management process? | You want to be sure that the CM can ensure that components are available when needed and that they are willing to inventory parts that may not be needed immediately. |
| How will you protect my intellectual property? | Your CM should have the systems in place that can ensure that your sensitive proprietary information is 100% secure. |
| Can you demonstrate expertise in manufacturing specifically to the technology in my device? | You should understand the specifics about the experience the CM has in working with various technologies, applications, and platforms. This means getting out on the production floor in addition to case study demonstrations and examples. |

# References

1. http://search.aol.com/aol/search?enabled_terms=&s_it=wscreen-smallbusiness -w&q=make+vs+buy+++pdf
2. Schwarting, D. and Weissbarth, R. Make or Buy Three Pillars of Sound Decision Making, 2011, http://www.strategyand.pwc.com/media/uploads/Strategyand -Make-or-Buy-Sound-Decision-Making.pdf.
3. http://globenewswire.com/news-release/2014/11/24/685770/10109613/en /Medical-Device-Outsourcing-Market-Worth-Is-Forecasted-To-Reach-50-37 -Billion-By-2020-New-Report-By-Grand-View-Research-Inc.html

4. Cirtec White paper. Cirtec is a full service contract manufacturer of Class II and III devices, http://cirtecmed.com/wp-content/uploads/2013/11/Best-Practices -in-Medical-Device-Contract-Manufacturing.pdf.

5. KPMG. Outsourcing in the pharmaceutical industry: 2011 and beyond, https://www.kpmg.com/Ca/en/IssuesAndInsights/ArticlesPublications /Documents/Outsourcing-pharmaceutical-industry.pdf.

6. http://www.resultshealthcare.com/media/116314/20131216_results_cro_pre sentation_for_rh_website.pdf

7. https://www.parexel.com/files/5013/9420/3451/2013_Strategic_Partnerships _Report.pdf

8. http://www.strategyr.com/Pharmaceutical_Contract_Manufacturing_Market _Report.asp

9. BioPlan Associates, *12th Annual Report and Survey of Biopharmaceutical Manufacturing Capacity and Production*. Rockville, MD, April 2015.

10. Langer, E. Biomanufacturing outsourcing globalization continues. *BioPharm International*, 28(5), 2015.

11. Outsourcing in the Pharma Industry—Experience, Expertise and Enthusiasm, http://www.alkermes.com/assets/content/files/Partnership_Whitepaper _August_2012.pdf.

12. Outsourcing the manufacturing of drugs. Taylor Wessing LLP, http://www .taylorwessing.com/synapse/may13.html.

13. Should YOU Manufacture Your Product? Sparton Corporation, http://vert assets.blob.core.windows.net/download/e2e4447f/e2e4447f-f3bf-4ea3-b2ca -33e207a0dcfa/spa_14080_make_vs_buy_wp_150210_final_client_approved.pdf.

# 11

## Patents versus Trade Secrets

### 11.1 Introduction

The world-famous Coca-Cola formula has been kept as a trade secret asset since 1889 because competitors cannot reverse engineer the exact Coca-Cola formula. If the inventor had patented the famous composition (and disclosed the ingredients and their exact proportions), then all intellectual property protection would have been lost forever upon the expiration of the patent. Interestingly, in May 2006, a Coke employee and two others were charged with stealing and trying to sell guarded Coke secrets to Pepsi. Pepsi quickly notified Coke of the breach and the FBI was called to investigate.

Both patents and trade secrets are part of intellectual property rights. **Intellectual property (IP)** is a legal concept that refers to "creations of the mind" for which exclusive rights are recognized [1]. In its broadest sense, intellectual property means the legal rights that result for intellectual activity in the industrial, scientific, literary, and artistic fields, and protection against unfair competition [2].

A **patent** grants an inventor exclusive right to make, use, sell, and import an invention for a 20-year period (on June 8, 1995, the new term took effect in the United States), in exchange for the public disclosure of the invention, and its practical application. An invention is a solution to a specific technological problem, which may be a product or a process. You cannot patent naturally occurring products in nature, scientific principles, laws of nature, mental processes, and mathematical formulas.

The birth of every patent starts out as a trade secret. At the time of conception, the idea or information can only be protected by keeping it secret. However, a subsequent decision needs to be made to determine whether or not to convert the trade secret asset into a patent asset. The traditional approach is based on the NUN factors: novelty, usefulness, and nonobviousness [3].

If the trade secret asset meets the patentability requirements, then the decision tree often dictates that the owner seek patent protection because a patent will provide greater protection for the duration of the patent life.

In the past, there was a great deal of variation of the term of protection afforded by patents in different countries. The members of the World Trade

Organization (formerly GATT) have now harmonized recognition of technology patents for a 20-year period that begins with the priority date.

A **trade secret** is a formula, practice, process, design, instrument, pattern, or compilation of information that is not generally known or reasonably ascertainable, by which a business can obtain an economic advantage over competitors or customers. The following are some techniques for creating and maintaining trade secrets:

- Keeping private and confidential documentation
- Restricting access to all forms of confidential information
- Establishing a security system for maintaining secrecy
- Controlling visitor's access to documents or facilities
- Requiring written employee secrecy agreements
- Conducting new hire and exit interviews emphasizing secrecy and confidentiality

## 11.2 Who Benefits from Intellectual Property Rights?

How can legal monopolies such as patents, trademarks, or copyrights benefit society? A monopoly that is rightfully obtained gives the owner the right to exclude others from (a) making, (b) using, or (c) selling the invention, and (d) using substantially similar "expressions." For example, a patent gives a benefit to an inventor and a benefit to the public, as shown below:

- A patent gives the public a set of detailed instructions that explain how the patent works. Thus, the inventor is teaching others and thus contributes to the promotion of national and societal progress.
- Anyone is free to use these techniques as inspiration or reference, or to make new contributions, as long as the results do not infringe the patent while it is in force.

A patent is a bargain between society and an inventor wherein the inventor discloses all inventions to the public in exchange for a time-limited monopoly. This ensures that society will be able to enjoy the full benefit of the invention after the expiration date of the patent. (A US Patent expires as of noon on the expiry date.)

### 11.2.1 Real Estate Analogy

Claims are considered legal property—that is, they can be bought, sold, rented, or allowed to lie fallow. Patent claims can be likened to the description of a parcel of land in a real estate deed as described in Table 11.1.

**TABLE 11.1**

Similarities between Patents and Real Estate Deeds

| Patent Terminology | Real Estate Terminology |
| --- | --- |
| Claim limits | Metes and bounds that locate and define the perimeter of the property |
| Exclusion | No trespassing sign; building a fence; limited access |
| Licensing or demanding a royalty | Charging a fee for entering the property Charging rent |
| Cross-licensing | Providing common access for mutual benefit |
| Infringement | Trespassing Entering into the property without permission |

*Source:* Modified from Maynard, J.T. and Peters, H.M. *Understanding Chemical Patents.* American Chemical Society, Washington, DC. p. 86, 1991.

## 11.2.2 Provisional Patents

For the entrepreneur/inventor trying to be as frugal as possible, a **Provisional Patent Application** may be your savior. Starting on June 8, 1995, the United States Patent and Trademark Office or USPTO has allowed inventors the option of filing a provisional application for **utility (mechanical, electrical, or chemical) patents**. The keyword here is "provisional." A provisional patent only gives 1 year of protection. After that, you must file for a nonprovisional patent or abandon your patent.

A provisional patent is a low-cost alternative, a *preliminary* step before filing for a regular patent that gives one additional year of protection or grace—maybe enough time to test market your invention before investing in the full cost of a regular patent. A provisional patent allows filing without any formal patent claims, oath, or declaration, or any information disclosure (prior art) statement.

- It provides the means to establish an early effective filing date in a nonprovisional patent application (also known as a docket).
- It also allows the term *Patent Pending* to be applied to your invention.

## 11.2.3 Time Limits

A provisional patent application can be filed up to 1 year after the date of first sale, offer for sale, public use, or publication of the invention. These prefiling disclosures, although protected in the United States, may preclude patenting in foreign countries.

Unlike a nonprovisional patent, the provisional patent is filed without any formal patent claims, oath, declaration, information disclosure, or prior art statement. What must be provided for in an application for a provisional patent is the (1) written description of the invention and (2) any drawings necessary to more fully understand the invention.

**TABLE 11.2**

Provisional Patents

| Advantages | Disadvantages |
| --- | --- |
| Relatively simple and inexpensive. | A provisional application automatically |
| The specifications will not be examined. | becomes abandoned when its pendency |
| More comprehensive disclosures can be | expires 12 months after the provisional |
| followed at a later time. | application filing date by operation of law. |
| Can claim priority to multiple provisional | Provisional applications will not mature into |
| applications, as measured from the earliest | a granted patent without further |
| filed application. | submissions by the inventor. |
| Once docketed, the term *Patent Pending* can | If not followed by a utility filing within |
| be used for business purposes. | 1 year, the inventor must cease using patent |
|  | pending to avoid charges of false marking. |
| The effective patent term is 21 years from | Examination is delayed up to 1 year. |
| filing date of the provisional application. |  |

If either of these two items is missing or incomplete, your application will be rejected and no filing date will be given for your provisional application.

### 11.2.4 Advantages and Disadvantages of Provisional Patents

There are several advantages and disadvantages to a provisional patents—the reader is well advised to seek competent patent counsel. A well-written provisional patent application should satisfy all formal and substantive legal requirements of the patent law. A provisional patent application should always be as complete as possible as compared to a nonprovisional patent application; however, you will not be required to file any claims. You can conveniently use that grace year to collect additional data that may form a basis for eventual claims.

The entrepreneur/inventor must carefully balance the plusses and minuses of provisional patents, as shown in Table 11.2.

### 11.3 The Special Case Involving Life Sciences Patents

> Life sciences and biotechnology are widely regarded as one of the most promising frontier technologies for the coming decades [4].

Research and development (R&D) in the life sciences is extremely costly and time-consuming. The pharmaceutical industry provides a good example of the time scales (8–10 years) and funding to bring a drug or biological product to market, and most biotechnology start-ups do not have the financial resources available to them to survive for that period.

The business model of biotech firms often relies heavily on intellectual property rights, in particular patents, as they are often the most crucial asset they own in a sector that is extremely research-intensive and with low imitation costs. Investors in biotech companies are generally well aware of the centrality of patents and the survival of such companies may very well depend on their ability to convince investors that they have a solid IP strategy and that risks are reduced to a minimum [5].

Why are patents so important for companies in the biotechnology sectors? It may be difficult to understand this without understanding how the industry operates. According to Estevan Burrone, a consultant for Europe's Small and Medium Enterprises (SME) Division [6], there are five major reasons:

1. Biotechnology is probably one of the most research-intensive industries. Compared with other major industries that also rely on R&D, such as the chemical industry, where the ratio of R&D expenditure to total revenues is approximately 5%, or the pharmaceutical industry, for which the equivalent figure is generally no more than 13%, biotechnology companies generally invest between 40% and 50% of their revenues in R&D. As in any research-based industry, the protection of research results becomes a major issue.

2. There are generally exorbitant costs for the development of new products and processes, but relatively low costs of imitation. The costs of performing biotechnology research are to be considered in the context of the high risks involved in any research project. It is hard to predict at the outset whether years of research will lead to breakthrough innovations with a great market potential or may simply leave a company empty-handed with results that are unlikely to bring revenues. Given the high costs involved in R&D, the relative ease of imitation is an issue that is of great concern. According to the founders of Nordic Biotech, "the present reality in drug development (...) is that almost any technology or compound can rapidly be reverse engineered" [7]. Adequate IP protection becomes a means to ensure that biotechnology companies can appropriate their R&D results and reduce the likelihood of imitation by competitors.

3. Contrary to traditional industries, where there is a clear distinction between the basic research performed in universities and public sector R&D institutions on the one hand, and the applied R&D undertaken by private enterprises on the other, in biotechnology, basic and applied research are often profoundly interlinked. Research undertaken in academic research institutions is often the basis for the establishment of biotechnology spin-offs. Similarly, biotechnology companies are often involved in (and are actively patenting) what some consider to be basic research.

4. The biotechnology industry, in most countries, consists mainly of recently established small enterprises, an important number of which have yet to take a product to market. In many cases, biotechnology SMEs are established on the basis of one or more patents developed within, or in partnership with, public research organizations or universities.

5. Finally, a point that derives from some of the issues discussed above is that for some biotech companies, intellectual property rights are actually the *final* product. It is not uncommon, in fact, to find biotechnology companies that develop innovative inventions, patent them, and then license them to larger companies that have the resources to take the product to market. Such companies may actually never sell a product themselves in the traditional sense but base their revenues on their ability to develop, protect, and out-license their innovations.

In addition, biotechnology patents are a breed onto themselves. For example, you cannot obtain general patent protection for DNA sequences of a novel gene in a number of species if you have only sequenced a single vertebrate or invertebrate example. Description of the species usually does not allow protection for the genus in patents in the biosciences. Also, DNA sequences for which no function has been demonstrated are generally not considered patentable. There are many laws and regulations that must be met, as shown below [8].

### 11.3.1  Genetic Engineering Patents

Isolated DNA sequences and proteins to which functions have been attributed and other metabolites are usually viewed in patent terms as chemical compounds, much like a new organic drug molecule. The unique sequence of the nucleotides or amino acids that you have uncovered constitutes a novel biological molecule (much like a novel chemical molecule) and may thus be patentable. In addition, vectors containing your nucleotide sequence and cells containing the vector/DNA may also be patented, provided they are considered new.

### 11.3.2  Microbiological Sciences Patents

Genetically modified organisms used in such processes may be eligible for patent protection. In addition, new microbes that you have isolated, purified, and cultured are generally considered patentable, provided they can fulfill the usefulness patent requirements.

### 11.3.3  Plant and Animal Sciences Patents

According to the patent laws of several countries, you cannot obtain biotechnological patent protection for plant or animal varieties, or essentially biological processes for the production of plants or animals. The United States is the exception to this and issues so-called *plant patents*. Similarly, biotech patent claims to animals obtained by traditional breeding methods are not allowable at most patent offices, but a genetically modified animal is considered patentable in the United Kingdom, Europe, and the United States. There is currently no equivalent in the animal sciences field to the protection offered by Plant Breeders' Rights [9].

### 11.3.4 Pharmaceutical and Chemical Sciences Patents

Novel purified chemical or pharmaceutical compounds are patentable, as well as their pharmaceutically acceptable isomers and salts. Crude extracts in which a compound is enriched may also be patentable, depending on the level of enrichment relative to the natural, unfractionated state. Importantly, novel pharmaceutical carriers may also be patented. Patent protection may also be obtained for pharmaceutical compositions containing your novel pharmaceutical compound.

### 11.3.5 Medical Sciences Patents

Because of the medical patent restriction on methods of treatment, diagnosis, or surgery mentioned above, surgical techniques are specifically excluded from patent protection in these regions. However, instruments for use in surgery, diagnosis, or therapy may be patented. In addition, diagnosis based on a sample obtained from the body is allowable and should, accordingly, be limited to in vitro applications in a patent application.

### 11.3.6 Microorganisms and Sufficiency of Description

In the complex field of biotechnology, it is not always possible to fully describe a microorganism in terms of physical, chemical, and genetic characteristics in a patent specification. The Budapest Treaty [10] provides a solution to this patent problem—patent applicants may deposit a sample of the organism (as claimed in the patent specification) at a recognized patent depository and in doing so may overcome patent examiners' arguments as regards insufficiency of description of the microorganism in the biotech patent application. The deposit number of the sample must be reflected in the patent specification and the deposit must have been made before or at the time of filing the patent application.

## 11.4 Practical Advice to the Entrepreneur/Inventor

> I'm not going to buy my kids an encyclopedia. Let them walk to school like I did.
>
> **Yogi Berra**

Patents do not merely protect inventions against imitators; they can also be used to block a competitor's technical progress. Thus, they are an integral part in your competitive advantage armamentarium.

These exclusive rights allow owners of intellectual property to benefit from the property they have created, providing a financial incentive for the creation of an investment in intellectual property, and, in the case of patents, attract investment capital.

The founder/entrepreneur needs to be fully aware of the time required to "prosecute" a patent, as shown in Figure 11.1.

Patents enable entrepreneurs to acquire financial capital under the most favorable terms in earlier founding rounds [11]. Firms of having larger patent portfolios enjoy a greater likelihood of sourcing initial capital and of achieving liquidity through an initial public offering. Given the lengthy government certification process, it provides a reliable "due diligence" signal for investors by which the quality of their investment can be quantified [12].

Given the fundraising importance of patent protection, the entrepreneur/investor must guard against making innocent mistakes that may prevent their ability to obtain a patent. An inventor has 1 year from the date of "first public disclosure" of the invention to file a patent application in the US Patent Office. "**First public disclosures**" are many, and surprisingly they include the following:

- Disclosures at presentations and poster sessions
- Prior public uses or demonstrations
- Prior conversations with potential partners
- Prior publications or interviews
- Prior sales of prototypes at beta sites

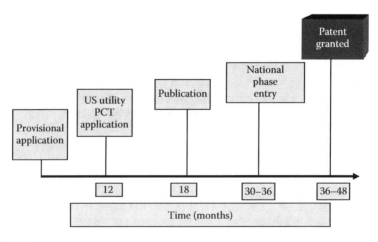

**FIGURE 11.1**
Patents are not a sprint; they are a marathon.

Also, keep in mind that if the US application is filed after the public disclosure, the inventor is not able to file or patent protection in many countries. There is only a 6-month "grace" period in Japan, Korea, and Russia. There is a 1-year grace period in Canada, Australia, and Mexico.

Also understand that the loss of foreign patent rights greatly diminishes the financial value of intellectual property in the eyes of investors. For that reason, and for your maximum protection, consider filing a patent application before embarking on any public disclosure.

- Is the patent in a subject area that is earning significant profits?
- Are there currently patent litigation cases in process in the subject area?
- Does the invention allow for reduced costs or increased performance?
- Are there any competitors that could directly benefit from your invention?
- Are there blocking or dominating patents in this area?
- Do you have freedom to operate?
- Do you have an inventorship/ownership policy in place?

In summary, a patent can help your company be more "investable." Fundamentally, investors will analyze the risks and potential rewards of a single investment. Owning one or more patents can reduce the risk of the company by strengthening the competitive advantage and providing an additional marketable asset.

## 11.5 Trade Secrets in the Start-Up Environment

**Trade secrets** are confidential and undisclosed business information that provides the owner with a competitive advantage. Virtually all types of information can be protected as a trade secret as long as reasonable and accepted measures are taken within the confines of the law. For example, the Uniform Trade Secrets Act, codified as Iowa Code Chapter 550, defines a trade secret as "information of nearly any kind that derives economic value from not being generally known or readily ascertainable by proper means, and is the subject of reasonable efforts to maintain its secrecy."

Examples of trade secrets include the following:

- Software, including source code
- Chemical formulations
- Customer lists

- Business plans
- Pricing models
- Marketing and sales strategies
- Manufacturing costs

A start-up needs to strongly consider whether to opt for patent protection or trade secret for certain innovations. Patent protection lasts for 20 years; a trade secret can last indefinitely unless (a) the information is no longer confidential, (b) the information has been discovered by legitimate means (such as reverse engineering), or (c) you do not maintain its confidentiality.

Thus, for certain innovations, the entrepreneur must decide a priori whether it will be economically more advantageous to seek a 20-year patent monopoly, or to maintain the information as a trade secret potentially indefinitely. Keep in mind that more than 80% of trade secrets are lost not only through employee disclosures but also through contractors, and insiders may inadvertently "spill the beans," as shown in Figure 11.2.

Unlike patents, state law governs the protection of trade secrets. Almost every state has adopted a variation of the Uniform Trade Secrets Act that generally provides protection to any formula, pattern, device, or compilation of information and provides a competitive advantage. The *"sine qua non"* of a trade secret is that the information is secret. The entrepreneur must also take reasonable steps to maintain the secrecy. However, trade secret protection does not protect the independent development of the secret [13].

### 11.5.1 Trade Secrets Must Be Kept Secret

The trade secret intrinsic value is generally established by showing that the secret is an advancement in the industry or offers a competitive advantage. As a practical matter, courts tend to protect information that was developed with a significant expenditure of time and money, is difficult to obtain, and is not generally known.

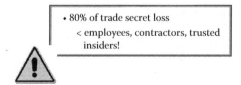

- 80% of trade secret loss
  < employees, contractors, trusted insiders!

- Departing or disgruntled employees
- Intentional (malicious)
- Inevitable (disseminated knowledge)
- Through ignorance

**FIGURE 11.2**
Eighty percent of trade secret loss.

Develop a trade secret protection policy

Advantages of a written policy:

– Clarity **(how to identify and protect)**
– How to reveal **(in-house or to outsiders)**
– Demonstrable commitment to protection → **important in litigation**
– Educate and train:
  • **Clear communication and repetition**
  • **Copy of policy, intranet, periodic training and audit, etc.**
  • **Make known that disclosure of a TS may result in termination and/or legal action**
– Monitor compliance, prosecute violators

**FIGURE 11.3**
Develop a protection policy.

Documenting steps taken to protect and develop a trade secret is accordingly crucial. Once trade secret protection is established, however, the owner should be able to prevent the following [14]:

1. Unauthorized disclosure by those formerly or presently in an express or implied confidential relationship with the owner
2. Discovery of the trade secret by improper or unethical means

Figure 11.3 summarizes ways you can develop a written trade secret protection policy.

## 11.5.2 Business Factors Affecting Your Decision

There are four types of intellectual property rights: patents, copyrights, trademarks, and trade secrets. Only two of these intellectual property rights protect information: patents and trade secrets. Patents protect information by dedicating the information to the public in return for a limited monopoly. Trade secrets protect information with independent competitive value derived from the secrecy of the information.

A start-up owner must weigh various factors other than just the legal scope of the different forms of protection in determining whether to maintain an invention as a trade secret or to apply for patent protection. Table 11.3 summarizes the alternatives.

## 11.5.3 Protecting Your Trade Secrets

As we have seen, trade secrets can include, but are not limited to, manufacturing processes, formulas, marketing and business strategies, customer lists, training programs, search algorithms, and recipes. The information

**TABLE 11.3**

Patents versus Trade Secrets

| Factors Favoring Patent Protection | Factors Favoring Maintaining Trade Secrets |
|---|---|
| 1. Patents provide a deterrent to competitors who otherwise might be tempted to make and sell similar products. | 1. The expense of obtaining the patent, which does not immediately provide a revenue stream (unless licensed) and, similarly, the potential for protecting the invention in foreign jurisdictions as a trade secret without the difficulty and expense of obtaining foreign patents. |
| 2. The protection it supplies for inventions that can be reverse-engineered. | |
| 3. The avoidance of any need to maintain complete security for inventions to be kept as an internal trade secret. | 2. The potential for product launch delay while a patent application is being filed. |
| 4. Patents furnish value as assets potentially useful for cross-licensing technology in settlement of patent infringement (or other) litigation. | 3. Disclosure in a patent provides a "roadmap" facilitating an unscrupulous competitor's copying your invention. |
| 5. Highly attractive to investors. | 4. The expense of enforcing a patent against an infringer through litigation. |
| 6. The ability to out-license the patent and derive immediate economic value. | 5. Negative know-how (what doesn't work). |
| 7. Can apply for continuations-in-part. | 6. Nonpatentable improvements. |
| 8. Competitive advantage. | 7. Attractive if patent protection is uncertain. |
| 9. Marketing and sales tool. | |
| 10. "Shelf life" is long. | 8. No government filing. |
| 11. Technology is easier to outsource. | 9. Immediate effect. |
| 12. Easier to enforce than trade secrets. | |
| 13. Legal monopoly. | |

can be a trade secret as long as it is of a business or technical nature and derives value from not being generally known and the information cannot be readily ascertainable by independent development or reverse engineering [15].

Finally, the owner of a trade secret must take steps to protect its confidentiality. Otherwise, it is not likely to be a secret. The following are two practical steps to ensure the maintenance of your trade secrets:

1. **Know what constitutes trade secrets.** Company leaders must examine their operations from top to bottom, documenting valuable information. As part of the trade-secret audit, companies must determine who has access to the information, where records relating to it are stored, and what the historic costs of developing it are. If an employee leaves and is believed to have taken company information, these audits place the company in a much better position to ask the courts to step in.

2. **Establish a culture of confidentiality.** After conducting an internal audit, business leaders must take an additional step: create a culture

of confidentiality. They can do this by instituting the following measures:

*Confidentiality agreements*—New employees who are likely to have access to trade secrets should be required to acknowledge—in writing—that they will be entrusted with such information and that they will safeguard it. This makes clear, at the beginning of the relationship, that confidentiality is something the company takes seriously.

*Covenants not to compete and nonsolicitation agreements*—These agreements are often combined with confidentiality agreements, but they provide additional protections to the employer. After all, what better way to ensure that an ex-employee does not use sensitive information against a former employer than preventing them from working in the same industry for some period and cutting off contact with former customers? Employers seeking to use such agreements must be careful. North Carolina law requires that covenants not to compete and nonsolicitation agreements be entered at the beginning of the employment relationship or as part of a change in duties or compensation. They also must be used to protect legitimate business interests. Courts routinely hold that the protection of trade secrets qualifies as a legitimate business interest.

*Training programs*—Eighteenth-century English writer Samuel Johnson said, "People need to be reminded more often than they need to be instructed." When it comes to trade secrets, regular instructions and directives from the front office serve to keep the need for confidentiality in the forefront of employees' minds.

*Computer and physical security*—Atlanta-based The Coca-Cola Co. does not leave its secret soft-drink formula on a table in the manufacturing room. Instead, it is locked in a vault that few people have access to. Companies should take similar measures when it comes to their secret information that competitors would love to have for themselves. Records should be segregated, and computer files should be restricted to only those with a need for them. Someone in human resources, for example, should not be able to access files that contain information regarding valuable manufacturing processes. Along these lines, companies should consider implementing computer-security measures that notify management when certain employees attach external devices to their computers or download or upload information. The number of recently filed lawsuits in which an employee, shortly before quitting, uploaded thousands of files to cloud storage or copied them to a flash drive is remarkable.

*Personal devices*—Work demands more of employees' time, so in an effort to provide the best service possible, employees frequently access work e-mail through a web service on their personal device, or they forward work e-mails to a personal account. "Bring Your Own Device" policies are born from the reality that more employees are conducting business on their personal devices. An employee losing his or her device, however, is a recipe for disaster. Additionally, when employees leave, company information on their phones go with them. Companies should therefore either prohibit employees from using personal devices for business purposes or mandate that employees submit to certain security measures such as password protection on the device and occasional audits of the device. Violations of these policies can be grounds for termination.

*Exit interviews*—When an employee who regularly had access to trade-secret information leaves, companies must take time to meet with that employee to remind him of his obligations to safeguard such information, including the duty to honor any confidentiality agreement and covenant not to compete that he signed. Companies must demand the immediate return of all their property, including not only company-issued phones, laptops, and other equipment, but work notes and other documents.

Start-up executives must understand and enforce their companies' trade secrets. To this end, executives should emphasize that trade secrets are composed of four information elements: (1) financial, (2) technical/scientific, (3) marketing, and (4) negative, as shown in Figure 11.4.

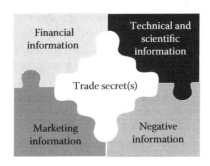

**FIGURE 11.4**
Trade secrets.

## 11.6 University Patents versus Trade Secrets Policy

Universities spend millions of dollars annually conducting basic research. The most visible rewards of this research are the host of publications, presentations, and graduate theses, which communicate these research findings to scientific colleagues throughout the world and provide the basis for educating students. Such broad dissemination of research results is unquestionably the primary goal of university research activities.

Sometimes, however, academic research also results in commercially important intellectual property that may be patentable. Intellectual property has always been an integral part of economic growth and in recent years has become critical to the US international competitiveness and industrial health. As a result, a large number of laws, as well as state and federal programs, have been developed to stimulate the inventive process and increase the rate at which valuable inventions move from the academic laboratory into the marketplace [16].

To be protected as a trade secret, the information or invention must be used in a business, and positive measures must be employed to keep it secret. Since a university's task is exactly the opposite, the dissemination of technical information, universities are seldom involved with maintaining trade secrets. This creates an inherent conflict.

### 11.6.1 The Academic "Research Exception"

University researchers thrive on free interchange of ideas and discoveries with scientific peers throughout the world. Why, in such an environment, would a university seek to patent the discoveries of its researchers, since a patent may be perceived as a restriction on the use of the discovery that is patented? There are four important reasons, among others:

- Traditionally, a "research exception" has been recognized as a limit on a patent's effectiveness. Generally, patents covering a technology do not limit academic research on that technology. Thus, patenting has been assumed not to prevent academic research by the inventor or by anyone else in the academic research community.

- Historical experience has shown that ideas that are not patented—which are instead "dedicated to the public"—tend not to be developed commercially. This is because few commercial businesses will invest the millions of dollars frequently required to develop a university-originated idea into a commercial product unless there is a sufficiently long period in which that investment can be recovered from a "protected" market.

- Commercial development of practical ideas has become more essential to the economic well-being of the nation and the state; the economic dominance once enjoyed by American companies continues to be eroded by nations more adept at commercializing new ideas—in many cases, new ideas that originated in the United States but were not protected through patenting.

- Ferocious competition for federal research grants has increased the importance of industrial research funding, which usually requires the resulting technology to be patent protected.

Since much state-of-the-art research is done at university laboratories, researchers within the university setting play an extremely crucial role in the technology commercialization process. However, if researchers act without regard to the patent implications of their activities, the value of this cutting-edge technology can be lost, and US opportunities to commercialize such technology can be severely compromised [17].

### 11.6.2 Can Academic Researchers Have Their Cake and Eat It Too?

With so many ways to lose patentability, researchers may infer that they cannot have both patents and publication freedom. THIS IS NOT NECESSARILY THE CASE. Patentability can be protected in a number of ways, while still allowing researchers to publish and collaborate. Baylor University recommends the following steps:

1. **File a Patent Application before Publication**

   Publication defeats patentability only if it occurs before filing for patent protection. Hence, one easy way of protecting patentability is to have a patent application on file before the publication, the poster session, the discussion at a scientific meeting, and so on.

   Invention Disclosure is the first step to filing a patent application. The proper Invention Disclosure form for Baylor University inventions are filed by the Office of the Vice Provost for Research. Thus, simply communicating before publication can make a significant difference. It is essential that researchers think of patentability before they publish. Given a modicum of advance notice, the Office of the Vice Provost for Research can make sure that all patent rights are protected and that publication can go forward without problem or delay.

2. **Use Confidential Disclosure Agreements**

   Publication means communication to persons with no obligation to hold the communication confidential. Thus, another way to protect patentability is to place such an obligation of confidentiality on the audience. This is unworkable with any large audience, but it is very easy with a small group—for example, a meeting with industry scientists interested in a researcher's work. Whether these scientists visit the university lab or the researcher travels to the company's labs. A simple one-page Confidential Disclosure Agreement can make the difference between retention and loss of patent rights.

Again, the Office of the Vice Provost for Research can provide these forms and assist in their use. Industrial people seldom object to the forms, since patentability ultimately helps them the most. So if a researcher is scheduling a technical meeting with people outside Baylor University, a quick call to the Office of the Vice Provost for Research is all that's needed to help protect any potential patent rights.

3. **Don't Disclose "Enabling" Information**

Since a communication must be enabling to defeat patentability, a researcher can also protect patent rights merely by giving a "tantalizing glimpse" of the technology without revealing technical details. This is not always appropriate, since a presenter at a scientific meeting is expected to answer technical questions from the audience. However, smaller or less formal meetings can easily show the results or benefits of a technology without revealing the details of how they are achieved.

As a general rule, complete technical information should not be volunteered. Abstracts or oral presentations can be "sanitized" to reveal only the general objectives and results of the work, without revealing significant, patentable details.

4. **When in Doubt, Mark "CONFIDENTIAL"**

As discussed in conjunction with research proposals to federal agencies, it never hurts to mark something as CONFIDENTIAL. It's not a guarantee, but it can help if the recipient of the information could be expected to hold information confidential on the basis of it bearing that message.

## 11.7 Summary

To patent or not to patent? That is the question. The answer is: it all depends on your specific circumstances. In addition to Coca-Cola, consider the following well-known cases [18]:

*The Big Mac Secret Special Sauce*: In 2004, McDonald's acknowledged privately that they had lost the recipe for the Big Mac special sauce. As it turns out, McDonald's changed the original special sauce recipe to cut costs and lost the original. When a returning executive wanted to return to the original special sauce, no one could find the recipe. The executive remembered the name of the California company that supplied the sauce 36 years ago. They still had the sauce in their record books, and McDonald's was able to recover the recipe.

*KFC Chicken Recipe*: In the entire company, only two KFC executives know the finger-lickin' recipe of 11 herbs and spices. A third executive knows the combination to the safe where the handwritten recipe resides. Less than a handful of KFC employees know the identities of the three executives, who are not allowed to travel together on the same plane or in the same car for security reasons. After being locked in a safe for 68 years, Colonel Harland Sanders' handwritten recipe was temporarily relocated to a secret-secure location as KFC modernizes its safekeeping. It was ceremoniously transported in an armored car and high-security motorcade.

*WD-40 Formula*: The formula for WD-40 spray lubricant and rust remover is locked in a bank vault and has only ever been taken out of the vault twice—once when they changed banks and once on the occasion of the CEOs 50th birthday. The CEO rode into Times Square on the back of a horse in a suit of armor with the formula. The company mixes WD-40 in a concentrated form in three locations—San Diego, Sydney, and London—and then sends it to aerosol manufacturing partners.

In 1953, a fledgling company called Rocket Chemical Company and its staff of three set out to create a line of rust-prevention solvents and degreasers for use in the aerospace industry. Working in a small laboratory in San Diego, California, it took them 40 attempts to get the water displacing formula worked out, but they must have been really good, because the original secret formula for WD-40— which stands for water displacement perfected on their 40th try—is still in use today [19].

Convair, an aerospace contractor, first used WD-40 to protect the outer skin of the Atlas Missile from rust and corrosion. The product actually worked so well that several employees snuck some WD-40 cans out of the plant to use at home. In 1968, as a goodwill gesture, kits containing WD-40 were sent to soldiers in Vietnam to prevent moisture damage on firearms and help keep them in good working condition.

*Lena Blackburne's Baseball Rubbing Mud*: There is this special baseball rubbing mud, and Major League Baseball absolutely depends on it. A brand new baseball just out of the box is slippery; so much so that a pitcher has no control when throwing one unless it's dirtied up a bit first. So, an umpire spends a lot of his time before a game rubbing mud into dozens of balls, but not just any mud works. Before the 1930s, teams tried all kinds of substances, including tobacco juice and shoe polish, but nothing really worked. Then, one day, Lena Blackburne, a no-name player turned coach, was taking a walk near his house in New Jersey when he stumbled upon some strange mud. Obviously having a "Eureka!" moment to rival Archimedes', Blackburne took some home and tried it out. Amazingly enough, it worked brilliantly.

By 1938, the American League was using Blackburn Rubbing Mud exclusively on all their balls. The National League wouldn't use it until the 1950s, mostly because Blackburn refused to sell it to them, but they've been using it ever since.

### 11.7.1 The Big Trade-Off

A trade secret can grant proprietary rights in perpetuity, or for as long as the owner is able to maintain the secrecy. A patent, on the other hand, has a shelf life of 20 years from the time an application is filed, and while a trade secret can remain an enigma, a patent application requires the inventor to describe exactly how his invention works [20].

Trade secrets can include an intangible process, technique, or method. A trade secret can be a quantifiable design, composition, formula, or pattern. It can be a physical device or mechanism. Chemical formulas, manufacturing processes, or business information can be considered trade secrets, and even if the ingredients in a chemical recipe like a soft-drink syrup or fried chicken batter are discovered, the exact ratios involved or the way they are combined can still remain a trade secret.

Until last year, American inventors could rely on the US Patent and Trademark Office to keep a patent application secret until it was granted. If the application was rejected, the invention remained confidential, but in 2011, the United States, following the rest of the world, initiated a new practice of publishing patent applications 18 months after the application is filed.

Anyone who makes commercial use of a trade secret and later decides to apply for a patent must do so within a year. After that, the invention is no longer eligible for a patent. An idea can, however, have a copyright and also be a trade secret. The US Copyright Office allows material to be divided so that some parts can be revealed while others are kept secret.

Since trade secrets are intellectual property, courts have ruled that software algorithms, customer lists, financial data, Wall Street formulas, names of suppliers, and even blueprints can qualify. What makes them unique as intellectual property is the economic value derived from their being kept secret, and corporations have been known to spend millions to defend them.

Or forsake millions. In the 1970s, Coca-Cola withdrew from India rather than comply with a law in that country that would have compelled the soft-drink manufacturer to transfer technology—in this case, its secret syrup formula—to an Indian-owned company.

There are disadvantages to trade secrets, compared with patents, because just about anything can be analyzed, reverse-engineered, and copied, and patents and trade secrets are not equals in a courtroom; patents are accepted as valid, whereas trade secrets must be authenticated first.

To defend a trade secret under most states' laws, the owner has to show that a reasonable effort has been made to maintain the secrecy. Companies can require employees, suppliers, and subcontractors to sign nondisclosure, confidentiality, or noncompete agreements. They can divide a process or formula among workers, making sure that no one has knowledge of the entire secret.

In most cases, the courts look at how many people inside and outside a business know about the secret, what kind of precautions the owner takes to preserve the secrecy, the value the owner gains against his competitors from holding the secret, and how much trouble and expense someone else would incur to crack the secret.

Patents, trademarks, and copyrights fall under federal law, but trade secrets are covered by state law. That practice can be traced to the 19th century, when common law protected trade secrets. Most states have adopted specific laws since then, which differ from place to place, though some still use common law. In 1996, the Economic Espionage Act made theft of trade secrets a federal crime.

Despite the increasing importance of trade secrets to world economies, there is no global law on trade secrets, or even a universal definition of a trade secret. Patents, copyrights, and trademarks are addressed in comprehensive international legal treaties; trade secrets are not included. What can be protected as a trade secret differs from country to country and, in some nations, trade secrets have no legal standing at all.

Global "harmonization" of intellectual property laws has been a top American policy priority in recent years, but trade secrets are still at a disadvantage. Germany and Japan require public trials for lawsuits, for example, and anyone seeking redress must first reveal his trade secret. In other countries, confidential data are revealed when submitted for government review of safety or effectiveness.

---

## References

1. Raysman, R., Pisacreta, E.A., and Adler, K.A. *Intellectual Property Licensing: Forms and Analysis.* Law Journal Press, 1998–2008. ISBN 973-58852-086.
2. *WIPO Intellectual Property Handbook.* WIPO Publication No. 489(E) 2004, http://www.wipo.int/export/sites/www/about-ip/en/iprm/pdf/ch2.pdf.

3. Halligan, R.M. Trade secrets vs patents: The new calculus. *Landslide*, 2(6), July/ August 2010. © 2010 by the American Bar Association, https://clients.kilpat ricktownsend.com/IPDeskReference/Documents/Trade%20Secret%20or%20 Patent%20Protection.pdf.

4. European Commission. *Life Sciences and Biotechnology—A Strategy for Europe*, 2002.

5. Burrone, E. Patents at the Core: The Biotech Business, esteban.burrone@wipo .int.

6. http://www.wipo.int/sme/en/documents/patents_biotech.htm

7. Medicon Valley Patent Guide, 2002. Medicon Valley is a Danish/Swedish organization, http://www.mva.org/media(3,1033)/Medicon Valley Patent Guide .pdf.

8. Hoffelner, C. Patents Biotech Biotechnology, http://www.svw.co.za/patents -biotech.html.

9. Wikipedia Plant Breeder's Rights, http://en.wikipedia.org/wiki/Plant_breed ers'_rights.

10. WIPO Biotechnology http://www.wipo.int/patent-law/en/developments/bio technology.html.

11. Hsu, D. and Ziedonis, R.H. Patents as Quality Signals for Entrepreneurial Ventures. Copenhagen, DRUID Summer Conference, Denmark, June 2007, http://www2.druid.dk/conferences/viewpaper.php?id=1717&cf=9.

12. Spence, M. Job market signaling. *Quarterly Journal of Economics*, 87, 355–374, 1973.

13. Toren, P.J. Patent Bar Review 2014, Patents vs trade secrets, http://www.ipwatch dog.com/2014/12/09/trade-secrets-a-viable-alternative-to-patents/id=52554/.

14. Kilpatrick Stockton Intellectual Property Desk Reference. Choosing between trade secret and patent protection, https://clients.kilpatricktownsend.com / IPDeskReference/Documents/Trade%20Secret%20or%20Patent%20 Protection.pdf.

15. Durham, J.B. Three steps business leaders must take to protect valuable information. *Business North Carolina*, 2013, http://www.poynerspruill.com/publica tions/Pages/3StepsBusLeadersTakeProtectInformation.aspx.

16. http://www.baylor.edu/research/vpr/files/inventionsandtechnologytransfer .pdf

17. http://www.baylor.edu/research/vpr/files/patentlawbasics.pdf

18. Benjamin, K. Secrets Only Two Living People Know (For Some Reason), http:// www.cracked.com/article/147_7-secrets-only-two-living-people-know-for -some-reason/.

19. http://wd40.com/cool-stuff/history

20. Chartrand, S. Patents; Many companies will forgo patents in an effort to safeguard their trade secrets. 2001, http://www.nytimes.com/2001/02/05/business /patents-many-companies-will-forgo-patents-effort-safeguard-their-trade -secrets.html.

21. Maynard, J.T. and Peters, H.M. *Understanding Chemical Patents*. American Chemical Society, Washington, DC. p. 86, 1991.

# 12

## Strategic Alliances

## 12.1 Introduction

Strategic alliances are a formal relationship formed between two or more parties to pursue a set of agreed upon goals or to meet a critical business need while still remaining as independent organizations. On many occasions, strategic alliances are partnerships formed between two organizations in response to an essential threat or opportunity in their business environment.

Strategic alliances are also called join ventures, interfirm collaborations, or consortium agreements. Table 12.1 summarizes the distinguishing characteristics among the alliance types.

Joint ventures and strategic alliances allow companies with complementary skills to benefit from one another's strengths. They are common in technology, manufacturing, and commercial real estate development, and whenever a company wants to expand its sales or operations into a foreign country. In a joint venture, the companies start and invest in a new company that's jointly owned by both of the parent companies. A strategic alliance is a legal agreement between two or more companies to share access to their technology, trademarks, or other assets. A strategic alliance does not create a new company [1].

## 12.2 The "Big Question"

Strategic alliances represent a way for aggressive companies to pursue growth by broadening product lines, penetrating new markets, and stabilizing cyclical businesses despite limited resources, but before embarking on any strategic alliance quest, management must answer the Big Question:

> Can we create organic sales growth versus sales growth through strategic alliances or acquisitions?

The firm can grow organically (by internal investment) or inorganically (by strategic alliances, i.e., cooperative ventures, joint ventures, joint ownership,

**TABLE 12.1**

Distinguishing Characteristics among Strategic Alliance Types

| Alliance Type | Distinguishing Characteristics |
| --- | --- |
| Informal cooperation | Mutual help in distribution, sharing space at industry meetings<br>No legal formalization |
| Formal collaborations | Uncertainty related to specific tasks<br>Clear need for flexibility<br>Success without losing independence<br>Legal documentation in place |
| Consortium agreements | Need for large size and technical skills<br>Need for large geographical coverage<br>Limited financial risk for each partner<br>Achieving goals without loss of identity |
| Joint ventures | Clear business need to form relationship<br>Specific allocation of resources<br>Legal formalization<br>Not tied to core technologies or geographical location<br>Independent business entities<br>Pooling resources to share risks, rewards, and control<br>Commercial purpose of defined scope and duration |

or mergers and acquisitions [M&A]). One theoretical way of approaching the Big Question is to look at the continuum of strategic alliance options interdependence as shown in Figure 12.1.

When two or more companies combined participate in a project, it is a **cooperative venture**. This participation can be in the form of sharing financial or technical resources for mutual benefit.

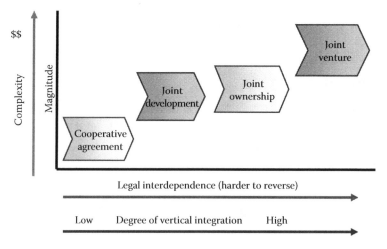

**FIGURE 12.1**
Strategic alliance options.

A **joint venture** (JV) creates a separate entity in which both firms invest. The JV agreement specifies investment rights, operational responsibilities, voting control, exit alternatives, and generally the allocation of risks and rewards. The entity could be a division or an entirely new business established for the venture.

In a **joint ownership** alliance, the parties agree to long-term licensing agreement, co-marketing agreements, co-development agreements, joint purchasing agreements, and long-term supply or toll agreements, with each party owning 50% of the intellectual property (IP) plus other nontangible assets.

Strategic alliances can be characterized as follows [2]:

- Relative bargaining power and ownership
- Degree of interfirm cooperation
- Individual contribution to the value chain
- Geographical reach
- Acceptable economic risk
- Legal interdependence (ability to walk away)

## 12.3 Advantages of Strategic Alliances

Strategic alliances represent an alluring means for start-ups to pursue high-growth strategies despite limited resources. The underlying rationale is that one plus one equals three. Alliances promise to provide the partners greater likelihood of success in a competitive context than if they were to go alone. If you are contemplating a strategic alliance, ask yourself the following preliminary questions:

- Why do you want to form a strategic alliance in the first place?
- What outcomes (benefits) do you envision from the alliance?
- Do you have other (or better) ways of achieving your goals?
- What makes the other party an attractive partner to you?
- Are your goals compatible with those of your potential partner?
- Are you and your potential partner a good match in terms of culture, background, experience organizational values, and strategic goals?

Traditionally, inorganic growth can be achieved by the judicious use of strategic alliances. In a strategic alliance, both risks and rewards are shared

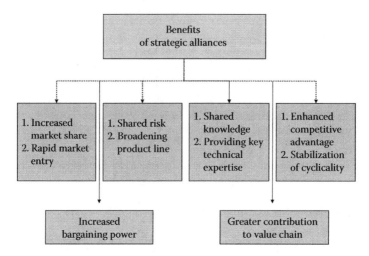

**FIGURE 12.2**
Benefits of strategic alliances.

and typically lead to long-term strategic benefits for both partners, as summarized below:

- Adding value to products
- Improving market access
- Strengthening operations
- Adding technological strength
- Enhancing strategic growth
- Enhancing organizational skills
- Building financial strength

In addition, strategic alliances display other advantages, such as those seen in Figure 12.2.

## 12.4 Pitfalls of Strategic Alliances

Although a properly planned and implemented strategic alliance can undoubtedly boost the growth and profitability of the participating partners, the route to a successful partnership is not without pitfalls.

One of the most common occurs when there is a substantial difference in the sizes of the two partner organizations. Such a disparity can easily

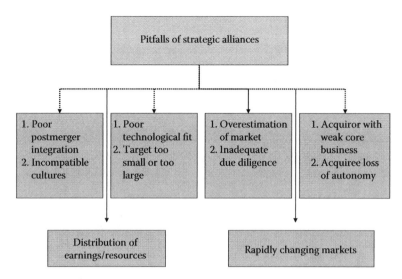

**FIGURE 12.3**
Pitfalls of strategic alliances.

generate conflict and misunderstanding [3]. Conflict does not have to be a roadblock to a successful alliance if you and your partnering alliance members are willing to resolve the conflict at the core level, in a timely manner. In fact, the resolved conflict can lead to a stronger relationship through improved communication. Unfortunately, conflict that is left unresolved will lead to fatal flaws that will erode the relationship [4].

Just because you're working with a company of integrity, it doesn't mean they will look out for you. Even in a partnering relationship, you are still accountable for your own success and well-being. Make sure your bottom-line expectations take into account that servicing the partnering agreement is going to require extra resources. Be certain of everybody's alliance partnering goals. Some of the more common areas of conflict in alliance relationships are shown in Figure 12.3.

## 12.5 Best Practices

Three are two schools of thought regarding strategic alliances. Practitioners of the first school argue that transactions are accomplished by the hubris of the two respective executives, with details negotiated at a later time by the respective company specialists. The second school of thought recognizes the intricacies of the transaction and develops a systematic methodology, thus increasing the likelihood of long-term success.

**TABLE 12.2**

Best Practices for M&A Negotiations

| Common Mistakes | Common Solutions |
|---|---|
| Unrealistic timetables and expectations | Select an acquisitions team experienced in cost/benefit time allocation |
| Inexperienced M&A negotiation team | Establish an acquisitions team with defined responsibilities and authority |
| Lack of structured transaction process | Clearly define team member roles<br>Be prepared to "walk away" from a bad deal |
| Disproportionate time spent on minor issues | Focus on outcomes, not activities<br>Set "drop dead" dates |
| Incomplete or irrelevant information | Obtain corroborating data |
| Inadequate or nonexistent due diligence | Engage industry experts |
| Inadequate sensitivity analysis | Perform financial and commercial sensitivity analyses<br>Set minimums |
| Overlooking integration issues | Thoroughly assess the impact of "culture clashes"<br>Can value be created? |
| Poor negotiating techniques | Preplan negotiation strategies, tactics, and strategic objectives |
| Naïve and inexperienced negotiators | Decide on deal breakers ahead of time |
| No meeting transcriptions or minutes | Include a "secretary" as note taker |
| Communications failures | Debrief other party on issues discussed and agreements reached |
| Long time to reach a Term Sheet agreement<br>Deals have a life. A lengthy negotiation for a Term Sheet is an early warning sign of impending impasse | This is the most significant document in the early stages. It should list price, form of payment, deal structure, and management issues. The Letter of Intent will follow the overall principles contained in the Term Sheet |
| Overreliance on a Letter of Intent by seller<br>It is merely "An agreement to agree" | Understanding that a Letter of Intent is a nonbinding agreement. While it is crucially important, an agreement to agree is not an agreement |

The establishment of a methodology for analyzing a potential M&A is the difference between an amateur and an experienced buyer. Table 12.2 presents a summary of best practices to be followed.

## 12.6 Strategic International Alliances

Strategic international alliances (SIAs) are sought as a way to shore up weaknesses and increase competitive strengths. Opportunities for rapid expansion into new markets, access to new technology, more efficient production and marketing costs, and additional sources of capital are all motives for engaging in SIAs [5].

An SIA is a business relationship established by two or more companies to cooperate out of mutual need and to share risk in achieving a common objective. An SIA implies (1) that there is a common objective; (2) that one partner's weakness is offset by the other's strength; (3) that reaching the objective alone would be too costly, take too much time, or be too risky; and (4) that together their respective strengths make possible what otherwise would be unattainable. In short, an SIA is a synergistic relationship established to achieve a common goal where both parties benefit.

Opportunities abound the world over but, to benefit, firms must be current in new technology, have the ability to keep abreast of technological change, have distribution systems to capitalize on global demand, have cost-effective manufacturing, and have capital to build new systems as necessary. Other reasons to enter into strategic alliances include the following:

1. Acquiring needed current market bases
2. Acquiring needed technological bases
3. Utilizing excess manufacturing capacity
4. Reducing new market risk and entry costs
5. Accelerating product introductions demanded by rapid technological changes and shorter product life cycles
6. Achieving economies of scale in production, research and development (R&D), or marketing
7. Overcoming cultural and trade barriers
8. Extending the existing scope of operations

The scope of what a company needs to do and what it can do is at a point where even the largest firms engage in alliances to maintain their competitiveness.

A company enters a strategic alliance to acquire the skills necessary to achieve its objectives more effectively, and at a lower cost or with less risk than if it acted alone.

For example, a company strong in R&D skills and weak in the ability or capital to successfully market a product will seek an alliance to offset its weakness—one partner to provide marketing skills and capital and the other to provide technology and a product. The majority of alliances today are designed to exploit markets and technology.

Of course, not all SIAs are successful; some fail and others are dissolved after reaching their goals. Failures can be attributed to a variety of reasons, but all revolve around lack of perceived benefits to one or more of the partners. Benefits may never have been realized in some cases, and different goals and management styles have caused dissatisfaction in other alliances.

## 12.7 Strategic Alliances and Partnerships

In an increasingly challenging marketplace, where mergers have failed to deliver R&D productivity gains, the importance of alliances has increased significantly [6]. In fact, research suggests that products co-developed by a pharmaceutical and biotech company are more likely to be commercialized than those that are developed by a single entity [7].

Demonstrating the growing importance of strategic alliances, "the 20 biggest pharmaceutical firms formed nearly 1,500 alliances with biotech companies between 1997 and 2002" [8]. In the highly competitive drug industry, effective alliance strategies have provided an opportunity to proactively manage risk.

### 12.7.1 International Alliances Examples

An interesting example of a successful alliance strategy may be the giant pharmaceutical company Merck, which has undergone a dramatic business development transformation. Long regarded as the pharmaceutical industry's best at internal R&D and admired for its ability to rely on its internal capability, Merck has changed corporate course and now aggressively pursues external licensing and alliance opportunities to feed its pipeline. Merck's partnership transactions have risen by almost 80%. In addition, Merck is actively engaging in co-promotion. In the past few years, three of four drug launches were co-promoted [9].

For example, the partnership between Roche and Genentech is often cited as the most successful strategic alliance to date in the industry. In 1990, Roche bought 10% of Genentech for $490 million, giving them a 60% stake and control. The agreement gave Roche a much-coveted access to Genentech's data after the completion of Phase II trials, with the option to decide if they wanted to commercialize the tested product.

While Genentech maintained its independence, Roche obtained ownership of a growing entrepreneurial company without fear of stifling innovation. Roche also gained access to a pipeline it could market outside the United States. The deal benefited Genentech by providing much needed funding and by freeing up management to focus on the core business rather than raising capital. In two separate deals, Roche's total investment in Genentech was approximately $7.7 billion. Overall, Roche raised about "$8 billion in cash after the IPO and they still own 54 percent of Genentech worth about $28 billion" [10].

In 2015, Roche maintained its strategic alliance momentum by partnering with US diagnostics firm GeneWEAVE BioSciences "superbug" diagnostics firm for up to $425 million. Roche planned to pay shareholders in the privately held Californian company $190 million upfront and up to a further $235 million depending on the future success of its products [11].

The deal gives Roche access to GeneWEAVE's "Smarticles" technology, which allows for the rapid identification of multidrug-resistant organisms direct from clinical samples, without the need for traditional preparation processes. Better testing is seen as central to fighting drug-resistant bacteria. It should allow doctors to make faster and more accurate diagnoses and give patients the appropriate drug to kill their particular infection. Roche has been building up its presence in antibacterial research since buying Switzerland's Polyphor, a developer of new medicines for resistant bacteria, in November 2013. Although Roche pioneered some of the more modern antibiotics, like many large drug-makers, it wound down its research at the end of the 1990s, given the poor returns in the antibiotics field compared to other therapy areas such as cancer.

## 12.8 Joint Technology Development Alliances

There is an increasing trend in business today toward the joint development of technology by two or more corporate partners. Whether these arrangements are called joint development agreements, joint ventures, corporate partnering, alliances, or other names, there are some basic legal considerations that must be considered when a joint development of technology is employed [12].

Typically, the motivating factor for a joint-development arrangement is that each of the parties brings a needed piece of the technology puzzle to the table. For example, one company may have excellent basic research, but not the practical development expertise needed to launch a successful product. Another common situation involves the joint adaptation of an existing product to a new market.

The joint-development arrangement is usually embodied in a written contract between two or more partners. The contract is the framework on which the relationship is built and must be negotiated and drafted carefully and completely in order to be effective. The contract may govern the relationship of the parties for many years and may be referred to when conflicts or other issues arise. Thus, it is important to raise and negotiate the major points at minimum of the contract in order to avoid uncertainty and potential time-consuming and expensive litigation.

One example of a possible resolution of the technology ownership question would be to determine that those inventions that are created as a result of work on the contract solely by an employee or employees of partner A are owned by partner A; inventions that are conceived during the term of the contract solely by an employee or employees of partner B are owned by partner B. In the case of inventions conceived jointly by an employee or employees of both partners, the invention can be owned in joint, undivided interests by partner A and partner B, meaning that either partner can practice the invention without accounting to the other.

## 12.9  Strategic Partnership Licensing

Licensing implies a legally binding agreement between parties who receive and exchange approximately equal benefits and value. A voluntary license must be a win–win arrangement in order to be successful [13]. Successful partnership licensing depends on five fundamental principles.

1. **Technology licensing only occurs when one of the parties owns valuable intangible assets, such as IP.** A license is a consent by the owner to the use of IP in exchange for money or something else of value. Technology licensing does not occur when there is no commercially viable IP.

2. **There are three different kinds of technology licenses.** Licenses may be for certain IP rights only (e.g., a license to practice an identified patent or to copy and distribute a certain work of authorship). Licenses may be for *all the IP rights of any kind* that are necessary to reproduce, make, use, market, and sell products based on a type of technology (e.g., a license to develop a new software product that is protected by patent, copyright, trademark, and trade secret law). A license may also be for all the IP rights necessary in order to create and market a product that complies with a technical standard or specification (e.g., a group of enterprises has agreed on a technical standard to ensure interoperability of devices—the group agrees to pool their IP rights and license to each other all rights each will need to manufacture and sell the product).

3. **Technology licensing occurs in the context of a business relationship in which other agreements are often important.** These agreements are interrelated, whether they are in distinct documents or integrated in one big document.

4. **Technology licensing negotiations, like all negotiations, have sides (parties) whose interests are different, but must coincide in some ways.** It is difficult to successfully negotiate a license where you wish to obtain the rights to technology if you have little to offer in return. Ideally, both sides to the negotiation will have different elements of value to offer, including, for example, skilled employees, a market that can be commercially exploited, know-how, research facilities and commitments, and some form of IP.

5. **Technology licensing involves reaching agreement on a complex set of terms, and advance preparation is essential.** In advance of the negotiation, before the other party has been approached, a party may spend many months defining business objectives, assessing leverage, researching the other party, deciding positions on key terms, preparing documentation, and protecting IP, among other tasks.

## 12.10 IP Joint Ownership in Strategic Alliances

An issue that arises in any joint-development arrangement is the contribution of each partner to the project. In the written contract, each partner's contribution can be set forth in a list or table that is either part of the main contract or an appendix to it. This can include the scope of the work, where the work is to be performed, a schedule for the completion of various tasks, and which partner will perform each portion of the work. An important consideration is the so-called background technology. Often, one or more partners will own patents or trade secrets that must be used if the joint development is to be a success. In this case, licenses may have to be granted under the contract, or if a new entity is formed for the joint development (such as a joint venture company), licenses may have to be granted to that new entity. As with any legal document, the more specific the listings of each partner's contribution, the better the contract.

Joint ownership often arises in connection with collaborative innovation, joint ventures, and more generally to any research project involving the co-development of IP [14]. Generally speaking, joint ownership, also called co-ownership, refers to a situation in which two or more persons have proprietary shares of an asset: they co-own a property.

Joint ownership of IP, in particular, frequently arises in collaborative projects. In most cases, one or both partners contribute IP rights to the project—usually called *background technology.* As the partners begin to work cooperatively, when the results—usually called *foreground technology*—have been jointly generated by the collaboration partners, the share of work is not easily ascertainable.

In this context, background technology means all confidential information and IP rights that are owned by a Party other than Foreground and that have contributed to the strategic alliance. Foreground technology means any inventions, improvements, and other innovations relating to the technology, developed by either party in connection with the collaboration project, plus all the related confidential information and IP rights. Table 12.3 clarifies what is being contributed by each partner.

**TABLE 12.3**

What Is Being Contributed?

- Intellectual property
- Patents, trade secrets, trademarks
- Background IP
- Foreground IP
- Available capital
- Capabilities (testing, access to technical expertise, manufacturing)
- Marketing expertise
- Sales and sales channels
- Related products outside core technology

**TABLE 12.4**

Roles Each Partner May Play in IP Co-Ownership

| Joint Inventor | Executor |
|---|---|
| Originally conceived the idea | Describes a hypothesis for proof of concept |
| Materially (technical, financial) contributes to the invention development | Follows instructions |
| Provides solutions to problems as they arise | Performs standard procedures |
| Provides the background innovation | Executes necessary P–O–C testing |

Even more precisely, for a work to be considered jointly owned, two basic requirements are needed:

1. **Originality**, in the sense that one partner's contribution could be considered as its own personal creation
2. **Indivisibility**, in the sense that one partner's contribution is not easily discernible from the other's contribution

Table 12.4 clarifies the roles each partner may play in IP co-ownership.

Many people confuse the concepts of the ownership of IP and the inventorship or authorship of creations, or sometimes they are simply not aware of their different nature. Yet, it is crucial to understand how to manage these rights as their improper handling could cause real problems, such as the validity of IP rights granted or the risks of legal disputes [15].

## 12.11 The Complex Issue of Modifications to the Background Technology

A very important, but often overlooked aspect of a joint-development arrangement is the ownership of any IP rights arising out of the development work. For example, during the term of the contract, if an employee of partner A and an employee of partner B jointly create an invention, who owns the resulting technology? There are a number of ways of resolving technology-ownership issues. The key point is that the issues must be raised in negotiations and that the resolutions are reflected in the language of the contract.

Of particular importance is the definition of modifications to the background. It is not always easy to draw a distinction between derivative work and new work made under collaborative effort. Once the parties have defined the joint IP expected to be generated as "project results," a clear mention about the ownership of the background modifications should be included within the contract.

As far as the jointly owned IP is concerned, there are several ways to apportion it. Normally, this should be in line with the scope of the project. Because the background technology is needed to achieve results through the partners' collaborating efforts, one of the most common structures is the equal share of foreground ownership between collaboration partners. A particularly common agreement is shown below:

- Each Party retains exclusive property of its own background.
- The modifications to or derivative works of the parties' background shall be the sole property of the contributing party.
- Foreground developed in connection with the collaboration project hereof shall be jointly owned in equal shares by parties.

## 12.12 Rights of Exploitation

Through joint ownership contractual arrangements, parties are able to define the terms by which each co-owner can assign, license, and in general exploit jointly owned foreground. Such activities can be done with or without the consent of the other parties, depending on the partners' interests.

One important issue to be agreed from the outset is the compensation that the other partners will have in respect of the exploitation of the joint foreground made by one party, as described below:

RIGHT OF EXPLOITATION—first option [consent required]

1. A Party shall not pledge, assign, sell, or otherwise dispose of its interest in the foreground to third parties without the other Party's prior written consent.
2. Licensing of foreground to third parties shall require written agreement between the Parties, setting out their respective rights and obligations, including but not limited to, the distribution of licensing costs and income.

RIGHT OF EXPLOITATION—second option [consent not required]

1. Each Party shall have the right to pledge, assign, or otherwise dispose of its interest in the foreground to third parties as they may desire notifying its intention to the other Party [...] days before the activity concerned.

2. Each Party shall have the right to grant [type of licenses] on the foreground to third parties as they may desire without accounting to the other Party.
3. The total income after deducting costs as derived from the licensing of the foreground shall be distributed [...%] to Party [...] and [...%] to Party [...]. According to the type of license granted, said distribution *ratio* may be adjusted upon written agreement by the Parties.

## 12.13 Management of the Jointly Owned IP

Management of the jointly owned IP refers to the protection, maintenance, and defense of the foreground generated under the collaboration project. That is to say, contractual rules should set forth how confidential information, IP rights filing, prosecution, and infringement should be dealt with by the co-owners.

### 12.13.1 IP Rights Prosecution

Starting with the assumption that the IP rights protection and maintenance costs can be equally shared between joint owners, parties may also establish the following:

- Who will decide to protect the IP generated or keep it as a trade secret
- Who will follow the procedures to register the IP rights
- Who will bear the costs of the IP rights prosecution and maintenance

Where the designated party might fail to, or decide not to, file an application for the granting of IP rights, contractual provision should allow other parties to take steps in place of the unfulfilling party.

A further consideration is territory for ownership of the invention. In some cases, one partner may want ownership of all inventions in a specific country created during the term of the contract, whether created by their company, the other company, or jointly. Finally, the contract may also specify that although one partner may own the invention, the other may have a license to use or practice the invention either for a royalty payment or royalty-free. The license can be either exclusive or nonexclusive.

Ancillary to the ownership issue is the responsibility of the partners to file, prosecute, and maintain patent applications on the inventions. Usually, the

**TABLE 12.5**

IP Applications Filing, Prosecution, and Costs

First option [shared management]. Sample clauses

1. The Parties shall decide, by mutual agreement, whether to file, prosecute, and maintain IP rights protection of the foreground. The Parties shall equally bear all costs resulting from these activities.
2. The Parties shall agree which Party shall conduct the activities thereof in the names of and on behalf of the Parties. The elected Party shall provide a copy of relevant documents relating to the activities thereof for the other Parties examination.
3. If a Party declines to bear its share of the costs associated with the activities thereof, the other Parties may conduct such activities in their own name and at their own expense. The declining Party shall retain its rights of use, but shall lose its rights of ownership and exploitation in respect of foreground.

Second option [single management]

1. Party […] hereto agrees to file, prosecute, and maintain IP rights applications of the foreground in a timely manner and at its own expense and after consultation with the other Parties.
2. Within […] days of receipt of filing, Party […] shall provide the other Parties with copies of the IP rights applications and all documents received from or filed with the relevant IP office in connection with the prosecution of such applications, for the other Parties' examination.
3. If Party […] elects not to file IP rights applications, it so informs the other Parties […] days before the expiration of any applicable filing deadline, priority period, or other statutory date, so that such other parties may elect to file and prosecute IP rights applications at their own expense. The declining Party shall retain its rights of use, but shall lose its rights of ownership and exploitation in respect of foreground.

owner of the invention is given the first right to file, prosecute, and maintain (as well as pay for) patents throughout the world. In the event of joint ownership, the partners may share in the costs of the patents. If the first right is not exercised, the contract usually requires that notice be provided to the other partner or partners, and the notified partner or partners then have the right to file, prosecute, and maintain the patents. In that case, it is conventional that the partner who undertakes the expense of filing, prosecuting, and maintaining the patents will assume ownership of them, as shown in Table 12.5.

### 12.13.2 IP Rights Infringement

Of extreme importance are also the defense of the IP rights and the consequent handling of infringement claims. Hence, joint owners should agree which of the parties will be responsible for monitoring and policing the joint IP and pay the expenses for any infringement in connection with it. The latter can arise either because the jointly owned IP infringes third-party IP rights or because it is the third party who infringes the co-owned IP, as shown below:

INFRINGEMENT CLAIMS. Sample clauses

1. Each Party shall be responsible for monitoring and defending the joint IP. Each Party will, however, notify the other Parties promptly if it has a reasonable basis for believing that the joint IP has been infringed by a third party or if the joint IP would infringe any IP right of a third party.
2. The Parties shall equally bear any costs in connection with the law prosecution of third-parties' infringement of the joint IP. Any accorded awards will be shared in equal parts.
3. The Parties shall equally bear any costs in connection with claims that the joint IP infringes third parties' IP rights.

### 12.13.3 Termination Clauses

Another major issue is termination. This issue is often avoided because it is akin to discussing with your future spouse what happens if you get divorced. Unpleasant as it may seem, full discussion concerning how a contract is to be terminated and the ramifications of such termination will avoid many later problems that can lead to costly and time-consuming litigation. Termination clauses must be drafted carefully and completely because it is those clauses that are the most carefully reviewed once a relationship starts to go wrong.

Termination clauses should specify how and when one partner can end the relationship. Often, the contract can be terminated only by breach of contract by the other partner, subject to a period (usually 30 days) to remedy the breach. The termination clause should set forth detailed procedures regarding how notices (preferably in writing) should be made to the other partners and, importantly, the effective date of the notice (i.e., effective upon sending the notice or effective when the other party receives the notice). There should also be clear provisions as to ownership of the tangible assets (e.g., pilot and laboratory equipment) brought to the arrangement. Furthermore, any continuing rights to use the background technology or technology developed during the term of the contract should be spelled out.

## 12.14 Summary Questions

Now that you have explored the intricacies of strategic alliances, you are in a better position to answer the following questions:

- Is your interest in the venture/alliance primarily strategic or financial in nature?

- What consequences would stem from a sale of your interests in the venture/alliance?

- Why does it make sense for you to partner on this project rather than go it alone?

- What opportunities will you forgo by entering into the venture/alliance?

- What is the scope of the noncompetition and exclusivity provisions that are envisioned?

- What are the strengths that each party brings to the table?

- What are the parties' bargaining powers, both up front and over time?

- How much money do you wish to invest in the venture, both up front and over time?

- What are the expected exit strategies and do all parties have a shared view of the likely exit scenarios?

- Have you adequately considered all that could go wrong with the venture/alliance and how to adequately protect its interests in such various downside scenarios?

## References

1. Marzec, E. http://smallbusiness.chron.com/difference-between-joint-venture-strategic-alliance-11922.html.
2. Root, F. *Entry Strategies for International Markets*. Lexington Books, 1987, http://teaching.ust.hk/~mgto650p/meyer/readings/9c/Root.pdf.
3. Irwin, T. http://www.tcii.co.uk/2013/04/04/avoiding-the-pitfalls-of-strategic-alliances/.
4. Rigsbee, E. The Pitfalls to Successful Strategic Alliances, http://www.rigsbee.com/ps5.htm.
5. International market entry strategies, http://highered.mheducation.com/sites/dl/free/0077122852/823243/gha22852_Ch11.pdf.
6. Cohen, J., Gangi, W., Lineen, J., and Manard, A. Strategic Alternatives in the Pharmaceutical Industry. Kellogg School of Management, https://www.kellogg.northwestern.edu/research/biotech/faculty/articles/strategic_alternatives.pdf.
7. Shalo, S. *The Art of the Deal*. BioPartnerships—A Pharmaceutical Executive and Biopharm International Supplement, October 2004, pp. 8–16.
8. Lam, M.D. Dangerous liaisons. *Pharmaceutical Executive*, 24(5), 72, May 2004.

9. Bernard, S. *Back to the Pharma Future*. BioPartnerships—A Pharmaceutical Executive and Biopharm International Supplement, October 2004, pp. 6–7.
10. Mills, L. Great science not all that matters developing treatments. *Financial Times*. 11/10/2004, p. 5.
11. http://www.reuters.com/article/2015/08/13/us-roche-diagnostics-bacteria -idUSKCN0QI0OA20150813.
12. Radack, D. Joint technology development arrangements. *JOM*, 49(2), 68, 1997. A publication of The Minerals, Metals & Materials Society, http://tms.org/pubs /journals/JOM/matters/matters-9702.html.
13. WIPO. Successful technology licensing, http://www.wipo.int/edocs/pubdocs /en/licensing/903/wipo_pub_903.pdf.
14. IP joint ownership. European IP Helpdesk. 2013, https://www.iprhelpdesk.eu /sites/default/files/newsdocuments/IP_joint_ownership_updated.pdf.
15. https://www.iprhelpdesk.eu/sites/default/files/newsdocuments/Inventorship _Authorship_Ownership_final_1.pdf.

# 13

## Deciding to Be Acquired

### 13.1 Introduction

As a start-up, you may decide to be acquired by an established strategic partner before launching your knowledge-based product. Many entrepreneurs no longer build companies for the long term; they build companies for the short term, hoping to sell their company for quicker exits.

When we use the term *merger*, we are referring to the merging of two companies where one new company will continue to exist. The term *acquisition* refers to the acquisition of assets by one company from another company. In an acquisition, both companies may continue to exist. However, throughout this chapter, we will loosely refer to mergers and acquisitions (M&A) as a business transaction where one company acquires another company. The acquiring company (the buyer, acquiror, or acquirer) remains in business and retains its corporate name. The acquired company (the seller, target) will be integrated into the acquiring company and, thus, the acquired company ceases to exist after the merger.

Every M&A deal has its own unique reasons why the combining of two companies is a good business decision. The underlying principle behind M&A is deceptively simple: 2 + 2 = 5. The joining or merging of the two companies should theoretically create economic value that we call "synergy" value. Synergy value can take three forms [1]:

1. **Expenses:** By combining the two companies, you will realize lower expenses than if the two companies operate separately. Thus, the hugely expensive launch of your first product can be better absorbed by the combination of the two companies.

2. **Revenues:** By combining the two companies, you will realize higher revenues than if the two companies were to operate separately.

3. **Cost of capital:** By combining the two companies, you will experience a lower overall cost of capital. Thus, the combined companies will have a stronger balance sheet.

Strategic M&A alliances allow money-hungry start-ups to pursue their individual strategies despite limited financial resources. These alliances allow the entrepreneur to pursue product launches with greater likelihood of commercial success.

## 13.2 Mergers and Acquisitions

**Mergers and acquisitions** are an aspect of corporate strategy, corporate finance, and management dealing with the buying, selling, dividing, and combining of different companies and similar entities that can help an enterprise grow rapidly in its sector or location of origin, or a new field or new location, without creating a subsidiary or another child entity or using a joint venture [2].

### 13.2.1 Mergers

Theoretically, a **merger** happens when two firms agree to go forward as a single new company rather than remain separately owned and operated. This kind of action is more precisely referred to as a "merger of equals." In practice, however, actual mergers of equals don't happen very often. Usually, one company will buy another and, as part of the deal's terms, simply allow the acquired firm to proclaim that the action is a merger of equals, even if it is technically an acquisition [2].

### 13.2.2 Acquisitions

Practically speaking, an **acquisition** is the process through which one company completely takes over the controlling interest of another company. Such controlling interest may be 100%, or nearly 100%, of the assets or ownership equity of the acquired entity. An "acquisition" usually refers to a purchase of a smaller firm by a larger one.

## 13.3 The Acquisition Courtship by Motivated Strategic Buyers

You have developed your initial idea into a knowledge-based product. It has taken a lot of sweat and hard work, and you have experienced and overcome many technical challenges. Strategic buyers are now taking note of your development and making inquiries.

A strategic buyer is a type of buyer in an acquisition that has a very specific reason for wanting to purchase the company. Strategic buyers look for companies that will create a synergy with their existing businesses [3].

Because strategic buyers (also known as synergistic buyers) may actually get more value out of an acquisition than the intrinsic value of the company being acquired, strategic buyers will usually be willing to pay a premium price in order to have the deal go through. You have arrived!! Right? Well, not quite.

According to Lior Zorea of startupPerColator [4], the potential acquisition courtship that starts with these preliminary conversations will be lengthy, complex, and potentially very disruptive to your business. It will take away significant management attention from the day-to-day operations, and leaks can affect your ability to retain your employees and, potentially, your customers.

Since deals have a life span, the longer the process takes, the greater the potential for a transaction to fall through. While the acquisition process is generally well established, time is not on your side. When the acquisition call comes in, you want to be ready. You have limited resources, but by focusing on a few key areas, you can make a big difference in accelerating the process and the likelihood of a successful transaction.

1. **Maintain good records on an ongoing basis.** Strategic buyers, particularly serial acquirers, have professional corporate development and/or acquisition teams. They have been through the process many times and approach it in a very systematic and serious fashion. You want to be ready to handle the detailed, lengthy, and invasive due diligence process. The pace can be overwhelming at times, but you can alleviate that dynamic by getting your records "due-diligence ready." Consult your legal and financial advisors to find a solution that is most appropriate for you.

2. **Maintain your credibility.** Acquirers do not expect start-ups to be perfectly oiled organizations, but they will nevertheless demand perfection, as if you are a multibillion dollar organization. As you well know, problems and issues come up with your business on a regular basis and acquirers know that. Some are less important and some are serious. You may have a disgruntled former co-founder, you may have imperfections or gaps in your IP title, you may have accounting or tax issues—whatever it is, own up to it.

   Acquirers with professional M&A teams will ultimately dig up these issues during due diligence. When they do and, particularly, when it is at the tail end of a lengthy transaction, it can be harmful to the relationship, potentially causing the acquirer to revalue your business or, if serious enough, kill the deal.

3. **Lean on your advisors.** Your key advisors in an M&A transaction are your legal and financial advisory teams. The process can be daunting and complex and you may not have the benefit of having venture capitalists or other professional board members with significant M&A experience. Talk to your advisors and educate yourself about the process. Set realistic expectations for how long the process will take. Your financial advisor's job is to create market interest for your business and, ultimately, to maximize your valuation. Both your bankers and lawyers are experts in structuring transactions—broadly speaking, bankers will focus on economics and lawyers on terms and post-closing liabilities. Work with each to maximize your understanding of the process and the deal structure that is optimal *for you and your team.*

4. **Maintain control of the process.** There are lots of players and each has its own set of interests. The key players are the executives driving the deal at the acquirer and members of your management team, but there are many other players, including the acquirer's finance, legal and M&A teams, the bankers, the lawyers, and the accountants. In most deals, a working group list is put together at the beginning of the process to allow for good communication among the parties. With all these players contributing to the process, sometimes deals, particularly larger deals, tend to gain a momentum of their own. It is a natural and welcomed result of the process.

   As the target-company chief executive officer (CEO), you may find it difficult to run your business and maintain firm control of the process. Lots of decisions are made in the negotiation process, some which you may not even be aware of. To assist you in the process, identify the key executives and advisors who will be your core M&A execution team and meet with them on a regular basis to make sure that the transaction is progressing in a manner you are comfortable.

5. **The devil is in the details.** When selling the business, the parties typically focus on the aggregate purchase price. However, hidden value or hidden costs can be buried in the deal terms and can have a significant impact on the bottom line economics. For example, is the portion of the purchase price that is paid in stock subject to vesting after closing? If so, under what conditions can stock be forfeited? Are the indemnification provisions for the benefit of the acquirer outside market norms, and do they expose the equity holders to potentially outsized clawbacks of the purchase price?

6. **Pigs get fat, and hogs get slaughtered.** Be thoughtful and aggressive (but realistic) in positioning your business in the marketplace and crafting your value proposition to potential acquirers [5]. Accordingly, private companies need to think long before dismissing overtures from strategically motivated suitors. Listen carefully

to your advisors (and follow their advice). They know the market well, and when an acquirer has a number of potential competing targets to choose from, you want to take reasonable action in light of all the facts available to you. If your acquirer turns negative on the deal and instead decides to buy one of your competitors and if at the same time other potential acquirers have also acquired certain of your competitors, your position as a viable acquisition target may diminish significantly.

## 13.4 The Enduring Questions

Before consummation of the transaction, the buyer and the seller find themselves in an adversarial position. Table 13.1 lists the 10 most frequently asked questions in buying or selling a business. Paradoxically, although the questions look similar, the answers are not.

The list below presents the 10 biggest risks/challenges faced by start-ups when contemplating being acquired by a strategic acquirer:

1. Amount of funding available to execute the product launch
2. Overcoming weak market acceptance
3. Successful integration of the cultures

**TABLE 13.1**

The Ten Most Frequently Asked Questions

| Seller ("Target") | Buyer ("Acquirer") |
|---|---|
| Why is their offering price so low? | Why is their asking price so high? |
| Are they bottom fishing? | Are they serious about selling? |
| Is it OK for us to shop around? | This should be a no-shop negotiation. |
| Why are they interested in us? | What do we really know about them? |
| Do we really need money now? | What will they do with our money? |
| Is this transaction for cash or shares? | What are their future financial demands? |
| Who should be part of our negotiation team? | Are we really negotiating with the decision-makers? |
| How much independence do we retain post-transaction? | How do we integrate them into our winning culture? |
| Could we do better on our own? | Do we really need them? |
| What happens if the deal collapses? How vulnerable do we remain? | What if we find deal-killers during due diligence? |
| What happens if our CEO is run over by the mythical train during negotiations? | How indispensable is their CEO? Do they have a succession strategy? |

4. Purchase price gap between target and acquirer

5. Possible turnover of key personnel

6. Technology transfer hurdles

7. Consolidation and integration of manufacturing

8. Credibility of technical and marketing forecasts

9. Competitive response to the contemplated merger

10. Tax implications and shareholder's reply

## 13.5 The Due Diligence Process

There is a common thread that runs throughout much of the M&A process. It is called due diligence. Due means "appropriate" or "warranted," and diligence means "careful assessment" or "detailed analysis."

Due diligence is a comprehensive and extensive evaluation of the proposed transaction. An overriding question is, "Will this merger work?" In order to answer this question, we must determine what kind of "fit" exists between the two companies. This includes the following:

- **Investment Fit**—What financial resources will be required, what level of risk fits with the new organization, and so on?

- **Strategic Fit**—What management strengths are brought together through this M&A? Both sides must bring something unique to the table to create synergies.

- **Marketing Fit**—How will products and services complement one another between the two companies? How well do various components of marketing fit together—promotion programs, brand names, distribution channels, customer mix, and so on?

- **Operating Fit**—How well do the different business units and production facilities fit together? How do operating elements fit together—labor force, technologies, production capacities, and so on?

- **Management Fit**—What expertise and talents do both companies bring to the merger? How well do these elements mesh together—leadership styles, strategic thinking, ability to change, and so on?

- **Financial Fit**—How well do financial elements fit together—sales, profitability, return on capital, cash flow, and so on?

## 13.6 Cultural Issues in M&A

The business world seems littered with integrated companies that have lost value for shareholders. The question that inevitably arises is, "What forces are powerful enough to counteract the value-creating energy of economies of scale or global market presence?" [6].

Culture has emerged as one of the dominant barriers to effective integrations. In one study, culture was found to be the cause of 30% of failed integrations [7]. Companies with different cultures find it difficult, if not often impossible, to make decisions quickly and correctly or to operate effectively.

### 13.6.1 What Is Corporate "Culture"?

In plain English, culture is "how we do things around here." Deal and Kennedy [8] created a model of culture that is based on four different types of organizations. They each focus on how quickly the organization receives feedback, the way members are rewarded, and the level of risks taken:

1. **Work-hard, play-hard culture:** This has rapid feedback/reward and low risk resulting in the following: Stress coming from quantity of work rather than uncertainty. High-speed action leading to high-speed recreation. Examples: restaurants, software companies, and ladies' shoe manufacturers.

2. **Tough-guy macho culture:** This has rapid feedback/reward and high risk, resulting in the following: Stress coming from high risk and potential loss/gain of reward. Focus on the present rather than the longer-term future. Examples: police, surgeons, politicians, and sports figures.

3. **Process culture:** This has slow feedback/reward and low risk, resulting in the following: Low stress, plodding work, comfort, and security; stress that comes from internal politics and stupidity of the system; and development of bureaucracies and other ways of maintaining the status quo. Focus on security of the past and of the future. Examples: banks, insurance companies, teaching hospitals, and universities.

4. **You-bet-your-company culture:** This has slow feedback/reward and high risk, resulting in the following: Stress coming from high risk and delay before knowing if actions have paid off. The long view is taken, but then much work is put into making sure things happen as planned. Examples: aircraft manufacturers, oil companies, and start-ups.

Culture consists of the long-standing, largely implicit shared values, beliefs, and historical assumptions that influence behavior, attitudes, and meaning in a company (or society). This definition has three important implications:

1. **Culture is implicit.** People who share in a culture find their culture challenging to recognize. The most insightful cultural observers often are outsiders, because cultural givens are not implicit to them.
2. **Culture influences how people behave and how people understand their own actions.** As a result, culturally influenced beliefs and actions feel right to people, even while their implicit underpinnings make it difficult for those people to understand why they act the way they do or why other ways of acting might also be appropriate.
3. **Culture is resilient and enduring.** Its elements are long-standing, not a matter of fads. The resilience of culture is supported by culture being implicit. It is difficult for people to recognize their own culture and how it exerts an influence on them. The staying power of culture is that it feels right to people; new cultural values that are imposed on people seldom replace their underlying values and beliefs in the long run.

According to Larry Senn [9], M&As are a fact of life in today's highly competitive global business environment. Unfortunately, statistics indicate that up to one-third of mergers fail within 5 years, and as many as 80% never live up to their full expectations. Deals go bad because of the reasons shown in Table 13.2.

A great deal of evidence indicates that the ultimate success of M&A and the amount of time it takes to get them on track is determined by how well the cultural aspects of the transition are managed. Best practices show how to systematically and consciously avoid cultural clash and gain the most synergy from any merger or acquisition.

M&As are a key part of many organizations' strategies. Often, billions of dollars are at stake as well as the very future of the organizations and the executives who are coordinating the merger. Unfortunately, more often than not, the benefits of mergers or acquisitions fail to materialize or fall short of expectations.

Learning to systematically and consciously avoid cultural clash is a necessary skill because mergers are a fact of life in business. One reason is the continuing consolidation of industries. Phone companies, cellular companies,

**TABLE 13.2**

Deals Can Go Bad Because…

| | |
|---|---|
| Cultural clashes and incompatibilities | 50% |
| Incompatible strategic rationale | 20% |
| Business model change | 20% |
| Synergies did not materialize | 10% |

utilities, oil companies, financial services companies, insurance companies, healthcare organizations, retailers, defense and electronic companies, and dozens of others are a part of this consolidation trend.

### 13.6.2 The Importance of Addressing the Cultural Clash

Since the human factor is so critical, it is important to understand the role of this phenomenon and to address it in each phase of the merger or acquisition process.

Over a period, organizations, like people, develop distinctive and unique personalities. This personality of the organization has been referred to most often as corporate culture. An individual's personality is made up of one's habits, beliefs, values, and behavioral traits. A company's culture is also made up of its habits, values system, customs, and norms that govern behavior within the organization. The culture reflects the unwritten ground rules of behavior, or simply "the way we do things around here."

As a result of all the personality conflicts, the term *cultural clash* has been coined to describe what happens when two companies' philosophies, styles, values, and habits are in conflict. That may, in fact, be the most dangerous factor when two companies decide to combine.

The "corporate culture" is frequently seen in the larger, better established buyer, and the "entrepreneurial (innovation) culture" is seen in the start-up seller, as explained in Table 13.3.

**TABLE 13.3**

A Clash of Cultures

| Corporate Culture "Buyer" | Entrepreneurial (Innovation) Culture "Seller" |
|---|---|
| Rewards ultraconservative decisions | Trial and error<br>"You will miss 100% of the shots you don't take" |
| Demands to wait for instructions<br>"It usually takes 3 weeks to prepare a good impromptu speech" | Rewards quick actions<br>"Don't punish failure; reward success" |
| Expects "no surprises" | Encourages new approaches that may fail<br>"Starting up is hard to do" |
| Collects information<br>"Paralysis of the analysis" | Expects decisions even under imperfect information<br>"Take risks, not chances" |
| Controls information<br>"Information is power" | Encourages open discussion<br>"Gentlemen do read each other's mail" |
| Structured decision-making process | Make decisions quickly<br>"Decide first, then repent" |
| Market centric | Technology centric |
| Bureaucratic | Democratic |

### 13.6.3 Key Human Problem Areas to Avoid

1. **Loss of key people.** Whenever acquiring an organization, remember that "the natives have the maps." Even if you need to downsize, if not handled right, the wrong people will leave and the venture can be jeopardized. A number of studies document the high exit rate from acquired companies. One survey indicated that only 42% of the managers remained with the acquired company for as long as 5 years ("Merging Human Resources," *Merger and Acquisition Magazine*).

   SBC's acquisition of Pacific Bell is an example of an exodus of senior talent. It was heralded as a merger of equals when the two chairmen announced the historic coupling. It didn't turn out that way. "Within months all six top officers were gone, having either retired or quit. Of its 35 corporate officers, just six remained," reported the article "Executive Exodus" in the *San Francisco Business Times*. Most of this was attributed to a clash in cultures and no attempt to bring the cultures together.

2. **Winners versus losers—"we" versus "they."** When companies are acquired or combined, people almost immediately start to focus on the differences in the companies. They also quickly begin to "keep score" on who are the winners and losers. It is typical in an acquisition for the acquiring company to see themselves as the winners and the acquired company as the losers. Typically, the controlling company wants to impose changes and views those in the acquired company as highly resistant to change.

   On the other hand, the most frequent complaint from employees of companies that are being acquired is that the new owners don't appreciate them. They often feel that they don't get any credit for what they've done well and what is working and that their new leaders only want to point out how the new way is better.

   In a newly merged or acquired company, the appointment of people to positions is closely watched. This is a specific area in which people immediately keep score, tallying which side won or lost on each issue or appointment.

3. **Judgment versus respect for differences.** There is a tendency for each group to be judgmental about the way things are handled by the other. Rather than respecting and building on differences, people frequently enter into right and wrong judgments.

4. **Fear of the unknown—insecurity is the enemy.** Uncertainty and insecurity are associated with almost all mergers or acquisitions. As a merger is announced, fears and anxieties are fueled by uncertainty about what the changes will bring. There is typically a feeling of personal vulnerability and loss of control. People often spend time updating their resumes and exploring their options. People fear the

unknown. It might be more accurately called "fear of the imagined," since people have a tendency to fill in the blanks of what they don't know by imagining the worst.

Whether a merger is for the better or worse, it throws relationships, norms, work behavior and support systems out of balance. If these psychological losses are not addressed early on, chronic problems in attitude and behavior can result.

5. **Loss of organizational effectiveness.** The uncertainty surrounding the change often causes the employees to lose enthusiasm about their work and their organization, and a drop in morale and organizational pride follows the merger. Countless hours are spent feeding the rumor mill, and large numbers of people adopt a wait-and-see attitude. Results usually suffer and customers are lost.

## 13.7 Guidelines for Creating a Successful Merger

The dustbin of business history is loaded with the stories of ill-conceived M&A, but while there are no magical solutions or silver bullets that ensure success, a process that is co-designed by the buyer and seller from the beginning will make the transaction appear seamless and fluid, with a high degree of positive, engaged energy throughout the organization [10]. To that end, below are nine specific recommendations:

1. **Retain your key leaders.** It is essential to identify those people critical to continued success and initiate a plan to ensure that these key people stay and remain engaged and aligned.

2. **Communicate your vision.** The sooner that some semblance of certainty about the future can be communicated, the sooner people will settle down. Once a new vision for the organization is created, new future targets are set, and new teams are connected and aligned, people can refocus their energy in a forward direction.

3. **Address the new organizational structure as early as possible.** Failed mergers are characterized by a tendency to have unclear reporting relationships and frequent changes in the reporting structure. In one study of merger successes and failures, it was found that 81% of the failures were characterized by frequent changes in the reporting relationship after the merger. Successful acquisitions were characterized by clear reporting relationships that were established early on and not changed ("Merging Human Resources," *Merger and Acquisition Magazine*).

4. **As the leader of an acquiring company, go out of your way to acknowledge as many positive aspects of the acquired company as possible.** At the same time, set clear expectations and create an environment in which there is a high level of openness to change.

5. **Avoid throwing out the baby with the bathwater by identifying which cultural factors have historically made an organization great.** For example, if a company had historically been successful based on its culture of service and quality, rapid and insensitive cost-cutting could begin to destroy what made that organization great in the first place. One example is the acquisition of a smaller, highly entrepreneurial company by a larger, more formalized one. That combination poses cultural challenges because it is hard to provide direction and additional structure. However, this must be done without killing the entrepreneurial goose that lays the golden eggs.

6. **Be clear about the nature of the union and be willing to talk about it.** Is it a true merger of equals, an acquisition that attempts to use the best of both, a stand-alone holding company, or just a stand-alone assimilation?

7. **Clearly communicate your mutual benefits.** Most people understand that M&A take place for business reasons. It is important at the outset to communicate the benefits of the merger. People may not like it, but if they see that it has a legitimate purpose, and the benefits are obvious, there is less resentment and employees are more likely to accept it.

8. **Make sure the acquiring company's leaders communicate in person as much as possible.** It is easier to be resentful toward an unknown, invisible giant than it is to be resentful about a person you have personally experienced as being real, rational, and concerned. Successful mergers only happen when senior managers make themselves visible and accessible to all employees affected by the merger and promote the benefits at all levels. Employees at all levels need to experience the buy-in and support of their leaders for the merger or acquisition.

9. **Create an integration plan.** Perform adequate due diligence on the cultures both before and after the merger. Create a specific cultural integration plan led by the CEO and the senior team, not just delegated to the HR team, or to chance.

### 13.7.1 Variations in the Human Nature of M&A

Specific steps needed to deal with the human side of the merger or acquisition are greatly influenced by the basis for the merger as well as the cultures of the organizations. For example, in a merger where the acquiring company is interested only in the physical and financial assets of a target company and expects to lay off most managers and employees, major efforts to manage culture are unnecessary. However, when a true "marriage of two equals" is the end goal, attention to the management of culture becomes critical and detailed planning is most crucial. The varying goals for merger outcomes are shown below in their most common forms.

1. **Autonomy or semi-autonomy.** In the "hands-off" scenario, the goal is to create mutual support and synergy without necessarily changing the nature of the organizations. It is unrealistic to assume that the acquiring company will not want some modifications. For example, there may be a desire to shift one or more qualities, such as innovation, bias for action, and a higher level of expectations. This is graphically shown in Figure 13.1.

   However, when the basis for the acquisition is autonomy or semi-autonomy, it is important to respect the reasons for the differences in culture and to proceed slowly with integration activities.

2. **Absorb and assimilate.** If the goal is to completely absorb and assimilate the acquired company, then the primary need is to educate the acquired employees in the rules of the new corporate culture. Edgar Schein [11] provides us with a working definition of the corporate culture: "a pattern of shared basic assumptions that the group learned as it solved its problems of external adaptation and internal integration, that has worked well enough to be considered valid and therefore, to be taught to new members as the correct way to perceive, think, and feel in relation to those problems."

   It should be remembered that they have been playing a different game under a different set of unwritten as well as written ground rules. Orientation to the new organization should include

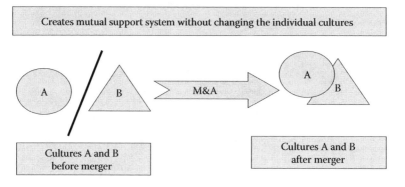

**FIGURE 13.1**
Autonomous M&A.

letting them know about the vision and values of their new organization. It is also important to focus on how the new game is going to be different and not on judging the past or telling them why what they were doing was wrong. This is graphically shown in Figure 13.2.

3. **Co-create a new entity (integrated cultures).** While avoiding cultural clash is always important, the greatest attention should be paid to successful cultural integration when a true marriage of equals is intended (see Figure 13.3).

The acquiring company must capture the full value of the merger by integrating carefully each element of both organizations. The development of an integrated culture is one of the critical factors for M&A success. The initial challenge for all organizations that consider a merger or acquisition is to

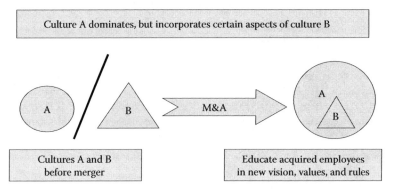

**FIGURE 13.2**
Absorb and assimilate.

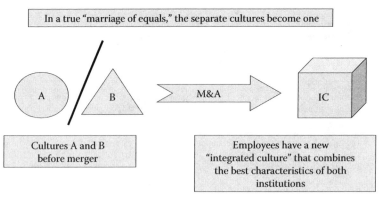

**FIGURE 13.3**
Integrated cultures.

understand that the culture has deep roots that cannot be easily pulled out, examined, and reprogrammed to create a new shared culture. As Beaudan and Smith admonish: creating an integrated culture involves careful discovery, inventing, reseeding, and letting go [12].

## 13.8 How to Successfully Integrate Cultures

This is easier said than done. To successfully integrate the two cultures, savvy acquirers first define the cultural objective in broad terms. This is invariably a job for the chief executives—and the CEO of the buying company as well as the founder of the target company must be willing to sustain their commitment until the objective is realized [13]. Integrating cultures can be achieved by adhering to the following activities:

1. **Integrate teams and shape culture.** Whenever new leaders or new teams at any level are put in place, processes to align those teams around the greater vision and direction are vital. Companies can no longer afford to take months to get acquainted and work out differences.

   Off-site sessions with the top leaders are vital as part of a process to begin reshaping the culture to a desired new state. This brings new teams together in a relaxed and collaborative environment to focus their energy in the same direction.

   Use of a more formal, customized culture-shaping process is often skipped owing to the demand of business. This leads to unintended loss of people and slow starts for teams, and wastes time and energy.

   A "cultural clash" is not hypothetical. It is real and it happens among people who have not taken the time to develop openness and trust. Think of a team of newly drafted ball players trying to play in the major leagues with no practice, no commonly understood signals, and no time to learn to play well together. It wouldn't matter how good the individual players were; they probably wouldn't succeed. A customized process can be used to embed the new values and shape the culture through values and guiding behaviors.

2. **Inspire and align people around vision, mission, and shared values.** During a merger or acquisition, people need to be inspired to move toward new goals and visions. In the absence of a compelling purpose for a new organization, people tend to stay locked in the past and to unhealthy speculation.

### 13.8.1 Role of the Senior Team

In a merger designed to create a new combined entity, the senior teams of each organization need to work together to clarify the new mission and the shared values, or behavioral ground rules by which they are all going to play.

In acquisitions that are assimilations, the acquiring company needs to have a clear vision and set of values and guiding behaviors and a process to orient employees of the acquired company. If the company is not clear about these things themselves, it is very confusing and disruptive.

Academic studies on culture point to a powerful phenomenon called the "Shadow of the Leaders." As leaders go, so goes the company and the merger. If leaders show up unaligned, the two merging companies will be unaligned. If they fight over turf, so will all those who look to them. That is why the leaders need to spend time coming together as "one team" and aligning vision and strategy.

The shadow leaders cast across the organization are a powerful form of communication. For that reason, it is critical that the new senior team be the first team to come together (beyond the transition planning team). Members should spend time in a series of well-designed off-site sessions. The alignment process described earlier can be used by the senior team not only to build the team but also to come together around the shared values and guiding behaviors for the merged entity. Because of its importance, this process is best handled with assistance from skilled and experienced outside facilitators.

The senior team can ease the clash of cultures by

- Recognizing there are culture differences between buyer and seller
- Expecting a clash to occur, and taking steps to ameliorate the disagreement
- Sensitizing staff to the culture clash dynamics
- Proposing mechanisms for learning about each company's culture
- Emphasizing the development of a new common culture

### 13.8.2 The Emotional Cycle of Change

The integration process should be entered into realistically with full knowledge of the obstacles that may be encountered. Most acquisitions considered to be successful follow a pattern described as the "merger emotion syndrome" or "merger syndrome" [14]. The syndrome encompasses executives' stressful reactions and the development of a "crisis management" atmosphere, as shown in Figure 13.4.

As shown in the chart, phase 1 is unbridled optimism, when people are excited about the new venture and have not as yet faced the challenges and complications. Phase 2 is informed pessimism when all of the issues, rumors,

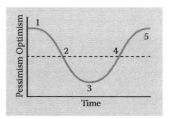

- Phase 1 unbridled optimism
- Phase 2 informed pessimism
- Phase 3 realistic outlook
- Informed optimism
- Rewarded completion

The merger emotion syndrome is a phenomenon that illustrates employees' predictable reactions after the announcement of an unexpected M&A deal

**FIGURE 13.4**
Merger emotion syndrome.

and disruptions are being faced. It can take one of two courses. Without a systematic plan, pessimism and rebellion can become a long-lasting reality.

In phase 3, realism sets in. The issues and challenges are understood and success requires determination. However, with a plan in place and continued commitment, the tide will begin to turn to phase 4, or informed optimism. In phase 5, rewarded completion, the benefits of the transaction start to become a reality.

The target company CEO can minimize the emotional cycle of change by taking the following proactive steps:

- Establish a transition team.
- Prepare your staff for a period of intense high-level activity.
- Rally the troops with your vision for a better and stronger organization.
- Operate in a way that says: "We are all in this together."
- Acknowledge everyone's uncertainty and concerns.
- Communicate, communicate, and communicate.
- Tell all you can, and always tell the truth.
- Orchestrate a master plan of priorities, problem areas, and synergies.
- Involve everyone in managing the transition.
- Empower teams with information, influence, guidance, and authority.
- Emphasize the benefits that each person will enjoy after transaction.

### 13.8.3 Merger Emotions Management

In the typical M&A transaction, many employees undergo a psychological trauma period that results in negative consequences for the organizations. Since the employees of the acquired company are more affected by the big changes, they are deeply shaken and respond with shock and strong emotional reactions.

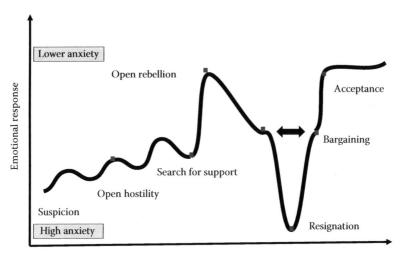

**FIGURE 13.5**
Nervousness Index.

The employees of the acquired company ask themselves many questions: "Would I still have a job?" "Will my job demands change unreasonably?" "How do I adapt to the new team?" "Do I still belong?" "Will I survive the changes?"

The predictable response can be called the "Nervousness Index," and is graphically shown in Figure 13.5. Anxieties, aggressions, and high stress levels may be managed by maintaining positive emotions [15].

Figure 13.5 depicts the seven "grieving" stages experienced by many employees of the acquired company, although it is also seen in those high-level executives of the acquirer who are not part of the decision-making group. The merger emotions of management can be summarized as follows:

- Fair and understandable personnel selection process
- Transparency of transition process
- Periodic communication of M&A status and goals
- Evoking and maintaining trust in the leadership
- Making senior management highly accessible
- Encouraging employee participation at all levels

### 13.8.4 Benefits of a Systematic Integration Process

One of the benefits that can come from systematically dealing with specific cultural aspects of mergers is that team members operate more quickly and effectively in their new or newly revised organization without loss of momentum. This is summarized in Table 13.4.

**TABLE 13.4**

Benefits of a Systematic Integration Process

| Cultural Aspects | Benefits |
|---|---|
| There are fewer defections. Usually the best people leave immediately. | People don't move on because of uncertainty or imagined concerns and issues. |
| Negative impact on morale is lessened or eliminated. | People don't waste countless hours on speculation or on feeling victimized. |
| Focus on the customer is not lost and customer disruptions are minimized. | All the planned synergies, such as cross-selling, are captured. |
| Consolidation of functions is done faster and more smoothly and the cost benefits of consolidation are better captured. | This leads to improved productivity and profitability in a shorter period. |
| The process of creating a vision, mission, and shared values creates excitement, inspiration, and commitment. | All people now working for a new future goal as opposed to living in the past. |
| A sense of community is created sooner among all individual stakeholders. | Shared vision and values link individuals to the organization and bind people together. |

## 13.9 What Are You Worth to an Acquirer?

Acquirers have deep pockets, but short arms.

Every founder believes in his heart of hearts that their venture is truly worth a fortune, and it will get funded appropriately. From the founder's perspective, it should be obvious to every acquirer what an outstanding opportunity is being offered. After all, you are at the threshold of introducing a world-beating innovative product. So why don't acquirers write a big check?

A business valuation is the process used by acquirers to determine the financial worth of a closely held (private) company. For our purposes, a closely held business is an organization owned and operated by a relatively small number of owners.

The valuation process begins with an understanding of your company, following a series of generally accepted valuation techniques, such as the following:

- Determining which business valuation(s) are most applicable to your company
- Analyzing the company's financial statements and pro-forma statements
- Assessing comparative and market statistical information
- Determining appropriate discounts and premiums
- Calculating current company valuation

### 13.9.1 Putting Lipstick on Your Pig: Value versus Price

Some men know the price of everything and the value of nothing.

**Oscar Wilde**

The **value** of your start-up is an economic theoretical concept. It is an estimate of the likely price at a given point in time. **Price** is the precise amount of
money asked in exchange for something. In your case, you are asking Angels
to invest $X$ amount of money into your start-up company in exchange for $Y$
percentage of ownership (based on shares).

Since traditional company values are based on objective measures, such
as gross revenues, net profits, cash flows, net assets, increased sales, and so
on, valuing a pre-revenue company is highly subjective. Complicating matters is the known "founder's syndrome," which is overvaluing their baby. It
all comes down to deciding if you will be satisfied with a slice of a rapidly
expanding pie (Figure 13.6).

Valuation is a particularly thorny problem for innovation-focused tech
acquisitions [16]. It is nearly impossible to apply traditional valuation techniques to companies in their early stages of development, when operating
histories are brief and there's little or no historical or predictable future cash
flow. Acquirers therefore must resort to other measurements to build the
case for a particular investment.

Their executives typically consult internal research and development and
product teams to determine the cost—in terms of both time and money—
of building a product or service internally. Very often, the acquirer has the
necessary capability, but the lead time to build the product or service is prohibitive, and an acquisition can significantly improve speed to market. Very
often, the acquirer has the necessary capability, but the lead time to build
the product or service is prohibitive, and an acquisition can significantly
improve speed to market.

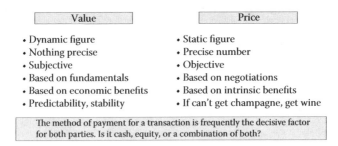

| Value | Price |
|---|---|
| • Dynamic figure | • Static figure |
| • Nothing precise | • Precise number |
| • Subjective | • Objective |
| • Based on fundamentals | • Based on negotiations |
| • Based on economic benefits | • Based on intrinsic benefits |
| • Predictability, stability | • If can't get champagne, get wine |

The method of payment for a transaction is frequently the decisive factor
for both parties. Is it cash, equity, or a combination of both?

**FIGURE 13.6**
Value versus price.

### 13.9.2 Maximizing Your Value to Strategic Buyers

When it comes to valuation, it's easy to focus on the consideration a buyer is paying instead of what the buyer is hoping to gain from the purchase. Understanding what the potential buyer is seeking from the transaction can help the seller better assess a potential transaction's impact on valuation [17]. We will discuss capabilities and geographic footprint as two important components of your company's valuation in the eyes of a potential strategic acquirer.

1. **Capabilities.** Certain strategic acquirers may want to purchase a firm to build a broader corporate capability or enter a new line of business. These buyers are usually in a related business and want to "buy instead of build."

   They may use cash flow as a buying method, but could put a relative premium on a valuation if your unique strength is valuable enough. This type of buyer often exclusively seeks out start-ups with knowledge-based products, unique capabilities, and exceptional human capital.

2. **Geographic footprint.** A buyer may consider a firm simply to enter a new market and leverage the firm's network and existing clients. This is another "buy versus build" strategy and can be an attractive point of entry for a buyer. *Potential impact on valuation:* "If your location is ideal for whatever the buyer's 'concept' is, you may command a premium."

   For example, is your pharma firm located in Cambridge, Massachusetts, more valuable than a firm in the rural Midwest? Since your location gives you quick access to world-class hospitals, does it command a premium? Perhaps, but there are plenty of "successful firms" in remote locations.

   When it comes to valuation, you may want to think about the reasons a buyer may be attracted to a firm and the subsequent implications for the "sale planning" process: The multiyear process to improve the value of your business in preparation to sell.

### 13.9.3 What Your Business Is Worth Depends on the Buyer

There is an old saying: your business is worth what a buyer is willing pay. Of course, the first step in placing a value on your business is identifying the "right buyer" [18]. The range of values that different buyers may be willing to pay is staggering. Buyers pay for opportunity. The buyer who perceives the greatest opportunity is the buyer willing to pay the most for your business. This is shown in Figure 13.7.

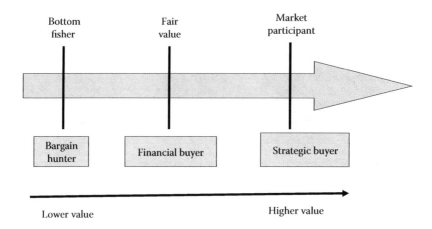

**FIGURE 13.7**
The value continuum and buyer types.

Identifying the right buyer requires understanding the four main classifications of buyers.

1. **The Strategic Buyer.** These are the very best buyers. They almost always pay cash and buy at a premium. Typically, public or very large private companies' decision to buy usually revolves around considerations of economies of scale, new channels of distribution, new innovative technologies, or other integration considerations. To be attractive to a strategic acquirer, your company should fit most, if not all, of the following criteria:

   • Sales in excess of $10 million
   • Proprietary product or process
   • Unique market presence or share
   • Synergistic fit with the acquirer
   • Suitable management willing to stay

2. **The Financial Buyer.** Financial buyers include private equity firms (also known as "financial sponsors"), venture capital firms, hedge funds, family investment offices, and ultra high net worth individuals. These firms and executives are in the business of making investments in companies and realizing a return on their investments. Their goal is to identify private companies with attractive future growth opportunities and durable competitive advantages, invest capital, and realize a return on their investment with a sale or an initial public offering [19].

Because these buyers have fundamentally different goals, the way they will approach your business in an M&A sale process can differ in many material ways.

While this might seem obvious, strategic buyers usually are more "up to speed" on your industry, its competitive landscape, and current trends. As such, they will spend less time deciding on the attractiveness of the overall industry and more time on how your business fits in with their corporate strategy. Conversely, financial buyers are typically going to spend a lot of time building a comprehensive macro view of the industry and a micro view of your company within the industry. It is not uncommon for financial buyers to hire outside consulting firms to assist in this analysis.

With this analysis, financial buyers might ultimately determine that they do not want to invest in any company in a given industry. Presumably, this risk is not present with a strategic buyer if they are already operating in the industry. As the seller, the risk of having a sale process fail owing to "industry attractiveness" factors is reduced by ensuring that you are soliciting strategic buyers.

## 13.10 M&A in Healthcare

In the healthcare field, Medtronic acquired Covidien in a $42 billion transaction. The combined Medtronic/Covidien organization is the largest medical device company in the world. Anthem's acquisition of WellPoint made it the largest healthcare management company in America. The question in each case is, "Can merging companies achieve the necessary synergy, or will their cultures clash?"

An article in the *Los Angeles Times* entitled "After Back-Slapping Wanes, Mega-Mergers Often Fail" concluded that "Perhaps more than anything else, senior management stumbles over cultural issues." They noted that: "The most important issue is **trust**. Along with cultivating trust, the keys to success in pulling together companies are crafting a shared vision, developing a precise transition plan, which includes more than structure and processes and avoiding the common pitfall of focusing so much on the merger details that customers (and employees) are neglected."

While it is clear that successful M&As must be based primarily on strategic, financial, and other objective criteria, ignoring a potential clash of cultures can lead to financial failure. Far too often, cultural and leadership style differences are not considered seriously enough or systematically addressed. Many acquisitions that looked very promising from a strategic or financial viewpoint ultimately fail and require major surgery or extensive subsequent hand-holding because these "soft" issues were neglected.

---

## References

1. Evans, M.H. Course 7: Mergers and Acquisitions (Part 1), http://www.exinfm .com/training/pdffiles/course07-1.pdf.
2. http://en.wikipedia.org/wiki/Mergers_and_acquisitions
3. Investopedia on Facebook: Strategic Buyer Definition | Investopedia, http:// www.investopedia.com/terms/s/strategic-buyer.asp#ixzz3k8rO6Dqm.
4. Zorea., L. M&A Tips for the Bootstrapped and Early-Stage Technology Startup, PerkinsCoie, 2015, http://www.startuppercolator.com/ma-tips-for-the-boot strapped-and-early-stage-technology-startup/?format=pdf.
5. Crafting your value proposition, MaRS Discovery District, November 2012, http://www.marsdd.com/wp-content/uploads/2012/12/Crafting-Your-Value -Proposition-WorkbookGuide.pdf.
6. Cultural issues in mergers and acquisitions. Leading through transition: Perspectives on the people side of M&A Deloitte Consulting LLP, 2009, http:// www2.deloitte.com/content/dam/Deloitte/us/Documents/mergers-acqisitions /us-ma-consulting-cultural-issues-in-ma-010710.pdf.
7. Dixon, I. Culture Management and Mergers and Acquisitions, Society for Human Resource Management case study, March 2005.
8. Deal, T.E., Kennedy, A.A. *Corporate Cultures.* Perseus Book Publishing LLC, HarperCollins Publishing, New York, 1982.
9. Cultural clash in mergers and acquisitions. Senn Delaney, 2004, http://knowledge .senndelaney.com/docs/thought_papers/pdf/SennDelaney_cultureclash_UK.pdf.
10. http://iveybusinessjournal.com/publication/seven-steps-to-merger-excellence/
11. Schein, E.H. *Organizational Culture and Leadership.* Jossey-Bass Inc., San Francisco, pp. 16–17, 1992.
12. Beaudan, E. and Smith, G. Corporate culture: Asset or liability. *Ivey Business Journal,* March 2000.
13. http://www.bain.com/publications/articles/integrating-cultures-after-a -merger.aspx
14. Marks, M.L. and Toder, F. When your company is acquired: The human aspect. *The Business Journal,* October 22, 1999, http://www.managementcontinuity .com/images/When_Your_Company_Is_Acquired_-_Fran.pdf.
15. Kusstatscher, V. Cultivating positive emotions in mergers and acquisitions. *Advances in Mergers and Acquisitions,* 5, 91–103, 2006, https://karhen.home .xs4all.nl/Papers/5/Cultivating%20positive%20emotions%20in%20mergers%20 and%20acquisitions.pdf.
16. Acquiring innovation strategic deal-making to create value through M&A. PWC, March 2014, http://www.pwc.com/en_US/us/advisory/business-strategy -consulting/assets/acquiring-innovation.pdf.

17. Taking steps to help maximize the value of your firm. Fidelity, https://fiws
.fidelity.com/app/literature/log?literatureURL=9857852.pdf.
18. How much is my business worth? Vanguard Resource Group, http://vrgsandiego
.com/how-much-is-my-business-worth.
19. Boyle, C. 5 Differences between Financial and Strategic Buyers, February 2014,
http://www.axial.net/forum/5-differences-financial-strategic-buyers/.

# Section III

# Product Launch

# 14

## Pricing Strategies

### 14.1 Introduction

Setting the "right" price for the launch of your innovative product is one of the most crucial marketing decisions you will ever face. Too high a price and it will not sell; too low a price and you will be out of business. Meeting the price of existing products is the easiest pricing goal to implement, but how do you price an innovative product, since, by definition, it does not currently exist in the market?

Pricing must be thought of in terms of the product and adoption life cycle. Keep in mind that pricing is the only part of the marketing mix that produces revenues; all the other elements produce costs [1]. Your selected pricing strategy will

- Define your product
- Help segment the market
- Incentivize customer adoption
- Signal your quality intentions to your competition
- Establish the gold standard

Figure 14.1 summarizes the recommended six steps in setting your product launch pricing policy.

### 14.2 Establishing Your Pricing Tactics

*Some people know the price of everything, and the value of nothing.*

Your pricing tactics should accurately reflect your strategic goals. As an innovative start-up, you should be thinking in terms of value, not just pricing. Value in new product pricing ensures that customers receive fair

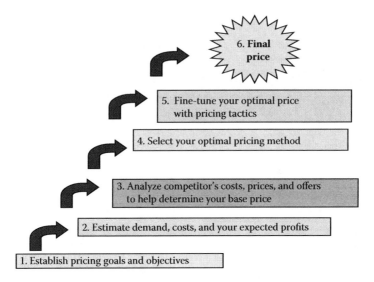

**FIGURE 14.1**
Setting your launch pricing policy.

value-based pricing, while enabling the entrepreneur to reach an industry price equilibrium that provides adequate revenue returns [2].

**Value** is the difference between what the customer gains from owning a product minus the costs of obtaining the product. **Quality** is the characteristics of a product/service that satisfy stated or implied customer needs. Value-based new product offerings can best be seen in terms of a price-quality continuum, as shown in Figure 14.2.

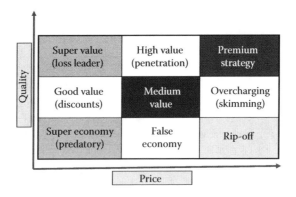

**FIGURE 14.2**
Value-based new products: the price–quality continuum.

## 14.3 The Complex Sale

*Focus on success, not failure avoidance.*

The complex sale is a type of selling (a) where a number of people must give their approval or input before the buying decision can be made and (b) that requires long and involved cell cycles [3]. The complex sales are primarily focused on business-to-business and business-to-government transactions, and can range from a few weeks to years [4].

Most innovative start-ups will face the challenge of the complex sale. The current business environment is characterized by four interrelated phenomena: (1) escalating customer requirements with increased complexity, (2) rapid commoditization leading to price erosion, (3) relentless competitive forces, and (4) need to respond within a tight window of opportunity. Commoditization is the pressure exerted by the customer to equalize the differences between suppliers, thus reducing their decision-making to the lowest common denominator: the selling price. This leads to the great margin squeeze as depicted in Figure 14.3.

The length of time that an innovation enjoys the advantage of being first in the market is getting shorter and shorter. For a start-up, the key to success is to differentiate your innovative offering. Differentiation allows for more profitable, preemptive, and effective product introductions.

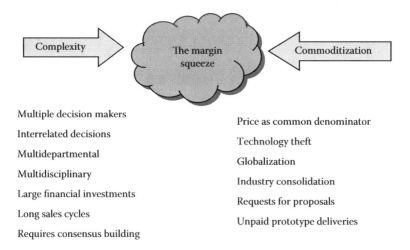

**FIGURE 14.3**
The great margin squeeze.

## 14.4 Sales Talking Points

If you are launching a knowledge-intensive product, you are inevitably faced with the intricacies of the complex sale. Sales talking points are a means of selecting best practices and communicating them to your salespeople. Sales talking points should concisely describe what the salesperson should do in different situations they might encounter in the field.

Sales talking points should be customized to a company's specific situation. A sales playbook for a company selling $5000 solutions over the phone will be very different from one for companies selling $5 million solutions in complex request for proposal (RFP) or request for quotation (RFQ) situations. Below are examples to illustrate the crucial differences.

### 14.4.1 Short Sales Cycles, Low Solution Prices

The sales talking points for a company selling a low-priced solution via a marketing campaign targeted at a specific customer segment with the goal of selling a specific solution might include the following:

- The e-mail campaign
- Titles mailed to specific groups
- Phone and e-mail scripts to use to follow-up
- Specific calls to action to move the prospect to the next stage (including sales tools such as case studies, analyst reports, etc.)
- Quick reference sheets for competitors
- Specific data updates based on call outcomes

The expectation is that these campaigns will be high volume and highly scripted. The sales talking points may outline the sales process from initial prospect engagement through close of sales by a purchase order.

### 14.4.2 Longer Sales Cycles, Higher Solution Prices

At the other end of the spectrum, salespeople selling higher-priced, more complex solutions (complex sales) generally follow a less scripted sequence. A salesperson in situations like this might have five phases of the sales process:

1. Prepare via external research how to approach companies in your prospect list.
2. Network within companies in your prospect list to locate a group within that company likely to have problems that make them great candidates for one of the solutions you sell.

3. Confirm for a specific group which problem they have and which of your solutions can overcome their problems.

4. For a group with a specific problem, move them from interest to active consideration, and then close the sale.

5. Do not sell products; sell solutions.

### 14.4.3 Preparation Steps for Your Sales Talking Points

Before embarking on your sales talking points, you should have completed these steps:

- Segment your market by different needs and priorities.
- Select the market segments that best match your differentiators with their needs.
- Study your competition—which segments they concentrate on and what their strengths and weaknesses are for those segments.
- Note key differentiators.
- Create qualification criteria for ideal prospects.
- Identify buyers' roles and typical titles encountered by role.
- Outline the sales process (sequence of steps, order in which roles are approached if relevant).
- Identify impediments to selling and sales strategies and processes to overcome them.
- Map out what supporting sales tools you need by sales stage, role, and segment.

### 14.4.4 What Maximum Price Can You Command?

*Do not price to sell; sell the price.*

With your positioning, you have decided how you will differentiate your product against the competition—this includes pricing. Specifically, you should answer the following questions:

- What maximum price can you ask?
- What pricing strategy will you adopt for optimum sales volume?

The price you can ask is the price (value) the customer is prepared to pay. This contradicts the widespread opinion that price is determined directly by cost. Of course, cost is a factor, but the cost/price ratio only becomes critical when the price that can be asked does not cover the costs.

This, by definition, means that the business is unattractive. Cost naturally also plays a role because the difference between cost and price defines the profit—and the ultimate goal of any commercial enterprise is to maximize profit.

The price you can ask depends entirely on how much the *benefit* of your product or service is worth to the customer. You have defined, and perhaps also quantified, the customer benefit in your business idea or product description.

---

## 14.5 What Pricing Strategy Will You Adopt?

Your pricing strategy depends on your goal: do you want to penetrate the market quickly with a low price ("penetration" strategy), or do you want to get the highest possible return right from the start ("skimming" strategy)?

**New standard:** When Netscape, for instance, distributed its Internet browser for free, it was able to set a new standard. Apple, on the other hand, followed a skimming strategy with the Macintosh, and thus missed the opportunity of establishing it as a standard.

**System-related:** Businesses with high fixed costs must find a large number of customers very quickly if they are to be profitable. FedEx is the classic example: air transport and sorting offices require similar investments, whether the company moves thousands or millions of letters.

**Competition:** Low-entry barriers make strong competition likely. A penetration strategy is the best way of securing a large market share more quickly than the competition. However, this raises the question as to whether a business of this sort is appropriate at all for a start-up company.

**Penetration:** Unlike a skimming strategy, a penetration strategy generally requires high initial investments to produce supply that is adequate to meet the high demand. Whenever possible, start-ups prefer to avoid this additional investment risk and adopt a skimming strategy, retaining the option to adopt a more aggressive approach when appropriate.

**Skimming strategies:** There are usually good reasons for new companies to pursue skimming strategies: The new product is generally positioned as "better," "more effective," "quicker," and so on; hence, its price can also be correspondingly higher.

Higher prices generally produce higher margins, thus enabling the new company to finance its growth itself. New investment can be financed out of profit, and there is no need for additional outside investors.

## 14.6 Typical Gross Margins

**Gross margin** is the difference between net revenue and cost of goods sold, or COGS, divided by revenue, and is expressed as a percentage. Generally, it is calculated as the selling price of an item, less the cost of goods sold (production or acquisition costs, essentially). Gross margin is often used interchangeably with gross profit, but the terms are different.

When speaking about a dollar amount, it is technically correct to use the term *gross profit*; when referring to a percentage or ratio, it is correct to use *gross margin*. In other words, gross margin is a % value, while gross profit is a $ value [5]. The purpose of margins is "to determine the value of incremental sales, and to guide pricing and promotion decisions" [6].

Gross margins vary widely from business to business, and they depend on various factors:

- The competitive situation in the market (strong competition produces low margins)
- The entrepreneur's business efficiency (improves the margins)
- The complexity of the product (increases margins), the quantity, throughput time, and stock levels (the higher the number of units and the shorter the throughput time, the lower the margins)

### 14.6.1 Gross Margins in Different Industries

Table 14.1 lists the average gross margins expected in different industries [7].

**TABLE 14.1**

Gross Margins Expected in Different Industries

| Industry | Average Gross Margins (%) |
|---|---|
| Legal | 93 |
| Healthcare | 91 |
| Banking | 91 |
| Telecom | 87 |
| Publishing | 77 |
| Computer design | 71 |
| Research and development | 64 |

### 14.6.2 Your Pricing Strategy Checklist

A business can use a variety of pricing strategies when selling a product or service. The price can be set to maximize profitability for each unit sold or from the market overall. It can be used to defend an existing market from new entrants, to increase market share within a market, or to enter a new market. Businesses may benefit from lowering or raising prices, depending on the needs and behaviors of customers and clients in your particular market niche. Finding your right pricing strategy is a crucial element in launching your product and running a successful and profitable business [8,9].

So how did you arrive at your pricing policy? Did you

- Determine the costs involved?
- Set prices for selling and profit?
- Fit pricing into sales forecast for cash flow projections?
- Consider clients' perception of value?
- Consider internal marketing strategies (the image you wish to project)?

Did you include the following factors into your pricing policy?

- Costs (Material + Labor + Overhead)
- Competition
- The competitive pricing strategy
- Ability to adjust pricing
- Ceiling prices
- Customers' buying behavior
- Your anticipated return on investment (profit margin)

Did you factor in any of the following overhead expenses into your pricing?

- Fixed expenses:
  - Rent
  - Vehicle
  - Bank charges
  - Insurance
  - Lease
  - Utilities
  - Salaries
  - Other
- Variable expenses:
  - Labor
  - Overhead
  - Materials

- Inventory
- Commissions
- Professional fees
- Vehicle Costs
- Materials
- Other

Did you perform a break-even analysis using the following formula?

- Units Break-Even = Annual Fixed Costs
- Unit Selling Price – Unit Variable Costs
- Sales Break-Even = (# Units to Break-Even) × (Selling price/unit)

## 14.7 Pricing High-Tech Products

The term *high technology* is a catchall category that includes any product manufactured with some type of an advanced technology, from computer electronics or wireless devices, to medical telemetry, to long-range missiles. However, there is no specific class of technology that is high tech—the definition shifts over time—so products hyped as high tech in the past may now be considered to have everyday or dated technology [10].

Every developer would like to set a high price for its high-technology products to cover their investments in research and development (R&D) or to prove the high quality of their innovative products, but there are some internal and external factors that put pressure on prices [11].

Forces affecting the price are varied and very strong: volatile short life cycle of the product, the rapidly changing market, big investments in R&D, compatibility with existing products, the Internet, competition, external networks, the cost of the first produced unit, price/performance ratio, and consumers' perception of the cost/benefits ratio for new technologies.

A key feature of advanced technology is the rapid changing rhythm that leads to a shortened product life cycle and the need for frequent rapid decisions. Pressures on the price/performance ratio are explained in a clear manner by Moore's law [12]: "Every 18 months, technology improvements double the product performance without a price increase." In other words, this type of improvement reduces the price by half for the same level of performance [13].

"Moore's law" is the observation that the number of transistors in a dense integrated circuit has doubled approximately every 2 years. The observation is named after Gordon E. Moore, the co-founder of Intel and Fairchild Semiconductor, whose 1965 paper described a doubling every year in the number of components per integrated circuit and projected that this rate of growth would continue for at least another decade [14].

His prediction proved accurate for several decades, and the law was used in the semiconductor industry to guide long-term planning and to set targets for R&D. Advancements in digital electronics are strongly linked to Moore's law: quality-adjusted microprocessor prices, memory capacity, sensors, and even the number and size of pixels in digital cameras

### 14.7.1 Skimming or Penetration Pricing?

According to Spann, Fischer, and Tellis, a skimming strategy is more profitable than a penetration strategy at the camera level. However, a strategy mix appears to be preferable at the portfolio level after taking into account demand and cost interdependencies between products [15].

The current market environment, especially for high-tech categories, is characterized with rapid introductions of new products. In this environment, the pricing of new products is a difficult and important task affecting the financial success of any company. On the one hand, if the price is set too low, a company not only gives up potential revenues but also sets a low value position for this new product, which can make future price increases difficult [16].

Conversely, a price set too high might harm the diffusion of the new product [17], limit gains from experience effects [18], or inhibit the product from reaching its critical mass for success [19]. The literature suggests two basic dynamic pricing strategies for new products, *skimming* and *penetration* strategy [20,21].

A skimming strategy ("cream rises to the top to be skimmed") involves charging a high introduction price, which may be subsequently lowered [22]. The rationale for this strategy is to *skim* surplus from customers early in the product life cycle in order to exploit a momentary monopolistic position or a low price sensitivity of innovators.

A penetration strategy involves charging a low price to rapidly *infiltrate* the market. The strategy works on the expectation that customers will switch to the new brand because of the lower price. Penetration pricing aims at exploiting economies of scale or experience. Further, if word-of-mouth is important in the market, then achieving large early sales increases word-of-mouth and enables rapid market penetration [23,24].

Penetration pricing is most commonly associated with marketing objectives of enlarging market share and exploiting economies of scale or experience [25,26]. The chief disadvantage, however, is that the increase in sales volume may not necessarily lead to a profit if prices are kept too low. Also, if the price is only an introductory campaign, customers may leave the brand once prices begin to rise to levels more in line with rivals [27].

The choice of the pricing strategy is particularly important for high-tech products such as digital cameras where new products are frequently introduced and life cycles are short. Differentiation by features leads to a proliferation of products in each price tier. Textbooks recommend a skimming strategy for differentiated products where companies have some additional source of competitive protection.

However, many textbooks also recommend a penetration strategy for price-sensitive markets where new products usually face strong competition soon after introduction [28], which is the case for digital cameras. Hence, while the normative literature on dynamic pricing strategy provides plausible guidelines under what conditions to choose which strategy, it falls short of offering guidance in markets where conditions favor both strategy types.

Unfortunately, many if not most markets for modern consumer durables (e.g., computers, mobile phones, TV sets, and digital cameras) present the same dilemma: extensive feature differentiation supporting a skimming strategy concomitant with strong competition supporting a penetration strategy. Moreover, popular examples support the success of either strategy.

In contrast, in the automotive industry, Lexus has been successfully competing with Mercedes and BMW in the US premium *luxury car* market with its penetration pricing strategy relative to these two brands.

## 14.8 Determining Your Price Parameters

The price of your high-tech product always fluctuates between two points: the price ceiling and the bottom price (see Figure 14.4). The market segment being addressed will ultimately determine the price ceiling; no customer will buy above this level, and this price ceiling will be translated into a zero market share [29].

The bottom (lowest) price is established by the cost structure of a product; below this price, the company loses money on every product sold, which leads to a negative return. With the specifications of high-tech products, a marketing manager must evaluate these two limits by analyzing the price elasticity of demand of your targeted market segments and by the costs' learning curve.

| | Price pointers | Actions | Pricing policies |
|---|---|---|---|
| Ceiling price | | | |
| | Market segment acceptance | Demand elasticity of price | Pricing to value |
| | Current market pricing | Competitor's list prices | Lowest bidding price |
| Bottom price | Product cost structure | Determine life cycle of product and learning cost | Your break-even price |

**FIGURE 14.4**
From bottom price to ceiling price.

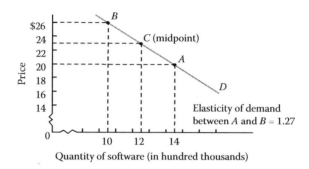

**FIGURE 14.5**
Elasticity of demand. This is an example of new software pricing versus expected demand.

### 14.8.1 Evaluating Your Price Elasticity of Demand

The price elasticity of demand in relation to price measures the variation of customer purchases according to price changes. Thus, if elasticity is high, demand for a product is heavily influenced by its price. Understanding demand elasticity for a product allows you to determine which products drive market penetration and thus require a low penetration price, and which products can be priced at a premium, like in the case of smart cellphones or broadband subscriptions. Figure 14.5 is a classical depiction of elasticity of demand for a new software product entry, showing that as price decreases, demand will increase.

Usually, innovative high-tech products have low elasticity. This means that high variation in price, an increase as well as a decrease, does not significantly modify demand. These high-tech products have few substitutes, meaning that the costs to switch to another product are high. Additionally, at the first stage of the technology, buyers—either innovators or forerunners—are less sensitive to price than to additional performance; they often have deep pockets or are ready to spend more for a new innovative and outstanding product (often referred to as early adopters). Furthermore, the high price of these products is often perceived as a sign of quality and reinforces a customer's confidence in the company.

### 14.8.2 Estimating Your Learning Curve Costs

Successful high-tech firms are constantly monitoring costs in order to keep these costs down. To show a profit that encourages future investments, a company must at least cover its variable costs that are linked to production volume and its fixed costs (salaries, rent, administration, and R&D) that are necessary to manufacture its product. Identifying and controlling these costs allow you to measure your learning curve.

This learning curve effect corresponds to the company's improved know-how as its production increases during the growth stage of the product life cycle:

- Purchasing optimization
- Design simplification for manufacturing purposes
- Output increase for production facilities
- Improvement of sales force
- Selection of distributors
- Increased performance of sales promotion campaigns

All these gains in productivity lead to a decrease in the average manufacturing unit cost. This decrease in cost could be passed on to the price in order to react to a competitor's actions or to increase price-sensitive demand.

The learning curve is valid for high-tech products because of the high level of R&D costs required by these products. Because the product life cycles are fairly short, these expenses must be written off very quickly (e.g., in 1 year for computers and in 2 years for robotics), and these R&D costs inflate the average unit cost at the beginning of the product's life, before decreasing very quickly. This unit cost variation is reflected in the changing unit price.

## 14.9 Pricing Pharmaceutical Global Launches

Pharmaceutical companies pursuing global product launches are faced with a choice between minimizing the time to market and maximizing prices. Limited intellectual property protection and stockholder expectations (among other factors) often suggest that the best product launch strategy is one that provides the fastest commercialization [30].

This strategy is appropriate in those countries where manufacturers are free to set innovator product price; however, in countries that require price negotiations before launch, such acceleration to enter the market risks sacrificing significant revenues over the product life cycle.

Of course, this choice is merely the first of many hurdles faced by manufacturers pursuing global product launches. Others include price maintenance, unilateral regulatory price changes, managing price negotiations, and sequential launch timing.

A successful global launch strategy includes far more than determining price. Typical launch issues, including product positioning, price determination, and reimbursement negotiations, must include an evaluation of all the factors that affect the launch and life cycle of the new therapy.

For example, a profitable global launch strategy must

- Demonstrate the clinical attributes of the therapy against products
- Protect against the possibility of a generic or new competitive entry
- Incorporate each country's healthcare system and physician prescribing patterns
- Comply with country-specific regulatory environments while successfully negotiating suitable prices

### 14.9.1 Practical Pharma Pricing Tips

Price is the amount of money charged for a product or service, or the sum of the values that consumers exchange for the benefits of having or using the product or service. Economic theory contends that the market price converges at a point where the forces of supply and demand meet [31].

Regardless of theoretical economic theories, price is one of the most controversial topics in pharmaceutical marketing, and is a frequent topic of media discussion. How much should you charge for a new pharmaceutical product? Charge too much and you will not sell—a problem that can be fixed relatively easily by reducing your price. Charging too little is far more dangerous: a company not only forgoes significant revenues and profits but also fixes the product's market value position at a low level, and as companies have repeatedly found, once prices hit the market, it is difficult, even impossible, to raise them [32].

Internal factors affecting pricing include the company's marketing objectives, marketing mix strategy, costs, and organizational considerations. External factors that affect pricing decisions include the nature of the market and demand, competition, and other environmental elements. Besides, a company may amortize its R&D cost over a period, which becomes an additional cost component [33].

In view of the peculiar characteristics of pharmaceutical industry, the different approaches applicable and practiced in the industry are as follows:

- Cost-plus pricing
- Break-even pricing
- Value-based pricing
- Competition-based pricing
- Economy pricing

### 14.9.2 Cost-Plus Pricing

Cost-plus pricing is a method for setting retail prices of medicines by taking into account the production cost of a medicine together with allowances for promotional expenses, manufacturer's profit margins, and charges and profit margins in the supply chain.

The manufacturing cost structure forms the basis of this type of pricing. The required profit margin is added to the cost of the product to arrive at the ex-factory price and then the trade price and market retail price. This type of pricing is usually done for old molecules where the market is very crowded, and a higher price cannot sustain the required market share. The objective of a company in such scenario is to either get some additional volume for their manufacturing facility or complement their existing product range.

### 14.9.3 Break-Even Pricing

Break-even pricing strategies are normally adopted for products specifically manufactured for government tenders and for institutional buyers. The objective is not profit, but either to (1) get volumes or (2) to gain entry into large hospital pharmacies so that the positive impact may come from out-of-hospital practice of the doctors who have to prescribe their brand in hospital because of inclusion in pharmacy. Normally, this type of pricing policies are never adopted for research-based high-profile molecules, so that there may not be a negative impact on their high in-market price.

### 14.9.4 Value-Based Pricing

This approach for pricing is most commonly used by multinational companies, especially in case of new chemical entities [34]. There are countless examples where the cost of product has no relevance whatsoever and the company has priced a product as per the perceived medical/therapeutic value.

### 14.9.5 Competition-Based Pricing

This is what most marketing-oriented companies attempt to do these days. They take into account not only the perceived value but also the value being offered by the competition and then arrive at a reasonable price, giving them good margin as well as keeping them competitive in the long run. It is extremely important to take into account not only current competitors but also expected competitors, which come with a much lower price and snatch the market share.

### 14.9.6 Economy Pricing

There are some companies that focus only on offering brands of established molecules at the lowest possible price. They base their price on cost and keep the margins to bare minimum. The reason this is being discussed separately is that the molecules selected have no impact whatsoever on the pricing strategy. They may even pick up a molecule where there is just one leading brand and price their "bioequivalent" at 75% lower price.

### 14.9.7  External Reference Pricing

External reference pricing (also known as international reference pricing) refers to the practice of using the price of a pharmaceutical product (generally ex-manufacturer price or other common point within the distribution chain) in one or several countries to derive a benchmark or reference price for the purposes of setting or negotiating the price of the product in a given country. Reference may be made to single-source or multisource supply products.

## 14.10  Differential Pricing in the Pharma Industry

Adapting drug prices to the purchasing power of consumers in different geographical or socioeconomic segments could potentially be a very effective way to improve access to medicines for people living in low- and middle-income countries [35].

Recent trends, however, are prompting the pharmaceutical industry to pay more attention to differential pricing, such as economic and demographic growth in some low- and middle-income markets, which has increased the potential market size of many low- and middle-income countries; greater recognition by the pharmaceutical manufacturers and their investors of the social responsibilities; stronger global advocacy for access to medicines; and growing competition from generic manufacturers in emerging markets.

Differential pricing allows pharmaceutical companies to signal that their pricing policies are socially responsible and consistent with their obligations to society and not just geared toward maximizing profits. In addition, differential pricing on select drugs opens opportunities to serve low- and middle-income markets and creates economies of scope for pharmaceutical companies

It is important to note that differential pricing is not a panacea to ensuring access. For patients with affordability levels lower than the marginal cost of manufacturing, donor subsidies and government support will continue to be required. Despite some evidence that differential pricing of pharmaceuticals can benefit manufacturers and poor countries without adversely affecting higher-income countries, the widespread and systematic use of such pricing has been limited to vaccines, contraceptives, and antiretrovirals mostly in low-income countries.

## 14.11 Regulatory Role in Pharma Pricing

The final responsibility of allowing a particular price resides with the regulatory bodies of each country. The objective of regulatory bodies is two pronged; on one hand, they have to ensure the protection of patients' rights and provision of quality healthcare of masses, and on the other hand, they have to allow companies to make reasonable profit so that they keep developing and manufacturing the medicines needed for the people.

The process of pricing at the company level goes through the same steps as it goes in case of any other product, but the matter becomes totally different when an application is filed with the regulatory bodies for allowing a specific price.

In most countries, the perceived potential for manufacturers to exploit a monopoly position when facing relatively inelastic demand for medicines has led many countries to regulate prices for at least some portion of the pharmaceutical market. Two countries with pluralistic coverage schemes— Canada and Mexico—have established price regulation for on-patent pharmaceuticals intended to assure that prices paid by any part of the population, insured or not, are not excessive [36].

Regulatory authorities use a common set of tools to limit the prices charged by pharmaceutical firms. The most commonly used methods involve comparing proposed prices for new products against those prices paid by other payers, a practice known as external price referencing, or against those prices already paid for products judged to be similar, a practice known as internal price referencing.

Pharmaco-economic assessment is used by some schemes as a means of making a formal judgment as to the value provided, in terms of benefits and costs. There are a limited number of other approaches used, including profit controls, which serve as an indirect form of price regulation. Pricing policies are not limited in focus to the payment received by pharmaceutical firms; regulation of the distribution chain is undertaken in many systems.

With the possible exception of profit controls, public and private payers and purchasers of pharmaceuticals use the very same approaches to define the acceptable payment or reimbursement price. In the context of reimbursement, so-called reference price systems are often used to set common reimbursement amounts for products judged to be equivalent or similar, leaving patients to pay any price difference out-of-pocket.

## 14.12 Medical Technology Industry

The medical technology industry is central to the development of medical devices and diagnostics that will provide the lifesaving and life-enhancing treatments of the future. Patient access to advanced medical technology generates efficiencies and cost savings for the health care system and improves the quality of patient care. Between 1980 and 2010, advanced medical technology helped cut the number of days people spent in hospitals by more than half and add 5 years to US life expectancy while reducing fatalities from heart disease and stroke by more than half. The industry is also an engine of economic growth for the United States, generating high wage manufacturing jobs and a favorable balance of payments [37].

The medical technology industry is composed of companies that develop and manufacture medical devices and diagnostics. These products are diverse, running the gamut from tongue depressors to the most complicated molecular diagnostic tests, advanced imaging machines, and cardiac implants.

Structurally, small firms are a key part of the medical technology industry. A 2007 study by the US International Trade Commission found a total of 7000 medical technology firms in the United States [38]. The US Department of Commerce estimated that 62% of medical technology firms had fewer than 20 employees and only 2% had more than 500 employees.

Small firms, often funded by venture capital, are particularly critical to the future of US scientific and technology leadership because they are the source of a disproportionate number of the breakthrough implantable technologies that drive medical practice and industry growth [39].

Whether created by large or small firms, medical technologies are characterized by a rapid innovation cycle. The typical medical device is replaced by an improved version every 18–24 months. To fuel innovation, the medical device industry is research intensive. US medical technology firms spend over twice the US average on R&D. Medical device companies specializing in the most complex and technologically advanced products devote upward of 20% of revenue to R&D [38].

In no small measure as the result of the diagnostics, treatments, and medical tools developed by the medical technology industry, the health advances of recent years have been breathtaking. According to the National Center for Health Statistics [40], between 1980 and 2010, medical advancements helped add 5 years to US life expectancy. Fatalities from heart disease were cut by 57%; deaths from stroke were reduced by 59%; mortality from breast cancer was cut by 31%; and disability rates declined by 25% [41]. Moreover, the pace of positive change has quickened. Between 2000 and 2010, life expectancy increased by nearly 2 years. Fatalities from heart disease were cut by 30%; deaths from stroke were reduced by 36%; and mortality from breast cancer was cut by 18%.

The dramatic improvements in health have gone beyond reduced mortality to improved quality of life. The proportion of the elderly with a functional limitation has declined and the years of disability-free life expectancy have increased [42]. To cite one example of technology's impact, patients who received total hip or total knee replacements typically transitioned away from disability within 1 year. Their risk of dying was cut in half and their risk of a new diagnosis of heart failure or depression was significantly reduced [43].

### 14.12.1 Medical Device Prices

The medical technology industry is highly competitive. A study of medical device prices from 1989 to 2009 found that they increased, on average, only one-fifth as fast as other medical prices and less than one-half as fast as the regular Consumer Price Index (CPI) [44]. Because the highly competitive market kept prices low, medical devices and diagnostics accounted for a relatively constant 6% of national health expenditures throughout the 20-year period despite a flood of new products that profoundly changed medical practice.

The US medical technology industry is also a source of economic growth and good jobs. The industry employs more than 420,000 people in the United States. It generates an additional four jobs in suppliers, component manufacturers, and other companies providing services to the industry and its employees, for every direct job—for a total of more than 2 million jobs nationwide [45].

### 14.12.2 Downward Pressure on Prices

If medical device manufacturers wish to avoid additional downward pressure on prices, the challenge for medical devices companies is to ensure that spending on medical technologies is seen not as a cost but as an investment, both in terms of patient outcomes and in terms of treatment times [46].

The medical devices (or medtech) industry, following the path of the pharma industry, is adapting to a healthcare ecosystem that increasingly values better health outcomes and effective cost-containment. It is no longer enough for medtech companies to rely on their traditional market access models, which tended to be focused on commercial or sales and marketing functions. To gain access and obtain optimum price reimbursement, medtech companies need to showcase innovations that can clearly demonstrate evidence of better health *outcomes* at reasonable costs [47].

### 14.12.3 Average Prices for Implantable Medical Devices

Bereft of the effective monopolies created by pharma patent protection, medical device companies have been far more exposed to the competition created by globalization and the rise of developing market producers. The rapid product cycle in the industry—akin to that in the smartphone or software sectors—has also made competition more intense.

Average prices for implantable medical devices paid by hospitals have declined substantially in recent years on an inflation-adjusted basis [48]. Table 14.2 reports the change in the average selling price for each category of device relative to the 2007 average price and after adjusting for inflation. The average selling price for each device category declined in real terms between 2007 and 2011. The size of this decline ranges from a 17% decline for artificial knees to a 34% decline for drug-eluting stents (corresponding to an average annual rate of decline of −4.6% and −10.5%, respectively).

**TABLE 14.2**

Price Decline in Inflation-Adjusted Prices

| Device Name | 2007 | 2011 | Total Percent Change |
|---|---|---|---|
| Cardiac resynchronization therapy defibrillators | 100% | 74% | −26 |
| Implantable cardioverter defibrillator | 100% | 76% | −24 |
| Cardiac pacemakers | 100% | 74% | −26 |
| Artificial hips | 100% | 77% | −23 |
| Artificial knees | 100% | 83% | −17 |
| Drug-eluting stents | 100% | 66% | −34 |
| Bare metal stents (not medicated) | 100% | 73% | −27 |

## 14.12.4 Practical Pricing Tips

According to HBS Consulting, pricing strategies need to balance the demands of the market, that is, what the customer needs and wants, with the needs of the company. Pricing objectives need to be closely linked with organizational and marketing objectives, as well as taking account of cash flow requirements, profit objectives, and return on investment. In addition, they must take into account the market's price sensitivity, which is defined as the relative importance of price in a purchasing decision. In view of the complexities involved in pricing, obtaining an efficient pricing strategy is an important issue for all medical device and diagnostic companies.

In HBS's 2006 publication [49], they argue that medtech companies should first recognize that there are few truly innovative, lifesaving devices being developed—most are developments on an existing technology and thus competition is high. Therefore, persuading a customer to purchase one technology in favor of another can be a difficult process.

The second reason is that most of the major medical device companies in the market have been established for generations, and rather than their pricing systems evolving smoothly, new processes have been built on top of old ones to create a highly complex mesh that hinders communication between the various processes. These systems are often put to the test when negotiating discounts and the addition of other products and services (bundling) to the deal in order to entice the customer to make a purchase, and they frequently break down.

Medtech companies need to establish a clear pricing policy based on the price influencers, as shown in Table 14.3.

## 14.12.5 Assessing Your Market "Pain"

Innovative medical devices with a high medical need (market pain) can frequently command privileged prices, especially in its launch phase. Table 14.4 illustrates the critical questions a company should ask in order to evaluate

**TABLE 14.3**

Price Influencers

| Pressures Influencing Pricing | Your Competitive Differentiators |
| --- | --- |
| Competitor's technology | Is your technology more effective? |
| Existing price structure | Should you match or exceed prices? |
| Reimbursement schemes | Is your product approved for reimbursement? |
| Procurement methods | What are your sales channels? |
| Global pricing trends | Falling or rising? |
| Customer identification | Who is your customer? The hospital? The patient? The healthcare provider? |
| Product brand strength | Can your brand protect your price? |
| Economic/medical value | Can you command a premium? |
| Company's financial strength | Can you afford to promote heavily? Can you afford to undercut? |

**TABLE 14.4**

Device Therapy Value and Its Price Result

| Therapeutic Value/Utility | Expected Price Result |
| --- | --- |
| Will severity of the disorder or the symptoms affect price sensitivity? Is the disorder disabling? | Disorder severity can either make price sensitivity high or low. |
| What is the position of the disease in the payer, provider, or the public's perception? | A high profile can either make the payer prepared to pay a premium or feel that price should be lowered to make the therapy widely available. |
| What does this disorder cost the health care system and society (direct, indirect, quality of life)? Can society afford the cost? | The more the disorder costs the health system (or society), the higher can be the price sought for the device. |
| What is the potential to reduce the healthcare cost with your product? | The greater the potential to reduce the cost, the greater the potential to increase the price, as long as the price doesn't exceed the ceiling of the decreased cost. |
| What information will be needed to document and demonstrate any savings? Are clinical trials necessary, or are published papers sufficient? | This can be information from clinical trials against competitive technologies combined with economic data using prices of the technologies and cost savings on patient care. |
| Is the product likely to be used as mono- or combination device? Combination problems require longer regulatory development time. | The whole of the cost of the therapeutic process needs to be considered and the prices combined if it is a combination device. |
| Will the value of the product be different for different potential indications? Are all stents born equal? | For example: Will a stent placed in a carotid artery have the same perceived value as a coronary artery stent? Is the brain more important than the heart? |

the medical need for its medical device and the effect this may have on its proposed price.

The answers to these questions are not always clear-cut. Ultimately, many companies find themselves in a position where they gather this information and then combine their marketing research and current market conditions to make a final pricing decision.

## References

1. Kotler P. *Marketing Management*. Simon & Schuster Company, Englewood Cliffs, NJ, 1994.
2. Bernstein, J. and Macias, D. Engineering new product success: The new product pricing process at Emerson. *Industrial Marketing Management*, 31, 51–64, 2002.
3. http://en.wikipedia.org/wiki/Complex_sales
4. Thull, J. *Mastering the Complex Sale*. John Wiley & Sons, Inc., 2000.
5. https://en.wikipedia.org/wiki/Gross_margin
6. Farris, P.W., Bendle, N.T., Pfeifer, P.E., and Reibstein, D.J. *Marketing Metrics: The Definitive Guide to Measuring Marketing Performance*. Pearson Education, Inc., Upper Saddle River, NJ, 2010. ISBN 0-13-705829-2.
7. http://research.financial-projections.com/IndustryStats-GrossMargin.shtml
8. https://en.wikipedia.org/wiki/Pricing_strategies
9. http://www.mindofmarketing.net/2008/10/your-pricing-should-be-influenced-by-your-customers-reference-point/
10. https://en.wikipedia.org/wiki/High_tech
11. Dovleac, L. Pricing policy and strategies for consumer high-tech products. Transylvania University of Braşov, http://webbut.unitbv.ro/bulletin/Series%20V/BULETIN%20V%20PDF/05_DOVLEAC%20L.pdf.
12. Moore, G.E. Cramming more components onto integrated circuits. *Proceedings of the IEEE*, 86(1), 1998.
13. Mohr, J., Sengupta, S., and Slater, S. *Marketing of High-Technology Products and Innovations* (3rd ed.). Prentice Hall, 358–366, 2010.
14. https://en.wikipedia.org/wiki/Moore%27s_law
15. Spann, M., Fischer, M., and Tellis, G.J. Skimming or penetration? Strategic dynamic pricing for new products, https://business.ualberta.ca//media/business/departments/mbel/documents/marketingseminars/2008-09/strategicdynamicpricingpaper.pdf.
16. Marn, M.V., Roegner, E.V., and Zawada, C.C. Pricing new products. *The McKinsey Quarterly*, 3(July), 40–49, 2003.
17. Golder, P.N. and Tellis, G.J. Pioneer advantage: Marketing logic or marketing legend? *Journal of Marketing Research*, 30(May), 158–170, 1993.
18. Tellis, G.J. Beyond the many faces of price: An integration of pricing strategies, *Journal of Marketing*, 50(October), 146–160, 1986.
19. Dhebar, A. and Oren, S.S. Optimal dynamic pricing for expanding networks. *Marketing Science*, 4(4), 336–351, 1985.

20. Kotler, P. and Armstrong, G. *Principles of Marketing*. Prentice Hall, Upper Saddle River, 2005.
21. Nagle, T.T. and Hogan, J.E. *The Strategy and Tactics of Pricing: A Guide to Growing More Profitably*. Prentice Hall, Upper Saddle River, NJ, 2006.
22. Dean, J. Pricing policies for new products, *Harvard Business Review*, 54(Nov–Dec), 141–153, 1976.
23. Clarke, F.H., Darrough, M.N., and Heineke, J.M. Optimal pricing policy in the presence of experience effects. *Journal of Business*, 55(4), 517–530, 1982.
24. Robinson, B. and Lakhani, C. Dynamic price models for new product planning. *Management Science*, 21(10), 1113–1122, 1975.
25. https://en.wikipedia.org/wiki/Penetration_pricing
26. Tellis, G.J. Beyond the many faces of price: An integration of pricing strategies. *Journal of Marketing*, 50(October), 146–160, 1986.
27. http://www.investopedia.com/terms/p/penetration-pricing.asp#axzz2ETtC9KCQ
28. Monroe, K.B. *Pricing—Making Profitable Decisions*. McGraw-Hill, New York, 2003.
29. Viardot, E. *Successful Marketing for High-Tech Firms*. Third Edition. Artech House, Norwood, MA, 2004, http://www.kolegjifama.eu/materialet/Biblioteka%20Elektronike/Artech_House_Successful_Marketing_Strategy_for_High-Tech_Firms_3rd.pdf.
30. Rankin, P.J., Bell, G.K., and Wilsdon, T. Global pricing strategies for pharmaceutical product launches. Chapter 2 of *The Pharmaceutical Pricing Compendium*, http://www.crai.com/sites/default/files/publications/Global-Pricing-Strategies-for-Pharmaceutical-Product-Launches.pdf.
31. http://www.investopedia.com/terms/m/market-price.asp
32. http://www.mckinsey.com/insights/marketing_sales/pricing_new_products
33. Khoso, I., Ahmed, R.R., and Ahmed. J. Pricing strategies in pharmaceutical marketing. *The Pharma Innovation Journal*, 3(7), 13–17, 2014, http://thepharmajournal.com/vol3Issue7/Issue_september_2014/14.1.pdf.
34. http://www.forbes.com/sites/forbesinsights/2012/06/11/value-based-health-care-fad-or-future/#29da073473ca
35. Yadav, P. Differential pricing for pharmaceuticals. U.K. Department for International Development (DFID). Review of current knowledge, new findings and ideas for action, https://www.gov.uk/government/uploads/system/uploads/attachment_data/file/67672/diff-pcing-pharma.pdf.
36. Pharmaceutical Pricing Policies in a Global Market. OECD Health Policy Studies. 2008, http://apps.who.int/medicinedocs/documents/s19834en/s19834en.pdf.
37. AdvaMed's Innovation Agenda: Background and Detail, http://advamed.org/res.download/839.
38. United States International Trade Commission. Medical Devices and Equipment: Competitive Conditions Affecting U.S. Trade in Japan and Other Principal Foreign Markets, March 2007, http://www.usitc.gov/publications/332/pub3909.pdf.
39. Platzer, M. *Patient Capital: How Venture Capital Investment Drives Revolutionary Medical Innovation*, 2007, http://www.contentfirst.com/past/Patientcapital/NVCA PatientCapital.pdf.
40. National Center for Health Statistics. *Health, United States, 2012: With Special Feature on Emergency Care*. Hyattsville, MD, 2013.

41. The Value of Investment in Health Care: Better Care, Better Lives. Report compiled for The Value Group by MedTap International, 2004. Data cited on disability rates is limited to 1982–2000.
42. Federal Interagency Forum on Aging-Related Statistics. Older Americans 2012: Key Indicators of Well-Being. Federal Interagency Forum on Aging-Related Statistics. Washington, DC: U.S. Government Printing Office, June 2012; D. Cutler, K. Ghosh, and M. Landrum. Evidence for Significant Compression of Morbidity in the Elderly U.S. Population. National Bureau of Economic Research, July 2013.
43. Medscape Medical News (by Kathleen Louden), http://www.medscape.com/viewarticle/781620.
44. Long, G. et al. Recent Average Price Trends for Implantable Medical Devices, 2007–2011, the Analysis Group, February 2013.
45. The Lewin Group. State Economic Impact of the Medical Technology Industry, June 7, 2010, and February 2007, http://www.socalbio.org/studies/MTI_Lewin_2010.pdf.
46. Value-based healthcare. Strategies for medtech, http://pages.eiu.com/rs/eiu2/images/MEDTEC%20Value based%20healthcare%20WEB.pdf.
47. Value-based healthcare. White paper from The Economist Intelligence Unit Healthcare, 2014, http://pages.eiu.com/rs/eiu2/images/MEDTEC%20Value-based%20healthcare%20WEB.pdf.
48. Long, G., Mortimer, R., and Sanzenbacher, G. Recent average price trends for implantable medical devices, 2007–2011 Advamed, 2013, http://advamed.org/res.download/365.
49. Pricing Strategies—The Outlook for Medical Devices and Diagnostic Companies. HBS Consulting, 2006, http://hbs-consulting.com/HBSStrategyReviews/Pricing.pdf.

# 15

## Product Launch Risk Analysis

### 15.1 Introduction

All start-up businesses entail huge risks; therefore, systematically analyzing your product launch risks will prepare you for the challenges you will face during your early years. Including a critical risk analysis is crucial because acknowledging inherent risks will allow you to establish a plan to overcome these risks.

Furthermore, having a plan to navigate around these critical risks will provide you will gain credibility, since you have not yet demonstrated your ability to survive in the fierce competitive knowledge-based environment. By understanding your critical start-up risks, you can offer creative and effective solutions to those risks if and when they occur, and thereby minimize their impact.

### 15.2 Critical Risk Analysis

Professor Michael Goldsby of Ball State University likens critical risk analysis to a flight simulator for pilots. It is a "what if" scenario for addressing the competitive dynamics of your chosen industry. It will prepare you for likely eventualities and provide a roadmap to counteract business adversities. A well-known "flight simulator" is Porter's forces of competition, a subject we will discuss in the following paragraphs.

In 1979, a *Harvard Business Review* article entitled "How Competitive Forces Shape Strategy" was published by industrial economist Michael E. Porter. Porter started a revolution in the field of strategic critical risk analysis and industry profitability. It provided a framework for anticipating and influencing competition and profitability over time. Porter argued that a healthy industry structure is as much of a competitive concern to strategists as their company's own position. This technique became known as "Porter's 5 forces analysis." (Since then, a sixth force has been added, namely, regulatory threats.)

**TABLE 15.1**

Modified Porter's Force Analysis

"An Industry's Profit Potential is Largely Determined by
the Intensity of Competitive Rivalry within That Industry"

1. Competitive rivalry within the industry
2. Threats of new entrants
3. Threats of substitutes products
4. Bargaining power of customers
5. Bargaining power of suppliers
6. Public authorities: Regulatory threats

Porter's "Five Forces of Competition" framework describes how the structural features of an industry influences the distribution of value created by firms within that industry.

- Ideally, firms in an industry would like to capture most or all of the economic value that they create.
- However, competitive forces operate to push that value "forward" to customers (in the form of lower prices) or, in some cases, "backward" to suppliers.

The classical Porter's 5 forces analysis represents the competitive environment of the firm. It is a strategic foresight to avoid putting the competitive edge at risk and ensure the profitability of products on a long term. For the company, this vision is quite important because the firm is able to direct its innovations in terms of choice of strategies and investments. The profitability of businesses within the industrial structure depends on the six forces, as seen in Table 15.1.

This is visually summarized in Figure 15.1.

### 15.2.1 The Competitive Rivalry within Your Industry

The competition between firms determines the attractiveness of your selected sector. Your competitors change based on sector development, diversity, and the existence of barriers to enter. In addition, it is an analysis of the number of competitors, products, brands, strengths and weaknesses, strategies, and market shares.

### 15.2.2 The Threat of New Entrants

It is in your company's interest to create barriers to prevent its competitors to enter the market. Your competitors are either new companies or companies that intend to diversify. These barriers can be legal (patent regulations) or industrial (products or single brands). The arrival of new entrants also

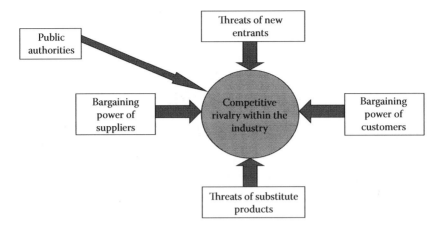

**FIGURE 15.1**
Modified Porter's force analysis.

depends on the size of the market (economy of scale), the reputation of a company already established, the cost of entry, access to raw materials, technical standards, or cultural barriers.

### 15.2.3 The Threat of Substitute Products

The substitute products can be considered as an alternative compared to supply on the market. Substitute products are attributed to changes in the state of technology or to the innovation. The companies see their products be replaced by different products. Substitute products often have a better price/quality report and come from sectors with higher profits. These substitute products can be dangerous and your company should anticipate coping with this threat.

### 15.2.4 The Bargaining Power of Suppliers

The bargaining power of suppliers is very important in a market. Powerful suppliers can impose their conditions in terms of price, quality, and quantity. On the other hand, if there are a lot of suppliers, their influence is weaker. One has to analyze the number of realized orders, the cost of changing the supplier, and the presence of raw materials.

### 15.2.5 The Bargaining Power of Customers

If the bargaining power of customers is high, they influence the profitability of the market by imposing their requirements in terms of price, service, or quality. Choosing clients is crucial because a firm should avoid being in a situation of dependence. The level of concentration of customers gives them more or less power. Generally, their bargaining power tends to be inversely proportional to that of the suppliers.

### 15.2.6 Public Authorities: Regulatory Threats

In many industries, government rules and regulations present a formidable barrier to commercialization. Regulatory agencies such as the US Food and Drug Administration (FDA) and the US Environmental Protection Agency present huge challenges, especially to start-ups. The cost of meeting FDA requirements can be overwhelming to undercapitalized start-ups. In the medical/pharmaceutical fields, the inability to obtain FDA approval is one of the main causes of bankruptcies.

## 15.3 Knowledge-Based Enterprises

The knowledge-based enterprise process encompasses the complete life-span of the enterprise and the career of the entrepreneur. Entrepreneurial knowledge-based ventures mimic the familiar pattern of life on earth in that there is a beginning and there is an end. Businesses open and sooner or later they close. The only question is how long they will survive—at least in their initial form.

Individuals undertake entrepreneurial ventures at different stages of their lives and careers. There is also a cycle of entrepreneurship that relates to what the entrepreneur is doing—which may not coincide with what is happening to your enterprise.

At one extreme, an enterprise may be thriving, but the founding entrepreneur may wish to leave it for a variety of possible reasons; at the other end of the spectrum, the business may fail and close but the founder remains an entrepreneur by starting a new venture.

### 15.3.1 Knowledge-Based Start-Up Classification

Hisrich and Peters [1] divided knowledge-based start-ups into three groups: lifestyle, foundation, and high-potential:

1. A **lifestyle firm** that exists primarily to support the owners. Privately owned, it achieves modest growth because of the nature of the business and the motives of the entrepreneur. These are typically micro-business with up to 10 employees.

2. A **foundation company** is created from research and development (R&D) and lays the foundation of a new industry. Its innovation changes the nature of an entire sector, for example, Apple

Corporation founded by Steven Jobs and Stephen Wozniak that turned computing from a specialized technology into a mass market.

3. A **high-potential venture** achieves rapid growth because of its innovative product/service in a large market and also receives greatest investment and public interest. For example, Boston Scientific changed the minimally invasive surgical world and became a multi-billion-dollar company.

### 15.3.2 Which Start-Ups Close and When?

The data on business closures indicate that there are two groups of start-ups that are most vulnerable to closure. Smaller enterprises—the very small microfirms are most likely to close as closure rates are lower among medium-sized and larger firms. The largest numerical segment of small and medium-sized enterprises—microenterprises—are most at risk of closure. This indicates that standing still and staying small are not a good survival strategy even though many business owners do not want to grow.

The next most vulnerable start-ups are young enterprises—the chances of survival improve as the business ages so that the most vulnerable are the very young, relatively new enterprises. The message to the founding entrepreneur is clear: the longer you can keep going and the more you can grow your business, the greater chance you will have of survival.

Drucker [2] made one of the earliest summaries of what is required to keep an enterprise going through the various stages of its life cycle and it stills seems valid today. He proposed that the four key factors, in chronological order, were likely to be as follows:

1. Focus on the market
2. Financial foresight, especially planning cash needs
3. Building a management team—before it is needed
4. Finding an appropriate role for the founding entrepreneur in a developed enterprise

### 15.3.3 The Entrepreneurship Process

The entrepreneurship process encompasses the complete life-span of a start-up and the career of an entrepreneur. This chapter will consider what happens to businesses as they grow and decline, as well as what happens to entrepreneurs as they enter into and exit from an enterprise. Life cycle models of an enterprise from start to finish typically describe five stages:

1. Product development/concept/test stage
2. Introduction (product launch)

3. Growth

4. Maturity

5. Decline or regrowth

These five stages in the conceptual life cycle of a start-up are depicted in Figure 15.2.

Such conceptual life cycle models have limitations as growth is rarely smooth and does not necessarily take place in the order of the model. Many enterprises reach steady state and never grow out of the introduction (product launch) phase. If the product is successfully launched, then the growth phase will be influenced by

- The founders—their motivation, previous management experience, demographics (age and education), and the number of entrepreneurs involved in the enterprise
- The enterprise—the legal form, age, and size of the business
- The management strategy—the market position, introduction of new products, devolution of management to non-owning managers, and sharing of equity
- The external business environment—the market sector or industry, competitive forces, and location

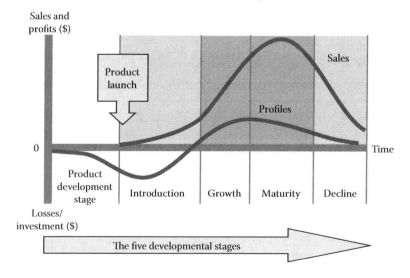

**FIGURE 15.2**
The entrepreneurship life cycle.

## 15.4 Why Do Most Product Launches Fail?

According to Schneider and Hall [3], the biggest problem they encounter is lack of preparation: Companies are so focused on designing and manufacturing new products that they postpone the hard work of getting ready to market them until too late in the game. Below is a list of the most common product launch mistakes:

### 15.4.1 Prelaunch Mistakes

- No prior market research on the product
- Budget used to develop product; little left for product launch or promotion
- Technically interesting but lacks market need
- Few key differentiators
- Needs extensive customer education
- Undefined target audience
- Product lacks sufficient testing to support claims

### 15.4.2 Launch Phase Mistakes

- Product lacks reliability
- Product aimed at wrong target audience
- Insufficient inventory to satisfy orders
- Claims cannot be verified
- A regulatory body orders the product withdrawn for market
- No "influencers" to promote product
- Product design is confusing to customers
- Product priced too high
- Poor product quality and reliability
- Product not yet ready to market and falls short of expectations
- Product revolutionary but there is no market demand

## 15.5 Approaches to Product Launch

A successful product launch depends on careful planning and preparation. It is the final stage in the product development process, which represents a significant investment in future revenue and profit for your small business. A successful product launch can take you into new markets or give you access to new customers, as well as increasing business with existing customers [4]. It's important to look at a product launch not as a single event but as a process, as shown below:

**Step 1.** Set measurable objectives for the launch. Prepare a comprehensive launch plan and allocate a budget to cover launch expenditure. Appoint a senior manager to coordinate launch activities. Identify risk and success factors in the launch and prioritize critical tasks that could affect success. A high proportion of product launches fail because of poor planning, according to pragmatic marketing.

**Step 2.** Complete the final product review. Ensure that the project team has evaluated product performance in line with market requirements. Check that the product meets all certifications and complies with any relevant product legislation. Complete the production of product documentation. Operate a test market before the launch. Ask selected retailers or distributors to stock the product and run a local promotional campaign. Evaluate test market results and feedback, and make any necessary adjustments to the launch program.

**Step 3.** Set up training programs for sales representatives. Brief the sales force thoroughly on the product, the target market, and the benefits of the product. Provide a comprehensive sales guide and a quick-reference guide to follow up the training. Hold a launch event to build enthusiasm and commitment to the launch. Set revenue targets for the launch period and offer incentives related to the launch targets.

**Step 4.** Thoroughly brief the distribution network on the timing and scope of the launch. Hold training programs or provide product guides for the network. Supply promotional material for local outlets.

**Step 5.** Establish a support infrastructure. Train technical service staff to teach, install, and maintain the product. Produce any essential customer support documentation. Set up a help desk (telecommunications) to handle support requests and queries during the initial launch phase.

**Step 6.** Prepare and distribute press releases to consumer and trade publications that serve your market. Invite journalists from important publications to a press briefing to improve coverage. Plan a launch advertising or direct marketing campaign in line with available budgets. Inform existing customers about the new product via the sales force or other direct communications. Your press release should contain the following information:

- What are you going to produce
- Name of your product

- What market will you serve with what features/benefits
- Why does the market need this product (push–pull)
- Who are the first adopters that will benefit the most
- How will you produce the product. Domestic or off-shore?
- Your launch team, and who to call to get answers

Some product launches are steeped in a philosophy called "If I build it, they will come." Many start-ups find themselves building a market solution that is based on one or two customer experiences. The reality is… without the proper market research, even the best launch plans can fail. To avoid this mistake, adequate research needs to be completed to ensure that your go-to-market plan is based on facts and substance [5].

It is imperative that you validate that there is a market out there. Does the market have a business need? Who are your best customers? Are there enough to sustain growth? How does this solution tie into the bigger growth picture for a business? Your product launch should proceed in two predictable phases: (1) planning phase and (2) execution phase, as shown in Figure 15.3.

### 15.5.1 High-Tech Industry Risk Profile

The high-technology industry is vast, feverishly paced, and extremely competitive. For high-tech companies, one thing is certain—today's new product is tomorrow's commodity. That is the main risk of a high-tech venture, and that is only one of the challenges of a high-tech enterprise.

High-tech entrepreneurs must face that risk and that challenge with imagination, innovation, and insight, but unfortunately, many do not—and cannot—bring the same creativity and competence to the management of their companies' business affairs.

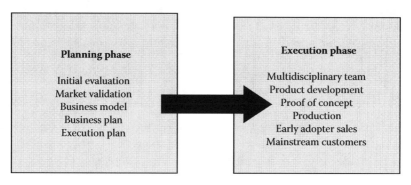

**FIGURE 15.3**
Start-up product launch.

As a result, promising high-tech companies often fail—not for lack of ideas, but for some very common reasons: lack of capital when they need it most, a naive understanding of the marketplace, poor forecasts of development and production costs, a botched product launch, and mismanaged rapid growth.

## 15.6 Keeping a Watchful Eye on Your Market

After you assembled the market analysis for your business plan, you identified your market and potential customer base and defined an initial launch strategy. Now, you need to refine that market analysis and select specific distribution channels and focus on specific key customers.

By the launch phase, you have developed and implemented a comprehensive marketing plan to guide you on an annual and a long-term basis. A thorough market analysis can assist you in your current development effort and help you position competitively for the future.

### 15.6.1 Monitoring Changes in the Marketplace

Prelaunch, you should monitor the market continually to assess the impact of changing competitive strategies. Keep a close eye on the functions, specifications, and features that the marketplace expects. Establish and maintain contact with your intended customers to get their feedback: what do they need? Be sensitive to how the market is changing, and incorporate those changes into your plans. It is important to keep your finger on the pulse of the marketplace to avoid the disaster of going to market with a nearly obsolete product.

However, beware of delaying your product to keep it absolutely state of the art: the way technology changes today, that might keep you out of the marketplace forever! To avoid that dilemma, you'll have to develop a strategy for future products and product enhancements, even before your current product hits the marketplace.

### 15.6.2 Selecting Your Optimal Marketing Channels

Analyze various marketing channels to determine which is best, for now and for later. Which channels are the most readily available, the most practical, the most cost-effective to use? Will you use a company sales force, contract with well-established manufacturers' representatives, or use some other channel to get your product to market? What is the predominant industry practice today?

### 15.6.3 Selling Strategies and Methodology

Long before you begin to ship, you need to determine your selling strategies and methodology. Think about

- Conditions and terms of sales.
- Forms of customer contracts.
- Policies and procedures for product warranty, credit and collection, and returns and allowances.
- Refining your product-service strategy. Who will service your customers? Your customers want to know this *before* they buy.
- How you intend to promote your product.
- What kinds of advertising, public relations, and other forms of marketing-support communications should be implemented to generate market awareness.

### 15.6.4 Production and Marketing Ramp Up

Now, you need to focus on setting up production facilities while you penetrate the market and consummate customer contacts. During this stage, you evolve from an engineering-oriented company to a market-driven one. You need to hire additional employees, particularly in the middle-management ranks.

You may need additional rounds of financing to support rising salaries for these extra layers of management, as well as to provide working capital for inventory and receivables.

During this stage, plan to address these important action items:

- Focus your marketing strategy.
- Plan and ramp up your production.
- Implement a strategy for future products.
- Manage the rapid growth of your company.
- Identify your information needs and develop accounting and management information systems to accommodate them.
- Begin to explore foreign markets.

## 15.7 Postlaunch Marketing Strategy and Approach

During this stage, marketing is key to your success and survival. The more focused your marketing strategy and the more proactive your approach to the changing market, the higher your chances of success.

A sound marketing strategy helps you use available resources in the best ways possible, because it gives you a good grasp of your opportunities and limitations. During this stage, you should return to your original marketing plan(s) developed in previous stages and complete the definition of your distribution channels. Remember that marketing plans constantly evolve.

### 15.7.1 Refine Pricing Policies

Refine your policies for pricing, terms, warranty, returns, credit, and collection. You already may have set a price for your product and established some initial benchmarks, but only when you are actually in the marketplace selling and servicing your product do these policies begin to work as an interactive process. Now, take a closer look at your initial policies in view of actual market conditions; they may need adjustment.

### 15.7.2 Refine Product-Service Strategy

Refine your product-service strategy. Decide how to service your product—through your own network, through your distributor's service capability, or through a third-party servicing organization.

Awareness of customer needs and satisfaction should be heightened. You should establish a mechanism for feedback from your distributors, service representatives, and customers. This information will help keep you abreast of product problems that may require you to modify your product, replace a component, or take other action. It will also keep you apprised of desirable product enhancements and changes that can improve your competitive position.

### 15.7.3 Actual Sales Performance

In the market description section of your business plan, you made initial sales forecasts. Now, you can develop and refine your methodology for creating realistic interactive sales forecasts. Your initial forecast was based on a somewhat idealized view of your environment, but now you can see the real market forces in action. This perspective will help you to formulate a methodology that can realistically capture the marketplace environment.

### 15.7.4 Production Processes and Facilities

Clearly, it is now time to concentrate on developing an efficient production process and facility. First, you should hire an operations executive, as well as other key production personnel, to round out your management team. In earlier stages, your concern was to set up an initial management framework and then to fill in the voids in the financial arena. Now, you need to fill out your employee roster with personnel who possess expertise in operations and production.

You should consider outside consultants to help determine the optimal facilities layout for efficient flow of the production process and for storage and movement of incoming materials and outgoing products. Your management consultant can scrutinize the process for unnecessary steps and inefficiencies that may raise your costs and help you design a smooth and efficient process. Study your production capacity and the capabilities and costs of expansion and contraction—next year and in the long term—taking into consideration your anticipated growth.

### 15.7.5 Inventory Management

Establish and implement procedures, policies, and systems to control your inventory, both of raw materials and of finished products. Establish policies that control engineering change orders. To achieve Just-in-Time production efficiency, you need to minimize inventory on hand, yet be able to supply your customers' needs promptly.

Adopt a policy for accounting for "field spares," plug-in components that will be replaced in the field and repaired back in the plant. Financial and tax accounting for inventory can be tricky and early planning can maximize tax benefits.

Revise and expand the sales forecast of your business plan, and use it as a strategic planning tool to help you monitor and adjust the production required to achieve those sales forecasts. This will also help forecast your material and labor requirements and procurement.

## 15.8 Balancing Limited Resources

As products change, the marketplace changes. You must refine your market strategy to keep your product apace with or ahead of marketplace dynamics. Then, you must reallocate resources to implement that strategy. Determine what financial, material, and human resources you will need to implement future product development, and balance that projection with current production needs. *Balancing is the key to success.*

### 15.8.1 Managing Rapid Growth

During this stage of your company's life cycle, you are beginning to grow rapidly. Growth is obviously good, but unmanaged growth can be disastrous. Your business organization is becoming increasingly complex and sophisticated; you may feel overextended and out of control of some aspects of the organization. The key concept here is to monitor: to put systems, policies, and procedures in place to *monitor* and help you manage, among other things, financial resources, sales, production, and your employees and their productivity.

### 15.8.2  Written Systems and Procedures

Establish sound accounting policies, and maintain good systems and financial controls. During this stage, you should continue to refine your financial-reporting methods: review your monthly budget-to-actual reporting of financial results and monthly financial statements, and implement strict spending authorization and revenue-recognition policies.

Does management have the key information it needs to evaluate current and future production? Identify all key accounting policies and procedures, write them up in a procedures manual, and make sure that your policy objectives are communicated to the appropriate members of your management team, as described below:

- Implement procedures to monitor and control financial performance.
- Inventories and production costs, and other service parts.
- Credit and collections.
- Service requests and calls.
- Quality control, both production and service.
- Sales returns and warranty problems.

### 15.8.3  Rapid Growth Risks and Pitfalls

As your growth accelerates and your business organization becomes more complex, it is crucial to resist making hair-trigger decisions or to react to immediate pressures without giving due consideration to the long-term consequences. Later, you may regret decisions made now without forethought or adequate information. If each action plan is not addressed thoroughly, you may encounter the following difficulties during this stage:

- Delays in initial product shipments
- Incomplete marketing and distribution-channel development
- Production bottlenecks: poor labor know-how; inefficient shop-floor layout
- Failure to develop timely product enhancements as dictated by the market
- Inadequate management information systems
- Chronic cash shortages
- Poor credit and collection procedures

- Improper accounting policies, particularly revenue recognition and inventory accounting
- Inadequate control over inventory and purchasing, leading to problems with vendor lead times; too much or too little key raw materials; or excess inventory
- Excessive sales returns and warranty claims
- Unrealistic shipping expectations
- Poor communication, leading to overlapping of tasks or neglect of crucial business needs
- Battles between sales and production departments

### 15.8.4 Managing Exponential Growth

By now, your company is truly taking off. Your products are well received and your venture is highly successful. You have good accounting systems, budgets, and continually updated business and marketing plans. To manage your burgeoning company, you must continue to use that plan as a guide.

Congratulations. You are experiencing the exponential growth phase and you may be considering branching out into new markets, new facilities, new development, and new products. You need considerable financing to expand into exciting new directions.

If you got off the ground at an earlier stage with seed capital, your investors may wish to realize some return on their investment, and you may be ready, as well, to reap some of the financial rewards of your labors.

During this exponential growth stage, your focus is *controlled* expansion. To avoid false starts and retain control, you should attend to these critical action points:

- Maintain your organizational effectiveness and ensure the attentive management of your business during the capital-raising process.
- Analyze your capital sources and determine the best for your company.
- Continue your R&D efforts to enhance existing products and develop future generations of products.
- Refine your marketing strategies and implement international expansion.
- Implement broad-based compensation plans to attract and retain employees.

By now, the financial rewards are considerable and you have ample management talent in place. Your financial environment is probably stable, well financed, and strong, and you have ready access to outside financing through credit lines, bank loans, and debt structures.

The emphasis of your compensation plan probably has moved to cash-oriented benefit plans or to sweeten existing cash-oriented plans.

In short, you *have arrived*. Now, your objectives are sustained growth and continued development of new products and expanded product lines. To achieve these objectives, you need to

- Reevaluate the direction of your organization
- Identify new directions for growth
- Improve cash flow and profitability
- Continue to attract, motivate, and retain key employees

These action items are not unique to knowledge-based companies but are common to most businesses that have reached this stage in the life cycle. They are essential to maintaining the strength of any business enterprise.

### 15.8.5 Continuing R&D

No matter how successful your initial products and marketing efforts may be, or how rapidly your sales may grow, you need to keep the R&D fires burning to enhance your existing products and develop future generations. In the high-tech market, it is very risky to be a "one-product" company.

The life expectancy of technology-based products can be extremely short, and you can be sure that the competition is always close behind. Multiple enhancements and fresh, marketable ideas will give your company staying power. From an R&D standpoint, you should continue to promote and reward creativity and innovation. From a tax standpoint, you should be on the lookout for R&D tax credit opportunities.

Particularly in knowledge-based industries, a business enterprise needs continual "tweaking" to respond to ever-changing markets and ever-increasing competition. Sound organizational planning is vital to help you identify problems and maximize the overall profits of your company in the early stages of your product launch.

Last, Figure 15.4 summarizes the five lessons you should follow to enhance your product launch success odds.

- Identify your key driving milestones
- Hit your milestones
- Time is more valuable than money
  - Your competition is hungry
  - Market changes on a dime
  - Knowledge-based technology moves at the speed of light
- Money is a commodity; brains are real value
- An idea is worth one dollar; execution of an idea is worth a million dollars

**FIGURE 15.4**
Lessons to be followed.

# References

1. Hisrich, R.D. and Peters, M.P. *Entrepreneurship: Starting, Developing and Managing a New Enterprise*, 3rd edition, Irwin Inc., Boston, 1995.
2. Drucker, P.F. *Innovation and Entrepreneurship*, Heinemann, London, 1985.
3. Schneider, J. and Hall, J. Why most product launches fail. HBR, April 2011, https://hbr.org/2011/04/why-most-product-launches-fail&cm_sp=Article -_-Links-_-Top%20of%20Page%20Recirculation.
4. Sun, L. Planning a Successful Product Launch, http://www.businessdictionary .com/article/257/planning-a-successful-product-launch/.
5. Grant, J. 7 Reasons Why a Great Product Launch Can Fail and How to Avoid It .Global Strategy and Analyst Relations, Telesian Technology Inc., http://www .massmac.org/newsline/0508/article02.htm.

# 16

## Commercializing Pharmaceutical Products

### 16.1 Introduction

The Economist Intelligence Unit projects that the US pharmaceutical market, the world's largest at $396 billion in 2011, will increase by 6.4% annually through 2016. Demographics and disease trends are expected to boost overall drug consumption. The expansion of insurance coverage to millions of uninsured Americans under the Affordable Healthcare Act (ACA) via health insurance exchanges and Medicaid expansion is forecast to increase revenue for drug makers. However, ACA-related pharmaceutical sector fees, a new medical device tax, and lower government drug prices could negatively affect growth.

To sustain their expected rates of growth, pharmaceutical companies have historically relied on successfully launching new drugs periodically. This pressure is only likely to increase, since many patents are expiring and product pipelines are shrinking. However, legislated austerity measures in many countries are increasing local and national hurdles for market access, and at the same time, launches are becoming more numerous, smaller, and more competitive.

Yet the drug launch track record is sobering at best. About two-thirds of new drugs fail to meet prelaunch consensus sales expectations for their first year on the market, and those that fall short typically continue to underdeliver. Improving that record requires pharmaceutical companies to recognize that the world has changed dramatically and adjust their drug launch strategy accordingly.

The August 17, 2015, issue of *Forbes* magazine [1] stated that expectations in the drug business have been getting extremely high. Hepatitis C drugs are generating some of the biggest annual sales ever. New medicines from Merck and Bristol-Myers Squibb that harness the immune system to fight tumors are stimulating new discoveries and opening new therapeutic and market avenues.

For a quick sense of what is possible in the pharmaceutical industry, the top drug multibillion-dollar launches, as compiled by pharma analysts at investment bank Evercore ISI [2], were Lipitor, Humira, Plavix, Enbrel, Advair, and Remicade. Included was the debut of Sovaldi, Gilead's hepatitis C medication, which hit $10 billion in sales its first year on the market—the fastest growth out of the gate of any pharmaceutical ever.

## 16.2 Idiosyncrasies of Pharmaceutical Products Approval

Pharmaceuticals are subjected to the strictest and most rigorous approval process of any product in the world. Because of regulatory requirements, it costs between $900 million to $1 billion (in year 2000 dollars) [3], and over 12 years of development to bring one pharmaceutical from discovery in a laboratory to the patient. For every one medicine that reaches the market-able stage, between 10,000 and 30,000 compounds must be screened, and the majority are discarded [4].

The complexity and cost of the regulatory approval process can be gleaned from Figure 16.1. The entire process typically takes 10–14 years, depending on the drug/disease matrix complexity [4].

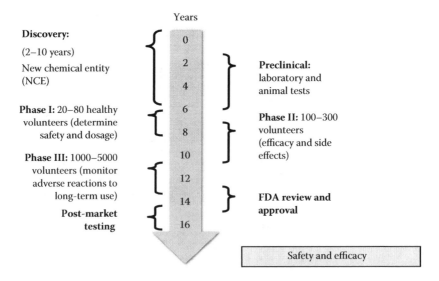

**FIGURE 16.1**
Pharma approval is risky and costly.

## 16.3 Pharmaceuticals and Biotechnology

Pharmaceutical companies develop synthetically derived chemical compounds, as well as plant-extracted products, to make medicines that cure or manage diseases, and protect us from infection [5]. The term *pharmaceuticals* is a catch-all category that includes many diverse products that together comprise the category. While many firms also produce animal health products, livestock feed supplements, vitamins, and a host of other products, we will focus solely on their drug products used to treat human illness.

Pharmaceutical companies deal in generic or brand medications and medical devices. They are subject to a bewildering variety of laws and regulations that govern the patenting, testing, safety, efficacy, and marketing of drugs [6]. The pharmaceutical industry is one of the most heavily regulated industries in the world.

### 16.3.1 Biotechnology Sector

Biotechnology is the applied knowledge of biology. It seeks to duplicate or change the function of a living cell to work in a more predictable and controllable way. The biotechnology industry uses advances in genetics research to develop products for human diseases and conditions. Several biotech companies also use genetic technology to other ends, like the manipulation of crops.

The biotechnology segment had a total revenue of $233 billion in 2012, representing an increase of 9.6% over the previous year. Focus therapeutic areas include oncology, autoimmune disorders, and infectious diseases [7].

The primary difference between biopharmaceuticals and traditional pharmaceuticals is the method by which the drugs are produced: biopharmaceuticals are manufactured in living organisms such as bacteria, yeast, and mammalian cells, whereas pharmaceuticals are manufactured through a series of chemical synthesis.

Biotechnology technology refers to the large and growing array of scientific tools that use living cells and their molecules to make biological products for many different industries. Human and animal health care, agriculture, forestry, environment, and specialty chemicals are among the industries that have benefited most from biotechnology.

The economic promise of biotechnology is extraordinary. At present, it is a $70 billion sector worldwide, and it is estimated to become a market of at least $120 billion annually by 2020. Although biotechnology is a high-growth sector, moving a promising research discovery to market is an exceedingly complex, costly, and challenging undertaking.

Biotech opportunities largely mirror those in the pharmaceutical industry. The key difference is that biotech firms are much more focused on research because they are still developing their initial products. Biotech firms tend to expand their marketing and sales forces when and if a viable product nears US Food and Drug Administration (FDA) approval. Biotech companies tend to be concentrated in geographical clusters, often near prominent research universities and leading hospitals.

The challenges of starting a biotechnology company in the United States include raising capital, building strategic partnerships, recruiting, and motivating and retaining top scientific talent and compliance with regulatory bodies. Commercializing a biotechnology product entails challenges in manufacturing, sales and marketing, reimbursement, and several other unique managerial challenges.

## 16.4 Pharma Launch Excellence

Launching products into the lucrative pharmaceutical market has never been more crucial and challenging for life science companies seeking to achieve high performance. A product launch nowadays has to be "faster"—enhanced uptake of top line sales, "better"—accelerated growth and higher peak sales, and "cheaper"—executed with fewer resources.

Research shows that many players in the life science industry are facing several market trends that increase the importance of delivering maximum value to customers and to the company with each new product or indication launch. The following trends and implications can be observed:

- Blockbuster patent expiry and weak pipeline enhancing the need to optimize replacement sales from pipeline products and the importance of successful new product launches
- Significant price erosion after patent expiry caused by intense generic competition requiring maximization of product value during patent protection period
- Increased focus on in-licensing requiring capabilities and flexibility to quickly ramp up resources to launch in-licensed products
- Changes in sales model increasing the need to sufficiently align and coordinate resources for launches
- Poor public perception enhancing the need to increase positive perception toward new products and pharmaceutical organizations
- Payer and authority pressures requesting the demonstration of superior product value and benefits
- Intensified and unpredictable health politics environment requesting to ensure an early launch uptake. In order to respond to these dynamics, life science companies need to establish an effective

product launch capability that ensures launch readiness and allows them to accelerate launch uptake to offset sales gaps from patent expiry and maximize sales throughout the patent protected product life cycle.

Despite the importance of an effective product launch process, many companies will experience launch shortcomings that, if not addressed, can threaten the company's future success. Addressing and overcoming these launch weaknesses are a key factor for success for life science companies to become high-performance businesses in the future.

### 16.4.1 Drivers of Launch Excellence

Understanding the drivers of pharma launch excellence can help companies close the gap between expectations and results. Ahlawat et al. [8] propose that consistent success with drug launches is a function of four interrelated elements: (1) winning launch mind-set, (2) establishing a launch academy, (3) excelling in one of five great decisions, and (4) ensuring a roadmap for fundamentals, as seen in Figure 16.2.

Additionally, management must "think backwards," that is, start from the end and work backward. The end is the optimal price that the new drug can command in the market. We can call this strategic launch excellence, as depicted in Figure 16.3.

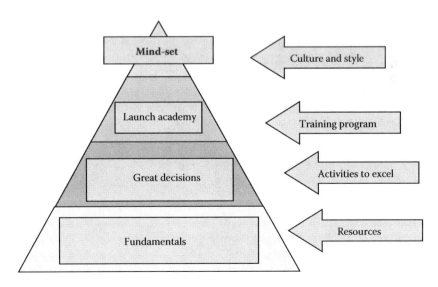

**FIGURE 16.2**
Pharma launch excellence. Strongly influenced by management. (Modified after DiMasi et al., *J. Health Econ.*, 22, 151–185, 2003.)

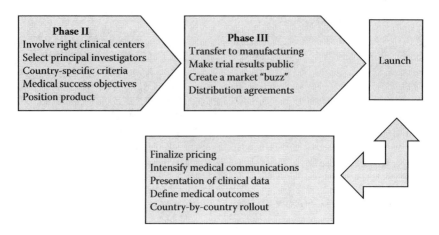

**FIGURE 16.3**
Key steps in drug launch process. Strategic launch excellence.

### 16.4.2 Launch Archetypes

Only 25% of pharma launches can be classified as "market disrupters" or "go for the gold" launches. These involve drugs that are strongly differentiated from competing products and treat diseases with a high perceived burden. Examples include Zytiga, Johnson & Johnson's prostate cancer treatment, and Januvia, Merck & Co.'s drug to lower blood sugar levels in people with type 2 diabetes.

At the lower extreme of differentiation, more than half of upcoming launches are "trend setter" products in well-established disease areas, and their priority will be to find a way to "stand out from the crowd."

These launches must find or create an edge that will allow the drug to be positioned effectively for particular patient segments and create clear differentiation from existing competitors.

Roughly 15% of launches are called "breakthrough therapies" by the FDA [9] and are the subject of a specific guidance document [10]. A breakthrough therapy is a drug

- Intended alone or in combination with one or more other drugs to treat a serious or life-threatening disease or condition
- That may demonstrate substantial improvement over existing therapies on one or more clinically significant end points (based on preliminary clinical evidence), such as substantial treatment effects observed early in clinical development

If a drug is designated as breakthrough therapy, FDA will expedite the development and review of such drug. All requests for breakthrough

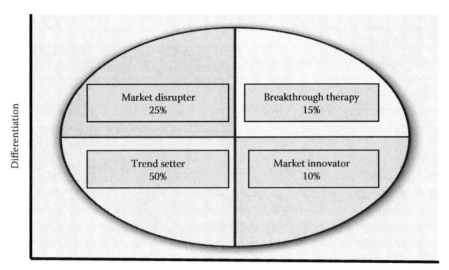

**FIGURE 16.4**
Launch archetypes. (Modified after DiMasi et al., *J. Health Econ.*, 22, 151–185, 2003.)

therapy designation are reviewed within 60 days of receipt, and FDA will either grant or deny the request.

The priority is to establish unmet needs effectively to ensure access for a targeted population to a well-differentiated treatment. Ahlawat et al. call these launches "category creators," for example, Gardasil, with its development and launch into the unestablished human papillomavirus market.

Finally, the remaining 10% of launches face the substantial challenge of launching an undifferentiated product in an unestablished disease area. Once the decision to market such a product has occurred, the priority for these "market innovator" launches will depend on securing access for the product and effectively establishing unmet needs.

Although no two launches are the same, even for drugs with similar profiles, knowing the four archetypes a product launch falls into can help companies identify the strategic choices they need to make to meet or exceed launch expectations. These four launch archetypes are presented in Figure 16.4.

### 16.4.3 Speed to Market

Speed to market is a key component to achieving success for any company launching a new product. It provides the distinctive opportunity to establish loyal customers and set the benchmark for consumer expectations. Timing is everything, and getting there first means capturing market share, revenue, profits, and customer mindshare.

Nowhere is timing more crucial than in the pharmaceutical industry. When drug patents expire, generic drug manufacturers play a waiting game with approvals from the FDA. Once approvals come through—often on unpredictable days such as Fridays or holidays—it's a sprint to the pharmacy shelf or the distributor's warehouse. The supply chain network must be ready to deliver when authorization comes, without wasting time or resources.

As the old adage says: Time is Money. The speedier the time to market, the lower the drug development costs. Critically, the failure rate for drugs in Phase III is too high—around 40%, according to a team of researchers at Sagient Research Systems and Biotechnology Industry Organization. From a value-creation perspective, this is perhaps the most inefficient outcome possible. Since the cost of research and development (R&D) increases sharply from one phase of clinical development to the next, failing in Phase III is a very inefficient use of capital that could have been better deployed on other assets.

This is diagrammatically seen in Figure 16.5, where time to marketing is illustrated. What is not easily seen is that as the product proceeds through the different phases, costs escalate exponentially.

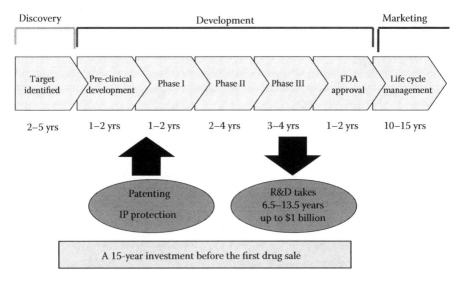

**FIGURE 16.5**
Time to marketing means lots of money.

### 16.4.4 Managing Launch Uncertainties

Over the next 3 years, pharmaceutical companies are expected to launch some 400 products and indications yearly, up 146% from 2005. By 2015, sales from products launched in the past 5 years should account for more than US $80 billion worldwide. In an era of patent cliffs and shrinking pipelines, capturing full value from every product launch is critical, but with only about a third of launches meeting or exceeding analysts' expectations, the challenge is considerable and unlikely to get any easier [11].

The importance of getting drug launch correctly the first time and the difficulty of recovering from a slow start suggest that there is an overwhelming need for a consistent and reproducible approach to ensure launch success.

In many ways, launch is like rocket science. Hundreds of activities all need to happen at exquisitely predefined moments to a certain standard. The three main sources of launch uncertainty are as follows:

1. *Regulatory and market access.* Launch preparation starts long before final decisions are taken on a drug's label or pricing and reimbursement. A product is commercialized almost immediately after its approval by the European Medicines Agency or FDA, leaving little room for a company to correct its course if payers make unexpected decisions.

    Changes in payers' priorities and policies, unpredictable label changes, and budget cuts can all have major consequences for a product's launch strategy, tactics, and eventual success.

2. *Clinical data analysis.* In principle, a pharma company enters the launch phase as soon as the clinical data from its Phase III registration trial is published. However, data analysis often continues, with subgroup analysis and statistical elaboration of efficacy and safety data.

    Findings from these analyses, as well as challenging interpretations of results by "antagonist" investigators, can have a considerable impact on a product's launch plan.

3. *Market reaction.* Competitors' clinical results, shifts in medical practice, disruptive innovations, and competitors' negative counter-messaging can radically alter a new product's market situation before launch and impair its eventual outcome.

### 16.4.5 New Drug Pricing and Reimbursement

In most markets, new drug pricing and reimbursement conditions are the single most important value drivers at the time of your launch. Although many country and regional payers are becoming increasingly sophisticated in their health economic assessments, market access conditions are in practice often influenced by a range of other factors including political agendas, informal social networks within institutions, and emotional drivers such as family members with a specific medical condition.

Pharmaceutical companies, on the other hand, tend to focus on pharmacoeconomic models and technical issues, failing to address the political and personal factors that play a part in payers' decision-making and thereby limiting the effectiveness of their value proposition.

By generating deep insights into your stakeholders' (regulatory, payers, hospitals, physicians, patients, societal values) attitudes and their approach to pricing and reimbursement decisions, companies can gain a better understanding of their priorities and concerns, shed light on how the process for updating formularies and protocols really works, weigh up the relative influence of different stakeholders in the final decision, and assess which arguments for articulating a product's value will resonate most with payers.

### 16.4.6 Tools into Payer's Priorities and Needs

Different tools exist for gaining insights into payers' priorities and needs: Your "persuading" armamentarium consists of the following:

- *In-depth interviews* are permissible in most countries. Interviews should be thoroughly prepared and carefully structured, with easy-to-use analytical and visual support materials that are detailed enough to enable interviewers to explore how payers actually reach their decisions. One effective approach is to show payers a range of different modules that might be used to launch the new brand and ask them to classify each module as strong or weak. By repeating this exercise with multiple payers, companies can identify which topics and arguments are most compelling and then use them in the value story they develop about their brand.

- *Focus groups* are allowed in some markets, although they can be harder to execute than interviews. Companies can use similar research techniques for payers as for physicians or patients. The advantage of focus groups over interviews is the opportunity to hear a range of views and opposing perspectives within the group.

- *Mock protocol committees*, often involving former members of payer bodies, are the most suitable forum for developing insights into budget impact analyses or the structure of pharmacoeconomic models, but less useful for deriving emotional insights.

- *Advance notification*, whether formal or informal, is becoming common practice in a number of countries throughout the world. Companies can use interactive modeling tools to help them understand a payer's financial constraints, approach to product evaluation, and decision-making priorities. These tools allow users to vary parameters such as price/volume trade-offs and population restrictions so as to test the payer's likely response to different scenarios [12].

## 16.5 Glocalization of Health Care

The global health care industry is going through a period of "glocalization," a term that combines the words "globalization" and "localization" to describe the adaptation of global products or services to accommodate the needs of people in a specific locale. The term first appeared in a late 1980s publication of the *Harvard Business Review*. At a 1997 conference on "Globalization and Indigenous Culture," sociologist Roland Robertson stated that glocalization means the simultaneity—i.e., the co-presence—of both universalizing and particularizing tendencies [13].

Typically associated with efforts by large consumer companies to boost sales by tailoring their products and menus to appeal to local tastes, glocalization also applies to health care: Industry issues are global, even if care is usually delivered locally. While the effects of these issues are influenced by local factors, many challenges are shared around the world to varying degrees, as are the opportunities to innovate.

Total global health spending was expected to rise by 2.6% in 2013 before accelerating to an average of 5.3% a year over the next 4 years (2014–2017). This growth will place enormous pressure on governments, health care delivery systems, insurers, and consumers in both developed and emerging markets to deal with issues such as an aging population, the rising prevalence of numerous chronic diseases, soaring costs, uneven quality, imbalanced access to care owing to workforce shortages, infrastructure limitations and patient locations, and disruptive technologies.

Across the globe, there have never been more health care challenges than there are today. However, these challenges can push stakeholders to innovate in new and exciting ways and to generate scientific, medical, and care delivery breakthroughs that can improve the health of people worldwide. This chapter examines the current state of the sector, describes the top issues facing stakeholders, provides a snapshot of activity in a number of geographic markets, and suggests considerations for 2016 and beyond.

### 16.5.1 Global Health Care Spending Patterns

No industry seems more out of step with prevailing efforts to reduce government costs than the health care sector [14]. Health care expenditures, for both providers and payers in public and private settings, is a very costly segment. The Economist Intelligence Unit estimates that global health care spending as a percentage of gross domestic product (GDP) will average 10.5% in 2014 (unchanged from 2013), with regional percentages of

- 17% in North America
- 11% in Western Europe
- 8% in Latin America
- 7% in Asia/Australasia
- 6% in the Middle East/Africa

Among developed nations, health is the second-largest category of government spending, after social protection programs (i.e., social assistance, health/unemployment insurance).

Most of the countries across the globe are facing a formidable challenge to manage the rapidly increasing cost of health care. Although spending rose by just an estimated 1.9% in 2012, it is expected to pick up again, with total spending rising by 2.6% in nominal terms in 2013 and by an annual average of 5.3% until 2017. Given projected population growth, spending per capita is anticipated to rise by an average of 4.4% a year from 2014 to 2017.

### 16.5.2 Effect of Income on Health Care Expenditures

Concurrently, the number of high-income households (those earning more than $25,000 a year) is expected to increase by approximately 10%, to more than 500 million, with more than one-half of that growth coming from Asia. Governments in many emerging markets are taking note of this economic growth and planning to roll out public health care services to meet consumers' rising expectations.

A glance at expenditures by country reveals a strong correlation between income levels and health outlays. Advanced economies like the United States, Europe, and Japan spend about twice as much of their income (12% of GDP) on health care as emerging/developing economies (6% of GDP, on average). Overall, about two-thirds of the $8 trillion in global health care spending occurs in advanced economies, with the United States accounting for $3 trillion, or 40% of the total, as seen in Table 16.1.

Health care spending varies disproportionately with income for two reasons. (1) Health care spending is a "superior" good, where demand rises more than proportionately with income [15]. As countries become richer, households are naturally willing to forego more discretionary consumption in favor of medical advances capable of extending life and improving its quality. (2) Advanced economies also tend to be older societies. The share of the population over 64 years of age is equal to approximately 24% of the population between 15 and 64 years in advanced economies.

**TABLE 16.1**

Health Spending and per Capita Income, Holding Other Factors Constant

| Percentile | GDP per Capita ($) | Health Care Spending Share of GDP |
|---|---|---|
| 25 | 12,000 | 7 |
| 50 | 20,000 | 8 |
| 75 | 35,000 | 9 |
| 95 | 56,100 | 10 |

### 16.5.3 Life Expectancy and Demand for Health Care

Life expectancy is projected to increase from an estimated 72.6 years in 2012 to 73.7 years by 2017, bringing the number of people over age 65 to approximately 560 million worldwide, or more than 10% of the total global population. In Western Europe, the proportion will hit 20%; in Japan, it will reach 27%. The aging population will create additional demand for health care services in 2017 and beyond.

Every year, health care expenditures rise appreciably owing to the growth and aging of the population. Although policymakers can do practically nothing to affect these factors, it is important to understand and anticipate the fiscal impact of such demographic changes [16].

With aging populations, an increase in the number of those inflicted with chronic ailments requires more health care spending, government initiatives to increase the access to care in both industrialized and emerging markets, and treatment advancements expected to drive sector expansion; thus, pressure to reduce health care costs remains and is escalating. Heavy government debts and constraints on tax revenue, combined with the pressures of aging populations, are forcing health payers to make difficult decisions on benefit levels.

Europe remains under particular pressure, and not just in those countries most affected by the regional economic crisis. After forcing through painful cuts to drug prices, wages, and staffing levels, some governments are now using the crisis as a chance to push through broader reforms to health care funding or provision. The goal is that these reforms may make increased health care expenditures more sustainable in the future.

### 16.5.4 Global Health Care Sector Top Issues

There are four major issues that governments, health care providers, payers, and consumers face: (1) aging population and chronic diseases, (2) cost and quality, (3) access to care, and (4) technology. As evidence of the trend toward glocalization, many of the challenges and opportunities emanating from each of these issues can be both global and market specific.

1. **Aging population and chronic diseases**

The shared, long-term trends of an aging population and an increase in people inflicted with chronic diseases are expected to drive demand for health care services in both developed and emerging economies in 2014 and beyond.

Aging populations and increasing life expectancies are anticipated to place a huge burden on the health care system in markets such as Western Europe, Japan, and—surprisingly—China, where it is expected to combine with a sharp decline in the number of young people. (China's decline may be related to the impact of family size policies.) The global population age 60 or above has tripled over the last 50 years and is expected to more than triple again over the next half-century, to reach nearly 2 billion in 2050.

Europe currently has the world's highest proportion of older individuals and is projected to retain that distinction for at least the next 50 years: About 37% of the European population is projected to be aged 60 or older in 2050. In contrast, only 10% of Africa's population is projected to be older than 60 years in 2050. The current growth rate of the older population, at 1.9%, is significantly higher than that of the total population at 1.2%, and the spread between the two rates is expected to become even larger as the baby-boom generation starts reaching older ages in several parts of the world. Mexico has a young population—nearly 30% were 14 years old or younger in 2011; however, by 2017, about 7.5% will be 65 or older, placing a greater strain on public health care services and boosting spending on chronic, age-related diseases.

Another shared demographic trend creating increased health care demand is the spread of chronic diseases—heart disease, stroke, cancer, chronic respiratory diseases, diabetes, and mental illness, among others—which is attributable to the aging population, more sedentary lifestyles, diet changes, and rising obesity levels, as well as improved diagnostics.

2. **Chronic diseases**

Chronic diseases are, by far, the leading cause of mortality in the world, representing 63% of all deaths. Cancer and heart disease are becoming major killers, even in emerging markets. Africa, the Middle East, Asia, and Latin America are experiencing epidemics in diabetes and cardiovascular illnesses. China, with 92 million diabetics, has overtaken India (80 million) as the world leader in diabetes cases, according to the International Diabetes Federation. The cost of treatment for diabetes and other chronic diseases—which may be out of reach for many consumers, especially in emerging markets—is expected to compel a more intense focus on disease education and prevention by governments and health care practitioners while life sciences companies continue to develop innovative new medicines to address many of these diseases.

The transformational changes taking place in the global health care sector can be disconcerting and challenging, but they can also push participants to innovate in new and exciting ways. Additionally, shared health care challenges may lead to shared solutions if individual countries endeavor to learn from other nations' successful practices and adapt them to local needs.

3. **Aging population and chronic diseases**

Many of the world's countries are working individually and collaboratively to address age-related care and cost challenges, and to control and prevent chronic diseases. The World Health Organization is endeavoring to create global awareness about chronic diseases and intervene against them; the organization has set a goal of achieving an additional annual reduction of 2% in the global mortality rate from chronic diseases in the next 10 years, which is projected to prevent 36 million premature deaths by 2015. Additionally, health plans and providers in the United States and other nations are collaborating to innovate in approaches to wellness and prevention. Lifestyle-related habits and chronic diseases contribute to 75% of health costs and patients often get off track in their treatment regimen.

### 16.5.5 Global Health Care Costs

In the global struggle to manage the cost of health care, payers, providers, and policymakers are transitioning from a focus on volume to a focus on value—improving outcomes while also maintaining or lowering costs. Concurrently, numerous countries are instituting cost-containment measures, such as new physician incentive models, prescription drug price cuts and controls, comparative effectiveness, and evidence-based medicine. Care continues to move outside costly settings such as hospitals to more affordable retail clinics and mHealth applications. Consumers value the convenience, and costs can be as little as one-third of a traditional health care site.

Most national health care systems have been encouraging greater use of generic drugs; in the United States, for example, the proportion of prescriptions filled by generics has risen from around half to 80% over the last decade. Brazil is making branded generics and proprietary drugs of greater interest to pharmaceutical companies, and in China, recent reforms have put intense pressure on the prices of all drugs, including generic and over-the-counter medicines. In another cost-containment approach, Germany and several other countries have turned to value-based pricing for new drugs, which allows a price differential from existing offerings—including generics—based on a new product's demonstrated superiority. Finally, some countries are increasingly mandating drug set prices: India, Brazil, and China, for example, have national lists of essential drugs with set prices.

### 16.5.6 Access to Care

Nations around the globe are taking steps to address patient access issues by helping to ease the health care workforce shortage. In the United States, for example, health care industry employment rose from 8.7% of the total US civilian workforce in 1998 to 10.5% in 2008, and is projected to increase to 11.9% (19.8 million) by 2018. Several US initiatives are planned at the federal level to address workforce-related issues: The National Health Care Workforce Commission, a 15-member committee appointed by the General Accountability Office, is required to review health care workforce supply and demand and make recommendations regarding national priorities and policy.

The National Center for Health Workforce Analysis is developing guidelines for a uniform minimum health data set across health professionals in order to improve data collection and comparisons over time. Also, competitive grants are provided to enable state partnerships to conduct comprehensive planning and carry out health care workforce development strategies at state and local levels. In Australia, the government has launched the Australian General Practice Training program to increase the number of trainee general practitioners. In 2011, the country's health minister reported that the administration was halfway to achieving its goal of adding another 600 to the program by 2014. China's Ministry of Civil Affairs has set an ambitious target to train 6 million caregivers by the end of 2020. The South African National Department of Health's 2012/2013–2016/strategic plan includes programs around equitable staffing, health workforce development, recruitment, and retention. Other tactics used by various countries' health systems include recruiting quality nurses from low-income and middle-income countries to meet staffing needs and identifying incentives to attract new providers to a specific hospital or to join the profession.

From an infrastructure perspective, hospitals in India are expected to add more than 1.8 million beds to achieve a target of two beds per 1000 people by 2025. The Saudi Arabian government has identified investment in health care infrastructure as a priority; the 2013 budget includes funding for 19 new hospitals, on top of the 102 currently under construction. The Chinese government has consistently increased its health care expenditure budget to expand its primary care infrastructure and insurance reimbursement coverage.

### 16.5.7 Health Information Technology

Health information technology and innovation are becoming important contributors to improve the quality of care, reduce the cost of care, and, most importantly, improve patient outcomes. Advancements such as electronic health records, mHealth applications, e-prescribing, and predictive analytics are being used to better understand diseases and potential treatments and to identify similarities across patients to improve the quality of care. Industry leaders are applying advanced analytics to improve disease management, to drive more focused sales and marketing efforts, and to build new analytics platforms that combine internal and external data to create new business models for coordinating care across the health care ecosystem. Looking a few years out, the power of technology could enable countries to experiment with virtual health care delivery systems.

## 16.6 The Typical Biotech Entrepreneur

The typical biotech entrepreneur who starts a company usually comes from one of four background types, although individuals from any background can start a biotechnology company—as long as they have the ideas, skills, and motivation. The four most common backgrounds of life science entrepreneurs include the following [17]:

1. The **Scientist/Physician/Bioengineer** who comes from an academic institution (University, Research Foundation, Nonprofit Research Institute)
2. The **Scientist/Physician/Bioengineer** who comes from within the life science industry such as another biotechnology company
3. A **Businessperson**, such as a former executive in the life science, pharmaceutical, or venture capital industry, who is not a Scientist/Physician/Bioengineer
4. A **Core Group of Individuals** that emanated from another life science organization within the industry group.

The biotech entrepreneur is usually an accomplished scientist, bioengineer, physician, or businessperson. Most often, but not always, they have a PhD, MD, MBA, or a combination of these educational backgrounds. These individuals usually have well-paying and secure positions, and are already experiencing some degree of success in their current position. Frequently, a biotech entrepreneur voluntarily leaves their comfortable world and steps into an industry that carries uncertainties and risks unique to any other business.

**Successful Biotech Entrepreneurs Share the following Characteristics:**

- Have a strong desire to take control and be independent
- Are not afraid to work hard and put in long hours to achieve personal and business goals

- Are highly optimistic about what the future holds for their businesses and for themselves personally
- Are very self-confident in their abilities
- Set goals and develop an action plan to reach their goals and then reward themselves when they have reached and exceeded those goals (big and small)
- Prepared to handle stress and welcome challenges
- Are not procrastinators, but proactive in their approach to completing jobs and tasks in full, correctly, and on time
- Have a competitive and winning spirit
- Are accountable, accepting personal responsibility for their decisions and actions
- Take the initiative, lead others, and are willing to delegate
- Are independent thinkers and workers
- Take calculated risks and understand that in the absence of risk, success is seldom if ever achieved
- Communicate exceptionally well and respect everyone's right to an opinion even when others disagree
- Are proficient time managers and use time-saving systems
- Are persistent and not easily discouraged
- Are highly organized
- Think and react logically and not emotionally
- Are knowledge hungry and never stop looking for ways to become better in all areas of business
- Have realistic business expectations
- Are great planners
- Are proficient problem solvers and decisive decision-makers
- Keep an open mind, are flexible, and are adaptable to change when change is beneficial
- Are good listeners

## 16.7 Struggle over Social Media

In 1 year alone—from 2012 to 2013—the number of social network users around the world rose from 1.47 billion to 1.73 billion (about 25% of the world's population), which is an 18% increase [18]. By 2017, the global social network audience is expected to total 2.55 billion [19]. More than 72% of all

Internet users regularly access social networking sites [20]. In the United States, people spend 16 min every hour using social media.

At issue here is the fact that start-up risk management policies and procedures are not designed for, quite literally, minute-by-minute monitoring of social media chatter to identify brand, strategy, compliance, legal, and market risks.

Among corporations, establishing a social media presence is now more than accepted—it is expected. Among Fortune 500 firms, 77% have active Twitter accounts, 70% have Facebook pages, and 69% have YouTube accounts. As a start-up attempting to commercialize a product, social media is a tempting target because of its reach and low cost. The impact of social media is discussed in the subsequent paragraph.

### 16.7.1 Interactive Social Media

The Internet and interactive social media provide an efficient, low-cost way to send fast messages to millions of people and to targeted patient populations, but pharma companies have been slow to take advantage of these methods, largely because of FDA rules that control what manufacturers can state about their products. FDA has been rolling out new guidelines for using interactive media in recent months [21].

The irony of the social media marketing debate is that patients increasingly turn to the Internet to search for health information, identify possible treatments, and confirm diagnoses. The FDA itself is a heavy user of social media.

In June 2014, the FDA issued its widely anticipated "Guidance for Industry Internet/Social Media Platforms with Character Space Limitations— Presenting Risk and Benefit Information for Prescription Drugs and Medical Devices." The draft guidance intended to describe FDA's current thinking about how manufacturers, packers, and distributors (firms) of prescription human and animal drugs (drugs) and medical devices for human use (devices) that choose to present benefit information should present both benefit and risk information within advertising and promotional labeling (sometimes collectively referred to in this guidance document as "promotion") of their FDA-regulated medical products on electronic/digital platforms that are associated with character space limitations—specifically on the Internet and through social media or other technological venues (Internet/social media).

Examples of Internet/social media platforms with character space limitations include online microblog messaging (e.g., messages on Twitter or "tweets," which are currently limited to 140 character spaces per tweet) and online paid search (e.g., "sponsored links" on search engines such as Google and Yahoo, which have limited character spaces as well as other platform-imposed considerations).

### 16.7.2 Social Media Increases Its Benefits

A recent survey of physicians [22] found that more than 50% of practices responding used Facebook as a platform, and 87% of those physicians under the age of 55 used some form of social media. With the Centers for Medicare and Medicaid Services requiring increased use of digitalized data under the Meaningful Use guidelines, the government is actively encouraging certain actors in the health care system to increase their use of technology to enhance patient engagement [23].

The draft guidance gives marketers some leeway to correct misinformation on drugs and medical devices posted on the Internet by independent third parties. Corrections of "user-generated content" have to be "truthful and not misleading," apply only to messages outside company control, and should not be used as "a springboard to engage in promotional messaging." Marketers should address only the specific misinformation cited, but are not expected to continually monitor the site and track further comments.

A final guidance is slated to address the FDA's concerns about using links to other Internet sites that discuss drug risks and benefits. FDA has warned against connecting to off-label information, and that a "one-click" process for linking to full risk and benefit information does not satisfy its requirements for fair balance and full disclosure.

Even with the new advisories, pharma companies may continue to lag far behind other industries in utilizing the Internet to communicate important information to the public. Drug makers have been using social media primarily for corporate operations—announcing financial reports, hiring employees, recruiting clinical trial investigators and participants, and disease awareness. Nonetheless, there is continuing disagreement over how effective the Internet is for detecting adverse drug events.

## 16.8 Pharma Launch Business Plan

The potential for value creation is a central driver of the high-risk, high-reward pharm business model. The odds are daunting, but historically, the companies that succeed in bringing breakthrough products to market—and the investors who back them—have reaped handsome returns. In doing so, these pharm transition from creating value to *capturing* it—generating revenues and earning profits.

Your strategy behind [24] producing a pharm business plan provides you with an excellent opportunity to consider all the facets of a business or a new venture, challenging feasibility and providing greater confidence in decision-making. The process will also help you identify and clarify future financing needs and is a necessary step in raising external finance.

Your business plan should define your strategy planning process and your new venture's competitive advantage and opportunities. Your business plan should detail the broad action points derived from strategy planning, establishing corporate goals, setting objectives, and how you propose to measure successful achievement of milestones.

For a biotech company, there can be three different strategy models. For example, in biopharmaceuticals:

1. Virtual company (few employees, mostly outsourced)
2. Fully integrated pharmaceutical company
3. Strategically partnered, royalty-based pharmaceutical company

### 16.8.1 What Is Different about Pharma Launches?

The engine driving pharma value capture is, of course, R&D—the years-long process of identifying and testing via sequential clinical trials. As a product journeys from the laboratory to the marketplace, there are discrete events—for instance, completed phases of clinical trials and strategic alliances—at which key stakeholders step up or step down its valuation or the valuation of its developer. These inflection points are critical for both companies and their backers, since value can only be captured if it is recognized and rewarded by others.

Writing a business plan is never easy. Writing one for a biotech company has additional complications (inflection points) owing to the particular characteristics of the industry, some of which we set out below:

- Technology—capturing and conveying the market potential of new technology is critical. Major technological leaps forward, protected by excellent patents, may be valueless without a clear route to market. Multiple applications from the same technology make it a "platform" from which to build even greater value. An understanding of the potential value of the sales from your technology is critical. It is essential to ensure that ownership of any intellectual property is well protected.

- Team—your team should be skilled in technology, proof-of-principle techniques, milestone management, and commercial goals. In short, the skills and experience of your team need to fit the strategy imperatives of the business.

- Timescales—unlike most development stage businesses, biotech companies can take years to get from concept, through proof of principle, to approvals, and finally product sales. It is not unusual for this to take 15 years for biopharmaceutical companies and 10 years for agricultural biotechnology companies.

- Strategy—the costs of developing a new drug are high and significant funding is required to develop a marketable product. Companies must have a dear strategy defining when and if they plan to enter into collaborative agreements in order to gain access to other technology or skills, to help with funding, and in time to provide assistance with marketing and distribution requirements. In the future, the company may need to seek access to public equity markets to raise the significant sums required to develop a marketable product. The timing of entry to such markets should be considered at an early stage.

- Transitions—a biotech company will develop through several stages, as the resource needs for progressing potential products increase. The costs of research trials geometrically escalate through the development phases. Expect management, cultural and cash requirement changes occur.

- Milestones—a journey of several years' duration can be difficult to plot. Funders want to know how you will reach your destination. Large investments in pharma are only made if there is clarity about intended usage and milestones, against which progress can be measured. Future funding will only happen if milestones are achieved.

- Value building—in technology terms, in IPR terms, in commercial terms, and in overall business terms, you are "building value." Financial investors, strategic partners, regulators, and payers all play a role in measuring a biotech product's value. However, the ways in which these groups award value are notoriously inefficient—in other words, there is a disconnect between the creation of value by a biotech company and the timing and extent to which this value is acknowledged by other parties.

- Clinical trials uncertainties—the slow and opaque process of clinical trials—in which results are revealed only at a few discrete points—means a development company's stakeholders have few mechanisms of measuring and recognizing the value that is being created along the way [25].

- Funding—often the most difficult cash is that which gets a company from concept, through proof of principle, and toward the stage when the next plan would have more solid commercial foundations. There are no easy answers to funding this money, but it has to be found by the start-up team if the funds of the later rounds are to follow.

- Deals—it is an inevitable fact that biotech companies will enter into "deals." They do them to acquire technology, to fund developments, share rights/risks, sail distribution rights, and speed up the building of a business. Deals are an important source of funds and an end point in the value chain to market. They are not easy, and doing deals correctly is a core skill for the team.

- Sales—no matter how hard you try to explain, there will always be a majority of people who don't understand how you can build a biotech business if you are not yet selling anything. The financial community that deals with biotech companies understands why sales are not present in most biotech financial projections; however, that does not mean that they don't think about sales. Indeed, assessing product sales potential is a key skill requiring careful market analysis, scientific advisory networks, and business evaluation models.

- Credibility/advice—venture capitalists and other funders take big risks with large sums of money in biotech. They will look very carefully at businesses that appear to have the potential to really create value. In the final analysis though, the team and its scientific and other advisers will need to have very high credentials and be recognized, probably internationally, as experts in their fields. If a team or plan lacks sufficient credibility, then it is unlikely to attract funding.

# References

1. http://www.forbes.com/sites/matthewherper/2015/07/29/the-top-drug-launches-of-all-time/
2. http://www.evercore.com/investment-banking/institutional-equities
3. http://www.ipi.org/docLib/20150414_HighCostofInventingNewDrugs.pdf
4. DiMasi, J.A., Hansen, R.W., and Grabowski, H.G. The price of innovation: New estimates of drug development costs. *J. Health Econ.*, 22, 151–185, 2003.
5. Lawlor, M. Difference between Pharmaceutical and Biotechnology, 2013, http://www.morganmckinley.ie/article/difference-between-pharmaceutical-and-biotechnology.
6. https://en.wikipedia.org/wiki/Pharmaceutical_industry
7. Deloitte's 2014 Global Life Sciences Outlook: Resilience and Reinvention in a Changing Marketplace.
8. Ahlawat, H., Chierchia, G., and van Arkel, P. Beyond the storm, launch excellence in the new normal, http://www.mckinsey.com/~/media/McKinsey/dotcom/client_service/Pharma%20and%20Medical%20Products/PMP%20NEW/PDFs/PMP_.
9. http://www.fda.gov/RegulatoryInformation/Legislation/SignificantAmendmentstotheFDCAct/FDASIA/ucm329491.htm
10. http://www.fda.gov/downloads/Drugs/GuidanceComplianceRegulatoryInformation/Guidances/UCM358301.pdf
11. Beyond the storm. Pharmaceutical and Medical Products Practice 2013, McKinsey & Co., http://www.mckinsey.com/~/media/McKinsey/dotcom/client_service/Pharma%20and%20Medical%20Products/PMP%20NEW/PDFs/PMP_Beyond_the_storm_Launch_excellence_in_the_new_normal.ashx.

12. For a broader perspective on using deep customer insights in pharma marketing, see *The Eye of the Storm*, McKinsey & Company, 2008.
13. https://en.wikipedia.org/wiki/Glocalization
14. https://www.carlyle.com/about-carlyle/market-commentary/2016-global -health-care-outlook
15. Hall, R. and Jones, C. The value of life and the rise in health spending, *The Quarterly Journal of Economics*, 2007.
16. Mendelson, D.N. and Schwartz, W.B. Health care costs. The effects of aging and population growth on health care costs. *Health Affairs*, 12(1), 119–125, 1993. doi: 10.1377/hlthaff.12.1.119, http://content.healthaffairs.org/.
17. What makes a biotech entrepreneur? http://www.springer.com/cda/content/doc ument/cda_downloaddocument/9781441900630-c2.pdf?SGWID=0-0-45-855351 -p173887155.
18. Culp, S. A Comprehensive Approach to Managing Social Media Risk and Compliance, http://www.accenture.com/sitecollectiondocuments/financial-ser vices/accenture-comprehensive-approach-managing-social-media-risk-com pliance.pdf.
19. Social Networking Reaches Nearly One in Four Around the World, eMarketer Inc., June 18, 2013, http://www.emarketer.com/Article/Social-Networking -Reaches-Nearly-One-Four-Around-World/1009976.
20. The Growth of Social Media in 2014: 40+ Surprising Stats [Infographic], *Socially Stacked*, January 23, 2014, http://www.sociallystacked.com/2014/01/ the-growth -of-social-media-in-2014-40-surprising-stats-infographic/#sthash.t4GoW1Bc .KxNuUnDR.dpbs.
21. Wechsler, J. Stuggle over social media continues. *Pharmaceutical Executive*, August 2014, http://www.pharmexec.com/social-media-struggles-continue.
22. Which social media tools are physician practices in love with? *Med City News*, http://medcitynews.com/2013/10/social-media-tools-physician-practices-love/.
23. http://www.forbes.com/sites/johnosborn/2014/05/13/fda-draft-guidance -takes-the-social-out-of-social-media/
24. Biobusiness Plan, http://www.masterclassbiobusiness.nl/downloads/BP.pdf.
25. http://www.ey.com/Publication/vwLUAssets/EY-beyond-borders-unlocking -value/$FILE/EY-beyond-borders-unlocking-value.pdf

# 17

## Launching Medical Device Products

### 17.1 Introduction

The United States remains the largest medical device market in the world with a market size of around $110 billion in 2012, and is expected to reach $133 billion by 2016. The US market value represented approximately 38% of the global medical device market in 2012. US exports of medical devices in key product categories identified by the Department of Commerce exceeded $44 billion in 2012, or more than a 7% increase from the previous year [1].

There are more than 6500 medical device companies in the United States, mostly small and medium-sized enterprises (SMEs). More than 80% of medical device companies have fewer than 50 employees, and many (notably innovative start-up companies) have little or no sales revenue. Medical device companies are located throughout the country, but are mainly concentrated in regions known for other high-technology industries, such as microelectronics and biotechnology. The states with the highest number of medical device companies include California, Florida, New York, Pennsylvania, Michigan, Massachusetts, Illinois, Minnesota, and Georgia. Other states with significant sector employment include Washington, Wisconsin, and Texas.

US medical device companies are highly regarded globally for their innovations and high-technology products. Investment in medical device research and development (R&D) more than doubled during the 1990s, and R&D investment in the domestic sector remains more than twice the average for all US manufacturers.

The United States also holds a competitive advantage in several industries that the medical device industry relies on, including microelectronics, telecommunications, instrumentation, biotechnology, and software development. Collaborations have led to recent advances including neurostimulators, stent technologies, biomarkers, robotic assistance, and implantable electronic devices. Since the industry is fueled by innovation and the ongoing quest for better ways of treating or diagnosing medical problems, the future growth of this sector remains positive.

## 17.2 Medical Devices Economic Activity

In measuring economic activity, such as the nation's production or national health expenditures, it is necessary to clearly define the boundary of the activity being measured. To develop a clear "device boundary," we adopted a working definition based on a standard dictionary definition of "device," something "made, particularly for a working purpose; an invention or contrivance, especially a mechanical or electrical one, and without pharmacological activity." The device boundary would have eliminated in vitro diagnostic substances (NAICS 325413). These commodities are "substances" rather than devices. Also included in the US Food and Drug Administration (FDA) definitions are in vitro diagnostic substances and equipment.

To further determine the "medical boundary," we use manufacturing categories in NAICS (the North American Industry Classification System) because the data from which the estimates were developed are from the federal government statistical system, and that system is currently based on NAICS for industry data. The medical boundary narrows the economic activity universe to the nine categories shown below with their NAICS codes.

334510—Electromedical and electrotherapeutic apparatus

334517—Irradiation apparatus

339111—Laboratory apparatus and furniture

339112—Surgical and medical instruments

339113—Surgical apparatus and supplies

339114—Dental equipment and supplies

339115—Ophthalmic goods

339116—Dental laboratories

We exclude dental equipment and supplies (NAICS 339114) and dental laboratories (NAICS 339116), either because complete corresponding data were unavailable for all elements of the analysis (in the case of dental laboratories) or because dental care and related expenses are typically financed through different health care insurance mechanisms than the other products considered in our analysis.

### 17.2.1 Innovating Medical Devices

Medical devices differ from drugs in that they do not achieve their intended use through chemical reaction and are not metabolized in the body. Medical devices range in nature and complexity from simple tongue depressors and bandages to complex programmable pacemakers, implantable artificial hearts, coronary stents, and sophisticated imaging systems.

According to Davidov [2], surgeons are often on the front line of medical device innovation because of their clinical background and hands-on use of devices. This experience also allows surgeons to clearly see the shortcomings of existing technology.

Whether it is a stapler that misfires, an awkward laparoscopic instrument, or a hard-to-implant bioprosthesis, the "end-user" surgeon quickly recognizes suboptimal performance. For this reason, surgeon-innovators have pioneered many successful surgical products, such as central line catheters, pulse oximeters, implantable pacemakers, pacemaker-defibrillators, balloon-tipped catheters, coronary stents, and so on. Because of their technical understanding of surgical needs and design, surgeons account for more than one-third of all medical device patents in the United States.

### 17.2.2 History and Overview

In the "good old days" (before the Medical Device Regulation act of 1976), bringing a new medical device to market was a lot easier. It was essentially a two-step process: (1) develop a product that met a perceived medical need, and (2) build a working prototype, display it in your booth at a medical show, and, if doctors like it, start selling the product.

Needless to say, that is not the case anymore. Nowadays, obtaining FDA approval is a multiyear process. Reimbursement issues and increased regulatory requirements are now front and center. While the FDA may approve the device as safe and efficacious, the Centers for Medicare and Medicaid Services (CMS) may withhold reimbursement. Thus, medical device developers must make a compelling case that the new device reduces health care costs.

The role of medical technology in health care costs has long been a source of debate and controversy. It has been widely asserted that health care technology can be cost increasing, owing to price and volume effects, both for medical technologies themselves and related services. Other findings have suggested that returns on spending on medical technologies can far exceed their costs, particularly when longer-term benefits are measured in terms of productivity and reduced disability. Yet, surprisingly, very little analysis has been conducted on the direct costs to the health system of medical devices themselves.

According to AdvaMed, an industry advocacy group, changes in medical practice attributed to medical technology encompass a variety of factors. These factors include (1) development of new medical procedures; (2) improvements in existing procedures; (3) increases in the number of procedures performed because of increased safety, effectiveness, or convenience; (4) development of new pharmaceutical products; and (5) development and use of new and improved medical devices and diagnostics.

While medical device spending has grown at about the same rate as national health expenditures overall, prices for medical devices have actually grown far more slowly than the Medical Consumer Price Index (MCPI) or even the overall Consumer Price Index (CPI). Over the 21-year period from 1989 to 2010, medical device prices have increased at an average annual rate of only 1.0%, compared to 4.7% for the MCPI and 2.7% for the CPI. This relatively slow rate of price increase suggests that the industry is highly price competitive.

During much of the 22-year period, 1989–2010, a significant driver of changed medical practice has been the development of new medical devices—from stents to implantable defibrillators, to artificial hips and knees, to new imaging modalities, to new diagnostic tests, to new surgical tools. In view of the conventional wisdom about the role of medical technology in driving up costs, it is surprising that the cost of medical devices has risen little as a share of total national health expenditures. It is also striking that, unlike most other areas of medicine, the prices of medical devices have actually been growing more slowly compared to not only the MCPI but also the CPI as a whole.

## 17.3 FDA Device Classification

The US FDA classifies medical devices into three classes based on the risk the device poses to the patient or the user and the intended use [3]. Consequently, class I devices are considered non–life-sustaining and class II devices are defined as more sophisticated and pose more risks than class I. Class III devices support or sustain life, and their failure would be life-threatening. They serve to prevent impairment of human health, or may present a potential risk of illness or injury [4]. Part 860 of 21 CFR provides detailed information on "medical device classification procedures," as seen in Figure 17.1.

| Classification | Examples | Required submission |
|---|---|---|
| Class I (low risk) | Bandages, gloves, surgical instruments | 510(k) |
| Class II (moderate risk) | Infusion pumps, wound dressings, catheters | 510(k) IDE possible |
| Class III (high risk) | Heart valves, stents, vascular grafts | PMA approval IDE probable |

**FIGURE 17.1**
FDA medical device classification.

In practice, to determine the class of a medical device, the applicant can search the device classification database, which was set up by the US FDA. Approximately 1700 different generic types of devices, grouped into 16 medical specialties, have been defined. Each of these generic types of devices is assigned to one of three regulatory classes based on the level of control necessary to assure the safety and effectiveness of the device.

## 17.4 Regulatory Pathways for Device Registrations

The device classification determines the marketing authorization process, which can be a premarket notification (PMN [510(k)]), a premarket approval (PMA), or an exemption from the aforementioned. These will be outlined in the following paragraphs.

### 17.4.1 Premarket Notification

A PMN, also known under the term "510(k)," is relevant for devices, for which no exemption is defined in the regulation and which are not subject to a PMA. It is applicable to most of the class II devices. The aim of a PMN submission is to demonstrate that a device, which is planned to be marketed in the United States, is "substantially equivalent" to a so-called predicate device, a device already legally marketed [5].

Determining whether a device is "substantially equivalent" involves an evaluation of the intended use and the technological characteristics. However, it does not necessarily mean that the devices must be identical. Once the FDA has confirmed that the device is substantially equivalent by sending a letter to the applicant, the device is considered as FDA "cleared" and can be distributed on the US market. 21 CFR, Part 807, Subpart E defines requirements, like content and format, for a 510(k) application [6].

### 17.4.2 Premarket Approval

The PMA process, which applies to all medical devices of class III, involves a scientific and regulatory review evaluating safety and effectiveness of a medical device. The aim of the PMA is to demonstrate that there is sufficient scientific evidence to assure safety and effectiveness of the device. This type of a device marketing application is the strictest one and is covered by 21 CFR, Part 814, Subpart B. A PMA process for a medical device runs through similar steps as the registration process for a medicinal product in the United States: 45 days after submission of the application, the US FDA will notify the applicant on the acceptance for filing. The review starts and after involvement of the advisory committee's recommendation, the process is finalized with an approval.

These two procedures, 510(k) and PMA, imply that all devices, which cannot be considered as substantially equivalent to a marketed device and which are not classified by the regulation, would have to go through a PMA procedure, like a class III device. For this case, the US FDA offers two further options: The so-called de novo process and device exemptions.

### 17.4.3 De Novo Process

The "de novo process" is applicable to low-risk devices. Devices for which applicants of a 510(k) receive a "not substantially equivalent" letter would be placed into the category of class III. In these cases, the applicant can request a "de novo classification" of the device into class I or II within 30 days from the receipt of the letter. If the US FDA classifies the device into class I or II, the applicant will receive an approval to market the device and the device is then considered a "predicate device" for other firms to submit a 510(k). If the result of the de novo process is that the device remains a class III device, the applicant has to submit a PMA [7].

Table 17.1 shows the review timelines for the three mentioned procedures, 510(k), PMA and the de novo process. However, the US FDA reveals on their website that a PMA review usually takes longer and can take up to 2 years [8].

### 17.4.4 Device Exemptions

Most devices of class I and some of the class II devices are exempted from the PMN requirements. Nevertheless, these devices are subject to other general control; for example, all medical devices must be manufactured under a quality assurance program, suitable for the intended use and have an "establishment registration" and device listing [9].

In addition to this, there is also a device exemption for "humanitarian use devices." This is similar to the principle of an orphan drug. If a device is intended to treat or diagnose a disease or condition that affects or is manifested in fewer than 4000 patients in the United States per year, the applicant needs to submit a PMA, but is exempted from some of the requirements [10].

**TABLE 17.1**

FDA Review Timeline Range

| Procedure | Review Timelines |
|---|---|
| 510(k) | 90–120 days |
| De novo | 60–90 days |
| PMA | 180–360 days |

## 17.5 Increased Regulatory Environment

Device manufacturers may face increased regulation from the FDA as the FDA reviews its 510(k) clearance program, sometimes referred to as the "fast track" approval process for medical devices. Most devices receive FDA approval through one of two review processes, 510(k) or PMA. PMA is the more stringent of the two approval procedures and requires the submission of clinical trial data. PMA approval can take up to 2 years, whereas receiving 510(k) approval can theoretically take as little as 3 months [11].

Device manufacturers decide which regulatory review course to pursue (PMA or 510(k)), but the FDA has 60 days to comment on the appropriate course of action. The majority of devices in the United States reach market through the 510(k) process. In response to numerous recalls of medical equipment approved through the 510(k) process, critics charge that this process is not as vigorous and robust as is necessary. The FDA's guidelines are vague with regard to which approval process should be followed for specific devices and this lack of clarity may have allowed high-risk medical devices to be approved through 510(k) rather than a more robust PMA process.

Critics also assert that the penalties for submitting inaccurate data are not severe enough, there are too few experts reviewing each 510(k) submission, and postapproval monitoring and surveillance is severely lacking. In September 2009, the FDA commissioned the Institute of Medicine to conduct a thorough review of the 510(k) process and recommend changes. The Institute of Medicine's recommended changes making the 510(k) approval process more rigorous, which will lead to higher costs, lengthen the time to market and lower approval rates for medical device manufacturers.

The FDA has already implemented some changes to the PMA advisory panels. From May 1, 2010, the FDA has required separate votes by outside experts on the safety and effectiveness of a medical device up for PMA review. Before, the FDA only required the expert advisory panel to simply vote on the approvability of the PMA application for the device. In addition, panels now vote by ballot, rather than by a show of hands, and the votes will be made public. The new balloting procedure is intended to allow panel members to vote without the immediate influence of other members [12].

In addition to the FDA implementing changes, the Center for Devices and Radiological Health (CDRH), which is responsible for ensuring the safety and effectiveness of medical devices, is in the process of implementing changes to keep the advisory panel members focused on the science as opposed to the regulatory issues. The medical device industry has issues with the panels in their current form as a result of inexperience, lack of expertise, and potential conflicts of interest of members sitting on the panels. However, the CDRH contends that the pool of qualified, experienced candidates that are interested in sitting on these panels is limited.

### 17.5.1 Global Regulatory Scrutiny

Across the developed world, makers of medical devices face a perfect storm of increased regulatory scrutiny, more stringent reimbursement requirements, and aggressive new procurement practices. In search of new top-line growth, manufacturers are looking to a land some call OUS, for Outside the United States, and others call BRIC, for Brazil, Russia, India, and China.

However, seeking salvation in emerging markets brings its own challenges, not least in talent recruitment, management, and retention, but how did we get here? Not so long ago, medical devices were seen as the less risky alternative to biotech in the race to apply innovative technology to health care. Devices typically faced lower regulatory hurdles, shorter time to market, and fewer outright failures than biopharmaceuticals.

In addition, acquisitions by big players often provided a quick exit strategy for founders and early-stage investors, but that has changed. Technological innovation is still prized, but it only gets a player a seat at the table. A series of high-profile recalls and other self-inflicted wounds have prompted politicians to view medical devices with a sharper eye and, in turn, urge the FDA to raise the bar on clinical trial outcomes.

Health care reform in the United States and diminished government revenues across the European market have netted tougher reimbursement protocols. At the same time, providers have become savvier bargainers, shifting major purchase decisions from surgeons to supply chain specialists schooled in the tough procurement protocols of heavy industry.

Factor the stagnation since the 2008 financial crisis, and it is no surprise that makers of medical devices face an unfriendly environment with no respite in sight. In this tough climate, the robust economic growth in Asia and parts of South America is like a bright light in the darkness, and device companies have focused on those markets, but making headway in what used to be called the Third World is not easy, and results have been variable.

### 17.5.2 Headwinds Hitting the Industry

When major newspapers like *The New York Times* or the *Washington Post* run front-page headlines about failing hip implants, faulty heart defibrillators, and overused arterial stents, politicians react, and despite the popular rhetoric about reducing regulations to benefit business, congress's inevitable reaction to these news stories is to publically criticize the FDA and to demand tougher legislation with device makers. FDA officials respond by asking for more detailed data, more relevant end points, and more clinical trials, all of which increases the cost and time required to bring a new device to market [13].

Approval times in the United States have become so protracted that many device makers now launch new products in Europe (or elsewhere) rather than wait for the FDA. In some cases, FDA review has taken so long that companies are already selling second- or third-generation devices abroad while still awaiting initial approval in the United States.

While regulatory delays have a negative impact on device companies' revenues, they also restrict patients' access to advances in health care technology. Industry leaders say that the FDA is well aware of these problems and its negative consequences.

In Europe, the headwind to medical device innovation is reimbursement. A CE Mark—indicating that the product has met the European Union (EU) safety or efficacy requirements—contrary to popular opinion—does not necessarily mean that the product is market-ready. Health care payers want more comprehensive trials to establish clinical efficacy and to demonstrate a compelling health care economic advantage. In other words, the new device must be shown to lower health care costs; otherwise, it will not be approved.

### 17.5.3 Need for Comprehensive Solutions

In such a market, product features and price alone do not drive the buying process. Sales executives must be able to address cost-of-care and efficiency improvements, value-added services, and comprehensive solutions. They must also understand the needs of varied stakeholders—including clinicians, procurement staff, hospital executives, and local policymakers—and be able to communicate effectively with each type of stakeholder. This requires not only solid relationship-building and negotiating skills but also a firm understanding of health economics and the mechanics of reimbursement.

Often overlooked, quality assurance is an area ripe for transformation. This is a critical function for all device companies, but of greatest significance in implants, where product failures can be tragic for patients, and reports of defects often make front-page news.

## 17.6 Hospital Spending and Payor Trends

Equipment and device manufacturers are significantly affected by the spending habits of their key customers, namely, hospitals. Hospital spending has declined over the past several years owing to the overall economic decline. S&P estimates that capital expenditures of publicly traded hospital chains will continue to decline [14].

Industry analysts reason that manufacturers of high ticket purchases (e.g., magnetic resonance imaging [MRI] and radiation therapy equipment) have proportionately been affected more by decreased spending than manufacturers of devices that may be implanted as part of a nonelective surgery (e.g., pacemakers, stents, etc.).

Cost containment and comparative effectiveness research (CER) continue to be major focuses of both public and private payors. The American Recovery and Reinvestment Act of 2009 set aside $1.1 billion for CER efforts, which will undoubtedly lead to further margin pressure as device manufacturers will be forced to defend their product's effectiveness and pricing versus that of alternative solutions. Such trends could spur additional industry consolidation as smaller manufacturers may lack the resources to rebut claims of a device's ineffectiveness.

### 17.6.1 Nonregulatory Policy Areas

There are a number of key nonregulatory areas that significantly affect the viability of the US medical device industry, ranging from financial investments to legislative changes to innovation and product convergence [15].

- *Reimbursement Rates:* Valuation and reimbursement of products by public- and private-sector financial entities are crucial to the success of the medical device industry. The US market is so large that reimbursement decisions made in the United States have the potential to impact the viability of manufacturing the product for other markets. In the United States, there are several unrelated government organizations involved in establishing reimbursement rates.

  The Department of Health and Human Services' Center for Medical and Medicaid Services (HHS/CMS) administers both the Medicaid and Medicare program that covers the reimbursement of medical devices. In addition, the Veterans Administration is the key agency responsible for negotiating an agreement with manufacturers/ distributors of medical devices (Federal Supply Schedules) for procurement of medical devices by certain government agencies.

- *Impact of Health Care Reform:* In March 2010, the US House of Representatives passed the Patient Protection and Affordable Care Act (H.R. 3590). The bill had been previously approved by the Senate in December 2009 and was subsequently signed into law by President Obama. Health care reform will have a wide-ranging impact and will impose new mandates on individuals, employers, medical service providers, and health product manufacturers.

- *Comparative Effectiveness and Benefits:* As policymakers contend with rising health care costs, it is likely that some form of comparative effectiveness, a system based on the relative benefits a product delivers, will be implemented or expanded both in the United States and abroad.

  Comparative effectiveness employs research that compares the clinical effectiveness of different drugs, devices, and procedures with an eye toward improving quality of care. However, issues